W9-AQG-430

THE GROWTH
OF
ECONOMIC THOUGHT

Duke University Press, *Durham, North Carolina*

HENRY WILLIAM SPIEGEL

Catholic University of America

THE GROWTH

OF

ECONOMIC THOUGHT

Revised and expanded edition

94-794

Library of Congress Cataloging in Publication Data

Spiegel, Henry William, 1911–
  The growth of economic thought.

  Bibliography: p.
  Includes index.
  1. Economics—History. I. Title.
HB75.S6854 1983   330'.09   82–24275
ISBN 0–8223–0550–X
ISBN 0–8223–0551–8 (pbk.)

2   3   4   5   6

To Cecile

PREFACE

It has been my aim to strengthen the link between economics and the humanities and to relate the history of economic thought to the intellectual tendencies of the various periods. This meant that a cultural approach was chosen rather than a technical one that would convert earlier ideas into mathematical models. The inclusion of biographical detail again underlines the humanistic orientation of the work and enhances the human-interest appeal. If attention is paid to the spirit of an age and to the personal history of a writer, new insights are opened up that disclose why economic thought took a certain turn at a given time.

An attempt was made to integrate the treatment of the various periods, especially the earlier ones, by systematically raising the question: How did a writer or his school propose to cope with the fundamental economic problem of scarcity? Some of the ancients faced this problem by proposing restrictions on the demand for goods, whereas others suggested public controls or recommended moderation. Side by side with these ideas there emerged the view that the economic problem of scarcity can be resolved by working on the supply of goods rather than the demand for them, a view that gained ground only gradually. The medievalists concentrated on consumer protection as a means to cope with the economic problem of scarcity, whereas the mercantilists attempted to resolve the problem by the pursuit of national gain at the cost of other nations. Smith suggested self-reliance, Malthus self-restraint.

The story of pre-classical economics is told at some length because it is replete with alternatives to the consumer economy, a matter of substantial current interest.

The treatment of the modern period is designed to be comprehensive and cosmopolitan. A great deal of attention and space are given to twentieth-century economics. In the economics of the last hundred years, there is distinguished a first phase, concerned foremost with the allocation of a given quantum of resources and treated in chapters devoted to Jevons and his forerunners, the Austrians, the Lausanne School, and the Cambridge School. Each of these chapters concludes with current developments; for example, that about the Cambridge School leads to monopolistic competition, welfare economics, and the income approach to monetary theory. The next phase in modern economics—the breakthrough of monetary and income analysis, as exemplified by the work of Keynes—is traced both to the Cambridge and the Scandinavian Schools. The third phase—the transformation of economics into econometrics—is documented in broad outline, with attention to the influence of such mathematicians as von Neumann and Wald and to contemporary currents of thought in France, where mathematical economics originated and where it may find a new direction.

The book is designed as a text for advanced undergraduate and graduate courses. When it is used in a two-semester course, it may be supplemented by the collateral readings—sources and interpretations—which are listed on pp. 677 ff. In a one-semester course, the collateral readings can be used more sparingly or dispensed with altogether, and the material presented in Chapters 4, 7, 9, and 15 may be presented in condensed form or omitted.

The lengthy bibliographical notes point to opportunities for further research.

Grateful acknowledgement is due to Provost John J. Murphy and Professor Walter Morton, who have made helpful comments on the manuscript of the first edition.

For the new edition, the bibliographical notes have been brought up to date and a new chapter, dealing with current concerns, has been added.

H.W.S.
Washington, D.C.

CONTENTS

CHAPTER 1

FROM THE BIBLE

TO PLATO

Founts of Western Civilization

History, it has been said, is that field of study in which one cannot begin at the beginning. If one were to trace all manifestations of economic thought, explicit in books, business records, wills, and letters as well as implicit in institutions and ways of life, one would have to go far back to prehistory. Coming closer to our own times, we could look for indications of economic thinking during the Stone, Bronze and Iron Ages. Still later, by about 3000 B.C., a flourishing urban civilization might be found in India, one that rivaled those of Egypt and Babylon. Although manufacture was advanced in these regions and trade prospered, the situation then was quite different in Europe north of the Alps. There barbarism continued for another two or three thousand years, and the forerunners of the Nordic race, kept in savagery, made a poor living from shellfish and game along the coast of the Baltic Sea.

The civilizations of ancient India, Egypt, Babylon, and other old cultures have disappeared. There is only a tenuous link between their value systems and achievements and those of our own Western Civilization. To be sure, if we would want to use the method of contrast to bring into sharper relief the characteristics of our own civilization, we could compare it with those built by early man or with the later ones of India, Egypt, or Babylon. This task, however, is one that in the academic division of labor is assigned to specialists other than students of economics. This is true also of comparisons of our own civilization with the economic life of today's primitive peoples, a subject under the jurisdiction of the anthropologists.

Western Civilization has its origin not in ancient India, Babylon, or Egypt but rather in the civilizations of the Hebrews of biblical times and of the Greeks of the Classical Age. Three world religions and the moral

law have sprung from the Hebraic heritage. Greece has inspired the love
of beauty and the search for wisdom. Indeed, it has been said that

3

> it was in the fifth century B.C. that we find the greatest single
> burst of intellectual and aesthetic activity that the world has ever
> known. . . . Small wonder that such great geneticists as Galton
> and Bateson have expressed their conviction that the climax of
> human evolution was reached by the Attic Greeks in the fifth
> century B.C.! It was, moreover, about the same time that the reli-
> gion of Israel reached its climactic expression in Deutero-Isaiah
> and Job, who represented a height beyond which pure ethical
> monotheism has never risen.[1]

With the Greeks of the fifth century begins the logical age of man, that is,
his emancipation from magic and astrology, transmigration of souls, divine
kings, and gods more human than divine. The logical age differs from the
prelogical age of the savages as well as from the immediately preceding
age of the civilizations of the Near East with their empirical stage of
logical thinking, "where the highest thought is quite logical as a rule, but
draws its sanctions from the results of experience and not from formal
canons of thinking."

The logical age of man also marks the rise of the individual, who
begins to "receive formal recognition in religion and literature, with personal responsibility proclaimed for the first time in ethical teaching." As
the same authority adds, "it is significant that no fundamental change in
man's highest achievement in modes of thought can be detected after the
fifth century B.C. For the past 2500 years civilized man has thought in much
the same fundamental ways." Statements such as these are by no means
the view of an isolated thinker. Gilbert Murray, an outstanding student of
classical civilization, shares Albright's opinion that "few new ideas in the
realms of metaphysics or morals have occurred to the human mind since
the fourth century before Christ."[2]

ECONOMIC THOUGHT OF THE BIBLE

Many passages of the Bible confirm the value of a good life. God
promises to bless the children of Israel with abundance in the land that is
flowing with milk and honey so that no one should be in need (Deut.

---

[1] William F. Albright, *From the Stone Age to Christianity*, 2d ed. (Baltimore: The Johns Hopkins Press, 1957), pp. 121–23. This is also the source of the
quotations that follow.

[2] Gilbert Murray, *Stoic, Christian and Humanist* (Boston: Beacon Press,
1950), p. 85.

3:8; 15:4). "The Law was given that a man should live by it, not die by it."[3] The central moral rule, "Thou shalt love thy neighbor as thyself," has been interpreted as implying that self-love is not only natural but good. "A sound morality must take account of our own interests equally with those of others."[4] Self-denial and austerity are not valued as ends in themselves. Enjoyment is not to be foregone because it is bad in itself but rather for the sake of others, the poor or the otherwise handicapped. At harvest time the faithful must not reap the field to its very corners nor gather the stray ears of grain. These are to be left to the poor and the strangers (Lev. 19:9).

Just as the poor are protected by a number of provisions that command acts of charity—their triennial claim to the tithe (Deut. 14:28), their participation in feast days (Deut. 16:11, 14)—so there are detailed regulations for the protection of the workingman. An employer must not deny him his wage at the end of the day (Lev. 19:13). He must not require unusually long hours of work even if he pays an unusually high wage. If a day laborer has finished his job before the day is over, he may be called upon to do only light work. A craftsman who has been hired to practice his skill need not perform other duties.

THE SABBATH

The cornerstone of biblical social legislation is the Sabbath, the weekly day of rest, relaxation, and good living, to be enjoyed by the master of the house and his family as well as by the slave, the maidservant, and the stranger within the gates. The institution of the weekend was a social invention that has no parallel in the civilizations of Greece, Rome, or other ancient cultures.

SLAVERY

Another unique feature of biblical law requires the periodic liberation of slaves of the Israelite race. They are to serve for six years, to be freed in the seventh, with their wives, and to be liberally furnished with food and other goods that will enable them to start out on a life of their own (Deut. 15:12). Israelites who are slaves must not be treated harshly (Lev. 25:46), and an escaped slave must not be handed over to his master. He is to live wherever he chooses and must not be molested (Deut. 23:16). This provision has been interpreted as the equivalent of the abolition of slavery. It is in line with the demands of Jer. 34:8–22 and Lev. 25:39. Not even an ox must be muzzled when it is treading out grain (Deut. 25:4),

---

[3] George F. Moore, *Judaism in the First Centuries of the Christian Era* (Cambridge: Harvard University Press, 1927), Vol. II, 107.
[4] *Ibid.*, p. 86.

whereas a Roman plantation slave wore a muzzle when employed at the mill stones.[5]

Other provisions, not limited in their application to Israelite slaves, aim at the slave's protection against violence by the hand of the master. These again form a stark contrast with the institutions of Rome, where the master could put a slave to death. Exodus 21:20, 26 provides that if a slave suffers immediate death as the result of the master's actions, the latter is to be punished; if a slave loses an eye or a tooth, he is to be given his freedom.

THE SABBATICAL YEAR

The seventh year, or Sabbatical Year, in which the slaves are to be freed, has additional significance. It is also the year in which debts are to be canceled (Deut. 15:2), and in which the land is to lie untilled and unharvested so that the poor may eat of it (Exod. 23:10). This expansion of the idea of the Sabbath is now interpreted as an ideal rather than as a practical reality in ancient Israel. Nevertheless the periodic liberation of slaves as well as the periodic remission of debt, even if not universally enforced, indicates a profound concern with the quality of a life that was not to be burdened unduly with the dead hand of the past. Instead, slave and debtor were given opportunities for redemption.

THE JUBILEE YEAR

The right of the landowner, restricted as it was by the requirement of the Sabbatical Year, was further limited by the institution of the Jubilee Year, which precluded the transfer of agricultural land for a period in excess of fifty years (Lev. 25:13). In all likelihood this provision was designed to prevent the acquisition of the land of smallholders by the owners of large estates. That such concentration of ownership nevertheless took place is attested by passages in Isaiah 5:8 and Micah 2:2. To avoid it, the faithful were instructed to abstain from selling agricultural land in fee simple but rather to dispose of it in the form of leases limited in time to a fifty-year period. In the fiftieth year agricultural land would revert to the lessor or his heirs.

The Sabbatical Year and the Jubilee Year might be interpreted as devices that would periodically release social tension built up by past misfortune or social conditions. As in so many provisions of the Bible, the rules applying to these institutions are now considered to have been in the nature of moral exhortations to be enforced primarily by an individual's conscience rather than with the help of other sanctions.

---

[5] Max Weber, *Ancient Judaism*, trans. and ed. Hans H. Gerth and Don Martindale (New York: The Free Press, 1952), p. 261.

PROTECTION OF THE WEAK

The economically weak are protected by a number of provisions of which the release from debt in the Sabbatical Year is only one. Under primitive economic conditions loans are often sought for consumption rather than for productive purposes, and when consumption loans are taken, the borrower's bargaining position is often a weak one. He may feel compelled to agree to an interest payment that exploits his needs. The Bible takes account of this possibility by outlawing interest-bearing loans to fellow Israelites (Deut. 23:20). Exodus 22:25–27 further insists on the compassionate treatment of a poor debtor. If a garment has been pledged as security, it shall be restored to the debtor before nightfall. A widow's garment must not be taken as a pledge (Deut. 24:17), nor a mill or an upper millstone—this would be taking a life in pledge (Deut. 24:6).

The Bible was a source of inspiration to the medieval scholastics, whose writings abound with references to its economic and other provisions. Later still, in the seventeenth century, many economic ideas propounded by the Puritan divines of the New England theocracies were again derived from biblical sources. There was visualized, as the basis of these communities, a covenant with God, similar to those concluded with Abraham, Isaac, and Jacob. The condemnation of idleness and the corresponding elevation of industrious labor to high virtue were often supported by references to the Bible, for example, Prov. 22:29, where it is said that a skilful laborer should stand before kings.

LABOR

Much emphasis is indeed given by the Bible to the dignity and worth of human labor. Rather than a curse, labor is considered a blessing that gives life (Prov. 10:16), and the dignity of human labor is derived from God's labor on man's behalf. Just as toil is honored, so is idleness condemned (Prov. 6:6–11; 24:30–34; Eccles. 10:18). The positive attitude to manual labor is at variance with the ideas of leading thinkers of ancient Greece who looked upon toilers with contempt. Pindar, the greatest lyric poet of Greece, who lived in the fifth century B.C., was so much impressed with the irksomeness of labor that in his description the torments of Hades consist of "toil that eyes dare not look upon." Plato, perhaps the greatest of Greek philosophers, linked "mean employments" and the "manual arts" and stated that both are debasing and involve disgrace.

ECONOMIC THOUGHT IN CLASSICAL GREECE

It has been said that "except for the blind forces of nature, nothing moves in this world which is not Greek in its origin." At the time this statement was made—by Sir Henry Maine, an outstanding jurist, in an address given in 1875—its truth was more obvious than it is now. Knowledge of Greek language and literature at that time was still the badge of an educated elite. Of the classical economists, probably only Ricardo had not studied Greek. Adam Smith's *Wealth of Nations* contains references to Pythagoras, Democritus, Epicurus, Zeno (one each), and Plato and Aristotle (five each). Malthus looked for support of his population theories in the works of Plato and Aristotle. Mill translated and supplied notes to four dialogues of Plato. Marx wrote his doctoral dissertation on the natural philosophies of Democritus and Epicurus. Lassalle in his youth authored a two-volume work on Heraclitus's philosophy. Up until the twentieth century the Greek experience was kept alive in the minds of educated people. Long Greek quotations can still be found in an article published in the *Quarterly Journal of Economics* for 1895. Those who studied the ancient writers could not fail to be stirred by a unique moral and aesthetic experience after which the world never seemed the same.

As the intellectual legacy of the Greeks is so rich, it is not surprising that parallels have been found between Greek ideas and economic thoughts developed more than two thousand years later. Since Aristotle's works cover virtually all fields of knowledge, his writings have been an especially fruitful source of such parallels.

The economic thought of the ancient Hebrews is embodied in the moral commands of the Bible. That of the Greeks is found in the discussions of the philosophers. The Bible appealed to the people at large. The public of the Greek thinkers, on the other hand, was a more selective group which consisted primarily of a well-educated elite. Whereas the economic thought of the Bible is inspired by religious impulses, the economic thought of the Greek philosophers is developed principally in connection with their political ideas.

THE CITY-STATE

The arena of Greek politics was the *polis,* or city-state, which found its highest flowering in Athens. The city-states formed alliances, but Greece itself never constituted a political unit during the classical period. The latter came to an end when the city-states collapsed as the result of perpetual internal strife among the citizens, protracted external conflicts among the cities, and the onslaught of foreign powers—first the Macedonians and later the Romans.

The Greeks were politically minded to an excess, and much of what otherwise might have been their working life was spent in political activities often required by the institution of direct democracy, such as was feasible in the relatively small community of the city-state. Athens, the largest of these communities, covered an area of approximately one thousand square miles, or one-half the size of the modern state of Delaware. If people were on jury duty one day, sat in the legislative assembly the next, and fulfilled some other civic function the following day, little time was left for productive work. Much of this was done by slaves and resident foreigners, without whom the system would not have been able to produce the surplus needed to maintain so many politicians. The slaves and resident foreigners formed the majority of the population. Full-fledged citizenship was strictly a matter of descent, not of residence. As the foreigners were not allowed to own land, many became active in trades and crafts.

Although the Greeks' standards of personal consumption expenditure in terms of housing, clothing, and food were modest ones, common enjoyment was fostered by what in our own terms would be called lavish standards of public consumption in the form of public buildings and festivals. Every town had its own theatre, and the environment abounded with temples, artwork, and sculpture whose remnants to this day give an intimation of a beauty attained by no other civilization. Much of the revenue for this arose from the payments of allies or defeated enemies, which contributed a large part of the state income. Calculations have been made that in one period around 440 B.C. the larger portion of the revenue of the city of Athens went for the construction of temples and artwork on the Acropolis, in addition to the financing of a substantial number of public festivals.

FOUR EVENTS IN GREEK ECONOMIC HISTORY

Four events stand out in the early economic history of Greece that were to have profound effects on the economic structure of the city-state.

The first was the adaptation of the Phoenician alphabet early in the ninth century B.C. Although it took almost another three hundred years before the laws of Athens were codified in writing by Draco in 621 B.C., the availability of the written word was a highly significant factor in the development of trade and the reshuffling of economic classes. As the economy became less primitive, the landowning aristocracy, which had long ruled the city, gradually found its position threatened by dissatisfaction among the poor as well as by the rise of merchants, traders, and new men of wealth.

The second event was the founding of Greek colonies around the Mediterranean Sea and the Black Sea late in the eighth century B.C. While the colonists were primarily inspired by the desire to settle on land that had become scarce within the boundaries of the city-state, the colonies, politically independent of the founding cities, became important trading partners of the latter, exchanging slaves, grain, and other staples. As they opened up a window to the materially more resplendent East, a richer pattern of life, going beyond the bare necessities of subsistence, became known to the Greek world, stimulating production and trade.

The third event was the invention of coined money in Lydia in Asia Minor early in the seventh century B.C., which soon spread to Greece. The use of coins signified a great advance over earlier types of money such as tools and cattle. Coins were more widely acceptable than tool money, which had exchange value but did not have the intrinsic value of precious metals. Coins were far more convenient units of account and means of exchange than cattle. Moreover, the introduction of coins marked the end of an era when wealth was primarily held in the form of land, cattle, oil, or other products that were perishable or could not be accumulated without limit. By making available an asset that could be more readily amassed, more readily also than highly valued bullion, the coinage provided a powerful stimulus to the accumulation of wealth.

The fourth event, which roughly coincided with the spread of coined money, was the rise of lending at interest. Credit transactions of this type, which earlier writers such as Homer and Hesiod had not mentioned in their works, began to be reported in the second half of the seventh century B.C. Interest probably originated with loans of cattle or seed corn, where nature would produce a return. As opportunities for the productive use of money became more plentiful, the idea was expanded to cover returns on borrowed funds.

ECONOMIC DEVELOPMENT

The promotion of trade and enterprise seems to have increased the cleavage between the rich and the poor in the city-state, between large landholders on the one hand and small proprietors and landless laborers on the other, and between the aristocratic landowners of ancient lineage and the new moneyed classes. While this cleavage became more pronounced, several factors continued to place a limit on economic development. Population growth was checked by late marriages and a high rate of infant mortality, and when it exerted pressure it found an outlet in emigration to overseas settlements rather than in increased production. Slavery impeded economic development because of the slaves' lack of motivation and skill and because of the restraint that the institution imposed upon consumption by a large part of the population unable to exert pressure in favor of higher standards of living, such as free laborers and their organizations would have been apt to do. Enterprise continued to be of small size and was carried on in a traditional fashion by landholders, artisans, traders, and shopkeepers. Warfare was an important economic activity because it yielded slaves and tribute from the defeated enemy. Except in connection with the discharge of mercenaries, little was heard of unemployment, for which the Greeks had no word. Economic ruin meant slavery rather than unemployment. The Greek language has no counterpart of our concept of competition, although what is now its antonym—monopoly—was known, practiced, and disapproved. There was no idea of protection of domestic industry, although restrictions on foreign trade were common, to produce revenue or to reserve goods for the home market.

Such economic development as did occur in response to the availability of the written word, the establishment of colonies, and the introduction of coinage often meant the replacement of personal relationships by the money nexus. Smallholders and farm laborers could no longer rely on the paternalistic liberality of the noble landlord when they were in need. Many fell into debt and were threatened by loss of land or of freedom when unable to meet obligations that were swollen by high interest charges. A farm laborer was allowed to retain only one-sixth of the harvest for himself and his family, and the other five-sixths had to be turned over to the landlord. This situation, in which slavery because of debt constituted an imminent threat to many citizens, was relieved by the reforms of Solon early in the sixth century B.C. His reforms mark a milestone both of the movement toward political democracy and of the narrowing of economic class divisions. Economically they included the cancellation of all mortgages and of other debts for which the debtor had pledged his own person, the liberation of all those who had become slaves because of debt, the abolition of slavery for debt in general and for the future, a limitation on the size of landed property, and the prohibition of the exportation of staples other than olive oil. Solon's economic reforms were a boon to small proprietors and landless laborers in that they gave them a measure of protection against loss of land and freedom. The prohibition of grain exports was designed to prevent shortages and rising grain prices in the city. Paired with these reforms Solon instituted a number of political innovations that set the stage for the rise of democracy in Athens. He divided the citizens into four classes, each with different rights and duties. The fourth and lowest class included the smallholders, who now could vote in the assembly and become members of the judiciary to whom the magistrates were responsible. Furthermore, the assignment to each class was based on property qualifications rather than on accident of birth, noble or common. Economic mobility, to a degree, was thus allowed to check the power of the noble families, and political privilege and advancement were opened up to talent.

THE ROAD TO DEMOCRACY

The march toward democracy had to take several detours in Greece, and it was not always true that, as in Solon's reforms, political democracy and economic equality advanced together. Some "tyrants" who at times replaced the aristocracy of the hereditary noblemen or the democratic leaders, while attached to an authoritarian form of government, nevertheless claimed to be men of the people, and their policies helped to bridge the gulf between the rich and the poor. This was true, for example, of Pisistratus, who rose to power during the declining years of Solon. When his political opponents had gone into exile, he divided their vacant estates and distributed them among the landless laborers, turning them into a class of peasant proprietors.

At the end of the sixth century B.C., Solon's political reforms were further advanced by Cleisthenes, who strengthened the forces of democracy by making politically irrelevant the ancient loyalties to tribe and clan and replaced them by "wards" or political subdivisions that were strictly based on geographical factors. In the fifth century B.C., when victory had been won over the Persians, Athenian democracy reached its full flowering. Service to the state was now remunerated, and with the poor able to fulfill political functions more freely, the influence of the great families continued to diminish. The political power of the common people was so pronounced that they could vote in their favor for grain distributions and other benefits. At this time, however, when these privileges made citizenship especially valuable, Athenian democracy—always closed to slaves and resident foreigners—removed itself still further from an open society by restricting citizenship to men whose parents had both been Athenians—not only the father, as had been the earlier rule. This meant that a still smaller minority enjoyed the by then plentiful rights of citizenship—perhaps thirty thousand out of a total population of four hundred thousand.

While on the march toward democracy, the Greek city-states had been able to avert the threat posed by the expansion of the Persian Empire in the middle of the fifth century B.C. Unceasing rivalry, however, continued between Athens, Sparta, Corinth, and Thebes, and at the close of the century Athens found herself ruined as the result of the Peloponnesian War. A hundred years later, by the end of the fourth century B.C., the Greek city-states succumbed to the Macedonians, and their decline was accelerated by continued strife among them. Politically the fate of the city-states was sealed when they fell under Roman rule in the middle of the second century B.C., but culturally Greek civilization spread over wide areas of the then known world, ushering in the Age of Hellenism. The cultural legacy of Greece was a priceless endowment to many generations long after Greece's political power vanished. Of this legacy, including, as it does, art and literature of the highest order, the teachings of the Greek philosophers form an integral part.

THE GREEK PHILOSOPHERS

The examination of the economic content of Greek philosophy is made difficult by the wholesale destruction of by far the larger part of Greek literature. Of the writings of the philosophers, only the dialogues of Plato and the major works of Aristotle have been preserved intact. Of the writings of all other Greek philosophers there exist only fragments, in some cases only a few lines, and most of these fragments have come down to us in the form of second- or third-hand reports or quotations. The picture of Greek philosophy that is impressed on the mind of the student is thus a distorted one. The writings that have been lost wholly or in part are only dimly seen in the background, while Plato and Aristotle hold the center of the stage.

Indeed, not a single statement of democratic political theory has survived and for this reason it has been said that the surviving literature is not representative of Athens, which was the cradle of democracy.

The central figure in Greek philosophy was Socrates (469–399 B.C.), who did not produce any writings at all and whose views are known only from the reports of others, mainly from the dialogues written by his pupil Plato. So important was Socrates' position that Greek philosophy can be divided into a pre- and a post-Socratic period. Almost all of the many schools of thought that emerged during the post-Socratic period claimed to be the intellectual heirs of Socrates—so rich was the legacy of his thought and so varied were the interpretations that could be given to it.

PRE-SOCRATIC PHILOSOPHY: PYTHAGORAS

Many pre-Socratic philosophers form a link between mythology and the rational discourse of the logical age. Much of their attention was given to cosmology, the study of the nature of the universe and of rules that guide it. The ideas of a few of them have influenced economic thought. One of these was Pythagoras (c.582–c.507 B.C.), all of whose writings are lost but who, according to a later Greek writer, "extolled and promoted the study of numbers more than any one, diverting it from mercantile practice and comparing everything to numbers." The same writer also attributed to Phythagoras the introduction of weights and measures among the Greeks. Phythagorean ideas served as the basis of the "mathematical" approach to the theory of the just exchange as developed by Aristotle. It is an open question, however, whether Pythagoras's quantitative bent was inspired by mercantile practice. It seems that he came to mathematics rather by way of music, and he is believed to have discovered the numerical ratios that determine the intervals of the musical scale. From these investigations the notion of harmony was derived, which in turn has an affinity with the concept of equilibrium that was to occupy a central position in the economic thought of later generations. To the Greeks harmony meant "the joining or fitting of things together,"[6] an idea that played an important part in Plato's discussion of the threefold division of the soul and of the state.

HERACLITUS

At first glance, harmony, balance, or equilibrium may seem entirely unrelated to, or even the opposite of, the notion of strife or competition, which as a fundamental principle of cosmic and social organization goes back to Heraclitus (c.535–475 B.C.), another pre-Socratic philosopher who was Pythagoras's junior by about fifty years. Heraclitus, who was given the byword "the Obscure" by the ancients, developed his thought in paradoxical

---

[6] W. K. C. Guthrie, *A History of Greek Philosophy* (Cambridge: University Press, 1962), Vol. I, 220.

terms. He taught that "war is the father of all things," an idea that has been interpreted to refer to the struggle of opposite forces that generates balance, equilibrium, or a harmonious order. The forms that this thought has assumed in intellectual history are legion. Our notion of a self-regulating market has its root in Heraclitus's philosophy. So does the nineteenth-century idea of social Darwinism with its belief that the competitive struggle secures the survival of the fittest. A related concept of Heraclitus is his paradoxical logic, or polarity of thought, which teaches in its extreme form that opposites are identical, and in a more moderate form that opposites can only be understood in relation to their opposites. Two thousand years later this notion was revived in the dialectics of Hegel (1770–1831), whose thought has been interpreted to imply that one concept, the thesis, will inevitably turn into its opposite, the antithesis, and that the interaction of the two generates a synthesis that in turn would be the first form of another triad. Hegel's dialectic idealism led to Marx's dialectic materialism, which, like the "System of Economic Contradictions" of Proudhon, another Socialist, has an affinity with the thought of Heraclitus.

DEMOCRITUS

Seminal ideas emerge also in the thought of Democritus (c.460–c.370 B.C.), a contemporary of Socrates who is chiefly remembered for his theory of the atom but whose numerous writings include a treatise on economics. Of all this nothing but some three hundred quotations have been preserved.

Although Democritus taught that moral values are absolutes, his theory of economic value was a subjective one. "The same thing," a fragment of his writings states, "is good and true for all men, but the pleasant differs from one and another." Not only was utility thus interpreted in subjective terms, but recognition was also given to its relative character: "The most pleasant things become most unpleasant if moderation does not prevail"—a thought that anticipates the notion of diminishing utility and of the transformation of goods into nuisances once saturation is reached. Democritus also had a notion of time preference that may be more judicious than that of some modern writers who, like Pigou, interpret our inclination to place a higher value on present than on future goods as the result of a "defective telescopic vision." "The old man was once young," Democritus says, "but it is not sure whether the young man will ever attain old age; hence, the good on hand is superior to the one still to come."

The subjective and relative character of utility is further recognized in a saying of Democritus to the effect that if only a few goods are desired, these will seem to be many, because a restrained demand makes poverty equivalent to wealth. This and similar thoughts are indicative of Democritus's intention to tackle the economic problem of scarcity by operating on the demand side. He did not fail, however, to take also the supply side into consideration and was one of the few Greek philosophers to pay his respects to the value and worth of labor: "Toil is sweeter than idleness when men gain what they toil for or know that they will use it." As to the disutility of labor, Democritus stressed the relevance of regular work habits which may diminish it.

In the matter of economic organization, Democritus underlines the importance of liberality and mutual aid as means to integrate society. "When the powerful champion the poor and render them service and kindness, then men are not left desolate but become fellows and defend one another." Democritus also attached a higher value to freedom than to the enjoyment of material goods. "Poverty in a democracy is as much preferable to prosperity under a despot as is freedom to slavery." He favored private rather than communal property, basing his argument on the superior effects of private property on incentive, thrift, and pleasure: "Income from communally held property gives less pleasure, and the expenditure less pain."

Although Plato never referred to Democritus, Aristotle not only was familiar with his writings but devoted several works of his own to Democritus's thought. It may well be that Aristotle's defense of private property (pp. 27 ff.) was inspired by Democritus's ideas. Democritus was a still more important source of inspiration to Epicurus (p. 38), but the latter was unwilling to acknowledge his debt. Marx was attracted by the materialistic philosophy of the two and wrote his doctoral dissertation, first published in 1902, on the differences between Democritean and Epicurean natural philosophy.

PLATO

The dialogues of Plato (c.427–c.347 B.C.) that contain economic ideas are his *Republic* and his *Laws,* although a few may also be found in his other dialogues. These works treat of subjects that fall under the heading of political science or jurisprudence. Such economic thoughts as they contain must be discussed within the context of the political ideas with which they are linked.

THE *REPUBLIC* The ostensible purpose of the *Republic* is to give an answer to a question that has haunted philosophers throughout the ages— What is justice? Before giving what he considers the correct answer, Plato rejects a number of misinterpretations. He is not impressed by the view that justice consists of telling the truth and paying one's debts. In connection with the discussion of this faulty interpretation of justice, Plato develops a few thoughts about wealth. He admits that wealth is known to be a great comfort and that all love money because of its usefulness. A distinction is then made between inherited and acquired wealth. Those who have made their own fortune are twice as much attached to it as are other people: their wealth is not only useful to them; it is also their own creation. But such people are bad company. They have nothing good to say about anything except wealth. Some hold that the highest value of wealth derives from the peace of mind of the wealthy man who is able to speak the truth and pay his debts. This may be correct, but according to Plato—speaking through Socrates—telling the truth and paying one's debts is not an exhaustive definition of justice.

Another interpretation of justice that Plato rejects is the social-contract theory which holds that individual conduct is restrained by convention in the interest of all. Such compacts and conventions are made because people realize that if somebody is wronged, the harm of the sufferer must be given more weight than the advantage of the doer. Thus, laws are made to avoid doing wrong and suffering wrong, and what the law prescribes is justice. Here again random remarks about economic subjects are inserted, such as the threefold division of goods. One class consists of harmless pleasures and enjoyments that we welcome for their own sake, which have no further consequences besides the satisfaction of the moment. Another class is made up of pursuits which in themselves are a burden and are not done for their own sake but because of their desirable consequences or results, such as doing one's job. The third and highest class is filled with good things that are valued both for themselves and for their consequences, such as knowledge and health. It may be noted that among the examples designed to illustrate the second class we do not find specifically mentioned manual labor and toil but rather activities to which today many would be inclined to assign a satisfying content in themselves: physical training and the healing arts. If these were considered disagreeable and a burden, what must have been the ranking of labor and toil!

Having rejected these and other interpretations of justice, Plato then turns to construction rather than critique and with the help of the method of successive approximation constructs an ideal state which to him constitutes the materialization of justice on earth. Plato's ideal state is the one in which the philosopher is king. This final result is reached as the outcome of a protracted analysis, which is applied to the city-state of Plato's own environment. The basis of the city-state is not a man-made compact but the natural inequality of man, who is endowed by nature with a variety of gifts and talents that are highly developed in some and less so in others. Division of labor, specialization, and exchange are thus natural and advantageous in view of man's inequality and lack of self-sufficiency.

THE DIVISION OF LABOR Plato's analysis is of interest to the economist because one of his central concepts, the division of labor, is of paramount importance in the history of economics. Two thousand years later the same concept was to serve as a cornerstone of Adam Smith's system of economics. There is a significant difference, however, in the context and in the emphasis that the two authorities place on division of labor. To Plato the all-important fact is human inequality, which gives rise to specialization. To Smith, the aspect of the matter to stress is the improvement in productivity that results from specialization. Smith's great concern is the "causes of the wealth of nations," whereas Plato searches for the structure of the ideal community. Smith rationalizes moneymaking; Plato, as will soon be seen, rationalizes class distinctions and the stratification of society.

Plato, of course, does not deny that specialization raises production. He emphasizes that goods are produced more easily and plentifully and are of higher quality when each person performs the function in the community for which his nature best suits him. The idea of division of labor is expanded also to consider the need for imports from regions beyond the limits of the city-state, as well as for exports to be given in exchange for imports. The logical priority in this reasoning is placed on imports. In addition to the farmers, craftsmen, traders, and hired laborers, shopkeepers are also needed in the marketplace, people who take the money of those eager to buy and transmit it to those eager to sell. If no such specialists were available, the farmers and artisans would have to waste their time at the market, waiting for customers. In a well-ordered community, Plato points out, the shopkeepers are usually chosen from those who lack the physical strength to be useful in other employments. As for the wage earners, they have the physical stamina required for heavy work, but their intellectual ability is so poor that they hardly deserve to be included in the society.

THE IDEAL STATE   This first "model" of Plato's ideal city-state ministers to basic human needs. In it, justice arises if each follows that occupation for which nature has best equipped him. In response to the objection that such a city would resemble a "community of pigs," Plato then complicates the model by allowing for luxury, luxury trades, and other refinements of civilization. This development will be restricted by the meager resources of the city-state. The country will be too small to support the artists, poets, dancers, makers of household gear and women's adornment, servants, barbers, cooks, confectioners, and extra physicians required by the new style of life. To provide a more nearly adequate economic basis for it, the city-state will be compelled to make war on its neighbors to cut off a slice of their territory, and these in turn, if they likewise abandon themselves to the quest for unlimited wealth, will pursue the same aim. "All wars," Plato states in another context, "are made for the sake of getting money" (*Phaedo,* 66 c).

In the second approximation of Plato's ideal state there thus arises the need for military strength to support aggression on the part of the city-state and to protect it from the aggression of others. In addition to the class of producers—farmers, artisans, traders, shopkeepers, and so forth—that form the citizenry in his first approximation, there is thus formed a second class, that of professional soldiers. In line with the principle of specialization, they will have to have a native aptitude for their calling, and they will be given complete freedom from other occupations.

In the third approximation Plato's ideal state emerges complete. Here the two-class system of rulers—soldiers—and ruled—producers—is modified by a differentiation of the ruling class into soldiers and those who will stand at the apex of the pyramid, the philosophers. The three classes of producers, soldiers, and philosophers reflect Plato's view of the human mind or soul, which is divided by him into three parts, "one that craves, one that fights, and one that thinks."[7] In the threefold stratification of Plato's ideal community the people who are apt to crave material goods must toil to produce them; those who are equipped with a pronounced courage and a fighting instinct will constitute the military; those who can think rationally and philosophically will be chosen to rule. Such harmonious ordering of society will constitute justice. There are detailed regulations about the upbringing and education of children, the emancipation of women, and, not too clearly, the movement of people from one class into the other. That Plato, while admitting such movement in principle, expected to keep it within narrow bounds is evidenced by his strong belief in the importance of inherited characteristics and personality traits. This belief inspired him to impose strict rules on the selection of marriage partners, which was to proceed in line with the principles of scientific breeding as applied in animal husbandry, with the weak and infirm to be destroyed. To enable the philosophers to obtain and hold on to power in the state, they are instructed to sway the population with the help of propoganda in the form of "white" or "medicinal" or "noble" lies relating to their own god-like origin and the inferior lineage of the other classes.

PRIVATE VERSUS COMMUNAL PROPERTY Little is said in Plato's second and third approximations about the producing class and its economic organization. As to wealth and poverty, the general observation is made that both have evil consequences. Wealth will produce luxury and idleness; poverty will result in mean standards of conduct and workmanship. Hence, the ruling class will have to keep a watchful eye on these matters. As for the two components of the ruling class—the soldiers and the philosophers —they are to be freed from the burdens of private property and family in order to devote their lives to the business for which nature has equipped them best, soldiering and ruling. Instead, in addition to the communal upbringing of the children, there is instituted for the two upper classes a community of property as well as of women.

This means that the members of the upper classes will have no private houses but will live together and share common meals. They will not be allowed to possess gold or silver, "that mortal dross which has been the source of many unholy deeds." If they should be unhappy about these and other deprivations, it is not the happiness of any special class that counts but the happiness of the community as a whole. Moreover, the lives that they will lead will befit their true nature. They will not tear the city asunder by stamping the mark of private property upon various goods that they would drag into their homes. They will not be exposed to lawsuits, family quarrels, and the ever-recurring vexations of a family father.

----

[7] Gilbert Murray, *Stoic, Christian and Humanist* (Boston: Beacon Press, 1950), p. 46.

The significance that Plato attaches to the requirement that the upper classes must own property only in common is brought into still sharper relief in his discussion of the causes that are responsible for the degeneration of the ideal state. Such a degeneration may occur mainly as a result of the operations of economic factors. The ruling classes will be corrupted if they acquire a taste for money and possessions, and the producing class, whose members by their very nature do have such a taste, will not be eager to usurp the position of the rulers if this precludes the accumulation of wealth. In his description of the conditions of degeneracy Plato depicts the economic strife characteristic of the Greek city-states of his time, a social malaise that the outlawry of private property for the rulers of the ideal city-state aims to prevent.

TYPES OF GOVERNMENT   Altogether Plato distinguishes five types of government—the aristocratic one of the ideal community ruled by the best, and four degenerate forms: timocracy or the rule of the soldiers; oligarchy or plutarchy, the rule of the wealthy; democracy; and despotism.

If the soldier class usurps power, ambition and the desire to excel that constitute the native endowment of the warriors are no longer restrained by the rule of reason. Allowed to run free, envy and rivalries are stimulated by the possession of land, homes, and other types of property. In the public's scale of value wealth comes to rank as the highest good, replacing virtue. When, reflecting this change in valuation, property qualifications come to be required for the exercise of political power, the latter is taken over by the wealthy, and plutocracy is established. The state is then divided into the rich and the poor, with each class plotting against the other. Some wealthy people will squander their money, fall into debt, and be ruined. The ranks of the pauper class are swollen in this way because a society that honors wealth above all cannot at the same time inspire in its members the proper sense of self-control which would protect them, nor can it provide for them adequate institutional arrangements aiming at the same purpose, such as the refusal to enforce the repayment of loans. As more and more wealthy people become impoverished, the pauper class in the end rebels, civil strife ensues, and when the poor win, democracy becomes established. There the unsatisfiable desire for wealth as the highest good is replaced by an unsatisfiable desire for liberty. Plato frowns on social arrangements under which everyone is allowed to talk and act as he likes, although he has to admit that a constitution under which all can develop to the fullest their diverse individualities may be the finest of all. Nevertheless he deplores a situation where the citizens are at liberty to pursue the fancy of the moment, where no one is under duty to wield authority or to obey it, where tolerance is paired with disregard for the authoritarian principles of government ruling the ideal community, where rulers behave like subjects and subjects like rulers, where there is no respect for authority, and where in the end the slave is as free as the master who has purchased him.

Eventually, economic strife will be the undoing of democracy, just as it has destroyed other forms of government. Society will be broken up into three classes—idle spendthrifts (*drones*) who furnish the leaders, wealthy persons who become the prey of the drones, and the large mass of the population with small means and no interest in politics, to whom the drones will throw part of their spoil. The demagogic leaders and the wealthy class are embroiled in denunciations and plots, and the plundered rich eventually become what the demagogues accuse them of being: reactionaries with revolutionary designs. In this situation a champion of the people arises. He is transformed into a despot because he is unable to hold on to power by means other than terror, being at war equally with the rich, whom he prosecutes as enemies of the people, and with the men of courage and the men of reason, who detest him. Once he has eliminated his internal enemies, he will stir up external wars to create conditions of permanent emergency in which he can prove his indispensability and which so impoverish the people that all their energies have to be devoted to the winning of their daily bread rather than to plots against the tyrant.

THE *LAWS* In one way or another, the fall of the ideal state is invariably related to the accumulation of wealth and to the inequalities and cleavages created thereby. The elimination of private property from the institutions applicable to the lives of those who count—the ruling class—is thus a cornerstone of Plato's system. That this is so is demonstrated also in the *Laws,* a work that Plato wrote when he was older, more disillusioned by ill-fated ventures into practical politics, and more willing to sacrifice principle to practicability. Here again he points out, and in words that are stronger still and more moving than those used in the *Republic,* that the best political community is the one made up of friends who share everything, women, children, and all possessions. A community, he says, in which all is done to cast away what the word *ownership* refers to, in which all is done to turn into common property even that which nature has made our own— our eyes, ears, and hands, which now see, hear, and act in the common service—such a community will be united in its attachment to the same system of values, and what gives pleasure or pain to one will give pleasure or pain to all. If such a city could ever be found on earth it would be peopled by gods or by the children of gods (V 739). However, in the *Laws* Plato all but abandons this ideal as being impractical, and in its stead sets forth the fundamental principles of organization which, though not the best, come closest to the best and are more likely to be approximated in the world of reality.

Again the picture he draws is one of a community limited in size, here to some five thousand family farms, each operated by a citizen and handed over on his death to a son, natural or adopted. The number of holdings is not allowed to vary and the population is to be kept stationary, if need be by sending out colonists or, but only as a last resort, by admitting immigrants. The life of the citizens is subject to numerous and detailed regulations designed to keep out "dangerous thoughts" and to prevent the rise of pronounced inequalities that might threaten social cohesion. Great attention is given to education and persuasion to bring about right conduct and to attach the people to the ideal of the good life. As to pleasures and enjoyments, proper education will not insist upon complete self-denial but on modesty and sobriety. Although right conduct and the good life (which fosters the harmonious development of all virtues—wisdom, moderation, respect for others, courage) are valuable for their own sake, they have in addition attached to them a pleasure premium. Right conduct and the good life are thus depicted not only as morally superior but also as involving more pleasure and less pain than their opposites. Pleasure and pain are described as "the very wires or strings" whose pull causes people to act. They prefer pleasure and are repelled by pain, and in their actions they try to strike a balance on the side of pleasure. Pain and pleasure have "dimensions"—frequency, duration, intensity, and so forth—which people will take into account when striking this balance.

The citizens may enjoy the products of economic activities, but arts, crafts, and trades cut into people's leisure time; they stimulate undesirable appetites and tend to demean a person—especially one engaged in manual labor and retail trade. Hence, the citizens may only engage in agricultural pursuits connected with their farm holdings. They are not allowed to practice a craft or a trade. Such "sordid callings" are reserved for the resident foreigners, who are admitted, if they possess a skill, for a period of twenty years and may possibly be allowed to stay longer as a reward for having rendered some signal service to the community.

The citizens may not possess gold and silver but only token money. Thus they are not permitted to accumulate wealth in the form of full-bodied money. They may travel abroad only with the permission of the government, and if they happen to acquire foreign moneys they must turn them over to the authorities. Credit transactions are discouraged; if they occur, they have to be based strictly on trust because the borrower has no legal duty to pay interest or principal. Prices and quality of goods are controlled by public authorities, as is foreign trade. Only necessities may be imported, and only goods that are not needed exported. An individual's wealth may not fall below a minimum—the family holding, which is inalienable—nor may it exceed a maximum, that is, the holding plus other property up to four times its value. In this manner, extremes of indigence and opulence will be avoided. The citizens will be protected against corruption resulting from commercialization. Economic inequalities will primarily result from differences in thrift and efficiency in the management of the farm rather than from trade or craftsmanship or from speculative windfall gains which enrich some and impoverish others. The very wealthy, Plato argues, cannot at the same time be good men. Care for wealth should rank third and lowest, after care for the soul and for the body.

APPRAISAL OF PLATO'S THOUGHT Those of Plato's ideas that have been discussed in our present context constitute only a small segment of his thought. His writings have cast their spell over countless readers for more than two thousand years. To this day Plato is the most widely read writer in college courses in philosophy in our country, holding a lead of two to one over others. Only a few have been able to resist the magic of his dialogues, which are addressed to perennial problems, besides being pieces of art of the highest order. One of the few was Thomas Jefferson, to whom Plato did not appeal and who marvelled at his persistent reputation, ascribing it to "fashion and authority." Jefferson expressed great satisfaction that "Platonic republicanism" had not obtained favor; otherwise, he said, "we should now have been all living, men, women, and children, pell mell together, like beasts of the field or forest."[8] Indeed, the plea for solidarity is driven to such an extreme by Plato—see particularly the passage of the *Laws* paraphrased on page 19—that its fulfillment would destroy the individual and transform him into a mere limb of the political organism.

Plato's political ideas are pronouncedly authoritarian. Although they may not appeal to a democrat, they should compel a searching of souls of all who are attached to the democratic way of life. As a contemporary author has pointed out, the answer to Plato's apprehensions about the weakness of democracy lies in our lives rather than in arguments.[9]

Imaginative and exalted as Plato's thought is, his ideas about economics label him a child of his time. The city-state of his environment had a population of which slaves constituted one-third, and slaves and foreigners together one-half. Slavery he does not question, and with slaves and resident foreigners available to do the bulk of economic activities, the economic problem did not impress him as a particularly urgent one for the full-fledged citizens of the city-state. It is these with whom he is concerned, not with a wider political community or with universal humanity. As for the citizen himself, his heart is with the aristocratic families of ancient lineage, of whom he himself was a scion, and who at his time were on the defense against new social formations that did not offer him and his kind the opportunity for a career in politics. The fate of his teacher Socrates further compounded his apprehension about the value of democratic institutions.

Plato's rejection of private property, his disdain for commercial activities, his proposals for the breeding of human beings, his "noble lies," his lack of respect for the private sphere of individuals—all these are features that his work shares with a number of modern political ideologies. It makes no sense, however, to label him a Fascist or a Communist. He was no Fascist because in the *Laws* he expressly and at great length rejects the notion that a victorious war is the highest social ideal. Instead, he wants the

---

[8] Letter to John Adams, July 5, 1814, in *The Adams-Jefferson Letters,* ed. Lester J. Cappon (Chapel Hill: The University of North Carolina Press, 1959), Vol. II, 432–34.

[9] William Ebenstein, *Great Political Thinkers,* 3d ed. (New Pork: Rinehart and Company, 1960), p. 12.

community to be organized for external and internal peace, insisting that this, rather than war, is its highest purpose. Furthermore, throughout his work, his appeal invariably is to reason rather than to violence and emotion. He was no Communist because he would have been aghast at the thought of having political power turned over to the self-appointed spokesmen of the toiling masses. The communal life that he proposes is both narrower and wider than that which forms part of the communist program. The communal life required in the *Republic* for the ruling class does not preclude private property of producer goods among the economically active class—the elimination of which stands high on the agenda of communism. Also, with the exception of a few nineteenth-century sects, communism does not reject the institution of monogamic marriage and does not require that women be held in common. Lastly, the motives that make Plato prefer communal property for the ruling class are quite alien to the utilitarian lineage of communism. It is not pleasure that he wishes the ruling class to share but austerity. Basic to him is a dualism of body and soul which deprecates the value of material goods and the strivings for them. This is an attitude profoundly different from the monism of the philosophical materialist who denies the dualism of body and soul and places no opprobrium on the craving for material goods.

Although Plato, as has been seen, does develop a sort of hedonistic calculus whose outward appearance seems to anticipate that of Bentham (see p. 20), he is far from identifying the pleasurable with the good. What at first glance may seem to be a utilitarian argument merely aims at putting up a second line of defense for a conclusion that is reached on other grounds: the good life and right conduct are preferable to the bad life and poor conduct.

Plato does not propose the sharing of goods in order to diffuse pleasure but because he considers private property a burden, conducive to internal strife endangering the equilibrium of society, and likely to bring out the worst of human qualities. In more positive terms, which stand out in the passage of the *Laws* referred to on page 19, he proposes the sharing of material goods and of everything else as a means of integrating society to an extent that he himself considers utopian—fit for a community of gods rather than of men.

CHAPTER 2

FROM ARISTOTLE

TO THE FATHERS

OF THE CHURCH

ARISTOTLE

It is the extreme form of unity or solidarity of the state as it was espoused by Plato that Aristotle (384–322 B.C.), his principal disciple, found fault with. He held that we should not aim at it, even if we could, because it would mean the destruction of the state. The chain of reasoning that leads to this result will be examined shortly.

Aristotle did not have his master's vision and imagination, nor was he as dogmatic and as much inclined to radical proposals for change. He was, however, equipped with a more penetrating analytical power, and at the same time he was more of an empiricist than Plato cared to be. Aristotle's origin was less aristocratic—his father had served as physician to King Philip of Macedon, the father of Alexander the Great, whom Aristotle in turn tutored.

Aristotle's writings cover the whole span of human knowledge. Only a few of them refer specifically to economic matters, and if they do it is in connection with political or moral matters or with an examination of the general art of reasoning. A mastermind himself, but also a disciple of another towering figure, Aristotle often finds fault with the teachings of Plato, and at times his criticism does not seem altogether fair.

Aristotle's contributions to economics do not constitute a coherent system of thought but lie in different fields and are not connected by any one principle of integration. Moreover, his ideas, although always profound, sometimes lack consistence.

Basically Aristotle's inclination is an aristocratic one, as was Plato's, and his belief in the fundamental inequality of human beings is as pronounced as was his master's. Unlike Plato, though, Aristotle does not propose as strict and severe a regulation of society, and his solution of the economic problem places more emphasis on moral improvement than on regimentation. People can be changed by the proper environment, by suitable institutions, and by the power of persuasion, and if they become better men, the economic problem of pervasive scarcity of material goods will be less oppressive. Moreover, as will be seen in connection with Aristotle's defense of private property, a point is made of the greater productivity of the latter as compared with Plato's proposed communal property, a consideration to which Plato would have given little weight.

In Aristotle's thinking change and growth play a more significant role than they do in the rigid categories of Plato. This is illustrated by the central role that he assigns to the concepts of "nature" or "natural." To Aristotle, something is natural or according to nature if it leads to the realization of a thing's final end or purpose. Thus the family, the village community, and the state are all natural in the sense that they are indispensable in enabling man to lead the full and rich life that puts all his capacities to use.

Aristotle's contributions to economics treat of the economic organization of society, communal versus private property, and value and exchange. Most of these ideas are found in his *Politics*, the first treatise on political science; some in his *Ethics*; and a few in his *Topics* and *Rhetoric*, in which he discusses the art of reasoning.

The word *economics* is of Greek origin and literally means "management of the household." It is in this sense that Aristotle uses the word in his *Politics*. The social relations relevant for the management of the household are those between husband and wife, parent and child, and master and slave. Discussing slavery, he admits that some consider the institution a mere convention made by man, contrary to nature and therefore unjust. This opinion he rejects because "from the hour of their birth, some are marked out for subjection, others for rule." The master, he argues, can foresee by the exercise of his mind; the slave can with his body give effect to such foresight. A man is by nature a slave if he participates in reason to the extent of apprehending it in another without possessing it himself, a subtle distinction which borders on hairsplitting. Aristotle admits that not all who happen to be slaves by virtue of the law of the land are slaves by nature, and in such cases it is only power that sanctions slavery. On the other hand, if the relationship is a natural one, master and slave form a community of interest and there is no reason why they should not be friends. Such a thought, whether meant to refer to an ideal or to actual practice, would have been strange to Plato.

THE ART OF ACQUISITION

From the management of the household there is conceptually distinguished the "art of acquisition." The former has the function of using what the latter provides. Different methods of acquisition correspond to different ways of life—altogether five, which may occur in pure form or in combinations: pastoral, farming, fishing, hunting, and, surprisingly enough, piracy. The practice of these arts of acquisition yields what nature has provided for man—true wealth that is limited in quantity by the needs of the household and the city. "Life is action, not production."

Aristotle then goes on to discuss other exercises of the art of acquisition, which are distinguished sharply from the "natural" ones considered earlier. The natural ones are functionally related to the satisfaction of needs and thus yield wealth that is limited in quantity by the purpose it serves—the satisfaction of needs. The unnatural exercises of the art of acquisition, on the other hand, aim at monetary gain, and the wealth they yield is potentially without limits. Why unnatural wealth of this type has no limit is explained by means of two not altogether compatible explanations. It is said that it has no limit because it becomes an end in itself rather than a means to another end—satisfaction of needs—which would set a limit to it. But Aristotle adds that such wealth has no limit because people's desire for material goods has no limit, whereby the acquisition of wealth is turned again into an instrument or means rather than into an end in itself.

USE AND EXCHANGE

In line with this reasoning Aristotle makes the important distinction between use and exchange, which later was to be expanded into the distinction between value in use and value in exchange. The true and proper use of goods, he argues, is the satisfaction of natural wants. A secondary or improper use occurs when goods are exchanged for the sake of monetary gain. Thus, all exchanges for monetary gain are labeled as unnatural. This includes specifically commerce and transportation, the employment of skilled and unskilled labor, and lending at interest. The exchange of money for a promise to pay back the principal with interest is considered the most unnatural one, and this for two reasons. Lending at interest yields gain from currency itself instead of from another exchange transaction which money as a medium of exchange is designed to facilitate. Money begets no offspring; if nevertheless there is one—interest—this is contrary to all nature.

The ideas here developed indicate that Aristotle shared Plato's rejection of commercialism and his low opinion of the qualities of hired labor. It should be pointed out, however, that not all exchange transactions are condemned by Aristotle but only those that aim at monetary gain. Barter is expressly exempt. A more dubious status is assigned to exchange transactions that involve the use of money, but only as a measure of value and not as a source of gain. It would seem that these must be considered natural if the consistence of Aristotle's thought is to be preserved. As will be seen later, he makes a strong point in his *Ethics* of the fact that the city is held together by mutual give-and-take, by each rendering to others something that is equivalent to what he receives from them. In the *Politics* this principle is referred to as "the salvation of states." Moreover, the *Ethics* treats specifically of justice in exchange, and if all exchanges were unnatural it is hard to see how some could have the quality of justice.

Basic to the difficulty is of course the very fineness of the distinction between natural and unnatural acts of acquisition, the criterion of the one being the limited character of human needs and of the other the unlimited character of human wants. Aristotle nowhere makes plain at what point a need turns into a want, and the difficulty can only be resolved by his general appeal for moderation, a moral rather than an economic principle.

MONEY

In conjunction with his discussion of the art of acquisition, Aristotle develops his theory of money. Money, he holds, is not "natural" in the sense of being indispensable for man's self-fulfillment but arises from law or convention. It came into use to serve the requirements of foreign trade, where distance made barter impracticable. First serviceable commodities were used as money, measured by size and weight. Later coins were used, where the stamp marked the value and dispensed with the trouble of weighing. With the use of coin there were established a medium of exchange and a measure of wealth that facilitated accumulation of the unnatural type. Nevertheless, money and wealth must not be confused. Money is not wealth because the replacement of one monetary commodity by another may make the former worthless. Money does not immediately satisfy the necessities of life, and who is rich in coin may be in want of food, as was the fabled King Midas, whose touch turned everything into gold.

In the *Ethics,* the discussion of money is further amplified. Money is a sort of representative of demand, which "holds all goods together." As money exists by convention, its value can be changed or canceled. Thus, while its value is not always constant, it is nevertheless more stable than the value of other goods. Money is further recognized as constituting a claim to goods that can be asserted in the future.

PRIVATE PROPERTY

Although Aristotle frowns on moneymaking and exchange transactions aimed at moneymaking, he nevertheless has left behind a spirited defense of private property, opposing not only its replacement by communal property but also restrictions on the maximum amount of private property to be held, such as had been proposed in Plato's *Laws.* His defense of private property was written as a critique of Plato's ideal *Republic,* in which the rulers are to own property in common.

Aristotle first takes up Plato's goal, the perfect unity of the state, which the abolition of private property for the rulers is to serve as a means. Such a perfect unity, he holds, runs counter to three principles—diversity, reciprocity, and self-sufficiency—and even if it were obtainable, it would mean the ruin of the state. The principle of diversity requires that a state be made up not only of so many men but of different kinds of men. How else would it be possible to live up to the principle of reciprocity, according to which the city is held together by the mutual give-and-take of the citizens, each rendering to the others an amount equivalent to what he receives from them. Moreover, the city must also aim at self-sufficiency, which makes life desirable and replete. This has been interpreted to mean that the city must be a place that is equipped with resources, material and others, adequate to enable the citizens to develop fully their personalities, without reliance upon outside resources. Self-sufficiency is inversely related to unity. An individual is all unity and least self-sufficient; the family has less unity and more self-sufficiency—and this is still more true of the city. If self-sufficiency is to be desired, the lesser degree of unity, according to Aristotle, is preferable to the greater one, because without diversity there can be no self-sufficiency.

Having thus shown that the extreme type of unity in the state is not desirable, Aristotle goes on to scrutinize the means proposed by Plato for the attainment of such unity, that is, communal property for the rulers. He compares communal property with private property and finds the latter superior on five grounds—progress, peace, pleasure, practice and philanthropy.

1. Private property is more highly productive than communal property and will thus make for progress. Goods that are owned by a large number of people receive little care. People are inclined to consider chiefly their own interest and are apt to neglect a duty that they expect others to fulfill. The greatest interest and care are elicited when a person is applying himself to his own property.

2. Communal property is not conducive to social peace because people, when involved in a close partnership, face all sorts of difficulties. They will complain that they have contributed more work and obtained a smaller reward than others who have done little work and received a larger return.

3. Private property gives pleasure to the owner. Nature has implanted in him, as in all other human beings, the love of self, of money, and of property. This feeling is frustrated when all persons "call the same thing mine."

4. There is an appeal to practical experience. If communal property were such a good thing, it would surely have been instituted long ago. The experience of the ages testifies to the widespread use of private property. To renounce it signifies disregard

for such experience. Things are not good just because they are new and untried. Rather the opposite is true, and the social cost of abolishing private property may weigh more heavily than the social cost of private property itself.

5. Private property enables people to practice philanthropy and provides them with training in the practical virtues of temperance and liberality. Instead of compulsion, there is an opportunity for moral goodness to develop among the citizens if the property of each is made to serve the use of all. Part of one's property may be devoted to one's own use, another part may be made available to friends, and still another part may be devoted to the common enjoyment of fellow-citizens. "Friends' goods are goods in common." People must have enough property to be able to practice both temperance and liberality, not only the former, as Plato taught in the *Laws*. Temperance without liberality tends to turn into miserliness, and liberality without temperance tends to turn into luxury.

Aristotle is also opposed to limitations on the amount of private property an individual is allowed to hold, and he describes the practical difficulties that such restrictions would face. In his words, "it is more necessary to limit population than property." The neglect of this matter is a never-failing cause of poverty, and "poverty is the parent of revolution and crime." Even if it were feasible to equip every citizen with a certain amount of property, it would be "more important to equalize people's desires than their properties." This might be accomplished with the help of education, but one that would have to take into account individual differences rather than offer the same program for all. Moreover, economic inequality, although an important cause of social unrest, is not the only such cause. Inequality of office or prestige are important as well, but they operate in a different manner: the masses are incited to revolution by an unequal distribution of property, whereas the elite is so incited by an equal distribution of office or prestige. Thus, whereas poverty may be said to be the parent of revolution and crime, Aristotle points out that both types of social malaise may well be the offspring of other than economic factors. Not all crimes are caused by want, especially not the greatest ones: "men do not become tyrants in order that they may not suffer cold." Hence, the economic factor, although important, is not the only one that operates in history.

It is the use to which property is put that is of the highest moral significance. People always want more and more; their desires are unlimited and are never satisfied. In this situation it is neither the abolition of private property nor its equalization that impress Aristotle as helpful. Instead he proposes a reliance on education and suitable institutions: the better sort of people, who are capable of receiving such training, should be taught to limit their desires and thus refrain from wanting more wealth, whereas those unable to absorb such training should be prevented from obtaining more wealth "by being placed in an inferior position but not subjected to injustice."

Thus, the welfare state of Aristotle, in which people share the use of property with their friends and leave some of it for the common enjoyment of the citizens, is designed to diffuse happiness by making material goods available. Indeed, Aristotle points out that the whole of the political community cannot be said to be happy unless all or most or at least some of its members are happy. It is a welfare state, however, in which some are doomed to be slaves, while others are "placed in an inferior position."

ARISTOTELIAN JUSTICE

The principle of moderation, which we have already mentioned, is indeed a central one in the thought of Aristotle. It underlies Aristotle's concept of virtue. The virtuous man, for example, will practice courage because by doing so his action will hold middle ground between certain excesses: daring on the one side and cowardly restraint on the other. Similarly he will practice liberality rather than be a miser or a spendthrift. The notion of mean or average thus assumes great importance in the *Ethics* of Aristotle, which, as in his other writings, absorbs many of the mathematical teachings of the Pythagoreans and other schools of thought. To these, the world seemed ordered by mathematical relationships which the reality either reflected immediately or at least in a symbolic or analogous fashion. No wonder then that such relationships were found in the analysis of social activities, including economic ones. Since persons, rather than goods, are linked in Aristotle's economic analysis, they will appear side by side with goods in the terms of mathematical formulas, in a manner not acceptable to modern students.

The mean or average in turn is linked with the notion of proportionality, and all these concepts are put to use in the Aristotelian analysis of justice. Various types of justice are distinguished, including distributive justice and corrective justice. Distributive justice deals with the sharing of wealth and honor in society. They are distributed not equally but in proportion to the individual citizen's merit or worth. As an illustration, Aristotle refers to the distribution of expenditures from the public treasury, which are divided in the same proportion that the citizens' contributions to the public fund stand to each other. If A and B are the contributors, and C and D are public expenditures

$$A:B = C:D.$$

This would, according to Aristotle, reflect a "geometric proportion" under which people who are unequal receive unequal shares.

While distributive justice differentiates in this manner, corrective justice equalizes. It relates to the judge's correction of wrongs by means of reducing the gain of one party and the loss of the other. This is accom-

$$A–C = C–B.$$

For example, if merchandise that has been sold for 10 units of money is found faulty and the buyer claims that the price should be reduced to 2 units of money, the arithmetic proportion would be $10–6 = 6–2$. The judge would set the price at 6 units of money, the arithmetic mean of the original price and the one the buyer claims the merchandise is worth.

JUSTICE IN EXCHANGE

It is subsequent to this discussion of distributive and corrective justice that Aristotle turns to an analysis of justice in exchange. The passage in which he expresses his thoughts on this matter is obscure, and to this day opinions are divided whether or not he meant to develop the argument in terms of a third type of justice, referred by some authorities as commutative justice, to cover this case.

Aristotle starts the examination of justice in exchange by introducing the notion of reciprocity, which to the Pythagoreans meant requital or retribution both in the biblical sense of "eye for eye, tooth for tooth" as well as in the sense of "one good turn deserves another." Men seek to return evil for evil, and good for good, the latter constituting the reciprocal element in exchange. Reciprocity of this type is an important element of integration of human society: "it holds the people of the city together."

Aristotle makes it clear that reciprocity in exchange does not imply precisely equal returns but "proportional" ones, and here the difficulties of interpretation begin. Side by side with the Pythagorean meaning of reciprocity there also exists another one, epitomized in the *Elements* of Euclid for example, and it is possibly this notion of reciprocity that underlies the ideas that Aristotle now develops. He says: If A is a builder, B a shoemaker, C a house, and D a shoe, and if the builder and the shoemaker wish to exchange their products, proportionate return will be secured by reciprocal action—each turning over his good to the other—provided there is proportionate equality of the goods before the exchange takes place. This will be so if the number of shoes exchanged for the house corresponds to the ratio of the builder to the shoemaker, or

$$A:B = xD:C.$$

The interpretation of Aristotelian justice in exchange in these terms, that is, in terms of an Euclidian "reciprocal proportion," immediately poses two questions. First, we will want to know how to determine the x in the right side of the equation—the number of shoes that is equivalent to the house. Second, we will want to know the meaning of the left side of the equation, the ratio of builder to shoemaker.

The answer that successive generations of interpreters of Aristotelian thought have given to the first question has reflected the economic thinking of their time. From the Middle Ages until the last quarter of the nineteenth century it was common to derive economic value from labor, that is, goods were believed to exchange in proportion to the amount of labor incorporated in them or commanded by them. Consequently, over this long period of time the usual interpretation placed on the Aristotelian theory of exchange was that the *x* would equate the labor of the shoemaker with that of the builder. In the course of the past hundred years, however, the "labor theory of value" has been discarded, at least by the economists of the Western world, although Marxists still tend to adhere to it and do so at the cost of considerable intellectual difficulties if the adherence is a substantial one rather than a mere matter of words. According to the view that gradually has come to replace the labor theory of value, the economic value of a good is interpreted subjectively and derived from its utility. This turn of economic theory, to which greater attention will be given on a later occasion, has not failed to affect the Aristotelian theory of exchange.

Some contemporary students of the matter would determine the *x* in such a way that it would equate the utility—rather than the labor—of the goods to be exchanged. Such an interpretation would do no less justice to the thought of Aristotle than did the alternative interpretation which has prevailed for so many years. This resilience constitutes a testimony to the breadth and depth of Aristotle's thought which in varying interpretations has retained its relevance over a period spanning two millennia. As for the words used by Aristotle, the interpretation in terms of utility appears to be based upon more solid foundations than the interpretation in terms of labor. As he says, the goods to be exchanged must somehow be equal, and they must therefore be measured by a common yardstick. This yardstick, he continues, is demand or need, "which holds all things together," with money serving as its representative: "if men did not need each other's goods at all, or did not need them equally, there would be either no exchange or not the same exchange."

That valuation in terms of utility was not alien to Aristotle can be documented with the help of a number of passages drawn from his *Politics* as well as from other works such as the *Topics,* which treats of the art of reasoning, and the *Rhetoric.* In *Politics* (1323 b 7) it is said that there may be too much of a useful thing, and if there is, it either will harm or will be of no use to the possessor. Interpreted with some generosity, such thoughts may be said to anticipate the modern notion of diminishing utility. In the *Topics* (117 a and 118 b) a statement may be found to the effect that the desirability of a good should be judged by the gain resulting from adding it to, or the loss resulting from subtracting it from, a group of goods; and this, again with some generosity, may be interpreted as an anticipation of the marginal principle.

The second question—the meaning of the left side of the equation—

has been especially puzzling to many students of Aristotelian thought. What did Aristotle have in mind when he wrote of the ratio of the builder to the shoemaker? To attempt a solution of this puzzle we must remember what we have noted already in connection with Aristotle's examination of distributive justice, that is, that in his equations persons will appear side by side with goods and that to him the relationship between persons is more significant than that between goods. Once xD is equated to C—in terms of labor or in terms of utility—and once the exchange has taken place, the relative position or standing of the two parties remains undisturbed. Moreover, if

$$xD = C, \text{ then}$$
$$A = B, \text{ and}$$
$$A + xD = B + C,$$

which might be interpreted to imply that the exchange of equivalents has made the partners equal in terms of satisfaction.

In the light of his theory of exchange it is not inappropriate to speak of Aristotle as a builder of mathematical models which have become so prominent in modern economic theory. The model that he has constructed applies only to an isolated pair of trading partners, not to a market made up of a larger number of traders. It is expanded, however, beyond the case of barter and covers the exchange of goods for money. If A is a house, B 10 units of money, C a bed; and if

$$A = \tfrac{1}{2} B \text{ and}$$
$$C = \tfrac{1}{10} B, \text{ then}$$

$$A = 5 \text{ units of money} = 5 \ C, \text{ and}$$

"it makes no difference whether it is five beds that exchange for a house, or the money value of five beds."

MONOPOLY

Aristotle's discussion of isolated exchange is expanded further to include the case of monopoly. This is done in the *Politics* in conjunction with his examination of the different types of acquisition. Several case studies are found there, which illustrate the collection of data as one aspect of the Aristotelian method of investigation. He reports a story told of Thales, the well-known philosopher, whom people reproached for his poverty which, they said, proved the uselessness of philosophy. In this situation Thales put his knowledge of metereology to practical use when, anticipating a heavy crop of olives, he rented for almost nothing all available olive presses early in the season. At harvest time his corner of the market for olive presses paid off because he then rented them out "at any rate which he pleased," making a lot of money and showing the world that philosophers can easily be rich if they want to be, but their aim is directed at other things.

The creation of monopolies, Aristotle adds, is practiced not only by private individuals but by the government as well, which when in need of funds may create a monopoly in provisions. No moral blame is expressly attached by Aristotle to this kind of money making. He does not mention operations by rings or trusts, which Greek law forbade.

CYNICISM, STOICISM, AND EPICUREANISM

The Greek thinkers who follow Plato and Aristotle labored in a different environment. By then the Greek city-states had been subdued, and with the fall of the old order new ideas emerged that appealed to a different world. It was a world in ferment, plagued by political disaster and war, whose very coming seemed to prove the inadequacy of the city-state. Hence, on more than one occasion the new thought encompasses and is addressed to a wider community, going beyond the ·narrow confines of Plato's and Aristotle's city-state and embracing all humanity. Cosmopolis, or the world as fatherland, was the watchword of the new thinkers. Many of them had not been natives of the Greek mainland but had come to Greece from the East, from Cyprus and the regions around the Black Sea and those bordering on India. The connection with Eastern thought had also been strengthened by Alexander and the tradition had been set by him. It is thus not surprising that there are strong parallels between the new philosophies, especially their asceticism, and the corresponding thought of Indian Brahmanism which disparages the needs of the body.

The cosmopolitanism of the new philosophies has as its corollary a pronouncedly individualistic tendency. The blend of ethics and politics, so characteristic of Plato's and Aristotle's work, had reflected the solidarity of the city-state. The new philosophies are no longer addressed to citizens bound in narrow solidarity but to individuals unrestrained by such allegiance. At the same time the aristocratic outlook of Plato and Aristotle gives way to an appeal to the poor and dispossessed who would be little impressed by the praise of the country-gentlemanly life.

In time of general and repeated political upheaval, as one Greek city after the other became the victim of destruction, the old threats to individual security and safety—slavery, exile, and the loss of one's possessions—had become the concern, if not the fate, of an ever larger number of people. The appeal of the new philosophies to the poor and dispossessed required a treatment of the economic problem quite different from that suggested by Plato and Aristotle who had faced the problem of scarcity in their own way: Plato by proposing strict regimentation, and Aristotle by elevating moderation to the status of high virtue. What we now find is a much stronger emphasis on restraining the demand for worldly goods, which, if accepted, would in a way resolve the economic problem and bring consolation and comfort to the philosophers' new clients—the poor and dispossessed.

As the Greeks despaired of the gods that had been unable to protect their cities, the hold of their traditional religion relaxed, to give way to the new thought that in many respects resembled a new religion, appealing not only to the reason of a well-educated elite but to the belief of the common man, much more so than had been true of the thought of Plato and Aristotle. In a sense, of course, the founders of Cynicism, Stoicism, and Epicureanism were Platonists or Aristotelians because they were all bark of the tree nurtured by the image of Socrates.

THE CYNICS

The Cynics, who represented the extreme variety of the new thought, adopted the name and the life of dogs. Their founder Diogenes (c.412–323 B.C.), who made a barrel his home, renounced the amenities of civilization and inured himself to hardships of all kinds—all with the aim of attaining in his way "freedom from want," not by producing goods but by extinguishing desire and relinquishing possessions. The Cynics, a modern observer has said, established the standard of the minimum, to demonstrate that life could be lived under the humblest and meanest of conditions.

Cynicism differed in motivation and precept from other movements with which it may have had an outward similarity. For example, Diogenes, in his fiftieth letter, refers to love of money as the cause of all evil. This thought seems all but identical with the observation in 1 Tim. 6:10. But the Cynics' self-denial is in its motivation quite different from that of the New Testament. Christian asceticism aims at salvation in the next world, or at salvation of the soul, whereas that of the Cynics aims at salvation of the body, or at freedom from dependence on worldly goods, to make life livable in this world.

Cynicism has been referred to as a religion of the proletariat, but again the parallel is deceptive. A religion of the proletariat in the modern sense of the word would preach revolution and insist on a drastic change in social institutions, which the Cynics did not do. When Diogenes adopted as his motto the maxim "debase the currency," this was meant to suggest a revaluation of all values rather than an upheaval of institutions. He preached anarchy rather than the rule of the proletariat.

THE STOICS

Stoicism, so called because its founder Zeno's (c.336–c.264 B.C.) place of lectures was the stoa or painted porch at Athens, was originally an offspring of Cynicism, but it eventually adapted itself to become the basis for the outlook on life of many of the high and mighty in the Roman Empire. This accounts for a number of ambiguities and inconsistencies in Stoic doctrine and practice. The Stoics taught that there is only one good, virtue, and that its practice, and its practice alone, ensures happiness. Virtue to them meant a conduct of life that was free of emotions and passions. By rejecting emotions and passions, an individual would attain a serenity of mind that external events could not disturb. Pleasure was neither a good nor the permissible end of an action but at most given recognition as the result of an action that the wise man might make use of without being dependent upon it.

Although this doctrine might imply an attitude of disdain for worldly goods, Stoicism, during its long career, came to accept the acquisition and care of property that might aid the wise in being virtuous. Chrysippus (280–207 B.C.), the second founder of Stoicism, had himself laid the foundation for the latitudinarian view by stating that "the wise man will turn three somersaults for an adequate fee." To all the new philosophers slavery appeared in a new and dubious light, but Chrysippus had a "stoic" attitude to inequality of status and position: "Nothing," he said, "can prevent some seats in the theatre from being better than others."

The stoic doctrine gave express approval to earnings from teaching, from serving the wealthy, and from government employment. Some stoic philosophers, however, went further and developed a moral casuistry that contained strange doctrines, making permissible the circulation of debased money, the sale of merchandise with concealed defects, and the jettisoning of slaves during times of food shortage when their maintenance would constitute too high an expense.

NATURAL LAW *Gravitas* was a characteristic that the Stoics had in common with the Roman jurists. Indeed, many of the latter felt attracted by the stoic doctrine. It was thus through Roman law that some contributions of the stoic philosophy were transmitted to posterity. One of these was the concept of a natural law, interpreted to embody the all-pervasive reason that governs the world and to reflect the nature of things. Natural law came to be used as a touchstone to test the validity of man-made, positive law, sometimes to reject it but more often to confirm it. The concept has survived to this day in jurisprudence and ethics, especially in those civilizations that are attached to the ideal of a universal humanity. Countries where the ideal of a romantic nationalism has been stronger, such as was true of the German tradition, have been inclined to disregard natural law. The United States Declaration of Independence, on the other hand, refers expressly to "the Laws of Nature and of Nature's God."

ROMAN JURISPRUDENCE The natural law that the Stoics developed was a common one in the sense of applying to all humanity. Thus the concept had a further significance in providing the foundation for a law of nations. It is indeed the work of the Roman jurists, upon whom stoic influence was so pronounced, that constitutes virtually the only Roman contribution to social thought in the wider sense. As the Romans were doers rather than thinkers, their contribution to economic speculation did not go beyond a few remarks about the advantages of a simple life, of agricultural pursuits, and of free as compared with slave labor. Roman law, on the other hand, was of such excellence that to this day it has been an important source of inspiration to the draftsmen of statutes in the "civil law" countries of continental Europe and Latin America. Of lesser albeit by no means negligible importance has been its influence on the "common law" of the English-speaking countries. For example, the origin of the idea embodied in Sections 9 and 10 of Article I of the Constitution of the United States, which forbid retroactive legislation, might be sought in the Roman principle *nulla poena sine lege*—"no penalty without law." Another example, overwhelmingly important in modern economic life, is the doctrine of the corporation, which requires a great deal of legal sophistication of which the Roman jurists were eminently capable. Under this doctrine the corporate assets are separated from the assets of the owners of the corporation, and while the owners change, the corporation remains the same. This principle can be traced back to Roman law, which in this matter as in others was inspired by stoic teachings, in this case relating to the unity of the whole in the face of diversity and change of its constituent parts.

Both civil and common law countries have felt the effect of the highly developed Roman law of property and of contract, the mainstay of all legal systems in the Western world. Compared with today's practice, which reflects the vanishing individualism and the growth of social restraints, Roman law was more nearly absolute in its protection of the property owner and of his right to use the property as he saw fit, as it also was in upholding freedom of contract. Some Roman jurists went so far as to interpret property, or at least some property, as instituted by natural law, a view that was restated by the English lawyer Bracton in the thirteenth century, which has helped to maintain the right of the property owner vis-à-vis the government. In a different garb, and still more potently, the idea recurs in the seventeenth century when John Locke, who as a young teacher in Oxford had led discussions on the law of nature, declared the protection of property to be the principal purpose of government. However, to Locke property was much more than a narrowly economic category. Rather it approximated what Jefferson later was to call inherent and inalienable rights: life, liberty, and the pursuit of happiness.

Another intellectual connection with the Stoics can be seen in the development of the commercial law, or law merchant, which by its nature must be uniform and worldwide and which the Romans founded on the law of nature evidenced by commercial usage. Furthermore, whenever modern legal provisions contain references to reasonableness—as they often do in the form, for example, of reasonable price, reasonable value, reasonable man—they echo an idea for which the Stoics have set the precedent.

EPICURUS

It is not, however, in the teachings of the Stoics but in those of Epicurus that the manner in which the schools of philosophy considered here approached the economic problem has found its most concise and most emphatic expression. In a letter to a pupil, Epicurus suggests: "If you wish to make a person wealthy, do not give him more money, but diminish his desire." Hence, like the Cynics and Stoics, Epicurus proposes to resolve the economic problem by reducing the demand for goods rather than by increasing their supply.

As the Epicureans saw it, peace and safety were the keys to the happy life, in which their master instructed them behind the walls of his garden. He advised his followers to avoid any ostentatious display of wealth, to withdraw from active participation in politics, and to lead a retired life, cultivating the pleasures of friendship. While this way of life would secure them freedom from fear, they would enjoy freedom from want by habituating themselves to a simple mode of life, evaluating every desire in the light of this criterion :"What will be the result for me if the desire is fulfilled, and what if it is not?" Desires are divided into three kinds. The basic desires are natural and necessary, others are natural but not necessary, and still others are neither natural nor necessary. Only the necessary desires and those natural ones that are not harmful deserve gratification. People were to attain happiness by emancipating themselves from the drift into a way of life uninformed by reason, self-discipline, and the careful weighing of the advantages and disadvantages of an action.

It is not desire that is unlimited, Epicurus holds. Rather, he argues, people's minds are captives of the erroneous notion that an unlimited quantity of goods is required to satisfy their wants. He does not advise his followers to make do with little under all circumstances. Instead he preaches contentment with little if there is no plenty. Epicurus was a pragmatist in that he taught people to condition their minds, and in the absence of control over external things to seek "adjustment" by controlling their own thought.

As Epicurus did not believe in immortality, he taught that life was the highest good and pleasure the aim of life. He considered pleasure a normal and natural component of life, equivalent in positive terms to health of mind and body, and in negative terms to absence of pain. Basic to his argument is a calculus of pleasure and pain anticipating that of Bentham two thousand years later.

By elevating pleasure to the aim of life for all humanity, Epicurus's philosophy differs sharply from the more austere ideas of Plato and Aristotle. These also assign to the government more power than Epicurus would be inclined to grant it, and espouse a much more active participation in political life than is compatible with the Epicurean ideal of safety. Epicurus's philosophy differs from that of the Cynics in that the type of man he envisages is sociable, courteous, and watchful of his good reputation. Although affinities are not missing between stoic and Epicurean thought, there are also sharp contrasts. The Stoics deprecated the search for pleasure. They rejected emotions altogether, and their ideal was the cold and severe *gravitas* of the Roman statesman rather than the tranquillity of a life that withdraws from public affairs.

Epicureanism gained a following in Rome, especially among writers and intellectuals. Lucretius, the Roman poet, propagated the doctrine in his work *De Rerum Natura*—"On the Nature of Things." Epicurus taught a sort of deism affirming the existence of gods who were unconcerned about the affairs of men and need not be feared, and because of this view the doctrine was often on the defensive. Lucretius's book was considered extremely controversial over a long period and at one time was accused of being responsible for an earthquake. It was not translated into English until 1675; an Italian translation was printed as late as 1797, and a Spanish one in 1892.

THE FALL OF ROME AND THE RISE OF CHRISTIANITY

Although all roads lead to Rome and some lead from there to us in language and law, the Roman legacy has been a meager one in the realm of ideas. Roman history was studded with economic problems, but no thought was given to speculation about economics. Education was strictly literary and rhetorical, and science had no place in the curriculum. Indeed, Rome produced no major scientist, and the scientific advances that had been made by the Greeks were in no way continued by the Romans. The Roman character was a peculiarly paradoxical one in that it combined a stern, warlike, and cruel disposition, which made for activism, with an obsessive belief in the forces of fate and fortune.

Initially Rome was a city-state, vying with other city-states for power in the Italian peninsula. Step by step, and by means of unrelenting warfare, Rome extended its dominion to cover first the whole of Italy and in the end the vast reaches of the Roman Empire. Agrarian struggles were a frequent occurrence in the Roman Republic, which came to an end with the principate of the emperor Augustus. The agrarian reform of the Gracchi brothers in the 130s and 120s B.C., who proposed to distribute farm land among smallholders, coped with problems that were not essentially different from those that Solon and Pisistratus had attempted to resolve four centuries earlier in Athens. As there were Greeks among the mentors of the older Gracchus, the parallelism of the solution may have been more than a mere accident. In the realm of ideas Greek influence was paramount in Rome, and her best minds were stocked with Greek thought.

When the inroads into the peasant holdings by the owners of great estates continued, these were operated at first as plantations by gangs of slaves. But since the landlords were absentees who wanted to be freed of personal care and attention to their estates, these—the *latifundia*—gradually came to be parceled out among tenant farmers recruited from the peasantry and from freedmen. The management that they adopted may have constituted a throwback to older and less efficient methods of cultivation than those practiced on the large plantations.

Territorial expansion played a singular role in Roman economic history. It widened the market, but at the same time it gave rise to new centers of production that competed with the old ones. In this manner the expansion of the Empire placed Italian agriculture in a precarious position, as it did Italian commerce and industry. Italy had attained great prominence as a producer and exporter of wine and olive oil, but the rise of wine and olive oil production in the provinces became responsible for overproduction in Italy. At the close of the first century A.D. the emperor Domitian attempted to salvage Italian viniculture by ordering the destruction of half of the existing vineyards and prohibiting the planting of new ones.

As civilization and urbanization spread over the conquered provinces, Italy lost her leading position in commerce and industry, and these, unlike viniculture, remained unprotected. Orders for military supplies, always of signal importance, were apt to be placed in the provinces close to the place of delivery rather than in distant Italy. Nevertheless industry continued to flourish as long as the Empire expanded and new markets developed. After the reign of Hadrian (117–138 A.D.) territorial expansion came to a standstill, and Italian producers for the market from then on had to rely on the purchasing power of the few relatively well-to-do people in the cities and of the ever-increasing numbers of urban and rural paupers.

The fall of the Roman Empire, one of the greatest events in the history of the world, was accompanied by grave economic disorders. Wars and invasions destroyed property and absorbed manpower. Taxes became more and more ruinous and were supplemented by requisitions and exactions in kind, forced services and forced labor that were so burdensome that many people tried to escape them by fleeing to the woods and deserts. The currency was debased and depreciated time and again, and inflation, first chronic, eventually became galloping. In Egypt, for example, for which suitable data exist, the price of wheat nearly tripled between the first and third centuries A.D., and at the end of the third century it was over a hundred thousand times what it had been two to three hundred years earlier. These disorders reflected the economic strain to which constant warfare exposed the Roman Empire, and constant warfare had become necessary not to expand but to hold on to its territories and avert invasions by the barbarians. In the end the Empire fell under the rule of competing military chieftains whose neglect of the rights and privileges of the individual in the face of the ostensible interest of the state did much to paralyze economic initiative and effort. The city elites were gradually absorbed by the masses, and in this process no group was left to fulfill the function of assimilating and civilizing the proletarians within and the barbarians without.

Under these conditions it is less surprising that the Roman Empire fell than that it survived as long as it did. To this day it has remained a matter of controversy among historians to what extent the various factors that accompanied the decline were symptoms or causes. Some authorities make much of the exhaustion of the soil, others of the decline of population in Italy, others of the effects of slavery. Next to these economic factors political ones are brought into play—the leveling effects of a worldwide state that stifled the civilizing capacities of the Greek city-states, and the failure of the Roman Empire to arrange for the participation of the broad masses of the population in its political life. Still other writers stress the biological factor and claim that the Roman Empire was destroyed by a perverse process of natural selection in which the best elements perished in warfare and civil strife, or by race suicide due to the failure of these elements to reproduce, or by miscegenation with alien races, or by lead poisoning. All these interpretations have obvious weaknesses.

A more profound interpretation of the fall of Rome, it seems, would emphasize the specific nature and limitations of its civilizing genius, which reached its fullest bloom in politics rather than in spiritual, cultural, or economic matters. It had established law and order within the confines of the Empire but exerted little or no civilizing influence on the barbarian tribes that roamed beyond its borders. Apart from the call for military surrender it had no message to offer them. Hence, the blessings of peace and prosperity that Augustus had brought to the Empire were to last for only a few centuries. Once the barbarian tribes began to move and violate the territorial integrity of Rome, profound disturbances ensued and the Empire died slowly. It took a new message to civilize the invaders and to bring them into the borders of a universal community. This new message was given by Christianity, the rise of which overlaps the decline of the Roman Empire. The new civilization that took the place of the Roman one and was soon to rally millions of people was inspired by an idea that was new, different from both the wisdom of the Greeks and the law of the Romans: the gospel of love.

CHRISTIAN TEACHING

Christianity constituted an organic growth in an environment that had become extremely favorable to the spread of its idea. Several factors account for this. Many Romans had been attracted to the mystery religions that flourished in the Eastern part of the Empire—Mithraism, Syrian sun worship, and the like. Some of these religions, especially the Semitic ones, had pronouncedly monotheistic tendencies. The westward spread of these ideas as well as the intermingling of cultures and races was promoted by a number of emperors who were of Semitic origin. Christianity also shared a number of features with the cynic, stoic, and Epicurean philosophies that were to become so prominent in Rome. The cynic ideals of poverty and asceticism, the Stoics' conception of natural law and their sharp distinction between virtue and vice, Epicurus's love of mankind—all found affinity, if not fulfillment, in Christian teachings.

In the sayings of Jesus no weight is attached to economic considerations because there is no need to care for production and material welfare in the Kingdom of God, whose coming is imminent. Jesus' followers relinquish their occupations and possessions (Matt. 4:18–22). When the Twelve are sent out to preach, they are not allowed to carry money (Matt. 10:9). The wealthy young man who inquires about the path to perfection is told to sell his property and give the money to the poor (Matt. 19:21; Mark 10:21; and Luke 18:22).

Indifference to economic considerations may also be found in the parable of the laborers in the vineyard, who are paid the same wage regardless of hours of work (Matt. 20:10) as well as in Jesus' admonition of Martha, who instead of listening to his teaching as does her sister Mary is absorbed in work (Luke 10:38 ff.). Indeed, not indifference to economic considerations but hostility and disapproval of wealth and the search for wealth is expressed in the Sermon on the Mount. Treasure is not to be stored up on earth but in heaven (Matt. 6:19–20). There is no need to care for life's necessities; the Lord maintains the birds of the air and the lilies of the field (Matt. 6:25–34). And, most forcefully: "No one can serve two masters. You cannot serve God and Mammon" (Matthew 6:24). The poor and the hungry are blessed, but evil will fall on the rich and on those who are full now (Luke 6:20–25). In the parable of the rich man and Lazarus, the latter after his death is carried to Abraham's bosom whereas the rich man is tormented in Hades (Luke 16:19–31). The same thought may be found in Jesus' saying: "How hard it is for the wealthy to enter the Kingdom of God! It is easier for a camel to go through the eye of a needle than for a rich man to enter the Kingdom of God" (Mark 10:23–31).

An especially passionate condemnation of the rich may be found in the Epistle of James.

> "If a man with gold rings and in fine clothing comes into your synagogue, and a poor man in shabby clothing also comes in, and you pay attention to the one who wears the fine clothing and say, 'Have a seat here, please,' while you say to the poor man, 'Stand there,' or, 'Sit at my feet,' have you not made distinctions among yourselves, and become judges with evil thoughts? Listen, my beloved brethren. Has not God chosen those who are poor in the world to be rich in faith and heirs of the kingdom which he has promised to those who love him? But you have dishonored the poor man. Is it not the rich who oppress you? Is it not they who drag you into court? Is it not they who blaspheme that honorable name by which you are called?" (James 2:2–7).
>
> "Come now, you who say, 'Today or tomorrow we will go into such and such a town and spend a year there and trade and get gain'; whereas you do not know about tomorrow. What is your life? For you are mist that appears for a little time and then vanishes. Instead you ought to say, 'If the Lord wills, we shall live and we shall do this or that.' As it is, you boast in your arrogance. All such boasting is evil. Whoever knows what is right to do and fails to do it, for him it is sin.
>
> "Come now, you rich, weep and howl for the miseries that are coming upon you. Your riches have rotted and your garments are moth-eaten. Your gold and silver have rusted, and their rust

will be evidence against you and will eat your flesh like fire. You have laid up treasure for the last days. Behold, the wages of the laborers who mowed your fields, which you kept back by fraud, cry out; and the cries of the harvesters have reached the ears of the Lord of hosts. You have lived on the earth in luxury and in pleasure; you have fattened your hearts in a day of slaughter. You have condemned, you have killed the righteous man; he does not resist you" (James 4:13–5:6).

Several passages in the Acts of the Apostles testify to the acceptance that the first Christians gave to Jesus' advice to the rich young man. "All who believed were together and had all things in common; and they sold their possessions and goods and distributed them to all, as any had need" (Acts 2:44–45). "The company of the believers were of one heart and soul, and no one said that any of the things which he possessed was his own, but they had everything in common. . . . There was not a needy person among them, for those who had lands or houses sold them and laid the proceeds at the apostles' feet; and distribution was made to each as any had need" (Acts 4:32; 34–35). Instant punishment was meted out to Ananias and Sapphira, who did not lay the whole price of their possession at the apostles' feet but kept back part of it (Acts 5:1–11).

As time passed, Christianity spread among different peoples and among different classes of society. The coming of the Kingdom of God gradually appeared less close at hand than it had to Jesus' original disciples. The life in this world had to be lived and arrangements had to be made to accommodate the earthly career of the faithful with the social and economic institutions of their environment. Slavery, property, and the coexistence of the rich and the poor were part of these institutions. Hence, in the teaching of Paul, the great missionary apostle, the need for productive activity is recognized. He stresses more than once the duty to do work and rebukes idleness. "If a man will not work, he shall not eat." The people are exhorted to do their work in quietness and to earn their own living (2 Thess. 3:10–12), with their hands, so that they may command the respect of outsiders and be dependent on no one (1 Thess. 4:11–12). The rich are not condemned unconditionally but are urged to do good (1 Tim. 6:17–19). Slaves are to render faithful service to their masters (1 Tim. 6:1 ff.), and these are to accord fair treatment to their slaves (Eph. 6:5–9).

CLEMENT OF ALEXANDRIA

Toward the end of the first century, a few decades after the death of Paul, as highly placed a man as the Roman consul Titus Flavius, a cousin of the emperor Domitian, embraced the new faith. The attitude to economic status and property and the question of the salvation of the rich became issues that challenged the thought of eminent men. One of these was Clement of Alexandria, a theologian steeped in the philosophic tradition of his native Athens, who lived toward the end of the second century in a community that was known for its commercial wealth. One of Clement's sermons, or pamphlets, uses as a text the passage in Mark 10:21 in which Jesus counsels the rich young man to sell all his property and give the money to the poor. In this sermon, which usually is referred to by its Latin title *Quis Dives Salvetur?*—"Who Is the Rich Man That May Be Saved?"—Clement establishes the Christian duty to free the minds of the rich from futile despair and to show them the way to their salvation. Scripture, Clement holds, must be interpreted allegorically rather than literally. If the rich young man is advised to sell all his belongings, this means that he is to cast from his mind all attachment to wealth and all longing for it. What Jesus counsels is not an external act but a purging of the soul. In itself, there is no special merit in being poor. If all were to renounce wealth, it would be impossible to practice the virtues of liberality and charity—an argument that echoes a similar idea of Aristotle's. Wealth is designated by Clement as a gift of God, furnished to promote human welfare. It is a tool, and as such can be used rightly or wrongly. To foster the right use of wealth, the rich should seek guidance from a man of God. These thoughts, especially the emphasis on the use of property as a criterion of its goodness, mark a doctrinal attitude that was to attain great prominence in the centuries to come. In a broader sense, the imposition of duties—to God and to various spiritual and temporal lords—upon those who held the right to the use of a good was to become a salient feature of the medieval economic system.

THE FATHERS OF THE CHURCH

To be sure, wealth as well as private property was at times denounced in strong terms by some Fathers of the Church. These denunciations questioned the righteous origin of wealth, and they were apt to characterize private property as a deviation from the economy of God, which provides for communal sharing. Thus John Chrysostom (c.347–407), the greatest of the Greek Fathers, praised the economy of God, which made certain goods common to be shared equally by men as brothers. Private property, arising from the defective nature of man, is responsible for much contention and strife. As to wealth, it is questionable whether it can be acquired without injustice either on the part of the owner or of those from whom he inherited it. The rich can redeem themselves only by distributing their property; if they retain it, they harm themselves and others. Basil (c.330–379), whose monastic rules made him a spiritual ancestor of Benedict, underlined the egalitarian ideal: "whoever loves his neighbor as himself, will possess no more than his neighbor."

Although it is not quite clear whether in John Chrysostom's economy of God all goods or only certain goods are held in common, Ambrose (c.339–397), whose preaching inspired the conversion of Augustine, rejected altogether the division of goods into public and private. Nature, he held, gives all goods in common to all men. Usurpation is responsible for the private right. Hence, charity is not a gift but may be claimed as a matter of right. The poor receive what really is their own; the rich discharge a debt. Jerome (c.347–c.419) shared the view of John Chrysostom that the rich man is either unjust himself or the heir of an unjust person. To Jerome all wealth appeared tainted with iniquity: one man's gain, he insisted, is bound to be another man's loss.

Augustine (354–430) declared wealth to be a gift of God and a good, but neither the highest nor a great one. Private property he considered responsible for various evils—dissension, war, injustice. Those who can, he said, should abstain from it, but those who cannot should at least abstain from the love of property.

Although much fault was found with wealth and private property, the conclusion drawn did not ordinarily propose the abolition of these institutions in an imperfect world. Such counsel was given only to those who sought perfection and would lead a life devoid of property under monastic rule. For the multitude of ordinary people, the conclusion drawn was not the institution of communal property but the need for charitable giving. On this the Fathers insisted in the strongest terms. Broadly speaking, doctrine and practice came into line with the thought of Clement of Alexandria. In the 340s a synod held in Gangra (Kiangri) of Paphlagonia condemned as erroneous the view that those of the faithful who are wealthy but fail to relinquish all their wealth have no hope for salvation.

Private property was tolerated but it was by no means sacrosanct. Augustine, in a reply to heretics who had complained about the confiscation of their property by the emperor, made it quite clear that he considered private property strictly a creation of the state, of human right rather than of divine right, and thus not exempt from forfeiture. "For by divine right," he said, " 'The Earth is the Lord's, and the fullness thereof.' The poor and the rich God made of one clay; the same earth supports alike the poor and the rich. By human right, however, one says, this estate is mine, this house is mine, this servant is mine. By human right, therefore, is by right of the emperors. Why so? Because God has distributed to mankind these very human rights through the emperors and kings of the world." The legitimacy of private property in the face of the natural-law doctrine of communal property was a problem with which the canonists had to wrestle during the Middle Ages until it was resolved by Saint Thomas Aquinas in the thirteenth century.

The toleration of private property had as its corollary also the recognition of the worth of certain economic activities. At first glance Jerome's statement that one man's gain is another man's loss might seem to imply the notion that all private economic interests are irreconcilably opposed to each other and that exchange transactions benefit just one rather than both parties. Not all economic activities, however, were considered as deserving censure. The worth and dignity of human labor was stressed by several Fathers of the Church. There are intimations even of the thought—to become so prominent in the writings of Adam Smith almost fifteen hundred years later—that economic activities pursued for the sake of private gain may turn out to the benefit of society. John Chrysostom, in spite of his denunciations of wealth, makes this point when he teaches that work for one's own advantage and for the benefit of others are so closely linked that no worker can earn his pay without producing something that satisfies the wants of others. The exchange economy thus conforms to God's plan in which men are connected with one another by their needs. That is why countries have been given different natural endowments, why they are linked by the ocean, and why people have been brought together in cities. Mutual interdependence creates society, and economic life, like all human life, is based on reciprocal giving and receiving.

In this light even the trader, though often depicted as stimulated by greed and tempted to the employment of fraud, could redeem himself. Augustine, in sentences that were frequently quoted in the centuries to come, gave approval to a distinction between the trader and his trade. Trade in itself, for example when it involved the transportation of goods, might be beneficial to society and deserving of a reward. It is only the iniquity of the trader by which the profession might become tainted, not by a defect inherent in itself. If such iniquity is absent, trade might 'well be honorable.

Thoughts such as these indicate a penetrating view of a world that had achieved a high degree of economic development, having passed from earlier stages to a full-fledged exchange economy. To some Fathers of the Church the world indeed seemed old and fully developed. Cyprian (c.200–258), the bishop of Carthage, a region that had seen civilizations come and go, thought the world overpopulated and considered overpopulation a cause of economic distress. "Be fruitful and multiply," the demand made in Gen. 2:28, had been addressed to a world that was young and sparsely populated. For his own world, mature and overpopulated, Cyprian endorsed the counsel of chastity given in Matt. 19:12.

CHAPTER 3

MEDIEVAL

ECONOMIC

THOUGHT

The Practice of Charity

and the Avoidance of Sin

The end of the ancient world marks the beginning of the Middle Ages, which in turn were to last until the Renaissance opened up the modern era in history, that is, broadly speaking, until the year 1500. But when exactly did the ancient world come to an end? This is a question about which well-informed people have different views. The selection of landmarks to signal the end of one epoch and the beginning of another often involves an element of discretion. Lines are blurred as one period runs into the other. History is like a house that has many windows, and the year chosen as the boundary line will depend upon the view of the observer.

To some the Middle Ages begin with the year 256 with the first onslaught of the German invaders on Rome. Others prefer the year 284, marking as it does the accession of the emperor Diocletian who prepared the ground for the division of the empire into the East and the West. Again others stress the importance of the year 476 when violent death came to the last Roman emperor and the rule of Rome in the West was brought to an end. It will forever be a matter of controversy which of these events constitutes the most complete break of the continuity of history. In our own time doubt has been cast upon the very concept of the Middle Ages as a link to span the vast length of time that lies between the ancient and modern periods of history. The gifted Belgian historian Henri Pirenne (1862–1935) denied that the continuity of Roman civilization was completely broken by the German invasions. He insisted that town life, while languishing, nevertheless continued up until the time of the Moslem invasions, which began in the eighth century and all but closed the Mediterranean to the West. According to Pirenne it was the Moslem rather than the Germanic conquest that marked the end of the ancient world. Although Pirenne's thesis has been the subject of searching criticism by his fellow-historians, who point out that trade in the Mediterranean was never completely interrupted, his view is apt to underline the momentous change in the locus and focus of ancient and medieval civilizations, the northward move from the sunny lands around the Mediterranean to the misty forests that stretched from the Alps to the Atlantic.

FEUDALISM

The continued struggle with invaders (to those already mentioned might be added the Northmen, or Vikings, and the Hungarians) accounts for the warlike character of early medieval civilization. After the earlier invaders had consolidated their rule in western and central Europe and after their conversion to Christianity had given them a measure of civilization that Rome had failed to bring them, they had to cope with the seemingly never-ending assaults of newcomers. In these struggles a premium came to be placed on cavalry as the decisive element in warfare, and this development in turn is closely linked with the rise of feudalism. Coming probably from China, the stirrup made its appearance in the West some time in the eighth century, after which mounted shock troops became an indispensable factor in war. This type of combat was costly. To equip only one mounted man required an outlay equivalent to that for about twenty oxen, or the farm equipment of some ten peasant holders. Moreover, substantial expenditure was again incurred in the maintenance and replacement of horses for knight and squire.

Under the system of feudalism, the prevailing social order in Western Europe from the time of Charlemagne until the rise of the national state, it was possible to "finance" the new type of warfare by imposing the duty of rendering military and other suitable services upon the holders of land, which at that time constituted the most important form of wealth. Under feudalism the ownership of land was not absolute and divorced of duties as it had been in Rome and as it was to become again in modern times. Instead, and the picture given here is somewhat simplified and idealized, the original title to land was held by the king, the lord paramount. He then donated it in large parcels to his foremost noblemen, the tenants-in-chief, who in turn could appoint subtenants. The tenants-in-chief and the subtenants did not acquire full property rights but merely a right to the use of the land, which tended to become hereditary. Their right was conditional upon the rendering of services of different kinds, military, personal, or labor services, or deliveries of produce.

The feudal system thus provided institutions that delivered armed combat troops and furnished their maintenance and replacement. But feudal property was not only subject to duties. It was also the basis of political power. Numerous governmental functions were vested in the feudal lords, an arrangement that stemmed from the weakness of the central authorities in a time of poor communications and general insecurity. Various judicial and administrative functions were viewed as part of the nobleman's endowment with land, and in practice he often constituted the highest authority in his territory. Thus in the medieval state great leeway was given to the centrifugal powers within society, and it was only the modern nation state that tamed these powers.

THE MANOR

Economically the feudal holding, especially in Northern Europe, was often organized in the form of the manor, an agricultural estate that tended toward self-sufficiency and was worked by various types of labor, villeins and serfs, who were attached to the land rather than to the person of the owner. These were allowed to have plots of their own, in return for which they rendered labor services to the lord's demesne. Although important changes occurred in the methods of agricultural production, the manorial system itself survived the end of the Middle Ages in a number of continental countries and was not dismantled in France until the eighteenth or in Prussia and Russia until the nineteenth century. In England the manorial system disintegrated at an earlier time under the influence of the commercialization of agriculture, which occurred between 1300 and 1500 and brought in its wake large farm holdings operated by tenants and laborers. One aspect of this so-called agrarian revolution was the enclosure movement, that is, the fencing or otherwise setting apart of former commonly used land for purposes of sheep raising or more intensive cultivation, a movement that had started in the twelfth century. It increased agricultural productivity and made available for sale in the market a larger amount than the manor had been able to produce. But it was a controversial matter because it brought great hardship to those who had been dependent on the use of the common land for their living and found themselves displaced by sheep—"man-eating" sheep as they were called.

CHANGES IN AGRICULTURAL TECHNIQUES

The link between changes in the art of war and the rise of feudalism is paralleled by changes in agricultural techniques and the spread of the manor. In Roman times, and in the south of Europe, the land had been worked with a scratch plough. Now that civilization had moved north and rich alluvial soils had been wrought from the dense forests, the heavy, wheeled plough came into use. It was pulled by two yokes of four oxen each, too many for an isolated peasant to have on hand but available within the larger organization of the manor.

As time went on, the plough team of oxen was replaced by draft horses, with beneficial effects on agricultural productivity. The use of horses was supported by innovations such as the nailed horseshoe, which appeared in the West around the year 900 in the wake of the modern harness. Two hundred years later plough horses had become common in northern Europe. They were heavy steeds, the result of breeding that had preceded that of cattle. With the horse's greater speed and power of endurance, as much land could be worked with one horse as with a pair of oxen.

Along with the harness and the nailed horseshoe went improvements in transportation and communication that provided quicker service at lower cost. Whereas in Roman times the overland haulage of bulky goods had been responsible for the doubling of their price after one hundred miles, the movement of grain in the thirteenth century over the same distance raised the price by only 30 percent. The market was thus widened, and agricultural supplies could be made available at distant places not accessible by means of water transportation. Improvements also occurred in the design of the primitive two-wheel vehicles, and by the middle of the thirteenth century they were well on their way to being replaced by four-wheelers.

In addition to the heavy plough and the draft horse, agricultural productivity was also raised by the introduction in the late eighth century of the three-field system of crop rotation, with one field devoted to winter crops, one to spring crops, and the third lying fallow each year. This system proved far superior to the two-field rotation common around the Mediterranean in Roman times. It extended the size of the area that a peasant could handle by an estimated one-eighth and added as much as 50 percent to his output. Moreover, the spring planting supplied oats for horses as well as legumes—peas—for man, and thereby made possible an improvement in the quality of the human diet that was to have far-reaching effects. Medieval man acquired new vigor, and his newly found stamina supported population growth, urbanization, and an all-around rise in industrial and commercial activities that brought the Middle Ages to their highest flowering in the thirteenth century. As has been said, "In the full sense of the vernacular, the Middle Ages, from the tenth century onward, were full of beans."

The horse not only made the peasant a more efficient producer and marketeer but also put an end to rural isolation in a number of regions. As commuting became feasible, the farm home no longer needed to be in the immediate vicinity of the fields. Beginning in the eleventh century we find a "balling" of peasants in the nearby villages and towns, from which they went to work in the more distantly located fields, a development that has its counterpart in ancient Greece as well as in modern times and that could only lift the level of civilization.

THE GUILD SYSTEM

As markets widened and towns grew, trading activities, which had earlier taken place only intermittently at periodically held markets and fairs, became a more regular and conspicuous feature of the citizens' daily life.

The household or village economy gave way to that of the towns, with each town aiming at a degree of self-sufficiency and isolation from the economy of other towns by means of local tariffs and regulations. The right to carry on trade was restricted to the members of the town's merchant guild, whereas craft guilds, made up of apprentices, journeymen, and masters, regulated in great detail the production and marketing of the town's workshops. The medieval craft guild has features in common with the modern labor union but there were important differences as well. The former was a strictly local institution; the typical labor union is a national organization. Membership in the craft guild was restricted to skilled artisans; contemporary industrial unions include employees of all grades of skill, including the unskilled. The medieval guild comprised the masters, employer-entrepreneurs such as can be found as members in only a very few modern labor organizations. The medieval guild was a semipublic body with responsibilities for the protection also of the consuming public. Membership in the craft guild was compulsory for any one who wanted to ply his trade; modern unions claim to be voluntary associations. To the extent to which in practice they have lost this voluntary character they have come to resemble more closely the medieval guilds.

With the growth of specialization the craft guilds lost their mercantile functions to other organizations, and still later the guild system gave way to the domestic system of production. Under this the artisan no longer owned both his equipment and material but was provided with the latter by an entrepreneur who also took over the disposal of the merchandise.

TECHNOLOGICAL CHANGE

During the later Middle Ages, from 1000 to 1500, artisans and entrepreneurs came to utilize mechanical power, first water and later wind. In the eleventh century water power was used by grain mills as well as for industrial purposes by fulling mills and forges. Windmills became a common sight at the end of the twelfth century; unlike watermills, they could operate during the freezing season and serve people located in flat, inland areas with neither tide nor stream nearby. From that time on the power of water and wind was used in a large variety of industrial processes, including textile and iron manufacturing, tanning, laundering, sawing, crushing, metal working, grinding, and polishing.

In the thirteenth century people in the West began to show interest in utilizing the power of expanding gases and vapors, first for toy-like contraptions and later for bellows and blowguns. In the late Middle Ages military interest stimulated the use of rockets, gunpowder, cannons, and handguns. With the cannon, a one-cylinder internal combustion engine, was born the grandfather of the modern motor, which uses liquid instead of powdered fuel. Military purposes were also responsible for the use of gravity, the power of weight, first in primitive torsion machines which operated by means of the twisting of fibers, and later in the formidable trebuchet, a large, mobile sling-beam. It is likely that it was the employment of gun-carrying ocean-going sailing ships that ushered in the 450-year period of European domination of Asia and of the seas, which began with the arrival of Vasco da Gama in Calicut in 1498.

Machinery and mechanical power were put to use by the English woolen industry, which next to tin mining was the first English industry to provide examples of large-scale enterprise. Its operations were based on the domestic output of wool, which was the most important raw material in medieval England, holding a position comparable to that of coal in the nineteenth century. As early as in 1265 English cloth was exported to Venice, the greatest commercial center of the Middle Ages.

NATIONAL ECONOMIC POLICIES

Foreign trade gave some impetus to the rise of national economic policies in the form of duties on exports and imports. In addition, to take England as an example, the national importance of the woolen industry was underlined by the appointment of officers by the crown to check on the quality and measure of cloth. There were national regulations also of the price of ale and of the weight of bread for the protection of the consumer, as well as regulations of the currency and of working conditions. The Statute of Laborers of 1351 came close to establishing maximum rates of pay, and an Act of 1495 set down what in effect approximates minimum hours of work. Attempts were also made to avert the dearth of provisions, a constant threat to the medieval economy, by outlawing the monopolistic practices of engrossing, forestalling, and regrating, that is, of buying up provisions ahead of the harvest, or on their way to the market, or at the market itself with the view of profitable resale.

SOCIAL STRUGGLES

On the whole medieval people were willing to accept their station in life. There were protracted struggles, however, between landlords and serfs, and on occasion the serfs rebelled, as they did in England in the great Peasants' Revolt of 1381, an early instance of class warfare. Under the spell of John Ball, an excommunicated priest who advocated ecclesiastical poverty and social equality, the masses were aroused by such couplets as

When Adam delved and Eve span
Who was then the gentleman?

MEDIEVAL
ECONOMIC
THOUGHT

Wat Tyler, the leader of the revolt, had impressed upon King Richard II his request for the abolition of serfdom, feudal services, and market monopolies, but when Tyler was killed the concessions were immediately revoked. Upheavals such as this one remained isolated events in medieval times, and it required special circumstances to provoke them, in this case the combined effect of the Statute of Laborers and a drastic increase in the poll tax.

Other instances of social revolt occurred where business enterprise had grown larger and where it employed substantial numbers of laborers. Both in Flanders and in Italy textile workers rose repeatedly in revolt during the fourteenth century. Their attempts at forming organizations were cruelly suppressed by capital punishment in Florence, and in Ypres striking workmen were exposed to such penalties as blinding and perpetual banishment.

CREDIT OPERATIONS

As agriculture became commercialized and as mercantile transactions increased in scope and became more common, the need for cash grew more pressing and was only haltingly met by gold supplies from the East. Coin thus became supplemented by credit. It was in Venice that the earliest instances of medieval credit operations—not for consumption but for business purposes—could be observed as early as the ninth century. In view of the medieval prohibition of interest, about which more will be said later, these transactions did not assume the form of outright loans but that of the *commenda,* a kind of partnership agreement under which the capitalist financed the trading expedition of a merchant sailor. In England, trading on the basis of loan funds became common in the thirteenth century, again often in the form of partnerships. The lending might be done not by individuals but by organizations, which could more easily evade the prohibition of interest taking.

SOCIAL ORGANIZATION

In a way the social organization of the Middle Ages put into practice the ideas of Plato as well as of the Stoics. In principle, society was organized into three classes, the clergy who prayed, the warriors who fought, and the peasants who toiled, a division that in a measure realized the dream of Plato. There was little social mobility, upward or downward, and as a corollary everyone enjoyed a measure of protection in maintaining the position in society into which he was born. The principle of organization, it has been said, was that of status rather than of contract.

Although medieval society was internally divided in this manner, medieval civilization was given unity by the idea of a universal community, a concept held dear by the Stoics and one that forms a stark contrast to both the city-state of the Greeks and the national state of modern times. The universal community of the Middle Ages was a community of believers, deeply concerned about salvation in the next world and assigning to the Church the vital role of mediator between man and God. The age was one of faith.

THE CHURCH

In addition to their spiritual functions, the medieval clergy preserved the light of learning in the Dark Ages when not even the kings had mastered the art of reading and writing and the head of the Holy Roman Empire was apt to sign state documents by drawing lines connecting the letters that formed his name. Furthermore, the Church was one of the great powers in medieval politics, and there were protracted struggles between popes and emperors, and princes of the Church and secular rulers. Donations and bequests of the faithful added to the wealth of the Church, turning it at times into the largest landowner in Christendom.

The economic doctrines of the Church were derived from the Bible, the teachings of the Greek and Latin Fathers and of Aristotle, whose prestige became so overwhelming in the thirteenth century that he was often referred to as "the Philosopher." Side by side with these influences was the evolving theological tradition that had been built up over a period of more than a thousand years when the Middle Ages reached their highest flowering. Another important source was Roman law and the ecclesiastical or canon law as embodied in the legislation of councils, popes, and bishops and enforced by ecclesiastical courts.

What then was the gist of medieval economic doctrine? With man viewed as tainted by original sin and the world corrupt, any panaceas of earthly reform or thoroughgoing social reorganization to resolve the economic problem would seem futile and pointless if not heretical; a world so tainted and corrupt could not be turned into a paradise. Man's material well-being in his earthly life seemed of little consequence in comparison with the great and overriding question of his salvation in the next world. In brief, the economic doctrines of the Church aimed at minimizing sin and maximizing charity, but not in a manner that would have precluded the important economic developments that took place during the later Middle Ages.

Relative to the resources of the time, charity was indeed practiced on a lavish scale during the Middle Ages, both by the Church, which devoted a substantial portion of her wealth to this purpose, and by the faithful as a means of grace. In a sense, charity was seen as the principal way toward the solution of the economic problem of scarcity in the Middle Ages, not as a perfect solution—the world being what it is, such a thought would have been considered reckless and repugnant—but as an approximation to its solution.

Besides calling for charity, the medieval theologians tried to set standards of righteous behavior whose observance would protect the faithful from falling into sin. Medieval economic thought was thus invariably mingled with theological considerations. It taught what ought to be, and its character was a normative one. This implies, for example, that there was no perfect correspondence between the teachings of the Church and the practice of the world. Such correspondence may have been closest with respect to the call for charity, a duty that is relatively pleasant and easy to fulfill, which was not imposed to such an excess as would endanger the donor's social status—rather its fulfillment may have served as an affirmation of such status. In the case of other duties the correspondence between what is and what ought to be was less close, medieval people, in spite of their religious fervor, being as weak as man is apt to be in the face of temptation.

The medieval order was an essentially static one, and the idea of progress was as yet not born to serve as a stimulus to drastic and relentless change. This does not mean, however, that change was absent in the medieval economy. On the supply side improvements were not lacking, and especially during the later Middle Ages there were many instances of technological advance, the most important of which have been mentioned. Though much thought has been given to tracing their effects on medieval society, the complete story of how they happened to have come about is as yet untold and perhaps will never be told in all details. Such important innovations as the use of gunpowder and magnets and printing were known elsewhere in the world long before they came to Europe. Perhaps they were brought there as the result of mercantile contacts, which increasingly came to link the different regions of the world.

Among the factors affecting the demand for goods, austerity and asceticism were confirmed as virtues in medieval thought, but as virtues of the select few. The wealthy were bound in duty to practice not only charity but liberality and munificence as well, that is, to use their riches in a generous manner and for the fulfillment of some great and noble purpose. From the economic point of view, the construction of mighty cathedrals and stately buildings, which sometimes took many centuries to complete and absorbed a substantial portion of available resources, may have served important economic functions in providing employment and in inducing further rounds of expenditure. But all-pervasive charity, practiced universally and reaching all corners of medieval life, stands out most conspicuously as the method of coping with the economic problem commended in medieval thought.

SAINT THOMAS

A complete and authoritative statement of medieval economic thought may be found in the writings of Saint Thomas Aquinas (1225–74), a great figure in medieval scholasticism whose system of thought was to become, and has remained to the present time, the official Catholic philosophy. Saint Thomas, born near the city of Naples, when a youth joined the Dominican order, much to the dismay of his family which was part of the highest Italian aristocracy. His studies brought him to Cologne and Paris, where he eventually became an outstanding teacher. Saint Thomas's writings constitute a consistent and all-embracing structure of thought that aims at the reconciliation of faith and rational knowledge, a synthesis of Christian doctrine as it had emerged after more than a thousand years and of Aristotelianism. Aristotle's thought had been studied again in the West with growing interest from the twelfth century, having been brought there by Arabic and Jewish thinkers.

In the method of scholasticism, which Saint Thomas carried to perfection, a question is posed, and this is followed with a fair exposition, detailed and with citation of authorities, of the view to be refuted or reinterpreted. Then the answer is given, and the contrary views are made the subject of searching criticism, again with ample quotations.

PRIVATE PROPERTY

Saint Thomas's economic doctrines cover such matters as the institution of private property, the just price, and the prohibition of usury, matters that indeed form the core of medieval economic thought. As to private property, Saint Thomas establishes that the institution is in accord with the law of nature, it may be regulated by the government, the owner is under duty to share the use of his possessions with others, and communal property is reserved for those who wish to lead a life of perfection.

PRIVATE PROPERTY NOT AGAINST NATURAL LAW

Saint Thomas was of course a theologian and philosopher, and when he discusses economic matters he does so incidentally and in connection with theological and moral questions. Some of his thoughts on private property are in his "Treatise on Law," which forms a section of his *Summa Theo-*

logica. The specific question under which the matter is treated is headed, "Whether the natural law can be changed?" Nature, so the Fathers of the Church had taught, gives all goods in common to all men. Aristotle, on the other hand, had written a spirited defense of private property. To reconcile these points of view, Saint Thomas explains that certain matters belong to natural law "because nature did not bring with it the contrary." He then cites an example: "We might say that for man to be naked is of the natural law, because nature did not give him clothes, but art invented them." "In this sense," he adds, "the possession of all things in common and universal freedom are said to be of the natural law, because the distinction of possessions and slavery were not brought in by nature, but devised by human reason for the benefit of human life. Accordingly, the law of nature was not changed in this respect, except by addition." Implied in this subtle and ingenious argument is a very effective critique of those who would consider private property as being against the law of nature: those so inclined would appear to hold the wearing of clothes as being against the law of nature.

REGULATION OF PROPERTY

In another passage of the "Treatise on Law" Saint Thomas approvingly refers to the regulation of property instituted in the Old Testament—the Sabbatical Year, the Jubilee Year, and the common use of certain goods—and he relates these matters to Aristotle's belief that the regulation of property is conducive to the preservation of the state. Saint Thomas thus approves of governmental regulation of property for the common good. In line with the hierarchical organization of medieval society, as well as with the thought of Aristotle, Saint Thomas indicates no preference for an egalitarian distribution of private property. Nor does he establish an absolute right of the property owner against the state, as was attempted by later writers.

THE STEWARDSHIP OF WEALTH

The matter of common use of certain goods is taken up again in another part of the *Summa Theologica,* where Saint Thomas treats of theft. There he holds that there are two aspects of possessions—first, their acquisition and disposal; second, their use. With respect to acquisition and disposal, private property is justified on the basis of the reasons given by Aristotle. With respect to the use of possessions, Aristotle's thought is fused with that of the Fathers when Saint Thomas insists that others must be allowed to share in it. This duty, which reflects the idea of the stewardship of wealth, may be discharged by acts of charity, liberality, and munificence. As an obligation, charity need not go so far as to endanger the donor's or his family's status in society.

Saint Thomas's discussion of the duty of sharing the use of one's possessions with others is followed by the celebrated passage in which the human law is suspended under conditions of evident and urgent need, when appropriation ceases to be theft—one of the rare occasions that Saint Thomas cites both Aristotle and Augustine among the authorities with whose views his own is at variance.

Although Saint Thomas lifted the shadow of doubt that the teachings of the Fathers had cast on private property, he nevertheless as a counsel of perfection upheld the earlier view that hallowed for a select few the choice of voluntary poverty, either in the form of communal living or, best of all, by begging one's daily bread.

THE REDEMPTION OF BUSINESS

To the rehabilitation of property was joined the rehabilitation of the businessman. Ecclesiasticus (27:2) had taught: "As a nail sticks between the joinings of the stones, so does sin stick also between buying and selling," and the Fathers had expressed with similar pungency their concern about the manifold temptations to which the trader's actions expose him. As has been seen, however, Augustine had not completely closed the door leading to the businessman's redemption when he approved the distinction between the trader and the trader's craft: avarice and fraud "are the vices of the man, not of the craft, which can be carried on without such vices."

During the later Middle Ages the legal and theological authorities were willing to give recognition to the functional importance of the trader in an economy that had become more highly developed and complex and could forgo the trader's services only at the cost of reverting to more primitive forms of economic life, such as barter and production for the immediate use of the producer. There is a more profound reason, however, for the willingness of the later medievalists to accept the trader and his services. The point is not so much that their attitude differed from the patristic tradition but rather that the teachings of the Fathers had been addressed to a world that was still pagan and only gradually ceased to be so. In this pagan world little restraint was placed on man's acquisitive propensities. Roman law, with its individualistic bent, had only underlined the absence of such restraint. Now Europe had become Christian, and the teachings of the medievalists were addressed to a world that, although it could not shed all its wickedness, was no longer pagan. There were now restraints, legal as well as spiritual, that curbed greed and avarice. Because the trader was one of the faithful and operated under all the restrictions imposed on the faithful, the community of believers could accept him.

In the thirteenth century, when Saint Thomas wrote his *Summa,* canonists and scholastics found no fault with those earnings of the trader that could be interpreted as a return for labor and expenses. Scripture had spoken of the laborer as being worthy of his hire, and justice called for his fair remuneration. This thought was applied to dependent labor as well as to independent artisans and craftsmen who performed services involving the tangible transformation of goods. In the case of mercantile activities where no such transformation took place, it was not difficult to extend the idea to the services of transportation and storage and care. Transportation of goods was viewed as the foremost function of the trader, one that he could often discharge only by assuming heavy risks, and risk indeed came to be recognized as another item chargeable to the trader's expenses.

A more difficult problem was the treatment of that part of business income that was not allocable to labor and expenses in the sense just described. Here again canonists and scholastics showed the way to the rehabilitation of business profits by establishing as a criterion the intention or motive of the trader. Three justifying motives came to be recognized: the use of profits for self-support, the use of profits for charity, and the intention to perform business as a service by providing the public with goods.

All these considerations were given their due in the writings of Saint Thomas. In the *Summa* the problem of the trader is examined principally in connection with the question, "Whether in trading it is lawful to sell a thing for more than was paid for?" Saint Thomas starts out by defining the function of the trader as the act of engaging in exchange. His reply is linked both to the Augustinian distinction between the trader and his craft, and to the Aristotelian distinction between "natural" exchange designed to meet the needs of life and exchange for profit. The first type of exchange is characteristic of heads of households and states. The second type of exchange is the function of trade, which, because it pursues unlimited gain, is considered "somewhat dishonorable." However, Saint Thomas continues, profit in itself is neither reprehensible nor praiseworthy but morally neutral. It becomes legitimate, or at least moderate profit does, if the trader pursues a necessary or even honorable purpose, such as self-support, charity, or public service.

THE JUST PRICE

Broadly speaking, both the medieval jurist and the scholastic followed the same path when they broke the way that led to the rehabilitation of the trader and his profits. The solution outlined in the preceding paragraphs came about as the result of the joint efforts of canonists and theologians. To be sure, the question of the legitimacy of trade and of trading profits would arise more often before the *forum conscientiae*, the "trader's conscience," to be resolved by his spiritual adviser or confessor, than before a civil or ecclesiastical court of law. This followed from the nature of the matter, which was more likely to arouse doubts in the minds of the faithful than to involve actual law cases.

The situation was different with respect to another important problem in medieval economics, the just price. Here the canon and civil lawyers had before themselves the tradition of the Roman law with its *laesio enormis,* "excessive violation," as expanded by medieval practice. Classical Roman law had in principle maintained freedom of contract and of bargaining and imposed little or no restriction on the price at which bargainers might arrive. *Laesio enormis* then was in the nature of a very narrowly circumscribed exception from this general rule, applying only to transactions in land and to prices that were unduly low. In the medieval legal doctrine and practice the rule of *laesio enormis* was greatly extended, and it became possible to bring before the courts and question the validity of any transaction where the buyer had been overcharged to the extent of more than 50 percent of the just price, or where the seller had accepted less than one-half of this price. As will be seen, the solution of the problem of the just price by the scholastic theologians followed different lines and was on the whole more strict. The divergence was a matter of considerable practical importance, because cases involving the just price would as likely turn up before the civil and ecclesiastical courts as they would before the court of one's conscience, and it was only the latter court that was to be guided by the theological doctrine of the just price.

Saint Thomas's discussion of the just price is found in the *Summa* under the heading, "Whether a man may lawfully sell a thing for more than it is worth?" The worth or value of a good is its just price, and if the sales price deviates from it, the buyer or the seller, as the case may be, owes restitution. The deviation from the just price need not be as great as is required by civil law, but it must be "considerable." This requirement is made because the just price is not something "absolutely definitive" but the result of an estimate.

The divergence between the civil law and the stricter provision adopted in the theological doctrine is ascribed by Saint Thomas to the fundamental difference between the human and the divine law. The former, to use the words of a modern jurist, postulates only an "ethical minimum," whereas the latter leaves nothing unpunished that is contrary to virtue.

Saint Thomas does not specify what a good's worth, value, or just price is. According to a convincing albeit controversial interpretation, he did not need to because he treated a matter about which lawyers and theologians had reached a well-established and well-known agreement. The just price was the current price prevailing at a given place and at a given time, to be determined by the estimate of a fair-minded person.

The requirement that the price be just is derived by Saint Thomas from the golden rule and from the nature of exchange. Scripture commands: "All things whatsoever you would that men should do to you, do you also to them" (Matt. 7:12). Since no one wishes to acquire a good at a price in excess of its worth, no one should try to sell it for more than it is worth. Moreover, and here references are found to Aristotle's *Politics* and *Ethics,* exchanges have been instituted for the common advantage of buyer and seller. They should not be more burdensome to the one than to the other, and the contract between them should be based on the equality of things. "The value of a thing which is put to human use is measured by the price given; and for this purpose money was invented, as is explained in *Ethics,* V, 5. Hence, whether the price exceeds the value of a thing or conversely, the equality required by justice is lacking." Only under exceptional circumstances, when the transaction does not serve the common advantage of both parties but turns out to the advantage of one party and to the injury of the other, may the price include a premium to reimburse the seller for the loss incurred in parting with the good.

As Saint Thomas links his doctrine of the just price with the Aristotelian theory of justice in exchange, the interpretation of his doctrine has produced controversies similar to those that have arisen in connection with Aristotle's examination of the matter. The general question, what justice is, and the special one, what a just price is, have never failed to impress thoughtful minds as vital issues. Often those who have examined Thomistic teaching have found in it an echo of the ideas prevailing during their own time. Some have said that Saint Thomas was a precursor of the labor theory of value, which was the accepted economic doctrine until the 1870s. Others have interpreted him as an exponent of the subjective theory of value, which considers the economic value of a good as derived from its utility. Again, as with Aristotle, there is not a word in the passages containing the treatment of the matter in the *Summa* that would lend explicit support to the former interpretation—that Saint Thomas meant to equate the value of a good with the amount of labor embodied in it. Moreover, the view that to Saint Thomas the value of a good reflected its utility is supported by Aristotle's emphasis on "demand" or "need," as well as by the patristic tradition. Augustine himself had in the *City of God* outlined a system of valuation that was based upon human needs and had said that "a different value is set upon each thing proportionate to its use."

THE MEDIEVAL PRICE SYSTEM

However, a few years before the *Summa* Saint Thomas had written a commentary on Aristotle's *Ethics,* as had his teacher Albert the Great. In these commentaries, differences in the value of goods are ascribed to subjective as well as to objective factors, that is, to differences in their want-satisfying ability and in the amounts of labor and expenses used in their production. These passages, taken in conjunction with the treatment of the matter in the *Summa,* have caused modern students of the subject to interpret the just price as a functional one, that is, as an instrument designed to facilitate the operation of the medieval price system. According to this view, Albert the Great and Saint Thomas envisage values emerging from the subjective valuations of the individual marketeers which become objective as a "common estimate," reflecting the objective qualities of the goods and measuring the value of the services embodied in them. Both assert that social life is based on specialization and exchange. There will be no exchange and society will fall asunder if producers do not receive a just price that covers their labor and expenses.

The just price thus becomes a device facilitating the discharge of specialized functions. Its tendency is to conserve the order of medieval society, with its customary occupational structure and the traditional levels of living of each noncompeting group, and to protect it from upheavals both by monopolists and by the forces of unrestricted competition. The notion of the just price thus helps to elucidate the difference between what might be called the medieval price system and the modern one. The price system as it is understood today is not normative, and no opprobrium is attached to the refusal to pay a price that covers the cost of production. Instead, the price system brings into relief the function of prices in the allocation of productive resources, specifically in changing this allocation. In the medieval price system, on the other hand, a just price that would cover the cost of production would serve as an instrument of stabilizing the allocation of productive resources along customary and traditional lines. But however great the difference, that it has been possible to link the idea of the just price with the modern concept of a price system underlines the resilience and viability of the idea.

PRICE REGULATION

It must be remembered that in the medieval world many prices were the subject of regulation by public authorities and occupational groups. Where such a regulated price was in force, adherence to it was generally considered a fulfillment of the requirement of a just price. Sometimes the regulation aimed at placing a ceiling on an upward movement of prices. An early example of this is the famous edict of 301 of the emperor Diocletian, which threatened violators with the penalty of death. Later on, however, regulation often served as a floor below which the price was not allowed to fall. To the extent to which regulation of prices tended to maintain the traditional structure of production, it gave further strength to the conservative tendency of the medieval price system.

THE SIN OF USURY

Just as the medieval doctrine of the just price constitutes a sharp break with the classical Roman law of freedom of bargaining, so does the medieval prohibition of interest run counter to the ideas of the Roman lawyers who had allowed a rate of 12 percent a year on money loans and 50 percent on loans in kind. The medieval doctrine of interest, which equated it with usury, was derived from the teachings of the Fathers, who in turn had found the confirmation of their views in several passages of the Old Testament as well as in the words of Jesus, cited in Luke 6:35: "Lend freely, hoping nothing thereby." The authority of Aristotle was used much later, and only to fortify a doctrine whose early formation in the patristic writings antedates by a thousand years the rediscovery in the West of the relevant writings of Aristotle.

The Fathers had attacked lay as well as clerical usury, and occasional condemnations of both can be found in the statements of popes and councils since the fourth century. In 325 the Council of Nicaea denied the clergy the taking of interest on loans of all kinds, and in 789 there occurred the first instance of secular legislation when Charlemagne, citing the tradition, prohibited clerical and lay usury as well. In 806, when he confirmed this, Charlemagne defined usury in broad terms as occurring when "more is demanded back than what is given." This formula, as well as the citation from Luke, was to resound through later statements on the matter. In the legislation of the Church the prohibition was gradually applied to lay people. Thus in 1139 the Second Lateran Council explicitly forbade usury to all. From then on canonists and theologians gave increasing attention to usury, interpreting it as a violation of natural law and justice or as a sin of uncharitableness or avarice.

The clerical attitude to interest cannot be explained in terms of narrow economic advantage of the Church. As the Church gathered wealth, the prohibition may have turned out to its economic disadvantage because on balance there were more clerical lenders than borrowers. As far as the economy at large is concerned, the early medieval society was a primitive and overwhelmingly agrarian one, for which the prohibition of interest may have been as much suited as it was for the earlier Hebrew society to which the rules of the Old Testament had first been applied. During the later Middle Ages, when opportunities for the productive use of capital increased at a rapid pace, the prohibition was interpreted in such a manner that it failed to forestall economic development and may actually have accelerated it.

Saint Thomas's restatement of the doctrine of usury in the *Summa* sharpens some of the arguments with which the canonists and theologians had supported the prohibition of interest. On the basis of concepts derived from Roman law, a distinction was made between *consumptible* and *nonconsumptible* goods, and between a loan and a lease. A house or a farm may be leased for rent because their use renders a *usufruct* or yield. Under the terms of a lease contract a lessor may receive not only the return of the leased good but rent as well. Not so in the case of a loan of consumptible goods such as wine or grain, which do not render a usufruct or yield as does a house or a farm. Instead, in the case of consumptible goods the use exists exclusively in their being "consumed," that is, destroyed or alienated. Thus if the lender of such goods would ask for a return consisting of more than what he lent, he would ask for something that does not exist, namely their yield over and above their use. By doing so, he would violate justice. Moreover, a loan of grain or wine, as distinguished from the lease of a house, involves a transfer not only of possession but also of ownership, a sale. If one were to sell wine and the use of wine, one would sell the same thing twice and again violate justice.

As for money, its principal purpose, as Aristotle had said, is to serve as a means of exchange by being expended, or consumed, in exchange. It is a consumptible good, and the lender of money is barred from asking for a return in excess of the amount lent, just as is the lender of wine or grain.

Saint Thomas was aware that prices change over time, but the notion that because of the mere passage of time future goods have a value different from that of present goods was alien to him, as was, of course, the present-day distinction between consumer goods and producer goods. Nevertheless, implicit in his treatment of usury is the idea that the borrower will usually be a person who is impelled by necessity, a word used in no less than three different contexts within his discussion of usury in the *Summa*. A necessitous borrower is more likely to be one who desires a loan for purposes of consumption than of production.

EXTRINSIC TITLES OF INTEREST

Saint Thomas's doctrine of usury is thus more immediately applicable to consumption loans than to arrangements designed to facilitate the productive use of capital. These were by no means precluded by the prohibition of usury because the capitalist, instead of making his funds available in the form of a loan, was free to chose other legal forms such as a society or a partnership, under which the partners would share losses and gains. Moreover, even if the arrangement took the form of a loan and no interest could lawfully be claimed under the *intrinsic title* of the loan itself, there were *extrinsic titles* under which the lender could receive a return over the principal. One of these extrinsic titles was derived from the doctrine of *damnum emergens*, "damage suffered," which was explicitly recognized by Saint Thomas and under which the lender could ask for compensation for losses that he incurred because of having parted with his funds. Saint Thomas himself excluded from such compensation the loss caused by the lender's forgoing the opportunity of putting the loan amount to profitable use— *lucrum cessans*, "escaped gain"—an extrinsic title that later authorities were inclined to recognize haltingly and under qualifying conditions which were relaxed gradually.

A related extrinsic title, and one explicitly approved by Saint Thomas albeit not in the *Summa*, was that of *mora*, "default." A borrower who failed to make payment when due owed the lender conpensation for the delay. Such an obligation might be lawfully contracted in advance in the form of a conventional penalty that would be forfeited if the debtor defaulted on the loan. The arrangement opened the door to evasions of the prohibition of usury, for example by means of simulating a short term of the loan and an early default of the borrower.

A fourth extrinsic title, *periculum sortis*, "risk," was allowed only in a very restricted sense. The risk for the assumption of which the lender could claim compensation was not the mere chance that the borrower might fail to return the principal. Against this contingency the lender could presumably protect himself by insisting on a pledge that would secure the loan. The risk for the assumption of which the capitalist was allowed to seek compensation was that of the failure of a joint venture, in which case his capital would be lost. It was a risk not arising from an outright loan contract but from a partnership agreement under which gains and losses would be shared.

THE PARTNERSHIP

The partnership thus became a preferred form of investment, and one that was not tainted by usury. It was exactly the assumption of the risk of failure by the capitalist that distinguishes the permissible partnership from the disallowed interest-bearing loan. In a loan transaction the debtor is not relieved of his debt if the venture, which he desires to carry out with the loan, fails. But if the transaction takes place in the form of a joint venture or partnership, the incidence of failure rests on all partners, including and foremost the capitalist. By outlawing lending at interest, the medieval doctrine of usury may have driven the capitalist to seek risk-sharing investment in a partnership, the lawful way to share also in the gain from the venture. Concentration on this type of investment rather than on the use of loan funds may have been a stimulus to economic expansion such as occurred on a wide front during the later Middle Ages. Far more than a loan contract would have done, investment in a partnership encouraged the active participation of the capital-owning partner in the management of the invested funds, bringing extra care and industry to a venture that otherwise would have rested only on the shoulders of the borrower. Concentration on the partnership thus had the effect of turning the capitalist into a risk-taking entrepreneur rather than a rentier occupied with clipping coupons.

As for the position of the partner without capital, he might have found it more attractive than that of a debtor, who in the case of failure of the venture would continue to be burdened by his debt. Moreover, if he had to pay interest, openly or surreptitiously, the fixed charge might easily exceed the returns from the use to which he put the borrowed funds, whereas the profits of the partners would exactly reflect the productivity of the joint venture.

ANNUITIES

Of course, some arrangement was needed to accommodate those who would not or could not assume the role of a risk-taking entrepreneur but wanted to earn a return on their money. Such a person could turn over his funds to a landowner, the state, or a clerical establishment, and he could thereby acquire an annuity, an annual return derived from a productive asset of the seller of the annuity, such as his land, his enterprise, or, in the case of a public agency, its tax receipts. Annuities were an important financial institution of the Middle Ages, and there were many variants of them. Saint Thomas was silent about them, and their delineation from loans was often far from easy. It was especially difficult to draw the dividing line when the annuity was not tied to a specific property of the seller but was founded on his general income-producing ability; or when the annual return was fixed rather than varying with the yield of the property on which it was founded; or when the annuity was for a stated time rather than for life or perpetual; or, finally, when the annuity could be redeemed by the buyer or the seller rather than be nonredeemable. That annuities on the whole received the approval of the medieval theologians was perhaps because the investment was one that was by no means free of risk. The base might fail to yield a return, a situation not unlike that in which the present-day owner of an income bond might find himself—a bond that requires servicing only if adequate income is earned. There was also always present the risk that the government might repudiate the annuity that it had sold.

DEPOSIT AND EXCHANGE BANKING

The holder of an annuity was allowed to sell it at discount to a third party, as was the creditor of a bad debt, especially of forced debts—on which interest was permitted—which the Italian city-states compelled their subjects to subscribe to. This was, however, a controversial matter for a long time, as was the propriety of deposit banking, which was practiced on a large scale during the later Middle Ages. Great merchant bankers in the Italian cities and elsewhere, but particularly in Florence, accepted deposits and paid a fixed rate of interest on them, sometimes unconditionally and sometimes if earned. The merchant bankers were engaged in far-flung trading and lending operations, and the greatest of them had an influence that extended to emperors and popes. Apart from deposit banking, they were deeply involved in foreign exchange transactions, which often incorporated or served as a cover for credit operations. Bills of exchange were widely used in the fourteenth century. For example, if an Italian trader wanted to purchase goods for a later sale at a French fair, his hometown bank would advance him the money and draw on him a bill of exchange, instructing him to make payment to its correspondent in France.

In a transaction known as *cambio sicco,* "dry exchange," a bill of exchange was drawn up to dissimulate an outright credit transaction. A bank might make an advance to a person and in return receive a bill of exchange drawn on a city where the drawer had no funds. When the bill arrived at that city, a correspondent of the first bank took it in payment and drew another bill on the original drawer, payable to the first bank. Once this bill had traveled back to the home city, it was presented for payment.

Bills of exchange fulfilled important functions by serving as a money substitute in a time when money ostensibly was full-bodied and its supply could not easily be expanded. Their use obviated the shipment of specie, which may not have been available, and even if it was, it was hazardous and costly to ship. Their use facilitated the adjustment of international payments. This was true particularly of the activities of the exchange dealers entrusted with the business of the papacy, whose financial interests were worldwide and greater than those of any other organization. If revenues for the papacy had fallen due, say, in Cologne, the papal exchange dealers would credit them to the papal account in Rome, while at the same time selling drafts on their correspondent in Cologne to importers of goods from that city or to other persons who had to settle accounts there.

In the contemporary writings of the theologians the activities of the exchange bankers were often depicted as usurious, although attempts were made to interpret them as purchases and sales, rather than as loans, or to justify them on other grounds. Robert of Courçon (d.1219), a cardinal and author of a *Summa,* when discussing advances made by papal exchange bankers to be repaid in a foreign currency at a fair, noted that a pope who would be persuaded to notarize the relevant documents would not know what he was doing. The most complete treatment of exchange banking may be found in the writings of Saint Antoninus (1389–1459), who as archbishop of Florence, then the center of the world's banking, was intimately familiar with the prevailing commercial usages and made them the subject of a searching analysis. He rejects as usurious foreign exchange transactions involving credit, including the banker's advance of funds in return for exchange payable abroad and at a later date, although he does not deny that they might serve the public interest and that they are tolerated in Rome.

The activities of the deposit and exchange bankers during the late Middle Ages indicate that there was a far from complete agreement between theological doctrine and financial practice. It was a situation that no doubt created some tension in the minds of the faithful, but the tension may have been bearable because the age of faith was gradually coming to an end. Moreover, the public saw the banker mainly as a deposit banker, one who paid interest rather than received it, and borrowing on interest was no sin. The exchange transactions were much too involved to be readily identified with usury in the public's mind. Apparently neither the public nor the bankers themselves felt that the transactions in question constituted the sin of usury in the strict sense of exploitation of the poor.

THE USURY DOCTRINE IN MODERN TIMES

After the close of the Middle Ages the scholastic doctrine gradually came to accept an increasing variety of returns on loans as justified, partly by applying the titles of *damnum emergens* and *lucrum cessans* more widely, partly by allowing a return for the risk of lending. It became recognized that parting with one's funds constitutes a loss, and that present money has a higher value to the holder than future money. As has been noted, many credit transactions such as bills of exchange and annuities were interpreted as purchases and sales rather than as loans, and thus were placed not under the rule of usury but under that of the just price, which allowed profit. Both the rule of the just price and the usury doctrine were eventually used as a device not to disallow interest but to keep it within moderate bounds. In the nineteenth century the taking of interest up to the maximum rate established by the law of the land was given implicit approval by the ecclesiastical authorities.

The reaction to the medieval usury doctrine has changed with the times. It met little understanding, and much fault was found with it, during those ages whose spirit was hostile to restraints on individual initiative. Adam Smith condemned an outright legal prohibition of interest, but where the law established a maximum rate he favored a low one, one that would hover slightly above the market rate on a good security. According to the interpretation that Keynes has given to this passage, Smith favored a low rate of interest because this would increase the chance for savings to go into new investments rather than into debts.

Keynes himself was convinced of the advantages of a low rate of interest, and he took a positive attitude to the efforts of the medieval Schoolmen. Some of the hazards of medieval business were apt to depress the businessmen's expected profits—the marginal efficiency of capital— while others would tend to raise the savers' desire to keep their funds in liquid form. "The destruction of the inducement to invest by an excessive liquidity-preference was the outstanding evil," so Keynes held, "the prime impediment to the growth of wealth." The Schoolmen tried to remove this impediment by a policy that encouraged productive and profitable invest- ment while at the same time keeping interest rates down. It is not sure whether Keynes would have endorsed the efforts of the Schoolmen as enthu- siastically as he did had he not recognized in them an echo of his own views. But this endorsement by the twentieth century's leading economist speaks well for the resilience and adaptability of their philosophy.

THOUGHTS ON MONEY

The medievalists' concern with interest and usury drew them also into discussions of the related matter of money. These were carried on mainly by the lawyers, but a French theologian, Nicholas Oresme (c.1320–82), brought together the various strands of thought of the contemporary doc- trine in an interesting synthesis. His book, *A Treatise on the Origin, Nature, Law, and Alterations of Money,* written in the mid-fourteenth century, was a tract for the times, a reflection on the disorders for which the ever-recur- ring debasement of the currency by the French kings had been responsible.

Paper money, according to Goethe an invention of Mephistopheles, was not used in Europe during the Middle Ages. Money then consisted of coin. In China, the Venetian traveler Marco Polo had observed the use of paper money in Kublai Khan's realm in the thirteenth century and had marveled at the ease of its emission—he likened it to the philosopher's stone that would turn worthless substances into gold. At the end of his report he had expressed the hope that his European readers would understand what he was talking about. In Europe, paper money did not emerge until the end of the seventeenth century, and its rise reflected the perpetual troubles that arose from the debasement of metallic currencies. In the 1740s, David Hume still spoke of "this new invention of paper," an invention that the Founding Fathers contemplated with profound suspicion when the century came to its close.

Medieval money thus consisted of coin and gave rise to endless disturbances—there never seemed to be enough of the metallic substances from which coins were made; coins, being produced by primitive methods, lost much weight from constant use, and in addition to this natural process their substance was not always equal to what it was supposed to be, either because of malpractices of the issuer or because of later manipulations subsequent to the issue.

The debasement of coin by underweight, clipping, or the admixture of base metals did not originate in medieval times. The story of debasement is as old as that of coinage. We have seen that coins came into use in the kingdom of Lydia in Asia Minor early in the seventh century B.C. A number of these early coins, which were made from an alloy of gold and silver, are still extant. They are all surprisingly standardized in weight and appearance, but analyses undertaken in modern times have shown that their metallic content varied greatly, the most full-bodied coin having a metallic content worth more than 50 percent over that of the least full-bodied one. It thus appears that the oriental despots did not introduce coinage for the convenience of the public but rather as a revenue measure. The public turned over precious metals to the treasury and in return received coins of substantially smaller metallic content. Nobody appeared to lose much as long as the coins were accepted at their face value, which possibly could be enforced by making them what is now called "legal tender," but this measure would not help when coins were used for purchases abroad and the foreigner refused to accept them at their face value.

There was, further, the alteration or devaluation of currency, practiced since time immemorial, when coins were called in by the monetary authority and replaced by new ones of lesser metallic value. In 594 B.C. Solon had reduced the metallic value of the Athenian currency by one quarter, thereby bringing about an all-around reduction of debts. Debasement and alteration so much ruined the Roman currency that in the third century A.D. unminted metal came to assume again the role it had played before coinage had been introduced in Lydia a thousand years earlier. The circle was almost closed. In the early Middle Ages, feudal duties were discharged in kind or in labor, and to this extent the economy was divorced from money altogether. Elsewhere a barter economy developed under which money continued to serve as a standard of value or unit of account but shed its function of a medium of exchange: obligations were stipulated in terms of money but could be discharged by equivalent deliveries of commodities.

When coins again came into wider use, the practices of debasement and alteration were invariably resumed by the monetary authorities and mint farmers, not so much of the gold coins, which served as an international currency and for large transactions, but rather of the petty coins in which people received their pay and which were used to purchase the necessities of daily life. These practices were condemned by the medieval canonists and theologians and by the secular writers of a later age. They treated the matter in much the same way as modern writers are apt to speak of inflation —it was an abomination that must never, or hardly ever, be allowed to occur. Although debasement was considered a sin, no recourse could be had before a court of law. The only court of competent jurisdiction was the prince's own conscience. Moreover, debasement was no sin if it was required in an emergency situation.

The scholastics' condemnation of manipulations with the metallic content of coin through debasement or alteration was a consistent application of their monetary theory, which in turn was closely linked with the usury doctrine. In crisp language, and with a conciseness nowhere surpassed, John Buridan, the great philosopher and teacher of Oresme at the University of Paris, analysed the nature of money in terms of the four Aristotelian causes. Its material cause, out of which it arises, is a rare substance. Its efficient cause, which produces money, is the government. Its formal cause, which turns the rare substance into money, is the symbol of value inscribed upon the face of the coin. Its final cause, or purpose, is to serve the needs of man by facilitating the exchange of goods. In this view, money was identified with coin, and the value of coin was that which it carried on its face—the *bonitas extrinseca* given to it by the prince. Money was viewed exclusively as a measure, and as one with a fixed and stable value. Saint Thomas himself, in a work of his youth, had said that if more money were received by a lender for the lesser amount given to the borrower, a different measure would be applied in giving and in receiving—an obvious inequity. When money was debased or altered, the scholastics had to face exactly this situation: money, the measure, was differentiated, not by borrowers and lenders but by the monetary authority itself. To maintain a view consistent with the usury doctrine, this was something that could not be tolerated, and indeed condemned it was, in the face of a practice that was rife with violations.

The reconciliation of practice with doctrine was no easy matter because it would have meant giving recognition to the *bonitas intrinseca*—the metallic value of the coin—and abandoning the principle of the fixedness and stability of the monetary measure. If the money was debased to begin with, that is, when it was not full-bodied at the time of issue, some authorities allowed a devaluation that would merely acknowledge the accomplished fact of debasement and make the new standard of metallic content equal to what the debased coin contained. Much attention was paid to the plight of creditor who had given full-bodied money and, in consequence of subsequent debasement or devaluation, received money of lesser substance. If the debtor was in default at the time of the alteration of the coin, he would owe compensation for its deterioration.

ORESME'S *TREATISE*

Having sketched this background of the medieval monetary situation, we can turn to an analysis of Oresme's *Treatise*. The strength of this little work of approximately seven thousand words, which is one of the earliest devoted to an economic matter, does not lie so much in its metaphysical considerations or legal subtleties as in its emphasis on the political and economic aspects of the subject. The criterion frequently employed by Oresme in resolving a question or in appraising a policy of the government is the common utility—*utilitas communis*—"on account of which money was invented and by which it is regulated." The prince, just as he is in charge of other weights and measurements, has the exclusive prerogative of coinage, but he does not own the circulating coin nor is he its master. Instead it belongs to those who have acquired it in exchange for goods and services, that is, to the community. To defray the expenses of coinage, the prince is allowed to levy a seignorage fee that will account for a small deviation of the intrinsic value of the coin from its face value.

The material from which money is made should be neither too scarce nor too plentiful. Gold and silver are suitable as are cheaper metals for petty coins. Alloys should be used only in the least precious metal from which small change is made, in which case "the suspicion is least, or the fraud is of the least importance."

Just as laws may not be altered without evident necessity, so must no alteration be made of the monetary system except under conditions of grave necessity or for the clear advantage of the whole community. Oresme distinguishes five different types of alteration of coin: form, bimetallic ratio, denomination, weight, and material. As a general rule, none of these alterations is allowed. Changing the name of a penny and calling it twopence would make it "necessary for goods to be bought or priced at proportionately higher rates," while the real value of pensions and rents fixed in money would decline. Changes in weight are an outright fraud. To prevent changes in material, a sample of a standard coin should be preserved by the public authorities.

The prince's profit from alterations is the community's loss. If he were allowed a small alteration, on principle he could not be refused a larger one. By means of repeated alterations he could imperceptibly extract almost all the wealth from his subjects and turn them into slaves. The profit from alterations, or debasement, is unjust because it is made at the cost of the community that owns the money. It also is unnatural because money is designed to serve as a certain measure, and no profit should derive from changing such a measure. Moreover, debasement is worse than usury, which at least occurs in the form of a free contract joined voluntarily by the debtor, whereas debasement is undertaken against the will of the citizens and comes close to robbery and extortion.

As a further consequence of debasement one can see in operation Gresham's law—bad money drives out good money—which Oresme introduced two centuries before Gresham. The alteration will tend to lessen the quantity of the monetary material in the country because gold and silver will be carried abroad where they command a higher price. There are other undesirable effects of debasement on the economy. External and internal trade will be hampered once money ceases to be sound. Incomes determined in money cannot be correctly taxed and valued. Money cannot be safely lent. The bad example of the sovereign invites imitation by counterfeiters, whose forgeries are not easily discovered if they circulate side by side with the debased coin. The alteration of money also affects the distribution of income adversely. Money changers, bankers, dealers in bullion, and speculators are likely to make gains, but other more deserving elements of the population become impoverished.

Oresme is well aware that the market value of the metals from which money is made may change. Under a bimetallic standard the ratio in which the market values of the two metals stand to each other will deviate from the mint ratio. This is a source of monetary disturbance that has plagued bimetallic systems up to the present time. In this case Oresme allows a change of the mint ratio in response to a substantial change of the market ratio. But to keep such alteration within proper bounds and prevent its exploitation by the prince, "the community alone has the right to decide if, when, how, and to what extent this ratio may be altered, and the prince may not in any way usurp it." Here we have the germ of the idea that monetary management is to be entrusted to an independent monetary authority rather than to the executive, and also, since debasement is in effect taxation, that there should be no taxation without representation. Oresme does not specify in what form the community's decision should be made. He may have had in mind action by the French States-General, a representative body made up of the three estates, clergy, nobles, and commons, which was convened on several occasions during the fourteenth century.

The second instance in which Oresme considers debasement permissible relates to an emergency situation when a large amount of bullion has to be transferred abroad, for example in war or as the prince's ransom. In such a situation the community may rob itself and debase its coin, an action that then has all the characteristics of a good tax. These are enumerated by Oresme in a manner similar to that of Adam Smith's four canons of taxation requiring taxes to be equal, certain, convenient, and economical. The earlier standard should, however, be restored promptly. The authority to undertake debasement under these conditions rests squarely with the community and cannot be delegated to the prince. A kingdom cannot survive if the prince is allowed to extract all the wealth from his subjects. Such a concentration of wealth would be as harmful as perfect equality. Here Oresme illustrates his thought with the help of an analogy:

> As in a chorus unison has no power to please and excessive or improper dissonance destroys and spoils the whole harmony, but a proportional and measured difference of tone is needed to produce the sweet melody of a joyous choir: So also, generally, equality of possessions or power in all sections of the community is inconvenient and inconsistent, but too great a disparity destroys and spoils the harmony of the state.

Note not only Oresme's view of the distribution of wealth but also his identification of property and power, and the profound suspicion with which he looked upon an undue concentration of power. His bestowal of the right to debase on the community rather than on the prince marks his work as a milestone not only in the development of economic but of political thought as well. What he says of the authorities' standard claim that their actions are in the public interest has a ring of realistic insight that resounds through the ages: if the prince "should tell the tyrant's usual lie that he applies the profit from debasement to the public advantage, he must not be believed, because he might as well take my coat and say he needed it for the public service."

Oresme, who ended his career as a bishop of Lisieux, was a courageous man of independent mind. His was a special bent apt to attack the weaknesses of his contemporaries. He opposed not only debasement but in other works turned against the widespread belief of his time in magic and astrology, preferring rational explanation over one that would employ demons, divination, or the movement of celestial bodies. He was the first to describe the universe in terms of a gigantic clock, set in motion by God and with "all the wheels moving as harmoniously as possible," a metaphor that was to become of seminal importance in the history of ideas and which in later formulations left its mark on mechanistic views of the economic universe. He attained great fame as the preacher of a Christmas sermon delivered in the presence of the pope in 1363, in which he denounced the evils in the church. A shadow cast by events yet to come, this sermon was reprinted several times during the Reformation.

Chapter 4

THE TRANSITION
OF THE 16TH CENTURY:
From Unity
to Diversity

The unity of thought that had been the hallmark of the Middle Ages began to vanish in the sixteenth century, to be replaced by a greater diversity of approaches. The multiformity of opinion reflected the growth of the various nation-states which colored the thinking of their citizens, the rise of a secular approach in place of the otherworldly, religious one, and the differentiation of the religious foundation itself into various branches. These movements were interrelated in turn since in many instances the nation-state was not only a territorial but also a denominational unit.

THE RISE OF THE NATION-STATE

The rise of the nation-state, which first took place in England and France and much later, in the nineteenth century, in Italy and Germany, brought consolidation and strengthening to the power of the central government and a corresponding loss of power of the feudal authorities in localities and regions. It laid the foundation for the successful pursuit of national economic policies and for the growth of nationalistic feelings, the strength of which was eventually to rival that of the old religious ties. Their decline was accompanied by the divorce of religion and morality from statecraft. Reason of state, rather than compatibility of public policy with ethical or religious norms, came to be the overriding test of government action.

THE AUTONOMY OF POLITICS

Nobody expressed this idea more forcefully and in a more extreme fashion than the Florentine diplomat Niccolò Machiavelli (1469–1527). His book *The Prince* took as its hero the cruel and treacherous Cesare

Borgia, the younger son of Pope Alexander VI and the murderer of his brother, of the husband of his sister, and of countless others. In this work the pursuit of power by the state is depicted as an end in itself, with an autonomy bestowed on the political sphere in which standards of ethics or religion have no place and in which only efficiency counts: that policy is good that contributes most effectively to the power of the state.

As a political philosophy Machiavellianism has invariably been a failure because in spite of its proclaimed realism it neglects man's undying love of freedom and his attachment to spiritual values. However, by separating his science of politics from morals and religion Machiavelli set a precedent that in later times was followed by the exponents of other social sciences, including economics, when they established their own specialties as similarly autonomous disciplines. Moreover, Machiavelli, with his emphasis on self-interest as the principal motive force and on the connection between ends and efficient means, may be considered a forerunner of tendencies that were to assume great importance in the economic thought of later generations. Machiavelli's method, a blend of empiricism and speculative, a priori rationalism, has its counterpart in the approach of representative economists. Although asserting that he based his findings on observation, he nevertheless starts out with a general postulate about the nature of human nature, which he considers as constant and given, regardless of differences in culture and environment, and which for purposes of analysis and in line with the theological thought of his time about the universal depravity of mankind he assumes to be wicked. Just as Machiavelli's empirical bent was later recognized by Francis Bacon, who saw in him a predecessor, so was his general postulate about human nature to find a parallel in Adam Smith's model of man driven by self-interest and equipped with "the propensity to truck, barter, and exchange," which Smith believed was "common to all men."

In view of these characteristics of Machivelli's thought—the autonomy of politics, the utilitarian and pragmatic bent, the combination of empiricism with a speculative view of human nature narrowed down for the purposes of his specific analysis—it is not surprising that contemporary students of intellectual history have labeled him the first social scientist of modern times.

THE DECLINE OF CHARITY

The breakup of the old faith, which was all but accomplished during Machiavelli's life, implied, first of all, that charity had lost the central position that it had held in the medieval economic system. To the reformers, salvation by faith was more acceptable than salvation by specific good works, a means of grace that to them seemed discredited by the widesperad traffic in indulgences. Moreover, the social domination of which charitable giving is an accompaniment could not have as strong an appeal to the independent spirit of the man of the Renaissance and his successors as it had to medieval man who was enmeshed in a network of feudal and hierarchical ties.

Gradually the more impersonal agency of government came to be the principal dispenser of relief to the poor and handicapped, not in the form of charity but by way of excuting the law of the land. The Elizabethan Poor Law of 1601, which accepted public responsibility for the care of the poor, marks a milestone in this development.

THE PURSUIT OF GAIN

With charity dethroned and with the nation-state emerging, the pursuit of national gain came into its own as the foremost means of resolving the economic problem of scarcity. The ascendancy of this device is commonly associated with the rise of merchantilism (the subject of the next chapter).

What is lawful and what is forbidden in the search for gain was in the sixteenth century still a matter about which the men of the cloth had the last word. Since the old faith had given way to a variety of denominations, there was now a corresponding variety of theological responses, and many topics about which the medieval thinkers had developed settled opinions became a matter of controversy. However, the new thought was by no means universally "progressive" in the sense of according acceptance to the manifestations of the more active and acquisitive economy that had sprung up during the later Middle Ages. Nor was it on the whole more lax than that of the medieval Schoolmen had been.

MARTIN LUTHER

Martin Luther (1483–1546), an erstwhile Augustinian monk of peasant origin, was alarmed by the commercialism of his time, and his views about economic activities were more attuned to patristic thought and the primitive economic life of the earlier Middle Ages than to the refinements of later times as reflected in the doctrines of the Schoolmen at the close of the Middle Ages. Luther upheld the substance of medieval economic thought, including the doctrines of usury and of the just price, the former in its most severe form and shorn of the "extrinsic titles" to interest, but his doctrine of the priesthood of all believers put an end to church authority in these matters. Instead, the enforcement of the old restraints now fell on the secular authorities, and since Luther's political doctrines were as conservative as his economic ones, allowing the subject no right to resistance even against an unjust governor—whom Luther considered the rule rather than the exception—they both are among the factors that explain the economic backwardness of German territories up to the time of the nineteenth century and the spirit of blind obedience and dependence on authority characteristic of so many phases of German political history.

Lutheran thought also provided a basis for the rise of mercantilism in Germany, not only because it assigned to the government important economic functions but also because it looked more favorably upon national than upon private gain and tolerated in government activities a spirit of enterprise and acquisition which it denied to the individual. Here again this had lasting effects, prolonging the hold of mercantilism over the German economy and making the country cling to institutions that retarded the reception of classical economic thought and frustrated its integration with the culture of the West.

Luther was firmly attached to the medieval idea of a hierarchically ordered society which assigned to each individual a permanent place and rank. He endorsed serfdom, even if the master happened to be an unbeliever. To the strife of competition, the activities of middlemen and financiers, the importation of "luxuries" from abroad, and to what would now be called economic mobility he was bitterly opposed.

The Lutheran priesthood of all believers marks the fall of the double standard of behavior for clergy and laity. Hence the requirements for saintly living become generalized and asceticism is turned into a duty for all. Asceticism calls not only for adherence to traditional standards of consumption but also for toil, which serves to discipline and punish man in his fallen state. Man has the duty to work, and work in turn produces private property—a thought that anticipates Locke if not Adam Smith.

JOHN CALVIN

While Luther's thought was especially influential in Germany, that of the Frenchman John Calvin (1509–64) spread over the entire Western world and affected particularly France, Switzerland, Holland, Scotland, England, and, in America, New England. Calvin resuscitated the ancient doctrine of predestination in a form opposed to that of free will, according to which the souls of the elect are preordained to be saved whereas those of others are abandoned. The doctrine of predestination, in conjunction with the doctrine of the "calling" that assigns to each believer an earthly function in which he has the opportunity to prove his worth, seemed to place a premium on earthly success, making it a sort of prima facie sign of grace.

The addition of so powerful a religious stimulus to ordinary economic incentives, combined with the duty to toil, may have been a potent motive force in favor of economic effort. Economic success now not only had its pecuniary rewards but could be interpreted as evidence of salvation. Since the Calvinists frowned upon ostentatious consumption, much of the economic gain would have no other designation than further investment, the accumulation of additional capital. This is the substance of the famous thesis, established by Weber and Tawney, of the Calvinist or Puritan origin of capitalism, which ascribes to Calvinists and Puritans an important role in bringing about the birth of the modern economic world.

This thesis has often been criticized, and since it is not susceptible to complete proof it should perhaps be introduced as a hypothesis rather than as a thesis. Its critics have pointed to the flourishing economy of the Italian cities and other regions not yet affected by Calvinist thought—or not affected by it at all—and to the role played by a number of great Catholic businessmen and their families in the fifteenth and sixteenth centuries, whose economic accomplishments, wealth, and influence were unrivaled in their time. Alternative interpretations of the origin of capitalism have emphasized the importance of immigrants and strangers, Puritan and other, in assuming entrepreneurial functions and promoting economic development. Still other interpretations would underplay the religious factor in the rise of capitalism, assigning to it and to its stress on the other world a rather negative importance as a force promoting economic activities, and they would make more of the growth of rationalism, secularism, and materialism as harbingers of the modern economy. On the whole, however, the original hypothesis has proved extremely fruitful by opening up new approaches to the study of economic history and by stimulating the prolonged discussion of alternative interpretations of so vital a matter as the origin of the modern economic world.

Whatever the eventual outcome of this discussion may be, nothing could be further from the truth than to consider Calvin's thought an example of broad permissiveness in economic matters. Unlike Luther, Calvin subordinated the state to ecclesiastical authority rather than vice versa. In the communities in Geneva and elsewhere, which were established under his rule and that of his followers, all aspects of the life of the faithful were strictly regulated and controlled by the church. They were expected to lead a life of saintliness, and the restraints imposed upon them were occasionally more rigorous than those called for by medieval economic thought. While expected to observe strict standards of fairness in his business dealings, to adhere to a just price, and to be satisfied with a moderate profit, the Puritan businessman, as has been seen, operated under the strong religious impulse to prove his preordained salvation in the next world by a successful career in this one. This situation was pregnant with tensions that have troubled many businessmen to this day.

In the matter of usury, Calvin's attitude was more conciliatory than Luther's, but in substance it was not much different from that of the late medievalists. Whereas the latter, on principle, had forbidden the taking of interest but had tolerated it in special circumstances, Calvin reversed the arrangement by allowing interest in principle, but this rule was hedged by so many qualifying restrictions that for practical purposes the result may often have been the same under either approach. However, from a doctrinal point of view, Calvin's attitude represented a definite turning point. To accommodate the business world, it was no longer necessary to stipulate what seemed to be exceptions from a general rule. Instead, the general rule was reversed, and further accommodation could be given merely by allowing the exceptions from the new rule to fall into oblivion.

The erosion of the usury doctrine formed part of a broader movement of thought away from the authority of Aristotle, which the medievalists had rarely questioned and which had been one of the sources of the medieval doctrine of usury. It was a sign of the time that Peter Ramus, who later became the century's most famous logician, earned his master's degree in Paris in 1536 by defending the thesis, "everything which Aristotle had said is false."

SIXTEENTH-CENTURY ECONOMIC LITERATURE

The problem of usury continued to agitate men's minds during the sixteenth century. Earlier controversialists might have sharpened a subtle point, perhaps in connection with "extrinsic titles," without calling into question the basic rule that prohibited interest on loans. This attitude now changed and the rule itself became the subject of challenge and doubt. Some writers defended the old order and others disputed it. On the whole, the controversy generated more heat than light, and as hardly any new thoughts could be wrought from the timeworn topic, most of the writers who contributed to the discussion are now forgotten.

Approximately forty of the 217 titles published before the year 1600 that are listed in the catalogue of the Kress Library of Business and Economics at Harvard touch in one way or another on the usury question. That the literature could become so voluminous in the sixteenth century was in no small measure due to the invention of printing from movable type. No other innovation did more to foster the spread of book learning among the laity, promoted as it was by the humanistic movement of the time. It also provided the economic basis for lay authorship. Before the invention of printing the price of a book was enormously high, a single law book costing perhaps the equivalent of an average person's maintenance during eighteen months. If an average-paid law professor of the time had spent his entire salary on nothing but purchases of professional books, he would have been able to acquire fewer than two volumes a year. It is thus not surprising that libraries of any substantial size could be found only in monasteries or perhaps in the prince's palace. Since the literature of the time was profusely documented and contained an abundance of citations and quotations, a lay person without access to a monastic or princely library could not ordinarily write a book.

The invention of printing changed all this. Whereas all medieval authorities in the field of economics had been clergymen, the sixteenth century witnessed the rise of an economic literature written by lay people. Gradually learning became secularized.

Most of the economic writers of the sixteenth century were law professors or government officials. In the seventeenth century this was again to change, most conspicuously so in England, where much of the mercantilist literature was written by businessmen, the only period in the history of economics when this was the case. On the continent, especially in Germany, the close connection between government and economics continued much longer. There the hold of the state was so strong and statecraft was so pervasive that economics developed as a branch of public administration. This did not change much until the nineteenth century when German economic thought haltingly came to stir under the influence of the classical school, but even then economics continued to be classified as one of the sciences of the state, as it is to this day.

None of the sixteenth-century writers on economics who will be considered here led an uneventful life. Economic thought was only a sideline of their other activities in law and government, which involved them in the religious and political struggles of their time. The expression of economic ideas was often equivalent to a political or religious commitment of far-reaching consequences for the career if not for the life of the author. The changing fortunes of war and of political events compelled some writers to seek temporary refuge in foreign lands. The breakup of the unity of Europe had opened up this safety valve, the very existence of which made for greater articulateness and independence of thought. Not a few authors of the time found it convenient to write their books in the form of dialogues. On occasion this method of presentation was more than an innocent fad in line with a tradition of classical antiquity which humanism had revived. By adopting the form of a dialogue an author could express dangerous thoughts without necessarily identifying himself with them and thus hope to frustrate persecution.

THOMAS WILSON

Those who tried to uphold the old order of things in the matter of usury fought a losing battle. One of these was Thomas Wilson (1525–81), an Englishman, whose *Discourse on Usury* was published in 1572. English legislation on this subject had wavered, at times allowing interest up to 10 percent and at other times outlawing it altogether. After much vacillation a compromise bill was passed in 1571 which made interest up to 10 percent lawful but unenforceable before the courts. Wilson in his book, which is written in the form of a dialogue between a preacher, a lawyer, a merchant, and a doctor of the civil laws, opposed all interest—except for some extrinsic titles—just as he had done as a member of Parliament when the bill of 1571 was debated, a view then already on the way out and supported by only one other member.

Wilson was steeped in the civil law that he had studied in Italy when seeking refuge at the time of the accession of Queen Mary I to the throne under Queen Elizabeth. His condemnation of interest reflects his civil-law training which made him a belated defender of the medieval order of things, and a deeply felt religious impulse which made him look with aversion on the commercial hustle and bustle of his time.

DUMOULIN

A writer to take a view diametrically opposed to that of Wilson was the great French jurist Charles Dumoulin, latinized Molinaeus, who is still remembered in legal history. In his *Treatise on Contracts and Usury,* published in Paris in 1546, Dumoulin attacked the very basis of the usury doctrine, denied that interest on loans was forbidden by divine law, and proposed the regulation of interest rates by public authorities. Dumoulin's view may reflect the influence of Calvin. As a result of the publication of the *Treatise* and of other controversial writings Dumoulin had to seek refuge at German universities. He was declared a heretic and his book condemned to be burned and put on the Index.

JOHN HALES

Only a few writers of the time went beyond the discussion of usury and broke new paths along other lines of economic thought. One of these was the author of a dialogue published in 1581 under the title *A Compendious or Brief Examination of certain ordinary complaints of diverse of our countrymen in these our days: which although they are in some part unjust and frivolous, yet are they all by way of dialogues thoroughly debated and discussed by W.S. Gentleman.* This was reprinted on several occasions, the most recent in 1893 under the title *A Discourse of the Common Weal of this Realm of England.*

The question of the authorship of the work has never been definitely settled. The richness of its thought and the vividness with which the speakers are portrayed in their roles of knight, merchant, doctor, husbandman, and craftsman gave some semblance of plausibility to the claim of an eighteenth-century publisher that its author W.S. was no other than William Shakespeare. But since Shakespeare was a youth of seventeen in 1581, this claim must be denied, and the weight of authority now supports the view that it was written by John Hales (d. 1571) in the mid-sixteenth century. Hales, a member of Parliament, was involved in a number of the controversies of his time, including the struggle about enclosures, which next to the usury problem was one of the great issues. He had to leave England during the reign of Queen Mary I and again during the reign of Queen Elizabeth I. There is some evidence that the leading figure in the dialogue, the doctor, has been modeled after the ill-fated Bishop Hugh Latimer, still remembered for his last words at the stake in 1655: "We shall this day light such a candle by God's grace in England as I trust shall never be put out."

A number of Hales's ideas have proved forward-looking and influential. Here was a man speculating about economic questions who was no theologian and, unlike Wilson, no jurist. Nor did he argue as a special pleader, promoting interests of his own or of his class, as the mercantilist writers of the next century were apt to do. The greatness of Hales consists of his awareness of the need to discipline this new inchoate thought by finding a place for it in the hierarchy of the sciences. This might be confining, but it also meant coherence, system, intellectual backbone, and the dignity of an honorific name.

Economic thought is unhesitatingly declared by Hales to be a branch of "moral philosophy." Hereby Hales established a tradition that was followed by the best minds in English thought, leading from Locke and Hume to Adam Smith, John Stuart Mill, Henry Sidgwick, and John Neville Keynes. By putting the philosopher in charge of an important department of thought on worldly affairs, the Platonic ideal of making him king was given its closest approximation. Even if he is not king, he is at least an indispensable expert who comes to the subject with special skill and experience and thus lifts it beyond the reaches of mere table talk. "What commonweal," Hales asks, "can be without either a governor or counselor that should be expert in this kind of learning?"

The promotion of economics to a branch of moral philosophy accounts in no small measure for the excellence of English economic thought and differentiates it sharply from the continental *Polizeiwissenschaft*. Philosophical as the new learning is, it is nevertheless definitely problem- or policy-oriented. "Most of this matter contains policy or good government of a commonweal." Its method is that unique blend of empiricism and speculative thought that up to the present time has been the hallmark of economic reasoning at its highest. "Let that then be set for a sure ground that experience does further wisdom, and take it as it were the father of wisdom."

The branch of moral philosophy of which Hales treats teaches "first, how every man should govern himself honestly and profitably; secondly, how he should guide his family wisely; and thirdly, it shows how a city or realm or any other commonweal should be well ordered and governed." The general hypothesis that serves as a basis for Hales's discussion is that man is driven by self-interest, and "every man will seek where most advantage is." Furthermore, "that thing which is profitable to each man by himself...is profitable to the whole community." This rule, however, does not point to an unqualified harmony of interests since it applies only if the pursuit of gain "is not prejudicial to any other" person. To Hales the harmony of interests is less obvious than it was to be to Adam Smith, and more than competition is required to to produce it. Perhaps legislation might help, but "it were hard to make a law therein (so many as have profit by that matter resisting it). And if such a law were made, yet men, studying still there most profit, would defraud the law by one means or other." The guidance of self-interest thus becomes an important concern of public policy. This was a matter to which thoughtful men gave much attention, and not all arrived at the same solution. Cardinal Pole, a contemporary of Henry VIII, reportedly suggested that people learn to identify their own long-run interest with that of the state and thus recognize that by promoting the public interest they promote their own.

Hales depicts the operation of economic incentives that prompt the movement of economic resources from less to more profitable employments. If it is desired to raise the production in the former, these must either be made more profitable or the latter less so. If a transfer is desired on grounds of public policy, it will be more effective to accomplish it by means of "allurement" and rewards than by compulsion.

In matters of international economics Hales is open-minded, but in a number of questions his arguments are tinged by the preconceptions of the mercantilists. A country's endowment with resources seems to him the gift of Providence. What one country lacks, another brings forth, and what "one country lacks this year, another has plenty thereof the same year," so "that one may know they have need of another's help, and thereby love and society to grow amongst all the more." The balance of trade, that exports must pay for imports, is clearly recognized. Hales frowns on the importation of "trifles" and of manufactures produced abroad from British raw materials. By exporting these items, foreigners "find an easier way to get treasure by things of no value than by any mines of gold or silver." Even if foreign goods are cheaper, it is still preferable "to pay more to our own people for those wares than less to strangers," otherwise the buyer's gain would be the country's loss. Hales also frowns on selling cheap and buying dear, which leads to impoverishment.

Economic development deserves promotion, especially the introduction of new arts and crafts "whereby the people might be set awork, with such things as should both find their workmen awork, and also bring some treasure or commodity into the country." Freedom of entry into crafts and trades will be of help, especially in the rehabilitation of depressed localities and areas. Three classes of "mysteries," that is, of trades and crafts, are distinguished: first, those that sell at home "wares growing beyond the seas" and bring out treasure; second, those that sell at home domestic products; and third, those that bring in treasure by selling their wares abroad. The first class is tolerable but not necessary; the third class is the one most cherished.

As was common among the writers of his time, Hales deplores the evils of debasement. In this connection, paper money is mentioned, albeit as an absurdity. Gresham's law, by then a commonplace, is stated. The prince or his subjects must accumulate treasure to have on hand in time of war or of dearth. But does not lucre drive men to all kinds of mischief? Yes, but whereas it may be commendable for a few to renounce it, "it is not necessary for the commonwealth that all men should do so, no more than for all men to be virgins, though privately in some it is commendable."

The special problem that is the subject matter of Hales's dialogue is the problem of a general increase in prices. This does not occur as a result of a deficiency of supply but instead poses the paradox of dearth in the midst of plenty. Those "that live by buying and selling" are the principal gainers from the increase in prices, "for as they buy dear, so they sell thereafter." Those who live on fixed incomes are the principal losers. What is the cause of the general dearth? Is it the husbandman who charges higher prices for his products? Or is it the gentleman who raises the rent? Or the merchant who asks more for his wares? "One thing hangs upon another, and sets forward one another; but one, first of all, is the chief cause of all this circular motion and impulsion." This chief cause Hales considers to have been the debasement of money.

Such was the wording of Hales's manuscript, written before 1565. The only important addition, found in the printed version of 1581, is a reference to another factor making for higher prices, one not relating to a deterioration of the quality of money but to an increase in its quantity, to "the great store and plenty of treasure..., far more in these our days than ever our forefathers have seen in times past. Who does not understand of the infinite sums of gold and silver which are gathered from the Indies and other countries, and so yearly transported unto these coasts?" Here new ideas are expressed, containing both the germ of the quantity theory of money as well as the statement of a historical cause responsible for the increase in prices that was noted throughout Europe from the sixteenth century on. However, credit for these new ideas is not due to Hales or to W.S. but to others, principally Jean Bodin, the greatest figure among sixteenth-century economic writers.

THE EMERGENCE OF THE QUANTITY THEORY OF MONEY

The emergence of the quantity theory of money in the second half of the sixteenth century constitutes an event of momentous importance in the history of economics. Implied in this theory is the application of demand and supply analysis to money. Prices are seen as determined by the demand for and the supply of money. If the demand for money, that is, the offering of goods for money, remains unchanged, and if the supply of money increases, the price level will rise. Conversely, if the supply of money falls, the price level will decrease. This is the theory in its simplest form.

In the course of time the quantity theory of money has been refined in various ways, and although it has met much criticism and has in recent decades been pushed into the background by the analysis of income and expenditure, it nevertheless has always had some following as an explanation of changes in the price level. Its importance in doctrinal history is so great because by implicitly involving the demand and supply apparatus it prepared the ground for the eventual emergence of demand and supply analysis as a general explanatory principle, a development that stretched over three centuries and culminated in the work of Alfred Marshall at the close of the nineteenth century.

Although nobody can deny the importance of the rise of the quantity theory in itself, the circumstances of its birth also shed light on the manner and conditions attending the evolution of new ideas in economic thought. As is true of many other such innovations, changes in economic conditions were an important factor in stimulating new thought. During the Middle Ages the inadequacy of the money supply had put a damper on economic expansion. Now, with the discovery of the New World, a never-ending stream of treasure arrived in Spain and was diffused over the whole of Europe. Prices rose, and as the traditional explanation of changes in the price level, which had made much of the debasement of money as the principal cause, did not seem to fit the changing circumstances as well as it had before, thoughtful people in many lands searched for a better reason.

Considerations of practical policy were a second factor that prompted the rise of new thought. If debasement was no longer the principal cause of increasing prices, greater stability of the price level would call for policies other than the mere shunning of debasement. Hales had ostensibly written his book to discuss the complaints of his countrymen about economic conditions, and their chief complaint was the increase in prices. His purpose was not merely to air and ventilate these complaints but to investigate ways to alleviate them. To do this, a new explanation, hypothesis, or "theory" had to be developed. Similarly, some Spanish theologians who pioneered in the formation of the quantity theory did so not for the sake of speculation but because they wanted to resolve some practical problems of business ethics.

Again, the sequence of events leading to the emergence of the quantity theory sheds light not only on the stimulation and motivation of those who advanced the frontiers of knowledge but also illustrates a typical case of the various steps that are involved in the making of important discoveries in economics. Like many a great discovery it was first observed by an outsider who apparently approached the matter from a wider perspective than did the experts laboring closer to it. That the outsider happened to be a genius, the great astronomer Copernicus, was only incidental. In the later history of economics the pioneer was sometimes a nondescript person or even a crank.

COPERNICUS

Copernicus was a universal genius who combined faithful service as a clergyman with expert knowledge in a number of sciences, including mathematics, canon law, and medicine. In 1522 he had explained to the Prussian diet the principles on which a sound currency is based, and on behest of the king of Poland he had put his observations into writing four years later. All this illustrates again the policy implications of new thought in economics. His relevant statement was this: "Money usually depreciates when it becomes too abundant." To this crisp formulation of the quantity theory he had added an illustration: "for example, when so much silver has been transformed into money that there is more demand for bars than for coins." This peculiar illustration may indicate that the diminution of the value of money accompanying an increase in its quantity was considered by Copernicus to occur mainly or exclusively in relation to the commodity value of the monetary metal rather than to the value of all other commodities. It is uncertain whether he meant to enunciate this more restrictive principle or whether he had in mind a more universally applicable theory.

Copernicus's tract was not published until the nineteenth century and may not have had much influence on the thought of his contemporaries. In any event, his discovery, whatever its range and effect may have been, is especially remarkable because chronologically it antedates the large-scale movement of precious metals from America to Europe. By the power of reasoning and by the ability to invent fruitful hypotheses, a great mind may discover relations that ordinary people can recognize only if driven by the stimulus of observation.

"Money usually depreciates when it becomes too abundant"—a great mind is apt to expand the frontiers of science by establishing a general truth, while ordinary investigators are more likely to see the concrete, noticing in this instance the arrival of treasure and connecting with it the rise in prices. The former procedure is closer to the method of deduction, deriving, as it does, general conclusions from the nature of money and of prices. The latter procedure is inductive; it arrives at general laws on the basis of observation of the concrete detail. But even the deductive reasoning process may be stimulated by experience. Although Copernicus may not have noticed the impact of Spanish treasure, there occurred at his time a less conspicuous but nevertheless substantial increase in the supply of precious metals from sources in central Europe, an event that may have set in motion the deductive reasoning process of his superior mind.

NAVARRUS

After Copernicus's rudimentary statement of the quantity theory in the 1520s, it was not until the 1550s that related brief references appear again in the literature. Since the immediate effect of the price revolution, as the long-term, upward movement of prices following the discovery of America is known, was first felt in Spain, it is not surprising that there were a few gifted observers of the Spanish scene who at an early date related the rise in prices to the arrival of precious metals from the New World. One of these was Navarrus, also known as Martin de Azpilcueta, a Dominican priest who had taught canon law at Toulouse and Cahors before joining the faculty at Salamanca. In 1556 he published a manual on moral theology with an appendix devoted to a discussion of usury.

One of the questions that Navarrus examines in this work is the lawfulness of foreign exchange transactions. Can financiers legitimately profit from disparities in the value of money, buying it cheap in one country and selling it dear in another? This question Navarrus in principle answers with a resounding yes. Among the various reasons he gives for disparities of the values of two moneys is their relative scarcity. "Money," he says, "is worth more when and where it is scarce than where it is abundant...; it becomes dearer when it is in strong demand and short supply." Where money is scarce, goods as well as productive services fetch low prices; where it is plentiful, as in Spain after the discovery of the Indies, prices are high. Navarrus thus developed the quantity theory of money in conjunction with a discussion of international prices. Differences in the value of money are anchored in differences in purchasing power, due to differences in the quantity of money.

It is no accident that it was a member of the school of Salamanca who did the pioneer work in the development of the quantity theory of money. Following Aristotle's hint that demand or human need is reflected in price, these writers mentioned both the subjective estimation as well as the cost of production as determinants of price, with varying shades of emphasis on either factor but often underlining the subjective one. They thus came close to a demand-and-supply theory, of which, as has been seen, the quantity theory of money is a special application. The connection between the demand-and-supply approach and the quantity theory of money can be clearly recognized in the words with which Navarrus introduces the matter: "All merchandise becomes dearer when it is in strong demand and short supply. Money, in so far as it may be sold, bartered, or exchanged by some other form of contract, is merchandise and therefore also becomes dearer when it is in great demand and short supply."

Navarrus's book was translated into Latin and Italian and his opinions enjoyed a high reputation among theologians and jurists, both Catholic and Protestant, of the sixteenth and seventeenth centuries. It was not until the 1940s, however, that his role in the discovery of the quantity theory of money was rediscovered.

JEAN BODIN

Credit for the discovery of the quantity theory of money is usually given to Jean Bodin (1530?–96), a French jurist, whose fame lies also in the fields of philosophy of history and political science—to the latter he contributed the theory of sovereignty. Bodin developed the quantity theory of money in 1568 in a *Reply to the Paradoxes of M. Malestroit,* a contemporary writer whose views about money and prices Bodin made the subject of a critical review. Whether Bodin was influenced by Navarrus, or Navarrus by Bodin, is an open question. Navarrus (1493–1586) was much the older of the two. Both had been students at the University of Toulouse, where Navarrus was also to serve as professor. Even if it could be shown that Navarrus's tenure as a teacher at Toulouse overlaps Bodin's residence as a student or that Navarrus was Bodin's teacher, it would prove little since students not only learn from their teachers but also have been known to suggest new ideas to them. Actually, however, the two resided at Toulouse in different periods of time. Navarrus left in 1524 to assume new duties as professor at Salamanca, and Bodin did not come to Toulouse until about twenty-five years later.

Bodin was a paragon of learning, and it is unlikely that Navarrus's book escaped his attention. In a way, communication in the scholarly world was easier in those days than it is now, simply because there was less to be communicated. Books, although not as highly priced as before the invention of printing, were still fairly expensive to produce and there were fewer of them. The channels of communication were not yet clogged up by a huge literary output of which it would have been difficult to keep abreast.

Bodin himself claimed to have been the first to attribute the prevailing high level of prices to the abundance of gold and silver. Apparently the idea was in the air at the time of his writing, and, as did many important innovations in economics, it made its appearance in the literature as a "multiple" rather than as a "singleton." It turns up in English works in the late 1570s, inspired perhaps by an English translation of Bodin's *Reply* said to have been made in 1569 on behest of the Lord Chancellor, of which, however, no trace has been left. Bodin recapitulated his ideas about prices in a section of his *Republic,* first published in 1576, which appeared in an English translation in 1606.

The early history of the quantity theory of money has been traced in some detail because it constitutes a typical example of the manner in which new insight has emerged in economics. An outsider has the first vision. Then, after some time has elapsed, the idea is restated by a number of people. Some discuss it briefly, rudimentarily, and in a context relating to extraneous matter. Others develop it more systematically, at greater length, and as a topic in its own right rather than incidentally in connection with other matters. It is these who have the greatest effect on the further trend of thought, cause the new idea to become assimilated to the main stream of conventional thinking, and earn credit for the innovation. The recognition given to Bodin in the history of economic thought conforms with this pattern.

There are two contrasting views of the nature of creative thought, the *heroic* and the *systematic* theories of invention. The heroic theory interprets an advance in thought as an accident, the spontaneous work of a great man who like a *deus ex machina* happens to appear on the scene. The systematic theory would lay stress on the environmental factors, the conditions of the time, and the work of predecessors, all of which combine to prepare the stage for the development of the new idea. The heroic theory might fit as an explanation of the vision of the outsider. The systematic sheds light on the fact that innovations in economics appear so often as multiples. It is also especially suited to explain advances in modern economics, which has become more analytical and technical but also more mechanical, making it possible for a young man to break a new path by going one step beyond the work of his predecessors.

A long way had to be covered before economics reached this stage. Bodin's thought is classificatory rather than analytical, and his main contribution is a classification of the factors that account for changes in the price level. Such changes in general prices are distinguished from changes in relative prices. Bodin's discussion is altogether sound and has withstood the test of time. He sees five causes of an increase in prices: abundance of gold and silver, monopolies, scarcity of goods caused by exports and waste, luxury of kings and noblemen, and debasement of the coin. What Bodin says about the luxury of kings and noblemen is especially noteworthy because he describes not only its immediate impact on prices but he brings in psychological considerations, pointing to the "demonstration effect" and to "conspicuous consumption": People, he says, "esteem and raise in price everything that the great lords like, though the things in themselves are not worth that valuation." The "snob effect" comes into play "when the great lords see that their subjects have an abundance of things that they themselves like." They then "begin to despise them," causing their prices to fall.

Since Bodin sees in the abundance of gold and silver the "principal and almost only reason" for the increase in prices, he is not much concerned with the further accumulation of treasure and his discussion is free of the mercantilist prejudices of a later age. He endorses foreign trade not only on economic grounds but also "to maintain communication and keep up a good feeling" among nations. Although exports may be responsible for higher prices, imports will have the opposite effect. To stabilize the supply of wheat and its price he proposes the founding of public granaries, to be replenished every year. And to prevent the competitive debasement of money, he suggests that countries join in an international agreement providing for the exclusive issue of full-bodied money.

Bodin was burdened with vast learning, the outpouring of which often stifled the development of his own thought. He was in many ways a typical exponent of an age of transition, torn between the old and the new, a writer about paradoxes and paradoxical himself. Suspected by his contemporaries, and not entirely without reason, of being a religious nonconformist, he nevertheless was ultraconservative in his views on interest: there is no difference, he held, between moderate and exorbitant usury—God forbade them both. His authority was without rival in economic questions, as it also was in the special branch of the law of his time that dealt with the legal subtleties involved in the prosecution of witches, demons, and sorcerers. And in an argument replete with astrological considerations and mystic figures, he refuted the view that mankind had degenerated from a golden age of the past, expressing instead his belief in the value and worth of his own age and coming close to enunciating what was to become one of the central ideas of modern times—the idea of progress.

Chapter 5

MERCANTILISM:

Economic Warfare

for National Gain

In the seventeenth and eighteenth centuries economic literature assumed the dimensions of a veritable flood. A great library specializing in this kind of material, such as the Kress Library at Harvard University, may list in its catalogue some two hundred entries of pamphlets and books written in the sixteenth century. In the seventeenth century this small trickle increases tenfold to some two thousand entries, and in the folllowing seventy-five-year period, which ends with the publication of Adam Smith's *Wealth of Nations* in 1776, the number of entries goes up to five thousand. There are some stout folios and many-volume works in the literature, but much of it consists of small tracts or essays covering a few dozen pages.

Before 1776, systematic works on economics, that is, treatises covering the whole subject in a consistent and comprehensive matter, were few. Instead, the bulk of the earlier literature was devoted to special phases or aspects of the subject. The writing was usually stimulated by the events of the day, and it was often designed to assist the public authorities in policy making or to influence them by special pleading.

Hence, economics, or "political economy"—the phrase occurs in 1615 in the title of an otherwise undistinguished book written by a French hardware manufacturer—was not systematized during the period under discussion. Nor did it become professionalized in the sense of being developed by a group of people banded together by special training and common functions. Rather, as a modern observer has put it, every one was his own economist. The writers of the period include public officials, journalists, scientists, philosophers—and especially businessmen.

MERCANTILISM:
ECONOMIC WARFARE
FOR NATIONAL GAIN

Nothing brings out more strikingly the break with the past than the fact that the leading economic thinkers of the period were apt to be leading businessmen. Child, an outstanding figure in the economic discussion, was the wealthiest Englishman of the seventeenth century. Both he and Mun, another outstanding writer on economic questions, were closely associated and had leading positions with the East India Company. Trade and pecuniary gain, which in an earlier age had been looked upon with so much suspicion, now came into their own. In the Middle Ages the Schoolmen had outlined a narrow path along which a businessman might travel without endangering his salvation. Much of what they had to say was designed to protect the economic position of the consumer. There were still enclaves in which the old order persisted, more than anywhere perhaps in the Puritan theocracy of New England, where there is on record the famous case of a Boston businessman who in 1639 found himself harangued from the pulpit for having committed the sin of overcharging and related offenses. But on the whole it was the businessman rather than the moralist who took office as judge of business behavior—his own—and of public policies affecting the economy. With the new judge there came new criteria to determine the appropriateness of action, and among these the attainment of power and plenty in this world came to weigh more heavily than the salvation of souls in the next one.

THE MAN OF THE RENAISSANCE

In a way the combination of thought and action represented by the career of Child or Mun, and still more so, as will be seen, by that of Petty, was a phenomenon typical of the Renaissance. Versatility rather than specialization was the hallmark of the ideal of the Renaissance, the "universal man" who was to develop his individual potentialities to the utmost and in all possible directions. This ideal was closely approximated by such great figures as Lorenzo de' Medici, the merchant prince and ruler of Florence who was also a reputable scholar and poet, and Leonardo da Vinci, the painter, sculptor, architect, musician, engineer, and scientist. On a much smaller scale it was pursued by Montchrétien (c.1575–1621), the French hardware manufacturer who besides authoring the *Traité de l'économie politique* in 1615 gained fame as a minor poet.

In the economic sphere the repudiation of specialization meant disavowal of the division of labor between the thinkers and the doers. As the thinkers of old had wielded not only the spiritual sword, powerful enough as is was, but had claims to obedience against those who wielded the temporal sword, the usurpation of thought by the businessman himself freed him from many fetters and made possible the pursuit of a Machiavellianism under which everything was allowed that helped to bring about one's goals.

ECONOMIC THOUGHT OF THE PERIOD

That so many businessmen attained stature as economic thinkers had its effects on the quality of economic thought. By the standards of their own time as well as by our own these men were well-educated, trained in the humanities, familiar with several languages—not excluding Latin and Greek—and able to draw on suitable authorities for quotations to support their arguments. Child, the staid businessman, was not averse to citing Hobbes, the bête noire among the philosophers of the age, if it fitted his purposes, but not without adding the saving clause: "how erroneous soever he may be in other things."

In general, the thought of the period was eminently practical and policy oriented, largely based on what was considered observation of reality but also on a few general principles. On the empirical side it often failed because of the tendency to interpret as cause-and-effect relationships mere sequences of events that followed each other in time. Such lapses into the fallacies of *"non-sequitur"* or *"post hoc, ergo propter hoc"* were common when writers attempted to make the bare facts speak. But observation of facts yields insight only if the facts are seen as part of a larger whole. The writers of the period were interested in a few special economic problems and they did not have on hand, nor did they try to construct, an integrated model of the economy showing the relationships among the relevant variables such as only the pursuit of systematic knowledge can produce. As they were usually concerned with a segment of the economy, their thought lacked this integration and was replete with contradictions.

As for general principles, these were frequently enunciated in the economic literature, with the view of buttressing concrete policy proposals. Rarely, however, was an attempt made to link the general principle with the policy proposal by means of a detailed and cogent process of reasoning.

NATIONAL CHARACTERISTICS

The observations made thus far apply especially to England, where the connection between economic thought and business was especially close. However, with all its shortcomings, English economic thought was far superior to that of other countries. The Dutch, whose flourishing economy contemporary observers never failed to admire and envy, produced no economic thinker of note. In the one exhaustive study of Dutch economic thought of the period, a study now over a hundred years old, the author commented on this discrepancy between the thought and the accomplishments of the Dutch and concluded that the more an economy prospers, the less is written about it. This observation, however, is not borne out by the facts. In Spain the decay of the economy failed to stimulate notable economic thought, whereas in prosperous countries such as Italy and France contributions of significance were made, in France mainly by statesmen and government officials. In Germany, still backward in large regions, developments took a course of their own under the tutelage of absolute territorial rulers, who established in Halle and Frankfurt an der Oder the first university chairs for their kind of economics in the first half of the eighteenth century, the one in Halle filled by a law professor named Simon Peter Gasser in 1727, the other by a historian.

SPECIAL PLEADING

The situation in England, where the businessman-economist was so prominent, calls for some further comment. Not seldom these men dealt in their writings with matters involving their own private interests, which in turn were bound to be affected by the policies advocated by them. Unlike the high official of General Motors who claimed that what is good for General Motors is good also for the United States, these men were aware of the possibility of conflict between their own interests and those of society. Some of their writings were envenomed by bitter invective, and if they had failed to show such awareness, their adversary in the debate would no doubt have made the most of it. Thus economic writings became suspect as special pleading. Attempts to allay suspicion were likely to breed only more of it. Such attempts usually assumed the form of a disclaimer in which the author affirmed his attachment to the interests of society and promised to place these above his own. So widespread did this practice become that even John Locke, the great philosopher and servant of the state, and not a businessman, felt compelled to open up his argument against a reduction of the interest rate with these words:

> I have so little concern in paying or receiving 'interest' that were I in no more danger to be misled by inability and ignorance than I am to be biased by interest and inclination, I might hope to give you a very perfect and clear account of the consequences of a law to reduce interest to four percent.

In another tract the same author affirms:

> I shall never knowingly be of any but truth's and my country's side; the former I shall always gladly embrace and own, whoever shows it me: and in these papers, I am sure, I have no other aim but to do what little I can for the service of my country.

The suspicion that the writer was a special pleader placed severe limits on the effectiveness of economic literature as an instrument that could influence public opinion and policy makers. A number of remedies were tried to remove this weakness. One was the blending of the verbal argument with quantitative, that is, presumably objective, considerations. The other consisted of a sharpening of the argument and its elevation to a higher level of abstraction, where it would seem to be removed from the struggles of the day. As will be seen, both remedies were tried by the foremost thinkers of the age.

MERCANTILISM

The first attempt to systematize the thought of the writers here considered, those of the seventeenth and the first half of the eighteenth century, was made in 1776 by Adam Smith in Book IV of the *Wealth of Nations,* which discusses the "Systems of Political Economy." By far the larger part of Book IV, more than 200 pages, contains a review of what Smith calls "the commercial or mercantile system." Smith's intent was principally critical. He held up the weaknesses of the mercantile system and exposed them in the strong light of his own system of economic freedom. To him the mercantile system was a fraud perpetrated by the business class on the public: "The interested sophistry of merchants and manufacturers confounded the common sense of mankind." What Smith called the mercantile system later became known as mercantilism.

Mercantilism is now understood both as a bundle of ideas and as an exercise in statecraft. The second aspect is primarily of interest to the student of economic history. In the present context it is principally the ideas of the mercantilists that call for discussion. These developed against a background of rivalry and warfare among the great powers of Europe, which were at peace in only a single year during the period from 1600 to 1667. England, once a backwater, had successfully challenged the Spanish Armada in 1588. In the seventeenth century, she took on the Dutch, then the strongest commercial nation of Europe, and early in the eighteenth she put an end to the expansion of France, then the most powerful military country of Europe. The rise of mercantilist thought thus parallels the rise of England and the British Empire as a world power.

ECONOMIC RIVALRIES

The Dutch, located at the crossroads of east-west and north-south trade, had made the most of the opportunities offered by geographic location and had developed a profitable carrying trade side by side with their seasonal fisheries. Both activities provided a reserve of naval strength and stimulated a host of auxiliary industries. The Dutch fisheries, which had been a minor enterprise in medieval times, expanded greatly after the early fifteenth century, when the capricious behavior of the Gulf Stream brought the herring from the Baltic Sea to the Dutch and English coastal waters. The herring became both a source and a symbol of Dutch commercial strength and of Dutch-English commercial rivalries, which a common religious preference did little to restrain. In the protracted conflicts that the troubling of the English waters by the Dutch brought about, there was born an economic literature dealing with matters of international trade and finance as well as the modern law of nations, which takes its starting point from the work of Hugo Grotius, the Dutch jurist, who in his *Mare Liberum* of 1609 asserted that the sea was free to all, provoking the English reply from John Selden in his *Mare Clausum* of 1635.

It was, however, not only international rivalry that formed the background of mercantilist controversies but also domestic conflicts of interest. Tracts and pamphlets were used as weapons by the spokesmen of the great chartered companies which were active in foreign trade and colonization. Of these there were two kinds, the regulated company whose members traded on their own, and the joint-stock company whose operations resembled those of the modern corporation. Both needed a charter and had to cultivate good relations with the king, high officials, and the public. They were often involved in bitter hostilities and jealousies among themselves. Thus the Society of Merchant Adventurers, the oldest and most widely known of the regulated companies, founded in 1359, might denounce the East India Company, the greatest of all of them, chartered in 1600, and both might find fault with the "free traders" or interlopers who carried on independent activities. On occasion, however, regulated companies, joint-stock companies, and interlopers were united in their complaints about merchant bankers and financiers. If they did not deplore high rates of interest, they accused them of manipulating foreign-exchange rates. Thus the usury controversy did not die down but was transformed from a moral into an economic issue.

THE BALANCE OF TRADE

The central doctrine in mercantilist thought is that of the "balance of trade," a phrase probably derived from accounting precedents, which seems to have come into usage in the 1610s. As enunciated by Francis Bacon in 1616, the doctrine states: "Let the foundation of profitable trade be thus laid that the exportation of home commodities be more in value than the importation of foreign, so we shall be sure that the stocks of the Kingdom shall increase, for the balance of trade must be returned in money or bullion." The underlying idea is an old one that in medieval times had served as the basis of a comprehensive system of "bullionist" regulations of individual import and export transactions, aiming at what a nineteenth-century writer was to call "balance of bargains."

By 1600 little was left of these regulations except the prohibition of the export of coin or bullion. It was about this matter that the first great controversy in English economic thought developed. At least one extremist, the diplomat and customs official Thomas Milles (c.1550–c.1627), wanted to restore the earlier system with its "staple," which restricted the export trade to certain companies and towns, its "hosting," which meant the supervision of foreign merchants by local "hosts," its "statutes of employment," which compelled the foreign seller to employ the proceeds from an import on the purchase of English merchandise, its Royal Exchequer, which was to be transformed into an instrument of exchange control, and other ancient institutions which had long fallen into disuse.

Milles was so much out of step with the time that his pamphlets had little influence, but as they contained attacks against the merchant adventurers, John Wheeler (c.1553–c.1611), the secretary of the society, replied to these in his *Treatise of Commerce* of 1601. This work is an apology for what would now be called *orderly competition* as carried on by the society's thirty-five hundred members. This state of affairs is much preferable to "the straggling and single merchant's trade," but it must not be confused with monopoly—of which the society had been accused. According to Wheeler, "monopoly is when one man alone buys up all that is to be got of one kind of merchandise, to the end that he alone may sell at his own lust and pleasure." Although denying that the society is a monopoly, Wheeler nevertheless is at pains to show up the advantage that the producer of export articles derives from the marketing by the members of the society who are "united and held together by their good government and by their politic and merchantlike orders," advantages that the interloper is unable to procure.

Milles found much fault with the regulated companies, as he did with the bankers. The object of his most violent denunciation was foreign exchange transactions. "Merchandise exchange," he said, "is that labyrinth of errors and private practice, whereby (though kings wear crowns and seem absolutely to reign) particular bankers, private societies of merchants, and covetous persons (whose end is private gain) are to suspend their councils and control their policies...thus making kings to be subjects and vassals to be kings."

MALYNES

Milles's prejudices against foreign exchange transactions were shared by Gerard de Malynes (fl.1586–1641), who proudly called himself a merchant and who had a part in a number of business adventures of the time, fortunate as well as unfortunate, one of the latter causing him to spend some time in the London debtors' prison. He was to generalize on the basis of personal misfortune and to ascribe the occasionally sad state of his own and national affairs to the machinations of the bankers. Interlaced with Malynes's business career were a number of important government positions, with the mint and as financial adviser. He has been described as a "perennial office-seeker," and as his name became more and more identified with the plea for exchange control, it is not surprising that he expected to be appointed controller if his proposals were accepted.

Because of the special importance that men like Milles and Malynes attached to the regulation of foreign exchange transactions, they have been christened "bullionists" by some later students of mercantilism. Malynes's picture of the world was in substance that of a medievalist who lived in an environment that he found difficult to accept. He was deeply suspicious of usury and his thought in this matter reflects the not always acknowledged influence of Thomas Wilson. Although grudgingly willing to tolerate some forms of the evil, he concentrated his ire on foreign exchange transactions, which to him seemed to serve as a cover for an especially vicious type of usury. His complaint that money, by nature a mere measure, had become an article of commerce, and his insistence that exchanges should be traded at par recall the medieval notions of money and of the just price. His ideal was an orderly, static, and well-regulated economic universe, in which the desire for gain was always to be restrained by public policy.

Malynes's long and active career as a writer begins with an eighty-page tract, *Saint George for England Allegorically Described,* published in 1601, in which Saint George—the king—comes to the help of the fair lady —his treasure—who finds herself threatened by a dragon, equipped with wings that stand for usury and a tail that represents fluctuations of the exchange rate. Saint George finds himself in an unhappy dilemma, however, because if he were to kill the monster at once, its end would mean the cessation of all usury, something the economy could not bear. He is therefore advised to proceed gradually and let the dragon die a lingering death. In another context usury is depicted as a wolf held by its ears, "dangerous to be kept and more dangerous to abandon."

Less replete with gothic tales and zoological analogies, and more profound in its economic analysis, is another work of Malynes's of the same year, a tract of some 120 pages which carriees the title *A Treatise of the Canker of England's Common Wealth.* It is "divided into three parts; wherein the author, imitating the rule of good physicians, first, declares the disease; secondarily, shows the efficient cause thereof; lastly, a remedy for the same." The economist appears here garbed in the clothes of the physician, a figure of speech that will often recur in the literature. In the manner of the time, which was to become a cliché, the commonwealth is depicted as a great household or family. Just as a family will suffer a decline in its wealth if its purchases exceed its income, so does a commonwealth if its foreign purchases exceed its foreign sales. "This is the unknown disease...."

THE TERMS OF TRADE

Malynes does not speak of the balance of trade in so many words but insists that a country should have "a certain equality" of its exports and imports. It should not suffer "an overbalancing of foreign commodities" with home commodities which will cause it to lose wealth. Such a loss may be incurred in three ways: by exporting bullion or coin, by selling domestic goods too cheaply, or by buying foreign goods at too high a price "wherein chiefly consists the aforesaid overbalancing." Malynes is thus concerned with more than the mere balance of trade, the relationship between exports and imports. "This overbalancing," he says, "consists properly in the price of commodities, and not in the quantity or quality," that is, the overbalancing is connected with what is now known as "terms of trade," the relationship between the prices of exports and imports.

The terms of trade have deteriorated because prices abroad have increased faster than English prices. The change in prices has come about —and here Malynes bases his argument upon the findings of Bodin, with whose work he was quite familiar—as the result of the diffusion of American treasure in Europe as well as of the alteration of foreign coin, a devaluation that raised foreign prices. Implied in this argument is the view that the diffusion of American treasure did not elevate prices everywhere in the same proportion, a matter discussed by Malynes in another work.

England thus buys dear and sells cheap. Would devaluation of the English coin, a measure always proposed by a few, be of help in this situation? Malynes rejects this remedy, stating that it would raise prices both at home and abroad, and abroad more than at home.

THE RATE OF EXCHANGE

When England's exports fell short of her imports, foreign claims on England would exceed English claims on foreigners. The demand for foreign exchange would exceed the supply, English exchange would fall, and foreign exchange would rise up to the specie export point. The latter would be substantially above parity, much more so than in modern times, because of the seignorage—a charge for coinage not abolished until 1666 —and the high cost of transporting, insuring, and smuggling coin or bullion out of the country, the whole transaction being unlawful. Once the foreign exchange rate had exceeded the specie export point, a merchant who had to make a payment abroad would find it to his advantage to ship coin or bullion rather than purchase foreign exchange. Of all this, Malynes was aware, but with the blindness and obstinateness of a fanatic believer in conspiracy theories, he closed his eyes to the fact that fluctuations of the exchange rate, which give rise to specie exports, reflect commercial operations. Instead, he attributed to the bankers the power to manipulate the rate of exchange for the sake of their own gain, and he denounced them as being responsible for the outflow of specie accompanying a rising foreign exchange. This, to him, was "the efficient cause of the disease of the body politic."

Malynes's mind had a speculative bent that enabled him to detect relationships—not only figments of his imagination but also real insights—that were beyond the grasp of his contemporaries. While attaching vital importance to the balance of trade, neither he nor they ever raised in so many words the question, what determines exports and imports? Nevertheless, 150 years ahead of Hume's theory of the automatic flow of specie and attending changes in prices, which was to bring the curtain down on mercantilist thought, he came close to providing the answer: The rise in the foreign exchange rate "causes our monies to be transported and makes scarcity thereof, which abates the price of our home commodities, and on the contrary advances the price of the foreign commodities beyond the seas, where our money concurring with the monies of other countries causes plenty, whereby the price of foreign commodities is advanced." The thought is not developed, however, and instead Malynes goes on to discuss the consequences of a low rate of foreign exchange, or what is the same, of a high English exchange.

Because a high rate of foreign exchange—or a low rate of English exchange—leads to an outflow of specie from England, one would think that a low rate of foreign exchange—or a high rate of English exchange—would bring specie into England. Normally an English exporter's factor might use the proceeds from the sale of English goods on the continent to purchase a bill of exchange on London, drawn by the London banker's foreign correspondent. If the London exchange were high enough, the factor would prefer to ship specie once the specie import point had been reached. But this is not Malynes's argument. If the English exchange is high, that is, if per unit of foreign balances little English money can be obtained, the proceeds from exports will be used neither for the purchases of bills of exchange on London nor for the importation of specie. Instead they will be spent on luxury imports procured by the bankers and their factors who follow the English merchants abroad "as the eagle follows her prey," charging them high prices and again causing "overbalancing."

Thus, according to Malynes, neither a low nor a high rate of English exchange will bring specie into the country. Again and again the fluctuations of the exchange rate are ascribed to the tricks of the bankers rather than to the movement of exports and imports. The remedy that Malynes proposes is the elimination of fluctuations of exchange rates by pegging the rates at mint parity, combined with a comprehensive system of exchange control.

Malynes is highly optimistic about the benefits that will follow from the adoption of his proposal. His list includes the following statement: "The commodities of the realm will be advanced in sale and price." It is not clear, however, how this would be so if the exchange were raised to mint parity, causing English goods to become more expensive to foreign purchasers. Perhaps Malynes considered the foreign demand for English goods—mainly cloth—inelastic, and this indeed is indicated in statements that he made elsewhere. In this situation a modern theorist might endorse the proposal for an appreciation of the exchange rate, even though domestic commodities would not be "advanced in sale" thereby. In any event, the flow of specie into England, which Malynes expected to take place if his proposal were adopted, would raise English prices. This in turn would improve the terms of trade and increase employment at home. It would "set not only more people on work to make our home commodities, but also other commodities now imported, having within the realm fit matter or stuff thereunto." Thus Malynes can be credited with an early use of the employment argument in favor of higher prices.

Malynes never lost his belief in the secret power of the banking fraternity and affirmed it, frequently with violence and bitterness, in his later writings. In 1622, some twenty years after the publication of the *Treatise of the Canker of England's Common Wealth* he published what some consider his greatest work, *Consuetudo vel Lex Mercatoria or the Ancient Law-Merchant,* which was reprinted several times and went into three editions. Unlike his other writings this is a stout folio, which served as a reference work for such matters as maritime and commercial law and accounting. It is divided into three long parts—the first discusses "commodities, compared to the body of traffic"; the second, "monies compared to the soul of traffic"; and the third, "exchanges for money by bills of exchanges, compared to spirit or faculty for the soul of traffic." These metaphors were in line with the thought of the time, which was groping for principles that would shed light on social life similar to those that ruled natural phenomena.

MISSELDEN

Malynes's views about the exchanges were challenged by the balance-of-trade theorists, such as Misselden and Mun, who played down the influence of bankers and who believed that the outflow of specie was not the result of a low English exchange but of an "unfavorable" balance of trade. Edward Misselden (fl.1608–54), a businessman with a checkered career, a merchant adventurer who at times also served the East India Company, tried to explain the causes of the business depression from which England was suffering in the early 1620s in a tract of approximately 130 pages, *Free Trade or the Means to Make Trade Flourish,* published in 1622. This tract was an apology for the merchant adventurers and an indictment of the East India Company, with which Misselden was not yet associated.

Like all mercantilists, Misselden is obsessed by the idea that England needs more specie. To obtain it, she must force exports and restrain imports. When Misselden employs the words "free trade," he by no means wants to endorse what the term connotes now, that is, absence of restrictions on imports. What he had in mind was "freedom from competition" as well as "freedom to export," that is, a trade that was neither disorganized, such as that of the competitive interlopers, nor monopolized by a joint-stock company, such as was the East India trade by the great East India Company. In line with what Wheeler had argued some twenty years earlier, Misselden tries to absolve the merchant adventurers, who each trade on his own account, of constituting a monopoly. More adequately than his predecessor he defines monopoly as "a kind of commerce, in buying, selling, changing or bartering usurped by a few, and sometimes but by one person, and forestalled from all others, to the gain of the monopolist and to the detriment of other men." Every monopoly turns upon two hinges: "the restraint of the liberty of commerce to some one or few, and the setting of the price at the pleasure of the monopolian to his private benefit, and the prejudice of the public." But while Misselden castigates the monopolist, he by no means favors pure or perfect competition in the modern sense. The orderly competition that he supports is a market structure most adequately classified as oligopoly, although he does not use this word. The term had been introduced by Saint Thomas More in his *Utopia* of 1518, but as it was not employed in the English translations of this Latin work, it did not come into common usage until some four hundred years later, after Chamberlin had published his *Theory of Monopolistic Competition* in 1933.

To carry on its trade with the Orient, the East India Company was licensed to export stated amounts of treasure. Its particular balance of trade was thus decidedly "unfavorable," a matter that was a source of irritation to many an early mercantilist and constituted Misselden's second line of attack against the company. He was aware that such export of specie "out of Christendom," unlike specie lost temporarily in trade with Eupopean partners, would never return but remained sunk in the bottomless pit of oriental treasure hoards. From Misselden to Mun and to Davenant, this controversial matter was now argued back and forth. It touches on an important point because it goes a long way to explain why the theory of the automatic flow of specie, which Malynes had come so close to enunciating, was so long in coming and had to wait until the mid-eighteenth century when Hume gained acceptance for it. The theory—prices rising in the country whose export surplus brings in specie, and falling in the country with import surplus and specie loss, with ensuing reversal of the specie flow because of the changes in domestic prices which turn the export surplus into an import surplus in one country, and vice versa in the other—simply did not fit the important oriental trade as long as the Indies were principally a source of merchandise imports rather than a destination of English merchandise exports and never seemed to return the specie brought to them.

Misselden thus made the most of the contrast between the merchant adventurers, who sold English woolen cloth on the continent, and the East India Company, which brought merchandise into the country. No one believing that it was wisdom to sell, and folly to buy, could fail to be impressed. In addition Missolden introduced a number of policy proposals, which included the devaluation of the English money, or "raising the coin," as the euphonious phrase went, always a controversial step and one that Malynes was opposed to. Misselden did not deny that debasement would be followed by a rising level of prices, but he argued that this "will be abundantly recompensed unto all in the plenty of money, and quickening of trade, in every man's hand." Since he also in a cavalier manner rejected Malynes's proposal for a restoration of exchange parity, Malynes felt compelled to reply to Misselden in a pamphlet published in the same year, 1622, under the title *The Maintenance of Free Trade*. Misselden in turn did not remain silent and a year later resumed the debate, which now became extremely acrimonious, in a tract entitled *The Circle of Commerce,* where the expression "balance of trade" occurs for the first time in print. This provoked an equally bitter reply from Malynes, *The Center of the Circle of Commerce* (1623), the *center* being gain rather than the balance of trade. (The titles of the two tracts refer to the difficulty of drawing a circle by hand and to the still greater difficulty of locating the center of such a circle).

The debate produced much heat but few new arguments. To Malynes it was the tricks of the bankers and the deviation of exchange rates from parity that caused that outflow of specie; to Misselden it was the unfavorable balance of trade. Malynes had copied from an Elizabethan manuscript, authored probably by Sir Thomas Gresham, a list of twenty-four "feats" or tricks of the exchangers, and he incorporated it in his *Lex Mercatoria* as well as in *The Maintenance of Free Trade*. Misselden accused him of plagiarism but he himself included an old balance of trade from the same source in his *Circle of Commerce*. This provided Malynes with the opportunity of questioning the usefulness of the balance of trade by casting doubt on the reliability of the estimates that purported to measure it. As they were based on official valuations that diverged from market values and had to include an arbitrary allowance for smuggling, this criticism was by no means unjustified, and subsequent writers often conceded the grounds on which it was based.

As for the East India Company, Misselden had accepted a position with it before writing his second tract, in which the company is seen in an entirely different light. It is now absolved from responsibility for the outflow of specie from England in an argument in which Misselden joins forces with Thomas Mun, a director of the company and the most outstanding among its spokesmen.

MUN

Thomas Mun (1571–1641) had broken into print in 1621 with *A Discourse of Trade from England unto the East-Indies*. His major work, *England's Treasure by Foreign Trade,* was published posthumously by his son in 1664. It attained great influence and went into several editions, the

"The title of Mun's book," Adam Smith was
to say, "became a fundamental maxim in the political economy, not of
England only, but of all other commercial countries." It gave perfect expression to the spirit of the age for which it was written, an age possessed
by desire for economic expansion and political power and often identifying
the two. When it came before the public in 1664, it carried the imprimatur
of Henry Bennett, then secretary of state and one of the principal architects
of the anti-Dutch policy, for which it provided powerful intellectual ammunition.

THE DISCOURSE OF TRADE

Mun's first work, a tract of some fifty pages, is principally a defense
of the East India Company. His second work, although probably completed
by 1630, is superior in style and presentation, more "modern" in its approach
to the bullionist controversy, and broader in perspective as well as in the
range of topics.

As the subtitle of the *Discourse of Trade from England unto the East-
Indies* indicates, it is designed to provide an answer "to diverse objections
which are usually made against the same." The East India trade, its
detractors claim, has not been beneficial to Christendom because it is
depriving Europe, especially England, of treasure. It has been wasteful of
men and materials and is responsible for the dearth of silver brought to the
mint for coinage.

The first objection touched a matter that intrigued many and was
discussed again by Davenant at the end of the seventeenth century with
results differing from Mun's conclusions. Is the East India trade really a
blessing if it drains Europe of specie? Mun's answer is a resounding yes.
Oriental drugs and spices are necessities; indigo is an indispensable dye; raw
silk provides employment for the poor; calicoes are a substitute for
linen imports and will bring their prices down. Before the seaway around
Africa was opened up, this merchandise had to travel over land and
was purchased from the Turkish middleman at three times what it costs
to buy it in India. Much of the difference goes into the cost of shipping the
goods from India to Europe, but this does not require "ready money" as
would payment to the Turk; it merely involves the use of domestic labor and
materials. It is true that the East India Company is licensed to export a certain amount of silver every year, but it also has the obligation to bring back
as much treasure as takes out. Actually the exports of silver have always
fallen short of the maximum allowed, and the company has brought back
more than it exported. It has also found new markets for English cloth,
lead, and tin, and expects to increase these sales. Some of the merchandise
imported by the company is retained in England and sold there much more
cheaply than in earlier times. But more than three times as much as is kept
in England for domestic use is reexported to other countries, and the export
surplus produced by the East India trade is larger than that produced by all
other trades together.

Admittedly the East India trade uses up English raw materials, such as timber. This, however, is the purpose of such materials. Shipbuilding provides employment for the poor, and the warehouses of the shipbuilder and of the company constitute an emergency reserve useful for the nation in wartime. If England were to relinquish her East India trade, the Dutch would soon get hold of it. This would only increase the outflow of specie because the Dutch would double the price or charge what they please for goods imported to England.

The true causes of the present economic distress include the devaluations abroad and the circulation there, at premium rates, of English coin. Against this Mun sees no easy remedy; devaluation of the English coin "would much empoverish the estates of particular men" and "prove a business without end" as it would only stimulate further devaluation abroad. Other factors include the abuse of the exchange, especially a low English exchange which causes exports of specie. "For in respect the prices of the exchange do rise and fall according to the plenty or scarcity of money which is to be taken up or delivered out, the exchange is hereby become rather a trade for some great moneyed men than a furtherance and accommodation of real trade to merchants, as it ought to be in the true use thereof." Furthermore, there have been variations in the weight of coins, and the heavier ones have been exported or turned into plate. The "excellent" statute of employment has not been properly executed. Merchants often lack experience and skill. Mun concludes his observations by advising restraint in the domestic use of imported commodities so that greater quantities will be available for reexport, stimulation of domestic production of import-competing goods and of the fisheries, and avoidance of the "common excesses of food and raiment." Although the expression "balance of trade" is not yet used, the underlying concept permeates the whole work.

ENGLAND'S TREASURE BY FOREIGN TRADE

Mun's first work dealt specifically with the East India trade; his second work is an elucidation of the significance of the nation's foreign trade in general for the national economy. The theory of the balance of trade is stated boldly in the beginning of the work: "The ordinary means to increase our wealth and treasure is by foreign trade, wherein we must ever observe this rule: to sell more to strangers yearly than we consume of theirs in value."

The cultivation of hitherto unutilized land can be instrumental in reducing import requirements for such goods as hemp, flax, and tobacco. The same purpose is served by reducing the domestic consumption of foreign goods. Mun praises the sumptuary legislation of foreign countries and the laws commanding the use of domestic manufactures. Here as in other contexts he shows moderation and tact: "All kind of bounty and pomp is not to be avoided, for if we become so frugal that we would use few or no foreign wares, how shall we then vent our own commodities?" But when speaking of the "industrious Dutch," he deplores "the general leprosy of our piping, potting, feasting, fashions, and misspending of our time in idleness and pleasure."

Frugal living will not only reduce imports but leave more goods that are available for exports. Mun does not preach frugality for frugality's sake but keeps always in mind the foreign-trade ramifications: "if in our raiment we have to be prodigal, yet let this be done with our own materials and manufactures...where the excess of the rich may be the employment of the poor, whose labors notwithstanding of this kind, would be more profitable for the Commonwealth if they were done to the use of strangers."

Exports may be derived either from "natural" or from "artificial" wealth. The former are mainly minerals or products of the soil, whereas the latter consist of manufactures and the carrying trade. England should make the most of both types of activities but should especially cultivate the latter:

> ...We know that our own natural wares do not yield us so much profit as our industry. For iron ore in the mines is of no great worth, when it is compared with the employment and advantage it yields being digged, tried, transported, bought, sold, cast into ordnance, muskets, and many other instruments of war for offense and defense, wrought into anchors, bolts, spikes, nails and the like.... Compare our fleece-wools with our cloth, which requires shearing, washing, carding, spinning, weaving, fulling, dyeing, dressing and other trimmings, and we shall find these arts more profitable than the natural wealth.

The cultivation of artifical wealth has further advantages. Natural wealth, although "most noble and advantageous, being always ready and certain," nevertheless makes people "careless, proud, and given to all excesses," whereas artificial wealth "enforces vigilance, literature, arts, and policy." Artificial wealth provides opportunities for greater "diversity of employments." The cloth trade is upheld as the backbone of England's commercial strength, but it needs supplementation to afford protection from the risks of specialization arising from the possibility that a foreign market may be closed by war or import prohibitions. Mun never fails to draw attention to the fisheries as a source of wealth, the "golden mine" of the Dutch on which all their political and economic power is based. "If this foundation perish, the whole building of their wealth and strength both by sea and land must fall," including their East India trade, the principal rival of Mun's company.

The promotion of exports requires that proper attention be given to commodity prices. A judicious price policy will reflect the type of market in which the sale takes place as well as the elasticity of the demand for exports. Goods that constitute necessities to the foreign buyer, who is unable to procure them from other sources, may be sold "dear, so far forth as the high price cause not a less vent in the quantity." As for other goods, we must "strive to sell as cheap as possible we can, rather than to lose the utterance of such wares." A reduction in price may cut into private profits but be of benefit to the public if there is an increase in total revenue, making foreign claims larger than they would otherwise be.

But commodities, important as they are, are not the only goods to be exchanged in foreign trade. Since much of the commodity trade from Europe to Asia was of the one-way variety, European traders would be eager to look for the export of services as a substitute or supplement of merchandise exports. Indeed, much of the network of Asian trade was serviced by European ships which plied between Japan, China, India, Southeast Asia, and Persia, carrying such goods as silver, copper, cloves, cotton textiles, silk, and carpets. An imaginative practitioner such as Mun could not fail to notice that the opportunities for gain from the export of merchandise are paralleled by opportunities for gain from the export of services. He presents a survey of the matter that comes close to being exhaustive.

INVISIBLE ITEMS

Mun calls attention to the importance of the service, or invisible, items in the balance of trade, and gives a virtually complete list of these, including shipping, fisheries, insurance, travelers' expenditures, remittances to Rome, merchant commissions, and so forth. He emphasizes the earnings from shipping services. When he wrote his book the Navigation Act of 1660, which restricted the use of foreign ships, had not yet been passed. He admits that "it is true that the commerce ought to be free to strangers to bring in and carry out at their pleasure, yet nevertheless in many places the exportation of victuals and munition are either prohibited, or at least limited to be done only by the people and shipping of those places where they abound."

The earlier argument in favor of the carrying trade—that goods brought in from India can be obtained more cheaply than if they were bought in Europe—is now generalized in this form: "We ought to esteem and cherish those trades which we have in remote or far countries, for besides the increase of shipping and mariners thereby, the wares also sent thither and received from thence are far more profitable unto the Kingdom than by our trades near at hand." From the public's point of view, the higher cost of shipping is immaterial: "all these in the Kingdom's account are but commutations among ourselves, and no privation of the Kingdom's stock." There is thus a gain of the kingdom, constituted by the prices fetched by these goods on reexportation, which cover the cost of bringing them in from distant places by means of English ships. The gain of the kingdom must be distinguished from the merchant's apparent profit, much of which really is cost of transportation.

Commercial policy should be so fashioned that manufactures made from foreign material can be relieved of export duties. This measure would lead to increased exports as well as give employment to the poor. Since larger imports of foreign materials would be required, the increased revenue from import duties would offset the loss of revenue from export duties. In general, export duties should not be too high lest they be responsible for so much of an increase in the prices of exports that sales will be discouraged. Import duties on goods designed for reexport should be low, whereas a higher burden should be placed on imports of goods designed for domestic consumption. All these measures are in line with the theory of the balance of trade.

PARTICULAR AND GENERAL BALANCES

England's Treasure by Foreign Trade, like Mun's earlier work, is essentially an apotheosis of the carrying trade, but since the East India trade does not monopolize the attention of the reader to the extent to which this is true of the earlier tract, the apologetic intent is nowhere nearly so obvious. The East India trade, with its passive balance, constitutes an apparent break with the balance-of-trade theory, which requires an excess of merchandise exports over imports. To demonstrate that the break is more apparent than real, Mun now distinguishes between particular and general balances of trade, the former representing commercial relations with another country, the latter trade with the rest of the world. It is the general balance that counts. A particular balance may be "unfavorable," reflecing triangular trade relations or other circumstances that turn out to be beneficial in the light of a favorable general balance.

TREASURE AND TRADE

A strong case is again made in favor of "the exportation of our monies in trade of merchandise" as "a means to increase our treasure." Money must be sent out "to enlarge our trade by enabling us to bring in more foreign wares, which being sent out again will in due time much increase our treasure." As vigorous an exponent of the balance-of-trade theory as Mun was, he nevertheless is not possessed by the "fear of goods" characteristic of some mercantilist writers. He had already in the *Discourse of Trade* insisted: "Let no man doubt, but that money does attend merchandise, for money is the price of wares, and wares are the proper use of money; so that their coherence is inseparable." This argument is now strengthened. Money must not be left idle but it must be employed as capital funds; it must be turned into merchandise and then again into money, whereby it is multiplied. "Those that have wares cannot want money." If the money is kept at home, merchandise exports will in the end decline because prices will rise and foreigners will buy less—a lesson for all to learn "lest when we have gained some store of money by trade, we lose it again by not trading with our money." This is about as close as Mun comes to the specie-flow theory of international prices, but the theory does not take shape in his mind because in the context indicated here he visualizes the proceeds from exports being sent out again rather than being allowed to raise domestic prices.

Unlike other mercantilist writers, Mun does not consider monetary expansion indispensable for the growth of the domestic economy, nor does he, in this context, favor rising prices. "Neither is it said that money is the life of trade, as if it could not subsist without the same." In ancient times there was barter; in Italy, banking operations and the transfer of bills of debt take care of domestic monetary requirements. The treasure that gave foundation to these credits is used in foreign trade, and domestic currency requirements are limited to petty expenses.

People's assets need only include a relatively small reserve of ready money. "The rest must ever run from man to man in traffic for their benefit, whereby we may conceive that a little money (being made the measure of all our other means) does rule and distribute great matters daily to all men in their just proportions." The monetary theory, the germ of which is implied in these remarks—especially the determinants of the proper supply of money, the motives for holding cash balances, and the velocity of circulation—was not explained by Mun but was developed more fully a few decades later by John Locke.

Mun recommends price restraint when considering the competitiveness of the export economy, but in a chapter entitled "Foreign trade is the only means to improve the price of our lands," he apparently forgets what he said before, and has no qualms about relating rising prices to rising exports and vice versa. Once a merchant has sold cloth and comes back for more, the price of wool and of other commodities goes up and so do landlords' rents and land prices as more money is brought into the kingdom and people are enabled to bid up the price of land. Seen in this light, Mun's emphasis on foreign trade and his policy proposals might become attractive to the landed interests, and this perhaps was his intention.

In Mun's theory of the balance of trade there is no other way to bring treasure into the country than by the export of merchandise and of services. Mun parts company with Misselden, who had advocated devaluation, and with Malynes, who had proposed exchange control and parity rates of exchange, by rejecting these proposals and the formerly endorsed statute of employment. All these measures Mun considers unnecessary if not worse.

Devaluation, or "raising the coin," people say, will cause coin to be brought into the country; debasement in fineness or weight will keep coin at home as foreigners will not accept it at face value. These arguments carry little weight with Mun. Instead he points out that a change of the measure of value always brings confusion. Moreover, "if the common measure be changed, our lands, leases, wares both foreign and domestic, must alter in proportion," a conclusion which seems to neglect the delay in the effect of a devaluation on domestic prices and the ensuing stimulation of exports. Furthermore, even if we could we should not enhance the value of treasure as this would bring special benefits to Spain, the guardian of American treasure, an argument similar to the present-day rejection of an increase in the price of gold because of the benefits thereby bestowed on the USSR or South Africa. Lastly, devaluation will be ineffective because foreign countries will follow suit and retaliate by the same means.

In opposition to Malynes, the exchanges are depicted as essentially passive and their variations are shown to reflect the movements of trade rather than the manipulations of the bankers. The twenty-four "feats" of the latter are critically reviewed and found unimpressive. "That which causes an under or overvaluing of monies by exchange is the plenty or scarcity thereof."

The statute of employment, which compels those who export goods to England to purchase English merchandise, directs trade into bilateral channels and is likely to make it shrink. It invites retaliation, which will reduce the volume of trade still further, and it causes the functions of the domestic exporter to devolve on foreigners, to the loss of English merchants, seamen, and shipping interests.

Unlike other mercantilists, especially Child, Mun, arguing against the background of a business depression, expects no stimulation of trade from a reduction of the rate of interest. Rates are low, he points out, since the demand for loan funds is reduced because of the slump in trade. Businessmen can find no use for their own money and thus do not require other people's money. Trade and the interest rate rise and fall together.

PUBLIC FINANCE

The concluding chapters of Mun's work are devoted to questions of public finance. Taxes "seem to be a rabble of oppression," but when all circumstances are considered they will be found necessary and even profitable to the commonwealth. They may help to build up a war chest and they have their counterpart in public expenditures to the benefit of the community. Moreover, taxes do not oppress the people as much as it may seem at first glance "for as the food and raiment of the poor is made dear by excise, so does the price of labor rise in proportion." Like other mercantilist writers, Mun adhered by implication to a subsistence theory of wages; if the subsistence became more expensive, wages would go up. If taxes constitute a burden, it is one that is placed on the wealthy who have "the use and are the great consumers of the poor's labor." When extraordinary revenue is required, it should be raised "with equality to avoid the hate of the people, who are never pleased except their contributions be granted by general consent."

How much treasure may the king lay up yearly? According to Mun, the controlling factor in this matter is not the excess of the king's revenue over his expenditures but the excess of exports over imports. This latter excess constitutes the maximum that the prince can properly add to his treasure in a year. If he should fail to abide by this rule, "all the money in such a state would suddenly be drawn into the prince's treasure, whereby the life of lands and arts must fail and fall to the ruin both of the public and private wealth." Thus, if the king feels compelled to lay up more treasure than the rule allows, he must increase the export balance. He must not fail to redistribute revenue if the revenue balance exceeds the export balance, his function resembling that of "the stomach in the body, which if it cease to digest and distribute to the other members, it does no sooner corrupt them, but it destroys itself."

Mun's enthusiasm for the accumulation of treasure by the king is furthed tempered by other considerations. He points to the need for "necessary provisions," which are "the princes' jewels, no less precious than their treasure, for in time of need they are ready. . . . We may account that prince as poor who can have no wares to buy at his need, as he that has no money to buy wares; for although treasure is said to be the sinews of war, yet this is so because it does provide, unite, and move the power of men, victuals and munition." Moreover, from remarks made in other contexts, it is quite obvious that Mun looks with disfavor on wars that consume treasure, "where we do not feed and clothe the soldier and supply the armies with our own native provisions, by which disorders our treasure will soon be exhausted." Wars of this type have bled Spain of her treasure. Mun compares them unfavorably to the war "which a prince makes upon his own confines, or in his navies by sea, where the soldier receiving money for his wages, must every day deliver it out again for his necessities, whereby the treasure remains still in the kingdom, although it be exhausted from the king."

Mun takes it for granted that the king will want to accumulate treasure. But his enthusiasm for this destination of the inflow of specie is so limited that the principal point he makes in the discussion is his insistence on the ceiling that must be placed on the annual addition to the king's treasure. His whole approach invites the conclusion that he introduced it mainly for the sake of completeness or for the good effect that it might have on his public, and his real concern was less with the king's treasure itself than with keeping it within proper bounds.

THE USE OF TREASURE

Mun's theories raise the question of the ultimate purpose or end of the inflow of specie which Mun is so eager to maximize. As has been noted, Mun was not among those who considered the expansion of the domestic money supply an indispensable instrument of economic growth; he believed that such an expansion would lead to higher prices which would discourage exports. Money was thus not to be accumulated to serve as a medium of domestic exchange. Nor was it meant to serve as a store of wealth, a purpose that is minimized in Mun's discussion of the king's treasure and in other contexts. Nor was Mun a monetary fetishist who was drawn to it by an irresistible attraction. The detached irony of his remarks about the "want of silver" in the *Discourse of Trade* contradicts such an interpretation. Such want, he thinks, "has been, and is, a general disease of all nations, and so will continue until the end of the world; for poor and rich complain they never have enough: but it seems that the malady is grown mortal here with us, and therefore it cries out for remedy: Well, I hope it is but imagination makes us sick, when all our parts be sound and strong."

It is an interesting observation also that Mun and some other English mercantilists have only lukewarm feelings about specie not produced by foreign trade. In a passage relating to the melting down of plate into coin, Mun says: "The treasure which is brought into the realm by the balance of our foreign trade is that money which only does abide with us, and by which we are enriched." Of course, the domestic output of precious metals was a matter of little practical importance to England, and the example of Spain, which put the death penalty on their exportation but lost them nevertheless as soon as they arrived from America, was not considered deserving of emulation. Locke, the great philosopher, goes perhaps further than any other English writer in distinguishing to their disadvantage gold and silver drawn from mines from gold and silver gained by trade. "Nor indeed," he maintains, "things rightly considered, do gold and silver, drawn out of the mine, equally enrich, with what is got by trade." Work in the mines absorbs the labor of a country; if it wants to raise its supply of precious metals to that of a neighbor or rival, twice as much would have to be produced by mining as by trade with the neighbor or rival. The Chinese followed a "wise policy" when they forbade that their mines be worked.

If money was not sought primarily as a medium of domestic exchange, as a store of wealth, or as a fetish, why then the quest for treasure? To Mun money is primarily valuable as a medium of international exchange, to "drive trade." Trade is a means to obtain treasure, and treasure is a means to enlarge trade. It is not unnatural that in the mind of the director of the East India Company trade comes close to being an end in itself. It produces private profit, and it contributes gain to the nation in the form of employment, merchandise, and treasure. The maritime trade specifically provides a training ground for sailors and stimulates shipbuilding and a host of other industries that help to strengthen the military position of a country. Although Mun says that "plenty and power do make a nation vicious and improvident," considerations of plenty and power are nevertheless not absent from his thought, as trade begets both of them.

THE BALANCE OF POWER

When Bacon, the leading light of the age, whose writings enjoyed a wide distribution, spoke of the balance of trade, he associated it with the "balance of greatness," or balance of power, and both balances were to become the foremost objectives of English policy. Underlying mercantilist thought was the notion that power, trade, and treasure are in the nature of fixed quantities. When one country increases its share of any of them, another country is bound to suffer a corresponding loss. When England enlarges her East India trade, Mun argues that she does so at the expense of the

Turkish middleman. If she gains acceptance for her manufactures abroad by relinquishing, as Mun suggests, duties on exports, "this manufacture would yet increase very much, and decrease as fast in Italy and in the Netherlands." What is true of countries also applies at a different level to the economic relations among individuals. To Mun, "one man's necessity becomes another man's opportunity," and, more crisply, "one man's loss is another man's gain."

THE CONFLICT OF INTERESTS

Both in the international and in the domestic field the mercantilists are far from envisaging a harmony of interests such as the classical school was to postulate. If in international relations one country's gain is another country's loss, and if it can be assumed that countries will strive to make gains and to avoid losses, then commercial policy specifically and foreign economic policy generally become instruments of economic warfare. In this sense the mercantilists may be said to have considered the pursuit of national gain the solution of the economic problem as they saw it.

Nor is there a necessary harmony of individual and national interests. In Mun's opinion the commonwealth may gain while the merchant suffers a loss, for example, when the carrying trade brings treasure into the country in excess of what was paid out in the initial acquisition of the merchandise but not enough to cover the expenses of the merchant. It is also possible that the merchant is the gainer and the commonwealth the loser, as when merchants' profits grow from increased imports for domestic consumption. By recognizing the possibility of conflict between private and public interests, the mercantilists are thus driven to endorse regulations and restrictions placed on the pursuit of private gain. In this they are not motivated by an aversion to private profits or by the belief that the economic universe needs a detailed ordering by authority. As a rule they oppose restrictions—for example, on the outflow of specie—that they consider harmful to the goal of an export balance, although they favor those they believe helpful in the attainment of this goal.

The mercantilists' belief in the potential incompatibility of private and public interests reflects their narrow view of productivity. Strictly domestic transactions between citizens of the same country are transfers of wealth, or what Mun calls "commutations," matters that are of little account for the balance of trade, which is "the rule of our treasure." Only the work of those who contribute to the export balance creates wealth and is truly productive. "The noble profession of the merchant," especially of the exporter, thus becomes, if not the only productive profession, then the most productive of all. But Mun was not only the prophet of commercial capitalism. His insistence on the cultivation of "artificial wealth" yielding import-competing manufactures and exports of high value mark him also a prophet of industrial capitalism, although this aspect was to receive a greater and a somewhat different emphasis by later writers.

Again, the mercantilists' concentration on production for export forms a sharp contrast to the thought of the classical school. Adam Smith believed that "consumption is the sole end and purpose of all production." "In the mercantile system," he said, "the interest of the consumer is almost constantly sacrificed to that of the producer; and it seems to consider production, and not consumption, as the ultimate end and object of all industry and commerce." Restrictions on imports, the stimulation of certain exports, the fostering of bilateral trade—as was done by the Methuen Treaty of 1703 with Portugal which favored imports from that country over those from other countries in the expectation of increased exports to the treaty partner—they all bestow benefits upon producers at the expense of the consumers.

THE FLOW OF SPECIE

"The producers," Smith says, "whose interest has been so carefully attended to, ... have been the contrivers of this whole mercantile system. ... Our merchants and manufacturers have been by far the principal architects." Mun was prominent among the latter, and it is not surprising that he failed to develop a specie-flow theory that would have destroyed the structure he so carefully built up. All the elements of such a theory can be found in his writings. He is well aware of the relation between the quantity of money and the level of prices: "It is a common saying that plenty or scarcity of money makes all things dear or good or cheap." He repeatedly stresses that high prices reduce exports: "When by the excessive price of wools our cloth was exceedingly dear, we lost at the least half of our clothing for foreign parts." His principal argument, so often stated, is that an export belance will bring specie into the country. But whereas he is cognizant of each of these relationships, he fails to link them together in a chain that would constitute the automatic flow-of-specie theory.

It will never be known whether his failure to develop this theory was an oversight or whether he considered such a theory inapplicable in the light of the special conditions stipulated by him. There are good reasons to support either interpretation, and it may even be that both are correct. Mun did not see what he did not want to see and what he did not want to see he did not want to make sense. It did not make sense because specie sent out to the East Indies seemed never to return: they "have no use of our wares." If specie failed to return from the Indies, it could not raise prices in England and thereby bring about its eventual outflow. Moreover, he visualizes that English prices would increase and exports would be discouraged if such specie as does flow into the country were allowed to remain there. Hence his insistence that it be sent out again to "drive trade." Here also his equivocations about the prince's treasure fall into place. English prices will not rise and the automatic specie flow will not be set in motion if the newly acquired specie, instead of being utilized in a trade drive, becomes inactivated in the coffers of the king.

Although Mun's thought has its flaws and contradictions, his all-pervasive notion of the balance of trade not only cast its spell over his own contemporaries but has rarely failed to find approval by the popular mind. It has served to back up commercial policy more often than did the free-trade doctrines of the classical school. The latter placed chief emphasis on the optimum allocation of productive resources throughout the world, ostensibly divorcing this matter from considerations of political power. Mun argued in terms of national gain, actual and potential, economic and political, which to him implied a corresponding loss to other nation. The classics assumed full employment, whereas Mun more than once points to the employment opportunities for "the poor" that are opened up by increased exports and reduced imports. Keynes, for one, was impressed with mercantilist thought. Writing in the depths of the Great Depression, he praised the mercantilist "contribution to statecraft," which "may have attained to fragments of practical wisdom which the unrealistic abstractions of Ricardo first forgot and then obliterated."

Chapter 6

BEYOND
MERCANTILISM:
The Rise of
Quantitative Methods

After Mun had laid the foundations of mercantilist thought, two tendencies emerged in the economic discussion of the time. One was the gradual liberalization of economic thought, a movement often at variance with the practice of the time, which adapted itself to the new ideas only haltingly. These proved eminently durable, however, and they found their culmination in the system of the classical economists who influenced the institutions of a large part of the world in the nineteenth century. The liberalization of economic thought will be considered in chapter 7. Here we are concerned with the other tendency in economic thought, which, however, proved considerably more short-lived, to be revived only at a later stage of the development of economics: the use of quantitative methods.

THE QUEST FOR MEASUREMENT

That quantitative methods came to be employed in economics during the seventeenth century was by no means a coincidence. The innovation met the needs of the time; it was sanctioned by philosophical thought; and it constituted a belated parallel to the rise of geography and private accounting. Double-entry bookkeeping had been invented by Leonardo of Pisa in 1202, and so important was this invention as an instrument of facilitating pecuniary calculation and accumulation that Werner Sombart, the economic historian, dates the beginning of capitalism at this time. In England, then a backwater, the great Domesday Book of the late eleventh century provided the record of a survey, made by order of William the Conqueror, that was designed to assess the feudal liabilities of his landholding subjects. As many of these were a *quid pro quo* that in turn was to be devoted to specific purposes rather than flow into a general fund, and as they were rendered in the form of services or of deliveries of goods in kind, there were obvious obstacles to the aggregation of these items which had neither a common purpose nor a suitable common denominator facilitating their summation. The later conversion of taxes and other obligations into monetary payments both encouraged and increased the need for quantitative aggregates either in the form of *ex ante* estimates or of records of the past. Statistics, in the original primitive sense, the collection and estimation of such data for purposes of the state, was thus a natural accompaniment of the rise of national taxes assessed and levied in the form of money, approved by legislative bodies, and designed to be received into a general fund.

In the field of foreign trade the old bullionist regulation of individual transactions had retarded interest in aggregate estimates of the value and volume of trade. With the emergence of the doctrine of the general balance of trade and its assumption of a central position in the thought and practice of the time, such estimates became an instrument of eminent relevance to serve as the touchstone of the success of commercial policies and to appraise what had been accomplished in the past and what should be expected in the future.

The gathering of quantitative data was further stimulated by the revival of cartography, which had started around the year 1500. Maps incorporated some of the quantitative information that went into their making; in addition, such information was often given in detail at considerable length under the map's legend.

The connection between the use of quantitative methods in economics and the philosophical tendencies of the time is a more complicated matter. Many great thinkers of the age were great mathematicians. In the seventeenth century Newton and Leibniz discovered differential calculus and Descartes fathered analytical geometry with its system of coordinates and curves that stand for equations and whose intersection indicates the common "solutions" of the latter. Another two hundred years, however, were to pass before techniques such as these came to find a place in economics, long after they had proved their value in natural science. What the economic thought of the seventeenth century absorbed was not so much technical mathematics as the mechanistic philosophy of the great thinkers of the time, and, connected therewith, the concept that many if not all things lend themselves to measurement.

DESCARTES, HOBBES, AND BACON

Philosophy in the seventeenth century had gradually come under the spell of Descartes (1596–1650), much of whose thought was shaped by a mystical experience, a dream he had in 1619 which revealed the universe as a mechanism that could be described in mathematical terms. Aristotle and the sages of old had developed their arguments in verbal terms, often implying that language alone might not provide a perfect clue to the mysteries of nature. Now mathematics proved a powerful instrument to unravel them and to secure for its findings the attribute of certainty.

However, Descartes did not apply mathematics to man's mind or to human relations. This was accomplished by Hobbes (1588–1679), whose mathematical mechanistic bent was mixed with a large measure of empiricism. Hobbes was the mathematics tutor of the future King Charles II in Paris, and earlier he had himself served as secretary to Francis Bacon (1561–1626), the apostle of inductive experimentalism, who had died from a cold caught when exploring the method of refrigeration by stuffing a chicken with ice.

Bacon underestimated both deduction and the power of mathematical reasoning, and the influence of his thought may be linked with the retardation of pure mathematical economics, which did not gain a foothold until the nineteenth century. The Baconian philosophy had, however, a definite place for measurement, and in this more modest shape "mathematics" came to dominate the thinking of great and small intellects. The idea of "panometry," which calls for measurement everywhere, was in the air. Spinoza, one of the most exalted minds of the age, proposed to develop ethics along geometric lines. A theological friend of Newton's, whose name is now fogotten, attempted to give shape to a mathematical theology. In the field of economics, Petty introduced the method of "political arithmetic," which he describes as follows: "Instead of using only comparative and superlative words and intellectual arguments, I have taken the course...to express myself in terms of *number, weight, or measure;* to use only arguments of sense, and to consider only such causes as have visible foundations in nature."

PETTY

Sir William Petty (1623–87), the son of a poor Hampshire clothier, was entirely a self-made man. Making the most of the local educational opportunities, he was a competent Latin scholar at the age of twelve. Two years later, when serving as a cabin boy and left stranded with a broken leg on the French coast by his shipmates, he put his knowledge to good use by addressing the Jesuit fathers of the University of Caen in excellent Latin and securing for himself admission to the university. He then supported himself as well as he could by tutoring and by trading in custom jewelry. With the pronounced interest in such matters that is often characteristic of those who have risen from poverty by their own efforts, he was later to tell how his initial capital, one shilling in 1636, rose to four shillings and sixpence, then to twenty-four shillings, then to four pounds, and eventually, when he was twenty, to seventy pounds. At that time, when the English civil war between the king and Parliament had intensified, he went to the Netherlands to study medicine and other subjects, and from there he went to Paris where he assisted Hobbes in anatomical studies and made a number of contacts among mathematicians and other scholars interested in new scientific developments. At the age of twenty-four he could be found in London, attempting to put to commercial use an instrument for double writing, for which he had taken out a patent. In London he was admitted to the circle of the virtuosi, an "invisible college" made up of men eager to expand the frontiers of science and technology.

A year later, in 1648, he joined others in the group and moved to Oxford, where positions had fallen vacant as the result of the removal of royalists from office by the Commonwealth party. In very swift order Petty became a fellow and vice-principal of Brasenose College, a doctor in physic, professor of anatomy at Oxford, and professor of music at Gresham College in London. The word "music" then connoted a broader range of cultural endeavors than it does now, and the combination of the apparently unrelated professorships was not without precedent.

Although Petty went beyond the call of medical duty by bringing back to life a young woman who had been hanged for the alleged murder of her child, his academic career at Oxford was terminated after about three years when in 1651 he obtained a leave of absence. Shortly thereafter he was on his way to Ireland to serve as physician to the English army. His residence in Ireland marks an important milestone in his life. From it dates his connection with the Cromwell family and other people of importance, his work as surveyor of a large part of Ireland, one of his great accomplishments, and his participation in the distribution of forfeited Irish lands among the English soldiers and the "adventurers" who had advanced the expenses incurred in suppressing the rebellion of 1641. By accepting land as part of his pay for the survey and by purchasing other titles to land from soldier claimants, Petty amassed large holdings in Ireland and laid the foundation of a substantial fortune. This was not accomplished, however, without cost. Petty became a somewhat controversial figure; he was drawn into interminable lawsuits with rival claimants and tax farmers, and he was exposed to persistent anxiety about the security of his properties after the Restoration when some of his lands were returned to their original owners, an anxiety that increased after the accession of James II, who sought to strengthen the Catholic party in Ireland.

Petty returned to London in 1659 and from then on lived alternately in Ireland and in England. He served as a member of Parliament for a few months, cultivated his earlier interests in science and technology, became a charter member of the Royal Society, and started writing the series of books that account for his fame in the history of economics and statistics. King Charles II took a liking to him and overlooked his service to the Commonwealth and his connection with the Cromwells. He was knighted in 1661, and in 1667 he married a widow much his junior, the daughter of a reprieved regicide who had died in jail—at the time of Petty's survey he had been major general in Ireland, and they had then formed a close business association. Although Petty made himself available for major office as tax administrator and surveyor, he held none except an admiralty judgeship in Dublin, no easy position for one not trained in the law, but it brought him into contact with the future King James II who served as chief of the admiralty in Ireland. On James's accession in 1685, two years before Petty's death, such advice as he gave the king was graciously received even if it was not followed. One of the last acts of James before his escape to France in 1688 was to make Petty's widow a peeress for life. Petty's great-grandson was the earl of Shelburne, who as King George III's secretary of state advocated a policy of conciliating the North American colonies and later as prime minister concluded in 1783 the Treaty of Paris, which granted independence to the United States. Later descendants, especially the sixth marquis of Lansdowne, who died in 1936, have done much to honor the memory of their great ancestor by publishing works by and about him.

Petty's interests in science and technology went far beyond the fields of economics and statistics. He was a great gadgeteer, and over long periods of time tried to promote a double-keeled ship. He expected much of a two-wheeled conveyence he designed for fast, comfortable, and economical travel. He had advanced ideas about domestic plumbing and has been credited, probably erroneously, with the invention of the water closet. He was an eminently practical man who, though well-educated and among the best Latin poets of his time, cared little for book learning. His writings show the work of an independent and original mind, full of wit and irony, an iconoclast, often coarse and inclined to what may be called economism, or paneconomics—a tendency to find economic aspects everywhere and to measure everything in terms of money. This was the way in which he gave expression to the panometric leanings of his time, one of the characteristics he shared with Benjamin Franklin, a kindred soul, who found in Petty's economic writings a source of inspiration for his own.

MAJOR WRITINGS

The only major work of Petty's that was published during his lifetime was *A Treatise of Taxes and Contributions* (1662). His *Political Arithmetic* (completed probably in 1676), *Verbum Sapienti* (1664) *Political Anatomy of Ireland* (1672), and *Quantulumcunque Concerning Money* (1682) were all published after his his death, the first in 1690, the next two in 1691, and the last in 1695. All these writings were occasioned by events of the time. They discuss changes in the revenue system, war finance, monetary reform, war potential of the great powers, and other current issues. Such general principles, apart from those relating to his method, as Petty did formulate —and they were among the most important contributions made to the substance of economics before Adam Smith—emerged incidentally to his discussion of concrete problems.

Petty's quantitative, statistical bent and his fact-finding approach to economics have their counterpart in his work as a surveyor. Habits of thought and action generated by this type of work were to find their echo in Petty's approach to economics, influencing him both in what he set out to do—express himself in terms of number, weight, or measure; use only arguments of sense; and consider only such causes as have visible foundations in nature—and in what he would not do. The quotation from the preface to his *Political Arithmetic,* given on page 122 and summarized here, continues as follows: "leaving those [causes] that depend upon the mutable minds, opinions, appetites, and passions of particular men to the consideration of others." Petty thus declines to leave the realm of tangibles to develop a theory of economic decision making on the basis of a mechanistic psychology such as that taught by his master Hobbes. And, as mathematically minded as he was, he was not a Cartesian—an exponent of pure mathematical economics—who would look for mathematical formulas to interpret inanimate or social mechanics. All he wanted was to measure. The statement about his method concludes with these words:

> Really professing myself unable to speak satisfactorily upon those grounds (if they may be called grounds), as to foretell the cast of a die; to play well at tennis, billiards, or bowls (without long practice) by virtue of the most elaborate conceptions that ever have been written *De Projectilibus & Missilibus,* or of the angles of incidence and reflection.

PETTY AS STATISTICIAN

As far as statistical techniques are concerned, the only device that comes close to these and is used in Petty's work is simple averages. In today's usage a statistician is one who employs special techniques to handle and analyse masses of quantitative data. Petty was not such a statistician. If statistics merely means the employment of quantitative data—as it did during its early period—then Petty was a statistician, and a pioneer one. As such data were difficult to obtain in Petty's time, he frequently used shortcuts to estimate them, and this was the substance of his method of political arithmetic, a method that has its obvious shortcomings and whose arbitrariness invites abuse. What comes closest to his approach in modern times is perhaps the ingenious detective work of Western specialists in Soviet or Chinese economics who are compelled to derive their estimates from fragmentary and dubious data.

A few examples of Petty's method shed light on its shortcomings. Not having census data of population changes in Ireland, he will argue on the basis of a 30 percent increase in exports that the population has grow in a similar proportion. To calculate the population of London, he will multiply the number of burials by thirty—presumably one person dying out of thirty every year—or, alternately, he will multiply the number of houses sometimes by six, sometimes by eight. From the product he then derives the population of England by multiplying the London estimate by a factor of eight, this being the proportion in which the assessment of the whole of England stands to that of London.

Petty was well aware that the appearance of precision that the employment of figures creates is often misleading, but he rarely presented his findings as tentative or hypothetical or supplied a suitable *caveat* explained in so many words. In at least one instance he was accused of having doctored his figures, and the one who made the charge was Sir Charles Davenant, the principal apostle of Petty's political arithmetic, who was more apt to stress Petty's merits than his faults. In his *Discourses on the Public Revenue and on the Trade of England* of 1698, he gave vent to the suspicion that in Petty's calculation of the relative strength of England and France that of the latter had been understated in order to please King Charles II: "he rather made his court than spoke his mind."

Until census data became more plentiful—which was not before the nineteenth century—the method of political arithmetic was bound to invite suspicion. Adam Smith expressed the consensus of eighteenth-century opinion when he said: "I have no great faith in political arithmetic."

THE NATIONAL INCOME

Petty made great contributions to the substance of economic theory. In the light of today's interest and emphasis, his outstanding achievement was the conceptual derivation of the national income, a step that was pathbreaking but of small influence on the thought of his contemporaries and of many subsequent generations of economists. It was a concept that was never entirely lost in the economic discussion, but there were no adequate statistical data to support it. Petty's own method of substituting shortcuts for the missing census material did not invite confidence, although it was occasionally emulated by lesser thinkers, most of whose names are now forgotten. The concept of the national income did not come to the fore in economics until the 1930s, when it emerged not only as a cornerstone of Keynesian macroeconomic theory but also as a systematic and continuous structure of national economic accounting.

Petty does not take pains to define or derive his concepts of wealth and income. His whole discussion of the matter in *Verbum Sapienti* covers just a few pages and these are replete with "political arithmetic," that is, shortcuts, the relevant concepts being taken for granted. He implies that the national income equals the national expenditure, and puts the latter—for "food, housing, cloths, and all other necessaries"—at £40 million per year. He then proceeds to estimate the national wealth, which he sets at £250 million. The wealth, or stock, yields, however, but £15 million. Hence, the remaining £25 million of national income must have another source, which

Petty finds in the labor of the people. He then goes on to capitalize the value of the latter and estimates it as £417 million, or £69 per capita.

Petty does not introduce the national income to measure its changes or to develop a theory of its determination. Income and wealth appear in his discussion because these matters are relevant to his argument in favor of a widened tax base. They serve as underpinning for his conclusion that taxes should be assessed on "land and stock" and on "people considered without any estate at all" in the same proportion in which tangible wealth stands to the capitalized value of labor, that is, in a proportion of three to five. In the light of this account, laboring people are underassessed. Petty argues that they should work harder and spend less, each by 20 percent, thereby being able to pay taxes in the amount of 10 percent of their income, this being the proportion in which the nation's taxes stand to the national income.

Petty's use of the national income concept calls for a number of comments. The implied equality of income and expenditure echoes Keynes's law, according to which everybody's income is someone else's expenditure, which thus with equal justice might be rechristened "Petty's law." Petty makes no allowance, however, for saving and investment, a deficiency that was soon to be removed by Sir Charles Davenant (p.141), whose national economic accounting system is surprisingly modern and who, standing upon the shoulders of another man, finds it easier to present clearcut definitions of concepts of which the pioneer was dimly aware.

Relative neglect of capital accumulation is indeed a feature of Petty's thought that is characteristic also of his other writings. To him population growth rather than investment is the principal force of dynamism that promotes economic progress. His calculation of such concepts as the money value of a man sheds light on this side of his thought. In this and other calculations of the value of an asset from which income flows, he employs a capitalization procedure based on either "years purchase" or interest rate, or both. The matter is not explained as distinctly as in Locke's formula (p.163), who uses as a first approximation a capitalization factor that is the reciprocal of the rate of interest.

"The wealth, stock, or provision of the nation" is considered by Petty to be "the effect of the former or past labor"—one formulation of his labor theory of value that was to resound in the classical literature of later times.

MULTIPLIER EFFECTS

It is not quite certain whether Petty's macroeconomics included secondary or induced effects of additional spending such as are epitomized in the modern concept of the multiplier. In the *Treatise of Taxes and Contributions* there is a famous statement about public works to provide employment: "Now as to the work of these supernumeraries, let it be without expense of foreign commodities, and then it is no matter if it be employed to build a useless pyramid upon Salisbury Plain, bring the stones at Stonehenge to Tower-Hill, or the like." He does not explicitly mention induced secondary rounds of spending as the beneficial effects of such useless expenditure, but he goes on to say: "for at worst this would keep their minds to discipline and obedience, and their bodies to a patience of more profitable labors when need shall require it." What it would do "at best" he does not say here. However, the secondary effects appear more distinctly in another context when Petty wants to quell the resentment that spectacular public works—"entertainments, magnificent shows, triumphal arches, etc." —might create. The tradesmen who work on these things are engaged in activities that seem vain and only an ornament, "yet they refund presently to the most useful [trades], namely to brewers, bakers, tailors, shoemakers, etc."

VALUE THEORY

Petty's microeconomics, his views about value and distribution, are again not developed systematically but are dispersed throughout his books as by-products of his pragmatic concerns—measurement and policy proposals. His theory of value, to begin with, is not an outright labor theory but one which places land and labor side by side: "labor is the father and active principle of wealth, as lands are the mother." This sentence in the *Treatise of Taxes and Contributions* is bracketed, and brackets in Petty's time had the function now served by quotation marks. Hence there is an implication of an earlier usage of the phrase, which, however, has been lost. The earth as mother was a symbol common to a number of early civilizations, and in the pseudo-Aristotelian *Oeconomica* it is said that as all derive sustenance from their mother, so men derive it from the earth.

THE DOCTRINE OF THE PAR

Shorn of its symbolism, Petty's doctrine singles out the original factors of production, land and labor, as the sources of economic value. As one who desires to make quantitative comparisons and measurements of economic variables, he then faces what in *The Political Anatomy of Ireland* he calls "the most important consideration in political economies," that is, "how to make a par and equation between lands and labor, so as to express the value of anything by either alone." Petty links the value of land with the value of labor by a common unit of measurement into which the product of land and that of labor can be converted. Such a common yardstick or measure of value he believes he has found in the average man's daily requirements of "the easiest-gotten food of the respective countries of the world."

As product of land Petty considers what land yields if utilized without human labor. For example, the gain in weight of a calf that is put on pasture would be the product of land as well as its rent. This product, converted into "days food," can then be compared with the yield of land to which human labor is applied, and the difference, again converted into "days food," would measure the value of the product of labor or its wage. However, Petty is aware that money rather than his yardstick is the commonly used measure of value, and he is at pains to show a way to convert the natural rent of land into money. This he does in the *Treatise of Taxes and Contributions,* where the annual yield of land, net of the expenses of production, which presumably measure the contribution of labor, is equated with the yield of a silver mine, again net of the expenses of production. Thus, if the "natural and true rent of land"—that is, its yield less the seed and what the cultivator has used for his own subsistence, directly or in exchange for other goods—is twenty bushels of wheat per average year, and if the same man, working a silver mine, would have twenty ounces of silver left after the deduction of a year's expenses of production, then a bushel of wheat fetches an ounce of silver.

Petty's first variant of the doctrine of the par—the day's food—thus enables him to convert the value of land into that of labor. His second variant yields a conversion of natural rent into money. In a third variant rent is related to interest: "simple natural interest," that is, pure interest net of a risk premium, cannot fall below "the rent of so much land as the money lent will buy." If the interest were less, the prospective lender presumably would prefer to purchase land to obtain a higher return.

In the doctrine of the par there are echoes of the concept of opportunity costs and of the equalization of factor returns, and the discussion is permeated by Petty's awareness of the general interdependence of economic variables. In addition, the doctrine contains a number of other ideas that were to become influential during later stages of the history of economic thought. Underlying Petty's references to land and its return is the view that there are some returns to land that are costless in the sense of not requiring the using up of resources, a view that was later stated so forcefully in Ricardo's phrase of the original and indestructible forces of the soil. Petty's "days labor," which he considers a yardstick as "regular and constant as the value of fine silver," anticipates the search of the classics for an absolute measure of value.

VIEWS ABOUT DISTRIBUTION

Petty's views about the relationship between interest and rent and his thoughts about wages contain only the bare rudiments of a theory of distribution. Interest is a compensation for inconvenience. Hence it need not be allowed in the case of loans that are payable on demand, a view that is in line with present-day United States commercial banking regulations which forbid the payment of interest on the demand deposit liabilities of the commercial banks. As for rent, it will reflect the prices of the products of the land, and if these rise, so will rents. If cultivation expands in response to an increase in demand for agricultural products, rents of the better located lands will increase. These considerations in the *Treatise of Taxes and Contributions* contain the germ of the Ricardian theory of differential rent, although Petty's emphasis is on differences in location and those in fertility are only given scant attention.

The remarkable feature of Petty's wage theory is not that it is a subsistence theory, which would merely conform to the thought if his time. To him the subsistence theory has a normative content, one that is warranted by the backward-sloping supply curve of labor. Again in the *Treatise of Taxes and Contributions* he argues that wages should be restrained in accordance with the statutory ceiling which should provide no more than subsistence. If more were allowed, labor would respond by proportionately reducing working time or effort. The backward-sloping supply curve of labor is also implied in a passage in the *Political Arithmetic*. Here the reference is to an increase in real wages, and Petty alludes to a paradox that in later times was to occupy the minds of Malthus and Ricardo: real wages will be high when food is plentiful, because money wages are relatively inflexible in the face of decreasing food prices. In order to avert the resulting decline in the quantity of labor supplied, Petty suggests that in the event of an unusually large harvest a part of the supply of foodstuffs be taken off the market and placed in storage.

VIEWS ABOUT POPULATION

Petty's overall view of the economy shows the reactions of an independent mind to the prejudices of his age. As other writers of the time, he makes much of population growth: "fewness of people is real poverty" he asserts in the *Treatise of Taxes and Contributions*. The reasons he gives have novel features: population growth is attended by increasing returns since the overhead, the cost of government, does not rise nearly so fast. Moreover, as the density of population goes up, significant improvements occur in the quality of the population. People shed the dullness of the easy life made possible by sparsity of settlement when the means of livelihood can be appropriated from nature. As the population grows, work and the acquisition of skills are encouraged, and on the basis of this training people become ready for intellectual tasks. Petty does not use this context to draw attention to the benefits flowing from specialization, but he does so in the *Political Arithmetic,* where he also discusses other aspects of the quality of the population. He argues that the dissenters from the established religious opinion are most likely to be the economically most active element in the population and supports this view by copious references to historical experience. He denies that trade is "fixed to any species of religion as such," and instead insists that it is "the heterodox part of the whole" that is the most enterprising one. Petty is thus a pioneer in the branch of economic sociology that traces the influence of religion on economic life. His thesis, while at variance with that of Weber and Tawney, has its counterparts among modern interpretations of economic development.

Petty expected so much of population growth that this, rather than national gain, may have impressed him as the foremost instrument of resolving the economic problem. In his writings and correspondence, population growth is an ever-recurring theme, and he considered the matter a solution both to national economic problems and to his own problems as owner of huge tracts of thinly settled land. Gain in the mercantilist sense, that is, at the cost of others, did not seem to him the highroad to economic progress. His attitude is illustrated by a deprecatory remark in the *Treatise of Taxes and Contributions*, where he speaks of "particular men" who "get from their neighbors (not from the earth and sea) rather by hit than wit, and by the false opinions of others rather than their own judgments." What may be considered a central idea in Petty's substantive economics—the advantages of a large and quickly growing population—has its parallel in the economic thought of Benjamin Franklin and its opposite in the views of Malthus.

THE BALANCE OF TRADE

In Petty's writings there is little of the enthusiasm for a favorable balance of trade that is so characteristic of his contemporaries. That he failed to let himself be carried by this current of the thought of his time was not due to his neglect of book learning, as some have surmised. More likely it was the outcome of his empirical testing of accepted opinion. Where his testing was most effective because it was informed by close familiarity with the matter—as was especially true of everything relating to the economy of Ireland—the test of the doctrine of the balance of trade could have only negative results. Nowhere are these more clearly stated than in the *Treatise of Taxes and Contributions*: Ireland, although she exports more than she imports, nevertheless does "grow poorer to a paradox" because the absentee landlords drain her of the trade surplus and bring nothing in return.

MONETARY THOUGHT

As for money, Petty agrees with contemporary opinion "that there is a certain measure or proportion of money requisite to drive the trade of a nation," but he goes on to say that not only a smaller but also a larger amount would be prejudicial to trade. In the latter case the excess might be sterilized by being placed in the king's coffers. These thoughts, which are developed in the *Treatise of Taxes and Contributions*, may be supplemented by remarks in *Verbum Sapienti*, where Petty insists that England should aim at having more money than her neighboring states. But unlike other writers he does not refer to money as the blood but as "the fat of the body politic, whereof too much does as often hinder its agility as too little makes it sick." Here Petty also works up an estimate of the desirable money supply and relates it to the velocity of circulation, considering the latter in turn as a function of people's pay periods. The matter is taken up again in the *Quantulumcunque Concerning Money*. If there is not enough money, founding a bank will help because it "does almost double the effect of our coined money" and an English bank would be equipped "to drive the trade of the whole commercial world," a prediction that indeed came true in the nineteenth century. If there is too much money, it may be melted down and turned into plate, or exported as a commodity, or lent at interest.

PUBLIC FINANCE All these considerations are intertwined with thoughts on government finance, the subject that was closest to Petty's heart and which he came closest to systematizing. Here again his knowledge of practical affairs influences every page of his writings. As an owner of vast tracts of land in Ireland he was involved in interminable lawsuits with the tax farmers, and at times he thought he might become a tax farmer himself or assume another high office in financial administration—expectations that, however, were not realized.

As for the various ways of raising public revenues, Petty compares the relative advantages of crown lands with a land tax and considers the latter "manifestly the better, the King having more security and more obligees, provided the trouble and charge of this universal collection exceed not that of the other advantage considerably." A land tax, to be levied on rents, would be especially suitable for a new country. Presumably it would immediately be capitalized and the price of land would be reduced accordingly. In a settled country the imposition of a tax on rents would have different effects depending upon the term of the lease. If the lease is for a short term, the landlord will raise the rent and the tenants the price of their products. In the case of a long-term lease the landlord cannot pass on the tax to the tenants, and as the rent is not increased, the amount of the tax, being a percentage of the rent, will be less than in the former case. His tenants' products, however, will fetch the same higher prices at which the short-term tenants sell their own products; thus the long-term tenants are better off now than they were before the imposition of the tax. The final burden of it, Petty holds, rests upon the long-term lessor and the consumers: "not only the landlord pays but every man who eats but an egg or an onion of the growth of his lands; or who uses help of any artisan which feeds on the same," the latter's subsistence wage presumably going up.

As a general rule, taxes should be proportionate and neutral with respect to the prevailing distribution of wealth. This idea of Petty's is based upon welfare considerations which demonstrate a penetrating psychological insight. Long before Veblen's conspicuous consumption and Duesenberry's demonstration effect, Petty held that "the *ratio formalis* of riches" lies "rather in proportion than quantity." What matters to people is more their relative status than the absolute size of their wealth and income. If taxation is proportionate, "no man suffers the loss of any riches by it. For men. . . , if the estates of them all were either halved or doubled, would in both cases remain equally rich." Petty's view that taxes should leave the relative position of the taxpayer undisturbed was not held dogmatically. In his writings he endorses other objectives of tax policy that might interfere with the proportionality of the levy. Nor was his view indicative of an intention to perpetuate the prevailing stratification of society. Instead, his insistence on neutrality of taxation vis-à-vis the distribution of wealth may be considered a corollary of his endorsement of an open society which would secure social mobility by means other than tax policies. "There is nothing in the laws or customs of England," he said, "which excludes any the meanest man's child from arriving to the highest offices in this Kingdom, much less debars him from the personal kindness of his Prince," a statement the truth of which was borne out by the career of this humble clothier's son, the founder of a great family and the father of a daughter whose grandson, the earl of Shelburne, did indeed attain the highest office in the land.

Petty's thoughts on public finance, which are found in the *Treatise of Taxes and Contributions,* may supplemented by a number of passages in his *Political Arithmetic.* Chapter 2 of this work carries the heading, "That some kind of taxes and public levies may rather increase than diminish the wealth of the kingdom." It is here that Petty expands his discussion to include consideration not only of the effects of taxation but also of the public expenditures financed by taxes. The requirement that taxes should leave the distribution of wealth or income undisturbed is now relaxed, and emphasis is placed instead on the favorable effects of a transfer of funds from an "ill husband" to an "improving hand." "Suppose that money by way of tax be taken from one who spends the same in superfluous eating and drinking; and delivered to another who employs the same in improving of land, in fishing, in working of mines, in manufacture, etc. It is manifest that such tax is an advantage to the state."

In line with this thought is Petty's favorable judgment of the Dutch system of taxation, where they do not "tax according to what men gain...but always according to what men spend." Here as well as in his rejection of crown lands as source of public revenues Petty echoes ideas developed in his master Hobbes's *Leviathan* in 1651. Hobbes offers a more profound defense of making consumption expenditures, rather than wealth or income, the basis of taxation. Like Petty he insists on the "equal imposition of taxes," but to him this equality does not depend on "the equality of riches, but on the equality of the debt that every man owes to the Commonwealth for his defense." "The equality of imposition," Hobbes goes on to say, "consists rather in the equality of that which is consumed than of the riches of the persons that consume the same. . . . When the impositions are laid upon those things which men consume, every man pays equally for what he uses: Nor is the Commonwealth defrauded by the luxurious waste of private men." The proposal to tax consumption expenditure rather than income, which in modern times has had the support of such eminent men as Mill, Marshall, Pigou, Fisher, and Kaldor, thus has its precedent in the writings of Hobbes and Petty. Its modern defenders consider the resulting encouragement of saving and investment the chief advantage of the proposal, and the same idea also underlies the thought of Petty.

A NEGATIVE INCOME TAX? The discussion of Petty's contributions to public finance may be concluded with another one of his suggestions, which has a strictly modern flavor. This is his proposal, made in the *Political Arithmetic,* to endow with "a regular and competent allowance by public tax" all those who would otherwise make a living by relying on charity or on crime. Petty argues that the state, if it has no employment for such persons, should be compelled to bear the whole charge of their livelihood. This arrangement, he asserts, would be more economical than allowing them to obtain from the credulous and the careless more than is required for their subsistence, and it would serve to prevent crimes engendered by bad discipline. This proposal also has its counterpart in Hobbes's *Leviathan,* where, however, it is recommended only for those who "by accident inevitable, become unable to maintain themselves by their labor," and where its justification is seen in "the hazard of... uncertain charity." What Petty meant was probably no more than a call for public relief for the poor in the form of money grants. His suggestion is so worded, however, that it is virtually indistinguishable from a negative income tax, a form of subsidization of the poor found in Scandinavian countries and supported in the United States by high authorities.

Indeed, a whole cornucopia of words and concepts, often of seminal importance in the history of economics, has sprung from Petty's fertile mind. Most of these can be culled from the *Treatise of Taxes and Contributions.* As his statistical bent makes him prefer averages over data for single periods, he comes across "cycles"—one of "dearths and plenties" or another within which "all contingencies... revolve," and therewith a new word and concept enters into economic literature. Another perennial that is rooted in Petty's work is the phrase "*ceteris paribus.*" He also writes of "politics and economics," an early use of the word that eventually was to displace the expression "political economy." He states that "almost all uses may be answered several ways," and that "almost all commodities have their substitutes," and in the *Political Arithmetic* he uses the words "full employment."

THE POWER OF GOVERNMENT

Petty went along with the Stuarts as he had with the regime of Cromwell, and his writings lack the sensitiveness of one who would have had scruples about the unlimited power of government. His outlook in these matters was much closer to Hobbes than to Locke. Some may argue that this is an attitude befitting the founder of aggregative economics, whose summations make the individual and his transactions disappear behind the total figures for the nation. In a way Petty's work in aggregative economics may have reflected the requirements of his time which, being a period of internal upheavals and external warfare, made the power of the government the overriding factor in public affairs. Many of his estimates are designed either to shed light on the relative strength of England and her rivals or to enhance that of England. It may thus not be surprising that work along the lines of aggregation came to a standstill early in the eighteenth century when domestic conditions had become more tranquil and wars rarer—just as its revival in the 1930s coincided with the end of laissez faire, with the upheaval of the Great Depression, and with preparation for war.

Nevertheless, in Petty's writings the Hobbesian view of an all-powerful government appears only in attenuated form because Petty sees the power of the state limited not so much by the rights of the citizens as by the laws of nature, which impose restraints on the effectiveness of the exercise of statecraft. Petty's laws of nature are thoroughly secularized, as they had become under the influence of Hugo Grotius, the Dutch jurist, who interpreted them as rational principles derived from the nature of man and society. In this sense Petty argues against restrictions on interest, referring to "the vanity and fruitlessness of making civil positive laws against the laws of nature." In this limited sphere, absence of government restraint thus becomes identified with a natural order of things. Thoughts such as this, as well as Petty's favorite quotation, the Aristotelian *res nolunt male administrari*, "the world refuses to be governed badly," foreshadow the rise of liberal ideas.

GRAUNT

Petty's name was often connected with a book published in 1662 under the title *Natural and Political Observations...Upon the Bills of Mortality* by John Graunt. Graunt (1620–74), a draper and a man of substance, had befriended young Petty and secured for him the professorship of music at Gresham College. During Graunt's later years, when his position became precarious because of his conversion to Catholicism and because of financial losses due to the Great Fire of 1666, their roles were reversed and Graunt became a protégé of Petty's, who tried to secure gainful employment for his old friend.

Graunt was strictly a one-book man, and apart from an essay on the growth of fish in numbers and size, he published nothing besides the *Observations,* which enjoyed a well-deserved fame and went through five editions. He discusses such matters as the relationships between male and female births and between death rates and such factors as age and residence. His great achievement was the strictly empirical demonstration of the regularity of social phenomena if studied in the mass and on the average, the causes of death, for example, which in individual instances occur haphazardly and unpredictably. Graunt was no economist, and the matters he discussed do not fall within the field of economics. But the importance of his empirical method and his application of the law of large numbers—of which he was only dimly aware—is obviously considerable in economics as well. The law of large numbers holds that in the observation of mass phenomena greater general validity and independence from accidental variations is attained as the number of cases under observation increases. It is one of the great principles on which statistical and actuarial science is based.

During Petty's and Graunt's lifetimes there were some who surmised that Petty in one way or another had assisted in the preparation of the book ostensibly authored by Graunt. Whether and to what extent Petty helped with counsel and suggestions is debatable. It has been said that Petty did not actually write the book because of the careful way in which its author handles figures. This question was resolved by means of a more decisive test only in the twentieth century, when statistical techniques were employed to shed light on the authorship of this early statistical work. This test demonstrated a subtantial difference between the length of the sentences in the *Observations* and in Petty's writings.

Graunt, as has been noted, was a strict empiricist who applied the law of large numbers but showed little awareness of its existence. Observing, for example, that death rates vary more widely from year to year in country districts than in London, he would ascribe the difference to climatic conditions, without noticing that the larger number of observations in London made for greater regularity whereas the wide swings in country districts reflected the limited size of the statistical population.

SÜSSMILCH

Graunt's work influenced and was continued by a number of theological writers who considered the regularity of demographic phenomena evidence of a divine plan. One of these, the Prussian pastor Johann Peter Süssmilch (1707–67), was probably the first to show a clear awareness of the law of large numbers. There are copious references to his book *Die göttliche Ordnung* of 1741, "The Divine Order," in all editions but the first of Malthus's *Essay on the Principle of Population*. The content of Süssmilch's work may be indicated by a more complete rendering of its title, which reads in English translation: "The divine order in the changes of the human species demonstrated by its birth, death, and propagation, wherein are proved the rules of order established by divine wisdom and goodness in the course of nature for the maintenance, increase, and duplication of the human species."

If certain demographic applications of the law of large numbers were made in the seventeenth century by the students of political arithmetic, it would be surprising if these attempts had not branched out into the field of life insurance, which is based on this law. Graunt's work does indeed include life as well as mortality tables which show survivors and deaths, at specified ages, of a group of people. The preparation of such tables met not only the requirements of the life insurance business, which up to this time had operated on a much more primitive actuarial basis, but also the more insistent needs of governments ready to obtain loans in return for life annuities. A correctly constructed life table reflects principles similar to those postulated by the mathematical theory of games of chance. Work along these lines required skill greater than that possesed by Graunt. It was foreshadowed by

Pascal and Huygens and, as far as the life table is concerned, brought to perfection by the great astronomer Edmund Halley in 1692. Halley, like Petty and Graunt a fellow of the Royal Society, took his cue from Graunt but brought the ability of genius to his task. Thus were the mathematical theories of games and of probability applied to a practical field bordering on economics, but only after the passage of two centuries were attempts made to link them with the mainstream of economic theory.

FLEETWOOD

Another branch of inquiry opened up by the quantitative leanings of the time was the study of price history. This was of considerable importance because of the price upheavals that had long beset some European countries. The persistent increase in prices posed all sorts of practical problems, such as the one responsible for the publication in 1707 of a book by William Fleetwood (1656–1723) entitled *Chronicon Preciosum; or an Account of English Money, the Price of Corn and other Commodities for the last six hundred years.* Fleetwood was concerned with the situation of a college employee whose fellowship was to fall vacant if he had an outside income of five pounds. This amount had been fixed some 250 years earlier, and Fleetwood, observing that in the meantime prices had increased about sixfold, argued in favor of the retention of the fellow whose outside income was over five pounds. Fleetwood's book contained the first systematic history of prices and was for a long time the only work of its kind. It has a place also in the history of index numbers, since Fleetwood employed averages of the prices of individual commodities. He may have been aware of the vexing problem of weighting but was able to avoid it by having the prices of all commodities rise in similar proportions.

Fleetwood may have belonged to the same clan that married into the Cromwell family with which Petty had prolonged contact. However, the connection with Petty is much stronger in the case of Davenant, the principal apostle of Petty's political arithmetic, who also forms the link to the liberal thought that gradually emerged, which is the subject of the next chapter.

DAVENANT

Charles Davenant (1656–1714), the son of a famous poet, playwright, and theatrical producer, was himself connected with theatrical enterprises in his youth—as heir to his father's interests, as author of a play produced at the age of nineteen, and later as official censor of plays. After having turned to the study of law, he started out on a notable career in politics and government administration, serving for some time as a member of Parliament, a commissioner of excise, and inspector general of exports and imports.

Davenant was not as profound as Locke and not as versatile and original as Petty, of whose quantitative approach he was an early exponent. He was not a businessman like Mun, Child, and North, and he was not as much involved in business affairs as Petty had been. His busy career did not prevent him from being a copious and influential writer. His most important contributions to economics date from the late 1690s, when the War of the Grand Alliance, fought by a coalition of European powers against France, came to its close, a war that had its counterpart in one of the French and Indian Wars in America and was there known as King William's War. Davenant's writings are devoted to the political and economic issues of his time. It is in connection with these concrete issues that he occasionally states general principles of a liberal hue, without however developing their full implication except for those he wants to use in support of or in opposition to a specific policy. Some of these principles are so advanced that they could have been written by Adam Smith, and indeed a future generation found his writings significant enough to sponsor a five-volume edition of his collected works in 1771, shortly before the publication of the *Wealth of Nations.*

As a politician and administrator, Davenant was a child of his time. As an intellectual, he was ahead of it. Perhaps he was ahead of it because he approached his subject as an intellectual rather than as an interested person. An intellectual may see things that others are unable or unwilling to see. Some of the principles asserted by Davenant could only help to undermine the hold of the mercantilist ideas once all their implications were made clear, as they were in the writings of later generations.

Davenant's work is of further importance also because it serves to illustrate that in England at least mercantilist thought was often at variance with mercantilist policy and the two must not be identified. Davenant will poke fun at a law ordering that the dead be buried in woolen cloth, and he opposes legislation that places restrictions on the importation and domestic use of Indian textiles.

TRADE AND POWER

In all his writings Davenant underlines the value of the mercantilist trade policy as a source of political power. In *An Essay on Ways and Means of Supplying the War,* published in 1695, he points out that the export surplus, mainly produced by the carrying trade, is indispensable in financing a protracted war and that the same trade enables England to be a great sea power. There was nothing better to clinch his argument than the English victory at La Hogue, which had almost ended the naval war in 1692. France, as Davenant indicated, did not participate much in the carrying trade, the source of England's treasure and power.

VIEWS ABOUT POPULATION

In the same work Davenant discovers a new aspect of the population problem. He asserts that population growth is beneficial because the greater density of population will provide an incentive to "invention, frugality, and industry." In countries that are sparsely populated "there is nothing but sloth and poverty." England should open her arms "to receive all the afflicted and oppressed part of mankind." With population growth, "the value of all land and rents would certainly rise." "General liberty of conscience" will attract immigrants. Religious toleration is not to be feared because "God can protect his own in the middle of a thousand errors." The "industrious frugality of foreign handicraftsmen" will serve as a spur to wholesome competition, a "good correction to the sloth and luxury of our own common people."

RESTRICTIONS ON TRADE

In the *Essay on the East-India Trade* of 1696 the issue is the proposed embargo on textile imports from India, considered a threat to the English wool industry. Davenant argues against the embargo since a sizable portion of the imports are reexported. If England were to relinquish this profitable trade, the Dutch would soon get hold of it. In support of his case, Davenant then makes this often-quoted statement: "Trade is in its nature free, finds its own channel, and best directs its own course: and all laws to give it rules and directions, and to limit and circumscribe it, may serve the particular ends of private men, but are seldom advantageous to the public." Nevertheless,

> governments, in relation to it, are to take a providential care of the whole, but generally to let second causes work their own way; and considering all the links and chains by which they hang together, peradventure it may be affirmed that in the main all traffics whatsoever are beneficial to a country. They say few laws in a state are an indication of wisdom in a people; but it may be more truly said that few laws relating to trade are the mark of a nation that thrives by traffic.

Trade must not be suppressed nor must it be encouraged if it is not based on natural advantage.

> Wisdom is most commonly in the wrong when it pretends to direct nature.... As it is great folly to compel a youth to that sort of study to which he is not adapted by genius and inclination, so it can never be wise to endeavor the introducing into a country either the growth of any commodity or any manufacture for which nor the soil nor the general bent of the people is proper.

Two years later, in 1698, Davenant published a two-volume work entitled *Discourses on the Public Revenue and on the Trade of England*. In this as in other writings Davenant shows himself a skilled specialist in the field of public finance, a field to which he had devoted much of his work as government administrator. With most authorities of his time he holds that the final incidence of all taxes rests upon the land.

POLITICAL ARITHMETIC

The first of the *Discourses* contains a discussion "of the use of political arithmetic," a new approach of which Petty is the acknowledged master. Davenant defines political arithmetic as "the art of reasoning by figures upon things relating to government," an art that as yet is practiced "by very few." Political arithmetic has many important uses, for example, in the estimation of the war potential of one's own country, of the enemy, and of the allied powers; in forecasting a country's economic growth or its decline; in connection with taxation and other public policies; and in facilitating "a true account of the balance of trade."

Just as Hobbes desired to found a scientific politics on the model of the exact sciences by means of geometry and mechanics, so did the exponents of political arithmetic try to purge their arguments of elements that would, they believed, detract from their validity. In a remarkable passage Davenant sheds light on the connection between Hobbes's secular and authoritarian state, which brooks no clerical interference, and the political arithmetic of Hobbes's pupil Petty. In connection with census taking, Davenant speaks of "the sin David committed in numbering Israel," and he thinks the sin "might be probably this, that it looked like a second proof of rejecting theocracy, to be governed by mortal aids and human wisdom. For without doubt it must very much help any ruler to understand fully that strength which he is to guide and direct."

Davenant possessed an elastic mind and was willing to discard earlier opinions that on mature reflection he found erroneous. In the *Essay on Ways and Means of Supplying the War* he had proposed to revive and expand the medieval price regulations known in England as the law of assize. This idea he firmly rejects in the *Discourses*. Only the prices of perfectly standardized commodities are suitable for control; such goods are uniform and do not lend themselves to improvement. The prices of other goods should remain "uncertain and free," to be capable of providing an incentive to those who think of turning out better goods.

MONETARY THOUGHT

In monetary matters Davenant was enough of a mercantilist not to play down the role of money in human affairs. "They who stand possessed of the ready money," he said, "have in all times and in all countries given the law and held the rest of the people in their power," a bland statement of economic determinism. He argues, however, against those mercantilist writers who consider gold and silver "the only or most useful treasure of a nation." They are "indeed the measure of trade, but the spring and original of it in all nations is the natural or artificial product of the country; that is to say, what their land or what their labor and industry produces." "Money is at bottom no more than the counters with which men in their dealings have been accustomed to reckon." Wealth "is a very hard thing to define," and

Davenant proceeds to enumerate its elements in a list the includes all sorts of goods and skills as well as "wisdom, power, and alliances."

The discussion of monetary matters is now amplified to include credit, a subject to which the second of the *Discourses* is devoted. By the time of Davenant's writing, the bill of exchange had emancipated itself from an underlying foreign exchange transaction; it had become negotiable and discountable and had been transformed into a money substitute useful for purely domestic purposes. A banking system had developed that discounted bills and issued circulating notes. Paper money became a widely discussed subject. The importance that Davenant assigns to credit and related matters reflects these changes. "No trading nation," he said, "ever did subsist and carry on its business by real stock." "The general trade of this country" is now "more carried on by credit than managed with the species of money." Coin has become so much debased that only petty transactions are settled by it. For "all great dealings" bills and notes are used. They have greatly added to the country's money supply and are for certain purposes as useful as, and for others more useful than, specie. In fact, "though money has hitherto been called the measure of trade, yet mankind may agree to set up any other thing in this room; and whatever it be...it may serve their turn as well as gold and silver." This was an early statement of the so-called cartalist view of money, which was to come to the fore among later writers. The cartalists opposed the views of the metallists who were exponents of a commodity theory of the value of money and who considered it essential that money consist of, or be covered by, metallic substances—commodities—and who derived the value of money from the value of these commodities.

Paper money was no doubt the greatest social invention of the late seventeenth century. It greatly increased the money supply and facilitated growth and change—as well as inflation—and the rise of new classes. In an open society, advocated by Child and Davenant, talented men might rise from obscure origins and advance to positions of leadership. Davenant was aware of this transformation of society, and he was perhaps the first economic writer to draw attention to the importance of the middle class—"the middle rank of men who subsist from arts and manufactures"—in whom, together with labor and gentry, "the strength of a government" lies.

As practitioner of political arithmetic, Davenant generally followed paths outlined by Petty. In line with the latter's suggestions he calculated, for example, the nation's money requirements or the national income. His definitions of the national income concepts are remarkably clear and workmanlike and have stood the test of time surprisingly well. National income comprises "the whole that arises in any country, from land and its product, from foreign trade and domestic business, as arts, manufactures, etc." National expenditure includes "what is of necessity consumed to clothe and feed the people, or what is required for their defense in time of war, or for their ornament in time of peace." The excess of income over expenditure is a "superlucration," "which may be called wealth or national stock," that is, stock of capital in the modern sense. The mercantilists frequently use the word "stock," but more often than not they have in mind a capital fund, that is, a stock of mony to be employed for productive use.

KING

Davenant contributed to quantitative methods not only by his own work but also by disseminating the important statistical findings of Gregory King (1648–1712). King's writings were not printed until 1802 and had been known only from excerpts in Davenant's *Essay upon the Probable Methods of Making a People Gainers in the Balance of Trade*, published in 1699. For a century King's demographic work, his estimate of the national income, and the statistical relation between the price of wheat and the quantity sold, which illustrates both the law and the elasticity of demand, could be found only in Davenant's *Essay*, from which Adam Smith culled a number of quotes. King was disinterested, humble, and self-effacing, and his work reflects these qualities. He was drawn to statistics and demography by a quantitative bent and by skills acquired when employed as a genealogist and topographer. His statement of the relation between the price of wheat and the quantity sold foreshadows the theoretical and statistical study of demand that was not realized until the twentieth century. His estimate, sometimes known as King's law, shows that a reduction of the harvest of wheat may be accompanied by an increase in its price in these proportions above the common rate:

REDUCTION OF HARVEST	INCREASE IN PRICE
1/10	3/10
2/10	8/10
3/10	16/10
4/10	28/10
5/10	45/10

Thus, at almost five times the customary price only one-half of the "normal" quantity would be demanded. Marshall constructed a demand curve on the basis of King's law, and Yule derived from it an equation stating explicitly the law of demand.

Remarkable as the achievements of Petty, Graunt, Davenant, and King were, the intellectual movement that they pioneered failed to endure and came to a halt early in the eighteenth century. Only a very few other contributions were made to economic science in these years, and the collapse of political arithmetic in a way reflected the dearth of economic thought in general during that period. The principal reason, however, why the founders of political arithmetic had no substantial following was the inadequacy of government statistics on which a quantitative science of economics could be based. Often the absolute regimes of the time insisted on keeping secret such data as were available. Systematic and periodic censuses did not make their appearance until the early nineteenth century.

143

BERNOULLI

But while economics proper was in the doldrums, pathbreaking advances were made by the great mathematicians of the time in a field that would now be considered mathematical economics of the pure variety, but which no one then related to economics. Thus the first application of calculus and of analytical geometry to a problem now recognized as an economic one was made in 1738 by Daniel Bernoulli (1700–82), the Swiss mathematician, in conjunction with his attempt to resolve the St. Petersburg paradox, as it became later known because Bernoulli had submitted his work to the St. Petersburg Academy of Sciences. The paradox is the discrepancy between the mathematical value of a chance and the lower value that people ordinarily place on it. For example, a gambler will only pay a few dollars for an admission ticket to a game that will yield him $1 if a coin shows heads in the first throw, $2 if it does so on the second, $4 if it does on the third, $8 if on the fourth, and 2^{n-1} if it does on the nth throw—although the mathematical value of his expectation is infinitely great. Another example is a lottery ticket which offers an equal chance to win nothing or twenty thousand dollars. According to the theory of probability the ticket may be worth ten thousand dollars, but a poor man, Bernoulli holds, might do well to sell it for nine thousand dollars, whereas a wealthy one would not be ill-advised to purchase it at that price.

Bernoulli thus introduces the subjective element as a determinant of value, the utility that "is dependent on the particular circumstances of the person making the estimate." Only by taking the particular circumstances of each person, especially his wealth, into account can problems such as the St. Petersburg paradox be resolved. But he goes much further and develops both the concept of marginal utility and the principle of diminishing marginal utility. "There is no doubt," he says, "that a gain of one thousand ducats is more significant to a pauper than to a rich man though both gain the same amount." He further assumes "that there is an unperceptibly small growth in the individual's wealth which proceeds continuously by infinitesimal increments," and he argues that it is highly probable that any increase in wealth "will always result in an increase in utility which is inversely proportionate to the quantity of goods already possessed." Thus, if x is a man's fortune, y its utility, and b a constant, then

$$dy = b\,\frac{dx}{x}, \text{ or } \frac{dy}{dx} = \frac{b}{x},$$

an equation whose left side is the marginal utility.

The curve of the utility of wealth or income that Bernoulli constructs is reproduced here as the earliest graph that elucidates a matter now considered to fall within the scope of economic science. The curve has a diminishing slope for accretions to wealth, but Bernoulli expressly recognizes that when a small sum is at stake the curve may be considered a straight line and, hence, the marginal utility constant—a thought that parallels Marshall's assumption of an approximately constant marginal utility of money in the case of demand curves for goods to which consumers devote only a small part of their outlay.

Bernoulli's work has other important implications for the theory of games, of insurance, and of progressive taxation, some of which were noted by Bernoulli himself. But before the 1870s economists were barely at all aware of the relevance of his findings for their science, and even Jevons came across them only in a secondary source and apparently arrived at his own

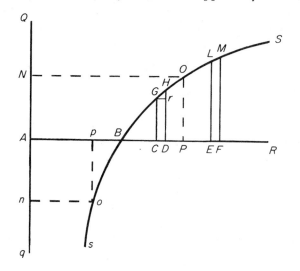

DANIEL BERNOULLI'S DIAGRAM OF 1738

AR measures wealth, AQ utility, Aq disutility. AB is the amount of wealth initially possessed, and BC, BD, etc., are additions to wealth. The curve sBS indicates the relationship between changes in wealth and changes in utility.

To gain the utility of PO would require an addition to wealth amounting to BP. This chance is only worth Bp because Bp is the loss of wealth accompanying a reduction of utility by po. PO = po, that is, the disutility of the loss is equal to the utility of the gain.

kindred doctrine of utility independently from Bernoulli. One reason for the neglect of Bernoulli's work by earlier economists was perhaps that his paper was originally published in Latin, with a German translation not available until 1896 or an English one until 1954. During the formative stage of economic science many economic writers were Latin scholars, but they cared little for mathematics; once they began to care for mathematics, many had ceased to be proficient in Latin.

Chapter 7

BEYOND

MERCANTILISM:

The Emergence

of Liberal Ideas

Petty's motto "The world refuses to be governed badly" and many of the aphorisms of Davenant form the link to the liberal component in seventeenth-century economic thought. This tendency found occasional expression in the writings of Child and, again in a different form, in those of Locke. It reached its full bloom in a small pamphlet by North which, however, failed to make a significant impression on North's contemporaries.

CHILD

Sir Josiah Child (1630–99) was like Mun connected with the East India Company, and his position was so powerful at times that he has been characterized as the virtual ruler of the company. Child wrote a number of tracts that he consolidated in a book published in 1693 under the title *A New Discourse of Trade*. This work went into numerous printings and editions, the last in 1804, and its influence was almost as great as Mun's.

Child's work contains discussions of an even wider range of topics than Mun's, including such matters as colonization, wage policy, population, and poor relief. His greatest concern is the interest rate, which he considers too high in England. The balance-of-trade theory is no longer discussed in great detail but is taken for granted, although Child is willing to admit the operational difficulties inherent in the concept, that is, the exact estimation of exports and imports. As for economic analysis, there are a number of shrewd remarks but also glaring contradictions.

> that merchants, artificers, farmers of land, and such as depend
> on them...are the three sorts of people which by their study and
> labor do principally, if not only bring in wealth to a nation from
> abroad; other kinds of people, viz. nobility, gentry, lawyers, physi-
> cians, scholars of all sorts, and shopkeepers do only hand it from
> one to another at home.

Child notes that the nation's economic and political goals are not
always compatible with each other. A policy may help the one at the
expense of the other. In such a situation he places power ahead of profit,
by endorsing, for example, the Navigation Act. A merchant might be
quoted lower freight rates for ocean transportation by the Dutch, but the
use of English shipping is required by defense considerations which call for
a strong merchant marine. "It seems to me absolutely necessary that profit
and power ought jointly to be considered." On fairly similar grounds his
attitude to foreign investments placed in England, a matter that now
gradually emerges in the economic literature, is one of strict reserve. Where
would such funds come from but from the Dutch? "Whatever money the
Dutch lend us, they always keep one end of the chain at home in their
own hands."

Child also points out the possibility of conflict between private interests and the interest of society and warns against confusing the two. As
examples of such confusion he cites the following statements: "We have
too many merchants already." "The stock of England is too big for the
trade of England." "No man should exercise two callings." Child thus
considered the monopolistic exclusions and restrictions of the guild age
hostile to the interest of the nation. He also notes Mun's case of the "poor
merchant" who does not cover his cost in foreign trade while the nation
gains treasure, and adds another instance of conflict: merchants may
become wealthy by following the rule of buying cheap and selling dear,
but for the nation's foreign trade the rule does not hold because foreign
competition requires sales as cheap as those made by others, or cheaper.

Child does not take up the question whether a reduction of the
interest rate, which he advocates so insistently, would lead to higher commodity prices and thus frustrate the drive for exports. Also he sees no
contradiction between his plea for a lowering of the legal rate of interest
and the principle of the competitive market: "They that can give the best
price for a commodity shall never fail to have it, by one means or other,
notwithstanding the opposition of any laws, or interposition of any power
by sea or land; of such force, subtlety, and violence is the general course
of trade." But he forgets this principle when he upholds the colonial system
that forbids the plantations in America to carry their sugar to "the best
markets" and compels them to send it to England.

There are liberal elements in Child's mercantilism in the sense that he was opposed to restrictions that constituted a leftover from the old order that was static and stable and under which trade was a small and local affair, closed to outsiders. As has been seen, he rejected the view that there were too many merchants in England, and he insisted that the joint-stock companies and regulated companies be open to all newcomers at a low charge of admission. "Liberty and property," he said, "conduce to the increase of trade and improvement of any country." "It would be for the advantage of the trade of England to leave all men at liberty to make what cloth and stuff they please, how they will, where and when they will, of any lengths or sizes."

Child thus proposes to reward inventors and innovators and he rejects laws that require service as an apprentice or limit the number of apprentices; laws that standardize woolen goods—fashions change; laws that restrict the number of looms or workers—they bring only sectional advantage; laws that prohibit a weaver from being a fuller, tucker, dyer, and so forth; laws against engrossing corn; and laws prohibiting the exportation of specie or bullion. He disapproves of price regulations of beer and ale—they bar improvement and prevent the imitation of foreign liquors made from corn; of excise taxes that place an equally high burden on exports and on domestic consumption; of export duties on native provisions; of laws restricting wages, admission of foreigners, or religious toleration—they restrain population growth, encourage emigration, and keep talented people out of the country. Child quotes with approval Hobbes's statement that all men are naturally alike. His is basically an open society in which he would like to see dissenters and nonconformists well treated.

Child was by no means opposed to all restrictions and controls but only to those that he considered harmful to the nation or to important interests. Thus he favors, besides a low legal rate of interest, the Navigation Act, the colonial system, restrictions on imports of goods that can be made at home or are made in countries that fail to purchase English goods. What he favors, he says, are laws that are not in opposition to nature but help nature along. "The midwifery of good laws" is indispensable, "the corrupt nature of man being more apt to decline to vice than incline to virtue." Whether a law is needed to help the natural order of things depends on historical circumstances and national traditions; every country will handle this matter in its own way.

VIEWS ABOUT POPULATION

Child's views about population growth constitute a marked change from earlier fears of overpopulation, fears that Malynes had expressed in Malthusian terms in 1622: "For unless the three impostumes of the world, namely wars, famine, and pestilence, do purge that great body; and kingdoms and countries become very populous, and men can hardly live in quiet, or without danger." In the course of the century, this attitude was gradually transformed into its opposite. Mun, emphasizing the military strength of a large population, argued that if the Dutch were deprived of their fisheries by the English, it "would mightily increase the breed of our people by this good means of their maintenance, and well enable us against the strongest enemy, and force likewise great multitudes of those Netherlanders themselves to seek their living here with us for want of better maintenance: whereby our many decayed sea-towns and castles would soon be re-edified and populated."

The title of a tract published in 1695 and attributed to Samuel Dugard reflects the mercantilist preference for large families. It reads: *A Discourse concerning the having many children. In which the prejudices against a numerous offspring are removed. And the objections answered.* According to this writer, the ideal number of children seems to be fourteen.

Child speaks of "the riches of a city, as of a nation," as "consisting in the multitude of its inhabitants." He welcomes population growth, which he considers related to economic conditions. High wages constitute "infallible evidence" of the riches of a country, as they "cause an increase in people which principally enrich any country." Population growth "necessarily follows from the increase of trade and improvement of lands, not that it causes married men to get more children but...a trading country, affording comfortable subsistences to more families than a country destitute of trade, is the reason that many do marry who otherwise must be forced to live single."

Child found no fault with high wages—if they raised cost, the latter might be reduced by a lowering of the interest rate—although he had in his mind an idea that corresponds to what is now known as the backward sloping supply curve of labor. The poor, he said, "in a cheap year will not work above two days in a week," only enough to maintain them in their accustomed condition. Rightly or wrongly the writings of the English mercantilists abound with complaints about people's indolence. To Malynes idleness is "the root of all evil." Mun deplores that "through lewd idleness great multitudes of our people cheat, roar, rob, hang, beg, cant, pine, and perish."

UNEMPLOYMENT AND POOR RELIEF   It is in the light of this commonly held view that the mercantilist policies affecting population, poor relief, and unemployment must be interpreted. The mercantilist writers were not so much concerned with plenty of people as with plenty of employed people. As Child said, "working more would make us richer." This is one of the reasons why Child and other mercantilists gave so much attention to the problems of poor relief and unemployment. When Child proposes the creation of an authority to put the poor into workhouses or deport them to overseas plantations, he has in mind a cure for the evil association of poverty and indolence which to him seem to go together. The mercantilists were indeed concerned with the avoidence of unemployment, but, different from the modern usage, the concept of unemployment that was basic to their thought did not unequivocally refer to involuntary idleness.

The discussion of population shows Child's power of analytical reasoning by offering him an occasion for developing an automatic mechanism of equilibrating adjustment. A decline in population, he says, will set in motion force that will bring about an eventual correction. "That decrease would produce its own remedy; for much want of people would produce greater wages, and greater wages if our laws gave encouragement, would procure us a supply of people without the charge of breeding them," that is, presumably, by immigration.

THE IMPERIAL ECONOMY

Continental students of mercantilism have emphasized its state-building function, a characterization that does not fit the English variant of mercantilism because there the national state was fully developed when the mercantilist writers appeared on the scene. What was state building on the continent was empire building in England. This was a matter to which Child gave considerable attention. A section of his book contains a reasoned defense of the colonial system with its Navigation Acts that established exclusive trading and shipping relations between England and her colonies.

Because of his views about the advantages of a large population, Child is much concerned with the question whether the American colonies have drained England of her population. On balance, emigration to North America has not been a net loss to England because, had there been no colonies, many of the people who went to America would have gone elsewhere: the Puritans to Germany and Holland, and the criminals to their penalties. Nevertheless, the ease of access provided by the colonies made more people leave England than would have departed had there been only foreign countries to receive them.

But since the plantations purchase English manufactures and employ nearly two-thirds of English shipping, "we have not the fewer but the more people in England by reason of our English plantations in America." On the West Indian plantations it is the custom to employ eight to ten colored people for one white man. "Every Englishman in Barbados or Jamaica creates employment for four men at home" engaged in producing provisions, clothing, and household goods, in shipping and shipbuilding.

All colonies whose trade is not confined to the mother country damage the latter. If the colonial trade were unrestricted, the Dutch would soon get hold of it because "their market is free" and they can sell cheapest and buy dearest. In a few years the benefits of the plantations would be wholly lost to the nation. The Dutch would get all the advantage, "leaving us only the trouble of breeding men and sending them abroad to cultivate the ground and have bread for their industry."

"New England," Child says, "is the most prejudicial plantation to the Kingdom of England." Unlike the other American plantations, which turn out sugar and other products complementary to the English economy, New England produces competitive products such as corn and cattle. New England does a flourishing trade with the island possessions and does so at the expense of the mother country. Child also views with alarm the prospect of increased shipbuilding in New England and he concludes his observations by deploring that, whereas one Englishman in the West Indies gives employment to four Englishmen at home, "of ten men that issue from us to New England...what we send to, or receive from them, does not employ one man in England." But in spite of all the fault he finds with the New England economy, the colonists to him are "a people whose frugality, industry and temperance, and the happiness of whose laws and institution do promise to themselves long life, with a wonderful increase of people, riches and power"—no mean prophecy in the seventeenth century.

Child compares the French and Spanish colonies in America with the English to the disadvantage of the former. "Property, freedom and inheritance being the most effectual spurs to industry," it is not surprising that the French plantations are not a success. The French planter does not become a freeholder as does the planter in the English colonies, instead he operates under the supervision and control of the plantation company and the French king. The Spaniards concentrate all their effort on the mining of gold and silver. Many of their people, "at least of their slaves," are destroyed in the mines. They neglect the cultivation of the earth and the production of agricultural commodities, "which might give employment to a greater navy, as well as sustenance to a far greater number of people by sea and land."

We shall postpone momentarily the discussion of the matter to which Child gives the most space in his writings—the interest controversy—and instead examine his role in the historical formation of three great ideas which have never lost their influence upon mankind. What he had to say in this connection may be a monument more lasting than his contribution to technical economics.

THE IDEA OF PROGRESS

In Child's work there is described for the first time in the economic literature an idea later taken for granted but then new, the idea of progress, which places the golden age in the future rather than in the past. If people look back to the past and praise it, "this proceeds from the frailty and corruption of human nature, it being natural for men to complain of the present and commend the times past." Child prefers a different attitude. To him "it is evident that this Kingdom is wonderfully fitted by the bounty of God Almighty for a great progression in wealth and power." Only the beginning of expansion has been seen. Trade is "not yet advanced to the one-fifth part of improvement that this land is capable of."

Since Child's time the notion of economic progress has been part of the inventory of great ideas of the Western world, and in our own days, in a "revolution of rising expectations," it has captured the imagination of the rest of mankind. Another general idea, first enunciated in the economic literature by Child, is that of continuity or gradualism, of change that proceeds steadily and relentlessly but without undue haste. This idea has left its mark on the political and economic thought of the English-speaking world. It has been the watchword of the Fabian Society, the intellectual arm of British socialism, and has served as the motto of Alfred Marshall's *Principles of Economics,* one of the most influential works in modern economics. Both Child and Marshall use virtually the same apothegm. Child's *Nec natura aut lex operantur per saltum,* "neither nature nor law proceed by a leap," becomes Marshall's *Natura non facit saltum,* "nature does not leap."

EXPERIMENTATION

A third strand of what was to become a great English tradition and is conspicuous in Child's thought is the empirical and undogmatic attitude to matters relating to the exercise of statecraft in the economic field. Child is willing to discard a host of antiquated laws and experiment with new ones. The ancient policy of maximum wages may have been right for its time; now new times call for different laws. A rationalist or dogmatic fanatic might insist that the whole world be built in his favored image. Not so Child, the empiricist: "that which is fit for one nation to do in relation to their trade is not fit for all." Here is the root of a quality at which foreign observers of the English scene have often marveled—the ability to combine political liberty and stability with varying degrees of economic experimentation and intervention.

THE INTEREST CONTROVERSY

Whereas the sixteenth century had come close to setting interest free, writers of the seventeenth century worked to try to tame it. Outlawing interest altogether was now out of the question. What was discussed, and often with great violence and vigor, was the ceiling that should be placed on interest rates. Child claimed that English merchants in commercial rivalry with the Dutch were unable to hold their own because of the higher rate of interest in England, which raised their cost over that of Dutch competitors. Projects of relatively low yield could attract Dutch entrepreneurs, while the English were precluded therefrom by the unfavorable interest rate. The Dutch might earn a return of 5 percent in the herring trade and be well satisfied; no Englishman could undertake such a venture if the opportunity cost—the interest that a goldsmith-banker would be willing to pay for a deposit—exceeded the return. High interest rates were declared responsible for a host of other difficulties, including some that were only tenuously related to the cost of borrowing. Child, to whom a low interest rate was a panacea that would eliminate all, or almost all, ills of society, insisted that it would reduce drunkenness.

Typically the seventeenth-century authors disclaim competence and intention to discuss the matter of interest from the point of view of the moral theologian, as had been the custom. The secular point of view is expressed in the *Tract against Usury,* a nineteen-page pamphlet which a learned country gentleman, Sir Thomas Culpeper, published in 1621 and which in later years was appended to the writings of Child. Culpeper starts his tract with the remark that he desires "to leave the proofs of the unlawfulness of usury to divines." Child, who showed greater concern about the height of the interest rate than any other leading mercantilist, insists like Culpeper that his argument is not a theological one, but to clinch it he cannot refrain from making the observation that if a rate of interest exceeding the Dutch has the bad effects on the English economy that he attributes to it, then it must be a sin, "although God had never expressly forbid it." Nothing would bring into sharper relief the progressive secularization of thought and the deification of the nation than the idea that what is harmful to the nation must be a sin.

Child's *Brief Observations Concerning Trade, and Interest of Money,* published in 1668, in which he proposes the reduction of the maximum rate of interest from 6 percent to 4 percent or less, was criticized by writers taking the opposite point of view, first by the unknown author of a twenty-four-page pamphlet, published in the same year, the title of which throws light on the principal argument made therein: *Interest of Money Mistaken. Or, A Treatise proving that the abatement of interest is the effect and not the cause of the riches of a nation, and that six percent is a proportionable interest to the present condition of this Kingdom.* Some may want to consider the author of this work an early exponent of the Weber thesis (see pp. 79–80) since he lists among the factors responsible for the growth of English trade the casting off of the Church of Rome. Child, who opposed this view, may appear as the first critic of the Weber thesis: "Our casting off the Church of Rome," he says, "did long precede our being anything in trade; moreover, in Italy, which adheres to the old faith, trade flourishes."

One year later Thomas Manley published a longer tract, *Usury at Six Per Cent Examined, and found unjustly charged by Sir Tho. Culpepper and J. C.* Manley, by the way, argued that a low rate of interest would cause an increase in drunkenness. In the *New Discourse of Trade* of 1693, the consolidation of his earlier writings, may be found Child's replies to Manley and the author of *Interest of Money Mistaken.*

What Child favors is not merely a low rate of interest but one as low or lower than the Dutch. Only in this manner will the competitive position of the English trader with his Dutch rival be maintained. When Manley insists that high wages rather than high interest cost spoil the English trade, Child replies that the Dutch pay higher wages, and he uses the opportunity to develop his theory of the beneficial effects of high wages.

BEYOND MERCANTILISM:
THE EMERGENCE
OF LIBERAL IDEAS

Whereas Manley suggests that wages be lowered, the author of *Interest of Money Mistaken* proposes still another alternative to a reduction of the English legal rate of interest: why not borrow from the Dutch? This idea finds no favor with Child. When lender and borrower are English, the interest payment is a mere transfer, but when the lender is a Dutchman, the payment becomes "a clear loss to the nation."

Child is aware that the importance of the interest rate varies in different trades. A trade that turns its merchandise over slowly and holds its inventory for long periods of time will be especially sensitive to a high rate of interest.

The apparent scarcity of money is ascribed by Child to "the trade of bankering which obstructs circulation, advances usury and renders it so easy that most men as soon they can make up a sum of £50 or £100 send it into the goldsmith; which does and will occasion, while it lasts, that fatal pressing necessity for money."

There are few good things that Child would not claim to be consequences of a reduction of the rate of interest. "Low interest is the natural mother of frugality, industry and arts." He does not seem to doubt that a reduced rate will bring forth a larger amount of loan funds because he argues that at a lower rate more people will be enabled to turn to trading. If there are more traders, their profits will decline and they will have to become more frugal. Since a low rate of interest encourages thrift, less will be spent on foreign goods.

If the interest rate is high, land values cannot be high also. Some claim that land sold for twenty years purchase when interest was 10 percent. "Will any man believe," Child asks, "that our fathers were so stupid as to lay out their money in land not to see it again in twenty years when at simple interest at 10 percent they might double their money in ten years, at interest upon interest in seven years?" The truth is that land and trade "wax and wane together." A reduction of the interest rate raises land values. It will also compel idle receivers of interest income to go to work, and if land values have risen, they will not be able to turn into country gentlemen.

To the author of *Interest of Money Mistaken* Child appears as the instigator of a conspiratorial scheme. He imputes to Child the "design of engrossing all trade into the hands of a few rich merchants who have money enough of their own to trade with, to the excluding of all young men that want it." Child is at pains to defend himself against this charge. A high rate of interest will "enrich a few greatly and empoverish the generality of trades;" a low rate conforms to a "diffusive principle." It may impose small losses on individuals but will constitute a vast gain to the nation. The East India Company is not in need of a reduced rate because it can take up as much money as it pleases at 4 percent, presumably because its credit standing is so high. "Money is not so much wanting in England as securities which men account infallible."

The great issue is "whether the abatement of interest be in truth the cause of the riches of any country, or only the concomitant or effect of the riches of a country." To Child the first alternative is obvious, whereas the author of *Interest of Money Mistaken* favors the second. As a concession Child admits that in line with the chicken versus egg controversy "the same thing may be both a cause and an effect." The reduction of interest causes an increase in wealth, and the latter may bring about a further reduction of the interest rate.

JOHN LOCKE

Child's *Brief Observations* of 1668 was responsible for bringing John Locke (1632–1704), the philosopher of freedom and founder of modern empiricism, into the discussion of economic matters. At that time Locke's patron, patient, and friend, Anthony Ashley Cooper, who later became the first earl of Shaftesbury, had been appointed chancellor of the Exchequer, and on his behalf Locke drew up a memorandum setting forth his views about interest and monetary policy. This memorandum of 1668 was published in enlarged and improved form in 1692, when the question of a reduction of the legal maximum of interest came again under debate, paired with problems of currency reform. The 1692 pamphlet, which has the title *Some Considerations of the Consequences of the Lowering of Interest and Raising the Value of Money*—the latter phrase referring to debasement or depreciation—was followed three years later by two others dealing mainly with currency questions.

Locke's *Considerations*, ostensibly devoted to two specific issues, contains enough general ideas, although badly ordered and diffuse, to constitute a treatise covering the highlights of economics. This subject was one of the various disciplines that challenged Locke's original and speculative mind. At his time a substantial economic literature had come into being, and Locke's large library of several thousand volumes included 115 titles on economics. The field then had no name, special method, or position of its own in the hierarchy of the sciences, although Petty, with his "political arithmetic," tried to provide all three. What later British writers were to call "political economy" was to Locke probably a peripheral part of the wider subject of politics, and politics in turn belonged to moral philosophy, defined by Locke as "the art of conducting men right in society, and supporting a community amongst its neighbors."

In the matter of interest, Locke had carefully perused Manley's tract and employed some of Manley's arguments. What, if any, personal contacts Locke had with Petty is not known, but he was acquainted with his writings and owned a copy of Petty's *Treatise of Taxes and Contributions*, first published in 1662. The labor theory of value, which Locke enunciated in his *Two Treatises on Government* of 1690, is mentioned in Petty's book, albeit briefly and indeed only parenthetically. Petty was Locke's senior by less than ten years, and both were in their twenties when they went to Oxford, Locke barely twenty and Petty twenty-six. But in 1652, when Locke entered Oxford, Petty, while precociously enough holding nominal office as vice-principal of Brasenose College and professor of anatomy, was actually on leave and had already moved on to a new stage of his many-sided career. Limited opportunities for personal contact between Locke and Petty came after 1668, when Locke was elected a fellow of the Royal Society, founded by Petty and eleven others in 1660. Petty was an active member when in London. He served intermittently on the council of the society and from 1674 as its vice-president, but at the time of Locke's joining the number of its members had increased to two hundred and opportunities for more than formal contact among them had become restricted.

In addition to book learning, Locke's manifold activities in the service of Lord Ashley had included at least one that provided him with experience in practical economics. In 1668 he had become secretary to the Lords Proprietors of Carolina, and a year later had helped to draft the *Fundamental Constitution for the Government of Carolina*. Later, in 1696, after his fame had spread and the Orange Revolution and the fall of the Stuarts had brought power and influence to Locke's friends, his career reached its peak when he was appointed one of "His Majesty's Commissioners for promoting the Trade of this Kingdom and for inspecting and improving the Plantations in America and elsewhere," a substantial and well-remunerated position that made him a master of colonial governors.

Locke, a careful and thrifty householder, had also been able to make a small paternal legacy grow through judicious and diversified investments in colonial and domestic ventures. His personal view about wealth is cited on page 165 in connection with the discussion of his theory of property. Locke was the grandson of a dealer in cloth; his nephew and heir, Peter King, the son of a grocer, ended his career as lord high chancellor of England and became the founder of a dynasty which flourishes to this day. Locke's own life as well as much of his thought mirrors the rise of the middle class which was propelled by faith in reason and science, belief in man's innate goodness and optimism about his future, and insistence on upholding in the face of the state the citizens' fundamental rights to political liberty, religious toleration, and private property. Locke's own life led him from modest circumstances to employment by the great and eventually to high office. Shaftesbury was as much his friend as his patron. But when Shaftesbury served as lord high chancellor of England, Locke sometimes had to walk with other retainers beside the coach that carried the great man to Whitehall. His career was not without vicissitudes and reversals, and he may have considered his life endangered by political upheavals that caused him to be spied upon at Oxford, deprived him of his academic post, and drove him into exile. Even though the Orange Revolution had put an end to the hated Stuarts, Locke thought it inopportune to admit authorship of the *Treatises on Government.* The fortunes of politics were unpredictable, and the fate of Algernon Sydney, another Whig theorist, who had been martyred for his cause, was forever a warning. Locke found temporary refuge in Holland and was safe and comfortable because of financial independence. Against the background of his own personal experience it is understandable that he considered property most important as a means of liberation from personal and political insecurity and dependence on others. In his writings more than once he raised the question, "What justice is there where there is no personal property or right of ownership?" and in his *Treatises on Government* he defined as "despotical power" one "over those who are stripped of all property."

LOCKE ON INTEREST

In Locke's *Considerations* the issue was the legal restriction on the size of interest. The discussion of this question led Locke to develop theories of money—its nature and functions, the demand for it, its relation to prices and to the rate of exchange—as well as a theory of demand and supply, both in general terms and in specific applications to money and land.

A high rate of interest, Locke admits, will be a handicap to trade. Sellers will be at a competitive disadvantage and the cost of money will eat into their profits. "There is no way to recover from this but by a general frugality and industry; or by being masters of the trade of some commodity which the world must yet have from you at your rate because it cannot be otherwise supplied." There is no other way because "the want of money...alone regulates its price." "The present state of trade, money and debts shall always raise interest" to its "true and natural value."

Regulating the market rate by legislation is an enterprise fraught with danger and should be avoided. Borrowers will find a way to evade the legal restraint, and prospective lenders who do not have the skill to obtain a return in excess of the legal one will put their funds into the hands of the bankers. These will monopolize the lending game and if the cost of holding money is low, will be induced to keep some in idleness. In the end, the supply of loan funds will be reduced, trade will shrink, and land values will fall.

If there is to be a legal rate, it is best to keep it close to the natural rate warranted by the "present scarcity" of money. The responsibility for a high natural rate of interest rests with two factors, (1) the small size of the money supply relative to debts, and (2) the small size of the money supply relative to the volume of trade. The first factor operates on rare occasions, such as in a financial panic when all creditors at once try to call in their funds. The second factor makes itself felt at all times.

Locke's theory of interest is thus a "monetary" one and interest is interpreted as the price of money. A change in the rate of interest causes no immediate change in the quantity of land, money, or commodities in

England and is therefore of no direct influence on prices; but indirectly, by affecting the quantity of money or the volume of goods in the country, it may have such effects.

MONETARY THOUGHT

Locke's views about money reflect the rise of paper money, to which his attitude, however, is considerably more cautious and reserved than, for example, Davenant's. He distinguishes two functions of money: as "counters" it serves as a measure of value, and as "pledge" as a claim to goods. Were it only to serve as counters, that is, as money of account, no gold or silver would be needed. Paper money might possibly also have its uses as a claim to goods in strictly domestic transactions, but for international transactions gold and silver are indispensable. Locke thus was an exponent of a qualified form of metallism.

The question why metallic moneys are required for international purposes is answered by Locke's "consent theory": "Mankind, having consented to put an imaginary value upon gold and silver...have made them by general consent the common pledges whereby men are assured...to receive equally valuable things...for any quantity of these metals." A domestic law may make paper money acceptable in domestic use but it cannot give it "that intrinsic value which the universal consent of mankind has annexed to silver and gold." The intrinsic value of the precious metals as used in commerce, Locke goes on to say, is identical with their quantity, "is nothing but their quantity."

In Locke's discussion of the desirable size of a country's money stock a distinction is made between international and domestic purposes. For international purposes, not simply "more gold and silver" is needed but "more in proportion than the rest of the world, or than our neighbors." Locke arrives at this conclusion by means of a process of gradual approximation. He starts with a highly unrealistic model, an "island separate from the commerce of the rest of mankind." On such an island, any quantity of money will be sufficient, as long as every resident has some, "there being counters enough to reckon by, and the value of the pledges being still sufficient, as constantly increasing with the plenty of the commodity." In the case of this isolated, imaginary economy, "any lasting material" might serve as money. Its value is determined by its quantity in relation to the volume of goods, that is, in line with the quantity theory of money.

How must this analysis be modified to fit the case of the real world or of any one country that is not isolated but is involved in foreign trade? In these situations, the quantity theory of money will continue to hold, both for the world as a whole and for a single country. In other respects, however, two important modifications of the theory applying to the isolated island economy have to be made. First, the substance of which money consists ceases to be irrelevant, and gold and silver come into their own as monetary metals, they alone being universally acceptable as means of international payments. Second, "any quantity" of money will no longer do. Instead there is required "a certain proportion" between a country's money stock and its trade.

Locke apparently means by this that the ratio of a country's money stock to its "trade" must not be "far less" than it is in other countries. Unless this is so, the country's commodities will not fetch prices "equal or at least near the price of the same species of commodities" abroad, and the country will suffer a loss in its trade. If the country's money stock is inadequate in the sense here described, alternate sets of adverse circumstances—Locke does not make clear which alternative is the more likely one—will ensue. In terms of the equation of exchange in its modern formulation, $MV = PT$ (where M stands for the money stock, V for its velocity, P for the average price, and T for the volume of transactions), the inadequacy or the decline of M is mirrored either by an inadequate or declining P or by a similar behavior of T.

Locke does not trace the decline of T in detail except for remarking that a great part of the country's trade must come to a standstill if there is not enough money in the country to pay for commodities "in their shifting of hands" at the higher prices prevailing abroad. Why this would be so he does not explain. If M were to fall by 50 percent, "half our rents should not be paid, half our commodities not vented, and half of our laborers not employed, and so half the trade be clearly lost." The decline in P, seen as an alternative to that of T, would mean that prices, wages, and rents would fall by 50 percent, or to one-half of what they are abroad. There will be no scarcity of domestic commodities, but these will be very cheap and foreign commodities very dear, "both which will keep us poor." Locke does not discuss the question whether English exports might not fetch prices substantially equal to those prevailing in the country of their destination, or whether foreign goods imported to England would have to sell there at prices not substantially higher than the English prices. He states that imports of foreign goods will be discouraged, and, worse, craftsmen, sailors, and soldiers will emigrate to countries where pay is better.

Locke's whole argument thus serves as a powerful underpinning of the mercantilist idea of a favorable balance of trade. A country must seek a favorable balance of trade lest its money stock fall behind that of other countries, a consequence that would have dire effects not only on trade but on agriculture, employment, wages, terms of trade, and population movements. The matter becomes one of still greater urgency because the world's money stock is continuously growing, both absolutely and relative to commodities. This implies both the idea of secular, worldwide inflation and the notion that a country that stands still will fall behind: as other countries' money stock rises, a country cannot afford merely to maintain its own but must forever seek to enlarge it.

BEYOND MERCANTILISM:
THE EMERGENCE
OF LIBERAL IDEAS

Locke's theory of money and prices thus diverges in important respects from the views of other mercantilists. He does not consider low prices a welcome stimulus to exports. Nor does he visualize a disappearance of treasure into the coffers of the king or into oriental hoards or into trade drives so that M in the equation of exchange would remain stable, with the corresponding stability of P. In his analysis, P, in the face of a rising M, could only remain stable if T were to increase, which is indeed the alternative feature of his argument. For completeness' sake it might be mentioned that Locke makes a statement asserting the importance of V, but he nowhere develops this thought at any length.

In a sense Locke's theory might be considered a backward step in that his thought is further removed from a theory of automatic specie movements than was that of earlier writers. This double paradox—that it was one of the few towering figures in the intellectual history of mankind who failed to see that a country is unable to a accumulate treasure indefinitely—is perhaps less mysterious if it is viewed in the light of Locke's opinion of a secular rise of the world's money stock. If this quantity "will daily grow greater" because "the mines supply to mankind more than [it] wastes and consumes in its use," the theoretical possibility is not precluded that all parts of mankind may see their own money stock grow. It may also be noted that whereas in one context he favors that a country acquire more gold "in proportion than the rest of the world," in the passages that contain the weight of his argument he expresses alarm about a situation where the country has "far less" money than others. He nowhere argues explicitly in favor of higher prices than those prevailing abroad—as would presumably be connected with the country's possessing more gold in proportion—but develops his argument on the assumption that prices have fallen substantially below the foreign level because the country's money stock falls short of that of other countries. It is thus possible to find embedded in Locke's argument two reasons why the automatic flow of specie might not be set in motion. According to the first, M's rise might be paralleled by one of T, a combination that would avert the necessity for a significant change in P. According to the second, M and P might increase together, both approaching but not exceeding the M's and P's abroad and thus failing to cause a reversal of the flow of trade.

In Locke's analysis of a country's foreign economic position the money stock has still another function besides maintaining prices and production at the desirable level. This function Locke develops in his theory of the foreign exchanges, where he points out that in addition to commodity movements there are other factors, albeit of secondary importance, that determine the exchange rate: a country's stock of money and the movements of capital. The latter are considered as quantitatively less significant and less volatile than commodity movements; moreover, they may be induced by prior commodity movements, as for example, when foreigners have acquired in merchandise trade a balance that they lend out in the country where they have earned it. The primacy of the merchandise trade as determinant of exchange rates, a matter on which the critics of the bullionists had insisted earlier and in such strong terms, is thus left undisturbed: "the merchant," Locke says, is "regulating the exchange, and not the usurer."

As for the country's money stock, if it is large relative to that of other countries it will, according to Locke, cause the country's exchange to rise above par, just as an export balance would do.

> These two together regulate the exchange, in all the commerce of the world, and, in both, the higher rate of exchange depends upon one and the same thing, viz. the greater plenty of money in one county than in the other: only with this difference, that where the overbalance of trade raises the exchange above the par, there is the plenty of money which private merchants have in one country, which they desire to remove into another; but where the riches of the country raises the exchange above the par, there is the plenty of money in the whole country.

The idea that a plentiful money supply will raise the exchange rate—and presumably draw still more money into the country, a conclusion that Locke, however, does not explicitly draw—leads him still further away from an approximation to the theory of the automatic flow of specie. In line with this theory, a plentiful money supply would revert the flow of trade and eventually cause an outflow of specie. Locke's theory implies the opposite, and although he himself made relatively little of it, it was to become a cornerstone of the inflationist theories of later paper money mercantilists such as Law.

Although Locke's views about a country's monetary requirements for international purposes are an extreme version of mercantilist thought, his theory of the demand for money for domestic purposes contains a statement of the transactions demand for money that is surprisingly modern. The size of a country's monetary requirements is again related to its trade, "but what proportion that is, is hard to determine, because it depends not barely on the quantity of money but the quickness of its circulation." He prepares estimates of the cash requirements of different economic groups —landholders, laborers, and "brokers," that is, merchants, but not of consumers because "there are so few consumers who are not either laborers, brokers, or landholders that they make a very inconsiderable part in the account." In each group the cash requirements are closely related to the length of the pay periods, and Locke pleads for a reduction of the longer ones so that less money "would do the business." The brokers—middlemen —whose activities enlarge the monetary circuit and whose profits eat into the earnings of laborers and landholders are at worst "worse than gamesters" since "they do not only keep so much of the money of the country constantly in their hands, but also make the public pay them for their keeping of it." Their work is compared unfavorably with manufacturing which "is driven with the least money" and "deserves to be encouraged."

Locke's general theory of value and price, which he repeatedly states, is a demand-and-supply theory. "The price of any commodity rises or falls by the proportion of the number of buyers and sellers." Supply, or quantity, is related to demand, or vent, in many formulations. "That which regulates the price...[of goods] is nothing else but their quantity in proportion to their vent." The subjective element in demand is stressed in this passage: "The vent of anything depends upon its necessity or usefulness; as convenience or opinion guided by fancy or fashion shall determine." It is "increased or decreased as a greater part of the running cash of the nation is designed to be laid out...rather in that than another [commodity]."

The quantity theory of money forms a special case of this general theory. The mercantilists were fond of the saying from Ecclesiastes: "Money answers all things." If, then, everybody is ready to accept money "without bounds" and to hold it, the demand or "vent of money is always sufficient, or more than enough." This indeed is Locke's conclusion, although in another connection he argues that the vent of money "varies very little... because the desire of money is constantly almost everywhere the same." The first formulation is more in line with Locke's view of the nation's monetary requirements for international purposes, the second with his domestic transactions demand. But regardless of whether the demand for money is unlimited or constant or both, Locke concludes that as far as money is concerned, the vent, or demand, is immaterial and its value, unlike that of other goods, is exclusively regulated by its quantity.

Locke then goes on to investigate the determinants of demand and supply. Goods in general are considered valuable because they can be exchanged or consumed. Their usefulness is a condition necessary but not sufficient to have a price placed on them. They must also be scarce. Thus air and water are useful but fetch no price "because their quantity is immensely greater than their vent." In his discussion of the determinants of demand, Locke demonstrates his familiarity with matters now known as "snob effect," "demonstration effect," and "conspicuous consumption."

> Fashion is for the most part nothing but the ostentation of riches, and therefore the high price of what serves to that rather increases than lessens its vent. The contest and glory is in the expense, not the usefulness of it; and people are then thought and said to live well when they can make a show of rare and foreign things, and such as their neighbors cannot go to the price of.

Certain goods are in demand because they yield a flow of income, and it is in connection with these that Locke develops an early theory of capitalization. The principal example is land, which has value because "by its constant production of saleable commodities it brings in a certain yearly income." The multiplier, known as "years purchase" in the early literature, which, if applied to a constant and perpetual annual return from land, yields the price of land is at first approximation the reciprocal of the interest rate. Thus, with an annual return of one thousand pounds, the value of land would be ten thousand pounds at an interest rate of 10 percent, twenty thousand pounds at one of 5 percent, and so forth, presumably because at the different interest rates the respective capital values would be needed to produce an annual return of one thousand pounds. This rule, which associates high land values with low interest rates and vice versa, Locke submits to an empirical test, and the results make him doubt its validity. Land in favorable locations, for example, in the vicinity of centers of manufacturing, has a scarcity value that results in premium prices.

The forces behind the demand for money are in part the same as those behind the demand for goods in general and in part similar to those behind the demand for land, depending upon whether money is wanted as a medium of exchange or as loanable funds. Money "is capable by exchange to procure us the necessaries or conveniences of life, and in this it has the nature of a commodity; only with this difference that it serves us commonly by its exchange, never almost by its consumption." As loanable funds "it comes to be of the same nature with land by yielding a certain yearly income which we call use or interest." For the use of land the tenant pays rent; for the use of loan funds the borrower pays interest. Interest and rent arise because of the unequal distribution of money and of land. The borrower or tenant has less money or land than he can or will employ; the lender or landlord has more of it.

LOCKE'S THEORY OF PROPERTY

The problem of inequality of wealth is one that Locke also touches upon—without, however, satisfactorily resolving it—in the *Two Treatises on Government* of 1690, his great contribution to political philosophy. It contains what his modern editor calls "perhaps the most influential statements he ever made," and what Locke himself, who openly admitted authorship of the then highly controversial *Treatises* only on his deathbed, claims to "have nowhere found more clearly explained" than in this book: his celebrated theory of property.

Locke develops his theory of property against the background of the state of nature, not necessarily a historical situation but one that would exist in the absence of civil society and government. To Hobbes, the state of nature had been a war of "every man against every man," where force and fraud made life "solitary, poor, nasty, brutish and short." To Locke, on the other hand, the state of nature was not a lawless one but was ordered by the law of nature. "Reason, which is that law, teaches all mankind who will but consult it that, being all equal and independent, no one ought to harm another in his life, health, liberty, and possessions."

The rule of reason is, however, neither self-interpreting nor self-enforcing, and men seek escape from the ills of the state of nature by establishing civil society by means of the social contract and by creating government as a trustee, the people being both trustor and beneficiary of the trust. The great end for whose sake the people call these instrumentalities into being is "the mutual preservation of their lives, liberties, and estates, which I call by the general name, property."

Locke thus uses the word *property* both in the broad sense indicated, in which it covers a wide range of human interests and aspirations, as well as in the narrower sense, in which it refers to material goods. The substance of his argument is that it is a natural right and that it is derived from labor. By making property a natural right that exists ahead of government, Locke differs from Hobbes to whom it is a creation of the sovereign state. By deriving it from labor, he differs from Grotius and other exponents of natural law who consider it dependent on general consent or contract.

THE LABOR THEORY OF VALUE According to Locke, nature has given the earth to mankind in common but has supplied every man with property in his own person. Just as his body is his own, so is "the labor of his body and the work of his hands." By applying labor to the products of nature man appropriates them and makes them his property. Labor not only is the origin of property but also "puts the difference of value on everything." Locke considers labor important enough to account for nine-tenths, perhaps even ninety-nine hundredths, of the value of goods, the rest being contributed by nature. The labor theory of value, which was to be one of the focal points in the thought of the classical economists, ruled without serious challenge until the 1870s and thus proved more enduring than Locke's labor theory of property, which soon found a rival in theories justifying private property on utilitarian grounds. But Locke's idea that property precedes government and his further conclusion that government cannot "dispose of the estates of the subjects arbitrarily" was one of the great formative forces of the modern age and to this day finds an echo in the fifth and fourteenth amendments to the Constitution of the United States which forbid that any person shall be "deprived of life, liberty, or property without due process of law."

LIMITS TO ACCUMULATION In the state of nature labor that creates property also contains in itself one of the limits to its accumulation: man's capacity to produce. The other limit is man's capacity to consume, and both are considered moderate enough to prevent goods from being spoiled and fellowmen from being despoiled. As Locke says:

> The measure of property nature has well set, by the extent of man's labor, and the conveniency of life: No man's labor could subdue, or appropriate all: nor could his enjoyment consume more than a small part; so that it was impossible for any man, this way, to entrench upon the right of another, or acquire to himself a property to the prejudice of his neighbor.

By means of these limitations on the accumulation of perishable goods and on the factors producing them it was possible to avoid what Locke considered an offense "against the common law of nature": waste. As goods of greater durability came to be introduced, those exposed to swift spoilage could be produced over the producer's personal needs and exchanged for goods of a more lasting character: plums for nuts, nuts for a piece of metal, sheep for shells, wool for a sparkling pebble or a diamond. One who accumulated property in this manner gave no offense, "the exceeding of the bounds of his just property not lying in the largeness of his possession but the perishing of anything uselessly in it."

The introduction of money marks the culmination of this process. Here was a "lasting thing that men might keep without spoiling, and that by mutual consent men would take in exchange for the truly useful but perishable supports of life." The introduction of money makes possible the unlimited accumulation of property without causing waste through spoilage. The same "tacit and voluntary consent" of mankind that gives value to gold and silver and sanctions their use as money also sanctions inequality of private property. "Gold and silver," Locke concludes, "may be hoarded up without injury to any one," since they do not spoil or decay in the hands of the possessor. With the introduction of money by consent there thus vanish the limits that the law of nature had originally placed on accumulation and inequality. Locke does not admit in so many words that there is a conflict between the law of nature and what mankind has arranged by consent. But he stresses that inequality has come about by tacit agreement on the use of money, not by the social contract establishing civil society, and that the law of the land may regulate property. Perhaps this implied that the government would function to moderate the conflict between the unlimited accumulation of property, sanctioned by consent, and a more nearly equal distribution of wealth, sanctioned by the law of nature. What principles the government should apply if it were to discharge such a moderating function, Locke does not say.

Was Locke, then, aware of this conflict? Or did he really believe that gold and silver may be hoarded without injury to anyone? In a private letter, written six years after the publication of the *Treatises,* he commented: "Riches may be instrumental to so many good purposes that it is, I think, vanity rather than religion or philosophy to pretend to condemn them." In the early 1660s, some thirty years earlier, he had written a series of essays on the law of nature, which, however, he had never allowed to be published. In one of these he had said: "When any man snatches for himself as much as he can, he takes away from another man's heap the amount he adds to his own, and it is impossible for any one to grow rich except at the expense of some one else." He was thus aware of a problem posed by unlimited accumulation but did not consider it his task to contribute to its solution. It is ironic that Child, the wealthiest Englishman of his time, took pains to proclaim his attachment to the "diffusive principle," whereas Locke, who was much less favored with worldly possessions, nowhere expressed such a thought. Moreover, Child, when he discussed his project for the employment of the poor, more than once indicated his concern with their "comfortable" maintenance. Such an idea never occurred to Locke. The proposals that he made as a commissioner for trade in this matter in 1697 were so harsh in substance and were expressed in such insensitive language that they did not appeal to his contemporaries, thick-skinned as they may have been. Able-bodied "begging drones" were to be impressed into naval service if caught without a pass, and the elderly or maimed would be sent to the house of correction to serve at hard labor. Begging children should be "soundly whipped," the argument implying that their duty to do productive work began at the age of three. A beggar who counterfeited his pass would have his ears cut off.

Locke's mind, steeped both in rationalism and in empiricism, was so fertile that not all elements of his thought form a consistent whole. Thus the labor theory of value of the *Treatises of Government* stands side by side with the demand-and-supply theory developed in the *Considerations*. Moreover, Locke anchors property in labor but in the end upholds the unlimited accumulation of wealth, a break in his thought that explains the appeal of his theory of property both to the rising capitalist class of his time and to the socialists of a later age. In his political philosophy Locke never failed to stress the limitations of governmental powers. By insisting on government by the consent of the governed, he prepared the ground for the English constitutional monarchy and for the work of the Founding Fathers of the United States. It is difficult to reconcile the liberalism of his political thought, which upheld the people's right to rebel against tyranny, with those of his economic views that were steeped in the mercantilist tradition. Locke saw no contradiction between the natural right of the property owner and the oppressive controls established in support of the mercantilist balance-of-trade theory. Such contradictory elements in one's thought were, however, not unusual at a time that had lost the integrated system of values of the Middle Ages and was groping for a new one. Davenant, whose general views about economic policy were more advanced than Locke's, was a deadly foe of the Whigs, with whose policies Locke was associated and to whom he owed preferment and position. North, in economic matters the most liberal of all mercantilist writers, consented to serve the Tories as a sheriff of London, an office that was procured for him in a rigged election, which he used to persecute the Whigs, driving Shaftesbury, Locke's patron, to rebellion and eventually into exile and death in Holland, a service for which he was knighted.

In the field of economics proper, Locke's most pronouncedly liberal conclusions relate to his opposition to the regulation of interest. Perhaps he hesitated to express himself in favor of liberal generalities, such as can be found in the writings of Davenant, because his penetrating mind was capable of visualizing the ramifications of such thoughts and their contradiction with the balance-of-trade principle.

Lord North, King George III's prime minister when Parliament in 1774 passed the "Intolerable Acts" that provoked the American Revolution, was the offspring of an old and notable family which a century earlier had included five brothers of whom all but one attained distinction in their chosen fields. The one who is best remembered is Sir Dudley North (1641–91). A failure at school at the age of twelve and with no penchant for book learning, he became a merchant and was sent to Turkey at the age of nineteen, equipped with a moderate capital by his family. He returned to England twenty years later, a wealthy man, and retired from business and spent his time in elective and appointive government positions.

Posterity would have forgotten Dudley had not his brother Roger North (1653–1734), a distinguished lawyer and man of letters, written a remarkable series of family biographies in which the accomplishments of his brothers are set forth with loving care and understanding. In these Roger traces Dudley's life in detail and draws attention to his unusual economic views as stated in the *Discourses upon Trade*. This brief pamphlet, which carries the publication date of 1691, was probably published early in 1692 shortly after Dudley's death. According to Roger, the tract "is, and has been ever since, utterly sunk, and a copy not to be had for money," that is, it was either suppressed or otherwise disappeared from circulation. The work subsequently fell into oblivion but was rediscovered in 1818 when James Mill read Roger's biography and came across the summary of the contents of Dudley's pamphlet. Copies of the pamphlet were eventually located, and a first reprint of the work was made in 1822.

Dudley's work appears to have exerted no influence on contemporary opinion, of which his views are indeed not representative. It is remembered in the history of economics as an early statement of the doctrines of free trade and laissez faire. Roger may have helped with the preparation of the manuscript, especially the preface, which, though ostensibly a summary of the work, contains views that go beyond its content.

Roger's biographies were first published in 1742. That it took almost another eighty years before they elicited attention to Dudley's work was no accident. Dudley's views were so much ahead of his time that they would find a sympathetic response only in a later age, one that had discarded the ideas of the mercantilists. The exponents of classical economics saw in his views a confirmation of their own. That Dudley was able to emancipate himself from the preconceptions and prejudices of his time may have been due to the deficiencies of his formal education. He never had much book learning and his mind never became a captive of the "traditional wisdom" of his time. The intellectual process that led to his discoveries was thus not so much one of emancipation—he did not have to emancipate his mind from what had never captured it—as of independent thought unshackled by what others would take for granted. His contribution thus provides another illustration of the observation that a new idea often will germinate in the mind of an outsider rather than of an expert. However, being merely an outsider is not sufficient in itself to enable one to see things in a new and penetrating light. More is needed. The outsider must have special qualities—in Sir Dudley North's case, the gift to develop thought on a high level of abstraction. Just as with other writers, however, the occasion that gave rise to such general thoughts was the concrete issues of the time: the interest problem and the reform of the currency—whether to acknowledge debasement by "raising the value of the coin" or to restore its old metallic content.

Other writers had discussed special aspects or emphasized special phases of trade—the trade with East India, the need for an export balance, the desirability to accumulate treasure. To North these concerns, which loom so large in the thought of the mercantilists, are obsessions, the results of vulgar and disorderly thinking that is unable or unwilling to grasp generalities. He proposes instead to treat of trade in general, to analyse it "philosophically," on the basis of a few "principles indisputably true," with things "reduced...to their extremes," a method of reasoning introduced by "Descartes's excellent dissertation *De Methodo*," which has caused "knowledge in great measure" to "become mechanical," that is, "built upon clear and evident truths."

To North, there is no difference between international and inter-regional trade. Both will operate best if left unhampered by regulation. If they are, every trade will redound to the benefit of the public. If they are not, regulations will be evaded, or if they are effective they may bring benefits to some sectional interests at the expense of others, leaving society no better off than before. The total volume of world trade is not fixed in the sense that the reduction of one nation's trade will be offset by the increase of another's. Contrariwise, when one country's trade declines, "so much of the trade of the world [is] rescinded and lost, for all is combined together."

North does not emphasize the function of trade to produce treasure but characterizes it as a "commutation of superfluities" in which people supply each other with "conveniences." Countries grow wealthy not by regulation but by being active and prudent producers, thereby attracting as much treasure as they need in exchange for their goods. "In this course of trade, gold and silver are in no sort different from other commodities, but are taken from them who have plenty, and carried to them who want or desire them, with as good profit as other merchandises." The mechanism of the market, of demand and supply, will thus provide a country with treasure, perhaps with more than its trade requires. "You have no more advantage by the being of it money, then you should have were it in logs or blocks; save only that money is much better for transportation than logs are." The same forces of the market that assure the country of an adequate money supply will also regulate the proportion of specie to bullion "without any aid of politicians." When specie is scarce, bullion and plate will be brought to the mint; when specie is plentiful, it will be melted down and turned into plate or bullion. "Thus the buckets work alternately, when money is scarce bullion is coined; when bullion is scarce money is melted."

North is sharply critical of sumptuary laws which discourage "industry and ingenuity." A nation "never thrives better than when riches are tossed from hand to hand." "The exorbitant appetites of men" are "the main spur to trade, or rather to industry and ingenuity." If men were content with bare necessities, "we should have a poor world." The thought behind the phrase with which Mandeville a few years later scandalized his readers, "private vices—public benefits," is expressed by North, albeit in a less provoking formulation: by the pursuit of the appetites of people like gluttons, gamblers, and misers, "other men, less exorbitant, are benefitted."

Locke took for granted the general trappings of mercantilist economic policy, whose very basis—the theory of the balance of trade—North questioned. Nevertheless there are a number of surprising similarities in their thought. Both reject a reduction of the legal rate of interest; both consider exchange and ready money the same thing; both treat "landlord and stock-lord,'" as North calls them, along parallel lines; both employ a demand-and-supply theory; both describe the demonstration effect. More surprisingly still, they both use the same curious phrase, Locke to show the absurdity of bullionist legislation and North to point out the futility of "policies" rather than "peace, industry and freedom" to bring trade and wealth: either one is an attempt "to hedge in the cuckoo." Nothing is more difficult than to trace priorities in the late seventeenth-century literature. Tracts often circulated for years in manuscript form, repeatedly to be amended and revised long before they were printed. Authorities were cited much more sparsely than they had been in the Middle Ages. In the case of North and Locke the situation is further complicated because both were on opposite sides of the political fence, North having been elected sheriff of London to pack the juries that had failed to indict Locke's patron Shaftesbury for treason. It is unlikely that either would have gone out of his way to acknowledge an intellectual debt to the other. An investigation as to whether North benefited from the perusal of Locke's work or vice versa would indeed be an attempt "to hedge in the cuckoo."

Chapter 8

THE RISE
OF PHYSIOCRATIC
THOUGHT:
Nature's
Circular Flow

The eighteenth century was to bring to prominence two schools of economic thought, the Physiocratic and the classical one. The Physiocrats were predominantly French, the classics Scottish and English. The Physiocrats had an important influence on Adam Smith, the founder of the classical system. Other influences were at work in shaping both systems, and it is with those affecting the rise of the Physiocrats that the first part of this chapter is concerned.

Bodin and Boisguilbert are the two leading figures in the economic thought of France before the advent of physiocracy. Bodin's great contribution has been noted in Chapter 4. To bring that of Boisguilbert, who in some respects was a precursor of the Physiocrats, into sharper relief, a few words are in order about French mercantilist thought, to which that of Boisguilbert and the Physiocrats formed the reaction.

No one had given more forceful expression to the fundamental assumption of the mercantilists than Montaigne (1533–92), the great French essayist, who in his twentieth essay developed at some length the theme indicated by its title: the advantage of one is the damage of the other. Merchants acquire wealth from young people's reckless spending, farmers from the dearth of grain, builders from the destruction of houses. Montaigne generalizes this thought and comes close to a concept of creative destruction—resuscitated in Schumpeter's view of competition—which is said to be nature's law: the rise and growth of one thing generates from the decline and decay of another.

LAFFEMAS

On the whole, French mercantilism was much more the work of doers —ministers of finance, and so forth—than of thinkers, and only a few writers have a claim to attention. One doer who was also a writer, albeit a minor one, was Barthélemy de Laffemas (1545–1611), a Huguenot tailor and *valet de chambre* to King Henry IV, by whose favor he was raised to the post of minister of finance. Laffemas discussed economic problems in numerous tracts in which he underlined the importance of manufacturing. Another writer was Antoine de Montchrétien (c.1575–1621), the poet and hardware manufacturer, who has already been mentioned as the author of a book embodying the words "political economy" in its title (1615). Montchrétien, who was killed in a Huguenot uprising, stressed the need for regulation and industrial education. He repeated the observation of Montaigne that one man's gain is another man's loss and applied it specifically to foreign trade.

COLBERT

State regulation and the promotion of manufacture reached fruition in the work of Jean Baptiste Colbert (1619–83), minister of finance under King Louis XIV, who is remembered as one of the greatest practitioners of mercantilist policy. He gave his name to the system of Colbertism, under which manufacture was encouraged by means of subsidies and tariff protection. Colbertism also brought a network of detailed regulations that aimed at quality and price control of manufactures and agricultural products and the elimination of barriers to the internal trade of France. Colbert also sought fiscal reforms, but his efforts were frustrated by the profligacy of the court and the expenses of the king's perennial warfare.

The French fiscal problem was aggravated by the erosion of the *taille,* a direct tax from which many noblemen, clerics, and office holders could claim exemption and which landowners were able to reduce by placing low valuations on their holdings. Its main burden fell on the rural population, who in addition had to meet feudal obligations of all sorts. Colbert attempted to lay greater stress on consumption taxes which the groups that escaped the *taille* would be unable to avoid. A friend of Colbert's, the marshal Vauban (1633–1707), the greatest military engineer of his time, also tried to solve economic problems, approaching them by means of "political arithmetic." More specifically he proposed a fiscal reform that would replace a number of taxes by a royal tithe—*dîme royale*—a kind of personal income tax that would be based on incomes from all sources and whose proportion would vary with fiscal requirements, 10 percent being proposed as an upper limit. There was even an attempt to make the tax progressive by reducing the percentage payable by certain groups, such as artisans. Vauban's book, whose title is identical with the proposed new tax, found no favor with Louis XIV, who had it condemned to public burning by the hangman. Vauban, old, disabled, and in disgrace, died the same day on which this judgment was executed.

The government's support of manufacture, its relative neglect of agriculture, and its inability to resolve the fiscal problem provided the background for the writings of Boisguilbert, a theorist of considerable accomplishments.

BOISGUILBERT

Pierre le Pesant de Boisguilbert, or Boisguillebert (1646–1714), a member of the French judicial nobility and a landowner, published a number of books, among them *Le détail de la France* in 1695 and *Factum de la France* in 1706, and also set forth his ideas in innumerable letters addressed to successive ministers of finance. In Boisguilbert's work a thought emerges that forms a stark contrast to the preconceptions of the mercantilists and was to reach its full development with the Physiocrats. This was the claim that agriculture and rural life are in many ways superior to manufacture and that manufacture should not be promoted at the expense of the rural population. In line with this thought Boisguilbert makes a vigorous plea for higher prices of farm products. In the interest of the urban population these had been depressed, he claims, by an embargo placed on the exportation of grains. In this connection he comes close to a grasp of the marginal principle and of demand and supply elasticities. A small change in agricultural exports or imports would have substantial effects on agricultural prices, and the change of these would in turn find a response in the form of greatly magnified variations of the quantity supplied domestically. The prohibition placed on the export of grain should be discarded because of its adverse effects on domestic prices and quantities supplied. Low prices of grain induce scarcity, high prices plenty. If the farmers are unable to recoup their expenses of production, they will respond by allowing cultivation to diminish and deteriorate. Scarcity will ensue, and the low price will beget a high price. Boisguilbert also comes close to enunciating the laissez faire formula when he pleads for freedom to export grain. "Nature," he says, "which is nothing but providence," has arranged things in such a manner that if it is left alone—*on laisse faire la nature*—there will be an equilibrium in which farmers will be adequately recompensed and sufficient supplies secured. Boisguilbert's attachment to laissez faire was, however, as ambivalent as that of some mercantilists inclined to make similar pronouncements. He favored economic freedom when it would seem to bring higher prices of grain, but he rejected it in favor of intervention by means of import duties to prevent prices from declining.

THE ECONOMY OF HIGH PRICES

The system Boisguilbert advocated was not so much one of laissez faire as one of high prices, and this feature of his work was further developed in his emphasis on consumption. Consumables, he thought, are more important than gold and silver. The effective demand of consumers would be strengthened by high prices, which he considered the equivalent of prosperity. With these thoughts he initiated an approach that has been influential in the history of economics. In contrast with the mercantilists he belittles the significance of the quantity of metallic money. A faster turnover of a given money stock goes hand in hand with rising consumer expenditures, and the former can accomplish as much or more as an increase in the quantity of money. However, when farm prices are low and the economy suffers from a depression, money tends to be hoarded. Boisguilbert's thought, developed along this line, then approaches the propensity to consume. He argues that money in the hands of the poor is a more effective instrument of expansion than money in the pockets of the wealthy. The former are apt to spend it and the latter to hoard it. Hoarding, to Boisguilbert, is the equivalent of theft.

As Petty had before him, Boisguilbert identifies the national income with consumption expenditure. Emphasizing always the role of consumption as a motor force of the economy, he recognizes the mutual interdependence that links all buyers and sellers in a "chain of opulence." If one potential buyer fails to recoup his cost of production, the chain is broken and *equilibrium*—Boisguilbert uses this word—destroyed. The failure of one potential customer to buy goods causes others to retrench their purchases, and the malaise soon spreads throughout the entire economy. In the light of these ideas it is not surprising that in France Boisguilbert is credited with having anticipated the theory of the multiplier. His writings also contain the germ of the idea of the stationary state, later developed by the classical economists. To Boisguilbert, economic evolution finds itself arrested when agricultural production has reached its maximum and can no longer be expanded.

With reference to fiscal reform, Boisguilbert proposed a royal tithe in a form related to that of Vauban, but more in the nature of a single tax, here again anticipating one of the central ideas in physiocratic thought.

As has happened to other theoretical thinkers, the circumstances of his time and his official duties did not always permit Boisguilbert to put his theories into practice. As an officer of the government he might have been compelled to fix the price of bread, although as a theorist he might have preferred to leave such matters alone. He seems to have been successful in his personal career and in his financial affairs, but his influence on contemporary opinion was severely limited by exaggerations and rash statements. He argued, for example, that one hundred units of money, given to the poor, would soon induce an expansion of consumption a hundred times that large. Or he claimed, in the subtitles of his works, that the remedy he offered would furnish the king within a month with all the money he needed and besides would make everybody rich; that he had on hand "very easy" means to increase the king's revenue by many millions as a result of "two hours of work" on the part of the ministers. To crown

French economic thought was carried further away from mercantilism by the writings of John Law and Richard Cantillon. Although the one was Scottish and the other Irish, the immediate effects of their work were felt more in France than elsewhere.

LAW

John Law (1671–1729), a famous financier in his time, is better remembered for his disastrous guidance of French financial affairs than for his contribution to economic thought, which, however, was quite substantial. After Louis XIV died in 1715, the Scottish financial wizard was invited to France to restore the economic health of the country. Law was eventually appointed minister of finance after having been converted to Catholicism. He founded a bank as well as the Mississippi Company, the first, among other things, to issue paper money, the second to develop Louisiana, then a French colony. Under Law's "system," as it came to be called, the bank's note issue greatly increased, and much of it was used for bidding up the prices of the shares of the Mississippi Company to fantastic heights. When the speculative frenzy came to a halt and the bubble burst, the few who had kept their heads and sold their shares reaped large profits, while thousands of others who had held on to their shares found themselves financially ruined. The disaster may not have been altogether the fault of Law, who had to leave the country—and spent his declining years as a professional gambler in Venice. He had to cope with the jealous hostility of the established financiers and operate under the irresponsible Philip of Orleans, who as regent of France had set him up in power.

In the history of economics, Law's thoughts, as set forth in his *Money and Trade Considered, with a Proposal for Supplying the Nation with Money* (1705), are important not so much as foreshadowing the ideas of the Physiocrats but rather as a further blow to those of the mercantilists. To be sure, Law was not one to play down the role of money; on the contrary, his views not only center around the concept of a managed currency but are grounded in the idea of using money and monetary policy to direct the economic affairs of the nation. The salient point that distinguishes him from the mercantilists is his preference for paper money and credit, which he considered better instruments to produce economic strength and expansion than metallic currencies.

In the history of economic thought Law is often characterized as a mere inflationist. But he was much more than that, having to his credit the then original idea that money can be created by the operations of banks. Earlier writers had been apt to equate banking operations with the activities of the goldsmiths, who accepted deposits from certain customers and then lent them out to others. With Law there emerges the idea that the bankers not merely transfer other people's money from one to another but are capable of creating their own money. Law also introduced the word *circulation* into the nomenclature of economics, borrowing it from physiology and setting a precedent that was followed a few decades later by a similar process of adaptation which brought into economics the physical science concept of equilibrium.

Law's "splendid but visionary ideas," as Adam Smith referred to them, may be sketched as follows. Metallic money is liable to fluctuate in value in line with the fluctuations of the prices of the metals from which it is made. Land, on the other hand, offers a constant yardstick of value, and it may be mobilized by means of paper money issued against the security of mortgages. Law proposes the establishment of a government bank to issue paper money and redeem it on demand in monetary metal, of which the monetary unit continues to represent a given quantity. The supply of paper money will thus expand and contract in accordance with the monetary requirements of the country. Private debts are payable in paper, but metallic money continues to be employed for the settlement of international obligations.

Law's proposal differs only in detail from a number of paper money projects advanced in England at the close of the seventeenth century. But Law goes further and uses the occasion for a remarkable analysis of economic value. Like Locke he develops a demand- and-supply theory, relating "quantity," or supply, to demand, employing the latter word where Locke speaks of "vent." Aristotle had distinguished between the use and the exchange of a good. This distinction Law expands, and like the classical economists later, he distinguishes between value in use and value in exchange. The classics, however, who adhered to a labor theory of value, developed only the theory of exchange value and discarded the concept of use value as soon as they had mentioned it. Law, on the other hand, combined both use and exchange value in a subjective theory that explains the exchange value of a good in terms of its usefulness and scarcity. Goods have value because they are useful, but how much value they have is determined by "the greater or lesser quantity [supply] of them in proportion to the demand for them." In the same manner, changes in demand and supply account for changes in the value of goods.

Law mentions as an illustration the value of water and of diamonds and explains it with the help of the same formula. Water, in spite of its pronounced usefulness, has a low value because it is available in quantities far exceeding the demand; diamonds are of little use yet of high value because the demand for them is much greater than their quantity. The classics, with their labor theory of value, did not have the analytical apparatus to explain what to them seemed a paradox, and when Smith returned to the water-diamond case, he merely mentioned it as an instance of an association of high use value and low exchange value and vice versa, with-

Law further expands his value theory to apply it to metallic money. He takes issue with Locke, who had spoken of the "imaginary value" of gold and silver. To Law, all economic values are subjective and in this sense imaginary, derived as they are from use. Thus precious metals have a value as commodities which arises from their use in art and in industry. If in addition they are employed to serve as money, this second use creates an additional demand and thereby an additional value. Thus the coin has a value that is higher than the value of an equal quantity of the same precious metal not employed as money.

CANTILLON

One of the few who was able to amass a large fortune—estimated at twenty million livres—under the regime of Law was Richard Cantillon, an Irishman active as a banker in Paris. Involved as he was in financial affairs, it may well be true that he had a passion for anonymity. Little is known of Cantillon's life, and even the year of his birth is uncertain, usually being given as between 1680 and 1690. Others place it as late as 1697, which would mean that he was many times a millionaire while in his early twenties. What is known is that he was a party in numerous lawsuits, that his daughter married two earls in succession, and that he died, a very wealthy man, in London in 1734, having apparently been murdered by a discharged cook.

In 1755, more than twenty years after Cantillon's death, there was published, ostensibly in London but more likely in Paris, an *Essai sur la nature du commerce en général,* said to be a translation from the English. This book, which contemporary opinion ascribed to Cantillon, was the work of a highly gifted and well-informed writer, equipped with profound analytical insight and knowledge of the world. The author was a well-read man, acquainted with the writings of Petty, Locke, Davenant, Boisguilbert, and many others. He in turn exerted considerable influence on the thought of the Physiocrats, but later his work fell into oblivion until attention was drawn to it by Jevons in 1881. In an article entitled "Richard Cantillon and the Nationality of Political Economy," Jevons called it "the first systematic treatise on economics" and "the cradle of political economy" and raised the question as to the nationality of a science founded by an Irishman with a Spanish name, who was in business in France and whose book had apparently been published in England. Since then Cantillon has gradually come to be recognized as a major figure in eighteenth-century economics. That recognition came so late was in part the result of the emergence later in the century of such towering figures as Quesnay and especially Smith, who overshadowed the others.

Cantillon was a first-rate theorist and much more of a systematizer than Petty, whom he emulated in other respects, especially in his political arithmetic. Cantillon frequently employed quantitative calculations, and there was an appendix to his work, now lost, which contained more of these. Like Locke, Cantillon was a model builder who used the method of abstraction and the process of gradual approximation to arrive at meaningful insights. Constructions such as Locke's "island separate from the commerce of the rest of mankind" have their counterpart in Cantillon's "owner of a large estate" to be considered "as if there were no other in the world." Petty had employed the *ceteris paribus* formula; Cantillon spoke of "other things being equal."

Concerned as they were with problems of the day, neither Petty nor Locke expanded his thoughts to form a system, a comprehensive and consistent whole in which the various elements of the economic process would fall into place. Petty came close to this by introducing the national income and by formulating his law according to which everybody's income is somebody else's expenditure. Cantillon goes further and describes in considerable detail the operations of a price system, modern in some features and bound to the conditions of his time in others.

He starts out by proclaiming land the source, or "matter," of all wealth and labor the "form" that produces it, giving an Aristotelian touch to the views of Locke and Petty, and with his emphasis on land anticipating the Physiocrats. Before showing his price system in operation he traces the development of economic institutions, an organization of material still followed in many a modern introduction to economics. When he sketches the transformation of primitive settlements into villages, towns, and capital cities, he finds opportunities for developing rudiments of a theory of location in connection with such questions as why farmers will meet merchants in market towns rather than have them come to their farms. He then postulates a law that was to reemerge in different garb in the thought of Marx and Wieser and Pareto—a law of concentration of ownership said to hold true in any type of economic society. Speaking specifically of land, he shows that ownership will invariably be concentrated among a few. Even if it were equally distributed to begin with, differences in the number of children and in their abilities would soon produce inequality.

Cantillon then gives a broad hint about the demand for products and factors. He will later show "that all classes and inhabitants of a state live at the expense of the proprietors of land." Since all artisans and entrepreneurs serve each other as well as the nobles and landowners, it is often overlooked, he says, that their upkeep falls ultimately on the landowners.

THE SUPPLY OF PRODUCTIVE FACTORS

With demand provisionally assumed as given, Cantillon next discusses the supply of productive factors. The supply price of the labor of artisans is higher than that of agricultural or common labor because of the higher expenses involved in acquiring the respective skills. Moreover, the supply is restricted because not all the children of an artisan are made to learn their father's trade. There will be variations in factor returns reflecting differences in skills, hazards, required abilities, and other circumstances attending different trades. Jobs will be filled in response to the demand. If a reduced factor supply raises the factor price, this will attract new-comers who will bring down the price. An increased factor supply, on the other hand, is accompanied by lower factor prices which an outward factor movement to other regions and occupations will correct. If this fails to take place because of inadequate factor mobility, the marriage rate among the regional or occupational segment will decline, infant mortality will increase, and the population will cease to grow. As a rule, however, factors "proportion themselves in number to the employment and demand for them." They are "always proportioned to the employment which suffices to maintain them."

The labor supply is thus directed by a self-regulating mechanism which does not require government intervention for its operation. Charity schools and special efforts to increase the number of artisans are useless, especially so since skilled labor is usually a complementary factor that becomes effective only in conjunction with the employment of capital. "If the King of France sent 100,000 of his subjects at his expense into Holland to learn seafaring, they would be of no use on their return if no more vessels were sent to sea than before."

Students of the history of economic thought have noted that Cantillon's price system operated in an institutional environment that was still a feudal one. This is true with respect to the role assigned to the land-owners as directors of production. But in other respects, especially with regard to the self-regulating mechanism that moves factors to and fro, Cantillon's thought was as far removed from feudalism as could be and much more akin to the liberalism and individualism of a new age.

PRICE THEORY

From factor supplies and factor prices Cantillon moves on to product prices. He distinguishes between the normal price, which he misnames "intrinsic value," and the market price. Normal price is a measure of the quantity and quality of the land and labor that have entered into the production of a good. It may exceed or fall short of the market price, which reflects consumption requirements and "the humors and fancies of men." For example, farmers may plant too much or too little, causing the market price to fall below or rise above the normal price. The latter is said never to vary, whereas the market price has a perpetual ebb and flow. However, in a well-ordered society the market price of articles whose consumption is fairly steady need not deviate much from the normal price, and it may be fixed by the magistrates, such as in the case of bread or meat.

Normal price is a measure of land and labor, but in the end it can be resolved into one of land only, or, for that matter, into one of labor only, but this was not the approach of Cantillon. As Petty had shown, it is possible to convert the value of labor into that of land and vice versa. Cantillon, like Petty before him, searches for the "par" and finds it by equating the value of a laborer with that of twice the produce of land that he consumes, allowing for variations of the laborer's quality and status. This will be necessary to maintain the laborer himself and secure a continued supply of labor by providing for two of his children during their dependent ages—it is assumed that one of them will survive. The required amount of land will vary with its quality and the mode of living in different countries. It may be a fraction of an acre in China, three acres in parts of France, ten to sixteen acres in England, or one hundred acres in the country of the Iroquois, who live by hunting. Thus, normal price reflects the amount of land used in the production of a good and the amount of land whose produce is allotted to the worker whose labor has turned out the good.

LANDOWNERS, ENTREPRENEURS, AND HIRED HANDS

By resolving the measure of the value of goods into quantities of land, Cantillon prepares the ground for the central idea of his work: "as all the land belongs to the prince and the land owners, all things which have this intrinsic value have it only at their expense." If the landowners would cease to cultivate their grounds, no one would have food or clothing. "Consequently all the individuals are supported not only by the produce of the land which is cultivated for the benefit of the owners but also at the expense of these same owners from whose property they derive all that they have." Everyone's means arise from the land, the "fountain head," whose produce yields three rents, each approximately amounting to one-third. One of these goes to the landowner while the tenant farmer retains two of them, one to cover his expenses of production and the other as his "profit." The landowner's rent serves to maintain his class and the city people catering to him, that remaining with the farmer maintains him as well as his suppliers. The landowners and the remainder of the population are in a relation of mutual interdependence. There are relatively few landowners and they have a highly effective demand backed up by substantial purchasing power. Because of this and because of the demonstration effect the landowner "is the principal agent in the changes which may occur in demand." As other groups try to emulate the consumption pattern of the landowners, the prices that the latter "offer in the market and their consumption determine the use made of the land just as if they cultivated it themselves." For this reason the landowning class is designated as independent and different from the dependent class, which is made up of "entrepreneurs" and hired people. The entrepreneurs, who therewith enter into the history of economic thought, have an unpredictable income because they transact purchases at certain prices and sales at uncertain ones. The hired people work for fixed amounts of income. As entrepreneurs come into money they acquire land from owners who have been ruined. Thus the class division is by no means a frozen one.

VIEWS ON POPULATION

The structure of the landowners' demand does not only determine the allocation of productive resources but also controls the factor supply, more specifically the growth of population. In line with the later thought of the classics, Cantillon considers income and population positively and causally correlated. "Men multiply like mice in a barn if they have unlimited means of subsistence." Thus, "if all land were devoted to the simple sustenance of man, the race would increase up to the number that the land would support." How many people the land will support depends on their mode of living and on the way the land is used. The use of the land, in turn, reflects the structure of the landowners' demand. "If by the prices they offer in the market for produce and merchandise they determine the farmers to employ the land for other purposes than the maintenance of man," there will be emigration, a declining marriage rate, and late marriages, and population will diminish. For example, the more horses the landowning class requires, the less food remains for the people, and the larger the amount of imports of foreign merchandise, the more produce must be sent abroad and land withdrawn from domestic subsistence. Conversely, "if the proprietors of land help to support the families, a single generation suffices to push the increase of population as far as the produce of the land will supply means of subsistence." What amount of subsistence is considered adequate will vary with the customs of the country, and Cantillon refuses to commit himself by resolving the question whether a large population, poor and badly provided for, is preferable to a smaller one living at greater ease. Such a question, he says, is outside his subject.

LANDOWNER SOVEREIGNTY

The first of the three untitled parts into which Cantillon's book is divided sheds a penetrating light on the operations of a self-regulating price system in which "consumer sovereignty" appears in the specific garb of "landowner sovereignty," a position to which the landowners are raised by their own superior purchasing power and by the desire of others to emulate their consumption pattern. In this system the normal price of goods reflects their cost of production as does the supply price of labor. The analysis is enriched by the introduction of the entrepreneur, who, however, plays a much more passive and adaptive role than he does in the modern discussion. Rather than initiate change, he responds to the pattern set by the landowners. With robbers, beggars, and chimney sweeps included in the group, he need not be a manager or a capitalist. Nor does Cantillon visualize him as an innovator as Petty, who was a gadgeteer and steeped in the technological and scientific lore of his time, might have done.

MONETARY THOUGHT

Whereas the first part of Cantillon's book generally depicts the "real" forces operating in the economy, the second introduces some complications which arise in a monetary economy. The discussion of market prices is expanded along the lines of a demand-and-supply analysis. Value theory is applied to money with the help of a quantity theory modified by a cost-of-production theory. After the precedent set by Petty and Locke, a careful estimate is made of a country's monetary requirements, with due regard to the velocity of circulation, commercial credit, clearing arrangements, and the interdependence of M and V. Money is said to pass always in return for services, and there emerges, dimly seen, the picture of two circular flows, one of money and the other of services, with each running in the opposite direction and with the money flow returning to the farmers the cash that they lay out in payments to the landowners and to the suppliers, the foundation of Quesnay's *Tableau*.

One of the highlights of part 2 of Cantillon's work is his analysis of what Keynes was to call "the diffusion of price levels," that is, "the fact that monetary changes do not affect all prices in the same way, in the same degree, or at the same time." Cantillon's contribution to this matter has been compared, not unfavorably, with that of Keynes, made two hundred years later in chapter 7 of his *Treatise on Money*. A case that Cantillon discusses in some detail is the diffusion of an increase in metallic money resulting from domestic mining operations. This accrues in the first instance to mine owners, their employees, and auxiliary industries. The incomes and expenditures of these rise, and as secondary rounds of expenditure ensue, the prices of agricultural products and manufactures increase. There is an initial decline in the real income of the landowners and other groups whose returns are fixed, but as time goes on leases and other contracts are renewed and the respective money payments are raised. As the increase in prices will in the end attract imports which compete with the products of domestic manufacturers, those who on balance are the only gainers of the increase in the money supply are the foreign manufacturers and the domestic mining interests.

Along similar lines Cantillon traces the diffusion of money flowing into the country as the result of a favorable balance of trade. This will raise employment, consumption, and prices, and in the end it will again invite imports from countries where money is tighter and the price level lower. Cantillon's book includes a theory of the automatic flow of specie and its effects on international prices, but it is embedded in involved arguments and not stated as crisply as it was by Hume, whose formulation was more influential on the further development of economic thought. Moreover, Cantillon weakens the effect of his ideas by repeatedly asserting the vital importance of a favorable balance of trade.

INTERNATIONAL TRADE

The third part of Cantillon's great work treats specifically of foreign trade and exchange, and contains further discussions of money, credit, and banking which are guided by his intimate familiarity with financial practice. Since Cantillon considers the produce of land the limiting factor in population growth, he opposes the international exchange of agricultural products for goods into which large amounts of labor have entered, a thought not uncommon at the time and fully developed by Sir James Steuart in 1767, who called for the importation of "matter" and the exportation of "work." With predilections such as these, Cantillon closed his eyes to the vast opportunities for improvements in output and productivity which a superior allocation of productive resources in line with international specialization would hold in store, conclusions later to be drawn by Ricardo.

THE PHYSIOCRATS

Although the Physiocrats by no means accepted all of Cantillon's views—they rejected, for example, his foreign-trade preferences— they assimilated such important ideas of Cantillon's as the circular flow and the special position of the landowning class into their own system.

With the Physiocrats there appears for the first time a school of economic thought with a recognized leader, a closely knit group of followers to exalt and spread the doctrines of the master, and a periodical to help in their dissemination. From the Physiocrats there dates the rise of schools of thought in economics—the classics, Marxians, historical economists, neoclassics, and Keynesians, to name but a few. Although new ideas often emerged outside the ranks of such schools, their absorption into the mainstream of economic thought usually required the active support of an informally organized group of scholars. Sometimes, as in the case of the Lausanne, Austrian, and Cambridge schools, there was a geographical basis for the intellectual link. But where the academic character of the school was less pronounced, as in the case of the Marxians, such a geographical basis might be lacking. As a rule, however, the formation of a school required a charismatic leader with a home base, and as the nineteenth century advanced, the latter was provided by a commanding academic position held for a substantial period of time. Roscher, Schmoller, Menger, and

Marshall, all founders of influential schools, devoted many years to their nurture. Such sustained and protracted leadership was lacking among the Physiocrats, and this is one reason why the school flourished for only about a dozen years, from the late 1750s to 1770.

QUESNAY

The head of the Physiocrats was François Quesnay (1694–1774), Louis XV's and Madame de Pompadour's personal physician, whose ability to win a following during a short span of time derived in part from the substance of his message, in part from his attractive personality, and in part from the aura of power and influence produced by his association with the highly placed persons under his medical care. Quesnay came to economics in his sixties, after he had made a name for himself as an outstanding physician and as an author of books on medicine, biology, and philosophy. The study of economics was but a passing phase of his intellectual career; after a few years his interest in economics lapsed and toward the end of his life he turned to mathematical investigations.

TURGOT

Next to Quesnay, the "Physiocrat" best remembered today is Anne Robert Jacques Turgot (1727–81), who after high positions with the French government served from 1774 to 1776 as one of the last ministers of finance under the *ancien régime*. Turgot, however, wanted to preserve his intellectual independence from the "sect," or school of the Physiocrats, or *économistes,* as they were called, and while closely allied with the group, he disclaimed membership in it. Another leading Physiocrat, not as watchful of his independence as Turgot, was Pierre Samuel Du Pont de Nemours (1739–1817), the publicist and editor of the school's journal, who founded an industrial dynasty of great renown and late in life came to the United States.

The sources of physiocratic thought are scattered over a large number of writings by Quesnay and his followers, incorporated not only in books but in periodical articles. Of Quesnay's works, a selection did not become available in an English translation until 1962, whereas Turgot's *Reflections on the Formation and the Distribution of Riches,* first published in 1770, was translated soon after its appearance, and again, in much improved form, in 1898. Thus, outside of France and the realm of the specialists, the image of the school's thought in doctrinal history has been formed not so much by the (at their time) more influential writings of Quesnay as by Turgot's compact and readable survey, originally written to give instruction to two Chinese students on their return to their homeland.

The system of the Physiocrats required a complete reconstruction of economics since they tore to shreds the entire fabric of mercantilist thought. Nothing is left of the primacy of foreign trade, which to them is but a "means of last resort" or "necessary evil." The hope for national gain at the cost of other countries is an illusion as the precarious gains are more than offset by the cost of the wars which are the result of policies harmful to other nations. "Monstruous systems" have made people believe that one can always sell without ever buying, or at least that one can always sell more than one buys. Trade is but the exchange of goods for goods; every sale is a purchase as well. In order to be able to sell, one has to buy. It is "the height of folly" to be always eager to dispose of goods for money without ever wanting to acquire them with money. Moreover, gold and silver do not constitute wealth but are merely "the effects of real production which has changed its form." The more there is of the latter, the less gold and silver are needed. Privations will not produce wealth; production will. The conclusions derived from the balance of trade are erroneous, and the doctrine that identifies the national advantage with the export surplus is a "chimerical idea." So runs the argument of Mercier de la Rivière in his *L'ordre naturel et essentiel des sociétés politiques* of 1767, which systematizes the thought of the school. What then did the Physiocrats offer to take the place of these discredited theories?

THE NATURAL AND THE POSITIVE ORDER

The Physiocrat's aim was to reorganize the French economy by means of tax reform and by promoting a system of efficient, large-scale farming. Quesnay's economic program was, however, presented as a part of a wider system of thought which extended over social and natural science and had its basis in natural law. From this emphasis, the name of the school is derived: physiocracy means *rule of nature*. Quesnay made a sharp distinction between the natural and the positive order, the one being made up of beneficial and self-evident rules, the other reflecting the inadequacy of the human legislator. Where the positive order deviates from the perfect and immutable natural order, the beneficial effects of the latter will not come into full play. But if the government is enlightened by reason, positive laws that are harmful to society will disappear. These thoughts reflect the stoic view of the world as a cosmos ordered by law, the optimism of the philosophy of Leibniz, and the belief of the French rationalists in the power of reason to derive truth from "self-evident" premises. Quesnay's view of the world and of science conform to the pattern of Cartesian rationalism as modified by the French philosopher Malebranche (1638–1715), of whom Quesnay was a faithful follower. Malebranche envisaged the cosmos as a variety of hierarchically and harmoniously arranged orders. Like Descartes, he distrusted data ostensibly established by the senses and instead extolled the immutable and eternal representations of the mind. These artifacts of reason have their counterparts both in Plato's ideas and in the abstract concepts and theoretical models employed in economics. As a Cartesian and follower of Malebranche, Quesnay thus became the founder of the rationalistic tradition in economics.

ECONOMIC INDIVIDUALISM

As for the substance of the natural order of soeiety, the Physiocrats visualized it as regulated by the principle of individualism. Turgot insisted that the individual is the best judge of his own interest, and to Quesnay the secret of a well-ordered society was that everyone works for others in the belief that he is working for himself. The Physiocrats thus postulated a perfect harmony of individual interests as well as of the interests of the king and of his subjects. It was in connection with the thought of the Physiocrats that the phrase *laissez faire, laissez passer* was coined, a maxim that to this day has served as an affirmation of economic individualism. The whole matter must, however, be viewed in the context of the fundamental dualism of physiocratic thought based, as it was, on the distinction between the natural and the positive order. Only in the natural order, the ideal, would harmonious individualism reach its full flowering. In the positive order of the world of reality the free play of individual forces might well be frustrated, with disadvantages that result in economic conflict rather than harmony.

PRIVATE PROPERTY

The individualism of the Physiocrats was complemented by a profound respect for the sanctity of private property. Quesnay derides the opinion that there is a natural right of everybody to everything. Such a right, he says, is similar to the right of each bird to all the insects that fly about in the air. In truth, this right is confined to all that it can catch. Similarly, although man has a natural right to goods suitable for his use, this right is confined to those goods that he can obtain through his labor. The endorsement of the Lockean labor theory of property is modified, however, by a consideration of social utility. Like Locke, Quesnay would found property on labor, but he also founds labor on property: it is the certainty of ownership, he says, that induces work necessary for the welfare of society.

The Physiocrats referred to a man's property as the measure of the freedom that he enjoyed. The protection of property rights was to them the foremost function of the positive order. That this in the end would mean the protection of the rich against the poor was a conclusion that the Physiocrats could not escape. Emphasized not so much by Quesnay himself as in the approved writings of his followers was the idea that liberty and equality are incompatible. In line with Cantillon's law of concentration, the Physiocrats explicitly endorsed inequality of possessions: If I have acquired the exclusive property of a good, no one else can be its proprietor at the same time—a thought that recalls the saying of an ancient philosopher that there are only a limited number of good seats in a theatre and that, once these are filled, others must be satisfied with lesser accommodations. In the physiocratic literature there can even be found a law of increasing concentration: As a society grows in wealth, so it does in inequality. The successful operation of the economic system as visualized by the Physiocrats required a good measure of inequality, and the latter, far from being considered obnoxious, was hailed as socially useful and natural, reflecting individual differences in ability and luck.

THE *PRODUIT NET*

As for the technical economics of the Physiocrats, they employ an equilibrium system in which the interaction of three economic classes—farmers, landowners, and artisans—produces the national income. The central idea of this system is the exclusive productivity of the farmer. By applying his labor to the land, he generates a surplus, or net revenue, *produit net,* in excess of his cost of production. This surplus has two unique characteristics. In the first place, it continually springs up afresh as a gift of nature that accrues to the farmer directly. "Nature," Turgot says, "does not bargain with him to be content with what is absolutely necessary" but yields him a physical product that exceeds both his expenses and his subsistence. In the second place, the surplus produced by the farmer serves to maintain the rest of society, that is, the "mixed" or "disposable" class of landlords that includes the king and the Church, and the "sterile" or "stipendiary" class of artisans, manufacturers, and traders.

Competition for leases enables the landlords to extract from the farmers the *produit net* in the form of rents, which become the income of the landlords. The latter are not productive in the strict sense since what they receive has been produced by the farmers. But they may claim the designation of a mixed class since they equip the farmers with capital and since they keep in circulation the net revenue, which in part is returned to the farmers to pay for their products and in part is spent for manufactures. The landlords do not have to work for a living and hence have leisure time; moreover, their money is not allocated in advance for specific purposes. Hence they form a disposable class in the double sense that they are available for public service and that their income can be used to defray public expenditures.

The artisans, manufacturers, and traders may work as hard as the farmers but they nevertheless are economically sterile since they only process materials originally produced by the farmers and in return receive no more than their subsistence. They are also known as a stipendiary class since they

TABLEAU ECONOMIQUE

Objets a considerer. 1º trois sortes de Depenses. 2º. leur Source. 3º. leurs avances, 4º. leur Distribution, 5º. leurs Effets, 6º. leur Reproduction, 7º. leurs Rapports entr'elles, 8º. leurs Rapports avec la population, 9º. avec l'Agriculture, 10º. avec l'Industrie, 11º. avec le Commerce, 12º. avec la masse des richesses d'une Nation.

DÉPENSES Productives	DÉPENSES DU REVENU	DÉPENSES Stériles
Relatives a l'Agriculture &c.	*l'Impôt compris se partagent a la Classe productive et a la Classe stérile*	*Relatives a l'Industrie &c.*
Avances annuelles *pour produire un Revenu de 2000ᵗ sont 2000ᵗ*	**Revenu** *Annuel de*	**Avances annuelles** *pour les Ouvrages des Dépenses stériles sont 1000.ᵗ*

2000ᵗ produisent net.......... 2000ᵗ

Productions   Ouvrages &c.

Productions			Revenu		Ouvrages &c.		
1000ᵗ	s.	d	reproduisent net..... 1000ᵗ s. d		1000ᵗ	s.	d
500	"	"	reproduisent net..... 500 " "		500	"	"
250	"	"	reproduisent net..... 250 " "		250	"	"
125	"	"	reproduisent net..... 125 " "		125	"	"
62	10	"	reproduisent net..... 62 10 "		62	10	"
31	5	"	reproduisent net..... 31 5 "		31	5	"
15	12	6	reproduisent net..... 15 12 6		15	12	6
7	16	3	reproduisent net..... 7 16 3		7	16	3
3	18	2	reproduisent net..... 3 18 2		3	18	2
1	19	1	reproduisent net..... 1 19 1		1	19	1
0	19	6	reproduisent net..... 0 19 6		0	19	6
0	9	9	reproduisent net..... 0 9 9		0	9	9
0	5	"	reproduisent net..... 0 5 "		0	5	"
0	2	6	reproduisent net..... 0 2 6		0	2	6
0	1	3	reproduisent net..... 0 1 3		0	1	3
0	0	8	reproduisent net..... 0 0 8		0	0	8

Total 2000ᵗ s. d   Total 2000ᵗ s. d   Total 2000ᵗ s. d

Il n'est pas nécessaire de s'attacher a l'intelligence de ce Tableau avant la lecture des 7 premiers Chapitres, il suffit a chaque chapitre de faire attention a la partie du Tableau qui y a rapport.

receive stipends out of the produce of the land. Thus both the farmers and the artisans, the two working and nondisposable classes, are left with an income depressed to the subsistence level by the process of competitive bargaining. The fundamental difference between the two is the productive character of the labor of the farmer, which, unlike that of the artisan, produces not only his own wage but also the surplus that maintains the rest of society.

THE *TABLEAU*

The relationship between the three classes was illustrated by Quesnay in the famous *tableau économique,* an early model of the circular flow of the "national income" and of its annual reproduction. There are several variants of the *tableau,* all of which, however, conform to two basic patterns. The one portrays successive rounds of spending and the other summarizes the results achieved thereby.

The *tableau* that depicts successive rounds of expenditure does so in the form of a zigzag diagram as shown on page 188. Basic to its understanding are two assumptions, one relating to the farmers' net revenue, which is supposed to be equal to the amount of their expenditure or income, that is, one dollar of cost incurred in the farm business yields one dollar of farm income and another dollar of *produit net.* The second assumption relates to the expenditure of any one of the three classes, which is always evenly divided among farm products and manufactures. Thus the landlords, for each dollar spent for manufactures, will spend another dollar for farm products; whereas the members of the two working classes, for each dollar spent for products of their own class, will spend another dollar for the products of the other class.

As the *tableau* shows, the farmers have produced in the previous year a net revenue worth two thousand livres, which has been turned over to the landlords as this year's rent. The landlords, in the first round of expenditure, spend one-half of this sum for farm products and the other half for manufactures. As the result of the first round of spending, the farmers find themselves with one thousand livres, which in their hands doubles, yielding a net revenue of another one thousand livres available to form part of the next payment to the landlords. Of the original one thousand livres, the farmers retain one-half for expenditures within the class—which are not shown in the *tableau*—while the other half is used for purchases of manufactures from the sterile class. The latter has in the meantime employed one-half of its receipts of one thousand livres from the landlords for intraclass purchases of manufactures—not shown—and the other half for purchases of farm products. Thus a second round of expenditure can start, in which both the farmers and the sterile class find themselves with five hundred livres. The farmers produce another net revenue equal to this amount, and each of the two working classes again spends one-half of the five hundred livres for its own products and the other half for the products of the other class. After approximately twelve such rounds of expenditure, each of the two working classes has reproduced its subsistence income or expenditure; in addition, the farming class has produced another net revenue of two thousand livres for the landlords.

The second variant of the *tableau* summarizes these findings. Here the farmers have produced a gross product worth five billion livres, three-fifths of which consists of food and two-fifths of raw materials. This they have on hand, and they also hold the entire money stock of the nation amounting to two billion livres. The landlord class has a rental claim of two billion livres against the farmers. The sterile class holds manufactures worth two billion livres. The distribution of the product begins when the farmers have paid the landlords' rental claim of two billion livres. One billion of this is returned by the landlords to the farmers for food, while another billion is spent for manufactures and accrues to the sterile class.

The farmers now hold one billion livres of money and four billion livres' worth of agricultural products. The landlords hold one billion livres' worth of food and one billion livres' worth of manufactures. The sterile class holds one billion livres of cash and one billion livres' worth of manufactures. The sterile class then uses its money to purchase one billion livres' worth of food from the farmers. These return the money to the sterile class for purchases of manufactures, and the sterile class employs this amount of money again for the purchase of raw materials from the farmers.

The farmers thus have recouped the money stock of two billion livres and have it ready for the next rental payment. Of the gross product of five billion livres, they have sold one billion livres' worth of food both to the landlords and to the sterile class, and to the latter also one billion livres' worth of raw materials. The sterile class thus finds itself with one billion livres' worth of food and another one billion livres' worth of raw materials, which it is ready to transform again into two billion livres' worth of manufactures. The farmers are left with two billion livres' worth of food-stuffs and raw materials and one billion livres' worth of manufactures. The two billion livres of foodstuffs and raw materials, their expenses of production, will yield another gross product of five billion livres, and the circle can start afresh.

The information given in Quesnay's *tableau* can without much difficulty be arranged in an input-output "*tableau*" such as has been constructed in our times by Leontief, who himself has alluded to the affinity of his construction with that of the Physiocrats. Such an arrangement sheds light on the underlying structure of the model, which in Quesnay's as well as in Leontief's case utilizes observed data. The presentation of these in the form of Leontief's *tableau* fails, however, to do justice to the distinctions between the three classes of physiocratic thought, and it presumes a "productive activity" of the landlords, consisting, perhaps, of their own public service or the service of their land. Here is an input-output tableau:

| PRODUCING SECTOR | PURCHASING SECTOR | | | TOTAL |
	FARMERS	LANDLORDS	ARTISANS	PRODUCTION
FARMERS	2	1	2	5
LANDLORDS	2	0	0	2
ARTISANS	1	1	0	2
TOTAL PURCHASES	5	2	2	9

To Quesnay the striking feature of the *tableau* was the light that it shed on the character of the three classes and on the productivity of agriculture. The landlord class sets the distributive process in motion by spending its rental income. The farming class produces its own income as well as the *produit net*. The income of the sterile class is generated by the expenditures of the landlords and farmers, and it is exactly offset by the expenses required to sustain the class and equip it with raw materials.

The *tableau* as thus far depicted shows the economy in equilibrium, that is, in a state where the national income exactly reproduces itself. But Quesnay also constructs cases in which "the *tableau* has lost its equilibrium." For example, the landowners may increase their expenditures for manufactures and reduce those for food, a change in the consumption pattern that the demonstration effect will spread throughout the economy. Initially the income of the sterile class will rise. In the years to come, however, the incomes of all classes will fall and universal ruin will ensue. The landlords' income will decline since it is derived entirely from the now diminished *produit net* of the farmers, as will the income of the sterile class, derived as it is from the expenditures of the two other classes.

Similarly undesirable effects are shown to result from restrictions on trade which depress agricultural prices, for example, from restrictions on the exportation of grain, and from "indirect" taxes levied on bases other than the rental income of the disposable class. Demonstrations such as these buttressed the principal policy proposals of the Physiocrats, namely, free trade, specifically freedom of exportation of farm products, and a "direct" single tax on the only surplus, the *produit net,* which becomes the rental income of the landlord class. With the other classes earning only their subsistence, the indirect taxes levied on bases other than the *produit net* would in the end still have to be paid out of the landlords' rental income. Hence the proposal for a straightforward single tax which would fall directly on the *produit net*. Such a tax, the Physiocrats insisted, could be collected with greater economy, and it would not depress the national income by reducing the productive expenses of the farmer or by causing other maladjustments.

In its substance the *tableau* in equilibrium may have been closer to the natural order of the Physiocrats than to the positive one. The Physiocrats were by no means unaware that the French economy of their time was replete with surpluses, that is, excesses of revenue over cost of production, in sectors other than the agricultural one. Such surpluses, however, they interpreted as the result of market imperfections produced by inappropriate public policies affecting foreign and domestic trade. They argued that if these were mended monopoly power would vanish as would the surpluses produced by it.

VALUE AND PRICE THEORY

Another apparent inconsistency, and perhaps a more serious one, derives from the inadequate value theory of the Physiocrats. The physical productivity of agriculture, as contrasted with its value productivity, was a well-established fact, and one on which earlier writers, including Cantillon, had often commented. The seed planted in the ground will multiply, perhaps as much as one hundred times. What the Physiocrats failed to demonstrate was the superior value productivity of agriculture. If the forces of competition would depress the prices of manufactures to their cost of production, and farm as well as manufacturing wages to the level of subsistence, why would the prices of agricultural products form an exception and remain high enough to yield the *produit net?* There are several possible answers to this question. It may be that the Physiocrats visualized so strong a pressure of population against the means of subsistence as to exempt agricultural prices from the general law of competition. It is difficult, however, to find a justification for such a view in the circumstances of the time, because the French farm economy normally produced an export surplus. It is more likely that what the Physiocrats had in mind was an active government policy of promoting a level of agricultural prices high enough to yield a substantial *produit net* in excess of the farmers' cost of production. The value productivity that they assumed thus had its basis not only in nature but in public policy as well, and their attachment to laissez faire was by no means so absolute as to preclude a political price for farm products. If they had been faced with a choice between laissez faire and intervention on behalf of farm-price supports, they would have chosen intervention. The means to resolve the economic problem that was foremost in their minds was the development of domestic agriculture rather than unconditional reliance on private initiative within a framework of competition. To prove this point, it would be necessary to show that the Physiocrats, in spite of the proclaimed general harmony of interests, the basis of the individualistic order of society, did come across an important case where the pursuit of private interest ran counter to that of society, as understood by them. Such a case will emerge presently.

LUXURY   The Physiocrats' gospel of high prices did indeed call for a *bon prix* of agricultural products, a price presumably high enough to enable the farmers to produce a net revenue of 100 percent, such as was assumed in the zigzag version of the *tableau*. Like Boisguilbert they identified large supplies sold at high prices with prosperity, whereas the same supplies sold at low prices constituted only the shadow but not the substance of affluence. Again in the manner of Boisguilbert they emphasized the desirability of strengthening consumer demand, while guiding it in the right direction. Quesnay taught that "in an agricultural country, frugality is the mother of poverty." He favored *luxe de subsistence,* high-level consumption of farm products while rejecting *luxe de décoration,* high-level consumption of manufactures, which would cut into the purchases of agricultural products.

REGULATIONS All this need not constitute a break with the laissez faire doctrine. The Physiocrats came closer to such a break when Quesnay and some of his followers pleaded for legal restrictions on the rate of interest for the benefit of the farmer, a matter that remained a subject of controversy and of which Turgot took the opposite view. A much sharper break was the Physiocrats' rejection of the exportation of manufactures, which the free play of economic interests might produce but which they considered harmful to the public interest because of allegedly unfavorable effects on agricultural prices. The Physiocrats made a sharp distinction between exports of farm products and exports of manufactures. The former they favored because of their wholesome effect on farm prices, and the demolition of restrictions on agricultural exports was an important point of their program of economic reform. But they associated exports of manufactures with a policy of cheap food designed to keep labor cost low, and since such a state of affairs would run counter to the gospel of high agricultural prices, they opposed the introduction of new manufactures destined for foreign markets. The glory of French manufacture had been luxury products, and these, the Physiocrats argued, could at best serve a foreign demand that was capricious and fragile. An adverse shift in the foreign demand would easily breed domestic unemployment; there would be food riots and with them would come insistent pleas for what the Physiocrats feared most: still lower prices of agricultural products. "Happy the land," Quesnay said, "which has no exports of manufactures because agricultural exports maintain farm prices at too high a level to permit the sterile class to sell its products abroad."

VALUE AND PRICE THEORY Quesnay's *bon prix* forms part of his value theory, which is not fully developed but has a number of interesting features. The *bon prix* stands in a certain relationship to the *prix fondamental,* which is equal to the cost of production. Market prices form a spectrum. On the one end they may fall short of the cost of production, in which case they will cause losses. On the other end they are "excessively high" and constitute a "burden." The *bon prix* is located between these extremes. It is a price that yields a gain and thus constitutes an incentive to maintain or expand production.

The *prix fondamental* forms the link between Quesnay's price theory and his theory of value. He distinguishes between value in use and value in exchange, the latter being referred to as *valeur vénale,* or "sales value."

Value in use reflects individual needs and desires and is only tenuously related to other values and prices. Quesnay thus discards the opportunity for developing a theory of use value. Instead he concentrates his attention on exchange value. Only goods that have *valeur vénale* constitute wealth, that is, value arises only in society. As to the forces that affect the *valeur vénale,* Quesnay seems to be reluctant to identify them in positive terms. He states explicitly that the *valeur vénale* "is by no means controlled by man's needs nor is it an arbitrary value or one constituted by the agreement among the contracting parties." He thus sheds more light on the factors that do not determine exchange value than on those that determine it, but he clearly eliminates from the latter the state of man's mind and the bargaining process. The factors that affect value do so without passing first through man's mind; they are objective rather than subjective. They are not only independent of the buyer's and seller's minds but they operate logically ahead of the exchange transaction, which may realize economic value but does not determine it.

This leaves the cost of production, the *prix fondamental,* as a determinant of value, but side by side with this is also mentioned the influence of foreign trade, to the Physiocrats a strategic factor in the formation of prices and values. With its stress on exchange value and its rejection of psychological determinants of value, Quesnay's cost-of-production theory of value is in line with the mainstream of doctrinal development, which was eventually dominated by the labor theory of value of the classics, not to be replaced by a subjective theory until the 1870s. The objective theory, although the ruling one, failed to satisfy everybody. During the eighteenth century several variants of a subjective theory of value had emerged, but because of the strong influence of the objective theory these had received little attention. One variant was developed by Turgot in an unfinished essay on "Values and Monies," written in the 1760s. To Turgot all valuations are subjective and relative; "they have nothing fixed and change from one moment to the other, following the variations of human desires." The *valeur estimative* mirrors the utility and scarcity of a good. An average of such *valeurs estimatives* of the parties to an exchange transaction constitutes the *valeur appréciative,* which in turn determines the price. A similar idea is hinted at also in Turgot's *Reflections,* where the market price is said to be "midway between the different offers and the different demands."

DIMINISHING RETURNS

Turgot was ahead of his time in many respects. He was the first to state the principle of diminishing returns and did so, in unexceptionable form, in the late 1760s, some fifty years before a number of English economists derived the same principle from practical experience. When developing this principle, Turgot speaks of incremental applications of the variable factor, thus anticipating the marginal principle as well. Successive applications of the variable input will cause the product to grow, first at an increas-ing rate, later at a diminishing rate, until it reaches a maximum. These thoughts were developed by Turgot in an obscure prize essay, and it is doubtful that they received much attention.

CAPITAL THEORY

Turgot pioneered in the development of the theory of capital, and as he did this in his *Reflections,* the influence of his thought in this matter reached further. Quesnay had already underlined the need for *avances* consisting of fixed and working capital which must be on hand in advance of the productive process. On this basis Turgot constructed a capital theory which later generations of economists found hard to improve. Savings, the excess of income over consumption, are supplied by the landowners when the satisfaction of their wants does not require all of their income. The other classes' ability to save is not strictly compatible with the physio-cratic view of their character because their members ostensibly earn no more than their subsistence. However, since competition is not keen enough to depress all incomes exactly to the level of subsistence, and since people differ in their attitude to thrift, prudent people will as a rule be able to accumulate a little nest egg, and some may even become capitalists: people who are rich without owning land and without working and who live on the income from their money or, if they lend it out, on interest.

The savings consist of *richesses mobiliaires,* stocks of goods or money. The demand for these arises because every kind of economic activity requires *avances* to be made available from previously accumulated *richesses mobiliaires.* Laborers have to be maintained before the product is ready for sale; farms and workshops need buildings, equipment, and raw materials. As for the relationship between saving and investment, Turgot speaks in one place of the "timid miser" who "keeps his money in a hoard," but when referring to what is apparently business saving, or retained business income, he says that this is converted "immediately" into real capital, or invested. Hence such savings, although they are usually made in the form of money, do not constitute a leakage from the income stream since they are returned to circulation at once. This view of Turgot's, which was echoed in Adam Smith's *Wealth of Nations,* was to rule economic thought for a long time. Although it was at times challenged during the nineteenth century, it came to hold a central position in the mainstream of traditional economic thought, with the challengers viewed as heretics. Not until the 1930s, with the ascendancy of the thought of Keynes, did the old orthodoxy give way to a new one which taught the opposite of what had been the leading doctrine.

Turgot distinguishes five different employments of capital—purchase of a landed estate, investment in agriculture, manufacture, commerce, and lending at interest—each of which yields a different return. The returns are interrelated in a way that will equalize the total advantage of the investor. Investments in land, because of their safety and ease, yield the least. The yield from loan funds will be somewhat higher because it includes a risk premium. Because of this, and also because of the care and attention required of the investor, capital invested in agriculture, manufacture, and trade will command still higher returns.

The returns on differently employed capital exercise a reciprocal influence on each other, and there exists between them "a sort of equilibrium, as between two liquids of unequal gravity which communicate with one another at the bottom of a reversed syphon of which they occupy the two branches; they will not be on a level, but the height of one cannot increase without the other also rising in the opposite branch." Similarly, if the return on one type of investment increases, the returns on the others will change in the same direction. The rising return on one attracts funds from other investments and raises returns there.

INTEREST Interest is payable as an opportunity cost because the lender, had he used his funds for the purchase of land, would earn a return, an opportunity he forgoes by lending out the money—an argument that goes back to Calvin's justification of interest. Turgot reinforces it with another consideration, based on the right of property, so dear to the Physiocrats: the lender is the owner of his funds; he can do with them as he pleases and no one has the right to claim their use for nothing.

With Turgot emerges the view that attaches to interest a strategic function in the economy. It is "the thermometer by which one may judge the abundance or scarcity of capital." Capital can only be employed in investments that yield as much as the interest rate. The latter can be considered a kind of "level beneath which all labor, all agriculture, all industry, all commerce come to an end." Turgot likens the interest rate to an ocean spread over a vast area:

> The summits of the mountains rise above the waters and form fertile and cultivated islands. If this sea happens to roll back, first the slopes of the hills, then the plains and the valleys appear and are covered with every kind of produce. It is enough that the water should rise or fall a foot to inundate immense tracts, or throw them open to agriculture.

EQUILIBRIUM AND CIRCULAR FLOW The word *equilibrium,* which Turgot employs in his capital theory, attracted other Physiocrats as well. They remark, for example, that the *tableau* "has lost its equilibrium" if the income, owing to adverse policies, fails to reproduce itself, or they speak of a "necessary equilibrium" of all prices. The context in which Turgot uses the word underlines its origin in physical science. That such borrowings from physics were more than an occasional turn of thought and that Turgot took mechanical analogies seriously may be demonstrated by a passage from his Eulogy on Gournay, where he speaks of "the unique and simple laws, founded on nature itself, in consequence of which all values that exist in trade are held in balance and settle themselves at determinate values, just as the bodies given over to their weight arrange themselves in the order of their specific gravity." Similarly Quesnay's circular flow idea, as portrayed in the general equilibrium system of the *tableau,* has its parallel in physical science. Quesnay was a medical man, and he actively participated in the lively discussions of circular processes which had been going on among physicians ever since Harvey had discovered the circulation of the blood early in the seventeenth century. Indeed, Quesnay has been described as a man obsessed by the mystery of the circle, which at the end of his life he tried to square. Earlier, the circle had impressed Greek philosophers and medieval astronomers as the perfect form, which has no beginning and no end. Circular movements, which in the opinion of these men propelled the celestial bodies of the cosmos, were now found to animate the human body and society as well.

The emergence of the equilibrium concept and of the circular flow in economic thought are milestones in the development of economic science. It is true that Quesnay could build on the foundations available in Cantillon's work, but the physiocratic constructions owe much to a fusion of economic thought with ideas borrowed from natural science. To the Physiocrats the natural order of society was a branch of physics. Their achievements in economics serve as an example of an advance made possible by the meeting of thoughts originally at home in different departments. Mercantilist thought had been enriched by the assimilation of business lore. That of the Physiocrats was stimulated by the adaptation of natural science ideas. The history of economics thus aptly illustrates Arthur Koestler's thesis, propounded in his *Act of Creation,* according to which great advances in thought arise as the result of a fusion of ideas originating in different disciplines.

Quesnay was a physician, as had been Petty, and the accomplishments of both men were nurtured by their familiarity with physical science. But what to Petty was only a passing phase of a great and varied career which soon removed him from medical practice and teaching was to Quesnay a lifelong and deep attachment. Both Petty and Quesnay were substantial landowners, and some of Petty's thoughts, especially his proposals relating to the peopling of Ireland, can easily be interpreted as a rationalization of his own economic interest. A similar interpretation of Quesnay's thought is much more dubious. He and his followers were spokesmen not so much of the landed interests as of those of the monarchy. During the physiocratic phase of his career Quesnay was attached to the royal household. He resided in Versailles, and his principal professional concern was the health of the king, a concern that soon came to include the latter's financial well-being, identified with the financial well-being of the nation. Quesnay's great aim was to increase the source of public revenue, which was to come out of the landlords' rents, enlarged by agricultural prosperity. This overriding aim is well brought out in Mercier de la Rivière's book, considered by Adam Smith the best statement of physiocratic doctrine, the economic part of which opens with the analysis of public revenue and of the single tax, matters that stand in the foreground of the discussion and to which all else is subordinated.

INFLUENCE OF THE PHYSIOCRATS

The close connection of the Physiocrats with the French court and their unconditional espousal of the absolute monarchy could not fail to make a profound impression abroad, especially on the "enlightened despots" of the age. It was a time in which the world looked up to French civilization and all things French as models worthy of admiration and emulation. There was considerable interest in the doctrines of the Physiocrats in foreign countries, but the pronounced individualism of their thought was not at all suited to the then "underdeveloped" regions of central and eastern Europe. There is an amusing report of an interview of Mercier de la Rivière with the empress Catherine the Great in Moscow. Catherine was interested in obtaining information that would help her in drafting legislation for her country, but all she received were references to the natural order. Thus Catherine asks:

"Sir, can you tell me the best way to govern the state well?"

"There is only one way, Madame, namely to be just, that is, maintain order and enforce the laws."

"But on what basis should the laws of a kingdom rest?"

"On one only, Madame, on the nature of things and men."

"Certainly, but if one wants to give laws to a people, what rules should one follow?"

"Madame, to make laws is a task which God has reserved for Himself. How can man be considered competent to impose laws on beings of whom he has no or only imperfect knowledge? And by what right would he impose laws on beings whom God has not placed in his hands?"

"To what then do you reduce the science of government?"

"To the study of the laws which God has so evidently engraven in human society when He created man. To seek to go beyond this would be a great calamity and a destructive undertaking."

"Sir, it has been a great pleasure to listen to you, and I wish you good day."

In France herself, as has been noted, the influence of the Physiocrats was extremely short-lived. The reforms undertaken on their behest had to be cancelled since the abolition of restrictions on the grain trade happened to coincide with serious harvest failures. But the principal reason for the decline of the school was the anachronistic character of its program, which was full of incongruities. The Physiocrats were eager to preserve what apparently could not be preserved, the ancient regime, and to accomplish this they developed a program with a number of distinctly medieval features, blended with surprisingly modern ones. Like medieval economic thought, their ideas were in substance normative ones which called for adherence to the natural order. Just as in medieval times economic power was to be tamed by the forces of religion, so it was now to be restrained by obedience to the natural order. Land, which had been the principal source of wealth during the Middle Ages, was to be restored to this position. Like the feudal lords of yore, the landowning class would enjoy a commanding position in society, and in return the members of this class would be liable not to feudal obligations but to the state's upkeep. At the helm of the ship of state would be an absolute ruler. Here, however, the parallel with medievalism ends. Quite unlike the medieval peasantry the farming class was to be free of all feudal duties and personal dependencies—services, deliveries in kind, and so forth—which were an essential feature of medieval society. Instead it was to be transformed into a prosperous class of large-scale efficient operators who would produce for a market that was unrestricted by regulations. Quesnay had little historical insight, and his rationalism prevented him from noticing the incongruous character of such a class in a world that in other respects was to be essentially medieval.

While professing attachment to laissez faire, the Physiocrats were undaunted in their belief in the virtues of absolute monarchy as the best form of government. And what they are best remembered for—their emphasis on agriculture—was already obsolete in an age that saw the dawn of the industrial revolution. Their opposition to manufacturing exports ran counter to the trend of the French economy which had produced such exports in excess of agricultural ones since the middle of the eighteenth century. When a belated attempt was made in England to rehabilitate the central idea of the Physiocrats, it was at once sharply rebuked. William Spence (1783–1860), not to be confused with the land reformer Thomas Spence, in 1807 wrote a tract, *Britain Independent of Commerce,* the thesis of which is amplified in its subtitle: *Proofs deduced from an investigation into the true causes of the wealth of nations, that our riches, prosperity and power are derived from sources inherent in ourselves, and would not be affected even though our commerce were annihilated.* In the following year, both James Mill, in *Commerce Defended,* and Robert Torrens, in *The Economists Refuted,* laid the physiocratic ghost to rest.

The Physiocrats' technical economics, as distinguished from their policy and philosophy, has, however, exerted far-reaching effects on the future course of economic thought. Adam Smith was profoundly influenced by it, especially by Turgot's contributions, although he did not develop the latter's attempt to form a subjective theory of value. Marx, who gave much attention to the *tableau,* found in it and in the Physiocrats' emphasis on the surplus produced by one class important inspirations for his own system of thought, whose central idea is again a surplus, this time produced by the workers rather than by the farmers. Today's mathematical economics, both in its econometric and in its purely theoretical variety, is foreshadowed in the work of the Physiocrats: Quesnay's *tableau* was designed to reflect observed or at least conjectural data, and in addition the school produced a geometric diagram with curves, after Bernoulli's the earliest in the economic literature. There are affinities also between the *tableau* and Leontief's input-output table, both of which represent a close union of theory and statistical observation, as well as between the geometric progression of the zigzag *tableau* and the multiplier. As for Quesnay and Keynes, whose names sound so similar and whose family origin can be traced back to Normandy, they are linked by strong ties of intellectual affinity in their work as the aggregative equilibrium of the one has its counterpart in that of the other.

Chapter 9

DISCORDANT
CURRENTS
OF THOUGHT:
Galiani
Hume
Steuart

The Physiocrats were not the only writers on economics who made a
name for themselves during the decades preceding the publication of Smith's
Wealth of Nations in 1776. There were others who contributed to economic
thought, and the discussion now becomes enriched by the rise of a variety
of points of view, especially about the right approach to the study of economics. In this debate the rationalism of the Physiocrats, who were guided
by reason rather than by experience, did not remain unchallenged. As an
alternative, the empirical approach had already emerged in the writings of
Hume in the 1740s and 1750s, before the Physiocrats. This rival approach
was stressed again by Galiani, a critic of the Physiocrats, in 1770, and it
was practiced on a substantial scale by Steuart in 1767. The second half of
the eighteenth century thus found the battle lines drawn between the followers of rationalism and those of empiricism in a first controversy about
methods that foreshadows the conflict between the Austrians and the
historical school a century later.

None of the three writers considered here developed a full-fledged
system of economics, nor did any of them found a school in the sense in
which Quesnay had. As for the substance of their thought, Galiani is mainly
remembered as a precursor of the subjective theory of value, and Hume for
his demolition of mercantilism. Steuart, "the last mercantilist," hung on to
ideas already obsolete in his time, but in displaying them in all their weakness he alleviated the birth pangs of new thought. What links the three is
their antirationalism, that is, in the context of the time, their opposition to
ideas held by the Physiocrats. Although Hume's writings precede those of the
Physiocrats, he expressed this opposition more forcefully than either Galiani

or Steuart because to him the empirical approach was part of a broad philosophy that he had developed at length before his economic writings. Galiani's methodological observations, which are more casual and aphoristic, were developed not for their own sake but *ad hoc* in connection with his critique of physiocratic policy. Steuart had little to say about methods, but his work is mainly an elaboration of economics along empirical lines.

GALIANI

The Physiocrats had advanced their opinions with a relentless dogmatism characteristic of true believers who consider themselves in the possession of absolute truth, self-evident to all except the wicked and the ignorant. They brooked no opposition and accused disbelievers of intellectual blindness. It was this feature of their work that seemed most dangerous to Ferdinando Galiani (1728–87), an Italian abbott in diplomatic employment in Paris, whose *Dialogues sur le commerce des blés* of 1770 contained an effective critique of physiocracy. Galiani condemned the dogmatic rationalism of the school from the point of view of historical relativism, and he called for flexible policies in line with historical and geographical conditions rather than for adherence to immutable principles of allegedly universal applicability. Galiani shows special concern about the honest enthusiasm that inspired the propagation of the physiocratic doctrine. Mountebanks and crooks are not to be feared as they will soon be exposed. But an honest man, whose views have become an obsession, is liable to be a danger to society. "The desire to do good," Galiani says, "is as much a passion as others."

Galiani's doubts about the power of reason to deduce eternal verities reflect the influence of Giambattista Vico (1668–1774), the great Italian philosopher of history and historian, who opposed the antihistorical rationalism characteristic of French Cartesianism. In his approach to history Vico stressed the evolution of social institutions and laid the foundation for a science of society developed on historical foundations. Like Vico, Galiani finds fault with the assertion of the rationalists that they are able to arrive at principles valid at all ages and places. "Men have the great weakness," he says, "to let themselves be guided by examples and reasons which do not fit at all the circumstances in which they find themselves." As will presently be seen, it was this principle of historical relativism that led Galiani to the discovery of the subjective theory of value.

When Galiani criticised the Physiocrats, he had already won fame as a brilliant intellect. Twenty years earlier, as a youth of twenty-two, he had written a remarkable treatise, *Della Moneta* (1751). For this precocious effort, which is without parallel in the early history of economics, he had prepared himself by translating Locke's economic tract. Galiani's book, a work of some three hundred pages, was to form part of a general treatise of political science, a project that Galiani, however, never completed. He was an original thinker of whom it has been said that, had he wanted to, he could have become an Adam Smith. He did not, however, have the disposition required for protracted intellectual effort, and although he was a sparkling conversationalist and fascinating correspondent as well as an effective diplomat and civil servant, his contributions to economics were peripheral and sporadic rather than the product of a lifelong devotion to austere scholarship.

Galiani's *Della Moneta* has a number of remarkable chapters, including one in which Galiani, after having constructed a model of a small communistic community, transforms this by what seems to be sheer magic, but is really a series of ingeniously formulated successive approximations, into the world of reality. This procedure brings into sharp relief the common structure of economic societies and the effects produced by the introduction of economic incentives, prices, money, and taxes. In another chapter Galiani traces the effects of a devaluation of money. He stresses the delay in public reaction to the reduction of the gold content of the monetary unit; domestic prices will rise only haltingly, especially if there is little foreign trade. In the meantime the supply of money has nominally been raised—one gold coin being worth, say, six lire instead of five—and this may stimulate economic expansion.

VALUE THEORY

These contributions, important as they are, are overshadowed by Galiani's theory of value. Like the classical theory of later times, his theory is based on the distinction between value in *use* and value in *exchange,* although Galiani does not introduce these concepts in so many words. The classics would mention use value but discard it almost immediately and develop a theory of exchange value based on labor. Galiani's procedure is different. He first develops at length a theory of use value and then derives exchange value from it.

Galiani's historical sense makes him see value not as an inherent quality of goods but as one that will vary with man's changing appreciation of goods. He recognizes the powerful effect of social forces and stresses the role of fashion as a determinant of man's desires and thus of value. Similarly he is aware of the significance of what Veblen was to call "invidious comparisons" and what is now known as demonstration effect. "After man has satisfied the desires which he has in common with the animals and which relate to the preservation of the individual and of the species, there is no stronger and more violent passion than that for distinction and superiority over others. . . . Goods which satisfy it have a very high value." In Galiani's analysis of value as a subjective relation between man's mind and external goods, utility and scarcity emerge as determinants of value. Utility is defined as "the aptitude of a good to make us happy." According to Galiani, "man is driven by passions which push him with unequal force. Satisfaction of these passions is pleasure. The possession of pleasure is happiness." Hence, any good that produces pleasure is useful. There are elemental passions or desires such as those for food, drink, and sleep. Once these are satisfied, others emerge which are just as strong. No line can be drawn between what is necessary and what ceases to be useful. "Man is so constituted that when he satisfies one desire, another one makes itself felt with equal force. He thus finds himself in a perpetual motion without ever arriving at complete satisfaction." Galiani hints at a number of principles that in a fully developed form are part of the modern subjective theory of value as it emerged in the 1870s. He knows of the substitution effect: "a good whose price falls is used in preference." In a general way he is aware of what was later to be known as diminishing marginal utility: "Somebody who has eaten his fill will consider bread the least useful of goods. He will then want to satisfy other needs." And he never fails to emphasize the strictly subjective and relative character of utility and of the ranking of goods derived from it.

Galiani's value theory was not developed into a full-fledged price theory, a task later attempted but not completed by Turgot, who shared Galiani's view about the subjective nature of value and referred to his book approvingly. A few decades earlier John Law had also taught a subjective theory of value, and in 1776, the year of the publication of *The Wealth of Nations*, Condillac, a French philosopher, had again enunciated such a theory, basing it on utility. There were thus at least four writers who developed subjective theories of value during the eighteenth century, a fact that again illustrates the principle that new scientific insights appear in the form of multiples. However, the views of these writers gained little following. Law's thought may have been discredited by the failure of his financial operations. Turgot's value theory does not form part of his *Reflections* but was developed as a peripheral essay that remained a fragment. Both Turgot and Condillac found fault with the Physiocrats but nevertheless the decline of physiocracy diminished their influence. Galiani's *Della Moneta* appeared in a second edition in 1780 and was reprinted several times during the nineteenth century, but with no translation available, its principal effect was felt in Italy only. Thus when Adam Smith fell back on the Lockean tradition and developed a labor theory of value, the ascendancy of the subjective theory was delayed for a hundred years.

Adam Smith's *Wealth of Nations* contains no trace of Galiani's influence. The only link between the two was the connection of both men with Hume, who, when appointed to a diplomatic post in Paris in 1763, frequented the same society of *philosophes* and *économistes* among whom Galiani was at home.

HUME

David Hume (1711–76), the famous Scottish philosopher, was the first great figure in economic thought to break the path leading to the establishment of economics as a constituent part of a wider social science. Such men as Petty, Locke, and Quesnay brought to economics the preconceptions and points of view of natural scientists. All three had been trained in medicine, at their time apparently the refuge of intellectuals eager to transcend the established boundaries of science and search for new ways of thought. Their first allegiance was to natural science—to physics, physiology, and related disciplines. As a young doctor, Petty had revived a person that had been hanged and given up for dead. Locke might be seen riding at dawn to gather for pharmaceutical research the roots of male peonies produced under a favorable constellation of the celestial bodies. This development culminated in the Physiocrats, who saw physical laws everywhere. They employed, as Mercier de la Rivière put it, "no other compass than the evidence of the laws of the physical order."

Such activities and thoughts were alien to Hume, who as a young man set out to construct a social science, a "science of man," as a moral agent and member of society that was to be based on "experience and observation." Before reaching the age of thirty he completed his principal contribution to philosophy, the *Treatise of Human Nature* (1739–40), which carries the significant subtitle *An Attempt to introduce the experimental Method of Reasoning into Moral Subjects*. The word *experimental* was then a synonym for *empirical*.

HUME AND THE PHYSIOCRATS

Both the Physiocrats and Hume were attached to economic individualism and liberalism, but their philosophies on which this attachment was based were entirely different. The views of the Physiocrats postulated a providential order of the world, harmonious, immutable, and beneficial. To Hume these were matters beyond human cognition, and his point of departure, unlike that of the Physiocrats, is the nature of man rather than that of the world. There is a profound difference also in the methods of Hume and of the Physiocrats. The Physiocrats were rationalists who set out to find self-evident truths in the light of reason rather than with the help of experience. Hume, on the other hand, was an empiricist who practiced the method of observation. He was aware of the limited opportunities for using genuine experiments in social science and thus placed much reliance on introspection and the lessons of history. Historical investigations would turn up certain regularities on which to base a science of politics and economics. Its findings, reflecting the varieties of human experience, are thus much more tentative than the allegedly immutable truths that the Physiocrats claimed to possess. The modern scientific approach that considers scientific truth a process rather than an immutable dogma has its forefather in Hume. Hume was also the first to make a sharp distinction between that which is and that which ought to be, that is, between positive and normative statements, a distinction that has become fundamental in modern social science.

Both the Physiocrats and Hume were utilitarians—they equated the useful with the good. To Quesnay, the moral law calls for adherence to a natural order which "self-evidently is the most advantageous one for mankind." The justice of this order is derived from its utility, and its immutable attributes are the natural rights to individual freedom and private property. Hume, however, was no believer in natural rights, and instead of the dogmatic utilitarianism of the Physiocrats he supports an empirical one. Private property deserves endorsement because it is socially useful under existing conditions, that is, when goods are scarce and when people place their own interests above those of others. If these circumstances were different, for example, if all goods were freely available in unlimited quantities, or if every person cared as much for others as he does for himself, the social utility, and hence the justification of private property, would vanish and it would become an "idle ceremonial."

Like the Physiocrats, Hume endorses the unequal distribution of property, but he does so in the course of a protracted discussion in which social utility is again employed as the overriding criterion. Perfect equality might seem "highly useful," since, wherever we depart from it, "we rob the poor of more satisfaction than we add to the rich." But the social cost of perfect equality would be prohibitive as it would destroy thrift and industry and thus lead to general impoverishment. The political consequences of perfect equality would be disastrous since either tyranny or anarchy would ensue: tyranny if the gvoernment were to enforce it, anarchy if the leveling of property would demolish the basis of political power. These thoughts are connected, however, with a plea for the diffusion of wealth. Each person, if possible, ought to enjoy the fruits of his labor. Such an equality "is most suitable to human nature" and it will strengthen the state by allowing a wide dispersal of the tax burden.

Hume's thoughts on property are partly found in his *Treatise,* partly in some of the essays that he published under the title *Political Discourses* in 1752. These essays contain Hume's contributions to technical economics, which he never presented in systematic form. His *Treatise,* to use Hume's own words, had fallen "deadborn from the press," and he may have hoped to find the public more receptive to short essays on a variety of subjects than to a lengthy systematic treatise. There is no doubt, however, that the essays represent an extension of his systematic thoughts on human nature as developed in the *Treatise.*

Hume's economic essays discuss such matters as commerce, money, interest, foreign trade, taxes, public credit, and population. They are written in an interesting, engaging style. Although Hume's *Treatise* was not published in a second edition until 1817, his essays were soon translated into French and in a modified and enlarged form were frequently reprinted during his lifetime.

THE PSYCHOLOGY OF ECONOMIC MAN

The connection with the general subject of the *Treatise* is especially noticeable in the attention that Hume gives to the psychological wellsprings of economic activities. Far from being an unqualified hedonist who would explain everything in terms of a desire for pleasure, he depicts people as being in search of an individually proportioned mixture of action, pleasure, and leisure. The fruits of their work not only gratify their desire for pleasure but the work itself meets their wish for action. Unlike the later classical writers, Hume does not visualize work as essentially painful and in the nature of a disutility but finds in it elements of fun and of a sporting spirit. As he puts it: "There is no craving or demand of the human mind more constant and insatiable than that for exercise and employment; and this desire seems the foundation of most of our passions and pursuits." In another connection he says: "Everything in the world is purchased by labor; and our passions are the only causes of labor."

ECONOMIC EVOLUTION: THE FLOW OF SPECIE

Next to psychology, history is the lodestar that guides Hume's economic investigations. History is replete with infinite varieties of human experience, but it also contains elements of constancy and regularity. Economic societies arise as the result of an evolutionary process which attaches to them unique features besides those that are common to all societies. As Hume's economic thought is grounded in history it is essentially genetic, and there is a certain affinity between his economics and the modern emphasis on economic development and growth. History is change, and the observation of change might open up vistas that are closed to the observer of static conditions. It is thus not surprising that a historically minded writer such as Hume was among the first to develop in a convincing form the theory of the automatic flow of specie. If country A, as a result of an export balance, gains specie, its price level will rise, while the opposite effect will take place in country B which has lost specie on account of its import balance. Prices in A are now too high to enable the country to maintain its export balance. A's high price level will attract imports from abroad while reducing its exports. The opposite will happen in B, and there will be a reversal of the flow of specie, which returns to B.

THE DEMONSTRATION EFFECT OF FOREIGN TRADE

Hume did not consider foreign trade a strategic device to produce specie, as the mercantilist writers had done, nor was it to him a necessary evil, as it had been to the Physiocrats. Instead he emphasized the role of foreign trade as a promoter of a country's economic development. Looking at evolutionary processes rather than at a momentary equilibrium, he points out the educational function of foreign trade, which acquaints men "with the pleasures of luxury and the profits of commerce," and carries them on "to farther improvements in every branch of domestic as well as foreign trade." This might be the chief advantage of foreign trade.

> It rouses men from their indolence; and presenting the gayer and more opulent part of the nation with objects of luxury, which they never before dreamed of, raises in them a desire of a more splendid way of life than what their ancestors enjoyed. And at the same time, the few merchants, who possess the secret of this importation and exportation, make great profits; and becoming rivals in wealth to the ancient nobility, tempt other adventurers to become their rivals in commerce. Imitation soon diffuses all those arts; while domestic manufacturers emulate the foreign in their improvements, and work up every commodity to the utmost perfection of which it is susceptible.

Once foreign trade has served its educational function, the resources devoted to it may be released and diverted to the production of goods for domestic use. As these observations indicate, Hume's analysis of the importance of foreign trade for economic development assigns considerable weight to such factors as the demonstration effect, the rise of a middle class, and the eventual reduction of foreign trade relative to the domestic sector of the economy. The picture that he draws is by no means unrealistic but has its counterpart in the history of many underdeveloped countries.

HUME'S COSMOPOLITANISM

Unlike the mercantilists Hume does not consider the volume of world trade as fixed. Nor is foreign trade to him a sort of economic warfare in which the expansion of one country's exports can only be obtained if the exports of another country decline. Instead of identifying a country's gain with the impoverishment of its neighbors, Hume advances the opposite point of view. Individuals as well as nations need not fear the prosperity of their neighbors; they can only benefit from being members of a prosperous community.

> The riches of the several members of a community contribute to increase my riches, whatever profession I may follow. They consume the produce of my industry, and afford me the produce of theirs in return. Nor needs any state entertain apprehensions that their neighbors will improve to such a degree in every art and manufacture as to have no demand from them.

Provided a country remains "industrious and civilized," such a contingency is precluded by the diversity of the world's endowment with resources. The faster the economy of a country grows, the larger will be its demand for the products of its neighbors. Hume concludes his observations with these famous words: "I shall therefore venture to acknowledge that not only as a man but as a British subject I pray for the flourishing commerce of Germany, Spain, Italy, and even France itself."

THE MIGRATION OF ECONOMIC OPPORTUNITY In this optimistic and cosmopolitan view, the economic interests of different countries are just as compatible with one another as are the economic interests of individuals. The fall in foreign demand for a specific good need not be fatal; if a country's resources are versatile and if it is enterprising and efficient, it will "easily" divert resources to the production of goods that the foreign market absorbs more readily. However harmonious this view of the international economic order may be, Hume's realism prevents him from closing his eyes completely to the possibility of economic conflict arising from the incompatibility of national economic interests. In the long run of history, "a happy concurrence of causes" makes it appear unlikely that a leading trading nation will be able to preserve forever its commanding position. To demonstrate this, Hume states what may be called a law of the migration of economic opportunity, which checks the growth of one country by opening up opportunities for growth elsewhere. Once a country has grown prosperous in trade, its price level may compare unfavorably with "the low price of labor in every nation which has not an extensive commerce, and does not much abound in gold and silver." This disparity then sets the stage for a diffusion of economic opportunities, causing, perhaps, stagnation in one country and expansion in another. As Hume puts it, manufacturers "gradually shift their places, leaving those countries and provinces which they have already enriched, and flying to others, whither they are allured by the cheapness of provisions and labor; till they have enriched these also, and are again banished by the same causes."

Hume's theory of the shifting center of global and regional economic strength rounds out his contributions to international economics. It may be tested by the historical experience of both old and New England, or by the domestic and international movements of industry, for example, of the textile industry. Hume's theory of the rise and relative decline of regional and national economies may be supplemented by his view of the significance of the international demonstration effect, the borrowing of one culture from another. In a perpetual circle of growth and decay there arises, on the shoulders of the pioneer, a newcomer, who, in the later interpretation of Veblen, makes the pioneer pay "the penalty for having been thrown into the lead, and so having shown the way." Veblen's analysis of the same matter is much more elaborate and includes consideration of factors other than international price differentials. But even these other factors can in the end be reduced to differences in cost and price. Veblen's approach, like Hume's, was genetic, and it shows the affinity of the two thinkers both in the chosen subject and in the method employed for its treatment.

Among Hume's contributions to domestic economics are his interest theory, his discussion of public loans, and his famous theory of beneficial inflation. Merely stating the final results of his thought does not do him full justice because he does not give conclusive answers but develops arguments rich in historical meanderings in which the matters under study appear as historical categories rather than as abstract entities not anchored in time and place. This relativism makes some of his statements appear ambivalent and even inconsistent, and it would seem to be the greatest obstacle to any attempt to systematize his thought. Such an attempt would be misplaced because Hume did not set out to construct an abstract system of economic principles; instead his economics is an expansion and illustration of his ideas of man as a social being and a further application of his empirical method which is grounded in psychology and history.

MONETARY THOUGHT

Often Hume's argument is presented in the form of an elaboration of the quantity theory of money, to which he ostensibly adheres but which he will employ as a peg to display his ideas of the more profound importance of changes in economic institutions. "The absolute quantity of the precious metals," he holds, "is a matter of great indifference. There are only two circumstances of any importance, namely, their gradual increase, and their thorough concoction and circulation through the state." It is a fallacy to ascribe to monetary factors consequences that really are the result of "a change in the manners and customs of the people." The mercantilists' monetary theory of interest, which makes the rate of interest vary inversely with the money supply, is an example of such a fallacy. Instead the interest rate will primarily reflect the demand and supply of real capital, factors that in turn are influenced by "the habits and ways of living of the people." Thus in an agricultural nation the interest rate will be high because the idle and pleasure-seeking landlords' demand for loans meets only a small supply. There is no class of savers or capitalists, and no loanable funds are accumulated because whatever money comes in, "the prodigal landlord dissipates it as fast as he receives it; and the beggarly peasant has no means, nor view, nor ambition of obtaining above a bare livelihood." The interest rate will be brought down in the course of economic development, when a class of merchants and manufacturers arises who acquire a "passion" for profits and practice frugality, making "the love of gain prevail over the love of pleasure." As capital is accumulated, "the plenty diminishes the price," and the rate of profit as well as of interest declines.

The relationship between the rate of interest and the rate of profit is not a causal one in the sense that a low rate of interest is the cause of a low rate of profit or vice versa. Either rate reflects the level of economic development and their relationship is one of mutual interdependence, a functional rather than a causal one. This statement of Hume's presages the later concern of economic science with functional rather than causal relationships, which was to emerge in the nineteenth century in the writings of Cournot but did not become common before the twentieth century. Both in the *Treatise* and in his essays Hume draws attention to the difficulties inherent in the interpretation of a situation where there is "the concurrence of a multitude of causes," and in the *Treatise* he goes as far as to say: "No questions in philosophy are more difficult, than when a number of causes present themselves for the same phenomenon, to determine which is the principal and predominant. There seldom is any very precise argument to fix our choice." Modern economic theory, with its functional approach, goes around this difficulty; Hume's thoughts on interest and profit showed the way.

Hume's essay on interest indicates the importance that he attaches to the rise of a commercial and manufacturing class. As agriculture is supplemented by commercial and manufacturing activities, the demonstration effect turns the peasants into independent and wealthy cultivators, while the diffusion of property among the commercial classes draws "authority and consideration to that middling rank of men, who are the best and firmest basis of public liberty." Hume's classes are economic categories that are mainly distinguished by the psychological characteristics of their members. The landlords are indolent and pleasure seeking, the peasants ignorant and without ambition, and among the merchants, "one of the most useful races of men," there is an "overplus of misers above prodigals."

THE PUBLIC DEBT Hume's heart is with the middle class, but with an active one and not one of *rentiers*. This is one of the reasons why he condemns, with unusual acerbity and firmness, the public debt, the greater part of which he sees in the hands of idle people who lead a useless and inactive life. The practice of contracting debts will invariably invite abuse, and in the end there loom three possible forms of collapse: repudiation, or the "natural death" of the debt; a "violent death," when the debt is serviced at the cost of neglecting vital functions of the state; death at the hands "of the doctor," when an attempt is made to service the debt with the help of a levy on capital, an attempt that will completely destroy what is left of the public credit. The fear that such destruction may be everlasting is, however, "a needless bugbear," because "so great dupes are the generality of mankind that notwithstanding such a violent shock to public credit...it would not probably be long ere credit would again revive in as flourishing a condition as before.... Mankind are, in all ages, caught by the same baits: The same tricks, played over and over again, still trepan them."

inflation starts out with an increase in the money supply, produced perhaps by an export balance. In line with the quantity theory of money, the increase in the money supply will tend to raise prices, but Hume now introduces a new idea, a time lag which occurs between the increase in the money supply and that of the price level. Prices will at first not rise at all, and later only haltingly and at different sectors of the economy. In this interval the beneficial effects of the increase in the money supply take place. They consist of an expansion of income and employment produced by successive rounds of additional expenditure. The exporters, to whom the new money accrues in the first place, will employ extra hands from a labor supply that initially is perfectly elastic; workers will have more money to spend, and second and third rounds of expenditure for consumer goods will ensue, only at gradually rising prices.

Hume thus takes up the matter discussed in Keynes's *Treatise* under the heading "the diffusion of price levels," the same matter to which Cantillon devotes a number of celebrated passages. Hume's striking conclusion—that the increase in the money supply will raise production as well as prices—is derived with the help of an analysis of expansion not unlike that offered by the theory of the multiplier. Much time was to pass, however, before Hume's idea gained wide acceptance. Malthus and Ricardo discussed his contribution and spoke of a "magic effect on industry," giving Hume credit for having been the first to observe it. But whereas Malthus was inclined to accept the idea, Ricardo was critical of it, and the Ricardian tradition was the stronger one until similar ideas gained wide currency much later under the influence of Keynes's *General Theory*.

Hume's short-run analysis of the beneficial effects of a rising money supply was noted with approval by Keynes. Because Hume here emphasized the transition, the path toward equilibrium rather than the equilibrium position itself, Keynes applauded what he considered a mercantilist streak in Hume's thought and praised him for having only "a foot and a half in the classical world." Hume's espousal of the merchant class was likewise in the mercantilist tradition, but his devastating critique of the mercantilist theories of money, interest, and balance of trade went far to discredit the mercantilist position.

HUME'S CONNECTIONS WITH THE PHYSIOCRATS AND SMITH

As for his relation to the Physiocrats, Hume's basic philosophy and his views about the economic role of the landowning class were so much at variance with their writings that there was no visible impact of his thought on theirs. Although Hume' *Discourses*, published in 1752 and soon translated into French, antedate the works of the Physiocrats, Du Pont, their first historian of economic thought, fails to mention Hume among the forerunners of the new science. Hume was personally acquainted with a number of Physiocrats and maintained a friendly correspondence with Turgot, with whom he debated the merits of the single tax. But he did not hide the low opinion he had of the Physiocrats, and in a letter written in 1769 he referred to them as a "set of men the most chimerical and most arrogant that now exist." He had no use for their metaphysics, their rationalism, and their dogmatism.

Hume was a close friend of Adam Smith's, and Smith, a fellow Scotsman, served as his literary executor after his death in 1776. The two carried on a lively correspondence, but there is little in it that sheds light on their respective ideas about economics. Hume lived long enough to congratulate Smith on the publication of *The Wealth of Nations,* praising its "depth and solidity and acuteness," but finding fault with Smith's treatment of rent. In a manner anticipating Ricardo's rent theory, he wrote: "I cannot think that the rent of farms makes any part of the price of the produce, but that the price is determined altogether by the quantity and the demand."

In *The Wealth of Nations* Smith adopted certain views of Hume's but failed to mention his theory of the automatic flow of specie, an omission that has puzzled many students of the history of economic thought. Hume's utilitarian philosophy, his espousal of economic individualism, his belief in the compatibility of the interests of individuals and of nations, and his critical attitude to mercantilist and physiocratic ideas were all shared by Smith. The great difference between the two was in their method. Hume had chosen the path of an empiricist, whereas in Smith's thought there is a great deal of abstract and deductive rationalism, albeit blended with a measure of casual empiricism. Although Smith made use of the lessons of history, he did so more incidentally and in a manner that would not obstruct his aim, the construction of a great system of primarily abstract thought. To the realization of such an aim Hume's genetic method did not lend itself. The historian and the theorist follow separate paths to knowledge, and the one chosen by the historian does not lead to a system. Even if Hume had been discouraged from further systematic work by the cool reception given to his *Treatise,* it is doubtful whether he could have constructed a systematic economics while remaining true to his empirical method. No economist who practiced the empirical method ever did construct a systematic economics. Some nineteenth-century historical economists promised to produce an inductive generalization of the contents of economic science on the basis of historical studies just as soon as these studies encompassed the experience of all mankind at all places and at all times. Obviously this promise has never been fulfilled. At best, the historical economists have been able to produce a classification of systems, but not a system itself.

One should not overstress the affinity of Hume's genetic method, his emphasis on the "change in the manners and customs of the people," with the approach of later schools of historical economics. Hume, an intellectual giant, was no mere collector of facts, and he might not cherish the connection with the lesser lights of the historical school, some of whom practiced a blind empricism devoid of any attachment to great principles. Many were narrow nationalists, and hardly any one of them would have shared Hume's utilitarianism, his individualism, or his cosmopolitanism. Among the institutional economists, Veblen comes closer to Hume in intellectual stature, in the grounding of his thought in philosophy, and in a skeptical outlook that borders on the cynical. What Veblen said of Hume—"he was gifted with an alert, though somewhat histrionic, scepticism touching everything that was well received"—might with equal justice be said of Veblen.

STEUART

In 1755, three years after the publication of Hume's *Discourses,* Sir James Steuart, an exiled fellow Scotsman, went to work on his *Principles of Political Economy,* which was eventually published in two stout volumes in 1767, just nine years before *The Wealth of Nations.* Steuart (1712–80) was a Jacobite who had been involved in Bonnie Prince Charlie's ill-fated attempt to restore Scotland to the Stuarts. After the battle of Culloden Moor in 1746 Steuart had to seek refuge on the Continent and was not allowed to return until 1762. Before his exile he had spent five years on the Continent, on the grand tour customary for a well-to-do young nobleman of his time. Thus he had been away from the British Isles during the major part of his adult life, and it was while in exile in Germany that he wrote the bulk of his *Principles.*

STEUART AND SMITH

Steuart's book was the first in English to carry the name of the new science in its title and the first also to develop it on a substantial scale. That the work had only a moderate success is not surprising because on many counts it compared unfavorably with *The Wealth of Nations.* It contained a number of nuggets but these were embedded in a proliferation of ponderous inanities that repelled the reader. Where Smith was lucid, Steuart was heavy and long-winded. Smith could approach his task with the equipment of a professional philosopher and student of literature; Steuart brought to it a legal training, not unlike that of many German cameralists. Having lived for so long an environment that was backward both economically and politically if compared with England, his thought was attuned more to German cameralism than to British liberalism. To Smith the individual was the prime mover of economic development, to Steuart it was the paternalism of an enlightened despot, of the "statesman," whom he supposes "to be constantly awake, attentive to his employment, able and uncorrupted, tender in his love for the society he governs, impartially just in his indulgence for every class of inhabitants, and disregardful of the interest of individuals when that regard is inconsistent with the general welfare." Steuart was the defender of the old order, Smith the prophet of a new age.

What integrates Steuart's book is not, as in the case of *The Wealth of Nations*, a pervasive principle such as that of economic individualism but rather his constant attention to matters of state action. His book thus approximates a system of economic policy rather than one of economics. It is the policy orientation of his thought that makes him never lose sight of the special historical and geographical circumstances that surround each country's economy. These limit the validity of general rules and of "systems" such as that of the Physiocrats which "mislead the understanding and efface the path to truth." "The variety of circumstances" is such that almost every practical conclusion derived from general principles is bound to be uncertain. Steuart's historical relativism makes him endorse the view that each country has its own "political economy," so great is "the variety which is found in different countries in the distribution of property, subordination of classes, genius of people, proceeding from the variety of forms of government, laws and manners." His attention centers on what List was to call "national economy," a name for economics that became current in Germany during the ascendancy of the historical school and has ever since been the preferred designation of economics in that country. It is not surprising that the appreciation of Steuart's work reached its peak in nineteenth-century Germany. In England, Malthus and Ricardo mentioned his name among the forerunners of the science, but Smith passed him over in complete silence. He may have felt reluctant to dignify by refutation the thought of a man who taught that in a state "all are children."

STEUART AND HUME

Steuart had read with care the *Political Discourses* of his fellow Scotsman Hume, whom he cites more often than any other authority. Hume, the empiricist, had wisely refrained from attempting to construct a system of economics on the basis of observation. Steuart, a man trained in the law but not in epistemology, sets out to inquire into the "principles" of the new science but at the same time never fails to insist that "concomitant circumstances...render general rules of little use." There is thus a break in his thought, of which he himself is dimly aware, speaking, as he does, of the "mortification" he always feels when confronted with the task of denying the validity of a general proposition. A mind greater than Steuart's was required to reconcile reason with experience. When he tries to resolve the two, the outcome is not always a happy one. Thus Hume, when speaking of the psychological wellsprings of economic activities, had singled out action, pleasure, and leisure as the three great motive forces, and had depicted people as being inspired by an individually proportioned combination of the three. This will not do for Steuart. He retains the idea of individual proportioning but to cover all possible varieties of human experience makes his list of motive forces so all-inclusive as to lose all meaning. "Man," he says, "we find acting uniformly in all ages, in all countries, and in all climates, from the principles of self-interest, expediency, duty, or passion. In this he is alike, in nothing else." Hume's statement sheds light on human behavior; Steuart's is a truism.

STEUART ON POPULATION

Steuart's work is divided into five books which discuss population and agriculture, trade and industry, money and coin, credit and debts, and taxes. Population growth is more carefully considered than it had been in the writings of Mun, Child, or Petty, who were apt to endorse it enthusiastically. Cantillon and others before him had recognized that it is limited by subsistence, and Cantillon had posed but left open the question whether a large population living in poverty is preferable to a smaller one living at ease. Steuart falls in line with the new thought. Man's generative faculty, he says, "resembles a spring loaded with a weight," the weight representing inadequate subsistence. Disease will check any tendency of the population to outrun the food supply. Population growth is still endorsed but not unqualifiedly: It is absurd "to wish for new inhabitants without first knowing how to employ the old." All this is still a far cry from the thought of Malthus, but matters were on the move towards the latter's fundamental reappraisal of population growth thirty years later.

Population growth proceeds on the basis of an agricultural output which exceeds the requirements of the farm population. It will be produced in response to a reciprocal demand, that of the nonagricultural population for foodstuffs and that of the farmers for manufactures. Industrial development thus becomes a prerequisite both of the expansion of production in the agricultural sector and of the growth of the population facilitated by such an expansion. The factor behind industrial development is the multiplication of wants, a matter like so many others that Steuart considers responsive to the manipulation of the statesman. The manipulation of wants is an equally important factor in the further stages of a country's economic development. Steuart distinguishes three of these: infant trade, foreign trade, and inland trade—the infancy, manhood, and old age of trading nations. To promote domestic economic development, luxury is encouraged during the first stage of infant trade. When the country engages in foreign trade, it enters the second stage. There luxury gives way to frugality in order to reduce the export-competing home demand and keep prices on a competitive level. Thrift is now encouraged at home and luxury abroad. The third stage, that of inland trade, Steuart calls "by far the most brilliant." It is to be initiated when a country finds itself threatened by an "unfavorable balance of trade," an expression contributed by Steuart to the vocabulary of economics, as was also "balance of payments." Now the wealth acquired by means of foreign trade comes to be circulated at home and luxury is to be encouraged again to restore the balance of domestic supply and demand, or, as Steuart calls it, the balance of work and demand.

Only if the world would form a single political unit under one government or if people's attitudes to luxury and frugality were the same in all countries could foreign trade be left free and unrestricted. In the absence of these conditions Steuart's statesman is under obligation to employ the entire arsenal of mercantilist policy, including subsidies and restrictions on imports and exports. One nation's gain is another nation's loss, Steuart holds, and he presents an extreme version of the so-called balance of labor, which places a special value on the exportation of labor embodied in manufactures. To provide employment and conserve a country's "natural wealth," the mercantilist writers had long expressed preference for this type of exports as compared with the exportation of "matter." In line with this tradition Steuart argues that "the matter exported from a country is what the country loses; the price of the labor exported is what it gains." He makes it a "general maxim to discourage the importation of work, and to encourage the exportation of it." To accomplish this end, the statesman, during the stage of foreign trade, must always see to it that wages are kept low. "The lowest classes of people," Steuart taught, "must be restrained to their physical-necessary." Rising wages and costs are the principal factors responsible for the transformation of the stage of foreign trade to that of inland trade. The extension of cultivation, required by a growing population's need for food, raises labor's cost of subsistence. At about the same time Turgot discovered diminishing returns resulting from the continued application of the variable factor to land, Steuart recognised that "in order to encourage the breaking up of new lands, the price of [subsistence] must rise."

PRICE THEORY

Steuart made notable contributions to the theory of price and demand. He distinguishes two elements of price, the "real value of the commodity" and the "profit upon alienation." The real value of a good is determined by the worker's subsistence and expense during the average working time required for the completion of the good—an idea that foreshadows Marx's socially necessary labor time—and by the value of material, which reflects again working time and subsistence. Steuart holds that price "cannot be lower...than the real value," whereas profit will fluctuate in response to the changing circumstances of demand.

Demand must be "effectual" or effective, that is, backed up by the power to supply what is reciprocally demanded. Steuart's theory of demand opens a window to what later was to become the theory of markets. His approach is not based on a polarity of competition and monopoly; instead the different market situations form a spectrum reflecting how "great" the competition—"an emulation to obtain a preference"—is among the buyers and among the sellers. If competition is great among buyers, price will be high; if it is great among sellers, price will be low. Competition is "simple" when it is stronger on one side of the market than on the other, "double" when there is competition on both sides. Demand is interpreted in the schedule sense—rising prices stop it, falling ones increase it. Under the influence of double competition the balance of supply and demand, called by Steuart work and demand, is "sustained in equilibrio," that is, the quantity supplied "is in proportion to the quantity demanded." The word *equilibrium,* already employed by the Physiocrats and others, has become part of the vocabulary of economics.

Steuart then goes on to discuss the effects of changes in demand or in supply. If there is a fall in demand, supply remaining the same, there either will be competition on the side of the sellers which will bring down prices, or, in the absence of such competition, there will be a surplus, an excess of the quantity supplied over the quantity demanded. Conversely, if there is an increase in demand, there either will be competition on the side of the buyers, raising prices, or, in the absence of such competition, there will be a shortage, with the quantity demanded exceeding the quantity supplied.

Changes in demand call for the intervention of the statesman. If there is a fall in demand, he must see to it that resources are diverted to other uses, or, in the case of a temporary misdirection of resources, he must provide guidance and assistance. In the case of an increase in demand, which is accompanied by rising prices and profits, the statesman must encourage the movement of resources into the industry. If the supply then rises, prices and profits will come down. But if the supply fails to rise and if prices and profits continue at high levels, there will be the danger that profits will become "consolidated with the real value of the merchandise," that is, the owners of the resources employed will become habituated to higher profits and to a higher standard of living. Such a transformation of profits into costs will have adverse effects on the competitiveness of the economy and will promote the transition from the stage of foreign trade to that of inland trade.

THE PAPER ECONOMY   Although Steuart fails to expand his price theory to a theory of factor prices or functional distribution, he shows how the distribution of wealth is affected by change in people's assets and how these changes in turn are facilitated by the introduction of "symbolic money," that is, "bank notes, credit in bank, bills, bonds, and merchants books." The circulation of money serves the acquisition of goods, services, or claims; among the goods, some are consumable, others, such as inexhaustible resources, are not. "The surface of the earth," Steuart says, "never can cease to be useful, and never can be lost," a formulation that may have influenced Ricardo's reference to "the original and indestructible powers of the soil." As long as people exchange one inconsumable good for another, there is no "vibration of the balance of wealth." Opportunities for the exchange of one's inconsumable assets for consumable ones invite changes in the distribution of wealth, and such opportunities are greatly enlarged by the introduction of symbolic money. Steuart becomes a prophet of what is now known as the "paper economy," which makes "land circulate as well as houses." The monetization of assets enables those "who have effects which by their nature cannot circulate (and which, by the bye, are the principal cause of inequality) to give an adequate circulating equivalent for the services they demand.... In other words, it is a method of melting down, as it were, the very causes of inequality, and of rendering fortunes equal." Had Steuart lived to see the rise of shares of stock and their diffusion he would have found a further illustration of the leveling effects of the paper economy.

Steuart's groping attempts to develop a theory of assets might have given direction to the later development of the theory of the firm. The latter, however, followed a different path and instead came to be based on the revenue-cost approach. Only in the twentieth century did Boulding propose a reconstruction of the theory of the firm that was to be based on the balance sheet. Some other ideas of Steuart's had earlier been incorporated into the tradition of economic thought, although it would be difficult to demonstrate his direct influence. These include his espousal of the introduction of machinery, his favorable view of long-term foreign investment, and his endorsement of the infant industry argument in support of protection. Steuart's approval of pervasive government intervention makes him a forerunner of neo-mercantilism and of the mixed capitalism of the twentieth century. In this sense he is more closely linked with the present age than he was with his own. In many instances in which Steuart conjures up the image of the statesman as a director of the economy, Smith would insist on allowing self-interest to be the guide. Steuart ostensibly uses the principle of self-interest as a "general key" to his inquiry, and he goes so far as to say that "it is the combination of every private interest which forms the public good." He has no faith in an economy in which individuals would pursue the public interest rather than their own. "Every one might consider the interest of his country in a different light, and many might join in the ruin of it, by endeavoring to promote its advantages. Were a rich merchant to begin and sell his goods without profit, what would become of trade?... Were people to feed all who would ask charity, what would become of industry?"

Although Steuart recognizes self-interest as a motive, he does not elevate it to the basic principle of an economy's organization. Instead it is the statesman on whom he unceasingly calls to check profits and prices, promote parsimony or luxury, impose import duties, grant subsidies, and regulate even the marriage rate. Steuart was no believer in self-regulating mechanisms, and he compares "modern states to watches which are continually going wrong; sometimes the spring is found too weak, at other times too strong for the machine: and when the wheels are not made according to a determined proportion..., they do not tally well with one another; then the machine stops, and if it be forced, some part gives way; and the workman's hand becomes necessary to set it right." To Steuart the watch was continually going wrong; to Smith it worked if left alone.

Chapter 10

ADAM SMITH'S
ECONOMICS
OF SELF-RELIANCE:
The Philosophical Background

The watch was a favorite symbol of the eighteenth century, but Steuart's image of society as a watch that would frequently require the attention of an earthly repairman was not in accord with the thought of the time. Under the influence of Newton a tendency developed to view the world as a harmoniously ordered mechanism of supreme quality, and the "Author of Nature" as a master craftsman or engineer whose work an earthly repairman would be unable to improve on. Hume, in his *Dialogues Concerning Natural Religion,* has one of the speakers say:

> Look around the world: contemplate the whole and every part of it: You will find it to be nothing but one great machine, subdivided into an infinite number of lesser machines, which again admit of subdivisions, to a degree beyond what human senses and faculties can trace and explain. All these various machines, and even their most minute parts, are adjusted to each other with an accuracy, which ravishes into admiration all men, who have ever contemplated them. The curious adapting of means to ends, throughout all nature, resembles exactly, though it much exceeds, the productions of human...intelligence.

The next step was to find a correspondence between the "general harmony of nature" and that of society, a step anticipated in mid-century by Colin Maclaurin, Newton's foremost interpreter, whom contemporary opinion considered second only to Newton himself. According to Maclaurin, Newton's natural philosophy was "chiefly to be valued as it lays a sure foundation for natural religion and moral philosophy." Maclaurin, professor of mathematics at Edinburgh, was one of the glories of Scottish academic life in the eighteenth century, when the English universities were in decay and the Scottish at the height of their fame. Scottish universities were in the forefront of those that spread the gospel of Newtonian philosophy. At about the same time that Maclaurin saw his readers "excited and animated to correspond with the general harmony of nature," Adam Smith, another Scottish scholar, in an *Essay on the History of Astronomy* wrote of Newton's system "as the greatest discovery that ever was made by man." It was Smith who was to bring to full fruition the work of applying to social and economic relations the idea of the world as a harmonious and well-ordered mechanism.

SMITH'S LIFE

The circumstances surrounding the life of Adam Smith (1723–90) were themselves orderly and harmonious. There were none of the disturbances that had troubled other great figures in the history of economics. Unlike Petty and Cantillon, Smith did not spend a single day of his life in jail. Unlike Locke, he was not spied upon, expelled from his academic post, or compelled to flee his native country. Unlike his great friend David Hume, he was not refused a university chair. Like Locke and Hume he never founded a family, but his biographers have little to report of romantic attachments, which at times loomed large in the lives of the two other philosophers. His most colorful characteristic seems to have been his absentmindedness, instances of which his contemporaries were fond of relating. When he did have a romantic attachment, he might fail to recognize its object at a party. Or, when showing a visitor around a tannery, he might fall in the tanning pit while expounding the advantages of the division of labor. When preparing his tea, he might put the buttered bread into the teapot and then complain about the poor quality of the beverage. Getting up in the morning, he might sniff the air in his garden and after some meditation find himself, in his dressing gown, fifteen miles away from home. When as a commissioner of customs he rated a present arms and had been so saluted on countless occasions, he might attempt to return the salute by performing an elaborate drill with his walking stick. Or, having to sign an official document, he might copy with care the signature of a fellow commissioner instead of writing his own name next to it.

Those who knew Smith realized that his absentmindedness had as its counterpart a highly developed gift of concentration which sustained him in his protracted intellectual pursuits. He was sober minded, composed, and possesed of a good measure of worldly wisdom, so much so that his colleagues at Glasgow College, where he taught moral philosophy, placed him in charge of finances and made him their dean and vice-rector. He was no hermit or introvert but enjoyed the pleasures of friendship and social life. "Society and conversation," he wrote in his *Theory of Moral Sentiments*, are "the best preservatives of that equal and happy temper, which is so necessary to self-satisfaction and enjoyment." He practiced what he preached and never tired of joining clubs.

Smith spent the greater part of his life in Scotland: in Kirkcaldy, a small town of fifteen hundred inhabitants not far from Edinburgh across the Firth of Forth, where he was born and to which he returned to work on *The Wealth of Nations*; in Glasgow, then the residence of twenty-three thousand people, as a student and professor; and, toward the end of his life, in Edinburgh as commissioner of customs. The circumstances of his life are quickly told. He was born a few months after the death of his father, a customs and law officer who had married into the family of a well-to-do landowner. He was very close to his mother, who made a home for him over long periods of his life and whom he survived by only six years. Young Smith entered Glasgow College and had the good fortune of benefiting from the contact with a great teacher, Francis Hutcheson, professor of moral philosophy, whose chair he was to occupy himself later on. At the age of seventeen he traveled to Oxford on horseback, and remained there for six years on a scholarship. Instruction at Oxford was perfunctory, and what he learned there came to him as the result of independent reading. Smith's stipend was meant to nurture future Episcopalian ministers, but as the Scots were Presbyterians the condition was not enforced and Smith got away without taking holy orders. On his return to Scotland in 1746 he was without regular employment until 1748, when at the age of twenty-five he began to give public lectures in Edinburgh on rhetoric and belles lettres as well as on jurisprudence and politics. He attracted large audiences, and when in 1750 the chair of logic fell vacant at Glasgow College, he was elected to fill it. He held it for one year only, and in 1752 he was appointed to the better-salaried chair of moral philosophy, a transfer that opened the way to Hume's unsuccessful candidacy for the opening in logic. By then Smith had become acquainted with Hume, and their acquaintance grew into a close friendship which lasted until Hume's death in 1776.

Smith was connected with Glasgow College from 1751 to 1764 and he considered the thirteen years spent there "as by far the most useful and therefore by far the happiest and most honorable period" of his life. Moral philosophy, Smith's subject, was the approximate equivalent of what is now known as social science. Smith divided it into four parts: natural theology—generally speaking, religion without revelation—ethics, jurisprudence, and "expediency," that is, politics and economics. In addition, Smith gave occasional lectures on rhetoric and belles lettres, fields that were under the jurisdiction of the professor of logic but with which Smith was acquainted from his Edinburgh lectures. Except for the part of the moral philosophy sequence that was devoted to natural theology, we have a fairly good idea of what Smith taught in the classroom because students' lecture notes were discovered that had been taken in his classes on rhetoric and belles lettres as well as on justice and expediency. As for the course on ethics, Smith himself published in 1759 his *Theory of Moral Sentiments,* which covers the same ground.

The book spread Smith's fame and secured him an appointment as tutor to a young nobleman, the duke of Buccleuch. This type of position was much desired by leading scholars of the eighteenth century because it paid well, offered opportunities for foreign travel, and established a useful connection with one of the great families of the kingdom. Hume had also held such a post, as had a number of Smith's colleagues. Smith's appointment, which caused him to resign his professorship, proved highly satisfactory for both the tutor and his charge. It provided Smith with travel expenses and an annual income for life amounting to three hundred pounds, nearly twice as much as his pay as professor had been. He now spent almost three years in France, where he made the personal acquaintance of the leading Physiocrats and other notables. While in Toulouse in 1764, he began "to write a book in order to pass away the time." This was to be the future *Wealth of Nations,* completed twelve years later after a retreat to Kirkcaldy and a few years' residence in London.

Smith's tutorial duties had been successfully discharged by the end of 1766, and he devoted the next ten years to the completion of his masterpiece. Away from the confusion of the world he spent long and lonely years on reflection and meditation. The work was an immediate success. Five editions were published during Smith's life, besides Irish and American editions and translations into French, German, Danish, and Italian. In 1778 the duke of Buccleuch, proud of his erstwhile tutor, secured him an appointment as commissioner of customs in Edinburgh, a post Smith held during the remaining twelve years of his life and which he considered "both easy and honorable," "though it requires a good deal of attendance." With a government pay of six hundred pounds a year, Smith's total income was now close to one thousand pounds, a "princely revenue" in the words of his biographer and in his own words a situation "fully as affluent as I could wish it to be. The only thing I regret in it is the interruptions to my literary pursuits, which the duties of my office necessarily occasion." So Smith wrote in a letter ten years before his death. In 1790, a week before he died, he insisted that sixteen volumes of his manuscripts be burned. A few *Essays on Philosophical Subjects* escaped destruction and were later published by Smith's literary executors. The variety of subjects treated in these attest to the breadth of Smith's intellectual interest, which exended all the way from the history of astronomy to the "affinity between certain English and Italian verses."

PRIVATE INTERESTS AND THE GENERAL GOOD

Smith's philosophical views reflect the spirit of the age with its belief in the Newtonian order of nature—a mechanistic universe whose harmonious and beneficial organization attests to the wisdom and goodness of its maker. Newton had found in gravitation or "attraction" the principle that unified the physical world. The British moralists of the eighteenth century, of whom Smith was one, had proposed several principles that would integrate the moral and social world in a similar fashion. The third earl of Shaftesbury (1671–1713), the grandson of Locke's patron and himself a pupil of Locke, considered man as being equipped with a "moral sense" enabling him to distinguish between right and wrong and to prefer the right action. Such action would constitute a perfect balance between man's egoistic and altruistic impulses; it would be pleasurable and also conducive to the welfare of society. Shaftesbury sees the harmony of nature reflected in a social order under which it is "according to the private interest and good of every one to work towards the general good."

That private interests might be made to serve the public interest and that they might do so without the intention of private parties was an idea not without antecedents in the intellecual history of mankind. Like Carl Becker's "heavenly city of the eighteenth-century philosophers" its roots may be traced to the theological thought of earlier generations. They may have evolved from the notion of a divine plan which the individual fulfills regardless of his intention. Thus in the patristic thought of the fourth century a close link is found between the work that a person does for his own advantage and the benefits that it yields to others. No worker, John Chrysostom taught, can earn his pay without producing something that satisfies the wants of others.

In the seventeenth century related ideas occur repeatedly. In Tommaso Campanella's *City of the Sun* (1623), a famous utopia, there is a reference to the Spaniards who conquered the Indies impelled by the desire for treasure but directed by Providence spread the gospel. Thus "we do not know what we are doing but are the instruments of God." Half a century later an economic application of the same fundamental idea may be found in the writings of the Jansenist Pierre Nicole, who in the third volume of his *Essais de Morale* (1675) specifically relates the pursuit of "enlightened self-love" to beneficial effects identical with those produced by charity. An example of this is trade: "By means of trade all needs of life are in some way satisfied, without the intervention of charity. Take the citizen of a state which does not admit charity because it bans the true religion. Such a citizen does not fail to live as much in peace, security, and ease as would the member of a republic of saints." Nicole was a widely read author. His *Essais* appeared in an English translation, and Locke himself tried to translate a few of them.

MANDEVILLE

The idea of the harmony of interests, and more specifically the notion that the pursuit of private interests would be beneficial to society, were thus in the air when Shaftesbury incorporated them in the mainstream of eighteenth-century British philosophy. Shaftesbury's thought, which may be said to identify private virtues with public benefits, was challenged by Bernard Mandeville (1670–1733), a Dutch physician who in his youth had settled in England and who scandalized the world with his *Fable of the Bees*

(1714–29), which has the subtitle *Private Vices, Public Benefits*. Mandeville was a mischief-maker and satirist, inclined to paradoxical formulations, who tried to pose as a strict and austere rigorist. All self-love, he taught, is vicious, only self-denial is virtuous, and there is no middle ground between vice and virtue. He thus castigates luxury and the pursuit of gain as vices but at the same time depicts them as indispensable prerequisites of economic prosperity. Thus private vices become public benefits, a formulation much more disquieting than Shaftesbury's identification of private virtues with public benefits. By inflating to the utmost the concept of vice, Mandeville makes the whole world appear wicked. From now on, "the profligate Mandeville," as Smith calls him in a communication to the last issue of the old *Edinburgh Review* of 1756, will be found in the path of every British moralist who had to refute his doctrine to uphold an acceptable theory of the harmony of interests. That Smith's "invisible hand"—which leads the individual, who seeks his own gain, to promote the public interest, "an end which was no part of his intention"—was inspired by Mandeville's ideas is extremely doubtful, as he could find a much more respectable forerunner in Shaftesbury. Moreover, the laissez faire implication, which is all-important in the thought of Smith, is entirely absent from that of Mandeville, who may have been a libertine but was no libertarian. In his *Letter to Dion* (1732), a reply to a critic, Mandeville insists that "the dexterous management of a skilful politician" is necessary to turn private vices into public benefits. Smith's idea that competition rather than "the wisdom of the politician" would be the instrument of this transformation has no counterpart in Mandeville's thought. Rather than being a forerunner of Smith, Mandeville is a precursor of those who held the so-called principle of the artificial identity of interests, under which the government will force or induce people to act in their own self-interest, a principle more in line with the thought of Bentham than with that of Smith.

Mandeville's emphasis on high-level consumption as a spur to prosperity and his view that "the fire of London was a great calamity, but if the carpenters, bricklayers, smiths," and others who would obtain employment on account of the rebuilding "were to vote against those who lost by the fire, the rejoicings would equal, if not exceed, the complaints" anticipate not Smith but much more recent developments in economic thought. There are, however, a few instances where Smith may have found stimulation in Mandeville's work, and of these the most important is the "division of labor," the expression itself as well as the analysis of the matter to which it refers, for which Mandeville set the precedent.

Mandeville was not the only critic of Shaftesbury. In the context in which Shaftesbury introduced the idea of the harmony of private and public interests it was bound to give offense not only to one who, like Mandeville, embraced rigorism as a sham but also, and much more so, to the genuine rigorists, the fundamentalist theologians, who were on the wane in England but whose position was still a strong one in Scotland. The Presbyterian divines who preached the doctrine of man's total depravity and who insisted on an austere asceticism would have found fault with a doctrine that considered virtue a balance between self-love and altruism, identified it with pleasure, and derived it from a moral sense rather than from theological precepts.

HUTCHESON

Because he offended the rigorists, Francis Hutcheson (1694–1746), who elaborated and emended Shaftesbury's ideas, got into trouble with the Glasgow Presbytery during the academic year 1737–38, when Smith was a first-year student at Glasgow College. "The never-to-be-forgotten Dr. Hutcheson," as Smith was to eulogize him in 1787, almost fifty years after the teen-age student's fleeting contact with the great man, was a major influence on Smith's intellectual development. Hutcheson was himself an ordained Presbyterian minister, as had been his father and grandfather, but the doctrines he taught as professor of moral philosophy at Glasgow College, which can be found in his writings, were sharply at variance with the somber asceticism exalted by the rigorist divines. He considered man by nature disposed to benevolence rather than to evil and the world more filled with happiness than with misery. His "moral Newtonianism" stressed both benevolence and utility as principles that would explain the harmony of interests in society. Our moral sense inclines us to benevolence to others and is thus conducive to actions that are both pleasurable and useful. Hutcheson identifies the virtuous with the benevolent, and as it gives us pleasure to be benevolent, "we undesignedly promote our own greatest private good" —happiness—by our benevolence to others. Hutcheson thus provided Smith with still another model of the invisible hand, which now works backwards, as it were, from the benefit of society to that of the individual agent. Hutcheson would not doubt that the virtuous action is useful, even though he would not derive its virtuous quality from its usefulness. But as he sees no conflict between virtue and utility, there is in effect little difference between him and the utilitarians, and many of his formulations sound utilitarian. It was indeed Hutcheson who anticipated Bentham with the famous utilitarian formula: "that action is best which procures the greatest happiness for the greatest number." Hutcheson also grounds natural law, now long secularized, in utility: what a law of nature commands is "no more than a conclusion from observation of what sort of conduct is ordinarily useful to society." Social utility also is the basis of the right of private property, "without which right we could scarce hope for any industry."

SMITH'S ETHICS

Smith's *Theory of Moral Sentiments* and his *Wealth of Nations* contain his own versions of moral and social Newtonianism, with the latter work expanding the idea to the field of political economy. Both works are thus in the tradition of the philosophy of the British moralists as illustrated by Shaftesbury and Hutcheson. *The Theory of Moral Sentiments* was one of a number of attempts to develop an ethics on the basis of a unifying principle —in this case, of sympathy—which would shed light on the harmonious and beneficial order of the moral world. As such it was of considerable interest to Smith's contemporaries who were groping for an ethics that would flow from man's impulses or sentiments rather than from his reason, from "innate ideas," or from theological precepts. If Smith had written only *The Theory of Moral Sentiments,* he would enjoy in the philosophers' hall of fame a niche not unlike that reserved for Shaftesbury or Hutcheson. That to posterity he is a man of much greater stature is because of *The Wealth of Nations*, a pathbreaking attempt to anchor the new science of political economy in a Newtonian universe, mechanical albeit harmonious and beneficial, in which society is shown to benefit from the unintended consequences of the pursuit of individual self-interest.

There is thus a considerable affinity between the structure of *The Theory of Moral Sentiments* and that of *The Wealth of Nations*. Each work is integrated by a great unifying principle. What sympathy accomplishes in the moral world, self-interest does in the economic one. Either principle, in its respective realm, is shown to produce a harmony such as the one that characterizes Newton's order of nature. Smith's ethics depicts man as being equipped with a fellow feeling that makes him share in the sentiments of others. As we sympathize with others, we approve of their feelings. Our fellowmen, being desirous of obtaining such approval, will want to be worthy of it and are thus impelled to practice propriety. We ourselves, in order to have our own behavior approved by the "impartial spectator" who resides within us, will want to behave decently. The judge who decides on the moral worth of our own actions and those of others thus speaks through the voice of our own inner conscience. Smith's ethics is one of self-command or self-reliance, just as is his laissez faire economics, and his ethics of self-command or self-reliance is typical of a man who had never known a father.

Smith rejects moral sense, benevolence, or utility as the basis of ethics. Moral sense, a new concept, is superfluous since it does not denote anything that cannot be derived from sympathy and approbation. Benevolence may be the sole principle of action in the Deity, but man, an imperfect creature, must often act from other motives. Utility, Hume's pervasive principle, is not a criterion of goodness; otherwise "we should have no other reason for praising a man than that for which we commend a chest of drawers." Man gives and seeks approval for actions considered right, not merely useful. Utility may also recommend approval, but only subsidiarily, as "an afterthought," which however, gives the approved qualities "a new value."

In Smith's ethics, sympathy and the desire for approval cause us "to restrain our selfish, and to indulge our benevolent effections." This "constitutes the perfection of human nature; and can alone produce among mankind that harmony of sentiments and passions in which consists their whole grace and propriety." The attainment of harmony, here as elsewhere, is due not to man's reason but to the "economy of nature," which endows man with an appetite for the means by which nature's end can be brought about, "for their own sakes and independent of their tendency to produce it." When we thus promote the end of nature, we must not impute this to our reason, "imagining that to be the wisdom of man, which in reality is the wisdom of God." A watch is admirably adjusted to show the time of day, yet no one would consider it as being endowed with a desire or intention to do so; we know that it is the work of the watchmaker. Nature's grand design is the happiness of mankind, which we promote when we follow the dictates of our moral faculties. Happiness is widespread indeed; "for one man who suffers pain or misery, you will find twenty in prosperity and joy."

How does the pursuit of self-interest fit into this grand design? Every man is by nature charged first with his own care and is in a better position to fulfill this function than anybody else. The impartial spectator will allow him "to be more anxious about, and to pursue with more earnest assiduity, his own happiness than that of any other person." He may in the race for wealth "strain every nerve and every muscle, in order to outstrip all his competitors. But if he should justle, or throw down any of them, the indulgence of the spectators is entirely at an end. It is a violation of fair play, which they cannot admit of." But, provided it stays within the bounds of prudence and justice, ambition deserves admiration. The world has little respect for a man who fails to exert himself in the pursuit of wealth when he can acquire it without meanness or injustice.

People seek wealth not because they are impelled by the necessities of nature. These will be supplied by the wages of the lowliest laborer. Instead, what motivates them is the desire to emulate those above them. Attention and approbation are the advantages that we pursue "by that great purpose of human life which we call bettering our condition." The final object of our desires is to attain the condition of the great. Thus men will accumulate wealth in toil and anguish, although they continue to be "always as much, and sometimes more exposed than before, to anxiety, to fear, and to sorrow; to disease, to danger, and to death." But it is this deceptive quality of wealth "which rouses and keeps in continual motion the industry of mankind." The rich "consume little more than the poor, and in spite of their natural selfishness and rapacity, though they mean only their own convenience, though the sole end which they propose from the labor of all the thousands whom they employ, be the gratification of their own vain and insatiable desires, they divide with the poor the produce of all their improvements. They are led by an invisible hand to make nearly the same distribution of the necessaries of life, which would have been made, had the earth been divided into equal portions among all its inhabitants; and thus, without intending it, without knowing it, advance the interest of the society."

231

It was thus from the tradition of British moral philosophy that Smith took the idea of a providential order of the universe in which man is but an instrument of the Author of Nature, promoting ends that are not of his intention. Interpreters of Smith's thought have raised the question of a conflict between the principle of sympathy, which orders the moral world, and that of self-interest, which fulfills a similar function in the economic one, and in this connection German scholars, in search of punctilious consistency, have spoken of the "Adam Smith problem." The problem is more apparent than real because Smith's ethics, as pointed out, assigns a legitimate function to the pursuit of self-interest within the limits indicated by the requirement of fair play. There is, however, a greater complacency, a more pronounced and bland optimism in *The Theory of Moral Sentiments* than in *The Wealth of Nations*. Beyond this, Smith's ethics and his economics are integrated by the same principle of self-command, or self-reliance, which manifests itself in economics in laissez faire.

NATURAL LIBERTY

Although the invisible hand has its precedents in British moral philosophy, the "obvious and simple system of natural liberty," of which Smith speaks in *The Wealth of Nations,* reflects several strands of thought that are not easily unraveled. Smith, who was not unconcerned about questions of priority—reportedly he would tell students that he hated scribblers when he saw them taking notes in his lectures—seems to have developed the basic idea very early in his career. Dugald Stewart, Smith's first biographer, had in his possession a paper read by Smith in 1755, in which Smith staked out his claim to priority in matters that he had already treated in his lectures in the late 1740s in Edinburgh. In this paper there are a number of allusions to the laissez faire principle. Stewart cites the following:

> Man is generally considered by statesmen and projectors as the materials of a sort of political mechanics. Projectors disturb nature in the course of her operations in human affairs; and it requires no more than to let her alone, and give her fair play in the pursuit of her ends, that she may establish her own designs.
>
> Little else is required to carry a State to the highest degree of opulence from the lowest barbarism, but peace, easy taxes, and tolerable administration of justice; all the rest being brought about by the natural course of things. All governments which thwart this natural course, which force things into another channel, or which endeavor to arrest the progress of society at a particular point, are unnatural, and to support themselves are obliged to be oppressive and tyrannical.

PUFENDORF AND LOCKE

The idea of laissez faire came early to Smith, but it is an open question whether and to what extent it was stimulated by his training in natural law at Glasgow College between 1737 and 1740. There he read Grotius—of whose work a copy, signed by Adam Smith who was then between the ages of fourteen and seventeen is still extant—as well as a Latin version of Pufendorf's *The Whole Duty of Man according to the Law of Nature*, which Hutcheson used as a text in his moral philosophy course. These writers were exponents of a secularized natural law, from which they derived the basic principles of jurisprudence. Their approach was basically a legal one. As they contrasted man's life in society with that in nature, they might give attention to the details of the state of nature and might even speak of the natural liberty prevailing there. In Pufendorf's thought—not so much, however, in the work that Smith studied as a text—there dimly emerges the idea of "natural rights" which the law of nature accords to man and to the citizen. The obligation of the ruler to honor such rights is characterized by Pufendorf, however, as imperfect, because if the human law forbids what the natural law orders, the citizen must obey the human law.

Samuel von Pufendorf (1632–94) was born the same year as Locke, and although he was steeped in the tradition of continental absolutism Locke studied his works with care and profit. In the writings of Locke and others, the natural rights approach reached its full development. Natural rights came to be considered inborn and inalienable, in contrast with acquired rights, and with them emerged the idea of a limitation of governmental functions, as epitomized in the English Bill of Rights and in Locke's *Second Treatise of Government* in the seventeenth century, and, in the eighteenth, in the bills of rights attached to the American state constitutions, in the French Declaration of the Rights of Man and of the Citizen, and in the first ten amendments to the Constitution of the United States.

Locke may have found more food for thought in Pufendorf than had Smith, who probably assimilated the natural rights idea in the Lockean version rather than in the incomplete form given to it by Pufendorf. What is more, when Smith could have found other provocative thoughts in Pufendorf, for example, in the latter's ideas about usefulness and scarcity as determinants of economic value, he made no use of them and instead embraced the Lockean labor theory of value. What then about Hutcheson, Pufendorf's interpreter in the classroom? He lectured without notes, and nobody knows what he taught in class. In his postumous works he does employ the phrase "natural liberty" and speak of it as a natural right. But his discussion is ambivalent and replete with qualifications:

> 'Tis plain each one has a natural right to exert his powers, according to his own judgment and inclination, for these purposes in all such industry, labor or amusements as are not hurtful to others in their persons or goods, while no more public interests

necessarily requires his labors or requires that his activities should be under the discretion of others. This right we call natural liberty. Every man has a sense of this right.

The sentiments expressed in the qualifying clause are underlined even more strongly in another statement of Hutcheson's:

> The populace often needs also to be taught, and engaged by laws, into the best methods of managing their own affairs and exercising their mechanic arts; and, in general, civil laws more precisely determine many points in which the Law of Nature leaves much latitude.

In Locke, Smith could find clearer statements about rights of the individual against government which gave expression to the popular aspirations of the time for the protection of life, liberty, and the pursuit of happiness. Locke himself speaks of "lives, liberties and estates, which I call by the general name, property," and he contrasts "natural liberty," under which man is ruled only by the law of nature, with the liberty of man in society, which is subject to the rule of government, but of one that is established by consent. Locke's guarantee of the liberty of man in society is secured by the requirements that government be established by the consent of the governed and by other conditions, including one that makes the government a fiduciary trustee authorized only to enact laws that are designed for the good of the people. Locke does not set forth in detail what constitutes the good of the people. Had he done so, his political philosophy would not have outlasted his time, because we know from his economic writings that he shared many of the mercantilist views which formed so sharp a contrast with the laissez faire idea. It was the greatness of the political philosophy of Locke that it provided the underpinning of the modern democratic state without committing it to any specific form of economic organization. The British Constitution and that of the United States are both shaped by the thought of Locke and have proved resilient in the face of momentous changes in economic organization and policy, from mercantilism to laissez faire and to the modern welfare state with its compensatory economy.

When Smith made his plea for natural liberty or laissez faire, he had behind him the tradition of Locke's political philosophy. The great idea that there are limitations to the legitimate functions of government he could find in Locke. On the substantive side, Locke's principal limitation would restrict legislation to that enacted for the public good. Whatever this may have meant to Locke, he was farsighted enough not to load his political philosophy with the economic preconceptions of his time. It was left to future generations to fill with specific content the notion of the public good in the light of the economic ideas of their time. To Smith, the public good required laissez faire because the pursuit of self-interest, guided by the invisible hand of competition, would produce it, whereas government intervention in the economic sphere would more often hinder than help it.

PARADOXES OF THE COMMERCIAL SOCIETY

Smith fused the political liberalism of Locke with his own economic liberalism and thereby became the prophet of the commercial society of modern capitalism, under which private enterprise, with the stimulus of the profit motive, put to use the technological exploits of the industrial revolution and did so in relative freedom from restraint by the government. But the commercial society, so convincingly rationalized for Smith's contemporaries in *The Wealth of Nations,* turns out to be a society that Smith finds marred by numerous blemishes of the most serious kind. *The Wealth of Nations* abounds with illustrations of such flaws. The division of labor, from which arises the wealth of nations and which is eulogized in Book I, is depicted in Book V, some seven hundred pages later, as being responsible, because of the monotony and simplicity of the workman's operations, for making him "as stupid and ignorant as it is possible for a human creature to become."

> The torpor of his mind renders him, not only incapable of relishing or bearing a part in any rational conversation, but of conceiving any generous, noble, or tender sentiment, and consequently of forming any just judgment concerning many even of the ordinary duties of private life. Of the great and extensive interests of his country he is altogether incapable of judging; and unless very particular pains have been taken to render him otherwise, he is equally incapable of defending his country in war. The uniformity of his stationary life naturally corrupts the courage of his mind, and makes him regard with abhorrence the irregular, uncertain, and adventurous life of a soldier. It corrupts even the activity of his body, and renders him incapable of exerting his strength with vigor and perseverance, in any other employment than that to which he has been bred. His dexterity at his own particular trade seems, in this manner, to be acquired at the expense of his intellectual, social and moral virtues. But in every improved and civilized society this is the state into which the laboring poor, that is, the great body of the people, must necessarily fall, unless government takes some pains to prevent it.

If such is the fate of the workman in the commercial society, one might expect to find compensating features among the other classes. This, however, is not the opinion of Smith. Of the landowners, he says that they, "like all other men, like to reap where they never sowed," and he speaks of their "indolence, which is the natural effect of the ease and security of their situation" and which too often renders them ignorant.

Employers he finds

> are always and everywhere in a sort of tacit, but constant and uniform combination, not to raise the wages of labor above their actual rate, . . .

a behavior that might well violate what Smith elsewhere considers a requirement of equity, namely, that they who feed, cloath and lodge the whole body of the people should have such a share of the produce of their own labor as to be themselves tolerably well fed, clothed and lodged.

Of merchants and master manufacturers Smith says that they

complain much of the bad effects of high wages in raising the price, and thereby lessening the sale of their goods both at home and abroad. They say nothing concerning the bad effects of high profits. They are silent with regard to the pernicious effects of their own gains. They complain only of those of other people.

Smith finds that

the interest of dealers...in any particular branch of trade or manufactures is always in some respects different from, and even opposite to that of the public. To widen the market and to narrow the competition, is always the interest of the dealers.

By narrowing the competition, dealers are enabled

to levy, for their own benefit, an absurd tax upon the rest of their fellow-citizens.

They are

an order of men, whose interest is never exactly the same with that of the public, who have generally an interest to deceive and even to oppress the public, and who accordingly have, upon many occasions, both deceived and oppressed it.

Smith speaks of the "meanness of mercantile prejudice," of the "mean rapacity, the monopolizing spirit, of merchants and manufacturers," whom he finds "in pursuit of their own pedlar principle of turning a penny wherever a penny was to be got," and he calls the accumulation of wealth in order to better one's condition "the most vulgar means." In a famous passage he says:

People of the same trade seldom meet together, even for merriment and diversion, but the conversation ends in a conspiracy against the public, or in some contrivance to raise prices.

He mentions the "excess of avarice of corn merchants"; the neglect, on the part of corporate directors, of "other people's money"; the inclination of lawyers who are paid by the length of their brief "to multiply words beyond all necessity"; and the fact that great wealth frequently is "an apology for great folly." He observes that

all for ourselves, and nothing for other people, seems, in every age of the world, to have been the vile maxim of the masters of mankind.

He does not underrate the difficulties that beset the path of those who oppose the "sophistry of merchants and manufacturers who are always demanding a monopoly against their countrymen":

The member of parliament who supports every proposal for strengthening this monopoly is sure to acquire not only the reputation of understanding trade, but great popularity and influence in an order of men whose numbers and wealth render them of great importance. If he opposes them, on the contrary, and still more if he has authority enough to be able to thwart them, neither the most acknowledged probity, nor the highest rank, nor the greatest public services, can protect him from the most infamous abuse and detraction, from personal insults, nor sometimes from real danger, arising from the insolent outrage of furious and disappointed monopolists.

The commercial society is replete with cleavages and conflicts, which threaten the "sacred rights of private property":

> Wherever there is great property, there is great inequality. For one very rich man, there must be at least five hundred poor, and the affluence of the few supposes the indigence of the many. The affluence of the rich excites the indignation of the poor, who are often both driven by want, and prompted by envy, to invade his possessions. It is only under the shelter of the civil magistrate that the owner of that valuable property, which is acquired by the labor of many years, or perhaps of many successive generations, can sleep a single night in security. He is at all times surrounded by unknown enemies, whom, though he never provoked, he can never appease, and from whose injustice he can be protected only by the powerful arm of the civil magistrate. . . . Civil government, so far as it is instituted for the security of property, is in reality instituted for the defense of the rich against the poor, or of those who have some property against those who have none at all.

Passages such as these indicate a certain break in Smith's position. On the one hand, he is the harbinger of commercial society with its natural liberty, on the other hand he is also a bitter critic of this same society, so much so that some of his strictures have a flavor not unlike that characteristic of the products of the vitriolic pen of a Marx or a Veblen. There thus appears what at first glance seems to be a paradox: how can the same thinker build in *The Wealth of Nations* a structure that in its essential features is modeled after the beneficent Newtonian pattern depicted with bland optimism in *The Theory of Moral Sentiments,* but which, once the scaffolding has been removed, impresses the observer with so many glaring deficiencies?

There are two possibilities of resolving this apparent paradox, one reinforcing the other, and both are rooted in the profound influence that Hume had on Smith's thought. When Smith wrote *The Theory of Moral Sentiments,* he was in his thirties. When he published *The Wealth of Nations,* he was in his fifties, a mature man who had seen the world, who had become acquainted with its greatness, and whose mind was stocked not merely with book learning and abstract patterns of thought but with a rich harvest gleaned from observation. In his second work he was in a much better position to practice what Hume preached, that is, to apply the lessons of experience. Of the three great principles that suffuse *The Wealth of Nations*—

the beneficial mechanism of the Newtonian universe, natural liberty, and the inadequacy of government—the third is indeed an empirical one. On countless occasions Smith employs in *The Wealth of Nations* the lessons of history and of contemporary experience to depict government as inefficient, corrupt, frivolous, wasteful, and subject to the pressure of vested interests.

Smith's work is a unique blend of rationalism and empiricism, of deduction and induction. His rationalism enables him to construct a great system of thought on the foundation of a few leading principles; his empiricism, which pervades the whole work, makes it realistic and endows him with the persuasive gift of supplying every general idea with a profusion of apt and convincing illustrations. Smith's empiricism not only made him see government in the light in which he perceived it but it also was responsible for disturbing the complacent view of the universe characteristic of his ethics and for the somber notes of discord which trouble the harmony of his economics. He had seen the world, had learned from what he had seen, and had found the commercial society less eligible to become perfectly harmonious and self-regulated than Newton's order of nature had intimated.

If Smith found the world of economics tainted by so many blemishes and nevertheless endorsed the idea of a commercial society with prophetic vigor and unparalleled intellectual strength, why did he do so? The clue to his intention may be found in certain passages of Hume's *Discourses* in which Hume stresses the civilizing effects of commerce and to which Smith refers as follows:

> Commerce and manufactures gradually introduced order and good government, and with them, the liberty and security of individuals, among the inhabitants of the country, who had before lived almost in a continual state of war with their neighbors, and of servile dependency upon their superiors. This, though it has been the least observed, is by far the most important of all their effects. Mr. Hume is the only writer who, so far as I know, has hitherto taken notice of it.

ECONOMIC EVOLUTION

Smith was a child of the age of Enlightenment and vigorously opposed to the feudal and ecclesiastical dependencies of earlier times. In his thought, commerce and manufacture emerge as indispensable instruments to bring their abolition. Smith's interpretation of this great historical change, which runs strictly in economic terms, is the following. As long as the great feudal proprietors found nothing to purchase with that part of their produce that exceeded their own limited requirements, they employed it to maintain a multitude of retainers and dependent tenants. On this their power was founded, and on this basis they came to mete out justice and command the military forces of their region. The power of the feudal lords was broken only by the rise of commerce and manufacture. These made them part of the market economy by furnishing them with products which they could purchase with their surplus produce and which they could consume themselves rather than share with their tenants and retainers. As they ceased to maintain these, they lost their power and authority over them. The great lords now produced cash crops for the market, and their tenants paid cash rents on the basis of long-term leases instead of rendering personal services. The lords spent the cash on the products of commerce and manufacture, maintaining directly and indirectly as many people in this manner as they had before. But whereas in the past each one of the retainers and tenants had been entirely dependent on one great lord, the lord now contributed only a minute share to the income of the workmen and their employers maintained by his purchases. This pluralism accounts for the much greater measure of independence of the people now maintained by him.

Smith's interpretation of historical change again illustrates his belief in the great providential principle which turns people, regardless of their intentions, into instruments of public service:

> A revolution of the greatest importance to the public happiness was in this manner brought about by two different orders of people, who had not the least intention to serve the public. To gratify the most childish vanity was the sole motive of the great proprietors. The merchants and artificers, much less ridiculous, acted merely from a view to their own interest. . . . Neither of them had either knowledge or foresight of that great revolution which the folly of the one, and the industry of the other, was gradually bringing about.

It is possible that Smith considered the civilizing influence of the commercial society, which brought liberation from feudal dependencies, important enough to make him accept its shortcomings for the sake of what he may have believed the greater good—political freedom and independence. This interpretation of Smith's intention would make him a foreunner of those who in modern times have asserted that political freedom cannot flourish without economic freedom. This view implies an economic determinism not unlike that characteristic of Smith's interpretation of the decline of feudalism and the rise of commercial society. This economic interpretation of history has no parallel in Smith's early lectures, and it may be that his views in this matter reached full maturity only after his visit to France.

SMITH AND THE PHYSIOCRATS

Regardless of whether Smith brought back from France a new view of historical change, it is certain that he did not return an exponent of absolutism. In this respect his thought stands in sharp contrast to that of the Physiocrats, whose influence on Smith has been the subject of protracted controversy. Moreover, still another contrast between Smith and the Physiocrats can be derived from the interpretation of Smith's intention as discussed in the preceding paragraphs. In the light of this interpretation Smith embraced laissez faire because it was to him an indispensable accompaniment of political liberty. The Physiocrats' intention was an entirely different one: they proclaimed laissez faire a means of perpetuating the absolutism of the *ancien régime*. Moreover, the laissez faire idea of the Physiocrats was modified by their insistence in a *bon prix* for agricultural products. Smith never shared their views about the desirability of high prices for farm products, exclusive productivity of agriculture, and the single tax.

However profound the differences in Smith's and the Physiocrats' intentions and in the elaboration of the laissez faire idea, their proclamation of a system of natural liberty may nevertheless have helped to fortify his own attachment to laissez faire, although he arrived at it independently. Smith himself intended to dedicate *The Wealth of Nations* to Quesnay and would have done so had not Quesnay died two years before publication. French writers have made the most of the alleged influence of the Physiocrats on Smith, beginning with Du Pont, the first historian of economic thought, who insisted that everything that is sound is *The Wealth of Nations* is derived from the Physiocrats, whereas everything added by Smith is faulty, a statements he came to regret. It seems certain that Smith arrived at the laissez faire idea independently of the Physiocrats because the germ of the idea can be found in the lecture of 1755, which points to a still earlier origin of the doctrine. As Quesnay's first economic publications date from 1756, what is involved here is a multiple discovery rather than the initial stimulation of the though of one by the other. Beyond this, Smith did read the physiocratic literature and there is no doubt that he profited from personal contacts with the leading Physiocrats in 1764 and after, as they did from personal contact with him. There are a number of passages in *The Wealth of Nations* that indicate the influence of the Physiocrats, but the basic idea of laissez faire may be considered Smith's own intellectual property.

THE INFLUENCE OF ROUSSEAU

Smith, like every thinker of his age, did not escape the pervasive influence of Rousseau, who deprecated the effects of civilization on mankind and contrasted life in civilized society with the state of nature to the advantage of the latter. Rousseau's views were the subject of conversation among men of letters everywhere. Hume, Smith's friend, had befriended Rousseau and invited him to England. Rousseau's influence on Smith is especially noticeable in Smith's view of the ill effects of the division of labor. What he says about these has its parallel in Rousseau's *Discourse on the Origin of Inequality*: "So long as men...confined themselves to such arts as did not require the joint labor of several hands, they lived free, healthy, honest and happy lives." All this changed "from the moment one man began to stand in need of the help of another; from the moment it appeared advantageous to any one man to have enough provisions for two." To Rousseau may be traced the idea of alienation, later developed by Hegel and by Marx, which considers man in society as being deprived of the freedom to be himself, alienated from himself by the need to adapt himself to the conventions of society and the requirements of the market. In Smith's version of this idea, man becomes dehumanized as a result of the division of labor, and to fend off these ill effects, government-sponsored education is depicted as indispensable. Smith's advocacy of the latter, which formed an exception from the laissez faire principle and became extremely influential in the history of education, may have required the strong underpinning provided by the somber passages about the dehumanizing effects of specialization, which makes people "stupid" and "ignorant."

SMITH AND THE ENGLISH TRADITION

In the tradition of English thought there was Locke's political philosophy, providing a framework into which Smith could fit the laissez faire idea. A strong strain of individualism had also been latent in the writings of not a few merchants who contributed to the literature of the seventeenth century. They may have called for the recognition or protection of the interest by which businessmen, or some businessmen, were led, implying the beneficial character of such an arrangement. But such claims were rarely more than assertions, which lacked the force of a fully developed theoretical argument. If words rather than the substance of thought would count, precedents could be found of Smith's laissez faire idea. Child had extolled the "liberty and property" of the merchants. Petty had employed as his motto the words "the world refuses to be governed badly" and in connection with the controversy about restrictions of the interest rate had spoken of "the vanity and fruitlessness of making civil positive laws against the laws of nature." Davenant had taught that "trade is in its nature free," arguing against the proposed embargo of textile imports from India. But, if we disregard the pamphlet of North's, which did not come before a wider public until the nineteenth century, these statements were half hearted and unsystematic and served to buttress a specific policy position rather than a general course of action.

CLASSICAL ECONOMICS

In Adam Smith's *Wealth of Nations* the laissez faire principle became the cornerstone of a system of thought and was anchored in a broad philosophy of which it formed an essential part. The laissez faire principle, competition, and the labor theory of value are outstanding features of the teachings of the classical school of economics, made up essentially of Smith himself, and of Malthus, Ricardo, and Mill. This school, the second in the history of economics, was in the lead, generally speaking, during the hundred-year period following the publication of *The Wealth of Nations* in 1776. Not all classical economics followed in all details the patterns established by Adam Smith. As natural law, natural rights, and the Newtonian order of nature gave way to other preconceptions, some writers came to place greater emphasis on the principle of utility as the foundation of laissez faire. Later still, others saw in competition not so much an individual's self-realization as a struggle along the lines of social Darwinism, with its survival of the fittest. In the matter of method, others might become more abstract, dogmatic, and doctrinaire than Smith, who refrained from using the phrase "economic laws" of ostensibly universal validity and whose empirical bent and historical sense permitted him to allow a number of important exceptions from laissez faire.

During the nineteenth century the classical school met three challenges, the first from the historical school, the second from the Socialists, and the third from the marginal utility economists of the 1870s. Although it survived the attacks of the historical economists and the Socialists, the third onslaught left its value theory shattered. In the twentieth century, Keynes's challenge of laissez faire shed doubt on the soundness of the very foundation of classical economics. Keynes's habit of denouncing all pre-Keynesians summarily as classics was therefore not entirely without justification. In his writings the epithet becames transformed from an accolade into a term of opprobrium: what was once meant to denote excellence now signifies old-fashionedness.

But what seemed old-fashioned to Keynes was revolutionary two centuries ago. What the classics proposed forms a sharp contrast with earlier trends of thought in economics. The medievalists had been inclined to rely on charity as a means of resolving the economic problem. The mercantilists had exalted the pursuit of national gain and had seen in it the clue to power and plenty. The Physiocrats in turn had made the most of agricultural reconstruction as a device to beat scarcity and poverty. With all these proposed solutions the classics found fault. The medievalists had called for good works; the reformers for faith. The classics demanded neither, their concern being thisworldly rather than otherworldly. Instead Smith drove home the demand for laissez faire, a system of natural liberty, as the best means of bringing about the wealth of nations. In such a system individuals could pursue their own self-interest, but, regardless of their intentions, a providential order would tend to turn the pursuit of self-interest into an instrument serving the interest of society.

Chapter 11

THE DETAILS
OF SMITH'S SYSTEM
AND ITS REORGANIZATION
BY SAY

Smith's *Wealth of Nations* is divided into five "books," which discuss in this order, generally speaking, production and distribution with special reference to labor, capital, economic development, the history of economics, and public finance. The first two books stand out as the most important on such matters as the division of labor, and the theories of value, price, wages, profits, and interest are all covered in them.

Smith's economics of self-reliance is grounded in "the desire of bettering our condition," a desire that "comes with us from the womb, and never leaves us till we go into the grave." To realize this desire, some will fawn upon their fellowmen and others will expect assistance from their benevolence. But man

> will be more likely to prevail if he can interest their self-love in his favor, and show them that it is for their own advantage to do for him what he requires of them. . . . It is not from the benevolence of the butcher, the brewer, or the baker, that we expect our dinner, but from their regard to their own interest. We address ourselves, not to their humanity, but to their self-love, and never talk to them of our own necessities but of their advantages.

By pursuing their own interests, people will generally promote the interest of society more effectively than when they really intend to promote it. "I have never known much good done," Smith says, "by those who affected to trade for the public good." People are usually better judges of their own interests than of those of society, but even the judgment of their own interests is far from perfect. For example, they tend to overvalue the chance of gain and undervalue that of loss, owing to "an absurd presumption in their own good fortune" which parallels "the overweening conceit which the greater part of men have of their own abilities." Economic rationality is far from perfect, but its very imperfection carries into the economic system an optimistic bias.

As regards the aim or end of economic activities, consumption is boldly stated to be the "sole end and purpose of production." From this it follows that "the interest of the producer ought to be attended to, only so far as it may be necessary for promoting that of the consumer." Although Smith declares consumption to be the purpose of all production, he does not develop a full-fledged theory of consumption and is principally concerned with production. Later on, when production had increased because of the industrial revolution and problems of economic conflict had become more pressing, distribution was to emerge as the central problem in the thought of Ricardo.

Smith's pervasive emphasis on production distinguishes his work both from medieval economics, which was consumer oriented also but which did not develop a doctrine of production, and from the mercantilists, whose first concern was with foreign trade and the accumulation of treasure resulting therefrom. The difference between Smith and the mercantilists is further underlined in the remarks that open up Smith's great treatise, in which he makes the per capita national income rather than aggregate income or national wealth the criterion of economic well-being and the starting point of his discussion:

> The annual labor of every nation is the fund which originally supplies it with all the necessaries and conveniences of life which it annually consumes, and which consist always either in the immediate produce of that labor, or in what is purchased with that produce from other nations.
> According therefore, as this produce, or what is purchased with it, bears a greater or smaller proportion to the number of those who are to consume it, the nation will be better or worse supplied with all the necessaries and conveniences for which it has occasion.

Macroeconomic concepts such as the national income did not therefore emerge in the 1930s with the Keynesian revolution and the statistical work accompanying it but were part of classical economics. They came to the fore again in Ricardo's macroeconomic theory of distribution but were pushed into the background between the 1870s and the 1930s by the individualizing tendency of marginal utility economics. Nor did these concepts originate with the classics, who could build on the foundations established by Petty, Davenant, and the Physiocrats.

THE DIVISION OF LABOR

Smith sees the per capita national income determined by two factors, the productivity of labor and the proportion in which productive labor stands to nonproductive. The idea that there is nonproductive labor he apparently derived from the Physiocrats, and he interpreted it to include all those engaged in services. As for the productivity of labor, Smith considers principally its connection with the division of labor, which emerges as the most important condition conducive to improvements of productivity.

The beneficial effects of the division of labor are illustrated in Smith's celebrated example of pin making:

> A workman not educated to this business (which the division of labor has rendered a distinct trade), nor acquainted with the use of the machinery employed in it (to the invention of which the same division of labor has probably given occasion), could scarce, perhaps, with his utmost industry, make one pin in a day, and certainly could not make twenty. But in the way in which this business is now carried on, not only the whole work is a peculiar trade, but it is divided into a number of branches, of which the greater part are likewise peculiar trades. One man draws out the wire, another straights it, a third cuts it, a fourth points it, a fifth grinds it at the top for receiving the head; to make the head requires two or three distinct operations; to put it on, is a peculiar business, to whiten the pins is another; it is even a trade by itself to put them into the paper; and the important business of making a pin is, in this manner, divided into about eighteen distinct operations, which, in some manufactories, are all performed by distinct hands, though in others the same man will sometimes perform two or three of them. I have seen a small manufactory of this kind where ten men only were employed, and where some of them consequently performed two or three distinct operations. But though they were very poor, and therefore but indifferently accommodated with the necessary machinery, they could, when they exerted themselves, make among them about twelve pounds of pins in a day. There are in a pound upwards of four thousand pins of middling size. Those ten persons, therefore, could make among them upwards of forty-eight thousand pins in a day. Each person, therefore, making a tenth part of forty-eight thousand pins, might be considered as making four thousand eight hundred pins in a day. But if they all had wrought separately and independently, and without any of them having been educated to this peculiar business, they certainly could not each of them have made twenty, perhaps not one pin in a day; that is, certainly not the two hundred and fortieth, perhaps not the four thousand eight hundredth part of what they are at present capable of performing, in consequence of a proper division and combination of their different operations.

Smith ascribes the favorable effects of the division of labor to three circumstances: the resulting increase in the workman's skill and dexterity, the saving of time which otherwise would be lost in passing from one species of work to another, and the invention of machinery which facilitates and abridges labor. Smith visualizes technological innovations as being made mainly by workmen who have become specialists along certain narrow lines of operations, a view of the circumstances attending technological progress that was challenged early and is not in accord with the facts of the history of technology.

The adverse effects of the division of labor Smith mentions in another context. In his systematic discussion he sees only the good that comes from interdependence and cooperation:

> It is the great multiplication of the productions of all the different arts, in consequence of the division of labour, which occasions, in a well-governed society, that universal opulence which extends itself to the lowest ranks of the people. Every workman has a great quantity of his own work to dispose of beyond what he himself has occasion for; and every other workman being exactly in the same situation, he is enabled to exchange a great quantity of his own goods for a great quantity, or, what comes to the same thing, for the price of a great quantity of theirs. He supplies them abundantly with what they have occasion for. . . .

Smith's view of the division of labor is thus broader than his example of pin making would indicate. He has in mind specialization not only by skills but also by occupations, functions, firms, and industries, and in a later context he will also refer to what may be called the territorial division of labor, the basis of interregional and international trade.

The division of labor did not originally arise from human wisdom or foresight but was the slow and gradual consequence of a propensity common to all men, "the propensity to truck, barter, and exchange one thing for another." Differences in human abilities are often not so much the cause as the effect of the division of labor.

This point of view was in line with the thought of the time, which emphasized nurture rather than nature as the determinant of human differences and caused Smith to disregard differences in native disposition as a factor making for specialization.

> The difference between the most dissimilar characters, between a philosopher and a common street porter, for example, seems to arise not so much from nature, as from habit, custom, and education.

Unlike Plato's *Republic,* the division of labor in *The Wealth of Nations* is not derived from any native inequality of men. Hence it does not serve as a principle requiring the stratification of society, as it does in Plato's *Republic* with its three classes. Instead it calls for economic mobility and freedom of entry into occupations closed to no one because of alleged native disabilities.

Smith closes his discussion of the division of labor by enunciating the great principle "that the division of labor is limited by the extent of the market." This is a statement that may sound trite today but, when it was made, it had all the freshness of an important new insight. Only by widening the market can the full benefits from the division of labor be realized. The Founding Fathers of the United States were among the first to practice what Smith preached when they insisted on the absence of internal barriers to trade and anchored the prohibition of internal tariffs in the Constitution of the United States. One hundred and fifty years later Europe followed by establishing the Common Market.

PRODUCTIVE AND UNPRODUCTIVE LABOR

Although few would find fault with Smith's exposition of the division of labor, his second factor determining the per capita national income, namely the proportion in which productive labor stands to unproductive labor, based, as it is, on the questionable distinction between the two kinds, became the subject of controversy not long after the publication of *The Wealth of Nations*. Those who upheld the distinction included Malthus, the Mills, and Marx. Ricardo did not commit himself, but Say, Lauderdale, McCulloch, and especially Senior seriously questioned it. It has served as a foundation of most disparate trends of thought. In the form given to it by Marx, the distinction became a precept of socialist economics and as such still controls the conceptual derivation and measurement of the national income of the Soviet Union. At the opposite end, the idea that the work of government is unproductive has inspired what Keynes called the Treasury view, a time-honored tradition calling for parsimony in government because the funds withdrawn from the taxpayer become unproductive in the hands of the government employees. In recent years new facets of the dichotomy of productive and unproductive labor have been discovered. With the contemporary attention to problems of economic development there has been a revival of interest in Smith's distinction, and some students of economic development view it more favorably than it was viewed at earlier times, when no special emphasis was placed on the promotion of economic growth as a criterion of economic activities.

Basically Smith's idea is to restrict the concept of production to the output of material goods which presumably have greater durability than do services. "Menial servants," government officials, military personnel, as well as "some both of the gravest and most important, and some of the most frivolous professions" are included in the unproductive category: "churchmen, lawyers, physicians, men of letters of all kinds; players, buffoons, musicians, opera-singers, opera-dancers, etc." These people, and this is a second reason for classifying them as unproductive, are maintained by the income of others, and they fail to reproduce their income, whereas productive labor "adds to the value of the subject upon which it is bestowed" and reproduces its income. Hence "a man grows rich by employing a multitude of manufacturers; he grows poor, by maintaining a multitude of menial servants." The possibility that a man may grow rich by employing people who render services to others Smith apparently discards.

Although unproductive labor earns an income kindred to the factor payments to others from which it is derived, it does not, in Smith's account, produce income in terms of output. The latter type of income, turned out by productive labor only, thus maintains those who have produced it as well as the unproductive part of the population and those who do not work at all.

THE LABOR THEORY OF VALUE

With the division of labor progressing, only a few wants of a person are supplied by his own labor. Instead, the greater part of his wants is supplied by exchange. "Every man thus lives by exchanging, or becomes in some measure a merchant, and the society itself grows to be what is properly a commercial society." But since one person's product may not meet the wants of another person, whose product the former desires, the commercial society requires money—a commodity "few people would be likely to refuse in exchange for the produce of their industry." Having introduced money to serve as a medium of exchange, Smith goes on to discuss "the relative or exchangeable value" of goods. He mentions both value in use and value in exchange, but after referring to what is now known as the paradox of value —a good may have a high value in exchange and a low use value, and vice versa: water and diamonds—value in use disappears from further discussion and Smith turns at once to value in exchange. He develops the labor theory of value:

> Every man is rich or poor according to the degree in which he can afford to enjoy the necessaries, conveniencies, and amusements of human life. But after the division of labor has once thoroughly taken place, it is but a very small part of these with which a man's own labor can supply him. The far greater part of them he must derive from the labor of other people, and he must be rich or poor according to the quantity of that labor which he can command, or which he can afford to purchase. The value of any commodity, therefore, to the person who possesses it, and who means not to use or consume it himself, but to exchange it for other commodities, is equal to the quantity of labor which it enables him to purchase or command. Labor, therefore, is the real measure of the exchangeable value of all commodities.

The exchange value of a good is determined by the amount of labor that the good can command in the market. Side by side with this theory of value in terms of labor commanded appears a "real-cost" theory of value, a theory of value in terms of labor pain, from which the former theory seems to be derived. Goods have the value of the labor they command in exchange because the owner, by exchanging them, can escape the pain of laboring himself to produce what he obtains in exchange. Smith continues:

> The real price of every thing, what every thing really costs to the man who wants to acquire it, is the toil and trouble of acquiring it. What every thing is really worth to the man who

has acquired it, and who wants to dispose of it or exchange it for something else, is the toil and trouble which it can save to himself, and which it can impose upon other people. What is bought with money or with goods is purchased by labor, as much as what we acquire by the toil of our own body. That money or those goods indeed save us this toil. They contain the value of a certain quantity of labor which we exchange for what is supposed at the time to contain the value of an equal quantity. Labor was the first price, the original purchase-money, that was paid for all things.

The "real," or "natural," value of all exchangeable commodities is measured in terms of labor commanded. Labor, however, is not a homogeneous quantity, since to different types of labor are attached different degrees of hardship and ingenuity. Hence labor defies exact measurement and cannot serve as the common denominator in which the value of goods is typically estimated. Instead adjustment takes place "by the higgling and bargaining of the market, according to that sort of rough equality which, though not exact, is sufficient for carrying on the business of common life." Thus the market price is explained in terms of labor commanded, and labor commanded in terms of the market price, an example of a kind of reasoning that interpreters of the thought of Smith have criticized as circular.

The intervention of money removes the estimation of the value of goods still further from the labor basis. In terms of labor expended, equal quantities of labor always have the same value, or "real price," but as the value of money is subject to change, so is the "nominal price" of labor and of commodities in terms of money. Labor as well as commodities thus has a real and a nominal price.

In Smith's development of the labor theory of value, labor is at times interpreted as labor commanded and at other times as labor expended, or labor cost. As society progresses there are further complications because Smith recognizes that labor then ceases to be the only determinant of value and that the price of goods produced with the help of labor, land, and capital includes not only a return to labor but also a return to capital and land.

> In that early and rude state of society which precedes both the accumulation of stock and the appropriation of land, the proportion between the quantities of labor necessary for acquiring different objects seems to be the only circumstance which can afford any rule for exchanging them for one another. If among a nation of hunters, for example, it usually costs twice the labor to kill a beaver which it does to kill a deer, one beaver should naturally exchange for or be worth two deer. . . .
>
> · In this state of things, the whole produce of labor belongs to the laborer.

But once capital comes to be employed in the productive process and land has become private property, the prices of goods resolve themselves into wages, profits, and rents. Thus Smith's labor theory of value becomes transformed into a cost-of-production theory. There is a great deal of ambivalence in all this. At times land and capital appear to be factors of production coordinated with labor. At other times the returns to land and capital are depicted as deductions from the product of labor, a thought that was to emerge with full force in the system of Marx, as did Smith's notion of the landlords in that of Ricardo: They "love to reap where they never sowed" and demand a rent even for the natural produce of land.

THE NATURAL PRICE

Smith speaks of the natural rate of wages, profits, and rent, the natural price of commodities, and their market price. Natural rates, also known as ordinary or average ones, are controlled by social forces. The natural price of a commodity is one that covers the natural rates of wages, profits, and rent. Market price, the one that goods fetch in the market, may deviate from the natural price. Market price is controlled by the quantity supplied and the effective demand of those willing to pay the natural price. If the effective demand exceeds the quantity supplied, market price will rise above the natural price; in the opposite case, it will fall below it. When the market price exceeds the natural price, the accompanying increase in factor payments will attract factor supplies, the quantity of the product that is supplied will increase, and rates and prices will be brought down to their natural levels. When the market price has fallen below the natural price, things will move in the opposite direction.

The natural price thus becomes "the central price, to which the prices of all commodities are continually gravitating." Nevertheless, fluctuations will ensue in those employments in which the supply does not adjust itself easily to demand, for example, in agriculture. In these, the market price changes not only with the less frequent variations in demand but also with the fairly regular variations in the quantity supplied. Moreover, monopolistic power, frictions, and lack of information may tend to maintain the market price above the natural one over long periods of time.

WAGE THEORY

That the natural price may be related to the level of output is a thought not considered by Smith. The implicit assumptions that underlie his argument are those of constant costs and fixed coefficients of production. In his theory there is no place for diminishing returns or factor substitution. Instead the natural price is functionally related only to factor returns. As Smith points out, the natural price varies with the natural rate of each of its components, that is, of wages, of profits, and of rent. The natural wage of labor, according to Smith, consists of the product of labor, which, before the appropriation of land and the accumulation of capital, belonged in its entirety to the laborer. With the rise of a class of landlords and of capitalist employers, he has to share his product with landlord and master. Laborers and masters are apt to form combinations to raise or to lower wages. The masters are usually more successful in these efforts than are the laborers, but the laborer's and his family's need for subsistence forms a floor below which wages cannot fall for any considerable length of time. An increasing demand for labor may raise wages substantially above the subsistence level, regarded by Smith as "evidently the lowest which is consistent with common humanity." However, the demand for labor can increase only in proportion to the increase of "the funds which are destined for the payment of wages." Thus appears the wages-fund, composed of surplus income and surplus capital in excess of the owner's personal and business requirements. Increasing income and increasing capital are the prerequisites of increasing wages.

An improvement in the economic position of labor due to higher wages Smith considers a clear gain to society:

> Servants, laborers and workmen of different kinds make up the far greater part of every great political society. But what improves the circumstances of the greater part can never be regarded as an inconveniency to the whole. No society can surely be flourishing and happy, of which the far greater part of the members are poor and miserable. It it but equity, besides, that they who feed, cloath and lodge the whole body of the people, should have such a share of the produce of their own labor as to be themselves tolerably well fed, cloathed and lodged.

Low wages are a symptom of stationary economic conditions, under which the wages-fund, large as it may be, fails to increase and thereby fails to stimulate a rising demand for labor. As for the relationship between wages and population growth, Smith holds that poverty will not discourage marriage and birth rates, and may even stimulate the latter, but it will have unfavorable effects on infant and child mortality rates. He recapitulates a thought by then well established:

> Every species of animals naturally multiplies in proportion to the means of their subsistence, and no species can ever multiply beyond it. But in civilized society it is only among the inferior ranks of people that the scantiness of subsistence can set limits to the further multiplication of the human species; and it can do so in no other way than by destroying a great part of the children which their fruitful marriages produce.

A high wage is the effect of increasing wealth and the cause of increasing population. "To complain of it, is to lament over the necessary effect and cause of the greatest public prosperity." In Smith's gospel of high wages these are further related to improvements of the productivity of labor. The idea of a backward-sloping supply curve of labor is not flatly rejected but is considered applicable to only a minority of the people.

Although Smith endorses high wages, he does not favor high prices. Unlike the Physiocrats, he associates low prices of provisions with plenty and prosperity, high prices with scarcity and distress. When provisions are cheap and plentiful, laborers may want to start businesses of their own and employers may want to hire more labor; with the demand for labor rising and the supply falling, the price of labor is likely to rise. When provisions are dear and scarce, events may take the opposite course.

Variations in the price of labor may run counter to variations in the price of provisions. However, since the money wage is regulated both by the demand for labor and the price of wage-goods, fluctuations of the price of wage-goods will not fail to exert an influence on money wages. This will have the effect of dampening the fluctuations of money wages, which are more rigid than the prices of provisions. As has been noted, when the prices of provisions are high, the demand for labor tends to decline as would the wage if this tendency of the wage were not checked by the high prices of wage-goods. And when food prices are low, the effect of the rising demand for labor on wages is again checked by the then prevailing low prices of wage-goods. Fluctuations of the prices of provisions thus have two effects on wages, one checking the other. They affect the demand for labor, and thereby the wage, in one direction, but the effect on the wage is offset, wholly or in part, by the countervailing effect of the same fluctuations—of the prices of wage-goods—pulling the wage in the opposite direction.

PROFIT AND INTEREST

While the increased accumulation of capital tends to raise the demand for labor and consequently the rate of wages, it will have a depressing effect on the rate of profit. As more and more capital becomes accumulated, competition among the owners of capital for profitable investment becomes more pronounced and capital is driven into employments of diminishing profitability. As for interest, "the compensation which the borrower pays to the lender, for the profits which he has an opportunity of making by the use of the money," it will tend to vary with profit.

In connection with wages and profits Smith develops the principle of equal advantage, according to which, under conditions of perfect mobility, the whole of the advantages and the disadvantages of different employments of labor will tend to equality. The same will be true of the different employments of capital. Differences in wages, for example, will compensate for differences in other advantages, such as the agreeableness of the job, the cost of learning it, the constancy of the employment, the chance—however small it may be in terms of mathematical probability—of unusually high rewards. The principle of equal advantage applies, however, only to a person's principal employment. If people cumulate jobs by what is now known as "moonlighting," the extra employment may be undertaken at a lower wage

In his rent theory, Smith vacillates between a number of explanatory principles on which to ground the payment of rent. It is to him "naturally a monopoly price," a designation that is explained by the observation that "it is not at all proportioned to what the landlord may have laid out upon the improvement of the land, or to what he can afford to take; but to what the farmer can afford to give." When Smith discusses commodity prices, he includes the rent of land as an element of cost and therefore presumably as a determinant of the product price, but in the chapter specifically devoted to rent he considers a high or low rent the effect of a high or low product price. As Smith did not change these passages in spite of Hume's criticism (see p. 214), he may not have found them inconsistent. It is possible that in his microeconomic price theory he considered the specific use of an individual plot of land as incurring cost in terms of alternative opportunities foregone, whereas in his macroeconomic theory of distribution land as a whole was viewed as having no alternative use.

Rent, furthermore, is interpreted as a differential that varies with both fertility and location. As for location, improvements in transportation will tend to equalize locational differences as well as rents.

In Smith's theory of economic development, a rising national income is associated with a rising share of the rental income of the landlord class. An increase in the national income, it will be remembered, is predicated by Smith upon the division of labor, to which manufacture is more susceptible than agriculture. Increasing specialization and, hence, productivity in the manufacturing sector of the economy will lower the prices of manufactures and increase the real value of rents. The rising share of the landlord class in the national income thus reflects improved terms of trade of the agricultural sector, in which productivity increases more haltingly than in manufacture. In the Ricardian theory, the strategic factor that produces a similar result is not so much the rising productivity in manufacture as the diminishing returns to land which raise agricultural prices and thereby improve the terms of trade of the agricultural sector of the economy and raise its share of the national income.

CAPITAL

Capital, or stock, is a requirement of the exchange economy with its division of labor. In this economy a person does not consume the products of his own industry but purchases the products of others with the price fetched by his own produce.

This purchase cannot be made till such time as the produce of his own labor has not only been completed, but sold. A stock of goods of different kinds, therefore, must be stored up somewhere sufficient to maintain him, and to supply him with the materials and tools of his work.

The division of labor cannot proceed without a previously accumulated stock, and as it proceeds more and more capital must be accumulated to accommodate labor, which has increased in quantity and productivity and can handle a larger amount of material. By capital Smith at times means an agglomeration of things, at other times an investment fund, and blended with these concepts is the idea, derived from the Physiocrats, that capital consists of "advances" made by the employer for the maintenance of his labor force.

Capital is accumulated as the result of a preceding act of saving, that is, of abstaining from consuming income. Hence,

parsimony, and not industry, is the immediate cause of the increase of capital. Industry, indeed, provides the subject which parsimony accumulates. But whatever industry might acquire, if parsimony did not save and store up, the capital would never be the greater.

Like Turgot, Smith does not visualize that savings may fail to be invested or that there may be a time lag between the act of saving and the act of investing. Instead he holds that the portion of income that is saved "is immediately employed as a capital." This was to become the leading doctrine for a period of more than 150 years, although critical undercurrents were soon to emerge which cast doubt on the invariably beneficial character of saving. To Smith, savings did not represent "leakages" from the income stream because he taught that what is saved is also consumed, not by the saver but by a different set of people, "laborers, manufacturers and artificers, who reproduce with a profit the value of their annual consumption." Smith belittles the possibility of hoarding money, and to him money is primarily a medium of exchange, with which people will want to part to acquire commodities. In contrast with the thought of the mercantilists, an inadequate money supply was not a problem to Adam Smith and the classics, who found themselves in an environment in which the introduction of paper money might seem to have stilled some earlier causes for concern. Those that nevertheless continued to operate were easily quieted by the assumptions of price flexibility and full employment. Say's law of markets is thus contained in the thought of Smith.

DOMESTIC AND FOREIGN TRADE

As for the different uses of capital, Smith, unlike the mercantilists, places no special value on its employment in foreign trade. On the contrary, he considers domestic trade more productive than foreign, since the capital employed in domestic trade will generally encourage and support a greater quantity of productive labor at home and raise the domestic national income more than would an equal investment in foreign trade. Nevertheless, foreign trade has an important function to fulfill because it opens up a market for goods produced in excess of domestic requirements and provides opportunities for the employment of capital accumulated in excess of the needs of the home economy. Once economic conditions favor exports these will be made, and they do not need special encouragement by public policies. Nor should the government interfere with imports and reserve the home market for domestic producers. Smith's free-trade doctrine is firmly grounded in the principle of absolute advantage.

It is the maxim of every prudent master of a family, never to attempt to make at home what it will cost him more to make than to buy. The taylor does not attempt to make his own shoes, but buys them of the shoemaker. The shoemaker does not attempt to make his own clothes, but employs a taylor. The farmer attempts to make neither the one nor the other, but employs those different artificers. All of them find it for their interest to employ their whole industry in a way in which they have some advantage over their neighbors, and to purchase with a part of its produce, or what is the same thing, with the price of a part of it, whatever else they have occasion for.

What is prudence in the conduct of every private family, can scarce be folly in that of a great kingdom. If a foreign country can supply us with a commodity cheaper than we ourselves can make it, better buy it of them with some part of the produce of our own industry, employed in a way in which we have some advantage. . . .

According to the supposition, that commodity could be purchased from foreign countries cheaper than it can be made at home. It could, therefore, have been purchased with a part only of the commodities, or, what is the same thing, with a part only of the price of the commodities, which the industry employed by an equal capital would have produced at home. . . .

Regulations that subvert this order reduce the national income below what it would be under free trade. Under free trade the allocation of productive resources is improved in the sense of yielding a higher income than would accrue under protection, with its monopoly of the domestic producer. Smith, however, is no doctrinaire exponent of an immutable dogma. He rejects the infant industry argument in favor of protection but upholds the defense argument, defense being always more important than opulence. He also grants that there may be an occasional use for retaliatory tariffs and that, if tariffs are to be eliminated, this is to be done gradually rather than in the form of a single drastic step that will doom all those who have invested in skills and capital.

THE TASKS OF GOVERNMENT

Smith never developed a full-fledged theory of government and his discussion of the functions of government is not influenced by any general principle other than that of laissez faire. But although he endorsed laissez faire, a careful examination of *The Wealth of Nations* reveals that he assigned to government a substantial variety of tasks. He opposes governmental restraints on the operation of the free market, that is, most but not all mercantilistic interferences with foreign trade, with the freedom of entry into occupations, and with the free play of competition. But he explicitly upholds the three general functions of government to provide protection, justice, and certain public works. More specifically he endorses the regulation of paper money banking, public enterprise in transportation, patents and copyrights, usury laws, public education, and even the grant of a temporary monopoly to a company in search of new trade in remote regions. As a rule, however, his criterion of the propriety of a government enterprise is its ability to yield a profit.

CANONS OF TAXATION

The best known of Smith's contributions to public finance is his enumeration of the four canons of taxation. Taxes, he holds, should be equal, certain, convenient, and economical. By equality in taxation Smith did not mean a formal equality which might well violate requirements of equity. Instead he had in mind taxation in accordance with the principle of ability to pay, the latter being measured by a person's income. Smith was aware that a given tax might not fulfill all four canons equally well but might live up to each of them in different degrees. He considered a substantial measure of inequality tolerable, but not even a small degree of uncertainty, which would put the taxpayer at the mercy of the tax-gathering authorities and open the door to corruption. Smith's discussion of this matter sheds light on an insight of a more general importance. The goals of economic policy are usually varied and are not always perfectly compatible. Hence the pursuit of one goal may involve cost in terms of the relative neglect of another.

INFLUENCE OF SMITH'S THOUGHT

Smith's book was an instantaneous success and the liberating effects of his thought were to be felt by many generations. T. H. Buckle, the English historian of civilization, considered *The Wealth of Nations* "in its ultimate results probably the most important book that has ever been written," one that has "done more towards the happiness of man than has been effected by the united abilities of all the statesmen and legislators of whom history has preserved an authentic account." According to Walter Bagehot, "the life of almost every one in England—perhaps of every one—is different and better in consequence of it." Profound and pervasive as the impact of *The Wealth of Nations* was, it took time to take effect. Thirteen years after its publication the French Revolution began, an earthshaking event whose impact was not limited to France. New thought was now looked upon with much suspicion everywhere, lest it be a forerunner of political upheavals. Many Englishmen discovered in Smith's doctrine of free trade and in his critical attitude to the institutions and public policies of the past a subversive spirit kindred to that which had fueled the fires of the French Revolution. The entire field of political economy came under suspicion as harboring dangerous thoughts inimical to the preservation of the old order. Hence, little was published during the remaining decades of the eighteenth century, and the next notable work to come out in England, that of Malthus, was free from any taint that would invite accusations of radicalism.

In France, Smith's message of economic freedom touched a sympathetic chord in the thought of some of the liberal *philosophes*. Condorcet, the great libertarian, whose ideas about the unlimited progress of mankind were to provoke the opposition of Malthus, studied *The Wealth of Nations* and wrote notes that were appended to some French translations of the work, of which several were published soon after 1776. Madame de Grouchy, Condorcet's widow, prepared a translation of *The Theory of Moral Sentiments*. During the French Revolution attempts were made to establish political economy as a subject of academic instruction, but under Napoleon the liberal taint of the new science, whose precepts ran counter to the emperor's economic warfare, prevented a resumption of these efforts. It was not until 1815, when Napoleon's rule finally came to an end, that political economy became acceptable as an academic discipline. In this year lectures on the subject were initiated at the Athénée of Paris, an institution offering higher adult education, and in 1820 a professorship—not of political economy but of the apparently safer "industrial economy"—was established at an institute of technology, the Conservatoire des Arts et des Métiers. This was followed in 1832 by the founding of a chair of political economy at the Collège de France.

SAY

The first professor charged with instruction in the new science at the three French institutions was Jean-Baptiste Say (1767–1832), the offspring of a Protestant family of textile merchants which after the revocation of the Edict of Nantes had sought temporary refuge in Switzerland. Say was a businessman, publicist, and man of letters, whose varied background had been enriched by travel in England and a career that led him from banking, life insurance, and newspaper and editorial work to entrepreneurial pioneering in the newly mechanized French cotton spinning industry. In 1788, at the age of twenty-one, he read *The Wealth of Nations*, but fifteen more years had to pass before he published in 1803 his *Traité d'économie politique,* a two-volume work which made him the principal apostle of Adam Smith in Europe and North America. When this work came out, Say held an important government post under the consulate, which he later lost because of his liberal views and independence of mind. After Napoleon became emperor in 1804, the authorities disallowed the publication of a second edition of Say's book, and Say himself left Paris for a period of several years to start a new career as a manufacturer. After his return to Paris a second edition of his work was eventually published in 1814, with three more to follow during his lifetime as well as translations into English, Italian, and Spanish. As academic instruction in economics began to spread, Say's work became a widely used textbook throughout Europe as well as in the United States. An English translation, published in 1821 under the title *Treatise on Political Economy,* which was later reprinted in many editions, was used at many institutions of higher learning, at Harvard as late as 1850 and at Dartmouth as late as 1870. Both Jefferson and Madison assured Say of hospitable reception in the United States were he to seek refuge there. Jefferson thought highly of Say and wanted to offer him the professorship of political economy at the newly founded University of Virginia. He considered his book "shorter, clearer and sounder" than *The Wealth of Nations.*

It was no accident that the book of a Frenchman would become the foremost instrument of propagating Smith's thought in the early nineteenth century. French writers have the great gift of orderly and coherent exposition, which displays logic and consistence in a manner especially suited for purposes of instruction. Thus Say found an eminently attractive and satisfying pattern in which the different parts of the new science fell into their places, a pattern that eventually became a tradition of long standing—the division of economics into production, distribution, and consumption, to which was later added circulation, or exchange. This arrangement was to be repeated countless times in the literature of economics, especially in the synthesis of textbooks, down to our own time.

As for the substance of Say's thought, it could not fail to reflect two facts: he was born almost half a century after Smith, and he was a man whose work was influenced by intimate knowledge of the business world, including the production side. Smith had been acquainted with James Watt, the great Scottish inventor, whose workshop stood in the shadow of Glasgow University. Joseph Black and James Hutton, the fathers of modern chemistry and geology, were close friends of Smith's and served as his literary executors. But Smith's very closeness to these men and their works prevented him from viewing the changes wrought by them in their full perspective. Say, being so much his junior, showed a much greater awareness of the profound scientific and technological advances of the time.

Say realized that he lived in a new age. All knowledge, he said, is of very recent origin. The direct stimulus exerted by science on industry is indispensable for industrial progress; besides, science promotes a rational view of the world which again gives an impulse to industry. Within the preceding hundred years, Say holds, scientific advances and techological progress have greatly increased productivity, that is, have caused the same input to yield a larger output or made it possible to produce the same output with a smaller input. Because Say is more impressed with technological progress than were the Physiocrats, the distribution of the fruits of this progress constitutes to him an issue of great relevance. The solution of this issue, he firmly believes, is low prices. His statements that "a country is rich and plentiful in proportion as the price of commodities is low" is in line with Smith's thought but sharply at variance with the physiocratic gospel of high prices. As a hypothesis designed to drive home his point of view, Say speaks of continued cost reductions, which eventually would bring the cost of production down to zero. Then all goods would become free goods like air and water, and the economic problem would be resolved. "Political economy would no longer be a science; we should have no occasion to learn the mode of acquiring wealth; for we should find it ready made to our hands." As yet such a status has nowhere been achieved, but along many lines of productive activity cost reductions have been impressive. What to Say was a hypothesis became a forecast, albeit a qualified one, in Keynes's essay entitled "Economic Possibilities for Our Grandchildren." Written during the depth of the Great Depression, this essay takes the optimistic view that in the absence of certain obstacles the economic problem of production might be solved within a hundred years. Still later, as Western societies grew more opulent, Galbraith's *Affluent Society* heralded the solution of the economic problem of scarcity in our own time.

Say finds fault with Smith for attributing only to labor the power of producing value. To Say, it is human industry, combined with nature and capital, that produces value. Say thus introduces the threefold division of the factors of production into labor, land, and capital, a division that was to become the standard in nineteenth-century economic literature. Say's view of value underlines the importance of utility, although he fails to develop a full-fledged theory based on this subjective element. Production, he argues, is not the creation of matter—only nature can create matter—but of utility. Value measures the utility of a good, price measures the value. Utility is created not only by those who produce tangible goods but also by those who render services, for example, in trade or transportation. These thoughts make Say a forerunner of the subjective theory of value, but a forerunner more of the thought than of the full-fledged theory, of which there were earlier pioneers in French economic thought.

Say's own experience with the rising industrial capitalism of his time makes him rediscover also the entrepreneur, of whom Cantillon had spoken, and who is now again introduced as—in the words of Say's translator:

the master-manufacturer in manufacture, the farmer in agriculture, and the merchant in commerce; and generally in all three branches the person who takes upon himself the immediate responsibility, risk, and conduct of a concern of industry, whether upon his own or a borrowed capital.

The entrepreneur will often employ some capital of his own, but his returns as an entrepreneur must be conceptually separated from his returns as a capitalist. The entrepreneur sets in motion every class of industry, but not every class requires the same great gifts of entrepreneurship. It is the scarcity of entrepreneurial talent and the risk that the entrepreneur bears—not only of loss of fortune but also of loss of character—that account for his high reward. When he employs outside funds, he must have connections and a good reputation. Regardless of the method of financing, entrepreneurship

> requires a combination of moral qualities that are not often found together. Judgment, perseverance, and a knowledge of the world as well as of business. [The entrepreneur] is called upon to estimate with tolerable accuracy the importance of the specific product, the probable amount of the demand, and the means of its production: at one time he must employ a great number of hands; at another, buy or order the raw material, collect laborers, find consumers, and give at all times a rigid attention to order and economy; in a word, he must possess the art of superintendance and administration. He must have a ready knack of calculation, to compare the charges of production with the probable value of the product when completed and brought to market. In the course of such complex operations there are abundance of obstacles to be surmounted, of anxieties to be repressed, of misfortunes to be repaired, and of expedients to be devised. Those who are not possessed of a combination of these necessary qualities, are unsuccessful in their undertakings; their concerns soon fall to the ground and their labor is quickly withdrawn from the stock in circulation; leaving such only as is successfully, that is to say, skilfully, directed. Thus, the requisite capacity and talent limits the number of competitors.

SAY'S LAW

Say is known as the writer who developed the law of markets, a law named after him which to this day figures prominently in the discussion of economic theory. In the American edition of Say's work, his law is stated in such versions as "it is production which opens a demand for products," or "a product is no sooner created than it, from that instant, affords a market for other products to the full extent of its own value." On the basis of this proposition, Say's thought is interpreted as having contained a denial of the possibility of general overproduction. According to Say, if there is overproduction of specific commodities, this is a result either of misdirected production or of a decline in the production of other commodities wherewith to buy the commodity of which there is overproduction.

Say's thoughts were endorsed by Ricardo and his followers but attacked by Malthus, Sismondi, and others. Throughout the various editions of his work, Say took note of these attacks and attempted to buttress his position by inserting new material and reformulating the old, a procedure that did not enhance the clarity of his presentation. To the present day the meaning of Say's law has remained controversial. Interest in the controversy has been heightened by the importance given to Say's law by Keynes, who employed it as a target in his attack against the classics, and by Patinkin, who considered it in connection with his critique of the logical adequacy of classical and neoclassical economics. Reasonable and definitive conclusions in these matters are difficult to produce, however, not only because Say's thought is not always free from obscurity but also because his thought is interpreted in the light of modern concepts and tools of analysis with which Say, of course, was entirely unfamiliar.

Those who employ Say's law as a target to attack classical economics usually interpret it as a tautological identity in the sense that the total demand for commodities is identical, that is, always equal to their supply. The implications and ramifications of the identity are then pointed out in the light of the barter argument, the invariant cash balances, the equality of saving and investment, the absence of the money illusion, the indeterminateness of the economic system, and the real-balance effect. A detailed analysis of all these matters would require a survey of modern monetary theory, and only a brief review can be given here.

The barter argument sheds light on the fact that Say's identity is unreservedly consistent only with an economic system in which barter prevails. In such a system commodities do indeed exchange for commodities and every "sale" of one commodity is a "purchase" of another. Such a barter economy may employ money as a unit of account but not as a store of value.

The argument drawn from the constancy of cash balances points out that in a monetary economy, which employs money as a medium of exchange and store of value, the identity will hold true only if people have no desire to change their cash balances, that is, if they purchase commodities only with the proceeds from the sale of other commodities and not from cash balances, and if they use such sales proceeds only for purchases of other commodities rather than add them to their cash balances.

The saving-investment relation will constitute no problem in such an economy, since only the invariant cash balances that people happen to desire serve as a store of value. The remainder of the money supply serves only as a medium of exchange. No one will want to "hoard" any part of it, and savings are immediately transformed into investments. In an alternative version, supply is said to create its own demand since the aggregate cost of production is spent for the aggregate product.

Since in this economy money and commodities are not in a relation of substitution, the relative prices of commodities are in no way affected by changes in the quantity of money. If the quantity of money changes, commodity prices will change equiproportionately. That is, if the quantity of money doubles, so will the money prices of all commodities. Such insensitiveness of individuals to changes in the price level is known as the absence of the "money illusion." Money is here considered a mere "veil" which conceals the action of the real forces in the economy. In an alternative version, money is said to be "neutral" since it does not affect the relative prices of commodities, these being the same as they would be under conditions of barter. In still another version, there is said to be a "dichotomy," or divorce, between the theory of relative prices and the theories of money and of the price level. This compartmentalization of the respective theories is supposedly a feature of classical and neoclassical economics, with consequences detrimental to their validity. In again another version, the relative prices of commodities are formed under conditions characterized by the "homogeneity postulate," that is, the demand functions for commodities, since they depend only on their relative prices, are, mathematically speaking, "homogeneous of degree zero in money prices." This means again that the prices of commodities will change in the same proportion in which the quantity of money changes.

(1) The indeterminacy argument stresses that a monetary economy in which Say's identity holds fails to have its prices determined by the market forces operating within the economic system. Regardless of the quantity of money, the money market is always in equilibrium as are the relative prices of commodities, however large or small they are in monetary terms. In the mathematical language of the Walrasian general equilibrium system, the system of equations cannot be solved and hence is indeterminate because the number of unknowns—the prices—exceeds by one the number of equations, one equation not being a genuine one but an identity—the demand for cash balances in excess of their invariant amount being identically equal to zero.

(2) The argument derived from the "real-balance" effect points to the possibility of removing the indeterminacy and the resulting contradictions. The indeterminacy can be removed by introducing a genuine equation containing information about people's demand for cash balances, either in the form of the equation of exchange $MV = PT$, or, if V is replaced by its reciprocal k, in the form of the Cambridge equation $M = kPT$. Empirical evidence demonstrates that the demand for cash balances is not invariant. Instead it will reflect changes in the price level that make themselves felt as the real-balance effect. According to the real-balance effect, people, in the face of changes in the price level, will want to maintain the real value of their cash balances, by adding to them if prices rise and by reducing them if prices fall. If they behave in this manner, they will violate both the homogeneity postulate and the related identity of Say: changes in the price level will induce people to substitute cash for commodities or commodities

for cash, with effects on the relative prices of commodities. Thus, once the real-balance effect is admitted, Say's law in the form of the identity cannot hold.

Those who are inclined to interpret Say's law as an identity in the sense here discussed can indeed find support for their view in a number of passages from Say and other classical writers. To Say, money is neutral or a veil: the value of money "plays no part in real, or even in relative variation of the price of other commodities. One product is always ultimately bought with another, even when paid for in the first instance in money." There is no demand for money as a store of value: "Money, even when employed as capital, is never desired as an object of consumption but merely as one of barter; every act of purchase is an offer of money in barter, and a furtherance of its circulation. The only part withdrawn from circulation is what may be hoarded or concealed, which is always done with a view to its reappearance."

Even here, however, Say makes allowance for people's desire to add to their cash balances from time to time, and in another context he qualifies a statement that "no act of saving subtracts in the least from consumption" by adding "provided the thing saved be reinvested or restored to productive employment." Elsewhere he discusses the painful circumstances that may attend the introduction of machinery, with the resulting "state of inactivity" of the capitalist's funds and distress among the unemployed workers, which he proposes to relieve through "the construction of works of public utility at the public expense." In the light of statements such as these it is doubtful whether Say meant to imply that the total demand for commodities is identical, that is, always equal to their supply. But if this is doubtful, a general principle of interpretation requires that he be given the benefit of the doubt and that his thought, if possible at all, be credited with a content less absurd than that implied by the identity. To produce such an interpretation, it is necessary only to transform his alleged identity into an equality that would hold true in equilibrium or would be indicative of a tendency. Say's law would then come to mean that the total demand for commodities is equal to their total supply in equilibrium, a situation that the forces operating in the economy would tend to approximate.

The difficulty with this interpretation, however, is that Say provides only the scantiest information about how the mechanism bringing about such an equilibrium position is supposed to operate. In fact, all he gives is a hint about variations in the rate of interest as an equilibrating factor. In a letter to Malthus he speaks of excessive savings and mentions that these carry their remedy with them. "Where the capitals become too abundant, the interests which the capitalists derive from them become too low to balance the privations they impose upon themselves by their savings."

It is Say's incomplete treatment of the mechanism of adjustment that is stressed by those who reject the interpretation of his law as an equality in the sense here indicated. What then is left of Say's law is a statement of the interdependence of total supply and total demand. The demand for anyone's product originates from the supplies of everybody else because these supplies, transformed into money, constitute demand. If everyone were to restrict his supply, the result would be a general restriction of demand. In this sense Say's law fits into the general pattern of his argument in favor of economic freedom and in opposition to restrictions on production imposed by public policy or private monopoly. His is a fight against what Veblen was later to call "capitalistic sabotage," the restriction of output characteristic of the monopolist. In this sense, Say's law also lends support to his free-trade argument. If unhampered domestic production is the best guarantee of a market for everyone's supply, so also is unhampered foreign production. Obstacles to a country's exports will vanish if it admits imports from its trading partners and if these do not restrict their own output. "The import of English manufactures into Brazil," Say holds, "would cease to be excessive and be rapidly absorbed, did Brazil produce on her side returns sufficiently ample; to which end it would be necessary that the legislative bodies of either country should consent, the one to free production, the other to free importation." Say did not recognize that more than "free production" might be necessary to stimulate economic growth in under-developed countries, but his insight that goods—imports—must pay for goods—exports—became an important part of nineteenth-century free-trade doctrine, an insight the validity of which few would doubt in the absence of widespread service trade and capital movements.

If interpreted as a recognition of the general interdependence of demand and supply, Say's law not only does not conflict with Keynes's law—everybody's income is someone else's expenditure—but the two laws actually coalesce. It was not, however, in this weak and restricted sense that Say's law was interpreted by those early nineteenth-century economists who were alarmed by what they considered an inadequacy of general demand and who opposed Say's view about the impossibility of general overproduction. These writers—Malthus, Lauderdale, and Sismondi—brought about sub-stantial transformations of the thought of Adam Smith in their search for theories of stagnation and crises. As time went on, it was not their approach that came to prevail during the nineteenth century but the opposing view of Ricardo and his followers. In this controversy, Say's law stood in the center. Malthus denied its validity, whereas Ricardo upheld it.

Say's law of markets, as stated by its author, was vague and invited a variety of interpretations—the three given here are by no means inclusive. But Say's very vagueness stimulated further thought and contributed to mak-ing his law the most alive part of classical economics—most alive because most widely discussed. Had he stated his thought unequivocally and in a cut-and-dried fashion, there would have been little comment on it.

Chapter 12

MALTHUS'S
POPULATION DOCTRINE
OF SELF-DENIAL

The economics of Thomas Robert Malthus (1766–1834) fall into two parts, one devoted to population problems and the other to the inadequacy of aggregate demand. The former are discussed in *An Essay on the Principle of Population,* published in 1798, whereas the deficiency of general demand forms the subject of Malthus's *Principles of Political Economy,* which appeared more than twenty years later in 1820. For a long time Malthus's fame was mainly derived from the *Essay,* the basic idea of which was endorsed by Ricardo and Mill. Only since the 1930s, when aggregate demand has once more been recognized as constituting a central problem in economics, has Malthus come into his own as the author of the *Principles* and received recognition as a forerunner of modern thought.

The message contained in Smith's economic of self-reliance had been one of moderate optimism: If people were allowed to arrange their affairs in accordance with their own interest, untrammeled by government, they would make a substantial contribution to the solution of the economic problem of scarcity. In the writings of Malthus much is done to dispel this optimism. Malthus does not question the laissez faire basis of Smith's economics but he is at pains to demonstrate that even under laissez faire a country would face severe obstacles to economic well-being, one of these obstacles being the pressure of population.

Malthus did not develop his thoughts in opposition to the moderately cheerful outlook of Smith but to the more extravagant variants of the spirit of optimism characteristic of the Enlightenment. The great Kant spoke of the Enlightenment as man's emancipation from a self-imposed nonage. Other thinkers of the age extolled the radiant prospects open to mankind once it attained maturity and allowed itself to be guided by reason. The French Revolution did indeed deify reason, and with reason enthroned, progress, it was hoped, would raise mankind to ever greater heights of material and spiritual well-being. There were prophets of progress in France and in England as well, where the French Revolution, which coincides with Malthus's formative years, was a matter of high hopes to the libertarians and a cause for alarm to the authorities and their allies. While Burke denounced the French Revolution in ringing phrases, Thomas Paine, whose *Common Sense* of 1776 had ushered in the Declaration of Independence, in the early 1790s shocked many Englishmen by attacking, in the *Rights of Man,* monarchy and aristocracy and proposing such radical economic reforms as a steeply progressive income tax with which to finance family allowances and old age pensions. There were mass demonstrations, and working class societies sprang up to promote manhood suffrage and other reforms. The government attempted to prosecute the agitators, but as some English juries refused to convict them, it eventually, in 1795, secured passage of the notorious Two Acts which severely restricted free speech and assembly.

In times as troubled as these, when the country was torn by dissension, opinions might vary even within a family. So they did in the Malthus family, headed by Daniel, a prosperous country gentleman with eight offspring, who led a life of leisure intermingled with varied intellectual pursuits that brought him in touch with Hume and Rousseau. His ancestors had passed on to him a substantial estate that was preserved by his father and grandfather, each of whom had only one child, but Daniel had broken this tradition. Daniel's son, Thomas, had been a student at Cambridge and after graduation with honors in mathematics had taken holy orders in the Anglican church, his ambition then being "a retired living in the country." In spite of some apprehension about an hereditary speech defect he was ordained at the age of twenty-two and subsequently became a fellow of one of the Cambridge colleges. Eight years later, in 1796, he left Cambridge and began service as a curate at the place of his father's residence. It was then that father and son came to talk about the burning questions of the time, the father, an optimist, siding with the two then best known prophets of progress and the son finding fault with their arguments. The son then put his thoughts on paper and published in 1798, with the fathers's encouragement, his *Essay on the Principle of Population, as It Affects the Future Improvement of Society, with Remarks on the Speculations of Mr. Godwin, M. Condorcet, and Other Writers.*

GODWIN AND CONDORCET

The history of ideas abounds with views that were formed in opposition to parental authority. Malthus as well as Godwin and Condorcet is an example of this. Just as Malthus, when rebutting Godwin and Condorcet, assailed the views of his father, so did Godwin and Condorcet develop their views of the world in conflict with their parents. Godwin, the grandson and son of dissident ministers and a lapsed cleric himself, was repelled by the narrow puritanism of his father and never forgot the reprimand he received when as a child he profaned the Sabbath by playing with a cat. Condorcet, educated by Jesuits after having been brought up by a devout mother who consecrated him to the Virgin and made him wear girls' clothes until he was nine, became an ardent follower of Voltaire in his twenties and outdid him in his anticlericalism.

The names of Godwin and Condorcet, the two prophets of progress with whom Malthus took issue in the first edition of his *Essay*, are now known only to specialists in intellectual history, but in the 1790s their fame was widespread and their writings made a profound impression. Godwin's and Condorcet's watchword was the perfectibility of man, whom they saw demeaned and shackled by vile institutions restraining the growth of his reason. In line with the motto of the French Revolution, "liberty, equality, fraternity," they were libertarians and egalitarians. William Godwin (1756–1836) was the husband of the first suffragette, the father of the author of *Frankenstein*, and the father-in-law of Shelley, who worshipped Godwin's ideas and by transforming them in his poetry secured for them an audience long after the dust had settled on Godwin's tomes. Godwin had many other enthusiastic disciples, among them Coleridge, Southey, and Wordsworth.

Godwin's principal work, *Political Justice*, was published in 1793, and two more editions followed during the 1790s. To forestall prosecution by the authorities, who recently had secured the conviction of Paine for seditious libel, the two-volume work was deliberately priced at three guineas, a sum large enough to restrict its sale and thereby reduce the risk of prosecution. The work did indeed contain a plethora of dangerous thoughts, but its author's lack of enthusiasm for representative democracy, the wave of the future, diminished its long-run influence. Godwin, a philosophical anarchist, found fault with all forms of organized government. Smith had taught that "if virtues were supreme among men, government would be unnecessary." Godwin believed that virtue could and would become supreme, relieving the need for government and enabling small communities to settle their affairs without coercion. Men can become virtuous by accepting the supremacy of reason. Reason, in turn, depends on knowledge, and "the extent of our progress in the cultivation of knowledge is unlimited." Social and technological inventions "are susceptible of perpetual improvement." Reason will induce men to share property and labor equally, making a daily half hour work by all sufficient to produce the necessities of life. Godwin's insistence on the gradual and nonviolent character of progress, on a revolution of opinion, is in line with the later development of British socialism, and his awareness of the potentially evil effects of democratic majority rule on minorities anticipates related thoughts of Mill.

In Godwin's opinion, the pressure of population constitutes no threat to the earthly paradise ushered in by the rule of reason. He speaks of "the principle of population," coining the phrase later employed in the title of

Malthus's *Essay,* and explains it in these words: "There is a principle in human society, by which population is perpetually kept down to the level of the means of subsistence." But where population pressure operates, it is the result of wicked institutions rather than of an inexorable refusal of nature to yield needed supplies. Under such institutions, agricultural production in Europe is restricted by "territorial monopoly." Were it not so, five times as many people could be maintained. Moreover, three-fourths of the inhabitable earth, taken as a whole, is uncultivated. With agricultural productivity on the rise, "myriads of centuries of still increasing population may pass away, and the earth be yet found sufficient for the support of its inhabitants." Godwin cites Benjamin Franklin's opinion that "mind would one day become omnipotent over matter," and as a conjecture, he anticipates that the growth of reason, having made man the master of his environment, will also make him the master of his body, improve his health, prolong his life, and teach him to master his passions. Thus, "when the earth shall refuse itself to a more extended population," he "will probably cease to propagate."

This conclusion of Godwin's—that there need be no undue concern about population pressure—was in substance not unlike the conclusion that Condorcet arrived at about the same time. The Marquis de Condorcet (1743–94), after remarkable accomplishments in mathematics and philosophy, had entered politics as a reformer and during the French Revolution had become president of the Legislative Assembly. Unlike Godwin, Condorcet was not an anarchist but a believer in representative government who gave much attention to questions of constitutional law. A close friend of Turgot and an associate of Paine, his thought reflected all facets of the age of Enlightenment. The coming age of liberalism was to bring to fruition many ideas which he espoused: civil liberties, abolition of slavery, emancipation of women, separation of church and state, and public education at all levels. His wife, the translator of Adam Smith and Paine, was the sister of the future marshal Grouchy, whose failure at Waterloo brought to an end the Napoleonic age. Condorcet was considered an extremist during the early stages of the French Revolution, but later, when moderation was dangerous, he was held to be a moderate, and as such became a victim of the Terror. Outlawed, in hiding, and under the shadow of the guillotine, he spent the last months of his life writing a universal history, depicting it as the story of man's progress to eventual perfection. In a reversal of opinion following the execution of Robespierre and the end of the Terror, this *Sketch for a Historical Picture of the Progress of the Human Mind* was after his death published at government expense in 1795, with an English translation appearing during the same year.

The last chapter of this work contains Condorcet's views about the future of mankind, which are marked by unbounded faith in the progress of science. Inequality among nations will vanish with the spread of enlightenment, which will bring to the underdeveloped world the fruits of European civilization. Public education will relieve inequality within a nation, as will economic reforms such as cooperative credit and old age security. Improvements in education will in turn stimulate scientific and technological progress. "Not only will the same amount of ground support more people, but everyone will have less work to do, will produce more, and satisfy his wants more fully." Man's life span will increase, as will his moral and intellectual capacity. Population pressure will not ring down a curtain over Condorcet's earthly paradise. As the population increases, the growth of knowledge will open up new methods of sustaining an ever larger number of people. Even if the population should approach the limits of subsistence, this day will be far off. Long before, the growth of reason will prevent man from peopling the world with numbers which it cannot support. However, Condorcet was a Frenchman, and, unlike Godwin, he does not derive this conclusion from faith in man's ability to master his passions. He speaks of man's duty to give happiness rather than existence to those as yet unborn, but about the method of implementing this duty he is silent.

During the nineteenth century, elements of Condorcet's thought were resuscitated by Saint-Simon and Comte, who saw in him a forerunner of their own ideas about the rational organization of society. In the England of the 1790s his views were highly controversial, so much so that a conservative such as Burke would include him in the "swinish multitude" who corrupted learning by disassociating themselves from the clergy and the nobility. In Scotland, where the connection with the continental Enlightenment was especially strong, the conservative reaction was even more severe. Dugald Stewart, professor of moral philosophy at Edinburgh and probably the first to teach a separate course on political economy in Britain, found it necessary to apologize for having mentioned Condorcet's name with respect.

PLEAS FOR EQUALITY

Many were particularly impressed, as others were offended, by Godwin's and Condorcet's pleas for greater economic equality. Such pleas were then also emerging from other sources, French and English: from land reformers such as William Ogilvie (1736–1819), erstwhile student of Adam Smith and later professor of humanity at Aberdeen, who advocated a single tax on land; from Thomas Spence (1750–1814), who agitated in favor of the expropriation of land owners; from still earlier French precursors of communism such as Morelly, an unknown author who espoused his ideas both in prose and in verse in the mid-eighteenth century; and from the Abbé de Mably (1709–85), Condillac's brother, who criticized the natural order of the Physiocrats as one of avarice, greed, and folly. Mably in turn inspired Babeuf (1760–97), who proclaimed a revolution greater than the original French one, and one to end all revolutions, whose conspiracy of the Equals opened up the history of modern socialism. This conspiracy had been suppressed by the French government and Babeuf had been executed when Malthus was at work writing his *Essay*.

THE FIRST *ESSAY*

Malthus' first *Essay* was a reply to the two prophets of progress. Where they had preached optimism, Malthus insists on pessimism. Their belief in the perfectibility of man finds him skeptical:

> A writer may tell me that he thinks man will ultimately become an ostrich. But before he can expect to bring any reasonable person over to his opinion, he ought to show that the necks of mankind have been gradually elongating; that the lips have grown harder and more prominent; that the legs and feet are daily altering their shape; and that the hair is beginning to change into stubs of feathers.

He then goes on to establish two postulates, first, that food is necessary to man's existence, and second, that the passion between the sexes is necessary and will remain nearly in its present state. On the basis of these postulates he concludes that "the power of population is indefinitely greater than the power in the earth to produce subsistence for man." This is so because population, when unchecked, increases in a geometrical ratio, whereas subsistence at best increases only in an arithmetical ratio. Nature, by making man's existence dependent on food, makes the two powers equal, and it does so by checking the growth of population whenever it presses against food supplies. The two checks are vice and misery.

> This natural inequality of the two powers of population, and of production in the earth, and that great law of our nature which must constantly keep their effects equal, form the great difficulty that to me appears insurmountable in the way to the perfectibility of society.... I see no way by which man can escape from the weight of this law which pervades all animated nature. No fancied equality, no agrarian regulations in their utmost extent, could remove the pressure of it even for a single century. And it appears, therefore, to be decisive against the possible existence of a society all the members of which should live in ease, happiness and comparative leisure; and feel no anxiety about providing the means of subsistence for themselves and families.

This is a summary of Malthus's principle of population, which he finds confirmed by experience, "the true source and foundation of all knowledge." Now, as Malthus admits, the lessons of experience are inadequate as far as the maximum growth of which population is potentially capable is concerned. No one knows how fast population could increase if there were absolutely no restraints on its growth. Never in history were manners "so pure and simple, and the means of subsistence so abundant, that no check whatever has existed to early marriages; among the lower classes, from a fear of not providing well for their families; or among the higher classes, from a fear of lowering their condition in life. Consequently in no state that we have yet known has the power of population been left to exert itself with perfect freedom."

If empirical evidence sheds no light on the potential maximum of population growth, an approximation must suffice. Such an approximation Malthus believes to have found in the demographic situation of the United States. There the means of subsistence have been more plentiful, the manners of the people more pure, and the checks to early marriages fewer than in Europe. In the United States the population has been observed to double in twenty-five years. Such an increase is "short of the utmost power of population," but as it approximates it and reflects actual experience, Malthus accepts it as the basis of his rule "that population, when unchecked, goes on doubling itself every twenty-five years, or increases in a geometrical ratio."

Again, in the matter of agricultural production, Malthus had no empirical data on hand which would show the maximum that could be accomplished. The most that he can conceive is growth by an equal increment that is added to agricultural output in each period, an increase in an arithmetical ratio. Taking the period as one of twenty-five years, he illustrates the two progressions to run as follows:

YEAR	1	25	50	75	100	125	150	175	200	225
POPULATION	1	2	4	8	16	32	64	128	256	512
SUBSISTENCE	1	2	3	4	5	6	7	8	9	10

That is, population, if unchecked, would increase 512 times after 225 years, the food supply only ten times.

Agricultural statistics at Malthus's time being virtually nonexistent, his empirical evidence for the arithmetical progression of the food supply is weaker still than that for the geometric progression of the population. To make his argument as convincing as possible in this situation, he insists that either estimate is a moderate one—the growth potential of the population, if it were truly unchecked, would go beyond the doubling every twenty-five years, and the assumed equal increment to the food supply during the same period exceeds what can be hoped for in reality. That relatively little can be hoped for Malthus ascribes—in substance but not in modern technical detail—to diminishing returns.

If on this showing the population tends to increase so much faster than the food supply, "the constant operation of the strong law of necessity" must keep population in check so that it does not outrun the means of subsistence. Moreover, population is controlled by subsistence in a still broader way. Not only does subsistence check its growth but where there is subsistence growth will occur: "Population does invariably increase where there are the means of subsistence." As a proof of this, Malthus again refers to the lessons of history. The general control of population by subsistence, in the sense that population will increase when the food basis makes an increase possible, is, however, an afterthought which Malthus introduces only incidentally. His principal argument relates to subsistence acting as an ultimate restraint on population growth. The means by which this restraint manifests itself are the two checks of vice and misery, "these too bitter ingredients in the cup of human life." If the population increases before the food supplies have expanded, food prices will rise and real wages will fall. In the ensuing distress, population growth temporarily comes to a halt. Meanwhile the reduction of wages encourages the increased employment of labor on the land, food supplies rise, and eventually a new stimulus to population growth sets in motion a renewed "oscillation."

The checks of vice and misery may affect either the birthrate, when they are known as "preventive," or the death rate, when they are "positive" or repressive. The positive check operates mainly in the poorer classes, among whom infant mortality is high and who usually suffer from inadequate nutrition, overcrowded conditions, and resulting ill health. The preventive check, most conspicuous among the upper classes, nevertheless permeates the entire society. People delay getting married because of fear of poverty or loss of status. Although there are passages foreshadowing a less restrictive view, Malthus considers such a delay productive of vice or misery.

From the principle of population Malthus derives the conclusion that public relief to the poor defeats its own purpose. Although well-intentioned and possibly alleviating somewhat the intensity of individual misfortune, it only spreads the distress by causing the prices of provisions to rise without adding significantly to their volume, which, should it increase, would only induce a further growth of population. Poor relief encourages sloth and waste. Poor laws embolden people to found families for which they cannot provide and therefore "create the poor which they maintain." What society gives to the poor it takes from others who are more deserving. Lest it be an incentive to sloth and waste, "dependent poverty ought to be held disgraceful." In connection with his discussion of poor relief, Malthus indicates that he favors the preventive check over the repressive one:

> Every obstacle in the way of marriage must undoubtedly be considered as a species of unhappiness. But as from the laws of our nature some check to population must exist, it is better that it should be checked from a foresight of the difficulties attending a family and the fear of dependent poverty than that it should be encouraged, only to be repressed afterwards by want and sickness.

But although the preventive check may have redeeming features compared with the repressive one, the world of the first *Essay* nevertheless is one of deep gloom. "To prevent the recurrence of misery is, alas, beyond the power of man." Godwin and Condorcet attribute responsibility for the evils of the world to social institutions, and these they propose to change. To Malthus the evils of the world are due to the condition of man, which is given and cannot be changed. Hence, Malthus rejects as pointless the reorganization of society urged by the two, and a large part of the *Essay* is devoted to showing up the inadequacy of their remedies. Greater equality will not relieve population pressure but rather aggravate its effects. If everyone could claim an equal share in the community's output, it would induce people to marry hastily and produce offspring for whom they would have no personal responsibility. Population would increase rapidly and would leave little to be divided.

By attributing to the condition of man rather than to social institutions a good deal of the world's unhappiness, Malthus was likely to give offense to those who wanted to uphold the benevolence of the creator. To fend off criticism, the last two chapters of the first *Essay* aim at the reconciliation of Malthus's principle of population with a view of the world assuming a providentially ordered universe. Want, he argues, stimulates exertion, and exertion favors the growth of the mind. Thus the evil produced by the operation of the principle of population is offset by "a great overbalance of good." Man "really is inert, sluggish, and averse from labor," and without the pressure of population he would never have emerged from the savage state nor would the world have been peopled. The principle of population prevents "the vices of mankind...from obstructing the high purpose of the creation."

With these thoughts the first *Essay* comes to an end. It was an essay in the true sense of the word: a brief test or trial of a particular idea. It was written cogently, with verve, and with the persuasive power of a man who has a message to offer to the world. As it touched on matters in which people took a profound interest—reason, man's perfectibility, social progress, in short, the basic ideas of the Enlightenment which were now questioned by those whom the course of the French Revolution had alienated—it immediately received a great deal of attention. Many readers were drawn to Malthus because he used William Godwin as his foil, a man at the height of his fame in the 1790s. By employing Godwin's thoughts as a peg on which to hang his own, Malthus could not fail to secure a wide audience.

The book was an enduring success, and Malthus kept it before the public by bringing out five subsequent editions during his lifetime. Having established himself as a writer in the field of economics, he relinquished his work as a clergyman—from 1803 to his death he was nominally in charge of a parish but did not reside there and had the work done by curates—and in 1804 he accepted an appointment as professor of history and political economy at the East India College, eventually located at Haileybury, an institution designed to train future employees of the East India Company. Among the small and unruly student body of the college Malthus was known as "Pop." His was the first chair in Britain to be distinguished by the name

MALTHUS'S
POPULATION DOCTRINE
OF SELF-DENIAL

"political economy," although in his case this was still blended with history. As his fame spread, he was elected to membership in the Royal Society, and similar honors were bestowed on him by the learned societies of Prussia and France. Sociable and affable, he was a charter member of the Political Eoconmy Club and of the Royal Statistical Society, which was founded in 1834, the year of his death. In 1811 he had introduced himself to Ricardo, and for the next twelve years, until Ricardo's death in 1823, the two great men were linked by a firm friendship and lively correspondence, in which they threshed out many doctrinal points on which they differed. Differences of opinion did not diminish their mutual attachment and respect, and when Ricardo died he left Malthus a small legacy as a token of his friendship.

REVISIONS OF THE *ESSAY*

The successive editions of the *Essay* are marked by the accretion of new material diminishing the prominence originally given to the views of Godwin and Condorcet, writers now no longer in vogue. The ideas of Paine and later those of Owen serve Malthus as new objects of criticism and rebuttal. If Owen was the first British socialist, Malthus may be said to have been the first academic critic of British socialism. As for other changes, the second edition of the *Essay*, published in 1803, was in many respect a new work, whose form, method, and substance set the pattern for the later editions. In the first *Essay*, a volume of some fifty thousand words, Malthus appeals to experience and pays his respects to it, but in spite of these protestations his argument is mostly a deductive one. As edition follows edition, the empirical material, taken from demography and history and gathered by means of reading and foreign travel, becomes more and more plentiful, making the second edition four times as large as the first and much harder to read and filling two or three volumes in the later editions. By far the most important change introduced in the second edition of 1803 is the supplementation of vice and misery by a third check, which Malthus calls "moral restraint." This was meant to refer to a preventive check consisting of the postponement of marriage, with continence observed during the delay, and a resulting restraint on the birth rate. Since the checks to population growth are no longer exclusively evil, the message of Malthus's second and later editions is not so gloomy and oppressive as had been the original version in the first *Essay*. Although it may not have been meant as one, the change is a concession to Godwin, who had sought out Malthus soon after the publication of the first *Essay* and had tried to impress on him the significance of prudence as a check to population growth, an approach in line with Godwin's belief in the power of reason over passion. There may have been an empirical basis for Malthus's new approach. He had become engaged in the meantime and did not marry until appointed to his academic post at the age of thirty-eight. The years of his protracted engagement may have taught him the lesson which he now enunciates: that such a status need not be marred by vice or misery.

Although Malthus may have had doubts about the extent to which the third check of moral restraint was in operation or could be put into operation, he made it the basis of his policy proposals. The aim of these is the reduction of poverty:

> The object of those who really wish to better the condition of the lower classes of society, must be to raise the relative proportion between the price of labor and the price of provisions, so as to enable the laborer to command a larger share of the necessaries and comforts of life.

Hitherto relief to the poor has given them encouragement to marry, with the result that the labor market has become overstocked. The labor supply has been increased where it should have been reduced. The possibilities of expanding food production, limited as they are, need not be neglected. But this effort alone will not bring about the desired increase in real wages. It must be combined with another effort:

> Finding, therefore, that from the laws of nature we could not proportion the food to the population, our next attempt should naturally be to proportion the population to the food.

Preventing the population from reaching the subsistence level is the only effective method of improving the condition of the poor. To achieve it, people must be imbued with the spirit of moral restraint. Malthus then goes on to consider four prerequisites for the growth of prudential habits: security of property, legal equality to accord dignity to the lower classes, the spread of representative government, and improvements in education. Like Adam Smith he sees man as being impelled by the desire to better his condition. Better knowledge, greater dignity, a feeling of personal responsibility, and the fear of degradation will induce man to live up to this impulse by following the commands of prudence. To Adam Smith self-reliance was the clue to the solution of the economic problem. To Malthus it is self-denial.

Viewed as a part of the pattern of his time, Malthus, the advocate of representative government and popular education, was not a reactionary but a progressive Whig. Like Jefferson he had a predilection for rural life and misgivings about cities. Although his views at times coincided with those of the spokesmen of the landowners, his own economic interests were not identical with theirs. In the *Principles of Political Economy* he referred to himself as one "who never received, nor expect to receive any [rents]."

The most striking part of Malthus's population doctrine was his two ratios. They were the most original as well as the weakest of his ideas and also, because of the impression of scientific exactness which they gave, those that perhaps more than others helped to make his book a great success. By concentrating on population pressure as the cause of poverty, and by holding the poor responsible for population pressure and the evils resulting therefrom, he shifted the responsibility for the most urgent social and economic problems from the upper classes and from government, which at his time still represented them, to the poor themselves. This transfer of responsibility constitutes another break with the ideas of Smith, who had blamed the bad practices of government for so many economic evils. Neither Smith nor Malthus was aware of the technological revolution that began during Smith's time and became so important during the nineteenth century. Malthus failed to anticipate the huge expansion of agricultural production, as he also failed to anticipate the spread of birth control.

FORERUNNERS OF MALTHUS

Malthus was aware that he had many precursors. That population must always be kept down to the level of subsistence he considered an obvious truth and one that had been observed by many writers. It was the skillful and systematic combination of many strands of thought, the dramatization of a vital issue, and the timeliness of the problem that secured for Malthus's work a much larger measure of recognition than had been accorded to his precursors. The clash between man's powers to generate and to find subsistence had been recognized as early as 1588 by the Italian Giovanni Botero in his *Greatness of Cities,* translated into English in 1606. That evil will produce good and, more specifically, that evil will restrain population growth were ideas discussed by Dr. Mandeville, the lover of paradoxes, who had included physicians and druggists among the checks to an increase of the population. Cantillon had ventured the opinion that, unless checked by the lack of subsistence, people would multiply like mice in a barn. Steuart had spoken of population growth in terms of a spring restrained by a weight representing the need for subsistence. Calculations of the time it takes a population to double had been attempted by a number of writers, including Petty and Benjamin Franklin. Malthus's check of prudence was suggested by Godwin as well as by the Italian Giammaria Ortes (1713–90), whose *Reflections on Population,* published in his native tongue during the year of his death, also anticipates Malthus's idea of a cleavage between the geometrically progressing population and the growth of subsistence. Ortes was rash enough to speak of three billion as an absolute limit to population growth. Whether Malthus was acquainted with his book is a matter of conjecture. He did not repeat Ortes's statement that children would serve as the nourishment of their parents.

In addition to a number of French writers on population during the eighteenth century, there was the Presbyterian minister Robert Wallace (1697–1771), Hume's opponent in a famous controversy about the question whether population had grown or declined since classical antiquity. Wallace, the author of a work entitled *Various Prospects of Mankind* (1761), was an egalitarian, but unlike Godwin and Condorcet a pessimistic one, who considered his ideally ordered society threatened by population pressure, which would occur in a distant time when the whole earth was cultivated like a garden. Godwin had taken Wallace to task for his pessimism, although to Malthus, who thought the threat imminent, he was not pessimistic enough.

INTERPRETATIONS OF MALTHUS

Different generations have placed different interpretations on Malthus's population doctrine, and not all interpreters have had a correct understanding of his work. A common misunderstanding relates to the point at issue between Malthus and Wallace: contrary to a widely held opinion, Malthus did not consider population pressure merely a matter for future concern but believed that "the period when the number of men surpass their means of subsistence has long since arrived" and that this cause of periodical misery has existed in most countries throughout recorded history. In spite of this view, and this leads to another common misinterpretation, Malthus was not an opponent of a large population nor of population growth as such. Instead he speaks of a large population as one of "the two grand *desiderata*," the other being the reduction of poverty and dependency. In the first *Essay* he had held that "population increases exactly in the proportion that the two great checks to it, misery and vice, are removed; and that there is not a truer criterion of the happiness and innocence of a people than the rapidity of their increase." Throughout his life he had to defend himself from attacks attributing different views to him:

> It is an utter misconception of my argument to infer that I am an enemy to population. I am only an enemy to vice and misery, and consequently to that unfavorable proportion between population and food which produces these evils.

Malthus, and this brings up another misinterpretation, never *advocated* vice and misery. If he was not immoral, was he then as hardhearted as many interpreters make him out? At times he presents his views so forcefully that he gives the impression of gloating over human misfortune. This is apparent in a famous passage of the second edition of the *Essay*, which he deleted in later editions:

> A man who is born into a world already possessed, if he cannot get subsistence from his parents on whom he has a just demand, and if the society do not want his labor, has no claim of *right* to the smallest portion of food, and, in fact, has no business to be where he is. At nature's mighty feast there is no vacant cover for him. She tells him to be gone, and will quickly execute her own orders, if he do not work upon the compassion of some of her guests. If these guests get up and make room for him, other intruders immediately appear demanding the same favor.

The report of a provision for all that come fills the hall with numerous claimants. The order and harmony of the feast is disturbed, the plenty that before reigned is changed into scarcity; and the happiness of the guests is destroyed by the spectacle of misery and dependence in every part of the hall, and by the clamorous importunity of those who are justly enraged at not finding the provision which they had been taught to expect. The guests learn too late their error in counteracting those strict orders to all intruders, issued by the great mistress of the feast, who, wishing that all her guests should have plenty and knowing that she could not provide for unlimited numbers, humanely refused to admit fresh comers when the table was already full.

Malthus objected to the construction of houses for the poor lest this encourage them to marry. He was relentless in his opposition to poor relief, of whose gradual abolition he was an untiring proponent. But he did all this because he considered poverty a symptom of population pressure, to be relieved by higher real wages resulting from a reduction of the labor supply. Like Smith he preached the gospel of high wages and accused of hypocrisy those who ostensibly were eager to lift up the poor but at the same time insisted on keeping wages down.

The close reader of Malthus's book will find in it not only a plea for free education for all but also, although displayed inconspicuously, the endorsement of free medical care for the poor (in "disastrous accidents, unconnected with habits of indolence and improvidence"), public assistance to emigrants, relief to poor families with more than six children (not as a reward but to relieve distress), and restrictions on child labor in factories.

Malthus has often been depicted as insensitive to the deeper feelings of man and to his need for love. Again, his attitude was the opposite. He exalts love and places it far above the enjoyments of the intellect:

Perhaps there is scarcely a man who has once experienced the genuine delight of virtuous love, however great his intellectual pleasures may have been, who does not look back to that period as the sunny spot in his whole life, where his imagination loves most to bask, which he recollects and contemplates with the fondest regret, and which he would wish to live over again.

Without love and affection the comforts of life lose half their attraction:

The evening meal, the warm house, and the comfortable fireside would lose half of their interest if we were to exclude the idea of some object of affection with whom they were to be shared.

It is love that gives dignity and happiness to human life:

The passion between the sexes has the most powerful tendency to soften and meliorate the human character, and keep it more alive to the kindlier emotions of benevolence and pity.

Considering then the passion between the sexes in all its bearings and relations, and including the endearing engagement of parent and child resulting from it, few will be disposed to deny that it is one of the principal ingredients of human happiness.

Malthus's doctrine must not be interpreted as containing an explicit or implicit approval of birth control. His check of moral restraint, the only one he advocated as a remedy against population pressure, referred exclusively to late marriages, with strict continence to be observed during the premarital period. Malthus in fact opposed birth control, the check to which Condorcet had alluded, as both immoral and an incentive to sloth. He did not elaborate on the moral issue but stressed the economic one by expressing fear that the indolence of the human race would be greatly increased if married people were able to limit the number of their children at will.

In 1820, when Godwin was in his sixties and forgotten by the world, he replied to Malthus at length in a discursive volume, *On Population*. In it Godwin denied the urgency of the population problem and anticipated that as time went on the food supply would increase and the birth rate would slow down. The book is a testimony to the strength of Godwin's intuition since it contains references to developments unheard of at Godwin's time such as the production of synthetic food, the utilization of the nutritive elements of the sea, and the introduction of machinery in agriculture.

FRANCIS PLACE

In 1822 the population problem was reviewed again, this time by Francis Place, the radical tailor and follower of Bentham, in his *Illustrations and Proofs of the Principle of Population*. Place (1771–1854), a self-made and self-taught man, had risen from poverty and obtained a respected position in the reform movement of his time. Himself the father of fifteen children, he had begun to study Malthus's doctrine soon after the publication of the first *Essay* in 1798. Through Ricardo he had borrowed Malthus's own copy of the fifth edition of 1817, and he studied it with the greatest care. He was now ready to comment on it, and his comments were those of a friendly critic. Place was under the spell of the radical views of Godwin and other reformers, but he had also become alarmed by Malthus's population doctrine. As a radical, he would not share Malthus's view which attributed poverty to population pressure arising from man's condition rather than to institutional arrangements and public policies which the radical program of reform wanted to change. As a disciple of Malthus, he was concerned about the complacency with which Godwin looked at the population problem. As a man of humble origin who had mixed with the lower class all his life, he had no confidence in the effectiveness of Malthus's third check, that of moral restraint.

Place was thus both a follower and a critic of Godwin and Malthus, and his book in a way tries to reconcile their views. He was impressed with both the need for reform and the immediacy of the population problem. Malthus would not induce him to abandon his program of social and economic reforms—the promotion of trade unionism and workers' education, freedom of the press, introduction of the penny postage, repeal of the corn laws, of the combination acts, and of the hated "taxes on knowledge" imposed on newspapers and periodicals—reforms which were eventually to change the social structure of nineteenth-century England. Nor would Godwin induce him to relax his efforts to reduce the pressure of population. And as he had no faith in Malthus's preventive check of moral restraint, he instead recommended another preventive check, one which Malthus would classify as vice, that is, contraception.

Place's book contains one of the earliest defenses of economically indicated birth control in the English language, albeit only in a handful of pages in a book containing some 270 pages. He brought into the open a matter that most of his contemporaries considered too delicate for discussion, and he recommended what the Church of England, that of Malthus, did not sanction until 1929 and what is still in substance forbidden by the Roman Catholic Church. Place was not the first writer to refer explicitly to birth control. Pierre Bayle, whose *Dictionnaire* of 1697 heralded the rise of modern rationalism, mentioned it as common in the sixteenth century and even more widespread in the seventeenth. Bayle's context is a medical one as he refers to the matter in an entry devoted to a prominent physician. In 1797, exactly one hundred years later, and a year before the publication of Malthus's *Essay*, the subject recurs in an economic context when Bentham, another outstanding exponent of rationalism and an inveterate social inventor, recommends birth control as a means of reducing the taxes levied to finance poor relief. James Mill, from 1808 a close associate of Bentham's, in 1818 had an article on "Colonies" in the supplement to the *Encyclopaedia Britannica*, where he recommended birth control, although ambiguously and in guarded language, as he was to do again in his *Elements of Political Economy* of 1821. Mill had known Place from about 1808; they became close friends and in 1812 Mill introduced him to Bentham. Through the help of Mill the manuscript of Place's *Illustrations and Proofs of the Principle of Population* was submitted to Ricardo in 1821, who thought it an able defense of Malthus and tried to interest a publisher in it. Place's ideas grew out of his own experience, the influence of Malthus, and his connection with the Benthamite circle, of which he became a leading member—the only one, however, to engage in a widespread campaign to disseminate birth control information by means of leaflets and letters. Place was one of the formative influences on young John Stuart Mill, who in 1823, at the age of seventeen, was caught by the police when distributing birth control handbills issued by Place.

From Place's book and still more so from his own and his followers' untiring propaganda activities there sprang the birth control movement of the nineteenth century in Britain and in the United States. Although birth control practices can be traced back to ancient times, organized propaganda in its behalf and the dissemination of relevant information did not develop until in the nineteenth century. In the 1860s the advocates of birth control became known as Malthusians, and in the 1880s as Neo-Malthusians, mis-nomers perhaps because Malthus had disapproved of contraception. But it was he who had sounded the alarm which made others agitate in favor of birth control.

MALTHUS AND DARWIN

Malthus's thought thus prepared the ground for the spread of a social invention that was to affect the habits of millions of people. His thought was also instrumental not in changing the world but in changing man's picture of an important aspect of it because Malthus had a decisive influence on the formation of the theory of evolution. The exponents of birth control saw in Malthus's population doctrine, shorn of its third check, the stark expression of biological necessity, of a determinism that made man a helpless victim of misery imposed on him by the inexorable forces of nature. This doctrine of necessity they rejected, rebelling against a determinism that to them was not ineluctable and from which man could escape by taking their advice. But the very thing they rejected profoundly impressed those scientists whose concern was not primarily the condition of man but the life of plants and animals and who found in the relentless working of the mechanics of Malthus's determinism an important stimulus for their own thought. Everybody had his own Malthus—the advocates of birth control one from whose biological determinism they desired to escape, and the natural scientists one whose biological determinism served as a model for their own theories. In this way, Malthus's "struggle for existence" and his geometric progression attained supreme importance in the development of nineteenth-century biology. Both Darwin and A. R. Wallace, each of whom arrived independently at the theory of evolution, have given a full and appreciative account of the debt they owed to Malthus when forming their own theories. When in 1836 Darwin returned to England after his voyage on the *Beagle,* he had, in his own words, "without any theory collected facts on a wholesale scale." Observing how man by artificial selection had successfully bred plants and animals, he was groping for a theory of evolution that would account for selection by nature. His thought had come to an impass when he happened, in October 1838, "to read for amusement Malthus on *Population.*" He was struck immediately by the light that Malthus's theory, especially the struggle for existence and the geometric progression, could shed on the evolution of plants and animals. Malthus had applied both ideas to man. By generalizing them and expanding them to cover the life of plants and animals, Darwin—and, in a similar fashion, Wallace—found the clue to the theory of evolution, according to which natural selection produces what Herbert Spencer was to call "the survival of the fittest." With the subsequent rise of social Darwinism, which applied these ideas again to the competitive struggles of man's social and economic life, the circle had made a full turn back to Malthus.

REACTIONS TO MALTHUS'S IDEAS

Marx, although he wanted to dedicate *Das Capital* to Darwin, completely rejected Malthus's biological determinism as applied to man. To him, as to Godwin and Condorcet, the ills of society were the result of bad institutional arrangements which he castigated in his critique of capitalism. There was no universally valid law of population, and what at his time appeared as a population problem was merely the symptom of other maladjustments of society curable by radical change. This view of Marx has had far-reaching effects on the population policies of his followers, and to it is due the hostile attitude of communist governments to birth control.

No nineteenth-century economist who wanted to take up the subject of population could escape the influence of Malthus. He had to come to terms with Malthus's doctrine and then might reject, accept, or modify it. In the 1820s and 1830s Nassau Senior and W. F. Lloyd, early holders of the newly instituted Drummond chair of Political Economy at Oxford, and Richard Jones, Malthus's successor at Haileybury, led the way to significant modifications of Malthus's doctrine by denying that his three checks were all-inclusive. These men were of a later generation than Malthus and their thought was already under the spell of nineteenth-century economic progress, which made class lines more fluid and dispersed what had been upper-class comforts first among the middle and eventually among the lower class.

Thus Senior added to Malthus's checks a "taste for additional comfort and convenience," which in a progressive society the laboring class would share. Lloyd thought that the desire to emulate others would lead people to prudence. Jones added "neutral checks" to those of Malthus and made them consist of the desire to satisfy unlimited "secondary wants," those in excess of the primary wants which produce physical suffering when unsatisfied. Jones noted that even the humblest agricultural workers did not spend all their wages on food and that among the higher income brackets expenditures for food constituted a declining proportion. Even the lowest income group did not press against subsistence but satisfied, however modestly, some secondary wants. Jones was an early member of the English historical school which made the propositions of the classics subject to the test of experience and raised doubts about their general validity regardless of the circumstances of time and place. He was critical of Malthus's concept of misery— Alexander the Great, he said, was miserable because there were no more worlds for him to conquer—and supplemented it with his distinction between primary and secondary wants, the latter having no limits and reflecting the everrecurring expansion of the horizon of consumption. Thus he formulated his own law of population: "As secondary wants multiply among the different classes of society, motives to prudence in regard to marriage multiply with them."

As the century wore on, the expansion of agricultural production and improvements in transportation cast doubts on the inadequacy of food supplies. Later still, when in the 1880s birthrates began their decline in western and northern Europe, an event that coincided with the spread of birth control information, Malthus's authority suffered an eclipse. However, it revived during the 1920s and again, after a lapse during the Great Depression, in the 1940s. By then Malthus's name no longer stood for his full-fledged theory but had become a symbol with which to warn the world of overpopulation. Thus Keynes, in *The Economic Consequences of the Peace* of 1919, would say:

> Before the eighteenth century, mankind entertained no false hopes. To lay the illusions which grew popular at that age's latter end, Malthus disclosed a Devil. For half a century, all serious economic writers held that Devil in clear prospect. For the next half century he was chained up and out of sight. Now perhaps we have loosened him again.

Keynes made an even more alarming statement in 1922, when for a newspaper article he supplied a photograph of "Malthus Island," a desolate rock packed with birds, with this legend:

> The guillemots on these islands off the coast of North-umberland sit shoulder to shoulder on their eggs, covering the entire superficies. If one more egg is laid another egg rolls off into the sea, by this ingenious social custom the population can be maintained in a state of stability.... The most interesting question in the world (of those at least to which time will bring us an answer) is whether, after a short interval of recovery, material progress will be resumed, or whether on the other hand, the magnificent episode of the 19th century is over.

Chapter 13

FURTHER
TRANSFORMATIONS
OF SMITH'S ECONOMICS:
The Concern
with Demand

Malthus is best remembered as a student of population, but he also has a claim to recognition as an outstanding contributor to general economic theory. This claim has been honored only grudgingly and belatedly because Malthus's transformation of Smith's economics, to which he devoted pamphlets, articles, and books published side by side with the revisions of his *Essay,* was contested by the rival transformation of Smith's ideas in the writings of Ricardo, Malthus's great friend. Contemporary opinion considered Ricardo the winner of this contest, and the Ricardian views eventually hardened into the orthodoxy of the nineteenth century, vigorously upheld by Ricardo's followers.

THE INTELLECTUAL ENVIRONMENT

The intellectual environment in which this contest took place was in many respects different from the world of Adam Smith and from that of Malthus's first *Essay.* The discussion of Malthus's contributions to general economic theory, often polemical, mirrored this new intellectual environment. There was more diversity of thought and more give-and-take. New channels of communication facilitated debate and provided outlets for the writings of the economists, who gradually acquired professional status. Smith had labored alone and unrivaled by antagonists, the latter either being in eclipse like the Physiocrats or dead like the mercantilists—the last of whom, Sir James Steuart, Smith could with impunity ignore in his great work: although physically still alive, his thought was dead. The early nineteenth century was replete with significant contributions to economics by Malthus, Ricardo, and many lesser figures. The world seemed full of economists who wanted to be heard and whose views would occasionally clash. A growing body of economic specialists took sides on general questions of theory and on practical issues of the day: the monetary effects of the Napoleonic Wars, the postwar depression, and the problem of continued protection for agriculture in an environment in which industry was growing rapidly. Opportunities for controversy arose, and they were made the most of in the great reviews which became a conspicuous feature of the intellectual life of nineteenth-century Britain: the *Edinburgh Review*, the *Quarterly Review*, and the *Westminster Review*.

THE GREAT REVIEWS

The *Edinburgh Review*, founded in 1802 by four young Whigs, espoused reform to a public that was willing to be roused from the intellectual lethargy that Tory rule combined with the fear of the ideas behind the French Revolution had instilled in it. Opportunities for reform were plentiful. Henry Brougham, one of the founders of the *Review*, listed them when seventy years later he spoke of Britain in the early 1800s:

> Protection reigned triumphant, parliamentary representation in Scotland had scarcely an existence—the Catholics were unemancipated—the test acts unrepealed—men were hung for stealing a few shillings in a dwelling-house, no counsel allowed to a prisoner accused of a capital offence—the horrors of the slave-trade tolerated, the prevailing tendencies of the age, jobbery and corruption.

By molding public opinion, the *Edinburgh Review* prepared the ground for the passage of the great Reform Bills later in the century. To many young intellectuals of the time, reform and political economy—the ideas of economic individualism and liberalism espoused by Smith—seemed bark of the same tree of liberty. It is not surprising that the pages of the *Edinburgh Review* abounded with articles about economics, and that most of the leading economists of the period contributed to it. The *Edinburgh Review* lent strong support to the views of Ricardo. Malthus was among its early contributors, but when later he disassociated himself more and more from the thought of his friend, his connection with the *Edinburgh Review* lapsed.

The *Quarterly Review* was started in 1809 as a Tory rival of the *Edinburgh Review*. It clung to the ideas of the past and had little use for the latest notions of economic freedom. Its discussion of economic matters was carried on by writers who, like the poet Southey, were distinguished in other fields but left no mark on the history of economics. Only sporadically, and not before 1820, did there appear among its contributors outstanding figures in the history of economics.

The third of the great reviews, the Benthamite *Westminster Review*, was founded in 1824. It pressed for reform more vigorously than the at times vacillating *Edinburgh Review*. On the whole the *Westminster Review* went along with the Ricardians in matters of economic theory, and in 1825 it published a most unfriendly criticism of Malthus's views by John Stuart Mill, who was then nineteen years old. As for Malthus's population doctrine, the *Quarterly Review* wavered in its attitude, but the others found no fault with this aspect of Malthus's work, Ricardo having endorsed it and the Benthamites converting its pessimism into an optimistic appeal for voluntary restraints on parenthood.

DECLINE OF SCOTTISH ECONOMICS

Nominally the *Edinburgh Review* was a Scottish establishment. All four of its founders had been imbued with the spirit of Adam Smith, the great Scotsman, the center of whose life had always been his native land. But three of them left Scotland permanently a few months after the publication of the first issue. Their move to England was a sign of the times, symbolizing the shift of the central fount of economic wisdom from the north to the south of the Clyde. To trace in detail the complex reasons for this shift would require a full-fledged intellectual history of the period. Political economy had become a Whiggish concern, one that in Scotland throve under the roof of the philosophy departments, and a secular one. The decline of Scottish political economy after the death of Smith mirrors unfavorable developments on all three counts—the Whiggish, the philosophical-academic, and the secular.

After the French Revolution the work of Whig-oriented political economists of Scotland was cramped by the pervasive suppression of dangerous thought by the Tory authorities. When the question "Will the revolution of France be of more advantage than disadvantage to Europe?" was put to a vote before a society of Edinburgh students in 1791, the response was an unanimous yes in favor of the revolution. The reaction to these attitudes of the young and of the not so young was a control of new thought and expression more severe than in England. This type of restraint was not conducive to the continuation of the Scottish tradition in political economy initiated by Hume and Smith. Smith's pupil Dugald Stewart (1753–1828), professor of moral philosophy at Edinburgh from 1785 to 1810, who began to teach a separate course on political economy in the winter of 1799–1800, was compelled to observe extreme caution in order to minimize the offense that his Whiggism gave to those in control of academic affairs. The Tory candidate who was appointed to his post in 1820 and held it until 1851 was a *littérateur*, ill prepared to teach moral philosophy and even worse equipped to resume work in political economy. An attempt made in 1825 to create a separate chair in political economy for McCulloch, the great champion of Ricardo, came to naught, and McCulloch had to look in London for an academic post.

By that time the curriculum of the Scottish universities came under fire, and unfavorable comparisons were made between the training of young

Scots in logic and moral philosophy—which had fostered the spirit of speculative inquiry of which political economy had been an offshoot—and the
emphasis of the great English universities on instruction in mathematics and
the classics. This attack, of course, did not strengthen the Scottish philosophy
departments. Still later Scottish university life was further disrupted by
sectarian dissensions, which again led to attacks, from a different direction,
on the teaching of the philosophy professors. An evangelical faction bore
down on the traditional secularism of Scottish moral philosophy, accusing
such of its exponents as Hutcheson and Smith of a "refined paganism,"
and when this faction succeeded in revamping the teaching of philosophy
in its own image, the field no longer offered much opportunity for the study
of a secular political economy.

THE POLITICAL ECONOMY CLUB OF LONDON

The founding in 1821 of the Political Economy Club of London serves
as an indication of the location of the new headquarters of political economy. The composition of the club's membership was symptomatic also of
another change: political economy, which during its flowering in Scotland
had been principally an academic concern, had now become a matter of
profound interest to businessmen, parliamentarians, publicists, and government officials. Among the thirty members of the Political Economy Club in
1821, Malthus was the only professor. The interest of the preponderantly
nonacademic component of this representative gathering of economists in
the program of the club—"mutual instruction" of the members, "and the
diffusion among others of just principles of Political Economy"—reflects the
fact that Adam Smith's message of economic freedom and individual self-
reliance had become a rallying cry for political action to resolve specific
issues. The public was aroused by these issues, especially by that of free
trade, which the founders of the club wished to promote and which was
indeed a matter of deep concern. The conflicting interests were eager to
buttress their case with the weight of economic opinion, presumably the
voice of scientific authority in this and other matters.

POPULAR POLITICAL ECONOMY

The reverential attention given to political economy in these years
and the high hopes that were placed in the dissemination of the eternal
verities presumably included in the discipline made it seem a fit subject of
popular instruction, especially of the young. Thus Mrs. Jane Marcet would
with great success publish 464 pages of *Conversations on Political Economy,
in which the Elements of that Science are familiarly explained,* a work that
came out in 1816, went through many editions—the seventh in 1839—and
established a pattern later followed by other writers. In the spirit of gallantry
for which the French are known, Say considered this work superior to those
of many male economists.

The efforts to spread popular economic education were paralleled by attempts to establish political economy as an academic discipline in the English universities. With university curricula notoriously inert, and with the Tories suspecting political economy of harboring radical ideas, it is not surprising that it took a long time to find the proper place for the new field. Malthus, the pioneer of academic economics in England, had to teach cadets, and many others made their contributions outside the halls of academe. For most of the nineteenth century, such academic positions as gradually became available at the English universities did not provide the basis for a life of undivided and sustained scholarly effort such as Smith had enjoyed. As a rule they offered sideline activities, part-time or short-term, poorly paid or not paid at all. It was not until the appointment of Alfred Marshall at Cambridge in 1885 that an academic school of thought did develop in England.

The story of economic instruction at Oxford and Cambridge, then still exclusive and sectarian and virtually the only institutions of higher learning in England, begins in 1816, the year in which Mrs. Marcet published her *Conversations*. Unpaid and with hours assigned in the afternoon lest there be interference with better established subjects, George Pryme, a young lawyer, began to deliver lectures on political economy at Cambridge. Never receiving a salary, he held this position for over forty years. He was made a professor of political economy in 1828 and thus became the first incumbent of the chair later held by Marshall. Three years earlier the banker and evangelist Henry Drummond had founded a chair of political economy at Oxford, which was endowed with an annual income of one hundred pounds but was tenable by any one holder for only five years, with the possibility of reappointment after two years. According to the terms of the endowment the professor had to deliver a minimum of nine lectures in a year, attract at least three students, and print—publish or perish!—at least one of his lectures each year, lest he forfeit the entire stipend. Nassau Senior, the first Drummond Professor of Political Economy, held this chair for two five-year terms, longer than any other incumbent during the early part of the nineteenth century.

Academic opportunities improved only slightly when in 1828 two institutions of higher learning opened their doors in London. University College was patterned after Edinburgh and was nondenominational; King's College was founded under Tory and Anglican auspices to counteract the influence of the other. The projectors of University College made provisions for a chair of political economy, with no endowment, which was held by John R. McCulloch from 1828 to 1832. At King's College the early experiences with political economy were not without incidents. Nassau Senior, who had relinquished his five-year professorship at Oxford in 1829 and two years later was appointed to King's, had to resign the post before making a start with his lectures. He had published a pamphlet suggesting a reduction of the finances of the Anglican establishment in Ireland, which maintained a large number of shepherds ministering but to a small flock. This suggestion angered the backers of the institution, who threatened to withdraw their financial support unless Senior resigned—the first academic freedom case in English economics. After this inauspicious beginning Senior's place was filled by the Reverend Richard Jones, who was appointed after much hesitation and not without doubts whether to inaugurate work in political economy after the distressing experience with Senior. The proposal was made to drop the dangerous word "economy" and instead sponsor a professorship of political philosophy, a proposal Jones averted by saying "that if the latter title were adopted he should feel himself at liberty to treat of political institutions—perhaps the ballot—which so alarmed the Conservatives that they gave way." Political economy, in the words of the same contemporary chronicler, was then "a subject of universal discussion" in London, and Jones's introductory lecture drew a large audience of about three hundred persons. The attendance fell rapidly, however, and when the third lecture was to be delivered, Jones found himself without an audience. He did not stay long at King's and after a year or two accepted an appointment as Malthus's successor at Haileybury.

With academic opportunities so limited, it is not surprising that Malthus was the only academician in the gathering of economists who founded the Political Economy Club in 1821. Among the other founder-members were such great figures as Ricardo and his mentor James Mill, and also Thomas Tooke, prominent as both a businessman and a historian of prices, and Colonel Robert Torrens, the joint discoverer of the theories of differential rent and comparative advantage. Senior was admitted to membership in 1823, and McCulloch six years later. Both Mill and McCulloch were more Ricardian than Ricardo himself. As the Ricardians were in the ascendancy in the great world of economics, so they were in this microcosm. Soon the battle lines were drawn. A year before the founding of the club Malthus had crowned his work in general economic theory by publishing the *Principles of Political Economy,* a serious challenge to Ricardo's thought, for which the Ricardians never forgave him. Their reaction is aptly described in the words of James Mill's biographer:

> The renowned Malthus, who made such a success in dealing with the one subject of population, was by no means regarded as a steady light on political economy at large. His manual of the general subject is certainly not a satisfactory performance. The survivors among the early members of the club well remember Mill's crushing criticisms of Malthus's speeches.

Malthus had not waited to launch his attack. At the very first meeting of the Political Economy Club he opened fire by proposing to debate a question bound to provoke the Ricardians, who would consider the negative a self-evident truth: "Can there be a general glut of commodities?"

MALTHUS'S CONTRIBUTIONS TO ECONOMIC THEORY

Malthus's *Principles* was the culmination of a long series of theoretical contributions, the beginnings of which are anchored in several chapters of the *Essay on the Principle of Population* of 1798. When discussing the poor laws in chapter 5, he traced the effects of changes in poor relief, that is, of transfer income, on prices, a matter to which he recurs in his *Investigations of the Cause of the Present High Price of Provisions* of 1800. In this pamphlet of twenty-eight pages, which received singular praise from Keynes, Malthus not only restates the view that relates changes in prices to changes in income but he also explicitly rejects the interpretation that sees in price changes first of all a monetary phenomenon. He considers changes in the quantity of money more likely to be an effect of price changes than their cause, and he traces the generation, by the banks, of means of payment to accommodate monetary requirements raised by higher prices and incomes. He does not fail to recognize, however, that once the quantity of money has increased, it will act as an obstacle to a return to lower prices. Malthus's view of inflation was at variance with contemporary opinion, which attributed the increase in prices to the activities of monopolists and speculators or saw in it merely a reflection of an increase in the quantity of money.

This early pamphlet by Malthus, which he wrote in two days, still has the verve and pithiness of the first *Essay*. Here Malthus the theorist is at his best as a speculative analyst, being willing to engage in what was later considered a special feature of Ricardo's rather than of Malthus's method—the construction of models based on "strong" or "extreme" cases:

> It appears to me that in the complicated machinery of human society, the effect of any particular principle frequently escapes from the view, even of an attentive observer, if it be not magnified by pushing it to extremity.

SAVING AND INVESTMENT

Chapter 15 of the first *Essay* also sheds new light on saving, which is interpreted more in line with modern ideas than with those of Smith, an interpretation that anticipates Malthus's later thought in the *Principles*. Smith, it will be recalled, had extolled the virtues of parsimony and taught that savings are "immediately" transformed into investments. Malthus now makes a distinction between Smith's frugal businessman and an avaricious miser who hoards his savings, with adverse consequences to the economy:

> The frugal man in order to make more money, saves from his income, and adds to his capital; and this capital he either employs himself in the maintenance of productive labor, or he lends it to some other person, who will probably employ it in this way. He benefits the state because he adds to its general capital; and because wealth employed as capital, not only sets in

motion more labor than when spent as income, but the labor is besides of a more valuable kind. But the avaricious man...locks up his wealth in a chest, and sets in motion no labor of any kind.

The hoarder, Malthus says, "locks up the power of producing" commodities. These contributions of Malthus—his emphasis on income, or "effective demand," as a determinant of prices and his interpretation of saving—are the more remarkable as they were made in 1798 and 1800, when he was a solitary thinker without the stimulation of the vigorous discussion of economic questions which had begun a few years later. In the 1810s when the problem of agricultural protection became a widely contested issue, Malthus wrote several pamphlets which stamp him as at best a lukewarm free trader and foreshadow the Ricardians' subsequent break with him.

CALCULUS IN ECONOMIC ANALYSIS

One of Malthus's pamphlets, the *Observations on the Effects of the Corn Laws,* published in 1814, contains what is probably the first reference in English economics to the usefulness of differential calculus for economic theory:

> Many of the questions both in morals and politics seem to be of the nature of the problems *de maximis et minimis* in fluxions; in which there is always a point where a certain effect is the greatest, while on either side of this point it gradually diminishes.

Malthus's reference to calculus was more than a casual whim. His interest in the matter went back to his student years at Cambridge, when he specifically mentioned, in a letter to his father, calculus as an important subject not adequately treated in the lectures, a subject of which he would attempt to acquire "a decent knowledge" by means of reading. In his later writings he occasionally made it a point to underline the related principle of balance or proportion, an idea he found relevant not only in economics "but throughout the whole range of nature and art." He himself did not follow up his suggestion of employing calculus in economics, perhaps because in mature years he became skeptical of mechanical tools of analysis. As he said in the *Principles,* "the science of political economy bears a nearer resemblance to the science of morals and politics than to that of mathematics." Malthus thus left it to others to carry out his suggestion about the utilization of calculus in economics, and indeed, in 1824, ten years after Malthus had alluded to the matter, Thomas Perronet Thompson published an article in the *Westminster Review* in which calculus was put to use in defining a maximum gain. Like Marshall in his *Principles* of 1890, Thompson took precautions not to alienate his readers with his mathematics, which was put into the footnotes. That such precautions were by no means inappropriate at the time is indicated by the dismal experience of Cournot, whose pathbreaking work on mathematical economics, published in 1838, was given a disappointing reception by his contemporaries.

RENT THEORY

The discussion of agricultural protection during the 1810s broadened out into an examination of related topics, especially of rent. During the Napoleonic Wars farm production had increased, as had rents as inferior land was taken into cultivation. Lest this land become idle, duties on wheat imports seemed indispensable. The issues of high rents and agricultural protection thus became interrelated; those who favored the one could not easily find fault with the other. The examination of rent absorbed the best minds in English economics, and in 1815 the modern theory of rent was born. The month of February saw the publication of no less than four pamphlets, each independently enunciating the principle of differential rent which was then in the air. Malthus may have a claim to priority since his *Inquiry into the Nature and Progress of Rent* was published early in the month ahead of the other pamphlets by Edward West, Robert Torrens, and Ricardo. He had given the matter attention in his lectures, and in the third edition of his *Essay,* published in 1806, inserted the statement that "universally it is price that determines rent, not rent that determines price." Ricardo, with characteristic generosity, acknowledged an intellectual debt to Malthus, but the theory of rent has come to be known as Ricardian rather than Malthusian, from which it does indeed differ in significant respects.

MALTHUS AND RICARDO

Malthus's *Principles of Political Economy,* published in 1820 and in a second, posthumous, edition in 1836, brought into sharp relief a number of doctrinal differences between Malthus and Ricardo, whose own *Principles* had appeared in 1817. The correspondence between the two, and Ricardo's *Notes* on Malthus's *Principles,* shows their protracted but unsuccessful attempts to reconcile these differences, which relate to the theories of value and of aggregate demand. Malthus wrestled with the theory of value in the *Principles,* in a subsequently published essay on *The Measure of Value* (1823), and in a book entitled *Definitions in Political Economy* (1827). Smith had offered a number of variants of the labor theory of value, and among these Malthus preferred "labor commanded" as a measure of value, whereas Ricardo emphasized "labor embodied." Since neither writer, however, denied that the price of a good also includes returns to factors other than labor, their views were perhaps not as far apart as they themselves may have believed—labor embodied, if conjoined with these returns, not being substantially different from labor commanded. Apart from the controversy about the adequacy of aggregate demand, those differences that remained relate to these three points: (1) Malthus included rent among the relevant returns making up the price of a good, whereas Ricardo excluded it, arguing on the basis of marginally produced goods. (2) The two differed in their choice of an unchanging, or nearly unchanging, measure of value, Ricardo preferring gold and Malthus the daily pay of common labor. Thus Malthus would convert the price of a good at a given time into the number of days of labor it could command at the prevailing pay and would repeat this procedure for other times. If at these the good would command, say, fewer days of labor, its value would be considered to have declined. What Malthus had in mind was a measure of changes in "real value" kindred to our index numbers. (3) Ricardo had no use for demand-and-supply analysis since it did not point directly to what to him mattered most as the fundamental determinant of value. Malthus, on the other hand, related cost of production to supply and fostered a demand-and-supply approach not unlike that of Marshall. "Of all the principles of political economy," he said, "there is none which bears so large a share in the phenomena which come under its consideration as the principle of supply and demand."

MALTHUS AND SAY'S LAW

By transforming the search for an absolute standard of value into an index number problem and by espousing a demand-and-supply analysis, Malthus came close to modern approaches in these matters at the cost, however, of alienating many of his contemporaries. What these found most fault with was Malthus's view of aggregate demand, and here again Malthus's opinion is more in line with modern thought than were the ideas of his opponents. By stressing the inadequacy of aggregate demand, Malthus not only differed from Ricardo and his followers but also from Jean-Baptiste Say, the French authority who had developed the law of markets named after him, which denies the possibility of general overproduction—a law of which James Mill was the co-discoverer and which Ricardo had endorsed enthusiastically.

The point at issue was, however, more than a mere denial of Say's law. By denying the validity of this law, that is, by refusing to accept a tendency of the economy to full employment and to full-employment income, Malthus shed light on an entirely new range of vistas in economic theory. In this new light there arose as a paramount task the development of a theory that would explain the determination of the national income, not merely its distribution under conditions of full employment, which was the task Ricardo had set for himself. Malthus's genius thus provided the opportunity for an entire redirection of economic thought. He broke a path, however, which at the time few cared to follow.

Malthus's theory of aggregate demand was an offshoot of the views on saving that he had stated earlier in the *Essay on the Principle of Population* as well as of his value theory with its emphasis on supply and demand. Without exploring more deeply the determinants of demand, Malthus assigned to it a place coordinated with supply in the formation of micro-economic values. He thereby laid the basis for the recognition of a further-reaching significance of demand in the determination of the total output of the economy. His own words indicate that there is a link between his micro-economics of demand and the use of the concept in macroeconomics. When "there is no effective demand for capital at home," he asks, "is it not a vain and fruitless opposition to that first, greatest, and most universal of all its principles, the principle of supply and demand, to recommend saving, and the conversion of more revenue into capital?" Saving, Malthus holds, is a national benefit or a national disadvantage according to the circumstances. In many instances it will be a sacred private duty, but there is no reason to call it a public duty. "The market for national capital will be supplied, like other markets, without the aid of patriotism."

MALTHUS'S *PRINCIPLES*

The great message of Malthus's *Principles* is the deliberate reduction of saving from an absolute to a relative virtue, a thought directly related to the passage of the *Essay* cited earlier in this chapter, where Malthus points to the adverse effects of hoarding. He admits that investment requires saving, but he also insists "that the principle of saving, pushed to excess, would destroy the motive to production. If every person were satisfied with the simplest food, the poorest clothing, and the meanest houses, it is certain that no other sort of food, clothing, and lodging would be in existence." The notion of an optimum propensity to consume (developed by Oskar Lange in 1938), was heralded by Malthus in these words:

> If consumption exceed production, the capital of the coun-try must be diminished and its wealth must be gradually destroyed from its want of power to produce; if production be in a great excess above consumption, the motive to accumulate and produce must cease from the want of an effectual demand in those who have the principal means of purchasing. The two extremes are obvious; and it follows that there must be some intermediate point, though the resources of political economy may not be able to ascertain it, where, taking into consideration both the power to produce and the will to consume, the encour-agement to the increase of wealth is the greatest.

In the light of Malthus's remarks about hoarding in the *Essay,* one might expect him to develop the thought that all savings are not necessarily invested. There are allusions to this idea in the *Principles* where, for exam-ple, he distinguishes between national and individual saving:

> National saving... considered as the means of increased production is confined within much narrower limits than indi-vidual saving. While some individuals continue to spend, other individuals may continue to save to a very great extent; but the

national saving, in reference to the whole mass of producers and consumers, must necessarily be limited by the amount which can be advantageously employed in supplying the demand for produce; and to create this demand, there must be an adequate and effective consumption either among the producers themselves or other classes of consumers.

Malthus also breaks with Smith's implicit assumption of neutral money that functions only as a medium of exchange and not as a store of wealth. He considers money "absolutely necessary to any considerable saving," and refers to several motives for holding money: to provide for children, to purchase an estate, to command labor in the future.

In another passage he speaks of "all the redundant capital which is confessedly glutting the markets of Europe in so many different branches of trade." The idea that savings may not lead to investments is, however, not fully developed by Malthus. He states, in a context relating to other matters, that "no political economist of the present day can by saving mean mere hoarding." This may not mean more than it says, that saving must not be identified with hoarding. What Malthus does develop more fully are elements both of an underconsumption theory and of an oversaving theory, which is based not so much on the failure of savings to become invested as on the excessive volume of saving and investment relative to demand. "If... commodities are already so plentiful that an adequate portion of them is not profitably consumed, to save capital can only be still further to increase the plenty of commodities, and still further to lower already low profits."

Malthus's views about oversaving secure him a place in both the history of business cycle theory and the theory of economic stagnation as they may be interpreted as rudiments of either type of theory. His views about the inadequacy of general demand are immediately derived from his theory of value: goods are valued in terms of the labor they command, and this may fall short of the labor embodied in them. In fact, there will be no demand for labor unless the value of its product exceeds the labor embodied in the product: no employing capitalist will put labor to work merely to recoup wages. Labor alone is not able to purchase the products of its industry since wages fall short of the value of the products. Hence, other classes must be relied upon to help dispose of the products, especially the idle rich and their servants. These "unproductive consumers" do not add to the supply of goods, and as they do not sell but only purchase goods, theirs is an important function in making general demand effective enough to dispose of the national product. Malthus's solution of the problem of overproduction is in line with his general preference for the landlord class, which he considers a civilizing force and an element of social and political stability. At the time Malthus was writing, the social value of this class had become a matter of dispute, and his solution of the problem of overproduction represents an attempt on his part to vest this class with the new dignity of an important economic function.

In the case of an acute depression, however, Malthus would not rely exclusively on the spending of the unproductive consumers to restore the full-employment income. In line with the ideas expressed in his pamphlet on the *High Price of Provisions* of 1800, he is skeptical about the chances of success of a merely monetary policy. Sudden contractions of the money supply should be avoided but efforts to maintain prices by a policy of plentiful money are futile. Abundance or tightness of money has generally followed and aggravated high or low prices, but seldom or never led them. The strategic variable is not the money supply but expenditure. The fiscal policies that Malthus considers indicate the independence of a mind far ahead of his time. He has his doubts about a policy of paying off the public debt from savings. He discusses the relative merits of a reduction of taxes and of an increase in government purchases of goods and services and assigns greater potency to the latter because the expansive effects of a tax reduction are limited by people's desire to save a considerable part of the remitted tax. Tax-financed public works are more effective than tax reductions if they create a greater and more certain demand for labor and commodities. Of public works, those are commended that do not produce marketable commodities which would compete with existing supplies that find no buyers. The disposal of goods in foreign markets will likewise be of help. Policies such as these will enable the capitalists "to save from steady and improving profits instead of from diminished expenditure."

MALTHUS'S MACROECONOMICS

However much or little one may think of Malthus's emphasis on the unproductive consumer as the savior of the economic order, there is no doubt that his posing the question of the determinants of total output places him in the first rank of economists. This was a question, however, not in agreement with the concerns of the economists of his time, and one that had to wait for its solution for another hundred years. That Malthus was not accorded a more generous reception when he posed the problem of the determination of the national income may be because he linked his macroeconomics with an espousal of the landlord class, a class that contemporary opinion considered destined for decline rather than ascension. At Malthus's time the landlord class was in the center of a value-loaded dispute, and Malthus's ideology was fundamentally opposed to that of other leading thinkers who did not share his preference for this class. They were repelled by the ideological taint of his macroeconomics, and rejecting his ideology as they did, they failed to appreciate the analytical possibilities that his view opened up. All this had nothing to do with questions of personal economic interest. As Malthus himself pointed out, he, who espoused the landlords, derived no income from land, whereas Ricardo, his great opponent, was the owner of large estates. If they had been guided by their personal economic interests, their roles in the dispute would have been reversed.

There remains the question of the compatibility of the thought of Malthus's *Principles* with that of his *Essay*. The *Essay*, originally published in 1798 but reprinted in revised editions both before and after the publication of the *Principles* in 1820, stresses the inadequacy of supply. The central idea of the *Principles* is the inadequacy of demand. In a formal sense the two ideas are compatible; as Malthus himself pointed out, the population doctrine of the *Essay* treats of the causes which depress population to the level of output, whereas the *Principles* treats of the factors determining output. The respective ideas are not irreconcilable, but there is a definite shift in emphasis from the inadequacy of supply in the earlier work to the inadequacy of demand in the later one. The easiest way to attempt an integration of Malthus's thought would be to interpret his population doctrine as a matter of the long run, and his view of demand as being concerned with the short run. However true this would be of Malthus's demand theory —in connection with which he called other writers to task for neglecting the short run, which might "amount to a serious sum of happiness or misery"— this interpretation nevertheless neglects the fact that Malthus considered the population pressure against food resources not a long-run tendency but an ubiquitous, permanent, and pressing problem, relevant to his own as well as to other times. It is true that both the population doctrine and the demand theory can be presented as parts of an integrated system, but there is no point in denying the break in emphasis.

Pushed aside as he was by the Ricardians, Malthus nevertheless was not entirely alone with his unorthodox views. There were two others who expressed concern about the adequacy of aggregate demand and transformed the system of Smith in a direction that led them away from Ricardo and his followers—Lord Lauderdale in Britain and Sismondi on the Continent.

LAUDERDALE

James Maitland, the eighth earl of Lauderdale (1759–1839), a member of the highest Scottish aristocracy, was a lifelong parliamentarian, who began his political career at the age of twenty-one as a pronounced Whig and ended it as an ultra-Tory and bitter opponent of the Reform Bill of 1832. He has been described as "violent tempered, shrewd, and eccentric" in his private life, and to his contemporaries and many subsequent generations of economists nurtured on the orthodoxy of Ricardian economics his economic writings seemed replete with capricious eccentricities. This is a judgment that cannot be upheld today, when his economic views appear forward-looking and informed by unusual independence and originality. Lauderdale was candid in his dissatisfaction with traditional thought and openly broke with "the superstitious worship of Adam Smith's name" in his *Inquiry into the Nature and Origin of Public Wealth*, published in 1804 and in a second edition in 1819. The book was severely criticized in the *Edinburgh Review,* and there were few who cared to associate themselves with the views of an author then considered highly unorthodox, although in modern opinion his work ranks "as perhaps the most substantial theoretical contribution in the score of years between Malthus' *Essay* and Ricardo's *Principles.*" The book found its public, however, which included Malthus, whose own work shows a number of parallels with that of Lauderdale. He referred to it in his *Principles,* keeping it at distance and deploring "the tendency to extremes," "one of the great sources of error in political economy, where so much depends upon proportions," one of his favorite ideas.

Lauderdale dismisses a number of Smith's central ideas. Labor, he holds, is no measure of value because its own value varies. The search for an invariable measure of value is as futile as was the alchemists' search for the philosopher's stone. The distinction between productive and unproductive labor has no validity. The division of labor is given a greatly exaggerated place by Smith; it is not the cause of the introduction of machinery nor do workers engaged in subdivided labor invent machinery. Capital is not adequately characterized by the statement that it puts labor into motion. Parsimony is no unqualified virtue. But Lauderdale did not spend his great gifts only on destructive criticism. On the positive side he, like Malthus, fosters a demand-and-supply approach, but unlike Malthus he fails to relate the supply to cost of production. As he derives value from utility and scarcity rather than from labor, he does not have to face the difficulties that made Smith shy away from unequivocally recognizing factors of production other than labor. Lauderdale is thus in a position to establish the trinity of land, labor, and capital as "sources of wealth" or factors of production, probably the first British economist to do so. This was again a multiple discovery, Say's threefold division of the factors of production having preceded that of Lauderdale by one year. As regards capital, it is Lauderdale's view that it does not consist of advances that set labor in motion but is a substitute for labor, rendering services that labor cannot perform at all or only at higher cost. This new view of capital enables Lauderdale to develop a productivity theory of the returns to capital which was later to receive qualified praise from Böhm-Bawerk. The upper limit to these returns is set by the wages of labor replaced by capital.

As the title of Lauderdale's book indicates, he was concerned with public or national wealth, which he refuses to identify with the aggregate of private riches. Public wealth is made up of all that is useful, whereas private riches consists of goods that have value. Since value is derived from scarcity, private riches will increase when goods become scarcer, in which case public wealth will decline. Thus if water were to become monopolized, or if there were to be a failure of a harvest, private riches and public wealth would move in different directions, the one going up and the other down.

Just as Lauderdale sees disharmony between public wealth and private riches, so he does between parsimony and the interest of society in a rising and stable income. His insistence on these disharmonies separates his thought from that of Adam Smith and makes him a forerunner of welfare economics, both of the Pigovian type which aims at the systematization of incompatibilities between private and social interests and of the new type which is concerned with the effects of different market situations on the welfare of society. Lauderdale himself did not break with laissez faire, but his themes could not fail to influence those who saw in a more active public policy a suitable instrument to reconcile public and private interests. Thus Daniel Raymond, the first American to write a monograph in the field of economics and an exponent of government promotion of economic development, would quote him with approval in his *Thoughts on Political Economy* of 1820.

Lauderdale's doctrine of oversaving is based on the consideration that land, labor, and capital are the sole sources of wealth and therefore the only means to increase it. Abstinence from expenditure and "accumulation" does not yield an addition to output. As for capital, there are limits to its usefulness, determined by the state of the arts and of technology and by the cost of labor:

> In every state of society, a certain quantity of capital, proportioned to the existing state of the knowledge of mankind, may be usefully and profitably employed in supplanting and performing labor in the course of rearing, giving form to, and circulating the raw materials produced. Man's invention in the means of supplanting labor may give scope in the progress of society for the employment of an increased quantity; but there must be at all times a point determined by the existing state of knowledge in the art of supplanting and performing labor with capital, beyond which capital cannot be profitably increased, and beyond which it will not naturally increase; because the quantity, when it exceeds that point, must increase in proportion to the demand for it, and its value must of consequence diminish in such a manner as effectually to check its augmentation. It is wonderful how the author of the *Wealth of Nations,* who successfully ridicules the indefinite accumulation of circulating capital by comparing it to the amassing of an unlimited number of pots and pans, did not perceive that the same ridicule is applicable to the unlimited increase of every branch of that description of the property of a country which constitutes its capital.

Unlike Malthus, Lauderdale did not develop these ideas during the depression following the Napoleonic Wars. Furthermore he is not alarmed by the mischief caused by thrift because he thinks that it is canceled by the prodigality of spendthrifts. Thus he can adhere to laissez faire because his principal concern is not with private thrift but with a faulty fiscal policy of the government, which desires to levy taxes with the view of retiring the public debt. If the government employs its tax revenue for the purchase of goods and services, the additional government expenditure will offset the reduction in the taxpayers' spending. But if there is no government expenditure to offset the effects of forced parsimony, aggregate demand and income must fall—the bondholders, whose securities the government has retired, are not going to spend the proceeds all at once. If they should later look for profitable investment opportunities, they will do so in vain, because the decline in aggregate demand and income has made capital redundant and destroyed such opportunities. This decline in aggregate demand—and here Lauderdale comes close to the idea of the multiplier—will be magnified by the fact that those who initially are affected by the reduction of purchases will have less to spend on purchases from others.

The association of savings with leakages—also found in Malthus's *Essay* of 1798—on which Lauderdale's doctrine of oversaving is based, was derived by him from Quesnay. Lauderdale had studied in Paris, and his work contains copious quotations from French authorities. Quesnay had taught that frugality is the mother of poverty, and Lauderdale quotes from the *Philosophie rurale* of 1763, written by Mirabeau in close collaboration with Quesnay:

> The revenue, then, properly speaking, is the groundwork of the expense. It is necessary that the revenue should be expended; for every saving in the revenue occasions a diminution of expenditure, and, by direct consequence, of production and of future revenue.

As has been seen, Lauderdale is not alarmed by private thrift because he considers it offset by private profligacy, but he does not demonstrate why the one should exactly, or almost so, cancel the other. Toward the end of his book, however, he introduces a new idea, that the distribution of wealth regulates both the direction of demand and its extent and that great inequality of wealth is the principal impediment to economic progress. In his own way he recognized that the propensity to consume reflects the distribution of income and that greater diffusion of income will raise the propensity to consume.

SISMONDI

Although Malthus and Lauderdale had their misgivings about the adequacy of aggregate demand, they nevertheless remained basically attached to the liberalism of Adam Smith, who refused to grant to the government more than a few narrowly circumscribed functions in the field of economic policy. This type of liberalism is now often characterized as *old-time* to distinguish it from the modern and more common use of the word *liberal,* which has come to mean almost the opposite. A liberal in the modern sense of the word will insist on civil rights and liberties which restrain the government vis-à-vis the individual, but he will be willing to rely on public policy for the solution of economic problems which in his opinion the market mechanism cannot overcome. The first liberal in this modern sense was Jean Charles Léonard Simonde, better known as de Sismondi (1773–1842), a name which he claimed as the offspring of an old

Florentine family, which had settled in France and then sought refuge from religious persecution in Geneva, where Sismondi was born, the son of a Calvinist clergyman. To him can be traced the bifurcation of liberal thought, and with him begins the new liberalism, which "invokes government intervention instead of reducing economics to the simpler and ostensibly more liberal maxim of laissez-faire."

These words, which Sismondi in 1827 put into the preface to the second edition of his principal work, *Nouveaux Principes d'économie politique,* first published in 1819, indicate that he was well aware of the break with the past which his thought represents. He refers to his work as an attack against an orthodoxy, and he became an early critic of industrial capitalism as it emerged in England. That the faults of the new order impressed him more than they did others reflects the greater detachment of this foreign observer, who visited England on several occasions and noticed changes not readily apparent to a permanent resident. In addition, Sismondi's awareness of social change was nurtured by a highly developed historical sense, which equipped him with an interest not only in the establishment of principles but also in historical detail and description. When he published his *Nouveaux Principes* in 1819, his reputation as a writer was already well founded. In 1801, while still in his twenties, he had published a study of Tuscan agriculture, which was followed later by many volumes of a history of the Italian republics and a history of the literature of southern Europe. Whereas these writings attest to his accomplishment as a historian and literary critic, he was also known as the author of a two-volume work on economics, published in 1803 under the title *De la richesse commerciale; ou Principes d'économie politique.* This work has a number of original features, for example, it includes an early statement ascribing the international exchange of goods to differences in factor endowments and factor prices—England, being plentifully endowed with capital, will import labor-intensive goods, such as lace from France, from countries where capital is relatively scarce and wages low. Sismondi here points the way to doctrinal developments that were brought to full fruition by Ohlin in the twentieth century but were overshadowed during the nineteenth century by the Ricardian doctrine of comparative cost, which was primarily designed to demonstrate the gains from trade.

On the whole, the *Principes* was an able exposition of the doctrines of Adam Smith and thus sharply at variance with the *Nouveaux Principes* published sixteen years later. The *Principes* brought Sismondi the offer of a professorship at the University of Vilna, and in 1819, the year in which he published the *Nouveaux Principes,* he received an offer from the Sorbonne. He turned down both and spent most of his remaining years in his native Geneva.

It is a contested issue among present-day students of economic history whether the economic position of the workers actually deteriorated during the industrial revolution in England. However this issue may be decided in the light of present knowledge, Sismondi, for one, was profoundly disturbed by what he considered the ravages of the factory system, which divorced ownership from work and created an industrial proletariat made up of unemployed and poorly paid employed laborers living in misery, toiling long hours, and continuously exposed to the double threat of machinery, which replaced them, and of competition, which depressed their wages. Employers, in turn, were in a position where they had to adapt themselves to technological change, cope with relentless competition, and face the increasing risk involved in catering to the capricious demand of wider and more distant markets. To stay in business, they were under pressure to cut prices, which they did by imposing further sacrifices on labor, the ranks of which were swollen by population growth and the employment of children. The severe depression that fell on England after the end of the Napoleonic Wars was an important factor in Sismondi's mind, and under its influence he drew a picture of the industrial economy much more somber than that contained in his *Principes* of 1803. He came to recognize the relevance of aggregate demand for the solution of the problem of overproduction, and he made a strong plea for bracing the purchasing power of the consumers to enable them to buy the national output. He not only advocated an underconsumption theory of economic fluctuations but he also raised the question of how to dispose of an increased national output among a population equipped with the smaller income earned in the preceding year, and he was thus one of the first to note the dynamic problem involved in breaking a path from one equilibrium position to another and from one period to another.

Sismondi's straightforward advocacy of economic interventionism and his policy proposals are thoroughly modern, and the eventual adoption of many of them in Western Europe and North America has gone a long way toward stabilizing the economy, breaking down the barriers between classes, instilling the working people with a middle-class mentality, and making them accept an economic order in which they have acquired a stake. They now tend to be taken for granted in the modern welfare state, but at the time Sismondi presented them they were new and radical. By means of legislation the worker is to be given a new "status," that is, dignity, and a guaranteed annual wage is to include allowances for such common hazards as illness, unemployment, and old-age dependency, which are to be considered part of the enterprise's cost of production rather than a burden on society at large. A ceiling is to be placed on hours of work, and a floor on wages. Profit sharing and other institutional arrangements are to provide opportunities for an upward mobility of the members of the working class. And to all this is added the remark—though not in the main body of Sismondi's work—that the government must cease its opposition to labor unions. This incidental proposal is, however, given less emphasis than the plea for solidarity which Sismondi sees replacing conflict between employers and employees if his proposals are adopted. The employing capitalist's property has no value without the workers' labor; the workers' economic existence depends on the property of the employer. Injury to the worker through occupational diseases and other hazards will be diminshed if the cost of such injury is placed on the enterprise—an idea basic to the workmen's compensation legislation of later years and, in a kindred form, to merit rating in unemployment compensation. Wages are not only a cost item but also a factor determining the demand for goods, and if they are not depressed, business firms will more readily dispose of their output.

Unlike Lauderdale and Malthus, Sismondi did not consider fiscal policy an instrument of economic stabilization, and he was aware of the difficulties which would remain even after the adoption of his proposals. Enterprise would still have to cope with the risks created by economic fluctuations and with the uncertainty inherent in production for distant markets. Besides establishing the principle of economic justice he finds himself unable to turn out a detailed blueprint that would provide for the solution of all economic problems. He may himself have considered his policy proposals more utopian than realistic, and there is a certain note of resignation in the concluding chapter of his work.

Although Sismondi's thought anticipates the modern welfare state and the modern concern with social justice, these were slow in coming, and during the nineteenth century many a reader of the *Nouveaux Principes* was more impressed with the faults that Sismondi found with capitalism than with his proposals for reform. Sismondi himself was no Socialist but had a romantic yearning for the simple and personal type of economic relationships characteristic of the rural economy of bygone days. He detested centralization and his suspicion of concentrated economic power made him a firm believer in widely diffused private property. But his bitter critique of capitalism was bound to provide food for thought for the Socialists. He wrote of factory labor as being divorced from ownership in the means of production, and he was one of the first writers to develop his argument not only against the background of two classes, employers and employees, but in terms of a *struggle*—the word is his—between these classes. He considered the workers *proletarians*—again his own word—who, without property, like the lowest class in ancient Rome, had only the function of providing "offspring," or *proles*—the Latin word from which the expression is derived—for the mills of capitalist society. As Marx was to note, Sismondi also spoke not of surplus value but of surplus products which the workers turn out and which are transformed into the employer's profit. He visualized difficulties obstructing the realization of profit and found them inherent in the unreconstructed capitalism which he desired to reform. Some of his thoughts and expressions could not fail to influence later Socialist writers. Their ways parted, however, when it came to Sismondi's reform proposals, because what he wanted to reconstruct the Socialists desired to abolish or saw doomed by the march of history. In the end, however, economic society in Western Europe and North America came to be organized along the pattern of Sismondi's thought rather than that of the Socialists.

During the period of political reaction that set in after the fall of Napoleon and the restoration of the continental monarchies, Sismondi's ideas found only a faint echo. His thought was too far ahead of his time to receive recognition, and disappointment turned him into an eccentric. As a token of his struggle against overproduction he would choose the feeblest and oldest worker for employment on his farm and have his house repaired by a laborer no one else would have wanted to hire. Defeated in his hopes he would write, shortly before his death in 1842: "I leave this world without having made the slightest impression, and nothing will be done."

Sismondi was the last of the three great figures in early nineteenth-century economic thought to express concern about the adequacy of demand and make this question a central point of his doctrine. Such matters as economic fluctuations, overproduction and underconsumption, and the saving-investment relationship now went underground, to be treated, if at all, in the twilight of Socialist economics and to be resurrected by conventional thought at a much later stage of the discussion. It was the commanding figure of Ricardo that came to dominate economic thinking, and in Ricardian economics aggregate demand and the determination of the national output constitute no relevant issues.

Chapter 14

RICARDIAN ECONOMICS:

Liberalism Enthroned

To be a son who rebels against parental authority may be part of the human condition. It is debatable whether this is a burden that rests more heavily on sons destined to attain greatness in later life or whether it is a common experience of ordinary people. With the exception of Adam Smith, who never saw his father, all the great classical economists had their share of rebellion against parental authority. Like Malthus before him and John Stuart Mill after him, Ricardo found himself only after having come to terms with his father. Ricardo's emancipation from the benevolent despotism of his father took the form of an outright though temporary break with his family and a permanent alienation from the faith of his ancestors. No one knows if Ricardo's early confrontation with authority in the microcosm of his personal life turned him into the advocate of laissez faire that he was to become later, one much more unqualifiedly attached to laissez faire than were Malthus and Mill, who never broke the ties to their fathers openly and abruptly.

RICARDO'S LIFE

There was little in Ricardo's early training to indicate that he was destined to become the leading economic thinker of his time. His first contact with economics—he "never thought of political economy" before— did not occur until he was twenty-seven, when at a resort he happened to come across a copy of *The Wealth of Nations*. As he later told an acquaintance, he "liked it so much as to acquire a taste for the study." This encounter symbolizes what was true of the lifework of all economists of

Ricardo's generation and of his own work as well: their thought was, first of all, a reaction to and transformation of Smith's great system. After his encounter with *The Wealth of Nations* it took ten years before Ricardo, in 1809, broke into print as an author in the field of economics. Within another ten years he reached the height of his fame. Three years later he died. Considering that Ricardo's life was short and filled with other pursuits and that his formal education was the most meager received by any great economist, his accomplishment as an economic thinker must have been due to genius.

David Ricardo (1772–1823) was born in London, the offspring of a family of orthodox Jews who had fled from the Iberian peninsula after the great wave of persecutions toward the end of the fifteenth century. They eventually settled in Holland, and from there Ricardo's father moved to London, where he prospered as a stockbroker—and presided over a large family. His son, David, the third of seventeen children, received a conventional education in local schools and from private tutors, and at the age of eleven he was sent to Amsterdam for two years to attend school, probably one that trained orthodox Jews in the Bible and the Talmud. At the age of fourteen his father began to employ him in the stock exchange. At the age of twenty-one he renounced the faith of his ancestors and married a young Quaker. The ensuing break with his family threw Ricardo on his own resources. However, a bank, impressed by the young man's reputation, came to his aid and enabled him to establish himself in a business of his own as a stockbroker, that is, a dealer and broker in government securities. Within a few years Ricardo became a rich man, and after 1814, when he was in his early forties, he gradually retired from business and turned to the life of a country gentleman. When he died in 1823, he left an estate estimated at seven hundred thousand pounds.

There are several, not necessarily consistent, stories about the rules that Ricardo observed in his speculations, the one most often repeated being that he followed these "golden rules": "Cut short your losses" and "Let your profits run on." He himself stated, although at a time when he was already a rich man: "I play for small stakes, and therefore if I'm a loser I have little to regret." Early in his business career Ricardo mainly bought and sold securities on his own account. Later he became a loan contractor who bid for new issues of government securities and distributed them among investors. During the Napoleonic Wars the fiscal requirements of the government rose substantially, and the changing fortunes of the war were accompanied by fluctuations of the prices of securities. An able financier who could anticipate the movements of the market might do extremely well. Ricardo did well and retained his integrity in the process. There had often been irregularities with loan contractors who had failed to pass on the securities to their subscribers in a rising market. There were no such complaints about Ricardo's handling of such matters, and on one occasion his subscribers presented him with a silver vase in appreciation of his integrity and "in testimony of their unanimous approval of his conduct as joint contractor."

Ricardo was not a captive of Mammon who would accumulate money indefinitely and enjoy the activity of the stock exchange. Having become a man of wealth, he withdrew to the country and cultivated his intellectual interests. In his twenties he had been attracted to mineralogy and science and in his thirties had joined the Geological Society shortly after it was founded. The decisive event in his intellectual career was, however, his acquaintance and subsequent friendship with James Mill, the follower of Bentham and philosophical radical, who was aware of the intellectual potential in his friend and goaded him to write the *Principles* and have himself elected to Parliament and would have made him a director of the East India Company if Ricardo had let him.

Mill, the son of a shoemaker, was a struggling journalist when Ricardo met him in 1808. He and the prosperous stockbroker had a common interest in current economic questions, one of which had been discussed by Mill in a pamphlet published the same year. There was more, however, that linked the two. Like Ricardo, Mill had abandoned his faith. He had been trained in his native Scotland for the Presbyterian ministry but after coming to London in 1802 he gradually lost his attachment to organized religion and became an agnostic. Mill's reform work brought him into contact with Quakers and Unitarians, a circle in which Ricardo moved as well because of his wife's connections, his geological interests which a number of Quakers happened to share, and his own affiliation with Unitarian chapels. Moreover, there was much that Ricardo admired in Mill, especially Mill's formal education, which he himself did not have. Mill had attended Edinburgh University and in the Scottish tradition received excellent training in philosophy and the classics, so much so that he would have made a splendid professor of Greek and at one time seriously considered becoming one.

Ricardo had begun his literary career in 1809 when he contributed an anonymous article to a newspaper. Other papers and pamphlets followed and formed the subject of discussions with Mill when they took walks together or corresponded with each other. The suggestion, and not the first one, that Ricardo start work on a comprehensive study of economics and also that he enter Parliament was made by Mill in August 1815. Ricardo, now rich—"Bless us all! nobody can tell *how* rich"—and with leisure time, owed it to humanity and to his own reputation, Mill wrote, to improve a science of such singular importance to the welfare of mankind. He was far better qualified than anyone else. Moreover, with his newly won leisure, Ricardo had no excuse for not going into Parliament to help improve it also. Ricardo, a modest man, remonstrated on both counts, claiming inadequate gifts of style and presentation, but after much anguish and with Mill's active help the *Principles of Political Economy and Taxation* was published in April 1817, less than two years after Mill had broached the idea. The work, of which 750 copies were printed, established the author as the foremost authority in his field, especially after a young Scotsman, John R. McCulloch, wrote a glowing appraisal in the *Edinburgh Review*.

RICARDO IN PARLIAMENT

It took Mill another two years to bring Ricardo into the House of Commons, which was then still unreformed and which Ricardo, like a few other outstanding liberals of his time, entered by having himself elected from a pocket borough, in his case one in Ireland, then united with England. Ricardo refused to undertake any obligation that would limit his freedom of action in Parliament, and he served for the five years preceding his death (1819–23) as an independent, conscientious, and respected member. Most of his speeches dealt with economic matters such as currency questions, the national debt, and agricultural distress. His proposal to levy a tax on capital and pay off the national debt was considered doctrinaire even by his friends and lost him much of his influence. In one speech he argued that "this would be the happiest country in the world, and its progress in prosperity would be beyond the power of imagination to conceive, if we got rid of two great evils—the national debt and the corn laws." Brougham, who was well disposed to Ricardo and had been an intermediary in the negotiations leading to his election to Parliament, suggested that "His hon. friend, the member for Portarlington, had argued as if he had dropped from another planet."

In political matters Ricardo invariably sided with the reformers, favoring parliamentary reforms—especially the secret ballot instead of the then prevailing open votes, a matter that he thought of greater importance than the extension of the suffrage—and the free discussion of religious opinions. He voted for a variety of libertarian measures, including a reduction of the then numerous offenses subject to capital punishment, the abolition of flogging, the maintenance of civil liberties, and support of Roman Catholic complaints about discrimination. In matters of parliamentary reform there was, of course, a certain ambiguity in the position of a parliamentarian who pleaded for the abolition of the very election procedures to which he owed his own seat—an ambiguity that an unfriendly critic did not fail to capitalize on. Here again the politicians would consider Ricardo a doctrinaire, a person who insists on the application of theories regardless of the practical problems arising from such application. In short, Ricardo's parliamentary career, although by no means a failure, was not nearly so overwhelming a success as were his careers as financier and economist. Ricardo's modesty and good disposition were features extolled by many of his contemporaries, but no one ever, even by implication, noted in him the gift of compromise, so highly valued in politics but alien to this straightforward thinker. His was the fate that so often falls on the man of thought who involves himself in politics, to be "treated as an ultra reformer and visionary," as he himself complained to McCulloch.

RICARDO'S APPROACH TO ECONOMICS

Ricardo's faults as a politician may have been his virtues as an economic thinker. With relentless logic he reduced the economic system to a few variables and then deduced conclusions which on the basis of his assumptions appeared self-evident. He was not trained in history or philosophy, but he had the sharpest of minds which enabled him to manipulate his abstractions as if they were marionettes. As one of his brothers pointed out in an obituary:

> He had not the benefit of what is called a classical education; and it is doubtful whether it would have been a benefit to him, or whether it might not have led his mind to a course of study, in early life, foreign to those habits of deep thinking, which in the end enabled him to develop the most abstruse and intricate subjects, and to be the author of important discoveries, instead of receiving passively the ideas of others.

With Ricardo, economics loses the empirical bent which had been so characteristic of Adam Smith's approach and instead becomes austere and abstract. With him economics also loses its touch with philosophy and becomes truly autonomous, that is, detached from any principles except those generated by the inner logic of its own system of thought. Ricardo was connected with the Benthamite circle through Mill and others. Bentham would say: "I was the spiritual father of Mill, and Mill was the spiritual father of Ricardo; so that Ricardo was my spiritual grandson." But whereas Ricardo's career as an economist was fashioned under the influence of Mill and he associated himself with the practical policy proposals of the Benthamites, there is in his writings no trace of an attempt to come to terms with the great questions about man and society which Bentham's philosophy had raised.

Ricardo's method was that of a stern logician arguing on a high level of abstraction, but what induced him to become an active participant and eventually the leader in the economic discussion of his time was his interest in the specific and concrete issues facing early nineteenth-century Britain. These issues arose, first of all, from the background of war finance generated by the country's involvement in the protracted Napoleonic Wars. Next to this was the shift in Britain's economic structure from agriculture to industry, a transformation more noticeable at Ricardo's than at Smith's time and one that shook British society to its foundations, welcomed by some and deplored by others. The latter were eager to retard the transformation while the former wanted to speed it up. In this issue Ricardo allied himself with the side that was to become victorious, and to the extent that ideas may be said to shape the course of history, he can be acclaimed as one of the architects of the economic order of the nineteenth century whose center was firmly established in England with a *Pax Britannica* based on the gold

THE BULLION DEBATE

From 1809 to 1813 Ricardo's economic writings—his publications and correspondence—dealt with the monetary controversy of his time. From then on his attention gradually shifted to the broader economic issues posed by the problem of protection for agriculture, and the treatment of these issues yielded a pamphlet and eventually the *Principles of Political Economy* in 1817. When Ricardo broke into print with an unsigned newspaper article on "The Price of Gold" in 1809, what has been called "the greatest of all monetary debates" was reaching its peak. Opinion was divided among the "bullionists," to whom wartime inflation was the result of monetary expansion, and the "anti-bullionists," who ascribed it to the operation of other causes. The famous Bullion Report of a Select Committee of the House of Commons, which was made a year later and on whose preparation Ricardo exerted some influence, took the side of the bullionists and advised early resumption of specie payments by the Bank of England to put a damper on monetary expansion. Gold payments had been suspended in 1797, and from then on, for almost a quarter of a century, the country was on an inconvertible paper standard. There were intermittent and on the whole moderate increases in the price of gold, foreign exchange, and commodities, and it was the interpretation of these manifestations of wartime inflation that concerned the growing troop of political economists. The matter was complicated by a number of factors which included the occasional failure of the grain harvest in England, requiring imports of grain, the continental demand for gold for purposes of monetary reconstruction after the disaster of the *assignats* in France, and the exigencies of war finance, which involved the maintenance of the army on foreign soil and subsidies to allies on the Continent.

THORNTON

When Ricardo entered the monetary debate, it had already been discussed in a number of valuable pamphlets and in an outstanding book, *The Paper Credit of Great Britain*. Henry Thornton (1760–1815), who had written it in 1802, was banker and parliamentarian, and with William Wilberforce a leader of the evangelical "party of the Saints," or Clapham Sect, which urged the abolition of the slave trade and other reforms. Like his father, who had been an early benefactor of Dartmouth College, Thornton was a great philanthropist, who gave six-sevenths of his income to charity before he assumed family responsibilities and who regularly overpaid his income tax in line with a scheme of graduation he had proposed in the House of Commons but which had failed to be adopted. Thornton's book was a pathbreaking work and was recognized as such by John Stuart Mill in his *Principles of Political Economy* of 1848. It was not a book with one great idea but a careful and balanced analysis of the circumstances attending the expansion and contraction of money in both their domestic and international aspects. Thornton traced in detail what since Marshall's time has been known as the indirect link between money and prices, that is, the effect of a change in the quantity of money on the interest rate and thereby on prices. In this connection, Thornton, in anticipation of Wicksell's distinction between the market rate of interest and the natural rate of interest, analyzed the effects of monetary expansion resulting from a divergency between "the rate of interest taken at the bank" and "the current rate of mercantile profit." In a speech delivered before the House of Commons in 1811, Thornton anticipated Irving Fisher's distinction between the real and the nominal rate of interest by pointing out that when prices are expected to rise, the temptation to borrow is stimulated by the reduction of the burden constituted by a nominally unchanged rate of interest. Like a few other writers of his time, Thornton related the quantity of money not only to the price level but also to output, visualizing the latter as rising with monetary expansion and falling with monetary contraction. Like Malthus, Bentham, and others, he espoused a variant of the notion of forced saving, and underlined the possibility of growth even under conditions of full employment: with a monetary expansion the rising level of prices enforces a reduction of consumption among those whose incomes lag and thus frees resources for investment.

In the field of international finance, Thornton was the first to note the inflow of short-term funds from abroad in response to an increase in the rate of interest. More importantly, he expanded Hume's mechanism of adjustment, operating, as it does, with the help of specie flows, to cover the case where the initial disturbance does not arise on the monetary side—Hume had emphasized changes in the quantity of money—but on the commodity side, for example, as the result of the failure of a harvest. The country will then import grain and the resulting unfavorable balance of trade will cause the exportation of gold. If there is an attending monetary contraction, lower prices may stimulate commodity exports, but such a contraction may restrain output.

RICARDO'S MONETARY THEORY

Ricardo's reaction to Thornton's ideas was a mixed one, and as he was a more forceful writer, pushing his argument by stressing a few variables, his influence on the further development of monetary doctrine over-shadowed that of Thornton. In various newspaper articles and pamphlets, most importantly in one on *The High Price of Bullion* of 1810, Ricardo espoused a narrow quantity theory of money. To him it was monetary expansion, and monetary expansion alone, that was responsible for wartime inflation, which could have been prevented if the Bank of England had remained under the discipline of the gold standard. He therefore endorsed an early resumption of specie payments and coupled this plea with a proposal for an "ingot plan," which resembled the gold bullion standard of the twentieth century. His adherence to a rigid quantity theory of money precluded the acknowledgment of a connection between changes in the quantity of money and changes in output, a connection that had to wait a century before it was rediscovered in modern monetary theory. Although he assimilated Thornton's view of the indirect link between money and prices via the rate of interest, he had no use for the idea of forced saving, to which he ascribed at most "trifling" effects. As for an unfavorable balance of trade, it could have no other cause but a "redundancy of currency" produced by monetary expansion. "The temptation to export money in exchange for goods, or what is termed an unfavorable balance of trade, never arises but from a redundant currency." To Thornton, the redundant currency might be the effect of an unfavorable balance of trade. To Ricardo, it can only be a cause: "If we consent to give coin in exchange for goods, it must be from choice, not from necessity. We should not import more goods than we export, unless we had a redundancy of currency, which it therefore suits us to make a part of our exports." Thus Ricardo denies the need for equilibrating gold movements: There is no need to export gold if its purpose is merely to lower prices in the exporting country and raise them in the importing country so that the gold will eventually return to the erstwhile exporter in exchange for commodities. Why not export commodities in the first place?

This impatience with a chain of adjustments that seems to obfuscate the eventual equilibrium is a characteristic feature of Ricardo's method of approach. This method makes him employ a sort of elliptic shorthand that suppresses facts that run counter to principles derived from the interest of the parties concerned. When taken to task by Malthus, Ricardo justifies his approach in these words:

> The first point to be considered is, what is the interest of countries in the case supposed? The second, what is their practice? Now it is obvious that I need not be greatly solicitous about this latter point; it is sufficient for my purpose if I can clearly demonstrate that the interest of the public is as I have stated it. It would be no answer to me that men were ignorant of the best and cheapest mode of conducting their business and paying their debts, because that is a question of fact, not of science, and

might be urged against almost every proposition in Political Economy.... When you say that money will go abroad to pay a debt or a subsidy, or to buy corn, although it be not super-abundant, but at the same time admit that it will speedily return and be exchanged for goods, you appear to me to concede all for which I contend, namely that it would be the *interest* of both countries, when money is not superabundant in the one owing the debt, that the expense of exporting the money should be spared, because it will be followed by another useless expense—sending it back again.

Some years later, in 1817, Ricardo brought his own procedure into still sharper relief by comparing it with that of Malthus:

It appears to me that one great cause of our difference in opinion, on the subjects which we have so often discussed, is that you have always in your mind the immediate and temporary effects of particular changes—whereas I put these immediate and temporary effects quite aside, and fix my whole attention on the permanent state of things which will result from them. Perhaps you estimate these temporary effects too highly, whilst I am too much disposed to undervalue them.

By driving matters to their ultimate conclusion, by stressing the long run, and by making time-absorbing adjustments appear to take place in-stantaneously, Ricardo at times expresses thoughts that border on the para-doxical. As he pointed out in a letter to Malthus in 1820, his object is to elucidate principles, and to do this, he imagines "strong cases." These characteristics of his approach, which stand out in his early work, have left their mark on all his writings.

However, it must not be thought that Ricardo's genius was capable only of carrying him to the heights of abstract speculation but failed when more earthbound pursuits of factual matter were concerned. He had, of course, the well-stocked mind of a successful man of affairs and was as much at home in the world of facts as he was in the world of ideas. That he was a master in marshaling huge amounts of factual material he demon-strated in his *Reply to Mr. Bosanquet's Practical Observations on the Report of the Bullion Committee* of 1811, in which he made short shrift of an attack against the bullionist position launched by an empiricist who claimed to have "irrefragable proofs of the discordance of the theory with former practice."

Ricardo returned to monetary problems in 1816, when he published his *Proposals for an Economical and Secure Currency;* in 1820, when he contributed the article "Funding System" to the *Supplement to the Encyclo-paedia Britannica;* and in 1823, the year of his death, when he prepared a *Plan for the Establishment of a National Bank,* which was published the following year. The *Proposals* reiterate his ingot plan. His last work con-tains a plea, similar to one made earlier in the *Principles,* to terminate the

Bank of England's profitable privilege of issuing paper money and transfer it instead to a government authority, an arrangement that would allow the profits from the note issue to accrue to the public.

THE GENESIS OF THE PRINCIPLES: WAGES AND PROFITS

Meanwhile the ideas that were to become the substance of his *Principles* of 1817 were gradually assuming shape in Ricardo's mind. From 1812 to 1814 he published nothing, but we know from his letters that in 1813 and in 1814 there developed in his thought a view of profits that later became the cornerstone of his system. This view was sharply at variance with the view Adam Smith had held. Smith had taught that as capital accumulates, competition causes the rate of profit to decline. Ricardo, on the other hand, related profits to wages and thereby ultimately to the cost of producing the laborer's subsistence. High costs of producing food would make for high wages and low profits; reduced costs would have the opposite effect. What interested him was apparently the empirical question of the actual course of profits during the period of the Napoleonic Wars, and this question was discussed in his correspondence with Malthus. In 1813 he wrote:

> That we have experienced a great increase of wealth and prosperity since the commencement of the war, I am amongst the foremost to believe; but it is not certain that such increase must have been attended by increased profits, or rather an increased rate of profits, for that is the question between us. I have little doubt, however that for a long period...there has been an increased rate of profits, but it has been accompanied with such decided improvements of agriculture both here and abroad...that it is perfectly reconcileable to my theory.

In March of the following year he reported to his friend, Hutches Trower, on the controversy, and concluded with these words: "Nothing, I say, can increase the profits permanently on trade, with the same or an increased Capital, but a really cheaper mode of obtaining food." And in October 1814, in a letter to Malthus, he expanded the idea and related it to what constitutes the germ of the differential rent theory:

> The accumulation of capital may be paving the way for permanently diminished profits. It appears to me important to ascertain what the causes are which may occasion a rise in the price of raw produce, because the effects of a rise, on profits, may be diametrically opposite. A rise in the price of raw produce may be occasioned by a gradual accumulation of capital which by creating new demands for labor may give a stimulus to population and consequently promote the cultivation or improvement of inferior lands,—but this will not cause profits to rise but to fall, because not only will the rate of wages rise, but more labourers will be employed without affording a proportional return of raw produce.

The next step Ricardo took was designed to make his theory of diminishing profits more convincing by relating it expressly to a full-fledged theory of differential rent. Of this latter theory, the principle of diminishing returns is an important corollary. Early in the nineteenth century, as England shifted from net exports of grain to net imports, awareness of this principle spread when attempts were made to raise domestic production. In the eighteenth century, the principle had been stated in an exemplary fashion by Turgot; Steuart had alluded to it; and a Scottish agricultural expert, James Anderson (1739–1808), had come close to enunciating the principle of differential rent. In the 1810s this matter assumed a new importance because of the great issue of protection for domestic agriculture. There was much searching for a formulation of the principle of differential rent, and in February 1815, Malthus, West, Torrens, and Ricardo (within the short span of three weeks and in this order) published pamphlets enunciating the new principle—all of them, with the exception of Torrens, referring to what later became known as extensive and intensive margins of cultivation.

The title of Ricardo's pamphlet aptly indicates the direction that his thought now takes. It reads: *An Essay on the Influence of a low Price of Corn on the Profits of Stock; Showing the Inexpediency of Restrictions on Importation.* Printers worked fast in those days, and the subtitle of his essay could refer to the pamphlet that Malthus had published the same month. In the introduction to his *Essay on Profits,* as the pamphlet is commonly called, Ricardo refers to his own "principles which regulate rent" as differing only "in a very slight degree from those which have been so fully and so ably developed by Mr. Malthus in his late excellent publication, to which I am very much indebted." In the *Essay* Ricardo employs the principle of differential rent to buttress his view that the growth of population and of capital will involve diminishing profits, a contingency he wishes to see averted by the unrestricted importation of grain from abroad.

Ricardo thus developed substantial parts of his theory of distribution covering profits, wages, and rent before he started writing his *Principles.* The *Essay on Profits* does not include a theory of value, however. In its place Ricardo employed a corn standard in which the agricultural product as well as the distributive shares are expressed in terms of corn—in the language of the time, of wheat or other grains. In terms of corn, Ricardo envisaged an increase in rent, constancy of wages, and declining profits, with the farmer's rate of profit controlling the rate of profit elsewhere in the economy. This left unanswered the question of why farm profits should have the controlling influence ascribed to them by Ricardo and why a higher money wage—reflecting a constant real wage but higher grain prices—would not raise product prices and thus leave profits untouched. The theory of value that Ricardo developed in the *Principles* and with which he then integrated his theory of distribution was to provide an answer. There is a hint to this theory of value in the *Essay* when Ricardo points out that "the exchangeable value of all commodities rises as the difficulties of their production increases."

319

PRODUCTION VERSUS DISTRIBUTION

Ricardo thus approached the study of general economics as a student of distribution, a shift in emphasis from Adam Smith who had placed the problem of production in the center. Ricardo was aware of this difference, and in a letter to Malthus in 1820 he commented on it: "Political Economy you think is an enquiry into the nature and causes of wealth—I think it should rather be called an enquiry into the laws which determine the division of the produce of industry amongst the classes who concur in its formation." The new stress on distribution was in line with the changing circumstances of the time. The transition from agriculture to manufacturing raised questions about the relative shares of landlords and capitalists, and the factory system, barely emerging at the time of Adam Smith, was well on its way, gradually bringing the labor problem to the fore. The stress on distribution was a new feature in the history of economic thought. To the Middle Ages, with its relatively immobile social order, distribution had posed no special problem, and economic thought was then primarily consumer oriented. To the mercantilists, the desire for national gain overshadowed all other considerations.

The quotation given in the preceding paragraph points to another break with the Adam Smith tradition, indicative of Ricardo's abstract generalizing method, which made him search for economic laws, a term Smith did not employ. An economic law may be the statement of an empirically observed regularity, but few economic laws, as they have emerged in the history of doctrine, are of this nature. Instead, and this applies especially to Ricardo's use of the term, they are logical constructions derived from definitions, premises, and deductions, the work of rationalism rather than of empiricism.

Ricardo's concern with distribution and his search for economic laws become immediately apparent in the preface to his *Principles of Political Economy and Taxation* of 1817. There he speaks of the three classes of society, the landowners, capitalists, and laborers, who receive rent, profit, and wages. "In different stages of society," he goes on to say, "the proportions of the produce of the whole earth which will be allotted to each of these classes...will be essentially different.... To determine the laws which regulate this distribution, is the principal problem in Political Economy." The writings of Turgot, Steuart, Smith, Say, and Sismondi, however valuable they are in other respects, have done little to resolve this problem, but with Malthus's and West's publication, in 1815, of "the true doctrine of rent," it has become possible "to understand the effect of the progress of wealth on profits and wages."

With his purpose of determining the laws that regulate distribution,

Ricardo then branches out into what constitutes the first part his work, which contains the substance of his general economic theory and includes chapters on value, rent, price, wages, profits, and foreign trade. The second and third parts, approximately of equal length, discuss taxation and miscellaneous subjects. The most important differences in the various editions consist of the addition of a new chapter, "On Machinery," to the third edition of 1821, the last published during Ricardo's life, and changes in the chapter on value.

THE THEORY OF VALUE

Ricardo's chapter on value begins with these words:

> The value of a commodity, or the quantity of any other commodity for which it will exchange, depends on the relative quantity of labor which is necessary for its production, and not on the greater or less compensation which is paid for that labor.

Ricardo's theory of value, which is summarized in this sentence, had assumed definitive shape during the preparation of the *Principles*. He wrestled with it for the rest of his life, but never relinquished its fundamentals. It forms the capstone of a structure of thought which in its essential features had been developed ahead of it, and which it now integrated and transformed into a full-fledged system, making it all but impregnable in the opinion of its author.

To Ricardo as to Smith, value is primarily exchange value rather than use value, and exchange value has three constituent elements—utility, scarcity, and labor—embodied in the good whose value is to be ascertained. As for utility, no good that fails to be useful can have exchange value, but utility does not measure exchange value. As for scarcity, it alone will determine the value of goods that cannot be reproduced by labor, such as paintings and statues that are masterpieces and rare books and coins. The value of these will reflect the strength of the demand of those who are eager to purchase them. But the number of such goods and their importance are small. Far more significant are those goods that can be reproduced in quantity by human labor, and it is to these, if produced under conditions of unrestricted competition, that Ricardo's theory of value applies, that is, their exchange value is regulated by the amount of labor embodied in them. Ricardo considers this doctrine "of the utmost importance in political economy; for from no source do so many errors, and so much difference in opinion in that science proceed, as from the vague ideas which are attached to the word value."

Ricardo rejects Smith's alternative version of the "standard measure of value," that of labor commanded. Labor embodied and labor commanded, he points out, are by no means equal, and labor commanded is a highly variable quantity, being subject to changes in the demand and supply of labor and in the prices of wage goods. He also has no use for the corn standard, which Smith had discussed, again because of the variability of such a yardstick, whose value will change with agricultural conditions, population, and public policies affecting its importation.

Ricardo then goes on to discuss a number of difficulties that the value theory of labor embodied must face. The principle that relative amounts of labor embodied rather than labor's wages determine the exchange value of goods, already qualified by the words "almost exclusively," now appears as "considerably modified" by the operation of certain factors. In the discussion of these Ricardo occasionally wavers between a theory of value aiming at the explanation of exchange ratios and one aiming at the explanation of changes in these ratios. The difficulties that the labor theory of value faces arise because of labor's lack of homogeneity and because of the employment of capital, which is associated with labor in a proportion that varies in different processes of production. There are variations also in the proportion of fixed and circulating capital, in the durability of fixed capital, and in the turnover rate of variable capital.

What all this amounts to is the recognition of the significance of the time element in the process of production—investors receive a return related to the length of time that elapses before the investment bears fruit in the form of marketable goods, and the exchange value of goods will be affected by this return to capital. Goods would exchange in proportion to the amounts of labor embodied in them if labor and capital were everywhere combined in the same proportion, if all fixed capital were of equal durability, and if the turnover rates of circulating capital were uniform throughout the economy. But since this is not so, changes in wages will affect the exchange value of goods. If wages change relative to profits, the exchange value of goods embodying a relatively large amount of labor will change in the same direction, whereas the value of goods embodying a relatively large amount of capital will change in the opposite direction, the change to be most pronounced if fixed capital with high durability and circulating capital with slow turnover are employed.

Ricardo's recognition that not only the amounts of labor embodied but wages and profits as well affect exchange values makes it possible to interpret his theory of value, not as is done conventionally as a labor theory but as a cost-of-production theory, albeit one that excludes rent. This interpretation has the endorsement of Alfred Marshall and a few others. Nevertheless, Ricardo himself, although he fully explained the modifications of his labor theory, considered them unimportant on the whole, and attached far greater importance to changes in the amounts of labor embodied as a factor responsible for changes in exchange values. Ricardo's great impact on the history of economics was made as an exponent of the labor theory of value, not of a cost-of-production theory.

Ricardo applies his theory of value to money as well by considering the value of money in terms of a commodity theory of money. If money is to be treated as a commodity, its value will reflect the amount of labor embodied in it, as in the case of other commodities. A change in wage rates would have the same effect on the price of gold as on other commodities and thus would leave relative exchange values untouched. Gold coins may be more valuable than the respective amount of bullion because they include the state's seignorage charge, which is again interpreted in terms of labor. As for paper money, "the whole charge...may be considered as seignorage."

In the *Principles* the value of money is thus interpreted in terms of the labor theory of value, whereas in Ricardo's earlier writings on monetary questions the value of money had been discussed in terms of the quantity theory of money. The change in emphasis may be due to changes in monetary conditions. When Ricardo wrote his currency pamphlets England was on a paper standard, while at the time of the publication of the *Principles* the gold standard was in the process of being restored and the need to insist on the limitation of the quantity of paper money had abated. In 1820 Malthus again brought the question of the value of paper money to the attention of Ricardo, who then seemed inclined to exempt it from the application of the labor theory of value because as a monopolized commodity it did not fall into the class of commodities to which his value theory was meant to apply.

THE INVARIABLE MEASURE OF VALUE

Side by side with developing a theory of the determinants of relative exchange value, Ricardo pursued a search for an "invariable measure of value," a yardstick with which to measure changes in what he referred to as "real," "natural," or "absolute" value. Real, natural, or absolute value was to him determined strictly by the quantity of labor sacrificed in the production of a good. If, as the result of modifications in labor requirements, the relative exchange value of two goods changes, the question arises as to which of the two goods experiences a change in its real value. For example, if a unit of cloth, which formerly exchanged for two units of corn, now exchanges for four units of corn, either cloth has become dearer or corn cheaper. Either more labor was required in the production of cloth—and this would indicate an increase in the real value of cloth—or less labor was required in the production of corn—then the real value of corn would have fallen. With the help of an invariable measure of value it would be possible to identify the good whose real value had changed.

However, the change in the relative exchange value of a good need not be the result of a change in labor requirements. As has been seen, such a change may also reflect a modification of the ratio between wages and profits. Here again an invariable measure of value would be helpful. Such a measure would make it possible to determine whether and to what extent a change in exchange value is paralleled by a change in real value, that is, in the amount of labor embodied, or whether the change in exchange value has left real value untouched and is the exclusive result of a change in wages.

Ricardo never abandoned the search for an invariable measure of value, a *chimera,* as a later student of doctrinal history has called it. He wrestled with it in successive editions of his *Principles,* discussed it in his correspondence with Malthus and others, and ruminated about it during the last few weeks of his life. Adam Smith had spoken of corn and labor as invariants. Malthus proposed the pay of a day's labor, whatever it happened to amount to in terms of money, because it would always purchase a constant quantity of labor. None of these ideas satisfied Ricardo, who came close to admitting that there was no good in existence that would satisfy the requirements of an invariable measure of value. His treatment of the matter in the third edition of the *Principles* concentrates on defining and describing these requirements, which are developed in such a way as to correspond to his theory of relative exchange value.

Hence, to be an invariable measure of value, a good would have to embody at all times the same quantity of labor; it would have to be produced with precisely the same combination of fixed and circulating capital as all other goods; and the durability of the fixed capital and the turnover rate of the circulating capital employed in its production would have to be the same as in the production of all other goods. Such a good cannot be found. However, it would greatly facilitate matters if it were possible to use gold as an approximation to a more perfectly invariable measure of value, because if this were so used, a change in the value of a good could be measured by its money price. This is the solution, tentative as it may be, proposed by Ricardo. Gold may serve as an approximation to the invariable measure of value if it can be assumed that its production requires always the same quantity of labor and that the two kinds of capital are employed in its production in a ratio coming close to the average used in the production of most other goods. A rise in wages would thus have different effects on goods, depending upon whether the employment of capital and its durability are above or below the average. The money prices of the former goods would fall, while those of the latter would rise, but the average price and the composite value of the total output would remain the same.

VALUE AND DISTRIBUTION

Ricardo was the first to develop a theory of value and integrate it with a theory of distribution and thus heralded what was to become the principal concern of nineteenth-century economic theory: value and distribution. The close link between value and distribution was to reemerge later in the work of Marx, and it was even preserved when a new theory of value, radically different from that of Ricardo and Marx, came to the fore during the 1870s.

As has been seen, it is possible to interpret Ricardo's theory of value as a cost-of-production theory, although both at his own time and later there was much reluctance to interpret it in this manner. The most profound reason for this reluctance is perhaps to be found in Ricardo's refusal to include rent among the costs of production or among the determinants of value. Thus, if his theory of value is interpreted as a cost-of-production theory, it would be one that leaves out the cost of using land resources in the process of production—not unlike a performance of *Hamlet* without the prince of Denmark. In the Ricardian theory of value and distribution the use of land is considered as costless, and rent figures as a transfer payment that is unrelated to any countervailing flow of services. Rent is paid because land is held in ownership, because it is limited in quantity, and because it differs in fertility and location. Unlike the payment of wages to the laborer and of profit to the capitalist, the payment of rent is not in the nature of an incentive necessary to elicit desired services. Instead, rent is paid "for the use of the original and indestructible powers of the soil," which are viewed as fixed in quantity and ready for utilization even in the absence of rent payments.

THE THEORY OF RENT

The theory of rent reflects the operation of both the differential principle and the marginal principle, which, related to cost of production, here makes its entry into economic theory. According to the differential principle, production costs differ for outputs produced on different plots of land as well as for outputs produced with the help of varying doses of inputs of capital and labor on the same plot of land. According to the marginal principle the exchange value of output is always regulated by the cost of production incurred under "the most unfavorable circumstances." The price of corn will thus cover the cost of production incurred at the extensive margin of cultivation, that is, on land least fertile and least favorably located but whose output is still needed to satisfy the existing demand. Alternatively, the price will cover the cost of production incurred at the intensive margin of cultivation, that is, for the output produced with the last dose of input of labor and capital required to satisfy the demand for the product.

In the light of this analysis, rent is a surplus that accrues to the owner of land which is cultivated under conditions of cost more favorable than those prevailing at the margins. It is "always the difference between the produce obtained by the employment of two equal quantities of capital and labor." Rent is not part of the cost of production, and "corn is not high because a rent is paid, but a rent is paid because corn is high." To demonstrate the process of rent formation, Ricardo starts out with the model of a new country, where land is a free good and where only the best land is utilized. No rent is paid in this first approximation of the model. Then second-grade land is taken into cultivation, resulting in the formation of rent on first-grade land, the rent being the difference in the costs of production on the two grades of land. With the utilization of third-grade land, second-grade land begins to earn rent and the rent on first-grade land rises, and so forth. Increased productivity in agriculture may temporarily arrest the rise in rent, but not for long, because as rent falls, profit moves upward, encouraging the growth of capital and of population, which in turn requires an expansion of agricultural production with a consequent increase in rent. Economic development is thus a process that works to the advantage of the landowners, and it does so in a twofold sense. They gain because they receive a larger share of the product, and they gain because of the increase in the product price.

THE THEORY OF WAGES

In Ricardo's picture of the world it is the niggardliness of nature that keeps man in fetters. Thus, "the same cause which raises rent, namely, the increasing difficulty of providing an additional quantity of food with the same proportional quantity of labor, will also raise wages." Rising food prices will tend to raise "the natural price of labor," the wage that enables laborers "to subsist and to perpetuate their race, without either increase or diminution." The market price of labor, as of other matters, reflects the forces of demand and supply and may deviate from the natural price, but it will tend to conform to it. Thus the market price of labor may exceed or fall short of the natural subsistence wage, but in line with what later came to be called the "iron law of wages," the natural wage will eventually reassert itself. High wages will encourage population growth, and when in consequence of this the supply of labor has increased, wages will be brought down. When wages are low, population and the supply of labor will fall, causing wages to rise.

There are additional features both of grimness and of hope in Ricardo's subsistence theory of wages. The subsistence or natural wage is not absolutely fixed but varies with time and place, reflecting habits, customs, and institutions that are subject to change. In Ricardo's world historical experience indicates an upward movement of the subsistence wage so understood, so that "many of the conveniences now enjoyed in an English cottage would have been thought luxuries at an earlier period of our history." Moreover, a grand exception from the usual rule of coalescence of natural and market wage is postulated for conditions of sustained economic growth. Under such conditions the market wage may indefinitely be above the subsistence wage, because the growth of capital will cause an upward drift of the demand for labor. When the supply of labor has caught up, another increase in capital may produce the same effect.

However, as the population grows, the increased cost of producing food will not entirely be compensated by rising money wages so that the wage will buy less food. There is a redeeming feature here, too, because according to Ricardo the rise in the prices of agricultural products, which are produced under conditions of diminishing returns, is accompanied by a decline in the prices of manufactures, manufacturing operating under conditions of increasing returns. Thus, "in rich countries a laborer, by the sacrifice of a very small quantity only of his food, is able to provide liberally for all his other wants."

THE THEORY OF PROFIT

Ricardo's theory of profit is developed as a corollary of his theories of wages and value. Money wages rise in the course of economic development, reflecting the rise in food prices which accompanies the increase in labor required for agricultural production. The prices of manufactures, on the other hand, remain at their established level—the production of these requires no additional quantity of labor. Hence, as money wages increase, profits are bound to fall. As Ricardo tersely puts it, "profits depend on high or low wages, wages on the price of necessaries, and the price of necessaries chiefly on the price of food." The fall in the rate of profits will in the end usher in what later writers called the stationary state. When profits approximate zero, there will be no further inducement to the accumulation of capital. Population growth will cease as no additional funds become available to sustain more laborers. "Almost the whole produce of the country, after paying the laborers, will be the property of the owners of land and the receivers of tithes and taxes."

Ricardo's theory of distribution may be illustrated by an arithmetical example which is a slight variant of one he himself employs in the *Principles*. In Table 14.1 production is shown to start on Grade I land (line 1), where ten men turn out a product of 180 bushels of wheat. At the going price of $4 per bushel, the product fetches $720. The wage rate is composed of the monetary equivalent of 3 bushels of wheat plus $12 for other wage goods. The wage bill for ten workers is ten times the wage rate, or $240. Profit, the difference between the value of the product and the wage bill, is $480. There is no rent.

Once Grade II land is taken into cultivation, diminishing returns set in, and the product of ten workers on this land falls to 170 bushels (line 2). According to Ricardo's theory of value, the product of the ten workers on Grade II land has the same value as the product of the ten workers on Grade I land, that is, $720. This implies that the wheat price now rises from $4 to approximately $4.24, the ratio of these prices being roughly equal to that of 170 to 180, or, what is the same, $720 is divided among 170 bushels rather than among 180. At a wheat price of $4.24 the wage rate rises to $24.72 and the wage bill to $247. Since the wage bill is higher, profits decline from $480 to $473.

The rates of profit and of wages on Grade II land, which now is marginal, set the rates of profit and of wages on Grade I land (line 3). Because of the higher product price the value of the product rises from

ILLUSTRATION OF RICARDO'S THEORY DISTRIBUTION

	VALUE OF PRODUCT	WAGE RATE	WAGE BILL	PROFITS	RENT
1. GRADE I	180 × $4.00 = $720	3 × $4.00 + $12 = $24.00	10 × $24 = $240	$720 − $240 = $480	0
2. GRADE II	170 × $4.24 = $720	3 × $4.24 + $12 = $24.72	$247	$720 − $247 = $473	0
3. GRADE I	180 × $4.24 = $763	$24.72	$247	$473	$ 43
4. GRADE III	160 × $4.50 = $720	3 × $4.50 + $12 = $25.50	$255	$720 − $255 = $465	0
5. GRADE II	170 × $4.50 = $765	$25.50	$255	$465	$ 45
6. GRADE I	180 × $4.50 = $810	$25.50	$255	$465	$ 90
7. GRADE IV	150 × $4.80 = $720	3 × $4.80 + $12 = $26.40	$264	$720 − $264 = $456	0
8. GRADE III	160 × $4.80 = $768	$26.40	$264	$456	$ 48
9. GRADE II	170 × $4.80 = $816	$26.40	$264	$456	$ 96
10. GRADE I	180 × $4.80 = $864	$26.40	$264	$456	$144

TABLE 14.1

$720 to $763. Wages and profits are as on line 2, and as they add up to $720, rent rises, in the amount of $43, the difference between the value of the product—$763—and the sum of wages and profits—$720.

If land of Grade III is taken into cultivation, ten workers produce only 160 bushels, and the product price rises to $4.50 (line 4). Grade II land now earns rent (line 5), and the rent on Grade I land rises (line 6). Wages rise and profits fall. Lines 7–10 carry the illustration a step further by indicating the results of an expansion of cultivation to Grade IV land.

The parasitic character of the landlords—of whom Smith had already said that they "love to reap where they never sowed," although in his opinion they shared this disposition with "all other men"—is fully brought out in Ricardo's theory of economic development. In the *Essay on Profits* the interest of the landlord was characterized as "always opposed to the interest of every other class in the community." "His situation," Ricardo continued, "is never so prosperous as when food is scarce and dear; whereas all other persons are greatly benefitted by procuring food cheap." However, rent accrues to the landlord not as the result of individual greed but in consequence of inexorable laws which make food prices coincide with the cost of production at the margin of cultivation. It would be no help if landlords would forgo their rents—"such a measure would only enable some farmers to live like gentlemen, but would not diminish the quantity of labor necessary to raise raw produce on the least productive land in cultivation."

THE PRINCIPLE OF COMPARATIVE ADVANTAGE

Ricardo, who had said of wages that "like all other contracts," they "should be left to the fair and free competition of the market, and should never be controlled by the interference of the legislature," would see no other remedy to stem the arrival of the stationary state than strict adherence to laissez faire. In the relevant context this would mean the abandonment, though a gradual one, of restrictions on the importation of agricultural products from abroad. In this manner it would be possible to avert the expansion of domestic production of food with all its accompanying effects on rents, wages, and profits. Thus Ricardo went on to develop the most powerful argument in favor of free trade, that based on the principle of comparative advantage.

Ricardo's discussion of foreign trade does not have as its foremost aim an elucidation of the factors giving rise to trade, although his theory of comparative advantage, which sheds light on these, has left its mark on the history of economics and continues to be singled out as his outstanding contribution to the theory of international trade. His principal concern was rather with the benefits that countries derive from foreign trade. Of such benefits two may be distinguished, the distributional and those relating to improved real income.

In line with Ricardo's general attention to the theory of distribution, his discussion of foreign trade starts out with an examination of the effects of the international exchange of goods on the distribution of income. Here as elsewhere in his work, the distributional aspects are the ones that stand in the center of his interest. As he was profoundly impressed by the long-term tendency of profits to fall, it is this aspect that has first claim to his attention. The question he raises is that of the effects of foreign trade on the rate of profit, effects which may be divided into direct and indirect ones. As profits can vary only in response to variations in wages, there can be no direct effects of foreign trade on profits. However, as an indirect effect of foreign trade, profits will increase if wage goods, especially food, are imported from abroad at prices lower than would be charged for domestically produced goods and if, in consequence of this, wages fall. No such effects will be produced by an increase in imports that do not constitute wage goods.

EFFECTS OF TRADE ON INCOME

However, regardless of whether or not distributional effects will ensue, foreign trade is always accompanied by desirable effects on real income. In line with his theory of value, Ricardo denies that foreign trade will affect values. As these reflect the quantities of labor embodied in goods, an increase in foreign trade will not add to them. Foreign trade, nevertheless, has a high worth of its own because an increase "will very powerfully contribute to increase the mass of commodities, and therefore the sum of enjoyments." This real-income effect of foreign trade is unrelated to any distributional effects and is considered by Ricardo as "quite as important to the happiness of mankind" as are the distributional effects. The real-income effects benefit all, because all are consumers. The distributional effects benefit only the producers by raising their profits. By laying stress on the real-income effects of increasing trade, Ricardo was thus in a position to give his free-trade argument a wider appeal and to buttress his case for free trade more strongly than would have been possible had he relied exclusively or preponderantly on the distributional effects. Wage earners might care little for these since they involved a reduction in money wages—an aspect that did not always endear a free-trade advocate to the masses.

To demonstrate the real-income effect of trade, Ricardo does not start out with the simple case of an absolute advantage which Adam Smith had discussed when he referred to the possible production of grapes in hothouses in Scotland to yield domestic wine at thirty times the expense of an imported product. Instead he makes his case more convincing by tackling a more difficult model, one that involves not merely an absolute advantage from which common sense could derive the benefit of trade, say, in products of the temperate zones and the tropics. To introduce a model displaying the features characteristic of comparative advantage, he assumes that in England the production of a unit of cloth requires the labor of 100 men for one year; that of a unit of wine, the labor of 120 men. In Portugal, the same unit of cloth is produced by 90 men, and the unit of wine by 80 men. Portugal then has an absolute advantage in the production of both cloth and wine. But her advantage is greater in the production of wine than in that of cloth: $\frac{80}{120}$ is less than $\frac{90}{100}$. England's disadvantage, on the other hand, is comparatively smaller in the production of cloth than in the production of wine; $\frac{100}{90}$ is less than $\frac{120}{80}$. Portugal thus has a comparative advantage in the production of wine, and England in the production of cloth.

In the absence of foreign trade a unit of cloth fetches 9/8 units of wine in Portugal but only 5/6 such units in England. An English seller of cloth will thus prefer to dispose of his ware in Portugal rather than in England. The Portuguese, on the other hand, at home have to surrender 9/8 of a unit of wine for a unit of cloth; they will prefer to sell their wine in England if there they can obtain the cloth for less wine. The English will thus specialize in the production of cloth for export, the Portuguese in the production of wine. On the assumption of constant costs, implied by Ricardo, the situation prevailing before and after trade is compared in Table 14.2 showing labor requirements for the production of the two commodities in the two countries. The table elucidates the rationale of the principle of comparative advantage.

	NUMBER OF LABORERS REQUIRED TO PRODUCE SPECIFIED UNITS OF	
	CLOTH	WINE
Before trade:		
England—1 unit each	100	120
Portugal—1 unit each	90	80
Total	190	200
After trade:		
England—2 units	200	—
Portugal—2 units	—	160
Total	200	160

TABLE 14.2

This comparison shows that in the absence of trade the production of the four units requires the labor of 190 + 200 = 390 men, whereas the equivalent can be produced by 200 + 160 = 360 men as the result of specialization and trade. The principle of comparative advantage thus demonstrates the saving of resources made possible by international trade, with the freed resources available "to increase the mass of commodities, and therefore the sum of enjoyments," as Ricardo put it. Gains from trade accrue even if, as in Ricardo's example, an imported commodity is produced abroad at higher cost than would be incurred by its home production—the cloth that Portugal imports from England requires a larger labor input in England than Portuguese cloth would require. The gains accrue because the resources going into a country's exports are lower in quantity than the resources the country would have to devote to the domestic production of goods which instead it buys with its exports. In England, the cost of cloth is less than the cost of domestically produced wine; in Portugal, the cost of wine is less than the cost of home-produced cloth.

DIVISION OF GAINS FROM TRADE

It is obvious that England will not send cloth to Portugal if it fetches there less wine than it does in England—5/6 of a unit; nor will Portugal send her wine to England if the cloth there costs more wine than it would in Portugal—9/8 of a unit. The cost ratios thus form the outside limits of a range of profitable trading relations. At a ratio of 5/6 only Portugal would gain from trade; at a ratio of 9/8, only England. At ratios that lie between these extremes, both countries share the gain. The exact distribution of this gain from trade among trading partners was a matter that Ricardo's discussion did not settle; it had to wait for John Stuart Mill's analysis. Ricardo implied that one unit of cloth would exchange for one unit of wine, which would allow both countries to benefit from trade.

FOREIGN AND DOMESTIC TRADE

In domestic trade the rule holds that goods will exchange in proportion to the amounts of labor embodied in them. A unit of cloth, requiring the labor of 100 men, could not be exchanged for a unit of wine requiring the labor of 80 men. In foreign trade, however, this rule does not apply because Ricardo considers labor and capital mobile only within the confines of a single country. They are thus unable to move to localities offering superior conditions of production if the move requires the crossing of international boundaries. With the international movement of factors thus precluded by assumption, opportunities are opened up for the movement of products.

DISTRIBUTION OF PRECIOUS METALS

Ricardo's analysis did not stop with the establishment of the principle of comparative advantage in real terms. Cloth, he said, cannot be imported into Portugal unless it fetches there a higher price in terms of gold than it does in England, and the same rule holds for the importation of wine into England. To make the principle of comparative advantage operational, it is necessary to translate comparative advantages into absolute differences in money cost or prices. A completely satisfying translation was achieved only by later economists, but Ricardo's analysis led the way. According to his view, the precious metals are distributed throughout the world in such a manner as to facilitate the same movement of goods that would come about under conditions of barter. Variations of the exchange rate and of domestic prices constitute the mechanism bringing about this distribution. Parity of exchange rates is the test of a distribution of the precious metals that is the right one in the sense of facilitating the flow of goods that would occur under barter.

VARIATIONS OF EXCHANGE RATES

To show the equilibrating process in operation, Ricardo starts out with a disturbance of the equilibrium arising from a change in the circumstances attending the production of wine in England. He assumes that the change affects England's comparative disadvantage in the production of wine and makes it advantageous for her to produce wine at home rather than import it. Under these circumstances England would divert resources from the production of cloth to that of wine. The price of wine would fall, whereas that of cloth would remain the same as before—Ricardo always implying constant costs of production. During an intermediate stage Portugal would continue to import cloth from England, but she would give money rather than wine in exchange for it, England no longer constituting a market for Portuguese wine. The increase in the quantity of money in England and its decline in Portugal would raise commodity prices in England and lower them in Portugal, so that in the end the exportation of English cloth would cease to be profitable.

Ricardo further demonstrates how variations in the exchange rate will make it unprofitable for the Portuguese importer to continue with his purchases of English cloth. Before the disturbance of the equilibrium, that is, before the change in the circumstances affecting the production of wine in England, the Portuguese purchaser of English cloth could settle his obligation by paying for it with a bill of exchange purchased in Portuguese money from the Portuguese exporter of wine. With wine exports ceasing, the bill of exchange, which the Portuguese importer of English cloth purchases, is sold at a premium covering the cost of transporting gold from Portugal to England. When this premium equals the Portuguese importer's profit on imported cloth, the importation of cloth will come to a stop.

The test of a restored equilibrium, as has been noted, is parity of exchange rates, not a "state of prices"—Ricardo and the great majority of his contemporaries did not employ the concept of a price level based on index numbers—or a value of money uniform throughout the different countries. Transportation costs, the existence of goods that are not involved in foreign trade, and other factors operate against such uniformity. As a corollary to the lack of uniformity of price levels, there will be inequality also in the distribution of precious metals throughout the world. What is the right amount for one country is not the right amount for another country. More specifically, countries excelling in the production of exportable manufactures will attract precious metals.

The principle of comparative advantage was again a multiple discovery which Ricardo shared with Torrens, who had enunciated it earlier but in inadequate terms without reference to the decisive cost ratios. With the establishment of the principle of comparative advantage, the laissez faire rule assumes an almost cosmic significance. It becomes applicable to international economic relations of the widest scope and resolves the conflict between nationalism and cosmopolitanism by pointing to a harmony of national interests. Ricardo extols it in these words:

> Under a system of perfectly free commerce, each country naturally devotes its capital and labor to such employments as are most beneficial to each. The pursuit of individual advantage is admirably connected with the universal good of the whole.... By increasing the general mass of productions it diffuses general benefit, and binds together by one common tie of interest and intercourse the universal society of nations throughout the civilized world.

RICARDO ON TAXATION

In view of Ricardo's attachment to a "system of perfectly free commerce" it is not surprising that he discussed the theory of taxation at considerable length, because to him, the unequivocal exponent of laissez faire, there were only a few legitimate exercises of statecraft in the economic sphere, and among these taxation would emerge as the most important. To those who assign to the government a variety of economic policies of wide scope, taxation is but one among various public functions. Not so to Ricardo, who would single out the matter for inclusion in the title of his book. There was a second factor attracting him to the theory of taxation, and this was his poor opinion of Adam Smith's treatment of a matter that Ricardo in his *Essay on Profits* characterized as "perhaps the most difficult and intricate of all the subjects on which political economy treats" and which constituted a challenge to his intellectual ingenuity. A third reason that made him turn his attention to the theory of taxation was the connection with his theory of distribution, a connection that left its mark on the substance of his thought on taxation. Without disregarding the link to Adam Smith, to whose great book the whole work of Ricardo was in the nature of a reaction and with whom he forever had to come to terms, Ricardo may be hailed as the founder of public finance in the narrower and old-fashioned sense of the term, which primarily includes matters of taxation. With characteristic modesty he refused to consider his own treatment of the subject as definitive and never ceased to urge others to cultivate this all-important field. It was indeed McCulloch, Ricardo's outstanding disciple, who in 1845 would write the first self-contained treatise on the subject, thereby witnessing the birth of this first subdiscipline among the fields of specialization in economics.

Ricardo's thoughts on taxation are integrated among themselves as well as with his theory of distribution by constant attention to the shifting and incidence of taxes. A tax on rent falls on the landlords and cannot be shifted since it fails to raise the price of the output produced at the margin, but such a tax would discourage cultivation. The incidence of other taxes will fall either on consumers or on the receivers of profit. In the case of a tax on wages, it will invariably be borne by profit since wages are at their subsistence level. Taxes on produce or land will be shifted to consumers as will taxes on the profits of specific manufacturers. A tax on the profits of all traders will, however, reduce profits.

Interwoven with Ricardo's analysis of the incidence of various taxes are sundry observations on the general nature of public revenues and expenditures. The following statement is characteristic of his general outlook:

> Taxes which are levied on a country for the purpose of supporting war, or for the ordinary expenses of the state, and which are chiefly devoted to the support of unproductive laborers, are taken from the productive industry of the country; and every saving which can be made from such expenses will be generally added to the income, if not to the capital of the contributors.

SAY'S LAW

Government expenditure is thus viewed as occurring at the cost of private expenditure, and every dollar spent by the government reduces private expenditure by the same amount. This idea, which later was to become known as the "Treasury view," against which Keynes launched powerful arguments, was to dominate the field of public finance for over a century. It is connected with Ricardo's espousal of Say's law and with his opinion that the demand for goods increases at the same pace as their production. When Malthus argued to the contrary and stressed the worth of unproductive consumption, Ricardo, in his *Notes* to Malthus's *Principles of Political Economy*, compared the alleged usefulness of unproductive consumption to that of a fire that would destroy goods stored in a manufacturer's warehouse. Ricardo's view of Say's law and of the controversy surrounding it was vigorously restated in a letter to Mill, dated July 9, 1821, in which he repeated his opinion that "when produced, commodities would always find a market, and some consumers would be found for them who had an equivalent to give for them."

In spite of this apparent intransigence, Ricardo's *Principles* did include from the beginning a chapter entitled "On Sudden Changes in the Channels of Trade," treating of "temporary reverses and contingencies" such as those of course of great importance at the time of his writing. Moreover, in the third edition Ricardo added an entirely new chapter, "On Machinery," in which he abandoned his old view—which was stated not in the *Principles* but elsewhere—that the introduction of machinery is beneficial to all classes of society, including labor. The new view was foreshadowed in his *Notes* to Malthus's *Principles:*

> It might be possible to do almost all the work performed
> by men with horses, would the substitution of horses in such case,
> even if attended with a greater produce, be advantageous to the
> working classes, would it not on the contrary very materially
> diminish the demand for labor?

He now held that the introduction of machinery may indeed displace labor, circulating capital becoming converted into fixed capital. But having constructed a strong case, he equivocated by underlining a number of qualifications which limit the practical importance of the new rule. To have the described adverse effect on labor, new machinery would have to be *"suddenly discovered and extensively used."* In practice, he held, its introduction is likely to be a gradual process, which, moreover, will raise profits and savings and thus make available new capital rather than divert capital from its actual employment. He summed up by expressing the hope that "the statements which I have made will not...lead to the inference that machinery should not be encouraged."

RICARDO'S SYSTEM

Ricardo's great contribution was the forging of a system of thought that, with all its blemishes and in spite of the burden its presentation throws on the reader, is majestic in its cogency and simplicity. In general, goods exchange at prices proportional to the quantity of labor embodied in them. Wages hover at the subsistence level. Lack of prudence makes for population growth that is restrained only by the bounds of subsistence. There are diminishing returns, which raise the cost of food production. With food prices set at the margin of cultivation, the growth of capital and of population causes them to increase with the expansion of this margin. In the course of economic development, money wages will go up, cutting into profits. Rent will rise as the difference between the cost of production at the margin and under superior conditions increases. As profits come to approximate zero, the accumulation of capital will cease. In the end there beckons the stationary state. Free trade can delay its coming. In line with the principle of comparative advantage, free trade also has beneficial effects on the national income. All this lends new and powerful support to the laissez faire idea.

Ricardo's contribution was an original one in many ways. Although there were others who shared in the discovery of differential rent and comparative advantage, the combination of these and other principles into a full-fledged system was entirely Ricardo's work. He was original also in his espousal of an abstract deductive method which pointed the way to modern economic analysis and yielded theorems that were eventually translated into mathematical terms. Original also was the economy that Ricardo observed with respect to the number of abstractions constructed by him. No one was a more abstract thinker than Ricardo, but no one was more faithful in the observation of the principle known to logicians as Occam's Razor, which forbids the unnecessary construction of new abstract concepts. It was Ricardo's economy in the creation of such concepts that gave force and coherence to his work. Original with him was the divorce of Ricardian economics from personal valuations and philosophical and political considerations. Malthus, when pressed, would have to admit that his lukewarm attitude to free trade was grounded in a profound attachment to the values inherent in country life. Ricardo, when pleading for free trade, did not have to fall back on personal valuations but could base his plea on considerations generated by the internal logic of his thought. Ricardian economics could thus claim scientific status for a system that was ostensibly tied neither to time nor to place nor to externally conditioned valuations.

A scientific undertaking carries risks of its own because scientific propositions, unlike valuations, are subject to testing and therefore may be proven wrong. Karl Popper, the philosopher of science, established a demarcation criterion according to which scientific propositions differ from valuations in that they can be intersubjectively tested and refuted by experience. Valuations—to be a Frenchman is better than to be an Englishman, or vice versa, or an agrarian society is preferable to an industrial one—cannot be tested or disproven. If economic questions were decided according to personal valuations, there would be no scientific appeal against Malthus's view because it is not possible to disprove it on empirical grounds. Precisely because Ricardo was a pioneer in scientific economics he had to pay the penalty for having been in the lead, and his analyses have repeatedly been subject to critical revisions His labor theory of value, since it stresses a single factor, was found to face insuperable difficulties in a multifactor economy. His theory of distribution was found incomplete since it is not supplemented by a fully developed theory of the demand for products, without which the setting of the margin of cultivation remains indeterminate. His refusal to include rent in the cost of production is incompatible with the many uses of land, uses which make its employment for agricultural purposes costly in terms of lost opportunities. His stress on diminishing returns in the historical dynamic sense has detracted from the realistic character of his theory in a world replete with technological change. His attachment to Say's law prevented him from seeing the relevance of income and employment theory.

What has remained of Ricardo's thought is, therefore, not so much its substance as his way of approaching the study of economics, his abstract-generalizing analysis. Even of the substance not all has been forgotten. The theory of rent, in a modified and generalized fashion, is still part of the main body of economic thought, and the substance of the message contained in the principle of comparative advantage, though its form has changed, has endured. All things considered, the influence of Ricardo has been lasting and profound. Every nineteenth-century economist had to come to terms with him. From him stems the foundation of Marxian economics. But his influence did not end with Marx. "Marshall," Joan Robinson reports, "pored over Ricardo all his life, and Keynes, though not a great reading man, drank Marshall in his mother's milk. So all three were trained in one tradition."

Chapter 15

FROM RICARDO
TO MILL:
Consolidation and Ferment

OVERALL VIEW OF THE PERIOD

From 1823, the year of Ricardo's death, to 1848, when John Stuart Mill published his *Principles of Political Economy* and emerged as a major influence on the ideas of his time, there was no towering figure whose image would impress itself on contemporary economic thought as had Ricardo and John Stuart Mill. The period was, however, replete with secondary figures who either consolidated the accomplishments of the past or pioneered in giving new direction to economic thought. Those who did the work of consolidation were all under the spell of Ricardo, but even among those who broke new paths many labored under his influence, using his work as a target for their criticism or as a basis on which to build new thought.

In Britain, which continued to be the homeland of classical economics, Bentham was still alive to spread the gospel of utilitarianism, which, more than his un-Ricardian technical economics, had its effects on James and John Stuart Mill. James Mill and McCulloch ably defended the Ricardian tradition. In addition, much *ad hoc* theorizing went on to grapple with the great practical issues of the time—political reform, free trade, colonization, factory legislation, the Irish question, and, especially, monetary stabilization. This last issue posed a challenge to economic thought and produced a protracted debate in which the great majority of the economists of the time participated. Robert Torrens, the co-discoverer of the theories of rent and of comparative advantage, was among those who contributed to this debate as well as to discussions about foreign trade and colonization. Both as a theorist and as an investigator of current economic problems Nassau Senior became a widely respected thinker, virtually the only one to probe deeply into the theoretical foundations of classical economics. Academic opportunities were few, but the Dublin and Oxford economists made the most of them and pointed the way to a new theory of value. At Haileybury, Malthus's old college, his successor Richard Jones attacked the nature and methods of classical thought and became England's first historical economist. Outside the halls of academe socialist thought began to emerge in the work of Robert Owen and in that of a motley crew of radical publicists later known as Ricardian Socialists, who drew conclusions from Ricardo's labor theory of value not unlike those that later served as the foundation of the theoretical system of Karl Marx.

As a major influence, however, socialist thought emerged first on the Continent, especially in France, where the art of political compromise was less highly developed than in England and where the intellectual tradition of rationalism created more favorable auspices for the construction of speculative schemes of social reorganization. It was thus that Saint-Simon and Fourier came to the fore as major figures in the economic thought of France during the first half of the nineteenth century. To be sure, classical economics found a persuasive apologist in Bastiat, but there was little scientific work that would have continued the tradition of Say. During this period Cournot in France and Thünen in Germany blazed new trails in theoretical economics but it was only toward the close of the century that the full significance of their contributions came to be realized and acknowledged.

In the United States a characteristically American brand of economics developed in the 1820s. A number of writers followed the general pattern of classical thought but took exception to specific theories, especially those of population and rent, which impressed them as especially unsuited for the New World. Others deviated still further from the mainstream of the classical tradition by opposing free trade and assigning to the government important functions in the promotion of economic development. Among these writers there was at least one who made a signal contribution to the theory of capital.

The economic thought of the period, although lacking a central outstanding figure, fills a vast panorama, rich in diversity and with many minor claimants to fame. We shall discuss those economists whose work, however peripheral, was firmly grounded in the thought of the classics and whose impact was mostly felt by their contemporaries rather than by later generations of economists. This leaves out and reserves for later discussion the work of the pioneers of historical, socialist, and mathematical economics.

BENTHAM

Jeremy Bentham (1748–1832), who was in his late twenties when Adam Smith published *The Wealth of Nations,* had become the revered head of the philosophical radicals and was known as a reformer and philosopher of reform rather than as an economist. He had, however, been an active student of economics during an earlier phase of his life and published, in 1787, a *Defense of Usury,* taking Adam Smith to task for allowing a legal ceiling on the rate of interest. Other economic studies that he wrote in the following decades remained in part unpublished during his life. They contain a number of original and forward-looking ideas, often running counter to what was to become the Ricardian tradition, but their impact on contemporary opinion was slight.

It was not Bentham's technical economics but his utilitarianism that exerted the greater stimulation on the thought of his time, and it was through the notions embedded in his utilitarianism that he affected the future development of economics. Here he broke new paths leading away from laissez faire, and here he also, by making utility a central concept in his plea for reform, significantly expanded an area of speculation that was to become a great concern of later generations of economists.

Bentham's reforms, which were grounded in his utilitarianism and which he tirelessly promoted during his long and active life, changed the face of nineteenth-century England. They covered a large variety of programs stretching from parliamentary to prison reform and prepared the ground for the adoption of such important social inventions as the civil service and statistical fact-finding. Bentham was, first of all, a student of law. He considered as his foremost task the reform of the law and the development of a science of legislation. This science, in turn, he attempted to derive from the principle of utilitarianism, which in the version he gave to it makes the happiness, not of an individual but of society, the *summum bonum,* or "highest good." "Nature," he wrote in a famous passage, "has placed mankind under the governance of two sovereign masters, *pain* and *pleasure.* It is for them alone to point out what we ought to do, as well as to determine what we shall do...They govern us in all we do." At first glance this statement seems to make Bentham an exponent of egoistic hedonism in its psychological variant—"man desires only his own pleasure"—or in its ethical variant —"man should desire only his own pleasure"—or in both. But this Hobbesian approach is not Bentham's. Central to his thought is not the individual's happiness but the "principle of utility" or greatest happiness principle, which considers as the highest good the greatest happiness of the greatest number. Each man's pursuit of his own selfish ends will not maximize the public happiness, that is, there is no natural harmony of interests such as the one that Adam Smith had postulated or which was later to emerge in the form of social Darwinism or related laissez faire doctrines connected with the theory of evolution. Instead the task falls on government to produce an artificial harmony of interests by means of legislation. To Bentham, it was the function of legislation and of the science treating of it to establish a system of punishments and rewards that would induce individuals to pursue actions leading to the greatest happiness of the greatest number.

Although Bentham had criticized Smith's willingness to permit a legal ceiling on the interest rate, his espousal of the maximum happiness principle did not commit him to laissez faire but rather had as its consequence the recognition of a substantial range of legitimate activities of the government. Bentham distinguished between the agenda of the government, the non-agenda, and *sponte acta,* that is, actions which individuals could be relied upon to undertake spontaneously. As derived from and "immediately subordinate" to the maximum happiness principle, he listed four great objectives of public policy, which he ranked in the order of subsistence, security, abundance, and equality, and which, he pointed out, may be "sometimes in a state of rivalry." Although Bentham called legislation a "necessary evil" and in spite of his exhortation to government to "be quiet," his classification of policy objectives and his discussion of "the art of government in matters of political economy" mark a new departure in the direction toward a theory of economic policy.

This departure carried Bentham far away from the strict laissez faire position and opened up new trends in economic thought. When he elevated equality to an objective of economic policy, even though to one ranking last, he broke a path on which John Stuart Mill, who developed new views about distribution, was to follow him. When he, in spite of his opposition to a ceiling on the rate of interest, proposed to place a similar ceiling on the price of corn, he demonstrated his unwillingness to rely always and invariably on the forces of the market. When he suggested that the government take over the life insurance business, he stated the germ of the idea of social insurance. Moreover, his opinions about monetary economics were completely at variance with those of Ricardo and resembled those of Thornton, if not Keynes. He stressed monetary expansion as a means to full employment, and his discussion of this problem shows his awareness of the relevance of hoarding, forced saving, the saving-investment relationship, the propensity to consume, and other matters which form the content of modern income and employment analysis. Much of the best of what he had to say about these questions he kept unpublished because of James Mill's and Ricardo's adverse criticism.

Of greater consequence than Bentham's monetary views was the close attention that he gave to the elaboration of the fundamental concepts employed in his model of utilitarian decision making. He decided that pleasures and pains can be ranked according to their value and that the value can be estimated by taking account of certain "dimensions" such as the intensity, duration, certainty or uncertainty, propinquity or remoteness, of a pleasure or a pain. Such ranking would suffice to estimate the pleasure content of an action affecting an individual. Another dimension, designated as extent, would be added if the matter involved a group of people rather than an individual. In this case, each person would count for one. This "felicific" calculus, Bentham held, would enable an individual or a policy maker to compare the pleasure content of alternative courses of action and decide on the one tending to produce a maximum of pleasure. What he had in mind was a formal model, a logically consistent abstract frame of reference, rather than an operational procedure employing numerical calculations.

As an ethic and even more as a psychology, utilitarianism no longer commands the substantial following that it had in Bentham's England. But the conceptual apparatus that Bentham used touches on many problems— such as the measurability of utility and interpersonal comparisons of it—that are still debated in utility theory and welfare economics. In view of Bentham's concern with utility it is not surprising that he pioneered also by stating, in several versions, the idea underlying the principle of diminishing marginal utility. If you give an individual a certain quantity of money, he said,

> you will produce in his mind a certain quantity of pleasure. Give him again the same quantity, you will make an addition to the quantity of his pleasure. But the magnitude of the pleasure produced by the second sum will not be twice the magnitude of the pleasure produced by the first. While the sums are small, the truth of this position may not be perceivable. But let the sums have risen to a certain magnitude, it will be altogether out of doubt.

Bentham's concern with maxima and minima of pleasures and pains set a precedent for the future employment of the maximization principle in the economics of the consumer and of the firm and for the search for an optimum in welfare economics.

Bentham's role in the economic discussion of his time was only a peripheral one—his flashes of insight were often submerged in the huge mass of his writings devoted to other subjects. It was not his technical economics but his utilitarianism that provided stimulus and challenge to the thought of John Stuart Mill. James Mill, otherwise so faithful a follower of Bentham, considered Bentham's monetary views an indication that this matter belonged to a subject that Bentham "ceased to study before he had probed it to the bottom."

JAMES MILL

Faithful to Ricardo rather than to Bentham in his economics, James Mill, John Stuart's father, referred to himself and to McCulloch as Ricardo's "two and only two genuine disciples." James Mill (1773–1836) left his mark on economic and political thought, on psychology, and, as a leader of Bentham's circle of philosophical radicals, on the history of nineteenth-century Britain. It was James Mill's economic thought that brought him to Ricardo's attention in 1808, when Mill published an antiphysiocratic tract, *Commerce Defended,* which contained, among other matters, an early statement of the idea behind Say's law. Whether Mill arrived at this independently or was influenced by Say's book is a matter of conjecture as is also the influence that Mill's statement may have exerted on the new versions of the law found in later editions of Say's book.

Ten years later, after assiduous work, Mill brought out a monumental *History of British India,* which led to fame and employment with the East India Company, where he eventually rose to a great position, one to which his son succeeded at a later period. Mill, of course, had never come closer to India than Ricardo had to a factory. Facts meant little to these men of principle, which in the case of Mill was that of utility, the test of everything, including the rank of a civilization. Thus Mill would proclaim: "Exactly in proportion as *Utility* is the object of every pursuit may we regard a nation as civilized." In the light of this narrow standard, Mill found little to admire in the Hindu civilization, and although his influence has been credited with important reforms in India, it sometimes had surprising results. Thus a utilitarian follower of his, when appointed governor-general of India, would consider the demolition of the Taj Mahal in order to sell its marble at auction, a plan that he abandoned only when an auction of materials from another palace turned out to be a disappointment.

As a writer on economics, Mill was first of all concerned with the dissemination of Ricardo's ideas, and with this in mind he published in 1821 his *Elements of Political Economy,* the first textbook on economics. This work follows on the whole the thought of Ricardo but at times paints with a heavier brush matters on which Ricardo touched only lightly—disciples often having the tendency to exaggerate the ideas of the master. Thus Mill came to espouse the labor theory of value more unqualifiedly than did Ricardo. He would attribute the increase in the value of aged wine to an increase of the labor expended on it and would refer to capital as "hoarded labor." In another matter, Malthus's view of population tending to outrun the production of food was paralleled by Mill's opinion that the growth of population tends to outrun the growth of capital. There then emerges what to Mill—himself the father of nine children—appears as "the grand practical problem," that is, "to find the means of limiting the number of births." Mill also drew drastic conclusions from Ricardo's theory of rent and initiated a line of thought which later reached fruition in Henry George's condemnation of the "unearned increment" accruing to the owner of land whose value rises in consequence of the growth of population and of capital. Mill suggests that

> this continual increase, arising from the circumstances of the community, and from nothing in which the landholders themselves have any peculiar share, does seem a fund no less peculiarly

fitted for appropriation to the purposes of the state, than the whole of the rent in a country where land had never been appropriated.

McCULLOCH

John Ramsey McCulloch (1789–1864), the young Scotsman whose enthusiastic review of Ricardo's *Principles* had helped so much to spread its fame, was in frequent correspondence with Ricardo, whom he met shortly before Ricardo's death. He wrote a biography of Ricardo, published his *Works,* and became an undaunted defender of the Ricardian tradition. McCulloch, who was trained in the law, became eventually, like so many Scottish intellectuals of his generation, a resident of London, and after some years divided between journalistic work and unprofitable teaching served for over one-quarter of a century as head of the government printing office. There are several facets to McCulloch's work as he was a tireless writer and editor. Like Mill, he wrote a text, *Principles of Political Economy,* of which the first edition was published in 1825. The appearance of this work coincided with an attack, by Samuel Bailey, on Ricardo's labor theory of value, a theory that McCulloch, like Mill, was at pains to uphold. Although the Socialists' critique of profits was still a matter of the future, McCulloch seemed to have anticipated the need for a more complete justification of profits, which Ricardo had depicted as a surplus of output over wages designed to compensate the capitalist for his trouble and risk in putting capital to productive use. Just as Mill had written of capital as "hoarded labor," so would McCulloch refer to it as "accumulated labor." To McCulloch, profits, in the final analysis, would resolve into wages, the wages of accumulated labor, and wages would in turn constitute the profits of "the proprietors of the machine called man."

As for wages, McCulloch distinguished between the market or actual rate, which he considered depending "on the proportion which the whole capital bears to the whole laboring population"—the wages fund theory— and the natural or necessary rate, equated with subsistence, which forms a floor for the market rate. McCulloch's espousal of the wages fund theory did not preclude his strong endorsement of high wages. "This is not a point," he wrote, "as to which there is any room for doubt. The experience of all ages and nations proves that high wages are at once the most powerful stimulus to unremitting and assiduous exertion, and the best means of attaching the people to the institutions under which they live." Moreover, McCulloch expressed strong disapproval of the Combination Laws, which forbade all combinations of workers aiming at higher wages and fewer hours of work and which Ricardo, in a letter to him (December 4, 1820), had characterized as "unjust and oppressive." In the long run, as McCulloch pointed out in his *Essay on the Circumstances Which Determine the Rate of Wages* of 1826, neither the suppression nor the operation of labor unions will have an effect on wages. If wages are depressed in a certain line of work, capital will be attracted and wages will rise. Labor unions, however, may shorten the interval before the forces of competition among employers produce such an increase in wages. He made light of the fear that the repeal of the Combination Laws would produce monopoly and thought that abuses would be self-correcting.

In 1845, McCulloch published a *Treatise on the Principles and Practical Influence of Taxation and the Funding System,* the first work to offer a separate treatment of public finance. Besides writing lesser works on economics proper, McCulloch was a pioneer student of the history of economics. He ranks with Foxwell, Menger, Hollander, and Keynes as one of the great book collectors in his field and published several collections of rare tracts as well as the first bibliography of economics, *Literature of Political Economy,* in 1845. There was still another side of his work. His huge compilations of commercial, geographical, and statistical information constituted a one-man economic intelligence service, the first of its kind serving a function now fulfilled by a host of government departments and private agencies.

WEST

Mill and McCulloch were Ricardo's principal followers; West and Torrens shared in some of his discoveries, both having independently detected the principle of differential rent and Torrens also that of comparative advantage. Of Edward West (1783–1828), whose *Essay on the Application of Capital to Land* of 1815 contains a superior statement of the principle of differential rent, Ricardo wrote to Malthus: "He is a barrister—a young man and appears very fond of the study of political economy." This Oxford man of great promise was soon lost to economics since he apparently found opportunities more attractive in the field of law. He published but one more tract on economic matters and died after only five and one-half years of tenure as a judge in India, one and one-half years short of the then prevailing average there, which was kept down by the unfavorable health conditions in that country.

TORRENS

Robert Torrens (1780–1864) is an elusive figure who defies ready-made classifications. His long and active career was filled with a fifty-year record of copious and not always consistent publications testifying to a diversity of interests which included economic theory, money and banking, commercial policy, colonization, an occasional novel, as well as efforts on behalf of Catholic emancipation to which he, an Irish Protestant and son of a minister, gave valiant support. Side by side with these activities was a distinguished military career and another one as a publicist and parliamentarian. Among the economists of his time, Colonel Torrens played no mean role. It was he who presided at the first meeting of the Political Economy Club in 1821, which was attended by such great figures as Ricardo, Malthus, and James Mill. His influence was, however, more pronounced on his contemporaries than on later generations of economists, who were daunted by the very bulk and diversity of his work, much of which was published in small editions that have become extremely scarce. It has been said of Torrens that "there is no figure in the history of the first half of the nineteenth century whose work is a more significant reflection of the main movement of economic thought." Forming part of the mainstream of economic thought, some outstanding contributions of Torrens were multiple discoveries for which credit had to be shared with others—Ricardo, Malthus, John Stuart Mill. It was Torrens's misfortune that his co-discoverers were the greatest figures in the economic thought of his time.

Much of Torrens's best work on general economic theory was overshadowed by his co-discoverers—his anticipation of the principle of comparative advantage in *The Economists Refuted,* an antiphysiocratic tract published in 1808 when Torrens was 28, and the more complete statement of the principle in the *Essay on the External Corn Trade* of 1815, which also contains the principle of rent arising on lands differing in quality and the idea of the culturally conditioned subsistence wage. Although in these matters Torrens's thought ran parallel with that of Ricardo, there was a break when it came to the theory of value set forth by Torrens in the *Essay on the Production of Wealth* in 1821. Torrens's theory of value contains both a critique, one of the earliest of Ricardo's labor theory of value, and as a positive contribution a value theory of his own. He denied the validity of the labor theory of value in a multifactor economy and, as Lauderdale had done before and as Bailey was to do again shortly, refused to participate in the search for an invariable measure of value. To him, value is a mere relation between goods, not between the quantities of labor embodied in them but between the quantities of capital, including the outlay for wages, invested in their production. If competition equates the rates of profit throughout the economy, then, so Torrens argued, goods must exchange in proportion to the capital invested in them, with an adjustment to take account of the different durability of capital.

Ricardo and his followers had no use for Torrens's theory of value, and to them his offense was compounded by his refusal to participate in the search for an invariable measure of value, which Ricardo considered of such vital importance. Without this measure, so Ricardo wrote during the last few weeks of his life, a change in the relative value of the quantities of capital employed in different enterprises would leave unanswered the question of which of the capitals had changed in value.

Torrens also made original contributions to the theories of commercial policy and colonization, but here again his discoveries were multiple ones and his co-discoverers are better remembered than he. In his *Letters on Commercial Policy* of 1833 and in later writings he drew attention to the opportunities that a country has of improving its terms of trade by means of a tariff and on this basis made a vigorous plea for reciprocity as the cornerstone of a country's commercial policy. A country, he insisted, should not lower its tariffs unilaterally but only if this step was accompanied by the tariff reductions of other countries. The priority for this idea, however, belongs to John Stuart Mill, who developed it in the first chapter of his *Essays on Some Unsettled Questions of Political Economy*, published in 1844 but written in 1829 or 1830. Concern about colonial tariffs as a potential threat to British exports caused Torrens to pursue the matter one step further and urge establishment of an imperial free-trade area. In connection with this and related matters Torrens also shed new light on the economic aspects of colonization, but here again his fame was overshadowed by others, especially by Wakefield.

Torrens's contributions to the monetary controversies of his time were manifold and were made not only to the bullion debate of the early decades of the nineteenth century but also to the second great monetary debate which was fought between the followers of the currency and the followers of the banking schools and which yielded Peel's Bank Charter Act of 1844, the basis of English monetary and banking institutions until 1914. During the bullion debate Torrens was an anti-bullionist, stressing, what Hume and Thornton had underlined and what Ricardo had denied, the beneficial effects of monetary expansion on production. Unlike Thornton, who found flaws in it, Torrens then stood close to the real-bills doctrine. This doctrine, which Adam Smith had espoused and which has had some following down to the present time, holds that if only "real" bills are discounted, that is, if the banks make advances only to finance short-term commercial transactions, they will remain in a liquid position and the money supply will expand and contract exactly as the "needs of the trade" require it. Torrens's *Essay on Money and Paper Currency* of 1812, parts of which were written while he was on active service in the icebound Kattegat, contains a highly original qualification of his endorsement of the real-bills doctrine. While others would point to the dangers of inflation arising from adherence to this doctrine, Torrens took exactly the opposite point of view and considered a monetary system organized in conformity with the real-bills doctrine as suffering from a chronic tendency to deflation. Such a tendency would develop because the return payment of money to the banks, the "reflux," would include not only the principal sums but interest as well, and it could be checked only by continued monetary expansion. Besides this monetary theory of potential economic stagnation Torrens made other contributions to the bullion debate, including one that develops the principle of self-justifying anticipations in connection with a pioneer analysis of the role of confidence in the determination of output: "An enlargement of confidence always produces that enlargement of the market which it anticipates."

THE CURRENCY VERSUS THE BANKING SCHOOL

After the bullion controversy had died down, there arose in Britain a second monetary debate in which all the leading economists again participated. To bring Torrens's role in this controversy into sharper relief, it is necessary to sketch the background and introduce the spokesmen of rival views. When the bullion debate took place, England was on an inconvertible paper standard. The second great monetary debate took place under a different monetary system. The gold standard had been restored and specie payments had been resumed. Nevertheless, complaints about monetary disorders never ended. There were painful price fluctuations, and periods of monetary expansion were sometimes followed by sudden reversals and runs on the banks. There were failures of financial houses of great repute, including in 1825 that of Henry Thornton's old banking firm, a disaster that affected more than forty provincial correspondent banks. In 1839, because of an external drain that posed the threat of a suspension of gold payments, the Bank of France had to come to the aid of that of England, a situation considered humiliating by many Englishmen.

There were protracted parliamentary debates and a flood of pamphlets—more than forty in 1837 alone—all devoted to the great question of monetary and banking reform. Apart from a number of Socialists, who had their own ideas about monetary matters, only a very few participants in this discussion would deny the desirability of a metallic standard, which by then had become an article of faith. There were advocates of silver and bimetallism, but only the Birmingham group would urge a return to an inconvertible paper standard. This group was led by the brothers Thomas (1783–1856) and Matthias Attwood (1779–1851), the spokesmen of the regional iron and brass industry, whose markets had shrunk after the Napoleonic Wars and which was plagued by periodic distresses in later decades. The Birmingham school fought against the gold standard and urged the expansion of inconvertible paper money as a means to full employment, but the time was not ripe for such ideas and the proposals of the Attwoods fell on deaf ears.

There were other suggestions for less drastic reforms, such as that of a tabular standard which would adjust contractual obligations to changing prices, the revival of an idea first aired by John Wheatley in 1807. In the end, however, the issue narrowed down to the proper organization of the convertible paper standard, and two schools of thought emerged, one adhering to the banking and the other to the currency principle.

The main point at issue between the two schools was the proper control over the supply of money. According to the currency principle, a currency made up of gold and convertible paper should behave exactly as would a currency consisting solely of gold—it should expand and contract to the same extent as gold moved into or out of the country. Such a behavior of money, the followers of the currency principle held, would not come about automatically but would require regulation of the quantity of paper money to make it conform to the principle.

The banking school, on the other hand, denied such a need for regulation and would instead leave the determination of the quantity of paper money to the practical wisdom of the banking community, disciplined by the requirement of convertibility. The banking school further denied that a purely metallic currency would behave in the manner postulated by the currency school, that is, expand and contract *pari passu* with international gold movements. Such movements, instead of replenishing or depleting the gold in circulation, might instead replenish or deplete "hoards" of gold, that is, the bullion reserves of the banking system. Still another weapon in the armory of the banking school was the theory of "reflux"—bank notes are issued against loans, and when these fall due an equal amount of notes as was issued will flow back to the bank. Thus if convertibility should fail to guarantee the proper limitation of the money supply, the reflux would insure it. Moreover, the banking school pointed out that what is now called the money supply consisted not only of gold, or gold and paper money, but also of bank deposits and bills of exchange. The banking school did not propose to regulate the quantity of bank deposits—this was a matter for which the time was not yet ripe. But by emphasizing that the currency school's proposal to regulate the note issue would apply merely to one part of the money supply and leave uncontrolled another part of it, the banking school tried to undermine the position of the currency school altogether.

The great debate came to an end with the passage of the Bank Charter Act of 1844, which separated the banking and currency functions of the Bank of England and restricted its note issue in accordance with the proposals of the currency school. This solution, enduring as it was, proved no panacea. Monetary disorders continued, and the Bank of England, left free in its banking functions, endeavored to expand its deposit business by means of low discount rates.

The victory that the Bank Charter Act brought to the currency school was in fact a vindication of the thought of Ricardo, which had inspired the principal ideas of that school. In Ricardo's posthumous *Plan for the Establishment of a National Bank* the proposal to divorce banking and currency functions had been launched, and it was Ricardo who in his contributions to the bullion debate had proposed to limit the issue of inconvertible paper money to such an amount as could be issued under conditions of convertibility. From this the currency school derived the related idea that a currency consisting of gold and convertible paper should be made to behave as if it consisted of gold only.

Torrens was among the leaders of the currency school, and the support that this indefatigable controversialist gave to the currency principle accounts in no small measure for its eventual victory. His position in the banking-currency school debate marks a sharp break with the anti-bullionist views that he had held during the earlier bullion debate. To this day the circumstances responsible for this break are not entirely clear.

TOOKE

The banking school was ably led by Thomas Tooke (1774–1858), a prominent businessman and financier, early promotor of free trade, and the moving force behind the founding of the Political Economy Club in 1821. Tooke's principal works are his *History of Prices...1793–1856,* which he published in six volumes from 1838 to 1857, the last two in collaboration with William Newmarch, and his *Inquiry into the Currency Principle* of 1844. Tooke's analysis of monetary matters contains important new insights which led him far beyond the quantity theory as espoused by Ricardo and his followers. Tooke refused to interpret changes in general prices primarily as a monetary phenomenon and instead attributed them to changes in the demand and supply of goods and services. Changes in the money supply thus appear as a passive reaction to changes occurring in the market for goods and services. Tooke's concern with the latter type of change, especially his desire to locate a criterion that would help to separate price changes reflecting monetary conditions from price changes reflecting the situation in the market for goods and services, turned him into an early student of what Marshall was later to designate as the elasticity of demand. Tooke's analysis also produced an early version of the income theory of prices, that is, of the approach that emerged much later in the writings of Wicksell, Aftalion, and Keynes. According to the income theory of prices, it is not the quantity of money as such that determines general prices but the national income and expenditure. This view, as well as an incipient formulation of the consumption function, is clearly stated in Tooke's *Inquiry into the Currency Principle:*

> It is the quantity of money, constituting the revenues of the different orders of the State, under the head of rents, profits, salaries, and wages, destined for current expenditure, that alone forms the limiting principle of the aggregate of money prices, the only prices that can properly come under the designation of general prices. As the cost of production is the limiting principle of supply, so the aggregate of money incomes devoted to expenditure for consumption is the determining and limiting principle of demand.

The effective demand for consumer goods is thus seen as determined by the level of income, and consumption expenditure, in turn, is a function of income: The "power of purchase by the consumers depends upon their incomes; and the measure of the extent and of the exercise of such power is...in that portion of their revenues which is destined for expenditures on objects of immediate consumption."

SENIOR

Another innovator who broke away from the Ricardian tradition was William Nassau Senior (1790–1864), who has already been mentioned as a critic of Malthus and as the first holder of the Drummond chair at Oxford and of a similar but abortive appointment at King's College in London. Senior shared an ancestry that was in part similar to that of Ricardo, but the environment in which he spent his formative years was quite different— he grew up in an Anglican vicarage and received the best formal education then available at Eton and at Oxford. He was not a full-time economist, and his professional life was divided between the successful practice of real-property law—chosen, in his own words, because "it will give me the command of my time," the advising of the Whig governments of the period, and economic studies, mainly lectures given at Oxford between 1825 and 1830 and again between 1847 and 1852, when he won another appointment to the Drummond chair. Senior traveled widely, and the "conversations with distinguished persons" that he published subsequently to his travels made him the inventor of the modern interview.

Senior is remembered for his contributions to economic theory and methodology as well as to applied economics, which are found in his published lectures, periodical articles, pamphlets, government reports, and in one full-length book, *An Outline of the Science of Political Economy* of 1836. He had pronounced views about the nature and scope of economics and the functions of the economist. Political economy, which treats of wealth, must be sharply distinguished from the science of legislation, which has happiness or welfare as its subject. Wealth and welfare are by no means identical matters, and the economist must always remember that considerations of wealth are not the only and not even the most important elements in the solution of policy questions. Thus the economist, who as such has professional competence in matters relating to wealth, is allowed to state his conclusions but must never propose a definite course of action, since the latter is to reflect a host of other considerations besides the economic ones. It is doubtful whether Senior himself in his work as a busy government consultant always adhered to this principle.

Senior longed to establish economics as a positive and deductive science of universal validity. He admitted that the practical application of economics requires large-scale fact-finding, but he insisted that economics itself depends on reasoning rather than on observation. Instead of basing economic analysis on hypothetical premises he made it rest on a few elementary propositions which he declared were the result of observation or consciousness and familiar to everyone. Senior's elementary propositions, the foundation of his positive and deductive economics, are the following: (1) man's desire to obtain additional wealth with as little sacrifice as possible; (2) man's propensity to increase in numbers, which is limited only by moral or physical evil or by fear of having to lower one's standard of living; (3) the productivity of capital; and (4) the principle of diminishing returns in agriculture. The inferences drawn from these propositions, Senior taught, are as generally valid as are the propositions themselves. Inferences relating to the nature and production of wealth are universally true; inferences relating to its distribution are liable to be affected by the particular circumstances of time and place—"institutions"—but even here it is possible first to establish general rules and then to indicate the influence of disturbing factors affecting their validity under special conditions. Senior's categorical economics would thus claim much greater certainty and universal applicability than modern hypothetical economics, of which John Stuart Mill was the founder and which operates with the help of assumptions and "models" that need not be realistic rather than on the basis of propositions that are allegedly of general validity.

Senior's contribution to the substance of economic theory includes a subjective theory of value, which like Say's derives value from utility and scarcity, considers utility as relative—he writes of "an endless diversity in the relative utility of different objects to different persons"—and comprises an incipient formulation of the principle of diminishing marginal utility: "Pleasure diminishes in a rapidly increasing ratio.... Two articles of the same kind will seldom afford twice the pleasure of one, and still less will ten give five times the pleasure of two." Senior's most influential contribution to the economic thought of his time, however, and the only one that John Stuart Mill incorporated into his *Principles,* was his interpretation of capital as the result of "abstinence"—"that agent, distinct from labor and the agency of nature, the concurrence of which is necessary to the existence of capital, and which stands in the same relation to profit as labor does to wages." Ricardo, hamstrung by his concern with labor as the source of value, had written of profits as compensation for the capitalist's trouble and risk but had failed to assign to capital a distinct role as a factor of production. Senior filled this gap and provided a solution which placed capital on an equal footing with labor, each incurring real costs in the process of production.

Senior was no dogmatic exponent of laissez faire but he aligned himself with the Whigs rather than with the philosophical radicals, and in his contributions to questions of economic policy he did not always ride the wave of the future. In his *Letters on the Factory Act* of 1837 he sharply objected to a statutory ten-hour day since this reduction of working hours would wipe out the manufacturers' profits, which he ascribed to the last two hours of a twelve-hour day, a view more in line with a labor theory of value than with Senior's utility theory. Unlike John Stuart Mill, Senior had no sympathy with labor unions since he believed that the individual laborer was the best judge of his own interests. He endorsed housing and health legislation, free elementary education, and the regulation of the employment of children, but not of adult women, whom he, like John Stuart Mill, considered as capable of managing their own affairs as are men. Senior was one of the architects of the poor law reform of 1834, which substituted indoor or workhouse relief for outdoor relief and established the principle of less eligibility, imposing on the recipients of relief living conditions less attractive than those of the lowliest independent laborer. These provisions, which were in force for nearly a century, may impress a modern reader as harsh. They were less so in the context of their time, when leading economists urged the complete repeal of the poor laws and exclusive reliance on private charity or even denied to the latter the character of an economic virtue. In the prevailing view the able-bodied poor were the victims of their own indolence or lack of self-denial rather than of social conditions over which they had no control. It would take another hundred years before certain important causes of poverty would be recognized as being beyond the responsibility of the poor and the state would assume the function of maintaining full employment.

WHATELY AND LLOYD

Senior's influence as a theorist was overshadowed by that of John Stuart Mill, who was a more faithful Ricardian and whose authority perpetuated the Ricardian theory of value. Attempts to undermine the labor theory of value were made not only by Senior but also by his successors at Oxford, first by Richard Whately (1787–1863), his former tutor and life-long friend, and subsequently by W. F. Lloyd (1795–1852). In his *Introductory Lectures on Political Economy,* published in 1832, Whately considered "labor not essential to value," and argued that "it is not that pearls fetch a high price *because* men have dived for them; but on the contrary, men dive for them because they fetch a high price." Lloyd, in his *Lecture on the Notion of Value,* published in 1837, gave a more complete account of the subjective theory of value, distinguishing, though not in these words, between total and marginal utility and making value commensurate with diminishing marginal utility.

Whately, who later became Anglican archbishop of Dublin, was interested in a variety of intellectual pursuits, including logic and rhetoric, but he considered economics of supreme importance and never failed to promote it. It was his conviction that "the world, as it always in fact has been governed by political economists of some kind, must ultimately be under the guidance of such as have systematically applied themselves to the science." He found political economy discredited by misunderstanding as well as by an ill-chosen name, and suggested instead the word *catallactics,* the

science of exchanges. When he moved to Dublin, he took great pains to
establish academic economics in Ireland and founded a chair of political
economy at Trinity College, where Senior's Oxford tradition of critical
independence from Ricardian thought was continued.

LONGFIELD

The first holder of the Whately chair was Mountifort Longfield (1802–84), an original and penetrating thinker, who made a number of outstanding contributions to economics during the five short years of his tenure. His *Lectures on Political Economy,* published in 1834, contain a wealth of new ideas that were later to come into prominence. Dismissing the Ricardian theories of value and distribution, Longfield assigns to cost only an indirect influence—via supply—on value, which he sees determined by demand and supply, interpreted in the schedule sense, with the price equating demand and supply. While pushing forward this general analysis of demand and supply and applying it to productive services as well, Longfield also pioneered in the development of special aspects of price theory. He attacked the problem of joint cost and showed the way to its correct solution, which requires that each of the jointly produced goods fetch a price equating the quantities demanded and supplied and that the sum of their prices cover the joint cost. Furthermore, he dealt with what Cairnes, a later Dublin economist and protégé of Whately, was to term noncompeting groups, pointing out that the productive services of labor are not interchangeable—bricklayers will not become barristers, and barristers not bricklayers.

But there was more to come. Longfield not only enunciated the marginal principle in distinct terms in connection with his value theory but, just as he had with demand and supply, presented it in a generalized fashion and thus became a pioneer both of the subjective theory of value and of the marginal productivity theory. As applied to value, the marginal principle indicates that "the market price is measured by that demand, which being of the least intensity, yet leads to actual purchases," a formulation that anticipates the later findings of Menger and Jevons. As for the marginal product, Longfield held that the level of profits "must be determined by the profit of that capital which is naturally the least efficiently employed," and that the profit yielded by that dose of capital is "equal to the difference of the quantities of work which the feeblest laborer would execute with and without its use." Just as profit or interest is regulated by the marginal physical product of capital, so are wages related to the productivity of labor. They do not depend upon subsistence but subsistence depends on wages. A historical tendency toward a lower rate of profit, derived from the tradition of Smith rather than of Ricardo, will encourage the formation of the more durable type of capital, including education, "which implies a present sacrifice to procure a future good."

Longfield's *Lectures on Political Economy* were followed by *Three*

Lectures on Commerce and One on Absenteeism, published in 1835, which shed new light on the theory of international trade. Longfield was the first author to expand the Ricardian principle of comparative advantage to include an analysis of more than two commodities. He draws attention to income as well as to price changes as factors responsible for the adjustment of a country's international balances, an emphasis characteristic also of later economists associated with Trinity College and one for which Longfield's work may have laid the foundation. Furthermore, the book contains passages that mark Longfield as a forerunner of the modern view which makes differences in countries' factor endowments and the resulting differences in factor prices the basis of international trade, a pioneer effort for which Ohlin, the founder of the modern view, has expressly given credit to Longfield. In addition, Longfield's concern with the economic problems of Ireland, in particular with that posed by the absentee landlords, made him aware of the special burden that the remittance of rents beyond the borders placed on the Irish economy. Others considered the problem resolved by the fact that such remittances would be made in the form of increased exports from Ireland. Longfield recognized, as did John Stuart Mill, that they would turn the terms of trade against Ireland and thus prepared the ground for the twentieth-century theory of international transfers.

Lloyd at times held the post of lecturer in mathematics at Oxford, and Longfield in his later years published "An Elementary Treatise on Series." Outwardly their contributions to economics were strictly literary in form, but the substance of their thought points to the influence of their training in mathematics. It may have been a coincidence that caused them to stumble on the marginal principle, but such a coincidence is more likely to happen to one adept in calculus, provided that otherwise he is equipped with the vision required for the generation of new thought. But the vision alone may even suffice, as is demonstrated by Senior, who had, in his own words, an "aversion" to mathematics.

High as the quality of the work of the academic economists at Oxford and Dublin was, their influence on contemporary opinion remained slight. If opportunities for sustained and full-time work in economics had been available to them, they might have had a following and formed schools. But as part-time professors on short-term appointments, they turned to other pursuits when their professorships came to an end, Lloyd to the ministry and Longfield to the law.

WAKEFIELD AND THE COLONIZATION DEBATE

Torrens contributed much to the monetary debate, Senior to factory legislation, and Longfield to the discussion of the Irish question. All of them were also concerned with the great issue of colonization, but here the leadership of the debate fell on Edward Gibbon Wakefield (1796–1862), one of the architects of the new British Empire.

Following the precedent set by Adam Smith, who depreciated the political and economic value of colonies, castigated the empire as a project "extremely fit for a nation whose government is influence by shopkeepers," and suggested its disbandment, economic opinion continued to show colonies in an unfavorable light. But thought and action followed different lines. Britain had lost her North American colonies, but she gathered naval bases, settlements for convicts or freed slaves, and military outposts—a new empire that after the close of the Napoleonic Wars stretched from Africa over Asia to the Antipodes and which, as a later Cambridge historian put it, had been brought together "in a fit of absence of mind."

After 1815, an ambivalent attitude to colonies emerged in the economic opinion of the time. Being attached to Say's law as both were, neither Ricardo nor James Mill, who contributed an article on colonies to the *Supplement to the Encyclopaedia Britannica* in 1823, would lend support to the idea that colonies might serve a useful function by providing markets for the products of the mother country. Ricardo pointed out, however, that by affecting the terms of trade "the trade with a colony may be so regulated that it shall at the same time be less beneficial to the colony and more beneficial to the mother country than a perfectly free trade." Mill, on the other hand, emphasized that it is the ruling few who derive benefits from colonies, which he characterized as providing "outdoor relief for the upper classes." Moreover, the ascendancy of the free-trade idea and the emerging industrial superiority of Britain both helped further to depreciate the value of colonial possessions or acquisitions, as did the rapid expansion of trade with the recently emancipated United States.

Meanwhile, however, Malthusian apprehensions about overpopulation brought a new point of view to the colonization debate. These apprehensions came to be more deeply felt because of several factors. To begin with, there was the urgency of the problem of oppressive poverty which plagued Ireland and called for relief. Then there was the depression which followed the Napoleonic Wars, the dislocation that industrialization brought in its train, and the attending political unrest. These factors explain why the idea gained ground that colonies might provide a welcome outlet for a surplus population of paupers. Malthus himself was skeptical about this proposed solution of the population problem, which he considered a temporary palliative rather than a remedy bringing lasting relief. But Torrens stressed in 1817 the importance of colonies as a "safety-valve" which would relieve distress, raise domestic wage rates, and quell political unrest. However, there were many objections. In a letter written in 1823, Ricardo pointed out that a pauper, if employed at home, could replace with profit the capital that England would lose by laying out money to assist emigration. Senior and others developed what has been called a "vacuum theory," according to which the void created by emigration would only encourage further population growth. Again others declared that emigration would deprive the country of the young and industrious and leave the old and infirm at home. In the midst of this debate the British government in the 1820s gave financial support to emigration from Ireland, but the matter continued to be a highly controversial issue, constituting as it did a breach, though sanctioned by the majority of economic opinion, with the laissez faire ideas of the age.

From 1815 to 1829 the "shovelling out of paupers," as a contemporary observer called it, stood in the center of the colonization debate. Then suddenly it was given a new and lasting direction by an anonymous work, published in a series of letters ostensibly written from Sydney, which first appeared in a leading London newspaper in 1829 and toward the end of the year in book form under the title *A Letter from Sydney, the Principal Town of Australia*. Wakefield, its author, was a gifted man with a clouded past, who had never been in Sydney but had written the letters while serving a prison sentence for the fraudulent abduction of a young heiress. After his release he devoted the remainder of his life to the propagation of his thoughts about the settlement of colonies, helped by his magnetic personality, wide contacts which extended from Quaker philanthropists to Benthamites, and the ability to employ pressures and "public relations" in the service of his cause.

Wakefield's thoughts, which he developed in the *Letter from Sydney* and in other writings and which involved what he termed "systematic colonization," can be summarized under three headings—land sales, selected immigration, and self-government. The first constitutes a sharp break with Adam Smith's view of free land as a boon to new countries, which protects the "inferior orders" from oppression, raises wages, and encourages the growth of population. Wakefield's views moved along different lines. To him, unrestricted access to land meant disaster. If everyone is free to acquire land, no one will want to accept employment as a hired hand. Settlements will be widely dispersed and isolated, each using only the small amount of capital that can be combined with the work of the owner. All will tend to produce the same and will do so with little efficiency. There will be no exchange, no division of labor and of occupations, in short, no "combination of labor," which is the basis of civilization. In earlier times, the employment of slave or convict labor prevented such developments. To avert them under modern conditions, Wakefield proposed a policy of a "sufficient price" for land in new territories, a price that would restrict the free access to the land and compel the immigrant to work a few years as a dependent laborer before he would be in a position to acquire land of his own. The proceeds from the land sales could in turn be gathered into a fund with which to assist emigrants in their move to new countries, a feature that would give the plan "self-regulating action."

Before Wakefield submitted his proposals, only the unskilled and those skilled in trades displaced by technological progress had been considered eligible for assisted emigration. Wakefield rejected this idea and claimed that there was "want of room for people of all classes" in the Old World and that their immigration would raise the level of civilization in the colonies, making them "extensions of older societies." Instead of paupers and convicts, the colonies should be peopled with able-bodied young couples. Wakefield gave little attention to the problems posed by the existence of natives. He held that a society formed on the basis of his proposals could soon be entrusted with self-government.

Wakefield's view that there was want of room for people of all classes in the Old World was a corollary of his opinion that there existed not only a surplus of people in Britain but one of capital as well, for which emigration could provide an outlet. With capital becoming redundant and with profits on the decline, colonies could avert stagnation and absorb the surplus capital. Free trade alone was not sufficient to assure the continued prosperity of a country whose capital increased faster than that of its customers abroad. With production abroad restricted by inadequate capital, there could be no equivalence between the value of the exports from the country richly endowed with capital and the value of the imports it received in return from countries lacking in capital, in other words, the terms of trade of the country suffering from redundancy of capital would be bound to deteriorate.

Wakefield's systematic colonization was to serve a variety of purposes:

> The objects of an old society in promoting colonization seem to be three: first, the extension of the market for disposing of their own surplus produce; secondly, relief from excessive numbers; thirdly, an enlargement of the field for employing capital.

The relation between capital redundancy, or stagnation, and colonization was underlined by Torrens, an early participant in the debate, who like Wakefield was actively connected with a number of colonization schemes and who became a supporter of Wakefield in the 1830s. After much wavering Torrens explicitly rejected Say's law and grounded the case for colonization in an empirically observed capital redundancy. Torrens based his plea for colonization on still another reason. Alarmed as he was by the threat posed to Britain's terms of trade by tariffs which her customers might levy on her exports, he argued that the expansion of colonial trade—which "resembles the home trade...in the security and permanence which it possesses" would avert or at least minimize this threat. He clinched his argument by proposing the formation of a colonial Zollverein or imperial free trade area. The larger this area, the smaller would be the scope for hostile commercial policies on the part of Britain's customers and rivals.

The reactions of others varied. Wakefield's ideas did not appeal to James Mill who had his own thoughts about the most suitable remedy for overpopulation and who did not share Wakefield's apprehension about surplus capital. Wakefield made a strong positive impression on John Stuart Mill and a negative one on Karl Marx, Mill endorsing his plea for colonization in spite of its connection with the idea of surplus capital, Marx devoting the last chapter of the first volume of his *Capital* to a sharp denunciation of Wakefield, whose systematic colonization he characterized as a "manufacture of wage workers" and to whose influence on British policy he ascribed the diversion of the stream of British emigration to the United States, where the policy of a sufficient price for land was not practiced.

THE REPEAL OF THE CORN LAWS

The economic problems of Ireland, which loomed so large in the colonization debate, were also an important factor in bringing about the repeal of the corn laws in 1846. The driving force in this struggle was the Anti-Corn Law League, founded under the leadership of Cobden and Bright as a Manchester group in 1838 and as a national one the following year. There were annual motions in Parliament in favor of free trade, but agricultural protection was withdrawn only as a result of a protracted debate when the effects of a harvest failure in Great Britain were compounded by the imminent threat of a famine in Ireland. As the movement for repeal had its center in the Manchester region which drew its livelihood from the export trade, Disraeli gave it the derogatory designation "Manchester School," a name that later was applied not only to the advocates of repeal but to the followers of laissez faire in general. Cobden and Bright, the leaders of the school, were high-minded and self-educated businessmen whose aspirations went far beyond the mere business aspects of free trade, which they considered an important instrument of international pacification. Bright exalted free trade as "the international law of the Almighty," and Cobden argued against wars and warlike policies on the ground that it was not victory in battle but the competition of the cheapest that was the decisive factor in international affairs. Both were humanitarians and reformers, pacifists and anti-imperialists, but their dogmatic attachment to laissez faire made them indifferent or hostile to factory legislation and trade unionism.

Although the agitation for repeal gained strength from the general free-trade position of the classical school, the case for free trade, as made by Smith and Ricardo, was hedged by a number of qualifications which called for gradual and partial repeal rather than lending support to the complete abandonment of agricultural protection. Smith had qualified his free-trade position by insisting on slow and gradual repeal and by upholding protective duties serving defense or offsetting a tax on the domestic product. In the corn law controversy, Malthus fell back on the national defense argument, while Ricardo denied its applicability but upheld the other two qualifications that Smith had made, pleading for gradual and partial repeal and supporting such action in Parliament. McCulloch, his faithful follower, took a similar stand, as did Torrens after he had become convinced of the need for reciprocity in commercial policy.

In the great controversies of the time, the economists were generally exponents of a laissez faire principle that was pragmatic rather than dogmatic, which allowed exceptions and had to compete with rival principles. Thus the economists would for the sake of economic stabilization sanction public control over the issue of money; they would haltingly endorse factory legislation; and to relieve distress they would be willing to have emigration assisted with public funds.

The more positive attitude to government intervention that these views reflect is characteristic of a more hopeful outlook concerning the ability of the government to initiate and execute worthwhile policies, and this outlook in turn mirrors the growth of nineteenth-century parliamentary reform. The unreformed Parliament, taken for granted during Smith's formative years, had become a subject of controversy during Ricardo's lifetime, and in 1832 the Reform Bill made a beginning in extending the suffrage and removing some of the evils which blocked Parliament from becoming a truly representative institution. James Mill and other philosophical radicals placed the highest hopes in the further extension of the suffrage and in the spread of education. To Mill, the community was capable only of pursuing the common good; the lower class, when enfranchised, would accept the enlightened guidance of the middle class. Such an optimistic outlook about the capacity of a democratic government was incompatible with continued insistence on narrow restrictions of the legitimate scope of public policies.

BASTIAT

In France, a dogmatic and doctrinaire laissez faire approach was espoused in the writings of Frédéric Bastiat (1801–50), who attempted to emulate the achievements of the Anti-Corn Law League and whose *Sophismes Économiques* and *Harmonies Économiques,* written during the last five years of his life, express his opposition not only against protectionism and all other forms of government intervention but also against the Socialists, whose views had become more of an issue in France than in England. Bastiat grounded his ultraliberal individualism in a religiously anchored and optimistic belief in a preestablished harmony of economic interests under which spontaneous development rather than coercive institutions would produce a wider diffusion of an increasing income. Government intervention could only disturb this harmony. Bastiat would reject not only protectionism but all types of social welfare measures, pointing out that when the state supplies the wants of the individual, the individual himself loses his freedom of choosing other than the state-provided means of satisfying his wants. Bastiat's contributions to economic analysis include a theory deriving value from the labor saved by the person acquiring a good and thus ultimately from "service." In this view, exchange is an exchange of services, and property becomes a bundle of services and is identical with justice. With the victory of interventionism and the rise of a more critical attitude to the facts of economic life these ideas have fallen into oblivion and Bastiat is mainly remembered for his unsurpassed ability to drive home his economic insights in the form of satires and parables. Perhaps the best example of his art is the "Petition of the Candlemakers," in which the manufacturers of lighting equipment urge Parliament to prohibit the construction of windows, through which the wicked competition of the sun brings light free of charge, a telling story designed to show up the nonsense of tariffs. Anti-protectionists made use of the ammunition that Bastiat supplied in this form in nineteenth-century America, and anti-Socialists have continued to do so down to the present time.

AMERICAN ECONOMIC THOUGHT

Bastiat had a counterpart, albeit one who eventually turned to pro-tectionism—Henry Carey in the United States. Carey's work formed the capstone of the early tradition in American economic thought which was grounded in the famous state papers of Alexander Hamilton, the architect of the "great American system" of a strong and diversified economy assisted by the government. The forerunners of Carey include Raymond and List.

RAYMOND

Daniel Raymond (1786–1849), a Baltimore attorney, provided in his *Thoughts on Political Economy* of 1820 a basis for an active public policy of promoting economic development by distinguishing between individual and national wealth and making the latter his chief concern. This distinction echoes that of Lauderdale but is differently constructed and defines national wealth as "capacity" to produce goods. To government is assigned the func-tion of enlarging this capacity with the help of a policy of protection, which was given greater emphasis by Raymond than the policy of subsidies on which Hamilton had placed principal reliance. In his plea for protective tariffs Raymond made use both of the infant industry and of the employ-ment argument, speaking explicitly of "full employment."

LIST

Frederick List (1789–1846) is remembered for his *National System of Political Economy*, which was published in Germany in 1841 but anticipated in his *Outlines of American Political Economy*, written in 1827 on behalf of the Pennsylvania protectionists during List's five-year residence in the United States. List's thoughts echo those of Raymond. He rejects the indi-vidualistic as well as the cosmopolitan point of view and embraces nationalism, placing squarely on the government the function of developing a nation's "productive powers," which he contrasts with its actual production. Once the productive powers are fully developed, a policy of free trade may be the proper one, but in the interim protection is indispensable.

CAREY

Raymond and List, while espousing incipient theories of economic development, paid little attention to the theory of distribution, which came into its own in the voluminous writings of Henry Carey (1793–1879), a Philadelphian, whose father was a self-made Irish immigrant who became a prominent publisher and left his son a substantial estate. Carey was largely self-taught; although his thoughts were undisciplined, his writings were forceful, and they made a profound impression not only in the United States but also on the "underdeveloped" continent of Europe where there were aspirations for industrial growth. His ideas were marked by nationalism, optimism, and belief in an underlying harmony of economic interests.

Carey's *Essay on the Rate of Wages* of 1835 contains the germ of his "law of distribution," which holds that with capital increasing more rapidly than population, and with increasing production, profits will rise absolutely and will do so without cutting into wages, which will rise absolutely and relatively as well. In his *Principles of Political Economy,* a three-volume work published in 1837–40, Carey developed a value theory similar to that later taught by Bastiat and expanded the harmony established in the *Essay* between the laborer and the capitalist to include also the landowner, whose return was interpreted to reflect the application of capital to land rather than the operation of the forces of nature.

Carey's theory of rent was further developed in *The Past, the Present, and the Future* of 1848, where he reversed the Ricardian sequence and on the basis of the American experience made cultivation expand from the worst to the better land, with increasing rather than diminishing returns. In this work he also broke with his own formerly held free-trade ideas and turned into a vigorous advocate of protection. Under protectionism the cost of transportation will be reduced and encouragement given to "commerce" rather than to "trade," the former providing a direct link between producers and consumers, the latter requiring a middleman. With commerce fostered, there will be fulfillment of his "law of association," which calls for the diversification of economic activities instead of narrow specialization, for the diffusion of an increasing population, and for a decentralized organization of society.

Carey's protectionism was in line with the American tradition but his harmony doctrine, restated in 1850 in a work characteristically entitled *The Harmony of Interests,* constituted a break with the ideas of Raymond, who had recognized the possibility of conflict between different economic groups and assigned to the government the function of arbitrating such conflicts.

Carey would proclaim his attachment to the ideas of Adam Smith while expressing violent opposition to those of Malthus and Ricardo. Like other American writers he found much to criticize in the classical theories of population and distribution, which seemed especially unsuited to the American environment where labor was scarce, land plentiful, and opportunities unlimited. His work seemed to confirm the often stated opinion that the new country required a new economics, one grounded in different political institutions and economic conditions than those prevailing in the Old World. With government more representative, there seemed to be less reason to distrust it and limit its scope. The rise of a new economics, characteristically American, thus posed a challenge to the classical system's claim to universal applicability, made most categorically by Senior.

CARDOZO, TUCKER, AND EVERETT

Not all American writers were protectionists, however, and since doctrine often reflected regional opinion, the Southern writers especially were inclined to uphold the Ricardo theory of free trade, as much fault as they might find with other features of classical economics. Thus Jacob Newton Cardozo (1786–1873), a South Carolinian with considerable gifts of abstract analysis, took the Ricardian theory of distribution to task in his *Notes on Political Economy* of 1826 and found it neglectful of "increased facility of production," which will cause both real wages and profits to rise as wage goods become available more cheaply and as "the old channels of commerce are constantly enlarged" by free trade.

George Tucker (1775–1861), the first teacher of economics at the newly founded University of Virginia, besides criticizing the Ricardian theory of distribution in his *Laws of Wages, Profits, and Rent* of 1837, pointed to a new theory of value by stating that "value, in its largest sense, means the feeling with which we regard whatever can render us benefit or afford us gratification." But although he characterized value as an "emotion of our minds," he failed to develop the idea any further and placed it side by side with a labor theory of value. Tucker was more of a pessimist than other American writers and visualized economic development as being attended by declining real wages and shifts in consumption to nutrients, the production of which requires less land, for example, from meat to cereals and from cereals to potatoes.

Few Americans found the Malthusian population doctrine convincing. Cardozo criticized it for neglecting institutional factors—"the entire structure of the social system"—which might give the preventive check—moral restraint—a strength equal to that attributed by Malthus to the stimulus to population growth. Malthus's error, he declared, consisted in proclaiming as a law of nature what "may be the result of an imperfect social organization," a statement that later, albeit with a different emphasis, was to resound among socialist and other critics of Malthus when they denied the existence of a "population problem" and interpreted it as a mere symptom of economic maladjustments.

While Cardozo placed his hopes in moral restraint, Alexander H. Everett (1790–1847), a Bostonian who attained prominence in public affairs, stressed another point of view in his *New Ideas on Population,* written in 1823 after a personal interview with Malthus. He ascribed to population growth favorable effects on specialization and productivity and considered them strong enough to yield greater abundance rather than scarcity.

RAE

Everett was one of the New England protectionists who in 1834 sponsored the publication of a remarkable book, *Statement of Some New Principles on the Subject of Political Economy,* which carried the provoking subtitle *Exposing the Fallacies of the System of Free Trade, and of Some Other Doctrines Maintained in the "Wealth of Nations."* The author was John Rae (1796–1872), then a resident of Canada, a solitary and restless thinker who was born in Scotland but spent most of his adult life in North America and some time in the Sandwich Islands, now known as Hawaii.

Rae's most important single contribution is his theory of capital, in which the different valuation of present and future goods, which is explained at length, plays a central role. "Instruments," as Rae terms capital goods, are designed to provide for future wants. Between their formation and consumption lies a time interval during which they yield a surplus, measured by the number of years it takes them to double the amount of labor expended in their formation. The formation of capital requires the sacrifice of a smaller present good for a greater future one. The readiness to make such a sacrifice Rae terms "the effective desire of accumulation," and under this heading he presents an original and masterly discussion of the causes that determine the accumulation of capital. The strength of the effective desire for accumulation is related to man's "social and benevolent affections," that is, to his ability to take a long-term view and to his intellectual powers. The two are interdependent, "the affections exciting the intellect to discover the means of producing good, the intellect opening up a channel to the affections by giving the power to do good."

Division of labor and technological progress will quicken the pace at which investments are returned. Thus a new function of government arises, that of equipping society more adequately with the means to satisfy future wants by fostering inventions and technological progress. What Rae proposed was realized a hundred years later, when the government assumed the major responsibility for financing research and development.

John Stuart Mill, for one, was aware of the nuggets hidden in Rae's rambling book, which was replete with lengthy digressions, but it soon fell into oblivion and was not rediscovered until the turn of the century. Mill was not only an attentive and appreciative reader of Rae but took note of virtually all currents of thought of his time. His own ideas reflected these influences but went beyond them and displayed an originality that is the mark of a master.

Chapter 16

JOHN STUART MILL:

Liberalism Redeemed

Unlike Malthus and Ricardo, John Stuart Mill (1806–73) left his mark not only on economics but on philosophy and politics as well. To this day students of logic are made to wrestle with his canons of induction, and his political thought posed questions still relevant to all to whom freedom is a vital issue. With Mill's claim to intellectual preeminence so widely staked, it is not surprising that he brought to his work in economics a perspective shared by few other nineteenth-century economists. It was this wider concern with man's position in the cosmos and in society, with the rules of his thought and of his actions, that gave new direction and focus to Mill's contributions to economics. In the broad vista of Mill's thought, purely economic tests stressing the growth of production or of efficiency give way to new and more comprehensive ones in which the quality of life and the full development of the individual stand out. Mill was a technical economist, and a master one, but his technical economics was informed by the concerns of the social philosopher.

Soaring as it did over so wide a range of matters, Mill's mind was always open to the stimulus of new ideas. It was a delicate instrument registering the influence of a multitude of intellectual tendencies alive during his time. His thought underwent a number of progressive transformations, some of which were not altogether painless and free from disappointments, but which, all in all, turned his own intellectual career into an illustrious and moving example of a drive toward a goal designated by Wilhelm von Humboldt, a German libertarian approvingly quoted by Mill, as "the object towards which every human being must ceaselessly direct his efforts," namely, "the individuality of power and development." The supreme importance of this idea permeates the whole work of Mill, including his economics. In another quotation, which Mill employed as a motto for his

Mill not only was convinced of the paramount importance of the full development of the individual but he saw in such a development humanity's only hope, a hope that he considered by no means impossible of achievement. Although Mill on the whole adhered to Malthus's population doctrine and to Ricardo's theory of distribution, the possibility of human regeneration, always stressed throughout Mill's work, took the sting out of the population dilemma, the subsistence wage, the stationary state, and other wearisome features of classical economics. Instead of the gloom spread by the economics of Malthus and Ricardo that of Mill carries the promise of a measured optimism. "No one whose opinion deserves a moment's consideration," he wrote in his *Utilitarianism*, "can doubt that most of the great positive evils of the world are in themselves removable, and will, if human affairs continue to improve, be in the end reduced within narrow limits." What Mill produced was thus more than a mere restatement of classical economics, to which he gave a new life, one which expired only as the nineteenth century came to its close.

Mill's measured optimism redeemed classical economics by making it compatible again with the belief in progress. He confounded those who like Thomas Carlyle castigated the exponents of classical economics as "the dreary professors of a dismal science." But he did more than this. Carlyle's view was that of a backward-looking authoritarian, a savage critic of liberalism and all its works, which he considered a fall from the state of grace prevailing in the golden age of the past. Others, however, would be more inclined to seek for the golden age in the future, and to them the house that Mill built offered better accommodations than those of Malthus and Ricardo. The eighteenth century had bequeathed to the nineteenth the belief in progress, and the nineteenth had strongly confirmed it by a multitude of scientific and technical advances. The spirit of the age was progressive, and Mill conformed to it more than Malthus and Ricardo had. Nothing illustrates the change better than the fact that Condorcet, the apostle of progress and the target of Malthus's attack, was among Mill's favorite authors, being designated by him as "one of the wisest and noblest of men."

MILL'S LIFE

Among the intellectual influences on Mill's mind the earliest was his father, the lieutenant of Bentham and mentor of Ricardo, who made his son the heir of the intellectual tradition of both. The story of John Stuart Mill's education has been told in his *Autobiography*, which was published shortly after his death in 1873. Tutored by his father he began to learn Greek and arithmetic at the age of three; Latin at the age of eight and somewhat later geometry, algebra, chemistry, and physics; logic at twelve and political economy at thirteen; all this accompanied by wide reading. A year later he was sent to France to round out his education, and at the age of seventeen he began, again under the tutelage of his father, his career with the East India Company, which led to high office and lasted for thirty-five years, terminating with his retirement at a then very comfortable annual pension of fifteen hundred pounds when the company was liquidated in 1858.

The severity of Mill's early education—"of playthings, I had scarcely any"—under the strictest of taskmasters instilled in him ambivalent feelings both against his father and against what his father stood for, a state of mind in which resentment was mixed with admiration, apparent between the lines of the version of the *Autobiography* as eventually published but more clearly described in a number of suppressed passages such as in the terrible indictment in which Mill complains that he grew up "in the absence of love and in the presence of fear."

The product of this education was an unusual young man, intellectually ahead of his own generation by perhaps a quarter of a century— he stood out among the geniuses of all time. A modern educational psychologist who explored the early mental traits of future geniuses, the three hundred greatest figures since the time of the Reformation, came to the conclusion that young Mill, with an estimated I.Q. of 190, stood in a class by himself. Mill put his talents to work, and his career as a writer began in his teens, lasted throughout his life, and yielded a shelf of books and countless articles in periodicals, in addition to editorial work and a huge correspondence. This achievement is the more remarkable since it was only during the last fifteen years of his life that he was free of the duties of office, and even two years of this period were absorbed by membership in the House of Commons.

MILL'S UTILITARIANISM

As a youth Mill was close to Bentham and Ricardo, intimates of his father, who intended to prepare him for the eventual leadership of the Benthamites, or philosophical radicals, as the followers of Bentham were known. However, at the age of twenty, when he was well on the way to attaining such a position, he went through a mental crisis, and from then on, at first only within his own mind but more openly after Bentham's and his father's deaths, which occurred within the next ten years, he assumed a more detached and critical attitude to Benthamism. His mature view, as stated in his *Utilitarianism* in 1861 (published as a book in 1863), was again more conciliatory, upholding Bentham's general position but modifying it in several respects. He agreed with the central idea of Bentham's, that actions are right in the proportion that they tend to promote happiness and wrong as they tend to produce the reverse of happiness. He considered as significant, however, not only the quantity of a pleasure, as Bentham had, but also its quality, and recognized "that some *kinds* of pleasure are more desirable and valuable than others." Bentham, in an often cited passage, had said: "Quantum of pleasure being equal, pushpin [a children's game] is as good as poetry." Mill, by assigning to pleasure a quality dimension, buttressed his utilitarianism against the attacks of those who insisted that this philosophy depicted human beings as unappreciative of the finer enjoyments of life and "capable of no pleasure except those of which swine are capable."

This concession, which Mill believed necessary, had several important consequences. Whereas to Bentham the pleasure of one person counted as much as that of another, Mill's approach opened the door to a discriminate evaluation not only of pleasures but also of the agents enjoying them. "A being of higher faculties," he said, "requires more to make him happy," thereby setting a precedent later followed by F. Y. Edgeworth in his *Mathematical Psychics* of 1881, whose utilitarian calculus took account of supposed differences of capacity for enjoyment and who wrote of the superior capacity of "man above brute, of civilized above savage, of birth, of talent, and of the male sex." However, the calculus of utility can be employed not only in support of inequality, but, in conjunction with the principle of diminishing marginal utility, also in support of exactly the opposite, that is, of equalizing policies of, say, taxation, an implication likewise stressed by Edgeworth, who developed this idea in his writings on the pure theory of taxation. This supposed consequence of the principle of utility has been vigorously opposed by Lionel Robbins, who in the second edition of his *Essay on the Nature and Significance of Economic Science* (1935) denied the *scientific* comparability of different individual experiences altogether, relegating interpersonal comparisons of utility to the realm of judgments of value rather than of facts.

Modern utility theory has on the whole followed Bentham rather than Mill in not querying the inherent quality of goods. It posits choice not between classes of goods but between units of goods at the margin. There has been a return to Mill's type of approach, however, in the writings of those critics of utility theory who, like John A. Hobson at the turn of the century and John K. Galbraith fifty years later, would want to rank goods by other criteria than those provided by the market, the former pointing out the "human cost" of "mal-consumption," and the latter stressing the bias created by advertising in favor of goods of private consumption and the consequent disregard of goods of public consumption such as clean air and water. If the forces of the market, where each participant has one vote, albeit one weighted by purchasing power, do not suffice to bring about a redirection of production in line with these ideas, it will be necessary to rely on a judgment presumably superior to that of the market—again a thought that was not entirely alien to Mill, who in his *Considerations on Representative Government* of 1861 proposed to give extra votes to individuals possessed of "mental superiority" and who in his *Utilitarianism* made it clear that "it is better to be a human being dissatisfied than a pig satisfied; better to be Socrates dissatisfied that a fool satisfied. And if the fool, or the pig, is of a different opinion, it is because they only know their own side of the question. The other party to the comparison knows both sides."

MILL AND CONTEMPORARY CURRENTS OF THOUGHT

The new forces that came to rival and overshadow Bentham's and Mill's father's influence over Mill's mind arose from a variety of sources. To begin with, there was Mill's French connection, grounded in a fourteen-month residence in the country at a most impressionable age, giving him proficiency in the language and providing contact with the richest civilization of the Continent. By means of correspondence and frequent visits Mill nurtured this contact throughout his life, and his death and burial in Avignon seem a symbol of his attachment. The specific influences of Mill's French connection on his economic thought emanated from the socialism of Fourier and especially from that of Saint-Simon and his followers, as well as from the positivism of Comte, the erstwhile secretary of Saint-Simon and the founder of sociology.

In addition to these influences Mill's mind was moved by the romantic tendencies of his age. These form a stark contrast with Bentham's more narrow concerns with man's reason, which, it seemed to Mill, did not make adequate allowance for the role of feelings and sentiments. Bentham had compared poetry to a childish game and ridiculed it: "Prose is when all the lines except the last go on to the end. Poetry is when some of them fall short of it." Mill was deeply appreciative of poetry and considered that of Wordsworth an important factor in his recovery from his mental crisis at the age of twenty. Moreover, although Mill, unlike Wordsworth and Coleridge, never shed his youthful radicalism, he welcomed in the conservative thought of Coleridge a supplementation of the views of Bentham. "The two men," he said, "are each other's 'completing counterpart'; the strong points of each correspond to the weak points of the other. . . . To Bentham it was given to discern more particularly those truths with which existing doctrines and institutions were at variance; to Coleridge the neglected truths which lay *in* them." Mill found stimulation even in the ideas of Carlyle, the substance of whose thought was so different from his own but whom he considered basically a poet and man of intuition and as such capable of perceiving things not readily accessible to his own mind.

The specific influences on the formation of Mill's economic ideas can easily be traced. He was impressed with the arguments of the Saint-Simonians when they favored the emancipation of women or found fault with the uncontrolled passage of wealth from the dead to the living. He took seriously the Saint-Simonian and other variants of socialism with which he became familiar and attempted to come to terms with them. Comte's ideas about the place of economics in the hierarchy of the sciences and the method proper to it served as starting points for the development of his own mature thought about these matters. The religion of humanity proclaimed by the French thinkers and its ministration by the good and the wise informed his own humanism and his attempts to assign to a mentally superior elite a special role in state and society. He made the second of Comte's watchwords, "order and progress," his own, rivaling the greatest happiness principle as the highest good. Comte's attempt to interpret history as the progressive development of the human intellect, leading from the metaphysical over the theological stage to positivism, stimulated Mill's own search for a philosophy of history. Mill's historical sense was also activated by the teachings of Carlyle and Coleridge who like Wordsworth had been exposed to the influence of German romanticism with its opposition to the rationalism of the Enlightenment, paired with love for the past and predilection for historical studies. Although Bentham's precepts would not have turned Mill into a dogmatic exponent of laissez faire, what he learned from Coleridge could serve as a confirmation of his own more pragmatic attitude. Referring to Coleridge, Mill said:

> He is at issue with the *let alone* doctrine, or the theory that governments can do nothing better than to do nothing: a doctrine generated by the manifest selfishness and incompetence of modern European governments, but of which, as a general theory, we may now be permitted to say, that one half of it is true and the other half false.

MILL AND HARRIET TAYLOR

Weighty as these influences and convergent ideas were, they were overshadowed by what to Mill was the greatest intellectual and emotional experience of his life—his friendship and his subsequent marriage to Harriet Taylor. When the two first met, Mill was twenty-five and Harriet twenty-three and they seemed destined for each other had Harriet not been the wife of another man and the mother of two children. In 1851, some twenty years later, after Harriet had become a widow and a proper interval been allowed to pass, they were married, and an end seemed to have been put to a long period of frustration and heartache. However, the union was to last for only a few years as Harriet died in 1858. Mill's relationship to Harriet, a moving story in itself, is important as well in the history of ideas because Mill acknowledged, on many occasions and always in exalted terms, an intellectual debt to her that seems to defy all attempts at sober appraisal.

In dedications of his books and in his *Autobiography* Mill spoke of her as "the inspirer, and in part, the author, of all that is best in my writings," extolled her "exalted sense of truth and right," and described her "as the most eminently qualified of all persons known to the author either to originate or to appreciate speculations on social improvement." Of himself he said:

> Were I but capable of interpreting to the world one half of the great thoughts and noble feelings which are buried in her grave, I should be the medium of a greater benefit to it, than is ever likely to arise from something that I can write, unprompted and unassisted by her all but unrivalled wisdom.

He compared her with Shelley—"but in thought and intellect, Shelley, so far as his powers were developed in his short life, was but a child compared with what she ultimately became."

The interpretation of the kind and measure of the intellectual debt that Mill so generously acknowledged has remained a matter of controversy. On the one side there are some who are inclined to take him more or less literally; on the other side there are those who believe that Mill's profound attachment to Harriet made him magnify her influence on his work. Although definitive conclusions about the matter are difficult to reach, there is no doubt that in his *Principles of Political Economy* he willingly submitted to her influence both in shaping important ideas and in changing their presentation as one edition followed the other. It was on Harriet's prompting, to mention but one example, that Mill took a more positive attitude to socialism in the later editions of his book.

CONTRIBUTIONS TO INTERNATIONAL ECONOMICS

Mill's earliest contributions to economics, which show him at the the height of his intellectual powers, are found in his *Essays on Some Unsettled Questions of Political Economy,* all but one of which were published in 1844 but had originally been written in 1829 and 1830, when Mill was not yet twenty-five. The first essay contains the substance of Mill's contributions to the theory of international trade, which competent judges consider Mill's greatest and most influential accomplishment in technical economics.

THE DIVISION OF THE GAIN FROM TRADE

To begin with what stands out as most important, Mill developed his ideas about the distribution of the gains from international trade. This was, and was meant to be by Mill, a further development of the theory of comparative advantage founded by Ricardo, "whose attention," Mill said with characteristic deference, "was engrossed by far more important questions, and who, having a science to create, had not time, or room, to occupy himself with much more than the leading principles. When he had done enough to enable any one who came after him, and who took the necessary pains, to do all the rest, he was satisfied."

Ricardo had demonstrated that there is a gain from trade but had left open the question of its distribution among the trading partners. His discussion points to the conclusion that the comparative cost ratios, 5/6 and 9/8 in his example, form the outer limits of a range of profitable trading. That is, all the gain from trade accrues to Portugal if a unit of English cloth fetches no more than 5/6 units of Portuguese wine; whereas all the gain accrues to England if the cloth fetches as much as 9/8 units of Portuguese wine. He further implied that the rate at which English cloth would actually exchange for Portuguese wine would lie somewhere in the middle between these extremes, perhaps being 1:1.

Mill placed the capstone on the theory of comparative advantage by developing what Torrens, whose contribution overlapped that of Mill, designated as the theory of reciprocal demand. Mill's theory elucidates the determination of the price ratio of exports in terms of imports, or what since the time of Marshall has been known as the terms of trade. According to the theory of reciprocal demand, English cloth will be traded for Portuguese wine at a price that lies between the cost ratios and is such as to elicit from Portugal exactly the quantity of wine that England will accept in exchange for cloth, and from England exactly the quantity of cloth that Portugal will accept in exchange for wine. The presumption is that at prices that make cloth cheap in terms of wine—or, what is the same, at prices that make wine dear in terms of cloth—England will offer less cloth than Portugal is willing to take, and Portugal will offer more wine than England is willing to take. Conversely, at prices that make cloth dear in terms of wine, England will offer more cloth than Portugal is ready to accept, and Portugal will offer less wine than England would be willing to purchase. At the equilibrium price there will be no such shortages and surpluses; instead, the quantities of imports demanded will be equal to the quantities of exports supplied.

To the question, What determines the quantities of cloth and wine being offered at various prices?, Mill replied by referring to the factors constituting the strength and elasticity of demand. The stronger the demand for a commodity, the more favorable are the terms of trade of the country producing it, and vice versa. Mill's discussion demonstrates that he understood demand as a schedule or function and that he was aware of the significance of the varying reactions of prospective buyers to changes in price, that is, of the elasticity of demand. By laying stress on the relevance of demand elasticity for international trade theory and by giving special attention to the "extreme case" where "of some given commodity a certain quantity is all that is wanted at any price," that is, to an example of inelastic demand, he developed some of the thought behind what is now known as the Marshall-Lerner condition, which, to make an exchange depreciation instrumental in restoring equilibrium in a country's international balance of payments, requires a sum of elasticities of foreign demand for exports and home demand for imports greater than 1.

Mill's theory of reciprocal demand, which was not seriously questioned until the 1920s, shows the ability of a great mind to arrive by means of verbal thought processes at insights equivalent to those later established with the help of mathematical techniques. As has been said, "the fact that Mill could and did use mathematical reasoning without mathematical symbols, is a tribute to his genius, and makes his achievement all the more impressive." The apparatus of reciprocal demand or offer curves, which Marshall later developed and which was refined by Edgeworth, was in Marshall's own words no more than "a diagrammatic treatment of Mill's problem of international values." These curves, he wrote, "were set to a definite tune, that called by Mill."

Mill was aware of the total revenue criterion of demand elasticity and distinguished the three kinds now designated as elastic, unitary, and inelastic demand. An increase in the price of a good, he wrote,

> will probably diminish the quantity consumed. It may diminish it so much that even at the increased price there will not be required so great a money value as before. It may diminish it in such a ratio that the money value of the quantity consumed will be exactly the same as before. Or it may not diminish it at all, or so little, that in consequence of the higher price a greater money value will be purchased than before.

TARIFFS AND THE TERMS OF TRADE

While developing these ideas Mill scored a second point, marking another advance in international trade theory. An import duty, he taught, will raise the price of imports in the importing country. At the higher price the quantity demanded will be reduced as will the total sales revenue earned by the foreigner, who receives not the sales price in its entirety but diminished by the amount of the duty. The sales revenue earned by foreigners, or the value of their exports, will no longer cover the value of their imports. They will lose gold and their prices will fall, whereas prices will rise in the country imposing the tariff. Thus the latter country will obtain imports cheaper—their price will exceed what it previously was by less than the full amount of the duty, which the foreigner pays in part—and secure a higher price for its exports. The terms-of-trade argument in support of a tariff, which Mill developed here, is one of the very few such arguments that can stand up under static conditions.

Mill's analysis, although it seemed to weaken the case for free trade, was nevertheless in the tradition of Ricardo, who had pointed out the possibility open to a metropolitan country of changing in its own favor the terms of its colonial trade. Mill emphasized, however, that the argument developed by him lends no support to a prohibitive tariff which would put an end to all trade and that the danger of retaliation, always elicited by the type of tariff under discussion, would place severe limits on its practical use. The reaction to Mill's idea has varied. Marshall presented a detailed analysis of the matter but considered it of little practical bearing. Edgeworth, when commenting on a new variant of Mill's argument which was developed by Bickerdike at the turn of the century, proposed that because of the danger of abuse it should be labeled "poison." Modern reaction has been more positive, and there is a direct connection between Mill's theory and contemporary efforts to develop a theory of an optimum tariff.

Assuming German exports of linen, English exports of cloth, and an English tariff on linen, Mill depicts the adjustment of the balance of payment, after it has been disturbed as a result of the imposition of the tariff:

> *Prices* will fall in Germany and rise in England; linen will fall in the German market; cloth will rise in the English. The Germans will pay a higher price for cloth, and will have smaller money *incomes* to buy it with; while the English will obtain linen cheaper, that is, its price will exceed what it previously was by less than the amount of the duty, while their means of purchasing it will be increased by the increase of their money *incomes*.

THE MECHANISM OF ADJUSTMENT

The emphasis that has been given to the words *prices* and *incomes* indicates that the mechanism of adjustment, as visualized by Mill, includes changes in both prices and incomes. Although Mill elsewhere in his work laid stress on price changes as the instrument yielding adjustment of the balance of payments, price and income changes appear here side by side. On the basis of the precedent set by Hume's theory of the automatic flow of specie, the classical theory of the adjustment is generally considered as having viewed price changes as the instrument of adjustment. Hume had taught that a passive balance of trade is responsible for movements of gold, and that these, in line with the quantity theory of money, will raise prices in the gold-receiving country and lower them in the gold-losing one, bringing a redress of the balance and a return of the gold. However, as has been noted, Ricardo, for one, did not identify himself with this view, and as for Mill, he appears to have given weight both to changes in prices and to changes in incomes.

The theory of the adjustment process that envisages changes in incomes rather than in prices as instrumental in restoring equilibrium has been in the lead only since the late 1930s after the publication of Keynes's *General Theory*. This theory is often characterized as "modern" and contrasted with the classical view, although references to changes in incomes as the equilibrating factor, or as one of them, can also be found in the earlier literature, classical and postclassical. In spite of these references, exemplified by the citation from Mill, there is a sound basis for drawing a line of demarcation between the classical and the modern view, since only as a result of the work of Keynes has it been possible to connect the theory of the adjustment process operating via income changes with a full-fledged theory of income determination, yielding such conceptual aids as the propensity to import and the foreign-trade multiplier. Unlike earlier discussions of adjustment via changes in income, the modern theory makes it possible to indicate the extent or the limitations of the adjustment produced by such changes.

UNILATERAL TRANSFERS

When Mill discusses unilateral transfers such as the payment of reparations or subsidies, he relies exclusively on price changes to secure the necessary adjustment. A fall of prices in the paying and an increase in the receiving country will bring about a reduction of the paying country's imports and an expansion of its exports so that its exports will exceed its imports by the amount of the unilateral transfer. Such a transfer thus involves a deterioration of the paying country's terms of trade. By implication, the same consequence would follow in the case of long-term capital movements from lender to borrower.

The modern view is not nearly as unequivocal as was Mill's. It does not exclude changes in prices and in the terms of trade but relates these and their extent to such factors as the behavior of incomes and expenditures in the paying (lending) and in the receiving (borrowing) country, to the latter country's propensity to spend the new receipts on imports, and to the way in which the banking systems will react to the transaction. Price changes will be minimized if expenditures and incomes fall in the paying (lending) country and rise in the receiving (borrowing) country, and if the latter uses the receipts for purchases in the former.

Many writers after Mill have made valuable contributions to the theory of international trade, but a century had to pass before Ohlin, in the 1920s and 1930s, and then not much older than Mill had been when he wrote his *Essays,* produced a tour de force comparable to Mill's in originality and influence. In his *Interregional and International Trade* of 1933, Ohlin offered a searching criticism of the doctrine of comparative costs, the central part of the classical theory of international trade, to which Mill had given its lasting form, and he opened up an entirely new view by grounding international trade in differences in factor endowment. No such revolution in thought was accomplished by Mill. As an economic theorist, his work was mainly one of consolidation and further development of established thought.

MILL AND SAY'S LAW

It was characteristic of Mill's approach to search for something of value even in opinions that he felt compelled to reject. Thus in the second of the *Essays,* which contains a discussion of Say's law of markets, he appealed to "those who direct their assaults against ancient prejudices" to see to it "that no scattered particles of important truth are buried and lost in the ruins of exploded error." The assaulter here was either Say or Mill's father, who stated his own version of the law of markets. The ancient prejudices were the opinions of Lauderdale, Malthus, and Sismondi, who had given reasons for the belief that the quantity of all goods demanded might fall short of the quantity supplied. Mill went a long way to reconcile these differences. Say had argued that whoever offers a commodity for sale desires to obtain a commodity in exchange for it and is therefore a buyer by the mere fact of being a seller. This view Mill held incontestable, but only on the assumption that there is a state of barter, when selling and buying are combined in a single, indissoluble operation. The use of money, however, divides this operation into two separate transactions, and these may be performed during different periods of time. He who sells "needs not buy at the same moment when he sells; and he does not therefore necessarily add to the *immediate* demand for one commodity when he adds to the supply of another."

With buying and selling separated, a situation of general oversupply may easily be possible, not as a result of overproduction but of lack of confidence. A general anxiety to sell without delay then coincides with a general inclination to defer purchases. Inventories will rise and prices fall. Although Mill states that commodies of all kinds may remain unsold "for a long time," he nevertheless insists, and he does so more than once and always in forceful terms, that the excess of all commodities is always a temporary one and will generally be followed by a brisk demand. Mill thus denies the possibility of chronic stagnation inherent in Malthus's argument and instead develops an incipient theory of the business cycle in which the state of confidence holds a strategic position. His interpretation of Say's law freed it of its paradoxical character and prepared the ground for the modern view that represents the relationship between demand and supply as one of equality rather than of identity. In fact, the argument drawn from barter, which Mill was the first to develop, has continued to play an important role in contemporary discussion.

MILL'S APPROACH TO ECONOMICS

Mill's ability to transform Say's law from a paradox into a statement acceptable to common sense was in no small measure due to the method of economic analysis practiced by him, which he discussed in general terms in the last of his *Essays*. According to Mill, an *economist*—the word is now used side by side and interchangeably with *political economist* and no longer connotes a physiocratic connection—is a student of a science rather than a practitioner of an art. Economics is a collection of positive truths rather than a body of normative rules, although such rules are founded on it. It informs us of the laws that regulate the production and distribution of wealth; consumption, according to Mill, is not to be singled out and coordinated with the two other components since its study forms an inseparable part of these. As he wrote before the upheaval of the 1870s which brought marginal utility and the subjective theory of value to the fore, he could say: "We know not of any *laws* of the *consumption* of wealth as the subject of a distinct science: they can be no other than the laws of human enjoyment."

Production is the subject matter both of economics and—as technology—of the natural sciences. The overlap is, however, more apparent than real because economics is a moral science, concerned with laws of the mind, whereas the natural sciences develop laws of matter which the economist will accept as data. As a rule, he will presuppose the existence of these data without giving them specific content, but at times, for example in the case of the principle of diminishing returns, he specifies their peculiarities, borrowing, as it were, a truth from the physical sciences. Among the moral or mental sciences, some lay stress on man as an individual, whereas economics, for example, considers him as living in a state of society where he forms part of a union or aggregation of human beings who systematically cooperate for common purposes. Economics does not treat of the whole of man's nature and conduct in society but has a scope that is more narrowly circumscribed: it considers him solely a being desirous of possessing wealth and capable of passing judgment on the comparative efficiency of the means for the attainment of this end. Man, however, is swayed by a plurality of motivations and feelings among which the desire to possess wealth is only one. On the whole, economics abstracts from these noneconomic considerations, taking into account but three, man's aversion to labor, his desire "of the present enjoyment of costly indulgences," and the principle of population, all of which have been incorporated into economics. But with so many other motivations and feelings still abstracted, economics will only produce approximate truth which may have to be modified by making proper allowance for the operation of other factors.

Mill thus constructs a *homo economicus* but does so fully aware that his artifice is an ideal type which rarely has its exact counterpart in the world of reality. Unlike Senior's, his economics is not categorical but hypothetical, with propositions that are true if no degree of influence is exercised by the factors not taken into consideration. He considers the exploration of these factors an indispensable prerequisite for explaining and predicting the phenomena of the real world.

Mill draws the conclusion that economics is essentially an abstract science, arriving at generalizations on the basis of hypothetical assumptions which need have no basis in fact. Unlike the natural sciences, economics offers only limited scope for controlled experimentation, and it is mainly for this reason that induction, that is, arguing upward from particular facts to general conclusions, cannot be properly employed as a method of arriving at general statements in economics. Induction, however, has an important function to fulfill when it comes to the verification of the general propositions that have been developed with the help of hypothetical assumptions. Indeed, when it comes to the application of economics and to practical policy proposals, verification is indispensable and there is much scope for the observation of the facts of life. The business of verification consists mainly of the elucidation of "disturbing causes," which may have laws of their own, again to be discovered with the help of generalizations based on hypothetical assumptions. Many of these causes may relate to noneconomic factors which fall within the province of other sciences, and here, Mill says, "the mere political economist, he who has studied no science but political economy, if he attempt to apply his science to practice, will fail."

Mill was himself a faithful follower of his methodological precepts. It was his awareness of the need for hypotheses to be tested that made him scrutinize the applicability of Say's law to a monetary economy and interpret it in a manner that would do no violence to the observed fact of an occasional oversupply of commodities in want of purchasers. Moreover, Mill recognized that disturbing causes are often elusive and that to locate them one has to be an impartial critic of one's own theories, be willing to admit the existence of facts previously overlooked, and be able to see things from the point of view of other students of the subject. Mill's attitude to his own later work and his readiness to correct it in response to reasons he considered compelling indicate how seriously he took the methodological precepts which he had elaborated in his youth.

Mill's thought about the limitations of the expert was later given another and more forceful version in his *Autobiography:*

> Political economy, in truth, has never pretended to give advice to mankind with no lights but its own; though people who knew nothing but political economy (and therefore knew that ill) have taken upon themselves to advise, and could only do so by such lights as they had.

Mill's own watchword was Goethe's "many-sidedness." He himself was no narrow specialist but a master of the philosophy and of the social sciences of his time. Since then, however, the growing riches and complexity of each branch of knowledge and its consequent division into subdisciplines have made it all but impossible to live up to Mill's watchword. To apprehensions about the limitations of economists who give advice without realizing its political implications has been added the broader concern about the cleavage between "two cultures," one humanistic-literary and the other scientific-technical, apprehensions that are only inadequately allayed by attempts at intra- and inter-disciplinary communication and cooperation. Mill thus posed a problem that was closer to a solution at his own time than in ours.

Mill returned to questions of economic methods in his *Logic* of 1843, which he wrote after the *Essays,* and the matter continued to occupy his mind during the 1840s when he went to work on his *Principles of Political Economy* of 1848. By then he had come under the influence of Auguste Comte (1798–1857), the French positivist, and his later views about the proper method of economics and its place in social science show his attempts to come to terms with Comte's ideas and, if possible, attain a reconciliation between his own thought and that of Comte. Comte's wide-ranging and influential system covers all sciences and all history, and in it profound and bizarre ideas stand side by side. Comte's system was a closed one, which its author considered so perfect that any thought of completion, correction, or improvement would appear to him as a preposterous presumption. He had made it a rule of his regimen of cerebral hygiene not to read other people's books, would brook no opposition to his own thought, and if Mill would fail to accommodate his ideas to his own, the two men would have to part, as in the end they did.

Of all of Comte's ideas that Mill found suggestive and stimulating, the two most relevant in the present context were Comte's theory of the consensus and his positive method. Comte's consensus, an immensely fruitful idea which foreshadows both the *Gestalt* of contemporary psychology and the Walrasian general equilibrium in economics, insists on the mutual interdependence of all social phenomena. The philosophical and religious tendencies of a time, its literary and artistic creations, its technology and its political and economic institutions do not merely stand side by side but form an integrated whole. They are linked by processes of interaction whereby any profound change in one sector is accompanied by related changes, leading, lagging, or coincident ones, in the other sectors. With this theory of the consensus the founder of sociology meant to undermine the existence of any specialized branch of social science, vesting in an all-embracing sociology the only clue that would reveal the laws regulating life in society. Moreover, there was Comte's positive method, which heralded induction as the only proper way to arrive at generalizations, which, however, once they were drawn from specific experience, might be tested by deduction. As for economics, Comte found fault with it on the grounds of the theory of the consensus and the requirement of induction. Its very existence violated the former, and its method did not satisfy the latter. Comte made a few complimentary observations about Adam Smith but on the whole saw nothing good in economics, which he found unduly narrow, unscientific, and concerned with the meaning of words rather than with reality—a branch of metaphysics, as he wrote disparagingly, rather than a true science.

The 1840s show Mill wrestling with the issues that Comte's intransigence had raised. Much later, in 1865, when wholehearted enthusiasm had given way to partial disillusionment, Mill would in a series of essays

In the meantime he attempted in various ways to arrive at an accommodation with the thought of Comte. Impressed as he was with the theory of
the consensus, which echoed his own idea of the limitation of the expert,
he nevertheless upheld the validity of departmental social sciences such as
economics but conceded that their findings are conditional on agreement
with those of sociology, Comte's general science of society. The latter,
he taught, should adopt the inductive method, whereas for economics
he preferred to adhere to his own method of deduction. Moreover, economics was to be supplemented by "ethology," a science of national character yet to be constructed, which would be of assistance in revising the
findings of the economists in the light of behavior patterns and responses
characteristic of different countries. English economists, Mill pointed out,
are apt to assume that everybody behaves as an Englishman would—an
assumption often running counter to the facts. Mill eventually abandoned
work on this projected science, whose name has returned in modern times
to serve another purpose. However, the thought that underlies his proposal
recurs in his *Principles of Political Economy,* especially in the separate
treatment of distribution theory and in the attention given to habit and
custom and national differences in economic institutions. In addition, Mill
tried to put Comte's apprehensions to rest by designating the findings of
his *Political Economy* as "provisional," a characterization that Comte
accepted, although both may have interpreted the crucial word in different ways, the one—Mill—meaning "subject to such changes in the economic
organization of society as may occur in the future," the other—Comte—
"subject to the replacement of economics by the science of general sociology
yet to be created."

MILL'S *PRINCIPLES*

Mill's *Principles of Political Economy* was written in a little over
two years, and even during this short time Mill had to lay the manuscript
aside for a period of six months when other work called for his attention.
The book was at once accepted as authoritative, Mill by then having
become known as a brilliant essayist and writer on logic. The work went
through seven editions, which often contained important revisions. There
were also low-priced people's editions, an abridged edition, which an
unfriendly critic referred to as "mutilated," for the use of American
students, and numerous translations. The success of the book was a sustained
one, and it continued to be used as a text by succeeding generations of
students through the early part of the twentieth century.

Nurtured on Ricardian economics as Mill had been since his early
youth, he set out to update what Ricardo had taught and to harmonize
"the principles previously laid down by the best thinkers on the subject"
with new ideas—on currency, foreign trade, colonization, and so forth—

which had emerged during the preceding thirty years. But this was not his entire goal, which was much wider and went beyond a mere restatement of Ricardo's thought. The complete title of Mill's book reads: *Principles of Political Economy, with Some of Their Applications to Social Philosophy*. It is especially the subtitle that hints at this broader purpose of Mill's work, which gave it a character of its own and a structure resembling that of *The Wealth of Nations* rather than of Ricardo's *Principles*. This indeed was his intention. Being concerned not only with the exposition of abstract principles but also with their practical application, he felt the need to take into account "far larger considerations than pure political economy affords," expressing again his apprehension about the limitations of the expert:

> Except on matters of mere detail, there are perhaps no practical questions, even among those which approach nearest to the character of purely economical questions, which admit of being decided on economical premises alone.

Mill's two-volume work, whose five hundred thousand words make its length rival that of *The Wealth of Nations*, is divided into five books, which discuss production, distribution, exchange, "dynamics," and the influence of government. There is no separate discussion of consumption which would coordinate the matter with these overall headings. Historical and institutional material and matters of policy are discussed throughout but given extended scope, amounting to one-tenth of the work, when Mill takes up questions of agricultural organization and land tenure in connection with his attempt to contribute to the solution of the economic problems of Ireland.

PRODUCTION AND DISTRIBUTION

The great innovation, which Mill underlines by placing it at the beginning of the work, is the distinction he draws between production and distribution. The principles regulating the production of wealth are grounded in laws of natural science and therefore beyond human control, whereas "unlike the laws of production, those of distribution are partly of human institution" and thus subject to change.

It is an open question whether the facts support a dividing line so sharply drawn between production and distribution. Mill may have meant to stress that nature places a ceiling on output, hanging on to the old idea of the niggardliness of nature, which seems to be less emphasized in other parts of his work. His treatment of diminishing returns, for example, which is included in a chapter entitled "Of the Law of the Increase of Production from Land," shows that he was aware that the ceiling on output is flexible and reflects technology and the state of the arts, and that these matters, in turn, are a function of education and other institutional factors labeled by Mill as "progress of civilization," which he discussed at length as checking the tendency to diminishing returns. Elsewhere Mill writes of "the perpetual, and so far as human foresight can extend, the unlimited growth of man's power over nature." This would point to a break in his thought—if production is so much influenced by the progress of civilization, it cannot fail to be "partly of human institution," just as is distribution.

Mill accentuated the disjunction between production and distribution by failing to employ as a link between the two the labor theory of value, the link that Ricardo had forged with this purpose in mind. Neither his book on production nor that on distribution contains his value theory, which instead appears later under the heading of "exchange." Mill's position seems distant both from the earlier views of Ricardo and from neo-classical thought, which coordinates production and distribution with the help of the marginal productivity theory, the demand curve for factor services being the curve of the marginal revenue product. The contrast with modern thought is, however, more apparent than real because modern analysis relates to production the functional rather than the personal aspect of distribution. If Mill's dichotomy is interpreted as referring to production and personal distribution, the contrast with modern thought vanishes.

This is indeed what Mill appears to have had in mind. Sensitive to all proposals for social change as he was throughout his life, he wanted to consolidate an open rather than a closed economic science, which not merely abstracted from the economic organization of his time but would have many mansions to accommodate other forms of social life. His distinction between production and distribution was thus meant to give resonance to the clarion call for economic reorganization and reform which resounds throughout his work. By pointing out the variability of the laws of distribution, the division of wealth arising under laissez faire appears as but one of several types of economic organization. Unlike Adam Smith, Mill views laissez faire not as a natural system of liberty but as a man-made institution and as such subject to the test of social usefulness.

Mill's approach to distribution embodies its recognition as a concrete historical category, reflecting at his time the property relations in a given historical setting. He thereby opened up a protracted debate about the extent to which economic categories are universally valid and to what extent they reflect a specific historical structure. Marx, in his critique of capitalism and of political economy, considered the latter a superstructure built on a given mode of production and thus laid stress on the second interpretation. Böhm-Bawerk took the opposite view, both with respect to interest, which he tried to uphold as a general category rather than as one arising from specific institutions, and in a broad appraisal of the respective roles of "power vs. economic law." Pareto resumed the debate by making personal income distribution appear as an invariant conforming to a dubious law that would hold regardless of institutional change. The unsatisfactory status of the modern theory of distribution, which contains hardly any propositions relevant to personal distribution, indicates that the debate is still far from closed and invites its continuation.

Although these considerations shed light on the intention underlying Mill's thought about the flexible nature of distribution, another reason impelled him to make production appear as inflexible. He never wavered in his firm belief in the necessity for controlling population growth, a belief that he had already professed when as a youth he distributed leaflets on birth control and which continued to inform his mature thought as set forth in the *Principles of Political Economy,* where the same idea was elaborated, albeit more discreetly, and given a prominent place in his system. Just as Mill's view about the flexibility of distribution lent support to his plea for open-minded receptiveness to proposals for social and economic reform, so did his insistence on the inflexible nature of production serve as a justification for his opinion of an ever present need for the limitation of births. It would be a serious matter, he held, "to mistake the permanent laws of production (such as those on which the necessity is grounded of restraining population) for temporary accidents arising from the existing constitution of society—which those who would frame a new system of social arrangements are at liberty to disregard." This view was challenged by Marx and his followers, who held exactly the opposite opinion, as it was by all those who denied the independent existence of a population problem as such and considered it a mere symptom of economic maladjustment calling for just that type of reorganization of society which according to Mill would fail to break the hold of the permanent laws of production. It remains an open question how Mill meant to reconcile his view with the belief that the progress of civilization could check the tendency to diminishing returns.

THE THEORY OF VALUE

Mill's sensitivity to the intellectual currents of his time did not extend to two doctrinal matters where he failed to perceive or react to new thought which seemed within his grasp. These were the theories of value and of monopoly. "Happily," he wrote, "there is nothing in the laws of value which remains for the present or any future writer to clear up; the theory of the subject is complete." This was written in 1848, when the Ricardian theory of value had already been challenged by the Oxford and Dublin economists, and it remained unchanged throughout all subsequent editions of the *Principles,* including the last one printed during Mill's lifetime (whose appearance coincided with the publication of Jevons's *Theory of Political Economy* of 1871, which introduced a new theory of value and ushered in the marginal revolution). That Mill's sensitive mind failed to register the shadow cast by this new thought has to do with his reluctance to develop side by side with the theories of production and distribution a theory of consumption, which would have provided the analytical framework for an alternative view of value. A clue to his attitude is provided by the aforementioned passage in the *Essays* in which he denies that the laws of the consumption of wealth are the subject of a departmental science and insists that they are "no other than the laws of human enjoyment." This points to the possibility that it was not only deference to Ricardo that made Mill adhere to the latter's theory of value but also that the development of a rival theory was obstructed by Mill's ambivalent attitude to Bentham's utilitarianism, which made him reluctant to plough again the field dealing with the laws of human enjoyment.

MONOPOLY AND COMPETITION

A much more elusive matter than the subjective theory of value was the theory of monopoly, which Cournot had developed in 1838 in a book that for a long time was little noticed and with which Mill appears to have been unfamiliar. The economic theory that Mill developed was not a general one which would claim validity in any kind of market, nor was it given alternative forms to reflect different types of markets. Instead it was valid only on the assumption of competition, a limitation of his theory which Mill never tired of underlining. In place of Ricardian absolutism Mill's economics thus acquires a relativistic coloring both because of his special view concerning distribution, which relates the latter to concrete historical institutions, and again because of the explicit assumption of competition, which relates the whole body of his theory to a given market situation. Mill also stressed the potential loss of realism involved in developing on competitive assumptions an economic theory that might well diverge from a reality shaped by the forces of custom and noncompetitive markets, forces not considered by the economics as he saw it. This view foreshadows the critical concern of later generations with the inadequacy of an economic theory grounded in the assumption of competition.

STATICS AND DYNAMICS

Just as Mill made the Malthusian population theory a cornerstone of his system but drew conclusions from it that had been unacceptable to Malthus, so he also incorporated the Ricardian theory of distribution in his *Principles* but again gave it an interpretation at variance with that of its author. Adapting an idea developed by Comte, Mill divided his economics into a static and a dynamic part and thereby set a precedent that opened up a new view of the subject, whose specific content has been debated ever since. Statics shows economic phenomena in their simultaneous coexistence; dynamics adds a theory of motion revealing the nature, laws, and ultimate tendencies of ever present change. That this change would, on the whole, be progressive, at least "in the more advanced portions of the race, and in all regions to which their influence reaches," was a thought again suggested by Comte, one with which Mill identified himself wholeheartedly but which required a modification of the Ricardian position, especially when it came to the discussion of the stationary state.

The formal distinction between statics and dynamics is more fully developed in Mill's *Logic* than in his *Principles,* and it is elaborated in a fashion anticipating such modern approaches as the one employing difference—not differential—equations. "It is necessary," Mill writes in *Logic,* "to combine the statical view of social phenomena with the dynamical, considering not only the progressive changes of the different elements, but the contemporaneous condition of each; and thus obtain empirically the law of correspondence not only between the simultaneous states, but between the simultaneous changes, of those elements."

This thought, however, is not further pursued in the *Principles.* Instead Mill's dynamics follows the main lines of Ricardian economics, with rents rising, profits falling, and wages remaining near subsistence. Emphasis is placed, as it is throughout Mill's book, on the role of population and the need for its control to provide a remedy against low wages and poverty. Mill, however, does not merely present the bare outline of the Ricardian system but adds a wealth of new ideas. In his discussion of the decline of profits, for example, he discusses at some length the factors that may check this tendency. To Ricardo, the removal of protection for agricultural products had stood out as such a factor. Now that the repeal of the corn laws was an accomplished fact, new points of view emerge in the discussion—the export of capital, "periodic revulsions," that is, business depressions during which capital is destroyed or sent abroad, and improvements in productive techniques which reduce the cost of wage goods—they will all assist in checking the tendency of profits to decline. Mill's survey of these factors, together with the stress that he lays on the population problem, put him in a position tantamount to the view that in the developed economies of Europe both population and capital had become redundant, this in spite of his qualified adherence to Say's law.

THE STATIONARY STATE

In the absence of countervailing tendencies, Mill believed, profits would within a short time be so low that the further accumulation of capital would cease and the stationary state would ensue. But with these tendencies in operation, the stationary state would in all likelihood not soon be reached in any of the great countries of Europe. When Mill comes to the assessment of the stationary state itself, he takes a position explicitly at variance with that of his predecessors. To Ricardo, the imminence of the stationary state was an alternative to the removal of agricultural protection, and since he favored such a removal he had no incentive to look for redeeming features of the stationary state. The picture that Mill unfolds of the stationary state is by no means displeasing. Provided always that the further growth of population is kept in check, it will be a boon rather than a bane for mankind to be relieved of the relentless pressure for increased production. Instead of operating under the stern necessity of economic incentives, mankind will in the stationary state find liberation from the strife for ever-increasing material wealth and will have its higher aspirations set free. Mill's view of the stationary state contains both a criticism of the blind pursuit of economic growth without regard for the quality of life under which this goes on and a foretaste of *The Affluent Society*. "It is only in the backward countries of the world," Mill writes, "that increased production is still an important object: in those most advanced, what is economically needed is a better distribution."

Mill concludes his treatment of economic dynamics with a chapter on the probable future of the laboring classes, in which he expresses the belief that in the course of time the organization of dependent labor, with its wage system, will give way to new social arrangements such as profit sharing, partnerships between laborers and capitalists—and, especially, cooperatives. Mill was a pioneer student of the economies of scale, and he considered the cooperative type of organization capable of safeguarding these economies and of adding to them advances in productivity facilitated by new incentives arising under the influence of the harmonious spirit of cooperation.

THE WAGES FUND THEORY

The wage system, for whose replacement Mill entertained reasoned but as yet unfulfilled hopes, was interpreted by him and many of his contemporaries in terms of the wages fund theory, which by that time had pushed the Ricardian subsistence theory into the background. Generally speaking, the exponents of the wages fund theory considered the demand for labor as determined by a fund of capital destined for the maintenance of labor—the wages fund—and the supply of labor as reflecting the size of the population, with both demand and supply referring to certain quantities rather than to schedules. In this view wages appear as a quotient, the dividend being the wages fund and the divisor the number of workers. To raise wages it is necessary to lower the divisor, that is, to control population growth, hence the pervasive influence of this matter in Mill's thought. Emphasis is placed on the divisor rather than on the dividend—the wages fund—because the latter is considered fixed, or more or less so, reflecting principally the amount of circulating capital destined for wage payments.

Historically the wages fund idea had come down from the Physiocrats' and Smith's view that the employer "advances" wage goods or their monetary equivalent, a point of view especially applicable to the main item of workers' subsistence, which becomes available once a year at harvest time and must then be reserved for the workers' maintenance until another harvest falls due. In this form the idea points to the contribution of the past to current production, to a "sacrifice" of the capitalist, and to dependence on his savings as a source of wages. The wages fund theory was characteristic of a stage of the discussion in which the relevance of productivity for the theory of factor returns was but dimly seen by such pioneers as Longfield and Thünen. Attention to the wages fund kept alive the interest in macroeconomics, and it prepared the ground for the later development of capital theory because of its implicit or explicit reference to the contribution made by the past to present output.

It was the weakness of the wages fund theory that the isolation of and the concentration on the fund caused the exponents of the theory to neglect other factors relevant to wage theory altogether or to consider them as remote causes operating behind the wages fund and best managed with the equivalent of the *ceteris paribus* assumption. The wages fund theorists lost sight of the substitutability between the capital in the fund and other forms of capital, and of the factors that affect the rates of profit and saving.

Mill adhered to the wages fund theory throughout the successive editions of his *Principles,* but in response to criticism by William Thornton, a friend and associate, he recanted in an article published in 1869. He did so, however, without changing his view about the need for the control of population and without modifying his presentation of the wages fund theory in the next edition of his *Principles,* which was to be the last published during his lifetime. Instead, in the preface he referred the reader to his article, declaring the results of the discussion as not yet ripe for incorporation in a general treatise. In his article Mill admitted that the wages fund was not fixed by the amount of circulating capital but that it might be supplemented by income of the employer which might otherwise go into saving or be spent on consumption. It was Mill's view that this doctrinal change had great practical consequences because it now seemed clear that combinations of workers could secure an increase in wages. Those under the influence of the wages fund theory had sometimes expressed the opinion that such an increase was bound to cut into somebody else's wages. This conclusion, however, was not invariably drawn because even under the wages fund theory collective action might be considered necessary to offset the superior bargaining power of the employer and to bring wages up to the competitive level or to reach this level earlier than it would be reached in the absence of collective bargaining. Mill had looked favorably on trade union activities in the *Principles,* provided that they be voluntary, and he now extended his blessings to include "social compulsion," which makes workers join unions.

If Mill had revised his *Principles* to reflect his newly gained conviction of the fallacious character of the wages fund theory, it would have required a major effort at reconstruction affecting not only his wage but his capital theory as well. He had developed the latter in the form of fundamental propositions regarding capital which were grounded in the Turgot-Smith tradition stressing the importance of saving, the adequacy of general demand, and the absence of difficulties arising from the savings-investment relation. His conclusions confirmed and complemented the wages fund theory. The relationship between the latter and his capital theory is conspicuous especially in the fourth proposition where Mill, in a formulation as famous as it is puzzling, declares that "demand for commodities is not demand for labor." Correctly interpreted, this again points to the wages fund —it is not purchase of commodities that immediately generates a demand for labor but the seller's act of saving, which does so by replenishing the wages fund.

THE ROLE OF GOVERNMENT

As for Mill's views about the role of government and the desirable organization of society, Mill did not share his father's unbounded belief in the identity of interests between the governed and a representative government responsible to them. Macaulay, the great Whig historian, had upheld "the higher and middling orders" as "the natural representatives of the human race" and had taken James Mill to task for endorsing universal— albeit only male—suffrage and majority rule on the basis of a few general premises. Who would doubt, Macaulay asked, that under such a regime the poor would despoil the rich? American democracy, Macaulay argued, is no example because where everyone has the chance to become rich himself, he is not going to plunder the rich. But even there Macaulay envisaged forebodings of change which would assimilate the new country to the general pattern. "As for America," he wrote in 1829, "we appeal to the twentieth century." Macaulay then depicted the consequences of repeated spoliations of the rich by the poor. "Is it possible," he asked, "that in two or three hundred years a few lean and half-naked fishermen may divide with owls and foxes the ruins of the greatest European cities—may wash their nets amidst the relics of her gigantic docks, and build their huts out of the capitals of her stately cathedrals?"

Macaulay's criticism of James Mill's theory of government made a deep and lasting impression on John Stuart Mill, as did later de Tocqueville's searching appraisal of the prospects of democracy in America. He became alarmed by the possibility of abuse of majority rule, and in his *Considerations on Representative Government* of 1861 made a number of proposals designed to restrain the tyranny of the masses and give special weight to the political functions of men of independence and exceptional capacity. As for material interests, he never failed to stress the overriding force of a self-directed humanity guided by firm moral convictions. "It was not by any change in the distribution of material interests, but by the spread of moral convictions," he wrote, "that negro slavery has been put an end to in the British Empire and elsewhere." Belief speaks louder than interests: "One person with a belief is a social power equal to ninety-nine who have only interests."

The skepticism and lack of enthusiasm characteristic of Mill's view of government and his intention to safeguard individual freedom against social pressure are further demonstrated in his *Essay on Liberty* of 1859. Here

Mill makes the famous and difficult distinction between self-regarding acts which affect only an individual's own good and other-regarding acts which affect the interests of others. Society, Mill holds, has no warrant to protect the individual from himself; its legitimate function is only the protection of others. Mill wanted to guarantee the individual freedom of conscience, thought, discussion, association, and freedom to fashion one's life in accord with one's preferences, liberties that he considered indispensable for arriving at rational truth and for enabling man to lead a life rich in diversity and self-fulfillment and as such of value both to the individual and to society: "The worth of a state in the long run is the worth of the individuals composing it. . . . A state which dwarfs its men in order that they may be more docile instruments in its hands even for beneficial purposes will find that with small men no great things can really be accomplished."

It is against this background of Mill's general view of the role of government that his ideas about the special functions of government vis-à-vis the economy must be appraised. The exercise of governmental powers, which he considered dangerous and inimical to man's best interests, has only a remote and indirect relationship to economic matters. Mill was a strict libertarian in matters affecting man's thought and discussion and man's freedom not to conform. He was a libertarian also in economic affairs, but much less strictly so, and here his libertarianism was not derived from principles loftier than a general suspicion of governmental inefficiency, meddling, and mischief-making. From these principles laissez faire would follow, not as a natural law but as a working rule conforming to experience and expedience and as flexible as these. Thus Mill's attachment to laissez faire did not prevent him from giving serious attention to legislative interference with the freedom to reproduce, from developing further his father's thought about taxing away the landowner's "unearned increment," or from proposing restrictions on the inheritance of wealth and on hours of work.

MILL'S VIEW OF SOCIALISM

Mill's attitude to socialism, which he examined critically and came to advocate, albeit waveringly and halfheartedly, did no violence to his pragmatic laissez faire view because the type of socialism that he regarded favorably did not require a strong and active government to assume the direction of nationalized industry. Mill's socialism was not that of Marx; although both lived in London their worlds were different, and there are no indications that Mill was acquainted with Marx's work. Socialism was to Mill a matter of the future, to be tested empirically and grounded in voluntary associations of the cooperative type, which would gradually emerge and would compete with each other. He explicitly rejected revolution as too costly in social and human terms, and he remained attached to competition as a principle of economic organization, as he did to private property if freed of abuses. All this points to significant differences from the type of socialism envisaged by Marx, who indeed had little use for Mill and wrote of him that "he attempted to reconcile the irreconcilable."

MILL'S INFLUENCE

Mill's intensely serious moral purpose and the persuasive self-assurance conveyed by the masterly prose of his *Principles* gave his book an influence shared by few other similar works, perpetuating its use long after much of the detail had become superseded by new thought. His own age richly honored Mill. Gladstone hailed him as the "saint of rationalism." The young Sigmund Freud, who had accepted a commission to translate a series of Mill's essays, characterized him as "perhaps the man of the century who best managed to free himself from the domination of customary prejudices." Later, when William James published his *Pragmatism,* he dedicated the book to the memory of Mill, "From whom I first learned the pragmatic openness of mind and whom my fancy likes to picture as our leader were he alive."

It was, however, the very openness of Mill's mind and his sensitivity to the intellectual tendencies of his age that gave him a Hamlet-like quality which seemed unattractive to less sensitive and more dogmatic minds. Mill, perhaps half in jest, said of himself that with utilitarians he was a mystic, with mystics a utilitarian, with logicians a sentimentalist, and with sentimentalists a logician. Similarly, liberals thought him a Socialist, and most Socialists a liberal. Although Fabians later would hail him as a forerunner and kindred thinker, it is doubtful whether all their works would have won his approval. He underlined the need for historical studies, but his abstract-generalizing approach set him apart from the rising generation of historical economists. Roscher, a founder of the historical school, would deny his sense of history and find fault with his mind for not being cast in a single mold. To the new generation of theorists who produced the marginal revolution in the 1870s his view of the completeness of the old theory of value seemed singularly ill-chosen. Thus Jevons would not only call him a bad logician but express only a slightly better opinion of his economics: "There is much that is erroneous in his *Principles*...but the book is not the maze of self-contradictions which his Logic undoubtedly is." This was Jevons's view in 1875, symptomatic perhaps of an attitude that was to affect wider circles but symptomatic also in that, years later, Jevons still continued to use Mill's *Principles* as a text in his classes and recommended it to others.

Mill's position in intellectual history has perhaps best been characterized by his godchild Bertrand Russell, who said of him: "He was unfortunate in the date of his birth. His predecessors were pioneers in one direction and his successors in another." With Mill classical economics reached its last glow and was soon to fall asunder under the onslaught of new ideas.

CAIRNES

At a time when economics gradually became professionalized, Mill held no teaching post, but his intellectual preeminence was so commanding that it penetrated the halls of academe from the outside, perhaps the last instance of such a phenomenon. Thus there arose the rudiments of a Mill school. Closest to Mill stood John Elliott Cairnes (1823–75), "the last of the classical economists," a respected teacher at Irish universities and in London, who in 1874 made a final attempt at holding the classical position in *Some Leading Principles of Political Economy Newly Expounded*. Cairnes retained the wages fund theory and rejected Jevons's newly developed subjective theory of value. He further elaborated Longfield's idea of noncompeting groups, which Mill had espoused and which was to reach full fruition in twentieth-century theories of monopolistic or imperfect competition. His most enduring contribution was the sketch of the evolution of a country's international economic position, which in the form of the sequence "immature debtor—mature debtor—immature creditor—mature creditor" has become part of the substance of economics.

FAWCETT

Another follower of Mill, also persevering in his attachment to the wages fund theory, was Henry Fawcett (1833–84), who after having been blinded by his father in a hunting accident as the age of twenty-five started out on an astounding career as the first paid professor of political economy at Cambridge—Marshall later becoming his successor—as a member of Parliament and as an outstanding postmaster general. Fawcett, although more dogmatic in his profession of laissez faire than his master Mill, nevertheless was instrumental in setting up the parcel post, against considerable resistance.

SIDGWICK

Fawcett did not have a philosophical flair, which was supplied by Henry Sidgwick (1838–1900), a Cambridge philosopher of wide influence with interests in economics, political science, and history. Sidgwick was the last great figure in English philosophy who made a name for himself in "moral science" as well. In this respect, and because he was a utilitarian, it was on him that Mill's mantle may be said to have fallen, although he was by no means uncritical of Mill. Utilitarianism lingered longer than classical economics and was given new life with the coming of the subjective theory of value. Like Mill, Jevons and Edgeworth were utilitarians, but their economics went beyond that of Mill and the classics.

Chapter 17

INTERLUDES
OF HISTORICAL
ECONOMICS:
Baconian
and Related Variants

The abstract-generalizing method in economics, of which John Stuart Mill was a self-conscious but outstanding exponent and which to this day has remained the principal vehicle of advances in economic thought, has repeatedly come under fire from those who want to see it complemented or replaced by an inductive, empirical, or historical method. Althought not all historical economists were influenced by Bacon or Hegel directly and in the same degree, it might be convenient to distinguish two principal variants of nineteenth-century historical economics, the Baconian and the Hegelian. Side by side with these there were other minor variants, the Comtean, for example.

Bacon, the seventeenth-century philosopher who had exalted the merits of induction and observation, was claimed as an ally by a number of nineteenth-century thinkers who found fault with utilitarianism and saw in the deductive method as practiced by Bentham and James Mill the utilitarians' weak point that made it vulnerable. Thus Macaulay, the great Whig historian, who in the 1820s criticized James Mill's a priori and deductive method of deriving political theory from a few assumed propensities of human nature, contrasted this method unfavorably with that employed in Bacon's "incomparable volume, the noblest and most useful of all works of the human reason, the *Novum Organum.*"

WHEWELL AND JONES

During the following decade Bacon's inductive method was again brought to the fore by William Whewell (1794–1866), another opponent of utilitarianism, who at that time began to publish a series of works on the history and philosophy of the inductive sciences. Whewell, an influential

Cambridge scholar, was a lifelong friend of Richard Jones (1790–1855), who succeeded Malthus as professor of political economy at Haileybury College. As young students Jones and Whewell, together with the astronomer John Herschel and others, had studied Bacon and propagated his views. It was Richard Jones who called for a new approach to economics, which he proposed to reconstruct with the help of Bacon's method of induction.

Jones developed his ideas in *An Essay on the Distribution of Wealth and on the Sources of Taxation* of 1831 and in a number of minor works published after Jones's death by Whewell in 1859 under the title *Literary Remains*. As in the work of other historical economists, the *Essay* offered a program that promised more than it fulfilled, being more of a call to arms than a crossing of swords. It begins with a statement of Jones's methodological aims and sets forth the ambitious plan of the work, which was to cover all phases of distribution but which in fact went no further than the treatment of rent, the rest never having been written.

Jones's methodology has its critical and its positive side. The principal object of his attack is Ricardo, whose hasty generalizations contain only hypothetical truths that are at variance with the conditions of the real world. Employing narrow and limited data, Ricardo constructed a system claiming an explanatory value of virtually universal scope. Jones wants to replace Ricardo's abstract procedure by a look-and-see approach which is to encompass both past and present experience. He proposes to examine "the statistical map of the world" but in fact offers little quantitative material.

On the substantive side, the bulk of Jones's work contains a classification and detailed description of rents in different parts of the world and at different historical periods. Depending upon whether or not the occupier of the land employs labor, he distinguishes farmer and peasant rents, and then goes on to depict meticulously the circumstances attending serf rents in Russia, Poland, and elsewhere—metayer rents in classical Greece, Rome, and France, ryot rents in India, and cottier rents in Ireland. Where he turns from history to analysis, in his emendations of Ricardo, for example, the cancellation of diminishing returns by technological progress rarely goes beyond similar statements of Mill's. He made an effort to deny the "gloomy notions" of the classics and to make class interests appear as harmonious rather than discordant. He found fault with Malthus, but even more with those whom he accused of having abused Malthus's theory by deducing from it the need for birth control. The checks to population growth are not resolvable into vice, misery, and moral restraint, as Malthus had taught. That there are other factors at work is demonstrated by the existence of differential birth rates—high among the poor and low among the rich. This observation of Jones's was a pioneer one, which was later confirmed by a host of statistical studies.

Jones would often pose interesting questions but the answers that he gave, correct as they may have been, were intellectually unsatisfactory. Being unable or unwilling to abstract from the abundant historical detail which he had assembled, he could at best produce classifications advising the reader that everything is possible. He would, for example, raise the question of the effect of higher wages on population, the reply being that "the population may or may not increase," and on the next page observe that "when wages are reduced, the population may or may not be reduced also."

Mill's *Principles* contained a few references to the factual material collected in Jones's *Essay,* but he considered the appeal to Bacon's authority entirely unsuited to justify any type of crude empiricism. He wrote of Bacon:

> The philosopher who labored to construct a canon of scientific induction, by which the observations of mankind, instead of remaining empirical, might be so combined as to be made the foundation of safe general theories, little expected that his name would become the stock authority for disclaiming generalization and enthroning empiricism, under the name of experience, as the only solid foundation of practice.

Mill himself by no means lacked historical insight, and his own approach was broad enough to satisfy those who desired to have abstract generalizations of economic theory supplemented by realistic material. Moreover, Mill's measured optimism met the psychological needs of those who found the pessimism of his predecessors uncongenial. Furthermore, Jones was a moderate protectionist, and in this respect his thought was out of tune with the aspirations of his time, which pressed for and finally obtained the repeal of the corn laws. It is not surprising that in academic economics Jones's fame and influence failed to spread in the shadow cast by Mill, whose work was more penetrating, complete, and appealing.

There is, however, another side to Jones's work, one on which more light is shed by the lectures and tracts gathered in his *Literary Remains* than by the *Essay.* It reveals that Jones had in mind the construction of a "Political Economy of Nations," an investigation both of the structure and the evolution of national economics and of the impact on the evolving structures of changes in property relations, the organization of labor, and social and political institutions. All these matters were to assume great importance in the later thought of Marx, as was Jones's tendency to make an economic interpretation of historical change. It was this side of Jones's work that attracted the attention of Marx and caused him to single out Jones for a degree of approval—given by Marx to few other economists of the period —this in spite of the conservative leanings of Jones.

Jones's work may be characterized as programmatic, critical, optimistic, relativistic, evolutionist, and interdisciplinary. It was programmatic in that it suggested a new approach to the study of economics, one free from the alleged blemishes of the classical approach, which Jones untiringly criticized as faulty in method and substance. It was relativistic in that it threw doubt on the general applicability of economic theory, and it was evolutionist in its hints at an evolving structure of national economies. The connection that Jones found between economic change and social and political factors made him foster an interdisciplinary approach rather than the narrow study of "wealth."

Jones's was not the only variant of historical economics in the British Isles, and several minor variants emerged in the mid-nineteenth century, when another generation of historically-minded economists became active. Their work shared the programmatic, critical, and relativistic character of Jones's, but their inspiration was no longer derived from Bacon. There was, to begin with, an Irish contingent, connected with Trinity College in Dublin and other Irish universities, whose principal spokesmen were John K. Ingram and Cliffe Leslie. Ingram was an ardent follower of Comte and Leslie a more moderate one, and the variant of historical economics represented by these men may be designated as Comtean. There was also a psychological variant, exemplified by Walter Bagehot, a quantitatively oriented variant, exemplified by Thorold Rogers, and a humanitarian one, by Arnold Toynbee. In varying degrees the position of these men was fortified by the rise of historical economics in Germany, where this approach had attained a status of singular eminence. They formed an epoch or generation of economists rather than a school, all, with the exception of Toynbee, having been born in the 1820s.

INFLUENCE OF MILL, COMTE, AND SPENCER

The new generation of historical economists labored in a *fin de siècle* atmosphere in which the dusk was settling over classical economics. A period seemed to be coming to its close, with new thought about to take the place of the old. What this new thought was destined to be no one could be sure of, but the historical economists were convinced that theirs was the wave of the future—mistakenly so, as the course of events was to demonstrate. They felt fortified in their views by some of the obiter dicta of John Stuart Mill, from whom indeed none of the British historical economists was disaffected, Ricardo rather than Mill serving as the object of their attacks. Mill, always responsive to intellectual influences, shared some of their preconceptions, but what to him had been adumbrations of minor or passing interest became to them matters of central importance. This was true of the impact of Comte, acknowledged by Mill and the historical economists of Dublin, especially Comte's theory of the consensus, his dynamics, and his rejection of the "metaphysical" abstractions of economic theory. It was also true of Mill's explicit recognition of historical and institutional factors as qualifications of economic theory and of his warning not to neglect other than economic considerations when deriving policy conclusions from economic theory. It was further true of Mill's pragmatic attitude to laissez faire, a rule he weakened by many exceptions.

Mill drew attention to all these matters, but his awareness of them did not prevent him from developing a body of economic theory, hemmed in as it was by these considerations. The historical economists, on the other hand, drew entirely different conclusions from them. Comte, who had been one of Mill's many influences, became to some of them the principal intellectual inspiration. If Comte were correct, they argued, then the departmentalization of social science was uncalled for, as was the abstract-generalizing approach. If the laissez faire rule had so many exceptions it should no longer be maintained but should be relegated to the museum of antiquities composed of other relics of the natural law tradition.

The new generation of historical economists in the British Isles found assurance also in the thought of Herbert Spencer (1820–1903), the philosopher of evolution, who applied the biological notion of evolution to society, proceeding in part independently and ahead of Charles Darwin (1809–82), whose *Origin of Species* was published in 1859. Darwin developed his ideas about the struggle for existence and natural selection under the influence of Malthus's population doctrine. This intellectual debt was now paid back, with Darwin and Spencer stimulating the thought of the historical economists and reassuring them that the genetic approach contained the clue to the riddles of society. However, when it came to Spencer's economic doctrines, most of the historical economists parted company with him. Spencer was a strict individualist and an exponent of extreme laissez faire, whose ethics linked morality with the "survival of the fittest" and who saw in the new liberalism of his time the forerunner of the "coming slavery." Just as the old liberalism had restrained the power of the monarch, so the new liberalism, Spencer insisted in *The Man versus the State* of 1884, should restrain the power of the legislature. Social Darwinism of this sort had no appeal to the historical economists, who wanted to break rather than uphold the laissez faire rule. Bagehot, however, came close to social Darwinism as far as international relations are concerned, which he saw settled by the rule of the stronger and by war.

HISTORICAL VERSUS ANALYTICAL JURISPRUDENCE

Some of the historical economists were trained in the law, a field that in the mid-nineteenth century was in an uproar similar to the one in economics. There a struggle went on between the exponents of analytical jurisprudence, led by John Austin (1790–1859)—a Benthamite, friend of James Mill and teacher of John Stuart Mill—and the followers of a historical jurisprudence that emerged under the influence of Sir Henry Maine (1822–88). Bentham, to whom the past was replete with errors and abuses, wanted to reconstruct the law in the light of rational principles of more or less general validity. The Benthamite exponents of analytical jurisprudence were concerned with legal theory, whereas to the historical jurists law was to be studied historically and comparatively. There was a parallel between the aspirations of the historical economists and of the historical jurists, and when the latter came to command greater attention during the second half of the nineteenth century the former claimed them as allies in the struggle against the dominance of abstract theory.

To Maine as well as to Spencer are due some broad disjunctions, classifications such as inspired students of history are apt to make, which shed a penetrating light on different phases also of economic history. Maine was a profound student of ancient and comparative law, and from him originates the often cited distinction between societies organized on the principle of status—the Middle Ages, for example—and societies organized on the principle of contract—employment or sales contracts, for example, which largely determine one's position in the modern economic order. Maine, in fact, spoke of a "movement from status to contract." In a similar vein, Spencer distinguished between military and industrial societies—the latter being organized by voluntary cooperation, a distinction that has its economic counterpart in that between the command economy and the market economy.

THE IRISH CONTINGENT : INGRAM

The ideas of Comte, Spencer, and Maine form the background for the rise of several variants of historical economics during and after the middle years of the nineteenth century. That some of the Irish economists were drawn to a historical approach is not surprising because their environment made them realize that England was not the world and that conditions differed in many places. This was, of course, a consideration of which the classics had not been entirely oblivious, and Mill especially had paid attention to the diversity of historical and institutional conditions as they affected both competition and the distribution of income. To Jones, a Welshman, historical diversity became a focal point of his thought, as it did to Ingram and Leslie, the Dublin economists. John K. Ingram (1823–1907), the son of an Anglican clergyman, was a student of law, literature, and the classics, an able mathematician, a founder of the Statistical and Social Enquiry Society of Ireland, and the first editor of *Hermathena,* a scholarly journal still in existence. He held distinguished posts at Trinity College, and when he died the *Times* of London quoted his associates as extolling him as "the best educated man of Europe." Ingram fell under Comte's spell as a young man, visited the sage in Paris in 1855, and never wavered in his attachment to him during the ensuing half century. Since his economic studies were only part of his many pursuits he published relatively little in this field, but he nevertheless held a commanding intellectual position, and when the British Association for the Advancement of Science met in Dublin in 1878 he was chosen to address Section F, which was concerned with Economic Science and Statistics.

Ingram's address, entitled "The Present Position and Prospects of Political Economy," contains a thoughtful statement of the claims of historical economics, enriched by an occasional new insight and influenced in part by ideas emanating from German historical economics, which by then had come into full flowering. There is a fourfold indictment of classical economics: It isolates the economic phenomena of society from the intellectual, moral, and political aspects; it develops "viciously abstract" concepts; it "immensely" exaggerates the function of deduction, and it presents its conclusions as absolutes. The shrill notes that Ingram at times strikes point to continental rather than to English habits of scholarly discourse, but the epithet "vicious" was less violent than it sounded because it apparently meant to imply that there were modes of abstraction that were not vicious. In the manner of Comte, sociology is depicted as presiding over the whole intellectual system, and sociology on occasion turns into sociologism when Ingram searches for the ideological content of classical economics and ascribes to it an apologetic character:

> The distrust of its doctrines manifested by the working classes is no doubt in a great degree owing to the not altogether unfounded belief, that it has tended to justify too absolutely existing social arrangements, and that its study is often recommended with the real, though disguised, object of repressing popular aspirations after a better order of things.

The description of conventional economics as arriving at hypothetical propositions is but a cloak to cover its dissonance with reality. The correct approach is the historical inductive one, of which Adam Smith is claimed as an outstanding practitioner and which is to be developed among lines that avoid the faults of the conventional one. That is, the study of economics should be systematically combined with that of the other aspects of social life, the excessive tendency to abstraction should be checked, the deductive method should be changed for the inductive one, and the economic laws and practical prescriptions founded on them should be expressed in a less absolute form.

Ingram's influence spread widely when he published in 1888 *A History of Political Economy.* The work filled an existing gap, was translated into ten foreign languages, and with later supplements served as a textbook through the 1920s. Its lasting success was due to Ingram's erudition as well as to the fact that he provided more than a mere narration of economic doctrines but was able to test their validity by the criterion of what to him seemed the only proper method—Comte's positivism. Ingram guided the reader with a certainty possessed by the true believer where other doctrinal histories would leave him to his own resources in the search for a criterion of validity amid the welter of conflicting doctrines and rival points of view. Ingram's doctrinal history was written from a definite point of view, resembling in this respect the doctrinal histories of Marx and his followers. However, the guidance that he offered the reader had its cost. Often the reader would not only be guided but misguided—for example, when Ingram would deny that Jevons's name would survive as the originator of new theoretical constructions or when he castigated Cournot's mathematical economics in terms that now seem absurd: "The great objection to the use of mathematics in economic reasoning is that it is necessarily sterile. . . . There is then no future for this kind of study, and it is only waste of intellectual power to pursue it." Although Ingram was favorably impressed by Jevons's empirical and quantitative work, he failed to foresee the rise of the econometric variant of mathematical economics, with which his own approach has a certain affinity. Instead he identified mathematical economics with its pure variant.

CLIFFE LESLIE

Ingram accorded to Cliffe Leslie (1826?–82) the honor of having been the first English writer to produce a systematic statement of the philosophic foundation of the historical method as the appropriate instrument of economic research. Leslie was a gifted writer of essays which were eventually published in two volumes, *Land Systems* in 1870 and *Essays in Moral and Political Philosophy* in 1879. Of the latter, a second edition, including a somewhat different collection and containing an early appraisal of economic thought in the United States, was published posthumously nine years later.

Leslie's background resembled that of Ingram. The son of an Anglican clergyman, he was educated at Trinity College and trained in the law. He held a professorship of jurisprudence and political economy at Belfast, but the duties of this office were light and made it possible for him to reside in London. He was a student of Maine's and had a friendly association with both Ingram and Mill, who considered him, next to Cairnes, one of the best economists of his time. It was on Maine's suggestion that Leslie turned to historical economics.

Most of Leslie's essays are replete with historical anecdotes and literary allusions, which are at times repeated but contain profound and forward-looking observations that attest to the independence and originality of his mind. In his writings emerges the germ of the idea of consumer sovereignty and of that emphasis on the theory of consumption which, neglected by Mill, was to manifest itself in Jevons's *Theory of Political Economy* in 1871. In an essay written ten years earlier, "The Love of Money," Leslie denounced the economists for having concentrated their attention on an elusive abstraction, the desire for wealth, at the cost of neglecting historical changes in the content and uses of wealth. He suggests to the economists

> the cultivation of a department of the philosophy of riches which
> has never been scientifically investigated. The laws which regu-
> late the value of the supply forthcoming from the producers have
> been almost exhaustively developed in political economy; but the
> deeper laws which regulate the demand of the consumers, and
> which give the love of money all its force and all its meaning,
> have never yet received the regular attention of any school of
> philosophers.

The same essay also contains the observation that consumers "elicit" what the producers turn out, a thought restated in a more complete fashion in an essay "On the Philosophical Method of Political Economy," published in 1876 and offering both a criticism of conventional economics and a program of historical economics along the lines to be developed in Ingram's address of 1878. Here Leslie writes of "the wants and desires of consumers" as the real motives for production, with "the demands of consumers determining the commodities supplied by producers." He notes with approval Jevons's attempt to develop a theory of consumption but insists that no such theory can be forthcoming "without a study of the history and the entire structure of society, and the laws which they disclose." The employment of abstractions such as the desire for wealth or the love of money is a regression to the realism of medieval philosophy which attributed real objective existence to universals. It beclouds the relevance of such factors as the love of ease, of luxury, of distinction, and of social position, which may counteract the desire for wealth or add to its force as a motive to industry and accumulation.

Leslie was among the first to raise doubts about the relevance of an economic theory which attributed to economic agents an amount of knowledge that he found nonexistent. In this connection, he questioned whether the degree of mobility in the economic system was sufficient to allow conclusions conventionally made about the equalization of profits and the incidence of taxes. All in all he was an important forerunner of later institutionalist critics.

BAGEHOT

Not all historically inclined economists agreed on the interpretation of the economic features of their environment. Whereas Leslie doubted that the degree of mobility existing in the English economy supported the conclusions of conventional economic theory, it was exactly the pronounced mobility of labor and capital that impressed Walter Bagehot (1826–77) as the distinct mark of the advanced type of economic organization characterized by the "great commerce" of the English economy. Bagehot, the son of a Unitarian banker, was educated at University College in London because his father did not want him to submit to the religious tests then in force at Oxford. He later studied law, entered his father's business, and, after his marriage to a daughter of the founder of the *Economist* and the death of his father-in-law, became the editor of this great financial weekly, which had been established in 1843 to lend support to the free-trade movement.

Bagehot's family connections gave him entrance to the highest financial and political circles and provided him with the opportunity to observe at first hand the operation of the English financial system and of the government. Bagehot, a master observer, took advantage of this opportunity, turning out not what he called "paper descriptions" but penetrating analyses of these institutions. His *English Constitution* of 1876 did for English government what his *Lombard Street* of 1873 did for the London money market: It established an image drawn so penetratingly and realistically that it continued to impress generations of students long after the reality from which the image was drawn had undergone profound changes.

Bagehot was of Huguenot extraction, and the brilliant style of his writings that to this day has set the standard for a high type of English journalism partakes of the Gallic *esprit*. He wrote wittily and often with an ironical detachment which at times would border on the cynical. He started as a literary critic but branched out into biographical studies, history, politics, economics, and sociology. To these tasks he brought an amazing psychological insight. Thus he would distinguish, for example, between the "dignified" and the "efficient" parts of the English constitution, the former inspiring loyalty and allegiance as well as helping to conceal the reality of the working rules established by the latter. Social psychology also emerges in his *Physics and Politics* of 1872, where progress is depicted as arising from the "seed of adaptiveness" residing in the "cake of custom" and making for change through imitation, suggestion, and contagion.

Bagehot's psychological insight also stands out in his economic writings, which in this respect have been compared with Keynes's. His contributions to general economics are only fragmentary and programmatic. They were collected after his death in a volume entitled *Economic Studies* (1880). Had he lived longer he might have carried out his plan of a three-part approach to economics that was to encompass economic theory, a critical history of doctrines, and biographical studies of the great economists. Of all this, his published work offers only samples.

Bagehot was no crude empiricist—he rejected both the "all case method," which calls for the complete enumeration of all historical experience, and the "single case method," which explores facts ostensibly without being guided by theory. The approach he admired as setting precept and standard was Ricardo's rather than Mill's. This would bring him into the ranks of the theoretical rather than of the historical economists, to whom he indeed belongs only marginally and peripherally—as a relativist, as a student of primitive economic institutions, and as a keen observer of human nature. His work is not readily classified, but if he is to be designated as a historical economist, the variant of historical economics connected with his name is most aptly characterized as a psychological one.

Mill, Bagehot argued, had widened the old political economy either too much or not enough. He had built a halfway house that was not a home for universally valid theory nor for one that explained only the great commerce of modern England. It was the latter type of economic theory—one restricted in its applicability—that Bagehot wanted to fashion and for which he considered the Ricardian approach the model, abstract and general as it ostensibly was. Bagehot would search for the reasons why this type of theory lacked appeal. Abroad, he wrote, the protectionist creed rises like a weed because every nation wishes to see some conspicuous industry flourish. About the costs it does not care, "indeed, it hardly knows, it will never read, it will never apprehend the refined reasons which prove those evils and show how great they are." Foreigners will say: "Your English traders are strong and rich: of course you wish to undersell our traders, who are weak and poor. You have invented this political economy to enrich yourselves and ruin us: we will see that you shall not do so." There is, further, the disfavor in which government action is held by the English political economy, an attitude that again brings no accession of popularity because "all governments like to interfere—it elevates their position to make out that they can cure the evils of mankind." And there is the cleavage between the businessman and the student of economics:

> People who live and move among the facts often or mostly cannot of themselves put together any precise reasonings about them. Men of business have a solid judgment, a wonderful guessing power of what is going to happen, each in his own trade, but they have never practised themselves in reasoning out their judgments and in supporting their guesses by argument; probably if they did so, some of the finer and correcter parts of their anticipations would vanish. They are like the sensible lady to whom Coleridge said, "Madam, I accept your conclusion, but you must let me find the logic for it."

From Bagehot's *Lombard Street* and from his articles in the *Economist* the rudiments of a business cycle theory can be culled which again stresses a psychological factor, that is, expectations, their changes, the accompanying expansion and contraction of credit, and—the words are Bagehot's—the "excess of savings over investments." Bagehot's *Lombard Street* was a call for stabilization policies, with the Bank of England, as lender of last resort and holder of the nation's banking reserves, to assume responsibility for these policies. *Lombard Street* was a worthy sequel to Thornton's *Paper Credit*. In it Bagehot developed a theory of central banking at a time when many considered the Bank of England substantially not different in its functions from other privately owned banks. In elaborating the functions of a central bank, Bagehot established the famous principle connected with his name which calls for different policies to cope with internal and external drains. In the case of a domestic run on the banks, the remedy is to lend freely. "A panic, in a word, is a species of neuralgia, and according to the rules of science you must not starve it. . . . In wild periods of alarm, one failure makes many, and the best way to prevent the derivative failures is to arrest the primary failure which causes them." In the case of an external drain, when the loss of gold threatens, the remedy is to raise the rate of interest high enough to attract funds from abroad. Here Bagehot explicitly draws attention to the fact that the international gold standard does not operate automatically but requires management by the central bank in the form of appropriate discount policies. When the foreign exchange threatens to become unfavorable, the interest rate must be raised, not only to attract foreign funds but also to set in motion "a slower mercantile operation" at home, whereby prices fall, imports diminish, and exports increase.

It was Bagehot who in a number of passages in *Lombard Street* prepared the ground for the conceptualization of the multiplier sixty years later. Chapter 6 of the work contains his treatment of the business cycle and is characteristically entitled "Why Lombard Street is often very dull, and sometimes extremely excited." Bagehot describes the interdependence of the various industries: if one is in difficulty, those that customarily sell to it will suffer and the effect will be propagated throughout the economy, to rebound in the end. So, as time goes on, the loss of one industry "spreads and multiplies through all." It was with explicit reference to Bagehot's probing of the matter that A. C. Pigou, the Cambridge economist, in his *Industrial Fluctuations* of 1927 resumed the discussion, attempting, although in vain, to conceptualize the underlying idea and inviting others to try again where he had failed, a suggestion heeded by R. F. Kahn, another Cambridge economist, who in 1931 succeeded in expressing the idea in the precise formula later made famous by Keynes.

Bagehot's authority in financial matters was without rival. He was an influential journalist, whose advice was sought and respected in the highest councils of the English government. Gladstone referred to him as "a sort of supplementary Chancellor of the Exchequer." To Bagehot's suggestion was due the introduction of the Treasury Bill, a short-term credit instrument which he modeled after a commercial bill of exchange. Bagehot also outlined the necessary steps leading toward a *Universal Money*, the title of a book published in 1869, and he proposed the establishment of a world currency resulting from the assimilation of the English and American units of account. Bagehot looked beyond being a mere student and observer, but his attempts to enter upon a career in Parliament were not successful.

ROGERS AND TOYNBEE

To complete the survey of historical economics in the British Isles two more figures call for attention, Thorold Rogers (1823–90) and Arnold Toynbee (1852–83), the first supporting a quantitative variant of historical economics and the second a humanitarian one. Rogers, who held the Drummond professorship at Oxford, raised questions that were more fully answered by the quantitatively oriented economic historian of modern times. He pioneered in the historical study of prices and wages, which yielded, among other works, a monumental *History of Agriculture and Prices in England*, published in eight volumes (1866–1902). Rogers's and the other historical economists' productive life coincided with a period in which economics was often placed on the defensive, being attacked either as too formal or as a rationalization of the free-trade policy. Thus Ingram, when addressing the British Association for the Advancement of Science, found it necessary to defend the very existence of Section F on Economic Science and Statistics, which an unfriendly critic had questioned. Bagehot, as has been mentioned, attempted to uncover the psychological reasons for the hostile attitude to economic studies. Rogers, who was friend and associate of Cobden, the archpriest of free trade, also had to defend his science. When at a dinner party he was told by a historian that economics was so much garbage, he replied: "Garbage, is it?—The very thing then for a hog like you."

Arnold Toynbee—whose nephew and namesake was to become a famous historian in the twentieth century—was a high-minded and compassionate humanitarian who during his short life made a profound impression on all who knew him. His was a voice of protest against the darker phases of an industrial civilization which the classics had failed to expose. Mill had clearly depicted the structure of the old political economy and its foundation in hypothetical assumptions, but he never attempted to ascertain from actual observation to what extent these assumptions coincided with the facts of the real world. It was from the knowledge so acquired that Toynbee proposed to state the laws of prices, profits, wages, and rent. Adam Smith believed that freedom would destroy monopoly; little did he anticipate that it would become a means to establish it. The classics exalted competition but failed to see that it often prevails not among equals but among unequals. Instead of being blindly worshipped, it should be harnessed. There are forebodings in Toynbee's thought of Joan Robinson's view of an invisible hand that may strangle. He did not live long enough to develop his ideas and is best remembered for a study of *The Industrial Revolution,* published with other writings posthumously in 1884, which gave currency to the term designated in its title. His personal example provided a stimulus to workers' education, social work, and the establishment of settlement houses in urban centers.

THEORISTS AND HISTORIANS

With the closing decades of the nineteenth century historical economics had spent itself in England. Rogers's successor at Oxford was F. Y. Edgeworth, and at Cambridge Alfred Marshall began his long and influential career in 1885, when he was elected to the professorship of political economy over the strong competition of a rival candidate who was a historical economist. Under the influence of these men, especially of Marshall, economic theory had its great ascendancy. Chairs of economic history were founded at the leading universities, but theoretical and historical studies were eventually separated and followed different paths. This was due in part to the cautious reserve of Marshall, who was unwilling to be drawn into controversies with economic historians. The theorists and the historians had their own preserves, and no one was to poach on that of the other. When John H. Clapham, the professor of economic history at Cambridge, published in 1922 the article "Of empty economic boxes," in which he criticized the categories of the theorists—increasing and diminishing returns, an "industry," and so forth—as being devoid of empirical content, he was sharply taken to task by Pigou, Marshall's successor, for having misunderstood the formal character of economic theory.

Only toward the mid-twentieth century did there develop a closer cooperation between economic theorists and economic historians. It was the quantitative orientation that many had in common, rather than the influence of the nineteenth-century historical economists, that brought them together. When with the ascendancy of the econometric approach theorists began to conceptualize in operational or measurable terms, historians found a rewarding field of work in the retrospective statistical testing of economic theory. The application of statistical techniques became a method cultivated by both economic theorists and historians, and it even ran over into the study of general history.

Chapter 18

THE HEGELIAN VARIANT
OF HISTORICAL
ECONOMICS

Just as there is little continuity between the work of the nineteenth-century English historical economists and the present-day approach of economic historians, so there is only a tenuous relationship between the latter and the German historical school, which at its time was more influential than the English historical economists, had a more lasting impact, and was grounded in a different philosophy. Although German historical economics had little influence on the later development of economic thought as it unfolded during the second half of the twentieth century, it was, however, part and symptom of wider intellectual tendencies which have cast their shadow over the history of mankind. Most of the German historical economists exalted the nation and the work of the government, and this attitude is again grounded in these wider circumstances.

GERMANY AND THE ENLIGHTENMENT

Historical economics was more successful and enduring in Germany than in England because the tender growth of German Enlightenment, which reached its summit with the great philosopher Kant, was all but uprooted during the nineteenth century. In its substance historical economics was a revolt against the Enlightenment, which had brought the enthronement of reason and the religion of humanity. During the late eighteenth century the Enlightenment struck a few roots in Germany, which was then a backward country, barely recovered from the ravages of the Thirty Years' War, under the absolute rule of a large number of princes, and especially in the eastern parts dominated by the landowning noblemen. In the West, however, contacts with France brought new ideas into the country, and from the University of Göttingen, a Hanoverian foundation which maintained close connections with Britain, the thought of Adam Smith spread and made its influence felt on those who pressed for the abolition of rural serfdom in Prussia. Compromised as the ideas of liberty and equality were by the Terror of the French Revolution, they as well as related institutional changes were nevertheless spread throughout Europe by Napoleon's armies. Many educated people would have welcomed these ideas, but as they seemed to be part of the equipment of conquering armies, they became tainted with an alien character and aroused ambivalent reactions. Democratic aspirations were given new life when the king of Prussia, in his fight against Napoleon, replenished the standing army by a draft of his people and solemnly promised a constitution. With the end of the Napoleonic Wars, however, absolutism returned in full strength, and the hope for constitutional and other reforms became dim under the restoration regimes of Metternich's Holy Alliance, which suppressed both progressive and national aspirations and placed thought and its expression, academic and otherwise, under the control of the police.

GERMANY'S RISE TO NATIONHOOD

Unlike the English and the French—and of course the Americans— the Germans, until 1848, had never dared to rebel against their rulers. When the revolution of 1848 failed to bring the desired results, the outcome convinced many Germans that they lacked political ability and should remain obedient to their rulers. Bismarck, who finally in 1871 united Germany and turned it into a nation-state under Prussian leadership, did his best to strengthen this belief by compromising and exploiting the then established façade of parliamentarism. Nationhood, of which many had dreamed for so long, had come after victory in battle—against Austria in 1866 and against France in 1870–71—and as a concession, as it were, of the German princes to Prussian discipline and efficiency. It became in popular opinion identified with an omnipotent state, externally superior in military prowess and internally continuing the full exercise of statecraft that had long been a German tradition.

During the anxious and troubled decades that preceded the attainment of nationhood, many a German patriot had looked to the past to find inspiration and guidance. Some were attracted by the institutions of the medieval empire, once ruled by German emperors; others turned their attention to local and regional customs and traditions. This made them aware of the variety of social formations that had flourished in the past. To them, the unhappy present did not appear as the Age of Reason and perfection, nor did the multifarious manifestations of the social life of the past lend credence to the belief that reason offered universally valid rules on which to found institutions. The temptation to interpret the present as the golden age itself or at least as an approach to it was weakened further by the spread of the idea that classical antiquity had established standards of beauty in art and architecture which had never been equaled, an idea that marked the intervening period as one of decline rather than of progress.

413

GERMAN HISTORICISM

Many tendencies of the time gave a powerful stimulus to historical studies, culminating in the rise of "historicism," the specifically German reaction to the Enlightenment, which refused to wring general rules from reason and instead insisted on observing the unique in its endless historical variation. German historicism has many scholarly achievements to its credit, so much so that during the closing decades of the nineteenth century the German universities enjoyed an unparalleled prestige and attracted students from all over the world. It was, however, a movement not without dangers, both to the Germans themselves and to all mankind. Historicism offered no principles to guide and restrain action. It was hostile both to the secularized natural law tradition of which Adam Smith's work was a belated offspring and to utilitarianism. Its spread coincided with a time of weakening religious influence, and what was left supported rather than checked the trend toward the secular idolatry of the nation and of the state, German Lutheranism having for a long time exalted the unquestioning obedience of the faithful to government authority. Thus in the end historicism could degenerate into an idolatry of naked power. There was not only an absence of general principles but a disdain for them, a cynical contempt for anyone who would appeal to the rules of humanity. No one has characterized the situation that had come to prevail in Germany at the close of the nineteenth century more aptly than the empress Victoria, an Englishwoman of liberal views, who was the wife of the emperor Frederick III of Germany. "Peace," she wrote, "toleration, charity, these things, the most precious which man has on earth, we saw stepped upon, ridiculed, decried as 'luxuries,' 'impracticable,' 'unsuited for the time,' vague dreams. . . . Blood and iron alone had made Germany great."

HISTORICAL JURISPRUDENCE

Historical economics was but one of the many manifestations of German historicism. It found a parallel, for example, in historical jurisprudence, which could not fail to have profound effects on the academic economists who in the traditional organization of the German universities were part of the faculty significantly designated as in charge of the "sciences of law and of the state." In its German variant historical jurisprudence derived the law of the nation not from the arbitrary will of a lawgiver but from a mystic "folk soul," which was interpreted as the embodiment of folkish experience and characteristics, conceived as distinct from that of other peoples' and manifesting itself in national and regional customs and mores. Historical jurisprudence took a stand both against the legislative attempts at reformist codification of the time, such as those made with great success by Napoleon, and, what is more important, against the universal rule of natural law. This latter attitude had lasting effects, with the result that the restraining influence of the natural law idea vanished completely from German jurisprudence, even more so than did economic theory from economics. It was only after the upheaval of two great wars, the loss of which had shaken the foundations of Germany, that in 1949 the then enacted preliminary Constitutional Code of the Federal Republic of Germany opened the door for the return of this great civilizing idea by including an oblique reference to it.

HEGELIAN PHILOSOPHY

German historicism reached its peak in the philosophy of Georg Wilhelm Friedrich Hegel (1770–1831), and since Hegel's ideas came to suffuse the other manifestations of German historicism, the German variant of historical economics might be designated as Hegelian. Like other exponents of historicism, Hegel considered the study of history the proper approach to the science of society, which would reveal certain underlying tendencies of historical development. But he went beyond this point of view with the moral positivism of his philosophy of success, which taught that everything that is real is also reasonable, and everything that is reasonable is real. In his philosophy, history not only offers the clue to the understanding of society and social change but becomes glorified as the world's court of justice.

In Hegel's interpretation, history reveals the progressive unfolding of liberty and justice, which are embodied in strong nation-states and reach their full flowering in the absolute monarchy of the Prussia of his time, considered by him to be the materialization of justice on earth. Hegel's moral positivism equates might with right and power with morality. To win out before history's world court, the state must prove itself in war, and war in turn preserves its moral health, protects the people from the corruption that everlasting peace would bring on it, and checks internal unrest. As the state is the realization of justice and liberty, and of reason as well, it is only as a member of the state that the individual has moral worth. Hegel rejects those interpretations of liberty that make it consist in the participation of the citizens in public affairs or in restraints placed on the exercise of governmental power. Instead he considers liberty as the conscious submission to the authority of the state, as obedience to the authority of the state, whose power and morality coalesce. In fact, Hegel comes close to identifying laws with liberties, as every law, being real, is also reasonable and embodies a liberty.

At his time, Hegel was considered the court philosopher of the king of Prussia. His influence went far to undo the influence of the Enlightenment in Germany. Hegel promoted his views through lectures and writings as well as through action, which required the ideological commitment of the academic community, universities in Germany traditionally being state institutions. He would report rival philosophers to the police, causing, for example, one of the few followers of Bentham in Germany to lose his teaching post. As for the quality of Hegel's thought, opinion has been divided to this day. Schopenhauer, his colleague, considered him a charlatan, and John Stuart Mill said that "conversancy with him tends to deprave one's intellect." A historian of philosophy, writing in 1965, refers to him as "the only modern to compare with Aristotle," but he also raises the question, "How could he have been so silly?" There can be no doubt, however, about Hegel's wide-ranging influence, his thought being attuned to the intellectual tendencies of nineteenth-century Germany. He left his mark out not only on the historical economists but also on Marx. Moreover, his view of liberty as submission to the authority of the state foreshadows the development of social thought and of political programs stressing social control and public policy. Since in Hegel's philosophy the hallowed concepts of justice and liberty are artfully constructed to serve as a cloak for the idolatry of the state, of its power, of the citizens' submission to it, and of war, his work itself serves as an early example of the use of language as a tool of social control.

THE INFLUENCE OF BURKE

On the whole, the historical economists of the British Isles did not worship Hegel's idols, although Bagehot, in his *Physics and Politics,* does not altogether escape the temptation. However, from the British Isles early German historicism received stimulation through the writings of Edmund Burke (1729–97), whose antirevolutionary fervor and idealization of the past and its traditions made a profound impression especially on the German romantics, who shared many of his sentiments. They were particularly impressed by Burke's plea for the restoration of the medieval idea of corporate representation, under which the citizen does not exercise his political rights as an individual but as a member of a guildlike social or economic group, an idea later endorsed by Hegel and still later by state socialists, syndicalists, and other reformers, until it became thoroughly discredited with its resurrection under national socialism and fascism in the twentieth century.

Although Adam Smith is reported to have said that "Burke is the only man I ever knew who thinks on economic subjects exactly as I do"—this referring possibly to their common suspicion of the aims and methods of businessmen—and although Burke had a high opinion of Smith, Burke did not look with favor on the works of the economists. In a famous passage in his *Reflections on the Revolution in France,* whose years of publication

HEGELIAN
VARIANT

coincides with that of Smith's death, he says: "The age of chivalry is gone. That of sophisters, economists, and calculators has succeeded, and the glory of Europe is extinguished for ever."

ECONOMIC ROMANTICISM

The attitude expressed in Burke's words may be designated as a manifestation of romanticism, a multifaceted movement that arose in opposition to the Enlightenment. Enlightenment with its reason had tamed sentiments and emotions; the romantics wanted to liberate them. In nineteenth-century England Burke's pique against the economists was shared by Southey, Coleridge, Carlyle, and others, and it found occasional expression in the pages of the *Quarterly Review* of the Tories. But there such thought was on the whole peripheral and more characteristic of the speculations of litterateurs than representative of the spirit of the age, which was echoed in the *Edinburgh Review* and the *Westminster Review*. These had no counterpart in the German countries of the Continent, where police and the censor would have stifled them. Here romanticism grew much stronger and branched out into politics. Thus political romanticism and historicism reinforced each other in their rejection of the claims of an autonomous and abstract economics. To the criticism of economics, romanticism added a criticism of the darker phases of the rising capitalist economy, stressing the insecurity of the proletarianized workers and their alienation in structures that anticipated those of Marx. It was no accident that Sismondi, the most bitter pre-Marxian critic of capitalism, was himself under the spell of the romantic idea. In art and literature, classics and romantics constituted opposites, as they did in the history of economics.

ADAM MÜLLER

Burke found an eloquent disciple on the Continent in the person of Adam Müller (1779–1829), an exponent of "economic romanticism," a movement so designated by the later historical economists of whom Müller was a forerunner. Müller was a vigorous defender of the restoration policies of Metternich's Holy Alliance, policies under which he found employment and which he untiringly upheld in his writing. His working habits were not always straightforward and might be illustrated by his proposal that he be allowed to launch a newspaper ostensibly of liberal democratic views to serve as the butt of attacks and be bested by another newspaper also edited by him. His operations in the atmosphere of the police state recall the story about the czarist secret police, an organization which at one time employed so many *agents provocateurs* that it could only with considerable difficulty avert the assassination of the czar, which was planned by its own agents. Müller found fault with the ideas of the Enlightenment, of rationalism, and of natural law and, as a bitter critic of Adam Smith's liberal views, did his best to frustrate the appointment of a follower of Smith at the University of Berlin, newly founded in 1809. In his writings Müller extolled the corporate state and other medieval institutions and suggested their restoration, deploring the liberal commercialism of the modern age and contrasting it with what he claimed to be higher spiritual values grounded in authority, tradition, and religion, with the state exalted as a mediator between man and God.

Müller may be classified as an early critic of capitalism, which he considered a threat to the viability of the absolute state. He found free enterprise and competition generating disorder and loosening traditional personal ties, objected to free trade as violating the ideal of a self-sufficient and independent state, and expressed opposition to the abolition of rural serfdom, then a burning issue in the eastern parts of Germany. It was his aim to "spiritualize" economic thought, and among his positive contributions were the exaltation of money as a creation of the state, a view that placed paper money on a footing similar to that of metallic money, and the recognition of the spiritual or intellectual capital accumulated in the form of cultural values and scientific experience as part of the national wealth.

FICHTE

Self-sufficiency was extolled also by the philosopher Johann Gottlieb Fichte (1762–1814), the first rector of the University of Berlin and the predecessor of Hegel, who made it the goal of his *Closed Commercial State,* published in 1800. Fichte's state is a corporate one, with a controlled economy and autarky. To insure the efficacy of domestic controls and maintain the value of money, the state must also regulate international economic relations —unless self-sufficiency has been achieved, perhaps as the result of the state's expansion into its "natural frontiers," and international trade can be dispensed with. Ideas such as these were to resound in Germany for 150 years.

LIST

Friedrich List (1789–1846), with Müller the principal forerunner of the historical economists and the author of the *National System of Political Economy* of 1841, was opposed to the cosmopolitanism of the classics and propagated, for certain phases of economic development, the need for protective tariffs. List was among the first to fashion one of the so-called stage theories of economic development, which from then on, and for a long time, were to obfuscate the study of economic history. He suggested a five-stage scheme, distinguishing between the primitive, the pastoral, the agricultural, the agricultural-manufacturing, and the agricultural-manufacturing-commercial stage. As List pointed out, this scheme had come to his mind as the result of his experiences in the United States, where economic development occurred at such a fast pace that the observer could not fail to notice the perceptible movement from one stage to another. The principal purpose of List's and other stage theories was to buttress the claim that classical economics did not adequately reflect the variety of conditions prevailing in different countries, especially those in Germany.

Stage theories are harmless when they are mere classifications, standing between description and analysis, and indicating possible courses of economic development. They invite misuse when what they depict is declared to be a necessary historical sequence. When developed in this form, they tempt the student of history to treat his material in such a manner as to make it conform to the previously established theory. List's scheme was designed to lead up to the agricultural-manufacturing-commercial stage as the high point of economic development, a goal attained in England and achievable in other countries by appropriate economic policies. He was a prophet of industrialization but, as his designation of the highest stage indicates, of an industrialization balanced by a flourishing agricultural establishment. Industrialization was to be achieved with the help of "educational" tariffs protecting the infant industries of suitable underdeveloped countries. List fully realized that such protection would entail costs, but he considered them the necessary price for the industrial education of the nation, one amply offset by the gain accruing to it from the development of its productive powers. This concept of productive powers formed the core of List's national economy. The classics, he argued, had neglected it, assuming that what was to be achieved —the full development of a country's productive powers—had already been achieved. List did not deny the cogency of the free-trade doctrine of the classics but believed it to be applicable only in the future, when countries had made the most of their economic capacities and attained the agricultural-manufacturing-commercial stage characteristic of the English economy. Once all countries had realized their economic potential, the time would be ripe for free trade, universal peace, and world federation, goals that List heartily endorsed for the future and did not see threatened by the trade wars and commercial rivalries which his proposed development policy would bring on.

List attached to his educational tariff certain restrictions often forgotten by those who later employed his thought to justify protective measures. Since his main concern was with the movement from stage 3 to stages 4 and 5, that is, toward industrialization, he explicitly excluded agriculture from protection, expecting it to be regenerated by the demonstration effect of an efficiently operating industry. He also excluded from his protective policy countries that because of location, climate, or other reasons would be unable to participate in the march toward industrialization.

If such countries were to perpetuate their position as producers and exporters of raw materials, the likelihood of their exploitation by their trading partners would be diminished if they had to face as customers a number of highly developed countries rather than a single one. It was this danger of the exploitation of underdeveloped countries, arising from their position as suppliers of raw materials and purchasers of manufactures, that List never failed to underline, and he saw the continental countries of Europe exposed to it in their dealings with England. To avert this danger, industrialization was imperative. What List really wanted was to revise creation and turn everyone, as far as possible, into an Englishman. He recognized clearly the close connection between liberal political institutions and economic growth of the English variety. His thought contained many forward-looking elements, including a criticism of the classical theory of international trade converging with that of Myrdal and others in our own time, as well as the idea that high or rising levels of consumption in an underdeveloped country might well be the pacemaker of increased production.

Unlike Müller, List was a liberal in politics, one who in early manhood had seen the inside of a jail and who had been exiled from his country for political reasons. He was one of the driving forces behind the formation of a customs union of the German states, the *Zollverein,* and behind the movement toward railroad construction in Germany. In his later career he never again secured an academic post such as he had held and lost as a young man and had to make an uncertain living as a journalist and promoter. List was neither tactful nor crafty, and when disappointments overwhelmed him, he put an end to his life.

In his own way, List had aimed at a synthesis of nationalism and liberalism, and this was also true of the three founders of the German historical school, two of whom, like List, had been victims of political persecution early in life. However, as time went on, German historical economics did not escape the general political tendencies that made themselves felt in Germany. Liberalism was driven into a defensive position and in the end all but vanished from the scene, whereas nationalism came to suffuse all phases of life, especially after liberalism's great foe, Bismarck, had achieved with "blood and iron" the unification of Germany under Prussian leadership, a success that stifled and confused whatever remained of the opposition of liberal patriots.

THE OLDER HISTORICAL ECONOMISTS

The three founders of German historical economics were Wilhelm Roscher (1817–94), Bruno Hildebrand (1812–78), and Karl Knies (1821–98). They initiated a tradition in German economics which was to last almost a hundred years but their figures have become dim and their individual contributions indistinct. Roscher started the trend in 1843 with the publication of a programmatic "Outlines of Lectures on Political Economy, Based on the Historical Method." He had been educated at the University of Göttingen, the Hanoverian foundation, where traces of Adam Smith's influence might have lingered and where history and the "sciences of the state"—which included economics—were traditionally taught by the same professor, and he had capped his training by attending the lectures of Ranke, the great historian, in Berlin. His main work, published in 1854 and reprinted later in many new editions, was translated into English under the title *Principles of Political Economy* in two volumes in 1882. For forty-six years, from 1848 until his death, he occupied an influential teaching post at the University of Leipzig, turning down offers from Munich, Vienna, and Berlin.

The background of Hildebrand and Knies was different from that of Roscher, and their careers, at least in their earlier phases, were more stormy. Like Roscher, they were sons of government officials, but they came from the lower social stratum of this group and rose from poverty. Like Roscher, they started out as students of history. Roscher throughout his life maintained a strong religious commitment to Lutheranism, which instilled in him obedience to government authorities. Hildebrand and Knies were active liberals and became victims of political persecution, the former as a student and again in the 1840s and 1850s, when he lost his professorship and went into exile in Switzerland to escape arrest. At that time he had already published his principal work, *The National Economy of the Present and of the Future* of 1848. Knies, some nine years younger than Hildebrand and the latter's student, also went to Switzerland after his suspension as an instructor and while residing there published in 1853 his *Political Economy from the Standpoint of the Historical Method*. Eventually both returned to Germany, the years dimming the memory of their turbulent past. Hildebrand accepted an invitation to the University of Jena, and Knies went first to Freiburg and later to Heidelberg, where he taught from 1865 to 1896. All three thus came to hold commanding teaching positions and did so over long periods of time. All three had a message, superficially the same in its essential points. To disseminate it, Hildebrand founded in 1862 a periodical, which is still in existence, *Jahrbücher für Nationalökonomie und Statistik*, edited after his death by his son-in-law Johannes Conrad. The ground was thus prepared for the rise of a school of historical economics.

ROSCHER

In its core the message of the historical economists stressed the programmatic-methodological element, which from then on was destined to become a distinct and ubiquitous feature of German economic thought. Much intellectual energy was spent on setting forth the aims and methods of economics, its scope and limitations—energy that often became lost to the task of building up the substance of economics. "The method of a science," Roscher declared, "is of greater significance by far than any single discovery, however amazing the latter may be." This approach forms a stark contrast to the English tradition, where the logical and chronological primacy of substance over method was never questioned. In many formulations and with happy similes Mill stressed that the so-called first principles of a science are in truth last principles, established not before but after its substantive truths have been collected, and he compared such principles to the wall of a city or the roots of a tree "which may perform their office equally well though they be never dug down to and exposed to light."

The historical economists' program was more easily stated than executed. It aimed at the reconstruction of an economics that was "based on the historical method." To Roscher, who promised most, this meant the establishment of laws of economic development, to be derived from the investigation of national histories, with attention given not only to their economic aspects but also to legal, political, cultural, and other aspects, all forming a whole made up of interdependent parts. Roscher's aim was one that the present classification of intellectual endeavors assigns to the philosophy of history: To unravel the secret of history, find the meaning of history, and establish laws of historical development. At the same time, however, Roscher considered the meaning and purpose of history a religious mystery and its core beyond human knowledge, but he nevertheless approached the matter as one providing food for serious thought aiming at the expansion of the limits of the knowable and at shrinking the periphery of the unknown.

Judged in the light of these goals, what Roscher actually delivered was extremely modest. It was, in substance, no more than a cyclical hypothesis, making nations and their economies pass through periods of youth, manhood, and senile decay. In addition, however, he offered in his voluminous *Principles* a fairly complete exposition of the same subjects that Mill treated in his own work on economics, augmenting it with a wealth of historical examples and illustrations which would confirm, modify, or state exceptions from, the theoretical content. Roscher's learning was immense, and his references included such faraway names as Thomas Cooper of South Carolina and George Tucker of Virginia.

Roscher's vaunted historical method did not do away with the theory of the classics but impressed the reader with its relative character, tying the theory to place and time. It was exactly because he combined with his new thought a useful exposition of classical economics that his work had a much wider appeal than did that of Hildebrand and Knies, which was differently designed. Moreover, Roscher was considered the pioneer of the movement, to whom Knies dedicated his book and whose fame during his lifetime overshadowed that of the two others. There were, however, tensions between the three, with Knies becoming estranged from his teacher Hildebrand, whom he judged intellectually dependent on Roscher; with Hildebrand failing to mention Roscher in his book; and with Roscher and Hildebrand criticizing each other's views.

HILDEBRAND

Unlike Roscher's work, which contained a systematically arranged statement of the substance of the conventional economics of his time as it was taught at a number of German universities, Hildebrand's was a critical history of economic thought, arranged by writers and condemning the views of both the classics and the Socialists. Knowledge of socialist thought, then essentially a French product, had spread in Germany as the result of the publication of Lorenz von Stein's *Der Sozialismus und Kommunismus des heutigen Frankreich*, which first appeared in 1842 and went through three editions within a few years and which acquainted the German public with the ideas of the French Socialists. Socialist thought became a target of the German historical economists as had English classical economics. Of the shadow cast by Marx, the then thirty-year-old coauthor of the *Communist Manifesto*, published in 1848 as was Hildebrand's book, the latter shows the first barely perceptible trace, mentioning him as the editor of an obscure periodical.

Hildebrand's book had been designated as the first of a number of volumes, but it remained the only one because he never followed it up with the promised methodological criticism of the work of his predecessors. His basic position was similar to that of Roscher's, and his aim was the establishment of laws of economic development. Like Roscher, he was inspired by the intellectual tendencies converging in the Germany of his time. These had, as an offpring of historical jurisprudence, also produced a historical philology, which was mainly the work of the brothers Grimm of fairy-tale fame. Historical philology interpreted language as a manifestation of a "folk soul" in a manner resembling the kindred interpretation of law by the historically-minded jurists. It fostered an approach that had far-reaching political consequences by preparing the ground for making language the criterion of one's nationality. Historical philology more than historical jurisprudence suggested to Hildebrand the fruitfulness of a new historical approach to economics.

Hildebrand never clearly stated the methodological principles that would guide such a historical approach to economics, and he nowhere came close to producing a body of doctrine that could have superseded that of the classics and accomplished what in his opinion the classics were unable to do, that is, secure the intellectual defeat of the Socialists. He would point to morals, religion, customs, and standards of propriety as factors affecting economic behavior, would underline the interrelation between economics and other social sciences, and would draw attention to the specific conditions surrounding the German economy. On all these counts he would find fault with the theory of the classics, especially that of Ricardo, taking it to task for being one-sided, incomplete, materialistic, and cosmopolitan. In its stead he proposed to look at the historical reality and explore it with the help of statistical fact-finding. It was not until 1864, sixteen years after the publication of his programmatic work, that Hildebrand made an attempt to approach more closely his stated aim, the establishment of laws of economic development, by propounding a stage theory which made the means of exchange the relevant criterion and distinguished between the natural, the money, and the credit economy. Unlike Roscher, whose cyclical theory of historical change with its ups and downs of youth, manhood, and decay carries, as do most cyclical theories, the badge of conservatism, the more liberal Hildebrand was a believer in linear progress, and he considered the movement from one of his stages to the next as progressive. He neither derived his scheme from empirical work nor developed it as a purely theoretical hypothesis because, as will be seen, the last stage was depicted as a goal for the economy.

KNIES

Knies was equipped with greater analytical gifts than the two other writers but the wealth of thoughts assembled in his otherwise poorly written book prevented it from becoming an immediate success. Like Hildebrand he believed in linear progress, and this was one reason for his rejection of social science laws kindred to those of the natural sciences. The unfolding of moral progress gave each historical sequence characteristics of its own which at best would make it analogous, that is, correspond in particulars with other sequences but never equal them. Hence, economics could produce only laws of analogy, which Knies sharply distinguished from the laws of absolutely equal cause-and-effect relationships allegedly typical of natural science.

Knies considered it faulty to ground an absolute economics in the self-seeking pursuit of private interest. Not only did moral progress transform motivations of this type, but their free play would decompose and run counter to the tendencies toward the national unity of Germany. Moreover, their recognition, and with it that of the self-regulating forces of competition and of the market, would stamp as pointless and futile the active economic policy of the state, hallowed, as it was in Germany, by a tradition of long standing.

Knies believed classical economics entirely unequipped to overcome the rising tide of socialism. Classical economics and socialism shared common preconceptions such as a utilitarian outlook and an emphasis on labor as a factor of production and determinant of value. Hence classical economics, far from containing intellectual ammunition suitable for the defeat of socialism, would only help it along to victory. The concentration of economic power and the industrial feudalism that the unrestricted competition of the classical model would bring in its train would only hasten the march to socialism.

Again, although Knies produced a methodological and political criticism of economic theory, he failed to construct a new economics, differing from both that of the classics and that of the Socialists, that could have taken the place of conventional economics. When Knies came to write about economic value and about money and credit, tasks that he later accomplished with great distinction, the influence of the historical method espoused in his earlier work had almost disappeared. And when he published a second edition in 1883, thirty years after the first, the title no longer promised a *Political Economy from the Standpoint of the Historical Method* but instead a *Political Economy from the Historical Standpoint,* Knies apparently having by then become aware of the nonexistence of such a method. In this second edition Knies underlined the lack of identity and the differences in the tasks of historians and economists, as much as he impressed on the latter the desirability of a historical point of view.

The historical view of economic theory meant that the latter was divested of its absolute character and instead considered a product of historical circumstances. Theory, in Knies's words, "grows in living contact with the total organism of a period of human or national history, out of the conditions of time, space, and nationality, co-existing with these and developing with the progressive evolution." The results of theory "have the character of historical solutions; its general laws are only a historical explication and a progressive manifestation of truth." Theory becomes a relative phenomenon, limited in its validity by time and space. The emphasis on the specific historical circumstances with which a theory is organically connected opens the way to the exploration of the historical and social determinants of theory, that is, to "historism," "sociologism," or the sociology of knowledge, an approach indeed foreshadowed by Knies, who spoke of the "earthy flavor" of theory as it arises as an emanation of national conditions.

THE RESULTS OF THEIR WORK

When it comes to a general appraisal of the work of the three historical economists, it must be admitted that they were not successful in their search for laws of economic development. It was left to Marx, who shared some of the intellectual influences under which they labored, to resume the search for a law of historical change. The historical economists anticipated a phase of his thought by stressing the importance of the economic factor in history and on occasion would come close to a materialist conception of history, without, however, developing the idea further.

Nor were the historical economists more successful in establishing a historical method for the study of economics. It is true that both Hildebrand and Knies strongly supported statistical fact-finding. However, the quantitative data so unearthed were not designed by them to verify economic theory but were presumably meant to speak for themselves, an impossible enterprise since there can be no measurement without theory. As the historical economists were unable to develop a historical method for the study of economics, they in the end wanted to have it both ways, that is, they let conventional theory stand but judged it from a historical point of view, interpreting it as relative. As a result there befell on theory what has aptly been called a paralysis—it ceased to be useful as a guide to action.

As the idea of the invisible hand of competition lost its sway no efforts were made to restrain monopolistic combinations, and the cartel movement was allowed to spread. Because there were few who understood the theory of comparative advantage, and fewer still who would seek guidance by it, the leading German economists failed to oppose Bismarck when in he shifted the policy of the Reich from free trade to protectionism. Thus economic policies of interventionism or noninterventionism came to be decided on an inadequate *ad hoc* basis, there being no firm principles to adhere to in the face of an all-pervasive relativism.

SOCIAL POLICY

On the practical side, the three historical economists pleaded for a "social policy" of ameliorating the position of the laboring class. Whereas Mill had tried to assimilate socialist ideas into his thought, the historical economists were relentlessly opposed to socialism and attempted to bring about its defeat—by social policy. Thus, for example, Hildebrand's third stage, that of the credit economy, was viewed by him as contributing to the solution of the social problem by endowing laborers with credit and, based thereon, with a proprietary interest in industry, an anticipation of the later idea of "people's capitalism" in the United States. Bismarck identified himself with the anti-socialist social policy of the historical economists when within a span of five years he launched both a program of political persecution of Socialists in 1878 and his social insurance program in 1883, the latter setting a pattern eventually emulated throughout the world. Although the general idea was quite in line with the thought of the historical economists, who did much to promote it, it seems, however, that the insurance program itself did not have its origin in a suggestion from academic circles but in the ideas of Karl Marlo, an obscure socialist writer.

SCHMOLLER

The next generation of German historical economists was led by Gustav von Schmoller (1838–1917), a masterful man, who ascended to an influential chair at the University of Berlin. Schmoller, whom the government honored with ennoblement, came to dominate academic economics in his country. His endorsement of a candidate for a university post carried great weight with the public authorities in charge of such appointments. Since he required the candidate's commitment to his own approach to economics, there were only meager opportunities for the development of economic theory in Germany.

To distinguish the school led by Schmoller from the school of the three earlier historical economists, it is usually designated as the younger one, a name implying more than the replacement of one generation by the next because under Schmoller historical economics became far more hostile to economic theory than it had been before. The younger school did not merely reject the alleged absolutism of theory but theory altogether. Economics then became identified with economic history, and all theorizing was relegated to the uncertain future when studies of economic history would be available in such abundance that general conclusions could be drawn from them. The type of economic history that Schmoller and his disciples carried on consisted mainly of microscopic descriptions of often distant and always minute detail, oriented toward political history and especially the history of public administration.

The Schmoller school continued the older historical economists' program of pacifying the laboring class by means of social policy and in 1872 was instrumental in founding the *Verein für Sozialpolitik,* "Association for Social Policy," to support this program. Modeled after this organization was the American Economic Association, established in 1885 under the leadership of young American economists who had returned from their studies in Germany imbued with attachment to social policy and opposition to laissez faire. The American Economic Association committed itself to these ideas in its original statutes, but after a few years these were changed in favor of a neutral line which made the organization acceptable to economists of all scientific and political persuasions.

THE SOCIALISTS OF THE CHAIR

With their active but unprincipled interventionism Schmoller and his followers found themselves exposed to attacks from various quarters. Their opposition to laissez faire was considered objectionable by old-time liberals and caused a brilliant journalist of this persuasion to refer to them as *Kathedersozialisten,* "socialists of the professorial chair," a name that has clung to them ever since. This designation, which was meant to be a term of opprobrium, was by no means entirely without justification, since the Schmoller group, in their desire to attach the loyalty of the laboring class to the Prusso-German monarchy, made features of the socialist program their own. Adolph Wagner (1835–1917), Schmoller's colleague in Berlin, who was a deputy of the Conservative party, would nevertheless favor the extension of public ownership, redistributive tax policies, and taxation of the unearned increment accruing to the owner of urban real estate, and he would refer to himself as a "state socialist." Wagner promulgated a "law of increasing fiscal requirements," which implied that the intervention of the state was bound to increase, one measure of public policy generating the need for the next.

Other conservatives would reject the Schmoller school's plea for social justice and consider concessions to labor and the leveling of wealth an unnecessary weakness contrary to social Darwinism. The Socialists in turn, as Rosa Luxemburg remarked, judged the work of the Schmoller group as futile, hemmed in by the anvil of the Prussian state and the hammer of the revolutionary movement. The Socialists of the chair, she said, with their studies of minute historical detail, "tear up the living stuff of social reality so much that it became possible to dissolve theoretically all great connecting strands and to make the capitalistic wood scientifically disappear behind the trees."

Intellectually the Schmoller school was placed on the defensive in the *Methodenstreit*, "controversy about methods," which it carried on with the Austrian economist Carl Menger, one of the discoverers of the subjective theory of value and of the marginal principle, who upheld the primacy of economic theory in works published in 1883 and 1884. The revival of economic theory heralded by the pioneers of the new theory of value—Menger, Jevons, and Walras—in the 1870s had, however, only a faint echo in Germany and did little to disturb the work of the historical economists, who carried on almost to the middle of the twentieth century. In 1897, when assuming office as rector of the University of Berlin, Schmoller delivered an address that he boastfully entitled "Changing Theories and Settled Truths in the Sciences of the State and of Society." Actually the historical approach did not yield settled truths at all, and what the German economists lacked were established principles from which to derive guidance. When Bismarck's move toward protectionism was debated before the Association for Social Policy in 1879, Schmoller in effect made science abdicate when he declared, after sketching the history of commercial policy at home and abroad, that Bismarck had probably again done the right thing, as he always had. The German economists, by then neglectful of economic theory for decades, had no effective advice to stem the tide of the great inflation after World War I, when one dollar came to be exchanged for four trillion marks. They failed again when a decade later the attempt was made to fend off the Great Depression with a policy of deflation.

On his deathbed Schmoller came to repent the decline of economic theory in Germany, deploring that his followers were no longer familiar with what under his leadership they had so aggressively fought against. But his own attitude during the height of his career is aptly characterized by the following story. At a statistical congress in Berne, Schmoller heard Pareto speak of "the natural laws of economics." Interrupting him, Schmoller informed the little man from Lausanne: "Sir, there are no natural laws of economics." Pareto then asked whether Schmoller knew Berne well. "Surely," said Schmoller. Pareto: "Do you know of any restaurant where one does not have to pay for one's meal?" Schmoller, almost feeling pity for the poor man: "No, certainly not, but there are cheap ones." Pareto: "Aha, here you have the natural laws of economics."

ENGEL AND BRENTANO

While economic theory was all but muted during the reign of the historical school, advances were nevertheless made in various directions, some in close connection with the work of the Schmoller group, others going beyond it. To begin with, economics branched out into a number of applied fields, such as agricultural economics. Then there were a few important empirical investigations like those of the statistician Ernst

Engel (1821–96), who established a law carrying his name which indicates the variations of the composition of consumer expenditure in different income brackets, one of the few empirical laws in economics. Considerable impetus was of course given to historical work, and although much of it was of questionable significance, some proved of more lasting value, such as Lujo Brentano's (1844–1931) pioneer history of English trade unions, which traced their origin back to the guilds, an interpretation that has remained controversial. Brentano, who taught at the University of Munich, had English connections and encountered in his formative years the liberal Catholicism of Lord Acton's circle. Throughout his life he attempted to retain his liberalism and his attachment to English institutions.

SPIETHOFF AND SOMBART

Those who went beyond Schmoller included his pupil Arthur Spiethoff (1873–1957), who attained international recognition for his contributions to business cycle theory, as well as Werner Sombart (1863–1941), who tried to combine the writing of history with theoretical analyses of the historical processes. His history was not always reliable and his theory was as a rule antiquated, but the wide sweep of his work, in an age characterized by narrow specialization, attracted many readers. Sombart started as a Marxist but ended as a wavering Nazi, having no principles to guide him and symbolizing in his own career a development for which Adolph Wagner, to whose chair in Berlin Sombart succeeded, had prepared the ground. Sombart wrote a multivolume history of modern capitalism, which offered besides historical description an investigation of the driving forces in economic history, whose role he further examined in a series of separate studies of bourgeois mentality and of the economic impact of war and luxury. Central in his thought was the notion of an economic "system," and he developed a conceptual scheme to explore the morphology, or structure, of different economic systems, classifying them by their "sprit," their "form," and their "technique." Thus he would characterize the spirit of capitalism as dominated by the ideas of acquisition, competition, and rationality; its form as a free, decentralized, market-oriented private enterprise system; and its technology as ever changing and geared to advances in productivity. Sombert also wrote a history of economic thought, in which the triadic division of the material, invariably chosen by him under the influence of Marxian dialectics, recurs in the form of a classification of the judging, the ordering, and the understanding approach to economics. That the scholastics adopt the judging approach and classical and neoclassical economics the ordering one will be patent. The "understanding" approach, which Sombart claimed for himself and other historical economists, requires an explanation.

The understanding approach arose in conjunction with a distinction, made by German philosophers, between the natural and the cultural sciences, whereby the former were characterized as *nomothetic*, or law-setting, and the latter as *idiographic,* or describing the unique and individual. With history included in the cultural sciences, and with economics, of which the philosophers knew little more than the historical variant, considered as a historical study, this disjunction would have precluded any generalizing study of economics. This classification illustrates the dangers inherent in premature work along methodological lines, dangers intimated by Mill when he spoke of the wall built around a city before the city has come into being. It was in opposition to this classification of all science as either nomothetic or idiographic that those who like Sombart were eager to theorize about historical phenomena came to foster another approach, which they designated as the understanding one. This new approach was also grounded in the distinction between natural and cultural sciences, but it rejected the identification of the former with the nomothetic and the latter with the idiographic method. Understanding was said to be the approach germane to the cultural, including the social, sciences. To illustrate the difference between natural science and the understanding approach, Sombart would compare the compounding of chemical elements which results in a new substance with a merger or consolidation of business firms (or the playing of kittens with the activities going on at a football field). In the first case—that of the chemical elements or the kittens— we may order the phenomena and observe other regularities, but in the end we face a puzzle or mystery, a limit to our knowledge which has been interpreted by a variety of scientific hypotheses.

The situation is quite different in the case of the corporate merger (or that of the ball players), which human knowledge can understand in a sense that does not apply to nature, because here man explores man, and subject and object of knowledge are identical. We understand something if we can attribute a meaning to it, that is, bring it into a connection of which we have previous knowledge and in the end relate it to our total experience.

MAX WEBER

Sombart's classificatory concepts and his notion of understanding reflect the influence of Max Weber (1864–1920), considered by many Germany's greatest social scientist of recent times. Weber's application of the understanding approach to social phenomena resulted, in his own words, in the *Entzauberung* of the world, that is, in the breaking of magical spells and liberation from illusions. In this sense, Weber interpreted history as a process of "rationalization" in which magic is replaced by the cold efficiency of matter-of-fact thought which becomes ever more orderly and systematic. Rationalization is embodied in the growing managerial and governmental bureaucracies and in the rise of the professional expert. Concomitant with the upsurge of large and efficient organizations, life becomes depersonalized, mechanical, and permeated by routine. Unlike Marx, Weber felt that "the dictatorship of the official and not that of the worker is on the march." Weber, who was close to the Schmoller group, was also the author of the Weber-Tawney thesis of the Calvinist origin of capitalism. He made important contributions to economic history but is mainly remembered as a sociologist and investigator of the epistemological foundations of social science.

Weber became a successor of Knies at Heidelberg but protracted ill health, largely mental in origin—his father had died shortly after a stormy argument with him—limited his activities in the classroom. His influence, nevertheless, was enormous, because of both the scope and quality of his written work and the impact of his powerful personality. Weber's own historical interests and the intellectual atmosphere of the German academic economics of his time prevented him from making a name for himself in economic theory proper, although he was well informed of its structure. In general he contributed not to economics proper but to "economic sociology," a discipline that sheds light on the origins and determinants of economic behavior rather than on the abstract framework designed to interpret economic behavior itself. Weber's investigation of the Protestant origin of capitalism falls into this range of work, as do his explorations of the socioeconomic impact of other great religions. This type of approach has assumed a new significance in connection with the current concern about underdeveloped countries. Here related questions have been raised, and here also interdisciplinary cooperation with history, sociology, and other fields has been recognized as necessary.

Weber made much use in his work of the notion of an "ideal type," which in spite of its name does not designate anything normative or praiseworthy but rather has an affinity with the "models" employed in modern economic analysis. An ideal type is a mental construction that does not portray reality but abstracts from it by exaggerating certain of its features and disregarding others. It facilitates the formulation of hypotheses and the systematization and classification of empirically observed material. As such an ideal type Weber would, for example, consider the *homo economicus,* or economic man of economic theory. According to Weber it would be a misunderstanding—one to which especially the historical economists were prone—to interpret the economic man's pursuit of self-interest as being derived from psychological considerations or from the empirical study of human action and then claim to have disproved the universal existence of self-seeking behavior because psychology and the observation of behavior point to other wellsprings of human action.

Instead, Weber says,

> economic laws are schemes of rational action, deduced not from the psychological analysis of the individual but from a theoretical construction of an objective situation, a reconstruction, by means of ideal types, of the price struggle in the market. Where this theoretical situation in all its purity has its exact counterpart in the real world, there the individual, who finds himself enmeshed

in the mechanism of the market, has only the choice between this alternative: adaptation to the market [that is, pursuit of self-interest, e.g., profit maximization] or economic ruin.

Unlike a hypothetical law of natural science, which must be considered as being grounded in a false hypothesis if disproved in a single case, the hypothetical laws of economics do not claim universal validity and are not falsified if in a given instance individuals pursue other motives than the ones assumed in a rational scheme, for instance, if they choose economic ruin.

Weber's most profound effect on twentieth-century social thought resulted from another of his methodological preconceptions, namely, his insistence on the strict observation of Hume's distinction between what is and what ought to be. Social scientists, he warned, will abuse their position —which indeed was a commanding one in the light of the reverential attitude with which Germans looked up to the academicians—if they present as scientific propositions what in truth are only their personal preferences or political valuations. Social science must be kept free from value judgments. Weber thus prepared the ground for that dichotomy between one's personal and one's professional or professorial attitude which was to become characteristic of modern social science. Eventually it came under attack both from the panideologists who considered social science suffused with ideology and from those who castigated the professional reserve that Weber wanted to impose on his colleagues as akin to schizophrenia and harboring great dangers, comparable in its effects to the practice of Hegel's moral positivism, which identifies the moral with the existing order and never undertakes to question the latter, however sordid it may be.

Weber was a strong German nationalist. He died in 1920, and no one knows whether he would have retained his professional reserve had he lived some twenty years longer, when mass murder and genocide became the public policy of his country. All this may be a matter of degree. Weber was not alone in his protest against the political professor. In 1927 another vigorous defender of reason and the intellect, the French philosopher Julien Benda, wrote his *Treason of the Intellectuals,* also denouncing the political professor who places his intellect in the service of political purposes rather than of reason. But Benda identified reason with universal spiritual values, with the service of humanity, an ideal that in Germany had long been replaced by nationalist historicism.

INFLUENCE OF THE HISTORICAL ECONOMISTS

The influence of the German historical economists was not restricted to their homeland, but when their thought spread abroad it was often domesticated by the moderating forces of different traditions and environments which took the sting out of the nationalism, the idolatry of the state, the political polarization, and the illiberalism which attended the growth of historical economics on its native soil and with which it had become inextricably connected. Because so many American students were attracted to German universities during the closing decades of the nineteenth century, the influence of historical economics was especially strong in the United States, resulting, as has been noted, in the founding of the American Economic Association after the model of the German Association for Social Policy. But just as the American Economic Association soon revised its statutes, so did many pupils of the German historical economists Americanize the lessons they had learned abroad, promoting, for example, the control of trusts rather than the cartel movements which their German teachers supported.

When the budding academicians returned to the United States, they would bring back a disdain for laissez faire paired with positive attitudes to social policy and other forms of interventionism, to statistical and historical fact-finding, and to the cultivation of various fields of applied economics. But the seeds so transplanted were to grow in an environment quite different from the one where they had sprung up. Although utilitarianism as a philosophy was never strong in the United States, natural law ideas and with them the idea of humanity had never lost their hold on the minds of men; the state was considered an agent, if not the servant, of the people rather than worshipped as a mystical entity that could do no wrong; energies that elsewhere pressed for imperial expansion were absorbed in domestic development; parliamentary government was no sham; democratic and liberal traditions were upheld in an order that was pluralistic rather than monolithically oriented toward the monarchical state; class divisions were fluid; and the two great parties did not exist in different political worlds.

Had the young students brought back from Germany not only the rejection of laissez faire and the endorsement of social policy but the whole political value system from which these ideas stemmed, the propagation of their newly learned lessons would have fallen on deaf ears. But as this was not the case, these ideas not only became influential in the United States but their influence was on the whole a healthier one than in the home country and, contrary to the fears of libertarians, did not open the gates to "the road to serfdom." That the influence was a healthier one was due both to the different political environment and to the continuing strength, in the United States, of theoretical economics. In this situation, theoretical economics not only kept the aspirations of the historically minded economists within proper bounds but was itself liberated from doctrinaire dogmatism by being compelled to submit its hypotheses to the tests of the fact finders.

Moreover, not all American economists who had been trained in Germany became exponents of historical economics. To name but one, John B. Clark was a student of Knies's in the 1870s and later became the first American economist to gain international recognition for his contributions to economic theory. Knies, although he preached a historical approach, was himself an eminent practitioner of economic theory. In 1855, in an article on value, he made the value of a good depend on the degree to which it is capable of satisfying human wants. In addition to Jevons, Menger, and Walras, Clark is considered an independent discoverer of the subjective theory of value and of the marginal principle. In 1896, some years after this discovery, he contributed an article entitled "The Unit of Wealth" to a volume of essays honoring his erstwhile teacher Knies, and he mentioned that "suggestions received from Professor Karl Knies led me to seek to discover a unit, by which all varieties of wealth might be measured." Edgeworth's quip about the historical economists—"those who denounce the inordinate use of deduction in economics are commonly open to the imputation of condemning 'sins they have no mind to' "—does not apply to Knies, who may well have been among the intellectual ancestors of the modern theory of value, just as were his contemporaries at Oxford and Dublin.

Chapter 19

SOCIALISM BEFORE MARX:

A Diversity of Views

In the middle of the nineteenth century the classical system was subjected to attacks on three fronts. First, there were the lingering effects of the thought of those early writers who had doubted the ability of the system to generate a demand strong enough to absorb the output of the economy. Second, the struggle was joined by the historical economists, who placed the nation in the center of their thought and questioned the ability of the classical system to account for national diversities. Third, an attack was launched by the Socialists, who gave expression to class rather than to national aspirations and found the system wanting in attention to the needs of the "poorest and most numerous class," the proletariat.

This was truly a new idea, one alien to the spirit of a Smith or a Ricardo, both of whom considered the free enterprise carried on by the emancipated middle class humanity's best hope. In Smith's vision of the classical system, the central problem of economics, that of scarcity, was to be attacked by the unfettered production of self-reliant individuals. Malthus, in his population theory, had added self-restraint to Smith's self-reliance as a prerequisite of economic progress. As Malthus's population theory had done, Ricardo's analysis of distribution revealed that there were serious obstacles besetting the path of economic progress, obstacles, however, which free trade might help to overcome. Ricardo never questioned the absolute virtues of industry and thrift, of self-reliance and self-restraint, which within the limits of his distribution theory would perhaps not make for a perfect world but for the best of all possible ones. Neither Smith nor Ricardo would question the ability of the economic system to dispose of its output, the suitability of the abstract-generalizing approach to economics, or the institutional framework of the free enterprise economy.

On these three counts the classical system now faced serious challenges, and the response was different in various parts of the world. Historical economics was victorious in Germany, and France became the homeland of revolutionary socialism. In England developments took a different turn. There the historical point of view was absorbed into general economics and socialism emerged along evolutionary rather than revolutionary lines. That matters turned out this way attests to the British genius for compromise, a genius so outstandingly exemplified in the thought of John Stuart Mill. The three counts on which the classical system was challenged related to subjects that Mill approached with an open mind, which he treated as unsettled questions calling for discussion and solution with the help of new ideas. His readiness to accommodate new thought and integrate it with his own blunted the attack of the historical economists and Socialists. In England, historical economics, instead of conquering, became tamed, and socialism arose as a doctrine of peaceful change and gradual adaptation. Obviously this was an outcome that must not be credited to Mill alone but to the historical circumstances and conditions which found expression in his thought and which differed from those prevailing in other parts of the world.

THE PROLETARIAT AND THE BOURGEOISIE

The social forces that found expression in socialism were generated by the aspirations of the rising working class, the proletariat, as some Socialists called it, a class that they sharply distinguished from the middle class, or bourgeoisie. When socialism began its march the world still reverberated from the French Revolution of 1789, the great upheaval that had been inspired by middle-class aspirations. Now, in the nineteenth century, these aspirations found gradual fulfillment in protracted struggles, leading to the emancipation of the middle class from aristocratic rule and the fetters of feudalism. But before this development had run its course new claims were made, this time on behalf of the laboring class, which were different from those pursued by the bourgeoisie and which the victory of the bourgeoisie had failed to satisfy.

In line with the precedent established by American revolutionists, middle-class aims were forcefully stated in the Declaration of the Rights of Man and of the Citizen of 1789, which proclaimed liberty, equality, the inviolability of property, and the right to resist oppression. The equality heralded in this great document was a legal and formal one which promised citizens equal rights under the law. Soon voices were heard that questioned the adequacy of an arrangement that, as Anatole France was to remark, forbade poor and rich alike to steal bread, beg in the streets, and sleep under bridges. Claims for substantive equality became more insistent once the progress of the industrial revolution had uprooted the small independent craftsman and created large conglomerations of factory workers in the cities. Dissatisfaction with oppressive social conditions, with the new stratification

of society, with poverty and economic insecurity, found expression in socialist
thought, which formed a reaction to liberalism and the laissez faire rule.
The institutional framework of the laissez faire economy, which the classical
economists had taken for granted, grounded as it was in the competitive
struggle by private enterprise for private profit, now became the subject of
bitter complaints.

VARIANTS OF SOCIALISM

No one man can be said to have founded socialism, and there have
been almost as many variants of socialism as there are Socialists. What stands
out as a common feature of their thought is a profound dissatisfaction with
an economic order in which the competitive struggle seemed to yield poverty,
inequality, and insecurity. Against this background there arose the idea of a
fundamental change in institutional arrangements, one that would transform
and improve society. Some early Socialists were primarily critics of the
existing order. Others gave special attention to the details of the society to
come. Still others mapped out the path leading to it.

SOURCES OF SOCIALIST THOUGHT

The sources of socialist thought were as diverse as socialist thought
itself. There was, to begin with, the influence of the Enlightenment, with its
belief in progress and perfectibility, ideas to which Condorcet and Godwin
had given currency in France and England and which now found an echo
in the socialist thought of both countries. There was, furthermore, the
activism that had emerged during the French Revolution, and on a different
level there was the activism implied in Bentham's science of legislation, with
its happiness principle, its agenda, and the inclusion of equality among the
goals of public policy. Some Socialists would respond to these calls for
action, while others, to whom German philosophy had disclosed the meaning
of history, would join what they discerned to be the march of history. Again,
some Socialists found stimulation in the natural law idea of humanity guided
by reason as interpreted by them, and some responded to religious impulses
and were turned into Christian Socialists by the gospel of love. Most Socialists were inclined to give weight to the economic factor in history, stressing
an idea that was not new but which hitherto had never stood in the center
of anyone's thought. In addition, there were the teachings of the classical
economists, especially of Ricardo, which derived economic value from labor
or measured it in terms of labor—teaching that provided a starting point for
a chain of reasoning yielding the conclusion that the wage system did not
return to the worker the full value of his product.

SOCIALIST AIMS AND METHODS

Most of the early Socialists wanted to replace the competitive struggle by different institutional arrangements, but what these were to be and how they were to be established were debatable matters. Some Socialists saw in the institution of private property the root of all evil, but there were others who wanted to preserve and diffuse property. Most Socialists were opposed to the pronounced inequality of wealth and income, but few were strict egalitarians. Many considered cooperation rather than competition the proper means to organize society and proposed the establishment of cooperative associations of working people. Others placed reliance on the trade union movement to shift the balance of bargaining power from the employer to the worker. Still others suggested monetary reforms that would endow producers with purchasing power commensurate with their productive capacity.

Views were similarly divided about the means to call the new society into being. There were those who proposed to rely on moral suasion, self-help, and voluntary action to secure the transition to the socialism of their choice. Others agitated in favor of violent upheavals brought off by conspiratorial groups. Most Socialists considered the state unsuited to produce desirable social changes, and some wanted to do away with organized government altogether. In appraising the attitude of the early Socialists to the state, account must be taken of the fact that representative democracy was still nonexistent in some countries or in its infancy in others. Hence, only few Socialists would place their hopes in the state to accomplish by legislative action and public policy the renewal of society. In countries that had not yet begun to establish the institutions of representative democracy, they might appeal to the authoritarian governments of the time to take sides with the laboring class rather than with the bourgeoisie, whereas in politically more advanced countries they might count on the spread of representative government to help in the realization of their goals. Evolutionary socialism, which employs the state as an instrument to bring about the gradual reorganization of society, did not come into prominence until a later period, when representative democracy had been established in many lands.

Thus the early Socialists, with the rich diversity of their thought, had various ideas about how to resolve the economic problem. Their thought is important because of the influence it had on the later development of socialism. Democratic and authoritarian, revolutionary and evolutionary socialism, all stem from it. Beyond this, early socialism brought out a number of ideas that were to become influential at a later period and had by then lost their connection with socialism—cooperation of all varieties, the social responsibility of property, educational reform, managed money, government by a managerial elite, the promotion of industrial development, and the idea of making work attractive.

Just as the thought of the early Socialists nurtured that of democratic socialism, so it also stimulated that of Karl Marx (1818–83), the most influential of the revolutionary Socialists. Marx was not the founder of socialism, which was already richly developed when he appeared on the scene. He was the founder of his own kind of socialism, which he labeled communism, a designation until then not used in sharp distinction to other socialisms. Because it was in part the same intellectual legacy that nourished the thought of Marx and that of other Socialists, their ideas often ran along parallel lines and sometimes converged. Marx incorporated some ideas of the rival Socialists into his own system. He rejected many others, but even these were catalysts in the development of his own thought.

SOCIALISM AND NATIONAL PATTERNS OF THOUGHT

As a rule, socialism professes to be cosmopolitan and directs its message to the proletariat wherever it can be found or even to all humanity. Nevertheless, national patterns of thought were important factors in shaping and coloring the variants of early socialism in their homelands. In England the last revolution had occurred in 1688, and democratic and libertarian aspirations had found a greater measure of accommodation than in the France of the Bourbons or in the German principalities run by petty despots. Homegrown socialism in England tended toward libertarianism and evolution and in its early phase stressed self-help and voluntary action rather than reliance on the government. French Socialists, who thought out programs of the richest variety and whose ideas reached soaring heights of imagination unparalleled elsewhere, would not exclude these means. But in France the revolutionary tradition, nurtured as it was by the memory of the great upheaval of 1789, was considerably stronger, and under its influence Socialists would join conspiracies aiming at violent uprisings. State Socialists, who would want to introduce socialist measures by legislation, could be found in France too, but this form of socialism was more typical of Germany, where a long tradition, from which only a few Socialists emancipated themselves, hallowed the exaltation of the state and reliance on it.

ENGLISH SOCIALISM

English socialism appeared in three variants, the Godwinian, of which Owen was the outstanding exponent, the Ricardian, composed of a group of lesser-known representatives who took their cue from the classical theory of value, and the Christian, whose followers were motivated by religious impulses.

OWEN

The commanding figure in early English socialism was Robert Owen (1771–1858), whose view of the world, resembling that of Godwin, made man appear as essentially good and perfectible but corrupted by evil institutions. Owen's influence affected a wide segment of the population and was felt on both sides of the Atlantic. He was a wealthy self-made manufacturer, who attained worldwide fame as the eminently successful co-owner of a model factory in Scotland. There, at the New Lanark textile mills, he restricted the labor of children and devoted special care to their education, raised wages, shortened hours, improved housing and sanitary conditions and the services of the company store, and made other provisions to enrich the life of the community. What he did at New Lanark was unheard of at his time and the more impressive since the factory continued to earn substantial profits.

Only after Owen had demonstrated to the world his ability as a doer and practical man of affairs did he approach the public as a thinker and agitator. His fame and wealth helped him to secure a respectful audience, one at first by no means drawn only from laboring people but including the aristocracy as well as leading clergymen and financiers. Later on, when the radicalism of his views had become apparent, this part of his audience diminished but his hold over the laboring classes grew stronger. He had early in his career been a leader in the drive for factory legislation and later became a leader also of the trade union and cooperative movements.

Although Owen continued to write and agitate until his death at the age of eighty-seven in the mid-nineteenth century, his most important ideas, clearly and forcefully stated and without later encumbrances, can be found in his early works, *A New View of Society,* the first part of which was published in 1813, and the *Report to the County of Lanark* of 1821. Owen was an effective critic of the business civilization of the rising industrialism, and his writings indicate his deep concern about the defects of a society that compelled small children to work long hours and allowed them to grow up warped in mind and body and without an adequate education. As adults so formed they would spend their lives in cramped and unhealthy quarters and fill the mean factory buildings of the time, prone to the temptations of crime and seeking release in drunkenness. The employers, in turn, were forced to persevere in the maintenance of a system imposed on them by the competitive struggle, a system making for disharmony and dooming the worker to a life that had lost its dignity. Under the influence of the depression following the Napoleonic Wars, this essentially social criticism of Owen's was later expanded to one more specifically directed at such economic ills as unemployment and insecurity.

Owen's central idea was that man is formed by the forces of his environment, and this point of view caused him to stress educational reforms and the creation of circumstances favorable for bringing out the best in man. Considerations such as these made Owen a pioneer in the promotion of investment in human capital as well as an effective anti-Malthusian. Addressing his fellow manufacturers, he remarked on the care they gave their lifeless machinery and then pointed out that it would be equally rewarding to improve their living machines. As he observed,

> it was natural to conclude that the more delicate, complex, living mechanism would be equally improved by being trained to strength and activity; and that it would also prove true economy to keep it neat and clean; to treat it with kindness, that its mental movements might not experience too much irritating friction; to endeavor by every means to make it more perfect; to supply it regularly with a sufficient quantity of wholesome food and other necessaries of life, that the body might be preserved in good working condition, and prevented from being out of repair, or falling prematurely to decay.

Owen was a firm believer in scientific and technological progress, and he argued that under suitable institutional arrangements man's productive powers could be greatly strengthened, so much so that in the ensuing age of plenty the economic problem of scarcity would disappear, as would the problem of overpopulation. Mr. Malthus, he said, "has not told us how much more food an intelligent and industrious people will create from the same soil, than will be produced by one ignorant and ill-governed. It is, however, as one to infinity." That scarcity of goods and excessive numbers of people were not a necessary part of the human condition but the result of defective institutional arrangements was a point of view that many later Socialists shared with Owen.

Owen was a believer in altruism and taught that man can add to his happiness only by endeavoring to increase the happiness of all around him. The individual pursuit of self-interest, which the classics had made the cornerstone of their doctrine, Owen considered the source of many evils. If individuals pursue their aims opposed to and in competition with their fellowmen, angry and malevolent passions are nurtured, the divisive forces in society are strengthened, and all superior and valuable qualities of human nature are repressed.

The reorganization of society that Owen proposed was one of voluntarily formed producer cooperatives, paired with a monetary reform that would do away with money bound to a metallic standard and replace it by money representing units of labor time and issued freely concomitant with the production of goods. Such a reform, Owen held, would unloosen the forces of production and put an end to unemployment and depressions. "That which can create new wealth is, of course, worth the wealth which it creates," he told his followers, and he urged them "to let prosperity loose on the country" by changing the standard of value.

Owen devoted a great deal of effort and money to the establishment of cooperatives, in his native country as well as in the United States, where he founded New Harmony in Indiana. On the whole, however, the later Socialist movement in Britain did not follow the cooperative path but placed much greater reliance on legislation and government action, instruments of social change that Owen rejected.

Owen had no use for class hatred and believed that "the rich and the poor, the governors and the governed, have really but one interest." When addressing the working classes in 1819, he told them that "no rational ground for anger exists, even against those who by the errors of the present system have been made your greatest oppressors and your most bitter enemies." This attitude again reflected his fundamental belief that individuals are formed by the circumstances of their environment and that they cannot be held responsible for things beyond their control.

THE RICARDIAN SOCIALISTS

Owen's reform proposals found a ready response among a group of English writers later designated as Ricardian Socialists. This group, which had its forerunner in Charles Hall, included Thompson, Hodgskin, Gray, and Bray. Although the starting point in the argument employed by these men was not the same as that used by Owen, they nevertheless arrived at similar conclusions. In the thought of the Ricardian Socialists the classical theory of value held a position of central importance, and it was on the basis of this theory that they arrived at opinions sharply at variance with those of the classical economists. Owen also adhered to the labor theory of value but another thought—that man is formed by his environment—formed the core of his argument.

As England was the homeland of classical economics, it is not surprising that the Ricardian Socialists were among the first to use important elements of the classical system as points of departure for the development of a socialist economics. From the labor theory of value they derived theories of exploitation and surplus value, arguing that the wage system deprived the laborer of the value of the whole product of his industry. To replenish this share was to them a requirement of justice as well as a means to secure the proper functioning of the economy. For the achievement of these ends they proposed to rely on cooperative organizations, the trade union movement, and monetary reform. Like Owen they rejected both revolution and government action. Their thought was tempered by the disciplined approach of the classical economists from whom they took their cue. Few of these writers commanded a wide audience but their influence was felt by John Stuart Mill as well as in the later development of socialist thought.

HALL AND THOMPSON

Charles Hall (c.1740–c.1820), a generation ahead of the other members of the group, was a physician whose practice had impressed on him the degradations from which laboring people suffered during the industrial revolution. In *The Effects of Civilization,* published in 1805, Hall stressed the contrast between the rich, whose wealth constituted power, and the poor, who were compelled to sell their labor on unfavorable terms, retaining only a small part of its product, estimated by Hall as the equivalent of one hour out of eight hours of work. Similar lines of thought were more fully developed in the 1820s by William Thompson (1775–1833), an Irish landowner and model landlord, "one of the idle classes," as he called himself, who rose against his background and became a Socialist of note. In his *Inquiry into the Principles of the Distribution of Wealth* of 1824 he followed one variant of the classical tradition by interpreting rent and interest as deductions from the product of labor, but unlike the classics he characterized these deductions as unjust. Thompson was the first writer to employ the expression "surplus value," the substance of which had already been noted by Hall, and he was also the first Socialist in England to give detailed attention to the problem of justice in distribution. His analysis of this matter brought to light a number of important problems posed by socialist economics. Thompson believed that productivity would be greatly increased if workers were to receive the full product of their industry, but such rewards, he pointed out, would violate the principle of equality. Thompson was thus aware of the potential clash between equality of rewards and efficiency of production, as he was of the impossibility of leaving all surplus value with the laborer, there then being nothing left to satisfy important social needs. Thompson's discussion of various distributive arrangements may have implanted in John Stuart Mill, who was acquainted with him, the idea of sharply separating production from distribution and interpreting the latter as subject to institutional regulation.

HODGSKIN

Whereas Thompson hoped to resolve the problem of distribution with the help of producer cooperatives, his contemporary Thomas Hodgskin (1787–1869), a naval officer who became a journalist, suggested instead that the trade union movement be used to realize the claims of labor. In *Labor Defended Against the Claims of Capital* of 1825, Hodgskin extolled labor as the only productive agent and denied the productivity of capital. He considered circulating capital to be only coexisting labor, which provides the worker with goods he does not produce himself, and fixed capital only skilled labor applied to the result of previous labor. Hodgskin's *Popular Political Economy* of 1827 was the first textbook of socialist economics. It expressly excluded consumption from the subjects treated by political economy and thereby set a precedent which John Stuart Mill followed shortly thereafter.

GRAY

The labor theory of value served as point of departure also for John Gray (1799–1883), whose *Lecture on Human Happiness* of 1825 suggests further-reaching reforms than reliance on the labor movement. Gray became acquainted with the activity of the commercial world as a clerk in a London wholesale house, and his early experiences turned him into a bitter critic of competition, which not only depressed wages but stifled production as well. In Gray's indictment of competition there are echoes of such modern complaints as that about poverty in the midst of plenty or about production for profit rather than for use. Although Gray was attached to the ideal of producer cooperatives in his early work, he later shifted his emphasis to the planned direction of production and to monetary reform which would provide cheap and easy money. As time went on Gray's protests mellowed, and since they ceased altogether after 1848 it was long believed that he had died around 1850. But he had in fact made his way in the world and attained a position of wealth and influence as a publisher, surviving for some thirty years the end of his career as a socialist writer.

BRAY

The last of the Ricardian Socialists, and the only workingman in the group, was John Bray (1809–97), who was born in Washington, D. C. Bray, the child of stage performers, spent most of his adult life in the United States, working as a printer, photographer, and farmer, and participating in the labor movement of his time. For twenty years, from 1822 to 1842, Bray resided in England, and it was there that his principal work, *Labour's Wrongs and Labour's Remedy,* was published in 1839. Again arguing on the basis of the labor theory of value, Bray considered the employment contract a sham and deceitful device under which the worker turns over to the capitalist the labor of an entire week in exchange for the value of a fraction of this time—in fact, in exchange for nothing, because what the worker receives is not a contribution by the capitalist but merely a part of the wealth obtained from the worker himself the week before. As for remedies, Bray rejected all those that would preserve the employer-employee relationship and instead extolled communal property. However, since he recognized the practical difficulties facing its institution he proposed as an intermediate solution the establishment of a network of corporations founded and owned by the workers and those willing to become their benefactors. To emancipate these corporations from the cash nexus, Bray suggested that they issue money representing labor time and serving as a medium of exchange in intercorporate transactions.

CHRISTIAN SOCIALISM

The mainstream of early English socialism had its source in rationalism, which particularly in the case of Owen became fused with hostility to religion. Some Socialists, however, were inspired by moral and religious impulses and attempted to forge a link between socialism and religion. Thus a short-lived Christian socialism would emerged in mid-century, when the outbreak of the continental revolutions and the agitation of the Chartists at home impressed a number of Anglican clergymen with the need to search for new ways to cope with the social problems of the time. The movement was led by Frederick Denison Maurice (1805–72), Charles Kingsley (1819–75), and John Ludlow (1821–1911), the latter, who had spent his formative years in France, bringing to it the democratic vigor of the French variant of Christian socialism. There was a rift, however, with such leaders as Maurice, who did not share the democratic aspirations of the period but was a conservative in his political leanings, anxious to preserve the ancient prerogatives of the monarch and of the aristocracy.

The Christian Socialists aimed at an alliance between the national church and a spiritually regenerated laboring class to liberate the latter from the evil working conditions of the sweatshops and other social ills. Their program resembled that of the Owenites in its stress on class reconciliation, cooperation, and unionism. Like the Owenites and unlike the Chartists, the Christian Socialists placed no hope in political reforms, which indeed some of their leaders opposed. Although the movement found little following among the working people and failed to survive the 1850s, it foreshadowed later instances of a convergence of socialist and religious aspirations in England.

FRENCH SOCIALISM

French socialist thought shared a number of features with its English counterpart but acquired characteristics of its own which connect it with the French Revolution of 1789. This momentous event not only heralded the ascendancy of the middle class but in addition provided a training ground for the practice of revolutionary tactics, and under its stir socialist claims were made for substantive equality which the bourgeoisie was unwilling to grant. As regards revolutionary tactics, the Jacobins, a small closely knit group of determined men, would demonstrate—and impress with this demonstration generations of revolutionists yet to come—that power was within the reach of such a conspiratorial group and that it could be attained with the help of a "dictatorship of opinion" and the support of the Terror. Although the Jacobins were inattentive to the economic needs of the masses, this matter formed the core of the "conspiracy of the Equals" of François Babeuf (1760–97) and his followers, whose programs of violent revolution to end all revolutions, of common property, and of a general duty to work anticipated the ideas of later revolutionists. Although Babeuf was executed and the conspiracy stamped out, the survival of Filippo Michele Buonarroti (1761–1837), a leading member of the group, linked the movement with nineteenth-century socialism.

In the further development of socialist thought in France a considerable variety of different points of view emerged. Those who placed their trust in conspiratorial movements to lead the march into socialism found rivals in the state Socialists who proposed to realize socialist aims by legislation. Others rejected both conspiracy and the state as instrumentalities of change and instead recommended reliance on voluntary action in the form of cooperation or monetary reform to bring off a new society. The vision of the new society would again differ sharply among the various thinkers. To some it was the planned expansion of industrial production under central direction that appeared as the ideal of the future, while others stressed the attractions of community life in small, semirural organizations. In the thought of some reformers, libertarian socialism, with its aversion to coercion by the state, gave way to anarchism, which rejected organized government altogether. These and other tendencies came to life in the thought of Blanqui and Blanc, of Saint-Simon and Fourier, of Proudhon and Bakunin. As in England, there was also a Christian variant of socialism, with Lamennais as its principal exponent.

BLANQUI

The conspiratorial tradition was continued by Auguste Blanqui (1805–81), a professional revolutionist who was an advocate—and practitioner—of the *coup d'état* or *Putsch* brought about by a self-appointed elite recruited from the most progressive members of the proletariat and the disaffected part of the bourgeoisie, whose aim was a proletarian dictatorship. His program included free education (of which he considered the proletariat badly in need), expropriation of large estates, control over factories, the right to work, social equality, and—the progressive income tax. Blanqui's method contrasts sharply with the later emphasis on the need for a proletarian mass movement to bring off the revolution. Although he visualized a struggle between the classes, he considered the mass of the proletariat unequal to the task of rising against its masters.

BLANC

While Blanqui regarded revolution and the capture of the state by the proletariat as indispensable prerequisites of socialism, Louis Blanc (1811–82) became the founder of a rival tradition which proposed to utilize the machinery of the existing government to assist in the transformation of society. Blanc, often labeled a state Socialist, set forth his ideas in his *Organisation du Travail*, first published in 1839. He postulated the principle "from each according to his ability, to each according to his needs," called for the recognition of the right to work, and proposed to implement these principles by means of "national workshops," producer cooperatives which would be established with the financial assistance of the government and would in time take the place of competitive private enterprise.

Blanqui, the conspiratorial insurrectionist, and Blanc, the state Socialist, had definite but disparate views about how to bring on the society to come. Each in his own way set a pattern for the *political* tactics of socialist movements of the future. Economic thought, but not economic analysis, stands out more prominently in the writings of Henri de Saint-Simon (1760–1825) and Charles Fourier (1772–1837), each of whom had a different broadly conceived vision, in which madness was blended with insight, of a new society. To set it off, Saint-Simon and Fourier suggested other means than a revolution. Fourier wanted to rely on the voluntary association of individuals who would form cooperatives, whereas Saint-Simon placed his trust in the operation of historical tendencies supported by propaganda and *organisation*. Fourier has sometimes been designated as an "associationist," and both writers have been labeled "utopian socialists." The latter label does not exactly fit them because they were exponents of social reform rather than of a socialism aiming at equality or the abolition of private property. What they proposed and the form that they gave to their proposals had its fantastic and bizarre side, but a number of their ideas left their mark on the future development of socialism, and others demonstrated a prophetic awareness of tendencies and issues which emerged only during later stages of the discussion and had by then lost their connection with socialist thought.

Saint-Simon, a declassed nobleman with a checkered career as a soldier, wealthy speculator, and poverty-stricken pamphleteer, was a tireless advocate of industrial development, full production, and the primacy of economics over politics. To place science and technology in the service of the state so reorganized as to achieve these goals, he assigned, in an early version of his proposals, a commanding position to scientists and engineers. In later versions the emphasis shifted to bankers and businessmen who as members of a sort of planning board were to constitute a managerial elite and assume the direction of the economy, transforming the anarchy of production into an organization of production. Saint-Simon has been hailed as a prophet of industrialization, of the managerial revolution, of technocracy, and of economic planning for growth and full employment. It was his aim to unleash the forces of production, of whose potential he had an awareness shared by only a few of his contemporaries. Like Say, with whom he was acquainted and in whose house John Stuart Mill met the "clever original," Saint-Simon was conscious of the scientific and technical revolution of the age. His interest in natural science turned him into an exponent of what unfriendly critics later designated as scientism, a view that calls for the pursuit of social studies with the help of the "positive" methods of natural science and often forms a transition to social engineering and social control.

Parallel with this scientistic streak there ran in Saint-Simon's mind a historicist one which made him search for general laws of historical change. In this search he became impressed with the importance of the economic factor in history, the role of social classes, and property relations. There emerges a third feature of Saint-Simon's vision, a collectivist one in which classes rather than individuals become the principal agents of economic development. However, Saint-Simon was no advocate of the class struggle. Instead he saw all producers, employers and employees alike, united in a huge class of "industrialists," with whom he contrasted the "idlers," continuing Babeuf's tradition of the worship of work. He upheld private property in strong terms but grounded it in social utility rather than in an absolute right. Socially useful property could fetch ample rewards—"from each according to his capacity, to each capacity according to its works" became a watchword of Saint-Simon's followers, some of whom became railroad magnates and great bankers. Saint-Simon failed to assign a special mission to the proletariat, but in a phrase that became famous he insisted that the improvement of "the most numerous and poorest class" be given special consideration. As for government, with the primacy of economics over politics it would lose its character as an oppressive force over men and be transformed into administration, "the action of men on things."

Since Saint-Simon considered the forces of the market as conducive to anarchy rather than as instruments of discipline, and since he was skeptical about the strength of the traditional religious impulses, he came to recognize the need for a new social ethic that would inspire planners and managers to socially desirable behavior. Groping for such an ethic, he found it first in a religion of science and later in what he designated as a New Christianity—a doctrine that would not excite the poor to acts of violence against the rich and the government but would demonstrate to the rich and powerful that the moral and physical existence of the poor could be improved only by means that would also increase the wealth of the rich. The problem that Saint-Simon posed has assumed a new significance with the rise of the large corporation, whose emancipation, in important respects at least, from the discipline of the market has impressed thoughtful students with the need for a social ethic to produce the restraints and inducements provided under other circumstances by the forces of the market. Here again Saint-Simon's thoughts anticipated modern ideas.

FOURIER

The vision of Fourier, who led the monotonous life of a clerk and commercial traveler, was in many respects the opposite of that of Saint-Simon. Instead of central planning there was to be decentralization; instead of industrialization a movement back to the land; instead of managerial direction the spontaneous self-assertion of individuals. Saint-Simon worshipped production and work, idols that Fourier refused to revere unless they had qualities gratifying certain innate propensities of man. These God-given propensities, or "passions"—for variety, adventure, and friendly association with fellowmen—Fourier considered frustrated by the commercialism of the modern world, which doomed man to a drab and monotonous existence, caused strife and disharmony, and involved waste of all sorts. There was waste in competition and in the toll levied by the middlemen of the distributive apparatus; there was waste of valuable time and effort in the chores of housekeeping and in the scramble to produce and acquire shoddy goods of limited durability and marginal significance.

Fourier wanted to reorganize society in a manner that would be conducive to social harmony and at the same time permit the gratification of fundamental psychological needs arising from the immutable nature of man and stifled in the commercial society of his time. For this purpose he recommended the voluntary formation of cooperative associations, each called a phalanx and made up of some four hundred families, large enough to offer a variety of specialized occupations but not too large for the cultivation of personal relationships. In connection with the organization of life in the phalanx, which Fourier described in minute detail, he introduced what was perhaps his most original and fruitful idea—to make work so attractive that it would be pursued not in response to the baleful incentives of greed and need but as a means to assuage the fundamental human penchant for friendly rivalry in the exercise of one's abilities. A detailed job classification would enable each member of the phalanx to find occupations suited to him, not just one but a variety of them, each of which he would pursue singly and for only a few hours. Thus would the sting be taken out of the division of labor, which would be practiced in a fashion conducive to high productivity and would cease to stultify men's minds and warp their bodies, as Adam Smith had feared. Work would acquire the features of play or sport, and since each individual would be a member of a large number of different teams, interests and loyalties would be diffused throughout the community rather than attached to any particular group within it.

Work was to be further divested of its character as a burden or duty by the guarantee of a minimum income to each member of the phalanx. Fourier, who always favored diversity and variety, had no objections to a disparity of incomes in excess of the minimum. These would indeed differ, reflecting the individual's talents and skills and the amount of his investment in the community. A leveling tendency for investment income was, however, introduced by the proviso that the rate of return on investments was to decline with their size, the equivalent of a progressive tax on income from wealth.

Fourier's ideas left many questions unresolved but they were suggestive enough to lead to the formation, in Europe and America, of a number of cooperative associations patterned after his model, of which Brook Farm in Massachusetts became a famous example. As a rule, these and similar types of settlements, sectarian and socialist, of which well over one hundred existed at one time or another in North America, did not survive for long either because they tended to attract intellectuals with little inclination for manual labor or because the second generation born in the community did not inherit the idealism that had inspired the original members. But regardless of the viability of Fourier's type of producer cooperative, the idea of cooperation, of which he was a pioneer, was strong enough to survive in other forms, and there are echoes of his thought in such modern concerns as town and community planning, industrial psychology, and personnel management. The guaranteed minimum income, which Fourier was among the first to suggest, is another matter widely discussed in modern times, although the grantor is now to be the state rather than a privately formed group.

PROUDHON

Fourier's reliance on voluntary action set the pattern characteristic of the labor movement in many countries, which relied on the strength of freely formed organizations rather than on government action in the pursuit of its goals. Moreover, Fourier's opposition to centralization and compulsion by the government made him a forerunner of the anarchists, who proposed to abolish organized government altogether. In both these respects—voluntarism and transition to anarchism—Fourier's position resembled that of Pierre-Joseph Proudhon (1809–65).

Proudhon was in fact the first social reformer to call himself an anarchist. He cherished the family and the neighborly ties within the local community but beyond these limits had no use for authority and condemned coercion in all forms, be it practiced by the government or by associations of the Fourierist type. He thus came to reject representative democracy as well as authoritarian socialism and communism and expressed disapproval of a revolution contrived by radical schemers and, indeed, of any violent upheaval launched by the proletariat, an instrument of social change in which he refused to place much confidence. On the positive side he espoused a loosely knit "federalism" among local and regional communities and a system of "mutualism" which called for reciprocal rights and duties grounded not in the compulsion of the law but in freely entered contractual agreements. He was silent about the machinery needed to enforce such agreements.

Proudhon was a paradoxical thinker who prided himself on his own inconsistency. He saw life enmeshed in a variety of contradictions or antinomies, problems to which there were no ready solutions other than "balance," or "equilibrium." Proudhon's refusal to accept such apparently clear-cut solutions as violence or reliance on historical necessity placed him in a special position among the radical thinkers of his time. As he wrote to Marx, he was unwilling to become one of "the leaders of a new intolerance." He was indeed suspicious of the role of intellectuals in social movements and throughout his life was proudly conscious of his own working-class background.

As a printer and proofreader, Proudhon had opportunities for wide reading, and he became the first Socialist in France to enter into a dialogue with the orthodox economic opinion of his time. In the title of a work published in 1840 he raised the question, *What Is Property?*—a question to which he gave the resounding answer, "Property is theft." Such an either-or solution was, however, alien to the complex thought of Proudhon, and closer inspection reveals that he did not mean to condemn property as such but rather the "unearned" rental and interest income of certain property owners. In fact, in later writings Proudhon was to insist on the social desirability of private property, argue in favor of its diffusion, object to an inheritance tax as a threat to the patrimony of the family, and acknowledge, in the manner of the liberals, the liberating function of the private ownership of property as an offset to the power of govenment.

It was monetary reform rather than the abolition of private property that Proudhon proposed to use as a lever to bring about the organization of society along new lines. Proudhon was a follower of the labor theory of value, and there was to be, in the new society, no functionless income which would curtail the share of the laborer and preclude him from purchasing the product of his industry. Moreover, there was to be no stringency of credit to hamper economic expansion and expose society to unemployment and instability. Instead, there was to be a liberation of money and credit from the tyranny of gold, from the selfish control of financial capital, and from the inept and capricious control of the state. An instrument was to be created that would freely and gratuitously, or almost so, provide for the monetization of all products of labor, a bank or credit union which would transform into money the claims of wage earners and sellers of goods and advance funds for investment.

Apart from extolling, in another context, the virtues of price fixing, Proudhon did not suggest how the monetary institutions proposed by him would cope with the problem of inflation and with the need for the efficient allocation of scarce resources. To orthodox opinion he appeared a monetary crank, to Marx a captive of petit bourgeois sentimentality. There is a link, however, between Proudhon's thought and that of later monetary reformers, such as Silvio Gesell, who claimed Proudhon as his master and was like Proudhon considered a monetary crank until rehabilitated by Keynes.

BAKUNIN

Much more direct, however, was the influence of Proudhon on the later development of anarchism. Michael Bakunin (1814–76), under whose influence a widespread anarchist movement arose, acknowledged Proudhon as his mentor. Bakunin was a master conspirator and advocate of terror and violence to destroy organized government. It was these features rather than Proudhon's libertarianism that came to characterize anarchism in later years. Bakunin himself was a powerful rival of Marx in the struggle for leadership of the First International (1864–78), which indeed foundered as a result of this rift. The ascendancy of Bakunin, a Russian nurtured by the barbarous despotism of his native country, marks the degeneration of one of the strands of European socialism. Anarchism, in the shape given to it by Bakunin, appealed especially to the backward and rural people in southern Europe and to conspiratorial groups in czarist Russia, regions that had been bypassed by the march of nineteenth-century civilization. There were upsurges of anarchism elsewhere as well, and its appeal persisted. During the 1960s restive students in France, Germany, and the United States would unfurl the black flag of anarchism, the symbol of disdain for organized government. They felt contempt for totalitarianism because of the outrages of the Nazi and Soviet regimes and were impatient with democracy because they considered it controlled by party machines and unresponsive to what they believed to be the popular will.

LAMENNAIS

On the other end of the socialist spectrum but also linked with Proudhon in his aversion to filling in the details of grandiose schemes of social reorganization was Félicité de Lamennais (1782–1854), the leading exponent of Christian socialism in France. Lamennais's thought differs from that of all other Socialists discussed here in that he based his hopes for the attainment of working-class objectives on the spread of political democracy. A Catholic priest who eventually broke with his church, Lamennais was aroused by the working people's plight, which he described in a language no less vehement than that employed by Marx in terms of a class struggle. But unlike Marx, and with considerable foresight, Lamennais believed that universal suffrage, which he unceasingly advocated, would make the working classes eventually win out over their masters. Lamennais believed that the extension of the vote, by vesting political power in the people, would also make inevitable their economic emancipation. They would press for the abolition of all laws restraining the freedom of association and subsequently by means of collective action achieve bargaining power commensurate with that of the employers. Class distinctions would further be leveled by equal opportunities in education, on which the people's representatives would insist. With the ensuing diffusion of property nothing could prevent the workers from becoming capitalists and forming cooperative organizations of their own. Lamennais made no plea for the social service or welfare state, but by relating the diffusion of property to the diffusion of economic power, and the latter in turn to the diffusion of political power, he depicted the operation of forces that were to emerge under modern democratic socialism. This was true particularly in England, where Ludlow took Lamennais's ideas. Lamennais thus set the precedent for a tradition in socialism rivaling and opposing that founded by Marx and more enduring than that of Marx in Western Europe. Democratic socialism, though not devoid of religious inspiration, was, however, in substance a secular movement, and what survived in it was Lamennais's faith in democracy rather than the faith of Lamennais the churchman, although in his own mind the two were fused.

Two exponents of early socialist thought in Germany were Ferdinand Lassalle (1825–64) and Karl Rodbertus (1805–75). There is an affinity, albeit a superficial one, between Lamennais's trust in the suffrage and a somewhat similar attitude of Lassalle's. Like Lamennais, Lassalle wanted to extend the suffrage, and as a means to this end he promoted the formation of a labor party. Being a gifted political leader, he became the founder of the General Association of German Workers, the forerunner of the German Social Democratic Party. The spread of political democracy had, however, a significance in the context of his thought different from that which motivated Lamennais. To the latter the extension of the suffrage was the means for the liberation of the workers from legal restraint on collective action. Freed from such restraint, the laboring class was to realize its goals through self-help. Lassalle, on the other hand, considered the spread of political democracy primarily a means to mobilize the power of the state and make it come to the aid of the laboring class. To him, the extension of political democracy was a prerequisite of state aid rather than of self-help.

The principal purpose for which Lassalle proposed to mobilize the aid of the state was the establishment of producer cooperatives to carry on large-scale enterprises which would yield to their laboring owners wages as well as profits. If wages alone constituted the return to the workers, the workers, so Lassalle believed, would never realize more than a subsistence wage, with the deviations from such a wage averaged out over the long run. That Lassalle held this view was due to his adherence to a Malthusian population doctrine, of which he was one of the few followers in the socialist camp. It was his opinion that if the laboring class had to rely on wages as the only return, these would inevitably fluctuate around subsistence, rising temporarily above it after the birthrate had declined in consequence of wages below subsistence, but falling again once the increase in wages had caused the birthrate to rise and had replenished the supply of labor. This was, in Lassalle's famous phrase, the iron law of wages.

RODBERTUS

The state was visualized as an engine of social progress by another state Socialist, Lassalle's fellow countryman Rodbertus, who looked to the Prussian monarchy as the pacemaker of reform, which in time—Rodbertus mentioned five hundred years—would lead to complete socialism with communal property. In the meantime Rodbertus advocated social legislation, especially measures that would raise the level of wages. This Rodbertus considered necessary because of the view he held about depressions—perhaps the most influential part of his doctrine. On the basis of the subsistence theory of wages Rodbertus argued that wages are inadequate to secure the disposal of the national output. Rising productivity causes the national income to grow, but labor's share in it, bound as it is to the subsistence wage, has the tendency to diminish. Goods are produced for which there is no effective demand, and depressions follow, which are related by Rodbertus directly to overproduction and indirectly to a faulty system of distribution.

Rodbertus may have been the first writer to draw attention to the potential income that would have been produced under conditions of full employment but was lost because of the idleness of productive resources. He employed this thought to reinforce his attack against the concentration of income. The argument that an equal distribution of income would leave each individual with only a small share he considered faulty: "the gain that would result from a distribution which would allow a full utilization of the productive forces of society ought manifestly to be included in the computation."

Both Lassalle and Rodbertus anticipated later concerns by pointing to the role of taxation as a factor that might aggravate or relieve social maladjustments. Lassalle was an effective critic of indirect taxes, at his time the major component of public revenues. His thoughts were given scientific precision by later students of public finance. These, on the whole, found more fault with indirect than with direct taxes and thus continued a tradition that Lassalle had founded and which still endures.

Chapter 20

MARX:

Salvation

through Revolution

Karl Marx (1818–83) had little use for his socialist forerunners and rivals. Those Socialists who believed the new society would arise under the influence of good will or of moral or religious considerations he characterized as sentimentalists and moralizers. Those who wanted to bring it off by conspiracies he eventually, after some wavering, came to consider intemperate fools. Those who depicted the details of the society to come but proposed to rely on means to establish it that Marx thought inadequate he called utopians. Nor was he willing, and this in spite of his German background, to place his trust in the state as an instrument of social transformation.

THE SUBSTANCE OF MARX'S THOUGHT

In brief, Marx's doctrine, designated approvingly as scientific socialism by his friend Engels, was this: He, Marx, had in his possession the clue to the riddle of history. Hitherto history had been the arena of class struggles. The rise and fall of classes were determined by economic factors. Just as the bourgeoisie had defeated the old feudal regime, so would the proletariat defeat the bourgeoisie. This would come about in a revolution to end all revolutions and usher in the classless society. In this society the state, an instrument of coercion employed by the ruling class, would lose its function and disappear. The upheaval of the bourgeois order was bound to come, since it would be produced by the ineluctable forces of historical necessity. A revolutionary mass movement of the class-conscious proletariat would have history on its side and could be helpful in facilitating the transition to the new society. In its broad outline, Marx's doctrine was but another variant of German historicism, a theory of economic stages or periods which he invoked in order to assert, not the peculiar character of the German economy as other historical economists had done, but the inevitability of socialism.

During the 1840s and 1850s Marx impatiently waited for the revolution to break out. At that time he was willing to lend support to a middle-class upheaval, in the hope of subverting it into a proletarian one. But when the revolutions of 1848 were suppressed and new ones failed to occur, Marx, in a gesture of resignation, turned to economics to buttress his philosophy of history and demonstrate with the help of these studies that the downfall of capitalism was inevitable. Logically and chronologically, Marx's philosophical and historical ideas had precedence over his economics, to which he was drawn relatively late to make it the capstone of the structure of his thought.

Marx was a single-minded fanatic who derived from the fusion of philosophy, history, and economics a message which he drove home with unrelenting zeal. Ostensibly his prophetic vision of the cataclysm of capitalism and of salvation through revolution was grounded in strict science, hence its designation as scientific socialism. It contains, however, many elements that defy scientific proof and give his message a character variously interpreted as that of a drama, of a mythology replete with demons and heroes, or of a secular, this-worldly religion.

Followers of Marx will deny such an interpretation, but the fervor with which they uphold his views and the zeal with which they attempt to stamp out heretical opinion are qualities of true believers to whom truth is not an evolving process resulting from new insight and the sifting of evidence but an authoritatively stated dogma, to be faithfully adhered to and obeyed by loyal action rather than tested by questioning thought. Marx's message contains both an interpretation of the world and an appeal to action. Unlike science, which demands detachment and objectivity, it calls for personal involvement. Marx's message, for which the faithful have been willing to die and to kill, has greatly added to the amount of hatred in the world—class hatred, hatred against unbelievers and dissenters, and hatred against Marxists.

Marx's doctrines articulated the dissatisfaction of the poor and disinherited urban masses who had flocked to the newly founded factories, were equipped with only incipient political rights, and suffered from the maladjustments brought about by a rising industrialism relieved as yet by only a few relaxations of the laissez faire rule. Marx's life spans a period of time that coincides with the spread of industrialization throughout Europe. The growth of factory employment and urbanization brought new problems with which liberalism coped only haltingly. In time a labor movement emerged to claim its role as spokesman of the new class of urban wage workers. For the aspirations of this class, Marx's message offered an ideological underpinning.

LIFE OF MARX

Marx was born in the Rhineland and in his youth his mind was shaped at German universities, notably that of Berlin. Although early in life he became a professed internationalist—"the working men have no country," he was to declare in the *Communist Manifesto*—and although he was uprooted himself and spent the greater part of his life in exile, he never shed all traces of his German background. Engels indeed referred with pride to his friend's "German scientific socialism." Marx had contempt for the Slavs of eastern and southeastern Europe and only late in life became converted to the view that something good might come out of Russia. Marx's attachment to order and discipline, his authoritarianism, his industry and dogged perseverance, may all have been part of the legacy of his homeland. Added to these were lack of modesty and moderation, contentiousness, and an immense self-righteousness and self-assurance that brooked no resistance and tolerated no rivals. To an unfriendly biographer he appeared as a "Red Prussian."

Marx was the son of an attorney and he himself chose the study of law, which he pursued as a subordinate subject along with philosophy and history. As a student in Berlin he came under the spell of the Hegelian philosophy, which by then had captured the imagination of many young intellectuals. Marx never escaped the influence of Hegel, and in 1873, in the preface to the second edition of *Das Kapital,* declared himself "the pupil of that mighty thinker." He earned a doctorate in philosophy at the University of Jena in 1841 with a dissertation which discussed the idealistic and materialistic elements in the doctrines of Democritus and Epicurus. Even then the young Marx was imbued with the spirit of rebellion against established authorities and accepted values. In the projected foreword to his dissertation, which in the end, however, he suppressed, he cited the words that Aeschylus put in the mouth of the arch-rebel Prometheus: "In short, I hate all gods." An academic career, for which Marx was now ready, might have tamed his unruly mind. In substance his situation was then not much different from that of Hildebrand or of Knies, who also had their troubles with the authorities, as Marx was to have them later. But unlike Hildebrand and Knies, Marx never secured the relatively safe haven of an academic position. Just when he was ready to assume a junior post, the Prussian authorities turned against the Hegelian Left, with which Marx was associated, and expelled Marx's patron and prospective sponsor of a university appointment from his own position.

After his failure to secure an academic appointment, Marx began a long and stormy career as a journalist. His first job came to an end when the Cologne newspaper that he edited was suppressed by the censor on behest of the Russian government, which Marx had offended in his articles. From then on Marx rarely had steady employment. He went to Paris, the center of the intellectual life of his time and a refuge of radicals from many lands. It was there that he became associated with Friedrich Engels (1820–95), the son of a well-to-do German textile manufacturer, with whom he was to form a lifelong friendship. It was in Paris also that Marx became thoroughly familiar with the thought of the French Socialists, which ranks next to German philosophy among the intellectual influences affecting his work.

In the 1840s Marx turned from a radical journalist into a communist agitator. He was expelled from Paris in 1845 but after a temporary stay in Brussels returned in 1848, the year of the European revolutions, and after Paris went to Cologne. A year later, after the failure of the upheavals, Marx went to London, where he resided for more than thirty years until his death, not even superficially integrated into English society and moving mainly in a circle of foreign radicals. His time was divided between study, writing, and the organization of the international Communist movement. As the London correspondent of the *New York Tribune* and from other journalistic jobs he made a precarious living, seldom enough to escape dire poverty. His and his family's main support was derived from the generosity of Engels, who helped unstintingly, more liberally in later years as his own financial condition improved, out of his earnings from a profitable textile business in Manchester.

THE *COMMUNIST MANIFESTO*

Marx's and Engels's most famous work is the *Communist Manifesto,* published under joint authorship in 1848 but mainly written by Marx. This rousing appeal for organized political action on the part of the proletariat contains an early statement of Marx's key ideas. As Engels wrote in the preface to the German edition of 1883:

> The basic thought running through the Manifesto—that economic production and the structure of society of every historical epoch necessarily arising therefrom constitute the foundation for the political and intellectual history of that epoch; that consequently (ever since the dissolution of the primeval communal ownership of land) all history has been a history of class struggles, of struggles between exploited and exploiting, between dominated and dominating classes at various stages of social

development; that this struggle, however, has now reached a stage where the exploited and oppressed class (the proletariat) can no longer emancipate itself from the class which exploits and oppresses it (the bourgeoisie), without at the same time forever freeing the whole of society from exploitation, oppression and class struggles—this basic thought belongs solely and exclusively to Marx.

What the modern reader of this document will perhaps find most striking is Marx's recognition of the accomplishments of the bourgeois revolution:

> The bourgeoisie, during its rule of scarce one hundred years, has created more massive and more colossal productive forces than have all preceding generations together. Subjection of Nature's forces to man, machinery, application of chemistry to industry and agriculture, steam-navigation, railways, electric telegraphs, clearing of whole continents for cultivation, canalisation of rivers, whole populations conjured out of the ground— what earlier century had even a presentiment that such productive forces slumbered in the lap of social labor?

Marx then goes on to depict the forces undermining modern capitalism, which has gigantic means of production but can no longer control them and finds itself exposed to the recurring threat of overproduction and periodic crises. The property relations on which bourgeois society is founded have become fetters which restrain the forces of production and which the proletariat must break. Marx then lists a number of intermediate measures designed to revolutionize the mode of production in the most advanced countries. Some of these—the abolition of property in land and the extension of nationalized industries—would still be considered radical today, but others—a heavy progressive income tax, free education for all, and the centralization of credit and of the means of communication and transport in the hands of the state—have by now shed the revolutionary implications they once had.

THE INTERNATIONALS

The *Communist Manifesto* concluded with the words, "Working men of all countries, unite!" and after a span of some sixteen years it ushered in the Communist movement with its sequence of Internationals. Although strong at times, in the end they all foundered—the First (1864–76) in consequence of a rift with the anarchists; the Second (1889–1914) because World War I showed national loyalties to be stronger than class allegiance; the Third (1919–43) because after the precedent set by the Russian Revolution had failed to be emulated elsewhere, the Soviets dissolved the Comintern as a gesture to their wartime allies. After the world wars the strength of communism as an international movement was seriously impeded by the rise of splinter groups—followers of Trotsky founded a Fourth International in 1938—as well as, in the West, of noncommunist socialism. After World War II, the growth of national diversity among the newly established communist regimes frustrated the rise of a new, monolithic Communist movement of worldwide dimensions, as did later the rift between China and the Soviet Union. While the West has moved closer to democratic socialism, the march of communism has been eastward: from London, where Marx founded the First International, to Germany, the homeland of the strongest component of the Second, then to the Soviet Union, the driving force behind the Third, and in the end to China.

Thus, although Marx meant to appeal to the workingmen of the world, his message was heeded only in countries where backward economic conditions and the absence of a democratic tradition had kept the mass of people in poverty, ignorance, and submission. No free and economically advanced country has ever turned communist on its own volition and without foreign intervention. As the West became free and prosperous, it emancipated itself from Marx's appeal, strong as the latter was during the nineteenth century. Marx's appeal vanished with the spread of the suffrage, the transformation of government from laissez faire to the social service and later to the welfare state, rising standards of living, greater economic stability, and the gradual leveling of class distinctions. It was strong in the West when these conditions were absent, and it is still strong in the underdeveloped countries, making for a division of the world, not, as Marx thought, into poor and rich individuals but into poor and rich nations.

DAS KAPITAL

The economic side of Marx's thought was further developed in *Das Kapital,* which Marx started to write in London after the failure of the continental revolutions. Of this work, which carries the subtitle *A Critique of Political Economy,* the first volume was published by Marx himself in 1867. After Marx's death Engels edited the manuscript of the second and third volumes and published them in 1885 and 1894. Only fragments were left of an intended fourth volume, which was to deal with the history of economic thought. These were later published under the title *Theories of Surplus Value.* In Marx's *Kapital,* English classical economics joins German philosophy and French socialism as the third seminal influence on his work.

MARX AND HEGEL

Marx's views about philosophy and history never received the systematic and full-fledged treatment he accorded to his economics in *Das Kapital.* They emerge from a large mass of casual writings and were supplemented and expanded by Engels, whose gifts of synthesis and exposition may have tempted him to formulations simpler and broader than Marx's own. Like Hegel, Marx claimed to have unraveled the secret of history, but unlike Hegel, who considered history the unfolding of the spirit, manifesting itself in the rise of nations and in their struggles, Marx interpreted the past experience of mankind as a struggle between classes. To Hegel, wars between nations carried out what historical necessity ordained; to Marx, this function was served by wars between classes. To Hegel, the Prussian monarchy was to bring fulfillment of man's quest for liberty and justice, whereas in Marx's thought this task had fallen on the proletariat. Liberty, indeed, was interpreted by Marx in the Hegelian sense as conscious and willing submission to necessity. In Marx's as well as in Hegel's thought, power and morality, might and right, coalesce, and the difference between what is and what ought to be becomes obfuscated by their belief in the identity of reality and reason, with the march of history interpreted as the unfolding of reason. To Marx, the prevailing precepts of morality were no more than bourgeois prejudices, and religion an opiate for the masses to keep them in submission.

Such was Marx's view of the world, an interpretation grounded not in science and thus lending itself to empirical testing but derived from speculations that defy scientific proof. The speculations, however, became the basis of predictions, and these, of course, can be tested by experience.

Many of Marx's predictions were of the self-fulfilling variety—they stood a chance of becoming true if enough people believed in them. That is, if enough working people can be persuaded that they are members of an oppressed class, that their oppressors are the capitalists, and that their historically ordained salvation can only come from the overthrow of an order in which property is held privately, they might actually overthrow this order. Marx indeed considered his message a fusion of thought and action, of theory and practice. The theory ostensibly was an elucidation of historical necessity, but in truth was prophecy; the practice consisted of revolutionary activities designed to make the prophecy come true. As Marx expressed it in a famous passage in his Theses on Feuerbach: "The philosophers have only *interpreted* the world, in various ways; the point, however, is to *change* it."

To give progressive change the appearance of inexorability, Marx adapted another idea of Hegel's to his own use, the dialectics or paradoxical logic, a form of thought that has long figured in the history of philosophy. In the Hegelian dialectics the struggle between opposite or contradictory elements is considered as the force making for progressive change and evolutionary development. These elements may at times become united but in the ensuing tension the union will eventually be dissolved, with one of the opposing forces emerging as the victor. The Hegelian dialectics is often interpreted, as it was especially by Engels, in terms of a triad consisting of the thesis, its negation or antithesis, and the negation of the negation or synthesis, but original texts of Hegel fail to authenticate this mechanical view of dialectic development. Hegel did have something to say about another dialectical process, the gradual buildup of quantitative changes and their eventual transformation into a qualitative change, and of this idea also there are echoes in the thought of Marx.

To Marx, history was indeed replete with inexorable dialectical processes serving as instruments of progress. Thus individual private property, founded on the labor of the proprietor, was seen as negated by capitalist private property, the result of the capitalist mode of production, and it would in turn beget communal property, the negation of the negation. The class struggle itself was a dialectical movement in which successive ruling classes were replaced by the classes that they dominated, a process that would culminate in the classless society. The ruling class itself called into being the forces of its own undoing: thus the bourgeoisie produced its own grave-diggers by setting the stage for the rise of the proletariat, educating its members politically and otherwise, arming them in the struggle with foreign bourgeoisies, and assembling them in large factories where they could join in collective action. Engels went even further than Marx and found dialectical processes in the realm of nature, an expansion of the idea not entirely in line with Marx's thought, in which consciousness or awareness of the historical situation ranks highly among the forces pressing for a turning point. It was this consideration that made Marx develop the notion of class consciousness and advocate a mass movement of the class-conscious proletariat.

THE ECONOMIC INTERPRETATION OF HISTORY

Marx was no blind follower of Hegel, and he differed from Hegel especially in his emphasis on the economic factor in history, a thought that he stated a number of times and in various formulations but never fully developed. The most concise statement of Marx's economic interpretation or materialist conception of history is found in the preface to his *Critique of Political Economy* of 1859:

> In the social production of their means of existence men enter into definite necessary relations which are independent of their will, productive relationships which correspond to a definite stage of development of their material productive forces. The aggregate of these productive relationships constitutes the economic structure of society, the real basis on which a juridical and political superstructure arises, and to which definite forms of social consciousness correspond. The mode of production of the material means of existence conditions the whole process of social, political and intellectual life. It is not the consciousness of men that determines their existence, but, on the contrary, it is their social existence that determines their consciousness.

Marx then goes on to explain, and this brings the dialectics into the materialist conception of history, how conflict arises between the material productive forces of society and the existing relations of production. As the productive forces develop, these relations become fetters which are eventually broken asunder by revolution.

Marx's economic interpretation of history is thus grounded in the sharp distinction between productive forces and the social relations built thereon. The former, which Marx describes as the mode of production of the material means of existence, generate or determine the social relations, that is, the political and cultural content of the superstructure, its law and politics, and its intellectual, moral, religious, and artistic life. Marx never denied that there is a realm of ideas, but he saw these determined by the mode of production.

Marx and Engels considered the economic interpretation of history a simple and fundamental truth about which there can be no diversity of opinion. They never, however, made an effort to elaborate more fully the key idea, the distinction between productive forces and social relations. At times Marx would hint at an interpretation of the productive forces in technological terms: the hand mill, he said, gives rise to society with the feudal lord; the steam mill, to society with the industrial capitalist. But again he did not develop this interpretation more fully.

If the mode of production is given this technological meaning, new difficulties arise because Marx's theory of the economic determination of history would leave unexplained the factors making for technological change. Whether stated as a cause-and-effect or as a dialectical relationship, the link established by Marx between the mode of production and the superstructure makes the former the determinant of the latter, but the argument discloses nothing about the determination of the mode of production. In the search for the factors determining the mode of production, what comes first to one's mind is science and the state of the arts, but if these, which form part of the cultural life of the superstructure, are admitted as determinants, the whole distinction between the mode of production and the superstructure falls to the ground.

Late in life Engels, in a letter to Joseph Bloch dated September 21, 1890, commented further on the economic interpretation of history. He declared it pedantic to ascribe each and all historical events to the operation of economic forces, and denied that either he or Marx had singled out the economic element as the only determining one. But he still insisted that "the *ultimately* determining element in history is the production and reproduction of real life." He admitted that other factors—especially political ones and "the traditions which haunt human minds"—have their role to play, but made clear that he did not consider these the ultimately decisive ones.

What is ultimately decisive in human history is likely to remain a matter that thoughtful people will not profess to know. Professional historians usually interpret history as an interplay of a variety of forces which include, side by side with the economic factor, geographic conditions, the quality of the population, national and religious loyalties, the work of great men—and a fortuitous element of chance. Marx and Engels showed little foresight in failing to recognize the strength of nationalism as a factor in history. However, the stress that they laid on the economic factor, although in itself a simplification, did much to free history from its earlier concern with dynasties and their wars and to stimulate the study of economic history, a task that Adam Smith had anticipated in *The Wealth of Nations*. Marx and Engels themselves were assiduous students of economic history. Under their influence this field branched out into social history, which gives special attention to the social conditions surrounding the life of the people. They were among the first to approach this task with the help of a new and rich source of information, the blue books, or government documents, containing the reports of factory inspectors, poor law authorities, parliamentary commissions, and related information on social and economic conditions.

THE CLASSES

Whereas the reader finds in Marx's works only short statements indicating Marx's view about the economic interpretation of history, Marx showed even greater restraint when it came to defining one of the central concepts of his doctrine, that of the *class*. The word recurs on countless pages of Marx's works, but what it stands for is mostly left to conjecture. The very last chapter of the third volume of *Das Kapital* carries the title "The Classes," but this chapter has remained a fragment and breaks off after only one and one-half pages.

Although Marx's chapter on classes forms part of a section on incomes and their sources, the context in which he employs the class concept makes it appear likely that to him it was foremost an expression of relations arising out of the realm of production rather than distribution. In other words, Marx presumably did not identify a class in terms of the income—wages, rents, or profits—of its members, as Ricardo might have done, but in terms of the position of its members in the process of production. To Marx, the fundamental distinction in the society of his time was the division between laborers and means of production or, in terms of property, that between people not equipped with ownership in productive assets besides their labor power and the owners of capital. In addition to this specific use of the word *class* in the context of nineteenth-century industrial society, Marx also employed it in a generic sense, such as is involved in his idea of history as the arena of struggles between an oppressed class and that which oppresses it.

Marx was aware that the two-class scheme does not exactly fit the farmers and, of course, the middle class, which he visualized as being mainly made up of small craftsmen and artisans—later designated as the old middle class—rather than of white-collar workers—the new middle class. Marx, however, nowhere insisted on a strict two-class division, and there are passages in his writings that contain more highly differentiated class schemes.

His point was rather that there are forces in the economic system that will make for an increasing polarization of society and eventually divide it into two classes, with the embattled middle class sinking into or siding with the proletariat. It was largely to demonstrate the existence of these forces that he developed his economic theories.

However, a class was to Marx more than an agglomeration of people living under the same objective conditions. To play its role in history, its members had to become subjectively aware of these conditions, that is, in the case of the proletariat, acquire a class consciousness that would cause them to rise against untenable conditions. Marx intended to foster class consciousness by means of propaganda and organization to speed up the proletarian revolution.

Marx, however, overrated the role of classes in modern capitalism, just as he underrated it in the communist society. His doctrine has provided the point of departure for the study of classes by modern sociologists who have shed light on aspects different from the ones Marx emphasized—for example, on social divisions grounded not in economic factors but arising from differences in the prestige of status groups varying in education, occupation, and ways of life. They further underline the leveling of consumption standards and, in general, the diminution of class stratification in modern capitalism. Neither the bourgeoisie nor the proletariat has developed into a homogeneous monolith, and the gulf between the two has not widened. Instead, greater differentiation within the classes and increased social mobility have turned society into a continuum of finely gradated groups, each of which shades imperceptibly into the others. It is especially the emergence of the new middle class of office and service workers, supervisors, managers, and technicians that has falsified Marx's predictions. He neither foresaw the ascendancy of this class nor the emergence of fascism, to which under certain conditions this class would lend mass support. As a prophet he proved singularly wrong when he expected the industrial proletariat to rise against the bourgeoisie. Instead of rising *against* it, members of the proletariat have much preferred to rise *into* the bourgeoisie or into the greatly expanded middle class.

However, where opportunities for this sort of rise have been meager, as particularly in the preindustrial societies of background countries, sharp class divisions between a thin layer of wealthy people and the large mass of poor persist, with the middle class too fragile to bridge the gulf between the two. When the poor have no chance to emulate the rich they will tend to fight them, and the ensuing conflict will be acerbated if the poor make foreign influences responsible for their lot. It is for these reasons that there is a readier response to Marx's message in underdeveloped countries than in the industrial societies of Western Europe and North America, where results that Marx failed to foresee have deprived it of its meaning.

Classes, so Marx taught, would disappear in the communist society, since the abolition of private property in the instruments of production would put an end to class divisions. This view neglects the fact that no industrial society can function unless it employs managers—persons who supervise the performance of the workers on the job, organize their work, hire and fire, secure supplies and arrange for the disposal of goods, make financial arrangements, and, in the absence of a market, assume the direction of production. Members of the managerial class are bound to have a status distinct from that of the rank and file; the latter, in turn, will continue to perform the same kind of operations regardless of whether the plant is the property of anonymous stockholders or of an equally anonymous community. In the Soviet Union, which however does not as yet consider herself fully communist but professes to be in a transitional stage called socialism, the incomes of the managerial class are much higher than those of the workers, and among the working class itself pay differentials are large.

THE STATE

Since Marx considered the state an instrument of coercion employed by the ruling class, he taught that in the classless society it would lose its function and disappear. In fact, however, in few societies known to man has the state wielded more brutal power than in those that claim to be on the march toward communism. In the modern democratic societies, on the other hand, Marx's view of the government as an executive committee of the ruling class has been falsified by the extension of the suffrage. The universal right to vote has made it impossible to describe the bourgeoisie as a ruling class that dominates the state. Instead, there are labor parties and labor governments in Europe, and although there is no national labor party in the United States, the political influence of organized labor and of employees in general has been strong enough to call into existence a body of legislation for the benefit and protection of the working people, strengthening their position in industrial relations, providing them with social security, and taking their side in countless other ways. So pronounced has this tendency been that the American economy has in fact been referred to as "laboristic."

MARX'S ECONOMICS

To convince those who might not subscribe to his philosophy of history, which was, after all, an esoteric product of German transcendentalism, Marx devoted many years of his life to the writing of *Das Kapital*, which was to confirm in the terms of the economic science of his time what Marx's philosophy of history made appear as inevitable—the eventual downfall of capitalism. It was his aim to reveal "the laws of motion of capitalism," that is, the principles controlling economic evolution, an aim for which Ricardo's unraveling of the course of the distribution of the national income had set a precedent, albeit one narrower in scope. In its general direction Marx's thought thus followed that of Ricardo. This affinity between the two thinkers is also pronounced when it comes to the substance of their thought and to their method. Marx's economic method, to begin with, is like Ricardo's grounded in the manipulation of a limited number of variables, whose behavior, based on strong assumptions, is interconnected with that of others. In this manner the various parts that form the structure of Marx's thought—the theories of value, of surplus value and exploitation, of the falling rate of profit, of increasing concentration, of the industrial reserve army, and of the increasing misery of the proletariat—all fall into place and constitute an integrated whole which at first glance appears impressive in its consistency. Marx's approach differs from Ricardo's in its polemical character, which dramatizes matters with the help of dialectic disjunctions, moral indignation, the use of fighting words, and abuse heaped on those whose views are criticized. It also differs in the abundance of quotations which attest to Marx's wide reading and, most important, in the interweaving of sequences of abstract thought with the presentation of a wealth of historical and descriptive detail in a manner recalling the approach of Smith rather than that of Ricardo.

The polemical character of Marx's economics, which is hinted at in the subtitle of his work, *A Critique of Political Economy,* arises from his view that bourgeois economics reached its zenith in the work of Smith and Ricardo. During part of Ricardo's life, but especially later on, with the emancipation of the bourgeoisie and the greater intensity of the class struggle, economics—so Marx held—relinquished the search for truth and lost its scientific character. Instead it placed itself in the service of the bourgeoisie and became vulgar apologetics for bourgeois interests or, when it attempted a reconciliation of the classes, a "shallow syncretism" of the type of John Stuart Mill's economics. Being entirely averse to the spirit of compromise, Marx with his critical type of economics meant to show up the fallacies of the bourgeois variant. His attitude to other economic thinkers is thus divided —those whose work falls into the period preceding the alleged degeneration of economics into apologetics he treats with a measure of respect, whereas later thinkers receive varying shares of abuse and as a rule are depicted either as wicked or as fools.

Those thinkers whom Marx holds highest are the Physiocrats, Smith, and Ricardo—although on occasion he will upbraid the latter two—and it is with the ideas of these men that important elements of his own thought are linked. Quesnay's *tableau,* which portrays the regeneration of the national income, has its counterpart in Marx's reproduction scheme. Smith's ambivalent attitude to the emerging business civilization led him to equivocating vacillations, for example, to his interpretation of the division of labor as a boon in Book I and as a bane in Book V of *The Wealth of Nations.* At times Smith viewed the emerging scene through rose-colored glasses and what he saw was harmony, at other times he depicted bleak discord. Marx assimilated the latter views of Smith but not the former. His doctrine of the increasing misery of the proletariat has been interpreted as echoing

Smith's gloomy reaction to the division of labor, and his view of government as the executive committee of the ruling class has its corollary in Smith's hint that the government protects the rich against the poor.

THE LABOR THEORY OF VALUE

As for Ricardo's influence, it is conspicuous especially in Marx's labor theory of value, which, with modifications, serves as the foundation of Marx's system and from which he drew far-reaching conclusions. Calling attention to Aristotle's approach to the value problem, Marx considers the exchange value of goods as more than a mere relation that links x numbers of good A with y numbers of good B. Instead he regards the goods as equal in value because both embody equal quantities of a common substance, called abstract labor by Marx. Aristotle, Marx holds, was precluded from this insight because Greek society was founded on slavery and therefore it was difficult to acknowledge the equality and equivalence of different quantities of human labor.

Marx equates skilled labor to common labor with the help of a multiplier reflecting the valuations of the market. This still leaves open the question of how to deal with labor of different degrees of efficiency. If, as Marx holds, goods exchange in the same proportion in which they embody labor time, a good produced by a slow worker will be more valuable than one produced in less time by a more efficient one. To resolve this difficulty, Marx employs the concept of "socially necessary labor time," which averages out different degress of efficiency and also denies value to goods resulting from misdirected production for which there is no demand.

Marx sharply distinguishes between labor, the constituent of the value of goods, and labor power, which the worker sells in the market and whose value, in turn, is defined as the subsistence for the maintenance and reproduction of the worker. Wages do not pay the worker the full value of his product but only the typically lesser value of his subsistence. His work may embody ten hours of labor; his subsistence only five. The difference between the wage and the value of the product Marx designates as "surplus value," the source, and the only one, of profit or interest and rent.

Marx divides the capital that the firm employs into a variable and a constant part. The variable capital (v) is made up of wages, the constant (c) of plant, machinery, and raw materials. Constant capital merely reproduces its value in the process of production—in the case of plant and machinery, it merely earns its appropriate depreciation quota. Only the variable capital, which goes into the payment of wages, yields additional or surplus value.

The Marxian analysis proceeds with the employment of three ratios, $\frac{c}{v}$, or the organic composition of capital, $\frac{s}{v}$, or the rate of exploitation, and $\frac{s}{v+c}$, or the rate of profit. The proportion in which the constant capital stands to the variable capital, $\frac{c}{v}$, will vary among different enterprises, some employing more and others less constant capital in combination with labor, and it will rise with the more extensive use of machinery as capitalism develops.

The proportion in which surplus value stands to the variable capital, that is, $\frac{s}{v}$, or the rate of exploitation, is affected by a variety of factors. For example, technological progress may cause the quantity of labor embodied in wage goods to decline, and if this happens, there will be a fall in v. If hours of work are lengthened, if labor is driven to a greater intensity of effort, or if women and children are drawn into employment, s will rise, as it will if the productivity of labor increases in consequence of labor being combined with a greater quantity of constant capital. In the aggregate, $\frac{s}{v}$ reveals the division of the national product into nonlabor and labor income.

The proportion in which surplus value stands to variable and constant capital is $\frac{s}{v+c}$, or the rate of profit. As for the behavior of the profit rate, Marx comments especially on two tendencies. At any one given time the rate will tend to uniformity, and over time it will tend to decline. The tendency of the profit rates of firms and industries to converge Marx ascribes to the forces of competition, which cause the withdrawal of resources from lines of activity in which the rate of profit is low and their movement into activities in which the rate is high.

THE TRANSFORMATION PROBLEM

Certain difficulties arise because it is logically impossible to have, at the same time, a uniform rate of profit, prices that are identical with labor values, and a varying organic composition of capital. If the organic composition of capital varies, prices that are identical with labor values will not yield to the firm a surplus value which would constitute a uniform rate of profit on $v+c$. Where v, the only source of surplus value and of profit, is relatively large, the rate of profit will be high; where c is relatively large, the rate of profit will be low. Only if the organic composition of capital is assumed to be the same throughout the economy will prices that are identical with labor values generate profits that constitute an equal rate on $v+c$. This is the assumption Marx employs in the first volume of *Das Kapital,* so that in the context of this volume the problem of a deviation of prices from values does not arise. In the third volume Marx no longer assumes an equal organic composition of capital, and since he postulates a uniform rate of profit, he is now compelled to allow for the deviation of prices from labor values. Marx's proposed solution of the "transformation problem," or of the problem of transforming values into prices, is in short as follows. Prices are equal to labor values where the organic composition of the capital employed by a firm is equal to the average organic composition of the entire capital employed in the economy. Prices exceed values where the organic composition of capital is above the social average, and they fall short of values where the organic composition of capital is below the social average. Thus the deviation of prices from values is so conceived that it will produce uniform rates of profit equal to the rate of surplus value to the entire capital employed in the economy. For the economy as a whole, the deviations of prices from values, if added algebraically, yield zero, that is, they cancel out, and the sum of prices is equal to the sum of values.

THE COURSE OF PROFITS

Like Smith and Ricardo before him, Marx holds that over time the profit rate will have the tendency to decline. Each of the three came to this conclusion for different reasons. To Smith the decisive factor was that the growth of capital would be accompanied by increasing competition among the capitalists, both in the sale of commodities and in the hire of labor. To Ricardo it was the increase in money wages, reflecting rising prices of wage goods, that would cut into profits. Marx, on the other hand, ascribed the tendency of the profit rate to fall to the rising organic composition of capital. Only variable capital generates surplus value, and it is from surplus value that profits are derived. As the variable capital becomes combined with the constant capital in a declining proportion, the rate of profit must fall, unless the rate of exploitation rises fast enough to offset the effects of the relative decline in variable capital. To cancel the tendency of the rate of profit to fall, the rate of exploitation would have to rise in the same proportion in which there is a relative decline in the variable capital. Although Marx gave attention to the factors making for an increase in the rate of exploitation—longer hours of work, employment of women and children, rising productivity of labor, and so forth—he did not consider them potent enough to offset completely the impact of a rising organic composition of capital on the rate of profit.

THE CONCENTRATION OF CAPITAL

Side by side with the tendency of the profit rate to decline Marx finds a tendency of capital to become more highly concentrated among large enterprises. Marx ascribes this tendency toward concentration to competition, to the economies of scale, to restrictions on the entry of new firms, and to the credit system. In the battle of competition producers try to reduce prices. They try to cut costs with the help of a rising productivity of labor, and the latter, in turn, reflects the scale of operations. Hence, Marx concludes, "the larger capitals beat the smaller," and in another context he writes: "One capitalist always kills many." Moreover, it is difficult to enter into lines of productive activity that require large amounts of capital. Newcomers will therefore crowd into fields where relatively little capital is needed. In these fields competition rages fiercely. Only a few of the new enterprises survive and resist the absorption into larger concerns. In addition, there is the credit system, which draws funds from a multitude of scattered sources and hands them over to individual or associated capitalists. All these forces are held responsible by Marx for a constant diminution of the number of the magnates of capital and for the rise of monopoly, "a fetter upon the mode of production."

While the bourgeoisie is thus put on the defensive by the decline of the rate of profit and by the growth of concentration, the working class is kept down to a subsistence wage and exposed to increasing misery.

THE INCREASING MISERY OF THE PROLETARIAT

The classical tradition had related the persistence of subsistence wages to the Malthusian population doctrine. Lassalle, following Ricardo, linked the size of the population to wages and with the help of the iron law of wages attempted to demonstrate that wages would oscillate around subsistence. This view of the behavior of wages is grounded in the Malthusian population theory, which depicts population as pressing against subsistence. Marx, on the other hand, expressed contempt for the Malthusian population doctrine and in this matter parted company with Ricardo and Lassalle. It was his view that a surplus population is not called forth by a lack of subsistence but by a lack of demand for labor, and to this "relative surplus population" he assigned the name "industrial reserve army." Marx's view of the industrial reserve army was influenced by Ricardo's chapter on machinery, in which the replacement of workers by machinery had been recognized as a theoretical possibility. But whereas Ricardo considered the matter of limited practical significance and emphasized the compensating benefits from the spread of machinery, Marx derived from it predictions of ever more severe unemployment and expressed scorn for the theory of compensation.

The conclusion of all the foregoing tendencies was to Marx a gloomy vision of an increasing misery of the proletariat. The substance of this immiserization, as it has been labeled by later students, Marx depicted in various formulations, one hinting at an absolute decline in wages, another at a relative decline, and a third stressing the deterioration of the quality of the life of the worker. In this last version the lot of the laborer, be his wage high or low, grows worse as capital accumulates. There is, corresponding with the accumulation of capital, "accumulation of misery, agony of toil, slavery, ignorance, brutality, mental degradation."

More dismal than the science of the classics, which other critics of economics had so labeled, Marx's economics precludes such avenues of escape as the classics had provided in the form of moral restraint or foreign trade. Limitations of births, Marx held, would aggravate the ills of capitalism rather than relieve them. They would, by reducing the supply of labor, be responsible for a temporary rise in wages, but the latter in turn would accelerate the use of machinery and thus eventually increase the ranks of that it might tend to raise the rate of profit, but he added that it would hasten the expansion of the scale of production and thereby cause the variable capital and the rate of profit to fall. The expansion of the scale of production at home would necessitate ever-widening markets, while in the underdeveloped countries "slaves, coolies, etc. permit a better exploitation of labor" with accompanying profits that attract foreign capital. It was from these considerations that followers of Marx later developed theories of imperialist expansion that would explain the delay in the breakdown of capitalism.

ECONOMIC CRISES

Since it was the pathology of economic life that attracted so much of Marx's attention, it is not surprising that his work abounds with suggestions about instability, crises, and cyclical disorders. In his vision of an economic evolution replete with dialectic relationships and contradictions, and indeed generated by these, many ideas were foreshadowed that found systematic development in later business cycle theories: underconsumption and overproduction, short and intermediate cycles of ten-year duration, the instability of investment, disproportions in the structure of an unplanned production, variations of profits, and the cyclical character of replacement expenditure— they all appear in the pages of *Das Kapital*. Marx, however, never developed a separate, full-fledged theory of the business cycle. Instead his whole work was but a variation of one ever-recurring theme, the instability of capitalism with its crises of increasing frequency and severity brought about under the influence of a declining rate of profit and inadequacy of consumer demand. Although he dissociated himself from the underconsumption theories of Rodbertus and others, he nevertheless referred to "the poverty and restricted consumption of the masses" as "the last cause of all real crises" and underlined the connection by linking the two phrases with the word "always." He had no use for monetary theories of the business cycle and criticized the view that "looks upon expansion and contraction of credit, which is a mere symptom of the periodic changes of the industrial cycle, as their cause."

MARX'S REPRODUCTION SCHEMES

Marx went beyond business cycle analysis with his reproduction schemes, which anticipate more recent work in income and growth theory and shed light on the behavior of macroeconomic variables. The so-called simple reproduction scheme is a two-sector model of the economy which reveals the conditions necessary for the reproduction of the national income. An expanded reproduction scheme, which Marx did not complete, was to demonstrate the conditions for economic growth under net investment.

In the simple reproduction scheme, the economy is divided into Department I and Department II, the first turning out capital goods and the second consumer goods. On the assumption of a stationary state in which capital is maintained but no net additions are made to it, the output of Department I, $c_1 + v_1 + s_1$, is devoted to the replacement of capital in both departments, that is, it is in equilibrium equal to $c_1 + c_2$. The output of Department II, $c_2 + v_2 + s_2$, consists of nonlabor and labor income and is equal to $(v_1 + s_1) + (v_2 + s_2)$. In the first equation c_1 cancels out, and in the second $v_2 + s_2$, so that both equations can be reduced to $v_1 + s_1 = c_2$. The right side of this equation—the demand for the replacement of capital in Department II—must be equal to the net output of Department I—the left side of the equation—to secure the maintenance of the net output of Department I. This equality is required only of the macroeconomic aggregates, and as long as it prevails, it does not matter whether each individual firm matches its depreciation charge with replacement expenditure. If the aggregates are not equal, that is, if depreciation charges exceed or fall short of replacement expenditures, contraction or expansion ensues. In the reproduction schemes there are reverberations of Keynes's law—everybody's income is somebody else's expenditure—as well as of later analyses of the requirements of steady growth.

CRITICISM OF MARX'S ECONOMICS

A criticism of the economic thought of Marx must begin with the labor theory of value, an analytical tool unsuited for a multifactor economy and for one with markets that fail to be competitive throughout. Marx would have conceded this last aspect but he insisted on ascribing all economic value to labor. He would acknowledge that the productivity of labor rises when it is combined with larger amounts of capital, but he refused to consider capital as productive. In his writings the labor theory of value assumes the character of an ideology designed to arouse the working class to political action. By defining all value in terms of labor Marx puts himself in a position where he can castigate all nonlabor income as unearned and the result of exploitation.

When Marx faces the transformation problem, he in effect abandons the labor theory of value as an explanatory principle shedding light on microeconomic relations while attempting to save it as a principle underlying aggregate values. This attempt, if successful at all, requires assumptions similarly restrictive as those employed by Ricardo in his search for an invariable measure of value, with which Marx's analysis has many parallels.

Marx's law of the declining rate of profit is grounded in his view of profits as flowing exclusively from surplus value arising from the employment of labor. This view is asserted and derived from definitions but is not demonstrated in a fashion that will convince those who are unwilling to accept the opinion that all nonlabor income results from exploitation. Moreover, Marx arrives at his law of a declining rate of profit with the help of a procedure the legitimacy of which is open to serious doubts. He assembles a number of factors and from these derives a law, selecting, however, only those factors that lend support to the postulated law, while a host of other important factors that do not support the law are pushed aside and characterized as opposing or countervailing tendencies. Marx's procedure would have a counterpart in a "law" of Galileo's to the effect that bodies rise but that there are opposing tendencies which make them fall.

As for Marx's law of concentration, it is sometimes considered verified by the advent of big business. Marx failed to recognize, however, that the large corporation, while facilitating the concentration of control, has at the same time been instrumental in diffusing property among many small capitalists.

Marx's view of the growth of the industrial reserve army of the unemployed gained considerable following during the protracted period of mass unemployment from which the world suffered during the Great Depression of the 1930s. Since then, however, depressions have as a rule been mild in the advanced countries, and public policies have evolved that are designed to avert mass unemployment.

In its strongest version, Marx's theory of the increasing misery of the proletariat, derived as it is from a tendency of wages to decline, is incompatible with his law of a falling rate of profit. Although attempts have been made with the help of highly restrictive assumptions to visualize a situation in which both wages and profits fall, these carry little conviction in the absence, in the Marxian scheme, of rising returns to another class, such as the landlords. The proletariat has in fact not been exposed to increasing misery, however defined; instead, affluence and leisure have spread among all classes of society in Western Europe and North America. Some students of economic development hold that the gulf between these parts of the world and the underdeveloped countries has widened as incomes have increased faster in the former than in the latter, but this is not what Marx had in mind. His analysis was meant to apply to class alignments within a given country rather than to the alignment of poor and rich nations throughout the world.

Marx's views about cyclical disorders contain a number of suggestive ideas but they lack consistency since he at times rejects and at other times underlines the role of underconsumption as an explanatory principle.

MARX'S INFLUENCE

In spite of the imperfections in Marx's thought, he has been characterized as the most influential thinker of the nineteenth century. In parts of Asia and Eastern Europe powerful and despotic regimes require the unconditional adherence of their subjects to their versions of Marx's doctrine. In the more highly developed parts of the world his influence either was never strong, as in North America, or has been on the decline, as in Western Europe. But even there his message and that of rival Socialists played a historical role among the forces that transformed capitalism during the past hundred years and thereby falsified his predictions. Marx's message was meant to arouse the proletariat and bring revolution, but it also had its effects on the bourgeoisie and thus induced concessions and reforms which averted the threat of revolution. Marx was not among the architects of the modern world of affluence and peaceful economic change, but his threat of demolition put the architects to work.

Marx was not the last critic of business civilization. The impact which his work exerted on more recent critics who made themselves heard in America and Europe during the second half of the twentieth century did not stem only from the specific contents of his message. As the capitalism which Marx had denounced was transformed and as the proletariat, to which he had addressed his message, was absorbed into the middle class, these critics would have to express their discontent in ways different from Marx's and they would have to find an audience different from his. The main thrust of Marx's impact on them was the precedent set by his denunciation of capitalism, which they might emulate without making the full content of his message their own.

THE SOCIETY TO COME

Marx considered it characteristic of the utopianism of his rivals to depict the details of the society to come and therefore gave no systematic shape to his thoughts about this society and about the specific means it would employ to resolve the problem of scarcity. At times he mentioned certain features that would emerge as state and classes vanish: communal property, work that was made attractive by variety and change, production and distribution in line with the principle, "from each according to his capacity, to each according to his labor," and eventually, after increased production had made scarcity disappear, "to each according to his needs." Marx was convinced that the revolution would create not only a new society but a new man as well. Unlike many eighteenth-century thinkers, Marx did not consider the nature of man as constant but as variable and evolving progressively with the changes in the environment effected, in turn, by man. "By acting on the external world and changing it," he wrote, "man changes his own nature."

In an early work Marx described what he thought the life of the new man in the new society would be:

> In communist society, where nobody has one exclusive sphere of activity but each can become accomplished in any branch he wishes, society regulates the general production and thus makes it possible for me to do one thing today and another tomorrow, to hunt in the morning, fish in the afternoon, rear cattle in the evening or criticize the dinner, just as I desire, without ever becoming hunter, fisherman, shepherd or critic.

Nothing could demonstrate more aptly the weakness of Marx as a constructive thinker than this idyllic picture of the society to come, which regulates production but in which everyone is freed from the drudgery of the division of labor and may do such work as he chooses. Marx's strength resided in his destructive criticism, not in his constructive ideas. In the light of these it is he rather than any one of his rivals who appears as the arch-utopian. Why did he excel in destruction? Because, as Bertrand Russell once put it, his aim was far more the unhappiness of the bourgeoisie than the happiness of the proletariat.

Chapter 21

SOCIALISM AFTER MARX:
Reform
Versus Revolution

The main variants of socialist thought since the 1880s may be classified under the headings of German revisionism, French syndicalism, Soviet Marxism, and British Fabianism. There were other, minor variants known as Austro- and Neo-Marxism, from which indeed stemmed a number of contributions to economic thought. On the whole, however, the harvest of economic ideas generated in the socialist camps was a meager one. Socialist thought tended to become institutionalized and its exponents connected with the various socialist parties which sprang up throughout the world. As a rule it mirrored the concerns of these organizations, which were more profoundly affected by questions of political tactics than by economic speculations. Moreover, those who professed to be orthodox followers of Marx would engage in such speculations only with considerable reluctance since in their opinion Marx had said the last word on the economics of capitalism and since he had frowned on any thorough examination of the economics of socialism. It is therefore not surprising that pioneer work on the study of the economics of socialism was done by an economist who was not a Socialist at all—Enrico Barone—and that men who stood outside the socialist camps and were social reformers rather than Socialists—John A. Hobson and Henry George—came to exert substantial influence on socialist thought about economic matters.

At the turn of the century, Marx's intellectual influence was mostly felt in Germany, where his followers were numerous and included the leaders of the Social Democrats. These came to constitute a mass party with a parliamentary representation which at the time of the outbreak of World War I outnumbered that of any other party. The German contingent, in turn, played the leading role in the Second International, which linked the Socialist movements of the various countries until it fell apart during the war.

Marx's intellectual influence was also strong among Russian radicals

SOCIALISM
AFTER
MARX

who busied themselves both at home and in exile with undermining the foundations of the czarist regime. Marx himself was in touch with a number of them and discussed with them the relevance of his doctrine for a backward country such as Russia, which as yet had not undergone a bourgeois revolution. After Marx's *Kapital* was published in the original German version, the first language into which it was translated was the Russian. The Russian Socialists formed part of the Second International, but unlike their western associates they had to operate underground in their homeland by conspiratorial means rather than with the help of the ballot and of parliamentary procedures.

Marx had little influence in England, which nurtured her socialist aspirations from other sources, and little also in the United States. Immigrants to the United States might bring along from their homelands their socialist beliefs and adhere to them for a while, but few were able to transmit them to their children who were eventually absorbed into the melting pot of the American environment with its unparalleled wealth of economic opportunity and unrestrained upward mobility. Marx himself had felt that his kind of revolutionary socialism might not fit the situation in England and America, and possibly elsewhere. When addressing a public meeting of workers in Holland in 1872 he had said:

> We know that the institutions, the manners and the customs of the various countries must be considered, and we do not deny that there are countries like England and America, and, if I understood your arrangements better, I might even add Holland, where the worker may attain his object by peaceful means. But not in all countries is this the case.

REVISIONISM

Twenty years later, after further extensions of the suffrage and of social legislation, and after repeated victories of socialist parties at the polls, Engels seriously considered the inclusion of Germany and France among the countries eligible for peaceful revolution by ballot and parliamentary procedures. As the founders of revolutionary socialism were willing to revise a crucial point of their doctrine, the stage was set for others to try their hand at more thorough revisions. It was no accident that revisionism, the systematic reexamination and emendation of Marx's doctrines, had its birth in Germany, because nowhere else were there as many professed followers of these doctrines.

BERNSTEIN

The leading revisionist was Eduard Bernstein (1850–1932), who in 1899 published a book later translated into English under the title *Evolution-*

ary Socialism. Bernstein had left Germany in 1878, shortly before the passage of Bismarck's anti-socialist legislation, and worked for the German socialist movement as a journalist and correspondent first in Switzerland and from 1888 to 1901 in London. He was profoundly impressed by the new environment with its air of freedom and political moderation and would marvel at the Queen's heading the list of a charity subscription for the widow of a deceased radical or at the complacency of the police who would allow him to address strikebreakers imported from Germany. He became acquainted with the leading Fabians and broke with orthodox Marxism after an attempt to uphold it in a lecture to the Fabian Society had opened his mind to the futility of such a pursuit. What he then taught was officially condemned by the German Social Democratic party, but since the substance of his thought expressed the reality of the conditions under which the party actually operated and since it brought into the open opinions held by many of his associates, he continued as a respected party member and served for nearly thirty years as a deputy in the German Parliament.

What Bernstein set out to do was to explore "just where Marx is right and where he is wrong"—no easy task for a man who had gone into exile and served for many years a party ostensibly owing undivided allegiance to Marx, a man whom the aged Engels had befriended and had in fact appointed one of his executors. Bernstein's *Evolutionary Socialism* did indeed describe in considerable detail and in systematic fashion what its title promised: a vision of socialism which in its essential features differed sharply from that of Marx. On the philosophical side Bernstein would shed the Hegelian dialectics and instead proclaim his belief in a gradual evolution toward socialism, which would arise not merely from the struggle of opposites but from a juncture of related circumstances. He would attempt to realign socialist aspirations with the Hebrew-Christian tradition of moral values, from which Marx had divorced them, and he did so by stressing the relevance of the ethical factor, which would turn socialism into an ideal worth striving for, rather than depicting it, as Marx had done, as the outcome of inevitable historical necessity. As for the details of the society to come, he did not, however, dispel the mist in which Marx had enveloped them. Instead he underlined the pragmatic character of a movement that more and more became absorbed in the day-by-day tasks of social and economic reform by proclaiming that "the movement is everything, the goal nothing."

Bernstein's economic thought reached no soaring heights of speculation—this was not his strength, and the intellectual atmosphere that surrounded the historical economics of his homeland was not conducive to it. He had, however, a profound sense of realism and a pronounced empirical bent and thus became the first Socialist to question, in a searching manner, the validity of Marx's predictions about rising concentration, increasing misery, growing intensity of the class struggle, and ever more severe crises. He did not ignore the fact that capitalism, instead of lapsing into its death throes, showed a far greater vitality and viability than Marx had been willing to concede, and he gathered a wealth of evidence demonstrating that the laboring class did share in the benefits flowing from economic expansion. Averse to abstract speculations, as Bernstein was, he had his doubts about the relevance of the theory of value. Marx's labor theory, he held, singled out one facet of the matter, the utility theory another one, and both were not incompatible but complemented each other, with Marx's concept of socially necessary labor time constituting the link to demand as a determinant of value. Surplus value and exploitation were empirical facts demonstrated by the existence of unearned income; they did not have to be deduced from Marx's theory of value.

In his politics Bernstein became the prophet of democratic socialism, which would rely on the peaceful work of labor unions and socialist parties to wrestle benefits from a capitalism that was bountiful enough to afford them. The representative democratic state was to bring gradual fulfillment to socialist aspirations. Contrary to Marx's predictions, it would not fade away but would provide the political framework of the society of the future. Bernstein sharply rejected and characterized as barbaric a "dictatorship of the proletariat," words that Marx had employed on a few occasions and which were to assume a sinister importance in the political tactics of his more radically disposed followers. But so strong was the spell of Marx that Bernstein, however much he might revise Marx's doctrines, still professed to be a Marxist, just as did the apostles of the dictatorship of the proletariat.

FRENCH REFORMISM

Bernstein's revisionism had its counterpart in French reformism, which flourished under the Third Republic and in 1899 brought the first Socialist into a bourgeois cabinet, a common enough experience in the twentieth century but at its time a highly controversial innovation, of which many Socialists disapproved. Although the French Socialists had their parliamentary representation as did the German, and although it offered them greater potentialities for constructive work than the sham parliamentarism of Bismarck's Reich, they were nevertheless as reluctant as the German Socialists to accept the reformist label, however well it might fit many of them. Then and later, French socialism was divided into a number of splinter groups, and among the influences on them there was not only Marx but also the tradition of anarchism as represented by Proudhon and Bakunin and the revolutionary élan of the Jacobins and Blanqui. Moreover, the French labor movement was detached from the socialist parliamentary parties, much more so than in Germany, and it generated in time an ideology of its own, known as syndicalism, which was radical, revolutionary, and contemptuous of the work of politicians and of the institutions of parliamentary democracy.

Syndicalism, literally translated, means no more than labor unionism, the French word *syndicat* standing for labor union. The doctrine of syndicalism, or revolutionary syndicalism, which sprang up from the French labor movement at the turn of the century, was that of a militant unionism, sworn to the relentless pursuit of the class struggle and designed to establish workers' control over factories. This struggle was directed both against the employers and the state, and it was to be carried on by unions whose principal function was not the achievement of economic gains for their members but the undermining of the political order by means of "direct action" guided by a "conscious minority." Examples of direct action were sabotage, boycotts, strikes, and, especially, the general strike which might usher in revolution. Like the anarchists, the syndicalists rejected organized government and the coercion of the state. They differed from the anarchists by considering as focuses of the society to come not the local communities but the labor unions.

SOREL

The leading theoretician of syndicalism was Georges Sorel (1847–1922), who, however, kept aloof from the movement itself and during his later career turned away from socialism altogether. Sorel espoused the cult of violence, and like his contemporary, Pareto, he emphasized the importance of the irrational factor in social life. He saw man moved by his emotions and passions rather than by reason, the proper object of manipulation by an elite which would employ imagery and myths to arouse people to action. Sorel's preferred myth was the idea of the general strike, which would give the proletariat a sense of power and mission and invigorate it in the class struggle.

Sorel's world of voluntarism and make-believe was not the world of Marx but that of fascism, whose rise he lived to see. But just as Bernstein refused to relinquish the Marxist label, so did Sorel claim to have preserved "what was truly authentic in Marxism." On the philosophical side, Bernstein wanted to suffuse socialism with Kant's moral imperative, whereas Sorel appealed to the *élan vital* of Henri Bergson.

Syndicalism was but one of the variants of pre-World War I French socialism, and although vestiges of it continued to characterize the French labor movement for a long time, French socialism, just as the German, eventually came to identify itself preponderantly with political democracy. This was also true of the Second International, in which the great socialist parliamentarians from Germany and France played the leading roles. These men and the parties they represented would profess to be the legatees of Marx, however little their daily work of parliamentary maneuvering in the service of social reform might resemble a class struggle aiming at revolution.

Their claim that they were the heirs of Marx was not seriously challenged before the split between socialism and communism at the close of World War I, when the ascendancy of the Soviets in Russia heralded the rise of a totalitarian despotism which pretended to be the authentic successor to Marx's estate.

SOVIET MARXISM

Of the additions that had been built to the structure of Marx's thought since his death, the Soviets would reject some and appropriate others. Among those that they appropriated, the doctrine of imperialism stands out. If imperialism means political expansion by the force of arms, the Soviets in time became its master practitioners, as they annexed, after 1939, an area with a population of twenty-five million, and placed a population of more than one hundred million under the control of communist regimes in Eastern Europe. The Soviets attempted, however, to identify capitalism with imperialism, and for this purpose they espoused a specious theory of imperialism. Marx-inspired theories of imperialism had gradually been evolving since the early 1900s, long before the advent of the Soviets. In fact, it was Bernstein who had set the discussion in motion by investigating the apparently unrelated question raised by the continued survival of capitalism, which seemed to flourish rather than to languish. This question occupied the minds of a number of socialist thinkers during the early decades of the twentieth century. Bernstein had stated the facts and demonstrated them with the help of impressive documentation. In attempting to explain them, he referred to such matters as the growth of the world market and the rise of monopolistic combinations, without, however, arriving at definitive conclusions about their respective roles. These ideas were further developed by the so-called Austro-Marxists and Neo-Marxists, who attempted to interpret the delay in the breakdown of capitalism with the help of various theories.

THEORIES OF IMPERIALISM: J. A. HOBSON

The crucial element in most of these theories was the introduction of "imperialism" as the factor bestowing on capitalism a new life. Imperialism had been examined by the English writer, John A. Hobson, in a book so titled and published in 1902. Hobson (1858–1940) was a critic of conventional economics and at that time of Liberal rather than Labour party persuasion. In his book he condemned the European powers' policies of imperial rivalry and colonial expansion and related them to such economic factors as the search for population settlements, raw materials, export markets, and investment outlets, as well as to the theory of oversaving, which he had developed twelve years earlier. He blamed the selfish interests of financial and commercial groups for the pursuit of these policies, and he described their effects on the indigenous populations as "exploitation" and "parasitism."

Hobson's views have remained controversial among competent students of the economic history of the late nineteenth century, the period to which his investigation was meant to refer. The economic factor as a force making for colonial expansion has been much overrated compared with such impulses as national prestige, the sense of mission, and considerations of military strategy. As a rule, trade does not follow the flag; more often, the flag follows trade. Colonies have not absorbed sizable numbers of European settlers nor has colonial trade constituted more than a small fraction of the total trade of the metropolitan powers. The flow of foreign capital into the colonies, far from being merely exploitative, has been instrumental in promoting much of the economic growth feasible under the conditions of the colonial environment.

An implicit conclusion from Hobson's views, which was later drawn by Marxist writers, was the assertion that the desire for economic gain is the principal or only cause of war. This assertion may be in line with a narrow version of the economic interpretation of history, but it is not supported by historical experience. There have been phases in the world's history, such as during the period of mercantilism, when imperial expansion was propelled by economic considerations, but even then these were inextricably mixed with considerations of power. Not all the great war lords of history were exclusively or even preponderantly driven by the desire for economic gain. It was the lust for power and the sense of mission that prompted their conquests. There may have been minor conflagrations which can be interpreted in economic terms, but on the whole economic conflicts are far more easily negotiable than the greater issues that have divided nations when they fought for their independence and for the maintenance of their values and institutions.

HILFERDING AND LUXEMBURG

In spite of its shortcomings, Hobson's analysis was before long taken up by a number of socialist writers who interpreted imperialism as the last phase of capitalism, with imperial expansion serving as the means both to prolong the life of capitalism and to secure its eventual demise. The first of these writers was Rudolf Hilferding (1877–1941), to whom, however, imperialism was a secondary issue, overshadowed by the role that he assigned to "financial capital." In his book *Das Finanzkapital,* first published in 1910, Hilferding depicted financial capital, represented by the banks, as pressing for investment outlets abroad and inciting governments to imperialist rivalries while at home promoting the organization of cartels and other monopolistic combinations among its industrial clients to safeguard them from the effects of unrestrained competition. Hilferding and other Neo-Marxists also pointed out the new role of protectionism, which no longer served to facilitate the growth of "infant industries" but instead freed domestic monopolists from foreign competition and enabled them to charge high prices at home and dump surpluses abroad, thereby again strengthening the trend toward economic warfare. Hilferding's book was followed in 1913 by *Die Akkumulation des Kapitals* by Rosa Luxemburg (1871–1919), who derived from a reinterpretation of Marx's reproduction schemes the argument that the capitalist economy was unable to dispose of its output of consumer goods at home and was thus forced into overseas expansion for the sake of the realization of surplus value.

LENIN

In 1917 V. I. Lenin (1870–1924) published his *Imperialism, the Highest Stage of Capitalism,* which depicted war as the result of the capitalists' desire to divide up the world in order to wrestle from the underdeveloped countries "superprofits" with which to bribe domestic labor leaders and the upper stratum of the labor aristocracy and make them acquiesce in reformist policies. Lenin's work had vast and sinister consequences, because the doctrine of imperialism, endorsed here by the master agitator and practitioner of revolution, was now destined to become an integral part of Soviet Marxism, to be reiterated time and again as a means to divide the world and claim the allegiance of allegedly exploited underdeveloped peoples. The work of demolishing Western Civilization, which Marx had started by setting class against class, was now given a new direction by inciting the have-not countries to riot against the haves.

SOVIET ECONOMIC THOUGHT

With Lenin begins the period of Soviet Marxism, in which the Soviet Union became the center of thought and action ostensibly inspired by Marx. Its economic thought developed in isolation from that of the West, which was denounced as bourgeois or revisionist. Its point of departure was not the economics of 1920, as it had passed through the marginal revolution and been consolidated in the works of such thinkers as Walras and Marshall, but the economics of the premarginalist era, which for non-Marxists had come to a close half a century earlier. Soviet economic thought had to claim derivation from and compatibility with the doctrines of Marx in order to escape from being labeled bourgeois, revisionist, or deviationist.

KONDRATIEFF

Technical work in economics that at first glance appeared innocuous and ideologically neutral would not escape various tests of its orthodoxy. If these were found wanting, disastrous consequences might ensue. A case in point was that of N. D. Kondratieff, an outstanding student of economic fluctuations, whose writings on long cycles were well known in the West. When Kondratieff announced his findings, competent critics would examine the substance of his thought but a number would also raise the question whether his employment of mathematical statistics in economics was legitimate in the light of Marx's doctrines. This question was answered in the affirmative on the basis of a letter that Marx had written to Engels in 1873 which contains these observations:

> Do you know those charts, where the movement of prices, discount rates, etc. . . .during the year, is plotted? To analyze the phenomenon of crisis, I have attempted several times to compute the formulas of those irregular curves (I think that is possible if sufficient reliable material can be made available) in order to determine mathematically the main laws governing the crisis.

Another question that critics would raise was the affinity of Kondratieff's ideas with those of bourgeois economists. In the end they would denounce his views as "apologetic" because the anticipated upturn of the long cycle, implied by his theory, foreshadowed a new prosperity phase of capitalism rather than its downfall. Under the relatively favorable conditions of the early and mid-twenties this might have been the end of the matter. But once thought control became more severe, Kondratieff lost his research position, was arrested on a charge of conspiratorial activities, and in 1930 was deported to Siberia without trial, never to be heard of.

MARX AND SOVIET ECONOMICS

Even under favorable conditions, the task facing a Soviet economist was a formidable one because Marx's doctrines resembled a storehouse more richly stocked with incendiary material suitable to set capitalism on fire than with building blocks with which to construct the socialist order. What complicated his task further was Marx's assumption that the new order would arise in a highly developed economy, plentifully endowed with capital that was concentrated in a few hands and peopled by an alert industrial proletariat. Marx had in fact visualized the socialization of the capitalist economy as a fairly easy matter compared with the earlier transformation of the feudal economy into a capitalist one. The "primitive capitalist accumulation" by means of which the pioneers of capitalism had first acquired economic resources he described as a protracted and violent process, involving such exploitative devices as force, robbery, and subjugation. He compared the two periods of transition:

> The transformation of scattered private property, arising from individual labor, into capitalist private property is, naturally, a process, incomparably more protracted, violent, and difficult, than the transformation of capitalistic private property,

already practically resting on socialized production, into socialized property. In the former case, we had the expropriation of
the mass of the people by a few usurpers; in the latter, we have
the expropriation of a few usurpers by the mass of the people.

The task that the Soviets imposed on themselves involved an upheaval
quite different from the expropriation of a few usurpers. Theirs was a backward country with small islands of industrialization which were all but
submerged by millions of peasant holdings. Instead of toppling and taking
over a fully grown industrial structure, as Marx had envisaged, the Soviets
faced the task of building one. The two key economic problems with which
they became increasingly concerned were those of accelerating economic
growth and of planning. Marx had said little about planning, and what he
observed about economic growth he placed in the context of his critique
of capitalism.

Although Marx had not given attention to the details of planning
under socialism, he had constructed an elaborate structure of thought on
general economic questions, and to it the Soviet planners would look for
guidance. But what they found were restraints rather than directions. To
begin with, they had to come to terms with the labor theory of value and
either deny its relevance for a socialist economy or attempt to rationalize
the divergence of their pricing system from labor values. There was, furthermore, Marx's interpretation of interest as functionless, unearned, and the
result of capitalist exploitation. The planners' adherence to this view caused
Soviet prices to reflect only inadequately the cost of capital. This brought
into the Soviet economy an element that from the Western point of view
seemed irrational, especially so in view of the great scarcity of capital in an
underdeveloped country.

The Soviet regime never tolerated free thought but at no time was
as oppressive as during the reign of terror unleashed by Joseph Stalin (1879–
1953), Lenin's successor. Relatively speaking, that is, within the framework
of the power structure's interpretation of Marxism, which no one would
have been allowed to question, opportunities for the expression of economic
thought were more favorable before and after Stalin. Soviet economic
thought may be divided into three phases, the Leninist, the Stalinist, and
the post-Stalinist. The Leninist came to its close during the years following
Lenin's death in 1924, when Stalin acceded to power, and the Stalinist some
twenty-five years later. Lenin's authority, which ranked next to that of
Marx and Engels, continued to be invoked after his death; not so Stalin's,
whose rule was described as cruel and despotic by his former associates after
he passed from the scene.

BUKHARIN

Under Lenin, Soviet economic thought went through a short-lived
"liquidationist" period during which Nikolai Bukharin (1888–1938), then
the leading theoretician, pronounced in 1920 the end of political economy

with its value and price relations and laws that existed independently of the will of individuals or groups. The Soviet economy was no longer to be regulated by the blind forces of the market and competition but by a consciously carried out plan. The revolution, so Bukharin expected, was to spread westward, especially to Germany, where wartime economic controls had accelerated the trend toward "organized capitalism" that financial capital and the trust movement had set in motion. There state control and regulation had further reduced the range of the market and prepared the ground for a communist take-over, which would fill the then existing organizational form with a new content.

When contrary to the expectations of Bukharin and others the revolution failed to spread abroad, a long controversy followed about the possibility of "socialism in one country." In Russia the pressure of adverse economic conditions became so strong that in 1921, under the New Economic Policy, the private sector of the economy was again given greater leeway. Planning continued to be a subject of discussion, but the revival of the private sector limited its practical significance.

THE INDUSTRIALIZATION DEBATE

As the twenties advanced, the foremost question of economic policy was the expansion of the state-controlled sector of the economy and, related thereto, that of the industrial establishment. Long before the revolution there had taken place a protracted debate between those radicals who desired to maintain the preponderantly agricultural character of the Russian economy and those who favored large-scale industrialization. In this debate the exponents of industrialization had won, and the buildup of a strong industrial establishment, with emphasis on heavy industry, became the primary goal of Soviet economic policy. Opinions were divided, however, about the means to attain it. In the "industrialization debate" of 1924–28 various points of view emerged about questions not unlike those that a generation later occupied the minds of Western students of economic development. Was agricultural development to provide the stimulus to industrial growth? Was growth to be balanced or unbalanced? What criterion should be used in the allocation of limited resources to investment projects? What was the optimal time structure of investment, the optimal technology, and the optimal capital-output ratio? How was inflation to be controlled if the country faced a multiplication of expenditures generated by new investment?

Bukharin, one of the leaders in the debate, had by then reversed his earlier liquidationist position and suggested the postponement of planning. Instead the government was to occupy the "commanding heights" of the economy and guide the forces of the market. Bukharin proposed to assign priority to the regeneration of the peasant economy, whose prosperity would stimulate industrial growth. These views were opposed by Eugene Preobrazhensky (1886–1937), who insisted that in the absence of capital imports the means for the construction of an industrial establishment would have to be extracted from the farmers. With the help of monopolistic price policies of the state industrial enterprises and related measures the domestic terms of trade should be turned against the peasants. If these received low prices for agricultural products and paid high ones for manufactures, resources would be shifted from the private farm sector to the state's industrial sector. These were the policies advocated by Preobrazhensky to accelerate industrial growth, and he stressed their drastic character by referring to them as "primitive socialist accumulation." This expression was meant to be a counterpart of Marx's "primitive capitalist accumulation," that is, the utilization of exploitative devices such as force, robbery, and subjugation, which according to Marx the early pioneers of capitalism had employed to acquire economic resources.

STALINIST ECONOMICS

Stalin's forced collectivization drive closed the industrialization debate. Following neither Bukharin's nor Preobrazhensky's counsel nor that of others, he instead expropriated the mass of peasants in an "agrarian revolution from above," which uprooted millions and in which many perished, and for which a contrived famine had been the signal. Parallel with these developments there began in 1928 the series of five-year plans, which over the years transformed the Soviet Union into an industrial power. The planning instrument, which had been shaped during the discussion of the twenties, was the method of "material balances." Under this method the top authorities would establish certain production goals in terms of physical quantities, and the planners would then draw up detailed budgets for materials, equipment, and labor, balancing raw material requirements, exports, and terminal stocks with output, imports, and initial stocks. Since production goals tended to emphasize heavy industry and munitions rather than consumer goods, the sacrifices imposed upon the consumers made possible a high rate of investment, high enough to allow for economic growth in spite of many inefficiencies in planning.

Writers and administrators would concern themselves with the details of plans and there would be continued denunciations of bourgeois economics, but after 1928 the discussion of fundamental economic questions subsided, to be resumed only after Stalin's death in 1953. Liquidationism returned, having been held in abeyance since the inception of the New Economic Policy. Now, under Stalin, its implications became sinister and it brought extinction not only to economics but to economists and other intellectuals as well. Not a few of those who had proclaimed their belief in the early withering away of the state faced the firing squads during the great purges of the thirties. The victims included Bukharin, Preobrazhensky, and other leading economists. No one dared express an independent opinion because any opinion might be labeled treasonable and invite persecution. During a period of twenty-five years no one would write a textbook on general economics, and at times instruction in economics at institutions of higher learning ceased altogether. The liquidationist trend affected even economic statistics, which suggested the uncertainty of chance events rather than evincing the certainties of a world in which everything proceeded according to the plan. Thus from 1931 to 1941 the Central Statistical Office changed its name and functioned as Central Office of National Economic Accounting.

Instances of terror continued during the postwar period, such as when in 1949 the former head of the planning office and author of a history of the Soviet war economy was executed for unknown reasons and notwithstanding the fact that his work had been awarded the Stalin Prize two years earlier. His book contained a number of observations on the operation of the law of value under socialism, an abstruse matter and yet one fraught with weighty implications regarding the limits of the power of the state and of the efficiency of the planners. The theme was taken up by Stalin, who, having asserted his authority in the field of linguistics in 1950, branched out into economics in 1952, a year before his death. Stalin's essay on economic problems was an exercise in evasion, claiming in effect the validity of economic laws for those sectors of the economy in which transfer of ownership occurs and their abrogation in the state-controlled producer goods sector.

DE-STALINIZATION

During the period of "de-Stalinization" and temporary "thaw," which, however, was not free of reverses, the discussion of economic theory became animated again and genuine thought replaced the reiteration of citations from the writings of Marx, Engels, Lenin, and Stalin, the "quotationism," as it was called disparagingly. The overriding issue continued to be the validity of economic laws in general and specifically of the law of value. What gave this issue its great practical importance was that its substance hinged around the search for criteria that in the absence of the market would guide the planning authorities' allocation of resources and price policies. A related issue was the centralization of planning and decision making, a legacy left behind by Lenin, who had been impressed by the tightly organized German war economy during World War I. As the Soviet economy had grown and become more complex, complaints about the inefficient character of these arrangements became more insistent, and as long as the conditions of the intellectual thaw prevailed, reform proposals could be aired more freely.

No one proposed that the planners' sovereignty be replaced by consumers' sovereignty or that the rate of investment be determined by the market rather than by the authorities. What stood at issue was the question posed by consumer prices which were inflated by heavy turnover taxes to bring demand more nearly in line with meager supplies, and the more urgent question posed by accounting prices for producer goods turned out by state enterprises, which did not adequately reflect relative scarcities and the cost of capital. In conventional Soviet practice prices had been fixed in average terms and in line with Marx's value concept, that is, in terms of $v + c + s$, denoting the wage bill, depreciation charge, and a markup containing profit and turnover tax and designated now surplus product rather than surplus value.

PLANOMETRICS

In the debate of the 1950s and 1960s, the followers of a more conservative line of thought proposed no more than a standardization of the markup in various rival formulations. Others suggested further-reaching reforms which, while proclaiming continued adherence to the labor theory of value, would nevertheless make prices the shadows of relative scarcities and cover charges for capital and rent. The determination of final output goals was to continue under the direction of the planning authorities. But once the goals were established, recourse was to be had to mathematical techniques, to input-output analysis to coordinate the plan and to linear programming to optimize it.

Like the method of material balances, input-output analysis singles out for emphasis intermediate goods, which are linked in physical quantities to physical quantities of final products. A change in the output of final products, say an increase in automobiles, requires not only more steel, and so forth, but more automobiles as well, and there are other repercussions and regresses which can be handled with the help of a system of simultaneous equations. The system is in equilibrium when just enough of each output is produced so that the input requirements of all the others can be satisfied. It does not presume a specific system of pricing and cannot readily shed the assumption of fixed coefficients of production.

Linear programming shares with input-output analysis the emphasis on the ends-means connection between goals and activities. Its basic idea is the maximization of a linear function of variables subject to linear inequalities. It goes beyond input-output analysis by yielding a variety of plans each of which can fulfill the output goal but only one of which provides the optimum solution with shadow prices reflecting relative scarcities.

When suggestions were made for the adoption of these techniques in the Soviet Union, they were already well known in the West, where input-output analysis had been under discussion since 1936 and linear programming since the late forties. The Soviet planometricians, however, claimed these techniques as their own discoveries. Linear programming, for the optimum use of equipment in a plant, had indeed been discovered by the Soviet mathematician, L. V. Kantorovich (born 1912), who published his findings in 1939, a number of years before the independent discovery of the technique by G. B. Dantzig and T. Koopmans in the United States. Kantorovich's work received little attention in the Soviet Union before the 1950s, as did input-output analysis. The Soviet priority claim for the latter, which is far more tenuous, rests on the fact that W.W. Leontief, the discoverer of input-output analysis and a member of the Harvard faculty since the early 1930s, was born in Leningrad, received his early economic education in the Soviet Union, and in 1925, as a youth of nineteen, published an article on the balance of the national economy of the USSR. This article, which was published after Leontief had already left the Soviet Union, treats of material balances but does not draw in the system of simultaneous equations, the core of the future input-output analysis. Long before the latter became known in the Soviet Union, it was put to important military use in the United States, where it helped to pinpoint bottlenecks and other weak spots of the German and Japanese economies during World War II.

The breakthrough of mathematical economics in the Soviet Union did not arise *ex nihilo* but reflects a long Russian tradition of mastery of Western thought, with achievements in mathematics and mathematical statistics which reach far back to the period antedating the Soviet regime. During the Stalin era opportunities for displaying this mastery were unfavorable, and its practitioners were driven underground, not a few literally so, as was Kondratieff. Another case that illustrates both the continuity of Western thought in Russia and its disappearance from the surface is that of E. E. Slutsky (1880–1948), who in an article published in an Italian periodical in 1915 contributed the basis for modern indifference-curve analysis with its income and substitution effects. Slutsky's achievement received belated recognition in the West; his later career in the Soviet Union was one of relative obscurity, but he was not forgotten and his article was published in a Russian translation in 1963.

The independent rediscovery of the substance of Slutsky's findings by Allen and Hicks illustrates again the multiple character of scientific discoveries in economics, as does the doctrinal history of linear programming. The history of economics abounds with examples of multiple discoveries, but here was one made in cultural environments and value systems as far apart as the Soviet Union of the 1930s and the United States of the 1940s. All else notwithstanding, gifted people with similar training, employing the same tools of science and pursuing similar goals, would make the same discovery. That the inner logic of scientific advance was strong enough to overcome all obstacles was due to the identity of the technical apparatus employed, a mathematics unencumbered by public values and private emotions and the same everywhere. This technical apparatus yielded rules that lent themselves equally well to the ascertainment of the best use of resources, be they those of a police force or a band of gangsters, of labor in the factory or labor in prison. In either case the goal was efficiency. If this goal could now be proclaimed in the Soviet Union, and if there was greater permissiveness as regards the penetration of economics by mathematics, this would seem to indicate that the older ideologies were now challenged by a new cult, that of efficiency, which brought in its train the computer to find a solution to the problem of large-scale organization, which threatened to become almost intractable. In 1962 a leading Soviet mathematician and expert in cybernetics calculated that the personnel requirements for planning and administration increase as the square of the national product, and he concluded his observations with an extrapolation of current trends, which by 1980 would require the employment in planning and administration of the entire adult population of the country. The alarm sounded by the mathematicians did its work, and three years later the authorities awarded the Lenin Prize to Kantorovich and his associates. But there was still no official commitment to their views, and a prize for economic work had been an ill omen to its author not so long ago. Soviet economics was still in flux.

Soviet planometrics has mainly been concerned with the search for efficiency, whereas Western econometrics and Western socialist economics have invariably stressed not only the optimum in terms of efficiency but in terms of welfare as well. There has been no comparable development in Soviet economic thought, aiming, for example, at the specification of an optimum rate of investment which would maximize economic welfare. The conventional Soviet doctrine is derived from Marx's reproduction scheme and observations of Lenin and grounded in the distinction between the two departments of the economy, Department I turning out capital goods and Department II consumer goods. Soviet economists have postulated a law according to which economic growth requires faster expansion of Department I than of Department II. They further hold that the growth rate is to be maximized by a rate of investment which makes the rate of consumption a residual containing no more than an indispensable minimum determined by political, psychological, and incentive considerations. It is an open question whether, as a Western student of the Soviet economy has suggested, the dynamics of the Soviet political system require the relentless mobilization of resources for maximum investment. A totalitarian dictatorship, it has been claimed, is compelled to justify its existence continuously by professing a mission and instilling in its subjects a sense of urgency through "campaigns" and similar drives. If the campaign is not a literal one, as in outright warfare, the battle of production aiming at industrial and military strength may do the job.

Soviet growth theory, rudimentary as it is, thus relies on a maximum rate of investment as the stimulus to growth. Other stimuli, some of which were discussed during the industrialization debate of the 1920s and to which attention was again drawn during the more recent period, are either de-emphasized or rejected. This holds, for example, for the stimulation of growth by means of increased productivity or by means of the production of exportable surpluses, say, from agriculture, to obtain imported machinery sooner than it can be produced domestically in plants yet to be constructed.

ECONOMIC THOUGHT IN EASTERN EUROPE

Soviet economic thinking often followed lines different from those pursued in the other countries of the Soviet bloc and in Yugoslavia. The intellectual ties between these countries and the Soviet Union have, however, exerted a favorable influence on the modernization of Soviet economic thought and have been among the factors responsible for the upsurge of mathematical economics in the Soviet Union. The ranks of the Polish economists included a few men of internationally known accomplishments, who after a career in the West returned to their homeland during the post-war period. The influence of these missionaries of modern methods of economics—Oskar Lange (1904–65) and Michal Kalecki (1899–1970)—was felt not only in Poland but beyond her eastern borders as well.

In the struggle for a greater measure of political independence from the Soviet Union, the communist countries of Eastern Europe developed their economic organization apart from the Soviet pattern. Each country attempted to shape its economic organization in its own way. Greater emphasis, as a rule, was placed on the market and on the individual management of farm enterprises rather than on collectivization, which in a number of cases was cancelled after having been introduced earlier. Economic thought in these countries became more detached from that in the Soviet Union and concerned with a wider range of questions. The matter of a welfare optimum, for example, became the subject of vigorous debate among economists in Yugoslavia, and significant contributions were made to such problems as that of the optimum rate of investment. The participants in these discussions might pay lip service to the thought of Marx, either as mechanical incantations or as a cloak of legitimacy for their own ideas. In one way or another they would have to come to terms with the labor theory of value, a stumbling bloc to be overcome by a writer's ingenuity rather than an aid to what had then become the prical concern—national economic planning.

SOCIALISM IN UNDERDEVELOPED COUNTRIES

Planning was a matter for which solutions were sought elsewhere as well, in the nations of the West and in the underdeveloped countries of the world, many of which attached to themselves a socialist label. From various backgrounds, often sharply differing in social structure, economic organization, and political ideals, there arose variants of national economic planning which were shaped by the exigencies of circumstances, the power play of political leaders, pragmatic experimentation, and ideologies barely hardened into economic doctrines.

Amid the welter of the ideologies of underdeveloped countries professing allegiance to socialism certain features emerged, which, however, were by no means universally represented in equal strength. Marx's anticapitalism now appeared in the form of anticolonialism and anti-imperialism, with a new demonology in which foreign economic interests more than the domestic bourgeoisie were indicted for real or imaginary wrongs. At times the national bourgeoisie might even be acclaimed as a leader of an anti-imperialist revolution. The idea of a domestic class struggle often gave way to the espousal of national or tribal solidarity. Indigenous religious attachments, instead of being rejected, were considered important sources of socialist aspirations and stressed as instruments of national and regional integration.

CHINESE COMMUNISM

The national socialisms of underdeveloped countries thus acquired features of their own which were sharply at variance with the ideas of Marx, even more so when the socialism had racist undertones which set up, not class against class, but race against race, or when it made a militant peasantry the bearer of the revolutionary message. Although the Chinese communists claimed to be the true heirs of Marx, their thought has even further departed from Marx's than that of the Soviets. The worship of power rather than reliance on the forces of history has emerged in both regimes, but no one accented voluntarism more strongly than Mao Tse-tung (born 1893), the leader of communist China, in his often quoted statement that "political power grows out of the barrel of a gun." The appeals to patriotism, launched in the Soviet Union by Stalin in 1931 when he spoke of "Mother Russia" as the "socialist fatherland," have their counterpart in the traditional Chinese view which considers the rest of the world, including the Soviet Union, as peopled by barbarians. In communist China, the attack against imperialism was expanded to include "cultural" and "intellectual" variants, of which missionary activities were rated an important manifestation. The link with the proletariat in the countries of the West, still espoused in Soviet ideology, was all but broken in communist China, where the Western workingmen were viewed as beneficiaries of imperialist exploitation rather than as allies in a common struggle. Mao was credited with a number of contributions to socialist theory by his followers, but these are far more elusive than the political tactics which brought him to power in his homeland and which were emulated in other underdeveloped countries: guerilla warfare, carried on by self-contained peasant groups, which laid siege to the cities and in the end overwhelmed them.

BRITISH SOCIALISM

Regardless of whether they invoked it or attempted to break it, most of the socialist thinkers hitherto considered labored under the spell of Marx. Although Marx spent the greater part of his adult life in England, he had little influence on the development of British socialism. British trade union leaders might affiliate with the First International, but when they did so the motive was not so much to foment revolution as to avert the importation of strike breakers from the Continent. England became in fact the homeland of a non-Marxian socialism that was pragmatic and democratic rather than doctrinaire and authoritarian. English socialism left its mark on continental revisionism and tended to converge with it as the latter moved further along the road toward social and economic improvement by parliamentary means, a road only dimly illuminated by the thought of Marx.

THE INFLUENCE OF HENRY GEORGE

The decisive impact on modern British socialism in its formative stage was made not by Marx but by the American social reformer, Henry George (1839–97), whose *Progress and Poverty* (1879) articulated the social protest of the time and channeled it into paths different from those that Marx had broken. George, a native of Philadelphia, tried his hand as a sailor, printer, publisher, and journalist, and after protracted struggles, which brought him face to face with dire poverty, he settled in California. When the success of his book had turned him into a figure of worldwide fame, he returned to the East and spread his doctrine there and in the British Isles, which he visited on several occasions. He entered politics, and labor groups twice secured his nomination as mayor of New York, the first campaign ending with his narrow defeat and the second with his death five days before the election.

George's message had been formed as the result of impressions that he gained during his westward travels. He saw thriving towns spring up in regions that shortly before had been wilderness, a transformation that filled the coffers of the owners of real estate, who in turn might further enhance the value of their possessions by withholding some from improvement. Their wealth had been created by the transformation of their environment; by means of contrived scarcity they attempted to enrich themselves further. All this George found a revolting violation of social justice, and he came to consider it the principal social problem of his time, whose solution would cure a host of other ills, and which he proposed to solve by taxing the "unearned increment." Later he emphasized that a tax on rental income such as he contemplated would constitute a "single tax" sufficient to finance all government expenditure.

Like Marx, George drew on Ricardian economics to find the theoretical basis for his doctrine, but unlike Marx he found it in the Ricardian theory of rent rather than that of value. If rent was paid for the service of land, and if land was original and indestructible, a tax imposed on rental income would appropriate to the community what was a gift of God rather than the product of the owner's effort. Furthermore, if rents rose in consequence of changes of the environment, society, so George argued, was entitled to recoup the increment created by social change rather than by the action of the owner.

Although both Marx and George drew drastic conclusions from Ricardo's theories, in other respects their doctrines were far apart. George did not espouse a class struggle nor did he aim at the upheaval of an economic order based on private enterprise. He took no exception to nonlabor income other than rent, and he affirmed the desirability of competition. He did not envisage the transfer to common ownership of the means of production, except for such natural monopolies as common carriers and public utilities. He brooked no opposition to free trade, writing an entire book in its defense. He appealed not to the forces of history but to social justice, natural rights, and the teachings of Christianity. Although professional economists drew attention to a number of flaws in George's message, it caused a considerable stir and found a following which included not only laboring men but also middle-class people and a few men of wealth who gave it financial support.

The impact of George's message was felt even more strongly in the England of the 1880s, where it coincided with a renascence of socialist strivings. There had been a lull of these after the mid-century agitation of the Chartists, Owenites, and Christian Socialists had been quenched by the rising prosperity of the Victorian age, one from which the "labor aristocracy" of skilled workers drew special benefits. For some years, working class aspirations had been satisfied by trade union activities, the spread of consumer rather than producer cooperatives, the benevolence of model employers of the type of Owen, and the further extension of the suffrage. In the 1880s, however, this period of calm came to an end when a business depression, followed by sharpened industrial conflict and unrest among the unemployed, set the stage for a revival of socialist stirrings.

George's anti-landlordism seemed particularly relevant to conditions in England, where land ownership was highly concentrated and tenant farming the rule, and even more so to conditions in Ireland, whose economic plight, ascribed by some observers to absentee ownership, was the subject of a never-ending debate. Both the Mills had drawn from the Ricardian rent theory conclusions the substance of which converged with the ideas of George, and still earlier instances of anti-landlordism could be found in eighteenth-century English literature. When George arrived in England to spread his doctrine, he could address organizations which had been formed with aims similar to his own.

There was the further fact that George's appeal to religion would strike a sympathetic chord among a new generation of Christian Socialists and among labor leaders who had exchanged the pulpit of the lay preacher for the rostrum of the union hall. Although it had its counterpart in the secularist rationalism of many Socialists who were indifferent to religion, the religious strand in British socialism came to the fore again.

WILLIAM MORRIS

To the religious element must be added the cultural discomforts expressed in the writings of William Morris (1834–96), a poet and craftsman, who deplored the aesthetically unsatisfactory aspects of modern life. The transition from the workshop to the factory meant that men were put to work turning out shoddy goods and needless gadgets. Instead of wasting their lives in the production of these, Morris wanted them to find fulfillment and happiness by devoting themselves to the production of beautiful objects by manual arts. He was in search of a socialism that would liberate man from drudgery and restore beauty to the life not only of the rich but of the average man.

Marxist and anarchist ideas, although by no means entirely absent from the English scene, were no match for these indigenous forces of British socialism. When an English translation of *Das Kapital* was finally published in 1887, there was already in existence a labor aristocracy with middle-class rather than proletarian aspirations, to whom Marx's ideas had little appeal. The whole structure of Marx's thought, grounded as it was in German metaphysics with its emphasis on uncompromising absolutes and doctrinaire either/or solutions, was alien to the pragmatic instinct of the British, their talent for compromise, and their attachment to hard won democratic processes.

THE FABIAN SOCIETY

The decisive step in the formation of a British kind of democratic socialism was the founding of the Fabian Society in 1884, which was joined shortly thereafter by George Bernard Shaw (1856–1950) and Sidney Webb (1859–1947). When Shaw was twenty-five, then an unknown critic and not yet a world-famous playwright, he happened to attend a lecture by Henry George, which impressed on him the importance of economic problems. The socialism to which he became converted soon after found expression in the *Fabian Essays in Socialism,* written by Shaw, Webb, and others, and published in 1889. "When I was thus swept into the great socialist revival of 1883," Shaw later wrote, "I found that five-sixths of those who were swept in with me had been converted by Henry George." Shaw's principal contribution to socialist economics was the expansion of the principle of differential rent and its application to capital and personal ability. The generalization of rent theory was in the air at that time and set forth by economists on both sides of the Atlantic. These, however, did not share Shaw's conclusion from the generalization of the principle of differential rent, namely, the socialization of economic rents through taxation or nationalization and their use for public purposes such as social insurance and the provision of capital for public investment. In its later development, British socialism did not exactly apply Shaw's early formula, which reflected an exaggerated view of the size of rents, nor did it follow him in his demand for perfect equality of incomes, a demand that he justified on the ground that there is no rational basis for the determination of unequal incomes. This opinion Shaw refused to abandon, although on other occasions he manifested an open mind and followed the judgment of professional economists. He discarded, for example, Marx's labor theory of value after P. H. Wicksteed had converted him to Jevons's utility theory.

THE WEBBS

Gradualness was the watchword of the Fabian Society, which derived its name from that of Quintus Fabius Maximus Cunctator, the "delayer," a Roman general known for his holding tactics. Sidney Webb, who later coined the phrase, the "inevitability of gradualness," did express his conviction of an inevitable development toward socialism, which however, unlike Marx, he visualized as gradual and experimental, proceeding by parliamentary means rather than as the result of an abrupt upheaval. Sidney Webb and his wife Beatrice (1858–1943), whom he married in 1892, became masters in the art of social engineering and economic experimentation. They wrote a great number of historical and empirical studies which diverted the discussion of economic problems from ideological concerns and the analysis of abstract concepts and brought it down to the level of facts, an approach rarely practiced in the older universities and for whose promotion Webb founded the London School of Economics in 1895.

In its effects the work of the Webbs was comparable to that of Bentham's a century before. It ranked high among the forces responsible for the transformation of England during the first half of the twentieth century, both by nonlabor governments and by those of the Labour party, of which the Fabian Society became an intellectual branch. To the Fabians the trend toward socialism meant the approximation of social justice by means of planning and control exercised by governments responsible to the electorate in a democratic system. In their early program they envisaged the establishment of public enterprises on the municipal, county, and national level, which were to be financed from taxes on rents. As these enterprises would not be burdened by rent and interest charges, they could offer better wages and working conditions than private concerns and would gradually hire away their workers. Side by side with this idea appeared the proposal to nationalize certain existing industries, mainly public utilities, common carriers, and those under the control of private monopolies. The public enterprises, they held, would enable the unemployed to exercise their right to work, which private enterprise denied them.

H. G. WELLS AND G. D. H. COLE

During its long history the Fabian Society went through a number of crises. The first occurred during the South African War of 1899–1902, when Shaw and the Webbs supported British imperial expansion as likely, in the absence of world government, to establish a rule more efficient, responsible, and beneficial to the world at large than that of the independent Boer Republics. The second crisis ensued when H. G. Wells (1866–1946), a famous novelist and socialist publicist, who had joined the society in 1903, withdrew from it six years later, having failed to persuade it to initiate a program of mass agitation. A third crisis coincided with the rise of guild socialism, a movement promoted, among others, by G. D. H. Cole (1889–1959), one of England's leading socialist academics, which flourished between 1915 and 1925. Guild socialism was the English counterpart of French syndicalism, though far less influential among working people and considerably gentler than syndicalism, shorn of its exclusive emphasis on revolution and the class struggle and divided as to whether or not to retain the overall authority of the state. Guild socialism aimed at "self-government of industry," exercised not by the control of the working class as such but by the workers attached to national guilds. Except for a National Building Guild, the movement produced few tangible results, and when the building guild failed, it faded away.

Guild socialism was principally an enterprise of intellectuals, some of whom felt attracted to the medieval craft guilds while others were drawn to it because its pluralism seemed to offer a return to spontaneity and an escape from bureaucratic centralization, government by experts, and the cult of efficiency, which the increasing intervention by the national government portended. The Webbs rejected workers' control of industry and looked to trade unions primarily as instruments of collective bargaining, a representation of producer interests operating under the watchful eyes of consumer cooperatives and of popular government at all levels, which they visualized as guardians of the interests of the consumers.

SOCIAL SECURITY

The gradualism that the Webbs espoused meant the vesting of an increasing number of functions in government at all levels, with the national government assuming a more and more commanding role. They proposed a "national minimum standard of civilized life," and in 1909 Beatrice Webb, in the Minority Report of the Poor Law Commission, wrote the charter for a comprehensive social security scheme, the first blueprint of the future welfare state. Compulsory and contributory insurance, Bismarck's earlier model which was eventually adopted by the English government, was rejected in this report, which instead favored the financing of social security out of general revenues, with benefits not made available unconditionally as a matter of right but dependent on the qualified behavior of the recipient.

THE CULT OF EFFICIENCY

Shaw and Webb had joined the Fabian Society when young men in their twenties. During their old age in the 1930s, when England and other countries suffered from the Great Depression, they were rash enough to express an unseemly admiration for the dictatorial regimes in the East and in the West, which claimed to tolerate no unemployment and made the trains go on time. Throughout their lives the Webbs and Shaw had vacillated between the cult of efficiency and that of a love more paternalistic than brotherly. As their lives seemed to run out, and as their world fell victim to serious economic disorders, impatience drove them to worship what seemed to be the idol of efficiency at the neglect of the other. That it was a sham idol became apparent with the outcome of World War II, when the vaunted efficiency of the fascist dictators failed its crucial test.

SOCIALISM IN THE AFFLUENT SOCIETY

After two world wars a large part of the program of the Fabians had become reality in Britain. The welfare state was established and a substantial portion of industry nationalized. All this had been accomplished by democratic means, and the central government, while reaching out into virtually all spheres of the economy, continued to be bound by the traditional reverence for civil rights and liberties. But the very triumph of democratic socialism raised questions to which no ready answers were at hand. Poverty had been reduced and economic opportunity widened. Incomes had risen, had become more stable, and were more widely diffused. The affluent society, heralded by an American writer, seemed on the march. The welfare state and the partial nationalization of industry were established facts. The former had ceased to be a partisan issue. It might be expanded and improved, but such activities would be marginal rather than fundamental and unlikely to kindle much enthusiam among the tax-burdened electorate. Nationalization of industry was still a contested issue, about which even socialists had become doubtful and which gradually became a political liability. It had done little to affect the daily life of the workers in the factories, and opinions were divided about its success in terms of economic criteria. With the old goals nearing fulfillment, socialism was groping for new ones. Socialism was in substance a movement of protest against poverty and inequality, and as these vanished, Socialists had to redefine their goals to attract working and middle-class people. One of the first steps in this direction, undertaken in England and by democratic Socialists elsewhere, was to renounce further nationalization.

The fulfillment of working class aspirations by her own kind of democratic socialism made England immune to communism. Although the split between communism and socialism after World War I brought into being sizable communist parties on the Continent, communist representation in the House of Commons was most of the time nonexistent and never exceeded two seats. These disparate trends continued after World War II, when communist parties again gained considerable following in Italy and France but not in Britain.

As England became the leading Western country to refurbish her institutions in the image of her own brand of socialism, socialist economics became the concern of a number of her economists. It was, however, on the Continent that the breakthrough occurred which opened up opportunities for the assimilation of socialist economics into the mainstream of modern economic analysis. This was the result of the work of Walras, who developed a general equilibrium system on a level of abstraction so high that it could cut across the diversity of institutions and include consideration of socialist variants. Walras also set forth the conditions under which the economic system would generate a maximum of social welfare. His ideas were elaborated by Pareto and by the latter's disciple, Enrico Barone, a colonel on the Italian General Staff, who in 1908 in an article entitled "The Ministry of Production in a Collectivist State" applied them to a socialist system with communal property in capital and land, and freedom of choice for jobs and consumer goods. To generate a maximum of social welfare, Barone taught, the Ministry of Production would have to emulate an idealized competitive system, and by means of trial and error establish prices that equal costs of production, with costs of production being at a minumum. For a long time there was little response to Barone's work, but during the 1930s, when the Great Depression caused a revival of interest in socialist planning, academic economists in the English-speaking countries were led to a reexamination of socialist economics, which yielded a number of works developing further Barone's basic idea. During the rising prosperity of the postwar decades interest in this matter abated and greater attention was given to Keynesian macroeconomics and fiscal policy rather than to the economic theory of socialism of the Barone type, the study of which converged with that of welfare economics.

In the postwar era, Western economists, except for those in France, on the whole showed little concern with Marx's technical economics—his theories of value and surplus value, the reserve army of the proletariat, increasing misery, and so forth, appeared to be of little relevance to the problems then current. However, Marx's thought, as well as that of Bakunin, Fourier, and other anarchists and early Socialists continued to reverberate in the minds óf radical sociologists and philosophers who found fault with the quality of life in modern industrial societies. Affluence seemed within the grasp of these societies, but its coming did not still man's quest for the ideal society. The prophets of the "New Left," of whom much was heard during the 1960's, had little to say about how to preserve the newly won plenty amidst the welter of violence, intolerance, and suppression of thought which formed part of their message.

Chapter 22

ECONOMICS RESTRUCTURED:

Marginalism

and Optimization

1.   FORERUNNERS AND JEVONS

THE MARGINAL REVOLUTION

Conventional economics as exemplified by John Stuart Mill's writings, against which Marx and his followers launched their attack, did not stand still but underwent during the closing decades of the nineteenth century a profound transformation often designated as the "marginal revolution." When this revolution had run its course at the turn of the century, both the structure of economics and its method differed sharply from the political economy of the classics. The labor theory of value was shed, and with the help of a new unifying principle there was accomplished the integration of the theories of the consumer and of the firm, as well as the integration of the theories of value and distribution, which had been only loosely connected in classical thought. The unifying principle, which was now at hand, was the marginal one. It proved serviceable also if applied to price theory and the theory of markets, and it pointed the way toward the establishment of theoretical optimum positions, or equilibria, at which consumers and producers would maximize such magnitudes as satisfaction or net revenue. There was less emphasis on economic growth, with which Adam Smith had been so greatly concerned. Instead, the attempt to locate equilibrium positions was made within a framework in which the total quantity of resources was given. Economics became the science treating of the allocation of a given quantum of total resources, which meant that little attention continued to be devoted to the question of how this quantum was determined and how it could be increased. No more than Ricardo did the new generation of economists attempt to develop a theory of the determination of total output.

The search for optimum positions within a framework of a given quantity of resources opened the door to mathematical modes of argumentation, and in this sense the marginal revolution marks the beginning of modern economic analysis. Relationships between economic variables came to be recognized as functional ones, which relate the change of one variable to the change of another, such as the change of the quantity demanded to the change in the demand price. Once these relationships were interpreted as functional ones, there was but a short step to their expression in the form of equations and to the graphic portrayal of the curves they represent. Thus the economic literature became interspersed with symbols and graphs. Simultaneous equations made their appearance, denoting, for example, demand and supply, and they were solved by finding their root, that is, the price equating the quantities demanded and supplied and indicated by the intersection of the respective curves.

The search for optimum positions made the pioneers of modern economic analysis aware of the opportunities opened up by the employment of the powerful tools of differential calculus. Thus they would define the marginal unit in terms of the first derivative, the infinitesimally small change of one variable attending the infinitesimally small change of another. Marginal utility, for example, was interpreted as the differential coefficient of utility with respect to the quantity of a good under a person's control. It was noted that when the first derivative reaches the value of zero a maximum or minimum position is attained, be it, for example, maximum total utility or revenue or minimum total cost. It became apparent also that another type of optimum position could be defined in terms of the equality of marginal values in different uses, for example, when the last unit of expenditure spent in different directions conveys the same incremental satisfaction, a change in spending would not add to the total satisfaction.

The economic discussion thus shifted its attention from total quantities to small changes in these totals. One of its central concepts became the equilibrium, which equated certain variables and maximized others. Since the equilibrium was primarily employed in microeconomics and centered around the consumer and the firm, such matters as the macroeconomics of national income determination and the economics of growth and development were not among the themes that ranked prominently in this discussion. They had to wait until attention was eventually accorded to them as the twentieth century progressed.

The designation of the transition to marginal analysis as a revolution may be considered a misnomer for two reasons. What occurred was not a sudden shift but a slow movement by fits and starts which stretched virtually over the entire nineteenth century. Moreover, the break with the past was not as pervasive as the word *revolution* implies. To be sure, more than once a solitary thinker would rediscover the new technique without being aware of the work of his immediate precursors. But in its broader pattern the new thought had strong links with the great ideas of the past—with Bentham's calculus of utility and with the incipient equilibrium economics and subjective theories of value developed in eighteenth-century

France and Italy. In matters of economic policy, there was continuity rather than a break with the ideas of the classics.

That the acceptance of marginal analysis was delayed for so long reflected inertia and resistance to the employment of mathematics as well as a twofold failure of communication—the lack of attention given to the contributions of those who worked outside an incipient scientific community that was in the process of attaining professional status and inadequate lines of information within that community and from one national branch to another. Outsiders ranked prominently among the pioneers of marginal analysis because its discovery required a perspective that the experts did not necessarily possess, especially since the new idea consisted of a fusion of two disparate elements, one stemming from conventional economics and the other from mathematics, albeit not at its higher levels but at the level that was understood by most well-educated people.

As for the economic element in the fusion, it could, and did, appear in several variants, depending upon whether the marginal principle would be related to the theory of the firm, the theory of production, or the theory of the consumer. The first of these variants would yield the concepts of marginal revenue and marginal cost; the second, marginal productivity; and the third, marginal utility. It was not until the 1870s that three academic economists, Jevons in England, Menger in Austria, and Walras in Switzerland, each working independently, drew attention to the third variant of the fusion, and the new idea began to be absorbed into the mainstream of the economic tradition, renewing and modifying it in a process that again took several decades. It was the work of these men that set off the marginal revolution. They had many precursors whose thought, however, had little effect on the opinion of their contemporaries.

The doctrinal history of marginal analysis in the nineteenth century provides a case study that shows the emergence and eventual acceptance of a new scientific idea of major importance. Multiple discoveries, of which the events of the 1870s constitute the prime example, abound also during the earlier history. Of the pioneers of whose work this earlier history consists, only a few can be mentioned here. The circumstances attending their discoveries lend support to the hypothesis that among the strategic factors responsible for the emergence of the new idea were the inner logic of economic science, the philosophical predilections of some of its students, and the practical requirements of applied economics.

FORERUNNERS

The story begins in 1814 with certain suggestions made by Malthus, in which he called attention to the potential usefulness of differential calculus for economics and related sciences. Here it was the inner logic of the science that enabled one of the masters, equipped with great gifts of intuition as well as with training in mathematics, to hit upon a new idea. Ten years later Perronet Thompson, who like Malthus had excelled as a student of mathematics at Cambridge, became the first writer in English economics to employ the calculus in economic analysis. The problem that Thompson posed was to maximize the gain of a government that purchases goods and services with paper money, the issue of which is attended by rising prices. His article "On the Instrument of Exchange" was published in the first issue of the *Westminster Review*, the Benthamites' newly founded periodical, of which Thompson later became co-owner and editor and whose title page he embellished after Bentham's death with a medallion of the latter and the motto *maxima felicitas*. Hence the first response to Malthus's suggested employment of the calculus, with its maxima and minima, came from a member of a group whose master, Bentham, made maxima of pleasure and minima of pain the cornerstones of his philosophy and who had indeed coined the words *maximize* and *minimize*. One of the roots of marginal analysis can thus be traced to the world of Bentham, who himself had hit upon the idea of diminishing marginal utility.

Thompson's article was meant to be a contribution to the practical problems of the time—the third factor that impelled the early pioneers of marginal analysis. Thus in 1815 a continental writer, Georg von Buquoy, who stressed the managerial side of economics, advised farmers to maximize their net revenue by holding production at a level at which the first derivative disappears and the second becomes negative. Later on, when new economic problems emerged with the operation of railroads, similar ideas were advanced. In 1839 Charles Ellet, a noted American railroad builder, applied calculus to determine an optimum tariff that would maximize profits.

COURNOT AND DEMAND THEORY

Malthus's pathbreaking suggestion, Thompson's response, and the attempts at practical application of calculus found only a dim echo. Of much greater, though delayed, consequence was the publication in 1838 of a book by Augustin Cournot, *Researches into the Mathematical Principles of the Theory of Wealth,* which contained the first systematic elaboration of the marginal principle as applied to the theory of the firm.

Cournot (1801–77) was a scholar with notable accomplishments in mathematics and philosophy, a college president, and high official in the educational administration of France. His work in mathematical economics, which received little recognition during his lifetime, stood at the periphery of a career that was crowned with success. He was led to this work when as a student of the economic literature he came across an earlier piece of mathematical economics, found it faulty, and decided to improve it. The outcome was the first sustained effort to construct a mathematical economics of the "pure" type, which yields general propositions of formal validity rather than operational ones suitable for statistical testing, such as fall into the province of the earlier political arithmetic or the later econometrics.

That in this work he went far beyond the accomplishments of his forerunners may be ascribed to the cumulative effects of two sets of circumstances which in his case converged: The approach that the inner logic of economic science impressed upon him conformed also to the philosophical tradition of French rationalism. The followers of Bentham would find guidance in the maximum happiness principle in their search for optimum positions. But Bentham's world was not the world of Cournot. His lodestar was not utilitarianism but the rationalism of the French philosophical tradition, which trusted in the powers of reason to reveal a mathematically ordered world. Descartes, from whom this philosophy stemmed, had also been the discoverer of analytical geometry, whose system of coordinates now became the parade ground for the display of the new approach to economics.

It was thus no accident that French scholars excelled in the field of pure mathematical economics and that their work was cumulative and progressive, reaching its full flowering in the thought of Walras, which was linked with that of Cournot. The reliance on reason rather than on experience distinguished their approach from political arithmetic and econometrics. Reason forms a contrast not only with experience but also with unreason, and rationalism is opposed to empiricism as well as to the voluntarism that often is the expression of an irrationalist philosophy. Those who conceive the world as rationally ordered usually show little inclination to extol the role of the human will. Thus the rationalism that provided the background for the approach of the French mathematical economists might find its explicit or implicit supplementation in an antivoluntarism extolling the automatic mechanism of the market rather than the conscious planning of a self-directed humanity. In the parametric function of prices, to which individuals and firms adjust, Smith's invisible hand reached out for a firm grasp on the new economics.

Much of the content of Cournot's economics, pathbreaking as it was at his time, seems commonplace now since in the form given to it later in the influential writings of Marshall and others it has shaped the basic structure of twentieth-century economics. There was, to begin with, Cournot's interpretation of such economic concepts as demand and cost as functional ones, in which physical quantities are related to demand prices and costs, a point of view that gave a new interpretation to matters that had long formed the inventory of economics but whose orderly treatment had been frustrated by inadequate techniques. With Cournot, demand schedules and functions and downward sloping demand curves enter into the literature of economics, as do the related concepts of marginal revenue and marginal cost. Starting with the single hypothesis that each person seeks to derive the greatest possible value from his goods or his labor, Cournot first develops the theory of monopoly, virtually in the same form that a century later became the standard doctrine. The monopolist, that is, the seller of a unique product, who is eager to maximize his net revenue, will charge a price at which marginal revenue equals marginal cost. By gradually increasing the number of sellers, Cournot eventually arrives at the competitive case, and his discussion yields a full-fledged theory of the firm operating in various types of markets. The theory of duopoly, which he develops in this context, was the first of many attempts to arrive at a determinate solution of this difficult case. In Cournot's model each of the duopolists proceeds on the assumption that when he maximizes his net revenue the rival will not react to this by modifying his policy regarding output which he has hitherto pursued. The reaction nevertheless takes place, and each duopolist engages in a series of successive adjustments aiming at the maximization of his net revenue under the conditions established by the policy of the rival. The equilibrium position, which is reached when further adjustments would bring no improvement, is characterized by a price lower than that charged by a monopolist and by an output exceeding that of a monopolist. As the number of sellers increases, price declines and output rises until the competitive case is reached.

The employment of equations and diagrams in Cournot's work alienated many readers. As he grew older, the lack of recognition accorded to his contribution induced him to publish new books on economics from which the mathematics was eliminated. These are now forgotten, but his original approach in his earlier work had a profound influence on later generations of economists. In the 1870s Walras put Cournot's systems of equations to new use and, following the path that Cournot had broken, reached out for still loftier heights of generalization. In the 1890s Marshall, who aimed at greater realism, would implant his own constructions on Cournot's theory of the firm, to whose basic structure he adhered in the essentials. In his own development of the theory of monopoly Marshall, however, followed a slightly different path, and this delayed the incorporation of the marginal revenue concept into the corpus of economic theory for another thirty years until it reemerged in the writings of a new generation of economists.

THÜNEN AND MARGINAL PRODUCTIVITY

Cournot's application of the marginal principle to the theory of the firm had its parallel in kindred scientific stirrings in Germany where, however, the marginal principle was primarily employed in the theory of production. The pioneer contribution here was by Johann Heinrich von Thünen (1783–1850), a learned estate owner, mathematician, and student of scientific agriculture, who on the basis of detailed farm records carefully and patiently maintained over a number of years wrote a series of volumes entitled *The Isolated State* (1826–63). Thünen searched for the empirical verification of certain leading ideas at which he had intuitively arrived at an early age. He had constructed the model of an isolated, or as he originally meant to call it, ideal state, when he was only twenty years old, and it dominated much of his further work, as did the later idea of a natural wage, denoted by $\sqrt{ap}$, where the one variable stands for the worker's subsistence and the other for his product, a formula considered so important by Thünen that he had it inscribed on his tombstone.

The isolated state was to serve as a model of a closed economy of uniform fertility, with a city forming its market center and with farm production specializing along optimal lines, reflecting the distance from the market, in a number of concentric circles around the city. As the distance from the city lengthened, production would gradually become more extensive and shift from market gardening over intermediate stages to pasture. This model constituted an early exercise in the theory of location and served as a starting point for the later science of regional economics.

In the present context, however, it is not Thünen's isolated state or his natural wage that calls for attention but the application of marginal analysis to the theory of production which recurs in several passages of his work and opened up a vista of the marginal productivity theory of distribution. Thünen's treatment anticipates what later came to be known as the principle of variable proportion and that of substitution. He varies labor inputs while holding capital constant, and vice versa, and underlines the impact of variations in factor and product prices on the optimum input mix. His analysis culminates in the statement that net revenue is maximized when the value of the marginal product (*Wert des Mehrertrags*) is equal to marginal factor cost (*Mehraufwand*). The road to the marginal productivity theory of distribution is opened by the remark that the productivity of capital must be measured by the marginal product that a constant labor input yields if combined with an increased capital input, and conversely that the productivity of labor is to be measured by the marginal product yielded by a constant capital input combined with an increased labor input. Although this discussion proceeds in verbal terms, it is nevertheless oriented in terms of calculus and partial derivatives, concepts to which Thünen explicitly refers.

Thünen's work was widely acclaimed during his lifetime, but as he himself complained, few readers appreciated the significance of his contribution to technical economics. Several generations had to pass before others would rediscover the marginal productivity theory and secure it a place in a refurbished economics. As with Cournot, Thünen's principal influence was felt by later generations of economists, more specifically by Marshall, who singled out Cournot and Thünen as the men to whose work he owed a substantial debt.

Much more than to the theories of the firm and of production, precedents abound that suggest the application of the marginal principle to the theory of the consumer. As has been noted, the marginal principle had been applied to income and wealth by Bernoulli in 1738, and other eighteenth-century writers considered value in terms of the utility of a good rather than in terms of labor. Galiani and a few others had a vision of marginal utility and its diminution. Later, and especially during the first half of the nineteenth century, Bentham and a number of academic economists at Oxford and Dublin stressed utility as a determinant of value and even pointed out that the utility of an incremental quantity of a good diminishes with an increase in the total stock. Because of Mill's disinclination to develop a full-fledged theory of consumption in coordination with the theories of production and distribution, these ideas failed to be absorbed into the mainstream of the classical tradition as modified by Mill's *Principles*. Mill's reluctance had its point because the development of the theory of the consumer along the principle of marginal utility would have undermined the labor theory of value, as it did later. Since Mill wanted to adhere to the structure of the classical system of which the labor theory of value formed the capstone, he was compelled to neglect the suggestions made by Bentham and by the Oxford and Dublin economists.

GOSSEN AND UTILITY THEORY

The first writer, and one entirely neglected by contemporary opinion, who developed a full-fledged theory of consumption and grounded it in the marginal principle was Hermann Heinrich Gossen (1810–58), a native of the Rhineland. His life seems to have been a series of frustrations and failures, culminating in the lack of attention to what he expected to be its crowning achievement, the publication in 1854 of a book entitled *Development of the Laws of Human Relationships and of the Rules to Be Derived Therefrom for Human Action*. Gossen's work differed from that of Cournot or Thünen in that it went beyond the development of scientific principles by proclaiming the writer's philosophy of life—a consequent utilitarianism, calling on man to maximize the pleasure attainable during his life and ascribing this purpose of man's earthly existence to the divine design. So firmly was Gossen convinced of the far-reaching importance of his message that he started his book by comparing it with the discoveries of Copernicus and ended it with the promise that the acceptance of his doctrines would turn the world into a paradise.

In its substance Gossen's analysis of utility anticipated that of Jevons, as did his curves, although the detail of his procedure showed certain peculiarities, for example, the x-axis generally measured time rather than quantities of a good, and the relationships portrayed by the curves were linear ones represented by straight lines and further illustrated by Gossen with the help of elaborate arithmetic examples. Gossen admitted that utility is not directly measurable but nevertheless considered it legitimate to have the y-axis represent it. He pointed out that the spatial relations elucidated by the principles of geometry do not require direct measurement and referred expressly to astronomy, in which the possibility of direct measurement is forever precluded. Gossen's analysis culminated in two propositions which in the later continental literature came to be designated as his first and second laws: (1) the marginal utility—or, in Gossen's phrase, the value of the last atom—of a perfectly divisible good diminishes as the quantity of the good increases; and, derived from this, (2) the total utility of a given quantity of a good that serves several uses is at its maximum when the marginal utility is equal in all uses.

Gossen's contribution was not recognized until 1878, twenty years after his death, when a colleague of Jevons brought Gossen's book to his attention. Jevons communicated the discovery to Walras, and both resuscitated the memory of their forerunner, Jevons in the preface to the second edition of his *Theory of Political Economy* of 1879 and Walras in a series of articles in which he drew attention to Gossen's work. In Gossen's German homeland, where the intellectual tendencies were, if possible, even more inimical to utilitarianism than to natural law, the historical economists had no use for Gossen's approach and for a long time treated his work with a mixture of condescension and ridicule. As late as 1929 Sombart referred to him as an "ingenious idiot," one responsible for much mischief.

JEVONS, MENGER, AND WALRAS

Far more consequential than the work of Gossen was the almost simultaneous publication in the 1870s of books by Jevons, Menger, and Walras, in which the marginal principle was again applied to the behavior of the consumer. Their work had far-reaching results, which included the replacement of the labor theory of value by one stressing utility; the derivation, from the principle of diminishing margial utility, of the law of demand, which Cournot had postulated as given by the nature of things; and the eventual recognition of the marginal principle as the central and unifying one in economics.

The new views did not gain ground immediately and recognition was slow in coming, especially for Walras, whose message, as far as novelty and scope of the theory were concerned, went beyond that of the others. Why they were successful where their predecessors had failed is a question that has been much debated but defies definitive conclusions. Relevant considerations include the fact that all three were academic economists whose works had a prima facie claim to attention, especially since their case was cogently and persuasively argued in presentations far superior to Gossen's, for example. Moreover, there was strength in numbers, or more exactly, in variety, since each of the three turned out a product that was somewhat different from that of the others and might appeal to readers inappreciative of the products of the others. This diversity enabled them to proceed along different fronts, as it were, and to reach a wider audience than the thrust of single-minded uniformity could have captured.

Mathematics, then something more likely to deter than to attract readers, was not employed by Menger, nor did he present his analysis as part of a utilitarian view of the world, a philosophy with little following in North America and on the continent of Europe. Jevons did employ mathematics but in his own environment could find extenuating circumstances in the fact that, notwithstanding the novel method of argumentation, the substance of his argument was a consistent development of the ideas of Bentham, still a living tradition in England. Furthermore, Menger had the good fortune of being able to find gifted and faithful pupils, who disseminated his message in distinguished works of their own. The early publication of English translations of these works brought Menger's message to readers in the United States and elsewhere to whom Jevons's mathematics and his utilitarianism would not have appealed.

As the economic doctrines of Marx began to spread on the Continent, Menger's followers became aware of the potentialities of the new subjective theory of value as an instrument for demolishing Marx's economics, derived, as it was, from the labor theory of value. Members of the Austrian school, as Menger and his group came to be called, constituted the earliest and most effective critics of Marx. Although Menger's own principal works antedate the spread of Marx's doctrines and although Walras was a Socialist of sorts, economists who were groping for intellectual ammunition against the ideas of Marx would find in marginal utility economics and in the subjective theory of value an alternative if not an antidote to these ideas, the more so since followers of Marx expressed strong opposition to the new economics. While on the Continent the new economics was drawn into the conflict between Socialists and anti-Socialists, developments followed a different course in England. There the influence of Marx was too slight to make adherence to the labor theory of value a matter of principle to British Socialists, some of whom became early converts to Jevons's version of the new theory of value. In the absence of a divisive struggle over the theory of value, influential members of a later generation of British academic economists such as Pigou and Mrs. Robinson could start their march into socialism without having to accept the ponderous legacy of the labor theory of value and without relinquishing the standard toolbox of academic economics.

If an attempt is made to assess the contribution of each of the three —Menger, Walras, and Jevons—a distinction should be made regarding the terms of reference of such an assessment. If the contribution of each is weighed in terms of its effectiveness in securing the acceptance of the marginal principle and of the subjective theory of value, the prize probably falls to Menger and his disciples because of their employment of conventional modes of argumentation and for reasons indicated in the preceding paragraphs. If, however, the scope and novelty of the contribution to economic theory are the test, the odds favor Walras because to him is due not merely a variant of marginal utility economics and of the subjective theory of value but also the general equilibrium system, a contribution in which the others had no share and one virtually without precedent in the previous doctrinal history.

Again, if it is not the contribution to economic theory in the narrower sense that counts but the originality of the writer's approach to economic studies, Jevons's claim as a pacesetter is stronger than that of the others. Neither the Austrians nor Walras, outstanding theorists as they were, had an empirical bent. It was only Jevons who excelled both as a theorist and as an empirical investigator and whose quantitative studies foreshadowed the rise of econometrics in the twentieth century. In this sense it was Jevons who, more than the two others, was the pioneer modern economics. Although he left no school to inculcate his approach on later generations of economists, his type of work had greater affinity with the principal concerns of economists a century later than did the pure theorizing of Menger and Walras. Significantly enough, Jevons not only anticipated the trend toward econometrics but also produced a "logical machine, "a remote ancestor of the modern computer, which can still be seen in the History of Science Museum at Oxford.

JEVONS

William Stanley Jevons (1835–82) left his mark not only on economics but on other disciplines as well. His works on logic served as textbooks for successive generations of students in many parts of the world and brought his name before an audience whose numbers originally exceeded by far the readership of his economic studies. Jevons's short life was filled with accomplishments which the eagerness and resolute devotion of an original and versatile mind was able to bring to fruition against many obstacles. He was born into the business patriciate of Liverpool, into a highly cultured family of nonconformists with wide connections, but the bankruptcy of the parental business in 1848 threw him on his own resources at an early age. Without completing his education at University College in London, he accepted while still in his teens a position as an assayer to the mint in Sydney and spent almost five years in Australia. When his savings seemed adequate to finance his further education, he relinquished the many opportunities that beckoned in the new country and went home. Even at that time he felt a sense of mission, which made him rise, not against failure, but against success in a work in which his genius would not find fulfillment.

On his return to London he resumed his studies and branched out from his previous specialization in mathematics and chemistry into logic and economics. Having to pay the price for being a pioneer and innovator, he was not first in his examination in economics but had to be satisfied with third or fourth place. Since he was drawn to research and writing, he hoped to make his way as a free-lance author after the completion of his studies. When he failed in this attempt, he became connected, through the friendly interest of a cousin, with Owens College in Manchester, now the University of Manchester and one of the glories of English higher education, but then newly founded and struggling to attract students worthy of its excellent six professors. Jevons served at Owens College from 1863 to 1876, first as a tutor to backward students and from 1866 on, when his writings had spread his fame, as professor of logic, mental and moral philosophy, and political economy. While at Owens College, Jevons married a daughter of the founder of the *Manchester Guardian,* a woman whose name curiously enough was the same as that of Mill's wife. His teaching was not free of frustrations since he felt it his duty to prepare his students for the examinations given by University College in London, which meant that their instruction had to be oriented along the standard doctrines based on Mill's writings rather than along his own ideas. In 1876 Jevons left Manchester and accepted a professorship of political economy at University College, which required lectures only once a week and gave him more time for research and writing. These were still his preferred tasks, and in 1880 he severed all teaching connections to devote himself to them full time. Two years later he met his death in a drowning accident—he was not yet forty-seven years old.

Jevons's scholarship followed a path on which from its beginning both reason and experience shed their strong light. He was equally attracted to the creation of formal structures of thought, in which the mind builds up its own world, and to the look-and-see approach of the empirical investigator who uncovers new facets of the external world. In Australia, as a youth of barely twenty, he carried on empirical studies which extended from meteorology to job classifications and social surveys—his studies in meteorology secured a permanent place for him in the scientific annals of that country.

At the same time, Jevons's wide reading led him to economics and statistics. About the structure of economics he soon formed ideas of his own, and in 1857, at the age of twenty-one, he included in the agenda listed in his diary the words "Write work on Formal Economics." A number of early remarks by Jevons made it appear likely that this work would be informed by mathematics, a field in which he had been trained by a master teacher and of whose potentialities he stood in awe. In 1858 he confided to his sister that he considered it his mission to apply himself to such subjects as economics, asserting an insight into the foundations and nature of the knowledge of man deeper than that of most writers. In 1860, when not yet twenty-five, he discovered the "true theory of economy," the utility theory, and in 1862 he submitted a brief paper, which in outline form contained all the essential elements of his system, to Section F of the British Association for the Advancement of Science, at whose meeting it was read without, however, striking a responsive chord. Disappointed in his expectations, Jevons then turned to other work and resumed the elaboration of his economic theory in the late 1860s, and then in great haste. By that time correspondence with Fleeming Jenkin, a noted engineering authority, made him aware that his priority might be threatened by parallel discoveries of Jenkin's, made public in articles that referred to demand and supply functions (1868) and contained demand and supply curves (1870).

The result of Jevons's work was the publication, in 1871, of *The Theory of Political Economy,* which constituted his principal contribution to economic theory, a new beginning since at that time he was not acquainted with the books of Cournot, Thünen, or Gossen. His own work, therefore, was not an organic development of the works of these men, although there may have been an indirect link to Cournot by way of Dionysius Lardner's *Railway Economy* (1850), known to Jevons since 1857 and singled out by him as a source of inspiration for the mathematical treatment of economics. Lardner, a brilliant popularizer, was a mediator between English and French thought, who had settled in Paris after relinquishing his professorship of natural philosophy and astronomy at University College in London in consequence of an elopement with the wife of a cavalry officer. Whether Lardner owed an intellectual debt to Cournot for some of the ideas developed in the *Railway Economy,* no one knows. There is no direct evidence that Lardner had ever read Cournot's *Researches.* All that is known of the Cournot-Lardner connection is that Cournot had translated another book by Lardner into French in 1835 and that both lived in Paris in 1850 when Lardner published his *Railway Economy.* The substance of Lardner's argument, to which Jevons approvingly referred, was an exposition of the equilibrium of the monopolist, accompanied by a graph and expressing ideas similar to Cournot's. However, beyond acknowledging the influence of Lardner's method, Jevons did not follow up the substance of the matter, and his work contains neither a theory of the firm nor demand and supply curves, although such curves and their intersection had been given attention in his lectures since 1863.

THE UTILITY THEORY

The starting point of Jevons's analysis was the theory of utility. From this he derived a theory of exchange, and he rounded out his book with chapters on labor, rent, and capital. Economics, he held, required a mathematical treatment because it deals with quantities. These he assumed to be subject to continuous variations, an assumption that makes possible graphic representation and the employment of differential calculus, with its infinitesimally small quantities. Jevons's reliance on mathematical forms of reasoning reflected his earlier training in natural science. He was eager to apply to economics the same methods that had proved so fruitful in physics and chemistry.

Jevons's utility theory contained frequent references to Bentham, and in line with Bentham's approach Jevons visualized economics as a "calculus of pleasure and pain." To the objection that units of pleasure or pain are difficult to conceive and that such feelings of the human heart cannot directly be measured, Jevons replied that the effects of these feelings are noticeable in the common transactions of everyday economic life and that "it is from the quantitative effects of the feelings that we must estimate their comparative amounts."

Jevons interpreted utility in subjective and relative terms, that is, not as an intrinsic quality of things but as "a circumstance of things arising out of their relation to man's requirements." Citing a number of forerunners, he argued that portions of the same commodity do not possess equal utility. Up to a certain quantity, a commodity may be indispensable. Further quantities have various degrees of utility, and beyond a certain quantity the utility gradually sinks to zero and may even become negative as further supplies become inconvenient and hurtful. In line with these observations, he distinguished between total utility and what Wicksteed and Marshall later called "marginal utility," the latter designated by him as "final degree of utility" and defined as "the degree of utility of the last addition, or the next possible addition of a very small, or infinitely small, quantity to the existing stock." In the language of differential calculus, final degree of utility is the differential coefficient of utility with respect to quantity. As each incremental quantity of a good satisfies a less pressing want, the final degree of utility declines as its quantity rises. Jevon's utility theory culminated in the theorem, equivalent to Gossen's second law, that the total utility derived from a good that has several uses will be maximized when the final degrees of utility are equal in all uses. In his analysis he employed equations as well as diagrams, mainly showing curves of falling marginal utility, with quantities of the good measured along the x-axis and utility along the y-axis and the area under the curve indicating total utility.

From Jevons's statement of Gossen's second law it required just a short step to arrive at the modern formulation of the equilibrium of the consumer, in which the latter so distributes his expenditure that the marginal utility of each good acquired stands in the same proportion to its price. The equality here is not one of marginal utilities but, as Pareto designated them, of weighted marginal utilities, that is, of marginal utility divided by price. When these weighted marginal utilities are equal, the last small unit of expenditure, spent in every direction, conveys the same addition to total utility, and total utility is at its maximum.

Jevons's utilitarianism was not absolute in the sense that the maximization of pleasure, which he declared to be the problem of economics, would override all other considerations. He in fact distinguished between the calculus of utility, relevant to economics, and the "higher calculus of moral right and wrong," and subordinated the former to the latter. Only in matters of moral indifference was the calculus of utility to rule supreme. Jevons was also aware of the possibility of divesting the utility concept of its utilitarian implications, a possibility hinted at by his occasional remark that any motive that attracts us to a certain course of conduct might be called pleasure, and any motive that deters us from that conduct, pain, a thought that, had he pursued it further, might have brought him close to Menger's position.

Jevons did not explicitly distinguish between cardinal and ordinal measurements of pleasure or utility, but the caution with which he approached the whole subject of measuring utility makes him a forerunner of the ordinal approach. He considered it "seldom or never" possible to express one pleasure as an exact multiple of another or to estimate the total amount of pleasure gained by the purchase of a commodity or from the return for a day's labor. His theory, he pointed out, did not require the comparison of total quantities of utility and instead was satisfied by comparisons of nearly equal small increments, for example, between the extra utility of a small additional purchase of a quantity of a good and its money price or between the small disutility of additional work and the similarly small utility of additional possessions derived from it. Jevons also refused to make interpersonal comparisons of utility, which in fact he considered impossible. "The susceptibility of one mind," he pointed out, "may, for what we know, be a thousand times greater than that of another." He insisted that his theory did not require such comparisons. Jevons's restraint in this matter contrasts with Bentham's straightforward egalitarianism, which makes each person count for one, as well as with the divergent Mill-Edgeworth tradition of according discriminate treatment to persons with different capacities for enjoyment.

Jevons's theory of exchange, which he grafted on his utility theory, contains as its "keystone" the proposition that the ratio of exchange of any two commodities will be the reciprocal of the ratios of the marginal utilities of the quantities of goods available for consumption after completion of the exchange, or, in mathematical symbols,

$$(1) \qquad \frac{\phi_1 (a - x)}{\psi_1 y} = \frac{y}{x} = \frac{\phi_2 x}{\psi_2 (b - y)} \ .$$

Since he ascribed an extraordinary significance to this proposition, the procedure by which he arrived at it will be traced step by step.

If A holds the quantity a of corn, and B the quantity b of beef, A will surrender units of corn in return for units of beef, and B units of beef in return for units of corn as long as each considers the loss of utility incurred by the surrender of a unit of the one commodity as less than the gain of utility attending the acquisition of a unit of the other commodity. After A has bartered x units of corn for y units of beef,

> A holds a-x units of corn, and y of beef, and
> B holds x units of corn, and b-y of beef.

The marginal utilities of the two goods are:

> to A: $\qquad \phi_1 (a - x)$ $\qquad$ and $\psi_1 y$;
> to B: $\qquad \phi_2 x$ $\qquad\qquad$ and $\psi_2 (b - y)$.

A and B will continue to barter by exchanging an infinitesimally small amount dx for an infinitesmally small amount dy as long as each can thereby add to his total utility. This will be so as long as A derives a greater marginal utility from dy than from dx, and B a higher marginal utility from dx than from dy. Continued exchange lowers the marginal utility of the good acquired and raises that of the good surrendered. When the marginal utilities of both goods have become equal, opportunities to add to total utility by further exchange cease. A attains the maximum total utility when

$$(2) \qquad \phi_1 (a - x) \cdot dx = \psi_1 y \cdot dy,$$

and B does so when

$$(3) \qquad \psi_2 (b - y) \cdot dy = \phi_2 x \cdot dx.$$

Equations (2) and (3) can be rearranged in this fashion:

$$(4) \qquad \frac{\phi_1(a-x)}{\psi_1 y} = \frac{dy}{dx}$$

$$(5) \qquad \frac{\phi_2 x}{\psi_2(b-y)} = \frac{dy}{dx}$$

If $\frac{y}{x}$ is substituted for $\frac{dy}{dx}$, a procedure permissible according to Jevons's law of indifference, the result is the equation of exchange (1).

Jevons's theory of exchange was designed to apply to a market defined by him as consisting of two or more persons dealing in two or more commodities and equipped with perfect knowledge as regards stocks, intentions of the exchangers, and the ratio of exchange. His market thus encompassed the entire range of situations extending from bilateral monopoly to competition. As a correlative to his market concept he introduced the notion of "trading bodies" on the buying and selling sides, made up of single individuals or aggregates of individuals. It was his intention to develop this monolithic theory of the market because he believed that the same principles of exchange, as elucidated in equation (1), control all markets, regardless of the number of buyers and sellers.

Jevons's law of indifference, which allows the substitution of $\frac{y}{x}$ for $\frac{dy}{dx}$, holds that in the same market all portions of a homogeneous good must be exchanged in the same ratio, any portion being indifferently usable in place of an equal portion.

Modern economic theory, which acknowledges that there is only one price in one market, has assimilated Jevons's law of indifference but not his construction of a trading body and his related view that the equation of exchange—an exchange that has trading bodies as its partners—sheds light on all types of market structures. If it is applied to the case of an isolated barter or bilateral monopoly, it leaves indeterminate the ratio of exchange, which Jevons assumed as given in a numerical example. Jevons also meant to apply the equation of exchange to the case of the competitive market, but here the solution requires a number of intermediary steps leading to the derivation of demand curves from utility curves, a problem that Jevons did not attack and which was resolved by Walras and Marshall.

JEVONS'S ANALYSIS OF REAL COST

Just as Jevons refrained from deriving demand curves from utility curves, so he refrained from the derivation of money cost and supply curves. Instead he developed more fully a theory of real cost, expressed in terms of feelings of disutility or pain, an analysis that, although not yielding a theory of the firm, did shed light on the determinants of the supply of labor. He visualized work as initially irksome but becoming pleasurable over a certain range of hours of moderate length. After this range was passed, labor would again become irksome, and increasingly so with a longer number of hours. Work would come to a stop when the falling marginal utility of the worker's product or of his wages was exactly offset by the increasing marginal disutility of effort. If work ceased earlier, the marginal utility of the product would exceed the marginal disutility of labor, that is, there would still be an opportunity to add to total utility by continued work. If work ceased later, the marginal utility of the product would fall short of the marginal disutility of labor, and total utility could be increased by a reduction of working hours. Jevons's analysis, ingenious as it is, has exerted little influence on modern economic thought because it is grounded in the unrealistic assumption that hours of work are under the control of the individual worker.

THE DEMISE OF THE LABOR THEORY OF VALUE

The rise of Jevons's utility theory marked the demise of the labor theory of value. As Jevons pointed out, the labor theory of value lacked generality since it was only meant to apply to goods that could be reproduced with the help of labor. Moreover, in the range of situations where it was supposed to apply, a glance at prices actually charged in the market demonstrated that these did not reflect the quantities of labor embodied in goods.

To these considerations might be added the diversity of circumstances that attended the inception of the labor theory of value and that prevailed at Jevons's time. When Locke alluded to the labor theory of value, he did so in the context of his labor theory of property, which was designed to buttress private property against arbitrary and despotic governments. Meanwhile two hundred years had passed, governments had been tamed, at least in Britain, and in the Victorian age, of which Jevons was a contemporary, the security of private property might well have appeared strong enough even to a prudent observer to make him inclined to discard the labor theory of property, which indeed by that time had largely been superseded by other theories. With the changed circumstances it was also time to discard its appendage, the labor theory of value, the more so since first the Ricardian Socialists and later Marx had completely changed the function of the labor theory, which in the Lockean context was designed to protect private property. Instead they had transformed it from an instrument of sanctification of private property into an instrument of denigration of private property, which the theory of surplus value depicted as the result of exploitation. Jevons's text does not indicate any awareness on his part of these considerations, but they help to explain the readiness with which the labor theory of value was discarded as the nineteenth century came to its close.

In Jevons's analysis, utility and scarcity replaced labor as determinants of value. Instead of the classics' divorce of exchange value from use value, both were interpreted by him in terms of utility, the latter denoting total and the former marginal utility. Instead of the classics' emphasis on supply and cost as affecting value, Jevons singled out the factors operating behind the demand side. In the classical analysis value was considered as arising from the conditions of the external world, hence the designation of the value theory of the classics as an objective one. Jevons's theory was subjective in the sense that he derived value from a "distinct feeling" or from the state of mind, albeit one influenced by the external factor of scarcity.

Since the classics taught that goods had value because they embodied labor, in their view the value of the product reflected the value of the productive service. Jevons, on the other hand, derived the value of the productive service from that of the product, holding, for example, that the value of labor "must be determined by the value of the produce, not the value of the produce by that of the labor." Although he did not fully develop a view of marginal productivity in the general sense, he did so with respect to interest, which he interpreted in terms of the marginal productivity of capital.

Jevons refused to designate labor as a direct determinant of value, but he nevertheless conceded that the value of a good might be indirectly affected by labor. The amount of labor devoted to the production of a good influences its supply, and supply in turn has its effects on the degree of utility of the good, which governs the ratio of exchange. Jevons expressed this chain of reasoning as follows:

Cost of production determines supply;
Supply determines final degree of utility;
Final degree of utility determines value.

Later students of economic theory have found fault with the argument implied in this chain because it points to a time sequence with cause-and-effect relationships rather than to a simultaneous relationship of mutual interdependence. The work of Walras, which stressed the second type of approach, rather than the work of Jevons, has served as the principal inspiration for modern economic analysis.

JEVONS'S EMPIRICAL STUDIES

Although Jevons's *Theory of Political Economy* presumed to investigate the condition of the mind of the individual, it contained passages that underlined the significance of economic aggregates and of average behavior and hinted at the derivation of statistical demand curves. Notwithstanding these references, however, the *Theory of Political Economy,* grounded as it was in utility theory, was not developed in operational terms which would facilitate measurement and statistical testing. Thus, as far as Jevons's principal contribution to economic theory is concerned, he was more an exponent of pure mathematical economics than an econometrician. The econometric side of his work stands out in a number of quantitative-empirical studies on which he began to work in the early 1860s, articles which after his death were collected in a volume entitled *Investigations* in *Currency and Finance* (1884). In addition, Jevons published a book, *The Coal Question* (1865), which likewise contained an integration of theoretical and empirical work.

The Coal Question was an early study of conservation and a message of pessimism similar to that of Malthus's population theory. In it Jevons enunciated a "natural law of social growth," which he presumed proceeded in a geometric progression. With the repeal of the corn laws, he pointed out, the progress of the British economy was no longer restrained by corn, as Malthus had taught, but by coal, an exhaustible resource which had become the kingpin of the British economy. The demand for coal, he warned, which had grown at a geometric rate, could at that rate not be satisfied for long. "So far, then," he concluded, "as our wealth and progress depend upon the superior command of coal we must not only cease to progress as before—we must begin a retrograde career."

The quantitative studies by Jevons that were assembled in *Investigations in Currency and Finance* have as their central theme the subject of economic fluctuations. Having early in his career been a practicing meteorologist, Jevons approached the study of the fluctuations of the economic climate with the meticulous care of the student of natural science. By means of patient and painstaking statistical work, which was accorded recognition only haltingly, and without the help of statistical clerks and calculating machines, Jevons succeeded in isolating the three great fluctuations whose rhythm determines the beat of the economy: seasonal movements, business cycles, and secular trends. His attempt, made late in life, to link the business cycle with ten-year variations of the sunspots contrasts with an earlier hint interpreting it in terms of fluctuations of investment. The critical attention that has been given to his sunspot theory has tended to muffle the acclaim owed to Jevons's quantitative-empirical work, which was further enriched by contributions to index-number theory and by precedent-setting innovations in graphic presentation, including ratio charts.

Seen from the vantage point of the *ex post* observer, Jevons's inductive studies indeed mark, as Keynes said, "the beginning of a new stage in economic science," which achieved a blend of theory and history never before accomplished. Although Jevons's contemporaries could not benefit from the historical perspective which would have opened their eyes to the epoch-making character of his work, his studies nevertheless received the approving attention of Cairnes, Fawcett, and, particularly, Bagehot, who was impressed by the combination of abstract arguments and quantitative fact finding. The inductive side of Jevons's work could not fail to strike a chord of response among the historical economists, however little they would appreciate his later work in pure theory.

JEVONS'S INFLUENCE

The publication of *The Coal Question* turned its author, then thirty years old, into a personage whose acquaintance was sought by Gladstone and to whom Mill referred in flattering terms in Parliament. Thus, when *The Theory of Political Economy* came out six years later, Jevons had already established a highly creditable record as an author. Nevertheless, his credentials were not strong enough to secure a favorable response to the new ideas submitted in the book. As could be expected, historical economists would find fault with his abstract-generalizing approach and with the mathematical garb in which he clothed his ideas, whereas followers of the classics would insist on the retention of the labor theory of value. It was more surprising that Alfred Marshall, who soon would redirect economic theory along a path similar to the one that Jevons had broken, did not welcome Jevons as a comrade-in-arms but instead criticized his work in harsh terms. But in spite of the unfriendly reception accorded to Jevons's book, his position by that time was strong enough to attain honors and recognition. In 1872, like Petty and Malthus before him, he was elected a fellow of the Royal Society; the University of Cambridge called on his services as an external examiner in 1874–75; and in 1880 he was chosen vice-president of the Statistical Society of London, the forerunner of the Royal Statistical Society. He did not live long enough to accede to honors in the Royal Economic Society, which was founded in 1890, eight years after his death.

Jevons was also fortified by finding, in the writings of others, views paralleling his own, although this meant that he had to relinquish his claim as sole author of the new discoveries. Walras generously recognized Jevons's priority in the matter of the equation of the exchange and spread the knowledge of his work on the Continent, where mathematical economics found a favorable response especially in Italy. When toward the end of his life Jevons noticed a more positive attitude to the mathematical approach in England, this largely reflected the rising influence of Marshall's teaching. Marshall was seven years Jevons's junior but survived him for forty-two years, and his work, more than Jevons's, was responsible for the eventual acceptance of a new economics fostering marginal analysis and mathematical methods. Unlike Marshall, Jevons did not assemble a group of able pupils who would have recognized him as the leader of an influential school. Even if Jevons had been a more enthusiastic teacher than he was, Owens College did not offer such opportunities for recruiting able followers as were available at Cambridge University, with which Marshall was associated intermittently from the 1860s to 1908. Jevons's connection with University College in London lasted only four years. When he died, he had no substantial academic following, but some of his views influenced the thought of Edgeworth and of Wicksteed. They were, however, by no means uncritical followers of Jevons, whose authority soon became overshadowed by the living force of Marshall's work. Their approach differed from Marshall's, the other great theorist in the England of their time, in a number of respects, but their chief badge of distinction was the prominent place given by them, but not by Marshall, to the theory of utility, and in this respect they were the true heirs of Jevons.

Edgeworth and Wicksteed were equipped with versatile minds such as are rarely encountered in the modern age of specialization. Unlike Jevons, whose approach to economics was in substance that of a student of natural science, the field in which his early training had been concentrated, Edgeworth and Wicksteed were steeped in the classics, and to this day Wicksteed is as much remembered as a Dante scholar as for his contribution to economics. By way of mathematics, in which Wicksteed was self-trained, they came to economics, the study of which was carried on by Edgeworth as the vocation of a respected academician and by Wicksteed as a sideline activity of a Unitarian minister.

Wicksteed would succeed in converting influential Fabians to the new theory of value, but on the whole he, like Edgeworth, was principally an economists' economist rather than a students' economist. Although their work was more esoteric than Marshall's and did not have the wide appeal of the latter's teaching and writing, it nevertheless lent powerful support to the redirection of economics that Marshall achieved. Marshall and Edgeworth eventually held the professorships at Cambridge and at Oxford, and while Marshall turned Cambridge into the headquarters of the new economics, Francis Ysidro Edgeworth (1845–1926) abetted him from Oxford, where he occupied the Drummond chair from 1891 to 1922, and as long-term editor of the *Economic Journal,* which was founded in 1891 as the organ of the Royal Economic Society. Laboring in the shadow of Marshall, whose authority he freely acknowledged, Edgeworth never attempted a comprehensive work or a systematic treatise. His contributions to economics are found in his *Mathematical Psychics* of 1881 and in numerous periodical articles, which enriched virtually all phases of economic theory. Like Jevons, he was a confirmed utilitarian, and the utilitarian philosophy imbued all his writings. It was his aim to apply mathematics to the social sciences, and in the pursuit of it he came to recognize an affinity between the structure of utility and of belief. In the attempt to bring measurement to both structures, he made the one the focus of his work in economics and the other the point of departure for his contributions to probability theory and statistics.

THE INDIFFERENCE CURVE

Edgeworth's contributions to economics left their mark on the theories of monopoly, foreign trade, taxation, and production. In production theory, earlier authorities had generally employed the concept of an average product to demonstrate diminishing returns. It was Edgeworth who insisted on the distinction between the average and the marginal product and who underlined the significance of the latter in connection with the identification of the maximum position. In his *Mathematical Psychics* he expanded Jevons's utility function by relating the utility of a good not only to the quantity of the good that an individual possessed or consumed but also to the quantities of all other goods possessed or consumed by the individual—the value that a person attaches to another unit of food reflects not only how well he is fed but also how well he is housed, clothed, and so forth. In the same work he also introduced the indifference curve, the locus of combinations of two goods conveying equal total utility. With the help of a "contract curve" drawn through the points of tangency of indifference curves he demonstrated the indeterminate outcome of a bargain among bilateral monopolists. Later on Pareto would present the indifference curve in the form in which it eventually became a widely used tool of modern analysis and purge it of its utility content, but it was Edgeworth, an unusually clever mathematician, who originally devised this instrument. It was a curious irony that this tool, employed by its inventor in the context of his utility theory and charged with utilitarian implications, was later used to exorcise utility from the theory of the consumer, if not from economic analysis altogether.

WICKSTEED

Philip H. Wicksteed (1844–1927) belonged to that group of able economists who in the 1890s developed variants of a marginal productivity theory of distribution and with that offered a general and systematic exposition of an analysis hinted at in the earlier writings of Ricardo, Longfield, and Thünen. Wicksteed's part in the multiple discovery of the marginal productivity theory of distribution, which occurred twenty years after the multiple discovery of the utility theory of value by Jevons, Menger, and Walras, was a particularly distinguished one. Others might interpret, as he did, each factor's share in the product as the partial derivative of the product with respect to the factor input. Others might join him in relating the marginal productivity theory of distribution to the work of the classics and consider it a generalization of the Ricardian rent theory. But what was strictly his own contribution was the question that he raised which stimulated a discussion not yet terminated—the question whether and under what conditions the total product would be "exhausted" if each factor received its marginal product.

Wicksteed's answer to the "adding up" problem was that the total product is equal to the sum of the factor inputs each multiplied by its marginal product. He derived this answer from a theorem named after Leonard Euler, the great eighteenth-century mathematician, according to which the exhaustion of the product required a linear and homogeneous production function, the so-called homogeneous function of the first degree. In economic terms this meant that the distributive shares would exactly add up to the product, provided the production function was such that an increase of all inputs by a given constant would raise the product in the same proportion. In Wicksteed's view the exhaustion of the product thus required constant returns to scale, or the absence of economies or diseconomies of scale. Wicksteed's solution to the problem posed by him met opposition from Edgeworth, Pareto, and others, who directed their criticism primarily against the requirement of a linear and homogeneous production function. Moreover, Walras, who had earlier developed a marginal productivity theory of distribution on the narrow assumption of fixed and constant coefficients of production, now claimed that Wicksteed had failed to acknowledge his, Walras's, priority, and furthermore that Wicksteed's result, the exhaustion of the product, should be attributed to the effects of competition, which would reduce average cost to a minimum. In consequence of these attacks, Wicksteed was induced to give a halfhearted and equivocal recantation.

In the later debate on the properties of the production function a number of authorities continued to adhere to the requirement of first-order homogeneity, qualifying it perhaps by the recognition of indivisibilities, whereas others rejected it and pointed out that the exhaustion of the product occurred only in equilibrium, when total revenue equals total cost. Indeed, if the sum of factor shares is equal to the product only in equilibrium rather than being identical with it, as it would be if the production function were a homogeneous function of the first degree, exhaustion of the product in this narrower sense occurs regardless of the properties of the production function.

Wicksteed developed his marginal productivity theory in the *Essay on the Coordination of the Laws of Distribution* of 1894. Earlier, in 1888, he had published an introduction to the mathematical economics of the utility theory under the title *Alphabet of Economic Science*. Although this work reflected primarily the influence of Jevons, Wicksteed's later publication, *The Common Sense of Political Economy* (1910), showed the impact of the thought of the Austrians as well as of Walras and Pareto. The assimilation of the ideas of these men had its cost since it removed Wicksteed from the mainstream of the English tradition and led him further away from Marshall, who by that time had reached the summit of authority. For demand and supply analysis, which figured so prominently in Marshall's work, Wicksteed had only limited use. Instead he proposed to interpret the supply curve as a demand curve of those who possess the commodity, that is, as part of a total dèmand curve registering the relative scale of estimation accorded to each successive unit of a commodity. Wicksteed's disfavor of supply had its corollary in his rejection of real cost as a determinant of value. With value considered exclusively in terms of utility, cost would come into play only in the sense of foregone alternatives. As Wicksteed stated:

> At every stage the cost incurred in making a thing is the relinquished possibility of making other things, and its extent or amount is determined by the value, or marginal significance on the collective scale, which those other things would have had.

Under the influence of the Austrians and of Pareto, Wicksteed relinquished Jevons's utilitarianism and instead developed his argument in terms of scales of preference, however motivated. His thoughts on the nature of economics foreshadowed later formulations developed by

Lionel Robbins (b. 1898) in his influential *Essay on the Nature and Significance of Economic Science* (1932), the leading treatise on economic methods before the advent of macroeconomics. Wicksteed taught that economics treats of the administration of resources in such a way as to secure their maximum efficiency for the purpose contemplated. His reference to "the purposeful selection between alternative applications of resources" was to resound later in Robbins's definition of economics as the science that treats of the allocation of scarce resources among different uses.

Wicksteed further reasoned that all life consists of choosing between alternatives and thus denied that there are special laws of economic life. Instead, economic resources are administered along the same principles as those that regulate the conduct of life in general, that is, in terms not employed by Wicksteed, the principles derived from the logic of choice. The elevation of the logic of choice to an all-encompassing rule guiding human behavior in all its aspects has encouraged later writers to claim for economics a far wider scope than is conventionally accorded to it. This trend of thought culminated in the work of Ludwig von Mises (b. 1881), who in his book *Human Action: A Treatise on Economics* (1949) identified the science of human action with economics. The trend, in turn, converges with the efforts of philosophers and other scholars who attempt to construct a general science of human action—praxeology—which, however, is not necessarily grounded in the logic of choice.

Chapter 23

ECONOMICS RESTRUCTURED:

Marginalism

and Optimization

2.   THE AUSTRIAN SCHOOL: ACCENT ON UTILITY

MENGER

In 1871, the year in which Jevons published *The Theory of Political Economy* in England, there appeared in Vienna Menger's *Grundsätze der Volkswirtschaftslehre,* translated into English in 1950 under the title *Principles of Economics.* Unlike Jevons, Carl Menger (1840–1921), the Austrian co-discoverer of the marginal principle and of the subjective theory of value, was a graduate of the faculty of law, which in the academic tradition of the German-speaking countries was also in charge of instruction in economics. After a short interlude in financial journalism and government service, the publication of the *Grundsätze* brought Menger an appointment as instructor at the University of Vienna, where he held the chair of political economy from 1879 until his retirement in 1903. At that time Vienna was still the political and cultural center of a four-hundred-year-old and far-flung empire, which held together a great diversity of nationalities, including Germans, Hungarians, Czechs, Slovaks, Poles, and residents of the Balkans.

Menger, who also served as tutor and confidant of the heir to the Hapsburg throne, eventually occupied a commanding position in the academic economics of his native country. As his literary output was smaller than Jevons's, did not branch out into other disciplines, and did not require time-consuming quantitative studies of the type cultivated by Jevons, he could and did give close attention to his teaching duties, which he discharged with great distinction. He gained a substantial following among the young economists of his time, and his fame was spread abroad by enthusiastic students. As his influence grew, he came to be recognized as the unchallenged leader of the Austrian school.

In the intellectual environment of his homeland Menger did not have the Benthamite tradition to draw on for nourishment and inspiration, as did Jevons, and in his theorizing he faced the opposition of the historical economists of Germany, one far more deeply entrenched and enduring than that which Jevons encountered in England. If in spite of these obstacles Menger made important contributions to the pure theory of economics by developing a utility analysis culminating in the subjective theory of value, this accomplishment may be ascribed to the convergence of a number of disparate sets of circumstances. There was, to begin with, in the German-speaking countries the strong tradition of the philosophy of Kant's idealism, paralleling and rivaling that of Hegel, an idealism that interpreted the phenomena of the external world as creations of the human mind. There was an affinity between this philosophy and the subjective theory of value, which derived economic value from man's state of mind. The intellectual atmosphere generated by Kant's philosophy would foster the development of a subjective theory of value, regardless of whether or not the economist enunciating such a theory was a full-fledged Kantian. Earlier nineteenth-century economic thought in Germany contained a number of hints pointing toward a subjective theory of value, and Menger, unaware as he was of Gossen's complete analysis, which stemmed from Bentham, was influenced by these.

For the further development of these ideas German academic economics offered no fertile ground since it was dominated by historically-minded economists who had no use for abstract economic analysis and proposed to replace it by descriptive studies of concrete historical detail. It was no accident that an Austrian rather than a German economist transformed these incipient ideas into a full-fledged and influential structure of thought because historical economics did not gain a foothold in Austria. The reasons for this must be sought in the Austrian intellectual tradition and in the political circumstances that surrounded academic life in Vienna at Menger's time. As for the former, both the natural law heritage and the influence of the Enlightenment, the wellsprings of economic theorizing, had greater powers of survival in Austria than in Germany, where they succumbed to the idolatry of power. However inefficient, paternalistic, and at times ruthless the Austrian rule turned out to be during the nineteenth century, it never relinquished its claim to enlightened despotism. Joseph von Sonnenfels (1732–1817), the great cameralist, who in 1763 became the first occupant of a chair of economics at the University of Vienna, was a humanist imbued with the spirit of the Enlightenment. His views tempered the absolutism of his age and prepared the ground for the great reforms of Joseph II. Sonnenfels's textbook on economics was used in Austrian universities until 1848, and he left behind a legacy of liberal thought in economics and politics, much of which was dissipated during the period of romantic reaction in the early nineteenth century but which was never entirely lost.

From Sonnenfels's legacy there stemmed a faith in reason and a willingness to postulate general principles valid for all mankind. These dispositions, hostile as they were to historicism, derived further strength from the natural law idea, which, although it lost its hold in Germany proper, survived in Catholic Austria, there to fulfill a function not unlike that rendered by utilitarianism in England—to serve as a paradigm for the construction of general principles of economics. John Stuart Mill's theorizing and his liberal bent would preclude any profound influence of his work in Germany, even though German historical economists might pay lip service to his authority. It was in Austria that his work struck a chord of response. There he found a translator and there was published what for a century remained the only complete edition of his writings.

If the Austrian intellectual tradition was not receptive to a German historicism that denied the validity of an abstract-generalizing social science, this tradition gained powerful support from the political circumstances that attended Menger's work in Vienna, then the capital of a multinational empire which was rent by centrifugal pressures and on which the impending dissolution had already cast its shadow. The meticulous attention to and glorification of the national past, as cultivated by the historical economists, might have been conducive to national unity in Germany, where a single nationality aspired to nationhood. In Austria, where a multiplicity of nationalities pressed for emancipation, the pursuit of historical economics, which underlined national diversity, would have been divisive. Much more in line with the logic of the situation was the development of an economics that purported to stress the element common to all humanity and proceeded on a level of abstraction high enough to make national diversities appear immaterial. It was to the development of such an economics that Menger devoted his great gifts when he prepared his *Grundsätze* to launch his university career. The Austrian school did not start out to rebut Marx, as some students of doctrinal history have surmised, but to fortify the multinational empire of the Hapsburgs.

Menger thus developed his ideas on a level of abstraction which removed them from considerations of time and space; however, abstract and general as his approach was, what led him on in his study of economics during the late 1860s was, if a report to this effect can be believed, a practical problem of the day. One of his duties in government service was the preparation of market surveys, and in the discharge of this duty he found it difficult to reconcile the conventional price theory with the facts of life. Hence his attempt to reconstruct the theory of value and price on a new foundation. As in other instances of "high theory," such as Ricardo's theory of profit and the whole structure of his thought derived therefrom, concrete reality provided the stimulus to abstract theorizing. In other circumstances, the reverse would come true: Propositions that at first glance appeared most abstract, remote from reality, and entirely impractical would be pregnant with profound implications for policy and the world of reality.

ECONOMIC GOODS AND THEIR VALUE

Menger gave a great deal of attention to definitions, an approach inspired both by his legal training and by the scholarly tradition in German-speaking countries. A cogently argued chain of reasoning carries the reader from "useful things" to "goods" and eventually to "economic goods." Much of this definitional matter, with its emphasis on the subjective and relative character of the relevant attributes of economic goods, did in time become part of the standard doctrine and was incorporated into elementary text-books throughout the world. Menger had a predilection for interpreting economic relations as causal ones, and in line with this view he defined goods as useful things that can be brought into a cause-and-effect relationship with the satisfaction of human needs. Unlike Jevons, he developed his argument in terms of subjectively felt needs rather than in terms of pleasure. The need-satisfying quality of a good and the needs themselves are not necessarily real but may be imaginary, with the latter contingency, in Menger's opinion, becoming less frequent as civilization progresses. "Goods of first order," such as bread, serve human needs directly, whereas "goods of higher orders," such as flour and baking utensils, grain mills, labor services of the farmer, and so forth, serve them indirectly. As Menger underlined, goods of higher order require complementary goods; without these, they lose their character as goods.

Goods are economic goods when "requirements"—the amount that a person must have to satisfy his needs—exceed the available quantity. Although Menger did not use this term, the implication is that economic goods are scarce. In connection with economic goods there arises the problem of economizing, that is, of choosing between needs, satisfying some and leaving others unsatisfied, and of doing so in a manner that will achieve an optimum result. Menger approached his task outside the utilitarian tradition, and his economizing man does not seek to maximize pleasure but to satisfy his needs in the most efficient manner.

NEEDS AND THEIR SATISFACTIONS

Needs and their satisfactions are of unequal importance as regards both the satisfaction of needs of different kinds and the more or less complete satisfaction of one and the same need. Needs and satisfactions can be graduated, beginning with vital needs and descending to needs of lesser importance, until eventually saturation is reached. Menger employed neither diagrams nor mathematical formulas to support his argument, and instead he presented a table consisting of hypothetical scales indicating the importance of the satisfaction derived from the consumption of successive units of ten different goods. The goods were labeled I to X, and the scales extended from 10, which denotes vital importance, to zero. The ten scales are reproduced here:

I	II	III	IV	V	VI	VII	VIII	IX	X
10	9	8	7	6	5	4	3	2	1
9	8	7	6	5	4	3	2	1	0
8	7	6	5	4	3	2	1	0	
7	6	5	4	3	2	1	0		
6	5	4	3	2	1	0			
5	4	3	2	1	0				
4	3	2	1	0					
3	2	1	0						
2	1	0							
1	0								
0									

Menger used columns I and V to illustrate the diminishing importance of an individual's need for food and tobacco respectively. If the vital need for food has been satisfied to an extent numerically indicated by the figure 6, the consumption of tobacco, although on the whole less vital, assumes an importance equal to the further satisfaction of the now less pressing need for food. In discussing this matter, Menger did not refer to diminishing utility but to the declining importance of needs and their satisfaction. He established the principle that people will first provide for those needs whose satisfaction has the greatest importance for them and will then make provisions for needs of lesser importance until all needs are satisfied up to an equal degree of importance. The next step in the argument, a crucial one, was the derivation of a subjective theory of value from the principle just enunciated. Menger raised the question of what the result would be if an individual were to lose one unit of a stock of homogeneous goods, and he declared it to be the loss of satisfaction of the least important need that could be provided for if the total stock were left unimpared. Hence, he concluded, the value to an individual of any one unit of the total quantity of a good is equal to the importance of the least significant satisfaction attained with the help of a unit of the total quantity of the good.

THE THEORY OF IMPUTATION

Value is not an inherent quality of goods but is *imputed* to them. Although, strictly speaking, only satisfactions have value because man's life and well-being depend on them, man nevertheless imputes value to the goods whose availability makes satisfactions possible. Menger then went on to expand this theory of imputation—*Zurechnung*—to goods of higher order, which satisfy needs only indirectly and whose value is determined by the anticipated value of the goods of lower order to be produced with their help. Menger's approach to the valuation of producer goods, that is, to the theory of distribution, yielded a marginal productivity theory of sorts, in which, however, the value of the productive service was interpreted not in terms of the change of the physical product or of the value of the physical product but in terms of the changing satisfaction of needs. In accordance with the loss principle employed earlier by Menger in the valuation of goods of first order, he identified the value of a good of higher order with the satisfaction potentially yielded by goods of lower order but lost because of the withdrawal of a unit of the good of higher order. The theory of imputation opened up a unified view of distribution. It related the value of the product to that of the productive services and integrated the theories of value and distribution. In all these respects it went beyond the treatment that the classics had accorded to factor earnings. In the later development, however, the theory of distribution would unfold itself along the lines sketched by Thünen rather than along Menger's ideas.

Like Jevons's, Menger's theory of value assigned no place to cost of production as a determinant of value. Both developed their arguments on the basis of a given stock of goods that has been produced at costs incurred in the past, which are now irrelevant. Referring to these, Jevons made the famous observation that "bygones are forever bygones; and we are always starting clear at each moment, judging the value of things with a view to future utility." In a similar vein, Menger pointed out that "whether a diamond was found accidentally or was obtained from a diamond pit with the employment of a thousand days of labor is completely irrelevant for its value." This extreme reaction to the value theory of the classics with its emphasis on labor or cost of production as determinant of value would later be corrected by Alfred Marshall, who coordinated cost of production with utility as determinants of value.

Menger's discussion of value and of the nature of goods filled about one-half of the content of the *Grundsätze*. The rest he devoted to an exposition of the theories of price and money. In his price theory he distinguished between different types of market situations and arrived, for example, at the conclusion that price is indeterminate under conditions of bilateral monopoly. His price theory remained fragmentary, however, since, like Jevons, he did not incorporate costs and supply in his analysis and, moreover, developed it in terms of barter rather than with the help of demand functions or curves.

MONETARY THEORY

In his analysis of money, included in the *Grundsätze* and in an encyclopedia article published in 1892, Menger applied the subjective theory of value to money. The origin of money, he held, is not to be sought in an explicit convention or in the action of public authorities. Instead, it was the interest of economizing individuals which led them to exchange their goods for other, more saleable, goods. Money is the most marketable, or saleable, good, and its value is determined in the same manner as that of other goods that are objects of exchange transactions. In this interpretation, money was not introduced by design and in consequence of a plan but as an unintended result of the unconcerted actions of a multitude of individuals pursuing their own interests. At first glance, Menger's concept of "organic," or "natural," that is, nonpurposive, social formations recalls Adam Smith's "invisible hand," which leads men to promote ends that are no part of their intention. There is, no doubt, an affinity between the two ideas, but they do not refer to exactly the same phenomenon. Smith had in mind the incidental effects resulting from the concurrence of simultaneous activities rather than the growth of institutions over time and in response to custom and tradition, an essentially Burkean idea, which was adopted by the exponents of historical jurisprudence and which Menger took over from them.

MENGER ON THE METHODS OF SOCIAL SCIENCE

Menger returned to nonpurposive social formations in his second principal work, a polemical study of the proper methods of economic science, which was originally published in 1883 and of which an English translation appeared in 1963 under the title *Problems of Economics and Sociology*. This work was both a denunciation of German historical economics and a spirited defense of Menger's own abstract-generalizing approach to economics. Beyond this, Menger's study of economic methods marked the beginning of a period in which economic theory was largely identified with microeconomics, just as Lionel Robbins's *Essay on the Nature and Significance of Economic Science* (1932), written fifty years later but stemming from a similar tradition, marked the end of this period. Having sponsored a subjective theory of value which interpreted value in terms of the state of mind of an individual, Menger declared it to be the principal task of economic theory to investigate the behavior of economizing individuals. The economic life of the nation, he held, is the result of innumerable economic efforts undertaken by individual agents. These are the true elements that constitute the national economy, and they form the proper subject matter of economic theory. Menger considered his methodological individualism confirmed by such nonpurposive social formations as the rise of money, of towns, of fairs and markets, and of the division of labor, interpreted by him as social structures that are the unintended outcome of the pursuit of individual interests.

Menger's methodological individualism, in which microeconomic phenomena are singled out for analysis, forestalled systematic attention to the behavior of economic aggregates, the determination of the national income, and the overall performance of the economy, which before the advent of Keynesian economics received only casual treatment by business cycle specialists. Moreover, methodological individualism assigns no significant functions to public policy in the economic sphere and by implication, if not explicitly, has its corollary in laissez faire and political individualism.

Modern economics has not adhered to the precepts of Menger's methodology and has instead branched out into macroeconomics. It has also failed to follow Menger's ideas in a number of other respects. Menger called for the interpretation of economic relationships in terms of causes and effects and rejected their interpretation in terms of mutual interdependence, which has become the standard approach in modern economics. Perhaps related therewith, because mathematicians study functional rather than causal relationships, Menger did not employ and had no use for mathematical economics. He considered symbols and figures inadequate tools for the exploration of the "essence" of things, that is, if his brief remarks may be so interpreted, inadequate for what to him appeared too profound, lasting, and rife with ramifications and qualitative attributes to allow for expression in the form of symbols with no empirical content or in that of figures of fleeting relevance.

WIESER AND BÖHM-BAWERK

Menger's most important followers were Friedrich von Wieser (1851–1926) and Eugen von Böhm-Bawerk (1851–1914). Classmates and friends, and eventually brothers-in-law, the two were not, strictly speaking, students of Menger's but came under his intellectual influence when in their early twenties they read Menger's *Grundsätze*. Because of Menger's early retirement, Austrians who later became prominent, including Hayek, Mises, and Schumpeter, were not students of Menger but rather of Wieser and Böhm-Bawerk, who held a variety of teaching posts in the far-flung Hapsburg empire of their time. Wieser taught briefly at Vienna, then at Prague, and eventually again at Vienna as Menger's successor, his academic work being interrupted by wartime service as minister of commerce. Böhm-Bawerk alternated between teaching, first at Innsbruck and later at Vienna, and work in the ministry of finance, which he headed during three periods.

The two junior members of the original Austrian group had quite different personalities. Böhm-Bawerk was an indefatigable controversialist and close student of the economic literature; Wieser was noted for olympic detachment from the controversies of his time and restricted his reading to a regimen of intellectual hygiene recalling that of Comte—his brother-in-law would in vain attempt to draw him into discussions about matters of professional concern. Nevertheless, Wieser's intellectual interests were broader than Böhm-Bawerk's or even Menger's and included work in sociology.

Distinguished as the accomplishments of Wieser and Böhm-Bawerk were, neither had a mind equipped with the creative originality of Menger. In their work they pursued a number of ideas that had been suggested by the founder of the school. Both kept burning the light of economic theory in the German-speaking countries, a light that the historical economists had all but extinguished in Germany proper. Both turned out brilliant restatements of the subjective theory of value which gained the new doctrine adherents at home and abroad. Both tried, albeit with the same inadequate means, to develop further Menger's price theory. Wieser in particular gave much attention to the elaboration of the theory of imputation, with which Menger had attempted to explain the valuation of producer goods. Wieser also expanded Menger's theoretical structure by incorporating in it a theory of cost, interpreted by him as indirect, or sacrificed utility, foregone because of the use of a resource for a given rather than for other purposes. The germ of Wieser's concept of opportunity cost was already contained in a seminar report he delivered in 1876, and although it was more fully developed in his own later publications as well as by Böhm-Bawerk and other writers, it was Wieser who pioneered in this important matter.

In the writings of Wieser and Böhm-Bawerk there emerged what from then on was to become a feature characteristic of the Austrian tradition in economics—a critical reaction to the work of Karl Marx. This reaction, which was relatively mild in the case of Wieser, became stronger in the writings of Böhm-Bawerk and the later Austrians, who expanded their attack to include not only Marxian socialism but also reform socialism and economic interventionism in general. In a world that had largely abandoned laissez faire, the later Austrians became its last defenders.

WIESER AND SOCIALIST ECONOMICS

In his *Natural Value* (1889, Eng. trans. 1893), Wieser attempted to demonstrate that economic value is a "natural" category in the sense that any rationally ordered society, regardless of its institutions, would have to make valuations. He drew the important conclusion, which set a precedent for the later study of the economics of socialism, that a socialist economy could not dispense with valuations:

> Wants there would still be, there as elsewhere; the available means would still be insufficient for their full satisfaction; and the human heart would still cling to its possessions. All goods which were not free would be recognized as not only useful but valuable; they would rank in value according to the relation in which the available stocks stood to the demand; and that relation would express itself finally in the marginal utility. Social supply and demand or amount of goods and utility socially compared with one another, would decide value. The elementary laws of valuation, as we have explained them, would be entirely and unlimitedly effective for the whole community.

Although Wieser stressed the relevance of the subjective theory of value for a socialist state, he as well as Böhm-Bawerk rejected the labor theory of value and subjected it to searching criticism, the latter in a volume entitled *Karl Marx and the Close of His System* (1896, Eng. trans. 1898), for a generation the leading criticism of the work of Karl Marx.

BÖHM-BAWERK AND INTEREST THEORY

Böhm-Bawerk made his principal contributions to the theories of interest and capital, and it was with these that he developed his most effective criticism of socialism. He went considerably further than Wieser, who left the question of the viability or desirability of socialism unanswered and merely underlined the validity of fundamental economic principles under both capitalism and socialism. Böhm-Bawerk's main argument was that the socialist criticism of capitalism was in fact a criticism of the human condition, that is, of the central problem of scarcity, with which socialism would have to cope just as did capitalism.

Böhm-Bawerk's views were set forth in *Capital and Interest* (1884, Eng. trans. 1890) and *The Positive Theory of Capital* (1889, Eng. trans. 1891). The former was a somewhat tendentious doctrinal history of interest theories, whereas the latter contained his own theoretical contributions, which attracted a great deal of attention and stimulated controversies that are far from being settled at the present time. People tend, Böhm-Bawerk argued, to overestimate future resources and to underestimate future wants; besides, goods available now will yield goods of higher value in the future. In the light of these "three reasons"—the first two psychological and the third technological—people will be inclined to place a higher value on present than on future goods of the same kind and quantity, and to induce them to exchange present for future goods they are to be paid an *agio,* or premium, which equates the value of present and future goods. This agio, or premium, is known as interest.

A few examples, which Böhm-Bawerk himself provided, will illustrate the meaning of the three reasons. People tend to overestimate future resources: If they suffer in the present from the lack of certain goods, they may have reason to hope to be more amply provided for in the future. Cases in point are temporary distress or calamity, as well as the situation of all those who look forward to a career that will better their economic status. People tend to underestimate future wants: They do so because of deficient powers of the imagination and of the will and because life is uncertain and short. Present goods will yield goods of higher value in the future: A person who needs drinking water may go to the spring and drink from his cupped hands. Or he may hew a log into a bucket and store a supply of water in his house, but this more advantageous situation requires time to procure an ax and fell a tree. For even greater convenience, he may construct a pipeline that conducts the water to his house. Here the road that leads from the expenditure of labor to the availability of water becomes longer and more roundabout, but the result is still more rewarding. It is on these grounds that people appraise presently available goods more highly than goods that will become available in the future.

Böhm-Bawerk's first two reasons for interest, the psychological ones, lend support to what came to be designated as the time-preference theory of interest, whereas the third appears to be a newly garbed productivity theory of capital. This latter interpretation, however, was not endorsed by Böhm-Bawerk, who recognized only land and labor as original factors of production and refused to consider capital a factor of production coordinate with these. In his analysis, capital enhanced the productivity of land and labor; its employment was "time absorbing" and required more "round-about" processes of production which lengthened the "period of production." By producing a net, a fisherman would greatly enlarge his catch, but the process of producing the final output now required a detour which made it more time-consuming and lengthy, beginning with the incorporation of land and labor inputs into the net and into the tools or machinery with which it was manufactured.

All parts of this analysis, which Böhm-Bawerk presented with great assurance, were challenged in time. It was pointed out that people might overestimate future resources but would do so only if they expected their incomes to rise, an assumption not necessarily implied within the framework of Böhm-Bawerk's stationary economy. His second reason pointed to a defective telescopic vision, which caused people to place a premium on present goods. But the family motive for accumulation and the demonstrable willingness of people to make provisions for an uncertain future, tendencies that might assert themselves even at zero interest rates, made it appear likely that some people were inclined to place a premium on future rather than on present goods. As for his third reason, which he considered suffi-cient in itself to explain interest, it was pointed out that in the absence of time preference, that is, of the psychological reasons, the third reason would not give rise to interest but would induce people to devote all present goods to the production of future ones. The fact that people did not behave in this manner was due to their time preference, to the psychological reasons.

Böhm-Bawerk's formulation of the third reason did not satisfy those critics who insisted that it demonstrated the productivity of capital. Some of them attempted to restore the conventional triad of productive factors, and others denied the validity of drawing dividing lines between classes of productive agents all of which contributed the same type of productive service or input. Considerable efforts were made to clarify Böhm-Bawerk's concept of a period of production, visualized as starting with the initial dedication of original factors of production—land and labor—to a process of production and ending with the emergence of the final product ready for consumption. The period of production, whose affinity with the capital-output ratio has been recognized in recent years, was apparently considered by Böhm-Bawerk as an operational concept that would lend itself to empir-ical verification. Critics denied this, and some went as far as to question the logic of its construction and to express doubt whether the period of production, as Böhm-Bawerk understood it, would be finite. To F. H. Knight, a well-known American critic of Böhm-Bawerk's, the reference to the original factors of production meant the conundrum of an infinite regress since he found it impossible to visualize the production of a consumer good turned out only with the help of land and labor and without recourse to capital goods.

In Böhm-Bawerk's analysis a sharp distinction was made between the explanation of the "Why?" of interest, a question resolved with the help of the three reasons, and the determination of the interest rate. This latter matter he approached in a manner recalling that employed by Marx, that is, with the help of a two-class model, in which the working class exchanges its labor—productive of future goods—against present goods taken from a subsistence fund—a concept related to the earlier wages-fund idea of the classics. With a given subsistence fund and at full employment, wages and interest are mutually determined. In equilibrium, workers receive the discounted value of their products, which exhausts the subsistence fund, and the rate of interest is equal to the marginal product of the roundabout process of production lengthened to the extent made possible by the given subsistence fund. At rates of wages or interest that deviate from the equilibrium rates the subsistence fund either would not be exhausted or would not be large enough to employ all workers, and the roundaboutness of production would be either not pronounced enough or excessive. Competition would secure proper adjustments to equilibrium rates.

Böhm-Bawerk's model of the distributive process, the substance of which is similar to the marginal productivity theory, did not include consideration of a return to the owner of land, which in the first approximation was assumed to be a free good. It also left unexplained the size and composition of the subsistence fund and thus remained a suggestive though fragmentary analysis.

BÖHM-BAWERK'S CRITICISM OF SOCIALISM

Since the three reasons Böhm-Bawerk used to explain the emergence of interest were based on psychological and technological considerations accounting for a higher value of present as compared with future goods, Böhm-Bawerk concluded that interest is a general category and a feature characteristic of all economic systems and does not arise, as the Socialists argued, from the exploitation of labor under specific economic institutions. The three reasons for interest, he insisted, are still present under socialism, which cannot simply abolish the difference in the value of present and future goods. If under socialism the attempt were made to pay the laborer the undiscounted value of his product, curious results would ensue. A forester whose work would yield oak trees a hundred years hence would receive a wage several hundred times that of a baker, whose product "ripens" in a day. If, on the other hand, both were paid at the rate of the baker, with the interest accruing to the community and redistributed by it, it would still be true just "as it is of our capitalist society that owners of present goods derive interest through the labor of those who are producing a future product." Socialism may effect a change in the persons who receive interest and in the quantities in which it is distributed, but it cannot change the fact that possessors of present goods, when they exchange them for future ones, obtain an agio. If the planning authorities did not place a lower valuation on future goods, productive resources would always be channeled into their technically most productive uses yielding output available in the immeasurably remote future, at the cost of present dearth and distress.

Böhm-Bawerk's insistence that interest is a general category and not one arising from specific historical institutions was meant to combat not only the exploitation theories of the Socialists but also the views of the historical economists, then reaching their peak of prominence in Germany, who were inclined to interpret economic arrangements as reflecting prevailing power structures rather than immutable laws and who placed an increasing reliance on government to revise these arrangements by public policies. The supremacy of economic laws over institutional factors was also stressed in Böhm-Bawerk's final publication, a famous article entitled "Control or Economic Law?" (1914). The question at issue here was the effectiveness of labor union power in raising wages. By drawing attention to the limits of such power, Böhm-Bawerk in effect questioned the possibilities of reform proposed by the adherents of both socialist revisionism and nonsocialist interventionism.

With Böhm-Bawerk's interest theory the unity of the Austrian school's message gave way to a measure of diversity, since his contribution remained controversial even among the other founder members of the school. The diversity became still more pronounced with the later Austrians, most of whom adhered to or magnified certain features of the Austrian tradition while shedding others. After the fall of the Hapsburg empire in 1918 and especially after the occupation of Austria by German troops twenty years later, the leading members of the younger Austrian school, as the pupils of Wieser and Böhm-Bawerk were designated, sought refuge elsewhere and continued their work in the English-speaking countries. Diversity was produced not only by varied reactions to the intellectual atmosphere of the new environment but also by the passage of time, which dimmed the influence of the founders and introduced new ideas generated by the progress of economic science.

THE YOUNGER AUSTRIANS: MISES

Among the Austrian-trained economists who attained prominence as the twentieth century advanced were Ludwig von Mises (born 1881), Friedrich von Hayek (b. 1899), and Joseph A. Schumpeter (1883–1950).

If purely theoretical work, undiluted by empiricism and free of mathematics, and methodological and political individualism were the hallmarks of the Austrian school, no one continued these tradition in a more forthright and uncompromising fashion than Mises. His criticism of socialism, an economic system that he considered impossible because it contained no rational method of pricing, was as influential and thought-provoking at its time as had been Böhm-Bawerk's a generation earlier. Like Böhm-Bawerk, but much more dogmatically so, Mises also questioned the viability of a regime of economic interventionism. His attachment to laissez faire was so strong that he refused to concede to the government a role even in the field of monetary policy, where such a role had for some time been accepted by the great majority of economists, however conservative they might be in other respects. As time went on, and especially with the expansion of public policies following the diffusion of the ideas of Keynes, the unyielding tenacity with which Mises adhered to his views placed him in an extreme position, remote from the mainstream of economic thought and considered utopian by many of his contemporaries.

HAYEK

Hayek, Mises's junior by almost twenty years, shared the latter's individualism and libertarianism but was more receptive to mathematical economics and was thus in a position to participate in the discussion of the technical economics of his time. In his mid-career he made notable contributions to business cycle and capital theories but in later life turned increasingly to broader questions of economic organization, doctrinal history, and economic philosophy. Hayek's contribution to business cycle theory was an overinvestment theory, in which a "capital shortage" in a twofold sense brought on the downturn: A depression ensues when investment funds cease to be readily available and thereby leave incomplete investment projects that have already been constructed but require complementary projects, the construction of which has come to a halt.

Hayek's principal methodological concern was not so much with the employment of mathematics as such as with the use of natural science methods in economics, which he characterized as "scientism" and which, in his opinion, presumed—and encouraged—the application of controls suitable for the inanimate objects of natural science but not for human beings. Instead of advocating the ideal of a self-directed humanity, he, like Mises, invariably preferred to rely on the impersonal discipline of the market; indeed, he defined theoretical economics as aiming "at explaining those uniformities in the economic activities of society which are not the result of deliberate design but the produce of the interplay of the separate decisions of individuals and groups," thereby excluding from it all non-market phenomena. This definition, rendered in 1950, was typical of Hayek's and other Austrians' attitude to the economics of Keynes, which called for purposeful action by means of public policies. Although to some the Austrian approach seemed old-fashioned and out of step with the time, others valued it as a means to keep alive the discussion of fundamental questions in an intellectual atmosphere characterized by the rise of a new Keynesian-oriented orthodoxy.

Hayek's identification of economics with the study of the market economy went far beyond Menger's teaching. Menger repeatedly pointed out that numerous social phenomena are not of an "organic" origin; they do not arise as nonpurposive social formations but are "pragmatic," that is, "products of the agreement of members of society, or of positive legislation, results of the purposeful common activity of society." Similarly, Mises's support of an absolute laissez faire ran counter to the teachings of Wieser who, referrring to the labor market, had written: "In view of the helplessness of the individual, the slogan of the liberal school, 'Laissez-faire, laissez-passer,' becomes almost a mockery."

SCHUMPETER

Whereas Hayek and Mises transformed the legacy of their masters in their own ways, Schumpeter went still further in emancipating himself from the work of his forerunners. Instead of projecting or magnifying certain tendencies apparent in their writings, he was receptive to a number of influences emerging outside the Austrian sphere, first of all that of Walras, whom he ranked above all modern theorists, and, second, that of the Anglo-American tradition, with which he was linked through early personal contacts. While still in his twenties, he broke the hold of his master by developing a theory of interest at variance with that of Böhm-Bawerk. More conspicuous still was Schumpeter's break with the Austrian tradition by his general approach, which has been characterized as one of "methodological tolerance." His work was not confined to the type of pure theory cultivated by the earlier Austrians but was vastly broader and reflected the high hopes that he placed both in mathematical economics and in empirical studies of quantitative orientation. He in fact once observed that if fate were to allow him to begin his studies afresh, he would want to become an economic historian. The broad range of his interests was indicated by the subtitle of his *Business Cycles,* which he described as *A Theoretical, Historical and Statistical Analysis of the Capitalist Process.*

The central idea, at which Schumpeter arrived while in his twenties and which permeated his entire future work, from *The Theory of Economic Development* (1912, Eng. trans. 1934) to *Business Cycles* (1939) and *Capitalism, Socialism and Democracy* (1942), was the importance of an entrepreneurial elite for change and growth, for the business cycle, and for the survival of capitalism. The strategic element in entrepreneurial activity was "innovation," that is, the application of new ideas in technique and organization which would bring about changes in the production function. Innovation would brake the circular flow of the stationary economy and generate economic development with a new equilibrium position at higher levels of income. In a dynamic economy of this type there would emerge interest, which Schumpeter interpreted as a sort of tax levied on the entrepreneurs by the bankers in return for inflationary credit. Bunches of innovation, reinforced by imitators and speculators, would make for cyclical movements, with the economy pulsating to the threefold rhythm of the three-year Kitchins, nine-year Juglars, and fifty-five-year Kondratieffs, so named by Schumpeter after their discoverers.

The downfall of capitalism, which Schumpeter foresaw in his *Capitalism, Socialism and Democracy* and which, unlike in Marx's scheme, would come about as a result not of the failure but of the success of capitalism, was again related to the fate of the entrepreneurial elite. As in Max Weber's analysis, the overriding factor here was the ascendancy of a rationalism, which made capitalism flourish but destroyed the social fabric in which it was embedded. Enterprise became large-scale and impersonal, and with large-scale enterprise, innovation, hitherto the prerogative of the captains of industry, became depersonalized and transformed into an administrative routine carried on by salaried people rather than by receivers of profit. A bourgeoisie made up of salaried people and absentee stockholders divorced from management loses its attachment to private property and freedom of contract: "Dematerialized, defunctionalized and absentee ownership does not impress and call forth moral allegiance as the vital form of property did." Moreover, the political ascendancy of the bourgeoisie over its former protectors, the old ruling classes of aristocracy, nobility, and royalty, vested political power in the business community, a group that Schumpeter considered unfit to rule because it lacked the mystic glamour that counts in the ruling of men. Here Schumpeter's nurture on continental European experience broke through, just as it had in Hayek's *Road to Serfdom* (1944), because Hayek visualized a strong state as an oppressive one, not one restrained by a powerful democratic tradition.

Schumpeter's exaltation of the entrepreneur colored his views on monopoly, about which he was apologetic, and on Keynesian economics, to which he was firmly opposed. He considered monopoly power a suitable incentive and fitting reward for the innovating entrepreneur, who would enjoy this power only a limited time, until it was broken and replaced in a chain of "creative destruction" by another innovator's monopoly. For similar reasons, and also because of his general reluctance to "follow the crowd," he remained hostile to the policy implications of the ideas of Keynes, which he considered a threat to what to him appeared as the driving force in the economy, that is, private initiative rather than public policy.

Deviation from accepted opinion also characterized many pages of the monumental doctrinal history presented in Schumpeter's posthumously published *History of Economic Analysis* (1954). This work was informed by an almost unparalleled erudition, unusual even in the light of the standards of earlier ages when economists were more adept in book learning than in mathematical techniques but in modern times matched only by Hayek's contributions to the history of ideas and by Jacob Viner's *Studies in the Theory of International Trade* (1937). The novel conception of Schumpeter's work, indicated by its title, was to be the stress on the rise of analytical techniques, a sort of temporal provincialism alien to Schumpeter's general attitude of methodological tolerance. Ostensibly, his approach to doctrinal history tended to measure the accomplishments of the past in terms of the type of economic analysis carried on in the mid-twentieth century, with this analysis serving as the absolute standard. This rather confining approach was, however, not followed in the actual execution of the work, which, the author's idiosyncracies notwithstanding, is likely to survive Schumpeter's other writings as a monument to the scholarship of an age now past.

Chapter 24

ECONOMICS RESTRUCTURED:

Marginalism

and Optimization

3. THE LAUSANNE SCHOOL: A GENERAL EQUILIBRIUM

WALRAS, FATHER AND SON

At this juncture we must retrace our steps to the 1870s when Jevons and Menger developed their subjective theories of value on the basis of the marginal utility concept. Their work converged with that of Léon Walras (1834–1910), whose *Elements of Pure Economics,* originally published in French in two parts in 1874 and 1877 and translated into English in 1954, included an analysis of value and marginal utility similar to that of Jevons and of Menger. When Walras formed these ideas, he was not acquainted with their works nor with Gossen's earlier book. What shaped his mind was the intellectual influence of his father, Auguste Walras, and of Cournot, a schoolmate of his father's, with whose work he became familiar in his youth.

Like Cournot, Auguste Walras (1801–66) worked as an educational administrator rather than as a professional economist, and his economic writings found only a dim echo in the academic economics of the France of his time. As Locke had before him, he grounded both property and economic value in the same principle, represented in his case not by labor, as in the writings of Locke, but by *rareté,* or scarcity, of goods relative to human wants. It was this notion of the older Walras that his son, of all the sons of economists the most faithful, transformed into the equivalent of marginal utility. As for Cournot, the younger Walras found in his work a demand function and a demand curve, which Cournot had introduced as an empirical datum but which Walras now derived from the utility function.

Unlike Menger, Walras was a theorist as well as a social reformer. In his reform ideas, which he diligently pursued throughout his life, he again followed his father. His proposals, which had an affinity with related ideas of the Mills, Gossen, Henry George, and the early Fabians, called for

In a progressive society, Walras held, land values would continue to grow at rising rates and yield the state an income in excess of the one whose capitalized value had been paid as an indemnity to its previous owners. The state, Walras argued, could then renounce taxation as a source of revenue and instead meet its expenses from the rent of the nationalized land. Since Walras, besides other reforms, also advocated the idea of cooperation, he has at times been described as a Socialist, a name that fits him in only a vague sense or not at all if an affinity of his thought with that of Marx is implied.

WALRAS AND COURNOT

Walras's theoretical contributions went beyond those of Jevons and Menger in the development of the idea of general economic equilibrium and in its expression in the form of a system of simultaneous equations. It was this feature of his work that came to constitute his principal achievement and for which he was extolled by Schumpeter and others. The great problem that Walras attempted to solve was that of linking the numerous markets of which the economy is made up. Cournot had gone far in exploring particular equilibrium positions in markets viewed as separate from other markets, but he realized that his analysis was incomplete since it did not consider the interdependence among the markets existing in the economy and the question of the compatibility of their particular equilibrium positions. He posed the problem but expressed doubt about the possibility of resolving it:

> So far we have studied how, for each commodity by itself, the law of demand in connection with the conditions of production of that commodity, determines the price of it and regulates the incomes of its producers. We considered as given and invariable the prices of other commodities and the incomes of other producers; but in reality the economic system is a whole of which all the parts are connected and react on each other. An increase in the income of the producers of commodity A will affect the demand for commodities B, C, etc., and the incomes of their producers, and, by its reaction, will involve a change in the demand for commodity A. It seems, therefore, as if, for a complete and rigorous solution of the problems relative to some parts of the economic system, it were indispensable to take the entire system into consideration. But this would surpass the powers of mathematical analysis and of our practical methods of calculation, even if the values of all the constants could be assigned to them numerically.

The last sentence of the quotation hints at the possibility that Cournot despaired of resolving the problem of general equilibrium because he considered it an econometric one which should yield numerical values for the unknown quantities and prices. Walras's aim, however, was not measurement but the construction of a logically consistent system of theoretical or formal validity, and this aim he found it possible to realize, albeit under restrictive assumptions. His system required perfect competition, freedom of entry, mobility, and price flexibility. The business firms' revenues would exactly be matched by their costs as would be the consumers' incomes by their outlay on products. In Walras's first approximation, neither saving nor capital formation occurs, and there is no uncertainty that would induce people to hold money. The system is a closed one, not affected by foreign transactions or by the operations of government accounts. In equilibrium, the equality of the quantities demanded and supplied clears all markets, and excess demand, positive in the form of shortages and negative in that of surpluses, disappears.

GENERAL EQUILIBRIUM

In constructing his system of equations, Walras started with the basic distinction between products markets and markets for productive services. In the products markets the consumers demand products that are supplied by business firms; in the markets for productive services rendered by labor, land, and capital, the consumers, who are also the owners of the productive resources, sell productive services to the business firms and in return receive sales revenues which constitute their incomes. The consumers thus appear as buyers in the products markets and as sellers in the markets for productive services. The business firms are buyers in the markets for productive services and sellers in the products markets.

The unknown variables in the system are the prices and quantities of the products and productive services, as well as the quantities of the productive services utilized in the production of each product, "technical coefficients" in the language of Walras. If there are m products, n productive services, m product prices, n prices of productive services, and mn technical coefficients, the total number of unknowns adds up to $2m + 2n + mn$. This total number Walras reduced by 1, leaving $2m + 2n + mn - 1$ unknowns, because one of the products serves as $numéraire$, that is as the system's measure of value in which all other prices are expressed and which itself has the price of 1.

In general, the various unknowns can be determined and their coexistence demonstrated when there are a number of independent equations equal to the number of the unknowns. In Walras's system the number of the latter is matched by $m - 1$ demand equations for products, m cost equations, n quantity equations for productive services, and mn technical coefficient equations, that is, altogether $2m + 2n + mn - 1$ equations.

In the demand equations the quantity demanded of a product is related to the price of the product as well as to the prices of all other products and of the productive services. The prices of the productive services affect the consumers' income and hence their demand for products; the prices of other products—substitutes or complementary goods—also influence their demand for a given product in varying and more or less significant degrees. The demand equations are derived from utility functions which are maximized when for each consumer prices are proportional to marginal utilities. They are first drawn up for individual consumers and then aggregated for all but one of the m products. The demand equation for one product must be discarded because it is not an independent equation but merely provides information which can be obtained by drawing inferences from the information contained in all the other equations. That is, if the demand for all but one of the products is determined, so is the demand for the one, provided the consumers' income is equal to their outlay for products. In the light of this equality, which is known as the budget equation, it is clear that what is spent on the one product is the difference between income and expenditure for all other products. The general proposition from which it follows that under certain conditions—here the budget equation—equilibrium or the absence of excess demand in $m - 1$ markets implies equilibrium or the absence of excess demand also in the remaining market has been designated as Walras's law. This law sheds light on the structure of the quantitative relationships involved and explains, for example, why the total number of equations in the system is $m - 1$, the discarded equation standing for the price of money.

In Walras's cost equations the product price is equated to the quantities of the productive services embodied in it, each multiplied by the productive service. That is, on the assumption of perfect competition, prices, in equilibrium, are equal to average cost and the firm neither suffers loss nor incurs profit. In this position, entrepreneurial income is earned only in consequence of the entrepreneurs' ownership of productive resources. Walras's cost equations give an example of his procedure. In this notation, $a_t, a_p, a_k \cdots b_t, b_p, b_k \cdots c_t, c_p, c_k \cdots d_t, d_p, d_k$ designate the quantities of each of the productive services—land (T), labor (P), and capital (K)—which are used for the production of one unit of each of the products (A), (B), (C), (D).... The prices of services and products are denoted by $p_t, p_p, p_k \cdots p_b, p_c, p_d$. Then

$$a_t p_t + a_p p_p + a_k p_k + \cdots = 1,$$
$$b_t p_t + b_p p_p + b_k p_k + \cdots = p_b,$$
$$c_t p_t + c_p p_p + c_k p_k + \cdots = p_c,$$
$$d_t p_t + d_p p_p + d_k p_k + \cdots = p_d.$$

In the quantity equations for productive services the quantities of productive services demanded are equated to the quantities supplied—in equilibrium, the market for productive services is cleared.

The supply equations for productive services relate the quantity supplied of a service to the prices of all productive services as well as to the prices of all products. This procedure explicitly recognizes that a quantity of labor, for example, which a worker stands ready to supply, is a function not only of the wage rate but also of his real income as affected by the product prices and by the prices of productive services other than labor. Walras also considered the possibility that consumers, instead of selling the services of productive resources that they own, consume these directly, for example, prefer leisure to work, and in this context he introduced the equivalent of a backward sloping supply curve, which might intersect the demand curve more often than once and thus yield multiple equilibria.

The technical substitution equations indicate the quantities of each of the productive services that will be combined in the production of a product. The combination will be determined by the prices of the productive services and it will be the one with lowest cost and with marginal productivities proportional to the prices of the productive services. Walras developed the marginal productivity theory with its variable factor proportions only in later editions of his work, having first, for purposes of simplification, adhered to the assumption of fixed coefficients of production.

In the later chapters of his work, and in formulations frequently revised in successive editions, Walras expanded his system and introduced additional unknowns and equations to account for saving, the formation of capital, and the holding of money. In doing so, he maintained the formal symmetry of his system by extending the utility analysis of the demand for consumer goods to saving and to money. When interpreting saving, he did not ground it in a comparison between present and future goods but derived it from the utility of a perpetuity which would yield a constant and perpetual net income, the demand for which paralleled the consumer's demand for products. Walras's monetary economy continued to be characterized by the absence of uncertainty since he derived the demand for money not from its ability to serve as a reserve against contingencies but rather from its ability to serve as a means to make payments that are certain.

Walras's system of thought brought order into chaos and transformed diversity into unity. To those able and willing to see, it demonstrated the power of mathematical analysis. Its capstone was Walras's attempt to show that a perfectly competitive economy would tend to approximate equilibrium positions, and with this in mind he developed his theory of *tâtonnements*—"gropings," or approximations—which would explain the progressive movement of the market to the equilibrium position. This theory presumes the announcement of an arbitrary price, at which buyers and sellers declare the quantities they stand ready to buy and sell. If the price were to fail to clear the market, another one would be announced, and this procedure would continue until equilibrium was reached.

WALRAS'S INFLUENCE

Like Jevons and Menger, Walras formed his views while in his twenties, but he had to wait longer for a favorable reaction. He received little recognition in his native France, where he never succeeded in obtaining an academic post. His life was replete with disappointments. As a youth, he was twice refused admission to the prestigious *École Polytechnique*, where the examiners were dissatisfied with his mathematical preparation. When he subsequently entered the *École des Mines,* his second choice, he found engineering not to his liking and eventually dropped out. He then made a number of attempts to establish himself in a variety of employments—in literature and journalism, and as an editor, lecturer, railway clerk, director of a bank for cooperatives, and, after the latter went out of business, bank clerk. Finally in 1870, at the age of thirty-six, he was, by a vote of four to three, offered the newly created post of professor of political economy at the Academy of Lausanne, later known as the University of Lausanne, where a lecture on taxation, which he had given ten years earlier, had made a lasting impression on an influential man. Walras taught at Lausanne for over twenty years and retired in 1892. He was convinced of the importance of his message and carried on a huge correspondence, much of it with fellow economists at home and abroad and in search of a response to his doctrine. Recognition came only late in life, and even then he may not have considered it commensurate with his pathbreaking intellectual accomplishment.

At the time of his death in 1910, Walras had a number of followers in many parts of the world, but in the great centers of academic economics of the period, Germany, Austria, and England, the reaction to his work was lukewarm at best. In the German universities, which were then at the height of their prestige, only the historical kind of economics was considered worthy of attention. In Austria, an influential school fostered pure theory, but the founders of the school had little knowledge of mathematics and disparaged the symbols and equations that studded Walras's pages. England had a mathematical economist of her own, Alfred Marshall, but his authority was jealously guarded by his followers, and although he had succeeded in gaining recognition for an economics that was mathematical in structure, his was closer to life than Walras's and displayed its structure less conspicuously. When acknowledging the gift of a new edition of Walras's *Elements,* Marshall would write: "the right place for mathematics in a treatise on Economics is the background." Even those who were receptive to the new and strange language in which Walras expressed his ideas might consider the latter as unduly abstract and remote from life, or even as sterile. A friendly critic in Italy, where Walras had his greatest following, would describe his work as an attempt to solve the housing problem by building castles in the air. Others saw in it a misplaced idealization of competition and laissez faire, and the aged Cournot, to whom Walras submitted his work, expressed his reaction in these words: "I have great fear that your utility curves will lead you only to pure laissez faire, that is, in the domestic economy to a land denuded of its forests, and in the international economy to the subjugation of the common run of peoples by a privileged one in line with the theory of Darwin."

Walras's general equilibrium economics reached a wider public during the interwar years when the Swedish economist Gustav Cassel (1866–1945), a scholar of great reputation at his time, presented a simplified version of it in his then widely read *Theory of Social Economy* (1918, Eng. trans. 1924 and 1932). As Walras's system of equations received attention from economists and mathematicians, some of the latter, notably Abraham Wald (1902–50), probed more deeply into the nature of his system and arrived at the conclusion that the equality of the number of unknowns and equations offered in itself no assurance of meaningful results in terms of economics. The system might, as Walras himself had realized, yield multiple rather than unique equilibria or it might yield no solution at all—the quantities demanded and supplied might fail to be equal at any price—or it might yield solutions with zero or negative values of doubtful significance for economic analysis. Hence, as these writers pointed out, it was important to consider not only the number of unknowns and of equations but also the nature of the functions expressed in the latter.

Walras's theory of *tâtonnements* was criticized by Edgeworth, who compared it unfavorably with his own theory of "re-contracting," which was in fact quite similar and in which purchases and sales contracts are depicted as tentative only and subject to revision until equilibrium is reached. Whatever its shortcomings, the trial-and-error procedure of the *tâtonnements* assumed an important role in the theory of the socialist market economy as developed by Barone and Lange, who modeled the establishment of prices in such an economy after the pattern of Walras's *tâtonnements*.

In connection with the Walrasian system questions arose about the existence of equilibrium, its stability, and the path along which equilibrium is reached. Walras attempted to give answers—he meant to demonstrate that equilibrium exists, that the downward sloping demand curve assures its stability, and that equilibrium is attained with the help of the *tâtonnements*. These questions, which also challenged Alfred Marshall, were again taken up in the 1930s and 1940s when Kaldor, Hicks, and Samuelson tackled this whole range of problems.

The Walrasian system provided the point of departure for still another contribution to economic analysis. As it presumably represented classical and neoclassical economics in its fullest development, it was given special attention by those who argued that in classical and neoclassical economics there exists a dichotomy or divorce between the theory of relative prices and the theory of money and of the price level and that in the Walrasian system the price level is indeterminate. Patinkin, the foremost exponent of this view, considered the Walrasian system in need of supplementation by the Pigou, or real-balance, effect, which makes individuals adjust their money balances to maintain a desired relationship between these balances and the expenditures on commodities. A price level below the equilibrium level, for example, implies a real value of the money balances so high as to induce the individual to exchange money for commodities and thereby to set in motion an upward movement of the price level toward equilibrium. In the absence of the real-balance effect, Patinkin held, Walras's law would assure equilibrium in the money market whenever the commodity margets are in equilibrium, that is, equilibrium in the latter is compatible with any price level, which, in fact, is indeterminate.

Although the continuing discussion of these matters demonstrated the relevance of Walras's thought for pure theory, doubt was cast for a long time on its significance for economic practice, especially in connection with the formation of economic policy. These doubts were grounded in part in the sharp distinction that Walras himself made between pure and applied economics, and they appeared confirmed by the essentially microeconomic character of his general equilibrium system. Some of the equations in this system are to be summed up, but the system still took its point of departure from individual preference functions which seemed to defy statistical verification. Compared with the broad aggregates that form the keystone of Keynesian economics, Walrasian economics seemed unable to acquire empirical content and become operational.

LEONTIEF

These doubts were dispelled by the input-output, or interindustry relations, economics developed in the 1920s and '30s by W. Leontief, which constituted a fusion of general equilibrium economics and modern matrix algebra. Input-output economics may be characterized as an ingenious development of Walras's technical substitution equations, yielding a general equilibrium system of production with full recognition of mutual interdependence. This approach was based on the idea that a transaction, from the seller's point of view, may be interpreted as a sale of output, whereas from the buyer's point of view, the same transaction is a purchase of input. A table may be constructed, as much or as little condensed as desired, in which, in the left-hand column, the various sellers of goods and services are listed—agriculture, manufacturing industries, public utilities, transportation and finañcial enterprises, construction, sellers of labor and of the services of other productive resources, and so forth. Along the top of the table the column headings list, in the same order, the various buyers of goods and services. Any entry in the table indicates how much a certain industry—listed in the headings—purchases from another industry—listed in the left column. Obviously, there exists a close relationship between the value of the output of any single industry—its sales—and the value of its input—its purchases. Less obvious, but existing nevertheless, is the relationship of interdependence which prevails between any single entry in the table and all other entries. For example, a change in the sales of any one industry will be attended by changes in the sales of industries that sell supplies to the former. These industries, in turn, will change their purchases from other industries, and so forth, until the effects of the initial change are diffused over the whole economy.

Input-output analysis gave numerical content to general equilibrium economics and demonstrated its practical usefulness in economic planning and forecasting. With it the Walrasian system, which hitherto had formed part of pure mathematical economics, became a significant component also of econometrics. These developments owed much to the employment of electronic computers, which permitted the solution of a far larger number of equations than was possible at Walras's time. Nevertheless, by means of aggregation the number of equations required in input-output analysis was reduced substantially below what would have been their level in Walras's original system, estimated by Pareto at 70,699 equations for every one hundred persons exchanging seven hundred goods.

In a sense, all econometricians who employed systems of equations were heirs of Walras, he having been the first to put this device to systematic use in economics. In other respects, however, much econometric work, although it operated with the help of equations, was actuated by purposes beyond the range of Walras's principal concerns. Much econometric work aimed at resolving problems relating to fluctuations in national income and economic growth, problems that became the focus of Keynesian and post-Keynesian economics and for which the Walrasian system, treating of the allocation of resources at a given level of income, as it did, provided no ready solution. It was therefore not surprising that much econometric model building received its orientation from the work of later theorists rather than from Walras. Walras's system yielded a still picture of the economy, whereas much of econometric analysis showed the economy in motion and used time series as data. Again, since its orientation was macroeconomic, it employed aggregates, which reduced the number of equations. In the Brookings econometric model of the United States, considered the largest of the world, there were about four hundred equations, a small fraction of the number required in a Walrasian system.

PARETO

The tradition of mathematical and general equilibrium economics, which Walras had established at Lausanne and which earned him the designation of founder of the Lausanne School, was continued there by his successor Vilfredo Pareto (1848–1923). When Pareto, an Italian nobleman and engineer, acceded to Walras's chair in 1893, he had behind him a career as a successful corporation executive in the railroad and heavy industry of Italy. He came to economics relatively late in life and apparently did not become acquainted with Walras's work until 1891. In the 1890s and early 1900s he published many periodical articles and a number of books, including *Cours d'économie politique* (2 vols., 1896–97) and *Manuale di economia politica* (1906; Fr. rev. ed., *Manuel d'économie politique,* 1909).

Pareto's second career, in economics, was followed by a third one, in sociology, which led to the publication of a *Trattato di sociologia generale* (1916; Eng. trans., *The Mind and Society*, 4 vols., 1935).

Opinions may be divided whether Leontief or Pareto was the authentic heir of the intellectual legacy which Walras left behind. Unlike Pareto, Leontief was not personally linked with Walras—he was born a few years before Walras's death—and he did not teach at the University of Lausanne. But the substance of Leontief's work was in many respects more firmly anchored in that of Walras than was Pareto's. In their broad outlines, Pareto's economic writings followed Walras's mathematical and general equilibrium approach, but in other respects there were enough differences between the works of these two incompatible persons to cast doubt upon the designation of the one as a follower of the other. After an initial period of harmony following their first meeting in 1891, they eventually fell apart and there is no record of communication after 1902. Walras had the optimistic outlook of an idealist and he was a progressive in politics. His policy recommendations did not appeal to Pareto, who took a somber view of the human condition and looked upon parliamentary democracy and its works with the disdain of a reactionary aristocrat. To a man of Pareto's cast, utilitarianism would appear as a shallow and erroneous doctrine.

Hence Pareto went to work to exorcise the vestiges of utilitarianism in Walras's system. Walras, it will be remembered, was not only the founder of general equilibrium economics but also, together with Jevons and Menger, the pioneer of the marginal utility approach. Although Pareto expanded the general equilibrium theory, he rejected the utilitarian implications of utility analysis and indeed proposed to cast out the very word *utility* and replace it with *ophelimity,* a derivation from the Greek which was meant to denote the power to satisfy wants. This proposal was based on the view that utility denotes usefulness; that usefulness is the opposite of harmfulness; that consumption of, say, potable spirits, might be harmful rather than useful; and that, in consequence, what appeared as utility included in fact harmful utility, a contradictory conjunction.

Whereas ophelimity never established itself in the language of economics, far more influential was the use to which Pareto put Edgeworth's indifference curve. By divesting it of its utility content and transforming it into an ostensibly empirical statement about combinations of goods equally acceptable to a consumer, Pareto led the way toward the replacement of utility analysis by indifference-curve analysis. After Pareto's follower Barone devised the budget, or price-ratio, line, an alternative method was available to determine the equilibrium of the consumer, which did not have to face up to the difficult question of the cardinal measurement of utility. For some thirty years this new method was known to only close students of mathematical economics, who then formed a small circle. After Hicks and Allen called attention to it under more favorable circumstances in the 1930s, and especially after Hicks incorporated the matter into his *Value and Capital* (1939), knowledge of it spread rapidly and it became part of the standard doctrine of economics.

PARETO'S OPTIMUM

Other features of Pareto's work had a far-reaching influence both on the economic analysis of socialism and on welfare economics. In line with a tradition of long standing, Pareto extolled the beneficial effects of perfect competition, which in his interpretation under certain conditions yielded a maximum of ophelimity. Although a complete analysis of the conditions that are required for the optimum use of resources appeared much later, in the 1930s and 1940s in the writings of Lange, Lerner, and others, the works of Pareto and Barone contained the starting point of this analysis. Pareto's hostility to socialism notwithstanding, it was from his work that the later discussion of the economics of socialism received considerable stimulation. Following Pareto's suggestions, Barone portrayed an idealized picture of an economic system operating under optimum conditions and then elucidated the task of a socialist ministry of production in bringing about equivalent conditions by means of trial and error—Walras's *tâtonnements*.

Pareto further elaborated his concept of maximum ophelimity and defined it as a position where it is impossible, by means of a small change, either to increase or to decrease the ophelimities of all individuals. He arrived at this conclusion by distinguishing several cases: a small move might increase, or it might decrease, the welfare of all individuals. In the first case the new position is more, and in the second case it is less, advantageous for all the individuals. This left open the case where the move increases the well-being of some individuals and diminishes that of others. Here, Pareto concluded, it is no longer possible to state unequivocally that the community as a whole benefits from the move. In the later discussion of the "new welfare economics," this case served as the point of departure for the development of the "compensation principle" by Kaldor (1939) and others, who pointed out that a policy measure could be endorsed on welfare grounds if it so much improved the economic position of some that their gain would suffice to compensate others for a loss suffered by them. As originally formulated, this principle does not require the actual payment of compensation, a question to be resolved by a political decision rather than by economic analysis. The principle ostensibly does not require interpersonal comparisons of utility, a matter that Pareto relegated to social ethics rather than economics. He in fact wrote of the existence of an infinite number of maximum-ophelimity positions, each reflecting a different distribution of income.

OTHER CONTRIBUTIONS TO PURE THEORY

Pareto's remaining contributions to pure theory were less original or less influential. In his utility theory he followed Edgeworth in interpreting the utility, or ophelimity, of a given good not merely as a function of the quantity of that good consumed or possessed by the individual but as a function of the quantities of all goods controlled by the individual. As regards markets, Pareto attempted to consider monopolistic situations in the context of general equilibrium analysis, a procedure that differed from that of Walras, who concentrated his attention on competition, as well as from that of Cournot, who had examined the partial equilibrium of the monopolist. Pareto held that certain oligopolistic situations are indeterminate and that they must be examined in the context of their institutional setting. This view opened up the possibility that the number of equations in the general equilibrium system would fall short of the number of unknowns, with the result that instead of one equilibrium position there would be a range of such positions. In his theory of production, Pareto refused to accept the assumption that coefficients of production are always fixed, and he also rejected the opposite assumption that they are always variable. Instead he insisted that the cofficients may be fixed under certain circumstances and variable under others, with variable coefficients possibly emerging with variations of the quantity of output or with the substitution, at the margin, of one type of input by another.

In Pareto's work two tendencies stood out which are rarely combined in the writings of one man—the striving for ever higher generalizations and, at the same time, the profound interest in empirical detail. In his search for generalization, Pareto laid bare the general structure common to all economic systems, an approach that by implication at least meant the abandonment of the belief, hitherto often proclaimed by economic writers, in the naturalness of a competitive order. Although Pareto extolled competition, he did not fail to point out that it does not secure maximum ophelimity when fixed costs are large. In the case of railroads, for example, where average costs fall over the relevant range of output and are above marginal cost, marginal cost pricing does not yield a revenue equal to cost. Unless the enterprise receives a subsidy it is unable to pursue a policy of marginal cost pricing, which in turn is a prerequisite for the optimum allocation of resources. This matter was later considered by a number of writers, some of whom would argue, albeit erroneously, that the fulfillment of the optimum conditions required only proportionality, not equality, of marginal costs and prices. Pareto's proposal to finance the fixed costs of the enterprises in question was reiterated, in a different form, in an article by Hotelling in 1938.

Pareto further generalized the general equilibrium approach by interpreting all economic equilibria as the outcome of an interplay between "tastes" and "obstacles." In this view the tastes, or ophelimities, of an individual encounter such obstacles as the tastes of other persons, the fixedness of the quantity of a good which is to be divided among different persons, the need for complementary goods which are required for the production of the desired good, the unavailability of a good at a certain place or at a certain time. In this arrangement, other persons appear exclusively as obstacles to the realization of one's own desires, a view more in line with the zero-sum game strategy of the mercantilists than with the interlocking efforts of a great society in which the work of other persons results in progressive improvements in productivity and thereby becomes a help rather than a hindrance to the satisfaction of one's own desires.

PARETO'S LAW

Pareto demonstrated his attention to empirical detail on many pages of his writings, which abound with historical illustrations and statistical data. The most famous result of this side of his work was his "law"—as he described it in paragraph 960 of the *Cours*—of income distribution. On the basis of statistical information drawn from many countries and relating to different periods of time, he came to the conclusion that the distribution of income conforms to an invariant pattern. He attempted to demonstrate this by plotting, in a double-log diagram, income against income receivers, yielding straight lines of equal slope. Pareto thus purported to show up the futility of policies aiming at the redistribution of income, policies that in his view would merely set in motion forces that would restore the original pattern of distribution. Only by raising the total income of society could an increase of the incomes of certain groups be achieved. This view and the statistical procedures from which it was derived encountered a great deal of criticism, which all but deprived Pareto's law of its validity. Nevertheless, Pareto's α, which measured the slope of the straight-line curve, found employment not as an invariant but as a measurement of income dispersion at different times and places. Moreover, regardless of the validity of Pareto's law, this side of his work made him a forerunner of quantitative-empirical studies such as came to the fore in twentieth-century economics. Pareto was, strictly speaking, not a practitioner of an econometrics that presupposes a hypothesis that is to be tested statistically. Instead he described his law as an empirical one, that is, as one derived from the observation of regularities emerging directly from the statistical data rather than confirming an a priori hypothesis. Empirical laws of this type are rarely found in economics, with Engel's law about changes in the composition of consumer expenditure at different levels of income providing one of the few examples.

PARETO'S SOCIOLOGY

There were further occasions for Pareto to consider questions of income distribution in his later years when he turned to sociology. Whereas in his pure economics he constructed a world ordered by rational behavior, his sociology portrayed mankind as irrational, driven by sentiments, follies, fears, and superstitions—"residues" of rational behavior which mankind attempted to rationalize and cloak in the garb of logical respectability. Either portrayal of man is, of course, an abstraction from reality and of no great consequence if considered as such and not confounded with reality. It was the great defect of Pareto's sociology that the distorted image of man depicted there was not labeled a caricature but was alleged to be an authentic portrayal. Having drawn a picture of an eternally self-deceiving humanity, Pareto went on to deride with corrosive irony its belief in democracy, progress, and humanitarian ideals and to advocate the rule of an elite by force and fraud. Ideas such as these supplied ammunition to the Italian Fascists, who in turn appointed Pareto a senator shortly before his death.

Pareto's sociological views deserve rejection by all those who identify civilization with the growth of reason and are eager to widen the realm over which reason rules rather than, as did Pareto, narrow it. In his sociology, he would invariably arrive at conclusions aiming to demonstrate the dethronement of reason. He would argue, for example, that a society determined exclusively by reason does not and cannot exist because the end that the society should pursue cannot be indicated with the help of reason. Similarly, when he came to questions of income distribution, he made "sentiment" the only criterion of a choice between a very rich community with large inequalities of income and a poor community with approximately equal incomes. The admirer of the "superman," he wrote, will attach a low value to the utility of the "lower classes" and prefer the first type of community, whereas the lover of equality will do the opposite and prefer the second type. "There is no criterion save sentiment for choosing between the one and the other."

Here and elsewhere in his sociological treatise Pareto failed to consider the vital importance of fact finding in expanding the rule of reason and make amenable to it matters that would otherwise be decided by "sentiment." As an able critic of Pareto has pointed out, adjudication or consensus of sentiments or value judgments is far more difficult to achieve than a reasoned debate about facts, and facts in themselves will have their effects on valuations. To take as an example Pareto's own "law" of income distribution— if it would really refer to a fact, it could not fail to impress upon thoughtful people the need to fashion their views about a desirable distribution of income in accordance with this fact. Egalitarians, lest they be utopians, would have to revise their valuations. Similarly, it is possible to transform what Pareto characterized as a clash of sentiments about the worth of supermen in relation to that of the lower classes into a reasoned debate by adducing facts about differences in human capacities, the effects of material conditions on the utilization of these capacities, and so forth. Such fact finding may not completely transform a clash about valuations into a debate about facts, but it is likely to modify valuations and make them less compelling.

Chapter 25

ECONOMICS RESTRUCTURED:

Marginalism

and Optimization

4. THE CAMBRIDGE SCHOOL: TRANSCENDING SUPPLY AND DEMAND

MARSHALL

During the closing decades of the nineteenth century the two strands of thought represented by the work of the Austrian and the Lausanne economists were joined by a third, the product of the mind of Alfred Marshall (1842–1924), who in 1885 acceded to the chair of political economy at Cambridge and who turned this institution into a center of economic studies of world renown. Marshall came to economics not as a graduate of the law school, as had the Austrians, nor as an engineering student, as Walras and Pareto had been, but as a professional mathematician, whose early teaching career had indeed been in mathematics. Perhaps because of his superior training in this field he was a far more cautious practitioner of mathematical economics, far more skeptical about its possibilities, and far more aware of the abuse to which it might lend itself than were the other pioneers of mathematical economics. In part this attitude reflected the high moral purpose with which Marshall approached the study of economics and which made him relinquish, albeit with regret, purely speculative exercises which smacked of *l'art pour l'art* rather than be of immediate help in improving the lot of humanity. An ardent philanthropist and humanitarian, he came to economics from ethics, "intending," as he wrote later when reflecting on his early career, "to stay there only a short while; and to go back, as soon as I was in a position to speak with my enemies in the gate, that is, with those men of affairs who dashed cold water on my youthful schemes for regenerating the world by saying 'Ah! you would not talk in that way, if you knew anything about business, or even Political Economy.' "

The pragmatic urgency with which Marshall approached his task made his economics more realistic and less abstract than the utility theory of the

Austrians or the general equilibrium system of Walras. He would not speculate, as the Austrians were apt to do, about the manner in which a Robinson
Crusoe might allocate his resources, nor would he, although he was aware
of the general interdependence of all economic phenomena, ascend to the
heights of abstraction in which Walras moved. He himself was no econometrician—not for lack of inclination but for want of opportunity. If he were
a rich man, he wrote in 1901, he would hire economists and statistical
clerks to fill his generalizations with empirical content. He prepared the
ground for the rise of econometrics, however, because his sense of realism
was so pronounced that a number of the concepts he developed proved
operational in the hands of later writers and stimulated empirical studies
of statistical demand curves and demand elasticity.

In addition, and unlike Jevons, Marshall brought to his task a profound attachment to the earlier tradition of British economic thought,
crowned as it was by the works of Ricardo and Mill, of whom he considered
himself the intellectual heir and whose legacy he wanted to salvage rather
than destroy. Continuity, not upheaval, was his watchword, as illustrated
by the motto *natura non facit saltum*, "nature does not leap," which adorned
the title page of his *Principles of Economics*. It was this sense of continuity
that made Marshall not only extol the accomplishments of the past but
underplay the novelty of his own thought. Imperceptibly such self-efface-
ment would run over into a scientific strategy, which helped Marshall gain
wider acceptance for his views because they did not appear in a new and
strange form. Walras's text, to give but one example, was studded with
symbols and formulas; Marshall, in his *Principles*, hid the diagrams in
footnotes and the equations in appendixes.

DEMAND AND SUPPLY

The substance of Marshall's thought differed from that of Jevons, the
Austrians, and the Lausanne economists in that he kept utility theory in the
background and, on the other hand, went much further in developing a
theory of supply. His demand theory was richer than Cournot's since he
did not merely postulate a demand curve, deriving it intuitively from experience, as Cournot had, but connected it with utility theory. But the treatment
of utility did not hold the center of the stage, as it did in Jevons's and
Menger's work, and was instead subordinated to demand analysis, to which
these two writers had contributed little. Demand and supply, the "Marshallian cross" of the two curves, thus emerged as the two pillars of the Marshallian doctrine, and they were the analytical devices that integrated his whole
work. His main concern was not the theory of the consumer, as it had been
in the writings of Jevons and Menger, nor the general equilibrium of the
whole economy, but the particular equilibrium of the firm and of the industry. What Marshall shared with Jevons, the Austrians, and the Lausanne
economists was the emphasis on the disposition of a given output by microeconomic decision making The factors, "real" and monetary, that influenced

the determination of this output and its fluctuations had to wait for examination by other writers—monetary theorists and students of the business cycle, the Scandinavians, and Keynes, who rediscovered, as it were, macroeconomic analysis.

As for Marshall's position in doctrinal history, he is often characterized as a neoclassical economist, a designation that fits his intention to preserve the legacy of the classics and to refurbish their thought in line with new ideas. But there are two images of Marshall, one consisting of what he himself considered his position in doctrinal history to be and the other reflecting how it appeared to many interpreters of his thought. To begin with the latter, a frequent and almost standard interpretation of his work makes it a compromise or reconciliation between the thought of the classics, which centered around cost and supply, and that of the Austrians and Jevons, whose utility analysis seemed to underlie Marshall's demand theory. Marshall himself invariably rejected this interpretation, which by implication contains a judgment about certain priority claims that are obfuscated by Marshall's slowness in publishing his views. Although he acknowledged his obligations to Ricardo and Mill, he disclaimed any significant influence on his work by the writings of Jevons or the Austrians. Apart from the classics, his masters, he insisted, had been Cournot and Thünen, not Jevons or Menger. He admired Cournot's analysis of demand and of the firm and Cournot's interpretation of economic relationships as functional ones of mutual interdependence rather than causal ones. He extolled Thünen's contributions to analysis and his mastery of inductive and deductive methods, and above all Thünen's philanthropic humanitarianism.

Marshall's sense of realism made him view his economics not as complete and absolute but as tentative and provisional, a link in the endless quest for truth. The chain of continuity that connected his own thought with the tradition of the past was extended forward as well, and he believed that in time there would be revisions and improvements transcending his own doctrine, tied, as it was, to the intellectual tendencies and historical conditions of his environment. Of these historical conditions Marshall was an assiduous student, although the incipient specialization among economists and the jealousy with which some economic historians watched over the frontiers of their subdiscipline made him reluctant to branch out into the field of economic history. In his theoretical studies, however, he let himself be guided by a vast knowledge of empirical detail and of the historical forces as he understood them to be at work in his time. It was this attention to the facts of life that differentiated his contribution to economic theory from those of Jevons, the Austrians, and the Lausanne economists. Instead of resembling the pure theory of these writers, Marshall's work recalled the inimitable blend of empiricism and analysis characteristic of *The Wealth of Nations*.

Although Marshall's sense of realism made him forgo general equilibrium analysis, he did not consider the analysis of partial equilibria, the approach that he advocated and of which he became the master, as ideal.

The mechanical analogies of this approach might be useful as a first approximation, but he hoped that they would eventually give way to new methods, similar to those of biology rather than of mechanics, in which the behavior of the economic variables would be interpreted in terms of evolutionary change and growth.

MARSHALL'S *PRINCIPLES*

Marshall's ascendancy coincided with the passing from the scene of Mill, Cairnes, Jevons, and the generation of English historical economists who had been born in the 1820s. His *Principles of Economics,* published in 1890, soon acquired an authority in English-speaking countries comparable to that of Mill's *Principles* of 1848 among earlier generations of economists. It went through eight editions during the lifetime of its author, the last of which was published in 1920 and continued to be used as a textbook for many years. It was, in a sense, a unique work since it was the last to contain an original treatment of almost the entire economic theory of its time. Later books of the "principles" type were synthetic works rather than original ones or, when they were original, they considered a part of economic theory rather than the whole of it. Moreover, the attentive reader of Marshall's book would find that, although it raised many questions, it did not have conclusive answers to all of them. In this sense, Marshall's work constituted a challenge to successive generations of economists, who responded with an abundance of comments and interpretations relating to all phases of Marshall's work.

Marshall's analysis, centering as it did around particular equilibria, was pervaded by the *ceteris paribus* assumption, which made it possible to single out for attention one segment of the economy while neglecting the links that connected it with others. Such a neglect of mutual interdependence did not oppose reality so long as adjustments within the segment under study were of an order of importance too small to affect significantly the behavior of variables outside it and to be affected by repercussions stemming from the outside. Even under these circumstances, however, Marshall's approach opened up questions some of which long defied conclusive resolutions.

DEMAND ANALYSIS

The Marshallian demand curve, an analytical tool that was of supreme importance in his system, relates changes in the quantity demanded to changes in the demand price, and only to changes in the demand price. Thereby the door is closed to the potential influence of other factors, which are instead assumed to stay constant. However, as Marshall was well aware, a movement along the demand curve will as a rule require outlays that differ in amount. By affecting the amount of money at the disposal of prospective purchasers, such a movement is bound to affect the marginal utility of money, which will vary rather than stay constant. Marshall attempted to resolve this difficulty with the help of the assumption that the purchases read off along the demand curve would absorb only a small fraction of the prospective buyers' total consumption expenditure so that the marginal utility of money could for all practical purposes be considered a constant.

Marshall never supplied a complete list of the variables that he assumed to be constant for the purposes of his demand analysis. According to the standard interpretation, they included the prospective buyers' tastes, their incomes, and the prices of other commodities. This would allow for variations of total money expenditures for all commodities as well as for variations of the quantities purchased of other commodities because, unless these are allowed to change, the Marshallian demand curve would always appear in the form of a rectangular hyperbola with unitary elasticity of demand throughout.

If the Marshallian demand curve is drawn on the assumption of an unchanging income of the prospective buyer, there arises the further question whether it is the money income or the real income that is to be considered as constant. In the conventional interpretation, it is the money income rather than the real income of the consumer that is kept constant. This interpretation has been challenged by Milton Friedman, who has pointed out that the assumption of an unchanging money income implies that each point along the demand curve is associated with a different productive capacity of the community. At a lower price, for example, the community's total output of commodities would necessarily be larger since either a greater quantity of the commodity in question would be demanded or, in the case of an inelastic demand for that commodity, greater quantities of other commodities. To avert this consequence, Friedman has proposed to replace the conventional interpretation of the Marshallian demand curve and to hold real rather than money income constant. A lower demand price would then be associated with compensating variations either of money income or of the prices of other goods so as to yield a constant real income. Since in this interpretation the prices of commodities not closely related to the commodity in question are allowed to vary, the *ceteris paribus* rule would have to be modified accordingly.

Although Marshall left these matters undecided, he enriched his demand analysis by developing with considerable precision such concepts as demand elasticity and consumer surplus. His construction of demand elasticity in the form of a double fraction connecting a quantity change with a price change brought to perfection a long tradition in doctrinal history, which linked his contribution with the earlier ones of Tooke, Mill, and Whewell. Marshall's construction proved eminently useful and suggestive, both in econometric work and as a pattern that influenced the derivation of a host of other elasticity concepts—arc elasticity, income elasticity, cross elasticity of demand, elasticity of substitution of factors, and elasticity of expectations, to name only a few. There is some doubt whether Marshall, with his preference for realism, would have approved all these constructions. He himself was even wary about the elasticity of supply and underlined the lack of symmetry between demand and supply elasticity, the latter requiring, more than the former, specification of the length of the run for which the curve was drawn.

CONSUMER AND PRODUCER SURPLUS

Marshall's formula for demand elasticity was his own, but the notion of a consumer surplus had been anticipated in the writings of Jules Dupuit, a French civil engineer, during the mid-nineteenth century. The underlying idea stemmed from the observation that the demand curve of an individual slopes downward and that many of the demand prices identified by such a curve will typically lie above the market price. Marshall employed as an example an individual's demand for tea. At a high demand price only a small quantity would be demanded, which would increase with falling prices. On all units of tea preceding the last unit purchased, whose demand price coincided with the market price, the consumer would have earned a surplus equal to the difference between the respective demand prices and the market price. The consumer surplus was to be measured by the area enclosed by the demand curve and the horizontal price line. In Marshall's analysis the concept was expanded to apply also to the market demand represented by aggregate demand curves, a procedure that required interpersonal comparisons of utility which Marshall justified on the ground that in the mass and on the average economic events will affect the different classes of society in about equal proportions: "so that if the money measures of the happiness caused by two events are equal, there is not in general any very great difference between the amounts of happiness in the two cases."

In Marshall's analysis the consumer surplus emerged as a result of the conditions of the environment faced by the consumer. The forces of the market made it possible for him to obtain a good at the market price rather than at a higher demand price which he would be willing to pay for it rather than go without it. In the competitive environment that Marshall had in mind, the strategic factor giving rise to consumer surplus was invariably the market price, not the demand price. Marshall did not acknowledge that the conditions of the environment might affect the demand price as well and that a consumer surplus might be created or enlarged by means of advertising, which would raise the demand price above the market price.

Marshall's consumer surplus had its counterpart in producer surplus, measured by the excess of the market price over the supply price of labor— "worker's surplus"—or of saving—"saver's surplus." Just as the downward slope of the demand curve served as a prerequisite of consumer surplus, so did the upward slope of a supply curve in the case of producer surplus. Workers and savers are rewarded for each hour of work and for each dollar of saving at the same rate as that payable for the last hour of work and for the last dollar of saving.

Marshall's analysis of producer surplus leads conveniently to a discussion of his views concerning cost and supply. Unlike many of his contemporaries, Marshall did not stress the interpretation of costs in terms of opportunities foregone but instead operated with concepts of "real" and money costs. Real costs were the psychological "discommodities" involved in the production of commodities, the exertions of the laborers, and the "abstinences," or "waitings," of the savers. Money costs were defined as payments necessary to induce laborers and savers to come forth with these exertions. There was a further division of money costs into "prime," or variable, and "supplementary," or fixed, a distinction derived from accounting procedure and at its time pathbreaking. In the English-speaking countries this distinction soon became part of the treatment of the theory of the firm in the standard textbooks, as did Marshall's further distinction between different time periods available for the adjustment of the supply: the market period, the short period, and the long period. The time element, the foundation of Böhm-Bawerk's theories of capital and interest, thus pervaded Marshall's theories of price and of the firm. The time concept relevant to Marshall's analysis was a strictly functional one, which referred not to clock time but to the definitions of the three periods, with no adjustment of the supply taking place during the market period, with the quantities of inputs that are responsible for variable cost adjustable during the short period, and with all inputs, including the plant, varying in the long period. Marshall introduced the famous simile of the pair of scissors when examining the question whether demand or supply has a more potent effect on price, but he nevertheless pointed out that the influence of supply would be more powerful in the long run but less so in the market and short periods.

To his cost analysis Marshall added the concept of quasi rent, a differential return that is price determined and accrues to the owners of equipment, special skills, and natural abilities. These resources are in fixed supply for short periods and thus yield their owners an income which, though short-lived, resembles in other respects the true rent from the permanently fixed supply of land.

Depending upon whether an increase in the demand for the product of an industry would lead to a new equilibrium position at higher, lower, or unchanged prices, Marshall distinguished between increasing, decreasing, and constant-cost industries. In line with an earlier tradition he was inclined to identify increasing-cost industries with activities that have to cope with the inelasticity of nature's response to increased effort, whereas decreasing-cost industries were those which could benefit from man's power of improved organization, which raised the efficiency of labor and capital. In situations where one set of circumstances would offset the other, constant cost would result.

Marshall was reluctant to describe the economic universe of his time in terms of competition, a word that in his opinion had acquired an antisocial flavor. He preferred the expression "economic freedom," which was designed to bring out the self-reliance, the forethought, and the element of deliberate and free choice he considered characteristic of the economy of his environment. Although his sense of realism made him aware of monopolistic tendencies, he was not ready to accept a broad trend toward monopoly. In spite of his stated preference for "economic freedom," a somewhat vague term, he organized his analytical universe on the basis of competitive behavior.

To this analytical universe the existence of decreasing costs posed a serious threat. If a firm operated under conditions of declining unit costs, it would, instead of moving toward a position of competitive equilibrium, tend to increase indefinitely and eventually turn into a monopoly. Marshall made an effort to avoid this conclusion and introduced a number of novel devices which included a biological analogy purporting to explain managerial behavior patterns as well as such concepts as the representative firm, external economies, and, hinted at, imperfect competition. He taught, to begin with, that firms passed through a life cycle consisting of successive phases of managerial vigor and decay and that the latter would check the growth of firms. Furthermore, he introduced the concept of a moderately sized representative firm to serve as a model of competitive behavior. Neither of these two innovations, however, found much following. The biological analogy did not fit the facts of a business world peopled more and more by corporate enterprise, and the representative firm was not readily assimilated into the general structure of Marshall's theoretical analysis.

INTERNAL AND EXTERNAL ECONOMIES

Greater acclaim was accorded to Marshall's distinction between the cost-reducing economies incurred by the firm, which he divided into internal and external ones. A firm received benefits from the internal economies which it was able to derive from ever narrower specialization, from the growing scale of its operations, and from improved management. There were, in addition, external economies, benefits flowing to the firm considered as part of a larger industry. As examples of such benefits Marshall mentioned the availability of trade papers with technical and other information and the advantages that a firm derives from being located in a region with many firms of its kind, where it can draw on a pool of skilled labor and have on hand suppliers of highly specialized machinery and a host of subsidiary industries. Marshall's concept of external economies proved a durable innovation, which in the modified form of "social overhead" and "infrastructure" was to assume considerable importance in the later studies of economic development.

Highly suggestive also was an incidental observation, which Marshall put into a footnote and which anticipated the structure of the later theory of imperfect competition under product differentiation. "When considering an individual producer," Marshall wrote, "we must couple his supply curve

—not with the general demand curve for his commodity in a wide market, but—with the particular demand curve of his own special market." The context within which Marshall developed this thought was the problem posed by falling supply prices of a firm resulting from internal economies of scale, a problem that defied solution in terms of a competitive equilibrium. Marshall attempted to salvage this solution by pointing out that the particular demand curve will generally be very steep, perhaps as steep as the supply curve.

FURTHER DEVELOPMENTS OF MARSHALLIAN ECONOMICS

The preceding survey has stressed only the major contributions made by Marshall. Later writers, at Cambridge and elsewhere, would develop his thought further and would often display the mathematical scaffolding with lesser reluctance than was characteristic of Marshall. Progress was made with the development of welfare economics by Pigou, Marshall's favorite pupil and his successor to the Cambridge chair. This was followed by the elaboration of theories of imperfect or monopolistic competition by Sraffa, Harrod, Robinson, and Chamberlin. From Marshall's work in the classroom and from his testimony before official commissions there evolved a Cambridge tradition in monetary theory, which emerged in the work of Robertson and also left its mark on Keynes, yielding contributions to monetary and business cycle theory and to a monetary economics. About these matters Marshall's *Principles* contained little—"we may throughout this volume neglect," he wrote, "possible changes in the general purchasing power of money."

The rise of imperfect-competition theory and of macroeconomics went far to diminish the significance of Marshall's demand-and-supply analysis. This tool proved eminently useful when put to work for the purpose for which Marshall designed it, that is, for work on competitive situations in a microeconomic framework. The supply concept met the needs of the competitive case, when changes in the quantity supplied are a function only of changes in the supply price. But when the theory of imperfect competition introduced monopoly elements into the analysis, it became necessary to relate changes in the quantity supplied also to changes in the elasticity of demand, and for this the conventional supply concept was not suited. Analysis in terms of marginal revenue and marginal cost, which covered a broader spectrum of market situations and thus offered greater generality, came to eclipse demand-and-supply analysis, which applied only to the special case of competition. The demand-and-supply approach proved of limited use also in macroeconomics, which introduced new tools of analysis and in which the Marshallian concepts, fashioned, as they were, for micro-analysis, found employment only in modified form. If demand and supply are related to all labor, or to all goods, or to other broad aggregates, they lose the specific content given to them by Marshall when he wrote of, say, the demand for tea. In a way, the aggregative analysis had greater affinity with the work of Walras than with that of Marshall. Walras adhered to methodological individualism but allowed broad aggregations built up from individual cases; Marshall's aggregates rarely went beyond a single industry, although he did refer, in the context of his distribution theory, to the national income or national dividend.

PIGOU AND WELFARE ECONOMICS

The concept of the national income, if not the words, can be traced back to Petty, Smith, Ricardo, and Mill, who employed such expressions as "annual proceed" or "produce." With Marshall the concept established itself in the literature of economics under its present name, and it eventually became, albeit in a different context, the focal point of the work of another Cambridge economist, John Maynard Keynes, who was Marshall's student in 1906. Another link between the two was Arthur C. Pigou (1877–1959), Marshall's pupil and Keynes's teacher, and the holder of Marshall's chair from 1908 to 1943. Whereas in Marshall's writings the national income, like Ricardo's and Mill's produce, had served as a convenient reference term to designate the dividend to be distributed among landowners, laborers, and capitalists, it was put to new and important uses in Pigou's *Wealth and Welfare* (1912), later transformed into *The Economics of Welfare* (1920). In Pigou's welfare economics, which was stimulated by concern about unemployment and other social problems, Marshall's national income assumed a central position. Pigou interpreted economic welfare as a subjective state of mind that was ordinally measurable and could be related to the measuring rod of money. Its objective counterpart was the national income, certain types of changes of which were identified with changes in economic welfare. The latter would improve with an increase of the national income, with its wider diffusion, and with its greater stability.

By giving attention to the size and to changes of total output, Pigou raised questions that Smith had posed but which had disappeared from the mainstream of the nineteenth-century doctrinal tradition, which Ricardo had established and which centered around the problems of value and distribution arising from a given national output. The marginal revolution of the 1870s had brought to the fore the efficient allocation of such an output, leaving untouched again the question of the determination of its size. Although it was Keynes and not Pigou who eventually developed the theory of the determination of total output, Pigou's work constituted a milestone on the road leading toward such a theory. This was true in spite of Keynes's attacks against Pigou in his *General Theory* and Pigou's hostile reaction to Keynes's book.

In addition to the three welfare criteria of the size, distribution, and stability of the national income, Pigou's welfare economics contained such novel concepts as the marginal social and marginal private net product. These concepts were designed to shed light on situations in which a private enterprise failed to be the recipient of all the returns from its operations or in which it incurred costs that were not entirely borne by it. In situations such as these, the pursuit of private interest did not optimize the welfare of society: Too little was invested in instances of the first type, and too much in instances of the second type. Cases in point were the tenant farmer, who was reluctant to sink money into improvements which at common law would become the property of the landlord; the prospective investor in a forest who would remain uncompensated for the climatic benefits and the protection from soil erosion and depletion enjoyed by the community at large; the railroad company or factory whose operations imposed costs upon a neighborhood that became covered with soot; and the newly opened dispensary of potable spirits, whose customers would require the attention of an enlarged police force.

In these cases the marginal social net product—defined as the total net yield of the marginal increment of a resource, regardless of to whom it accrued—diverged from the marginal private net product—that part of the yield just described which accrued to the private owner of the resource. If such a divergency occurred, it would frustrate the attainment of an ideal optimum output, that is, of maximum national income. The attainment of the optimum required the fulfillment of two conditions. The marginal social net product would have to be equal in all uses of a resource—otherwise the transfer of resources from a use yielding a lesser marginal social net product to one in which this product was higher would raise total output. The second condition required equality of the marginal social net product with the marginal private net product. This meant that the private investor would have to receive all the yield from an investment and that he would have to bear its entire cost. Otherwise, when the marginal social net product exceeded the marginal private net product, a smaller than the optimum amount of resources would be devoted to a given use, whereas in cases of cost not borne by the investor, more than the optimum quantity would be invested.

The former type of divergency required public subsidies or tax privileges to raise the marginal private net product to the level of the marginal social net product; the latter type required special taxes to impose on private enterprise the equivalent of that part of its cost otherwise not borne by it. Pigou's analysis included a case of far more questionable merit, one to which Marshall had already given his attention and which set in motion a lively discussion. This was the case of decreasing-cost industries, supposedly not investing enough and eligible for subsidies, as contrasted with increasing-cost industries, presumably investing too much and liable to special taxes. In this case the policy of subsidies and taxes would result in lower prices, combined with rising output of the decreasing-cost industry and falling output of the increasing-cost industry. Marshall had discussed this matter in terms of consumer surplus, whereas Pigou approached it with the help of the private and social net product analysis, but neither produced convincing evidence that welfare could be improved by taxing one group of people and restraining their consumption of a good while using the tax revenue to stimulate the consumption of another good which the former group might not want.

Pigou's welfare economics was designed to reveal instances in which the pursuit of private gain did not redound to the welfare of society, and it included a larger number of cases than are recounted here. It offered, in fact, a systematic treatment of such instances, many of which, albeit in isolation, had been the subject of treatment by earlier writers, who had pointed out specific exceptions from the laissez faire doctrine of harmonious interests. Pigou's work transformed what had hitherto been isolated exceptions into a full-fledged system and thus represented a far sharper break with the harmony doctrine. It opened up a wide range of opportunities for public policy and constituted an early attempt at developing a principled theory of such a policy. Pigou's welfare economics, with its support of a wider diffusion of income, had its counterpart in the welfare state, which provided for social security and made opportunities for consumption along such lines as education, housing, and health care more nearly equal. In Pigou's native England, the institutions of the welfare state came to be paired with socialist measures resulting in the nationalization of substantial sectors of industry. These measures were not rejected by Pigou, as they would have been by Marshall, who favored some aims of the Socialists but was opposed to public enterprise. In his *Socialism versus Capitalism,* published in 1937, Pigou in fact took a position close to the Fabian Socialists. He suggested that with the changing circumstances and with the rise of the public corporation Marshall might have changed his mind.

PIGOU AND KEYNES

As Pigou grew older, his fame was overshadowed by the new doctrines of his Cambridge colleague Keynes. The relationship of his own work to that of Keynes was complex and ambiguous. At the outset he appeared as critic of Keynes's *General Theory* and held on to the opinion that wage cuts would restore employment, an opinion at variance with Keynes's emphasis on wages as a factor affecting the demand for goods. Although Pigou was a critic of Keynes, his own work contained a number of stepping-stones toward the edifice that Keynes built. As has been mentioned, he made the national income a central concept in his thought, subjecting it to a searching analysis as regards the measurement of its changes and its usefulness as an indicator of economic welfare. Furthermore, in his study of *Industrial Fluctuations* (1927), he laid stress on the psychological factor later referred to under the heading of "expectations," on "the mutual generation of errors of optimism and pessimism," and he was searching there also, albeit in vain, for a formal structure into which to fit what eventually became known as the multiplier. Moreover, in earlier writings Pigou opposed what later, under the name of "Treasury view," became a target of Keynes's attacks. This view, which can be traced to Ricardo and which has a measure of validity only on the assumption of full employment, denied that public works expand production and employment; instead it asserted that public works merely diverted to public use funds that otherwise would remain in private hands and be spent by private agencies.

Pigou, who took exception to this view as early as 1908, may thus be classified as both a critic and a precursor of Keynes, but this observation does not exhaust all aspects of the connection between his work and that of Keynes. In the 1940s and 1950s other facets of Pigovian economics received increasing attention and were employed as ammunition for a counterattack against Keynesian economics. Whereas Keynes stressed the relationship between income and expenditure, Pigou postulated a more complex relationship between wealth and expenditure. This view, in which price flexibility assumed an important function, yielded the Pigou effect, or real-balance effect, an analytical device with an adjustment mechanism which later opponents of Keynes compared favorably with the Keynesian analysis of income and expenditure. If there is unemployment attended by a decline in prices, there is an increase in the real value of that part of people's wealth or assets that is held in the form of money or of securities embodying money claims. This will induce people to reduce their rate of saving and stimulate their rate of expenditure since they will presumably want to hold constant or nearly constant the real value of their money holdings. With expenditures on the rise, prices, production, and employment will again increase, making for a return to a full-employment position. With the help of the real-balance effect some students of economics attempted to resuscitate the vanishing belief in the economy's tendency toward full employment, a tendency that Keynes denied. Others belittled the practical significance of the effect. Evidence was produced that it would require a massive price fall to work in the direction indicated by Pigou, and it was further pointed out that in the deflationary situation there would be generated expectations of continued decline, which would operate against an expansion of expenditures.

Just as Pigou's ideas provided a link with Keynes's macroeconomics, so did his welfare economics set a precedent which stimulated further work along similar lines. This work was carried on at Cambridge and elsewhere, and as it ceased to be the concern of a localized school it entered into the mainstream of economic doctrine.

NEW WELFARE ECONOMICS

The new welfare economics, as the post-Pigovian variants were designed, became the concern, albeit rarely the exclusive one, of a score of writers, whose works opened up a variety of views. Many approaches remained tentative and suggestive without yielding settled conclusions. With new vistas and emphases emerging every few years, the matter was in flux and constituted a challenge to further thought.

The new welfare economics was more diffuse than Pigou's also because the different variants took their points of departure not only from his ideas but alternatively from those of Pareto and Marshall. As for practical applications, some of the new approaches were far less promising than Pigou's. Pigou, nurtured as he was on the tradition of Marshall, attempted to construct a welfare economics that would lend itself to such applications. Like Mill before him, he was fond of citing Bacon's distinction between scientific works that bear fruit and those that shed light, and he was inclined to place the former above the latter. Some of the new welfare economics, in contrast, was developed on a very high level of abstraction, and its problems were shaped not so much by practical requirements as by the techniques employed. Another difference between Pigou and some later welfare economists was their reluctance to engage in comparisons of the welfare implications of changes in the distribution of income. Moreover, Pigou's egalitarianism made him favor a diffusion of income, a point of view not shared by those who instead followed the Mill–Edgeworth tradition.

THE COMPENSATION PRINCIPLE

The aim of the new welfare economics was to arrive at principled judgments which would rank alternative positions of the economy in terms of better or worse. In this manner, it was hoped, welfare economics could be of assistance to the policy maker by instructing him about the relative merits of different policies. The influence of Pareto was noticeable among those writers who took their departure from an optimum situation defined in such terms that a deviation from it could not improve the position of every member of the community without causing the deterioration of the position of at least one person. Much thought was given to the compensation principle developed by Kaldor and endorsed by Hicks in slightly modified form in the late 1930s, according to which a policy adversely affecting the income of some citizens could be justified, provided the policy resulted in an increase in income elsewhere in the economy sufficient to compensate those adversely affected.

Attempts were also made to construct a theoretical measurement of compensation, and for this purpose Hicks, in the 1940s, revived Marshall's concept of consumer surplus, now expressed in terms of indifference-curve analysis. It was to be employed for the measurement not, as in Marshall's case, of the difference between the market price and the demand price but of the compensation payable to the consumer in order to restore him to a level of satisfaction that had been adversely affected by changes in price or income. There was a protracted discussion also of the characteristics of collective indifference curves, drawn not for an individual but for a community, and Samuelson in particular subjected this concept to cogent criticism. The same writer also stressed the difficulties facing the unequivocal evaluation of changes in real income made up of disparate goods and services, a matter treated by earlier students under the heading of "index-number problem."

THEORY OF THE SECOND BEST

The question whether the step-by-step fulfillment of optimum conditions in segments of the economy would enhance economic welfare led to the development of a "general theory of the second best," which inquired into the ranking of less-than-optimal situations arising from violations of the optimum conditions. The optimum allocation of resources might be distorted by monopolies, tariffs, taxes, or subsidies, and the piecemeal removal of some of such obstacles would have effects that were far from unequivocal. For example, in a world of monopolies the abolition of public support for the prices of agricultural products might not lead to an improved allocation of resources, nor might the establishment of a free-trade area of limited spatial extent have such effects.

PUBLIC GOODS

In the field of public finance, welfare analysis brought considerable advances leading to the development of a theory of public goods. Such goods differ from private goods in a number of important respects. They bestow benefits that are often so widely diffused that it is impossible to allocate their costs to the individual beneficiaries in a commensurate proportion. Moreover, in the case of pure public goods their enjoyment by some will not curtail their enjoyment by others. The market will not produce such goods for a variety of reasons, but chiefly because if everyone can enjoy what is produced for someone else, no one will want to reveal his demand for a public good. Market demand curves for private goods result from the horizontal addition of the quantities demanded by individuals, whereas if an attempt were made to construct an aggregate demand curve for public goods, it would require the vertical addition of the prices that individuals are willing to pay for varying quantities of the public good.

COST-BENEFIT ANALYSIS

Goods and services not made available by the market will be rendered by public authorities, but this statement leaves open the question of how a public authority can ascertain whether to undertake one project in preference to another. The solution of questions of this sort, posed by Dupuit in

1844 in a paper on the utility of public works, was brought nearer by modern cost-benefit analysis, or project appraisal, which established procedures paralleling those that underly private investment decisions. Cost-benefit analysis was designed to yield estimates of the costs and benefits of a public investment project. Among the problems encountered in this work was the selection of an interest rate to discount the value of future benefits and to amortize the capital employed, the inclusion or exclusion of secondary, or spillover, costs and benefits, and the valuation of intangible benefits such as scenic beauty or the saving of human life.

The analysis of public goods and of costs and benefits of public investments went beyond the work of Marshall and Pigou, but much of the new welfare economics was nevertheless pervaded by Marshall's external economies and Pigou's divergence between social and private return, reflecting the spillover of benefits for which the beneficiary did not pay or the imposition of injury for which the damaged party received no compensation. These matters were treated in the new welfare economics under the heading of "externality," and they were drawn into the wider perspective of public policies affecting the quality of the environment, health, education, the renewal of cities, unemployment, stability of prices, and economic growth.

THE PARADOX OF VOTING

The new welfare economics seemed to offer the promise of a self-directed humanity, one that could escape with impunity the often misdirected discipline of the market. But looming in the paradise of a rationally determined optimum of welfare there was a serpent, of which Condorcet, the early prophet of perfection and target of Malthus's attacks, had been aware and of which Kenneth J. Arrow in his *Social Choice and Individual Values* (1951) gave warning. Arrow, who pursued his argument with the help of symbolic logic rather than with the hitherto conventional differential calculus, indicated certain flaws in collective decision making, which might frustrate the goals so carefully laid out by the welfare economists. An individual may be assumed to order his preferences transitively, that is, if he prefers A to B and B to C, he will also prefer A to C. But what is true of an individual may not apply to the community. Community preference might not express itself unequivocally but yield a "paradox of voting." Assume three alternative policies, A, B, and C, and three groups of citizens, equal in numbers, 1, 2, and 3. Then

> group 1 may prefer A to B and B to C,
> group 2 may prefer B to C and C to A,
> group 3 may prefer C to A and A to B.

The situation is paradoxical in that A is preferred to B by a majority (groups 1 and 3), as is B to C (groups 1 and 2), whereas another majority (groups 2 and 3) prefers C to A.

Arrow's book drew attention to the related structure of voting and of the market, and it stimulated further pathbreaking work which cut across interdisciplinary lines and applied analyses developed within the confines of economics first to political science and eventually to sociology. In the 1960s a theory of politics, with a mathematical structure similar to that of economics, appeared, an important advance which like most acts of creative scholarship consisted of the convergence of ideas hitherto unrelated.

IMPERFECT COMPETITION: SRAFFA

Marshall's concern with decreasing cost, shared by so many students of welfare economics, set in motion still another train of thought, which in time brought to fruition theories of imperfect or monopolistic competition. To trace the development of these theories it is necessary to return to the Cambridge of the 1920s where a young Italian economist, Piero Sraffa (b. 1898), was now heard and where he published in 1926 a seminal article entitled "The Laws of Returns under Competitive Conditions."

Sraffa's great accomplishment, achieved at the age of twenty-eight, signaled the chance for making such contributions that the changing approach to economic science gave to youth. As economics became more technical and pure it acquired a structure not unlike that of mathematics and the natural sciences, where great advances are often the work of people in their twenties. In contrast, a far longer period of gestation was involved in the works of economists who kept closer to the humanities and whose writings reflected the gathering of experience and worldly wisdom. Smith's *Wealth of Nations,* Marshall's *Principles,* and Keynes's *General Theory* were the accomplishments of mature men, who had already reached life's midpassage at the time of the publication of their principal works. On the other hand, the great contributions to pure theory by Menger, Jevons, Cournot, and Walras were made when these men were in their thirties, and earlier still in the case of Jevons if preliminary progress reports rather than the great work itself serve as the criterion.

CHAMBERLIN AND ROBINSON

In the twentieth century substantial contributions were made by writers who in their twenties were able to produce accretions to the work of their elders. This was true of other founders of the theories of limited competition. Like Sraffa, Edward H. Chamberlin (1899–1967) was twenty-eight when he submitted a dissertation later transformed into *The Theory of Monopolistic Competition* of 1933, the same year in which Joan Robinson, then barely 30, published her *Economics of Imperfect Competition.*

The gist of Sraffa's article was a plea for an analysis of the firm in terms of monopoly rather than of competition. With decreasing costs widespread, the obstacle to an increase in the sales of a firm was not the threat of rising costs but the unwillingness of the market to absorb larger quantities without either price reductions or increased "marketing expenses." Sraffa considered this situation common enough to require an adequate analytical model, and he adopted Marshall's suggestion of particular demand curves of special markets. Such a particular demand curve would slope downward like the demand curve facing a monopolist. It could be so drawn because buyers would not be indifferent in their choice between the products of particular firms but would, within limits, prefer one over the others. The causes of such preference were manifold and included trademarks, names, and "such special features of modelling or design in the product as—without constituting it a distinct commodity intended for the satisfaction of particular needs—have for their principal purpose that of distinguishing it from the products of other firms." A buyer's demand price for a product so distinguished reflected not only the valuation that he placed on this product but also the prices at which similar products could be purchased from other firms.

The work of Mrs. Robinson, who was connected with the University of Cambridge as a student and as a teacher, stemmed from that of Sraffa and was linked with the Cambridge economists' concern about decreasing costs. Chamberlin, a student and a teacher at Harvard University, formed his ideas without direct dependence on these strands of thought and had indeed arrived at them prior to the publication of Sraffa's article. However, several of his teachers, among whom there were such outstanding American theorists as Allyn Young and Frank Knight, had participated in the discussion of Marshallian and Pigovian ideas, and their work formed a link in the transmission of thought from one Cambridge to the other.

Robinson and Chamberlin tackled a range of largely identical problems. Their works overlapped in significant respects and differed in others, which Chamberlin in particular never tired of emphasizing. Marshallian economics had brought to the fore the analysis of the industry, one composed of many firms producing perfect substitutes. In the works of Chamberlin and Robinson the analysis of the industry gave way to that of the firm. Since the latter had a clientele that preferred its product over that of other firms, it faced a demand curve that sloped downward, as did the demand curve of the monopolist. Such a firm would engage in "non-price competition" through special services and features of its product rather than reduce its price competitively. Instead of defining the equilibrium position in the hitherto conventional terms of an intersection of curves, Chamberlin and Robinson, although in not exactly the same manner, posited an equilibrium position in terms of the "tangency solution," that is, of the tangency of the demand and average total cost curves. Since the downward falling demand curve would touch the cost curve at a point higher and to the left of its minimum, there would be "excess capacity," a capacity output being defined as one taking place at minimum average total cost.

Chamberlin and Robinson differed in their treatment of marginal revenue, a tool of analysis that Chamberlin employed only sparingly but which permeated Robinson's analysis. They differed further in their attention to market situations where sellers are few, a matter excluded by Mrs. Robinson from her analysis but discussed by Chamberlin under the heading of "oligopoly," a designation which soon became common usage. Chamberlin also included in his formal analysis of the equilibrium of the firm such variables as the product itself, that is, its "quality," and selling costs as distinguished from costs of production. There were further differences in the social philosophy of the two writers. Chamberlin was impressed by the diversity of products and opportunities for choice made available by monopolistic competition, whereas Mrs. Robinson stressed its waste, criticized it from the welfare point of view, and pleaded for government intervention. Chamberlin, in later writings, berated trade unions, whereas Mrs. Robinson considered them as instruments capable of fending off monopsonostic "exploitation," which she defined in terms of the wage or the marginal revenue product of labor falling short of the value of its marginal product. In the further course of their careers, Chamberlin devoted his life to buttressing and consolidating his theory of monopolistic competition. Mrs. Robinson's interests were wider in scope, and she became in time one of the foremost interpreters of the economic theories of Marx in English academic economics as well as a leading exponent of Keynesian economics, which she enriched with such concepts as "disguised unemployment" and "beggar-my-neighbor remedies for unemployment." She made noteworthy contributions to such varied fields as the theory of the foreign exchanges and the analysis of growth and development when this subject aroused the attention of economists during the period following World War II.

The simultaneous publication of the works by Chamberlin and Robinson in 1933 constituted again an example of a multiple discovery of the type so frequently found in the history of economics. Besides the two, there were a host of other writers then at work who attempted to shed light on the no-man's-land lying between competition and monopoly. A related multiple discovery, at which many minds were at work during the late 1920s and early 1930s, was the concept of marginal revenue, which had been known to Cournot as a mathematical expression a hundred years earlier and which occasionally, albeit nameless or under a different designation, had appeared in the literature. It was again introduced by Roy Harrod in 1930, then under the name of "increment of aggregate demand," and came into prominence with Mrs. Robinson's book, the new and lasting designation "marginal revenue" having been coined by her husband, E. A. G. Robinson.

Chamberlin's view of market situations as a spectrum with pure competition and monopoly forming the extremes and with competition and monopoly blended in between was before long incorporated into the leading textbooks, as was the marginal revenue and marginal cost apparatus, which permeated Mrs. Robinson's work. Further analyses of markets were attempted by numerous writers, but much of this work was only tenuously related to the theories of monopolistic and imperfect competition. On the whole these failed to serve as starting points for important further advances along theoretical or empirical lines. Being purely formal, they did not lend themselves to verification in quantitative terms, nor did they assist the policy maker. They continued to be presented in the textbooks for decades in very much the same form that the founders had given to them. After the mid-1930s Keynesian macroeconomics cast its spell on many who considered its further development a more challenging task than work on microeconomics. Later there arose still another challenge in the form of such rival approaches to the conventional pattern of microeconomics as game theory and mathematical programming.

The theory of monopolistic competition was accorded outright rejection only by the members of the Chicago school, who had conservative leanings both in politics and in matters of doctrine. Frank Knight and, among a later generation, George Stigler and Milton Friedman, proposed to adhere to the old-established dichotomy between competition and monopoly. They upheld competition as the norm of socially desirable business behavior and denied that the theory of monopolistic competition was equipped with predictive power. They were dissatisfied in particular with Chamberlin's concept of a "group" of firms selling differentiated products, a concept that they found lacking in precision, and with his assumption of uniform cost and demand curves of the firms constituting the group, an assumption that facilitated the tangency solution. Doubts about the tangency solution were also expressed in other quarters. As Roy Harrod pointed out, firms would be reluctant to charge prices that by yielding a net revenue would attract newcomers, whose entry would in turn push the demand curve downward until it become tangent to the cost curve.

On the whole, however, the emergence of the theory of monopolistic competition marked the beginning of an era in which there was increasing willingness among economists to shed the model of pure and perfect competition of its normative implications for socially desirable behavior. Schumpeter, as has been noted, took an apologetic attitude to monopoly. J. M. Clark suggested a new norm consisting of "workable" or "effective" competition, which he characterized by such features as the number of firms in a market and the share of each, the size of profits, readiness to introduce new technologies, and freedom of entry, without, however, explicitly indicating which of these features was to be the one to count. In again another version monopoly was given a measure of rehabilitation in John Kenneth Galbraith's theory of "countervailing power," in which monopoly power on one side of the bargaining table was considered offset by monopoly power on the other side.

MONETARY THEORY: MARSHALL

The pursuit of the evolving theories of imperfect competition and of later developments in the study of markets has again removed us from the Cambridge of Marshall's time. There remains for discussion the monetary thought of the Cambridge school, a subject that calls for a return to the closing decades of the nineteenth century when Marshall's ideas about these matters took shape. Marshall, never a hasty writer, was particularly reluctant to put these ideas into print. They could be gleaned from the evolving oral tradition at Cambridge, from Marshall's occasional presentation of material before official commissions of inquiry, and eventually from his *Money, Credit and Commerce,* which was not published until 1923, a year before his death.

Marshall's productive life coincided largely with the Victorian period of prosperity and expansion when monetary problems did not loom as large as they had during the bullion debate of the early nineteenth century and during the subsequent controversy between the followers of the banking and currency schools. Later in the century bimetallism posed new problems, which gave rise to a discussion among economists from many countries but which were not nearly so pressing as those that had been faced earlier or as those that cast their shadow over the last few years of Marshall's life. It was in the 1920s, when Britain and others countries found themselves exposed to the grave monetary disorders caused by the war, that a new monetary debate ensued, which continued with even greater vigor during the next decade when conventional monetary thought and practice were challenged by a worldwide depression of unprecedented severity. In these debates a new generation of Cambridge economists took a leading part, notably Dennis H. Robertson (1890–1963), who was connected with Cambridge during most of his life and succeeded Pigou to Marshall's chair in 1944, Ralph Hawtrey (b. 1879), who after an education at Cambridge served the British Treasury as an economic adviser, and, of course, John Maynard Keynes (1883–1946). Keynes's contributions to monetary theory were overshadowed by his later income and employment theory, which introduced new trends of thought, alien to the organon fashioned by Marshall and his followers and marking the end of the Cambridge school as an instrument serving this organon.

THE CASH-BALANCE APPROACH

The legacy of monetary thought that Marshall left to the new generation of Cambridge economists consisted principally of the "cash-balance," or liquidity approach, considered by Marshall a refinement of the quantity theory of money, which he, generally speaking, endorsed. In the later development, which can be traced here only in its broadest outlines, the Cambridge economists devoted much effort to the elaboration of the cash-balance approach, but they rejected the quantity theory and replaced it with an income theory—milestones on the road toward Keynes's macroeconomics.

Among the determinants of the money supply and, within the framework of the quantity theory, of the price level, Marshall's cash-balance approach singled out the public's desire to hold a fraction of income in the form of cash balances. Side by side with this Marshall also referred to a fraction of assets that the public wanted to hold in the form of cash, but this thought was not followed up in the early formulation of the cash-balance approach. Marshall's analysis, which he developed in verbal terms, was subsequently pursued with the help of symbols and equations. In its simplest formulation it yielded the equation $M = kY$, where M represented the quantity of money, Y the money income, and k the portion of the public's money income that it desired to hold in the form of cash.

At first glance it seemed difficult to differentiate the cash-balance approach from the quantity theory, developed at the time by Irving Fisher in terms of an equation of exchange which related the quantity of money and its velocity, M and V, to the price level. It was pointed out that the Marshallian k was but the reciprocal of V. For example, if the public desired to hold cash balances equal to its income for two months, $k = 1/6$ and $V = 6$. There was, however, a fundamental difference between these two approaches since the Cambridge economists, by stressing the importance of k, concentrated attention on changes in the public's desire for cash balances, or for liquidity, as a strategic factor affecting prices. As it was also recognized that liquidity had its cost in terms of interest foregone, the ground was prepared for the later conceptualization of the functional relationship between interest rates and desired cash balances in Keynes's liquidity preference theory of interest.

HAWTREY'S INCOME APPROACH

The gulf between the Cambridge approach and the quantity theory of money widened when Hawtrey in 1913 began to advocate a monetary theory that combined the cash-balance with an income approach. This latter approach, of which Tooke had been an exponent in the mid-nineteenth century, now found followers in many countries, including Wieser and Schumpeter in Austria, Wagner in Germany, Aftalion in France, and Wicksell in Sweden. The quantity theory set forth the determinants of the price level in terms of the quantity and velocity of money, whereas the exponents of the income theory looked to income and expenditure as factors affecting the price level. Keynes, who adopted the income theory in 1930, underlined the difference between the two approaches in this way: The quantity theory makes stoutness the effect of letting out one's belt; the income theory acknowledges that a stout person requires a larger belt.

In the pursuit of the income approach, which related the price level to expenditures, Hawtrey traveled a road at the end of which beckoned such concepts as the total output of the economy and the total demand for goods. Pigou, who investigated the effects of a reallocation of resources on total output, reached a similar destination by a different route. In Pigou's analysis the behavior of "real" factors and the resulting changes in real income stood out, whereas Hawtrey's model was that of a money economy, the performance of which was determined by streams of money expenditure. This was a novel approach, which contained more than one indication of the direction in which economics was to move in the 1930s.

In sentences that in the 1910s anticipated the core of the later macro-economics, Hawtrey characterized "the aggregate of all money incomes" as "the total effective demand for all finished commodities in any community." By stating that "all costs of production are someone's income," he gave his own version of what later became known as Keynes's law. Hawtrey's approach, which emphasized the pervasive influence of monetary phenomena on the level of output, marked a sharp break with the methods of the classics and of Marshall, who accorded to money only a subsidiary role in explaining economic change. Their analysis stressed the real factors, while putting aside the "distorting veil of money." Hawtrey may have exaggerated the importance of his own approach when, for example, he supported a business cycle theory that singled out the monetary factor as responsible for this type of economic fluctuations. But he opened up a new perspective when he insisted that "the distorting veil of money cannot be put aside. As well. . . play lawn tennis without the distorting veil of the net. All the skill and all the energy emanate from the players and are transmitted through the rackets to the balls. The net does nothing; it is a mere limiting condition. So is money."

In Hawtrey's monetary theory of the business cycle the downturn was attributed to the policy of the banks, which would contract credit once they found themselves exposed to a shrinking cash position. This was but one among many business cycle theories developed during the early decades of the nineteenth century when an increasing number of economists gave attention to this matter. The business cycle theorists looked, albeit from a special point of view, at the overall performance of the economy, and their work formed another link with that of Keynes, who developed a general theory of the subject in 1936.

ROBERTSON

Robertson's theory of the business cycle, formed when the author was in his twenties and published in 1915, combined the monetary factor with such real phenomena as harvest cycles, partial overproduction, and the temporary exhaustion of investment opportunities. Here and in his later writings Robertson envisaged cyclical fluctuations as part of a wider process of economic growth. He was a forerunner of later growth theories as well as a pioneer student of dynamic period analysis leading to an equilibrium over time and developed in terms of a "day" in which income is earned and another day in which it is spent. Other concepts he employed anticipated the later saving-investment analysis and the distinction between *ex ante* and *ex post* categories. Robertson was a student and associate of Keynes, but the two became estranged in the 1930s and were only superficially reconciled when their wartime work brought them together in the 1940s. Whereas earlier their paths had seemed to converge, Robertson became a persistent critic of Keynes's *General Theory*. He took a dim view of

Keynes's saving-investment analysis, of the multiplier, of fiscal policy, and of the liquidity-preference theory of interest, which he considered less adequate to account for thrift and industry than the loanable-funds theory. Although Robertson had early in his career rejected the so-called Treasury view, according to which expenditures for public works necessitate a corresponding reduction of private expenditures, he was dissatisfied with the general character of Keynes's macroeconomics, with its emphasis on the short run and with its policy implications, which to him appeared as illiberal and tending to inflation and which he characterized as offering for nourishment what in truth was a medicine to be taken sparingly. Keynes's thought, so it appeared to Robertson, was hardening into a new orthodoxy that became increasingly intolerant and rigid.

But, however much Robertson might attempt to salvage the Marshallian heritage in writings that sparkled with wit and ingenuity, a large part of it was dissipated when the 1930s came to their close. In microeconomics Marshall's demand-and-supply approach was rivaled by the marginal revenue and marginal cost approach. Marshall's "industry" was considered relevant only for the limiting case of a purely competitive market. Microeconomics itself, with its analysis of particular equilibria, was pushed into the background by the rise of a macroeconomics that concentrated on aggregative equilibria and took cognizance of the influence of monetary factors. Instead of the earlier emphasis on "value and distribution"—the allocation of a given quantity of resources—questions were now raised about the factors that influenced the determination of that quantity itself, that is, the level of income and employment. In part the new problems emerged in consequence of a logical extension of Marshall's thought; in part they were generated not by the logic of science but by the changing circumstances of the time, which called for increasing attention to monopolistic markets and to fluctuations in income and employment and which became more sensitive to the demands for social justice.

OXFORD ECONOMISTS: HARROD AND HICKS

Marshall's and Keynes's association with Cambridge accounted for its unique stature in the world of academic economics during the first half of the twentieth century. Economic work of great distinction was, however, also carried on at other English universities. After an interval following Edgeworth's death, Roy Harrod (b. 1900) and John Hicks (b. 1904) emerged as the leading Oxford economists. Harrod's influence was felt in the discussion leading to the conceptualization of marginal revenue and in international trade and business cycle theory. His crowning achievement was the construction of a model of steady growth, which set forth the conditions under which additional productive capacity, generated by new investment, would be absorbed by the additional income likewise generated by the new investment. Side by side with this work in theory, other Oxford economists cultivated empirical studies. With the help of the survey method, long established in sociological work but new in economics, attempts were made to test the empirical relevance of theoretical models by inquiring into the sensitivity of management to changes in the interest rate and into the extent to which managerial decisions were based on calculations in terms of marginal values.

Hicks was a leader among those responsible for the resuscitation and refinement of indifference-curve analysis and for the assimilation of the general equilibrium approach into English economics. He made other notable contributions to welfare economics, which he attempted to reconstruct on the basis of Marshall's consumer surplus, to the marginal productivity theory, to the classification of innovations, and to growth theory.

THE LONDON SCHOOL OF ECONOMICS

At the London School of Economics, the leading economist for many years was Edwin Cannan (1861–1935), a student of doctrinal history and a somewhat captious critic of the classics. Cannan, an exponent of the commonsense approach to economics, viewed the technical economics of Alfred Marshall with skeptical detachment. For some time academic economics at the London School, originally a foundation of Fabian Socialists, came under influences that were conservative both in economic thought and in politics, and the school acquired a status similar to that of the University of Chicago in the academic economics of the United States. Among the great teachers who were associated with it in the 1930s and later, Lionel Robbins (b. 1898) and F. A. Hayek (b. 1899) stood out. Both were erudite and urbane scholars, more philosophers than technicians, who kept alive the link between economics and the humanities and made important contributions to doctrinal history. Robbins's influential *Essay on the Nature and Significance of Economic Science* (1932) supported the famous definition of economics as a science treating of the allocation of scarce resources; to Hayek, economics was primarily concerned with nonpurposive social formations, that is, the phenomena of competitive markets, which arise as the unintended consequences of individual or group action. Their economics offered scant accommodation to aggregative analysis, quantitative-empirical studies, and government intervention, which played an ever greater role in mid-twentieth-century economics.

Chapter 26

FROM WICKSELL TO KEYNES:
The Upsurge
of Monetary
and Income Analysis

NEUTRAL MONEY

The marginal revolution of the 1870s left in its wake a refurbished economics of the consumer and of the firm. Much attention was given to the behavior of relative prices but no contributions of similar significance were made to the analysis of money and of the price level. Here the rule of the quantity theory of money continued unabated, and since in this field little had been destroyed, there was little opportunity for reconstruction. Attempts were made to make money the subject of the same type of microeconomic utility analysis that was applied to commodities in general, but these attempts had the result of understating the role of money in the economy rather than bringing to the fore its commanding influence. Walras, the most ambitious system builder of his time, introduced the *numéraire*, which singled out the value-measuring function of money but abstracted from its other important functions. Marshall discarded monetary influences on the economy by constructing his *Principles* on the assumption of a stable price level. Something important was missing from the structure of the economy that the architects of the marginal revolution had built. It was a structure that resembled an imaginary barter economy more closely than the money economy of the modern world. Money was considered primarily as "neutral" instead of as an active instrument affecting the level of output and the distribution of income.

This weakness of neoclassical economics was only inadequately relieved by recourse to the quantity theory of money, which an American economist, Irving Fisher, expounded in the form of the "equation of exchange," $MV = PT$—the quantity of money times its velocity equals the price level times the physical volume of trade. The quantity theory of money, it was hoped, would supply the "multiplicative factor," which would determine the price level and supply the system of relative prices with an absolute dimension. The equation of exchange, however, far from forming part of a complete theory of the price level, merely provided an overview of some of the factors related to it. The behavior of M, the quantity of money, could only be brought into a causal relationship with the price level under the most stringent of *ceteris paribus* assumptions, which required that V, a highly volatile element, be considered as a constant.

Monetary questions again became a subject of discussion during the closing decades of the nineteenth century when a worldwide decline of commodity prices coincided with efforts aiming at the remonetization of silver and the establishment of a bimetallic monetary standard. Marshall's contributions to monetary theory, which were meant to be in accord with the quantity theory of money but went beyond it, were a product of this debate, and from Marshall's views Hawtrey and Robertson took their point of departure. Originally the new monetary debate was primarily concerned with the behavior of prices. As it went on, it became intertwined with the analysis of cyclical fluctuations. As the overall performance of the economy became a subject of study, attention was given not only to the behavior of prices but to income and employment as well, aspects that came to the fore in the work of Keynes.

WICKSELL

When the Cambridge economists started out on their search for new ways in a territory on which the quantity theory of money shed only a dim and uncertain light, they were not fully aware that this territory had already been mapped out and that a path had been opened by someone else. The pathbreaker was the Swedish economist Knut Wicksell (1851–1926), whose principal works, written at the turn of the century, were for many years available only in German and did not appear in English translation before the mid-thirties when Keynes's *General Theory* was ready for publication. Wicksell's writings and those of other Swedish economists, such as Myrdal and Lindahl, constituted guideposts on the road toward a theory of income and employment, but they became more widely known in the English-speaking countries only after Keynes had arrived at his own version of such a theory.

Generally speaking, Wicksell was a contemporary of the architects of the marginal revolution as well as of Marshall, Böhm-Bawerk, and Wieser. But he turned to economic studies in a later period of his life and was thus able to use their work as a base from which he would branch out into new and untried directions. Although he was an exponent of an economic theory that was as pure as that of Walras and of the Austrians and purer than Marshall's, his career was far more stormy than that of these sedate and dignified academicians, and it did not exhaust itself in academic work.

Unlike Marshall, who abhorred all controversy, Wicksell actively sought it, but his chosen field of battle was a wide range of social and political problems, often rather sensitive ones, rather than academic economics. Unlike the Austrians, who adhered to views that made them eligible for the highest positions in government, Wicksell was a nonconformist whose opinions often gave offense to the public authorities and who did indeed at the age of fifty-eight serve a sentence of two months' imprisonment.

Wicksell's advocacy of unorthodox views brought him much notoriety and was of no help in his later teaching career. But it was precisely his interest in social problems, more specifically the population problem, that made him turn to economic studies in the 1880s when he was already in his thirties and had earned degrees in mathematics and natural science. Although the issues on which he was to take a stand included such diverse matters as alcoholism, prostitution, civil marriage, freedom of speech, and the institution of the monarchy, he considered overpopulation a central problem and, following Mill rather than Malthus, persevered in the advocacy of birth control.

Beginning in 1885 Wicksell set out to study economics in England, France, Germany, and Austria, as well as in his native country, and earned a meager livelihood as a journalist and lecturer. The first teaching appointment did not come his way until 1899, at the age of forty-eight, and then only after he had obtained an additional degree, in law, as was required of academic economists, who were members of the law faculty. At that time he was already the author of the three works that together with one published a few years later constitute his great achievement: *Value, Capital and Rent* (1893, Eng. trans. 1954), a book on the theory of public finance entitled *Finanztheoretische Untersuchungen* (1896), and *Interest and Prices* (1898, Eng. trans. 1934). In 1900 Wicksell obtained an interim appointment at the University of Lund, which a deeply divided faculty regularized a year later. At Lund he taught until his retirement in 1916, and there he published two volumes of *Lectures on Political Economy* (1901, 1906; Eng. trans. 1934–35).

During his years as a wandering scholar, Wicksell became acquainted with the various approaches to economics then in vogue in different European countries—the historical economics of the Germans, the pure theory in its Austrian and Walrasian variants, and the more realistic analysis of Marshall. He reacted to them in his own way. With Marshall he shared a thorough training in mathematics, but he lacked Marshall's touch with reality and his intimate knowledge of historical conditions. Whereas Marshall attempted to obliterate the dividing line between theoretical and applied economics, Wicksell, on the whole, adhered to the distinction that Walras had drawn between pure, applied, and "social" economics, and he cultivated especially the pure branch. His approach had a greater affinity with that of the Austrians and of Walras than did Marshall's, and unlike Marshall he did not praise the efforts of the German historical economists. In its broad outline what Wicksell attempted was a fusion of Austrian and

Walrasian thought, in which a version of Böhm-Bawerk's capital theory, modified in line with the marginal productivity theory, was to be fitted into the general equilibrium system.

In the pursuit of this attempt Wicksell introduced numerous refinements and corrections, some of which paralleled contemporary work by other scholars, for example, his marginal productivity theory, developed one year ahead of Wicksteed, and his transformation of utility into demand functions. Wicksell, however, was virtually the only economist of note to criticize the view, advanced by some of the architects of the marginal revolution, that competitive prices denote a social optimum. Instead he pointed out that in the presence of pronounced inequalities of income an exchange between the rich and the poor might yield a larger total utility when effected at a price suitably fixed than at the competitive price, and he cautiously expanded the argument to apply it to minimum wages and maximum hours of work established by legislation or by labor unions. Wicksell favored government intervention in a number of instances, suggested marginal cost rather than full cost pricing for public utilities and common carriers, and developed thoughts from which support for the selective nationalization of certain industries could be drawn. He introduced the principle of marginal utility into his analysis of public finance and supplemented the conventional theory of the shifting and incidence of taxation with many new insights relating to the effects of taxes on the distribution of income, to questions of social choice and decision making in these matters, and to the general problem of justice in taxation.

THE INCOME APPROACH TO MONETARY THEORY

These contributions were distinguished enough to earn Wicksell recognition as a thinker of substance and originality, but the contribution for which he is best remembered is the development of a monetary theory which went beyond the conventional quantity theory and with which business cycle and income theory could eventually be integrated. Wicksell took as his point of departure Tooke's income theory of prices, enunciated in 1844, according to which it is not the quantity of money but the national income designed for expenditure that determines the price level. Following Tooke in employing such macroeconomic concepts as the general demand and supply of goods, Wicksell related changes in the price level to the general monetary demand for goods exceeding, or falling short of, their supply and set himself the task of explaining how and why this would occur.

WICKSELL'S INTEREST THEORY

In his explanation of changes in the price level Wicksell fell back on the rate of interest, in itself not a startling idea since there was a tradition of long standing, extending from Ricardo to Marshall, which recognized, besides the direct influence of the quantity of money on prices, an indirect one which operated via the rate of interest. If the quantity of money increased, so this argument ran, low interest rates would be accompanied by an expansion of credit, and borrowers would bid up prices when putting their new financial resources to use. High and low rates are relative terms, however, and the argument did not provide a standard that could serve as a criterion whether the interest rate was high or low. Such a criterion Wicksell made available by distinguishing between the "natural" rate of interest and the loan rate. The natural rate was the expected return from newly constructed capital, whereas the loan rate was that which borrowers were charged by the banks. As the two rates diverged, for example, if the natural rate exceeded the loan rate, a "cumulative process" ensued in which prospective investors, eager to maximize profit, bid up the prices of productive resources, causing in turn money incomes and the prices of consumer goods to rise. In the case of an excess of the loan rate over the natural rate, the cumulative process would move in the opposite direction.

Wicksell's theory of the two rates opened up a wealth of new insights. It contained an explanation of the investment decision in line with the maximization principle as well as an allusion to the role of expectations. And, as it later became apparent, his natural rate of interest was an analogue to Keynes's marginal efficiency of capital. Like Keynes, Wicksell considered investment determined by the relationship between the loan rate of interest and the expected return from newly constructed capital. Pathbreaking as Wicksell's achievement was, much remained to be done to transform it into a full-fledged theory of income determination. His concern was with price changes occurring at full employment rather than with changes in income and employment, and what he produced was an analysis of the cumulative process rather than an analysis of income determination. In this analysis principal attention was given to investment rather than to consumption and saving, and it contained neither the consumption function nor the multiplier. Wicksell's policy goal was the stabilization of prices rather than the attainment of full employment. Although he intimated that the public's desire for cash balances was related to the interest rate, this matter did not form a central point in his analysis. He was not aware of the limitations that the liquidity trap would impose on a policy of monetary expansion and did indeed place main reliance on banking policy as a stabilization device. His analysis was formal and did not invite statistical testing, a shortcoming that gave him cause for concern and to which he alluded at the end of his life when he urged upon a new generation of economists the importance of empirical work. Wicksell's principal achievement was that of a pioneer explorer who mapped out the broad outlines of a new territory, leaving it to others to fill in some of the detail that he saw beckoning in the distance.

WICKSELL'S CONTEMPORARIES

During his later years Wicksell's work received generous acclaim, and he became the leading figure among the growing number of economists in Sweden and other Scandinavian countries who left their mark on economic science. There was David Davidson (1854–1942), Wicksell's early mentor, who taught at the University of Uppsala and was involved with Wicksell in a running controversy about the respective merits of stable prices and of prices declining in accord with rising productivity, Wicksell being in favor of the former and Davidson of the latter. There was Gustav Cassel (1866–1945), professor at Stockholm and a rival of Wicksell's, of worldwide repute at his time, who advocated an economics that was solely concerned with prices, received its orientation from the "scarcity principle," and rejected utility analysis and value theory as futile. Although Cassel was a trained mathematician and an exponent of general equilibrium economics, he had a respectful audience among the German historical economists, who shared his aversion to the utility theory of the Austrians. Cassel's influence was felt in international economics, where he developed a controversial purchasing power parity theory, according to which the equilibrium rate of exchange equates the domestic purchasing power of a currency with what it can buy abroad if exchanged for a foreign currency. Cassel also made a noteworthy contribution to the theory of interest, which lent support to the view, later held by Keynes, albeit for different reasons, that there is a floor below which the rate of interest is unlikely to fall. To Cassel this thought was a necessary consequence of the limited length of the human life span. At a rate of interest below, say, 2 percent, the length of people's productive life would be too short to make it possible for them to provide for their old age, and with the desire for accumulation thus stifled there would be little incentive to save.

THE NEXT GENERATION

The next generation of Swedish economists included a number of Wicksell's and Cassel's pupils who ranked high among the economists of their time: Johan Åkerman (b. 1891), Bertil Ohlin (b. 1899), Erik Lindahl (1891–1960), and Gunnar Myrdal (b. 1898). Åkerman, a perceptive and erudite scholar, heeded the injunction of the aged Wicksell not to neglect the study of history. In a sweeping synthesis that rew on the resources of economic theory, history, and statistics, he set out to explore the historical causes responsible for the "structure" of an economy and its changes and thus came close to the goal pursued by historical economists—the theoretical explanation of historical change. Åkerman's elevation of the concept of an economic structure to a central position had its counterpart in the works of Sombart, Eucken, and Spiethoff, in which the economic "system" or the economic "style" served as a principle of classification. But he went beyond these writers since his principal purpose was not classification but the investigation of change and growth. Åkerman's work supplemented Marshall's study of the long run and set a precedent for later econometric analyses of long-term changes. His approach struck a more resonant chord of response in continental Europe, especially in Germany and France, than in the English-speaking countries, since he accorded to the microeconomic and later macroeconomic analysis that was pursued there only a subordinate position, relevant to the study of a given economic structure but of no help in explaining how this structure came into being and how it changed.

OHLIN

Ohlin attained worldwide recognition with his reconstruction of the theory of international trade in *Interregional and International Trade* (1933), which integrated the theories of domestic and foreign trade and derived both of them from a spatial location theory that considered trade the result of an unequal endowment of regions and countries with productive resources. Where Ricardo had started out with a demonstration of the gain from trade, Ohlin's point of departure was the investigation of the reasons for trade. His work and that of other Swedish economists stimulated further studies of location theory in Germany and in the United States and the type of regional analysis that emerged at mid-century.

In the 1920s and early 1930s Ohlin, Myrdal, and Lindahl contributed to the further development of Wicksell's monetary theory by applying it to conditions of less than full employment and in their own way arrived at results partly anticipating and paralleling the income and employment analysis of Keynes's *General Theory* of 1936. The Stockholm school, as it came to be known, operated with the help of a new equilibrium concept, which like Keynes's aggregate equilibrium and unlike the conventional microeconomic equilibrium was no longer defined in terms of a maximum position. The Stockholm school's "monetary equilibrium" referred to a situation characterized by equality of the natural and the loan rates of interest as well as—and this was somewhat controversial—by stability of the price level. Unlike the conventional microeconomic equilibrium, the monetary equilibrium was neither stable nor indicative of a tendency leading toward it. Disequilibrium was explained in terms of Wicksell's cumulative process, which would cause a movement further and further away from equilibrium.

The Stockholm school fostered a dynamic period, or sequence, analysis of income determination, in which expectations figured prominently and which preferred to employ *ex ante* and *ex post* concepts—plans and their realizations—rather than instantaneous adjustments. These concepts proved of great value in the later discussion of Keynes's *General Theory* when it came to the elucidation of the meaning of the equality of saving and investment, on which Keynes insisted. As was then noted, *ex post,* or realized, saving was equal to investment if both are defined as the difference between income and consumption during the same period, whereas *ex ante* saving, defined as the difference between consumption in one period and income in the preceding period, differed from investment and became equal to it only in equilibrium, after changes in income had produced appropriate changes in *ex ante* saving.

MYRDAL

Myrdal, who in his youth played a leading role in the discussion of the saving-investment relationship, became, after Keynes's death, perhaps the world's best known economist. This was due to the moral appeal of his work and to the widening scope of his interests, which ranged from technical economics to broad questions of scientific method, economic policy, international trade, economic development, and the American race problem. Myrdal's *Political Element in the Development of Economic Theory* (1930, Eng. trans. 1953) was the first great contribution by an economist to the emerging sociology of knowledge, which explores the social conditioning of scientific thought. It demonstrated the penetration of political valuations into classical and later economic thought and its suffusion with normative elements grounded in the great philosophies of natural law and utilitarianism, and it ended with a plea for the explicit introduction of political valuations into economic analysis, which would make it possible to draw political conclusions on a scientific basis.

Myrdal originally believed that it would be feasible to eliminate all metaphysical elements from economics, with the resulting emergence of a body of positive doctrine independent of all valuations. Later he abandoned this view and in the preface to the English translation of his work he characterized it as "naive empiricism." He then insisted that there is an a priori element in all scientific work, that even the selection of a problem for investigation involves a valuation, and that facts become relevant only within the framework of a theoretical pattern. Myrdal's thoughts about the value problem were further developed in the methodological appendixes to *The American Dilemma* (1944), a comprehensive study of the race problem in the United States. In his contributions to international economics and to economic development, Myrdal questioned the applicability of the conventional theory of international trade to commercial relations among advanced and underdeveloped countries and pointed out that the latter do not receive benefits from trade commensurate with the expectations generated by this theory. In his *Asian Drama: An Inquiry into the Poverty of Nations* (3 vols., 1968) Myrdal challenged the methods as well as a number of policy proposals characteristic of conventional development economics. He appealed for profound institutional changes in the underdeveloped countries, the principal means, in his opinion, to accelerate economic development. The policy orientation that pervaded Myrdal's work and its appealing ethos, grounded as it was in a frank support of humane values, made it stand out among the flood of narrowly technical and quantitative studies of the period.

When the contributions of the Stockholm school to income and employment analysis became available in English translation during the late thirties, Keynes's *General Theory* was already the subject of a lively discussion in which the pros and cons of the new doctrine were heatedly debated. Keynes's was a work that offered a complete statement of the theory of the determination of income and employment; it was striking in its novelty, written with the author's customary vigor, and it originated from Cambridge, the font of so much economic wisdom. Its author, then in his fifties, had already left his mark on the economic thought of his time and was known throughout the world as a writer of originality and penetrating power of analysis. Under these circumstances it is not surprising that attention tended to be concentrated on Keynes's work rather than on the parallel efforts of the Stockholm school and that a far greater neglect fell upon similar attempts made by German writers, students of engineering who turned to economics in the thirties and attempted the development of macroeconomic systems.

KEYNES

With John Maynard Keynes (1883–1946) there emerged the twentieth-century counterpart of the towering figures that had shaped and given direction to economic science in the eighteenth and nineteenth centuries. Although his work was widely contested, its influence was soon felt since it offered answers to the burning questions of the time which conventional economics left largely unresolved. Anyone who compared two standard textbooks on economics, one written around 1930 and the other twenty years later, could glean the prodigiousness of his influence. In the former the reader would search in vain for the systematic treatment of macroeconomics dealing with the determination of the great aggregates of income and employment. In the latter such a treatment would be accorded a prominent place coordinate with that of microeconomics and would perhaps overshadow it, and there would be other far-reaching changes indicative of the influence of Keynes affecting the chapters on monetary theory, public policy, taxation, government expenditure, and international trade and finance. Keynes's influence was not limited to the English-speaking countries but extended to the entire non-Communist world, more so, of course, to the highly developed countries which faced similar problems of economic stabilization, but with modifications also to the underdeveloped countries as they became concerned with the behavior of their income within a framework of economic growth. Growth theory was largely post-Keynesian, but it arose from the macroeconomic pattern of thought linked with Keynes.

Although there were precursors of Keynes and contemporary efforts paralleling his own, the revolution in thought that he set off was far more the work of one man than the marginal revolution of the 1870s had been. Keynes was able to bring it off alone because his thought was more than a logical extension of the scientific legacy of the past and constituted a solution to the needs of the time, more so than had been true of the work of the architects of the marginal revolution. Beyond this, fate had been unusually generous to Keynes by endowing him with genius and by placing him in an environment that nurtured his talents and was prodigiously favorable to their unfolding.

Keynes grew up in the academic atmosphere of Cambridge, the son of a logician and college administrator who also pursued economic studies and wrote a widely read book on the structure of economic science. He was educated at Eton and Cambridge, and after having been trained in mathematics and philosophy he was persuaded by Marshall to make economics his lifework. What reverses there were in the early career of this gifted youth did not compare with the uphill struggles of Jevons or Walras, but there was a defeat of expectations when a youth of such great promise could not secure first place in his examinations or obtain a fellowship at first try. These defeated expectations in time brought their own reward. Had Keynes obtained the desired fellowship, he might have turned to logic and become lost to economics; had he secured first instead of second rank in the civil service examination, he might have been drawn into a lifetime career with the Treasury instead of accepting, for a short time, a less desirable position with the India Office, the only domestic job then open. The result was that Keynes in 1908 resigned from the India Office and accepted a lecturership which was financed by Pigou, the newly elected professor of economics, who continued Marshall's tradition of paying out of his own funds the salaries of two lecturers. In the following year Keynes was elected to a fellowship at King's College in Cambridge, a position that he held until his death in 1946.

Keynes's great gifts were conspicuous even in his youth. A magnetic personality, well aware of his superior abilities, he became the center of any group with which he chose to associate. Fellow students remembered him as one of the cleverest of men. Half a century later his former teacher at Eton would recall Keynes's "formidable combination of intellectualism and aestheticism," alluding to a disposition that made him seek the company of writers and artists, some of whom became his intimate friends, and which later turned him into a patron of painting, of the theatre, and of the ballet. When Keynes left Eton, he was already a self-assured and accomplished public speaker. His public presence would shine everywhere, from the classroom to the House of Lords. He became an outstanding teacher with a far greater appeal—albeit also with greater opportunities—than that of Jevons or Walras. He did not allow his mathematics to affect the style of his prose, and he was indeed a master of the written word—his style had no equal among economists and has been compared with Churchill's. Although a great writer and an avid collector of books, he was not bookish, not a retiring scholar, but a man of the world and of affairs, a devotee of cards and of roulette, a practitioner of economics who was as successful a manager of an investment trust and director of an insurance company as he was in his own speculations, which in time and after reverses made him a millionaire in dollars if not in pounds. His influence as an economist stemmed not only from his teaching and writing but also from counseling great political figures and working intermittently for the government, which at the end of his life he represented in international negotiations of the highest importance and which rewarded him with the peerage.

As Bertrand Russell, a contemporary and acquaintance of Keynes, wrote in 1941, "the eighteenth and nineteenth centuries were a brief interlude in the normal savagery of man; now the world has reverted to its usual condition." Keynes's life coincided with the cataclysmic upheavals that upset the modern world, whereas the classics had labored under conditions that, though they were replete with stupendous changes—the French Revolution, the emancipation of the North American colonies, the Napoleonic Wars and their aftermath—ushered in the orderly progress of liberal capitalism and the stability of the *Pax Britannica*. Nor did the architects of the marginal revolution live in a world that was free of disturbances. Menger completed his great work after the defeat of his country by the armies of Prussia, and these were on the march again when Walras traveled through war-torn France on the way to his post at Lausanne. However, eventful as these times were, they were as yet not darkened by the shadows cast by the great upheavals of the twentieth century, which brought two world wars, the fall of ancient empires, the rise of new despotisms unparalleled in their barbarism, unprecedented mass unemployment in the interwar period, and the exhaustion of Britain, which after the two world wars could no longer uphold the *Pax Britannica*.

These upheavals and their economic implications posed a serious threat to the survival of liberal capitalism in the Western world, whose civilization Keynes cherished and in whose restoration to health his lifework played a considerable role. Unlike Marx he chose to salvage capitalism, not to bury it. "How can I adopt a creed," he wrote in 1925, "which, preferring the mud to the fish, exalts the boorish proletariat above the bourgeois and the intelligentsia who, with whatever faults, are the quality in life and surely carry the seeds of all human advancement?" This task of saving a capitalism that seemed doomed constituted a far greater challenge than the problems that had beset the path of earlier generations of economists—the free-trade controversy, for example, or the exhaustion of natural resources, a threat that so impressed Jevons that he laid up a supply of writing paper large enough to meet the needs of generations yet to come. This task also required a man less inhibited and hemmed in by the Victorian conventions of his time than was Marshall, who wanted to steer clear of all controversy and who felt guilty when he engaged in the harmless recreation of a game of chess. A new era with new tasks required a different type of economist, a man more rude and less circumspect than the polite classics and one who would relentlessly and vigorously question conventional patterns of thought and replace them with new ones, pertinent to the overriding issues of his time. Such a man was Keynes.

As a young student of philosophy, Keynes was exposed to the influence of Bertrand Russell and Alfred North Whitehead, who were then in their ascendancy at Cambridge and whose work, with its discovery of new dimensions of logic and of the logical structure of mathematics, ushered in the empiricist, analytic, and linguistic philosophy which emerged in the English-speaking countries during the twentieth century. In later years Russell became the heir of Mill and Voltaire as the great intellectual figure of his time to champion individual liberty. Russell's main impact on Keynes, however, was by way of his technical philosophy, which made itself felt on the work of Keynes's youth, prepared while he was a student and fledgling teacher but not published until 1921, his *A Treatise on Probability*.

Keynes's philosophical views were also shaped by another Cambridge philosopher, George Edward Moore, whose *Principia Ethica* of 1903 made a profound impression on contemporary opinion. Moore supported an "ideal utilitarianism," which came close to identifying the moral duty to perform an action with the action's capacity to produce the greatest possible amount of good in the universe. When it came to an explanation of the nature of goodness, Moore gave great leeway to intuition by declaring good to be indefinable, and he characterized as "naturalist fallacy" the attempt to derive ethical precepts from nonethical premises. Moore's ethical intuitionism made the individual the judge of his moral obligations, and from it support could be drawn for the refusal to conform to convention. Keynes would in later years comment on the shortcomings of Moore's philosophy, which left out "the life of action, and also the pattern of life as a whole," but in his youth he and the circles in which he moved were deeply affected by it and welcomed it as a rationalization of a way of life that exalted what Moore considered as the greatest good—"the enjoyment of beautiful objects" and "the pleasures of human intercourse."

At the cost of some simplification, it may be said that Bertrand Russell influenced Keynes's early work in probability theory and that from George Moore's philosophy he derived support for his way of life and for a nonconforming attitude that was willing to challenge accepted doctrines and conventions. As for Keynes's economics, it was in its early phase shaped by Marshall and Pigou, however little Marshall might appeal to him as a person. Keynes's break in later years with the thought of his early masters was a break also with Marshall's reverence for the mainstream of the tradition of English economics. Whereas Marshall had looked up to Ricardo and Mill and had attempted to link his thought with theirs, Keynes recognized the affinity of his own ideas with those in Malthus's *Principles of Political Economy* and in other unorthodox writings which questioned the adequacy of general demand, and he expressed admiration for Jevons's earlier revolt against the tradition of Ricardo and Mill. But however much the substance of Keynes's thought might diverge from Ricardo's, there was a similarity of intellectual achievement, as each built an imposing structure of thought that was abstract and general but responsive to the conditions of their time, designed to influence policy in a manner that would affect the fate of their own country if not of the world and made up of a few variables fusing the parts of the edifice. Both forged a structure whose unity, apparent simplicity, and ironclad logic commanded assent but was laden with implications providing food for thought for future generations.

A TREATISE ON PROBABILITY

Of Keynes's seven major works only one, *A Treatise on Probability*, was outside the field of economics, although with later developments, which introduced the study of expectations and of economic decision making under conditions of uncertainty, the theory of probability came into a closer relationship to economics than it had during the early decades of the century. Keynes's work was concerned with an age-old philosophical problem to which Aristotle had alluded and which had been debated by Hume, Mill, and Jevons—that of the nature of empirical knowledge arrived at by means of induction. Such knowledge would fail to yield perfect certainty because it was derived from an incomplete enumeration. In other words, however often two events might have been observed to occur together, there was no definite assurance that they would always occur together. Keynes made a widely acclaimed contribution to this debate by attempting to appraise the truth content of inductive knowledge with the help of the theory of probability. In an interpretation of probability that has remained highly controversial he broke with the frequency theory, which holds that the probability of an event, under given conditions, is the relative frequency with which it occurs under these conditions. Instead he supported the view that probability is a logical relation and that it can neither be defined nor in general be measured numerically. He came close to interpreting probability in terms of the strength of belief, informed not only by empirical knowledge but by intuition as well.

Keynes's discussion of these matters was not directly related to economics, but his refusal to follow the frequency theory had its later parallel in the writings of G. L. S. Shackle, an English economist who developed an ingenious theory of decision making under conditions of uncertainty and who, like Keynes but for different reasons, found the frequency theory unacceptable. Shackle considered each managerial decision a unique event, one not embedded in a series of such events and hence not tractable by the frequency theory. On the whole, however, economists and, particularly, econometricians will be inclined to accept the frequency theory as a more congenial theory of probability than other such theories because of its historical link with statistics and because it shows the way to numerical results. For this and for other reasons, references to Keynes's work on probability are rare in the economic literature treating of decision theory and related matters, and it has continued to appeal more to professional philosophers than to economists.

All of Keynes's major writings in economics were prompted by the economic problems of his time and constituted attempts to develop general principles from which to derive solutions for these problems. His first book, *Indian Currency and Finance* (1913), was an offshoot of his work with the India Office and contained an able analysis of the monetary standard known as the gold-exchange standard, under which a country pegs its currency to that of a gold standard country. From this work, published when Keynes was barely thirty, stemmed his interest in monetary economics, which he maintained for the remainder of his life. His expert knowledge of the gold-exchange standard stood him in good stead when this standard became widely used in the 1920s.

During World War I Keynes served in the Treasury and was soon placed in charge of Britain's foreign exchange requirements. A story is told that sheds light on Keynes's working habits. On one occasion there was an urgent need for Spanish pesetas, and Keynes reported to the secretary of the Treasury that with difficulty he had been able to get hold of a small amount. The secretary expressed gratification about what he considered to be a temporary solution. " 'Oh no!' said Keynes. 'What!' said his horrified chief. 'I have sold them all again: I am going to break the market.' And he did." Keynes could be as rude as he was daring and resourceful. Traveling with a Treasury deputation to France, he listened to Lloyd George, then chancellor of the Exchequer, state his views about the business at hand. When it came Keynes's turn to comment, he said: "With the utmost respect, I must, if asked for my opinion, tell you that I regard your account as rubbish."

THE ECONOMIC CONSEQUENCES OF THE PEACE

At the peace negotiations in Paris, Keynes served as the Treasury representative, but eventually he resigned from his official position in protest against what he considered excessive reparation requirements imposed on Germany by the Allies. He published his views in *The Economic Consequences of the Peace* (1920) and in *A Revision of the Treaty* (1922). The first of these books was a bitter indictment of the Allied peacemakers, who, Keynes argued, had drawn new political frontiers but had left unresolved the economic problems of postwar Europe and aggravated them by imposing on the vanquished peace terms that were impossible of fulfillment. The victors, Keynes insisted, had been revengeful rather than magnanimous and had failed to honor previous commitments. To his analysis he added highly uncomplimentary portraits of the "Great Four" who represented the Allies at the peace negotiations, especially of President Woodrow Wilson.

Keynes's thesis was brilliantly argued, and the book, written in purple prose, treated of a matter on which the attention of the world was concentrated. Its appeal was wide, and with its publication and with German and

French translations, which followed promptly, Keynes became an influential public figure known throughout the world. His thesis, highly controversial at the time, has remained so. Keynes's view lent support to those who attributed the evil consequences of the war not to those who had brought it on but to the peace settlement, which he described as a "Carthaginian peace." The vanquished found in Keynes's views a justification for their failure to acknowledge their guilt and for their ever more vehemently expressed indignation about the "dictate of Versailles." Among the victors Keynes's work had the effect of making more profound their disillusionment about the postwar situation, a feeling of disappointment that became widespread especially in the United States and led to a rejection of the peace treaty and of membership in the League of Nations. No one knows how the course of history during the fateful interwar years would have been changed had the United States thrown her weight behind the League instead of withdrawing into isolation.

Keynes's insistence on the difficulty, if not the impossibility, of making large-scale reparation payments ushered in a debate about the transfer problem, which took place during the late 1920s and the 1930s and in which some of the outstanding economists of the time participated. By then Keynes had become the foremost opponent of reparations outside of Germany, and he was at pains to provide a theoretical underpinning for his views. He stressed the price adjustments ostensibly required if the paying country were to generate export surpluses in amounts sufficient to discharge its obligations on reparations account, and he drew attention to a secondary burden imposed on that country by the attending deterioration of its terms of trade. Beyond this, he expressed pessimism about the strength of demand elasticity needed to bring about the required export surpluses even at greatly reduced prices. Keynes's argument was never submitted to an empirical test; when after World War II a similarly pessimistic attitude about demand elasticities in international trade emerged, it proved, on the whole, unfounded. Ohlin, Keynes's principal opponent in the transfer debate, changed the focus of the argument by placing emphasis not on price changes but on changes in income attending the payment of reparations. The changes in income, he asserted, would lead to shifts in demand in the paying and in the receiving country, and these shifts would bring about the transfer of goods. Ohlin, however, did not give adequate consideration to the need for divergent domestic policies in the two countries—contraction in the paying and expansion in the payee country—without which the transfer along the lines he indicated could not take place. Keynes's position reflected, on the whole, the doctrinal tradition of Thornton and Mill, whereas Ohlin's views followed a pattern established by Ricardo and Bastable.

Keynes's predictions about the impracticability of reparations became fulfilled, albeit in a manner not envisaged by him, when Germany was able to obtain loans from the United States in excess of her reparation payments, so that on balance she paid nothing on her reparations account.

When Germany, her power restored and greatly enlarged in less than twenty years, again went to war, Keynes's views were challenged by a young Belgian economist, Étienne Mantoux, whose book *The Carthaginian Peace, or the Economic Consequences of Mr. Keynes* was published in 1946, after Mantoux himself had been killed in action the year before.

Keynes's work cast doubt on the wisdom and practicability not only of reparations but of the imposition of monetary obligations on wartime Allies as well. His strong plea for the cancellation of the inter-Allied debts incurred during World War I, in conjunction with the difficulties encountered in the attempts to settle these debts, difficulties that were in turn related to the frustration of reparation payments, generated in time an attitude favorable to new methods of war finance and to the replacement of inter-Allied loans by grants. An example of the new method was the lend-lease arrangement during World War II, which in turn established a pattern for the later Marshall Plan, under which United States grants rather than loans were applied to the postwar reconstruction of Europe. In subsequent years it became apparent that loan financing of the Marshall plan might have averted or allayed the balance-of-payments problem which the United States encountered later on.

Keynes's appeal to the victors to be magnanimous and to the creditors to renounce their mutual claims thus had far-reaching effects, foreseen and unforeseen, on the thought and action of the time. To these appeals Keynes added a third, which found no response after World War I but whose underlying idea, though under modified conditions, was carried into practical application thirty years later. To offset the fragmentation of the Continent by the borders of the new states, Keynes proposed the formation of a European free-trade union, of which Germany and the successor states of the dismantled Hapsburg and Ottoman empires were to form the nucleus and which England and France were invited to join. Here again Keynes set in motion a chain of thought that in the end led to curious consequences. Here was an Englishman who after the end of World War I suggested the formation of an European economic community, but when such an organization was actually founded after World War II, Britain was refused admission.

A TRACT ON MONETARY REFORM

Although Keynes, in *The Economic Consequences of the Peace,* took it on himself to question widely accepted modes of thought about reparations and war debts, his *A Tract on Monetary Reform,* written in 1923 against the background of the monetary disorders that World War I left in its wake, contained an attack against a more formidable target. In this work Keynes broke with the long-standing tradition that considered as self-evident the desirability of the gold standard. In Keynes's opinion, the conditions that had favored the gold standard in the nineteenth century had undergone profound changes. Moreover, like other economists of the time, he extolled the ideal of stable prices, a goal not always compatible with stable rates of exchange. If a choice had to be made between stable prices and stable exchange rates, he would prefer the former. A country that submitted to the discipline of the gold standard jeopardized its freedom to pursue an independent domestic policy. Inflation elsewhere in the world, especially in a leading nation, would cause it to gain gold and would make inflation spread within its borders; deflation elsewhere would have the opposite effect. The monetary authorities had in fact under the gold standard pursued policies supporting its operations or averting certain consequences of it. Hence the gold standard was not automatic but required management, such as did a managed currency, under which exchange rates would be allowed to vary more freely than if they were pegged to gold.

Shortly after Keynes published *A Tract on Monetary Reform,* Winston Churchill, then holding office as chancellor of the Exchequer, not only restored the gold standard but also the prewar parity of $4.86 to the pound. Sterling was thereby overvalued and the competitive position of Britain in foreign markets was seriously threatened. In a pamphlet entitled *The Economic Consequences of Mr. Churchill* (1925) Keynes called attention to these dangers, which in the end could only be averted at the cost of a painful deflation of domestic prices, with attending social unrest culminating in a general strike. At the same time Keynes also published another pamphlet, *The End of Laissez Faire,* which raised the debate to a more general level and underlined the need for management and control of the economy.

A TREATISE ON MONEY

Keynes's *A Treatise on Money,* a two-volume work which appeared in 1930, contained a comprehensive exposition of monetary theory and policy, but its impact remained limited because it was overshadowed by Keynes's *General Theory* of 1936. The further direction of Keynes's thought was indicated by his critical attitude to the quantity theory of money and to the cash-balance approach and by his support of an income approach. While not neglecting the rate of interest, he used as a starting point for the development of a theory of prices not the quantity of money but the flow of money income earned by the production of consumption goods and investment goods and expended on consumption and saving. In the *Treatise* Keynes attempted an analysis of the saving-investment relationship, which was to reappear, in different form, in the *General Theory.* Furthermore, the *Treatise* contained notable contributions to (1) the analysis of the motives for holding money, (2) the public's relative preference for holding its assets in a more or less liquid form, and (3) the anticipated yield of new capital. These ideas would reach full fruition in the *General Theory,* where the first reappeared under the headings of the classification of the motives for holding money, which have since become the standard, the second as liquidity preference, and the third as the marginal efficiency of capital. The *Treatise,* however, did not include consideration of the consumption function, and though it shed a penetrating light on the relation between money, prices, and interest rates, it did not contain a theory of the determination of the national income such as was to be proffered in the *General Theory.* Keynes's greatest achievement was yet to come, and compared with it the *Treatise,* although it was an outstanding work, was but a halfway house, which contained a number of building blocks that Keynes put to use again, and in modified form, in the *General Theory,* where they were embedded in the framework of a theory of output.

Within different contexts Keynes renewed his plea for management and control and expanded the idea to the international field by proposing the establishment of a supranational monetary authority of a type similar to the organization created at Bretton Woods twenty-five years later. He reiterated apprehensions that he had expressed earlier in periodical articles about the undesirable consequences of the uncontrolled flow of capital over international boundaries. Foreign investments, he pointed out, were made in response to higher interest rates abroad. They might not lead to adjustments in the form of increased commodity exports because the flow of these reflected disparities in cost rather than in interest rates. Foreign investments might cause interest rates at home to rise, might frustrate the reduction of domestic unemployment, and might require the assumption of unwarranted risks. In order to prevent the diversion of funds from domestic to foreign investment, Keynes suggested differential terms for the two, possibly a subsidy for the former and a tax on the latter. During the 1930s Keynes also became apprehensive about the effects of free trade on a country such as Britain, which found it difficult to equilibrate a balance of payments in which commodity imports loomed so large. Instead of allowing herself to be forced on the way of deflation and wage cutting, Britain might pursue a policy of tariff protection. In an article published in 1933 he went even further and suggested that a policy of greater self-sufficiency and economic isolation might reduce otherwise unbearable costs of adjustment.

A number of miscellaneous articles by Keynes were collected in the 1930s in two volumes, *Essays in Persuasion* (1931) and *Essays in Biography* (1933). One of the pieces included in the former, "Economic Possibilities for Our Grandchildren," written during the Great Depression, opened up an optimistic view of the future which anticipated the "affluent society" heralded by later writers. The other collection included a reprint of a famous obituary which Keynes had written about Alfred Marshall and, besides appraisals of contemporary figures, one of Malthus, whose views about the inadequacy of general demand Keynes compared favorably with Ricardo's adherence to Say's law. Keynes's biographical sketches did not only discuss doctrinal matters but showed his human interest in the life and time of the men he wrote about. Of the great figures of the past, Keynes singled out Malthus and Jevons. It was they who had made their influence felt on his own work and whose doctrine or approach he had found most congenial.

607

THE GENERAL THEORY

Keynes's career as a writer reached its peak with the publication of *The General Theory of Employment, Interest and Money* in 1936. Although the initial reaction to this work was by no means universally favorable, much of its substance soon became part of the standard doctrine of economics. An increasing number especially among the younger generation of economists acclaimed Keynes as the master economist of the age. During the remaining ten years of his life he worked only intermittently because of poor health. In World War II he published a tract entitled *How to Pay for the War* (1940), in which he developed the concept of an "inflationary gap" and proposed forced loans, alternatively described as compulsory savings or deferred pay, as a means to finance the war. Later he represented Britain at the conference held at Bretton Woods, New Hampshire, in 1944, at which the design of the International Monetary Fund and of the World Bank was debated, and in other international negotiations. Keynes favored an international financial organization with a substantial potential for monetary expansion—his plan failed to be adopted at the time but came to partial fruition later.

In the history of economics the appearance of Keynes's *General Theory* was an event comparable with the publication of Smith's *Wealth of Nations,* Ricardo's *Principles,* or Marx's *Kapital.* The liberal capitalism of the modern age, which Smith had heralded, whose victory Ricardo had proclaimed, and which Marx sought to destroy, was transformed by Keynes and given a new life. When Keynes published the *General Theory,* the world was still suffering from the protracted mass unemployment of the Great Depression. There was widespread despair about an economic order that left so many people without work. Conventional economics counseled further deflation, wage cuts, and budgetary restraint, but these remedies were found to aggravate the malaise instead of relieving it. Voices were heard announcing the doom of capitalism and hailing the fulfillment of Marx's predictions. With an unprecedented proportion of the labor force thrown out of work, the sinister appeals of communism and fascism gained strength. Keynes pointed the way to a different solution, and his work provided a theoretical framework that contained both a diagnosis of the principal economic ills of the time and the suggestion of a cure. His thought gradually conquered economic opinion, and under its influence full employment became a goal which was explicitly endorsed by the governments of many countries and pursued by policies suggested by him. In the decades following World War II, depressions in the highly developed countries of the Western world gave way to mild and short-lived recessions, a transformation that many thoughtful observers ascribed to the effectiveness of Keynesian economics.

In the development of Keynes's thought the ideas expressed in the *General Theory* represented a shift from price stabilization as the goal of public policy to the stabilization of income and employment at high levels. Although the content of the *General Theory* taxed the minds of readers habituated to the economics hitherto accepted as conventional and although the work had its share of complexities and paradoxes, its substance can be stated in a few sentences: The national income equals expenditures for consumption and investment. A national income at less than full employment indicates that expenditures are deficient. Among expenditures for consumption and investment, those for consumption are more passive and and tend to change in response to changes in income. Changes in income are generated by, and reflect in a magnified form, changes in investment. Investment expenditure is determined by the relationship between anticipated rates of return from investment and the rate of interest. The rate of interest reflects the public's preference for holding assets in the liquid form of cash. Expenditure that is deficient—inadequate to generate full employment—may be augmented by the stimulation of consumption and investment. Private investment may be supplemented by public investment, that is, by the compensatory spending of public authorities, with a resulting "compensatory economy" and the partial socialization of investment.

Keynes constructed this theory with the help of an analytical apparatus which was impressive in its originality, coherence, and power to stimulate further thought.

There was, first, the consumption function or propensity to consume, a functional relationship between consumption and income. It was stated in average or marginal form and had its counterpart in the propensity to save, both propensities adding up to income or unity. The relationship between consumption and income was envisaged as fairly stable if not proportional, and it facilitated the making of predictions about the amounts that consumers would disburse out of different hypothetical incomes.

A second element was the multiplier, inversely related to saving and defined as the reciprocal of the marginal propensity to save, which indicated how a change in investment generated a multiple change in consumption expenditure and therewith in income. This tool of analysis, at which Bagehot had hinted and which Pigou had attempted to forge, was the work of Richard Kahn (b. 1905), a noted Cambridge economist and, like Mrs. Robinson, an outstanding pupil of Keynes's. With the propensity to consume given, the multiplier made it possible to appraise changes in income generated by changes in investment.

A third element in Keynes's analytical apparatus was the relationship between saving and investment, newly considered in the *General Theory*. Whereas in the *Treatise* saving and investment were defined as unequal, they were made equal by definition in the *General Theory* since both were described as the difference between income and consumption during the same period. Without affecting the substance of Keynes's argument, many interpreters of Keynes's thought preferred, however, a different formulation, one more in line with the ideas of Robertson and the Stockholm school, in which a distinction was made between *ex ante,* or planned saving, and *ex post,* or realized saving. In this interpretation *ex post* saving was defined, like investment, as the difference between income and consumption of the same period and hence was by definition equal to investment, whereas *ex ante* saving was defined as the difference between consumption in one period and income in the preceding period. *Ex ante* saving might fall short of or exceed investment; in the former case, income and the saving made therefrom would rise during the ensuing periods until *ex ante* saving, *ex post* saving, and investment were equal at equilibrium income. In the latter case income, and with it saving, would decline during the ensuing periods until it had fallen to the equilibrium level.

A fourth part of Keynes's analytical apparatus was the inducement to invest, reflecting the schedule of the marginal efficiency of capital, or anticipated rate of return on different amounts of investment, and the rate of interest. This analysis assigned a prominent place to the role of expectations, and it underlined the volatile character of investment, whose fluctuations would in turn affect income. It also coordinated the investment decision with the main body of microeconomic theory since it interpreted this decision in terms of the maximization principle. With a falling schedule of anticipated marginal returns as the amount of hypothetical investment increased, returns would be maximized by an investment expenditure whose marginal rate of return was equal to the rate of interest. If a larger expenditure were incurred, cost would exceed the returns; if a smaller, investors would fail to exhaust the opportunities for earning returns in excess of cost.

In his interpretation of interest, Keynes adhered to the liquidity preference theory, a monetary theory of interest which explains the phenomenon in terms of money as distinguished from "real" theories such as the time-preference theory or the productivity theory of interest. In this view, the rate of interest is functionally related to the amount of cash balances the public desires to hold, with a falling schedule of interest rates as the hypothetical cash balances increase. The liquidity-preference function reflects the various motives for holding cash balances—the transactions motive, the precautionary motive, and the speculative motive. The speculative motive induces people to prefer cash to securities if they expect, in contrast with the prevailing opinion of the market, the price of securities to decline or, what is the same, the rate of interest to rise. The monetary authories, by equipping the people with larger cash balances, are able to bring the interest rate down, thereby stimulating a larger volume of investment. The "liquidity trap," so designated by Robertson, puts a limit on this opportunity, however, because once the interest rate has declined to a very low level, a further increase in cash balances may fail to reduce it further. At this low level, holders of assets believe that only an increase in interest rates or a decline in security prices can be expected, and they are willing to sell securities to the monetary authorities at the prevailing prices so that the interest rate will remain what it is. Hence, a purely monetary policy of coping with a depression may be abortive, and recourse must be had to fiscal policy—public works or tax reductions.

FURTHER DEVELOPMENT OF KEYNESIAN ECONOMICS

In the decades following the publication of the *General Theory* much work was done to elaborate and refine the ideas of Keynes. Considerable attention was given to the consumption function. The broad aggregate of consumption expenditures was broken up, and significant differences were discovered in the relationship between income and consumption expenditures for durable and nondurable goods. Apart from this disaggregation new variables were introduced to shed light on consumer behavior. For example, it was discovered that consumption expenditure was not only related to current income but also to income earned in the past. This work, which was carried on by James S. Duesenberry and Franco Modigliani, who developed their ideas independently during the late 1940s, was paralleled by Friedman's "permanent income" hypothesis. In *A Theory of the Consumption Function* (1957), Friedman distinguished between income considered as transitory and income considered as permanent by the householders, and he attempted to demonstrate that consumer spending mainly reflects permanent income, whereas transitory income is saved.

Keynes's analysis did not include a theory of distribution, but it provided the starting point for such a theory as developed by Nicholas Kaldor (b. 1908), an economist associated with Cambridge University. This theory demonstrated that under certain assumptions the share of profits in the national income was determined by the ratio of investment to output and that under still more restrictive assumptions—zero marginal propensity to save on the part of wage earners—profits equaled the sum of investment and of consumption by the receivers of property income, with wages constituting a residue. The gist of this macroeconomic theory of distribution could be expressed in these words: "Capitalists earn what they spend, and workers spend what they earn."

In the further elaboration of the multiplier concept, several variants came to be distinguished, and the application of the concept also proved fruitful in the field of international economics. The propensity to import linked changes in imports to changes in income, and the export multiplier related changes in exports to changes in income. Ways were found to demonstrate the interaction between the multiplier and the acceleration principle, which shows how changes in output generate magnified changes in investment. This subject was explored in a notable article by Samuelson. Multiplier analysis also provided the basis for the theories of steady growth which were developed by Harrod and Domar.

In the 1940s the fiscal policy implications of Keynesian economics began to take shape in the form of "three ways to full employment"—an increase in government purchases of goods and services with an attending budget deficit, a reduction of taxes, which would require a larger deficit, and an increase in equal amounts both of government expenditures for goods and services and of taxes, with a balanced budget. The respective merits of the three policies formed the subject of a wide-ranging discussion, in which attention was also drawn to the factors that might limit the effectiveness of fiscal policy. In time the debate on the relative merits of public spending versus a reduction of taxes became intertwined with the discussion of other than strictly fiscal issues. Those who advocated policies aiming at the reduction of poverty, urban renewal, cleaner air and water, and other extensions of public consumption favored a fiscal policy stressing government purchases of goods and services and suitable for the pursuit of other goals in addition to full employment. Consequently they considered a fiscal policy consisting of tax reductions as less desirable and characterized it as "commercial Keynesianism." In a further extension of Keynes's thought fiscal policy was also placed in the service of antiinflationary campaigns, with a reduction of government purchases and an increase in taxation vying with policies of monetary restraint.

ECONOMICS BEFORE AND AFTER KEYNES

The extent to which under the influence of Keynes old ideas gave way and new ideas gained ground can be gleaned from the following survey of representative changes in economic thought before and after Keynes. He set off a veritable revolution in economic thinking.

Before Keynes, economic analysis was concerned with the efficient allocation of resources, a matter treated under the headings of price theory, value and distribution, and partial and general equilibrium. After Keynes, these theories were supplemented by the analysis of the determination of total output, yielding income and employment theory.

Before Keynes, by far the greater part of economic theory had only a formal validity, that is, it could claim logical consistency on the basis of certain assumptions but did not lend itself to empirical testing. Virtually all microeconomic concepts were *ex ante* notions which reflected subjective estimates of the future. They were not suited to statistical verification. After Keynes, much economic theory became operational in the sense of being developed in terms that lent themselves to empirical measurement. The rise of macroeconomics, consisting of such *ex post* aggregates as the various national income concepts, stimulated the development of national economic accounting. Governments throughout the world assumed a task in which private scholarship had pioneered—the systematic derivation of the various national income concepts and their regularly recurring estimation. Keynes was primarily a theorist, although occasionally he would marshall empirical data in support of his argument, for example, when he attempted to demonstrate the impact of population growth on the demand for capital. But his analysis, much of which was developed in operational terms, provided a powerful stimulus to econometrics and enabled economists to produce numerical results.

Before Keynes, economic policy primarily aimed at the stabilization of prices and was pursued principally in the form of monetary policies. These, in conjunction with wage cuts, were also considered suitable to relieve unemployment and to bring about full employment, a position interpreted in terms of an equilibrium toward which the economy would tend to move in line with Say's law. After Keynes, the reliance on the operation of automatic forces that would secure full employment vanished, and the stabilization of employment emerged as a goal of public policy. After Keynes it became recognized that the national income might be in equilibrium while unemployment persisted. In view of the limitations of purely monetary policies, these were supplemented by fiscal policy. Wages were considered as a factor affecting cost as well as demand, and wage cutting and deflation were no longer relied upon as means to full employment.

Before Keynes, a strong tradition in economic thought considered money as neutral in the sense of not affecting the level of output. After Keynes, variations in cash balances were associated with variations in the rate of interest. Since the latter was an important determinant of investment in Keynes's theory and since investment was a strategic variable affecting the levels of employment and income, the latter were indirectly linked with money.

Before Keynes, a time-honored tradition had elevated thrift to an absolute virtue, which was to be practiced at all times by private citizens and public authorities alike. Fiscal propriety was interpreted as requiring a balanced budget. Keynes taught that expenditure generates income and employment, and after him it became recognized that when income and employment are unduly low, public or private thrift ceases to be a virtue. With Keynes, the view that under certain conditions planned savings might be redundant and self-defeating, a view hitherto held by only a small number of economic "heretics," became respectable, and Keynes himself attempted to rescue the memory of "the brave army of heretics," among whom he included Mandeville, Malthus, Gesell, and Hobson.

Keynesian economics, with its rich harvest of new ideas, nevertheless had its limitations. Keynes's theory of output, though ostensibly a general one, was primarily relevant to conditions in which the economy operated at less than full capacity. Under conditions of full employment, such tools of analysis as the multiplier would register what were not real but monetary changes. Under such conditions the old-line microeconomic approach, with its emphasis on the allocation of resources, would again move closer to the center of the stage, monetary policy would be rediscovered as one of the means to cope with inflation, and thrift would be hailed as a virtue. Furthermore, the aggregative economics of the *General Theory,* especially when evolving into a fiscal policy of commercial Keynesianism, did not constitute a conceptual apparatus from which could readily be drawn questions and answers relevant to such problems as the quality of the ecological environment and the emerging issues of the cities and race. These matters, which became such overriding concerns thirty years after the publication of the *General Theory,* did not weigh on Keynes's mind when he wrote his great book. Although he did not fashion a corpus of economic doctrine directly responsive to these types of issues, he was, however, by no means insensitive to them and never lost sight of the quality of life as mankind's paramount concern. When pleading for government support of the arts in 1938, he characterized the view that "the utilitarian and economic—one might almost say financial—ideal" is "the sole, respectable purpose of the community as a whole" as "the most dreadful heresy, perhaps, which has ever gained the ear of a civilized people." He deplored the fact that such matters as education and public health only become a matter of public concern when they "creep in under an economic alias on the ground that they 'pay'."

With Keynes's work, economic wisdom did not reach its end. The light that he kindled illumined a new province of economics, and at its boundaries new frontiers could dimly be seen, beckoning the explorer and waiting to be conquered in the endless quest of science. In commenting on the long-run validity of the quantity theory of money Keynes once remarked that the long run is a misleading guide to current affairs. "In the long run," he wrote, "we are all dead." His approach to macroeconomics did indeed single out for attention the short run. It was also largely a static approach, in which the variables were not given a time dimension. Moreover, the relationship that he stressed was that between *employment* and output, whereas the influence of other variables, productivity changes, for example, and the host of institutional factors behind these, was not taken into account. That his work had these characteristics is not surprising and followed from the nature of things. He set out to find a solution for the burning issue of the day, not for long-run problems. By developing a static analysis, he prepared the ground for dynamic approaches. By concentrating on a limited number of variables he clothed his system in a simple and coherent garb and gave it a persuasive strength which enabled his novel thought to gain adherence.

The very limitations of Keynes's analysis indicated the directions in which further work would move, and those who carried on this work did so while standing on Keynes's shoulders. From his static macroeconomics of the short run there stemmed attempts at developing long-term and dynamic analyses. His study of the relationship between employment and output inspired the search for a more comprehensive theory of growth, wide in sweep and encompassing a large number of variables that influence output.

Chapter 27

ECONOMIC THOUGHT
IN THE UNITED STATES:
Orthodoxy and Dissent

When Keynes was invited to the economic seminar that the Federal Reserve sponsored in Washington during the early 1940s, he expressed amazement about the large number of economists in attendance. There were as many in the room, he was reported to have observed, as could be found in all of the British Isles. By that time American economics had attained a leading position in the world, unsurpassed in the number of economists, the quantity of their output, and the quality of their average effort. American economics had come into its own, but it had in the process produced no towering figure comparable in stature to the great classics, no Marx, Jevons, Walras, or Keynes.

That this was so may be explained in terms of differences in preoccupations and intellectual roots of the Old World and of the New. In the Old World as well as in the New, the spirit of 1776 brought to the fore the advocacy of natural rights, but the rights claimed in *The Wealth of Nations* were different from those exalted in the Declaration of Independence. Smith's concern was with the emancipation of business, Jefferson's with the emancipation of the nation. Both great men responded in their own way to the different challenges posed by the conditions of their environment. Later on, when Malthus and Ricardo had completed the structure of classical thought, the new nation occupied itself with building up a world replete with open spaces and beckoning with opportunities, a world that placed a premium on action rather than on thought and was little impressed with the relevance of Malthus's and Ricardo's principal concerns. Americans might attempt to revise the classical system, as did Carey by questioning some of its assumptions and George by drawing extreme conclusions from it, and they might attain worldwide fame by doing so, but no Marx would arise from their ranks to demolish what the classics had built. Carey in fact claimed adherence to the thought of Smith, and George's conclusions might have been drawn by Ricardo and were in fact drawn by James Mill. Just as Americans had not been prominent among the architects of the classical system, so they did not set out to destroy it. The land of plenty and opportunity would not produce a Marx. Moreover, there was in the United States no living tradition of a utilitarian philosophy such as had nurtured the thought of Mill and Jevons; nor was there the spirit of French rationalism from which Cournot and Walras had drawn strength in constructing a mathematical counterpart of the world of reality.

As the twentieth century advanced, the absence of these intellectual traditions in the New World no longer constituted an obstacle to the rise of magisterial thought in American economics because by then they had weakened in the Old World as well. Arising from similar pragmatic concerns with measurement and aiming at scientific status, economic thinking in the New and in the Old World converged. In the 1930s when the American economy posed problems not unlike those of the European countries, conditions might have favored the rise of an American Keynes. If he did not emerge, this may have been because there was no American Marshall or Pigou to train him and because geniuses are rare. But by the laws of chance those who are strongest in numbers and in other ways are favored by the same circumstances that prevail elsewhere are most likely to have a genius in their midst, so that conditions bid fair for an American to emerge as the next great figure in the history of economics.

Of the two early American economists who commanded worldwide attention, neither Carey nor George was an academician. Academic economics in the United States came into its own only after the Civil War, when it ceased to be a peripheral concern of professors who combined the teaching of moral philosophy, belles lettres, political economy, and the evidences of Christianity—as did, for example, the Reverend John McVickar, who retired from Columbia in 1864—and instead was assigned a separate professorship, first at Harvard and later at other institutions of higher learning. Thus the age of the specialist began and that of the generalist came to its end. The age of the polymath had advantages of its own since it gave a brilliant scholar, adept in another discipline, the chance to approach economics from a new and wider perspective, one closed to the narrow specialist. The last such polymath was Simon Newcomb (1835–1909), a mathematician and astronomer of great distinction, whose *Principles of Political Economy* (1885) broke new ground.

NEWCOMB

From Newcomb stemmed the basic distinction between a "flow" and a "fund," income and capital, for example, and he developed the idea of a wheel of wealth, designated by him as "societary circulation," made up of flows of money and of goods and services running in opposite directions. Newcomb considered "demand as the director of industry," and in the monetary field he constructed an equation of exchange which served as the basis for the later work of Irving Fisher. Although Newcomb's theoretical innovations were forward-looking, his economic philosophy was a backward one. Steeped in a vanishing laissez faire tradition that at his time was already on the defensive, he bitterly denounced the interventionist views of the younger generation of economists who founded the American Economic Association. "It is a great mistake," he insisted, "to suppose that the enormous inequalities which we see in wealth imply anything wrong in the system which permits them." Charity, he held, would only increase the number of beggars and "degraded classes." "If the children of the degraded classes could be taken in infancy, before their bad habits have had time to form, and trained to earn a livelihood, a certain proportion of them would be redeemed. If those who could not be so trained were allowed to starve, the number to grow up a burden on society would be diminished." Newcomb's social Darwinism, extreme as it was, did not prevent him from calling on the government to create an instrument that was to render powerful assistance in the exploitation of the country's natural resources. As one of the nation's leading scientists, he was prominent among those who supported the founding of the Geological Survey in 1879.

WALKER

At the time of the publication of Newcomb's *Principles* the foremost American economist was Francis A. Walker (1840–97), an outstanding leader and an able administrator, who had been brevetted brigadier general at the age of twenty-four and appointed superintendent of the census at the age of thirty. In the 1880s and 1890s Walker served as president of the Massachusetts Institute of Technology, of the long-established American Statistical Association, and of the newly founded American Economic Association, which benefited greatly from his leadership. Between 1876 and 1883 Walker wrote books on wages, rent, money, and general economics, books which excelled more in common sense than in theoretical subtlety. Unlike Newcomb, he was moderate in his views on laissez faire and recognized various conflicts of interest—"imperfect competition," for example—which required intervention by public authorities. In his distribution theory, Walker generalized the rent concept and applied it to entrepreneurial returns, with wages remaining as a residual. Walker's overall view of distribution gained little following, but he was an effective critic of the wages-fund theory, which now disappeared from the body of accepted economic principles. In *International Bimetallism* (1896), Walker's last book, he stressed the inadequacy of the supply of gold in a world characterized by economic expansion and underlined the advantages of a "moderate, progressive increase of the money supply and a general upward tendency of prices." Walker's antideflationary point of view had a greater affinity with later twentieth-century opinion than with the antiinflationary concerns of his contemporaries, such as the Austrians and Wicksell and Davidson, who preferred a stable or a declining price level as a means to distribute the fruits of rising productivity.

Much of the best in late nineteenth-century American economics was provoked by the challenges that Carey and George hurled at conventional thought. Newcomb's interest in economics was spurred by the fame of Carey; he read Carey's works and the result "was much like a slap in the face." George's proposals were responsible for sharp reactions on the part of Walker, who, though usually a man of moderation, judged them a "precious piece of villainy" and "steeped in infamy." While the Austrians were busy rebutting the challenges of Marx and in the process producing such works as Böhm-Bawerk's theory of interest and capital, American economists found themselves similarly challenged by George's ideas and responded to them in their own writings. This was also true of certain phases of the work of John Bates Clark (1847–1938), the first American exponent of the conventional type of economic theory to obtain worldwide recognition and as much acclaimed in his domain as were Carey and George in theirs.

J. B. CLARK

Compared with Walker, who insisted on the scientific character of economics and stated that the task of the economist was "to teach and not to preach," Clark was more a figure of transition, whose work linked the earlier age of an American economics that was religiously inspired and taught by clergymen with the modern technical economics that was ostensibly free of valuations. Clark himself had felt drawn to a clerical vocation, and when instead he chose a career in economics, he produced work that had some of the evangelical undertones characteristic of an earlier generation of New England divines who had turned from the pulpit to the classroom.

Clark's evangelism underwent a curious transformation: In his *Philosophy of Wealth,* published in 1885 but based on a series of earlier articles, he found much to condemn in modern capitalism and its conventional interpretation, whereas in his *Distribution of Wealth,* published in 1899 and again derived from earlier contributions to periodicals, he discovered in the prevailing system of distribution, as did Hegel in the Prussian monarchy, the materialization of justice on earth. The earlier work reflected the influence of Clark's study in Germany, where he, like so many of his generation, had received instruction from the socialists of the chair. In the later work these influences had vanished and the evangelical fervor of the critic had been replaced by that of an apologist. By then Clark had moved on to Columbia University, where he taught with great distinction for many years.

These two books constituted Clark's achievement as a technical economist. The first contained an oblique version of the marginal utility theory of value, which Clark had originally published ten years after the appearance of Jevons's and Menger's works, independent of these but perhaps inspired by ideas of his teacher Knies. The second contained Clark's principal contribution, a comprehensive and detailed statement of the marginal productivity theory of distribution, which he had developed in a series of pathbreaking articles approximately concurrent with the related attempts of Wicksteed, Wicksell, and other scholars. The hallmark of Clark's version of the theory was that he developed it not merely as a consistent logical structure but made further-reaching claims which came close to identifying the theory with a description of the real world and to vindicating a society ostensibly living by the rule "to each what he creates." These claims did not go unchallenged, and Clark was denounced for confounding theory and facts and for neglecting the influence of inherited wealth and inequality of opportunity on the distribution of income.

Clark was a theorist of considerable subtlety and impressive analytical power. From his work stemmed the seminal distinction between "functional" and "personal" distribution, the generalization of the principle of diminishing returns, which was shown to be applicable not only to land but to any factor held constant and combined with varying doses of another, and the consequent generalization of the principle of differential rent. In his analysis of marginal productivity Clark made a point of demonstrating that the homogeneous intramarginal units, which receive the same return as the marginal, are not exploited, as they seem to be in Thünen's and Böhm-Bawerk's variants of the theory. He showed that what appears to be a higher productivity of these units is in truth due to their combination with a larger portion of the fixed factor. As the units of the variable input are increased, they become associated with an ever-diminishing share in the fixed factor, and it is the efficacy of this factor that declines as it is diffused over a larger quantity of the variable input.

Clark had found in certain passages of Henry George's work the stimulus that made him develop the marginal productivity theory of distribution. There was a curious connection also between Clark's generalization of the rent concept and George's attack against the "unearned increment" allegedly accruing to the owners of land. If every type of income can be interpreted as a differential surplus akin to ground rent, the latter loses those distinct characteristics that invited George's attacks. Conversely, however, income from capital, if viewed as a differential surplus, can be made the target of attacks similar to those that George launched against income from land. It was this other side of the coin to which Hobson and the Fabians called attention when they undertook to generalize the principle of differential rent at about the same time as this was done by Clark.

As a controversialist, Clark was the peer of Böhm-Bawerk, and it was in opposition to Böhm-Bawerk's views that Clark developed his own ideas about the nature of capital. He insisted on a sharp distinction between "capital" as an abstract fund and concrete "capital goods," and he characterized the one as permanent and mobile and the others as perishable and embodied in specific forms. There were obscurities and paradoxes in Clark's presentation, which caused Böhm-Bawerk to refer to it as a "mythology of capital." However, Clark's insistence on the permanence of the capital fund meant no more than that the concrete capital goods yield a return that includes allowances for their maintenance and replacement. From this he concluded that the lifetime of capital is virtually endless and not bounded by a "period of production" such as Böhm-Bawerk envisaged.

As a corollary of Clark's view of the nature of capital, he developed what has been called a "synchronization economics" in the place of the more conventional "advance economics." From Turgot to Böhm-Bawerk it had been the prevailing view to characterize capital as an advance that tides the producer over an interval of waiting until his own product is ready for use. Clark broke with this view and instead declared that the existence of the permanent capital fund makes it possible to consider production and consumption as synchronized. One of his illustrations that shed light on the synchronization principle related to a family's supply of firewood from a nearby forest. Each year a row of trees is cut, and a new row is planted. Planting and cutting occur simultaneously; one does not plant a sapling and wait for it to mature to make a fire. Once there is a permanent forest, there is no need to wait for the fuel. In a broader perspective Clark illustrated the principle as follows:

> On the ranches of Montana cattle are breeding, among the forests of Pennsylvania hides are tanning, in the mills of Brockton shoes are finishing; and, if the series of goods in all stages of advancement is only kept intact, the cowboy may have today the shoes that he virtually creates by his efforts. This result is attainable because of the existence of a complete stock of capital goods. We must have growing cattle, hides, tanned leather, partly made shoes and finished shoes, all maintained in a constant quantity, in order that a certain number of shoes may each day be taken for use. With sheep in the pastures, wool in the mills, cloth in the tailoring shops, and ready-made garments on the retailers' counters, the labor of the people can, as it were, instantaneously clothe the people. With a series of capital goods of the right kinds once established, the work of today yields its results today in the shape of completed clothes.

Clark's capital theory, as most of his theoretical work, was more apt to shed light than to bear fruit. It did not include an examination of the investment process nor did it lead to a business cycle theory, but it opened up a new view of the capital concept and the whole process of production and consumption.

What was perhaps the most enduring legacy of Clark's work was the search for an economic dynamics, which he himself pursued and which became the concern of many outstanding economists of the following generations. Clark considered his own analysis static and hence incomplete and preliminary since it abstracted from the important changes in population, capital, technology, consumer wants, and industrial organization. He

attempted a dynamic analysis in his *Essentials of Economic Theory* (1907),
in which he set out to "examine seriatim the effects of different changes, to gauge the probability of their continuance, and to determine the resultant of all of them acting together." The outcome, however, was not an economic dynamics in which the varibles would be dated or which would trace the path from one equilibrium position to another—as dynamic analysis was later understood—but a comparative statics showing different equilibrium positions. Although later generations of economists would define static and dynamic analysis in terms different from those employed by Clark and although their attempts at forging an economic dynamics would differ from Clark's, it was his work that had shown the way toward a new goal in economic theory.

FISHER

As in the Old World, the mode of communication employed by the economists of the New World was gradually changing. Visual means of presentation had been employed by Carey in the form of statistical charts, and these were further developed and perfected by Walker in connection with his work for the census. Clark made use of analytical geometry and even printed a few three-dimensional graphs. The mathematical method of presenting economic ideas was more fully employed by Irving Fisher (1867–1947), whose tenure at Yale overlapped in part Clark's at Columbia. Fisher came to economics as a well-trained mathematician, and he brought to his tasks great gifts of patient and pedagogically effective exposition. His teachers at Yale included Willard Gibbs, a great physicist, and William Graham Sumner, a social scientist of ultraconservative leanings with an attachment to laissez faire so strong as to prevent him from joining the controversial American Economic Association. It was because of Sumner's influence that Fisher turned to mathematical conomics, then a field at the frontiers of science. When Sumner suggested that Fisher write a dissertation on mathematical economics, Fisher replied: "I have never heard of such a subject."

Fisher's economics was more orderly and disciplined than that of the verbalists, and since his approach had the greatest affinity with what was to become the standard a century after his birth, he has been described, not without justification in terms of this standard, as America's greatest economist. A less generous appraisal would accord him recognition for having pioneered in what were to become the accepted methods of approaching scientific economics but would find his legacy of original contributions to the substance of this science less replete with profound and comprehensive ideas than was Clark's.

As economics became more disciplined in the writings of Fisher, it also became more prosaic and apparently failed to absorb all of his creative energy. Thus he pursued with much vigor a great many sideline activities, campaigning for prohibition, public health, eugenics, healthful living, the League of Nations, and monetary reform. He was the successful inventor of a visible card index file system and from this earned a fortune, most of which, however, together with his wife's, was lost in the great stockmarket crash of 1929. Fisher was active as a financial adviser and forecaster, but like many other experts he did not foresee this event and on October 15, 1929, just two weeks before the sharp break of the market, made the famous observation: "Stock prices have reached what looks like a permanently high plateau." He might have found consolation in the thought that a greater scientist than he, the renowned Isaac Newton, who in his youth assiduously studied the laws of probability and the mathematics of games of chance, was not markedly successful when trying his hand at such games and, a disappointed man, stopped playing cards for forty years. Fisher's conspicuous failure as a forecaster must, however, have been a tragic blow to a man who in 1892 in his doctoral dissertation, when mapping out the path of his own work, had cited with approval the words of the revered Newcomb: "To ultimately expect from political economy results of such certainty and exactness, that it can present the legislator with numerical predictions...is by no means hopeless."

UTILITY THEORY

Fisher's doctoral dissertation, which he entitled *Mathematical Investigations in the Theory of Value and Prices,* again illustrated the observation that scientific advances are made in the form of multiples. The work contained a rudimentary exposition of equations of general equilibrium worked out by Fisher in 1890, about fifteen years after the appearance of Walras's book, which was unknown to Fisher when he wrote his own version. It also contained the indifference curve, rediscovered by Fisher a decade after the publication of Edgeworth's *Mathematical Psychics,* which came to Fisher's attention only after he had completed the relevant part of his book. Thus, even if Walras and Edgeworth had failed to make these discoveries, the relentless logic of science would have stimulated another pioneer to produce them a few years later.

Fisher's utility theory, to the development of which he devoted a large part of the *Investigations,* had certain features in common with Edgeworth's, although in other respects it went beyond it. Both took their point of departure from Jevons's work. As Edgeworth had before, Fisher recognized that the utility of a commodity to an individual may not only be interpreted as a function of the quantity of that commodity, which had been Jevons's interpretation, but the utility function may be generalized to encompass the functional relation between the utility of a commodity and the quantities of all commodities held by an individual. Fisher went beyond Edgeworth by considering still another utility function, which would relate the utility of a commodity to an individual with the quantities of that commodity consumed by all persons in the market. This line of thought, which was approximately concurrent with Veblen's related ideas about conspicuous consumption, had already been hinted at by Petty and more explicitly stated by Rae, to whom Fisher paid homage in another connection and who wrote of "commodities the estimation of which depends wholly or in part on their power to mark the possession of a certain relative superiority," with pearls serving as his example whereas Fisher mentioned, among other things, diamonds and other articles of fashion.

The highlight of Fisher's *Investigations* was an operational theory of cardinal utility, in which he proposed to measure utility in terms of utils and defined a util as the marginal utility of an arbitrarily selected quantity of a reference commodity B. To measure the marginal utility of commodity A, he prepared a schedule listing the varying increments of A that the consumer stood ready to accept in lieu of equal increments of the util. This schedule could be transformed into another one made up of the total and marginal utilities yielded by equal increments of A. In later years, Fisher and Ragnar Frisch, the Norwegian econometrician, developed this approach further and made attempts at the numerical measurement of cardinal utility on the basis of empirical data.

In a number of respects, Fisher's *Investigations* stood halfway between Edgeworth's earlier work and Pareto's later work. As Pareto was to do, Fisher attempted to cleanse utility of utilitarian connotations and interpreted it as desiredness with no implication regarding the usefulness of the object of the desire. But unlike Pareto and in spite of the fact that he had given shape to the outward form of the modern indifference curve, Fisher attempted the cardinal measurement of utility. Fisher's *Investigations* constituted a notable contribution to the econometric theory of the consumer and was recognized as such among the small circle of scholars appreciative of mathematical economics at the time. Even among those not all appreciated the teaching machine, consisting of hydraulic tanks, with whose help Fisher, a man of a mechanistic bent of mind, proposed to elucidate the conditions of general equilibrium.

Fisher's *Investigations* was the work of a youth in his early twenties, and as is often true of mathematicians he attained the height of his intellectual powers at that early age. However, his later contributions reached a far wider public than the *Investigations*. It was on his subsequent publications that Fisher's growing reputation rested.

CAPITAL AND INTEREST THEORY

Fisher's later contributions fell under the headings of capital and interest theory, and monetary theory and policy. In *The Nature of Capital and Income* (1906) he acknowledged that such concepts as capital and income did not spring up from nowhere but reflected certain accounting conventions, with which he attempted to link the respective concepts as employed in economics. Adopting Newcomb's distinction between a fund and a flow, he demonstrated how the interest rate links the flow of income with the fund of capital. The value of capital then appeared as the present value of a flow of discounted future incomes. Capital generated income, but the value of capital reflected the values of the future income translated into present values by discounting.

Of lesser importance than Fisher's clarification of these fundamental relationships, but more controversial, was his formulation of an income concept equivalent to what is commonly called consumption—"psychic income" in the words of Frank A. Fetter, from whom the idea originated. Fisher used this uncommon definition to buttress his proposal of the exemption of savings from the income tax. This is an idea which under certain conditions has merits of its own and which on the grounds of such merits— but not in consequence of a mere definition—has had the approval of such authorities as Mill, Marshall, and Pigou.

Fisher's *Theory of Interest* (1930), the mature version of a subject that he had treated earlier in 1896 and in 1907, was largely a clarifying restatement of ideas developed originally but less cogently by Böhm-Bawerk, to whose memory, together with John Rae's, the work was dedicated. Its subtitle indicated that Fisher considered the interest rate "as determined by impatience to spend income and opportunity to invest it." The book contained a masterly integration of the time-preference and productivity theories of interest. The distinction between a "nominal" rate of interest and a "real" rate, which corrected the former for price changes, a distinction that since the time of Thornton had frequently been made in the literature, figured prominently in Fisher's work, as did the concept of a "rate of return over cost," like Wicksell's natural rate of interest a forerunner of Keynes's marginal efficiency of capital and recognized as such by Keynes. The rate of return over cost, later designated by Boulding as the "internal rate of return," was the hypothetical rate of discount at which the investor would exactly recoup, through the present worth of the returns from an investment, the present worth of its costs. The rational investor would make use of an investment opportunity if it yielded a rate of return over cost greater than the market rate of interest.

Fisher's interpretation of interest proceeded in terms of nonmonetary factors—time preference and productivity of capital—and was thus at variance with the soon-to-emerge monetary theory of interest in terms of liquidity preference. However, there were observations in Fisher's book that pointed to the short-run validity of a monetary theory of interest:

> While the main object of this book is to show how the rate of interest would behave if the purchasing power of money were stable, there has never been any long period of time during which this condition has been even approximately fulfilled. When it is not fulfilled, the money rate of interest, and still more the real rate of interest, is more affected by the instability of money than by those more fundamental and more normal causes connected with income impatience, and opportunity, to which this book is chiefly devoted.

It was for this reason that Keynes, the exponent of the liquidity-preference theory of interest, would refer to Fisher as "the great-grandparent, who first influenced me strongly towards regarding money as a 'real' factor" in the determination of the interest rate.

MONETARY THEORY

Fisher's principal contribution to monetary theory was his *Purchasing Power of Money* (1911), a careful restatement of the quantity theory of money. Adopting Newcomb's algebraic statement of the equation of exchange, Fisher fitted the quantity theory into the formula $MV = PT$, that is, the money stock in circulation times its velocity equals the price level times the volume of trade. To account for bank deposits, he properly expanded the left side of the equation. Although the work contained many valuable insights and broke new ground especially along econometric lines— it included statistical estimates of the various terms of the formula—Fisher's approach left out much that to other students seemed relevant to the determination of prices or pushed such matters into the background, where they tended to disappear behind the elements of the formula. He did not ignore the fact that V is volatile, that the level of prices varies directly with the quantity of money in circulation only if V and T are constant, and that it varies in the same proportion only in an "ultimate" and "normal" sense. But he made light of these and related disturbing circumstances by assuming them away or by placing them as "indirect influences" behind the terms of the equation which he recognized as "direct influences." In spite of the wealth of up-to-date statistical material his approach impressed many as unreal and antiquated, and it was superseded before long by the cash-balance and income approaches.

REFORM PROPOSALS

There was a link between Fisher's adherence to the quantity theory of money and the proposals for monetary reform which he with equal persistence supported throughout his mature life. They were as simple as the basic idea behind the quantity theory, and Fisher might have hoped that their very simplicity would gain followers for them. Before the advent of the Great Depression he was a vociferous exponent of the stabilization of purchasing power, an aim much in vogue at the time, which he proposed to attain by means of a "compensated dollar." This plan, which resembled Marshall's tabular standard and still earlier suggestions, provided for lowering or raising the price of gold in the same proportion in which prices increased or decreased. The coming of the Great Depression, which followed a period of relatively stable prices, might have convinced Fisher that a stable price level was no assurance of economic well-being and might in fact hide serious maladjustments.

During the Great Depression Fisher supported Silvio Gesell's plan for "stamped money," which was also favorably considered at that time by Keynes, a plan that was designed to discourage the hoarding of money by requiring that stamps be purchased and affixed to money to preserve its value. Later still Fisher campaigned for the "hundred percent reserve" plan, which a group of economists from the University of Chicago had launched and, which can be traced back to earlier ideas of Walras and Mises. This plan was designed to wrest from the banking system its power to create deposit money by requiring that demand deposits be backed, dollar for dollar, by cash. All these plans, of dubious value, came to naught, and Fisher's backing of them added little to his stature.

CONTRIBUTIONS TO BUSINESS CYCLE THEORY AND STATISTICS

Profoundly attached to monetary panaceas, as Fisher was, he also ascribed business fluctuations, which he considered as less regular and periodic than did other students of the business cycle, to monetary influences. In his "debt-deflation theory of great depressions," he attempted to explain business depressions in terms of "over-indebtedness" and "deflation." In this view, the liquidation of an excessively large debt would be followed by a contraction of money and a decline in prices. Under the ensuing deflation, the burden of the debt would become all but unbearable. These thoughts did not constitute a complete theory of the business cycle, but they were more apt to elucidate the conditions prevailing during the Great Depression than the more finely spun theories of others who pleaded for further deflation.

Throughout his work Fisher aimed at developing his theories in operational terms that would lend themselves to numerical measurement. From econometrics he branched out into the allied field of statistics, to which he made a number of contributions, by popularizing, for example, the use of the ratio chart, a device earlier employed by Jevons. In Fisher's *The Making of Index Numbers* (1922), he attempted to describe the characteristics of an "ideal" index and believed he had found it in the geometric mean of the Laspeyres and Paasche indexes, which use weights of the base period and of later periods respectively. In more recent decades index-number theory came to de-emphasize the statistical aspects, with which Fisher was concerned, and instead became involved with the economic aspects of the measurement of utility and welfare, on which this study of Fisher's shed no light. Of more lasting impact was his pioneer investigation of the statistical treatment of "distributed lags," which arise when the effects of an economic cause do not make themselves felt at once but are distributed over time. Fisher's discussion of the matter in 1925 stimulated further work by a large number of scholars, who found his ideas fruitful in a variety of economic contexts.

Except for writing an elementary text, Fisher did not bring his contributions to economics together in a book of the "Principles" type. Schumpeter referred to them as "the pillars and arches of a temple that was never built," adding, however, that the pillars and arches would be visible long after the work of others had fallen into oblivion. This was true because Fisher's mathematical approach represented the wave of the future, more so than did the approaches of his contemporaries.

Fisher's life spanned a period during which the number of American economists began to increase phenomenally. Membership in the American Economic Association, less than two hundred in 1886, exceeded ten times that number by 1911, rose to five thousand in 1947, the year of Fisher's death, and doubled within the next twelve years. In its earlier stage, the expansion of the economics profession reflected the spread of academic instruction in economics in the United States, where courses in economics attracted large numbers of students, who took them as part of their general education. The situation here was, and continues to be, quite unlike that in most other parts of the world, where courses in economics are taken as a matter of choice by the relatively few students who aspire to become professional economists and as a matter of compulsion by the students of law, who have to take them because they form part of the required curriculum. In its later stage, the increase in the number of professional economists in the United States reflected the widening range of opportunities in government service—mainly since the Great Depression—and in business —mainly since World War II.

FISHER'S CONTEMPORARIES

With such an abundance of talent devoting itself to the economics profession, the task of the chronicler becomes perforce highly selective. Among the many contemporaries of Fisher who served their profession honorably and with distinction one could single out such men as Frank W. Taussig (1859–1940) of Harvard, an expert in international economics and tariff history, who directed a number of investigations of the ways in which a country's international balance of payments finds adjustment, made by students who were to become leaders of the next generation of economists; Frank A. Fetter (1863–1949) of Princeton, who aspired to revise the study of economics in line with new trends in psychology; J. Laurence Laughlin (1871–1933), founder of the department of economics at the University of Chicago, a conservative but broad-minded in tolerating divergent opinion, under whose leadership the Chicago group acquired its unique position in American economics; and Herbert J. Davenport (1861–1931) of Cornell, part of the establishment but highly skeptical of its conventional wisdom, which he wanted to see restricted to a narrow price theory and supplemented by a type of economics different from the orthodox one and taught by "institutional" economists, his teacher Veblen in particular. Davenport considered much of conventional economics as apologetic, and by restricting it to price theory he hoped to purge it of moralizing tendencies. He scandalized the profession by insisting on the inclusion of unlawful activities among the productive ones—burglars' jimmies, he wrote, are wealth just as much as are other forms of capital. He pleaded for a new economics that was to be not "a system of apologetics, the creed of the reactionary, a defense of privilege, a social soothing sirup, a smug pronouncement of the righteousness of whatever is."

INSTITUTIONAL ECONOMICS

Davenport formed the link between the "orthodox" group, of whom Clark and the scholars mentioned in the preceding paragraph were the leading exponents, and the band of dissenters who became known as institutional economists and among whom Thorstein Veblen (1857–1929), John R. Commons (1862–1945), and Wesley C. Mitchell (1874–1948) were the outstanding figures. What the group of protestants had in common was their opposition to the type of economics then in vogue and exemplified by the work of Clark and also of the Austrians, who were at that time at the height of their influence and with whom many American economists attempted to come to terms. Pure theory in general and, more specifically, the pure theory of comparative statics as developed in the utility analysis of consumer behavior and in the marginal productivity theory of distribution became the principal targets against which the institutional economists launched their attacks. Only Veblen, however, wanted to destroy the conventional approach by root and branch, whereas the other two took a somewhat more conciliatory position. And only Veblen was a critic not just of conventional economics but of the business civilization of his time, which he condemned in strictures as bitter and severe as those embedded in the work of Marx.

The institutional economists shared the critical attitude to conventional economic theory characteristic of the German historical economists, whose views were diffused by their former students after their return to the United States. The link between institutional economics and German historical economics was especially pronounced with Commons, who came to share his teacher Ely's attachment to the German approach. It was less strong with Veblen, who likewise, but for a briefer period, was a student of Ely's and who judged Ely's views more critically. Of the three master institutionalists only Mitchell spent some time as a student in Germany, but he went to Austria as well and neither experience seems to have profoundly affected his future work.

In a sense, institutional economics formed a counterpart to historical economics, but it was a characteristically American movement with unique features of its own, lent to it by its connection with the American philosophy of pragmatism. Veblen was a student of Charles Peirce's and a colleague of John Dewey's—Peirce, Dewey, and William James were the leading exponents of pragmatism. Mitchell was a student both of Veblen's and Dewey's. There was no such personal link between the great pragmatists and Commons, but the currents of thought generated by them made themselves felt also in his work. Together with related movements in law, history, and other disciplines, pragmatism and institutional economics formed parts of a wider, and again characteristically American, movement of thought which has been interpreted as a "revolt against formalism," that is, the formalism of abstract deductive reasoning in the social sciences. This revolt appealed to experience rather than to universally valid reason, to evolutionary change rather than to the search for "normal" or "natural" conditions, and to man as an active agent rather than as a passive instrument registering the impact of pleasure and pain. The pragmatic revolt thus constituted a sharp break with the natural law tradition, which had enthroned universally valid reason, with the utilitarians' interpretation of human behavior in terms of a calculus of pleasure and pain, and with the economists' concern with the equilibria of comparative statics, indicative ostensibly of tendencies toward normalcy or naturalness.

Under the influence of Darwin the pragmatists stressed the biological aspects of evolution and assigned to social science the task of explaining man's adaptation and survival under the ever-changing conditions of social, political, and economic life. Hence, evolutionary change was one of the watchwords of the pragmatists. Another one was the unity of thought and action in an experimentalism that tested ideas by applying them in practice. A third was the rejection of a priori abstract reasoning and its replacement by empirical studies. The institutional economists, each in his own way, followed the programs indicated by these watchwords and fashioned their work in line with them. Veblen set out to depict, in broad strokes, the evolutionary change of culture. Commons allied himself with the forces of economic reform and aided them with his work as a social inventor. Mitchell pursued painstaking empirical studies along quantitative lines and explored the evolutionary change of the modern economy in terms of business cycles, with one phase generating the next. None of the three had use for the marginal utility approach, which they considered tainted by utilitarianism, for the natural law tradition, which emphasized unity and stability rather than diversity and change, or for the quest for normalcy characteristic of the conventional economists' concern with comparative statics.

Darwin's thought, however, influenced not only the pragmatists and institutional economists but also the social Darwinists. The pragmatists and institutionalists rejected laissez faire and instead taught that natural selection in the struggle for his existence would enable man to learn the art of adjustment to new conditions by deliberate public policies. The social Darwinists, on the other hand, adhered to laissez faire, under which the fittest were guaranteed survival. In this manner, pragmatists and social Darwinists arrived at diametrically opposite conclusions, both ostensibly deduced from the thought of Darwin. Both interpretations left their mark on Veblen, and this brought a measure of ambivalence into his own work. He was influenced not only by the views of the pragmatists but also by the opposite views of his teacher Sumner, one of the leading exponents of social Darwinism and of laissez faire, the same scholar who started Irving Fisher on his way to mathematical economics. From Sumner, Veblen learned that man's power to change social structures by deliberate action is severely limited, and it was perhaps under Sumner's influence that Veblen abstained, until late in life, from proclaiming a program that called for action. Sumner's influence also explains Veblen's lifelong support of free trade, a support as steadfast as that found in the writings of the great exponents of the classical tradition in economics.

Veblen, Commons, and Mitchell fought conventional economics from within the academic bastion rather than as outsiders, but only Mitchell's career was an unqualifiedly distinguished one throughout and without reverses, leading him from Chicago to Berkeley, which gradually emerged as a Western rival of the great academic enterprises of the East, and eventually to Columbia. That Mitchell's career was an undisturbed one was because of his engaging personal qualities and the greater affinity of his work with conventional economics. Commons likewise had engaging personal qualities and, like Mitchell, became the educator of a host of future economists. But he never earned a Ph.D. and his early academic career was filled with painful reverses. After a period that to all appearances had ended in failure, he was at the age of forty-two given a new opportunity at the University of Wisconsin, where he found himself and where his and his associates' work put the economics department into the front rank of comparable institutions. Veblen's career was made dismal by his difficult personality, marital problems, and dislike of teaching, which, compounded with his unconventional views, taxed the patience of university authorities at Chicago, Stanford, and Missouri and prevented his advancement beyond the rank of associate professor. Faithful friends attempted to help him over difficulties, aided him financially, and in his declining years secured him a teaching position at the New School for Social Research in New York. Unlike Commons and Mitchell, Veblen never held office as president of the American Economic Association. When he was sixty-eight an attempt was made to nominate him for this post, but he declined the honor as coming too late.

VEBLEN: CRITIC OF BUSINESS CIVILIZATION

Veblen was the child of two cultures, in neither of which he felt at home. Born in Wisconsin, the son of Norwegian immigrants, he grew up in one of Minnesota's Little Norways, and when at the age of seventeen his father enrolled him at Carleton College he went as an alien who spoke broken English and preserved detachment from the influence of the Congregationalist spirit which the college was designed to spread in the Midwest. Even at Carleton Veblen withdrew into the shell of "sardonic humour" that became the hallmark of his later work. Not everyone recognized his great gifts, but among those who did was John Bates Clark, Veblen's teacher of economics at Carleton, one of the way stations in Clark's academic career. After his graduation Veblen spent a year teaching elementary school. Then, after a short sojourn at Johns Hopkins, where he failed to obtain a scholarship, he went to Yale to study philosophy and earned a doctorate in 1884. Veblen, a "Norskie" with dubious religious views, was now ready for a teaching post, but in spite of the good recommendations of his professors none came his way and he had to return to the family farm, dissatisfied with the world and with himself. After seven long years he reemerged in 1891 at Cornell where, wearing a coonskin cap and corduroy trousers, he introduced himself to J. Laurence Laughlin, the professor in charge of economics, and asked for an opportunity to continue his studies. He was given a fellowship, and when a year later Laughlin accepted an appointment to head the department of economics at the University of Chicago, which had just been launched on Rockefeller's millions, he took Veblen along. There Veblen joined the faculty and in slow stages rose to assistant professor in 1900, at the age of forty-three.

In 1899 Veblen published his first book, *The Theory of the Leisure Class,* which was later followed by some ten others but remained his best-known work. Here as in his other writings, including a large number of articles, Veblen drew on the resources of philosophy, anthropology, psychology, history, and natural science to elaborate the ever-recurring theme of his works: Life is an evolutionary process in which man demonstrates his power to survive. In this process of natural selection and adaptation certain institutions are shaped, defined by Veblen somewhat vaguely as "habits of thought" or "prevailing or dominant types of spiritual attitude and aptitudes," but since these are perpetuated by the forces of custom and fashioned by the past, they do not invariably fit the requirements of the present. Lags arise, which bring tension and need for continued adjustment and change. Economic institutions more specifically are "habitual methods of carrying on the life process of the community in contact with the material environment in which it lives."

The study of economic institutions was to be the hallmark of the economics that Veblen advocated, an evolutionary science that explored the cause-and-effect relationships involved in the process of cumulative change. In this task it could not arrive at settled truth: "The outcome of any serious research," Veblen asserted in an address in 1908, "can only be to make two questions grow where one question grew before." What Veblen proposed was no less than a thorough revamping of economics. In an essay published in 1898 he raised the question, "Why is economics not an evolutionary science?" and characterized the conventional approach to economics as taxonomic, that is, concerned with classification, aiming at systematization in line with natural laws while pushing aside "disturbing factors," elements that did not fit into the system, and as depicting human behavior in hedonistic terms, passive, inert, and reflecting an immutably given human nature. In a passage that exemplifies his style at its best, Veblen wrote:

> The hedonistic conception of man is that of a lightning calculator of pleasures and pains, who oscillates like a homogeneous globule of desire of happiness under the impulse of stimuli that shift him about the area, but leave him intact. He has neither antecedent nor consequent. He is an isolated, definitive human datum, in stable equilibrium except for the buffets of the impinging forces that displace him in one direction or another. Self-imposed in elemental space, he spins symmetrically about his own spiritual axis until the parallelogram of forces bears down upon him, whereupon he follows the line of the resultant. When the force of the impact is spent, he comes to rest, a self-contained globule of desire as before.

An excerpt from the same article, where Veblen attempts to denigrate conventional economics by employing the nomenclature of botanical classifications, shows his style at its worst:

> If we are getting restless under the taxonomy of a monocotyledonous wage doctrine and a cryptogamic theory of interest, with involute, loculicidal, tomentous and moniliform variants, what is the cytoplasm, centrosome, or karyokinetic process to which we may turn, and in which we may find surcease from the metaphysics of normality and controlling principles? What are we going to do about it? The question is rather, What are we doing about it?

What Veblen put in the place of conventional economics was an exposure of the modern business civilization, which illustrated, as a sort of test case, man's frailty in the midst of institutions that had fallen on him as part of the legacy of the race and had ceased to serve him well. Veblen depicted human evolution as having passed through the savage, barbarian, handicraft, and machine-process cultures. Savages, he asserted, are peaceable and poor, and among them is found little differentiation of employment and distinction of classes. Savagery gives way to barbarism as predatory habits of life—warfare, big game hunting—become common, and with them there emerges ownership, first of women, then of slaves, and later of inanimate things. Aggressive prowess becomes an object of admiration and emulation, and invidious comparisons are made between exploits and other worthy employment on the one hand and productive work on the other, the latter being associated with weakness and submission to a master. Labor becomes irksome because it is considered an unworthy employment, whereas the possession of wealth is in the nature of a trophy and confers honor. The root of ownership and accumulation is emulation and invidious distinction rather than the search for subsistence and physical comfort. Since the possession of wealth confers honor, the desire for it has no limits. Wealthy people want to put their affluence in evidence, and they do so by means of conspicuous consumption, conspicuous leisure, and conspicuous waste.

Waste was to Veblen as obnoxious as it had been to Locke, and he imputed it not only to consumption but to production as well. The captains of industry, who presided over production, strove not for a maximum output of goods and services but for pecuniary rewards, and they obtained these by financial manipulations and monopolistic restrictions of output—designated as sabotage by Veblen—rather than by expanding output. A parasitic and predatory culture was kept going because it was sanctioned by an elaborate make-believe—labor, social utility, or natural rights theories of property, theories of distribution such as Clark's, and so forth—which confirmed the underlying population in its low opinion of the worth of its employments and in its eagerness to emulate the exploits and wasteful consumption of the superior ranks. Redemption would come, if it was to come at all, from an upheaval of the members of the technical engineering class, whose matter-of-fact working habits made their minds less susceptible to the make-believe that impressed the working class, and who might assume the direction of production.

Such was, in its barest outline and in part in Veblen's own words, the message that can be distilled from his work. Defects there were many—such as Veblen's disdain for all firm rules guiding human behavior, be they derived from the natural law tradition or from utilitarianism; his elitist claim to superior insight, enabling him to discover ubiquitous make-believe; his false disjunction between the captains of industry and the productive technicians; his insipid hope that the latter might save the world; his apparent belief that in the United States manual labor is considered unworthy and that a leisure class flourishes there; his advocacy of increased output as the only true test of economic well-being; his mercantilist notion that one man's gain is another man's loss, a notion entirely inappropriate in an environment where increasing productivity is the rule. But in spite of these and many other defects, Veblen's work had a profoundly disturbing effect on many American economists, who may have taken it more seriously than did Veblen himself. This effect was felt with special intensity during the Great Depression, the moment of truth when conventional economics was put to its most severe test. Considering such advice as that of Fisher, who was presumably the country's greatest economic theorist and who insisted that with the stamina of the American people strengthened by prohibition there was no need to be afraid of a severe depression, it was not surprising that many found Veblen's views more to the point, in particular his opinion, stated in *The Theory of Business Enterprise* (1904), that in modern times short-lived depressions had given way to more chronic stagnation: "Dull times," he wrote, "are, in a way, the course of nature; whereas brisk times are an exceptional invention of man or a rare bounty of Providence."

Veblen did not live to see it, but his work, in conjunction with the trauma of the Great Depression, placed the economics profession in a position that resembled that of the farmer with an empty sack, whom Veblen once encountered just after he had come across a hornets' nest. Veblen asked to borrow the sack, went away, put the hornets in, and then returned it to the farmer with a "thank you." The farmer, it is said, is still looking for Veblen.

MITCHELL AND THE STUDY OF BUSINESS CYCLES

Veblen's distinction between workmanship and what has been called the wastemanship of the captains of industry was echoed in the writings of Wesley C. Mitchell, whose distinction between making goods and making money served as the starting point for his lifelong study of business cycles. To Mitchell, the salient feature of the modern economy was its character of a money economy, in which money is used not merely as a medium of exchange but in which economic activities occur in the form of making and spending money incomes. Whether a person is rich or poor in economic terms is not determined by his ability to turn out useful goods or husband his supplies but by his ability to command an adequate money income and practice pecuniary thrift. Whereas conventional economists might evoke an invisible hand or map out an idealized pattern of a competitive economy in which rational economic behavior would tend to maximize welfare, Mitchell's dichotomy between making goods and making money was grounded in the explicit recognition that there are various ways of making money that do not contribute anything to the nation's welfare or which affect it adversely. The "real" factors—national resources, mechanical equipment, industrial skill—Mitchell considered necessary but not sufficient conditions for the nation's well-being. In the money economy these factors will be utilized only if the men in command of production expect a monetary profit from their use.

The idea that the private pursuit of gain might frustrate the achievement of maximum national welfare was stated by Mitchell in his *Business Cycles* of 1913, the first of a series of pioneer investigations devoted to this subject. At that time this idea began to interest other economists, and it stood in the center, for example, of Pigou's concurrent work on welfare economics. But whereas in Pigou's writings it served as the basis for the theoretical classification and systematization of cases in which private gain and public welfare were incompatible, Mitchell did not stress this aspect of the matter. Unlike the conventional economists he did not employ equilibrium analysis, and in his *Business Cycles: The Problem and Its Setting* (1927) he characterized such concepts as "the normal state of trade" as a "figment." Instead he moved on to a empirical exploration of the overall performance of the economy, whose inherent instability he attributed primarily to the process of moneymaking. The self-generating business cycle thus became, in Mitchell's writings, a synonym for the historical movement of the money economy of modern capitalism, in which production depends on realized or expected profits, and these, in turn, on the relation between costs and prices and a host of other factors, all interrelated and thus responsible for the spread of maladjustments.

Although Mitchell was a profound student of the various business cycle theories that single out specific elements—monetary factors, weather cycles, oversaving, underconsumption, overinvestment or underinvestment, and so forth—and employ these on a priori grounds as principles of explanation, Mitchell approached his task without reliance on any of these theories and instead proposed to begin with a factual study of the matter. He gathered the statistical facts in the most painstaking manner, and when the task proved beyond the ability of a single investigator he helped to organize the National Bureau of Economic Research in 1920 and guided its work as the first director of research for a quarter of a century. Since then there have been prepared under the National Bureau's sponsorship a great number of studies on those phases of the economy that lend themselves to quantitative exploration. Although at times, and especially in more recent years, the bureau has sponsored research of a more theoretical type, it has, on the whole, been faithful to Mitchell's empirical approach.

Mitchell's patient gathering of facts in the form of statistical time series, of which he assembled, with the bureau's help, over a thousand, impressed unfriendly critics as a futile exercise in naive empiricism, as limited in its explanatory value as "measurement without theory" was bound to be. Embedded in Mitchell's work and obfuscated by its plethora of statistical data there were, however, many of the analytical tools considered relevant in modern business cycle theory. Thus Friedman was able to distill from Mitchell's 1913 volume such ideas—expressed verbally rather than mathematically and varying in explicitness—as the multiplier and the principle of acceleration, waves of optimism and pessimism, the drain of cash from the banking system, and the decline of the yield expected from new investment, the latter idea belonging to the same family as Wicksell's natural rate of interest, Fisher's rate of return over cost, and Keynes's marginal efficiency of capital.

Although Mitchell was primarily a student of business cycles, he made a number of other important contributions. His first book, *A History of the Greenbacks* (1903), was an authoritative study of Civil War inflation. In the early 1920s, several decades before work of this type was recognized as a public responsibility and undertaken by the government, Mitchell was the coauthor of a National Bureau study devoted to the conceptualization and estimation of the national income. A student's lecture notes taken in Mitchell's course on *Types of Economic Theory* in 1934–35 were, until the publication of Schumpeter's *History of Economic Analysis,* the only record of the sweep of doctrinal history as seen by one of America's master economists. The leading item in a collection of Mitchell's essays, *The Backward Art of Spending Money* (1937), and the one from which the book derived its title, showed the limited extent to which the rationale of economic calculation applied in the field of consumption, where the art of buymanship was far less developed than that of salesmanship.

Throughout his work, Mitchell upheld the goal of an objective scholarship and insisted on the separation of scholarly science from reformist policy making, which involved valuations instead of the ostensibly neutral "job of finding out as definitely as possible what happens under specified conditions." In line with this approach, which converged with Max Weber's methodological ideas rather than with Gunnar Myrdal's skepticism about a value free social science, the National Bureau was forbidden in its bylaws to append policy recommendations to its findings.

COMMONS AND LABOR ECONOMICS

The disjunction between scholarship and reform that Mitchell advocated made his approach contrast sharply with that of John R. Commons, the other member of the institutionalist triad. Soon after Commons joined the department of economics at the University of Wisconsin in 1904, he became associated with the progressive government of the state, then headed by Robert M. La Follette, and in a sequence of memorable experiments helped to draft legislation which often incorporated new ideas and which after a period of trial on the state level was emulated by other states and on the federal level. Counseled by Commons, the state of Wisconsin became a laboratory for the testing of precedent-setting innovations in public utility regulation, workmen's compensation, and unemployment insurance. Commons's pioneer work as a practical reformer encompassed not only labor legislation and industrial relations but a wide range of subjects falling under the broad headings of public administration and "government and business."

The drafting of legislation required preparatory fact-finding, which Commons and his students undertook in the form of field work. Their exploration of facts and opinions resembled that of a legislative committee, the principal differences being the far lesser formality of their proceedings and the fact that the interrogators examined the witnesses in the field and on the site instead of meeting them only in the halls of the legislature. Commons and his associates became quite proficient in their type of fact-finding, to which Commons, never at a loss for a name, referred as "investigational economics" and which he, as "analytical studies," delineated from the "schedule studies" of the exponents of statistical fact-finding. It was an approach that was more impressionistic than the latter or the survey method which later came into vogue in economics, but it was more flexible' than these and apt to reveal more if practiced by a master intuitionist.

Side by side with these activities Commons pursued a far-flung program of historical studies which in time made him the chronicler of the history of American labor. This program began in 1909 with an article about "American Shoemakers, 1648–1895," in which Commons related the evolution of workers' organizations to changes in the market for their products. It was followed a year later by a monumental *Documentary History of American Industrial Society*, edited by Commons and his associates in ten volumes, and it culminated in 1918 in a four-volume *History of Labor in the* *United States,* of which Commons was the senior coauthor. Commons's engrossing concern with the history of labor yielded in time a genetic approach to current labor problems, which were interpreted in the light of their past evolution rather than with the help of conventional equilibrium economics. This approach became the hallmark of the Wisconsin school of labor economics over which Commons presided. Many of Commons's achievements in labor history and labor economics were the results of teamwork, as were his contributions to reform legislation. Thus, several years before the founding of the National Bureau of Economic Research, Commons pioneered in organizing research as an enterprise carried on by a group of devoted and enthusiastic followers. In the 1930s, when the government and the great foundations began to sponsor large research projects, teamwork in economic research proved to be the wave of the future.

Unlike the mathematical economists, who were apt to make their contributions early in their career, Commons's general ideas were shaped by long years of experience. Late in life, and as the crowning achievement of his work, he published *Legal Foundations of Capitalism* (1924) and *Institutional Economics* (1934). As a draftsman of reform legislation, Commons had become aware of the influence of the law on economic life and had found that the ideas of economists and lawyers about value were not always the same. In the law there had evolved the concept of reasonableness. Public utility regulation was concerned with reasonable value, labor law with reasonable wage, workmen's compensation with reasonable safety, and public officials and private citizens were expected to live up to the requirement of reasonable conduct. Commons found little in the writings of the economists that would shed light on the nature of reasonableness. It was the courts that filled the concept with substantive content, and the Supreme Court, which had the final say in the matter, had become the "first authoritative faculty of political economy in the world's history."

By stressing the impact of legal institutions on economic life Commons made his work reflect the growing interventionism of the modern age. During the era of laissez faire economists would proceed on the assumption of severely restricted functions of government, which appeared to them as an instrument that protected the rich against the poor and as a guardian of property rights and contractual obligations. Now, with an increasing range of governmental functions, the state had ceased to be a mere night watchman, and the effects of various types of legislative interference on the economy were waiting for analysis. Commons's interest in legal institutions reflected a phase of economic interventionism is which the latter made itself felt primarily in the form of regulation rather than through measures of fiscal policy that would point toward central planning. As regards such planning, Commons, in his *Institutional Economics,* expressed doubts about the competence of democracy and representative government to manage it. He has rightly been characterized as a "conservative reformer."

In Commons's *Institutional Economics,* the vista widened and encompassed not only action on the governmental level but all "collective action" such as that undertaken by organizations of labor, farmers, business, and other bodies that constitute the pluralistic universe of the American economy in the twentieth century. In this work Commons defined an institution as "collective action in control of individual action" or, more specifically, as "collective action in restraint, liberation, and expansion of individual action." The older economics had disregarded institutions because it envisaged economic relations as prevailing not between man and man but between man and nature—between human labor and the resistance of nature's forces, as in classical economics, or between the quantity wanted of nature's forces and the quantity available, as in marginal utility economics. The older economics had constructed a pure theory based on the physical exchange of materials and services but had neglected the fact that what counted were not physical entities but property rights. This point of view of the older economics Commons contrasted with his own, which called for attention not to individuals and nature's forces but to the mutual transfers of property rights, out of which human beings got their living. Commons's institutional economics was conceived as a broad synthesis of law, economics, and ethics, which recognized both conflicts of interest and their mutual dependence as well as the need for security of expectations or order. The basic concept of institutional economics was not the commodity or the exchange but the "transaction." Of the latter Commons wrote:

> Transactions intervene between the production of labor, of the classical economists, and the pleasures of consumption, of the hedonic economists, simply because it is society that, by its rules of order, controls ownership of and access to the forces of nature. Transactions, as thus defined, are not the "exchange of commodities," in the physical sense of "delivery," they are the alienation and acquisition, between individuals, of the *rights* of future ownership of physical things, as determined by the collective working rules of society. The *transfer of these rights* must therefore be negotiated between the parties concerned, according to the working rules of society, before labor can produce, or consumers can consume, or commodities be physically delivered to other persons.

With considerable powers of construction, Commons filled in the further details of his far-flung conceptual scheme of institutional economics. There was a far lesser response, however, to this aspect of his work than to his activities as a reformer and initiator of the study of applied fields of economics. Students of Commons and their students in turn would cultivate these and add to the master's legacy by drafting the social security legislation of the 1930s. But Commons's theoretical message, made public in 1934, although it did not exactly fall on deaf ears, was soon forgotten and not followed up by allied efforts aiming at the redirection of economics. His message was more relevant to the regulatory phase of interventionism, when the legal merits of the regulatory measures formed the subject of a heated debate, than to its later phases, when the great legal issues had been resolved and fiscal policy rather than regulation moved into the foreground of public policy. The impact of Commons's *Institutional Economics* was weakened by the publication, only two years later, of Keynes's *General Theory*, which overshadowed all other work. There are limits to the capacity of a profession to absorb new ideas; coming to terms with Keynes strained this capacity to the utmost.

The question may be asked why institutional economics as developed by Veblen, Mitchell, and Commons remained a unique feature of American thought, which found few parallels elsewhere. There were, to begin with, the specific characteristics of the American intellectual atmosphere which provided a fertile ground for the rise of institutional economics. Abroad, these characteristics were absent, and apart from this there were in the various countries factors in operation that stemmed the rise of kindred thought. In Germany the historical economists were in control for almost the whole century preceding World War II. Since conventional theory was deposed and had hardly any followers, there would have been no suitable target for an attack along institutionalist lines. A target was missing also in France, where economics was in the doldrums during the period in which institutional economics flourished in the United States and where the great pioneers of mathematical economics received only scant recognition at that time. The only French economist whose work converged with that of the institutionalists was François Simiand (1873–1935), who applied similar methods to the study of the long-range movement of prices and wages.

In England, Marshall's theory was less pure than that developed by Clark and the American followers of the Austrians, and except for the one-man crusade of John A. Hobson (1858–1940) there was no revolt against it comparable to that which took place in the United States. Hobson had little influence on academic economics in England, but to him was due an early formulation of the idea of oversaving, then—in 1889—universally rejected by respectable economic opinion but later memorialized by Keynes, and the first exposé, in 1902, of imperialism, one later exploited by Lenin and other followers of Marx in their denunciations of capitalism.

The generations of American economists who succeeded Veblen, Commons, and Mitchell included only a few who would claim to be institutional economists. In fact, standard economic theory became ever more pure instead of descending to a lower level of abstraction, as the institutionalists had suggested. Although conventional theory did not surrender to the institutional approach, it nevertheless purged itself, by the devices of its own logic, of some features that the institutional economists had found particularly offensive. Thus the pure theory of consumption was emptied of utilitarian content, the spectrum of monopolistic competition replaced the polarity of competition and monopoly, and macroeconomics added a social dimension to individualizing microeconomics. Moreover, as least one great figure who was steeped in pure theory—Schumpeter—went beyond the confines of conventional theory and raised broad questions about the future evolution of capitalism, questions of the type that institutional economists liked to raise and for which their approach supposedly provided answers. There was also the study of the economic development of backward countries, to which an increasing number of economists were drawn after World War II. Some of this work proceeded along the lines of pure theory, but it also opened up opportunities for studies on a lower level of abstraction, for the exploration of development problems within the contexts of varied cultures, and for the interdisciplinary utilization of the resources of such allied sciences as history, anthropology, sociology, and political science, approaches closer to the institutionalist program than to conventional theory.

J. M. CLARK

Leading American economists whose work linked them with the institutionalists in one way or another included John M. Clark (1884–1963), Simon Kuznets (b. 1901), John Kenneth Galbraith (b. 1908), and Kenneth Boulding (b. 1910). Clark worked under the influence both of his father's tradition and that of the institutionalists. Although he adhered to the framework of conventional theory, he considered it overly pure and attempted to make it more realistic and socially useful. With this aim in mind, he developed the concept of workable or effective competition, designed to serve as a standard of socially acceptable business behavior. Among Clark's contributions to theory was his discovery, in 1917, of the principle of acceleration of derived demand, according to which changes in consumption or output bring about magnified changes in investment. This was again a multiple discovery, credit for which Clark shared with the French economist Albert Aftalion, who explained—but did not name—the operation of the principle in 1909.

KUZNETS

Like other scholars connected with the National Bureau for Economic Research, Kuznets continued Mitchell's tradition of statistical fact-finding. Whereas Mitchell devoted his life to the study of business cycles, Kuznets turned to other fluctuations—seasonal ones and secular movements—then to national income estimation, and later to studies of economic growth. The Kuznets cycle, an intermediate wave with a duration of fifteen to twenty-five years, was discovered by Kuznets and was named after him.

GALBRAITH

Galbraith's criticism of the "conventional wisdom" echoed Veblen's strictures. His works, written with enthusiasm and wit and replete with political implications, appealed to a large public and were more widely commented upon than the writings of other contemporary economists. The key words of Galbraith's most influential writings were "countervailing power," "affluent society," and "technostructure." Oligopoly, he argued, was under

the discipline of countervailing power, which compelled one oligopolistic
concern to bargain with another—a steel producer, for example, with an
641
automobile manufacturer. The affluent society provided plentifully for the
satisfaction of wants created by advertising, but it starved the supply of
public services that would keep air and water clean, make cities livable,
improve education, and so forth. Many productive activities, Galbraith
pointed out, derived their social value not from the production of useful
goods but from the employment that they provided and from the income
that they generated. To the technostructure rather than to owners and
managers Galbraith attributed decisive power in the "industrial society," in
which consumers' sovereignty was replaced by the large concerns' control
over the market and in which the power of the latter over society was
checked not by labor unions but by the educational and scientific estate.

BOULDING

Discontent with conventional economics was also expressed in the
writings of Boulding, whose bill of particulars included the lack of integration of economics with the other social sciences and the absence of a macroeconomic theory of distribution. Boulding's *Reconstruction of Economics*
(1950) contained proposals for the removal of these and other faults.
Although he was critical of the work of the institutional economists, his own
ideas, with their biological and physiological analogies and his search for a
unified social science, had a certain affinity with theirs.

AMERICAN SCHOOLS OF THOUGHT

Of the scholars mentioned in the preceding paragraphs, Kuznets and
Galbraith were members of the Harvard faculty, as were Schumpeter,
Chamberlin, and Leontief, whose contributions have already been assessed.
Besides a number of other scholars of great renown, the Harvard department
included Alvin H. Hansen (b. 1887), the leading exponent of Keynesian
economics in the United States, who lent his support to the propagation of
the new ideas long before they had become accepted as part of the standard
doctrine. The Harvard group formed no school; its eminence was based
on the variety of the points of view outstandingly represented by its members.

THE CHICAGO SCHOOL

The followers of Keynes in the United States formed no school because
their point of view within a short span of time was absorbed by what soon
became a new orthodoxy to which the great majority of the profession
adhered. Some of those who took exception to Keynesian economics and to
the theories of monopolistic competition did, however, constitute a closely

knit group, and since its base of operations was the University of Chicago, it became known as the Chicago school. This group, which at different periods included Frank H. Knight (b. 1885), Jacob Viner (1892–1970), Henry Simons (1899–1946), George Stigler (b. 1911), and Milton Friedman (b. 1912), stood out as conservative in politics as well as in science. On the positive side, members of the group favored a redirection of monetary policy, first by means of the 100 percent reserve plan and later with the help of a rule requiring an annual increase of the money supply by a given percentage. Libertarians all, they preferred rules to authorities and the impersonal forces of the market to their deliberate direction, and they viewed with alarm the increasing scope of governmental activities in the economic sphere. Knight and Viner, the two senior members of the group, made pathbreaking contributions to the theory of the firm. The source of what later became the standard diagrammatic exposition of the theory of production, with total, average, and marginal cost curves, was a graph in Knight's *Risk, Uncertainty and Profit* (1921), and the source of what later served as the standard portrayal of cost curves was Viner's celebrated article on "Cost Curves and Supply Curves," published in 1931. From Knight's work stemmed the fundamental distinction between risk, which is calculable and insurable, and uncertainty, to which the probability calculus cannot be applied and which gives rise to profit. Viner's article contained an early reference to "marginal revenue"; another of his articles, published in 1921, twelve years ahead of Chamberlin's *Monopolistic Competition,* discussed the "differentiation of products." Knight's philosophical penetration, his advocacy of reason and tolerance, and the subtlety with which he handled a wealth of ideas made him an intellectual force whose impact was felt by several generations of economists. Viner was without peer in the field of international economics and as a chronicler of intellectual history.

SAMUELSON

Of the ever-increasing penetration of economics by mathematics the work of Paul A. Samuelson (b. 1915) became an outstanding example. Samuelson's sparkling intellect was nourished by several of the great traditions in American scholarship. As an undergraduate he was a student of Knight and Viner; as a graduate, he went to Harvard and was taught by Schumpeter and other illustrious men. Samuelson's teaching career at the Massachusetts Institute of Technology coincided with the ascendancy of this great institution in the field of academic economics. Samuelson was not a man of a single overmastering idea but one whose many contributions to mathematical economics added sparkle to numerous facets of economic theory. In the words of Isaiah Berlin—"the fox knows many things, but the hedgehog knows one big thing"—Samuelson must be counted a fox rather than a hedgehog unless his mathematical approach is considered the one big thing. To say that his contributions aimed at clarification and refinement would not do justice to them. But their very profusion makes it difficult to synthesize them and present more than an enumeration of the highlights—at least until the passage of time creates better opportunities for a more detached judgment.

In 1938, at the age of twenty-three, Samuelson started to develop his ideas about "revealed preference," a challenge to the conventional utility and indifference-curve approaches to the analysis of consumer behavior. One year later he published an article, soon to become famous, about the interactions between multiplier analysis and the principle of acceleration. In the early 1940s he contributed pioneer articles about dynamics and comparative statics, which were later incorporated into his *Foundations of Economic Analysis* (1947). In this work Samuelson set forth his view of comparative statics as a special case of dynamic analysis, with the stability conditions evolving only within the framework of dynamic theory. He also gave direction to future work by employing systems of differential and difference equations in dynamic adjustment processes, the former for the "rate analysis" of continuous processes involving flows and the latter, "perhaps of even greater importance for economic theory," for discrete processes treated in "period analysis." Like other great theorists, Samuelson was drawn to the theory of international trade, to which he made many important contributions. These included a definitive criticism of community indifference curves, an investigation of the equalization of factor prices under free trade, an exploration of the influence of international trade on the functional distribution of income, an interpretation of the gain from trade measured in terms of the difference between prices in a freely trading world and autarchic prices, and examinations of the transfer problem and the impact of the trade in intermediate products on the conventional theory of international trade.

Samuelson is equipped with both penetrating powers of analysis and great gifts of exposition. He is eminently proficient not only in the language of mathematics but also in verbal expression. He wrote an introductory text of which more than one million copies were sold throughout the world and helped to establish new standards of economic instruction at home and abroad.

Samuelson's work formed a link with econometrics, to which he and other American economists made great contributions and which, at the twentieth century's midpoint, had become the favorite and most prestigious approach to economics, a wave of the future that engulfed the present.

Chapter 28

FROM ECONOMICS
TO ECONOMETRICS

The survey of econometrics that is presented in the following pages offers an inventory rather than a critical appraisal such as can successfully be attempted only at a later time when current events can be viewed in a broader perspective and when the econometric phase of economic thought is linked with the next one. Moreover, a complete account of the accomplishments of the econometricians during the past few decades would require a whole book as their work affected virtually all aspects of economics and in the process transformed economics itself. Economics, to begin with, was brought under a new discipline, one more rigorous than the looser standards of scientific procedure applicable to verbal methods of expression. Under this new discipline, assumptions had to be carefully stated, concepts defined in concise and consistent terms, and so forth.

As mathematics came to discipline economics as it had before disciplined the natural sciences, the dividing line between social and natural science methods became ever more fluid, especially when the pioneers of mathematical approaches were found knocking at the doors of politics and sociology as well. The conquest of the social sciences by mathematics thus opened the way to the restoration of the unity of all science, which had prevailed until the nineteenth century. In the words of George Sabine,

> Reason, essentially the same everywhere, was believed to validate the majestic system of Natural Law, which was accepted as the clue to order everywhere in astronomy and physics as well as in religion, ethics, politics, jurisprudence, and economics.[1]

In the nineteenth century this unity was dissolved when the historicists claimed that social studies required an approach of their own, a historical

---

[1] "Logic and Social Studies," *Philosophical Review*, March, 1939, p. 155.

method rather than the systematic generalization that had hitherto been characteristic of all science. Historical economics set out to explore the diversity of concrete circumstances; mathematics brought out what they had in common and what was true of all of them. Whitehead, when explaining the meaning of abstraction in mathematics, put it in these words: "The nature of the things is perfectly indifferent, of all things it is true that two and two make four." The rise of mathematical economics meant defeat for historical economics and removed the threat that historicism had posed to the unity of science.

However, as the discipline of mathematics made economics more rigorous, opportunities for economists to carry on the type of wide-ranging social speculations, which had been considered part of their work in previous years, diminished. The "end of ideology," which was predicated of all the social sciences, meant a transformation of the work of the economist, which more and more came to resemble that of the engineer. If mathematics, as has been said, is a language, then those who speak this language and think in its terms employ a vehicle suitable for thinking and expressing the kind of thoughts for which their language makes provision.

The penetration of mathematics into economics conforms to an important intellectual tendency of the age. As mathematics has pervaded economics, it has pervaded other sciences as well—psychology and biology, for example. Critics of this general tendency have labelled it "reductionism" and charged to it the view

> that the only scientific method worth that name is quantitative measurement; and, consequently, that complex phenomena must be reduced to simple elements accessible to such treatment, without undue worry whether the specific characteristics of a complex phenomenon, for instance man, may be lost in the process.[2]

Mathematical economics emerged in two variants, of which one, the pure type, was concerned with quantitative relations in the abstract, yielding a model or theoretical structure which, like all such structures, did not perfectly reflect reality with its wealth of concrete detail. What distinguished pure mathematical economics from conventional economic theory was its quantitative character and the mathematical mode of expression. The other variant, known as econometrics, aimed at developing models or theories, again in terms of quantitative concepts, but designed to be operational or measurable and thus subject to statistical testing. Numerical measurement thus became the hallmark of econometrics. Cournot's theoretical demand analysis and originally also Walras's general equilibrium system were examples of pure mathematical economics. Petty's calculation of the national income had the components of an exercise in econometrics since his estimate was not the result of crude empiricism but presupposed a measurable con-

---

[2] Arthur Koestler and J. R. Smythies, eds., *Beyond Reductionism*, New York, The Macmillan Company, 1969, p. 427.

cept, however implicit and rudimentary. Econometrics has been hailed as a union of rationalism and empiricism: Reason, supported by experience and intuition, would develop a hypothesis, which experience would test.

The word *econometrics* is of recent origin, having been coined in the late 1920s by Ragnar Frisch, the Norwegian economist and statistician, as an analogue to biometrics and similar neologisms designed to bring out the connection of a science with measurement. When Frisch, together with Irving Fisher and other scholars, founded the Econometric Society in 1930, the word gained a wider currency. The society, an international organization of which Fisher was first president, declared as its aim "the advancement of economic theory in its relation to statistics and mathematics" and the "unification of the theoretical-quantitative and the empirical-quantitative approach." An affiliated research organization was founded in 1932. This was the Cowles Commission, later changed to Cowles Foundation, for Research in Economics, named in honor of Alfred Cowles, who provided it with funds. The coordination of theoretical with empirical work distinguishes the econometric approach from that of the National Bureau of Economic Research, which stresses fact-finding rather than construction of theoretical models.

In practice, the division between pure mathematical economics and econometrics has often been obliterated. Work of both types has frequently been pursued by the same scholar, and work labeled as econometric did not invariably yield numerical results. Thus econometrics has at times been employed as a word broadly synonymous with mathematical economics.

That econometrics came into its own during the twentieth century was no accident but resulted from the convergence of favorable circumstances. Scientific advances often occur when there are opportunities for a fusion of hitherto disparate elements that are embedded in different disciplines. When the econometricians set out to fuse the theoretical-quantitative and empirical-quantitative approaches, they had on hand, as regards the former approach, the pure mathematical economics of Cournot and Walras, contributions of the French genius, which were supplemented by a number of Marshallian concepts amenable to measurement. On the empirical-quantitative side, there were on hand the series of great advances in statistical method, which began during the closing decades of the nineteenth century. Apart from notable Russian contributions to probability theory, these were largely the work of Englishmen—Galton, Edgeworth, Pearson, Weldon, Yule, and, especially, R. A. Fisher—and most of them were made in connection with research in the natural sciences.

AMERICAN PIONEERS OF ECONOMETRICS

Generally speaking, econometrics originated from the fusion of French mathematical economics with English statistics. As was true of modern statistical methods, econometrics eventually became an approach practiced on a worldwide scale. However, from its beginning econometrics appealed strongly to an American mind that was predisposed to quantification, pragmatic, and weary of historical diversity. Thus, Americans stood out among the pioneers of econometrics during its earlier phase, which roughly coincided with the first third of the twentieth century. During its next phase, the shadow cast by the political upheavals and persecutions preceding World War II brought to the United States a number of European scholars who excelled in econometric work. With American econometrics enriched by their contributions and with econometrics so strongly appealing to the American mind, it became the dominant theme in American economics at mid-century. By then the circumstances attending the war and its aftermath had ushered in a period during which the American scientific establishment and its prestige attained the highest rank throughout the world. As American influence spread abroad, so did the econometric approach.

MOORE AND SCHULTZ

Besides Irving Fisher, the American pioneers in econometrics included Henry L. Moore (1869–1958), Henry Schultz (1893–1938), and Paul H. Douglas (b. 1892). In a letter to Walras, dated April 10, 1908, Moore described his program as follows:

> I wish I might have your opinion, sometime, as to the wisdom of attempting, by modern statistical methods, to bring a number of the conclusions of pure economics to a statistical test. It has been my feeling for sometime that one of the chief reasons why the pure science of economics does not attract students is the absence of inductive demonstrations of its fundamental tenets. I have, therefore, assumed that the present generation of scholars could render most effective service by attacking inductively the problems which you and others have treated so brilliantly in a deductive manner.

Moore, who taught as Columbia University from 1902 to 1929, attempted to test statistically Clark's marginal productivity theory of distribution, developed a business cycle theory in terms of weather cycles affecting the yield of farm products and thereby agricultural prices, tried to forecast the yield and price of cotton, and in connection with these investigations undertook the statistical derivation of demand curves, work that proved of lasting importance. Moore was not the first to attempt to derive demand curves statistically, but the earlier work of European scholars was interrupted by World War I and did not converge, as did Moore's work in the United States, with similarly oriented studies by agricultural economists and policy makers. Moore's statistical demand analysis was continued on a larger scale and with the help of an apparatus of statistical clerks and other assistants by his student Henry Schultz. This type of research procedure set a precedent for later econometric research, which often went beyond the capacity of a single researcher and required cooperative efforts as well as

DOUGLAS

Clark's marginal productivity theory, the statistical verification of which had formed the subject of Moore's first book, served as the point of departure also for the econometric work of Paul Douglas, who was trained at Columbia University, where Clark and Moore taught. During his later career at the University of Chicago Douglas became an influential teacher, who organized a multitude of cross-section and time-series studies, undertaken by him and his pupils and designed to test statistically the marginal productivity theory of distribution. He found a collaborator, the mathematician Charles E. Cobb, and their work yielded the Cobb-Douglas production function, which indicated, broadly speaking, that a one percent increase in labor input would raise the product by two-thirds of one percent, whereas a one percent increase in capital input would raise it by one-third of one percent. This result, which conformed with the observed division of the national income among labor and capital, was, however, not without its paradoxical side since it seemed compatible only with constant returns to scale and a competitive structure of the economy.

On the later phase of econometrics Leontief's input-output studies left their mark, as did the application of linear programming and game theory to economic problems. Leontief's work has been mentioned in preceding chapters devoted to the Physiocrats' *tableau économique*, Soviet economics, and Walras's system of equations. In connection with Soviet economics, mention was also made of mathematical programming.

VON NEUMANN AND GAME THEORY

In its later phase, substantial advances in econometrics as well as in pure mathematical economics stemmed from the work of John von Neumann (1903–57), a great figure in twentieth-century mathematics. The history of mathematics and of the natural sciences abounds with examples that illustrate the fruitful results of the interplay between these disciplines, with advances in mathematics frequently being generated by and responsive to the requirements of the sciences. Von Neumann was the first outstanding figure in the history of mathematics to take a pronounced interest in economic theory. He did so in the expectation that a mathematician's attention to the social sciences would have favorable repercussions on the development of mathematics and would generate new thought as did the earlier mathematicians' attention to the natural sciences.

Von Neumann, a native of Hungary, belonged to that galaxy of illustrious men whose work illumined the eclipse of the ancient Hapsburg empire. Like Freud's reflections on the human condition, like Kelsen's pure theory of law, like the pure economics of the Austrians, the contributions of these men excelled, if not in pure theory, then in thought relevant to the circumstances of all humanity and transcending the national and historical differences that were tearing asunder the unity of the Hapsburg empire. Considered in perspective, the disintegration of that ill-fated empire foreboded the fate of all humanity, whose unity might be refreshed by the unity of a science that exalted what mankind had in common rather than its diversity.

When von Neumann came to the United States in 1931, he had already published, three years earlier at the age of twenty-five, one of the two short articles on which his influence on economic thought was founded. Six years later, in 1937, he published the other. Von Neumann's contributions to economics were but peripheral to a wide range of creative work in mathematics and physics, work for which he was accorded signal honors.

Von Neumann's 1928 article heralded the arrival of a new branch of mathematics known as game theory. Mathematicians had long examined the structure of games of chance, of roulette and dice for example, and this work had in the end yielded the mathematical theory of probability. Von Neumann's principal concern was not with games of chance but with games of strategy, the outcome of which depended not only on the action of one player but also on the action and reaction of the other participants. In such situations, rational behavior could not be defined in terms of the straightforward pursuit of a maximum since the maximum varied with the actions and reactions of the partners. For example, A may have a choice of several strategies, each yielding a variety of different payoffs, with each of the variants reflecting the strategy chosen by B. B may be in a similar position. Von Neumann's solution centered around the concepts of minimax, from the Latin *minimum maximorum,* the smallest among the largest, and of maximin, from *maximum minimorum,* the largest among the smallest. To elucidate this matter, potential payoffs may be rectangularly arranged in a matrix. If there are two players, A and B, and if each can choose between three strategies, the outcome or payoff of each strategy of A is shown in horizontal rows of numbers, whereas the three vertical columns indicate the strategies open to B. Each entry denotes a payoff, that is, a gain to A and a loss to B.

	STRATEGIES OF B		
STRATEGIES OF A	I	II	III
I	6	12	3
II	7	10	8
III	5	2	6

A may feel inclined to select strategy I, which has a potential payoff of 12, larger than any other. But in this case B might choose strategy III, which would give A a payoff of 3 rather than of 12. A will do best to select strategy II, where in the worst case his payoff will be 7, the largest among the smallest payoffs resulting from the alternative strategies, or the maximin. B will choose strategy I, because any other course of action may be responsible for a larger loss. By pursuing strategy I, B protects himself against incurring a loss larger than 7, the minimax or smallest among the largest possible losses, which are 7, 8, and 12 respectively. The entry 7 is known as a "saddle point"; it is both the maximin and the minimax, the largest number in its row and the smallest in its column. There is thus a determinate outcome of such a game of pure strategy.

Von Neumann's major mathematical contribution rested on the further demonstration that a saddle point, and with it a determinate result, could always be shown to exist in a zero-sum, two person game, transforming the game of pure strategy into one of mixed strategy, that is, by admixing an element of chance. In a game of mixed strategy, the players would pursue a probability strategy, which on the average would yield them optimal results, with minimax and maximin coalescing. For example, if they were to match pennies, they would randomize the results by tossing the coin before showing it rather than by showing heads or tails in a definite pattern that might reveal itself to the partner.

The mathematical structure of games, which von Neumann discovered, has its parallels in conflict situations such as they arise in economics, politics, and war when the parties must decide on courses of action the outcome of which depends on the courses of action pursued by others. Moreover, when the game involves more than two partners, opportunities open themselves up for the formation of coalitions, and the structure of these may again be studied with the help of game theory. In order to demonstrate the relevance of game theory in this wider context, von Neumann joined forces with Oskar Morgenstern, a gifted economist teaching at Princeton University, and they published in 1944 their pathbreaking *Theory of Games and Economic Behavior*. There they called attention to the interpretation of certain market situations, especially oligopoly, in terms of game theory, and since then these and other applications of game theory, including political and strategic ones, have been explored by a large number of investigators. These are very recent developments, and only the future can tell whether game theory will grow into an instrument as powerful and indispensable in the social sciences as the mathematical theory of probability has proved to be in the natural sciences. Opportunities are on hand for another mathematical genius to develop the theory of games along certain lines, for example, by modifying its pessimistic bias about the possibility of preserving the secrecy of one's strategy or by mapping out a strategic approach that is aggressive rather than defensive. The newly emerging decision theory contains developments that point to these directions.

In the field of economics proper, the theory of games shed new light not only on oligopolistic situations and bargaining processes. In addition, it left its mark on the theory of utility, provided stimulating suggestions for the construction of a decision theory, and has a common root with the new theory of mathematical programming. In utility theory, neoclassical theory aimed at the cardinal measurement of utility, whereas the indifference-curve approach yielded an ordinal ranking in terms of preference. To these approaches von Neumann and Morgenstern added a new type of so-called cardinal utility theory, which they developed in connection with their treatment of games of mixed strategy. There the choice among strategies involving risks required the construction of a utility index to yield a person's preference scale, with numerical ranking, for certain strategies involving risks. Unlike neoclassical theory, this utility index was not designed to measure the intensity of feelings, and its cardinal character existed only within the context of game theory and not within that of neoclassical theory.

DECISION THEORY

The nature and scope of decision theory are still the subject of current discussions, which have not as yet yielded settled conclusions. Decision theory has been developed by psychologists and by students of all the social sciences, as well as by mathematicians and statisticians. Using the utility index constructed by von Neumann and Morgenstern, psychologists made a number of experiments designed to test whether man behaves in a rational fashion, that is, whether he uses effective means to satisfy his wants. Their approach has at times converged with that advocated by economists, who attempted to develop a theory elucidating the making of economic decisions under conditions of uncertainty. In this work, many of the concepts developed in game theory have proved useful. Unlike in game theory, however, attention has been concentrated on situations in which there is complete uncertainty as regards the countermoves that threaten the outcome of a course of action—"games against nature." The decision rules that have been considered as relevant for this type of situation include again the maximin as well as the far more aggressive maximax—choosing the strategy with the largest payoff—and intermediate criteria holding middle ground between these extremes. Various application of probability theory have also found employment in the theory of decision making, including the Bayes criterion, named after an eighteenth-century mathematician, which recommends, among courses of action potentially frustrated by equally uncertain contingencies, the choice of the one with the largest payoff. Decision theory also led to a reexamination of the foundations of statistics, which was interpreted as a game against nature. The great figure here was Abraham Wald (1902–50), whose work converged with that of von Neumann in other respects-as well.

MATHEMATICAL PROGRAMMING

Linear programming stands side by side with input-output analysis and game theory in the forefront of the new econometric approaches. As has been seen, linear programming resulted from a multiple discovery made first by

L. V. Kantorovich, a Soviet mathematician, in 1939, and independently
a few years later by George B. Dantzig (b. 1914), an American mathematical
statistician, and by Tjalling C. Koopmans (b. 1910), a Dutch economist
who found a new home in the United States. There was also a connection
between linear programming and von Neumann's work in game theory
since the matrix game is solved with the help of the same mathematical
procedures as are certain linear programs.

Like differential calculus or the theory of games, mathematical programming forms part of mathematics rather than of economics. It was,
however, devised as a technique specifically designed to assist in the solution of economic problems. Linear programming as developed in the United
States was to solve certain scheduling problems which arose in connection
with the far-flung procurement program of the Air Force. Since its inception
it has proved useful for the numerical solution of a number of practical economic problems facing business management. It has, for example, facilitated
the routing of products made in the various plants of a corporation to different markets at the least cost of transportation and the production of specific types of gasoline from various blends, again at minimum cost. When
employed in production processes, linear programming is sometimes designated as "activity analysis."

Programming means planning or decision making, not, as might be
presumed, the preparation of a program for electronic computers, although
these have found useful employment in linear programming. The programming is known as *linear* because it involves the manipulation of linear functions, that is, of functions in which only the first power of the variables
appears and which are represented by straight lines. In conventional microeconomic theory, the typical relations are depicted as nonlinear and are
represented in curvilinear form. Linear programming has come to the fore
because, typically, microeconomic theory has a formal character and does
not facilitate numerical calculations of the variables involved. To apply
linear programming techniques to relationships between microeconomic
variables, these may be visualized as being transformed into linear ones by
having the conventional curves of microeconomic theory broken up into
small linear segments.

Like differential calculus, which underlies microeconomic theory, linear
programming yields maxima and minima of profits and costs, for example.
However, in linear programming the maximization or minimization is subject
to certain restraints known as "side-conditions" or "inequalities"—limited
storage space, limited number of machines, minimum labor requirements to
man the machines, and the like. These side-conditions reflect more fully
the actual environment in which business firms operate than does conventional microeconomic theory, which is more abstract and general. The
inclusion of the side-conditions in the apparatus of linear programming adds
to the realism of the numerical calculations yielded by it.

Besides linear programming other variants of mathematical programming, of different degrees of complexity, have been developed to cope

with special situations. Nonlinear programming has been devised to handle situations involving diminishing returns and integer programming for cases with indivisibilities requiring calculations in terms of whole numbers.

The great advances of econometrics along the lines of input-output analysis, game theory, and mathematical programming are all linked by a common core of mathematical operations, which connects them also with other advances in mathematical economics. These do not at first glance invite practical applications and are related to the mathematical aspects of equilibrium theory. The signal contributions to this matter were made in a series of articles by Wald in 1935–36 and in von Neumann's article of 1937.

WALD AND EQUILIBRIUM THEORY

Wald, a distinguished mathematician in his own right, left his native Rumania in the late 1920s and went to Vienna, where he worked with the mathematician Karl Menger, the son of the economist. He came to the United States in 1938 and became known for his great work in statistical decision theory and sequential analysis of sampling and quality control. Most of Wald's contributions to pure mathematics and mathematical economics antedated this period and were made earlier during Wald's residence in Vienna, where mathematical economics was attracting the attention of Karl Menger and other scholars. It was then that Wald wrote a number of fundamental articles of great complexity, in which he explored the existence and uniqueness of economic equilibria and pointed out that more was involved than the mere counting of equations.

As so often happens in intellectual history, there were others who were attracted by problems similar to those that occupied Wald. His work converged with the emerging interest in England and the United States in related aspects of economic equilibria, their stability and the relationship between statics and dynamics, work that yielded Hicks's *Value and Capital* (1939), a number of articles by Samuelson later incorporated in his *Foundations of Economic Analysis* (1947), and other notable contributions. Samuelson's work contained the famous "correspondence principle," which underlined the formal dependence between comparative statics and dynamic analysis.

Wald's attention to the mathematics of economic equilibria was paralleled also by similar efforts of von Neumann, culminating in his 1937 article. There von Neumann constructed, under highly restrictive assumptions, an equilibrium model of a steadily growing economy characterized by unlimited supplies of natural resources and absence of diminishing returns. Such an economy, as von Neumann demonstrated, would expand at a rate equal to the rate of interest. Von Neumann's model had certain features in common with Adam Smith's "early and rude state of society which precedes both the accumulation of stock and the appropriation of land"; but, paradoxical as it may seem, aspects of the model had their counterpart in the economies of underdeveloped countries operating under conditions of ostensibly unlimited supplies of labor and disguised unemployment. Von Neumann's article exerted a profound influence on later mathematical theories of economic growth, which employed such concepts as "golden growth equilibrium," sometimes defined as a state in which the output of all goods and the labor force expand in equal proportions. These theories, in turn, led to the "turnpike theorems" developed by Samuelson and his associates, which elucidated the relationship between different growth paths and the one that maximizes steady growth—the turnpike.

ECONOMETRICS IN EUROPE

The direction of econometric studies points to the present frontiers of economic science and is illustrative of the profound transformation that economics has undergone in recent decades. A galaxy of scholars carry on econometric work in many lands. In the Netherlands, Jan Tinbergen (b. 1903) pioneered in econometric business cycle research. His investigations, which employed the system of equations of general equilibrium economics and dynamic relationships, established an influential precedent for this type of work. Norwegians who have excelled in econometric work include Ragnar Frisch, who with Tinbergen in 1969 shared the first Nobel Prize in Economic Science, and Trygve Haavelmo, the leading exponent of the probabilistic approach to econometrics, in which the data of the past become parameters of the probability distributions of the future data. The flowering of mathematical economics in Norway and in the other Scandinavian countries, exemplified by the work of Zeuthen in Denmark and the Stockholm school in Sweden, reflects in part the lasting influence of Wicksell.

The mathematical approach also spread in Germany, where before World War II it was a specialty cultivated by only a few scholars, notably Erich Schneider (b. 1900) and Heinrich von Stackelberg (1905–46), who made well-known contributions to the theory of monopolistic markets. The changes in political and intellectual orientation that attended the end of World War II broke the hold of historical economics in Germany. Since that time, mathematical economics has been in the ascendancy. The same is true of Japan and, as noted earlier, of the Soviet and Soviet-type economies.

FRANCE

Of particular interest was the postwar upsurge of econometrics in France, the homeland of the masters of pure mathematical economics, who were so haltingly accorded recognition there. French econometricians who did yeoman work during the interwar years included François Divisia (1889–1964), René Roy (b. 1894), and Robert Gibrat (b. 1904). Divisia's work, much of which was developed within the framework of the quantity theory of money, had features in common with that of Irving Fisher in the United States. Like Fisher, Divisia also contributed to index-number theory. Of Roy's many contributions, his statistical demand analysis stood out. Gibrat's work included the law of the proportionate effect, known as Gibrat's law, which holds that the expected rate of growth of a firm is independent of its size and which has proved an eminently fruitful hypothesis, tested by a number of American and English investigators.

After World War II, a new era started with the work of Pierre Massé (b. 1898) and Maurice Allais (b. 1911), under whose influence econometric studies were carried on by a growing number of young scholars, disciples, in particular, of Allais. Allais himself acknowledged Irving Fisher as his master, and like Fisher gave special attention to the theory of interest. An engineering graduate with wide interests and an imaginative bent of mind, he had turned to economic studies during the war and, without the aid of libraries and the give-and-take of academic discussion but with a copy of Fisher's *Theory of Interest* on hand, had reconstructed on his own the main body of modern economic theory. His two-volume work *Économie et intérêt,* published in 1947, was a study of the conditions required by an intertemporal optimum and moved along paths similar to those pursued by the growth theorists. But whereas the latter expressed their ideas in the form of hypothetical models grounded in certain assumptions, Allais's was a program for action, in which the assumptions were converted into policy proposals, including the maintenance of a zero rate of interest.

Like Allais, many French econometricians were trained as civil engineers and graduated from the prestigious École Polytechnique. They filled the ranks of administrators in charge of national planning, the operation and investment programs of the nationalized industries, and the management of public utilities, and for the problems that they encountered they sought econometric solutions, an approach for which their training in engineering equipped them well. Theoretical work has been produced in response to practical needs, and the close relation between the two may be illustrated by the fact that Massé, who after experience in the management of the nationalized electrical industry became the chief officer of the French planning organization, is also the author of an authoritative study of *Optimal Investment Decisions* (1959, Eng. trans. 1962). In connection with the price and investment policies of public enterprises, French econometricians made significant contributions to the theory of marginal cost, for example, by distinguishing between the marginal cost of expansion and that of contraction, which may not be symmetrical, and by developing a principled policy of peak-load pricing for electricity, with a new, so-called "green tariff," under which peak demand was discouraged and investment in generating plants substantially reduced. On a higher level of abstraction, and continuing the work of his teacher Allais, Edmond Malinvaud explored the intertemporal connections between competitive equilibrium and the Pareto optimum, branching out into both welfare economics and capital theory.

Nothing confirms more impressively the triumph of the mathematical approach than its victory, after considerable delay, in France. The mathematical approach, however, may not signal the ultimate perfection of a final stage of economic science. No one knows how lasting the victory of econometrics will turn out to be and when there will emerge a rival approach at the endless frontiers of science. In the English-speaking countries the critical discussion of the value of the mathematical approach to economics and of its limitations is largely a matter of the past, but in France this discussion still goes on. For this reason, and also because it was the French genius from which mathematical economics stemmed, the question may be in order whether a new phase of economic science, one yet to come, will again have its roots in France. No one can foretell what this new phase will look like, whether new ideas will further develop the mathematical approach or lead away from it. The great ideas embodied in input-output analysis, game theory, and linear programming came to the fore some thirty years ago and since then have not been followed up by new advances in mathematical economics comparable to them in seminal importance.

If productive ideas emerge outside mathematical economics proper, it is possible that they may influence mathematical economics and set off a fusion of elements hitherto considered disparate. The potential for such a fusion is embodied in the work of François Perroux (b. 1903), professor at the Collège de France and a leading figure, with considerable following, in French economics. Like the American institutionalists, Perroux has been critical of neoclassical economics, and he has produced work with an institutionalist flavor. Like Schumpeter, who has influenced him and to whose thought he devoted a book-length appraisal, he has not shied from developing an economics in which social speculation about the great issues of the time finds a place. Again like Schumpeter, he has taken a positive attitude to mathematical analysis and, far less skeptical about these than Schumpeter, devoted a book to a review of quantitative techniques of planning. Moreover, in the foreword to the great synthesis of his work, *L'Économie du xxe siècle* (1961, sec. ed. 1964), he has announced his intention to recast his thought, hitherto expressed verbally, in the form of algebraic models.

Perroux's principal complaint about neoclassical economics was grounded in the observation that it precluded attention to certain vital aspects of the economy by its very structure, especially by the equilibrium concept, which formed its core. Equilibrium economics presumed action on the part of economic agents that were coordinated by a substantial measure of equality. Reciprocal give-and-take would produce adjustments and corrections of disturbances. Perroux rejected this approach as running counter to the facts and concealing the role of economic power in the market. Instead he supported an economics not of coordination among equals and their functional interdependence but of subordination, with the dominating economic agent on the one side and the dominated one on the other. Just as Schumpeter had disclosed the dynamics of innovation, so Perroux set out to reveal the dynamics of inequality. He did not ignore the fact that there were established theories of monopolistic market situations that paralleled his own ideas, but he insisted that these theories covered only a special aspect of a matter that called for treatment by means of a general theory. Perroux's theory of the "domination effect" stressed the asymmetrical and irreversible character of the relations between dominant and dominated economic agents. This lack of symmetry and reversibility, Perroux argued, made power relations operating in the market essentially different from the interdependencies encountered in equilibrium economics. Instead of re-establishing equilibrium and automatically correcting disturbances, the domination effect was apt. to produce protracted and cumulative changes.

Perroux developed his theory of the domination effect at various levels. At the level of the firm, the dominant firm integrated its operations, which yielded it a surplus swollen from ever-rising sales to and ever-diminishing purchases from the outside, and by an attendant market position securing it favorable prices. The surplus further enhances its power by equipping it with means suitable for internal financing, for the acquisition and control of other enterprises, and for financing or otherwise manipulating the demand for its products. Another illustration of the domination effect is the preponderence, within the framework of modern macroeconomics, of the investor over the saver. Those who control investment decisions are in a dominating position relative to those concerned with saving. At other levels, the domination effect makes itself felt in the "macro-decisions" of the government, the principal instrument of coercion, and of other collective entities. At the international level Perroux took up the subject of the dominant economy and shed on it new light. His own theory differed from the theories of imperialism by making irrelevant—as he did throughout his analysis of the domination effect—any intention on the part of the dominating power.

The thoughts sketched in the preceding paragraphs offer only a sample of the many contributions that Perroux made to a new type of economic theory, less pure and closer to reality than the conventional one. As an alternative to equilibrium economics, his work may be a milestone on the road to a new phase of economics. If it should become fused with mathematical economics, there might arise an econometric institutionalism or institutional econometrics, raising new questions and providing new insight into the age-old problems of economics.

Chapter 29

AN EXPANDED PROFESSION

IN SEARCH OF NEW FRONTIERS

THE ECONOMICS PROFESSION

During the last five years of the 1960s the increase in the number of professional economists, as measured by membership in the American Economic Association, was larger than the total number of American economists in 1940. This rapid expansion, which began after World War II and had its parallels in Western Europe, came to a halt in the 1970s. While it lasted, it mirrored changes in the academic world and in the world at large. Student enrollment rose, and so did the number of institutions of higher learning, while there were increased opportunities for the employment of economists in government and industry.

The market forces, which strengthened the demand for the services of economists and which in turn elicited the increase in their supply, received powerful support from changes in public policy and social mores that opened up more widely the doors to the academic world and the economics profession to groups whose members had found entry difficult or impossible in the past. This movement, the "inclusion of the excluded," as it is called in Joseph Alsop's memorable phrase, began in the 1930s and affected at first religious and ethnic groups and eventually that half of the population made up of women. It has changed profoundly the composition of the economics profession and enriched it in many ways by bringing into it talented people of varied backgrounds.

The inclusion of the excluded set an example for the rest of the world. It had its counterpart in the relaxation of standards of restriction and exclusion elsewhere, with millions of foreign workers admitted to jobs in northern and western Europe and with an enhanced spirit of cosmopolitanism that brought an Indian scholar to the prestigious Drummond chair of economics at the University of Oxford and a German sociologist to the directorship of the London School of Economics.

Windows were also opened up to the East when Japan joined the Western world in the pursuit of advanced economic studies and shared in the legacy of a common tradition of economic thought. What was true of the Japanese became true also of other nations in the Orient and elsewhere. At the same time, geographical mobility increased over wide parts of the world, bringing with it opportunities for an interchange of thought with people of different nationalities and backgrounds who occupied jobs in places far away from their original homes.

An important factor of integration that united economists, both domestically and on the international scene, was the common training in mathematics that became part of their standard education during the postwar decades. Mathematics became the *lingua franca* of the economics profession, linking those of different mother tongues just as Latin had linked the medieval scholars and French the diplomats in more recent times. Similar effects must also be ascribed to the computer and statistical techniques as training in their use came to be common among economists everywhere.

It is no accident that the expansion of the economics profession was accompanied by the ascendancy of mathematical economics and econometrics. To shed light on this connection, it may be recalled that long before the onset of these scientific movements America had been more hospitable to quantification and measurement than other countries, and this in turn can be related to the character of the United States as a "melting pot" and as a society harboring large numbers of people. Similarly the shift from literation to numeration in economics accommodates a multiethnic profession replete with members that have diverse backgrounds and do not share a common historical experience other than that of mankind at large.

While the common concern with mathematical techniques facilitated communication among economists, the very size of the profession became an obstacle to communication that was overcome by a profusion of new organizations and scholarly periodicals. As long as the number of professional economists had been fairly small, a single national organization could serve them adequately and a mere handful of periodicals provided sufficient outlets for publication. With the growth of the profession, organizational ties became diffused among numerous newly founded organizations, some cultivating a special approach, others catering to regional needs, and still others specializing along the lines of a subdiscipline. Many of these organizations sponsored new professional journals, which together with new periodicals with no organizational ties became so plentiful that the perception of their contents went beyond the capacity of the human mind and required the memory of a computer.

What have been the outstanding accomplishments of the enlarged economic profession? A discussion of the Nobel awards in economics will provide an answer to this question.

THE NOBEL AWARDS

Alfred Nobel's will of 1895 singled out five fields for prizes that would recognize and reward persons who have "rendered mankind the greatest benefit." Economics was not included in these five fields. But the names of economists have occasionally turned up in connection with Nobel prizes for other achievements, most notably that of Walras, who was an active candidate for the peace prize during the last five years of his life.

It was only in 1968 that the Nobel Memorial Prize in Economics, as it is officially designated, was instituted by the Central Bank of Sweden to celebrate the bank's 300th anniversary. Since 1969 prizes have been awarded every year, with at times two recipients sharing one. The table that follows provides information about the awards that have been granted so far.

No one can doubt that the awards represent a professional mainstream economics whose practitioners have varied backgrounds but who are united by a mathematical or quantitative bent. Only a very few Nobelists owe their reputation to work that does not employ numbers or mathematical symbols. More than half of all the Nobelists reside in the United States, with the rest distributed among the United Kingdom, Sweden, Norway, the Netherlands, and the Soviet Union.

The Nobel prizes have not been uncontroversial, and at one time Gunnar Myrdal, himself a Nobelist, pleaded for their abolition, claiming that economics is not a "hard" science such as physics or chemistry but a "soft" one in which research relates to human behavior and which is charged with political and social valuations. However, neither literature nor peace, for achievements in which Nobel prizes have long been awarded, are hard sciences. On the whole it is difficult to find fault with the inclusion of any one of the great scholars chosen for the Nobel prize, although it goes without saying that with every year that passes more and more of the undisputable choices have been made and the selection process becomes more discretionary. Judicious observers have wondered why Joan Robinson and François Perroux have been passed over, the one renowned for her theory of imperfect competition and attack against the marginal productivity theory, the other the only living economist who developed a theoretical system rivaling conventional equilibrium economics.

Some Nobelists have to their credit a breakthrough or revolution in economics. For example, except for the pioneers of game theory, most of the great figures who led the march into mathematical economics and econometrics are included among the Nobelists. By age, all Nobelists are beyond life's midpassage. The prizes they have received typically reward past achievements rather than the promise of great accomplishments in the future. The breakthrough that each may have succeeded in bringing about is a thing of the past. There is no certainty whether among the Nobelists there is any one whose work contains the germ for an incipient breakthrough or future revolution.

Whether a breakthrough is imminent is an important question because, as

The Nobel Awards in Economics

YEAR OF AWARD	NAME OF NOBELIST	VITAL STATISTICS	NATIONALITY	PRINCIPAL ACHIEVEMENTS
1969	Ragnar Frisch	1895-1973	Norway	Pioneering econometric studies; planning
	Jan Tinbergen	b. 1903	Netherlands	Pioneering econometric studies; bus. cycles
1970	Paul A. Samuelson	b. 1915	US	Mathematical reformulation of econ. theory
1971	Simon Kuznets	b. 1901	US	Income concepts; measurement of growth
1972	Kenneth J. Arrow	b. 1921	US	Paradox of voting; information theory
	John R. Hicks	b. 1904	UK	Modern microeconomic theory
1973	Wassily Leontief	b. 1906	US	Input-output analysis
1974	Gunnar Myrdal	b. 1899	Sweden	"American Dilemma," "Asian Drama"
	Friedrich A. v. Hayek	b. 1899	UK	Pol. philosophy, monet. & bus. cycle theory
1975	Leonid V. Kantorovich	b. 1912	USSR	Linear programming
	Tjalling C. Koopmans	b. 1910	US	Linear programming
1976	Milton Friedman	b. 1912	US	Founder of monetarism; libertarian approach
1977	Bertil Ohlin	1899-1979	Sweden	New approach to international trade theory
	James E. Meade	b. 1907	UK	International economic policy
1978	Herbert A. Simon	b. 1916	US	Organization & decision theory; rationality
1979	W. Arthur Lewis	b. 1915	UK	Development studies
	Theodore W. Schultz	b. 1902	US	Farm economics: human capital
1980	Lawrence Klein	b. 1920	US	Econometric models & forecasting
1981	James Tobin	b. 1918	US	Macroeconomic & portfolio theory
1982	George J. Stigler	b. 1911	US	Microeconomic theory; critique of regulation

**AN EXPANDED
PROFESSION IN SEARCH
OF NEW FRONTIERS**

will be seen, there is much dissatisfaction with conventional economic thought. In this context the question may be raised whether there is any standard definition of a breakthrough or revolution in economics, or, in the absence of such a definition, how to go about defining the concept. To resolve this question, a more extended discussion is required.

A DIGRESSION ON REVOLUTIONS IN ECONOMIC THOUGHT

Major changes in the substance or method of economic thought are often referred to as breakthroughs or revolutions. They occur only rarely and are usually set off by the work of a master economist rather than being the result of cumulative accretions that work their way slowly and gradually through the efforts of numerous patient laborers. Of course, even the master economist stands, as the saying goes, on the shoulders of others, and there is typically some degree of continuity of thought, however slight, that links the ideas of the master economist with those of his predecessors.

Modern philosophers of science tend to interpret a revolution of thought in terms of the rise of a new "paradigm," a concept introduced by Thomas Kuhn in 1962. As is often the case with weasel words, the term caught on and in the course of two decades a whole literature has come into being interpreting and applying it not only in the context of natural science, for which it was originally designed, but along a whole range of other intellectual pursuits stretching from economics to political science, sociology, and even theology.

What is a paradigm? Kuhn defines it, apparently unambiguously and in a straightforward fashion, as "universally recognized scientific achievements that for a time provide model problems and solutions to a community of practitioners." In spite of the apparent precision of this definition, interpreters of Kuhn have found a large variety of different shades of meaning of the term, twenty-one or even more, that they have located in Kuhn's work itself.

The discussion of these matters is especially lively in the realm of natural science, which is replete with mementous changes and upheavals. It has produced an alternative concept in the form of "scientific research programmes" or clusters of theories, a concept designed by Imre Lakatos. No ready definition of this term is at hand, but Lakatos has in mind conglomerations of interconnected theories that have a "hard core" which its exponents refuse to have refuted, and a "protective belt" that is subject to testing. Lakatos further distinguishes between progressive and stagnating research programmes. In the case of the former, theoretical growth precedes empirical growth and provides a base for successful predictions of novel facts. In the case of stagnation, the sequence between theoretical and empirical growth is reversed and there are only "*post hoc* explanations of either chance discoveries or of facts anticipated by, and discovered in a rival programme."

Attempts have been made at interpreting the history of economics both in the context of the theories of Kuhn and Lakatos, with such revolutions emerging as the Smithian, stressing economic individualism, laissez faire and the market, the marginal revolution of the 1870s leading to the search for optimum positions, the Keynesian revolution emphasizing macroeconomic aggregates, and the mathematical revolution that changed the language and method of economics.

No one knows when to expect the next revolution in economic thought and what it may bring, but one may speculate whether or not one is beginning to take form. There is no ringing of bells marking the onset of a revolution, and those who live in one need not be aware of it. To be sure, the Smithian and Keynesian revolutions were recognized as such and widely acclaimed from the start. Not so the marginal revolution, whose message eager followers were able to spread only in Austria but which elsewhere was responded to only weakly and haltingly, if at all, for some time. Thus it may well be that at present there are stirrings of thought ready to usher in fundamental changes in economic science without their potential being recognized as such by the profession at large.

Stirrings of thought there are, but they have principally occurred in the form of criticism of conventional economic thought, which in itself can hardly be said to constitute a new paradigm or scientific research programme. Such criticism helps to undermine existing structures, but does not build new ones. If criticism were sufficient to bring about a breakthrough, there was plenty of it in the early 1970s.

CRITICISM OF CONVENTIONAL ECONOMIC THOUGHT

The year 1972 was a high-water mark in two senses. It marked, for the first time, the appointment of an academic economist to the high office of Secretary of the U. S. Treasury, an unparalleled token of the public esteem then enjoyed by the profession. It marked also, within the profession, a flood of criticism, unprecedented in its extent, of conventional economic thought. No less than six prominent scholars published articles in such prestigious journals as the *American Economic Review, Economic Journal,* and *Journal of Economic Literature,* all deploring the inadequacy of conventional economics. The very titles of the articles indicate the concern the authors felt about the unsatisfactory status of economic science. Nicholas Kaldor wrote of the irrelevance of equilibrium economics, Oskar Morgenstern listed thirteen critical points in contemporary economic theory, E. H. Phelps Brown referred to the underdevelopment of economics, G. D. N. Worswick raised the question, Is progress in economic science possible? Joan Robinson spoke of the second crisis in economic theory, and Gunnar Myrdal gave special attention to the weakness of development economics.

Kaldor referred specifically to the dominating role played in real life by increasing returns, whose coexistence with competition economists are at a loss to explain; in general, and alluding to the papers by Phelps Brown and Worswick, he wrote: "On the one hand it is increasingly recognized that abstract mathematical models lead nowhere. On the other hand it is also recognized that 'econometrics' leads nowhere." We gather data and apply advanced statistical techniques, but lack "any basic understanding of how the actual economy works." He interpreted the new fashions that emerge every few years—the revival of the quantity theory of money, finely tuned fiscal policy, the Phillips curve—as symptoms of a "pre-scientific" stage when everything is tried because nothing can be rejected with assurance. Phelps Brown in his presidential address to the Royal Economic Society declared that the most conspicuous developments in economics during recent decades have only made small contributions to the solution of contemporary problems, and ascribed this to the employment of unverified assumptions about economic behavior. Economists must employ numbers as well as study historical detail, but at its present stage the science is not yet ripe for mathematization. There is much need for empirical studies of human behavior. Worswick, in his presidential address to Section F of the British Association for the Advancement of Science, deplored that economists concentrate their attention on what he called "abstract games of little relevance" and "meretricious quantification." Joan Robinson characterized the great depression of the 1930s as the first crisis in economics. The second crisis, in her opinion, is the lack of a theory of distribution. "We have nothing to say on the subject which above all occupies the minds of the people whom economics is supposed to enlighten." Myrdal found fault with the inadequate attention to the equality issue in development economics as well as in the economics of advanced countries, and underlined the connection between inequality, poverty, and low productivity.

Morgenstern, who with John von Neumann had developed the application of game theory in economics, delivered the most detailed bill of particular complaints. It touches on virtually all phases of economic theory and is difficult to summarize. Here are his thirteen critical points:

1. Economic agents are rarely in control of the variables that they are supposed to manipulate in the pursuit of an optimum.

2. Revealed preference does not reveal the preference of people of means.

3. The Pareto optimum is not optimal for a person who resents being left behind by some one else whose income rises.

4. Walras's *tâtonnements* may yield collusion or cooperation rather than competitive equilibrium.

5. People interact rather than react to given parameters as is supposed in Walrasian general equilibrium. The economists' concern with the latter is in the nature of a "fixation" or obsession.

6. The market may not be the only instrument capable of putting resources to their best use.

7. Goods may be substitutes, but their value may depend on their usefulness as complementary goods.

8. Demand may be interdependent rather than additive.

9. The indifference curve is such a poor tool of analysis that it will disappear from economics in another generation (see also the observation of Paul Samuelson, cited below, p. 672).

10. The theory of the firm applies to the production of physical output rather than of services, which now constitute 60 percent of GNP.

11. Analysis in terms of aggregates is a step backward rather than forward.

12. The marginal productivity theory of distribution does not account for power, exploitation, bargaining, etc.

13. Morgenstern closes his criticism with a remarkable table that relates market types to theory relevance and which supports his conclusion that much of the content of economic theory is irrelevant. As the table indicates, economic theory tends to concentrate on the study of market behavior that has only a faint counterpart in the world of reality. For example, much attention is given in theory to free competition in the market for physical output, a constellation virtually absent from the real world, while relatively little attention is paid to markets containing few sellers and perhaps also buyers in physical goods or service industries, situations that are more typical of reality.

The preceding summary does not do justice to the wealth of ideas embodied in Morgenstern's article. His observations provide plentiful food for thought, even if all the points he attempts to score are not equally well taken and even if the reader is aware that Morgenstern is disposed to construct cases that invite the application of game theory rather than more conventional analysis.

As the 1970s went on, there were insistent complaints about the apparent inability of the economics profession to come up with a solution to the problem of inflation-cum-stagnation or stagflation, about the unreliability of econometric forecasts, and about the alleged sterility of many exercises in mathematical economics and econometrics. As Robert Heilbroner puts it: "The prestige accorded to math has given economics rigor, but alas, also mortis." It was recalled also that the reaction of Keynes, the last master economist of the age, to mathematical economics and econometrics had been ambivalent at best. He did not refuse to support what at his time were attempts at pioneering with a new method, but when it came to fundamental theoretical arguments, he questioned the assumptions of the new approach and rejected the transformation of economics into a pseudo-natural science. Although himself an occasional practitioner of mathematical economics, he criticized in the *General Theory* "symbolic pseudo-mathematical methods of formalizing a system of economic analysis . . . which allow the author to lose sight of the complexities and interdependencies of the real world in a maze of pretentious and unhelpful symbols." This view, however, ran counter to the temper of the time, and many followers and interpreters of Keynes's substantive economics refused to abide by his methodological precepts and instead became leaders of the mathematical revolution.

What has been the response, if any, to the critical objections reviewed in the preceding pages? While criticism in itself does not constitute a breakthrough, it has on occasion served as a catalyst that gave direction to and set in motion important changes. An example is the impetus which the institutional economists earlier in the century provided for a redirection of economic thought, making it shed its pervasive concern with utility, perfect competition, and microeconomics, and provoking the rise of indifference-curve analysis, imperfect-competition theory and macroeconomics. A discussion of current alignments in economic thought will shed light on the nature and extent of the response to recent criticism.

**AN EXPANDED
PROFESSION IN SEARCH
OF NEW FRONTIERS**

CURRENT ALIGNMENTS IN ECONOMIC THOUGHT

It may be convenient to divide current alignments in economic thought into mainstream economics and peripheral movements.

MAINSTREAM ECONOMICS

Mainstream economics is not as monolithic as it was during the postwar decades, when a standard brand of Keynesianism constituted a new orthodoxy. It now encompasses several schools of thought that extend all the way from the monetarists to the neo-Keynesians. A detailed account of these movements would require a textbook on contemporary economic thought. Only a brief sketch can be given here.

1. The monetarists, ably led by Milton Friedman, constitute a reaction against the emphasis on investment, fiscal policy, and the consumption function as it prevailed under the influence of the Keynesian revolution, whose followers were not overly impressed with the importance of monetary changes. To the monetarists, on the other hand, "money matters," that is, monetary changes are supposed to have profound effects on general economic conditions.

The monetarists have resuscitated and attach great importance to the quantity theory of money, according to which price changes reflect changes in the quantity of money. To the monetarists the quantity theory is a theory of the demand for money, to be supplemented by information about the supply of money and its velocity. Monetary changes are subject to control by the central bank, which should allow a constant rate of growth of the monetary aggregates. Because of the lagged effects of policy changes and for other reasons the monetarists oppose a discretionary monetary policy.

Although the monetarists gained considerable following in recent decades, many precepts of the theory outlined in the preceding paragraphs continue to be the subject of lively controversy, especially the definition and measurement of monetary aggregates. The monetarists, in turn, reject Keynesian macroeconomics and the policies derived from it. Their laissez faire view and libertarianism spill over into neo-Austrian and supply-side economics.

2. Various brands of Keynesian economics constitute the other branch of mainstream economics. Its followers may be designated as conventional Keynesians, pure Keynesians, and neo-Keynesians. The conventional Keynesians gained a wide following during the postwar years until they were challenged first by the monetarists and later by exponents of rival brands of Keynesianism. They still constitute the leading school of economic thought, but their following is not as widespread as it used to be.

Conventional Keynesians teach the standard brand of macroeconomics (and, of course, microeconomics as well) as it has come to be embodied in the leading introductory texts by Paul Samuelson and others. The pure Keynesians, a small minority, challenge them on various grounds, the principal being that much of what goes on under the name of Keynesian economics is an incrustation that has been imposed by interpreters of Keynes on his doctrine and which keeps under cover vital parts of his message. This is said, for example, of the Hicksian and other diagrammatic representations of a macroeconomic equilibrium that converts Keynes's analysis into comparative statics, endows his disequilibrium economics with a tendency towards equilibrium, and deprives it of the element of uncertainty and the dynamism of a time dimension. Hicks himself, it may be noted, has misgivings about his early formalization of Keynesian economics, and refers to it as a "potted version" ("potted" is British slang and means shallow or superficial). The pure Keynesians argue further that a more faithful reading of Keynes discloses his awareness of the importance of monetary policy and changes in the price level, and of an upward drift in wages that requires the restraint of an incomes policy. They also consider the analysis embodied in the Phillips curve an excrescence, especially the tortuous attempts to modify it to make it conform more closely to reality.

The neo-Keynesians go much further and some of their thoughts spill over into radical economics. They claim on rather narrow grounds to have demolished the marginal productivity theory of distribution and want to refurbish Keynesian economics with a theory of distribution that draws on the thought of Kaldor and Kalecki. They stress the monopolistic elements in the economy rather than competition, and are doubtful about the ability of the market economy to generate steady growth. The leaders of this group include Joan Robinson, and its headquarters is at the University of Cambridge, while their principal opponents are located in Cambridge, Massachusetts, not, alas, at Harvard but at the Massachusetts Institute of Technology.

PERIPHERAL MOVEMENTS: RADICAL ECONOMICS

Fringe movements that are at the periphery today may include the orthodoxy of tomorrow. Only the future can tell whether this is true of the three peripheral movements here considered: radical economics, neo-Austrian economics, and supply-side economics.

In the immediate postwar period there was just one avowed follower of Marx teaching economics in the United States. In the 1960s and '70s radical economics came into greater prominence as the student disorders and traumatic effects of Vietnam and Watergate seemed to forebode a revaluation of existing values. A Union for Radical Political Economics, founded in 1968, was reported eventually to include some 3,000 members. As the 1970s came to a close, academic life became calmer again and the politicization of students gave way to career orientation. Interest in radical economics faded among a new generation of students, but persisted among some teachers, who brought the temper of the time of their own youth into an age quite differently disposed.

Radical economics passed through a number of stages marking attachments to Leninism, Maoism, Castroism and other isms that receded as disillusionment set in. At times its orientation was anarchist rather than Marxist, although the latter component has as a rule been strong. Radical economists stress what they consider weaknesses of capitalism—its class structure, instability of prices and employment, the profit motive, producer-created wants, private ownership of the means of production, inequality, "alienation," etc. Often they are as much opposed to the market as they are to the bureaucracy, and fail to recognize that less reliance on the one instrument requires greater reliance on the other. Depending on the degree of their radicalism, they are as a rule not reform-oriented but aim at a more thorough reorganization of society. Defenders of capitalism may point to the glaring defects of other types of economic organization such as the illiberalism, drabness, and low standard of living in Soviet and Soviet-type economies, the dependence of the Soviet Union on imports of foodstuffs from the capitalist world, the near-bankruptcy of some Soviet-type economies, the Soviet Union's path of imperial expansion, etc. But radical economists will invariably reply that the organization with which the defenders of capitalism find fault does not embody the true brand of Marxism, communism, or socialism which the radical economists want to see established. Many radical economists favor the nationalization of industry, or of some industries. In Western Europe, where substantial parts of the national output are produced by nationalized industries, such measures are as a rule not considered to have been a success, although there are exceptions to the rule, for example, in countries where government service is idealized and attracts the best minds.

The impact of radical economists on the profession has been slight, but occasionally Marxist-inspired research about the economics of education, the work place, or discrimination has met praise. As far as the impact on students is concerned, it is difficult to generalize. Not all are likely to respond as this one did: radical economics has "broadened my perspective and sharpened my critical faculties. And I believe all this should help when I eventually go into banking" (*U. S. News & World Report,* Jan. 25, 1982, p. 43).

NEW AUSTRIAN ECONOMICS

The Keynesian revolution gave the government a greater role in the economy; the mathematical revolution promoted pervasive quantitative studies. The return to the teachings of the Austrian economists was propagated in order to undo both revolutions. The 1970s brought vigorous promotional efforts aiming at the rebirth of Austrian economics, particularly in the extreme version in which the Austrian tradition was continued by Ludwig von Mises. A group of economists, some of whom had been students of Mises at New York University, undertook a well-organized effort to spread Mises's message: espousal of the market, unequivocal individualism in economics and politics, laissez faire, rejection of public policies (including, in some version, monetary policy), rejection of quantitative studies in economics. Attempts were made to impress a new generation of economists with this message by means of lectures and publications, but since substantially nothing new was added to a message that had been around for a long time without being accepted widely, no great consequences could be expected from making it more resounding.

Supply-side economics developed in the 1970s as a reaction to Keynes's emphasis on demand. Unlike the followers of Keynes who would consider in the first line the effects of a tax cut on demand, supply-side economists argue that the first-line effects are on supply. Some of them claim intellectual lineage from Say's law, according to which supply creates demand—not the other way around. Unlike Keynesian macroeconomics that would attempt to cope with inflation by *increasing* taxes in order to restrain the demand for goods and services, supply-side economics attempts to harness inflation by stimulating the expansion of production by means of a *reduction* of marginal tax rates. The benefits from such a tax policy, which under the administration of President Ronald Reagan was adopted as the policy of the United States government, accrue primarily to the upper-income groups, whose increased saving and investment, it was argued, would lead to the desired expansion of production.

Support for supply-side economics has been more readily coming forth from politicians and journalists than from professional economists. Among academic economists the leading exponents of supply-side economics are Robert Mundell, a specialist in international economics at Columbia University, and Arthur B. Laffer of the University of Southern California, noted for the construction of a curve named after him, which seeks to demonstrate that tax revenues rise with increasing tax rates, reach a maximum, eventually decline and fall to zero at ever higher rates of taxation. Mundell is not a doctrinaire supporter of the supply-side view, who would be willing to uphold it under all circumstances. Instead he has endorsed Keynesian policies for periods of mass unemployment. In an inflationary situation Mundell proposes "to split monetary and fiscal policies, using monetary restraint to check inflation, and tax reduction—which would reduce the upward wage pressure—to increase employment." He argues that monetary and fiscal policies have different effects on the economy, monetary policy affecting expectations in a manner different from fiscal policy.

The chances for an expansion of output, the pragmatic test of supply-side economics, were, however, dimmed by unusually high interest rates, which existed side by side with the tax cuts and which helped to bring down inflation but discouraged investment and instead brought many enterprises to the brink of bankruptcy and beyond. Initially at least, the tax cut did not lead to an expansion of output, but its principal effect was a restraining influence on government spending, lest the budgetary deficit become unmanageable.

Few professional economists are persuaded that a reduction in marginal income-tax rates will significantly increase people's willingness to work, save, and invest. Conservative economists will criticize supply-side economists primarily on this ground and also because some supply-side economists are not deeply concerned about budget deficits resulting from lower tax revenue. Liberal economists disapprove of the preference which the tax cuts accord to the upper-income groups, a policy that breaks with the liberal aim of diffusing income and wealth and that in the words of James Tobin has the sure effect "to redistribute wealth,. power, and opportunity to the wealthy and powerful and their heirs."

**AN EXPANDED
PROFESSION IN SEARCH
OF NEW FRONTIERS**

NOTABLE INDIVIDUAL CONTRIBUTIONS

The principal alignments in contemporary economic thinking do not reveal any new thought that would constitute a systematic response to current criticisms. Neither do they contain the promise of a breakthrough. There remain to be discussed the efforts of individual thinkers that are notable in themselves but which so far have not resulted in a reordering of the main lines of economic thought.

THE NEW HOUSEHOLD ECONOMICS

The classics considered the study of population problems an important task for economists. Later, and especially during the twentieth century, population became the subject of study for demographers and sociologists, although not all economists relinquished the field. In recent decades Gary S. Becker has made a vigorous attempt at restoring the lost province to economics. The essence of the new household economics as developed by Becker is the application of Hicksian microeconomic analysis to fertility, marriage, divorce, and related matters hitherto considered beyond the economists' jurisdiction, the latter not extending to behavior that is outside of the monetary economy and the market. Becker has, for example, conceptualized the price and income elasticities of demand for children, and expanded his approach, with economic theory "providing a unified framework for *all* behavior involving scarce resources, nonmarket as well as market, nonmonetary as well as monetary, small group as well as competitive."

Becker's work is still highly controversial but has found a wide following and stimulated a lively discussion. Some critics doubt that it is desirable to extend the scope of economics in a manner that submits the details of family life to the economic calculus. Others take a more pragmatic point of view but deny that the new approach provides a better explanation of reality than more conventional ones. Paul Samuelson, for one, criticized the new household economics in harsh terms, referring to "rather sterile verbalizations by which economists have tended to describe fertility decisions in terms of the jargon of indifference curves, thereby tending to intimidate non-economists who have not misspent their youth in mastering the intricacies of modern utility theory" (*Population Studies*, 1976 p. 244).

Becker's approach recalls Petty's paneconomics or economism. Both Petty and Becker share the temper of a time that looks for measurement everywhere and upholds the adage that "science is measurement." Becker's approach also fits into the mold of economics as defined by Mises, who made "human action" the province of economics. One of Becker's books carries the title *The Economic Approach to Human Behavior* (1976). An isolated effort, apparently not connected with Becker, goes even beyond *human* behavior and applies economic analysis to the behavior of animals—rats—whose demand curves for food are reported to be negatively sloped.

Becker's approach does not constitute a revolution in economics since it treats of matters peripheral to the core of economics. It may well, however, constitute a revolution in population studies or in other fields extraneous to economics to which economic analysis is being applied—crime, law, political theory, moral philosophy, etc.

A RECONSTRUCTION OF MICROECONOMICS

The generous but by no means uncritical response that has been accorded to the new household economics is as yet still lacking in the cases of other accomplishments of individual scholars, some of which are too recent to permit a definitive judgment about their impact. This is true of the reconstruction of microeconomics attempted in Harvey Leibenstein's *Beyond Economic Man* (1976).

Microeconomic analysis on the whole still follows the pattern established by Hicks in the late 1930s. While Becker expands the application of microeconomics, putting to new use analytical tools considered rather brittle by many thoughtful observers, Leibenstein aims at reforming microeconomics by refurbishing its tools. He challenges a number of basic assumptions of conventional microeconomic theory that have remained unquestioned over a long stretch of time but which run counter to human behavior as observed in the world of reality. One of these is the assumption that there is a single decision-making agent in households and firms, an assumption that Leibenstein proposes to replace by group behavior. He makes the latter the subject of an ingenious analysis of the interaction among the individuals that make up the group. Drawing on the resources of psychology and sociology he recognizes the element of interdependence among the decisions of the members of the group as well as among the decisions an individual makes both as a consumer and producer. The theory of human motivation which brings life into Leibenstein's analysis is further expanded and applied to the distinction between the activities of principals and agents. The model of rational economic man is superseded by that of a model characterized by selective rationality, a procedure that has its precedent in an early proposal of Herbert Simon to replace the assumption of behavior that leads to a maximum by behavior that brings satisfaction. Leibenstein's theory sheds new light on the inertia and resistance to change often observed in large organizations and among agents. Its explanatory value compares favorably with the standard analysis.

SOCIAL LIMITS TO GROWTH

Much attention has been given to physical limits to growth. Fred Hirsch, in a book so titled, shows that there are also *Social Limits to Growth* (1976). Hirsch attempts to resolve what he calls "the paradox of affluence," that is, the paradox that people are not entirely satisfied with economic advancement even if all of them aspire to it and most of them achieve it. He resolves the issue by distinguishing between "material" and "positional" goods. The former become available more plentifully with economic growth, while the latter are limited in their supply, which does not readily increase with economic growth. Houses with a view, services of the top surgeon, and domestic service are examples of positional goods, and so are positions of prestige in the social or occupational hierarchy. This is of course not an entirely new idea. Already the ancient stoics made the point that there are only a limited number of good seats in the theatre, and, as Gilbert and Sullivan put it: "When everyone is somebodee, then no one's anybody!" But Hirsch places his thoughts in the context of a profound analysis that is informed by economics and social philosophy. The conundrum arises because, as basic needs are met, positional goods become more important and more highly valued; but since their supply does not rise, there is no attending increase in real income. Other paradoxes to which Hirsch calls attention and which he tries to resolve are the modern concern with distribution (rather than with the size of the output that is distributed) and the reluctant reliance on public policy in economic matters, which coincides with people's insistence on untrammeled personal freedom in other matters.

THE RISE AND DECLINE OF NATIONS

What forces put a halt to the flowering of Chinese civilization after it had given the world silk, printing and movable type, gunpowder, the stirrup and the wheelbarrow, the magnetic compass, and other technological marvels? What explanations are there of the fall of Rome? Of the rise of Western Europe? Can the long period of western dominance over Asia simply be explained in terms of ocean-going vessels that were equipped with powerful guns? These are awesome questions that challenge the imagination. Only rarely have economists felt qualified to come up with answers to them. Even the more limited search for an explanation of the postwar rise of Japan and the Federal Republic of Germany poses questions that defy a ready solution. It is a rare event in the history of economics when an economist ascends to the intellectual heights at which Hume and Smith moved when they tried to resolve such questions.

In our days Mancur Olson grapples with these problems in *The Rise and Decline of Nations* (1982) by bringing to them the resources of contemporary economics. He develops a theory of increasing organizational rigidity that singles out as strategic factor the operations of associations or combinations that engage in lobbying, cartelization, and related collective action. In the political arena they secure legislation that affords benefits to special interests and in the marketplace they pursue policies aiming at monopoly prices. Under conditions of political stability the element of time is on their side, enabling them to build up their positions and place an ever growing burden on the economy at large: monopolistic restrictions, prices above the competitive level, special benefits, restrictions on entry, resistance to new technologies and other changes, reduction of geographical and occupational mobility, increasingly burdensome regulation, rising prices, etc. Boundary changes, political upheavals and wars tend to break their hold.

Within this framework which contains many refinements and special feature that cannnot be summarized here, Olson provides persuasive explanations for such events as the postwar rise of the Japanese and German economies, the stagnation of Great Britain, and the rapid growth of the West and South of the United States relative to the Northeast and the older Middle West. Olson's work will no doubt set in motion a lively discussion that will test his hypothesis and bring back into economics the consideration of great issues of worldwide importance that has always occupied the best minds in the long history of economics.

NEW THOUGHT ABROAD

To complete the story, a few words may be added about new thought abroad. On the continent of Europe, no breakthrough seems imminent that would challenge the principal alignments of economic thought recorded above. Nevertheless, lively and stimulating contributions are being made, and nowhere in greater plenty than in France. In the field of history bordering on economic history, the magisterial writings of Fernand Braudel are without equal anywhere in the world. Braudel is an offspring of the *Annales* school—*Annales d'histoire économique et sociale*—which was founded by Marc Bloch and Lucien Febvre in the 1920s and which is concerned with *mentalité,* an approach that yields a science of human societies which depicts the environment in which people live, their reaction to it, or their way of life. Phases of this approach run over into economic history, but it is more broadly conceived, encompasses geography and social and technological history, and draws on the resources of social psychology. Examples are Braudel's monumental *The Mediterranean and the Mediterranean World in the Age of Philip II* (1975) and his equally impressive *The Structures of Everyday Life: The Limits of the Possible,* of which the first volume, *Civilization and Capitalism 15th–18th Century* was published in 1982. They conjure up the picture of an age or region that overwhelms the reader with its richness and breadth.

Braudel is a master of detail, who writes with verve and clarity and does not summon the reader to accept a message. Another writer, erudite and on occasion profound, but obscure and repetitive in his highly abstract prose, is Michel Foucault. His writings, in one way or another, treat of the exercise of various forms of power in society, hidden or overt. The two books that are relevant in the present context are *The Order of Things* (1970), which carries the subtitle *An Archeology of the Human Sciences,* and *The Archeology of Knowledge* (1972), with an appendix *The Discourse on Language,* Foucault's inaugural lecture at the Collège de France, where both he and Braudel hold chairs. In these works Foucault explores, among other things, the origins of the science of economics, connects its rise with that of the other "human sciences"—biology and linguistics—and attempts to explain why the rise happened to occur at a particular turning point of history. To Foucault, the human sciences, a recent invention, are the result of a mutation that perhaps now is drawing to its close. He investigates a number of shifts of the human sciences and interprets them with the help of the notion of "episteme," a concept similar to Kuhn's paradigm. For example, he argues that during the sixteenth century the human sciences operated with the help of analogies, an insight that, as far as economics is concerned, a look at the titles of Misselden's books (above, p. 101) will confirm.

During the seventeenth and eighteenth centuries, analogy and similitude were replaced by representation and classification as central concepts. Here the transition from metallic to paper money illustrates the new episteme governing the field of economics. In the nineteenth century, dialectics, history, and energy emerge as the focal points of the human sciences, and Foucault demonstrates how they are accommodated in the thought of Ricardo and Marx.

Another concern of Foucault's is the system of controls that define the authenticity of scientific pursuits during a given period. In his view scientific discourse is disciplined not only by censorship but also by other constraints that operate partly without conscious design and which suppress, dismiss, or neutralize dangerous thought. These considerations are permeated by Foucault's absorbing interest in the manifestation of power, an interest that is evident also in his writings about other subjects.

Foucault refuses to be labeled a student of the history of ideas; the concept that he prefers he designates as archeology of knowledge. His thoughts about economics have an affinity with Gunnar Myrdal's sociology of economic knowledge—the study of the social and political determinants of economic doctrines—as well as with Myrdal's concern about miseducation as expressed in *Asian Drama.*

In conclusion, one may mention another French writer, the author of a book with an odd title: *Bruits: essai sur l'économie politique de la musique* (1977), which reads, in English translation, *Noise: An Essay on the Political Economy of Music,* and deals with the relations between developments in music and economic history, broadly conceived. One could pass it by as a curiosity, were it not for the fact that its author, Jacques Attali, holds a high position as an economist with the French government and that he has for a number of years served as economic advisor to François Mitterand, now the President of France. His book is a testimonial to a civilization that accommodates a combination of high practical expertise with flights of fancy into abstruse matters—here the philosophy, politics, and sociology of music. Which other civilization would nurture that type of achievement? More than any one else, the French seem to be mindful of Mill's saying that people who know nothing but economics know that badly.

Collateral

Readings

COLLATERAL READINGS

Material for collateral reading was drawn from the twelve books listed below.

Cole, G. D. H. (intro.), *Classics in Economics*. New York: Philosophical Library, 1960. Rpt. Port Washington, N. Y.: Kennikat Press, 1971.

Gherity, James A., ed. *Economic Thought: A Historical Anthology*. New York: Random House, Inc., 1965.

Grampp, William D. *Economic Liberalism*. 2 vols. New York: Random House, Inc., 1965. Rpt. Magnolia, Mass.: Peter Smith, Publisher, Inc.

Keynes, John M. *Essays in Biography*. New York: W. W. Norton & Company, Inc., 1963. Rpt. *Collected Writings,* Vol. 10, New York: Cambridge University Press, 1972.

Lekachman, Robert, ed., *The Varieties of Economics*. 2 vols. New York: The World Publishing Company, Meridian Books, 1972. Rpt. Magnolia, Mass.: Peter Smith, Publisher, Inc.

Malthus, Thomas Robert, *Population: The First Essay,* with a foreword by K. E. Boulding. Ann Arbor, Mich.: The University of Michigan Press, Ann Arbor Books, 1959.

Monroe, Arthur Eli, ed., *Early Economic Thought*. Cambridge, Mass: Harvard University Press, 1924. Rpt. New York: Gordon Press, Publishers.

Needy, Charles W., ed., *Classics of Economics*. Oak Park, Ill.: Moore Publishing Company, Inc., 1980.

Rima, Ingrid H., ed., *Readings in the History of Economic Theory*. New York: Holt, Rinehart & Winston, Inc., 1970.

Schumpeter, Joseph A., *Ten Great Economists*. New York: Oxford University Press, 1951.

Smith, Adam, *Selections from the Wealth of Nations,* ed. George J. Stigler. New York: Appleton-Century-Crofts, Crofts Classics Series, 1957.

———, *Representative Selections from the Wealth of Nations,* ed. Bruce Mazlish. Indianapolis: Bobbs Merrill Company, Inc., 1961.

COLLATERAL READINGS BY CHAPTERS

ORIGINAL SOURCES	INTERPRETATIONS	CHAPTER
Lekachman, Vol. 1, 301–4 (Plato)		1
Monroe, pp. 2–29 (Aristotle) _____, pp. 32–49 (Xenophon)	Grampp, Vol. 1, 3–47 (The Stoic Origins of Liberalism) Rima, pp. 1–8 (Gordon)	2
_____, pp. 52–77 (St. Thomas) _____, pp. 80–102 (Oresme)	Gherity, pp. 4–23 (Dempsey) _____, pp. 23–41 (De Roover) Rima, pp. 9–21 (De Roover)	3
_____, pp. 104–20 (Molinaeus) _____, pp. 122–44 (Bodin)		4
_____, pp. 144–67 (Serra) _____, pp. 170–97 (Mun) _____, pp. 222–43 (von Hornick) _____, pp. 378–99 (von Justi) Needy, pp. 4–9 (Mun)	Gherity, pp. 43–66 (Coleman) _____, pp. 67–95 (Viner) Rima, pp. 22–31 (Gould)	5
Monroe, pp. 200–220 (Petty) Lekachman, Vol. 2, 173–84 (Petty)		6
_____, Vol. 1, 185–87 (North)	Grampp, Vol. 1, 48–97 (The Mercantilists as Liberals) Rima, pp. 32–47 (Chalk)	7
Monroe, pp. 246–77 (Cantillon) _____, 340–48 (Quesnay) _____, pp. 350–75 (Turgot) Needy, pp. 10–14 (Quesnay)	Gherity, pp. 98–114 (Higgs) _____, pp. 115–49 (Meek) _____, pp. 150–58 (Phillips) Rima, pp. 48–63 (Meek)	8
Monroe, pp. 280–307 (Galiani) _____, pp. 310–38 (Hume) Lekachman, Vol. 1, 142–46 (Steuart)		9
Smith, *Selections*	Grampp, Vol. 2, 3–72 Rima, pp. 64–74 (Rosenberg)	10–11
Malthus, *Population*	Keynes pp. 81–124 (*Coll. Wrtgs.*, pp. 71–108) Rima, pp. 75–84 (Grampp)	12–13
Lekachman, Vol. 1, 244–51 (Ricardo) Needy, pp. 63–74 (Ricardo) Cole, pp. 29–34 (Ricardo)	Gherity, pp. 160–245 (De Quincey) Rima, pp. 85–94 (Cassels)	14

ORIGINAL SOURCES	INTERPRETATIONS	CHAPTER
Lekachman, Vol. 1, 202–18 (Bentham) ———, Vol. 1, 235–41 (J. Mill) ———, Vol. 1, 274–76 (Cobden) ———, Vol. 1, 278–88 (Senior) Cole, pp. 57–66 (McCulloch)		15
Lekachman, Vol. 1, 253–63; Vol. 2, 26–33 (Mill) Needy, pp. 74–88 (Mill)	Rima, pp. 95–107 (Breit and Pigou)	16
Lekachman, Vol. 1, 57–66 (List) ———, Vol. 2, 252–56 (Toynbee) ———, Vol. 2, 282–91 (Weber) Needy, pp. 165–74 (List)		17–18
Lekachman, Vol. 1, 320–40 (Owen) ———, Vol. 1, 341–47 (Saint-Simon) ———, Vol. 2, 79–94 (Bakunin)		19
———, Vol. 1, 349–52; Vol. 2, 75–77 (Marx) Needy, pp. 86–108 (Marx) Cole, pp. 67–72 (Marx & Engels)	Schumpeter, pp. 3–73 Rima, pp. 108–16 (Sowell)	20
Gherity, pp. 493–511 (George) Lekachman, Vol. 2, 35–44 (S. Webb) ———, Vol. 2, 258–63 (S. & B. Webb) ———, Vol. 2, 129–39 (Lange)		21
Gherity, pp. 345–52 (Jevons) Lekachman, Vol. 2, 149–51 (Jevons) Needy, pp. 113–31 (Cournot, Jevons) ———, pp. 248–67 (Wicksteed) Cole, pp. 100–110 (Wicksteed)	Keynes, pp. 225–309 (*Coll. Wrtgs*, pp. 109–60) Gherity, pp. 328–45 (Robbins) ———, pp. 266–82 (Fisher) Rima, pp. 136–44 (Kauder)	22
Lekachman, Vol. 2, 143–47 (Menger) ———, Vol. 1, 264–71 (Hayek) Gherity, pp. 284–302 (Böhm-Bawerk) ———, pp. 302–26 (Wieser) Needy, pp. 131–39 (Menger) ———, pp. 381–405 (Schumpeter, Hayek) Cole, pp. 277–85 (Hayek)	Schumpeter, pp. 80–90 (on Menger) ———, pp. 143–90 (on Böhm-Bawerk)	23
Gherity, pp. 354–74 (Walras) ———, pp. 375–429 (Pareto) Needy, pp. 139–46 (Walras) ———, pp. 238–48 (Pareto)	———, pp. 74–79 (on Walras) ———, pp. 110–42 (on Pareto) Rima, pp. 145–53 (Friedman)	24

**COLLATERAL
READINGS
BY CHAPTERS**

ORIGINAL SOURCES	INTERPRETATIONS	CHAPTER
Lekachman, Vol. 2, 158–63 (Marshall)	Keynes, pp. 125–217 (*Coll. Wrtgs*,	25
Cole, pp. 4–10,41–56 (Marshall)	pp. 161–231)	
Needy, pp. 220–33 (Marshall)	Schumpeter, pp. 91–109	
———, pp. 267–84 (Pigou)	Gherity, pp. 432–70 (Shove)	
———, pp. 285–316 (Chamberlin	Rima, pp. 154–63 (Wolfe)	
and Robinson)		
Gherity, pp. 547–54 (Wicksell)	Rima, pp. 231–42 (Alexander)	26
Lekachman, Vol. 1, 47–55, 167–74		
(Keynes)		
———, Vol. 1, 175–82 (Myrdal)		
Needy, pp. 233–38 (Wicksell)		
———, pp. 324–52 (Keynes)		
———, pp. 353–81 (Hicks)		
Cole, pp. 119–33, 204–212, 285–91		
(Keynes)		
———, pp. 167–81 (Hicks)		
Gherity, pp. 515–26 (Commons)	Schumpeter, pp. 191–221 (on Taussig)	27–29
———, pp. 526–44 (Veblen)	———, pp. 222–38 (on Fisher)	
Lekachman, Vol. 2, 116–28 (Veblen)	———, pp. 239–59 (on Mitchell)	
———, Vol. 2, 56–69 (Galbraith)	Gherity, pp. 472–90 (Fetter)	
———, Vol. 2, 194–207 (Mills)	Rima, pp. 164–75 (Mann)	
———, Vol. 2, 209–21 (Mitchell		
and Burns)		
Needy, pp. 146–61 (Clark)		
———, pp. 174–88 (Veblen)		
———, pp. 188–98 (Mitchell)		
———, pp. 198–212 (Commons)		
———, pp. 405–34 (Samuelson)		
———, pp. 434–46 (Arrow)		
———, pp. 447–85 (Friedman)		

Bibliographical Notes

684

CHAPTER 1

• Freeman, Kathleen, **The Pre-Socratic Philosophers** (Oxford: Basil Blackwell & Mott Ltd., 1946), is useful for the extensive treatment of Heraclitus (pp. 104–32) and Democritus (pp. 289–326). Chapters 2 and 7 of Philip Wheelwright, **Heraclitus** (Princeton, N.J.: Princeton University Press, 1959), treat of the matters discussed in the text. Cyril Bailey, **The Greek Atomists and Epicurus** (London: Oxford University Press, Clarendon Press, 1928), contains an extensive survey, with quotations, of Democritus's ideas about value, utility, wealth, and labor (pp. 186–212), wherefrom the citations in the text have been culled. For an appraisal of Herodotus see Joseph J. Spengler, "Herodotus on the Subject Matter of Economics," **The Scientific Monthly**, Vol. 81, No. 6 (December, 1955), 276–85. See also Edward Hussey, **The Presocratics** (London: Duckworth, 1972); Charles H. Kahn, **The Art and Thought of Heraclitus** (New York: Cambridge University Press, 1980).

• Ginzberg, Eli, "Studies in the Economics of the Bible," **Jewish Quarterly Review**, new series, Vol. 22, No. 4 (April, 1932), 343–408, contains a discussion of the provisions of the Old Testament regarding slavery, the Sabbatical Year, and the Jubilee Year. See also Otto Weinberger, **Die Wirtschaftsphilosophie des Alten Testaments** (Vienna: Springer-Verlag kg, 1948), with extensive bibliography; Max Weber, **Ancient Judaism** (New York: The Free Press, 1952); Robert Graves, "Mammon: Remarks of a Poet about Money," **Encounter**, June, 1964, pp. 21–29, in which the author relates the economic thought of the Bible to that of the Greeks and Romans. A new work is Aryeh Ben David, **Talmudische Oekonomie**, 2 vols. (Hildesheim: Georg Olms, 1969–70). See also Yehoshua Liebermann, "Elements in Talmudic Monetary Thought," **History of Political Economy**, Vol. 11, No. 2 (Summer, 1979), 254–70.

• Heichelheim, Fritz M., **An Ancient Economic History**, 3 vols. (Leiden: A. W. Sijthoff N. V., 1958–70), is the leading work on the subject. The author maintains that "the disturbances of our twentieth century which have produced several global revolutions already have close historical affinity to the catastrophic centuries of the Early Iron Age before and after 1100 B.C. or so. . . , the period during which Ancient Oriental Civilization vanished from our globe or was mummified. This development of three or so millennia ago, it is true, was characterized by a marked change-over from collectivism and planning to laying stress upon liberty, individualism, small scale refinement, and the individual conscience, which is exactly the opposite of the changes which modern man experiences, even if he has the good luck to live in a libertarian Western state. Owing to this modern trend to central planning the so-called Decline and Fall of Graeco-Roman civilization. . . has striking analogies to our own life experiences also. . . ." (vol. 1, p. 295). Another outstanding work, Mikhail I. Rostovtzeff, **Social and Economic History of the Hellenistic World**, 3 vols. (London: Oxford University Press, 1941), has a chapter on "The Ancient World in the Fourth Century," that is, the classical age of Greece. Other useful works on economic conditions include Jean-Philippe Lévy, **The Economic Life of the Ancient World** (Chicago: The University of Chicago Press, 1967); Alfred Zimmern, **The Greek Commonwealth: Politics and Economics in Fifth-Century Athens**, 5th ed., rev. (London: Oxford University Press, Clarendon Press, 1931); H. Michell, **The Economics of Ancient Greece**, 2nd ed. (New York: Barnes & Noble, Inc., 1958). An old work still deserving attention is August Boeckh, **The Public Economy of Athens**, translated from the second German edition by A. Lamb (Boston: Little, Brown and Company, 1857). Special topics are treated by A. M. Andreades, **A History of Greek Public Finance**, Vol. 1 (Cambridge, Mass.: Harvard University Press, 1933); M. I. Finley, ed., **Slavery in Classi-**

cal **Antiquity** (Cambridge, Eng.; W. Heffer and Sons, 1960), a useful collection of essays.

See also by Finley, the leading ancient historian of our time, **The Ancient Economy** (Berkeley: University of California Press, 1973); **Democracy Ancient and Modern** (New Brunswick: Rutgers University Press, 1973). Finley has doubts about the use of quantitative "data" to interpret the ancient economy and questions the suitability of modern economic analysis for a society that "did not have an economic system which was an enormous conglomeration of interdependent markets" (**Ancient Economy**, p. 22). See also Finley's **Economy and Society in Ancient Greece**, ed. Brent D. Shaw and Richard P. Saller (London: Chatto & Windus, 1981), a collection of essays.

• Laistner, M. L. W., **Greek Economics: Introduction and Translation** (New York: E. P. Dutton & Co. Inc., 1923), is devoted to economic thought and contains a valuable selection of excerpts from the Greek sources and a general introduction of some forty pages by the editor and translator, who was a well-known scholar in the field of ancient history. A general survey of the field may be found in a doctoral dissertation, Albert A. Trever, "A History of Greek Economic Thought" (University of Chicago, 1916). The same subject is covered by August Suchon, **Les Théories économiques dans la Grèce antique** (Paris: Librairie de la société du recueil général des lois et des arrêts, 1898). For short articles, see E. Simey, "Economic Theory among the Greeks," **Economic Review**, Vol. 10 (October, 1900), 462–81; S. Todd Lowry, "Recent Literature on Ancient Greek Economic Thought," **Journal of Economic Literature**, Vol. 17, No. 1 (March, 1979), 65–86.

Special phases of Greek economic thought are discussed in the following works: K. Singer, "Oikonomia: An Inquiry into Beginnings of Economic Thought and Language," **Kyklos**, Vol. 11 (1958), 29–57, on the origin and early use of the word "economics", R. L. Lind, "Economic Man in Ancient Athens," **Classical Journal**, Vol. 35, No. 1 (October, 1939), 27–38; Clifford H. Moore, "Greek and Roman

Ascetic Tendencies," in Herbert W. Smyth, ed., **Harvard Essays on Classical Subjects** (Cambridge, Mass.: Harvard University Press, 1912), pp. 97–140; Arthur T. Geoghegan, **The Attitude towards Labor in Early Christianity and Ancient Culture** (Washington, D.C.: The Catholic University of America Press, 1945); Hannah Arendt, **The Human Condition** (Chicago: The University of Chicago Press, 1958), a difficult book that examines the Greek and modern systems of values, with special emphasis on "labor," "work," and "action." Labor, that is, effort necessary to meet basic needs, and work, that is, the making of tools and objects for use, were looked down upon by the Greeks, who exalted action, that is, "the doing of deeds and the speaking of words" through which man is linked with his fellow man and that integrates society. In the modern order of things, Miss Arendt holds, the ranking of the three values has been reversed, as illustrated by Adam Smith's refusal to consider as productive the rendering of "services"—of public servants, churchmen, lawyers, physicians, men of letters, musicians, and so on.

• Plato, **The Republic**, translated with introduction and notes by F. M. Cornford (New York: Oxford University Press, Inc., 1945), is a work by the outstanding Plato-scholar of his time. The translation is superior to all others in compactness and accuracy. Cornford's **The Unwritten Philosophy and Other Essays** (New York: Cambridge University Press, 1950), contains a chapter on "Plato's Commonwealth" and in another presents a critique of "The Marxist View of Ancient Philosophy" with its stress on the pervasive relevance of the economic factor. As an example of this approach, A. D. Winspear, **The Genesis of Plato's Thought** (New York: Russell & Russell Publishers, 1956), may be cited.

The Laws was translated with an introduction by A. E. Taylor (New York: E. P. Dutton & Co. Inc., Everyman's Library, 1960). Most of the passages of economic interest are found in Books 5, 8, and 9. The most complete commentary on this work is Glenn R. Morrow, **Plato's Cretan City: A Historical Interpretation**

of the Laws (Princeton, N.J.: Princeton University Press, 1960).

Robert S. Brumbaugh, **Plato for the Modern Age** (New York: Crowell-Collier and Macmillan, Inc., 1962), places **The Republic** and **The Laws** within the wider framework of Plato's philosophy, to which they serve as a suitable introduction. Specifically devoted to Plato's political ideas is R. H. S. Crossman, **Plato Today**, rev. ed. (London: George Allen & Unwin Ltd., 1959), an interpretation by a British political scientist and M.P. (Labour) in the light of the modern world of the 1930s. He has thought-provoking chapters on "Plato looks at Communism" and "Plato looks at Fascism."

The most influential critique of Plato's thought by a contemporary philosopher is K. R. Popper, **The Open Society and Its Enemies**, 3rd rev. ed., enlarged, 2 vols. (Princeton, N.J.: Princeton University Press, 1957). Vol. 1 treats of "The Spell of Plato." A more apologetic view is represented by R. B. Levinson, **In Defense of Plato** (Cambridge, Mass.: Harvard University Press, 1953). A survey of the controversy may be found in Renford Bambrough, "Plato's Modern Friends and Enemies," **Philosophy**, Vol. 37, No. 140 (April, 1962), 97–113. Collections of statements illustrative of both sides of the question are to be found in Thomas L. Thorson, ed., **Plato: Totalitarian or Democrat?** (Englewood Cliffs, N.J.: Prentice-Hall, Inc., Spectrum Books, 1963), and in Renford Bambrough, ed., **Plato, Popper and Politics: Some Contributions to a Modern Controversy** (Cambridge: W. Heffer and Sons, 1968). See also A. H. M. Jones, **Athenian Democracy** (Oxford: Basil Blackwell & Mott Ltd., 1957), which is the work of a historian, with chapters on "The Economic Basis of the Athenian Democracy" and "The Athenian Democracy and Its Critics." Sir Ernest Barker, **The Political Thought of Plato and Aristotle** (New York: Dover Pubications Inc., 1959) is a standard work.

• Tozzi, Glauco, **Economisti greci e romani** (Milan: Feltrinelli Editore, 1961). This is a scholarly and detailed work of more than 500 pages in which the author reviews, in chronological order, the contributions of Greek and Roman thinkers to economics.

CHAPTER 2

• **Eryxias**. This dialogue, of unknown authorship and modeled after the writings of Plato, discusses with much hairsplitting the relationship between wealth, virtue, and happiness. The wisest man is said to be the richest because he can guide his life successfully by knowing what is good and what bad. Wealth is defined relative to place and person as being useful and indispensable for man's bodily needs. The richest man is said to be the most unhappy one because he has the greatest and most numerous needs. Perhaps the most remarkable thing about the dialogue is the definition of wealth in terms of utility and the stress on its relative character. For a detailed analysis of the dialogue, which has been translated by Laistner (pp. 41-64), see D. E. Eichholz, "The Pseudo-Platonic Dialogue 'Eryxias,'" **Classical Quarterly**, Vol. 29, No. 3 (July-October, 1935), 129–49.

• **Oeconomica**. Of this work, which is of unknown authorship and probably was written by a number of people including a member of Aristotle's school, only two brief chapters are preserved. The first treats mainly of household management; the second contains a number of anecdotes about dubious ways of money making. Some passages in Chap. 1 have apparently served as an inspiration to later writers. Agriculture is said to rank ahead of other employments because of its justice: it does not take anything away from men, either with their consent, as in business, or against their will, as in war. This idea is echoed in Benjamin Franklin's "Positions to be Examined Concerning

National Wealth" of 1769, which conclude with the remark that agriculture is the "only honest way"—war being robbery and commerce cheating—"for a nation to acquire wealth." Agriculture furthermore is said to be "natural" because as all infants derive their sustenance from their mother, so men derive it from the earth. This may have inspired Sir William Petty's reference to land as "the mother of wealth," labor being the father—**Economic Writings**, ed. C. H. Hull, 2 vols. (London: Cambridge University Press, 1899), Vol. 1, 68—a figure of speech that has found a psychoanalytical interpretation in Walter A. Weisskopf, **The Psychology of Economics** (Chicago: The University of Chicago Press, 1955). A translation of **Oeconomica**, by E. S. Forester, may be found in Vol. 10 of **The Works of Aristotle**, W. D. Ross, ed. (London: Oxford University Press, Clarendon Press, 1921).

• Aristophanes, Greece's greatest comic poet who lived during the second half of the fifth century B.C. and the early decades of the fourth, has written a number of comedies that reflect on economic matters. In the **Ecclesiazusae**, or **Women in Parliament**, the women take over the government and institute a communistic regime modeled probably after Plato's **Republic**. In **Plutus**, the god of wealth is introduced as blind; he then recovers his eyesight and a more equitable distribution of wealth commences. Victor Ehrenberg, **The People of Aristophanes** (Cambridge, Mass.: Harvard University Press, 1951); New York: Schocken Books, Inc., Schocken Paperbacks, 1962), is, in spite of its restrictive title, by far the best survey of economic life in Athens during the fifth century B.C. On the economic ideas of Aristophanes, see Giuseppe Nicosia, **Economia e Politica di Atene attraverso Aristofane**, 2nd ed. (Milan: Sperling & Kupfer, 1935). Yves Urbain, "Les idées économiques d'Aristophane," **L'Antiquité Classique**, Vol. 8 (May, 1939), 183–200, makes great claims for Aristophanes as an economic thinker and considers him a forerunner of the subjective theory of value. In the **Frogs** there are certain lines that ring like Gresham's law: The full-

bodied gold and silver coins that are the pride of Athens "are never used," while the mean brass coins pass from hand to hand (725).

• Aristotle, **Ethica Nicomachea**, trans. W. D. Ross, Vol. 9 of **The Works of Aristotle** (London: Oxford University Press, Clarendon Press, 1925), is the standard edition. The discussion of justice in exchange will be found in the fifth book of the work. Older commentaries include Sir Alexander Grant, **The Ethics of Aristotle: Illustrated with Essays and Notes**, 2nd ed. (London: Longmans, Green & Co. Ltd., 1866); J. A. Stewart, **Notes on the Nicomachean Ethics of Aristotle**, 2 vols. (London: Oxford University Press, Clarendon Press, 1892); John Burnet, ed., **The Ethics of Aristotle**, with introduction and notes (London: Methuen & Co. Ltd., 1900); Henry Jackson, ed., **The Fifth Book of the Nicomachean Ethics of Aristotle** (London: Cambridge University Press, 1879). More recent discussions are found in H. H. Joachim, **Aristotle, The Nicomachean Ethics: A Commentary** (London: Oxford University Press, Clarendon Press, 1951). The author, who lectured at Oxford on the ethics of Aristotle regularly for fifteen years, gives a detailed survey of Aristotle's thoughts on justice in exchange. He remarks: "How exactly the values of the producers are to be determined, and what the ratio between them can mean, is, I must confess, in the end unintelligible to me" (p. 150). See also M. I. Finley, "Aristotle and Economic Analysis," **Past & Present**, No. 47 (May, 1970), 3–25, who comments: "I must confess that, like Joachim, I do not understand what the ratios between the producers can mean" (p. 13). The article is reprinted in Finley, ed., **Studies in Ancient Society** (London and Boston: Routledge and Kegan Paul, 1974).

For comments by the highest modern authority on Greek mathematics see Sir Thomas Heath, **Mathematics in Aristotle** (London: Oxford University Press, Clarendon Press, 1949), where justice in exchange is discussed on pp. 274–76. The author doubts that Aristotle had in mind a formal reciprocal proportion in the technical sense as developed by

Euclid but rather that he meant "retaliation" or "requital" in the broader Pythagorean sense. The controversy hinges on the interpretation of the Greek word "antipeponthos," or reciprocity. On the Euclidian reciprocal proportion see the same author's **The Thirteen Books of Euclid's Elements**, 2nd ed. (New York: Dover Publications, Inc., 1956), Vol. 2, 188f.; on the theory of proportion and means in general see Heath, **A History of Greek Mathematics** (London: Oxford University Press, Clarendon Press, 1921), Vol. 1, 84ff.

Modern students of the history of economic thought who have examined Aristotle's theory of exchange are inclined to interpret his ideas as anticipating the subjective theory of value. The most complete treatment is Joseph Soudek, "Aristotle's Theory of Exchange: An Enquiry into the Origin of Economic Analysis," **Proceedings of the American Philosophical Society**, Vol. 96, No. 1 (1952), 45–75, who finds a parallel with Jevons's theory of exchange. See also S. Todd Lowry, "Aristotle's Mathematical Analysis of Exchange," **History of Political Economy**, Vol. 1, No. 1 (Spring, 1969), 44–66. Joseph J. Spengler, "Aristotle on Economic Imputation and Related Matters," **Southern Economic Journal,** Vol. 21, No. 4 (April, 1955), 371–89, contains a critical examination of the extent to which Aristotle anticipated Menger's and Böhm-Bawerk's views on subjective value, the marginal principle, and the principle of diminishing utility. He reproduces the relevant passages from the **Topics** and the **Rhetoric.** On the same subject see Emil Kauder, "Genesis of the Marginal Utility Theory," **Economic Journal**, Vol. 63 (September, 1953), 638–50, who also reprints the passages from the **Topics** and parallel ones from Menger and Böhm-Bawerk. The parallelism was originally discovered by Oskar Kraus, "Die aristotelische Werttheorie in ihren Beziehungen zu den Lehren der modernen Psychologenschule," **Zeitschrift für die gesamte Staatswissenschaft**, Vol. 61 (1905), 573–92. See also Johann Zmavc, "Die Werttheorie bei Aristoteles und Thomas von Aquino," **Archiv für die Geschichte der Philosophie**, Vol. 12 (1899), 407–33; Zmavc, "Die Geldtheorie und ihre Stellung innerhalb

der wirtschafts- und socialwissenschaftlichen Anschauungen des Aristoteles," **Zeitschrift für die gesamte Staatswissenschaft**, Vol. 58 (1902), 48–79, Aristotle on money; for comments on this see also A. R. Burns, **Money and Monetary Policy in Early Times** (New York: Alfred A. Knopf, Inc., 1927).

Barry J. Gordon, "Aristotle and the Development of Value Theory," **Quarterly Journal of Economics**, Vol. 78 (February, 1964), 116–28, examines the subjective and objective elements in Aristotle's theory of value and concludes "it would seem that Aristotle stands at the head of both traditions. . . . Aristotle is most properly thought of as a forerunner of Marshall" (p. 128). On Aristotle as a founder of the metallist tradition in monetary theory see the same author's "Aristotle, Schumpeter, and the Metallist Tradition," **Quarterly Journal of Economics**, Vol. 75 (November, 1961), 608–14, and for a comparison of Aristotle and Hesiod, "Aristotle and Hesiod: The Economic Problem in Greek Thought," **Review of Social Economy**, Vol. 21 (September, 1963), 147–56.

For further discussions of Aristotle's views about justice in exchange see D. G. Ritchie, "Aristotle's Subdivisions of 'Particular Justice,'" **Classical Review**, Vol. 8, No. 5 (May, 1894), 185–92, who favors the view that justice in exchange must be kept separate from distributive and corrective justice and christens it "catallactic" or "commutative" justice; Giorgio Del Vecchio, **Justice**, ed. A. H. Campbell (New York: Philosophical Library, Inc., 1953), the work of an oustanding Italian jurist, in which emphasis is placed on the continuity of Aristotelian and Roman thought concerning justice, with *suum cuique,* or giving everybody his due, becoming the basis of jurisprudence in the whole civilized world. Del Vecchio's copious references to the continental literature are of special value. Hans Kelsen, considered by many the greatest legal philosopher of modern times, in an essay on "Aristotle's Doctrine of Justice"—**What Is Justice?** (Berkeley and Los Angeles: University of California Press, 1957), pp. 110–36—maintains that Aristotle only has stated the problem of justice without giving an answer that would go beyond the mathematical formulation of the well-known principle *suum cuique,* leaving it to the positive law to determine what is everybody's due. Aristotle's concept has no definite content and legitimizes the given social order. Eric A. Havelock, **The Liberal Temper in Greek Politics** (New Haven, Conn.: Yale University Press, 1957), the work of a classical scholar, makes an ingenious attempt to separate the liberal and authoritarian elements in Aristotle's thought.

Politics. The most useful edition is the translation with an introduction, notes, and appendixes by Ernest Barker (London: Oxford University Press, Clarendon Press 1946). Among the periodical literature the following contributions may be mentioned. W. J. Ashley, "Aristotle's Doctrine of Barter," **Quarterly Journal of Economics**, Vol. 9 (April, 1895) 333–42; J. Cook Wilson, "Aristotle's Classification of the Arts of Acquisition," **Classical Review**, Vol. 10, No. 4 (May, 1896), 184–89 (on the place of mining and forestry); L. von Bortkiewicz, "War Aristoteles Malthusianer?" **Zeitschrift für die gesamte Staatswissenschaft**, Vol. 62 (June, 1906), 383–406; Wladimir Gelesnoff, "Die oekonomische Gedankenwelt des Aristoteles," **Archiv für Sozialwissenschaft und Sozialpolitik**, 1923, pp. 1–33. Karl Polanyi et al., **Trade and Market in the Early Empires** (New York: The Free Press, 1957), contains a chapter on "Aristotle Discovers the Economy" (pp. 64–94), which interprets his work as a link between the ancient economies that were "embedded" in the social order by means of blood ties, legal compulsion, religious obligation, fealty or magic, and the "disembedded" economy that regulates itself by means of price-making markets. See also T. J. Lewis, "Anxiety and Acquisition: Aristotle's Case Against the Market," **Canadian Journal of Economics**, Vol. 11, No. 1 (February, 1978), 69–90; Henry W. Spiegel, "A Note on the Equilibrium Concept in the History of Economics," **Économie Appliquée**, Vol. 28, No. 4 (1975), 609–17, where the distinction between Platonism and Aristotelianism is applied to the history of economics.

• Barker, Ernest, **From Alexander to Constantine** (London: Oxford University Press, Clarendon Press, 1956), pp. 392–480, offers a complete discussion, with citations from the sources, of the social and political ideas of the Christian church down to the age of Constantine. The significance of Clement of Alexandria is documented on pp. 424–30. See also Clement of Alexandria, "The Rich Man's Salvation," Fragment of an Address to the Newly Baptized, **The Exhortation to the Greeks**, trans. G. W. Butterworth (Cambridge, Mass.: Harvard University Press, Loeb Classical Library, 1919). See also Herbert A. Deane, **The Political and Social Ideas of St. Augustine** (New York: Columbia University Press, 1963), pp. 104–15 on St. Augustine's views about property and slavery; Hans Kelsen, "The Idea of Justice in the Holy Scriptures," in **What Is Justice?** (Berkeley and Los Angeles: Univ. of California Press, 1957) pp. 25–81, especially pp. 49–53 (teachings of Jesus) and pp. 74–75 (teachings of Saint Paul); Hans Lietzmann, **A History of the Early Church**, trans. Bertram Lee Woolf, 4 vols. in 2 parts (New York: The World Publishing Company, Meridian Books, 1961); John A. Ryan, **Alleged Socialism of the Church Fathers** (Saint Louis: B. Herder Book Co., 1913). A detailed interpretation of the views of Saint Basil, Saint Ambrose, and Saint Jerome, which concludes that all the church fathers "admitted private property to be just, although less perfect than common ownership, and they declared that private owners did wrong when they refused to distribute their surplus goods among the needy" (p. 81). For a more comprehensive exposition see Ignaz Seipel, **Die wirtschaftsethischen Lehren der Kirchenväter** (Vienna: Mayer & Co., 1907), which also contains a section on the alleged communism of the church fathers. Pp. 108f. cite the sources of Saint John Chrysostom's views about the exchange economy. A more analytical treatment will be found in Ernst Troeltsch, **The Social Teaching of the Christian Churches**, 2 vols., trans. Olive Wyon (New York: The Macmillan Company, 1931). Chapter 1, pp. 39–200, treats of the early church. See especially p. 174, where Troeltsch develops the view that "it is a mistake to found the economic doctrine of the Gospel upon the story of the Rich Young Ruler, and certain familiar words which are connected with it concerning rich people. . . . The words about the spiritual danger of riches are quite clear when we understand the fundamental point of view of Jesus, and they contain no negation of property, nor indeed any asceticism at all. . . . Jesus' attitude towards the question of possessions is clear enough, namely, to seek first the Kingdom of God and not to be anxious for the morrow. . . . But the young man wants to do something special, so Jesus invites him to take part in His missionary work, and to sell all and give to the poor. . . . Without the recognition of the fact that Jesus did summon His disciples in the narrower sense, or the missionaries and messengers of the Kingdom of God, to tasks which were harder than those which are laid on the mass of His followers, the whole Gospel cannot be understood." See also Jacob Viner, **Religious Thought and Economic Society** (Durham, N.C.: Duke University Press, 1978), Chap. 1 on the economic doctrines of the Christian Fathers.

• Heitland, W. E., **Agricola: A Study of Agriculture and Rustic Life in the Greco-Roman World from the Point of View of Labor** (London: Cambridge University Press, 1921), includes appraisals of the works of the Roman writers on agriculture—Cato, Varro, Cicero, Columella, Pliny, and so on. See also F. Harrison, [A Virginia Farmer] **Roman Farm Management in the Treatises of Cato and Varro**, trans., with notes of modern instances (New York: The Macmillan Company, 1913). Other translations of these works are also available (Cambridge, Mass.: Harvard University Press, Loeb Classical Library). They are full of curious lore—recipes for myrtle wine and remedies for loose bowels, tapeworms and other afflictions in Cato (234 B.C.–149 B.C.), information about the origin of bees, which according to Varro (116 B.C.–27 B.C.) is found in the putrefied bodies of cattle, recipes for pickling olives (Columella, first century A.D.), and advice to take chicken brain in wine to overcome the poison of serpents (Pliny, A.D. 23–A.D.

56)—but their economic content at best serves to illustrate farming practices rather than ideas. The mean streak in Roman civilization is exemplified in this recommendation of Cato's: "Sell the old work oxen, the wool, the skins, the old wagon, the worn-out iron tools, the aged slave, the slave that is diseased, and everything else that you do not need." Many of these writings, especially those of Pliny, enjoyed a high reputation during the Middle Ages. Of the work of Palladius (fourth century A.D.) **On Husbandry**, the only English translation was produced during the fourteenth century. The translator put it in verse form. See the edition by Barton Lodge, **Publications**, No. 52 (London: Early English Text Society, 1872).

• MacKendrick, Paul, **The Roman Mind at Work** (New York: Litton Educational Publishing, Inc., Van Nostrand Reinhold Company, Anvil Books, 1958) has an informative section on Roman law, with excerpts from the sources (pp. 70–75 and 164–69). The same subject is covered in H. F. Jolowicz, **Roman Foundations of Modern Law** (London: Oxford University Press, Clarendon Press, 1957). On "The History of the Law of Nature," see the article by Sir Frederick Pollock, originally published in 1900 and reprinted in his **Jurisprudence and Legal Essays** (New York, St. Martin's Press, Inc., 1961), pp. 124–56. See also F. de Zulueta, "The Science of Law," in **The Legacy of Rome**, ed. Cyril Bailey (London: Oxford University Press, Clarendon Press, 1923), pp. 173–207: "The Roman Empire, as it developed, created the idea of a supernational state, which since has never wholly left men's hearts. The creation of that idea would have been impossible without the creation of a supernational law, and neither creation would have been possible without the Roman character, the national *gravitas,* which enabled the Roman jurists to take reason, with its witness, the common customs of mankind, as the principle of their expansive interpretation, without indulging in the construction of speculative Utopias" (p. 182). Later developments arising from Roman law are discussed in John Henry Merryman, **The Civil Law**

Tradition (Stanford, Cal.: Stanford University Press, 1970).

• Rostovtzeff, Mikhail I., **The Social and Economic History of the Roman Empire**, 2nd ed., rev. P. M. Fraser, 2 vols. (London: Oxford University Press, Clarendon Press, 1957), is the leading work on the subject and its discussion of the causes of the decay of ancient civilization (Chap. 12) has served as basis for the exposition here. Rostovtzeff concludes his great work with the statement that "the main phenomenon which underlies the process of decline is the gradual absorption of the educated classes by the masses and the consequent simplification of all the functions of political, social, economic, and intellectual life, which we call the barbarization of the ancient world. . . . The evolution of the ancient world has a lesson and a warning for us. Our civilization will not last unless it be a civilization not of one class, but of the masses. . . . But the ultimate problem remains like a ghost, ever present and unlaid: Is it possible to extend a higher civilization to the lower classes without debasing its standard and diluting its quality to the vanishing point? Is not every civilization bound to decay as soon as it begins to penetrate the masses?" (Vol. 1, p. 541).

Late in the fourth century A.D. the eastern and western parts of the Roman Empire became divided, with the former—the Byzantine Empire—continuing until the fall of Constantinople to the Turks in 1453. Phases of the long history of Byzantium are characterized by economic prosperity as well as by conflicts between large and small landowners. Toward the end of the empire, Gemistus Plethon (1355–circa 1450) proposed its reconstruction in part along lines suggested by Plato and in other parts in line with later ideas of John Locke. He suggests that the produce of all labor should be assigned to three different recipients, first to the laborer himself, second to the person who provides the stock for the laborer, and third to the person who ensures security for the whole community. Land should be the common property of all inhabitants who are free to use it as long as they cultivate it with the proper care. See Ernest Barker, **Social and Political Thought in Byzantium**, translated with an introduction and notes (London: Oxford University Press, Clarendon Press, 1957), pp. 196ff.

For a new appraisal of the factors responsible for the decline of the Roman Empire, and for a comparison of the relevant conditions in the Western and Eastern Empires see A. H. M. Jones, **The Later Roman Empire**, 2 vols. (Norman, Okla.: University of Oklahoma Press, 1964). According to Jones, "the basic economic weakness of the empire was that too few producers supported too many idle mouths" (Vol. 2, 1045). Moreover, compared with the Eastern one, "the Western Empire was poorer and less populous, and its social and economic structure more unhealthy. It was thus less able to withstand the tremendous strain imposed by its defensive effort. . . But the major cause of its fall was that it was more exposed to barbarian onslaughts which in persistence and sheer weight of numbers far exceeded anything which the empire had previously had to face" (1067f.).

S. C. Gilfillan, "Lead Poisoning and the Fall of Rome," **Journal of Occupational Medicine**, Vol. 7 (February, 1965), 53–60, holds that lead poisoning, caused by the use of leaden household utensils, was responsible for the Roman upper classes' loss of stamina. J. Donald Hughes, **Ecology in Ancient Civilizations** (Albuquerque, N.M.; University of New Mexico Press, 1975), considers the abuse of the environment as a factor responsible for the decline of ancient civilizations. See also Arnaldo Momigliano, "Declines and Falls," **American Scholar** (Winter 1979–80), pp. 37–49; Max Weber, **The Agrarian Sociology of Ancient Civilizations** (Atlantic Highlands, N.J.: Humanities Press, 1976), and the review of this work by Momigliano, **Times Literary Supplement**, April 8, 1977, p. 435, where Weber's interpretation of the fall of Rome is restated.

• Oates, Whitney J., ed., **The Stoic and Epicurean Philosophers** (New York: Random House, Inc., Modern Library, Inc., 1957), contains the complete extant writ-

692

ings of Epicurus, Epictetus, Lucretius, and Marcus Aurelius. On the Cynics, see Donald R. Dudley, **A History of Cynicism** (London: Methuen & Co. Ltd., 1937); Farrand Sayre, **Diogenes of Sinope: A Study of Greek Cynicism** (Baltimore: J. H. Furst Company, 1938). On Stoicism, see R. D. Hicks, **Stoic and Epicurean**, originally published in 1910 (New York: Russell & Russell Publishers, 1962); E. Vernon Arnold, **Roman Stoicism**, originally published in 1911 (London: Routledge & Kegan Paul Ltd., 1958); Gilbert Murray, **Stoic, Christian, Humanist** (Boston: Beacon Press, 1950), Chap. 2: The Stoic Philosophy; John Rist, **Stoic Philosophy** (London: Cambridge University Press, 1970). On Epicurus, see Norman W. De Witt, **Epicurus and His Philosophy** (Minneapolis: University of Minnesota Press, 1954). A valuable older study of the whole group is Eduard Zeller, **The Stoics, Epicureans and Sceptics**, trans. Oswald J. Reichel (London: Longmans, Green & Co. Ltd., 1870). See also Paul Nizan, **Les matérialistes de l'antiquité** (Paris: François Maspéro Editeur, 1968), which relates the thought of the Stoics and Epicureans to Democritus; J. M. Rist, **Epicurus: An Introduction** (New York: Cambridge University Press, 1972); F. H. Sandbach, **The Stoics** (New York: W. W. Norton and Company, 1975).

• Xenophon (c. 430 B.C.– c. 355 B.C.) was a disciple of Socrates who attained prominence in politics and as a military leader. Some of his writings touch on economic subjects. The **Cyropaedia**, trans. Walter Miller, ostensibly an account of the education of a Persian prince, contains a statement anticipating Adam Smith's dictum that the division of labor is limited by the extent of the market: "In small towns the same workman makes chairs and doors and plows and tables, and often the same artisan builds houses, and even so he is thankful if he can only find employment enough to support him"; in the large towns "many people have demands to make upon each branch of industry," and "one trade alone, and very often even less than a whole trade, is enough to support a man" (New York: The Macmillan Company, 1914), Vol. 2, 333.

The Economist, trans. Alexander D. O. Wedderburn and W. Gershom Collingwood, with a preface by the editor, Bibliotheca Pastorum, ed. John Ruskin, Vol. 1 (London: George Allen & Unwin Ltd., 1876) assembles the thoughts of a gentleman-farmer and soldier on the management of the household and farm. Interspersed are notions about property and wealth. A man's property is only what benefits him or what he knows to use. A true gentleman should not practice mechanical arts but rather agriculture and war. Mechanical arts are injurious to mind and body—that is why in some states citizens are not allowed to engage in them. Ruskin in his introduction praises the work highly, especially the "faultless definition of wealth and explanation of its dependence for efficiency on the merits and faculties of its possessor; a definition which cannot be bettered; and which must be the foundation of all true political economy" (p. xxxix). Laistner reproduces the opening chapters that contain the enquiry into the meaning of wealth (pp. 28–40).

Ways and Means to Increase the Revenues of Athens (Laistner, pp. 10–27) makes a number of suggestions designed to realize the purpose indicated in the title. Among other things, Xenophon proposes to attract increasing numbers of resident foreigners, improve the port, build markets and inns for visitors, establish a government-owned merchant fleet, increase the production of silver by the government-owned mines at Laurium, and have the city acquire slaves to be hired out to private users. Eventually there should be three slaves to every Athenian citizen—probably the reverse of the actual proportion. In discussing mining, Xenophon expresses the view that the silver ore will never give out and that silver will never lose its value, whereas "when an abundance of gold makes its appearance, its value depreciates and it sends up the price of silver" (p. 17). The last observation may have been in line with actual events at the time, following upon the freer circulation of Persian gold coins in Greece. See K. von der Lieck, "Die xenophontische Schrift von den Einkünften" (dissertation, Cologne, 1933), and A. R. Burns, **Money and Monetary Policy in Early Times** (New York: Alfred A. Knopf, Inc., 1927) which contains an appendix, pp. 467–72, on "Monetary Theory in Early Times," with a discussion of the views of Plato, Aristotle, and Xenophon. Dr. Burns is inclined to admit

the plausibility of Xenophon's view about the relative value of gold and silver because of the disappearance of silver into hoards, its exportation, and the wear and tear on the coinage. See also J. K. Anderson, **Xenophon** (New York: Charles Scribner's Sons, 1974).

CHAPTER 3

• Ashley, W. J., **An Introduction to English Economic History and Theory**, Vol. 1 in 2 parts, 4th ed. (London: Longmans, Green & Co. Ltd., 1906–9), devotes two lengthy chapters (Part 1, Chap. 3 and Part 2, Chap. 6) to medieval economic thought. This work by a prominent student of economic history served as the basis of other studies of medieval economics, of which the last, in book length, was published sixty years ago by an authority on the economic history of Ireland: George O'Brien, **An Essay on Medieval Economic Teaching** (London: Longmans, Green & Co., Ltd., 1920). In O'Brien's view the teaching on usury was an application of the theory of the just price (p. 35), an interpretation that is open to criticism because the usury doctrine referred specifically to loans. It was exactly by transactions being interpreted as sales rather than loans that they could escape the usury doctrine and be made legitimate (see John T. Noonan, Jr., **The Scholastic Analysis of Usury** (Cambridge, Mass.: Harvard University Press, 1957), pp. 397f.). In addition to O'Brien's work, there are also a number of books by an English Dominican, Bede Jarrett: **Social Theories of the Middle Ages, 1200 to 1500** (Boston: Little, Brown and Company, 1926); **Mediaeval Socialism**, originally published in 1913 (London: Burns & Oates Limited, 1935). Much of the detail of these older works is superseded by the more recent studies by Baldwin on the just price and by Noonan on usury (see pp. 694, 696 below). This applies also to the still older standard work on the subject by a legal historian, Wilhelm Endemann, **Studien in der romanisch-kanonistischen Wirtschafts- und Rechtsleh-**

re bis gegen Ende des 17. Jahrhunderts, 2 2 vols. (Berlin: Dr. Walter Gruyter & Co., 1874–83), which has recently been reprinted. This work is still unexcelled in broadness of coverage and familiarity with the sources.

A number of briefer surveys are more up-to-date. Gabriel Le Bras, a distinguished French student of legal history, has contributed a chapter on "Conceptions of Economy and Society" to **The Cambridge Economic History of Europe** (London: Cambridge University Press, 1963), Vol. 3, "Economic Organization and Policies in the Middle Ages," Chap. 8, pp. 554–75. See also J. Ibanès, **La Doctrine de l'Église et les réalités économiques au xiiie siècle: L'Intérêt, les prix et la monnaie** (Paris: Travaux et Recherches de la Faculté de Droit et des Sciences Économiques, 1967). The connection with economic thought is emphasized by Raymond de Roover: "Scholastic Economics: Survival and Lasting Influence from the Sixteenth Century to Adam Smith," **Quarterly Journal of Economics**, Vol. 69, No. 2 (May, 1955), 161–90, in which the author links the thought of the Schoolmen with the later, secularized natural-law doctrine and through this with Adam Smith. See also, by the same author, **La Pensée économique des Scolastiques: doctrines et méthodes** (Montreal: Institut d'Études Médiévales, 1971), and Jacob Viner, **Religious Thought and Economic Society** (Durham, N.C.: Duke University Press, 1978), Chap. 2 on the economic doctrines of the Scholastics. Ernst Troeltsch, **The Social Teaching of the Christian Churches**, trans. Olive Wyon (New York: The Macmillan Company, 1931), Vol. 1, Chap. 2, 201–445 on "Med-

694

ieval Catholicism," has much to offer to those readers who are mainly interested in the religious and theological implications of the matter. R. H. Tawney, **Religion and the Rise of Capitalism** (New York: Harcourt, Brace & World, Inc., 1937), Chap. 1 on "The Medieval Background," is inimitable in its verve and profundity and may serve as an excellent introduction to medieval economic thought (New York: The New American Library, Inc., Mentor Books, 1947).

• Baldwin, John W., "The Medieval Theories of the Just Price," **Transactions** of the American Philosophical Society, new series, Vol. 49, Part 4 (Philadelphia, 1959), is the standard work on the subject, with a complete bibliography of primary and secondary sources. The author is a specialist in medieval history, who has investigated the original material with great care. For interpretations reflecting various points of view see Vigo A. Demant, ed., **The Just Price: An Outline of the Medieval Doctrine and an Examination of Its Possible Equivalent Today** (London: Student Christian Movement Press, 1930). Rudolf Kaulla, **Theory of the Just Price**, translated from German by Robert D. Hogg (London: George Allen & Unwin Ltd., 1940), is a general treatment that devotes only a few pages to the medieval doctrine. Two articles, one by a Jesuit father who was a well-trained economist, and the other by an outstanding student of the history of economic thought, discuss the functional role of the just price. The first one is Bernard W. Dempsey, "Just Price in a Functional Economy," **American Economic Review**, Vol. 25 (September, 1935), 471–86. The second article is E. A. J. Johnson, "Just Price in an Unjust World," **International Journal of Ethics**, Vol. 48 (January, 1938), 165–81. A recent contribution to the protracted controversy about the relationship of the just price to cost of production on the one hand and to the market price on the other may be found in Samuel Hollander, "On the Interpretation of the Just Price," **Kyklos**, Vol. 18, No. 4 (1965), 615–34. For a readable survey by a student of economic history who was a well-informed expert on medieval economics,

see Raymond de Roover, "The Concept of the Just Price: Theory and Economic Policy," **Journal of Economic History**, Vol. 18 (December, 1958), 418–34. The same author also has written a study that traces the development of the theory of monopoly back to the scholastic authorities: "Monopoly Theory Prior to Adam Smith: A Revision," **Quarterly Journal of Economics**, Vol. 65 (November, 1951), 492–524. See also Franz-Ulrich Willeke, **Entwicklung der Markttheorie: Von der Scholastik bis zur Klassik** (Tübingen: J. C. B. Mohr [Paul Siebeck], 1961); Joseph Höffner, **Wirtschaftsethik und Monopole** (Stuttgart: Gustav Fischer Verlag, 1941); same author, **Statik und Dynamik in der scholastischen Wirtschaftsethik** (Opladen: Westdeutscher Verlag GMBH, 1955). James Healy, **The Just Wage 1750–1890** (The Hague: Martinus Nijhoff's N.V., 1966). S. T. Worland, **Scholasticism and Welfare Economics** (Notre Dame, Ind.: University of Notre Dame Press, 1967); same author, "Justum Pretium: One More Round in an 'Endless Series'," **History of Political Economy**, Vol. 9, No. 4 (Winter, 1977), 504–21; G. W. Wilson, "The Economics of the Just Price," same journal, Vol. 7, No. 1 (Spring, 1975), 56–74; Odd Langholm, **Price and Value in the Aristotelian Tradition** (New York: Columbia University Press, 1979).

• Baron, Salo W., "The Economic Views of Maimonides," in Salo W. Baron, ed., **Essays on Maimonides** (New York: Columbia University Press, 1941), pp. 127–264. Medieval civilization was, of course, not exclusively Christian. There were the Jews, now a widely dispersed, struggling, and often persecuted minority, and the Moslems, founders of an empire that at its height reached from Central Asia to Spain. The towering figure in the Hebrew thought of the Middle Ages was Maimonides (1135–1204), often cited as "Rabbi Moyses" by the Schoolmen. In his general philosophy Maimonides was as much under the spell of Aristotle as were the Schoolmen, but his economics was confined to an exegesis of the biblical law. Adherence to this offered a better means to preserve the Jewish identity in exile than reliance on Aristotelian politics and economics, which had developed in an environment so different from the one in which the Jews now found themselves. Maimonides's economic ideas parallel those of Saint Thomas in many respects, but there are also important differences. Both are exponents of social solidarity and have much to say about usury and the just price; but Maimonides, being under the influence of a different tradition, does not praise poverty as such (p. 142), does not trouble to justify private property, which is taken for granted as "an eternal and God-given institution" (p. 146), and has no compunction about commerce as "a necessary and unobjectionable human institution" (p. 171). On the positive side, Maimonides teaches the faithful to lead lives that combine intellectual and economic pursuits. He "stresses in particular the obligation of every Jew to earn a livelihood rather than become a public charge. Even the highly desirable devotion to intellectual pursuits is no excuse for economic inactivity. . . . On the other hand, economic pursuit should merely be secondary, and, if at all possible, man should devote most of his time to study" (p. 141). "Learning a trade and teaching it to one's children is declared by Maimonides to be one of the major obligations of every Jew" (p. 248). "The obligation to work is coupled in rabbinic theory with a sort of moral, if not legal right to work, emanating from the obligations of every Jew, as well as of the community at large, to supply employment to needy coreligionists" (p. 249). See also the work by Aryeh Ben David, cited above, p. 684, and, for the development of economic doctrine under Islam, Ibn Khaldun, **The Muqaddimah: An Introduction to History**, translated and with an introduction by Franz Rosenthal, 3 vols., Bollingen Foundation (New York: Random House, Inc., Pantheon Books, Inc., 1967); Joseph J. Spengler, "Economic Thought of Islam: Ibn Khaldun," **Comparative Studies in Society and History**, Vol. 6 (April, 1964), 268–306; Jean David C. Boulakia, "Ibn Khaldun: A Fourteenth-Century Economist," **Journal of Political Economy**, Vol. 79, No. 5 (September-October, 1971), 1105–1118; L. Haddad, "A Fourteenth-Century Theory of Economic Growth and Development," **Kyklos**, Vol. 30, No. 2 (1977), 195–213. President Ronald Reagan has cited Ibn Khaldun as supporting the view that a reduction in tax rates will generate larger tax revenues (News Conference, October 1, 1981).

• **The Cambridge Economic History of Europe** contains detailed and up-to-date background material on medieval economic history. The first three volumes of this monumental work, which already have been published, all treat of the Middle Ages (London: Cambridge University Press, 1942, 1952, 1963). Those who look for a readable survey rather than a reference work will find useful Henri Pirenne, **Economic and Social History of Medieval Europe** (New York: Harcourt, Brace & World, Inc., 1937, same publisher, Harvest Books, 1956). See also M. M. Postan **The Medieval Economy and Society: An Economic History of Britain, 1100–1500** (Berkeley: University of California Press, 1973). On a special phase of medieval economic history see the fascinating study by Lynn White, Jr., **Medieval Technology and Social Change** (London: Oxford University Press, Clarendon Press, 1962; also Oxford Paperbacks, 1964), which for the most recent period may be supplemented by Carlo M. Cipolla, **Guns, Sails and Empires: Technological Innovation and the Early Phases of European Expansion, 1400–1700** (New York: Random House, Inc., Pantheon Books, Inc., 1965). See also Lynn White, Jr., **Medieval Religion and Technology** (Berkeley: University of California Press, 1978); Jean Gimpel, **The Medieval Machine: The Industrial Revolution of the Middle Ages** (New York: Holt, Rinehart & Winston, Inc., 1976).

• McKeon, Richard, "The Development of the Concept of Property in Political Philosophy: A Study of the Background of the Constitution," **International Journal of Ethics**, Vol. 48, No. 3 (April, 1938), 297–366, includes a treatment of the medieval writers, as do the relevant chapters in **Property: Its Duties and Rights**, essays by various writers with an introduction by the bishop of Oxford (London: Macmillan & Co. Ltd., 1913), especially pp. 117–32; Richard Schlatter, **Private Property: The History of an Idea** (New Brunswick, N.J.:

696

Rutgers University Press, 1951), pp. 47–76. Specifically devoted to Saint Thomas Aquinas, and written with special emphasis on the philosophical principles involved is William J. McDonald, **The Social Value of Property according to Saint Thomas Aquinas** (Washington, D. C.: The Catholic University of America Press, 1939).

• Noonan, John T., Jr., **The Scholastic Analysis of Usury** (Cambridge, Mass.: Harvard University Press, 1957), is the standard work on the subject. The author, trained in law and in Scholastic philosophy, has made an exhaustive investigation of the original sources. According to his interpretation, the doctrine of usury has its origin neither in law nor in economics but is a theological creation aiming to build a moral code on rational grounds. The last chapter of the work contains a critical survey of alternative interpretations that see the origin of the doctrine in the view that money is barren, or relate it to the labor theory of value, or make it a part of the theory of just price, and so on. For a study that lays greater stress on the economic connotations on the subject, see Thomas F. Divine, **Interest: An Historical and Analytical Study in Economics and Modern Ethics** (Milwaukee: Marquette University Press, 1959), a work originally written in 1938 by a Jesuit father as a doctoral dissertation under the direction of Lionel Robbins. Benjamin N. Nelson, **The Idea of Usury** (Princeton, N.J.: Princeton University Press, 1949), is an interesting sociological study of the history of the double standard established by Deuteronomy 23:19–20 that forbids lending on interest to brothers but allows the taking of interest from others. This is traced to modern times. According to the author, the transformation of clan comradeship to universal society has occurred at the cost of an "attenuation of love" (p. 136). Bernard W. Dempsey, **Interest and Usury**, with an introduction by Joseph A. Schumpeter, (London: Dobson and Company, 1948) based on the Harvard dissertation of a Jesuit father, offers a comparison of modern theories of interest with the usury doctrines of three Scholastics of the sixteenth and seventeenth centuries. Sources of equilibrium as identified by

some contemporary theories are interpreted as usury—"institutional," not personal—and related to the thought of the late Schoolmen. This is a view compatible with that of J. M. Keynes, who had this to say about the medieval usury doctrine: "I was brought up to believe that the attitude of the medieval church to the rate of interest was inherently absurd, and that the subtle discussions aimed at distinguishing the return on money loans from the return to active investment were merely Jesuitical attempts to find a practical escape from a foolish theory. But I now read these discussions as an honest intellectual effort to keep separate what the classical theory has inextricably confused together, namely, the rate of interest and the marginal efficiency of capital. For it now seems clear that the disquisitions of the Schoolmen were directed towards the elucidation of a formula which should allow the schedule of the marginal efficiency of capital to be high, whilst using rule and custom and the moral law to keep down the rate of interest"—**General Theory of Employment, Interest and Money** (New York: Harcourt, Brace & World, Inc., 1936), pp. 351–52. The view Keynes was brought up to believe had indeed been that of Alfred Marshall, **Principles of Economics**, 8th ed. (New York: The Macmillan Company, 1920), p. 586.

Still a different interpretation of the usury doctrine is given in the paper by W. Stark, **The Contained Economy** (London: Blackfriars Publications, 1956). He sees in the stiffening attitude to usury, which in the twelfth century became forbidden to all and then was considered a sin against justice rather than against charity, the awareness of a distant but noticeable threat to the medieval ideal of a harmoniously ordered society. The price system was an integral part of this order. "But the price system can only remain in its quasi-legal fixation and fixity if no strong dynamizing agency becomes active in the economic sphere. Capital, however, is such a dynamizing agency; in fact, it is the dynamizing agency par excellence, and capital, in turn, is brought into being and stung into action through the payment and the promise of interest. No wonder that the guardians of the medieval order of values were up in arms against it. . . It has been said more than once that the Doctors did not understand the phenomenon of capital, but that is decidedly less than fair. Certainly, they did not have an express theory of it, but they realized, however dimly, what its true nature is—to be the spring of economic change and advancement, to be the motor force of progress. . . We think economic progress desirable, whatever the cost; they counted the cost and found it excessive. Only Almighty God can say who is the wise man and who is the fool in this business" (pp. 18–19). See also J. Melitz, "Some Further Reassessment of the Scholastic Doctrine of Usury," **Kyklos**, Vol. 24, No. 3 (1971), 473–91.

• Oresme, Nicholas, **The De Moneta and English Mint Documents**, trans. from Latin with introduction and notes by Charles Johnson (Camden, N.J.: Thomas Nelson & Sons, 1956). This is the first complete translation of Oresme's **Treatise** into English. A translation of the substance of the work may also be found in Arthur Eli Monroe, **Early Economic Thought** (Cambridge, Mass.: Harvard University Press, 1924), pp. 79–102. See E. Bridrey, **La Théorie de la monnaie au xive siècle: Nicole Oresme** (Paris: M. Giard et E. Brière, 1906), entries on Oresme in Palgrave's **Dictionary of Political Economy** and the **Encyclopaedia of the Social Sciences**, and the entry on "Debasement of Coin" by F. Y. Edgeworth in the former. Oresme's work was "rediscovered" in the nineteenth century by an historical economist, but doubt was cast upon his find by the oustanding authority on the economic doctrines of the canonist writers, who questioned both Oresme's alleged originality and the claim that he had fallen into oblivion.

New light on the social utility of debasement is shed by Carlo M. Cipolla, **Money, Prices, and Civilization in the Mediterranean World: Fifth to Seventeenth Century** (Princeton, N.J.: Princeton University Press, 1956). Given the inability of the monetary authorities to control the supply of petty coins and the inelastic character of the supply of precious metals,

Professor Cipolla argues that the debasement of the petty coins on balance did more good than harm. It averted a disastrous shortage of this type of currency and a deflation of appalling dimensions. Debasement of the petty coins also facilitated the maintenance of the weight and fineness of the gold coins that were used in international transactions. The two sorts of money, the petty coins and the ones from gold, tended to circulate among different social classes, and the chronic debasement of the petty coins with their resulting depreciation in terms of gold coins and commodities depressed real wages, at least in the short run, and raised the profits of the entrepreneurs.

Professor Cipolla also has studied recurring fluctuations of the supply of petty coins. After debasement they were issued in large quantities because the issuing agencies profited from the disparity between face value and metallic content. The large supply forced down the value at which the coins were accepted by the public (that is, commodity prices rose in terms of the debased coin), and once the current value had reached the value of the metallic content, the supply of petty coins contracted because there was no longer any gain to be obtained from striking them. Then a new debasement occurred, the supply increased again and another cycle started (pp. 32–35).

On all these matters see also the posthumous publication of a work by Marc Bloch, the great French expert on medieval economic history: **Esquisse d'une histoire monétaire de l'Europe** (Paris: Librairie Armand Colin, 1954), and Raymond de Roover, **Business, Banking and Economic Thought in Late Medieval and Early Modern Europe** (Chicago: University of Chicago Press, 1976).

• Saint Thomas Aquinas, **Summa Theologica**, 1267–73. The questions of the **Summa** treating of usury and the just price,—*Secunda Secundae*, that is, the second part of the second part, Questions 77–78—are translated in Monroe, **Early Economic Thought**, pp. 52–77. This may be supplemented by some passages in **Basic Writings of Saint Thomas Aquinas**, edited and annotated, with an introduc-

697

698

tion, by Anton C. Pegis, 2 vols. (New York: Random House, Inc., 1945), a selection that does not contain the questions translated by Monroe but does include some others of economic relevance, especially in the Treatise on Law in the first part of the second part, Questions 90–108 (Vol. 2, 742–978): Q. 94, Art. 5 on property and natural law (779f.); Q. 105, Art. 2 on the regulation of property (932f.). Neither of these works includes the important passages in which Saint Thomas distinguishes between the acquisition and disposal of property, on the one hand, and its use (*Secunda Secundae,* Q. 66, Art. 2) and in which he discusses the moral issue of theft by needy people (Art. 7). The reader who wishes to consult these texts must turn to the complete version of the **Summa** in the translation by the Fathers of the English Dominican Province (New York: Benziger, Inc., 1947).

For a modern interpretation of the thought of Saint Thomas by a leading exponent of Thomistic philosophy, see the works of Jacques Maritain, especially **True Humanism** (New York: Charles Scribner's Sons, 1938), pp. 177–89 on property, and **Freedom in the Modern World** (New York: Charles Scribner's Sons, 1936), pp. 193–214, on the same subject. According to Maritain's interpretation of Saint Thomas's views about property, "individual ownership is based on a spiritual foundation, on the capacity of the rational being as an intellectual subject to give form to matter" (**Freedom in the Modern World**, pp. 211f.). Property is an extension of a person's "proprietary right over himself." It is of the very essence of the proprietary activity "to imprint on matter the mark of rational being." This can best be accomplished if a person has the rights and privileges commonly associated with private ownership (p. 198). The modern industrial system, with its wage workers and corporate employers, "has given rise to such serious abuses that normal administration would seem to require us to return to a type of industrial ownership in which a group of technicians, workers, and sleeping partners would all be co-owners of the concern" (p. 204).

As to the common use of private property that Saint Thomas requires, this is derived "in the first place from the prime universal purpose of material goods," which are dedicated "not to individual men but to man, to humankind" (p. 206). In Maritain's interpretation, common use implies much more than the surrender of surpluses. It is a universal rule requiring that an individual act of consumption or enjoyment be governed by reason rather than by greed. Such an act, since it sustains the individual's physical or intellectual mechanism, is common use by virtue of the "fact that this mechanism must itself serve the common good" (p. 207). But the principle of common use also calls for a management of private property that serves the common good (p. 208). In this connection Maritain emphasizes "the necessity of an organization—a social structure—that will ensure a certain measure of employment for all and also a certain administrative responsibility for all" (p. 209). The law of common use "can only be inadequately safeguarded by the state, its spiritual foundation resting in the last resort on human personality and on love" (p. 211).

For a pronouncedly critical appraisal of modern economic organization and the institution of private property in the light of the teachings of Saint Thomas see A. Horvath, O.P., **Eigentumsrecht nach dem heiligen Thomas von Aquin** (Graz: Moser, 1929), who derives the right to private property from labor. Labor is interpreted broadly as any human activity designed to facilitate common enjoyment. Private property is to serve as an organizational device for the natural, common use of goods. The book contains proposals for the distribution of the social surplus. For discussion, see **Bulletin Thomiste**, Vol. 7 (1932), 373f., 602–6.

Two other leading theologians of the Middle Ages who contributed to the development of economic thought were Saint Bernardine (1380–1444) and Saint Antoninus (1389–1459). Both were well acquainted with the commercial practices prevailing in the flourishing Italian cities of their time and gave much attention to questions of business ethics. The interpretation of their work by later thinkers has varied; some have considered them as forerunners of a labor theory of value, others make the utility theory stem from them, and still others see in them precursors of both theories of value. In a very advanced fashion, which, however, found little following, they interpreted the value of a good as being derived from the existence of a subjective desire for it (*complacibilitas*), its objective ability to satisfy such a desire (*virtuositas*), and its scarcity (*raritas*). See Bede Jarrett, **S. Antonino and Mediaeval Economics** (London: B. Herder, 1914), who recounts this theory of valuation on p. 69, but who on p. 64 says: "S. Antonino insists on the principle rightly understood, which Karl Marx in recent years has made so popular, that the value of things commercial (i.e., exchangeable) depends upon labor, whether of head or hand." In line with this thought, Richard H. Tawney declared: "The true descendant of the doctrines of Aquinas is the labor theory of value. The last of the Schoolmen was Karl Marx"— **Religion and the Rise of Capitalism** (New York: Harcourt, Brace & World, Inc., 1937), p. 36. For a critique of this view, see Noonan, **Usury**, pp. 396f.; Raymond de Roover, **San Bernardino of Siena and Sant 'Antonino of Florence: the Two Great Economic Thinkers of the Middle Ages**, Publication No. 19 of the Kress Library of Business and Economics (Boston: Harvard Graduate School of Business Administration, Baker Library, 1967), who concludes that the two theologians "should perhaps be considered as the originators of utility theory." On Saint Antonino and Saint Bernardine see also August Pfister, "Die Wirtschaftsethik Antonins von Florenz" (Dissertation, Fribourg, 1946); Carl Ilgner, **Die volkswirtschaftlichen Anschauungen Antonins von Florenz** (Paderborn: Ferdinand Schöningh, 1904); A. A. Crosara, **La Dottrina di S. Antonino di Firenze** (Rome: Editrice Studium, 1960); A. G. Ferrers Howell, **S. Bernardine of Siena** (London: Methuen & Co., Ltd., 1913); Alberto E. Trugenberger, **San Bernardino da Siena: Considerazioni sullo sviluppo dell' etica economica cristiana nel primo Rinascimento** (Bern: A. Francke Verlag AG, 1951).

Saint Antoninus's writings contain an observation to the effect that when gold is hoarded it becomes scarce and more goods will be given for the same amount of money—an early anticipation of the quantity theory of money. See Arthur E. Monroe, **Monetary Theory before Adam Smith** (Cambridge, Mass.: Harvard University Press, 1923), p. 26.

Some points made by the Franciscans of the British Isles may also be noted. John Duns Scotus (1265–1308), known as the "Subtle Doctor," identified the just price with cost of production rather than with the current price and thereby established a tradition that gained some following. Had this been the leading view it would have buttressed further the conservative tendency of the medieval price system because of the difficulty of dislodging producers who could claim, as a matter of justice, recovery of their cost. William of Occam (died c. 1349), the "Invincible Doctor," did not directly contribute to economic doctrine, but his influence and that of his followers on the development of English thought and specifically of the social sciences must not be underrated, because his nominalism broke with the prevailing philosophy of "realism" or universalism. This was a controversy that treated of the relationship between general concepts and individual things. The realists were inclined to attach logical priority and independent existence to general concepts. The nominalists taught that universals such as collective entities and general concepts have no independent existence but are mere generalizations of individuals, artifacts constructed by the human mind. The tradition of British philosophy and of modern social science, with their stress on individualism, empiricism, and measurement, has been nurtured by the thought of the nominalists. Modern economic thought is strictly nominalistic; no economist would deny that such concepts as the price level, the demand for goods, or the supply of money are constructions of the human mind that have no independent or "real" existence of their own. On this matter see Karl Pribram, **Conflicting Patterns of Thought** (Washington, D.C.: Public Affairs Press, 1949). On Duns Scotus and William of Occam see Max Beer, **Early British Economics** (London: George Allen & Unwin Ltd., 1938), pp. 45–51, 54–56.

CHAPTER 4

• Bodin, Jean, **The Response to the Paradoxes of Malestroit and the Paradoxes**, translated from the French 2nd edition (1578) by G. A. Moore (Chevy Chase, Md.: The Country Dollar Press, 1946). Sections of the book are translated also by Arthur E. Monroe, **Early Economic Thought** (Cambridge, Mass.: Harvard University Press, 1924), pp. 121–42, and in **Introduction to Contemporary Civilization in the West,** a source book prepared by the Contemporary Civilization Staff of Columbia University (New York: Columbia University Press, 1946), Vol. 1, 350–63. An especially valuable edition, with a long introduction by the editor, is that by Henry Hauser, **La Vie chère au xviᵉ siècle: La Response de Jean Bodin à M. de Malestroit** (Paris: Librairie Armand Colin, 1932). The standard work about Bodin is Henri Baudrillart, **Jean Bodin et son temps** (Paris: Guillaumin et Cie., 1853), reprinted 1963. Bodin's economic views have been discussed by a member of his family, Jean Bodin de Saint-Laurent, **Les Idées monétaires et commerciales de Jean Bodin** (Bordeaux: Y. Cadoret, 1907). This author points out that the influence of American treasure on European prices was first noted by Noël du Fail in 1548, twenty years ahead of Bodin (pp. 34f.), a view endorsed by the authority of Edwin R. A. Seligman, "Bullionists," **Encyclopaedia of the Social Sciences** (New York: The Macmillan Company, 1930), Vol. 3, 61. See also, above, p. 699, on Saint Antoninus as precursor of the quantity theory.

On Bodin as an economist see also Ernst Oberfohren, "Jean Bodin und seine Schule: Untersuchungen über die Frühzeit der Universalökonomie," **Weltwirtschaftliches Archiv**, Vol. 1 (April, 1913), 249–85; Paul Harsin, "L'afflux des métaux précieux au xviᵉ siècle et la théorie de la monnaie chez les auteurs français," **Revue d'histoire économique et sociale**, Vol. 15 (1927), 321–50; Henri Hauser, "Un précurseur, Jean Bodin, Angevin," **Annales d'histoire économique et sociale**, Vol. 3 (1931), 379–87; Jean-Yves le Branchu, "La théorie quantitative de la monnaie au xviᵉ siècle," **Revue d'économie politique**, Vol. 48 (1934), 1241–56.

Book 6 of Bodin's **Republic** treats of questions of public finance. There are enumerated such sources of public revenue as public lands, tributes from defeated enemies, donations from abroad or from the country's own citizens, contributions of allies, public trading, duties on foreign trade, and taxes. Bodin endorses public trading with the remark that it is better if the prince is a trader than a tyrant and that it is better for the noblemen to trade than to steal. Among the taxes Bodin favors special-purpose taxes because, since the connection between these taxes and the benefits is conspicuous, they meet with less resistance than general taxes. On his views about public finance see M. E. Kamp, **Die Staatswirtschaftslehre Jean Bodins** (Bonn: Ludwig Röhrscheid, 1949).

Bodin's contributions to political thought are ably discussed by William Ebenstein, **Great Political Thinkers**, 3rd ed. (New York: Holt, Rinehart & Winston, Inc., 1960), pp. 344–48; George H. Sabine, **A History of Political Theory**, 3rd ed. (New York: Holt, Rinehart & Winston, Inc., 1961), pp. 399–414; John Plamenatz, **Man and Society** (New York: McGraw-Hill Book Company, 1963), Vol. 1, 89–115. His connection with the rise of the idea of progress is illuminated by J. B. Bury, **The Idea of Progress** (New York: The Macmillan Company, 1932), pp. 37–44, who says: "he comes nearer to the idea of progress than any one before him; he is on the threshold" (p. 43).

• Copernicus, Nicholas, **Monetae cudendae ratio** (1526). A reprint of the Latin text, with a French translation, may be found in M. L. Wolowski, ed., **Traictie de la première invention des monnoies de Nicole Oresme** (Paris: Guillaumin et Cie., 1864). Another French version is in Jean-Yves le Branchu, ed., **Ecrits notables sur la monnaie (xviᵉ siècle) de Copernic à Davanzati** (Paris: Félix Alcan, 1934), Vol. 1, 5–27. For comment, see J. Jastrow,

"Kopernikus' Münz- und Geldtheorie," **Archiv für Sozialwissenschaft und Sozial-politik**, Vol. 38 (1914), 734–51; J. Dmochowski, "Nicolas Copernic, écono-miste," **Revue d'économie politique**, Vol. 39 (1925), 100–126; E. Lipinski, **De Copernic à Stanislas Leszcynski—la pen-sée économique et démographique en Pologne** (Paris: Presses Universitaires de France, 1961). See also T. Guggenheim, "Some Early Views on Monetary Integra-tion," in **The Economics of Common Currencies**, ed. H. G. Johnson and A. K. Swoboda (Cambridge: Harvard University Press, 1973) on Copernicus, Bodin, and others.

• Dumoulin, Charles (Molinaeus), **Trea-tise on Contracts and Usury**. The original edition of 1546 contains around 360 pages. A brief selection is translated by Monroe, **Early Economic Thought**, pp. 103–20. Whether and to what extent Dumoulin was influenced by Calvin is an open question. In the beginning of Dumoulin's work there is an obscure allusion to forerunners. Calvin's thoughts on interest can be found in interpretations of the Bible published in the 1550s and in a letter dated November 7, 1545, which was published for the first time in 1575. Böhm-Bawerk, Tawney and others refer to this letter as addressed to the German reformer Oecolampadius, but the latter had died in 1531, fourteen years before Calvin's letter was written.

For a brief appraisal of Dumoulin by a famous nineteenth century economist who authored a distinguished doctrinal history of interest theories, see Eugen von Böhm-Bawerk, **Capital and Interest**, first published in 1884 (South Holland, Ill.: Libertarian Press, 1959), Vol. 1, 18–22. On Dumoulin's treatment of money as a standard of deferred payments see Walter Taeuber, **Molinaeus' Geldschuldlehre** (Stuttgart: Gustav Fischer Verlag, 1928).

• Hales, John, **A Discourse of the Commonweal of This Realm of England** (1581), ed. Elizabeth Lamond (London: Cambridge University Press, 1893). For an appraisal of Hales see E. A. J. Johnson, **Predecessors of Adam Smith** (Englewood Cliffs, N.J.: Prentice-Hall, Inc., 1937), pp. 19–37, where the self-taught Hales is characterized as a human-ist: "Stylistically and textually Hales' **Dis-course** is a humanist document: man is in the center of his thought, the object of his solicitude" (p. 21). The authorship of Hales is still a controversial matter. An earlier suggestion that the **Discourse** was written by Sir Thomas Smith has been discussed and rejected as having "no great probability" by Miss Lamond in the intro-duction to her edition (pp. 28–29). More recently it has been given support by le Branchu, **Monnaie** (p. 700, above), Vol. 1, lxi-lxxx, as well as by Mary Dewar, **Thomas Smith** (London: Athlone Press of the University of London, 1964). Dewar also has published a new edition of the **Dis-course** (Charlottesville: University Press of Virginia for the Folger Shakespeare Library, 1969).

• Hegeland, Hugo, **The Quantity Theory of Money** (Göteborg: Elanders Boktrycke-ri, 1951), contains the most complete and up-to-date discussion of the rise of the quantity theory of money. Hegeland dis-tinguishes three principal variants of the quantity theory. The first variant is an arithmetic relation of proportionality be-tween the quantity of money and the value of the monetary unit: "Ceteris pari-bus, average prices are always in propor-tion to the quantity of money." The second variant adds an element of causal-ity: "if other things remain the same, changes in the quantity of money *cause* proportionate price changes." In the third variant, considered by Hegeland to be the correct one, changes in the quantity of money are related to the velocity of circulation, while the effect on prices "is a secondary question" (pp. 1f.). Hegeland considers it likely that Locke was the true founder of the quantity theory, but he endorses the view that Bodin "did in-fluence its *formulation*, so that the kernel of the theory was misunderstood" (p. 17). See also Arthur E. Monroe, **Monetary Theory before Adam Smith** (Cambridge, Mass.: Harvard University Press, 1923), esp. p. 58; Paul Lambert, **La théorie quantitative de la monnaie** (Paris: Edi-tions Sirey, 1938).

• Keynes, John M., **A Treatise on Money**, 2 vols. (New York: Harcourt, Brace & World, Inc., 1930). Here Keynes comments on the importance of American treasure for the economic development of Europe in the sixteenth and seventeenth centuries. He considers the ensuing profit inflation in the European countries as a stimulus to economic growth (Vol. 2, 148–63) and remarks: "Never in the annals of the modern world has there existed so prolonged and rich an opportunity for the businessman, the speculator, and the profiteer. In these golden years modern capitalism was born" (p. 159). For critical comments see E. Lipson, **The Economic History of England**, Vol. 2, 6th ed. (New York: Barnes & Noble, Inc., 1956), xviii.

• Machiavelli, Niccolò, **The Prince**, first published in 1532, with English translations available in many editions (e.g., London: Oxford University Press, World Classics, 1935). Machiavelli is chiefly remembered in the history of political thought. With one exception, the incidental remarks that he makes about economic matters are not noteworthy. The exception is found in a statement that concludes Chap. 8 of the **Prince** and that indicates that Machiavelli had recognized the principle of diminishing utility. He advises the prince to commit necessary cruelties at once, while distributing benefits over time: "Injuries should be done all together, so that being less tasted, they will give less offence. Benefits should be granted little by little, so that they may be better enjoyed."

• Merton, Robert K., "Priorities in Scientific Discovery: A Chapter in the Sociology of Science," **American Sociological Review**, Vol. 22, No. 6 (December, 1957), 635–59; "Singletons and Multiples in Scientific Discovery: A Chapter in the Sociology of Science," **Proceedings**, of the American Philosophical Society, Vol. 105, No. 5 (October, 1961), 470–86; "Resistance to the Systematic Study of Multiple Discoveries in Science," **European Journal of Sociology**, Vol. 4 (1963), 237–82. These articles, the first of which was the author's presidential address read before the American Sociological Society, treat of the sociological significance of multiple discoveries, of which the quantity theory of money and many other contributions to economics may serve as illustrations. Professor Merton has established the

hypothesis "that all scientific discoveries are in principle multiples, including those that on the surface appear to be singletons" ("Singletons and Multiples," p. 477).

• Navarrus [Martín de Azpilcueta], **Comentario resolutorio de usuras** (1556). Sections of this work are available in an English translation by Marjorie Grice-Hutchinson, **The School of Salamanca: Readings in Spanish Monetary Theory 1544–1605** (London: Oxford University Press, Clarendon Press, 1952), pp. 89–96. Excerpts from the writings of other members of the Spanish school as well as a general appraisal of its contributions may be found in the same book. More recently the same author published **Early Economic Thought in Spain, 1177–1740** (London: Allen & Unwin, 1978), which is broader in scope and in the time period covered than the earlier work.

Information about the respective times spent by Navarrus and Bodin at the University of Toulouse was supplied by the librarian of the university in a communication dated May 15, 1964. That relating to Navarrus was drawn from **Dictionnaire d'histoire et de géographie ecclésiastique**, art. "Azpilcueta," Vol. 5, Col. 1368; that relating to Bodin from an unpublished thesis by Maurice Duby, "Jean Bodin et Toulouse," (Faculté de Droit de Toulouse, 1944). Bernard W. Dempsey, S.J., "The Historical Emergence of Quantity Theory," **Quarterly Journal of Economics**, Vol. 50, No. 1 (November, 1935), 174–84, draws attention to the Spanish school, which he considers as unjustly neglected by historians of economic thought. He does not point out, however, the significance of Navarrus, whose book antedates that of Bodin by twelve years, but mainly that of Luis Molina (1535–1600), whose discussion of the influence of American treasure on prices dates of the 1590s. See also "Comments" by Earl Hamilton, **Quarterly Journal of Economics**, Vol. 50, No. 1, 185–92. Hamilton's **American Treasure and the Price Revolution in Spain** (Cambridge, Mass.: Harvard University Press, 1934), is the authoritative work on the subject indicated by the title. Hamilton mentions another Spaniard, Francisco López de

Gómara, as having recognized the price-raising effects of this influx of American precious metals as early as about 1558.

On Juan de Mariana, still another Spanish writer, see John Laures, S.J., **The Political Economy of Juan de Mariana** (Bronx, N.Y.: Fordham University Press, 1928), with a foreword by E. R. A. Seligman. Seligman remarks: "In the field of the history of economics there are still vast tracts untilled and even uncleared. Among the more important of these unreclaimed stretches is the economic literature of Spain" (p. 5). The publication of Grice-Hutchinson's books has been of help in bringing the gap to a close. See also José Larraz López, **La época del mercantilismo en Castilla (1500–1700)** (Madrid: Ediciones Atlas, 1943), 2d ed.; Dmetrio Iparraguirre, S.J., "Las fuentes del pensiamento económico en España en los siglos xiii al xvi," **Estudios de Deusto**, Vol. 2, (1954), 79–113; Alberto Ullastres Calvo, "Martín de Azpilcueta y su comentario resolutorio de cambios; las ideas económicas de un moralista español del siglo xvi," **Anales de Economia**, Vol. 1 (1941), 375–407, and Vol. 2 (1942), 52–95.

• Schmoller, Gustav, "Zur Geschichte der nationalökonomischen Ansichten in Deutschland während der Reformations-Periode," **Zeitschrift für die gesamte Staatswissenschaft**, Vol. 16, Nos. 3 and 4 (1860), 461–716. This is a survey of the economic thought of the German reformers, especially of Martin Luther, by the leading member of the "younger" historical school of economics. "Liberation from authority was the watchword of the reformation . . . but in all matters that were not ecclesiastical, especially in the political ones, the reformers clung to the traditional authorities with a tenacity recalling the Schoolmen. Thus, when economic matters are involved, they like to return to Aristotle" (p. 470). Luther and the reformers praise agricultural activities, whether carried on by noblemen or by peasants, and deprecate crafts and trades. Luther claims to be unable to understand how any one can make real gain from anything but cattle and land because "goods are produced by God's grace rather than by human wit," an attitude which

Schmoller compares with that of the Physiocrats (p. 474). Luther's ideal is price fixing by public authorities (p. 493). He condemns the great trading companies as monopolies (p. 496). When wages lagged behind rising prices, Luther stands out among those who condemn pleas for higher wages as inspired by selfishness and insolence. Laborers must be treated with strict discipline (p. 513). In conclusion, Schmoller interprets the economic thought of the German reformers as follows: "In many respects it represents a step backwards, but only apparently so, compared with the views preceding the Reformation, which in some respects were freer. The ideal-transcendent one-sidedness of the Middle Ages, which had its basic principle in an exclusively otherworldly faith representing a break with material reality, had long ago been destroyed by the secularization of this principle in science, politics, and art. The positive powers of reality, among which the economic life of nations stands out, had penetrated into life and fought for recognition, but had thereby negated the basic principle of the Middle Ages and undermined and destroyed the structure of medieval culture. The ensuing decomposition required a new, inner reconciliation of the spirit and of the world, of ideal and reality, and found this in the principle of Protestantism as it affected at first only ecclesiastical matters. The application of this principle to all fields of life is a task for centuries, one for the whole modern era. . ." (p. 714). See also F. Edward Cranz, **An Essay on the Development of Luther's Thought on Justice, Law and Society**, Harvard Theological Studies 19, issued as an extra number of the **Harvard Theological Review**, 1959.

• Shipton, Clifford K., "The Hebraic Background of Puritanism," **Publications** of the American Jewish Historical Society, Vol. 47, No. 3 (March, 1958), 140–53. On the Puritans' exaltation of the Old Testament and the Law of Moses. See also Harold Fisch, **Jerusalem and Albion** (New York: Schocken Books, Inc., 1964); Joseph Gaer and Ben Siegel, **The Puritan Heritage: America's Roots in the Bible** (New York: The New American Library Inc.,

1964); Louis Israel Newman, **Jewish Influence on Christian Reform Movements** (New York: Columbia University Press, 1925), pp. 631ff., on "Hebraic Aspects of American Puritanism;" Milton R. Konvitz, **Judaism and the American Idea** (Ithaca, N.Y.: Cornell University Press, 1978).

• Weber, Max, **The Protestant Ethic and the Spirit of Capitalism**, transl. Talcott Parsons, with a foreword by R. H. Tawney (New York: Charles Scribner's Sons, 1930). Originally published in German (1904–5), this study by the then greatest social scientist in Germany was to have far-reaching effects on the thought of economists and historians. Here Weber (1864–1920) develops his famous thesis of the Calvinist influence on the rise of capitalism. Weber studied the relation between religion and economics in a number of other important works. He also gave some thought to the question whether the chain of causation runs from religion to economic conditions or the other way around. In his work on the Protestant ethic he says: "Here we have only attempted to trace the fact and the direction of its influence . . . in one, though a very important point. But it would also further be necessary to investigate how Protestant asceticism was in turn influenced in its development and its character by the totality of social conditions, especially economic. . . . It is, of course, not my aim to substitute for a one-sided materialistic an equally one-sided spiritualistic causal explanation of culture and of history. Each is equally possible, but each, if it does not serve as the preparation, but as the conclusion of an investigation, accomplishes equally little in the interest of historical truth" (p. 183).

Those who have criticized Weber's thesis of the relation between capitalism and Calvinism often represent him as much more dogmatic than he really was. "We have no intention whatever," he said, "of maintaining such a foolish and doctrinaire thesis as that the spirit of capitalism . . . could only have arisen as the result of certain effects of the Reformation, or even that capitalism as an economic system is a creation of the Reformation. . . . We only wish to ascertain whether and to what

extent religious forces have taken part in the qualitative formation and the quantitive expansion of that spirit over the world" (p. 91).

Just as influential as Weber's book was the subsequent elaboration of the theme by R. H. Tawney, **Religion and the Rise of Capitalism**, originally published in 1926 (New York: Harcourt, Brace & World, Inc., 1937; The Times Mirror Co., The New American Library Inc., 1947). Tawney (1880–1961) was one of England's leading economic historians, whose verve of style and profound moral sense give his writings an inimitable touch. His views about the matter are no more dogmatic than were Weber's. "The capitalist spirit," he says, "is as old as history, and was not, as has sometimes been said, the offspring of Puritanism. But it found in certain aspects of later Puritanism a tonic which braced its energies and fortified its already vigorous temper" (pp. 226f.).

Tawney's work is continued by the economic historian Christopher Hill, **Society and Puritanism in Pre-Revolutionary England** (London: Martin Secker & Warburg Ltd., 1964). For a brief statement by the same author, see "Protestantism and the Rise of Capitalism," **Essays in the Economic and Social History of Tudor and Stuart England: in Honour of R. H. Tawney**, ed. F. J. Fisher (London: Cambridge University Press, 1961), pp. 15–39, where he says: "There is nothing in Protestantism which leads automatically to capitalism; its importance was rather that it undermined obstacles which the more rigid institutions and ceremonies of Catholicism imposed" (p. 36). Hill's essay has been reprinted in his **Change and Continuity in Seventeenth-Century England** (London: Weidenfeld & Nicolson, 1974).

For an interpretation of the matter by a student of religious thought see Ernst Troeltsch, **The Social Teaching of the Christian Churches** (New York: The Macmillan Company, 1931), Vol. 2, on Protestantism. On "The Lutheran Ethic and Economic Questions," see pp. 554–60; on "The Ethic of Calvinism," pp. 602–17. See also Troeltsch's **Protestantism and Progress** (Boston: Beacon Press, 1958). One of the Catholic contributions to the debate reflects the views of Weber and Troeltsch; see George O'Brien, **An Essay on the Economic Effects of the Reformation**, originally published in 1923, (reprinted Westminster, Md.: The Newman Bookshop, 1944). O'Brien considers both capitalism and socialism as "the result of the Protestant Reformation" (p. 170).

On Calvin's economic ideas there is a full-length study by André Biéler, **La Pensée économique et sociale de Calvin** (Geneva: Librairie de l'Université, Georg & Cie., 1961). As others have done before him, Biéler points out that a distinction must be made between the thought of Calvin and that of his followers in later times. "It is not allowed to attribute to Calvin and to original Calvinism the influence, which for good or bad their later descendants could have exercised on the development of capitalism" (p. 512). "There is no doubt that Calvin has assigned to economic activity and to money a place which they did not hold before . . . but it is not possible in honesty to attribute to Calvin the responsibility for the evolution of capitalism in its historical form. This could develop, in this form, among the Protestant peoples, only under the influence of a relaxation of the Reformed doctrine and ethic" (pp. 513f). For a detailed discussion of Calvin's views on interest see pp. 453–76. Calvin's letter of 1545 may be found in his **Opera quae supersunt omnia** (Braunschweig: C. A. Schwetschke & Sohn, 1863–1900), 59 vols., Vol. 10, 245.

The German economic historian Werner Sombart criticized Weber at least by implication in developing a number of alternative interpretations of the rise of capitalism—for example, the growth of economic rationalism. "Economic activities are ruled by cold reason, by thought. As we have already seen, that has always been the case; it showed itself in the making of plans, in considering whether any policy was likely to be successful or not, and in calculation generally. The modern capitalist spirit differs from its predecessors only in the degree in which this rule is obeyed. Today the rule is strictly, one might almost say sternly, enforced. The last trace of traditionalism has vanished"—**The Quintessence of Capi-** talism, trans. and ed. M. Epstein (New York: E. P. Dutton & Co., Inc., 1915), p. 182. For a reply see Max Weber, **Protestant Ethic and Capitalism**, pp. 75–78. See also Sombart's article on "Capitalism," **Encyclopaedia of the Social Sciences** (New York: The Macmillan Company, 1930), Vol. 3, 195–208, and Frank H. Knight, "Historical and Theoretical Issues in the Problem of Modern Capitalism," **Journal of Economics and Business History**, Vol. 1, No. 1 (November, 1928), reprinted in **On the History and Method of Economics** (Chicago: The University of Chicago Press, 1956), pp. 89–103.

A related view places the beginnings of capitalism in the medieval monasteries, especially the Benedictine ones, whose members were bound by a strict discipline that imposed on them a life of regularity and hard work and which brought with it the use of clocks, record keeping, efficient administration and accumulation of capital. Success invited imitation. See the article by H. E. Hallam in Eugene Kamenka and R. S. Neale, eds., **Feudalism, Capitalism and Beyond** (New York: St. Martin's Press, 1976). However, other authorities stress the change from monasticism to mendicant poverty — L. K. Little, **Religious Poverty and the Profit Economy in Medieval Europe** (Ithaca, N.Y.: Cornell University Press, 1978) —or the recognition of purgatory, proclaimed in 1254, as a refuge of the sinful usurer. See Jacques Le Goff's contribution to a publication of the Center for Medieval and Renaissance Studies, University of California, Los Angeles, **The Dawn of Modern Banking** (New Haven: Yale University Press, 1979), and his **La Naissance du purgatoire** (Paris: Gallimard, 1982).

The role of the thought of the Jansenists—sometimes referred to as Catholic Calvinists—deserves further exploration. In the writings of Pierre Nicole (1625–95) society is interpreted alternatively in terms of charity and self-interest; cf. below, p. 729. The Jansenists shared the belief in predestination with the Calvinists, but their doctrine of a calling was substantially different. For this reason it has been denied that their thought has played a role in the development of capitalism; see

Paul Honigsheim, "Die Staats- und Sozial-lehren der französischen Jansenisten im 17. Jahrhundert" (historical dissertation, Heidelberg, 1914), pp. 139–55.

A critique of Weber's view that emphasizes the role of the Jesuits rather than that of the Calvinists is H. M. Robertson, **Aspects of the Rise of Economic Individualism** (London: Cambridge University Press, 1933), which in turn was criticized by James Brodrick, S.J., **The Economic Morals of the Jesuits** (London: Oxford University Press, 1934). Written also from a Catholic point of view, but quite different in its interpretation, is the work of A. Fanfani, who later was to become Premier of Italy: **Catholicism, Protestantism and Capitalism**, first published in 1934 (New York: Sheed & Ward, 1955). Fanfani considered the spirit of capitalism as alien to any kind of religion. If Protestantism had an effect on economic development, it did so because it brought about a release from religious inhibitions.

The idea that it was not religion but secularism and materialism that have ushered in the modern economic world is expressed also by Lewis S. Feuer, **The Scientific Intellectual: The Psychological and Sociological Origins of Modern Science** (New York: Basic Books, Inc., Publishers, 1963). Related views, directly aiming at the refutation of the Weber thesis, are found in Kurt Samuelsson, **Religion and Economic Action** (New York: Basic Books, Inc., Publishers, 1961). "Mercantilism, the Enlightenment, Darwinism, economic liberalism—all these systems of thought, in which a central role was played by economic expansion and the belief in a better future for nations or men through the increase of capital and the raising of the standard of welfare—cut across all religious creeds, or went over or around them." The verses from the Sermon on the Mount condemning the gathering of treasure "are fundamental to the Christian outlook. No matter what the church or sect, the guiding principle is the renunciation of the world" (pp. 151f.). It is doubtful whether Samuelsson does justice to the finer shades of thought of the writers he criticizes.

How suggestive and fruitful the Weber thesis has been is illustrated by the fact that the idea still resounds in the social-science literature. See, for example, David Riesman, **The Lonely Crowd** (New Haven, Conn.: Yale University Press, 1950), whose types of inner- and outer-directed motivation echo the work of Weber, the former type of motivation reflecting the influence of the Puritan ethic. Another illustration is Vianna Moog's **Bandeirantes and Pioneers** (New York: George Braziller, Inc., 1964), a comparative history of the United States and Brazil that contrasts the motivations and institutions of the Portuguese and Spanish colonizers with those of the North American settlers. See also J. E. Crowley, **This Seba, Self: The Conceptualization of Economic Life in Eighteenth-Century America** (Baltimore: Johns Hopkins University Press, 1974); Gordon Marshall, **Presbyteries and Profits: Calvinism and the Development of Capitalism in Scotland, 1560–1707** (New York: Oxford University Press, 1980).

For some fresh thought on the matter see also Jacob Viner, **Religious Thought and Economic Society** (Durham, N.C.: Duke University Press, 1978), Chap. 4 on Protestantism and the rise of capitalism; Herbert Lüthy, **From Calvin to Rousseau** (New York: Basic Books, Inc., Publishers, 1970); Agnes Heller, **Renaissance Man**, trans. by Richard E. Allen (New York: Schocken Books, Inc., 1981), who refers to the Italian philosopher Pietro Pomponazzi (1462–1525), who in his **Treatise on the Immortality of the Soul** discussed division of labor as a device to facilitate self-realization and thereby increase human happiness. For a selection of writings by Weber, Troeltsch, Sombart, Tawney, Robertson, Fanfani, and other contributors to the debate see Robert W. Green, ed., **Protestantism and Capitalism: The Weber Thesis and Its Critics** (Lexington, Mass.: Raytheon Education Company, D. C. Heath & Company, 1959). See also Gabriel Kolko, "Max Weber on America: Theory and Evidence," **History and Theory**, Vol. 1, No. 3 (1961), 348–70.

• Wilson, Thomas, **A Discourse Upon Usury** (1572), edited, with an historical introduction, by R. H. Tawney (London: G. Bell & Sons, Ltd., 1925). In an introduction of some 170 pages, Tawney places Wilson's work into the setting of its time. He discusses the principal types of credit transactions and public policy vis-à-vis the moneylenders. Of Wilson he says: "The economic outlook, the preoccupation with morality which he inherited, was that of the Middle Ages, and his target was the individualism which was destroying it." Wilson belonged to a tradition "whose social philosophy was based ultimately on religion," which "saw in the economic enterprise of an age which enclosed land and speculated on the ex-

changes, not the crudities of a young and brilliant civilization, but the collapse of public morality in a welter of disorderly appetites" (pp. 14f.).

Tawney's account of foreign-exchange transactions may be supplemented by Raymond de Roover's **Gresham on Foreign Exchange** (Cambridge, Mass.: Harvard University Press, 1949), which ostensibly treats of the Elizabethan financier whose name is connected with the famous "law," but which actually constitutes a full-fledged treatise on the difficult subject of foreign exchange in thought and practice during the sixteenth and seventeenth centuries.

CHAPTER 5

• Angell, James W., **The Theory of International Prices** (Cambridge, Mass.: Harvard University Press, 1926), is the standard work on the history of the subject. The mercantilists' thought is linked, on pp. 10-24, both to predecessors and subsequent schools. A more detailed discussion may be found in Chi-Yuen Wu, **An Outline of International Price Theories** (London: Routledge & Kegan Paul Ltd., 1939), pp. 13–74.

• Ashley, W. J., "The Tory Origin of Free Trade," **Quarterly Journal of Economics** (July, 1897), Vol. 11, 335–71, reprinted in **Surveys Historic and Economic** (London: Longmans, Green & Co. Ltd., 1900), pp. 268–303. Ashley claims Barbon, Child, Davenant, and North as Tory forerunners of the free-trade policy. Actually, Child was a Whig, and neither he nor Barbon and Davenant were free traders in the modern sense. On Child see also S. Helander, "Josiah Child," **Weltwirtschaftliches Archiv**, Vol. 19 (1923), 233–49.

• Beer, M., **Early British Economics** (London: George Allen & Unwin Ltd., 1938). Chaps. 6–12 contain a readable survey of mercantilist economics. Beer says of the doctrine that it "will no doubt strike the modern mind as crude, or, perhaps, as utterly irrational." But it "must have answered the interests and

logic of its age." He proposes to show "how the doctrine grew quite naturally, that is, with necessity, out of the commercial, political, and ethical conditions of the realm" (p. 62), an unusually determinist view that might be contrasted with that of Heckscher. For the economic history of the period, see E. Lipson, **The Economic History of England**, Vols. 2 and 3, The Age of Mercantilism, 6th ed. (New York: Barnes & Noble, Inc., 1961). The introduction to Vol. 2 summarizes the material on 150 pages. Lipson has a generally favorable opinion of mercantilism, but he refuses to consider the "planned economy" of the mercantilists as the sole or main factor responsible for the notable advances of the English economy in the seventeenth and eighteenth centuries. He mentions a number of other factors, including the quality of business leadership, the relaxation of traditional restraints, the reign of law, political stability and freedom from invasion, endowment with natural resources such as wheat, wool and coal, favorable location, the spirit of adventure that encompassed the globe, scientific discoveries, the settlement of aliens, the fiscal and banking system, and the cumulative effects of uninterrupted growth (p. 97), to which might be added the weakness of the administrative apparatus designed to enforce mercantilist regulations, which thus lost some of their

708

sting. See also Philip W. Buck, **The Politics of Mercantilism** (New York: Holt, Rinehart & Winston, Inc., 1942); C. H. Wilson, "Trade, Society and the State," in **The Cambridge Economic History of Europe**, Vol. 4, The Economy of Expanding Europe in the Sixteenth and Seventeenth Centuries (London: Cambridge University Press, 1967), 487–575, which includes a survey of the literature of the time.

• De Roover, Raymond, **Gresham on Foreign Exchange** (Cambridge, Mass.: Harvard University Press, 1949). While ostensibly devoted to the analysis of a manuscript ascribed to Gresham, this work contains the best modern discussion of the bullionist controversy. The term "bullionists" was coined by Richard Jones, an exponent of the English historical school in the first half of the nineteenth century and although the usage was endorsed by Seligman, it has not been universally accepted. See Richard Jones, "Primitive Political Economy of England," **Edinburgh Review**, April, 1847, reprinted in his **Literary Remains**, ed. W. Whewell (London: John Murray [Publishers] Ltd., 1859), pp. 291–335; E. R. A. Seligman, "Bullionists," **Encyclopaedia of the Social Sciences**, Vol. 3 (New York: The Macmillan Company, 1930), 60–64; **Curiosities of Early Economic Literature**, privately printed (San Francisco: John Henry Nash, 1920), pp. 7–11. See also Lynn Muchmore, "Gerrard de Malynes and Mercantile Economics," **History of Political Economy**, Vol. 1, No. 2 (Fall, 1969), 336–58.

The phrase "Gresham's law" was coined by Henry D. MacLeod, **Elements of Political Economy** (London: Longmans, Green & Co., Ltd., 1857), p. 477, but the underlying idea was expressed by a number of earlier writers and can in fact be traced back to Aristophanes. See also Frank W. Fetter, "Some Neglected Aspects of Gresham's Law," **Quarterly Journal of Economics**, Vol. 46 (1931–32), 480–95.

• Furniss, Edgar S., **The Position of the Laborer in a System of Nationalism**, originally published in 1920 (reprinted New York: Augustus M. Kelley, Publishers, 1957), is the standard work on mercantilist policies affecting labor and employment. Furniss compares the position of the laborer under mercantilism with that under a regime of laissez-faire. Under the latter wages are related to productivity as appraised by the employer, and labor's social utility is also defined in terms of productivity. Under mercantilism labor is valued as an instrument designed to attain national goals, and the social value of a laborer bears "no logical connection with the value of his services to individuals" (p. 199). Hence the allocation and remuneration are determined more by public policy than by the forces of the market. See also D. C. Coleman, "Labour in the English Economy of the Seventeenth Century," **Economic History Review**, 2nd series, Vol. 8, No. 3 (1956), 280–95, reprinted in E. M. Carus-Wilson, ed., **Essays in Economic History**, Vol. 2 (London: Edward Arnold [Publishers] Ltd., 1962), 291–308; T. E. Gregory, "The Economics of Employment in England, 1660–1713," **Economica**, Vol. 1, 37–51 (January, 1921), reprinted in **Gold, Unemployment, and Capitalism** (London: P.S. King and Son, 1933); N. G. Pauling, "The Employment Problem in Pre-classical English Thought," **The Economic Record**, Vol. 27, 52–65 (June, 1951).

• Grampp, W. D. "The Liberal Elements in English Mercantilism," **Quarterly Journal of Economics** (November, 1952), Vol. 66, 465–501, draws attention to the liberal elements found in the writings of a number of mercantilists and insists that mercantilist thought must be distinguished from mercantilist practice. For an earlier study of the same topic see A. Schatz and R. Caillemer, "Le mercantilisme libéral à la fin du xviie siècle," **Revue d'économie politique**, 1906, pp. 29–70, 387–96, 559–74, 630–42, 791–816. See also Alfred F. Chalk, "Natural Law and the Rise of Economic Liberalism in England," **Journal of Political Economy** (August, 1951), Vol. 59, No. 4, 332–47, which traces natural-law ideas to the dualism of mercantilist doctrine, which favored the extensive use of statutory law for purposes of economic control but at the same time contains expressions holding up "natural" liberties and reliance on the market. One very advanced writer, who, however, was apparently neglected by his contemporaries, was Isaac Gervaise, who was rediscovered by Foxwell and to whom Jacob Viner has called attention. See the new edition of his work, originally published in 1720, **The System or Theory of the Trade of the World**, with an introduction by J. M. Letiche (Baltimore: The Johns Hopkins Press, 1954). See also Joyce Oldham Appleby, **Economic Thought and Ideology in Seventeenth-Century England** (Princeton: Princeton University Press, 1978) for a survey of mercantilist thought by a professional historian.

• Hamilton, Earl J., ably reviews the work of the Spanish Mercantilists in two articles, "Spanish Mercantilism before 1700," **Facts and Factors in Economic History**, articles by former students of Edwin Francis Gay (Cambridge, Mass.: Harvard University Press, 1932), pp. 214–39, and "The Mercantilism of Gerónimo de Uztáriz: A Reexamination," **Economics, Sociology and the Modern World**, essays in honor of T. N. Carver, ed. Norman E. Himes (Cambridge, Mass.: Harvard University Press, 1935). Additional references may be found in these articles. About Uztáriz (1670–1732) Professor Hamilton says: "No other Spanish economist has received comparable recognition or adulation either at home or abroad" (p. 126). Yet, "one finds in Uztáriz's **Teórica** strikingly few acute generalizations, no discoveries of economic laws, and no penetrating analyses of economic phenomena such as abound in the works of, say, Sir William Petty and Richard Cantillon. . . .Uztáriz's outstanding achievement as a theorist was his unequivocal contention that population depends upon economic conditions rather than vice versa" (p. 128). However, in 1724, when Uztáriz's **Teórica** appeared, this thought was no longer new. Sir Josiah Child had already argued that "the increase of trade and improvement of lands" stimulates population growth. "Not that it causes married men to get more children, but . . . a trading country affording comfortable subsistences to more families than a country destitute of trade, is the reason that many do marry, who otherwise must be forced to live single"— **A New Discourse of Trade**, 2d ed. (London: Sam Crouch, 1694), p. 58. On the

spread of economic doctrines in Spanish America see Eduardo Arcila Farías, "Ideas económicas en Nueva España en el siglo xviii," **El Trimestre Económico**, Vol. 14, No. 1 (April-June, 1947), 68–82.

• Heckscher, Eli F., **Mercantilism**, rev. ed. E. F. Söderlund, 2 vols. (New York: The Macmillan Company, 1955). This great work interprets mercantilism as a unifying system, a system of power, a system of protection, a monetary system, and as a conception of society. It was written by a Swedish scholar equally at home in the fields of economic history and economic theory, who had a liberal outlook but was nurtured by German scholarship, especially in the field of economic history. Heckscher more than any other writer constructed an all-pervasive system of thought and policy, albeit one upon which he, an exponent of economic liberalism, looks with little sympathy. For a briefer version of Heckscher's ideas see his article on "Mercantilism," **Encyclopaedia of the Social Sciences**, Vol. 10 (New York: The Macmillan Company, 1933), 333–39. Charles W. Cole, the historian of French mercantilism, notices in Heckscher's work "The Heavy Hand of Hegel"—see his essay of the same title in Edward Mead Earle, ed., **Nationalism and Internationalism** (New York: Columbia University Press, 1950), pp. 64–78. By this Cole refers to the tendency to personify abstractions and allow them to become operative entities. Heckscher "makes mercantilism a real entity that brooded immanently over Europe for four or five centuries. . . . As a matter of fact, mercantilism was never an entity, never a system, never a coordinated or coherent body of policy or practice. It varied drastically in different periods and different countries. Those who practiced and preached it never thought of themselves as a school. The very name 'mercantilism' was invented by its opponents when the old ideas were already on the wane" (p. 75). Cole underlines the differences in the "mercantilism" of the various countries. He shows "that Portuguese mercantilism in the sixteenth century was focused on the spice trade, while Spanish mercantilism from 1550 to 1650 centered in American bullion; and Dutch mercantilism in the seventeenth century was built around the carrying trade, while English mercantilism after 1660 was based on colonial commerce" (p. 76).

A related feature of Heckscher's work is its rejection of any form of determinism, that is, its tendency to see economic policies reflect economic ideas rather than be determined by economic conditions. This tendency has been praised by some and criticized by others. On the whole, economic historians have found more fault with Heckscher than have historians of economic thought; see, for example, the review article by Herbert Heaton, **Journal of Political Economy**, Vol. 45 (1937), 370–93; also A. V. Judges, "The Idea of a Mercantile State," **Transactions** of the Royal Historical Society, 4th series, Vol. 21 (1939), 41–69. The latter concludes that mercantilism had neither a coherent doctrine nor an adequate number of accepted principles and that it was an imaginary system, the construction of which compels the student to reconcile ideas that in fact are disparate. In a more recent critique, "Eli Heckscher and the Idea of Mercantilism," **The Scandinavian Economic History Review**, Vol. 5, No. 1 (1957), 3–25, D. C. Coleman, an economic historian, underlines the shortcomings of the work as a study of economic history but concludes that "as a contribution to the history of economic thought, there can be no doubt whatsoever that Heckscher's work remains outstanding, still invaluable to the student of the period" (p. 25). For a reply to Coleman, see A. W. Coats, "In Defense of Heckscher and the Idea of Mercantilism," **The Scandinavian Economic History Review**, Vol. 5, No. 1, 173–87. See also D. C. Coleman, ed., **Revisions in Mercantilism** (London: Methuen & Co. Ltd., 1969), which reprints several contributions to the debate; C. G. Uhr, "Eli F. Heckscher, 1879–1952, and His Treatise on Mercantilism," **Economic History**, Vol. 23, No. 1 (1980), 3–39. For a review of different approaches to the study of mercantilism see also Charles Wilson, " 'Mercantilism': Some Vicissitudes of an Idea," **The Economic History Review**, 2nd series, Vol. 10, No. 2 (1957), 181–88. For a brief introduction to the substance of mercantil-

ism see also the same author's **Mercantilism** (London: for Historical Association, Routledge & Kegan Paul Ltd., 1958), and, for the historical background, his **Profit and Power: A Study of England and the Dutch Wars** (London: Longmans, Green & Co. Ltd., 1957). For an overall view seen through different eyes consult R. W. K. Hinton, "The Mercantile System in the Time of Thomas Mun," **The Economic History Review**, 2nd series, Vol. 7, No. 3 (1955), 277–90. See also Walter E. Minchinton, ed., **Mercantilism: System or Expediency?** (Lexington, Mass.: D. C. Health and Company, 1969); L. R. Muchmore, "A Note on Thomas Mun's 'England's Treasure by Foreign Trade'," **Economic History Review**, Vol. 23, No. 3 (December, 1970), 498–503, about Mun as spokesman of the East India Company.

• Johnson, E. A. J., **Predecessors of Adam Smith** (Englewood Cliffs, N.J.: Prentice-Hall, Inc., 1937). The first and major part of this work contains a series of valuable studies of individual writers beginning with Hales and ending with Steuart. The second part, entitled "A Primitive Theory of Production," is devoted to scholarly studies of the mercantilists' views about population quantity and quality, and about idleness and luxury, as well as of the transformation of the balance-of-trade doctrine into one of balance of labor or employment, aiming at the "exportation of work" and the earning of "foreign-paid incomes." See also the same author's **American Economic Thought in the Seventeenth Century** (New York: Russell & Russell Publishers, 1961).

• Keynes, J. M., **The General Theory of Employment, Interest and Money** (New York: Harcourt, Brace & World, Inc., 1936), Chap. 23, pp. 331–53, contains Keynes's favorable appraisal of mercantilist ideas in the light of his "criticism directed against the inadequacy of the theoretical foundations of the laissez-faire doctrine, upon which I was brought up and which for many years I taught— against the notion that the rate of interest and the volume of investment are self-adjusting at the optimum level, so that preoccupation with the balance of trade is a waste of time" (p. 339). For a critique of

Keynes's appraisal of mercantilism see Heckscher, **Mercantilism**, Vol. 2, 340–58.

• Knorr, Klaus E., **British Colonial Theories 1570–1850** (Toronto: University of Toronto Press, 1944). This standard work on the subject may be supplemented by a briefer study that stresses the historical background rather than economic ideas—C. R. Fay, **Imperial Economy and Its Place in the Formation of Economic Doctrine, 1600–1932** (London: Oxford University Press, Clarendon Press, 1934); also Richard Pares, "The Economic Factors in the History of the Empire," **Economic History Review**, Vol. 7, No. 2 (1937), reprinted in E. M. Carus-Wilson, ed., **Essays in Economic History**, Vol. 1 (London: Edward Arnold [Publishers] Ltd., 1954), 416–38. See also M. Merle, ed., **L'Anticolonialisme européen de Las Casas à Karl Marx** (Paris: Librairie Armand Colin, 1969), a collection of source readings.

• Laspeyres, Étienne, **Geschichte der volkswirtschaftlichen Anschauungen der Niederländer** (Stuttgart: S. Hirzel Verlag KG, 1863). This study has remained the sole interpretive examination of Dutch economic thought of the period, which was surprisingly barren. The author, who is also remembered for his index-number formula, has interesting comments on this aspect of the matter, and his work includes an analysis of Grotius's and Spinoza's contributions to economic thought. On economic thought in Holland during a much later period see Irene H. Butter, **Academic Economics in Holland 1800–1870** (The Hague: Martinus Nijhoff, Publisher, 1969).

• Letwin, William **The Origins of Scientific Economics** (Garden City, N.Y.: Doubleday & Company, Inc., 1964), shows the mercantilist writers grope for a standard of scientific objectivity. The "old style" of such men as Child and Barbon gives way to the "new style" of Petty, Locke, and North who fortify their arguments with the help of quantitative methods, philosophy, and deductive theory. By introducing the methods of historical scholarship and by utilizing unprinted manuscript material on a scale hitherto unparalleled, the author himself has brought new standards to the study of the history of economics.

• Locke, John. Locke's economic tracts may be found in his **Works** as well as in a reprint of J. R. McCulloch's **Principles of Political Economy**, to which they were appended (London: A. Murray and Son [Publishers] Ltd., 1870). His theory of property can be found in Chap. 5, pp. 303–20, of the second of his **Two Treatises of Government**, of which the best edition is by Peter Laslett (London: Cambridge University Press, 1960). See also the valuable introductory remarks by the editor (pp. 100–106). Locke's **Essays on the Law of Nature** were published in Latin and English in an edition by W. von Leyden (London: Oxford University Press, Clarendon Press, 1954). Locke's idea of wealth as fixed fund is expressed in Essay 8, p. 211. References to Locke's work in economics as seen against the broader background of his life and career may be found in the standard biography by Maurice Cranston, **John Locke** (London: Longmans, Green & Co. Ltd., 1957). The quotation illustrating Locke's personal view about riches is on p. 407; the definition of "moral philosophy" on p. 428. On Locke as an economist see Letwin, **Scientific Economics**, Chapt. 6, pp. 158–95; W. Stark, **The Ideal Foundations of Economic Thought** (London: Routledge & Kegan Paul Ltd., 1943), Chapt. 6, pp. 1–26; Peter Laslett, "John Locke, the Great Recoinage, and the Origins of the Board of Trade," **William and Mary Quarterly**, 3rd series, Vol. 14, No. 3 (July, 1957), 358–69; James Bonar, **Philosophy and Political Economy**, 2nd ed. (New York: The Macmillan Company, 1909), Bk. 2, Chap. 5; Alberto Bertolino, **Locke Economista** (Siena: Tipografia Ex-combattenti Cooperativa, 1928). Karen Iversen Vaughn, **John Locke: Economist and Social Scientist** (Chicago: University of Chicago Press, 1980). On his monetary views see Ignaz Emrich, **Die geldtheoretischen und geldpolitischen Anschauungen John Lockes** (Munich: B. Heller, 1927); A. H. Leigh, "John Locke and the Quantity Theory of Money," **History of Political Economy,"** Vol. 6, No. 2 (Summer,

1974), 200–219. Locke's views on property have elicited more comment than his contributions to economic theory. See Paschal Larkin, **Property in the Eighteenth Century** (London: Longmans, Green & Co. Ltd., 1930); Walton H. Hamilton, "Property—According to Locke," **Yale Law Journal**, Vol. 41 (April, 1931), 864–80, who is critical of extensions and amplifications of Locke's doctrine; J. W. Gough, **John Locke's Political Philosophy** (London: Oxford University Press, 1950), a collection of eight studies; Chapter 4 is devoted to Locke's theory of property; C. B. Macpherson, **The Political Theory of Possessive Individualism: Hobbes to Locke** (New York: Oxford University Press, Inc., 1962), of which there is a review article by Jacob Viner, **Canadian Journal of Economics and Political Science**, Vol. 29, No. 4 (November, 1963), 548, with rejoinder and reply; J. P. Day, "Locke on Property," **Philosophical Quarterly**, Vol. 16, No. 64 (July, 1966), 207–20. Lawrence C. Becker, **Property Rights: Philosophic Foundations** (London and Boston: Routledge and Kegan Paul, 1977); C. B. Macpherson, ed., **Property: Mainstream and Critical Positions** (Buffalo, N.Y.: University of Toronto Press, 1978); James Tully, **A Discourse on Property: John Locke and His Adversaries** (New York: Cambridge University Press, 1980).

• McCulloch, J. R., ed., **Early English Tracts on Commerce**, originally published in 1856 (London: Cambridge University Press, 1954). The tracts by Mun, North, and other writers may be consulted here in their original versions. Other accessible sources are made available in the series of **Reprints of Economic Tracts**, initiated by Jacob H. Hollander (Baltimore: The Johns Hopkins Press). Monroe: **Early Economic Thought**, includes selections from Serra, Mun, Petty, and von Hornick. Separate printings of Mun's tracts have also been published: **England's Treasure by Foreign Trade** (Oxford: Basil Blackwell & Mott Ltd., 1949); **A Discourse of Trade** (New York: Facsimile Text Society, 1930). A reprint of Child's **Brief Observations** is appended to William Letwin, **Sir Josiah Child**, Publication No. 14 of the Kress Library of Business and Economics (Boston: Harvard Graduate School of Business Administration, Baker Library, 1949). Wheeler's **Treatise of Commerce** is available in two reprints, both with notes by George B. Hotchkiss (New York: Columbia University Press for the Facsimile Text Society, 1931; New York; New York University Press, 1931). The latter edition is the better one. Malynes and Misselden are elusive to modern readers, but a selection from the first may be found in R. H. Tawney and Eileen Power, eds., **Tudor Economic Documents** (London: Longmans, Green & Co. Ltd., 1924), Vol. 3, 386–404 (from **The Canker of England's Commonwealth**), and an extract from Misselden's **Circle of Commerce** in Philip C. Newman, Arthur D. Gayer, and Milton H. Spencer, eds., **Source Readings in Economic Thought** (New York: W. W. Norton & Company, Inc., 1954), pp. 43–48.

• Monroe, Arthur E., **Monetary Theory before Adam Smith** (Cambridge, Mass.: Harvard University Press, 1923), gives detailed attention to the thought of the mercantilist writers, as does Douglas Vickers, **Studies in the Theory of Money, 1690–1776** (Philadelphia: Chilton Book Company, 1959). More specialized are Hugo Hegeland, **The Quantity Theory of Money** (Göteborg: Elanders Boktryckeri, 1951); M. W. Holtrop, "Theories of the Velocity of Circulation of Money in Earlier Economic Literature," **Economic History**, Vol. 1 (January, 1929), 503–24. References to the views of Locke and other writers of the period may also be found in Arthur W. Marget, **The Theory of Prices**, 2 vols. (Englewood Cliffs, N.J.: Prentice-Hall, Inc., 1938 and 1942). The currency controversies of the time, which led to the founding of the Bank of England and the introduction of paper money, are traced in detail by J. Keith Horsefield, **British Monetary Experiments, 1650–1710** (Cambridge, Mass.: Harvard University Press, 1960). On the interest controversies of the time see G. S. L. Tucker, **Progress and Profits in British Economic Thought 1650–1850** (London: Cambridge University Press, 1960), Chaps. 1–3.

• Roscher, Wilhelm, **Zur Geschichte der englischen Volkswirtschaftslehre im 16. und 17. Jahrhundert** (Leipzig, 1851–52). Nineteenth-century English thought adhered for long to the opinion of the classics, epitomized in Book 4 of Smith's *Wealth of Nations,* who had seen little good in the "mercantile system." In Germany on the other hand, the historical school, with its emphasis on nationalism and statecraft rather than cosmopolitanism and laissez-faire, felt greater affinity with the mercantilists than with the classics. Roscher, a founder of the historical school—see below, p. 761—went to work on a scholarly and sympathetic examination of the contributions of the early English writers. Thereby he set the stage for the rehabilitation of the mercantilists in the writings of subsequent generations of German economists and of English economic historians who had received their training in Germany. These historians had fallen under the spell of the German academic influence, which reached its peak in the late decades of the nineteenth century. Another German appraisal, Gustav Schmoller's **The Mercantile System**, was published in 1884 (trans. New York: The Macmillan Company, 1897). In this book Schmoller illustrates the historical significance of the mercantile system from Prussian history, specifically from the economic policy of Frederick the Great. This led him to the conclusion, often reiterated in the later literature, that mercantilism, by overcoming the particularist power of the lower political subdivisions, was state making, that is, brought about the modern unified state. This interpretation never fitted the English case, where the state had been formed before the time of the mercantilists and where their work was a rationalization of empire building rather than of state building. In a similar vein, the English economic historian W. Cunningham, in his **Growth of English Industry and Commerce**, first published in 1882 (3rd ed. London: Cambridge University Press, 1903), described the mercantile system as "a national system of economic policy" (Vol. 2, 16). The development culminated in Heckscher's work, who starts out his interpretation with a characterization of mercantilism as a unifying system but appraises it in the light of his own laissez-faire predilection.

• Seligman, E. R. A., **The Shifting and Incidence of Taxation**, 5th ed. (New York: Columbia University Press, 1926), Bk. 1, Chaps. 5 and 6, treats of the mercantilist ideas about taxation.

• Serra, Antonio, **Brief Treatise on the causes which can make gold and silver plentiful in kingdoms where there are no mines**, originally published in Naples in 1613, may be found in English translation in Monroe, **Early Economic Thought**, pp. 143–67. This work, which preceded the bullionist controversy in England by some ten years, forms part of a similar discussion in Italy. Like Misselden and Mun, Serra considers the exchanges as passive, and their variations as reactions to the flow of trade. It is thus futile to expect to hold or gain specie by exchange control; what is important are exports and imports. These will be influenced by a country's endowment with human and natural resources.

Serra's work is mainly one of classification. He lists six determinants of a country's ability to produce an export balance. These are its capacity to produce a surplus of agricultural products over and above domestic consumption, its locational advantage, the volume of its manufacturing production, the quality of its population, the extent of its carrying trade, and the regulation of trade by the government. Serra is unaware of the quantity theory of money, and, unlike Mun, fails to relate the supply of money to the price level and the volume of exports to export prices. He thus moves nowhere in the direction of the specie-flow theory. An interesting idea that he develops is the superiority of manufacturing over agricultural production. He comes close to postulating increasing returns to the former and diminishing returns to the latter. There is less of a risk element in manufacture than in agriculture because manufacture does not depend upon the weather. As manufacture does not utilize a factor that is fixed, such as land, its product can be multiplied "and with proportionately less expense." Manufacturing products are not perishable, and they can be sold in distant markets. Manufacturing activities fetch higher rewards than agriculture.

Serra's treatise had no influence and was soon forgotten, to be rediscovered only around 1780. The work was written while the author was in prison, accused of counterfeiting. He was incarcerated again four years later, apparently on account of his economic views, which ran counter to the official policy in the matter of the exchanges. An appraisal of Serra may be found in G. Arias, "Il pensiero economico di Antonio Serra," **Politica**, Vol. 16 (1923), 129–46.

• Sewall, Hannah R., **The Theory of Value before Adam Smith**, Publications of the American Economic Association, 3rd series, Vol. 2, No. 3 (New York: The Macmillan Company, 1901), contains a survey of the value theories of the mercantilist writers. See also Louise Sommer, "Mercantilisme et théorie de la valeur," **Revue d'histoire économique et sociale**, Vol. 15 (1927), 5–24; Marian Bowley, "Some Seventeenth-Century Contributions to the Theory of Value," **Economica**, new series, Vol. 30 (May, 1963), 122–39; and, with special reference to Petty's and Locke's espousal of the labor theory of value, Emil Kauder, "The Retarded Acceptance of the Marginal Utility Theory," **Quarterly Journal of Economics**, Vol. 67 (November, 1953), 564–75. According to Kauder, "it was no coincidence that the members of the Italo-French subjective value school were Catholics and that the defenders of the cost theory of value were Protestants." See also the same author's "Genesis of the Marginal Utility Theory," **Economic Journal**, Vol. 63 (September, 1953), 638–50.

• Silberner, Edmond, **La Guerre dans la pensée économique du xvie au xviiie siècle** (Paris: Editions Sirey, 1939). On the role played by war and war preparation in the thought of the mercantilists.

• Small, Albion W., **The Cameralists** (Chicago: The University of Chicago Press, 1909), is the only comprehensive treatment of the subject in English, with copious excerpts from the writings of the seventeenth- and eighteenth-century authors. Small draws attention to the relation between the thought of these men and attitudes and valuations still current in twentieth-century Germany. The Cameralists were holders of office in the prince's chamber—*camera*—or official or self-appointed advisers to such officeholders in matters relating to the management of public affairs. Their writings reflect such features of their environment as the protracted absolutist rule and the disastrous economic effects of the Thirty Years' War (1618–48). Most Cameralists were concerned with the promotion of population growth, which in turn required rural and urban reconstruction, and with ways and means to satisfy the revenue needs of the prince. To some of them the satisfaction of revenue needs constituted the principal aim, in whose pursuit care had to be taken to ensure the economic well-being of the tax-paying subjects. Most mercantilists would have endorsed the opinion of Veit Ludwig von Seckendorff (1626–92) that "a country's richest treasure is its number of well-nourished people," an attitude that has been compared with that of a breeder of livestock.

The point of view from which these matters are discussed is as a rule that of a practitioner of public administration, in line with the training of most Cameralists in law. An exception is Johann Joachim Becher (1635–82), who had a background in surgery and chemistry and is remembered as one of the founders of the phlogiston theory of combustion. His **Political Discourse** (1668) and the lesser-known **Moral Discourse** (1669) contain ideas that, like those of other Cameralists, were to fade under the influence of eighteenth-century enlightenment, but that returned during nineteenth-century romanticism and during the national-socialist period of twentieth-century Germany.

Like Petty before him and Boisguilbert later, Becher underlies the strategic role of consumer expenditure as generator of income. "One lives from the other." Consumption is "the soul" of the three economic groups into which Becher wants to divide economic society—peasants, artisans, and merchants—and because of its great importance it must be promoted by the government. In other respects Becher's ideas often are interchangeable with those of the Nazis of the 1930s. He shares their lower-middle-class outlook, their vicious anti-Semitism (the Jews are blamed for alleged thriftiness, which frustrates Becher's goal of stimulation of consumption), their suspicion of all forms of the market (monopoly maintains one person at the expense of a hundred others, while competition—"polypoly"—lets a thousand live miserably where a hundred might live decently), their dislike of the middleman (whose function is to be taken over by government-operated distribution centers), their predilection for government price control and publicly regulated occupational groupings, their search for national self-sufficiency, and their hatred of the tyranny of money (an institution that keeps people in poverty.)

Like his brother-in-law Philipp Wilhelm von Hornick (1638–1712), the author of **Austria over all, if she only will** (1684), Becher would forbid merchandise imports altogether. To these writers, internal development is a more important goal than foreign trade and the accumulation of treasure.

Of the eighteenth-century Cameralists, the best known are J. H. G. von Justi (1717–71) and Joseph von Sonnenfels (1732–1817). The former systematized the field in his **State Economy** of 1755, in which the happiness of the subjects, the common happiness, and the happiness of the state are alternatively declared to be the guiding principle of public policy. Sonnenfels, to whom Beethoven dedicated a sonata, had on the whole a liberating influence. His thought was seasoned by the ideas of the enlightenment, and his works became the bible of enlightened despotism as practiced in Austria, where their authority was rarely questioned for the better part of the nineteenth century. With him the period comes to an end.

There are selections from Hornick and Justi in Monroe, **Early Economic Thought**, pp. 221–44, 377–99. For an appraisal of Sonnenfels see Robert A. Kann, **A Study in Austrian Intellectual History** (New York: Encyclopaedia Britan-

nica, Inc., Frederick A. Praeger, Inc., 1960), pp. 146–258, especially pp. 166–72 on his political economy; also Wenzel Lustkandl, **Sonnenfels und Kudler** (Vienna: Manz, 1891); Felix Spitzer, "Joseph von Sonnenfels als Nationalökonom". (dissertation, Berlin, 1906); G. Deutsch, "Joseph von Sonnenfels und seine Schüler—ein Beitrag zur Geschichte der Nationalökonomie," **Oesterreich-Ungarische Revue**, 1888, pp. 65–85; K. H. Osterloh, **Joseph von Sonnenfels und die österreichische Reformbewegung im Zeitalter des aufgeklärten Absolutismus**, Historische Studien No. 409 (Husum: Matthiesen Verlag, 1970). The standard works, in German, on the Cameralists are Kurt Zielenziger, **Die alten deutschen Kameralisten** (Stuttgart: Gustav Fischer Verlag, 1914); Louise Sommer, **Die oesterreichischen Kameralisten**, 2 vols. (Vienna: C. Konegen, 1920 and 1925); Erhard Dittrich, **Die deutschen und österreichischen Kameralisten** (Darmstadt: Wissenschaftliche Buchgesellschaft, 1973). A bibliography, **Bibliographie der Kameralwissenschaften**, by Magdalene Humpert (Cologne: Pick, 1937), includes 14,040 titles. See also A. Tautscher, **Die Staatswirtschaftslehre des Kameralismus** (Munich: A. Francke Verlag, 1947), and I. Bog, "Der Merkantilismus in Deutschland," **Jahrbücher für Nationalökonomie und Statistik**, May, 1961, pp. 125–45.

• Stangeland, C. E., **Pre-Malthusian Doctrines of Population** (New York: Columbia University Press, 1904), Chaps. 4 and 5, reviews the population doctrines of the period. See also James Bonar, **Theories of Population from Raleigh to Arthur Young** (London: George Allen & Unwin Ltd., 1931); R. Gonnard, **Histoire des doctrines de la population** (Paris: Nouvelle Librairie Nationale, 1923). An interesting special study is R. R. Kuczynski, "British Demographers' Opinions on Fertility, 1660–1760," **Annals of Eugenics**, Vol. 6, Pt. 2 (June 1935) 139–71, reprinted in Lancelot Hogben, ed., **Political Arithmetic** (London: George Allen & Unwin Ltd., 1938), pp. 283–327.

• Tucker, G. S. L., **Progress and Profits in British Economic Thought, 1650–1850**. Chap. 2 treats of "The Problem of Interest in the Seventeenth Century." See also Jelle C. Riemersma, "Usury Restrictions in a Mercantile Economy," **Canadian Journal of Economics and Political Science**, Vol. 18, No. 1 (February, 1952), 17–26; William D. Grampp, "The Controversy Over Usury in the Seventeenth Century," **Journal of European Economic History**, Vol. 10, No. 3 (Winter, 1981), 671–95.

• Viner, Jacob, "English Theories of Foreign Trade before Adam Smith," **Journal of Political Economy**, Vol. 38 (1930), 249–310, 404–57, reprinted in **Studies in the Theory of International Trade** (New York: Harper & Row, Publishers, 1937), pp. 1–118, stands out as the best introduction to the most important part of the mercantilist doctrine. See also, by the same author, "Power versus Plenty as Objectives of Foreign Policy in the Seven-teenth and Eighteenth Centuries," **World Politics**, Vol. 1, No. 1 (October, 1948), 1–29, reprinted in **The Long View and the Short** (New York: The Free Press, 1958), pp. 277–305, where it is argued against Heckscher, Cunningham, and others that power as well as wealth were ultimate ends of mercantilist policy. On **The Theory of the Balance of Trade** see also a book of the same title by Bruno Suviranta (originally Helsingfors, 1923; reprinted New York: Augustus M. Kelley, Publishers, 1967); Frank W. Fetter, "The Term 'Favorable Balance of Trade,' " **Quarterly Journal of Economics**, Vol. 49 (1935), 621–45; W. H. Price, "The Origin of The Phrase 'Balance of Trade,'" **Quarterly Journal of Economics**, Vol. 20 (1905), 157–67; Charles Wilson, "Treasure and Trade Balances: The Mercantilist Problem," **Economic History Review**, 2nd series, Vol. 2, No. 2 (1949), 152–61.

CHAPTER 6

• Bernoulli, Daniel, "Exposition of a New Theory on the Measurement of Risk," **Econometrica**, Vol. 22, No. 1 (January, 1954), 23–36. This is an English translation, by Louise Sommer, of Bernoulli's article on the Saint Petersburg paradox, which contains his thoughts on utility, marginal utility, and the principle of diminishing marginal utility, as well as a diagram depicting the relationship between utility and wealth. The article, published originally in Latin in 1738, was translated into German by Alfred Pringsheim under the title **Die Grundlagen der modernen Wertlehre: Daniel Bernoulli, Versuch einer neuen Theorie der Wertbestimmungen von Glücksfällen** (Berlin: Duncker & Humblot, 1896), which contains valuable notes of the translator, a distinguished mathematician, supplemented by an introduction from the pen of an economist, Ludwig Fick. More recent appraisals may be found in the bibliography appended to Sommer's translation as well as in Reghinos D. Theocharis, **Early Developments in Mathematical Economics** (New York: St. Martin's Press, Inc., 1961), Chap. 3; Ross M. Robertson, "Mathematical Economics before Cournot," **Journal of Political Economy**, Vol. 57, No. 6 (December, 1949), 523–36, especially 524f.; George J. Stigler "The Development of Utility Theory," **Journal of Political Economy**, Vol. 58 (August-October, 1950), 307–27, 373–96. Paul A. Samuelson, "St. Petersburg Paradoxes: Defanged, Dissected and Historically Described," **Journal of Economic Literature**, Vol. 15, No. 1 (March, 1977), 24–55.

• Davenant, Charles, **Two Manuscripts**, hitherto unpublished, ed. G. H. Evans, Jr. (Baltimore: The Johns Hopkins Press, 1942), includes income estimates and supplements his other works as listed in the text. For appraisals see Willy Casper, **Charles Davenant** (Stuttgart: Gustav Fischer Verlag, 1930); D. Waddell, "Charles Davenant (1656–1714): a Biographical Sketch," **Economic History Review**, 2nd series, Vol. 11, No. 2 (December, 1958), 279–88; R. M. Lees, "Parliament and the Proposal for a Council of Trade, 1695–96," **English Historical Review**, Vol. 54 (January, 1939), 38–66.

• Hobbes, Thomas, **Leviathan**, first published 1651. His economic ideas may be found in Chapters 24 and 30, the latter containing his views about taxation. See Aaron Levy, "Economic Views of Thomas Hobbes," **Journal of the History of Ideas**, Vol. 15 (1954), 589–95; Dudley Jackson, "Thomas Hobbes' Theory of Taxation," **Political Studies**, Vol. 21, No. 2 (June, 1973), 175–82; L. S. Moss, "Some Public-Choice Aspects of Hobbes's Political Thought," **History of Political Economy**, Vol. 9, No. 2 (Summer, 1977), 265–72.

• King, Gregory, **Two Tracts**, with an introduction by G. E. Barnett (Baltimore: The Johns Hopkins Press, 1936), contains a reprint of his work in convenient form. See also G. U. Yule, "Crop Production and Prices: A Note on Gregory King's Law," **Journal of the Royal Statistical Society**, Vol. 78 (1915), 296–98, where an equation calculated on the basis of King's law is given, H. Guitton, **Essai sur la loi de King. Étude des relations entre les mouvements de l'offre et les mouvements des prix** (Paris: Éditions Sirey, 1938); G. H. Evans, Jr., "The Law of Demand: The Roles of Gregory King and Charles Davenant," **Quarterly Journal of Economics**, Vol. 81, No. 1 (August, 1967), 483-92.

• Petty, Sir William, **The Economic Writings**, 2 vols., ed. C. H. Hull (London: Cambridge University Press, 1899), with a valuable introduction of around ninety pages by the editor. Formerly unpublished writings of Petty's are collected in **The Petty Papers**, 2 vols., ed. the Marquis of Landsdowne, a descendant of Petty, has also edited **The Petty-Southwell Correspondence** between Petty and his most intimate friend and literary censor (London: Constable & Co., Ltd., 1928), and has authored a book, **Glanerought and the Petty-Fitzmaurices** (New York: Oxford University Press, Inc., 1937), which sheds light on a number of phases of Petty's career: the land survey of Ireland, his interests in iron manufacture, fisheries, Irish properties, and so on. Another member of the family, Lord Edmond Fitzmaurice, has written the standard **Life of Sir William Petty** (London: John Murray [Publishers] Ltd., 1895). Another readable biography is E. Strauss, **Sir William Petty: Portrait of a Genius** (London: The Bodley Head Limited, 1954). A brief appraisal of Petty, by Sir Irvine Masson and A. J. Youngson, may be found in Sir Harold Hartley, ed., **The Royal Society: Its Origins and Founders**, published on the occasion of the tercentenary of the Society (London: The Royal Society, 1960), pp. 79–90. The wide range of Petty's interest is shown by Geoffrey Keynes, **A Bibliography of Sir William Petty, F. R. S. and of Observations on the Bills of Mortality by John Graunt, F. R. S.** (New York: Oxford University Press, 1971).

On the relation between Petty, Graunt, and Süssmilch see Hull's introduction to Petty's **Economic Writings**, where also the authorship of Graunt's **Observations** is discussed. On this matter see also M. Greenwood, "Graunt and Petty," **Journal of the Royal Statistical Society**, Vol. 91 (1928), 79–85, and Vol. 96 (1933), 76–81; G. U. Yule, "On Sentence-Length as a Statistical Characteristic of Style in Prose: with Application to Two Cases of Disputed Authorship," **Biometrika**, Vol. 30 (1939), 363–90.

On the capitalization of human earning power by Petty and later writers see B. F. Kiker, **Human Capital in Retrospect** (Columbia, S.C.: University of South Carolina, Bureau of Business and Economic Research, 1968).

• Spengler, Joseph J., "Quantification in Economics: Its History," in Daniel Lerner, ed., **Quantity and Quality** (New York: The Free Press, 1961), pp. 129–211, comments on pp. 140–42 on the work of the political arithmeticians and assigns them a place within the wider context of quantitative economics. See also the same author's "On the Progress of Quantification in Economics," in Harry Woolf, ed., **Quantification: A History of the Meaning of Measurement in the Natural and Social Sciences** (Indianapolis: The Bobbs-Merrill Co., Inc., 1961), pp. 128–46. Of great value are also the investigations of G.N. Clark, **Science and Social Welfare in the Age of Newton**, 2nd ed. (London: Oxford University Press, Clarendon Press, 1949).

Chapter 5 treats largely of the quantitative approach of Petty and other writers. The author raises the question why the movement towards a quantitative social science, which at the beginning of the seventeenth century "seemed to have an established position and a great future. . .was hardly more than a false start " (pp. 140, 144). Social thinking in general had to wait until the late eighteenth century for a new start. The lapse is ascribed to the inadequacy of the statistical material, to the slack in scientific thought in the central eighteenth century that paralleled the slack period in social thought, to administrative inertia in England—but not in France—that failed to explore social facts, and, most importantly, to the isolation in which the quantitative method was kept by its exponents. "The attempt was made to apply it separately, not as one element in an all-round examination of human and social life by all the methods which can explain them. Quantitative study did not begin as part of a comprehensive social science, embodying the knowledge which ethics, political thought, and theology had already attained. It was not continuous with the main tradition of thought on human problems; it even deliberately broke away" (pp. 145f.).

• Studenski, Paul, **The Income of Nations** (New York: New York University Press, 1958). The first part of this work contains the definitive history of national income estimates and concepts. Petty, King, and Davenant are discussed on pp.

26–40. As the author notes, "after its brilliant start in the seventeenth century, further development of political arithmetic and work on national income estimates in England came to a stop in the beginning of the eighteenth century. The general sense of domestic well-being and the relaxation of international tension contributed, no doubt, to the decline of interest in national income estimating" (p. 40). This interpretation might supplement that by Sir George Clark cited in the preceding paragraph, **Science in the Age of Newton**.

• Westergaard, Harald, **Contributions to the History of Statistics** (London: P. S. King and Son, 1932), contains a discussion of the work of the political arithmeticians and of the rise of probability theory. See also Frederick S. Crum, "The Statistical Work of Süssmilch," **Quarterly Publications of the American Statistical Association**, Vol. 7 (September, 1901), 335–80, where a comparison of the ideas of Süssmilch and Malthus may be found; E. S. Pearson, ed., **The History of Statistics in the 17th and 18th Centuries.** Lectures by Karl Pearson (New York: Macmillan Publishing Co., Inc., 1978).

• Yamey, B. S., H. C. Edey, and H. W. Thompson, **Accounting in England and Scotland, 1543–1800. Double Entry in Exposition and Practice** (London: Sweet & Maxwell Ltd., 1963). A review, with extracts, of the early literature on double-entry bookkeeping.

CHAPTER 7—SEE BIBLIOGRAPHICAL NOTES TO CHAPTER 5.

CHAPTER 8

• Bloomfield, Arthur I., "The Foreign-Trade Doctrines of the Physiocrats," **American Economic Review**, Vol. 28, No. 4 (December, 1938), 716–35. This excellent survey of the foreign-trade doctrines of the Physiocrats shows how their views were at variance both with mercantilist and classical thought. While the Physiocrats demolished the basis of the mercan-

tilist theories, they failed to recognize the benefits derived from international specialization. They considered foreign trade principally as a necessary evil that might support their policy of high agricultural prices.

• Bowman, Mary Jean, "The Consumer in the History of Economic Doctrine,"

American Economic Review, Vol. 41, No. 2 (May, 1951), 1–18. A valuable article, based on original sources, which contains a discussion of the views of Cantillon and of the Physiocrats.

• Cantillon, Richard, **Essai sur la nature du commerce en général** (1755). Edited with an English translation and other material by Henry Higgs, and published for the Royal Economic Society (London: Macmillan & Co. Ltd., 1931). For those who wish to read Cantillon's book in English translation, this edition, which has been reprinted in 1959, is the best. It contains a reprint of W. Stanley Jevons's article on "Richard Cantillon and the Nationality of Political Economy," first published in the **Contemporary Review**, January, 1881, supplemented by more recent findings of Higgs. A new French edition of Cantillon's work, ed. Alfred Sauvy, includes valuable contributions by Anita Page, A. Fanfani, Louis Salleron, Joseph J. Spengler, and the editor. (Paris: Institut National d'Études Démographiques, Presses Universitaires de France, 1952). A German translation of Cantillon's book (Stuttgart: Gustav Fischer Verlag, 1931), contains a valuable introduction by F. A. von Hayek. Supplementary information is contained in an article by J. Hone, "Richard Cantillon," Economist— Biographical Note," **Economic Journal**, Vol. 54 (1944), 96–100, and in one by Luigi Einaudi, "A Forgotten Quotation about Cantillon's Life," same journal, Vol. 43 (1933), 534–37. The best appraisal of Cantillon's work is Joseph J. Spengler, "Richard Cantillon: First of the Moderns," **Journal of Political Economy**, Vol. 62 (August–October, 1954), 281–95, 406– 24. See also Robert F. Hébert, "Richard Cantillon's Early Contribution to Spatial Economics," **Economica**, Vol. 48, No. 189 (February, 1981), 71–77, and, about Cantillon and other predecessors of Thünen, P. Dockès, **L'Espace dans la pensée économique du XVIe au XVIIIe siècle** (Paris: Librairie E. Flammarion & Cie. 1969).

• Cole, Charles W., **French Mercantilist Doctrines before Colbert** (Peterborough, N.H.: William L. Bauhan, Inc., 1931); **Colbert and a Century of French Mercantilism**, 2 vols. (New York: Columbia University Press, 1939); **French Mercantilism, 1683–1700** (same publisher, 1943). These works contain the standard history of French mercantilism in English. See pp. 63–112 of the first book on Laffemas, pp. 113–61 on Montchrétien. The work devoted to Colbert treats of his ideas in Vol. 1, 335–55. Pp. 231–67 of the third book take up Boisguilbert and Vauban. The standard work on Boisguilbert is J. J. Spengler et al., **Pierre de Boisguilbert et la naissance de l'économie politique**, preface by Alfred Sauvy, 2 vols. (Paris: Institut National d'Études Démographiques, Presses Universitaries de France, 1966). An appraisal in English is Hazel Van Dyke Roberts, **Boisguilbert** (New York: Columbia University Press, 1935). On the "stationary state" in Boisguilbert's writings see Michel Lutfalla, **L'État stationnaire** (Paris: Gauthier-Villars et Cie., 1964), Chap. 7, and on the "multiplier," M. Leduc, "Le Mécanisme du multiplicateur chez les mercantilistes de langue française du xviiie siècle," **Revue d'économie politique**, 1960, pp. 229ff. On the connection of his thought with that of Vauban see J. H. Bast, **Vauban et Boisguillebert** (Groningen: P. Noordhoff Ltd., 1935). On Boisguilbert's and later writers' national-income concepts see J. Molinier, **Les Métamorphoses d'une théorie économique: Le revenue national chez Boisguilbert, Quesnay et J.-B. Say** (Paris: Librairie Armand Colin, 1957). French mercantilist thought was influential also in Spain; see the references on p. 709, above.

• Du Pont de Nemours, Pierre-Samuel. About Du Pont see J. J. McLain, **The Economics Writings of Du Pont de Nemours** (Newark, Del.: University of Delaware Press, 1977); Ambrose Saricks, **P. S. Du Pont de Nemours** (Lawrence, Kansas: University of Kansas Press, 1965).

• Einaudi, Luigi, "The Physiocratic Theory of Taxation," in **Economic Essays in Honour of Gustav Cassel** (London: George Allen & Unwin Ltd., 1933), pp. 129–42. This article by the great Italian economist and statesman contains a novel and original interpretation of the single tax of the Physiocrats. The latter did not consider taxation, if kept within rational limits, as a burden but as a condition toward the maximization of the national income, which is attained when an adequate portion of income is allocated to the maintenance of the governing class. The tax thus "is born out of its very utility." Rather than being a problem of a burden, taxation, to the Physiocrats, constituted a problem of distribution among the factors of production, which include the state and the governing class.

• Hamilton, Earl J., "Prices and Wages at Paris under John Law's System," **Quarterly Journal of Economics**, Vol. 51 (November, 1936), 42–70. This article constitutes an installment of the definitive study of John Law that Professor Hamilton had been preparing for many years. So does the same author's "The Political Economy of France at the Time of John Law," **History of Political Economy**, Vol. 1, No. 1 (Spring, 1969), 123–49. The best edition of Law's works is that by Paul Harsin, ed., **Oeuvres complètes**, 3 vols. (Paris: Éditions Sirey, 1934); see also Paul Harsin, "La banque et le système de Law," in J. G. van Dillen, ed., **History of the Principal Public Banks** (The Hague: Martinus Nijhoff's N.V., 1934), to which is appended a comprehensive bibliography. H. Montgomery Hyde, **John Law: The History of an Honest Adventurer** (London: W. H. Allen, 1969), is an interestingly written and well-informed biography. See also Douglas Vickers, **Studies in the Theory of Money, 1690–1776** (Philadelphia: Chilton Book Company, 1959), pp. 111–40, for an appraisal of Law's economic ideas that is more balanced and up-to-date than that of Charles Rist, **History of Monetary and Credit Theory from John Law to the Present Day** (London: George Allen and Unwin Ltd., 1940). Law's stress on the money-creating ability of banks has not always been appreciated by earlier interpreters. For efforts similar to Law's, see J. Keith Horsefield, **British Monetary Experiments, 1650–1710** (Cambridge, Mass.: Harvard University Press, 1960).

• Labrouquère, André, **Les Idées coloniales des Physiocrates** (Paris: Presses Universitaires de France, 1927). In general, the Physiocrats considered the economic development of France more important than colonial expansion, in which they saw little good. This traditional interpretation of their doctrine is not accepted by the author, who develops an alternative one on the basis of previously unpublished documents.

• Landauer, Carl, **Die Theorien der Merkantilisten und Physiokraten über die ökonomische Bedeutung des Luxus** (Munich: M. Steinebach, 1915). The mercantilist theory of luxury is compared with that of the Physiocrats and found to reflect a certain view of production: fixed in quantity in the case of the mercantilists, and capable of being expanded in that of the Physiocrats.

• Maverick, Lewis A., "Chinese Influences upon the Physiocrats," **Economic History**, Vol. 3, No. 13 (February, 1938), 54–67. Eighteenth-century Europe tended to idealize Chinese thought and institutions, whose influence on the Physiocrats is traced in detail in this article as well as in other publications by the same author; see his **China a Model for Europe** (San Antonio, Tex.: P. Anderson Co., 1946), which contains a translation of Quesnay's essay on China's enlightened despotism. See also Adolf Reichwein, **China and Europe: Intellectual and Artistic Concepts in the Eighteenth Century**, trans. J. C. Powell (New York: Alfred A. Knopf, Inc., 1925); Michel Lutfalla, "La Chine vue par quelques économistes du xviiiᵉ siècle," **Population**, 1962, pp. 289–96; and Donald F. Lach, **Asia in the Making of Europe** (Chicago: The University of Chicago Press, 1966, 1977), Vols. 1–2. These volumes carry the story to the sixteenth century; additional volumes will cover the period of the Physiocrats.

• Meek, Ronald L., **The Economics of Physiocracy** (London: George Allen & Unwin Ltd., 1962). The first part of this book contains translations from the works of Quesnay, the second reproduces interpretive essays on the *tableau*, the Physiocratic concept of profit, early theories of underconsumption, and the relationship between Physiocracy and classicism. The concluding essay critically reviews various interpretations of Physiocratic thought. In the author's opinion, "in interpreting Physiocracy, the significant fact is surely not so much that the theory was subject to certain 'feudal' limitations, as that the Physiocrats so often and so brilliantly managed to transcend these limitations" (p. 398). See also, edited by Meek, **Precursors of Adam Smith, 1750–1775** (Totowa, N.J.: Rowman & Littlefield, 1973), with extracts from the Physiocrats and other early writers. For other appraisals see Max Beer, **An Inquiry into Physiocracy** (London: George Allen & Unwin Ltd., 1939), in which the essentially medieval features of the Physiocratic system are underlined; Henry Higgs, **The Physiocrats** (London: Macmillan & Co. Ltd., 1897), which contains six lectures on the rise of the school, its doctrines, its activities, its opponents, and its influence. Higgs considers the school not only the first but also "the most compact school to be encountered in the history of economics" (p. 144); Norman J. Ware, "The Physiocrats: a Study in Economic Rationalization," **American Economic Review**, Vol. 21, No. 4 (December, 1931), 607–19, where the Physiocratic system is interpreted as an instrument to serve the interests of the land-owning class; Thomas P. Neill, "The Physiocrats' Concept of Economics," **Quarterly Journal of Economics**, Vol. 63, No. 4 (November, 1949), 532–53, which points to cleavages in the thought of Quesnay and his disciples and considers him as a follower of inductive methods. See also Elizabeth Fox-Genovese, **The Origins of Physiocracy** (Ithaca, N.Y.: Cornell University Press, 1976), the work of a professional historian.

On the natural-law doctrines of the Physiocrats see O. H. Taylor, "Economics and the Idea of 'Jus Naturale,'" **Quarterly Journal of Economics**, Vol. 44, No. 2 (February, 1930), 205–41, reprinted in his **Economics and Liberalism** (Cambridge, Mass.: Harvard University Press, 1955), pp. 70–99; Michel Lutfalla, "L'Évidence, fondement nécessaire et suffisant de l'ordre naturel chez Quesnay et Morelly," **Revue d'histoire économique et sociale**, Vol. 41 (1963), 213–49; B. Raynaud, "Les Discussions sur l'ordre naturel au xviiie siècle," **Revue d'économie politique,** 1905, pp. 132–48, 354–73; same author, **La Loi natu-**

relle en économie politique (Paris: Domat-Montchrestien, 1936). On the philosophical background, Wilhelm Hasbach, **Die Allgemeinen philosophischen Grundlagen der von François Quesnay und Adam Smith begründeten politischen Ökonomie** (Berlin: Duncker & Humblot, 1890); on their contribution to mathematical economics, which includes a geometric diagram, Henry W. Spiegel, ed., **Pierre Samuel Du Pont de Nemours On Economic Curves** (Baltimore: The Johns Hopkins Press, 1955).

The leading French authority on the Physiocrats was Georges Weulersse. His works, treating of different periods, follow a common pattern: first, the history of the school is traced; second, its economic program; third, its politics and philosophy; fourth, the execution of its program; and fifth, the attacks against, and the defense of the school. See **Le Mouvement physiocratique en France de 1756 à 1770,** 2 vols. (Paris: Félix Alcan, 1910), of which an abbreviated version was published under the title **Les Physiocrates** (Paris: G. Doin & Cie., 1931); **La Physiocratie à la fin du règne de Louis xv (1770–1774)** (Paris: Presses Universitaires de France, 1959); **La Physiocratie sous les ministères de Turgot et de Necker 1774–1781)** (Paris: same publisher, 1950).

• Oncken, August, **Die Maxime "Laissez-faire, laissez-passer," ihr Ursprung, ihr Werden** (Bern: K. J. Wyss, 1886), traces the rise of the famous phrase. See also D. H. Macgregor, **Economic Thought and Policy** (London: Oxford University Press, 1949), Chap. 3 on "The Laissez-Faire Doctrine," for a discussion of Oncken's findings. For a similar history of the expression "political economy," see J. Garnier, "De l'Origine et de la filiation du mot 'Économie politique,'" **Journal des Économistes**, Vol. 32, 300–316; Vol. 33, 11–23 (1852). On this matter see also J. E. King, "Origin of the Term 'Political Economy,'" **Journal of Modern History**, Vol. 20 (1948), 230–31. G. Stollberg, "Zur Geschichte des Begriffs 'Politische Ökonomie'," **Jahrbücher für Nationalökonomie und Statistik**, Vol. 192, No. 1 (June, 1977), 1–35.

• Quesnay, François. The best edition of

Quesnay's works may be found in Vol. 2 of **François Quesnay et la physiocratie**, 2 vols. (Paris: Institut National d'Études Démographiques, Presses Universitaires de France, 1958). The first volume of this work contains more than ten interpretive articles as well as a bibliography. For an English translation of selections from Quesnay's works, see Meek, **Physiocracy**. For a discussion of the various editions of the *tableau* see Marguerite Kuczynski and Ronald L. Meek, **Quesnay's Tableau Économique** (Clifton, N.J.: Augustus M. Kelley for the Royal Economic Society and the American Economic Association, 1972). For interpretations of the *tableau* see R. Suaudeau, **Les Représentations figurées des physiocrates** (Paris: Éditions Sirey, 1947); Henri Woog, **The Tableau Économique of François Quesnay** (Bern: A. Francke Verlag, 1950); Shigeto Tsuru, "On Reproduction Schemes," in Paul M. Sweezy, **The Theory of Capitalist Development** (New York: Oxford University Press, Inc., 1942), pp. 365–67; Leslie Fishman, "A Reconsideration of the *Tableau Économique*," **Current Economic Comment** (University of Illinois), Vol. 20, No. 1 (February, 1958), 41–50; A. Bilimovic, "Das allgemeine Schema des wirtschaftlichen Kreislaufes," **Zeitschrift für Nationalökonomie**, Vol. 10 (1944), 199–241; Las Herlitz, "The Tableau économique and the Doctrine of Sterility," **The Scandinavian Economic History Review**, Vol. 9, No. 1 (1961), 3–55; I. Hishiyama, "The tableau économique of Quesnay," **Kyoto University Economic Review**, April, 1960, pp. 1–46; Herbert Lüthy, **François Quesnay und die Idee der Volkswirtschaft** (Zürich: Polygraphischer Verlag, 1959). J. R. Boudeville, "Les physiocrates et le circuit économique," **Revue d'économie politique**, 1954, pp. 456–81. V. S. Nemtchinov, "Le Tableau économique de F. Quesnay," **Cahiers de l'Institut de science économique appliquée**, Vol. 23, No. 173 (May, 1966), 11–37. A Phillips, "The Tableau Économique as a Simple Leontief Model," **Quarterly Journal of Economics**, Vol. 69, No. 1 (February, 1955), 137–44. J. Nagels, **Genèse, contenu et prolongements de la notion de reproduction du capital selon Karl Marx, Boisguillebert, Quesnay, Leontiev** (Brus-

sels: Université Libre de Bruxelles, 1970). T. Barna, "Quesnay's *Tableau* in Modern Guise," **Economic Journal**, Vol. 85, No. 339 (September, 1975), 485–96. Same author, "Quesnay's Model of Economic Development," **European Economic Review**, Vol. 8, No. 4 (December, 1976), 315–38. W. A. Eltis, "François Quesnay: A Reinterpretation," **Oxford Economic Papers**, Vol. 27, No. 2 (July, 1975), 167–200, and Vol. 27, No. 3 (November, 1975), 327–51 (on the *tableau* and on growth theory). See also Thomas P. Neill, "Quesnay and Physiocracy," **Journal of the History of Ideas**, Vol. 9, No. 2 (1948), 153–73, for a general appraisal.

• Samuels, Warren J., "The Physiocratic Theory of Property and State," **Quarterly Journal of Economics**, Vol. 75 (February, 1961), 96–111; also, by the same author, "The Physiocratic Theory of Economic Policy," same journal, Vol. 76 (February, 1962), 145–62. The first article draws attention to utilitarian elements in the Physiocratic theory of property and to social claims that restricted the right of the owner of property. In the second article, the author develops the view that "laissez-faire has a place only within the broader dimensions of the Physiocratic theory of economic policy, the latter deriving its basic character from its activism as a theory and program of social change and social control" (p. 145).

• Shafer, R. J., **The Economic Societies in the Spanish World (1763–1821)** (Syracuse, N.Y.: Syracuse University Press, 1958), refers to the occasional influence of Physiocratic thought on the work of organizations designed to promote agricultural development in Spanish America. See also, on the economic ideas prevailing in that part of the world, the article by Farías cited above, p. 709. In North America Physiocratic influences can be noted in a few remarks by Benjamin Franklin, who wrote in 1768: "Agriculture is truly productive of new wealth; manufactures only change forms, and, whatever value they give to the materials they work upon, they in the meantime consume an equal value in provisions." Jefferson's agrarianism may reflect Physiocratic influence, but his political thought differed profoundly from that of the Physiocrats. On these matters as well as on Jefferson's connection with Du Pont, see Henry W. Spiegel, **The Rise of American Economic Thought** (Philadelphia: Chilton Book Company, 1960), pp. 10, 39, 191.

• Spengler, Joseph J., **French Predecessors of Malthus** (Durham, N.C.: Duke University Press, 1942). This standard work includes a complete analysis of the population doctrines of the Physiocrats. On other aspects of Physiocratic thought see also Spengler's important article "The Physiocrats and Say's Law of Markets," **Journal of Political Economy**, Vol. 53, No. 3 (September, 1945), 193–211. The purpose of this article is "to describe in some detail the Physiocratic theory of consumption or expenditure and to indicate how this theory, together with the associated theory of production, both anticipated and contributed to the formulation of the Say-Mill 'Law of Markets,' This so-called law, in turn, gave a direction to economic analysis, one unintended outcome of which was Lord Keynes's 'general theory.' In a sense, therefore, it is in the Physiocratic conception of circular flow that Say's law and Lord Keynes's theory had their origin, even as did Marx's scheme of simple reproduction" (p. 193).

• Turgeon, Charles, and Turgeon, Charles-Henri, **Premières études: La valeur d'après les économistes anglais et français depuis Adam Smith et les physiocrates jusqu'à nos jours**, 3rd ed. (Paris: Éditions Sirey, 1925). Chap. 9 of this valuable work treats of the contribution of the French economists to the theory of value.

• Turgot, Anne R. J., **Reflections on the Formation and the Distribution of Riches (1770)** (New York: The Macmillan Company, 1898). This is the translation by W. J. Ashley of Turgot's principal contribution to economics. Turgot's essay on "Valeurs et monnoies" may be found in his **Oeuvres** (Paris: Delance, 1808), Vol. 3, 265–93, and an English translation of Turgot's statement developing the principle of diminishing returns in Edwin Cannan, **A History of the Theories of Production and Distribution from 1776 to 1848**, 3rd ed. (London: Staples Press Limited, 1953), p. 116. For a study of Turgot's life and work, see Léon Say, **Turgot**, trans. G. Masson (London: Routledge & Kegan Paul Ltd., 1888). A recent investigation of the authorship of an early English translation of Turgot's **Reflections**, which attributes it to Adam Smith, is I. C. Lundberg, **Turgot's Unknown Translator** (The Hague: Martinus Nijhoff's N.V., 1964). For new appraisals and translations of Turgot see P. D. Groenewegen, **The Economics of A. R. J. Turgot** (The Hague: Martinus Nijhoff, Publishers, 1977) and Ronald L. Meek, **Turgot on Progress, Sociology and Economics** (New York: Cambridge University Press, 1973).

• Will, Robert M., "Economic Thought in the *Encyclopédie,*" **Southern Economic Journal**, Vol. 32, No. 2 (October, 1965), 191–203, reviews the contributions of Quesnay to the French *Encyclopédie*.

CHAPTER 9

• Galiani, Ferdinando, **On Money** (1751). A translation of **Della Moneta** by Peter R. Toscano (Ann Arbor, Mich.: University Microfilms International, 1977). For a French translation of selections from Galiani's principal contribution to economics see **De la Monnaie**, translated and analyzed with bibliography, introduction, and notes by G. H. Bousquet and J. Crisafulli (Paris: Marcel Rivière & Cie., 1955). The theory of value is in Bk. 1, Chap. 2; the model of an economic society that is gradually transformed into reality in Bk. 2, Chap. 1; the analysis of devaluation in Bk. 3, Chap. 3. An English translation of the substance of Bk. 1, Chap. 2 may be found in Arthur E. Monroe, **Early Economic Thought** (Cambridge, Mass.: Harvard University Press, 1924), pp. 280–99. For a critical edition of Galiani's Dialogues on the Grain Trade see F. Galiani, **Dialogues entre M. Marquis de Roquemaure, et Ms le Chevalier Zanobi**. The autograph manuscript of the "Dialogues sur le Commerce des Bleds" diplomatically edited with introduction, notes and appendices by Philip Koch (Frankfurt am Main: Vittorio Klostermann, 1968) (**Analecta Romanica**, Heft 21). For an appraisal of Galiani by an outstanding Italian economist of modern times see "Einaudi on Galiani," Henry W. Spiegel, ed., **The Development of Economic Thought** (New York: John Wiley & Sons, Inc., 1952), pp. 61–82. This article contains English translations of a number of important passages from Galiani's work. See also Eduard Ganzoni, **Ferdinando Galiani: Ein verkannter Nationalökonom des 18. Jahrhunderts** (Zurich: H. Girsberger, 1938; W. E. Biermann, **Der Abbé Galiani als Nationalökonom, Politiker und Philosoph nach seinem Briefwechsel** (Leipzig: Veit & Companie, 1912); Wilhelm Weigand, **Der Abbé Galiani** (Bonn: Ludwig Röhrscheid, 1948), which gives a complete account of Galiani's life. For a comparison of the values theories of Galiani, Turgot, and Condillac see A. Dubois, "Les théories psychologiques de la valeur au xviiie siècle," **Revue d'économie politique**, Vol. 11 (September, 1897), 849ff., 917ff.; Hannah Robie Sewall, **The Theory of Value before Adam Smith**, Publications of the American Economic Association, 3rd series, Vol. 2, No. 3 (New York: The Macmillan Company, 1901), 91–113. Condillac's value theory may be found in his **Le commerce et le gouvernement, considérés relativement l'un à l'autre** (Paris, 1776). About him, see Paul Meyer, **Etienne Bonnot de Condillac, ein Wegbereiter der ökonomischen Theorie und des liberalen Gedankens** (Zurich: H. Girsberger, 1944).

• Hume, David, **Essays: Moral, Political, and Literary** (New York: Oxford University Press, Inc., 1963). This is a convenient source of Hume's economic essays. A separate publication of these may be found in David Hume, **Writings on Economics**, edited and introduced by Eugene Rotwein (Madison, Wis.: University of Wisconsin Press, 1955), which includes relevant extracts from Hume's correspondence. An appraisal of Hume's contribu-

tions to economics may be found in the editor's introduction to this work. A review article by Marcus Arkin, "The Economics Writings of David Hume—A Reassessment," **South African Journal of Economics**, Vol. 24 (September, 1956), 204–20, has been reprinted in Joseph J. Spengler and William R. Allen, eds., **Essays in Economic Thought** (Skokie, Ill.: Rand McNally & Co., 1960), pp. 141–60. See also Valentin F. Wagner, "Hume als Nationalökonom," **Zeitschrift für schweizerische Statistik und Volkswirtschaft**, Vol. 79, No. 6 (1943), 1–12; Thomas Mayer, "David Hume and Monetarism," **Quarterly Journal of Economics**, Vol. 95, No. 1 (August, 1980), 89–101; E. A. J. Johnson, **Predecessors of Adam Smith** (Englewood Cliffs, N.J.: Prentice-Hall, Inc., 1937), Chap. 9 on "Hume, the Synthetist," where Hume's work is interpreted as an attempted synthesis of earlier doctrines. In doing so, Hume "demonstrated, better than any other writer, the contradictions which were contained in the economic thought of his age and prepared the way for a new set of doctrines consciously designed to replace the traditional teachings of Adam Smith's predecessors" (p. 181). Albert Schatz, **L'Oeuvre économique de David Hume** (Paris: Arthur Rousseau, 1902), contains the definitive appraisal of Hume's work as an economist and relates it to his philosophy. Schatz underlines the unity of Hume's economic and philosophical thought. "The primary given to passion over reason in Hume's theory of knowledge and in the direction of our activities, the search for happiness, considered as a moral end and as realized in society, have transformed philosophy from a handmaiden of theology into a servant of social science" (pp. 51f.). See also the same author's magnum opus, **L'Individualisme économique et social** (Paris: Librairie Armand Colin, 1907), pp. 113–95 on Hume and Smith. For a discussion of the disputed authorship of **An Abstract of a Treatise of Human Nature** (1740), with which Adam Smith has been credited erroneously, see the introduction by J. M. Keynes and P. Sraffa to their edition of this pamphlet (London: Cambridge University Press, 1938).

• Steuart, Sir James, **An Inquiry into the Principles of Political Economy**, 2 vols. (London, 1767), is available in a photomechanical reprint. A new edition in two volumes, edited and introduced by Andrew S. Skinner, contains about two-thirds of the original text as well as biographical and analytical introductions (Edinburgh: Oliver and Boyd, Scottish Economic Classics, 1966). For a balanced appraisal of Steuart's thought, see Johnson, **Predecessors of Adam Smith**, pp. 209–34, who refers to his work as "the best summation of pre-Smithian British economic theory" (p. 234). See also S. R. Sen, **The Economics of Sir James Steuart** (London: G. Bell & Sons, Ltd., 1957), who considers as Steuart's main contribution "his economics of social control." According to Sen, the only writer who came near to appreciating the true importance of this contribution "and on whom Steuart has perhaps more influence than is commonly realised was Karl Marx" (p. 187). For a somewhat different interpretation see P. Chamley, "Sir James Steuart, inspirateur de Lord Keynes?" **Revue d'économie politique**, May–June 1962, pp. 303–13. Chamley also has explored the Steuart-Hegel connection. See his **Économie politique chez Steuart et Hegel** (Université de Strasbourg, Faculté de Droit. Paris: Erudita, 1963). See also along lines emphasizing the policy aspects of Steuart's work, R. L. Meek, "The Economics of Control Prefigured by Sir James Steuart," **Science and Society**, Vol. 22, No. 4 (1958), 289–305, and for further biographical information, W. L. Taylor, "A Short Life of Sir James Steuart," **South African Journal of Economics**, Vol. 25 (December, 1957), 290–302; Paul Chamley, **Documents relatifs à Sir James Steuart** (Paris: Librairie Dalloz, 1965). For an early comparison see S. Feilbogen, "James Steuart und Adam Smith,"

Zeitschrift für die gesamte Staatswissenschaft, Vol. 14 (1889), 218–60, and for a study of one aspect of Steuart's thought, Walter F. Stettner, "Sir James Steuart on the Public Debt," **Quarterly Journal of Economics**, Vol. 59 (May, 1945), 451–76. Kenneth Boulding's attempt at constructing a theory of the firm on the basis of the balance sheet may be found in his **A Reconstruction of Economics** (New York: John Wiley & Sons, Inc., 1950), Chap. 3. On Steuart's methodology and his interest in method, which, like the substance of his thought, was probably also stimulated by his long residence on the Continent, see Andrew Stewart Skinner, "Economics and the Problem of Method: An Eighteenth-Century View," **Scottish Journal of Political Economy**, Vol. 12, No. 3 (November, 1965), 267–80. Skinner, Steuart's modern editor, is the author also of a number of other articles devoted to Steuart; see his "Sir James Steuart; Economics and Politics," same journal, Vol. 9 (February, 1962), 17–37; "Sir James Steuart: International Relations," **Economic History Review**, Vol. 15 (April, 1963), 438–50; "Sir James Steuart: Author of a System," **Scottish Journal of Political Economy**, Vol. 28, No. 1 (February, 1981), 20–42. See also Robert V. Eagley, "Sir James Steuart and the Aspiration Effect," **Economica**, Vol. 28 (February, 1961), 57–61; M. A. Akhtar, "Sir James Steuart on Economic Growth," **Scottish Journal of Political Economy**, Vol. 25, No. 1 (February, 1978), 57–74; same author, "An Analytical Outline of Sir James Steuart's Macroeconomic Model," **Oxford Economic Papers**, Vol. 31, No. 2 (July, 1979), 283–302. Max J. Wasserman and Ray M. Ware, **The Balance of Payments** (New York: Simmons-Boardman Publishing Corp., 1965), devotes Chap. 1 to a history of the balance-of-payments concept (pp. 1–45).

CHAPTER 10

• Cannan, Edwin. Cannan, who taught at the London School of Economics from 1895 to 1926, was the leading student of classical economics in the England of his time. His detailed investigations viewed the classics from a highly critical perspective antedating modern technical economics. See his **History of the Theories of**

Production and Distribution from 1776 to 1848, 3rd ed. (London: Staples Press Limited, 1953), and A Review of Economic Theory (1929), with a new introduction by B. A. Corry (London: Frank Cass & Co. Ltd., 1964), which relates the classical school both to its forerunners and to later developments. For more recent interpretations of classical economics see Paul A. Samuelson, "The Canonical Classical Model of Political Economy," Journal of Economic Literature, Vol. 16, No. 4 (December, 1978), 1415–34, who constructs a dynamic model of equilibrium, growth, and distribution shared by Smith, Ricardo, Malthus, and Mill; D. P. O'Brien, The Classical Economists (New York: Oxford University Press, 1975), whose work centers around the classics' view of growth. As he writes: "Their focus was above all on the problem of growth, and the macro-economic distribution conclusions which followed from their view of growth" (p. 53); Robert V. Eagley, The Structure of Classical Economic Theory (New York: Oxford University Press, 1974), a mathematical restatement of the theories of the classics in their entirety from the Physiocrats to Walras, with special emphasis on the concept of capital as a central point of classical theory; Thomas Sowell, Classical Economics Reconsidered (Princeton, N.J.: Princeton University Press, 1975), who develops a system of classical economics into which the contributions of the individual authors are integrated; James L. Cochrane, Macroeconomics Before Keynes (Glenview, Ill.: Scott, Foresman and Company, 1930), Chap. 3 on classical macroeconomics; T. W. Hutchison, On Revolutions and Progress in Economic Knowledge (New York: Cambridge University Press, 1978), on the Smithian and other revolutions in the history of economics.

• Clark, John Maurice, et al., Adam Smith, 1776–1926, lectures to commemorate the sesquicentennial of The Wealth of Nations (Chicago: University of Chicago Press, 1928). This contains authoritative interpretations of the contribution of Smith in the light of the economic thought of the 1920s. Half a century later the bicentenary of the publication of The Wealth of Nations brought a number of new appraisals, including Andrew S. Skinner and Thomas Wilson, eds., Essays on Adam Smith (New York: Oxford University Press, 1976), which contains some thirty articles by high authorities on diverse aspects of Smith's thought. Another collection, by the same editors, includes papers given at the University of Glasgow on the occasion of a bicentennial conference honoring Smith's memory; The Market and the State (New York: Oxford University Press, 1976). Skinner, the co-editor of these volumes, has assembled a number of his own articles about Smith in a volume titled A System of Social Science (New York: Oxford University Press, 1979). The title underlines the idea that Smith considered his contributions to a variety of subjects as parts of a wider system of social science—in Smith's own words "an imaginary machine invented to connect together in the fancy those different movements and effects which are in reality performed." Other worthwhile collections of essays include Gerald P. O'Driscoll, Jr., ed., Adam Smith and Modern Political Economy (Ames: Iowa State University Press, 1979), based on lectures delivered at the University of California, Santa Barbara, in 1976; Fred R. Glahe, ed., Adam Smith and The Wealth of Nations: 1776–1976 (Boulder: Colorado Associated University Press, 1978), with contributions by Milton Friedman, Harry Johnson, and others.

Book-length interpretations of Adam Smith or The Wealth of Nations as seen through the eyes of a single scholar include the dissertation of Eli Ginzberg, "The House of Adam Smith" (New York: Columbia University Press, 1934); Samuel Hollander, The Economics of Adam Smith (Buffalo: University of Toronto Press, 1973); E. G. West, Adam Smith: The Man and his Works (New Rochelle, N.Y.: Arlington House, 1969); Clyde E. Dankert, Adam Smith: Man of Letters and Economist (Hicksville, N.Y.: Exposition Press, 1974); J. R. Lindgren, The Social Philosophy of Adam Smith (The Hague: Martinus Nijhoff Publisher, 1974).

On special aspects of Smith's economic thought see the following: N. Rosenberg, "Adam Smith on Profits—Paradox Lost and Regained," **Journal of Political Economy**, Vol. 82, No. 6 (November–December, 1974), 1177–90; V. Foley, "The Division of Labor in Plato and Smith," **History of Political Economy**, Vol. 6, No. 2 (Summer, 1974), 220–42; E. G. West, "Adam Smith's Two Views on the Division of Labor," **Economica**, February, 1964, pp. 23–32; same author, "Adam Smith's Public Economics: A Re-Evaluation," **Canadian Journal of Economics**, Vol. 10, No. 1 (February, 1977), 1–18; V. W. Bladen, "Adam Smith on Productive and Unproductive Labor, **Canadian Journal of Economics and Political Science**, Vol. 24 (1960), 625–30 (who takes a favorable view of the distinction); Philip L. Williams, **The Emergence of the Theory of the Firm: From Adam Smith to Alfred Marshall** (New York: St. Martin's Press, 1979); Warren J. Samuels, **The Classical Theory of Economic Policy** (New York: The World Publishing Company, 1966): David Laidler, "Adam Smith as a Monetary Economist," **Canadian Journal of Economics**, Vol. 14, No. 2 (May, 1981), 185–200; H. Myint, "Adam Smith's Theory of International Trade in the Perspective of Economic Development," **Economica**, Vol. 44, No. 175 (August, 1977), 231–48; William D. Grampp, "Adam Smith and the American Revolutionists," **History of Political Economy**, Vol. 11, No. 2 (Summer, 1979), 179–91; A. L. Macfie, **The Individual in Society** (London: George Allen & Unwin Ltd., 1968).

On the stage theories—hunting, pasturage, agriculture and commerce—of Smith and other writers see Ronald L. Meek, **Social Science and the Ignoble Savage** (New York: Cambridge University Press, 1976), who stresses the materialist conception of history derived from such stage theories, with the different modes of subsistence generating different institutions.

On Smith's failure to employ Hume's specie-flow theory in his attack against mercantilist writers, see F. Petrella, "Adam Smith's Rejection of Hume's Price-Specie-Flow Mechanism: A Minor Mystery Resolved," **Southern Economic Journal**, Vol. 34, No. 3 (January, 1968).

• Cropsey, J., **Polity and Economy: An Interpretation of the Principles of Adam Smith** (The Hague: Martinus Nijhoff's N.V., 1957). This is an original and closely reasoned study of Smith's intention. Earlier interpreters of Smith's thought usually have listed Smith's strictures of the commercial society without providing an explanation of this apparent break in his thought. According to Cropsey, Smith advocated capitalism because it makes freedom possible. "Smith's position may be interpreted to mean that commerce generates freedom and civilization, and at the same time free institutions are indispensable to the preservation of commerce. If the advantages of commerce can be sufficiently impressed upon the general mind, freedom and civilization will automatically follow in its train, and mankind will perhaps even be disposed to defend civilization, not necessarily out of love for freedom but out of love for commerce and gain" (p. 95). Smith's ambivalent position is discussed also by Michel Bernard, **Introduction à une Sociologie des doctrines économiques des physiocrates à Stuart Mill** (Paris: Mouton & Co., 1963), Chap. 2: "One cannot imagine the distortion which Smith's thought underwent at the hands of his heirs in the beginning of the nineteenth century. . . . In what sense was he a precursor of the enthusiasm for industry of those who claim him as one of theirs? No social class is treated worse in his great work than that of the manufacturers and traders. . . .All of Smith's theories are replete with equivocations; to reduce them to the lucid interpretations of his successors means to mutilate them" (p. 36). Smith's equivocations are explained as a result of caution and desire for respectability. According to Élie Halévy, **The Growth of Philosophic Radicalism**, trans. Mary Morris (London: Faber & Faber Ltd., 1928), Smith's attachment to laissez-faire in the face of his view that the interest of the merchants and manufacturers runs counter to that of the public finds its interpretation by the fact "that the theories relative to the distribution of wealth between the three economic classes were introduced into Adam Smith's doctrine too late, and, as it were, from outside," that is, from the teachings of the Physiocrats. "They are like a foreign body which the organism is constantly tending to eliminate" (p. 103). Furthermore, Smith's "liberal thesis found a powerful auxiliary in . . . [the] inertia and weakness" of the governments of his time (p. 104). G. L. S. Tucker, **Progress and Profits in British Economic Thought, 1650–1850** (London: Cambridge University Press, 1960), on the other hand, holds that Smith was fortified in his attachment to laissez-faire, the incompatibility of the public interest and that of the merchants and manufacturers notwithstanding, by "his idea of the willingness of government to legislate on the advice of merchants and manufacturers," the very groups who would be liable to propose policies running counter to the public interest (p. 72). For a different interpretation, with special emphasis on the views of Montesquieu and Steuart, see Albert O. Hirschman, **The Passions and the Interests: Political Arguments for Capitalism** (Princeton: Princeton University Press, 1977).

On Smith's divergent views about the division of labor see the article by West in **Economica**, February, 1964. On the origin of his pessimistic view in the matter see Jacob Viner, **Guide to John Rae's Life of Adam Smith** (New York: Augustus M. Kelley, Publishers, 1965), p. 36, who mentions Rousseau's influence and the alienation issue. Alienation is traced to Rousseau in Hans Barth, "Über die Idee der Selbstentfremdung des Menschen bei Rousseau," **Zeitschrift für Philosophische Forschung**, Vol. 13 (1959), 16–35.

That certain interpretations of the classical school made its thought appear unduly doctrinaire, dogmatic and reactionary is the thesis of Lionel Robbins, **The Theory of Economic Policy in English Classical Political Economy** (New York: St. Martin's Press, Inc., 1952).

• Hasek, C. W., **The Introduction of Adam Smith's Doctrines into Germany** (New York: Columbia University Press,

1925), treats of the resistance facing the absorption of Smith's liberal economics on the Continent, where absolutism and backward economic conditions prevailed longer than in England. The first German translator of *The Wealth of Nations* was a cousin of Schiller's, the national poet, who espoused the ideals of liberty and humanity. The translator of Hutcheson was supposedly Lessing, the foremost exponent of humanitarianism and the enlightenment in Germany. On the reception of Smith's thought in Germany see also the further references on p. 764, below.

See also Melchior Palyi, "The Introduction of Adam Smith on the Continent," in Clark et al., **Adam Smith**, pp. 180–233; R. S. Smith, "The *Wealth of Nations* in Spain and Hispanic America, 1780–1830," **Journal of Political Economy**, Vol. 65 (April, 1957), 104–25.

On Smith's first Russian disciple see A. H. Brown, "S. E. Desnitsky, Adam Smith and the Nakaz of Catherine II," **Oxford Slavonic Papers**, new ser., Vol. 7 (1974). Desnitsky, who studied in Glasgow in the 1760s, acquainted the Empress Catherine with Smith's ideas about finance. She in turn embodied them in a state paper that was made public eight years ahead of **The Wealth of Nations**.

• Hayek, Friedrich A., **Individualism and Economic Order** (London: Routledge & Kegan Paul Ltd., 1949). In the first essay reprinted in this collection, "Individualism: True and False," Hayek distinguishes between the British tradition of individualism with its nonpurposive social formations that arise as the unforeseen results of individual action, and the individualistic tradition of French and other continental writers that traces all discoverable order to deliberate design, based on the powers of Reason. The British point of view manifests itself in the works of Locke, Mandeville, Hume, and Smith. The French, grounded in Cartesian rationalism, came to the fore with Rousseau and the Physiocrats, and, according to Hayek, tends to develop into socialism and collectivism. Hayek speaks of "the decisive importance of Mandeville in the history of economics," referring to "his full account of the origin of the division of labor" and of money, and quoting his statement, "we often ascribe to the excellency of man's genius, and the depth of his penetration, what is in reality owing to the length of time, and the experience of many generations, all of them very little differing from one another in natural parts and sagacity" (p. 9). For a somewhat different interpretation of Mandeville's influence on the laissez-faire doctrine see Jacob Viner's introduction to Bernard Mandeville, **A Letter to Dion** (1732), The Augustan Reprint Society, Publication No. 41 (Berkeley and Los Angeles: University of California, William Andrews Clark Memorial Library, 1953), who refers to Mandeville's emphasis on the need for "the skillful management of the clever politician," and concludes that Mandeville, "in contrast to Adam Smith, put great and repeated stress on the importance of the role of government in producing a strong and prosperous society, through detailed and systematic regulation of economic activity" (pp. 13f.). Viner's introduction to this work has been reprinted in his **The Long View and the Short** (New York: The Free Press, 1958), pp. 332–42. For an interpretation that denies the applicability of the distinction between interventionism and laissez-faire to the thought of Mandeville see Nathan Rosenberg, "Mandeville and Laissez-Faire," **Journal of the History of Ideas**, Vol. 24, No. 2 (April–June, 1963), 183–96. Mandeville's "primary interest was not in interfering with the processes of the market place, but in assuring that such processes worked out to socially desirable ends" (p. 196). " 'Dextrous management' is not to be taken as the advocacy of a policy of continuous government intervention in domestic market processes; rather it is a way of stating that the welfare of society has been most advanced by the introduction and diffusion of laws and institutions which best utilize man's basic passions and which channel his energies into socially useful activities" (p. 188). See also A. Chalk, "Mandeville's *Fable of the Bees:* A Reappraisal," **Southern Economic Journal**, Vol. 33, No. 1 (July, 1966), 1–6; M. J. Scott-Taggart, "Mandeville: Cynic or Fool," **Philosophical Quarterly**, Vol.

16, No. 64 (July, 1966), 221–32; F. A. Hayek, **Dr. Bernard Mandeville**, Lecture on a Master Mind, British Academy (London: Oxford University Press, 1966); Hector Monro, **The Ambivalence of Bernard Mandeville** (New York: Oxford University Press, 1975); Thomas A. Horne, **The Social Thought of Bernard Mandeville** (New York: Columbia University Press, 1977; W. Hasbac, "Larochefoucault und Mandeville," **Schmollers Jahrbuch für Gesetzgebung** etc., Vol. 14, No. 1 (1890), 1–43.

Mandeville's **Fable of the Bees** is available in a magnificent modern edition by F. B. Kaye, 2 vols. (London: Oxford University Press, 1924). The editor ascribes to Mandeville a far-reaching influence on the laissez-faire doctrine (pp. 48ff.). See also the selection from the **Fable of the Bees**, ed. with an introduction by Philip Harth (New York: Penguin Books, 1970).

Echoes of the laissez-faire idea with its invisible hand may be found in Émile Thouverez, **Pierre Nicole** (Paris: Librairie Victor Lecoffre, 1926), which contains excerpts from Nicole's **Essais de morale** with their parallel of charity and self-interest. An early English translation of the **Essais** was published in four volumes under the title **Moral Essayes** (London: Samuel Manship, 1696). About Nicole's views see Anthony Levi, **French Moralists** (London: Oxford University Press, 1964), pp. 225–33; about the influence of the Jansenists, B. Groethuysen, **The Bourgeois: Catholicism vs Capitalism in Eighteenth-Century France** (New York: Holt, Reinhart & Winston, Inc., 1968).

Max Weber, **Gesammelte Aufsätze zur Wissenschaftslehre**, 2nd ed. (Tübingen: J. C. B. Mohr [Paul Siebeck], 1951, p. 33 has drawn attention to a parallel idea expressed in Milton's **Paradise Lost** (1667), where Mammon has this to say (Bk. 2, 257ff.):

Our greatness will appear
Then most conspicuous, when great things of small,
Useful of hurtful, prosperous of adverse,
We can create, and in what place soe'er
Thrive under evil, and work ease out of pain
Through labor and endurance.

Montesquieu, in **The Spirit of the Laws**, first published in 1748, argued that under a monarchy honor would restrain self-interest: "Thus each individual advances the public good, while he only thinks of promoting his own interest" (Bk. III, Chap. 7).

Related ideas are expressed in Goethe's **Faust**, where Mephisto refers to himself as

Part of that power which would

The evil ever do, and ever does the
good

as well as in Hegel's concept—possibly inspired by Smith's invisible hand—of the "cunning of reason," which equips man with unreasonable passions to realize ends which are not of his intention (see J. N. Findlay, **Hegel: A Reexamination** (New York: The Macmillan Company, Collier Books, 1962), pp. 252–53, 310, 334), and in Kant's nonpurposive formations. In Kant's philosophy of history the "unsocial sociability" of man is depicted as an instrument of progress. The desire for honor, power, or wealth makes him develop his talents, which in the end produce civilization. See W. H. Walsh, **An Introduction to Philosophy of History** (London: Hutchinson & Co. [Publishers] Limited, 1951), p. 125.

For the origin of the phrase "invisible hand" see Joseph J. Spengler, "Adam Smith on Population Growth and Economic Development," **Population and Development Review**, Vol. 2, No. 2 (June, 1976) 167–80, who calls it a seventeenth-century metaphor and refers to Joseph Glanvill (1636–80), Chaplain of King Charles II, who wrote: "Nature works by an invisible hand in all things" (**Variety of Dogmatizing**, 1661, p. 180, as cited by Basil Willey, **The Seventeenth-Century Background** [Garden City, N.Y.: Doubleday and Company, 1953, Anchor Books, first published 1934], p. 188). This does not refer to unintended consequences of human actions but to mechanical interrelations in nature that are hidden to the senses. Fontanelle, also cited by Willey, illustrated this in terms of hidden stage machinery.

For the historical derivation of individualism and laissez-faire see Albert Schatz, **L'Individualisme économique et social**, (Paris: Librairie Armand Colin,

1907), pp. 113–95 on Hume and Smith: Jacob Viner, "The Intellectual History of Laissez-Faire," **Journal of Law and Economics**, Vol. 3 (October, 1960), 45–69; same author, **The Role of Providence in the Social Order** (Philadelphia: American Philosophical Society, 1972), a discussion of providential elements in commerce, social inequality and the invisible hand; James L. Clifford, ed., **Man versus Society in Eighteenth-Century Britain** (New York: Cambridge University Press, 1968), with a contribution by Jacob Viner; Ronald L. Meek, **The Rise and Fall of the Concept of the Economic Machine**, (Leicester: Leicester University Press, 1965); Guido de Ruggiero, **The History of European Liberalism**, trans. R. G. Collingwood (New York: Oxford University Press, Inc., 1927; Boston: Beacon Press, 1959); Maurice Cranston, **Freedom: A New Analysis** (London: Longmans, Green & Co. Ltd., 1953); F. A. Hayek, **The Constitution of Liberty** (Chicago: The University of Chicago Press, 1959).

• Koebner, R., "Adam Smith and the Industrial Revolution," **Economic History Review**, Vol. 2, No. 11 (April, 1959), 381–91. Smith had personal contacts with James Watt, the great inventor, when the latter was mathematical instrument maker to Glasgow College, and Watt even made an ivory bust of Smith with his sculpture machine. But Smith showed little awareness of the Industrial Revolution that went on at his time and of which later interpreters were to hail him as a prophet. His system of laissez-faire prepared the ground for the innovators who put to practical use the newly developing technologies of the time.

• Pufendorf, Samuel von, **De Officio hominis et civis juxta legem naturalem libri duo**, (New York: Oxford University Press, Inc., The Classics of International Law, Publications of the Carnegie Endowment for International Peace, 1927). Vol. 2 of this work contains a modern English translation of the book used by Smith as a text when a student at Glasgow College. For an interpretation of Pufendorf's natural law and the bridge that it formed to natural rights see Otto von Gierke, **The Development of Political Theory** (New York: W. W. Norton & Company, Inc.,

1939): "The theory that the state exists only for the guaranty of security and legal protection, which had been made popular by Pufendorf, Locke, and Boehmer, offered a fitting handle whereby the scope of the rights untouched by the state-contract could be gradually widened. When Locke made personal liberty and property prior to all social organization, and treated these as the two inviolable rights that are entrusted by the individual to the state simply for protection, the groundwork was laid for a future theory of purely individualistic economics" (p. 108). See also H. J. Bittermann, "Adam Smith's Empiricism and the Law of Nature," **Journal of Political Economy**, Vol. 48 (August–October, 1940), 487–520, 703–34. Leonard Krieger, **The Politics of Discretion: Pufendorf and the Acceptance of Natural Law** (Chicago: The University of Chicago Press, 1965).

• Rae, John, **Life of Adam Smith** (London: Macmillan & Co. Ltd., 1895). New edition with an introduction by Viner (New York: Augustus M. Kelley, Publishers, 1965). This is the standard biography of Smith, which may be supplemented by R. B. Haldane, **Life of Adam Smith** (London: Walter Scott, 1887), or Francis W. Hirst, **Adam Smith** (London: Macmillan & Co. Ltd., 1904). A new biography, **Life of Adam Smith**, by Ian Simpson Ross (New York: Oxford University Press) is in preparation. W. R. Scott, **Adam Smith as Student and Professor** (Glasgow: Jackson, Son and Company, 1937), contains many hitherto unpublished documents. There is a lengthy review of this book by J. M. Keynes, **Economic History**, Vol. 3, No. 13 (February, 1938), 33–46. See also two books by C. R. Fay, **Adam Smith and the Scotland of His Day** (London: Cambridge University Press, 1956) and **The World of Adam Smith** (Cambridge: W. Heffner & Sons Ltd., 1960); also Walter Bagehot, "Adam Smith as a Person," **Fortnightly Review**, new series, No. 115 (July 1, 1876), 18–42, reprinted in his **Biographical Studies**, ed. R. H. Hutton (London Longmans, Green & Co. Ltd., 1881), pp. 247–81. Those interested in the contents of Adam Smith's library may consult James Bonar, **A Catalogue of the Library of Adam Smith**, 2nd ed. (London: Macmillan & Co. Ltd., 1932); T. Yanaihara, **A Full and Detailed Catalogue of Books which belonged to Adam Smith** (Tokyo: Iwanami Shoten, 1951). Hiroshi Mizuta, **Adam Smith's Library: A Suplement to Bonar's Catalogue with a Checklist of the Whole Library** (New York: Cambridge University Press for the Royal Economic Society, 1967.

• Randall, John Herman, Jr., **The Career of Philosophy: From the Middle Ages to the Enlightenment** (New York: Columbia University Press, 1962). This great work, the only modern history of philosophy written in English and developing its theme fully, treats in its fourth and last part of "The Order of Nature" (pp. 563–984). This provides an unparalleled background portrait of the philosophical environment of Smith's ideas. On Shaftesbury, see pp. 740–54; on Mandeville, pp. 754–61; on Hutcheson, pp. 775–89; on Smith himself, pp. 790–801. See also W. L. Taylor, "Eighteenth-Century Scottish Political Economy: The Impact on Adam Smith and His Work of His Association with Francis Hutcheson and David Hume," **South African Journal of Economics**, Vol. 24 (1956), 261–76; W. R. Scott, **Francis Hutcheson** (London: Cambridge University Press, 1900); William T. Blackstone, **Francis Hutcheson and Contemporary Ethical Theory** (Athens, Ga.: University of Georgia Press, 1965); Stanley Grean, **Shaftesbury's Philosophy of Religion and Ethics** (Athens, O.: Ohio University Press, 1967); Louis Schneider, ed., **The Scottish Moralists on Human Nature and Society** (Chicago: The University of Chicago Press, 1968); David Daiches, **The Paradox of Scottish Culture: The Eighteenth-Century Experience** (London: Oxford University Press, 1964). Carl L. Becker, **The Heavenly City of the Eighteenth-Century Philosophers** (New Haven, Conn.: Yale University Press, 1932), is an unexcelled albeit controversial introduction to the spirit of the age. See also Henry W. Spiegel, "Adam Smith's Heavenly City," **History of Political Economy**, Vol. 8, No. 4 (Winter, 1976), 478–93.

Gladys Bryson, **Man and Society: The Scottish Inquiry of the Eighteenth Century** (Princeton, N.J.: Princeton University Press, 1945), specifically treats of the Scottish intellectual background. See also her articles, "The Emergence of the Social Sciences from Moral Philosophy," **International Journal of Ethics**, Vol. 42 (April, 1932), 304–23; "The Comparable Interests of the Old Moral Philosophy and the Modern Social Sciences," **Social Forces**, Vol. 11 (October, 1932), 19–27. See also, for a modern appraisal of Smith's philosophy, O. H. Taylor, **A History of Economic Thought** (New York: McGraw-Hill Book Company, 1960), Chaps. 3–4; A. L. Macfie, "Adam Smith's *Moral Sentiments* as Foundation for his *Wealth of Nations*," **Oxford Economic Papers**, new series, Vol. 11 (October, 1959), 209–28; same author, "Adam Smith's *Theory of Moral Sentiments*," **Scottish Journal of Political Economy**, Vol. 8 (1960), 12–27. R. Anspach, "The Implications of the "Theory of Moral Sentiments' for Adam Smith's Economic Thought," **History of Political Economy**, Vol. 4, No. 1 (Spring, 1972), 176–206. T. D. Campbell, **Adam Smith's Science of Morals** (London: Allen & Unwin, 1971).

On "Adam Smith as Sociologist," see an article with the same title by Albert Salomon, **In Praise of Enlightenment: Essays in the History of Ideas** (New York: The World Publishing Company, Meridian Books, 1963), pp. 202–18; Albion W. Small, **Adam Smith and Modern Sociology** (Chicago: The University of Chicago Press, 1907). David A. Reisman, **Adam Smith's Sociological Economics** (New York: Barnes & Noble, 1976).

On **Adam Smith's Politics** see a book with the same title by Donald Winch (New York: Cambridge University Press, 1978). About Smith's jurisprudence see Knud Haakonssen, **The Science of a Legislator: The Natural Jurisprudence of David Hume and Adam Smith** (New York: Cambridge University Press, 1981); Peter Stein, **Legal Evolution**, same publisher, 1980.

• Smith, Adam. To celebrate the 1976 bicentenary of **The Wealth of Nations**, the University of Glasgow commissioned a six volume, complete and definitive edition of Smith's works and correspon-

dence, with two additional volumes to be published in association with the series. The **Glasgow Edition of the Works and Correspondence of Adam Smith** consists of **The Theory of Moral Sentiments, The Wealth of Nations, Essays on Philosophical Subjects (and Miscellaneous Pieces), Lectures on Rhetoric and Belles Lettres, Lectures on Jurisprudence,** and **The Correspondence of Adam Smith**, all published New York: Oxford University Press, 1976 ff. The two volumes published in association with the series are **Essays on Adam Smith**, ed. Andrew S. Skinner and Thomas Wilson, same publisher, 1976, and the forthcoming **Life of Adam Smith** by Ian Simpson Ross.

An excellent and less expensive edition of **The Wealth of Nations** is that by Edwin Cannan, which contains an introduction and valuable notes (New York: Random House, Inc., Modern Library, 1937; also available in an edition published by Chicago University Press, 1977). Selections from **The Wealth of Nations** have been published by Ludwig von Mises (Chicago: Henry Regnery Co., Gateway Editions, 1953); George J. Stigler (Des Moines, Iowa: Meredith Corporation, Appleton-Century-Crofts, 1957); and Andrew Skinner (New York: Penguin Books, 1970). All three carry interesting introductions by the editors.

For listings of older bibliographies of works by and about Smith, and of older studies of Smith's moral philosophy see the Bibliographical Notes in the first edition of this work, pp. 708, 712.

• Whitaker, Albert C., **History and Criticism of the Labor Theory of Value in English Political Economy** (New York: Columbia University Press, 1904). The first four chapters of this standard work on the subject are devoted to Adam Smith. See also Paul H. Douglas's article in Clark et al., **Adam Smith**; V. W. Bladen, "Adam Smith on Value," in H. A. Innis, ed., **Essays in Political Economy in Honour of E. J. Urwick** (Toronto: University of Toronto Press, 1938); Ronald L. Meek, **Studies in the Labour Theory of Value** (London: Lawrence & Wishart Ltd., 1956), Chap. 2; H. M.

Robertson and W. L. Taylor, "Adam Smith's Approach to the Theory of Value," **Economic Journal**, Vol. 67 (June, 1957), 181–98. The last item contains a discussion of Pufendorf's and Hutcheson's views on value.

• Young, Allyn, "Increasing Returns and Economic Progress," **Economic Journal**, Vol. 38 (December, 1928), 527–42. A discussion of Smith's theorem that the division of labor is limited by the extent of the market, which is characterized as "one of the most illuminating and fruitful generalizations which can be found anywhere in the whole literature of economics" (p. 529). See also George J. Stigler, "The Division of Labor Is Limited by the Extent of the Market," **Journal of Political Economy**, Vol. 59, No. 3 (June, 1951), 185–93, who points to the rise of monopoly as an implication of the theorem: "Either the division of labor is limited by the extent of the market, and, characteristically, industries are monpolized; or industries are characteristically competitive, and the theorem is false or of little significance" (p. 185).

CHAPTER 11*

• Becker, Gary S., and William J. Baumol, "The Classical Monetary Theory: The Outcome of the Discussion," **Economica**, new series, Vol. 19 (November 1952), 355–76. An able review of Say's law and its implications for the classical monetary theory. The authors reject the interpretation of Say's law and its implications for the classical monetary theory. The authors reject the interpretation of Say's law as an indentity and instead propose to consider it as an equality, an interpretation that in turn was criticized by Patinkin in his book noted below because Say failed to specify the equilibrating mechanism that would make his law valid (pp. 475f.). See also Baumol, "Say's (At Least) Eight Laws, Or What Say and James Mill May Really Have Meant," **Economica**, Vol. 44, No. 174 (May, 1977), 145–62; William Fellner, **Towards a Reconstruction of Macroeconomics** (Washington: American Enterprise Institute for Public Policy Research, 1976), points out that "the proposition that has become known as Say's Law . . . was considered valid by a long line of economists belonging to the classical school, beginning with Adam Smith," and refers to Bk. II, Chap. III of **The Wealth of Nations** — receipts saved are spent as regularly as those which are not saved; Thomas Sowell, **Say's Law: An Historical Analysis** (Princeton: Princeton University Press, 1972), an able survey with interesting material also about Sismondi.

See also André Paquet, **Le Conflit historique entre la loi des débouchés et le principe de la demande effective** (Paris: Librairie Armand Colin, 1953); B. J. Gordon, "Say's Law, Effective Demand, and the Contemporary British Periodicals, 1820–1850," **Economica**, new series, Vol. 32, No. 128 (November, 1965), 438–46; P. Lambert, "La loi des débouchés avant J.-B. Say et la polémique Say-Malthus," **Revue d'économie politique**, 1952, pp. 5–26; A. Macchioro, "Say, Ricardo e Malthus," **Rivista Internazionale di Scienze Economiche et Commerciali**, Vol. 13, Nos. 8–9 (July–September, 1966), 658–75, 881–95.

• Keynes, J. M., **The General Theory of Employment, Interest and Money** (London: Macmillan & Co. Ltd., 1936). Keynes interpreted Say's law as an identity according to which "the aggregate demand price of output as a whole is equal to its aggregate supply price for all volumes of output." So stated, Say's law is "equivalent to the proposition that there is no obstacle to full employment" (p. 26).

• Lange, Oskar, "Say's Law: A Restatement and Criticism," in **Studies in Mathematical Economics and Econometrics: In**

* These bibliographical notes contain only references to J. B. Say. For the literature relating to Adam Smith see the bibliographical notes to Chapter 10.

734

Memory of Henry Schultz, eds. Oskar Lange, Francis McIntyre, and Theodore O. Yntema (Chicago: The University of Chicago Press, 1942), pp. 49–68. This article, which opened up the contemporary discussion of Say's law, states it as an identity and includes a full consideration of the implications of this interpretation. "Either Say's law is assumed and money prices are indeterminate or money prices are made determinate—but then Say's law and hence the 'neutrality' of money must be abandoned. Say's law precludes any monetary theory" (pp. 65f.).

• Leontief, W. W., "The Fundamental Assumption of Mr. Keynes' Monetary Theory of Unemployment," **Quarterly Journal of Economics**, Vol. 51 (November, 1936), 192–97. This is the first statement of the homogeneity postulate as being a characteristic feature of classical economics. See also Leontief's article, "Postulates: Keynes' *General Theory* and the Classicists," in **The New Economics**, ed. Seymour E. Harris (New York: Alfred A. Knopf, Inc., 1948), pp. 232–42.

• Lerner, A. P., "The Relation of Wage Policies to Price Policies," **American Economic Review**, Vol. 29, Supplement (1939), 158–69, reprinted in William Fellner and Bernard F. Haley, eds., **Readings in the Theory of Income Distribution** (Homewood, Ill.: Richard D. Irwin, Inc., Blakiston Books, 1946), pp. 314–29. Lerner, a follower of Keynes, here gives a new interpretation of Say's law, different from the one given to it by Keynes himself. Say's law is not an identity. It points out that "the demand for output of any industry (or firm or individual) comes from the supplies of all the other industries (or firms or individuals). This is because the supplies translated into money constitute the demand for the output of the first industry (as well as for each other's output)" (p. 315). As regards the relationship between Say's law and Keynes's law, "these parallel laws meet" (p. 316). For a related interpretation, see D. H. Macgregor, **Economic Thought and Policy** (New York: Oxford University Press, Inc., 1949), pp. 111–16.

• Patinkin, Don, **Money, Interest, and Prices** (Evanston, Ill.: Row, Peterson and Company, 1956). Note L, "On Say's Law," pp. 472–76, contains a discussion of alternative interpretations of Say's law. Say's identity and its implications for classical economics are considered on pp. 119–21, 249–55. Patinkin's work aims at the integration of monetary and value theory, theories which he considers divorced by the dichotomy of the classics. For a different interpretation of the classical views, see Arthur W. Marget, **The Theory of Prices**, 2 vols. (Englewood Cliffs, N.J.: Prentice-Hall, Inc., 1938), 1942).

• Say, Jean-Baptiste, **A Treatise on Political Economy**, translated from the 4th French edition in 1821, and reprinted from the printing of 1880 (New York: Augustus M. Kelley, Publishers, 1964). For a book-length appraisal of Say see Ernest Teilhac, **L'Oeuvre économique de Jean-Baptiste Say** (Paris: Félix Alcan, 1927). Say's **Letters to Malthus**, trans. (London, 1821), have been reprinted, with a preface by Harold J. Laski (London: George Harding's Bookshop, 1936; later New York: Augustus M. Kelley, Publishers, 1965). See also G. Koolman "Say's Conception of the Role of the Entrepreneur," **Economica**, Vol. 38, No. 151 (August, 1971), 269–86.

• Smith, Adam; see bibliographical notes to Chapter 10.

• Schumpeter, J. A., **History of Economic Analysis** (New York: Oxford University Press, Inc., 1954). The late Professor Schumpeter offers a masterly analysis of Say's law on pp. 615–25. He interprets it as an equality rather than as an identity and reviews the various formulations of the identity interpretation, including two not mentioned in our text: one, according to which a seller's sales revenue is identical with the buyer's outlay, and another one, which, although stemming from Say himself, makes even less sense: overproduction is impossible because production is defined as "output, the receipts of which cover its cost." Thus wrote Say in a letter to Malthus, driven in a corner by the latter's attack and trying to uphold his law by restricting the meaning of production.

• Bonar, James, **Malthus and His Work**, 2nd ed. (New York: The Macmillan Company, 1924). This book, though now old and published originally in 1885, was for many years the standard study of Malthus. A more recent thorough appraisal of Malthus's theories and economic ideas by a professional sociologist is William Petersen, **Malthus** (Cambridge: Harvard University Press, 1979). The definitive biography is Patricia James, **Population Malthus: His Life and Times** (London and Boston: Routledge and Kegan Paul, 1979). Jane S. Nickerson, **Homage to Malthus** (Port Washington, N.Y.: Kennikat Press, 1975), is a popular introduction. See also G. F. McCleary, **The Malthusian Population Theory** (London: Faber & Faber Ltd., 1953). Briefer essays include Bonar, "The Malthusiad: Fantasia Economics," in his **The Tables Turned** (London: P. S. King and Son, 1926), where the ghost of Malthus is confronted with a modern critic; Gertrude Himmelfarb, "Malthus," **Encounter**, Vol. 5, No. 2 (August, 1955), 53–60, who wants to judge Malthus as a moralist, "reluctant to introduce any change that would lower prices, ease the condition of the poor, and bring out the old Adam in them, the sin of sloth" (p. 59); H. J. Habakkuk, "Thomas Robert Malthus, FRS (1766–1834)," Royal Society of London, **Notes and Records**, Vol. 14, No. 1 (June, 1959), 99–108, who characterizes Malthus in these words: "He was a man of fertile and strong intuition; ideas came to him swiftly, almost involuntarily, and he had a capacious grasp of evidence so that he could furnish his insights with a generous amount of illustration and employ them to illuminate wide tracts of history, But he was less proficient—or perhaps less inclined—to explore the logical implications of his ideas. Like Adam Smith and unlike Ricardo, he was not disposed to make the heroic abstractions from the facts which are necessary to make working theories out of illuminating generalizations" (p. 107); Bonar, C. R. Fay, and J. M. Keynes, "A Commemoration of Thomas Robert Malthus," **Economic Journal**, Vol. 45, No. 2 (June, 1935), 221–34, written on the occasion of the centenary of Malthus's death. See also Lionel Robbins, "Malthus as an Economist," **Economic Journal**, Vol. 77 (June, 1967), 256–61; F. Hoyle, **A Contradiction in the Argument of Malthus** (Hull: University of Hull Press, 1963).

• Bury, J. B., **The Idea of Progress** (New York: The Macmillan Company, 1932). Chaps. 11 and 12 are on Condorcet, Godwin, and Malthus, who is considered as having corrected but not denied the idea of progress by Élie Halévy, **The Growth of Philosophic Radicalism** (London: Faber & Faber Ltd., reprinted 1949), pp. 225–48. On the idea of progress see also Robert Nisbet, **History of the Idea of Progress** (New York: Basic Books, 1979); R. V. Sampson, **Progress in the Age of Reason** (London: The Heinemann Group of Publishers Ltd., 1956), and several articles in Herman Grisewood et al., **Ideas and Beliefs of the Victorians** (London: Sylvan Press, 1949). These books shed light on strands of thought that Malthus criticized rather than on his own position. Condorcet's work is available in a new edition, **Sketch for a Historical Picture of the Progress of the Human Mind**, by Antoine-Nicolas de Condorcet, trans. June Barraclough, with an introduction by Stuart Hampshire (New York: Noonday Press, 1955). On Condorcet see J. Salwyn Schapiro, **Condorcet and the Rise of Liberalism** (New York: Harcourt, Brace & World, Inc., 1934); Keith Michael Baker, **Condorcet: From Natural Philosophy to Social Mathematics** (Chicago: University of Chicago Press, 1975), who traces the term "social science" to Condorcet. William Godwin's **Enquiry Concerning Political Justice** has been published in a modern edition by F. E. L. Priestley, 3 vols. (Buffalo: University of Toronto Press, 1946). See also the same work, edited with an introduction by Isaac Kramnick (New York: Penguin Books, 1976). Interpretations of Godwin's thought are given by John P. Clark, **The Philosophical Anarchism of William Godwin** (Princeton: Princeton University Press, 1977); Don Locke, **A Fantasy of Reason: The Life and Thought of William Godwin** (London and Boston: Routledge and Kegan Paul, 1980); D. H. Monro, **Godwin's Moral Philosophy** (London: Oxford University Press, 1953), who starts out with the discussion of a moral issue the posing of which brought much notoriety to Godwin: whether to save from a burning house Archbishop Fénelon or one's mother. Godwin decided in favor of the Archbishop, because he was more likely to contribute to general happiness. On the reception of Godwin's ideas see Burton R. Pollin, **Godwin Criticism** (London: Oxford University Press, 1969).

• Eversley, D. E. C., **Social Theories of Fertility and the Malthusian Debate** (London: Oxford University Press, 1959), discusses the Malthusian and other population theories in their historical setting. For other views about population see J. Overbeck, **History of Population Theories** (Rotterdam: Rotterdam University Press, 1974); C. E. Strangeland, **Pre-Malthusian Doctrines of Population** (New York: Columbia University Press, 1904); James Bonar, **Theories of Population from Raleigh to Arthur Young** (New York: The Macmillan Company, 1931); R. Gonnard, "Les doctrines de la population avant Malthus," **Revue d'histoire économique et sociale**, 1929, pp. 58–84, 213–39; and, for the French ones, Joseph J. Spengler, **French Predecessors of Malthus** (Durham, N.C.: Duke University Press, 1942). For the Italian ones, see G. Arias, "La théorie de la population en Italie avant Malthus," **Revue d'histoire économique et sociale**, 1933, pp. 319–36; A. Breglia, "A proposito di G. Botero 'economista,'" **Annali di economica**, Vol. 4 (1928), 87–129; R. Gonnard, "Un prédécesseur de Malthus, Giammaria Ortes," **Revue d'économie politique**, 1904, pp. 638–66. For post-Malthusian developments see Sydney H. Coontz, **Population Theories and the Economic Interpretation** (London: Routledge & Kegan Paul Ltd., 1957). For applications of Malthusian ideas to current population problems see Jacob Oser, **Must Men Starve?** (London:

Jonathan Cape Limited, 1956); E. F. Penrose, **Populaton Theories and Their Application** (Stanford, Calif.: Stanford University Press, Food Research Institute, 1934); Kenneth Smith, **The Malthusian Controversy** (London: Routledge & Kegan Paul Ltd., 1951). Neil W. Chamberlain, **Beyond Malthus** (New York: Basic Books, 1970), who is concerned with the effects of differential rates of population growth that threaten stability; Thomas McKeown, **The Modern Rise of Population** (New York: Academic Press, 1976), a judicious and well-informed explanation of the population explosion by a professor of social medicine.

• Glass, D. V., ed., **Introduction to Malthus** (London: C. A. Watts & Co. Ltd., 1953). This useful volume contains a reprint of Malthus's **Summary View of the Principle of Population** of 1830, which forms part of an article that Malthus had written for a supplement to the **Encyclopaedia Britannica**, and of his **Letter to Samuel Whitbread** of 1807, in which Malthus opposes the construction of houses for the poor. In addition, there are valuable articles and a bibliography. One of the articles, by H. L. Beales, treats of "The Historical Context of the *Essay* on Population." See also J. Fréville, **L'Epouvantail malthusien** (Paris: Éditions Sociales, 1956); J. Stassart, **Malthus et la population** (Liège: Faculté de droit de l'Université, 1957).

• Griffith, C. Talbot, **Population Problems of the Age of Malthus**, (London: Cambridge University Press, 1926), explores the historical setting of Malthus's population doctrine. So do T. H. Marshall, "The Population Problem during the Industrial Revolution," **Economic History**, Vol. 1 (1929), 429–56; same author, "The Population of England and Wales from the Industrial Revolution to the World War," **Economic History Review**, Vol. 5 (1935), 65–78; and M. C. Buer, **Health, Wealth and Population, 1760–1815** (London: Routledge & Kegan Paul Ltd., 1926).

• Keynes, J. M., **Essays in Biography**, new edition by Geoffrey Keynes (New York: W. W. Norton & Company, Inc., 1963), contains on pp. 81–124, Keynes's famous essay on Malthus. This brilliant piece, originally written in 1933, did much to restore Malthus to a place of honor in English economic thought. Referring to Malthus's views about aggregate demand, Keynes says: "If only Malthus, instead of Ricardo, had been the parent stem from which nineteenth-century economics proceeded, what a much wiser and richer place the world would be today!" (p. 120). To avoid misinterpretations, this quotation should be placed side by side with another saying of Keynes: "Ricardo was the greatest mind that had found economics worthy of it" (cited by Roy Harrod, **Times Literary Supplement**, July 24, 1969).

• Malthus, Thomas Robert, **First Essay on Population** (1798), with notes by James Bonar. Reprinted for the Royal Economic Society (London: Macmillan & Co. Ltd., 1926). This is the best modern edition of the original version of Malthus's **Essay on the Principle of Population**, his only book relevant in connection with the present chapter. (References to his other works are in the bibliographical notes to Chapter 13.) A reprint of the last (6th) edition of the **Essay** revised by the author, with a biography, full analysis, and critical introduction was published by G. T. Bettany (London: Ward Lock & Co. Limited, 1890). Of modern reprints, T. R. Malthus, **On Population**, edited and introduced by Gertrude Himmelfarb (New York: Random House, Inc., Modern Library, Inc., 1960), reproduces the entire **First Essay** and copious selections from the 7th edition, published posthumously in 1872. The 7th edition can also be found without appendixes in **An Essay on Population**, 2 vols. (New York: E. P. Dutton & Co., Inc., Everyman's Library, n.d.). Other reprints include T. R. Malthus, **An Essay on the Principle of Population**, ed. with an introduction by Anthony Flew (New York: Penguin Books, 1970); same work, ed. Philip Appleman (New York: W. W. Norton and Company, 1976, Norton Critical Editions Series), which contains the text of the first edition of the **Essay**, background material, contemporary opinion, and critical essays, assembled by a Professor of English; **Population: The First Essay** has a foreword by Kenneth E.

Boulding (Ann Arbor, Mich.: The University of Michigan Press, Ann Arbor Books, 1959). In his foreword, Boulding says: "The Malthusian system, given the premises, is as irrefutable as a syllogism, and no amount of mere experience can stand up against a watertight logic" (p. x). At another place, Boulding has expressed Malthus's thought in the language of modern economic analysis; see his "The Malthusian Model as a General System," University College of the West Indies, **Social and Economic Studies**, Vol. 4 (September, 1955), 195–205. For a similar attempt see Alan T. Peacock, "Theory of Population and Modern Economic Analysis I," **Population Studies**, Vol. 6, No. 2 (November, 1952), 114–122. A reprint of Malthus's **Summary View of the Principle of Population** of 1830 forms part of **On Population** (New York: The New American Library, Inc., Mentor Books, 1960).

• Meek, Ronald L., ed., **Marx and Engels on Malthus** (New York: International Publishers Co., Inc., 1955), contains selections from the writings of Marx and Engels dealing with the theories of Malthus. The editor, a Marxist, closes his introduction with these words: "The struggle against Malthusianism is an integral part of the struggle for peace in the world today" (p. 50). See also Meek's "Malthus—Yesterday and Today," **Science and Society**, Vol. 18, No. 1 (Winter, 1954), 21–51; Samuel L. Levin, "Marx vs Malthus," Michigan Academy of Arts and Letters, **Papers**, Vol. 22 (1937), 243–58.

• Petersen, William, **The Politics of Population** (Garden City, N.Y.: Doubleday & Company, Inc., 1964). This valuable work by a professor of sociology contains chapters on the Malthusian theory, on Keynes's theories of population, on Marx versus Malthus, and on the socialist position on birth control. Professor Petersen holds that, "though Malthus' population theory suffers from inconsistencies and ambiguities, his principle of population has been one element in almost every subsequent theory, and many of the later reformulations were no great improvement in either logical or empirical terms" (Garden City, N.Y.: Doubleday &

738

Company, Inc., Anchor Books, 1965) p. 45. See also, for studies of special aspects of Malthus's work, J. M. Pullen, "Malthus' Theological Ideas and Their Influence on His Principle of Population," **History of Political Economy**, Vol. 13, No. 1 (Spring, 1981), 39–54; N. B. de Marchi and R. P. Sturges, "Malthus and Ricardo's Inductivist Critics: Four Letters to William Whewell," **Economica**, November, 1973, p. 387, where the possible application of calculus, first pointed out by Malthus in 1814, was taken up again and in similar words in 1829; Albert Fishlow, "T. R. Malthus and the English Poor Laws," **Social Science**, Vol. 33, No. 1 (January, 1958), 45–51; S. M. Levin, "Malthus' Conception of the Checks to Population," **Human Biology**, Vol. 10 (1938), 214–34; same author, "Malthus and the Idea of Progress," **Journal of the History of Ideas**, Vol. 27, No. 1 (January–March, 1966), 92–108, who quotes Malthus's observation in a letter to Ricardo, "I really think that the progress of society consists of irregular movements" (p. 93); Ernest Rubin, "The Quantitative Data and Methods of the Rev. T. R. Malthus," **The American Statistician**, February, 1960, pp. 28–31; Kingsley Davis, "Malthus and the Theory of Population," in Paul F. Lazarsfeld and Morris Rosenberg, eds., **The Language of Social Research** (New York: The Free Press, 1955), pp. 540–53, on the combination of deduction and induction in Malthus's work. How close an observer of the contemporary scene Malthus was can be seen in **The Travel Diaries of T. R. Malthus**, ed. Patricia James (London: Cambridge University Press, 1966).

• Place, Francis, **Illustrations and Proofs of the Principle of Population**, ed. Norman E. Himes (London: George Allen & Unwin Ltd., 1930), is a modern edition of Place's defense of Malthus against Godwin, which opened up the campaign for birth control in England. The standard biography of Place, Graham Wallas's **The Life of Francis Place**, which was originally published in 1898, barely mentions this delicate matter (London: George Allen & Unwin Ltd., 1925), 4th ed. See also **The Autobiography of Francis Place**, ed. Mary Thale (New York: Cambridge University Press, 1972). On Neo-Malthusianism see Himes's **Medical History of Contraception** (Baltimore: The Williams & Wilkins Co., 1936); James A. Field, **Essays on Population and Other Papers** (Chicago: The University of Chicago Press, 1931); also a number of articles by Himes: "Jeremy Bentham and the Genesis of English Neo-Malthusianism," **Economic History**, Vol. 3 (February, 1936), 267–76; "Benjamin Franklin on Population: A Reexamination with Special Reference to the Influence of Franklin on Francis Place," **Economic History**, Vol. 3 (February, 1937), 388–98; "McCulloch's Relation to the Neo-Malthusian Propaganda of His Time," **Journal of Political Economy**, Vol. 37 (February, 1929), 73–86; "John Stuart Mill's Attitude Toward Neo-Malthusianism," **Economic History**, Vol. 1, No. 4 (January, 1929), 457–84; "The Place of John Stuart Mill and Robert Owen in the History of English Neo-Malthusianism," **Quarterly Journal of Economics**, Vol. 42 (August, 1928), 627–40. Of all great figures in the recent history of economics, the most outspoken Neo-Malthusian was Knut Wicksell. See the introduction by Erik Lindahl to his **Selected Papers on Economic Theory** (London: George Allen & Unwin Ltd., 1958), and Torsten Gardlund, **The Life of Knut Wicksell**, translated from the Swedish by Nancy Adler (Stockholm: Almquist & Wiksell Gebers Foerlag AB, 1958), Chap. 3. See also Rosanna Ledbetter, **A History of the Malthusian League** (Columbus, Ohio: Ohio State University Press, 1976).

• Senior, Nassau W., **Two Lectures on Population** (London, 1829), is illustrative of the contemporary discussion of Malthus's population doctrine. It contains an appendix with the correspondence between Senior and Malthus.

• Spengler, Joseph J., "Malthus's Total Population Theory: A Restatement and Reappraisal," **Canadian Journal of Economics and Political Science**, Vol. 11 (February–May, 1945), 83–110, 234–64. This is an attempt to integrate the Malthusian population doctrine of the

Essay with that of the *Principles*. Professor Spengler holds that Malthus discovered the importance of effective demand in consequence of his analysis of the checks to population growth, which made him observe that poverty and absence of population pressure against resources may exist side by side.

Professor Spengler also has contributed a number of articles on the reaction to Malthus's views in the United States. See his "Population Doctrines in the United States," **Journal of Political Economy**, Vol. 41 (August–October, 1933), 433–67, 639–72; "Malthusianism in Late Eighteenth-Century America," **American Economic Review**, Vol. 25 (December, 1935), 691–707. Some of these articles are reprinted in Spengler's **Population Economics: Selected Essays**, compiled by Robert S. Smith et al. (Durham, N.C.: Duke University Press, 1972). See also George J. Cady, "The Early American Reaction to the Theory of Malthus," **Journal of Political Economy**, Vol. 39 (October, 1931), 601–32. On Benjamin Franklin's views about population, which may have influenced Malthus, see Lewis J. Carey, **Franklin's Economic Views** (Garden City, N.Y.: Doubleday & Company, Inc., 1928), and Henry W. Spiegel, ed., **The Rise of American Economic Thought** (Philadelphia: Chilton Book Company, 1960), pp. 9–10, 19–23.

CHAPTER 13

• Checkland, S. G., "The Advent of Academic Economics in England," **Manchester School**, Vol. 19, No. 1 (January, 1951), 43–70. The scope of this account goes beyond the geographical limits indicated in the title and extends to developments in Scotland, Ireland, and France. The chronological order in which academic instruction in political economy was offered in the United States is not entirely clear and it is beclouded by the rival claims of different institutions. It seems that the College of William and Mary included lectures based on the *Wealth of Nations* in the moral-philosophy curriculum as early as 1784. Harvard followed in 1820. Separate courses on political economy were offered at Columbia College—apparently in 1818—and at South Carolina College six years later. The professor in charge of the subject usually taught a variety of other disciplines in addition to political economy and a separate professorship of political economy did not come into being until 1871, when it was established at Harvard. Most of the early teachers of economics were clergymen and at times presidents of their institutions. The first texts were **Outlines of Political Economy**, by Rev. John McVickar, Professor of Moral Philosophy and Political Economy at Columbia College (New York, 1825), and **Lectures on the Elements of Political Economy**, by Thomas Cooper, M.D., President of South Carolina College and Professor of Chemistry and Political Economy (Columbia, S.C., 1826). Cooper was not a clergyman but an erstwhile English radical, whose tenure at South Carolina College was disturbed by a celebrated academic-freedom case. For detail see Henry W. Spiegel, **The Rise of American Economic Thought** (Philadelphia: Chilton Book Company, 1960), pp. 65f., 78f., 192.

• Clive, John, **Scotch Reviewers: The 'Edinburgh Review' 1802–1815** (London: Faber & Faber Ltd., 1957); on the **Westminster Review** George L. Nesbitt, **Benthamite Reviewing** (New York: Columbia University Press, 1934). For a listing of Frank W. Fetter's articles identifying the anonymous authors of review articles see the Bibliographical Notes in the first edition of this book, p. 719.

• Grampp, William D., "Malthus on Money Wages and Welfare," **American Economic Review**, Vol. 46, No. 5 (December, 1956), 924–36. This is an able and interesting discussion of Malthus's paradoxical wage theory, of its historical setting, and of its ramifications in the light of modern economic theory. Malthus developed this theory in 1814 and 1815 in his pamphlets on the Corn Laws and on

Rent. It was commonly believed at that time that money wages rise and fall with the price of corn, "corn" standing for grain, bread, or necessities. Malthus drew the conclusion—which buttressed his stand against free trade in grain—that high prices of corn benefit the working classes because "if they are able to command the same quantity of necessaries and receive a money price for their labor proportioned to their advanced price, there is no doubt that, with regard to all the objects of convenience and comfort, which do not rise in proportion to corn (and there are many such consumed by the poor) their condition will be most decidedly improved" (**Inquiry into the Nature and Progress of Rent**, 1815, pp. 48–49, cited by Grampp, p. 932). Malthus's logic was unimpeachable. What was questionable was the assumed relationship between money wages and corn prices, and the further assumption of other prices lagging behind corn prices. See also Joseph J. Spengler, "Malthus the Malthusian vs Malthus the Economist," **Southern Economic Journal**, Vol. 24, No. 1 (July, 1957), 1–11. According to Professor Spengler, Malthus set little store by this wage theory, which does not appear in his two principal works. Instead, "Malthus's case for high corn prices and agricultural protection rested upon his fear that low corn prices and cheap corn imports might, because of their long-run impact on population growth, retard improvement in the condition of the lower classes" (p. 8).

• Hollander, J. H., and T. E. Gregory, eds., **David Ricardo's Notes on Malthus' 'Principles of Political Economy'** (Baltimore: The Johns Hopkins Press, 1928). The manuscript of Ricardo's notes on Malthus's *Principles of Political Economy,* which came to light in 1919, is here reproduced for the first time, together with a valuable introduction by J. H. Hollander. On p. lxxix Hollander traces the origin of the oversaving and underconsumption doctrine to Quesnay. A more recent edition of Ricardo's **Notes** is in Vol. 2 of **The Works and Correspondence of David Ricardo**, edited by Piero Sraffa with the collaboration of M. H. Dobb (London: Cambridge University Press,

1951). Vols. 5–8 of this edition contain Ricardo's letters, including his correspondence with Malthus.

• Lauderdale, Earl of, **An Inquiry into the Nature and Origin of Public Wealth** (1804), edited with an introduction and revisions appearing in the 2nd edition (1819) by Morton Paglin. (New York: Augustus M. Kelley, Publishers, 1962). According to Professor Paglin, Lauderdale's contemporary critics "missed the drift of some highly significant arguments on consumer choice, utility, and demand, and on the effects of saving, spending, taxes, and debt retirement on national output. Malthus, in contrast, picked up a number of Lauderdale's basic ideas, but he failed to acknowledge his intellectual indebtedness" (p. 7). However, there are traces of the idea of oversaving already in Malthus's **First Essay** of 1798.

On Lauderdale, see also A. V. Cole, "Lord Lauderdale and his 'Inquiry,'" **Scottish Journal of Political Economy**, Vol. 3 (June, 1956), 115–25; F. A. Fetter, "Lauderdale's Oversaving Theory," **American Economic Review**, Vol. 35 (June, 1945), 263–83; Morton Paglin, "Fetter on Lauderdale," same review, Vol. 36 (June, 1946), 391–93; Morton Paglin, **Malthus and Lauderdale: The Anti-Ricardian Tradition** (New York: Augustus M. Kelley, Publishers, 1961). A. H. Hansen, **Business Cycles and National Income** (New York: W. W. Norton & Company, Inc., 1951), pp. 229–40; Maurice Mann, "Lord Lauderdale: Underconsumptionist and Keynesian Predecessor," **Social Science**, June, 1959, pp. 153–62; and Professor Mann's doctoral dissertation, "Keynes and His Underconsumption Predecessors" (Syracuse University, 1955); P. Lambert, "Lauderdale, Malthus et Keynes," **Revue d'économie politique**, January–February, 1966, pp. 32–56. B. A. Corry, "Lauderdale and the Public Debt: A Reconsideration," in Maurice Peston and B. A. Corry, eds., **Essays in Honour of Lord Robbins** (London: Weidenfeld & Nicolson, 1972), pp. 153–59.

• Malthus, T. R., **Principles of Political Economy**. A reprint of the 2nd edition, originally published in 1836 (New York: Augustus M. Kelley, Publishers, 1951).

This contains a biographical memoir by Bishop Otter, one of Malthus's friends. Of Malthus's third book—besides the **Essay** and the **Principles**—a modern reprint also is available: **Definitions in Political Economy** (1827), with an introduction by Morton Paglin (New York: Augustus M. Kelley, Publishers, 1963). Of Malthus's most important pamphlets, J. H. Hollander has edited **Observations on the Effects of the Corn Laws** (1814), and **Inquiry into the Nature and Progress of Rent** (1815) (Baltimore: The Johns Hopkins Press, 1932 and 1903, respectively). Harry G. Johnson has introduced and reprinted Malthus's **Investigation of the High Price of Provisions** (1800), in "Malthus on the High Price of Provisions," **Canadian Journal of Economic and Political Science**, Vol. 14, No. 2 (May, 1949), 190–202. A collection of articles written by Malthus for the *Edinburgh Review* and *Quarterly Review* may be found in Bernard Semmel, ed., **Occasional Papers of T. R. Malthus** (New York: Burt Franklin, 1963), which also contains an unsympathetic appraisal of Malthus by John Stuart Mill and a biographical note by William Empson. Another collection of periodical articles, in part overlapping with the former, has been edited by Cyril Renwick, **Five Papers on Political Economy by T. R. Malthus**, University of Sydney, 1953, No. 3 in a Series of Reprints of Works on Economics and Economic History, issued by the Faculty of Economics. No. 2 in the same series contains a reprint of Malthus's article on the bullion controversy.

• Paglin, **Malthus and Lauderdale**; see above p. 740. A discussion of Malthus's and Lauderdale's theories of value, rent, and effective demand, with a concluding chapter on the failure of the anti-Ricardian tradition. According to Professor Paglin, Malthus and Lauderdale were on the right track, but their theories lacked precision because they missed the concepts of marginal utility and of the consumption function. The ideas of the Ricardians were intellectually more attractive and not tainted by attachment to protectionism. "There was no organized opposition to Ricardianism, but quite the

reverse was true for Malthus" (p. 159). See also O. Pancoast, "Malthus versus Ricardo," **Political Science Quarterly,** Vol. 58 (1943), 47–66; James J. O'Leary, "Malthus and Keynes," **Journal of Political Economy,** Vol. 50, No. 6 (December, 1942), 901–19; same author, "Malthus's General Theory of Employment and the Post-Napoleonic Depression," **Journal of Economic History,** Vol. 3 (1943), 185–200; V. E. Smith, "Malthus's Theory of Demand and Its Influence on Value Theory," **Scottish Journal of Political Economy,** Vol. 3 (October, 1956), 205–20; S. Hollander, "Malthus and the Post-Napoleonic Depression," **History of Political Economy,** Vol. 1, No. 2 (Fall, 1969), 306–35; G. S. L. Tucker, **Progress and Profits in British Economic Thought, 1650–1850** (London: Cambridge University Press, 1960), Chap. 7; B. A. Corry, **Money, Saving and Investment in English Economics, 1800–1850** (New York: St. Martin's Press, Inc., 1962); Robert G. Link, **English Theories of Economic Fluctuations, 1815–1848** (New York: Columbia University Press, 1959). S. Rashid, "Malthus' Model of General Glut," **History of Political Economy,** Vol. 9, No. 3 (Fall, 1977), 366–83; Michael F. Bleaney, **Underconsumption Theories: A History and Critical Analysis** (New York: International Publishers, 1976), a Marxist analysis of underconsumption theories of Malthus, Sismondi, and others; W. A. Eltis, "Malthus's Theory of Effective Demand and Growth," **Oxford Economic Papers,** Vol. 32, No. 1 (March, 1980), 19–56; S. Rashid, "Malthus' 'Principles' and British Economic Thought, 1820–1835," **History of Political Economy,** Vol. 13, No. 1 (Spring, 1981), 55–79.

• Marcet, Jane. Mrs. Marcet and five other lady economists are the subjects of Dorothy Lampen Thomson, **Adam Smith's Daughters** (Jericho, N.Y.: Exposition Press, 1973).

• Political Economy Club, founded in London, 1821. **Minutes of Proceedings, 1899–1920, Roll of Members, and Questions discussed, 1821–1920, with Documents Bearing on the History of the Club** (London: Macmillan & Co. Ltd., 1921). This centenary volume brings together a wealth of material that sheds light on the rise and growth of nineteenth-century English economic thought.

• Say, Jean Baptiste, **Letters to Robert Thomas Malthus on Political Economy and Stagnation of Commerce** (1821), with a historical preface by Harold J. Laski (London: George Harding's Bookshop, 1936). A reissue of an English translation of Say's letters to Malthus, criticizing the latter's views about aggregate demand. For Malthus's reaction to Sismondi's doctrines and other matters see G. W. Zinke, "Six Letters from Malthus to Pierre Prévost," **Journal of Economic History**, Vol. 2 (1942), 174–89.

• Sismondi, J. C. L, Simonde de, reprints of his Encyclopedia article **Political Economy**, which Sismondi incorporated into his **Nouveaux Principes,** and of a collection of his essays published under the title **Political Economy and the Philosophy of Government** (1847) (New York: Augustus M. Kelley, Publishers, 1965). The **Nouveaux Principes** have never been translated into English. A German summary of this work as well as of the earlier **Principes** was published by Alfred Ammon, **Simonde de Sismondi**, 2 vols. (Bern: A. Francke Verlag, 1945, 1949). The standard biography and a book-length appraisal by an outstanding modern economist are—in French—Jean R.

de Salis, **Sismondi 1773–1842** (Paris: Honoré Champion, 1932); Albert Aftalion, **L'Oeuvre économique de Simonde de Sismondi** (Paris: Éditions Pédone, 1899). New material about Sismondi's algebraic model of national-income determination may be found in Thomas Sowell, **Say's Law: An Historical Analysis** (Princeton: Princeton University Press, 1972), Chap. 2; same author, "Sismondi: A Neglected Pioneer," **History of Political Economy**, Vol. 4, No. 1 (Spring, 1972), 62–88. See also Henryk Grossman, **Simonde de Sismondi et ses théories économiques** (Warsaw: Bibliotheca Universitatis Liberae Polonae, No. 11, 1924); Mao-Lan Tuan, **Simonde de Sismondi as an Economist** (New York: Columbia University Press, 1927); Élie Halévy, **Sismondi** (Paris: Félix Alcan, 1933), a selection of texts with an introduction, available in an English translation in Henry W. Spiegel, ed., **The Development of Economic Thought** (New York: John Wiley & Sons, Inc., 1952), pp. 253–68; William E. Rappard, **Economistes genevois du xixe siècle** (Geneva: Librairie Droz S.A., 1966). The Marxist reaction to Sismondi is exemplified by V. I. Lenin, who devoted a whole book to the refutation of his doctrines. English translation under the title **A Characterization of Economic Romanticism** (1897) (Moscow: Foreign Languages Publishing House, 1951).

CHAPTER 14

• Berg, Maxine, **The Machinery Question and the Making of Political Economy 1815–1848** (New York: Cambridge University Press, 1980), discusses the views of Ricardo and others on this important matter.

• Blaug, Mark, **Ricardian Economics** (New haven, Conn.: Yale University Press, 1958). A wide-ranging survey of the thought of Ricardo and of that of his followers and critics. The author is a profound student both of doctrinal history and of economic theory, who in another work, **Economic Theory in Retrospect**, third ed. (New York: Cambridge Univer-

sity Press, 1978) has offered a penetrating appraisal of doctrinal history in the light of modern economic analysis. Chapter 4 of this work, which treats of Ricardo's system, claims Ricardo as the inventor of the method of comparative statics. There is an older, still readable appraisal by Jacob H. Hollander, **David Ricardo** (Baltimore: The Johns Hopkins Press, 1910), which traces his life, his work, and his influence. For an exhaustive textual and theoretical analysis for advanced students by a modern authority see Samuel Hollander, **The Economics of David Ricardo** (Buffalo: The University of Toronto Press, 1979). For a brief survey see Michael J. Gootzeit, **David Ricardo** (New York: Columbia University Press, 1975). David Weatherall, **David Ricardo** (The Hague: Martinus Nijhoff Publisher, 1976) is strictly biographical. Oswald St. Clair, **A Key to Ricardo** (London: Routledge & Kegan Paul Ltd., 1957), the labor of love of a retired business man, offers the reader reliable guidance through the main parts of Ricardo's **Principles**. A bibliography has been attempted by Burt Franklin and G. Legman, **David Ricardo and Ricardian Theory** (New York: Burt Franklin, 1949).

• Checkland, Sydney G., "The Propagation of Ricardian Economics in England," **Economica**, new series, vol. 16, No. 61 (February, 1949), 40–52; R. L. Meek, "The Decline of Ricardian Economics in England," same journal, Vol. 17, No. 65 (February, 1950), 43–62. An interesting discussion of the fate of Ricardian economics, seen in terms of a victory by Checkland and in terms of a decline by Meek, as well as of the role of Say's law within the Ricardian doctrine. Since Ricardo held that only a rise in wages but not the accumulation of capital can lower profits, his doctrine did not require Say's law and was not based on it, but it provided a helpful corollary of his ideas. Thus, Say's law plays only a modest role in Ricardo's **Principles.** It had, however, a more lasting survival power than other elements of the Ricardian doctrine, such as the labor theory of value for example, which were put to use by radicals and social critics and which constituted a challenge to the belief in harmonious progress. Hence, the labor theory of value came under fire soon after Ricardo's death and, apart from the Socialists, was upheld almost solely by McCulloch. On this aspect of the matter see also R. D. Black, "Trinity College, Dublin, and the Theory of Value, 1823–63," **Economica**, new series, Vol. 12 (August, 1945), 140–48; Barry Gordon, "Criticism of Ricardian Views on Value and Distribution in the British Periodicals, 1820–1850," **History of Political Economy**, Vol. 1, No. 2 (Fall, 1969), 370–87; Frank W. Fetter, "The Rise and Decline of Ricardian Economics," same review, Vol. 1, No. 1 (Spring, 1969), 67–84. S. Hollander, "The Reception of Ricardian Economics," **Oxford Economic Papers**, Vol. 29, No. 2 (July, 1977), 221–57. All matters discussed in these articles are relevant also for the subjects considered in Chapter 15.

• Gordon, Barry, **Political Economy in Parliament, 1819–1823** (New York: Barnes & Noble, 1977), is an able treatment of Ricardo's role as parliamentarian. Frank W. Fetter, **The Economist in Parliament, 1780–1868** (Durham, N.C.: Duke University Press, 1980), covers a wider span of time. See also Fetter and D. Gregory, **Monetary and Financial Policy in Nineteenth-Century Britain** (Dublin: Irish University Press, 1973).

• Hutchison, T. W., "James Mill and the Political Education of Ricardo," **Cambridge Journal**, Vol. 7, No. 2 (November, 1953), 81–100. Professor Hutchison traces the influence of Mill on Ricardo's scientific method and on his liberalism, and compares the latter with that characteristic of Adam Smith. He finds the Mill-Ricardo connection paralleled by the Burke-Smith connection and sees in the Mill-Ricardo approach a forerunner not only of Marxian economics, but of Marxian political analysis as well. He urges that "much more emphasis should be placed on the contrast, or even conflict, between the methodological and political principles" of Smith and Ricardo (pp. 96f.). See also, by the same author, "Ricardo's Correspondence," **Economica**, new series, Vol. 20 (August, 1953), 263–73; "Some Questions about Ricardo," same journal, new series, Vol. 19 (November, 1952), 415–32; **On Revolutions and Progress in Economic Knowledge** (New York: Cambridge University Press, 1978).

• Marshall, Alfred, **Principles of Economics**, 8th ed. (New York: St. Martin's Press, Inc., 1920), Appendix I, "Ricardo's Theory of Value," pp. 813–21. A sympathetic interpretation of the classical theory of value by the founder of neoclassical economics. The link of Ricardo's theory of value with John Locke is underlined by Gunnar Myrdal, **The Political Element in the Development of Economic Theory** (London: Routledge & Kegan Paul Ltd.,

743

BIBLIOGRAPHICAL NOTES CHAPTER 14

1953), Chap. 3, on "The Classical Theory of Value," pp. 56–79. On the technical economics of Ricardo's value theory see G. A. Caravale and D. A. Tosato, **Ricardo and the Theory of Value, Distribution and Growth** (London and Boston: Routledge and Kegan Paul, 1980). See also, on related aspects of Ricardo's thought, George Stigler, **Essays in the History of Economics** (Chicago: The University of Chicago Press, 1965), pp. 156–97, 326–42; J. R. Hicks, "Ricardo's Theory of Distribution," in Maurice Peston and Bernard Corry, eds., **Essays in Honour of Lord Robbins** (London: Weidenfeld & Nicolson, 1972), pp. 160–67; Hicks and S. Hollander, "Mr. Ricardo and the Moderns," **Quarterly Journal of Economics**, Vol. 91, No. 3 (August, 1977), 351–69 (on Ricardo's growth model); G. S. L. Tucker, **Progress and Profits in British Economic Thought, 1650–1850** (New York: Cambridge University Press, 1960), Chap. 6 on Ricardo's theory of profit; S. Hollander, "Ricardo's Analysis of the Profit Rate," **Economica**, Vol. 40, No. 159 (August, 1973), 260–82, with reply by J. L. Eatwell and further discussion, same journal, Vol. 42, No. 166 (May, 1975), 182–202; S. Maital and P. Haswell, "Why Did Ricardo (Not) Change His Mind on Money and Machinery?" **Economica**, Vol. 44, No. 176 (November, 1977), 359–68; P. A. Samuelson, "Correcting the Ricardo Error Spotted in Harry Johnson's Maiden Paper," **Quarterly Journal of Economics**, Vol. 91, No. 4 (November, 1977), 519–30 (on rent); H. Brems, "Ricardo's Long-Run Equilibrium," **History of Political Economy**, Vol. 2, No. 2 (Fall, 1970), 225–45; Stephen C. Rankin, "Supply and Demand in Ricardian Price Theory," **Oxford Economic Papers**, Vol. 32, No. 2 (July, 1980), 241–62; Arthur I. Bloomfield, "British Thought on the Influence of Foreign Trade and Investment on Growth," **History of Political Economy**, Vol. 13, No. 1 (Spring, 1981), 95–120.

• Ricardo, David, **The Works and Correspondence**, ed. Piero Sraffa with the collaboration of M. H. Dobb, 10 vols. and a later published General Index volume (London: Cambridge University Press, 1951–55). This is the standard edition of Ricardo's works, enriched by the publication of hitherto unavailable letters and penetrating editorial comment. No other economist has been honored by a similarly magnificent edition of his works. The **Principles**, reprinted in Vol. 1, contains an editorial introduction of some 50 pages that sheds new light on many facets of Ricardo's thought. There are more editions of the **Principles** (New York: E. P. Dutton & Co., Inc., Everyman's Library, 1912; Homewood, Ill.: Richard D. Irwin, Inc., 1963, with an introduction by William Fellner; and New York: Penguin Books, 1971, with an introduction by R. M. Hartwell).

• Samuelson, Paul A., "A Modern Treatment of the Ricardian Economy," **Quarterly Journal of Economics**, Vol. 53, Nos. 1–2 (February–May, 1959), 1–35, 217–31. A penetrating analysis of Ricardian economics in the light of modern analysis. Samuelson indicates the difficulties encountered by a one-factor theory of value in a multi-factor world, and points out that the Ricardian system lends itself to an interpretation not only in terms of Ricardo's labor theory of value but also in terms of a "land theory of value."

• Sayers, R. S., "Ricardo's Views on Monetary Questions," **Quarterly Journal of Economics**, Vol. 67 (February, 1953), 30–49, reprinted in T. S. Ashton and R. S. Sayers, eds., **Papers on English Monetary History** (London: Oxford University Press, Clarendon Press, 1953). This article sheds light on Ricardo's monetary theories and on his participation in the bullion controversy. On the latter see also Jacob Viner, **Studies in the Theory of International Trade** (New York: Harper & Row, Publishers, 1937), Chaps. 3–4, pp. 119–217; Edwin Cannan, **The Paper Pound of 1797–1821**, 2nd ed. (London: P. S. King and Son, 1952), which contains a reprint of the Bullion Report; Frank W. Fetter, **Development of British Monetary Orthodoxy 1797–1875** (Cambridge, Mass.: Harvard University Press, 1965), Chaps. 1–3; B. A. Corry, **Money, Saving and Investment in British Economics, 1800–1850** (New York: St. Martin's Press, Inc., 1962).

• Shoup, Carl S., **Ricardo on Taxation** (New York: Columbia University Press, 1960), is the standard treatise on the subject. For a brief treatment of the same matter as part of a **Theory of Public Finance** see the book by Richard A. Musgrave (New York: McGraw-Hill Book Company, 1959), pp. 385–92.

• Thornton, Henry, **An Enquiry into the Nature and Effects of the Paper Credit of Great Britain (1802)**, edited with an introduction by F. A. Hayek (New York: Holt, Rinehart & Winston, Inc., 1939). This is the modern edition of Thornton's classic. For comment see Jacob Viner, **Canada's Balance of International Indebtedness, 1900–1913** (Cambridge, Mass.: Harvard University Press, 1924), Chap. 9, which called attention to Thornton's contribution to international economics; Costantino Bresciani-Turroni, **The Economics of Inflation**, trans. Millicent E. Sayers (London: George Allen & Unwin Ltd., 1937), originally published in 1931, and referring to Thornton's views about inflation; Friedrich A. Hayek, **Prices and Production**, 2nd ed. (London: Routledge & Kegan Paul Ltd., 1935), Chap. 1, "Theories of the Influence of Money on Prices"; same author, **Profits, Interest and Investment** (London: Routledge & Kegan Paul Ltd., 1939), Chap. 7 (on the development of the doctrine of forced saving); Fritz Machlup, **Essays on Economic Semantics** (Englewood Cliffs, N.J.: Prentice-Hall, Inc., 1963), pp. 213–40 (same subject); John Hicks, **Critical Essays in Monetary Theory** (London: Oxford University Press, 1967), pp. 174–88; D. A. Reisman, "Henry Thornton and Classical Monetary Economics," **Oxford Economic Papers**, Vol. 23, No. 1 (March, 1971), 70–89; Charles F. Peake, "Henry Thornton and the Development of Ricardo's Economic Thought," **History of Political Economy**, Vol. 10, No. 2 (Summer, 1978), 193–212; Philippe Beaugrand, **Henry Thornton: Un précurseur de J. M. Keynes** (Paris: Presses Universitaires de France, 1981). A contemporary review article of Thornton's book by Francis Horner, the co-founder of the **Edinburgh Review** and coauthor of the Bullion Report, has been reprinted in

The **Economic Writings of Francis Horner**, edited with an introduction by F. W. Fetter (London: The London School of Economics and Political Science, 1957).

• Viner, Jacob, **Studies in the Theory of International Trade** (New York: Harper & Row, Publishers, 1937), offers in Chap. 8, pp. 437–526, the definitive treatment of the history of the comparative-cost doctrine. Viner's analysis includes demonstrations that the comparative-cost doctrine can be expanded to apply not only to constant costs, which Ricardo assumed, but to increasing and decreasing costs as well, and that it need not be tied to a labor or production-cost theory of value. On this matter, see also Gottfried von Haberler, **The Theory of International Trade** (New York: The Macmillan Company, 1936), esp. pp. 175–98. There is a translation of the theory of comparative advantage into the mechanics of linear programming in Robert Dorfman, Paul A. Samuelson, and Robert M. Solow, **Linear Programming and Economic Analysis** (New York: McGraw-Hill Book Company, 1958), pp. 31–38. For discussions of the mechanism of international adjustment see Chap. 6 of Viner's book; James W. Angell, **The Theory of International Prices** (Cambridge, Mass.: Harvard University Press, 1926), Chap. 3; Chi-Yuen Wu, **An Outline of International Price Theories** (London: Routledge & Kegan Paul Ltd., 1939), Chaps. 3–4. For a general survey of the classical theory of international trade and its relations to later writers see John S. Chapman, "A Survey of the Theory of International Trade: Part 1, The Classical Theory," **Econometrica**, Vol. 33, No. 3 (July, 1965), 477–519. On the transfer problem as treated by Ricardo, Mill, and others, see Will E. Mason, "Some Neglected Contributions to the Theory of International Transfers," **Journal of Political Economy**, Vol. 63 (December, 1955), 529–35; "The Stereotypes of Classical Transfer Theory," same journal, Vol. 64, No. 6 (December, 1956), 492–506; "Ricardo's Transfer Mechanism Theory," **Quarterly Journal of Economics**, Vol. 71, No. 1 (February, 1957), 107–15; H. G. Grubel, "Ricardo and

Thornton on the Transfer Mechanism," same journal, Vol. 75 (May, 1961), 292–301. See also S. Hollander, "Ricardo and the Corn Laws, **"History of Political Economy**, Vol. 9, No. 1 (Spring, 1977), 1–47 (on adjustment to free trade); Arthur I. Bloomfield, "The Impact of Growth and Technology on Trade in Nineteenth-Century British Thought," same journal, Vol. 10, No. 4 (Winter, 1978), 608–35.

CHAPTER 15

• Barton, John, **Economic Writings**, with an introduction by G. Sotiroff, 2 vols. (Regina, Sask.: Lynn, 1962). A pamphlet by Barton (1789–1852), published in 1817, was cited approvingly by Ricardo in the chapter "On Machinery" inserted in the third edition of his **Principles**.

• Bastiat, F., **Economic Harmonies**, translated from French by W. H. Boyers, ed. G. B. de Huszar (New York: Litton Educational Publishing, Inc., Van Nostrand Reinhold Company, 1964). What was designed as Bastiat's principal contribution is made available here in a new edition to the modern reader, as are also his **Economic Sophisms,** trans. and ed. A. Goddard, and **Selected Essays on Political Economy,** trans. S. Cain, ed. G. B. de Huszar (same publisher and year). These volumes, which carry introductions by F. A. Hayek and Henry Hazlitt, were sponsored by the William Volker Fund to serve as an antidote to modern interventionism and socialism. See also George Charles Roche 3d, **Frederic Bastiat: A Man Alone** (New Rochelle, N.Y.: Arlington House, 1971), a volume in the "Architects of Freedom" series; Dean Russell, **Frédéric Bastiat: Ideas and Influence** (Irvington-on-Hudson, N.Y.: Foundation for Economic Education, 1963). This foundation also has sponsored a new translation of Bastiat's **The Law**, 1950.

• Bentham, Jeremy, **Economic Writings**, critical edition based on his printed works and unprinted manuscripts by W. Stark, published for the Royal Economic Society (London: George Allen & Unwin Ltd., 1952–54), 3 vols. This is the standard edition of Bentham's economic writings, culled together from a variety of printed and unprinted sources, with instructive introductions. It is only in this edition that a complete picture of Bentham as an economist emerges. A critical edition of

The Collected Works of Jeremy Bentham is forthcoming (London: University of London, Athlone Press). See also W. Stark, "Liberty and Equality, or: Jeremy Bentham as an Economist," **Economic Journal**, Vol. 51 (April, 1941), 56–79 and Vol. 56 (December, 1946), 583–608; T. W. Hutchison, "Bentham as an Economist," **Economic Journal**, Vol. 66 (June, 1956), 288–306; Jacob Viner, "Bentham and J. S. Mill: The Utilitarian Background," **American Economic Review**, Vol. 39 (March, 1949), 360–82; James Bonar, "In Memoriam: Jeremy Bentham (1748–1832)," **Economic History**, Vol. 2, No. 8 (January, 1933), 536–52; Wesley Clair Mitchell, "Bentham's Felicific Calculus," **Political Science Quarterly**, Vol. 33 (June, 1918), 161–83, reprinted in his **The Backward Art of Spending Money** (New York: McGraw-Hill Book Company, 1937), pp. 177–202; Oskar Kraus, **Zur Theorie des Wertes: Eine Bentham-Studie**, (Tübingen: Max Niemeyer Verlag, 1902); Lionel Robbins, **Bentham in the Twentieth Century** (London: University of London, Athlone Press, 1965), who speaks of the greatest-happiness principle in these words: "If we consider it, not as the ultimate solution to all problems of ethics and valuation . . . but rather as a working rule by which to judge legislative and administrative projects affecting large masses of people, it still seems to me better, more sensible, more humane, more agreeable to the moral conscience if you like, than any other I can think of" (p. 12).

For a considerably more critical evaluation of the greatest-happiness principle, based on a denial of the commensurability of Bentham's "dimensions," see John Plamenatz, **The English Utilitarians,** 2nd ed. (Oxford: Basil Blackwell & Mott Ltd., 1958): "Even an omniscient God could not make such calculations, for the very notion of them is impossible. The intensity of a pleasure cannot be measured against its duration, nor its duration against its certainty or uncertainty, nor this latter property against its propinquity or remoteness" (pp. 73f.). Bentham's **Introduction to the Principles of Morals and Legislation**, which contains a statement of the greatest-happiness principle, has been reprinted (New York: Hafner Publishing Co., Inc., 1948); it also appears in his **A Fragment on Government with An Introduction to the Principles of Morals and Legislation**, ed. Wilfrid Harrison (Oxford: Basil Blackwell & Mott Ltd., 1948), and in **The Utilitarians** (Garden City, N.Y.: Doubleday & Company, Inc., Dolphin Books, 1961).

Bentham's philosphy is sympathetically considered by David Baumgardt, **Bentham and the Ethics of Today** (Princeton, N.J.: Princeton University Press, 1952), which includes scholarly detail tracing the greatest-happiness principle to Francis Hutcheson, Adam Smith's teacher, and still earlier writers (pp. 33–63). Baumgardt also draws attention to the negative reaction to Bentham in Germany. While Bentham's fame spread through the world, he found little response in Germany, where hostility both to utilitarianism and to the rival natural-law philosophy stifled economic theorizing. There was only one contemporary philosopher of name in Germany who expressed admiration for Bentham, and him Hegel had expelled from his position at the University of Berlin. Even a "liberal" such as Goethe referred to Bentham as a "highly radical fool" (pp. 4f.). Paul A. Palmer, "Benthamism in England and America," **American Political Science Review**, Vol. 35, No. 5 (October, 1941), 855–71, investigates the reasons for the relative lack of response to Bentham in the United States. Among other factors he mentions the more deeply entrenched natural-law philosophy.

For general appraisals of Bentham see Leslie Stephen, **The English Utilitarians** (London: Gerald Duckworth & Co. Ltd., 1900), Vol. 1; Élie Halévy, **The Growth of Philosophic Radicalism**, trans. Mary Morris (London: Faber & Faber Ltd., 1928); J. L. Stocks, **Jeremy Bentham** (Manchester: Manchester University Press,

1933); Shirley Robin Letwin, **The Pursuit of Certainty** (London: Cambridge University Press, 1965), Part 2; Mary P. Mack **Jeremy Bentham: An Odyssey of Ideas, 1748–1792** (London: The Heinemann Group of Publishers Limited, 1962), a biography of the early period; Charles W. Everett, **Jeremy Bentham** (New York: Dell Publishing Co., Inc., 1966), with selections from Bentham's writings; D. J. Manning, **The Mind of Jeremy Bentham**, (London: Longmans, Green & Co. Ltd., 1968); Gertrude Himmelfarb, **Victorian Minds** (New York: Alfred A. Knopf, Inc., 1968); **A Bentham Reader**, ed. Mary P. Mack (New York: Pegasus (Publishers), Inc., 1969).

• Black, R. D. Collison, **Economic Thought and the Irish Question, 1817–1870** (London: Cambridge University Press, 1960). The definitive treatment of economic opinion about how to cope with the problems of the Irish economy, which shows the willingness of the economists of the time to compromise with the laissez-faire principle. There was more inertia in government circles, and consequent failure to avoid a great deal of terrible harm. As Jacob Viner says in the foreword: "A greater prevalence of uncalculating compassion and sympathy with suffering may at times be a better instrument of reform than the most carefully reasoned weighing of prudential pros and cons in deciding whether immediately helpful expedients would in the long run do more good than harm" (pp. vii f.). See also Cecil Woodham-Smith, **The Great Hunger: Ireland, 1845–1849** (New York: Harper & Row, Publishers, 1962), which contains a frightening quotation attributed to Senior (Los Angeles: The Times Mirror Co., The New American Library, Inc., Signet Books, 1964), p. 373. See further R. D. C. Black, "The Classical Economists and the Irish Problem" **Oxford Economic Papers**, new series, Vol. 5 (March, 1953), 26–40.

Professor Black also has written a study of the development of economic thought in Ireland; see his "Trinity College, Dublin, and the Theory of Value, 1823–63," **Economica**, new series, Vol. 12 (August, 1945), 140–48, which treats of Whately, Longfield, and others. See also

748

Mary S. Shields, "Some Irish Contributions to the History of Economics," an abstract of a thesis, (Washington, D.C.: The Catholic University of America Press, 1955), which carries the story forward to Cairnes, Bastable, and O'Brien.

• Grampp, William D., **The Manchester School of Economics** (Stanford, Calif.: Stanford University Press, 1960). A study of the English free-trade movement of the nineteenth century. The author underlines the tenuous connection between the Manchester School, which promoted repeal of protection, and economic opinion. "The names of none of the well-known economists appear in the register of the Manchester School." He argues that "neither the economists themselves nor their doctrines had any lasting connection with the repeal campaign" (p. 16).

• McCulloch, John Ramsey. The first full-scale study of McCulloch is D. P. O'Brien, **J. R. McCulloch: A Study in Classical Economics** (New York: Barnes & Noble, 1970). O'Brien also has edited McCulloch's **A Treatise on the Principles and Practical Influence of Taxation and the Funding System** (Edinburgh: Scottish Academic Press for the Scottish Economic Society, 1975), the first separate treatise on public finance. On the history of this subject see Harold M. Groves, **Tax Philosophers: Two Hundred Years of Thought in Great Britain and the United States**, ed. Donald J. Curran (Madison: University of Wisconsin Press, 1974); R. A. Musgrave and Alan T. Peacock, eds., **Classics in the Theory of Public Finance** (London: Macmillan & Co. Ltd., 1958); and various writings by Fritz Karl Mann: **Steuerpolitische Ideale** (originally published 1937; reprinted Stuttgart and New York: Gustav Fischer Verlag, 1978); "Geschichte der angelsächsischen Finanzwissenschaft," in Wilhelm Gerloff and Fritz Neumark, eds., **Handbuch der Finanzwissenschaft**, 2nd ed. (Tübingen: J. C. B. Mohr, 1952), pp. 469–88; "Abriss einer Geschichte der Finanzwissenschaft," same publication, 3rd ed. (same publisher, 1975), pp. 77–98.

• Mill, James, **Selected Economic Writings**, ed. Donald Winch, (Chicago: The University of Chicago Press, 1966); **History of British India**, new edition, with an introduction by J. K. Galbraith, 2 vols. (New York: Chelsea House Publishers, 1968). The standard biography of **James Mill** is by Alexander Bain (London: Longmans, Green & Co. Ltd., 1882). See also Stephen, **English Utilitarians,** Vol. 2; Halévy, **Philosophic Radicalism,** pp. 342–72 on Mill and McCulloch; T. W. Hutchison, "James Mill and the Political Education of Ricardo," **The Cambridge Journal**, Vol. 7, No. 2 (November, 1953), 81–100, who considers Mill a forerunner of Marx and of modern managerial totalitarianism: "We do not refer simply to the incidental account of 'the class struggle' which Mill and Ricardo saw emerging in the early 1820s; nor to Mill's extreme progressivist historicism; nor to his burning *Ressentiment* and his wholesale attribution of the most sordid motives to all contemporary political leaders. We refer rather to such broader notions as that of a corrupt or exploiting class . . . . Then we have Mill's idea of legislation or policy being an exact science . . . . From this idea it immediately follows that honest disagreement and doubt are impossible, and that political freedom should disappear" (p. 95); Joseph Hamburger, **James Mill and the Art of Revolution** (New Haven, Conn.: Yale University Press, 1963). William J. Barber, "James Mill and the Theory of Economic Policy in India," **History of Political Economy**, Vol. 1, No. 1 (Spring, 1969), 85–100, same author, **British Economic Thought and India 1600–1858** (New York: Oxford University Press, 1975); S. Ambirajan, **Classical Political Economy and British Policy in India** (New York: Cambridge University Press, 1978); W. O. Thweatt, "James Mill and the Early Development of Comparative Advantage," **History of Political Economy**, Vol. 8, No. 2 (Summer, 1976), 207–34.

• Rae, John, **The Sociological Theory of Capital**, ed. Charles W. Mixter (New York: The Macmillan Company, 1905). This was the title under which Rae's **New Principles**, in a rearranged form, were again brought to the attention of the economics profession. Since then the original work has been reprinted, among others by R. Warren James, **John Rae: Political Economist**, 2 vols. (Toronto: University of Toronto Press, 1965). Irving Fisher called the work "truly a masterpiece, a book of a generation or a century" and dedicated his own **Rate of Interest** (New York: The Macmillan Company, 1907), "To the memory of John Rae who laid the foundations upon which I have endeavored to build." See also J. J. Spengler, "John Rae on Economic Development: A Note," **Quarterly Journal of Economics**, Vol. 73 (August, 1959), 393–406, Craufurd D. W. Goodwin, **Canadian Economic Thought** (Durham, N.C.: Duke University Press, 1961), pp. 122–27.

• Robbins, Lionel, **the Theory of Economic Policy in English Classical Political Economy** (New York: St. Martin's Press, Inc., 1952), contains an evaluation of the attitude to laissez-faire among the economists considered in the present chapter. See also Warren J. Samuels, **The Classical Theory of Economic Policy** (Los Angeles: The Times Mirror Co., The World Publishing Company, 1966); George J. Stigler, "The Economist and the State," **American Economic Review**, Vol. 55, No. 1 (March, 1965), 1–18, who discusses the proposition "that the classical economists objected chiefly to *unwise* governmental intervention in economic life" (p. 5); John B. Brebner, "Laissez-Faire and State Intervention in Nineteenth-Century Britain," **Journal of Economic History**, Supplement 8, 1948, pp. 59–73. W. D. Grampp, "The Economists and the Combination Laws," **Quarterly Journal of Economics**, Vol. 93, No. 4 (November, 1979), 501–22; Michael Brock, **The Great Reform Act** (Atlantic Highlands, N.J.: Humanities Press, 1973).

• Seligman, Edwin R. A., "On Some Neglected British Economists," **Economic Journal**, Vol. 13 (September–December, 1903), 335–63, 511–35, reprinted in his **Essays in Economics** (New York: The Macmillan Company, 1925), pp. 64–121. A famous article in which attention was called to the contributions of Torrens, Bailey, Lloyd, Whately, Longfield, and others. On these see also Mark Blaug, **Ricardian Economics** (New Haven, Conn.:

Yale University Press, 1958); Robert M. Rauner, **Samuel Bailey and the Classical Theory of Value** (Cambridge Mass.: Harvard University Press, 1961); R. F. Harrod, "An Early Exposition of 'Final Utility': W. F. Lloyd's Lecture on 'The Notion of Value' (1833) Reprinted," **Economic History** (Supplement to the **Economic Journal**), Vol. 1 (May, 1927), 168–83; Laurence S. Moss, **Mountifort Longfield** (Ottawa, Ill.: Green Hill Publishers, 1976); W. D. Grampp, "Edward West Reconsidered," **History of Political Economy**, Vol. 2, No. 2 (Fall, 1970), 316–43.

• Senior, Nassau William, **An Outline of the Science of Political Economy** (London: George Allen & Unwin Ltd., 1938). This is a reprint of Senior's systematic contribution to economics, first published in 1835. A collection of his hitherto unpublished writings has been made available under the title **Industrial Efficiency and Social Economy**, ed. S. Leon Levy, 2 vols. (New York: Holt, Rinehart & Winston, Inc., 1928). The editor of this work also has written an enthusiastic appraisal of **Nassau W. Senior: The Prophet of Modern Capitalism**, (Boston: Bruce Humphries, 1943). The standard work about Senior is Marian Bowley, **Nassau Senior and Classical Economics** (London: George Allen & Unwin Ltd., 1937), a distinguished interpretation that relates Senior's thought to that of continental writers. In view of the espousal, by Senior and others, of a subjective theory of value, Miss Bowley holds that "either it must be recognized that there were two different and more or less contemporary schools even in England, the classical or Ricardian and the utility schools, or the term classical must be disassociated from its narrow sense" (p. 17). See also George J. Stigler, **Five Lectures on Economic Problems** (New York: The Macmillan Company, 1950), Lecture 3, pp. 25–36, which contains an appraisal of the Report of the Commissioners on the Handloom Weavers, of which Senior was apparently the principal draftsman. Using this report as a test case, Stigler makes the point that "in writing their treatises. . .the classical economists have employed an apparatus which is different, and in modern eyes

750

inferior, to that which they employed to analyze concrete problems" (p. 26). In the report "the demand curve is subjected to detailed study, income effects are recognized, the firm-household is the unit of analysis, the law of substitution enters, imperfections of competition are duly examined" (p. 34). Thus "the technical apparatus of the classical economics was best precisely in those areas, and on precisely those subjects, where the issues were posed by concrete problems of the day." When dealing with such problems, "the theorists' eternal, and proper, striving for generality is disciplined by the facts"; moreover, "most of our modern economics of price was deemed by the classical economists to be pedestrian stuff, inappropriate to a treatise . . . . For us, they would say, there are greater problems: the true basis of value, the laws of distribution of national income, the foundations of national prosperity, the growth and decline of nations" (pp. 35f.).

On the debate about the poor laws, in which Senior played a prominent role, see J. R. Poynter, **Society and Pauperism** (London: Routledge & Kegan Paul, 1969). N.C. Edsall, **The Anti-Poor Law Movement 1834–44** (Totowa, N.J.: Rowman & Littlefield, 1971); Michael E. Rose, **The Relief of Poverty 1834–1914** (London: Macmillan and Co. Ltd., 1972). On Senior's position regarding restrictions on hours of work, see Orace Johnson, "The 'Last Hour' of Senior and Marx," **History of Political Economy**, Vol. 1, No. 2 (Fall, 1969), 359–69.

• Spiegel, Henry W., **The Rise of American Economic Thought** (Philadelphia: Chilton Book Company, 1960), contains selections, with comment, from the works of Carey, Raymond, Everett, Cardozo, List, Rae, Tucker, and other American writers, as well as further references. For a more detailed interpretation see Joseph Dorfman, **The Economic Mind in American Civilization**, Vol. 1–2 (New York: The Viking Press, Inc., 1946); Paul K. Conkin, **Prophets of Prosperity: America's First Political Economists** (Bloomington: Indiana University Press, 1980); Michael Hudson, **Economics and Technology in Nineteenth-Century American Thought:**

The Neglected American Economists (New York: Garland Publishing Inc., 1975). Hudson also has edited, with new introductions that are reprinted in the above volume, some 46 works of early American economists (same publisher, 1970s). See also Charles P. Neill, **Daniel Raymond** (Baltimore: The Johns Hopkins Press, 1897); Margaret E. Hirst, **Life of Friedrich List and Selections from His Writings** (London: Smith, Elder and Company, 1909); Melvin M. Leiman, **Jacob N. Cardozo** (New York: Columbia University Press, 1966); A. D. H. Kaplan, **Henry Charles Carey** (Baltimore: The Johns Hopkins Press, 1931); Tipton R. Snavely, **George Tucker** (Charlottesville, Va.: The University Press of Virginia, 1964); same author, **The Department of Economics at the University of Virginia, 1825–1956** (Charlottesville, Va.: The University Press of Virginia, 1967). See also below, pp. 759–60, on List.

• Torrens, Robert, **Letters on Commercial Policy**, with an introduction by Lord Robbins (London: The London School of Economics and Political Science, 1958). In addition to this reprint of a work published first in 1833, there is available also a book-length appraisal by Lionel Robbins, **Robert Torrens and the Evolution of Classical Economics** (New York: St. Martin's Press, Inc., 1958), a distinguished work in which Torrens's position is summed up in these words: "It is clear that as an economist he was not in the first rank. He had neither the soaring speculative powers of Ricardo nor the strong intuitions of Malthus. Nor had he the exalted moral passion or the wide powers of synthesis of J. S. Mill. But among the men of the next grade his standing was not negligible. He had obviously much greater analytical breadth than James Mill or McCulloch, though he lacked the concentration of the former and the wide factual knowledge of the latter. The comparison with Senior is more difficult. Senior perhaps had more culture and probably better practical judgment; Torrens more originality and deeper analytical insight, less capacity for concise exposition, more for the moment of vision and the communication of *élan*" (p. 258).

See also S. A. Meenai's studies of Torrens: "Robert Torrens and Classical Economics," **Federal Economic Review** (Karachi), Vol. 2 (October, 1955), 155–200 and Vol. 3 (July, 1956), 18–40; "Robert Torrens and Classical Economists," same journal, Vol. 6–7 (July, 1959–January, 1960), 86–123; "Robert Torrens, 1780–1864," **Economica**, new series, Vol. 23 (February, 1956), 49–61; also Frank W. Fetter, "Robert Torrens: Colonel of Marines and Political Economist," **Economica**, new series, Vol 29 (May, 1962), 152–65; D. P. O'Brien, "The Transition in Torrens' Monetary Thought," same journal, new series, Vol. 32 (August, 1965), 269–301.

D. P. O'Brien and A. C. Darnell, "Torrens, McCulloch and the 'Digression on Sismondi': Whose Digression?" **History of Political Economy**, Vol. 12, No. 3 (Fall, 1980), 383–95, an article that resolves the question of authorship by means of a statistical test. For a similar attempt, undertaken in 1939 in connection with the Petty-Graunt problem, see above, p. 717.

The Correspondence of Lord Overstone, ed. by D. P. O'Brien, 3 vols. (New York: Cambridge University Press, 1971) deals with another leader of the currency school.

• Viner, Jacob, **Studies in the Theory of International Trade** (New York: Harper & Row, Publishers, 1937). This great work contains in Chapter 5, pp. 218–89, the definitive account of the controversy between the banking and currency schools. A more recent treatment can be found in Frank W. Fetter, **Development of British Monetary Orthodoxy, 1797–1875** (Cambridge, Mass.: Harvard University Press, 1965), which lives up to the standards set by Viner. There is a briefer study by Marion R. Daugherty, "The Currency–Banking Controversy," **Southern Economic Journal**, Vol. 9 (October, 1942–January, 1943), 140–55, 241–51. See also T. E. Gregory, **An Introduction to Tooke and Newmarch's "A History of Prices"** (London: The London School of Economics and Political Science, 1962), originally published in 1928. H. Rieter, **Die gegenwärtige Inflationstheorie und ihre Ansätze im Werk von Thomas Tooke** (Berlin:

Walter de Gruyter & Co., 1971); David Laidler, "Thomas Tooke on Monetary Reform," in M. Peston and Bernard Corry, eds., **Essays in Honour of Lord Robbins** (London: Weidenfeld & Nicolson, 1972), pp. 168–86. The London School of Economics and Political Science has made available reprints of Thomas Tooke, **An Inquiry into the Currency Principle**, 1844 (1959); **Economic Writings of James Pennington**, ed. R. S. Sayers (1963); and of **Selected Economic Writings of Thomas Attwood**, ed. Frank W. Fetter (1964). On the Attwoods see also Sydney G. Checkland, "The Birmingham Economists, 1815–1850," **Economic History Review**, 2nd series, Vol. 1, No. 1 (1948), 1–19. The background of the gradual evolution of regulating principles in English banking practice is explored by J. K. Horsefield, "The Duties of a Banker," **Economica**, new series, Vol. 8 (February, 1941), 37–51, and Vol. 11 (May, 1944), 74–85; reprinted in T. S. Ashton and R. S. Sayers, eds., **Papers in English Monetary History** (London: Oxford University Press, 1953).

• Wakefield, Edward Gibbon, **A Letter from Sydney and Other Writings on Colonization**, with an introduction by R. C. Mills (New York: E. P. Dutton & Co., Inc., Everyman's Library, 1929), offers a selection from Wakefield's works. Far wider in scope is M. F. Lloyd Prichard, ed., **The Collected Works of Edward Gibbon Wakefield** (London: Collins, 1969). Wakefield's biography has been written by Paul Bloomfield, **Edward Gibbon Wakefield** (London: Longmans, Green & Co. Ltd., 1961); it is worth studying. The colonization debate is ably discussed by Klaus Knorr, **British Colonial Theories, 1570–1850** (Toronto: University of Toronto Press, 1944), especially Chaps. 8 and 9, the standard work on the subject. See also Donald Winch, **Classical Political Economy and Colonies** (Cambridge, Mass.: Harvard University Press, 1965); Edward R. Kittrell, "The Development of the Theory of Colonization in English Classical Political Economy," **Southern Economic Journal**, Vol. 31, No. 3 (January, 1965), 189–206; H. O. Pappe, "Wakefield and Marx," **Economic History Review**, 2nd series, Vol. 4, No. 1 (1951),

88–97; Bernard Semmel, "The Philosophical Radicals and Colonialism, **Journal of Economic History**, December, 1961, pp. 513–25; E. R. Kittrell, "Bentham and Wakefield," **Western Economic Journal**, Vol. 4, No. 1 (Fall, 1965), 28–40; Craufurd D. W. Goodwin, **Economic Enquiry in Australia** (Durham, N.C.: Duke University Press, 1966), pp. 60–91; Bernard Semmel, **The Rise of Free Trade Imperialism** (New York: Cambridge University Press, 1970); H. J. M. Johnston, **British Emigration Policy 1815–1830: 'Shovelling Out Paupers'** (New York: Oxford University Press, 1972).

• Ward, J. T., **The Factory Movement, 1830–1855** (New York: St. Martin's Press, Inc., 1962). A social and political history of the struggle for factory legislation in Britain.

CHAPTER 16

• Anschutz, R. P., **The Philosophy of J. S. Mill** (London: Oxford University Press, 1953). This is one of the few book-length appraisals of the entire field of Mill's thought, written by a professional philosopher. Professor Anschutz, while pointing out the contradictions in Mill's thought, suggests that some of them arise from the matters treated rather than from a disorderly mind. He also speaks of "two strains in Mill. The sensitive temperament, that craved for sympathetic support and responded so delicately to every trend of the age was balanced, or almost balanced, by a strong and thoroughly trained will, which was never content to absorb influences but always persisted in systematizing them from a radical point of view which had in it something of the moralist but a good deal more of the scientist" (p. 6). See also, for works similar in scope, Alan Ryan, **John Stuart Mill** (London and Boston: Routledge and Kegan Paul, 1974); H. J. McCloskey, **John Stuart Mill** (London: Macmillan & Co. Ltd., 1971, in the Philosophers in Perspective series); K. Britton, **John Stuart Mill** (Harmondsworth, Middlesex: Penguin Books Ltd., 1953). For briefer, essay-type appraisals of Mill see first of all that by his godson Bertrand Russell, "John Stuart Mill," **Portraits from Memory and Other Essays** (London: George Allen & Unwin Ltd., 1956), pp. 114–34, who believes that "Mill, both in his prophecies and in his hopes, was misled by not foreseeing the increasing power of great organizations" (p. 120), but who finds himself in agreement with Mill's values: "I think he is entirely right in emphasizing the importance of the individual in so far as values are concerned. I think, moreover, that it is even more desirable in our day than it was in his to uphold the kind of outlook for which he stands. But those who care for liberty in our days have to fight different battles from those of the nineteenth century, and have to devise new expedients if liberty is not to perish. From the seventeenth century to the end of the nineteenth, 'Liberty' was the watchword of the radicals and revolutionaries; but in our day the word has been usurped by reactionaries, and those who think themselves most progressive are inclined to despise it . . . So far as any one person is responsible for this change, the blame must fall on Marx, who substituted Prussian discipline for freedom as both the means and the end of revolutionary action. But Marx would not have had the success which he has had if there had not been large changes in social organization and technique which furthered his ideals as opposed to those of earlier reformers. What has changed the situation since Mill's day is, as I remarked before, the great increase of organization" (pp. 124f.). Other essays about Mill include Maurice Cranston, **John Stuart Mill** (London: Longmans, Green & Co. Ltd., 1958); Noel Annan, "John Stuart Mill," in **The English Mind: Studies in the English Moralists presented to Basil Willey** (London: Cambridge University Press, 1964), pp. 219–39, who holds that Mill's rationalism was destroyed by Marx: "It was Marx who denied that social phenomena could be reduced to laws about human nature. Mill, standing at the end of the positivist explanation of social behavior, was still arguing that since men make their own environment and traditions, their institutions and customs must be explicable in terms of the mind and of human nature . . . This was the theory that Marx destroyed . . . Man was the product of society and a slave to the impersonal laws of history that governed society" (pp. 226f.). Together with other material, Russell's and Annan's essays are reprinted in **Mill: A Collection of Critical Essays**, ed. J. B. Schneewind (Garden City, N.Y.: Doubleday & Co., Inc., Anchor Books, 1968). See also Isaiah Berlin, **Two Concepts of Liberty** (London: Oxford University Press, 1958); and **John Stuart Mill and the Ends of Life** (London: Council of Christians and Jews, 1959); Basil Willey, **Nineteenth-Century Studies** (New York: Columbia University Press, 1949), Chap. 6; Shirley Robin Letwin, **The Pursuit of Certainty** (London: Cambridge University Press, 1965), Part 3; Thomas Woods, **Poetry and Philosophy: A Study in the Thought of John Stuart Mill** (London: Hutchinson Publishing Group Ltd., 1961). John M. Robson, **The Improvement of Mankind: The Social and Political Thought of J. S. Mill** (Toronto: University of Toronto Press, 1968). Gertrude Himmelfarb, **On Liberty and Liberalism: The Case of J. S. Mill** (New York, Alfred A. Knopf, 1974), attempts to resolve certain inconsistencies in Mill's thought. John M. Robson and Michael Laine, eds., **James and John Stuart Mill: Papers of the Centenary Conference** (Buffalo: University of Toronto Press, 1976).

• Chipman, John S., "A Survey of the Theory of International Trade: Part 1, The Classical Theory," **Econometrica**, Vol. 33, No. 3 (July, 1965), 477–519. This article contains a new appraisal of an extension of Mill's law of international value inserted in the third edition of the *Principles* and hitherto judged unfavorably. The standard discussion of Mill's theory of international adjustment and of his reciprocal demand is to be found in Jacob Viner, **Studies in the Theory of International Trade** (New York: Harper

& Row, Publishers, 1937), pp. 30ff., 446ff. For earlier comments on reciprocal demand see F. Y. Edgeworth, **Papers Relating to Political Economy** (London: Macmillan & Co. Ltd., 1925), Vol. 2, 3ff., on "The Pure Theory of International Values"; Alfred Marshall, **Money, Credit and Commerce** (London: Macmillan & Co. Ltd., 1923), pp. 155ff. and Appendix J. See also, on the terms-of-trade argument for a tariff, Edgeworth, **Papers**, pp. 340ff. A more recent discussion was initiated by Nicholas Kaldor, "A Note on Tariffs and the Terms of Trade," **Economica**, new series, Vol. 7 (November, 1940), 377–80, reprinted in **Essays on Value and Distribution** (London: Gerald Duckworth & Co. Ltd., 1960), Vol 1, 146–50. The discussion was resumed by Harry G. Johnson, "Optimum Tariffs and Retaliation," **Review of Economic Studies,** Vol. 21, No. 2 (1953–54), 142–53, reprinted in **International Trade and Economic Growth** (London: George Allen & Unwin Ltd., 1958), pp. 31–55. On Mill's somewhat reluctant endorsement of the infant-industry argument in favor of tariffs see M. C. Kemp, "The Mill–Bastable Infant Industry Dogma," **Journal of Political Economy**, Vol. 68 (February, 1960), 65–67. For Cairnes's and Sidgwick's contributions to international-trade theory see Chi-Yuen Wu, **An Outline of International Price Theories** (London: Routledge & Kegan Paul Ltd., 1939); James W. Angell, **The Theory of International Prices** (Cambridge, Mass.: Harvard University Press, 1926); Viner, **Studies**; and J. Melitz, "Sidgwick's Theory of International Values," **Economic Journal**, Vol. 73 (September, 1963), 431–41, for an interpretation differing from the preceding ones.

• Hamburger, Joseph, **Intellectuals in Politics: John Stuart Mill and the Philosophic Radicals** (New Haven, Conn.: Yale University Press, 1965). A detailed study of the political achievements of the philosophical radicals, and of Mill's leadership and eventual disenchantment. See also William Thomas, **The Philosophical Radicals** (New York: Oxford University Press, 1979).

• Hayek, F. A., **John Stuart Mill and Harriet Taylor** (London: Routledge &

Kegan Paul Ltd., 1951). A collection of letters between Mill and Harriet Taylor, with perceptive commentary. Professor Hayek holds that Harriet Taylor's influence on Mill's thought and outlook was just as great as Mill asserts, but that it acted "in a way somewhat different from what is commonly believed. Far from having been the sentimental, it was the rationalist element in Mill's thought which was mainly strengthened by her influence" (p. 17). For a different interpretation see H. O. Pappe, **John Stuart Mill and the Harriet Taylor Myth** (Melbourne: Melbourne University Press, 1960). See also Josephine Kamm, **John Stuart Mill in Love** (London: Gordon & Cromonesi; New York: Atheneum, 1977).

• Mill, John Stuart, **Principles of Political Economy**, edited with an introduction by Sir W. J. Ashley (London: Longmans, Green & Co. Ltd., 1909). This edition, which is available in a reprint, is the most useful one, since it indicates the most important changes made by Mill in successive editions and contains a valuable introduction and bibliographical appendixes by the editor. A more recent edition, in two volumes, was published in 1965 as part of the **Collected Works of Mill** (Toronto: University of Toronto Press). It carries an informative introduction by V. W. Bladen. See also another edition, edited with an introduction by Donald Winch (New York: Penguin Books, 1970).

Mill's **Essays on Some Unsettled Questions on Political Economy**, originally published in 1844, have been reprinted (London: The London School of Economics and Political Science, 1948). There are several editions of Mill's **Autobiography**, one edited by Harold J. Laski (London: Oxford University Press, World Classics, 1924), another edited by J. J. Coss (New York: Columbia University Press, 1924), and a third by Jack Stillinger, **The Early Draft of John Stuart Mill's Autobiography** (Urbana, Ill.: University of Illinois Press, 1961), which contains material hitherto not available in print. Although they do not directly relate to Mill's economics, the following reprints will appeal to those interested in the wider background of his work: **J. S. Mill: Philosophy of Scientific Method**, ed.

Ernest Nagel, with an introduction (New York: Hafner Publishing Co., Inc., 1950), which contains mainly selections from Mill's **Logic;** J. S. Mill, **On the Logic of the Moral Sciences: A System of Logic, Book 6**, ed. H. M. Magid, with an introduction (Indianapolis: The Bobbs-Merrill Co., Inc. for the Library of Liberal Arts, 1965); Marshall Cohen, ed., **The Philosophy of John Stuart Mill: Ethical, Political, Religious** (New York: Random House, Inc., Modern Library, Inc., 1961); J. S. Mill, **On Liberty, and Considerations on Representative Government**, ed. R. B. McCallum, with an introduction (Oxford: Basil Blackwell & Mott Ltd., 1946); J. S. Mill, **Utilitarianism, On Liberty, and Considerations on Representative Government**, ed. with an introduction and notes by H. B. Acton (London: J. M. Dent & Sons Ltd., Everyman series, 1976), which contains extracts from **Auguste Comte and Positivism**; J. S. Mill, **On Liberty**, ed. with an introduction by Gertrude Himmelfarb (New York: W. W. Norton and Company, 1975), with annotated text, sources and background, and criticism, in the Norton Critical Editions series; James M. Smith and Ernest Sosa, eds., **Mill's Utilitarianism: Text and Criticism** (Belmont, Calif.: Wadsworth Publishing Company, Inc., 1969); J. S. Mill, **Essays on Politics and Culture**, ed. Gertrude Himmelfarb, with an introduction (Garden City, N.Y.: Doubleday & Company, Inc., Anchor Books, 1963). The introductions to these works are among the best interpretive writings about Mill.

• Mueller, Iris Wessel, **John Stuart Mill and French Thought** (Urbana, Ill.: University of Illinois Press, 1956). A scholarly appraisal of the influence of Comte, the Saint Simonians, and de Tocqueville on Mill. See also M. Apchié, "Les sources françaises de certains aspects de la pensée économique de J. S. Mill," (thèse, Paris, 1931); Richard Pankhurst, **The Saint Simonians, Mill and Carlyle** (London: Sidgwick & Jackson Ltd., n.d.), and, on Coleridge, another important influence on Mill, William F. Kennedy, **Humanist versus Economist: The Economic Thought of Samuel Taylor Coleridge** (Berkeley and Los Angeles: University of California Press, 1958).

• Packe, Michael St. John, **The Life of John Stuart Mill** (London: Martin Secker & Warburg Ltd., 1954). This is the standard biography of Mill. See also Alexander Bain, **John Stuart Mill: a Criticism** (London: Longmans, Green & Co. Ltd., 1882), which is based on firsthand impressions; W. L. Courtney, **Life of John Stuart Mill** (London: Walter Scott, 1889); Herbert Spencer et al., **John Stuart Mill: His Life and Works** (Boston: Osgood and Company, 1873); Horace N. Pym, ed., **Memories of Old Friends, Being Extracts from the Journals and Letters of Caroline Fox**, 2 vols., 3rd ed. (London: Smith, Elder and Company, 1882); John Morley, **Critical Miscellanies**, Vol. 3 (London: Macmillan & Co. Ltd., 1886), pp. 37ff; Ruth Borchard, **John Stuart Mill the Man** (London: C. A. Watts & Co. Ltd., 1957).

  Bruce Mazlish, **James and John Stuart Mill: Father and Son in the Nineteenth Century** (New York: Basic Books, 1975), a psycho-history. According to the author, sons adopted a different posture toward their fathers some time between the late eighteenth and early nineteenth century. There was then a more intense filial rebellion that did not often fizzle into submission. Mazlish ascribes the change to the industrial revolution and the rise of new ideas that coincided with a demographic revolution with increases in young age groups. There is no mention of the related cases of Ricardo and Malthus. See pp. 98–111 with psycho-historical comments on James Mill's **Elements**, and pp. 351–76 with similar comments on J. S. Mill's **Principles**.

• Plamenatz, John, **The English Utilitarians**, 2nd ed. (Oxford: Basil Blackwell & Mott Ltd., 1958). Chapter 8 contains an analysis of Mill's utilitarianism viewed in the perspective of the English philosophic tradition. See also Élie Halévy, **The Growth of Philosophic Radicalism**, trans. Mary Morris (London: Faber & Faber Ltd., 1928); Leslie Stephen, **The English Utilitarians**, Vol. 3 (London: Gerald Duckworth & Co. Ltd., 1900), on John Stuart Mill; William C. Havard, **Henry Sidgwick and Later Utilitarian Political Philosophy** (Gainesville, Fla.: University of Florida Press, 1959). Anthony Quinton,

Utilitarian Ethics (New York: St. Martin's Press, 1973), with comments on Mill and his critics; J. J. C. Smart and B. Williams, **Utilitarianism: For and Against** (New York: Cambridge University Press, 1973).

• Taussig, F. W., **Wages and Capital** (Des Moines, Iowa: Meredith Corporation, Appleton-Century-Crofts, 1896). Reprinted with a new introduction by the author (London: The London School of Economics and Political Science, 1932). This work carries the subtitle, "An Examination of the Wages Fund Doctrine," and contains a detailed analysis of Mill's position. Francis A. Walker, another American economist, had before, in his **Wages Question** of 1876, subjected the wages fund theory to a devastating critique. The most important passages are reprinted in Henry W. Spiegel, ed., **The Rise of American Economic Thought** (Philadelphia: Chilton Book Company, 1960). See also W. H. Hutt, **The Theory of Collective Bargaining** (London: P. S. King and Son, 1930); William Breit, "The Wages Fund Controversy: A Diagrammatic Exposition," **Canadian Journal of Economics**, Vol. 33, No. 4 (November, 1967), 523–28; R. B. Ekelund, Jr., "A Short-Run Classical Model of Capital and Wages: Mill's Recantation of the Wages Fund," **Oxford Economic Papers**, Vol. 28, No. 1 (March, 1976), 66–85; E. G. West and R. W. Hafer, "J. S. Mill, Unions, and the Wages Fund Recantation: A Reinterpretation," **Quarterly Journal of Economics**, Vol. 92, No. 4 (November, 1978), 603–19, with discussion, ibid., Vol. 96, No. 3 (August, 1981); Alfred Marshall, **Principles of Economics**, 8th ed. (London: Macmillan & Co. Ltd., 1920), Appendix J; A. C. Pigou, "Mill and the Wages Fund," **Economic Journal**, Vol 59 (June, 1949), 171–80; and, for recent discussions of Mill's view that "demand for commodities is not demand for labor," F. A. Hayek, **The Pure Theory of Capital** (London: Routledge & Kegan Paul Ltd., 1941), Appendix 3; Harry G. Johnson, "Demand for Commodities is _Not_ Demand for Labor," **Economic Journal**, Vol. 59 (December, 1949), 531–36.

• Viner, Jacob, "Bentham and J. S. Mill: The Utilitarian Background," **American**

Economic Review, Vol. 39, No. 2 (March, 1949), 360–82; V. W. Bladen, "John Stuart Mill's **Principles**: A Centenary Estimate," **American Economic Review**, Vol. 39, Supplement (May, 1949), 1–12; James Bonar, "John Stuart Mill, the Reformer 1806–73," **Indian Journal of Economics**, Vol. 10 (April, 1930), 761–805; Abram L. Harris, **Economics and Social Reform** (New York: Harper & Row, Publishers, 1958), Chap. 2. These general appraisals of Mill's position in the history of economics may be supplemented by Abram L. Harris, "J. S. Mill on Monopoly and Socialism: A Note," **Journal of Political Economy**, Vol. 67, No. 6 (December, 1959), 604–11; same author, "Mill on Freedom and Voluntary Association," **Review of Social Economy**, Vol. 18, No. 1 (March, 1960), 27–44; Pedro Schwartz, "John Stuart Mill and Laissez-Faire: London Water," **Economica**, new series, Vol. 33 (February, 1966), 71–83; same author, **The New Political Economy of J. S. Mill** (Durham, N.C.: Duke University Press, 1973), the only book-length treatment of Mill's economics; N. B. de Marchi, "The Success of Mill's 'Principles'," **History of Political Economy**, Vol. 6, No. 2 (Summer, 1974), 119–57; S. Hollander, "Ricardianism, J. S. Mill, and the Neo-classical Challenge," in Robson and Lane, eds., **James and John Stuart Mill**, cited earlier, pp. 67–85; Bela A. Balassa, "John Stuart Mill and the Law of Markets," **Quarterly Journal of Economics**, Vol. 73, No. 2 (May, 1959), 263–74, with comment by Laurence C. Hunter, same journal, Vol. 74, No. 2 (May, 1960), 158–62; L. C. Hunter, "Mill and Cairnes on the Rate of Interest," **Oxford Economic Papers**, new series, Vol. 11 (February, 1959), 63–87; Bela A. Balassa, "Karl Marx and John Stuart Mill," **Weltwirtschaftliches Archiv**, Vol. 83, No. 2 (1959), 147–63. See also, for a list of doctrinal innovations credited to Mill, George J. Stigler, **Essays in the History of Economics** (Chicago: The University of Chicago Press, 1965), pp. 6–11 —for some of these, however, Longfield might have a safer claim to priority. See pp. 355–56 above.

CHAPTER 17

• Bagehot, Walther, **The Collected Works**, ed. Norman St. John-Stevas (Cambridge, Mass.: Harvard University Press, 1965ff.). This new edition of Bagehot's writings has been sponsored by the **Economist** in honor of its erstwhile editor. Altogether twelve volumes are projected, with the economic writings forming Vols. 9, 10 and 11. An earlier edition of the **Works and Life of Walter Bagehot**, ed. Mrs. Russell Barrington, Bagehot's sister-in-law, was published in ten volumes (London: Longmans, Green & Co. Ltd., 1915). A still earlier edition of Bagehot's **Works** was published in five volumes (Hartford, Conn.: Travelers' Insurance Company, 1891). It was edited by Forrest Morgan, the Travelers' librarian and editor, as a labor of love, and sold for the nearly nominal price of $5. St. John-Stevas, the editor of the most recent collection of Bagehot's works, has also published **Walter Bagehot: A Study of His Life and Thought, together with a** Selection from His Political Writings (Bloomington, Ind.: Indiana University Press, 1959), as well as **Bagehot's Historical Essays** (Garden City, N.Y.: Doubleday & Company, Inc., Anchor Books, 1965). There are biographical appraisals by Mrs. Barrington in Vol. 10 of her edition of the **Works**, by Alastair Buchan, **The Spare Chancellor: The Life of Walter Bagehot** (London: Chatto & Windus Ltd., 1959), and by William Irvine, **Walter Bagehot** (New York: Longmans, Green & Co. Ltd., 1939), which is principally concerned with Bagehot as a literary critic.

Bagehot's economic writings are available in these recent reprints: **Lombard Street**, with a new introduction by Frank C. Genovese (Homewood, Ill.: Richard D. Irwin, Inc. 1962); **Economic Studies**, ed. Richard Holt Hutton (Stanford, Calif.: Stanford University Press, Academic Reprints, 1953). There is an early edition of **The Postulates of English Political Economy** (New York: G. P. Putnam's Sons,

1894), with a preface by Alfred Marshall. This contains Bagehot's studies of the mobility of labor and capital, which are reprinted also in **Economic Studies**. Marshall, in his preface, said of Bagehot: "Though he has shown more clearly than perhaps anyone else the danger of a careless application of theory, he saw with great distinctness the need of its aid in dealing with complex economic problems. 'If you attempt to solve such problems,' he says, 'without some apparatus of method, you are as sure to fail as if you try to take a modern military fortress–a Metz or a Belfort–by common assault'" (p. 6).

For appraisals of Bagehot as an economist see T. E. Gregory, **The Westminster Bank** (London: Oxford University Press, 1936), Vol. 2, 237–73; Sir Robert Giffen, "Bagehot as an Economist," **The Fortnightly Review**, new series, Vol. 27 (April, 1880), 549–67; John M. Keynes, "The Works of Walter Bagehot," **Economic Journal**, Vol. 25 (September, 1915), 369–75; same author, "Bagehot's **Lombard Street**," **The Banker**, Vol. 1, No. 3 (March, 1926), 210–17; Walt W. Rostow, "Bagehot and the Trade Clycle," in **The Economist, 1843–1943; A Centenary Volume** (London: Oxford University Press, 1943), pp. 155–74, reedited in Rostow's **British Economy of the Nineteenth Century** (London: Oxford University Press, 1948), pp. 161–78. On Bagehot and the multiplier theory see Hugo Hegeland, "On the Genesis of the Multiplier Theory," in **Money, Growth and Methodology, and Other Essays in Economics in Honor of Johan Åkerman**, ed. Hugo Hegeland (Lund, Sweden: AB C. W. K. Gleerup Bokfoerlag, 1961), pp. 213f.

Keynes, in his article in the **Economic Journal**, repeatedly stresses Bagehot's psychological bent. He speaks of Bagehot "as a psychologist—a psychological analyzer . . . primarily of businessmen, financiers and politicians" (p. 369) and comments on *Lombard Street* in these words: "Perhaps the most striking and fundamental doctrine in *Lombard Street* . . . is, in a sense, psychological rather than economic. I mean the doctrine of the Reserve, and that the right way to stop a crisis is to lend freely." (pp. 371f.).

He makes a similar observation of Bagehot's appraisals of the work of other economists: "All this is not so much economics as the psychology of economic writings; just as *Lombard Street* is the psychology of finance, not the theory of it" (p. 373).

• Clapham, J. H., "Of Empty Economic Boxes," **Economic Journal**, Vol. 32 (1922), 305–14, with a reply by Pigou, a rejoinder by Clapham, and subsequent discussion by D. H. Robertson–same journal, 458–65, 560–63; Vol. 34 (1924), 16–30—reprinted in **Readings in Price Theory: Selected by a Committee of the American Economic Association** (Homewood, Ill.: Richard D. Irwin, Inc., 1953), pp. 119–59. This is the famous discussion of the empirical content of economic theory, a resumption of the nineteenth-century controversy between theorists and historians. Since that time economic history has become more quantitatively oriented, concentrating on measurable processes or developments rather than on institutions.

• Grossman, Henryk, "The Evolutionist Revolt against Classical Economics," **Journal of Political Economy**, Vol. 51 (October–December, 1943), 381–96, 506–22. Grossman stresses the evolutionary approach of Richard Jones as a link between theory and history and considers Jones as a forerunner of Marx. Other aspects of Jones's work are treated in Nai-Tuan Chao, **Richard Jones: An Early English Institutionalist** (New York: Columbia University Press, 1930); Hans Weber, **Richard Jones, ein früher englischer Abtrünniger der klassischen Schule der Nationalökonomie** (Zurich: H. Girsberger, 1939); M. L. Miller, "Richard Jones's Contributions to the Theory of Rent," **History of Political Economy**, Vol. 9, No. 3 (Fall, 1977), 346–65. Cliffe Leslie, Ingram, and other Irish economists form the subject of a study by Sister Mary Silverius Shields, "Some Irish Contributions to the History of Economics" (dissertation, The Catholic University of America, Washington, D.C., 1955), of which an abstract was printed in the same year. John Kells Ingram's **History of Political Economy** was published in a new and enlarged edition, with a supplementary chapter by William A.

Scott and an introduction by Richard T. Ely (London: A. & C. Black Ltd., 1915). James E. Thorold Rogers's **Six Centuries of Work and Wages** was reprinted with a new preface by G. D. H. Cole (London: George Allen & Unwin Ltd., 1949). Arnold Toynbee's **Lectures on the Industrial Revolution of the Eighteenth Century in England** has been reprinted in a paperbound edition (Boston: Beacon Press, 1956). About Toynbee see also George N. Clark, **The Idea of the Industrial Revolution** (Glasgow: University of Glasgow, 1970).

For a later phase of English historical economics see G. M. Koot, "H. S. Foxwell and English Historical Economics," **Journal of Economic Issues**, Vol. 11, No. 3 (September, 1977), 561–86.

CHAPTER 18

• Clark, Evalyn A., "Adolf Wagner: From National Economist to National Socialist," **Political Science Quarterly**, Vol. 55, No. 3 (September, 1940), 378–411. An article by Wagner, translated by C. F. Dunbar, was published under the title "Wagner on the Present State of Political Economy" in the **Quarterly Journal of Economics**, Vol. 1 (October, 1886), 113–33. Clark offers this statement of "Wagner's law": It "declared that state control would continue to increase, because this is a natural and necessary corollary of increasing national might, a sign of the growth of the *Kulturstaat*—just as the growing role of the army was. He envisages calmly (and prophetically!) as a final result of this tendency increased expenditures and taxation for a greater army, navy, diplomatic wars, permanent war staffs, munitions, factories, till finally the state becomes a state of functionaries and the military organ exercises a dominant control over national economy and finances" (p. 397). Clark's article sheds light on the nature of the historical economists' vaunted appeal to morality, which often served as a cloak for the most brutal power politics and, in Wagner's case, also for racism.

• Dorfman, Joseph, "The Role of the German Historical School in American Economic Thought," **American Economic Review**, Vol. 45, No. 2 (May, 1955), 17–28. Professor Dorfman closes his article by underlining "the fundamental distinction in political outlook between the Historical School in its native land and its American heirs" (p. 28). See also Henry W. Farnam, "Deutsch-amerikanische Beziehungen in der Volkswirtschaftslehre," in S. P. Altman et al., **Die Entwicklung der deutschen Volkswirtschaft im neunzehnten Jahrhundert**, Gustav Schmoller . . . dargebracht, 2 vols. (Leipzig, 1908), Vol. 1, Chap. 18; Jurgen Herbst, **The German Historical School in American Scholarship** (Ithaca, N.Y.: Cornell University Press, 1965). On the founding of the American Economic Association see the autobiography of Richard T. Ely, **Ground Under Our Feet** (New York: The Macmillan Company, 1938); Henry W. Spiegel, **The Rise of American Economic Thought** (Philadelphia: Chilton Book Company, 1960), pp. 184–85. Ely (1854–1943), the first secretary of the Association, was a student of Knies and did much to spread the influence of German historical economics in the United States. He was instrumental in bringing to prominence the department of economics at the University of Wisconsin, and his work forms a link between German historical economics and American institutional economics. See Benjamin G. Rader, **The Academic Mind and Reform: The Influence of Richard T. Ely in American Life** (Lexington, Ky.: The University Press of Kentucky, 1967); memorial articles about Ely by H. M. Groves and E. W. Morehouse, **Land Economics**, Vol. 45, No. 1 (February, 1969), 1–18. See also Henry R. Seager, **Labor and Other Economic Essays**, ed. Charles A. Gulick (New York: Harper & Row, Publishers, 1931), pp. 1–29. This article, on "Economics at Berlin and Vienna," was written in the early 1890s by a young American student who later became a distinguished economist and served as president of the

American Economic Association in 1922. The article shows that enthusiasm about the historical economists was by no means universal among their American students.

• Eucken, Walter, **The Foundations of Economics,** trans. T. W. Hutchison (London: William Hodge and Company, 1950). Eucken (1891–1950) was a German neo-liberal, who attempted to integrate the historical and theoretical approaches. This is a translation of his principal work, wherein much use is made of the concept of "economic systems" which are classified from various points of view. For a sympathetic account of Eucken's work see Frederic C. Lane, "Some Heirs of Gustav von Schmoller," in Joseph T. Lambie, ed., **Architects and Craftsmen in History: Festschrift fur A. P. Usher** (Tübingen: J. C. B. Mohr [Paul Siebeck], 1956), pp. 7–40, especially pp. 28–40. See also Eucken's **This Unsuccessful Age**, with an introduction by John Jewkes (New York: Oxford University Press, Inc., 1952), and, for the whole school of neoliberalism founded by Eucken, F. Bilger, **La pensée économique libérale dans l'Allemagne contemporaine** (Paris: R. Pichon et R. Durand-Auzias, 1964).

• Hayek, F. A., "Comte and Hegel," **Measure**, Vol. 2, No. 3 (Summer, 1951), 324–41, reprinted in Hayek's **The Counter-Revolution of Science: Studies on the Abuse of Reason** (New York: The Free Press 1955). Professor Hayek points to parallels in Comte's and Hegel's ideas and traces the influence of each on economic thought. See also, about Comte, H. Waentig, **August Comte und seine Bedeutung für die Entwicklung der Sozialwissenschaft** (Berlin: Duncker & Humblot, 1894); R. Mauduit, **Auguste Comte et la science économique** (Paris: Félix Alcan, 1929); W. M. Simon, **European Positivism in the Nineteenth Century** (Ithaca, N.Y.: Cornell University Press, 1963). Among the German historical economists, Schmoller was acquainted with Comte's work. The older historical economists do not seem to have known him when they wrote their programmatic works in the 1840s and 1850s. Knies expressly stated this in the second edition of his work, published in 1883 (Simon, p. 242).

Positivism in a broad sense, covering the approach of Comte and more recent thinkers, is made the subject of a searching critique in Ben B. Seligman, "The Impact of Positivism on Economic Thought," **History of Political Economy**, Vol. 1, No. 2 (Fall, 1969), 256–78.

• List, Friedrich, **The National System of Political Economy**, trans. S. S. Lloyd, with an introduction by J. S. Nicholson (London: Longmans, Green & Co. Ltd., 1904)—the English translation of List's principal work. List's ideas were grist for the mills of the American protectionists, and an early translation of this work was published in the United States in 1856. Margaret E. Hirst, **Life of Friedrich List and Selections from His Writings** (London: Smith, Elder and Company, 1909), contains, among other material, excerpts from List's **Outlines of American Political Economy,** written on behalf of the American protectionists during his residence in the United States. For a selection and additional references see Spiegel, **American Economic Thought**, pp. 83–88 and 192. On List's promotion of the German customs union see W. O. Henderson, **The Zollverein**, originally published 1939 (Chicago: Quadrangle Books, Inc., 1959); Arnold H. Price, **The Evolution of the Zollverein** (Ann Arbor, Mich.: The University of Michigan Press, 1949). There is a large List literature in Germany, and a society designed to perpetuate his memory and spread his ideas. See A. Meusel, **List und Marx** (Stuttgart: Gustav Fischer Verlag, 1928); H. Ritschl, **Friedrich Lists Leben und Lehre** (Tübingen: Rainer Wunderlich Verlag Hermann Leins, 1947); Carl Brinkmann, **Friedrich List** (Berlin: Duncker & Humblot, 1949). Harald Randak, **Friedrich List und die wissenschaftliche Wirtschaftspolitik** (Tübingen: J. C. B. Mohr, 1972); W. O. Henderson, "Friedrich List and the Social Question," **Journal of European Economic History**, Vol. 10, No. 3 (Winter, 1981), 697–708.

On the stage theories of the historical economists see Gertrud Kalveram, **Die Theorien von den Wirtschaftsstufen** (Leipzig: Buske, 1933); Artur Sommer, "Uber Inhalt, Rahmen und Sinn älterer Stufentheorien (List und Hildebrand)," in **Synopsis: Festgabe für Alfred Weber**, ed. Edgar Salin (Heidelberg: Lambert Schneider Verlag GMBH, 1948) pp. 535–65. A current example of a stage theory is W. W. Rostow's **The Stages of Economic Growth** (New York: Cambridge University Press, 1960), which distinguishes five stages: the traditional society, the preconditions for take-off, the take-off, the drive to maturity, and the age of high mass consumption.

• Menger, Carl, **Untersuchungen über die Methode der Sozialwissenschaften, und der politischen Oekonomie insbesondere** (Berlin: Duncker & Humblot, 1883); English translation by Francis J. Nock under the title **Problems of Economics and Sociology,** edited and with an introduction by Louis Schneider (Urbana, Ill.: University of Illinois Press, 1963); also, by the same author, **Die Irrtümer des Historismus in der deutschen Nationalökonomie** (Vienna: Alfred Hölder, 1884). These works, by the famous Austrian economist, contain both a statement of the method proper to economic science—which has retained its validity to the present day— and a critique of the approach of the historical school. For more extended comments on Menger's approach see below, p. 798. See also, for related views critical of the historical economists, Richard Schüller, **Die klassische Nationalökonomie und ihre Gegner** (Cologne: Carl Heymanns Verlag KG, 1895); **Die Wirtschaftspolitik der historischen Schule** (Cologne: Carl Heymanns Verlag KG, 1899). The whole "controversy about methods" is reviewed by Gerhard Ritzel, "Schmoller vs Menger," a Basel dissertation (Offenbach: Bollwerk–Verlag, 1951).

• Oppenheim, Heinrich, **Der Kathedersozialismus** (Berlin: Oppenheim, 1872). A book written by the liberal journalist who coined the phrase "socialists of the chair" as a designation for the Schmoller group. Other liberal writings include Ludwig Bamberger, Theodor Barth, and Max Broemel, **Gegen den Staatssozialismus** (Berlin: Simion, 1884); John Prince-Smith, **Gesammelte Schriften**, 3 vols. (Munich: F. A. Herbig Verlagsbuchhandlung, 1877–80). See Julius Becker, **Das deutsche Manchestertum** (Karlsruhe: G.

Braun, 1907); Georg Mayer, **Die Freihandelslehre in Deutschland** (Stuttgart: Gustav Fischer Verlag, 1927); D. Rohr, **The Origins of Social Liberalism in Germany** (Chicago: The University of Chicago Press, 1963).

• Popper, K. R., **The Open Society and Its Enemies**, 2 vols., revised and enlarged edition (London: Routledge & Kegan Paul Ltd., 1957). Vol. 2, Chap. 12, pp. 27–80, severely criticizes Hegelian historicism and traces its influence on German social thought. See also, by the same author, **The Poverty of Historicism**, 2nd ed. (London: Routledge & Kegan Paul Ltd., 1960), based on articles published first in **Economica**, new series, Vol. 11, Nos. 42–43 and Vol. 12, No. 46 (1944–1945). There are outstanding German studies of historicism, including those by Troeltsch and Meinecke. The titles of these refer to "Historismus" rather than historicism. Thus, what in English is known as historicism, that is, the view that the study of history is the method of the science of society, is in Germany designated as **Historismus.** In English usage historism and historicism are different things, historism denoting the view that scientific knowledge is historically determined. This at least is the usage adopted by Popper. Ernst Troeltsch wrote **Der Historismus und seine Probleme** (Tübingen: J. C. B. Mohr [Paul Siebeck], 1922), reprinted in 1966 under the title **Der Historismus und seine Überwindung.** A remarkable lecture by Troeltsch, which sheds light on the German tendency to reject the natural-law approach, has been translated into English under the title "The Ideas of Natural Law and Humanity in World Politics" and published as an appendix to Otto Gierke's **Natural Law and the Theory of Society, 1500 to 1800**, translated with an introduction by Ernest Barker, 2 vols. (New York: Cambridge University Press, 1934). In Friedrich Meinecke's **Historism: The Rise of a New Historical Outlook**, trans. by J. E. Anderson, with an introduction by Isaiah Berlin (New York: Herder & Herder, 1972), historicism is referred to as the second great contribution of Germany to Western thought after the Reformation. Its core is the replacement of the generalizing view by the individualizing one, but it does not exclude the search for generalities and regularities. Since the time of antiquity, natural law had instilled in people the idea of the stability of human nature, especially of reason, which may be disturbed by passion and ignorance, but when liberated is held to be the same at all times. This natural-law belief became fused with Christianity and served as a polestar, shedding a central and guiding light. But when natural law was used to justify a great variety of different things, reason lost its timeless character and became historically variable. Meinecke treats of an early period of German historicism, considering Herder, Goethe, and Ranke rather than Hegelian historicism. In his interpretation the great historian Ranke, who refused to taint historical study with personal or ideological commitment, represented the highest development of German historicism. See also Friedrich Engel-Janosi, **The Growth of German Historicism** (Baltimore: The Johns Hopkins Press, 1944); G. A. Wells, **Herder and After: A Study in the Development of Sociology** (The Hague: Mouton en Co. N.V., 1959), which has copious extracts not only from Herder but also from exponents of the Hegelian brand of historicism; Leonard Krieger, **The German Idea of Freedom** (Boston: Beacon Press, 1957); Georg G. Iggers, **The German Conception of History** (Middletown, Conn.: Wesleyan University Press, 1968); Peter Hanns Reill, **The German Enlightenment and the Rise of Historicism** (Berkeley: University of California Press, 1975); Isaiah Berlin, **Vico and Herder** (London: The Hogarth Press, 1976), pp. 143–216 on "Herder and the Enlightenment;" same author, **Against the Current** (New York: The Viking Press, 1980), pp. 1–24 on "The Counter-Enlightenment."

The relevant ideas of Hegel were mainly developed in his "Encyclopaedia of the Philosophical Sciences," his "Philosophy of History," and his "Philosophy of Law." See **Hegel: Selections**, ed. J. Loewenberg (New York: Charles Scribner's Sons, 1929). See also **The Philosophy of Hegel**, edited with an introduction and notes by Carl J. Friedrich (New York: Random House, Inc., Modern Library,

Inc., 1954); Herbert Marcuse, **Reason and Revolution: Hegel and the Rise of Social Theory** (Boston: Beacon Press, 1960); William Ebenstein, **Great Political Thinkers**, 3rd ed. (New York: Holt, Rinehart & Winston, Inc., 1960), Chap. 21, pp. 589–600; John Herman Randall, Jr., **The Career of Philosophy**, Vol. 2 (New York: Columbia University Press, 1965), Chaps. 14–15, especially pp. 319–21 on Hegel's socialized conception of freedom and its influence on social thought and action.

On the general philosophical foundations of nineteenth-century economic thought in Germany see James Bonar, **Philosophy and Political Economy** (New York: The Macmillan Company, 1893), Book 4; A. Friedrichs, **Klassische Philosophie und Wirtschaftswissenschaft** (Gotha: F. A. Perthes, 1913); Hans Freyer, **Die Bewertung der Wirtschaft im philosophischen Denken des 19. Jahrhunderts** (Leipzig: W. Engelmann, 1921). Alfred Ammon, **Nationalökonomie und Philosophie** (Berlin: Duncker & Humblot, 1961), treats of the relevant period only incidentally, his "retrospect" in Chap. 1 ending with J. S. Mill and being followed by a discussion of selected topics.

Besides Popper's, other noteworthy critiques of historicism include Ludwig von Mises, **Theory and History** (New Haven, Conn.: Yale University Press, 1957), especially Chap. 10, and Leo Strauss, **Natural Right and History** (Chicago: The University of Chicago Press, 1953), who argues that the denial, by the historicists, of the possibility of transhistorical thought is in itself a transhistorical statement. This view, which marks the historicists' claim as contradictory or paradoxical, can be applied also to the panideologists who find ideologies everywhere. The dilemma has a long history in logic, where it has found a famous formulation in the statement of a Cretan: "All Cretans are always liars."

• Roscher, W., **Principles of Political Economy**, trans. John J. Lalor, 2 vols. (Chicago: Callaghan & Company, 1882). An English translation of the principal work of one of the three older German historical economists. The works of

762

Hildebrand and Knies, which are cited in the text, are available only in the original version. The best modern appraisal of the three is Gottfried Eisermann, **Die Grundlagen des Historismus in der Deutschen Nationalökonomie** (Stuttgart: Ferdinand Enke Verlag, 1956), which places them in the political, economic, social, and intellectual setting of their time and whose views have influenced the interpretation by the present writer. A briefer and less critical appraisal is Walter J. Fischel's "Der Historismus in der Wirtschaftswissenschaft: Dargestellt an der Entwicklung von Adam Müller bis Bruno Hildebrand," **Vierteljahrschrift für Sozial- und Wirtschaftsgeschichte**, Vol. 47, No. 1 (March, 1960), 1–31.

For a highly favorable assessment of Roscher by his intellectual heir see "Schmoller on Roscher," in Henry W. Spiegel, ed., **The Development of Economic Thought**, abr. ed. (New York: John Wiley & Sons, Inc., 1964), pp. 221–36. Max Weber's critique of Roscher's and Knies's methods is in his **Gesammelte Aufsätze zur Wissenschaftslehre**, cited below, p. 765.

Roscher was familiar with Richard Jones's historical economics, but his occasional citations of Jones refer to matters of detail and do not indicate a more profound influence of the earlier writer. Knies knew of the existence of Jones's book but had not read it.

• Schmoller, Gustav, **The Mercantile System and Its Historical Significance: Illustrated Chiefly from Prussian History** (New York: The Macmillan Company, 1897). This is Schmoller's interpretation of mercantilism. Looking at it from a narrowly regional point of view, he underlines its state-building function. Schmoller was a copious writer and the above is not his principal work, although it illustrates his approach. In spite of his influence on the economics of his time, very little of Schmoller's work has been translated into English, apparently because its content was not particularly illuminating outside of its native environment. Another translation, that of Schmoller's appraisal of Roscher, has been cited in the preceding entry.

About Schmoller, see Carl Brinkmann, **Gustav Schmoller und die Volkswirtschaftslehre** (Stuttgart: W. Kohlhammer Verlag GMBH, 1937); Joseph A. Schumpeter, "Gustav von Schmoller und die Probleme von heute," **Schmoller's Jahrbuch für Gesetzgebung, Verwaltung und Volkswirtschaft im Deutschen Reich**, Vol. 50 (1926), 337–88; A. Spiethoff, ed., **Gustav von Schmoller und die deutsche geschichtliche Volkswirtschaftslehre** (Berlin: Duncker & Humblot, 1938). This is a memorial volume written on the occasion of the centenary of Schmoller's birth and edited by his outstanding pupil. The contributors include more than twenty prominent social scientists of the time.

There is an account, in English, of Schmoller's controversy with the conservative historian Treitschke, who opposed the social policy of the historical economists as running counter to social Darwinism. See Albion W. Small, "The Schmoller–Treitschke Controversy," **American Journal of Sociology**, Vol. 30 (1924–25), 49–86. Small, a pupil of Schmoller, later became a well-known American sociologist. American appraisals of Schmoller include the contribution by Pauline R. Anderson to Bernadotte E. Schmitt, ed., **Some Historians of Modern Europe** (Chicago: The University of Chicago Press, 1942), pp. 415–43, and the considerably more critical review article by Thorstein Veblen, "Gustav Schmoller's Economics," reprinted from the **Quarterly Journal of Economics**, Vol. 16 (November, 1901), in Veblen's **The Place of Science in Modern Civilization** (New York: The Viking Press, Inc., 1919). Veblen offers here a still valid assessment both of the earlier and later historical economists.

Schmoller's encounter with Pareto is reported by M. Pantaleoni, "In occasione della morte di Pareto: riflessioni," **Giornale degli economisti**, Vol. 64 (January–February, 1924), 13.

A searching and critical account of the work of the entire Schmoller group, comparable to that by Eisermann of the older historical economists (cited above, p. 762), is not available. Shehan's book about Brentano, which goes into considerable detail—see next entry—serves in part the functions of such a work. There is a history of the Association for Social Policy, written by its erstwhile secretary: Franz Boese, **Geschichte des Vereins für Sozialpolitik**, Schriften des Vereins für Sozialpolitik, No. 188 (Berlin: Duncker & Humblot, 1939); an earlier account written by a member of the school, Hans Gehrig, **Die Begründung des Prinzipes der Sozialreform** (Stuttgart: Gustav Fischer Verlag, 1914), as well as a few other appraisals, such a F. Lifschitz, **Die historische Schule der Wirtschaftswissenschaft** (Bern: Verlag Staempfli & Cie., 1914); Gerhard Wittrock, **Die Kathedersozialisten**, Historische Studien No. 350 (Berlin: Emil Ebering, 1939), which is written from the Nazi point of view. Fritz Völkerling, "Der deutsche Kathedersozialismus," a Halle dissertation (Berlin: Verlag die Wirtschaft, 1959), is well documented and critical enough, but the critique is inspired exclusively by the Marxist point of view; A. Müssiggang, **Die soziale Frage in der historischen Schule der deutschen Nationalökonomie** (Tübingen: J. C. B. Mohr [Paul Siebeck], 1967).

On the politics of imperial expansion of the historical economists, which found support even among the more liberal contingent of the group, see A. Ascher, "Professors as Propagandists: The Politics of the *Kathedersozialisten*," **Journal of Central European Affairs**, Vol. 23, No. 3 (October, 1963), 282–302. About their rejection of liberal pacifism see Edmund Silberner, **The Problem of War in Nineteenth-Century Economic Thought**, trans. A. H. Krappe (Princeton, N.J.: Princeton University Press, 1946), pp. 189ff.

• Sheehan, James J., **The Career of Lujo Brentano** (Chicago: The University of Chicago Press, 1966). This is a carefully documented and thorough study of a leading, albeit unconventional, member of the younger historical school, written from the point of view of a historian rather than of an economist. It traces not only the career of Brentano but brings in, if only peripherally, many other aspects of historical economics. The work is the only full-fledged study of a historical economist available in English. Translations of Brentano's own writings include his **On the History and Development of Gilds and the Origins of Trade Unions** (London: Trübner & Co., 1870).

• Sombart, Werner, **Die Ordnung des Wirtschaftslebens,** 2nd ed. (Berlin: Springer Verlag, 1927). This gives on sixty-five pages a survey of Sombart's principal ideas about economic systems, their spirit, form, and technique. Sombart's method can be seen in application in his article "Capitalism," **Encyclopaedia of the Social Sciences**, Vol. 3 (New York: The Macmillan Company, 1930), 195–208. Sombart's principal work is **Der moderne Kapitalismus**, 3 vols. in 6, Vols. 1 and 2 in 4th ed. (Berlin: Duncker & Humblot, 1921–27), which has influenced Frederick L. Nussbaum's **History of the Economic Institutions of Modern Europe** (Des Moines, Iowa: Meredith Corporation, Appleton-Century-Crofts, 1933). An early study of Sombart's examines the reasons for the lack of response to socialism in the United States: **Why Is There No Socialism in the United States**, ed. C. T. Husbands, trans. by Patricia M. Hocking and C. T. Husbands, forew. by Michael Harrington (White Plains, N.Y.: M. E. Sharpe, Inc., 1976; originally published in 1906).

English translations of other works by Sombart include the following: **The Quintessence of Capitalism**, trans. and ed. M. Epstein (London: George Allen & Unwin Ltd., 1915), which investigates the specific capitalist mentality; **Luxury and Capitalism**, with an introduction by Philip Siegelman (Ann Arbor, Mich.: The University of Michigan Press, 1967); **The Jews and Modern Capitalism,** trans. M. Epstein, new edition with an introduction by Bert F. Hoselitz (New York: The Macmillan Company, Collier Books, 1962); **Socialism and the Social Movement**, trans. M. Epstein (London: J. M. Dent & Sons Ltd., 1909); **A New Social Philosophy**, trans. and ed. Karl F. Geiser (Princeton, N.J.: Princeton University Press, 1937), based on Sombart's **Deutscher Sozialismus**, his endorsement of Nazism.

For an interpretation of Sombart's historical studies, see Wesley Clair Mitchell, "Sombart's *Hochkapitalismus*," in **The Backward Art of Spending Money** and Other Essays (New York: McGraw-Hill Book Company, 1937), Chap. 13; about Sombart's later work, see Abram L. Harris, **Economics and Social Reform** (New York: Harper & Row, Publishers, 1958), Chap. 6, based on his article "Sombart and German (National) Socialism," **Journal of Political Economy**, Vol. 50 (December, 1942), 805–35. There are accounts of Sombart's work also in Joseph T. Lambie, ed., **Architects and Craftsmen in History: Festschrift für Abbott Payson Usher** (Tübingen: J. C. B. Mohr [Paul Siebeck], 1956)–articles by Frederic C. Lane and Edgar Salin under the general heading "The German Design for Social History." See also Arthur Mitzman, **Sociology and Estrangement: Three Sociologists of Imperial Germany** (New York: Alfred A. Knopf, 1973), about Sombart and others.

Sombart's concern with economic systems was shared by Walter Eucken, referred to earlier in this section, and has a parallel in the economic anthropology of Maurice Godelier (see below, p. 778), which aims at the comparative analysis of different economic systems and the construction of a formal model of an economic system.

• Spann, Othmar, **The History of Economics**, translated from the 19th German edition by Eden and Cedar Paul (New York: W. W. Norton and Company, Inc., 1930). This is an English translation of a German textbook on the history of economic thought that was originally published in 1910 and during the following decades came to be the most widely used book of its kind in Germany, selling more than 100,000 copies. The author opposed conventional economic thought as mechanistic and individualistic and in its stead advocated a "universalist" approach that was grounded in Adam Müller's romanticism. His assessment of Müller on pp. 154–70 may serve as a sample of the copious German literature on the subject. See also Melchior Palyi, "Die romantische Geldtheorie," **Archiv für Sozialwissenschaft und Sozialpolitik**, Vol. 42 (1916–17), 89–118, 535–60; Goetz A. Briefs, "The Economic Philosophy of Romanticism," **Journal of the History of Ideas**,

Vol. 2, No. 3 (June, 1941), 279–300; Fritz Karl Mann, "The Romantic Reaction," **Zeitschrift für Nationalökonomie**, Vol. 18, No. 3 (1958), 335–57; H. G. Schenk, **The Mind of the European Romantics** (London: Constable & Co. Ltd., 1966); Jacques Droz, **Le Romantisme allemand et l'état** (Paris: Éditions Payot, 1967); R. W. Harris, **Romanticism and the Social Order, 1780–1830** (New York: Barnes & Noble, 1970). About Spann see an article by John Haag in Leo Baeck Institute, **Year Book**, Vol. 18 (London: Secker & Warburg, 1973).

On later exponents of a different brand of romanticism—Carlyle and Ruskin—see James Clark Sherburne, **John Ruskin, Or the Ambiguities of Abundance** (Cambridge: Harvard University Press, 1972); William D. Grampp, "Classical Economics and Its Moral Critics," **History of Political Economy**, Vol. 5, No. 2 (Fall, 1973), 359–74.

On the opposition of the romantics to the spread of the ideas of Adam Smith in early nineteenth-century Germany, see Wilhelm Treue, "Adam Smith in Deutschland," in **Deutschland und Europa: Festschrift für Hans Rothfels**, ed. Werner Conze (Düsseldorf: Droste Verlag und Druckerei GMBH, 1951), pp. 101–33; Graf Henning von Borcke-Stargordt, "Aus der Vorgeschichte zu den preussischen Agrarreformen," **Jahrbuch der Albertus Universität zu Königsberg/Pr**, Vol. 8 (Würzburg: Holzner Verlag, 1958), 122–42, an article dedicated to the memory of a German follower of Adam Smith, Christian Jakob Kraus (1753–1807).

There are only four brief references to John Stuart Mill in Spann's book, all relating to Mill's monetary views, and there is no general exposition of his thought, although his **Principles,** available in an early German translation, is included among the books recommended to the student. At the time when Spann wrote his widely used text, the ideals for which Mill stood counted no longer as relevant in Germany. This marks a significant change from earlier nineteenth-century attitudes, when liberal thought still found an echo in Germany. Roscher often referred to Mill, and invariably with the greatest respect. Schmoller wrote of his affection for Mill. But in the twentieth century Mill's influence all but vanished.

• Spiethoff, Arthur, "Anschauliche und reine volkswirtschaftliche Theorie und ihr Verhältnis zu einander," in **Synopsis: Festgabe für Alfred Weber,** ed. Edgar Salin (Heidelberg: Lambert Schneider Verlag GMBH, 1948), pp. 567–664. The mature judgment of Schmoller's most distinguished disciple about the relationship between economic theory and history. For an appraisal see F. Redlich, "Arthur Spiethoff on Economic Styles," **Journal of Economic History**, Vol. 30, No. 3 (September, 1970), 640–52. Spiethoff's contributions to business-cycle theory are reviewed in Alvin H. Hansen, **Business Cycles and National Income** (New York: W. W. Norton & Company, Inc., 1951), pp. 292–300. See also Lane, "Social History," cited in the entry before the last. For English translations of works by Spiethoff, see his "Business Cycles," **International Economic Papers**, No. 3 (1953), pp. 75–171, which is based on his famous article on "Krisen" in the **Handwörterbuch der Staatswissenschaften**, 1923; "The 'Historical' Character of Economic Theories," **Journal of Economic History**, Vol. 12, No. 2 (1952), 131–39.

• Vogel, Walter, **Bismarcks Arbeiterversicherung** (Braunschweig: Georg Westermann Verlag, 1951). An account of Bismarck's social insurance scheme, which established a pattern followed in many countries. The idea may be traced back to Sismondi and Marlo. Early in the nineteenth century Sismondi had underlined the need for special arrangements helping workers to cope with the financial incidence of old age, sickness, and unemployment. He apparently had in mind a guaranteed annual wage, making the cost of these hazards part of the expenses of production of the firm (see above, p. 304). Mandatory and contributory social insurance against old age, sickness, and financial misfortunes, coupled with survivors' insurance—paid-up membership in the insurance fund being a prerequisite of the right to marry—was part of a comprehensive reform scheme proposed by Karl Georg Winkelblech (1810–65), a German chemistry professor and exponent of socialist ideas. Under the pen name Karl Marlo he published **Untersuchungen über die Organisation der Arbeit, oder System der Weltökonomie**, 3 vols., 1848–59. This work, which was published during a period of political apathy following the abortive revolution of 1848, seems to have had little influence on contemporary opinion; however, interest in Marlo's ideas revived after 1870, when Albert Schäffle (1831–1903), another reformer with socialist tendencies, who for some months in 1871 served as minister in the Austrian cabinet, called attention to them and propagated some of Marlo's proposals in his own writings. When the Association for Social Policy was founded in 1872, the idea of social insurance was already in the air and from then on became a matter of public discussion.

• Weber, Max, **Gesammelte Aufsätze zur Wissenschaftslehre**, 2nd ed. by Johannes Winckelmann (Tübingen: J. C. B. Mohr [Paul Siebeck], 1951). This contains Weber's methodological essays, including his critique of Roscher and Knies. The translation, **On the Methodology of the Social Sciences**, trans. and ed. Edward A. Shils and Henry A. Finch (New York: The Free Press 1949), does not contain the latter. Max Weber's work on the Calvinist origin of capitalism has been referred to above, p. 704. He also wrote a **General Economic History**, trans. Frank H. Knight (New York: The Macmillan Company, Collier Books, 1961). One of his more important works on economic sociology, **Wirtschaft und Gesellschaft**, 2nd ed., 2 vols. (Tübingen, J. C. B. Mohr [Paul Siebeck], 1925), is available in English translations in parts; see **The Theory of Social and Economic Organization**, trans. A. M. Henderson and Talcott Parsons, with an introduction by Talcott Parsons (New York: Oxford University Press, Inc., 1947). **From Max Weber: Essays in Sociology**, translated, edited, and with an introduction by H. H. Gerth and C. Wright Mills (New York: Oxford University Press, Inc., 1946), contains a well-chosen selection. References to Weber's concepts of understanding and ideal type can be found on pp. 55–61 of the introduction. Another selection is

765

Weber: Selections in Translations, ed. W. G. Runciman, trans. by Eric Matthews (New York: Cambridge University Press, 1978).

The standard biography is Marianne Weber, **Max Weber: A Biography**, trans. and edited by Harry Zohn (New York: John Wiley and Sons, Wiley Interscience, 1975; originally published in 1926). About Weber's Heidelberg *milieu* see Martin Green, **The von Richthofen Sisters** (New York: Basic Books, 1974).

The interpretive literature about Weber is huge. See, for example, Talcott Parsons, **The Structure of Social Action** (New York: McGraw-Hill Book Company, 1937), Chaps. 14–17; H. Stuart Hughes, **Consciousness and Society** (New York: Alfred A. Knopf, Inc., 1959), Chap. 8; J. P. Mayer, **Max Weber and German Politics** (London: Faber & Faber Ltd., 1944); Raymond Aron, **German Sociology** (London: William Heinemann Ltd., 1957); Reinhard Bendix, **Max Weber: An Intellectual Portrait** (Garden City, N.Y.: Doubleday & Company Inc., 1962), which mainly deals with his substantive sociology and has little on his method. For appraisals that contain also critical views, see **Max Weber and Sociology Today**, ed. Otto Stammer, trans. by Kathleen Morris (New York: Harper & Row, 1971), especially the report by Herbert Marcuse on "Industrialization and Capitalism" with discussion (pp. 133–86), and that about the work of the committee on methodological questions (pp. 209–20). See also W. G. Runciman, **A Critique of Max Weber's Philosophy of Social Science** (New York: Cambridge University Press, 1972); M. L. Lachmann, **The Legacy of Max Weber** (Berkeley, Calif.: Glendessary Press, 1971);

Donald G. MacRae, **Max Weber** (New York: The Viking Press, 1974, Modern Masters series); W. D. Hudson, ed., **The Is-Ought Question: A Collection of Papers on the Central Problem in Moral Philosophy** (New York: St. Martin's Press, 1969); A. Schweitzer, "Typological Method in Economics: Max Weber's Contribution," **History of Political Economy**, Vol. 2, No. 1 (Spring, 1970), 66–96. The tensions in Weber's thought are stressed in Arthur Mitzman, **The Iron Cage: An Historical Interpretation of Max Weber** (New York: Alfred A. Knopf, Inc., 1970).

Georg Simmel, a contemporary of Weber and well-known sociologist, wrote **The Philosophy of Money**, first published in 1900, trans. by Tom Bottomore and David Frisby (London and Boston: Routledge and Kegan Paul, 1978). In Simmel's own words, "not a single line" of this work is about economics. It was interpreted as a "philosophy of our times" by one of Simmel's contemporaries.

On the distinction between natural and cultural sciences and the work of the German philosophers Wilhelm Windelband and Heinrich Rickert relating thereto, see Maurice Mandelbaum, **The Problem of Historical Knowledge**, (New York: Liveright Publishing Corp., 1938), pp. 119–47, where a section is also devoted to Wilhelm Dilthey who was influential in fostering the understanding approach (pp. 58–67). See also H. A. Hodges, **Wilhelm Dilthey** (London: Routledge & Kegan Paul Ltd., 1944); Heinrich Rickert, **Science and History**, trans. George Reisman, ed. Arthur Goddard (New York: Litton Educational Publishing, Inc., Van Nostrand Reinhold Company, 1962), especially the introduction by F. A. Hayek.

CHAPTER 19

• Beer, Max, **A General History of Socialism and Social Struggles**, 5 vols. in 2 (New York: Russell & Russell Publishers, 1957). This work, originally published in the 1920s, is based on a wide interpretation of socialism and carries the story of social struggles from antiquity to modern times. The fourth volume is

devoted to the period from 1750 to 1860. G. D. H. Cole, **A History of Socialist Thought**, 5 vols. in 7 (New York: St. Martin's Press, Inc., 1953–60), covers developments since 1789 and is worldwide in scope. Vol. 1 is entitled "The Forerunners, 1789–1850." Both are scholarly works, written from a sympathetic point of view by men who participated in the socialist movement of their time. Cole (1889–1959) was an outstanding socialist academic who taught at Oxford for forty years. A more detached view, paired with sparkling wit, may be found in Sir Alexander Gray, **The Socialist Tradition: Moses to Lenin** (London: Longmans, Green & Co. Ltd., 1946), who is especially attentive to the economic aspects of socialist thought. A useful survey is offered in Harry W. Laidler's **History of Socialism** (London: Routledge & Kegan Paul Ltd., 1969). George Lichtheim, **The Origins of Socialism** (New York: Encyclopaedia Britannica, Inc., Frederick A. Praeger, Inc., 1969), is the best general review of socialist thought before Marx.

More up to date than these works, and composed of a variety of valuable contributions, is **Histoire générale du socialisme**, ed. Jacques Droz, 4 vols. (Paris: Presses Universitaires de France, 1972–78), which is best on the French material. The story is told in chronological order, with the last volume devoted to the period since 1945.

A standard critique, written by a famous economist of conservative leanings, is Vilfredo Pareto, **Les Systèmes socialistes**, originally published in 1902, 2nd ed. (Paris: Giard, 1926). A more recent critical work, written by a professional philosopher and specifically devoted to Marxism rather than socialism, is Leszek Kolakowski, **Main Currents of Marxism: Its Rise, Growth, and Dissolution**, 3 vols. (New York: Oxford University Press, 1978). Vol. 1 is devoted to Marx and his forerunners, Vol. 2 to the period of the Second International, and Vol. 3 to the years from 1920 to 1970.

Outstanding studies of regional scope include Carl Landauer, **European Socialism: A History of Ideas and Movements from the Industrial Revolution to Hitler's Seizure of Power**, 2 vols. (Berkeley and Los Angeles: University of California Press, 1959); Donald Drew Egbert and Stow Persons, eds., **Socialism and American Life**, 2 vols. (Princeton, N.J.: Princeton University Press, 1952). A documentary history that assembles a great variety of elusive material is Albert Fried, ed., **Socialism in America: From the Shakers to the Third International** (Garden City, N.Y.: Doubleday and Company, 1970).

A comprehensive reader is **Socialist Thought**, ed. Albert Fried and Ronald Sanders (Chicago: Aldine Publishing Company, 1964). Selections mainly from French and Italian writers are included in Gian Mario Bravo, ed., **Les Socialistes avant Marx**, 3 vols. (Paris: Maspéro, 1970). Other readers include Irving Howe, ed., **Essential Works of Socialism** (New York: Holt, Rinehart and Winston, 1970; Bantam edition, 1971); **Socialist Economics**, ed. Alec Nove and D. M. Nuti (New York: Penguin Books, 1972).

• Bestor, Arthur E., Jr., **Backwoods Utopias** (Philadelphia: University of Pennsylvania Press, 1950), is an account of the communitarian settlements in North America. The same topic is treated in Mark Holloway, **Heavens on Earth** (London: Turnstile Press, 1951); William E. Wilson, **The Angel and the Serpent: The Story of New Harmony** (Bloomington, Ind.: Indiana University Press, 1964); Everett Webber, **Escape to Utopia** (New York: Hastings House, Publishers, Inc., 1959); Charles Gide, **Communist and Cooperative Colonies**, trans. by E. F. Row (London: George G. Harrap & Co. Ltd., 1930); Gairdner B. Moment and Otto F. Kraushaar, eds., **Utopias: The American Experience** (Metuchen, N.J.: Scarecrow Press, 1980). Reprints of firsthand reports of early observers include Charles Nordhoff, **The Communistic Societies of the United States**, first published in 1875 (New York: Hillary House Publishers, 1961); John Humphrey Noyes, **History of American Socialisms**, first published in 1870 (New York: Hillary House Publishers, 1961).

• Carr, Edward Hallett, **Studies in Revolution** (London: Macmillan & Co. Ltd., 1950; reprinted London: Frank Cass & Co. Ltd., 1962), contains chapters on Saint-Simon, Proudhon, and other socialists.

• _____ , **Michael Bakunin** (London: Macmillan & Co. Ltd., 1937). Bakunin, although a visionary, had enough good sense to express scepticism about the effective exercise of political power by the working class as anticipated by Marx. He hinted at the rise of a managerial elite, "a new and not very numerous aristocracy of real or spurious savants," a "new privileged scientific political class" with interests diverging from those of the common people. These ideas were later on more fully developed by the Polish-Russian radical Waclav Machajski (1866–1926), to whom Max Nomad has called attention in various writings, for example, in his **Aspects of Revolt** (New York: Noonday Press, 1961), with an introduction by Edmund Wilson, Chap. 5. Machajski taught that the classless society that the radical intellectuals promised, "was meant only as propaganda, as a sort of proletarian religion . . . The socialism which the socialist parties really aspired to was a hierarchical system under which all industries were owned by the government, the private capitalists having yielded place to officeholders, managers and engineers, whose salaries would be much higher than the wages paid for manual labor and who henceforth would constitute the new and only ruling class" (p. 100).

After Bakunin, the leading figure in anarchism was Peter Kropotkin (1842–1921), whose principal work, **Mutual Aid** (1902), underlined solidarity and communal work as more important factors in biological evolution than competition and the struggle for existence. On the basis of a study of animal life he concluded that those species that willingly abandon sociability are doomed to decay.

About anarchism see James Joll, **The Anarchists** (Boston: Little, Brown and Company, 1964); George Woodcock, **Anarchism** (New York: The World Publishing Company, Meridian Books, 1962); Alan Ritter, **Anarchism: A Theoretical Analysis** (New York: Cambridge University Press, 1981); April Carter, **The Political Theory of Anarchism** (New York: Harper & Row, 1971); Paul Avrich, **The Russian Anarchists** (Princeton: Princeton University Press, 1967); Paul Thomas, **Karl Marx and the Anarchists** (London and Boston: Routledge and Kegan Paul, 1980); Leonard L. Krimerman and Lewis Perry, eds., **Patterns of Anarchy** (Garden City, N.Y.: Doubleday & Company, Inc.,

Anchor Books, 1966); Irving L. Horovitz, ed., **The Anarchists** (New York: Dell Publishing Co., Inc., 1964). The last two items contain selections from anarchist writings. The earlier literature has been reviewed by Max Nettlau, **Bibliographie de l'anarchie**, first published in Brussels in 1897 and reprinted (New York: Burt Franklin, 1969). Recent anthologies in French include Daniel Guérin, ed., **Ni dieu ni maître. Anthologie historique du mouvement anarchiste** (Lausanne: La Cité, 1969); Bernard Thomas, ed., **Ni dieu ni maître: Les anarchistes** (Paris: Tchou, 1969). The former contains long selections in historical order, the latter comprises brief quotations around a number of key topics.

About Bakunin see Anthony Masters, **Bakunin: The Father of Anarchism** (New York: Saturday Review Press, E. P. Dutton, 1974); Arthur Lehning, **From Buonarroti to Bakunin** (Leiden: E. J. Brill, 1970); Michael Bakunin, **Selected Writings**, ed. Arthur Lehning (New York: Grove Press, 1973); **Bakunin on Anarchy**, ed. Sam Dolgoff (New York: Alfred A. Knopf. 1972).

About Kropotkin see George Woodcock and Ivan Avakumović, **The Anarchist Prince: Peter Kropotkin** (New York: Schocken Books, 1971; first published in 1950); Martin A. Miller, **Kropotkin** (Chicago: University of Chicago Press, 1979); P. A. Kropotkin, **Selected Writings on Anarchism and Revolution**, ed. Martin A. Miller (Boston: MIT Press, 1970); **The Essential Kropotkin**, ed. Emile Capouya and Keitha Tompkins (New York: Liveright, 1975).

About **Contemporary Anarchism** see a book by that title, ed. Terry M. Perlin (New Brunswick, N.J.: Transactions Books - Rutgers The State University, 1979); also Gerald Runkle, **Anarchism Old and New** (New York: Dell Publishing Company, 1972); **Reinventing Anarchy**, ed. Howard J. Ehrlich et al. (London and Boston: Routledge and Kegan Paul, 1979).

• Fourier, Charles, **Selections from the Works of Fourier**. With an introduction by Charles Gide, trans. Julia Franklin

(London: Swan Sonnenschein and Company, 1901). This translation has been reprinted under the title **Design for Utopia: Selected Writings of Charles Fourier**, with a new foreword by Frank E. Manuel (New York: Schocken Books, 1971). For other selections see **The Utopian Vision of Charles Fourier**, ed. and trans. by Jonathan Beecher and Richard Bienvenu (Boston: Beacon Press, 1971); **Harmonian Man: The Selected Writings of Charles Fourier**, ed. Mark Poster (Garden City, N.Y.: Doubleday and Company, 1971, Anchor Books). Early English translations of works by Fourier include **The Passions of the Human Soul, and Their Influence on Society and Civilization**, 2 vols. (London: Baillière, Tindall & Cassell Limited, 1851), and **The Social Destiny of Man** (Philadelphia: C. F. Stollmeyer, 1840), the latter an exposition by Albert Brisbane, a leading Fourierist in the United States. The standard work on Fourier was for a long time Hubert Bourgin, **Fourier: Contribution à l'étude du socialisme français** (Paris: Société Nouvelle de Librairie et d'Édition, 1905), to which now may be added Émile Lehouck, **Fourier aujourd'hui** (Paris: Les Éditions Denoël, 1966); Nicholas V. Riasanovsky, **The Teaching of Charles Fourier** (Berkeley and Los Angeles: University of California Press, 1970). Fourier's works are being reprinted, and some of his manuscripts published for the first time (Paris: Editions Anthropos). **Théorie des quatre mouvements**, with preface, notes and commentary by Simone Debout, has also been reprinted (Paris: Éditions Jean-Jacques Pauvert, 1967). The same publisher has made available a selection from Fourier's works under the title **L'Attraction passionnée,** ed. René Scherer (1967). An appraisal of Fourier, designating his thought as anarchist, is Edward S. Mason, "Fourier and Anarchism," **Quarterly Journal of Economics**, Vol. 42 (1928), 228–62. On related aspects of Fourier's work see David Zeldin, **The Educational Ideas of Charles Fourier** (London: Frank Cass & Co. Ltd., 1969); Daniel Bell, "Charles Fourier: Prophet of Eupsychia," **The American Scholar**, Vol. 38, No. 1 (1968–69), 41–58. George Lichtheim, "Socialism and the Jews," **Dissent**, July-August, 1968, pp. 314–42, about the vicious anti-Semitism of Fourier, Proudhon and other socialists.

• Manuel, Frank E., and Fritzie P., **Utopian Thought in the Western World** (Cambridge: Belknap Press, 1979). A monumental work. See also, ed. by the Manuels, **French Utopias: An Anthology of Ideal Societies** (New York: Free Press, 1966; Schocken Books, 1971), which contains selections from a wide variety of sources.

• Mason, Edward S., "Blanqui and Communism," **Quarterly Journal of Economics**, Vol. 44 (1929), 498–527. This article contains an analysis of Blanqui's economic views as well as a comparison of the revolutionary theories of Babeuf, Blanqui, and Lenin. See also A. B. Spitzer, **The Revolutionary Theories of Louis Auguste Blanqui** (New York: Columbia University Press, 1957); Maurice Dommanget, **Auguste Blanqui: Des origines à la révolution de 1848** (Paris: Mouton, 1969); Samuel Bernstein, **Auguste Blanqui and the Art of Insurrection** (London: Lawrence & Wishart, 1971). On Babeuf see David Thomson, **The Babeuf Plot** (London: Routledge & Kegan Paul Ltd., 1947); M. Dommanget, **Sur Babeuf et la conjuration des égaux** (Paris: Spartacus, 1970; Bibliothèque socialiste); R. B. Rose, **Grachus Babeuf: The First Revolutionary Communist** (Stanford, Calif.: Stanford University Press, 1978); John A. Scott, ed. **The Defense of Grachus Babeuf Before the High Court of Vendôme**, with an essay by Herbert Marcuse (New York: Schocken Books, 1972). About Babeuf's companion Filippo Buonarroti see John M. Roberts, **The Mythology of the Secret Societies** (New York: Charles Scribner's Sons, 1972). See also James H. Billington, **Fire in the Minds of Men: Origins of the Revolutionary Faith** (New York: Basic Books, 1980), which traces the revolutionary movement of modern times to the secret socities of the eighteenth century. See also Christopher H. Johnson, **Utopian Communism in France: Cabet and the Icarians, 1839–1851** (Ithaca, N.Y.: Cornell University Press, 1974).

• McKay, Donald C., **The National Workshops** (Cambridge, Mass.: Harvard University Press, 1933). The history of the ill-fated attempt to establish national workshops in line with the ideas of Louis Blanc during the French Revolution of 1848. See also J. A. R. Marriott, **The French Revolution of 1948 in Its Economic Aspect**, Vol. 1, **Louis Blanc's Organization du travail** (London: Oxford University Press, 1951); L. A. Loubere, **Louis Blanc** (Evanston, Ill.: Northwestern University Press, 1961).

• Menger, Anton, **The Right to the Whole Produce of Labour**, trans. M. E. Tanner, with an introduction and bibliography by H. S. Foxwell (London: Macmillan & Co. Ltd., 1899). This work includes an appraisal of the Ricardian socialists. Its value is enhanced by Foxwell's introduction, of which selections are reprinted in Henry W. Spiegel, ed., **The Development of Economic Thought** (New York: John Wiley & Sons, Inc., 1952), pp. 269–96. Some of the original writings of the Ricardian socialists were reprinted (London: The London School of Economics, 1931). There is a later reprint of Thomas Hodgskin, **Labour Defended**, originally published in 1825 (London: Hammersmith Bookshop, 1964), and a first publication of John Francis Bray's **A Voyage from Utopia**, edited with an introduction by M. F. Lloyd-Prichard (London: Lawrence & Wishart Ltd., 1957). Appraisals of individual members of the group include Élie Halévy, **Thomas Hodgskin**, trans. A. J. Taylor (London: Ernest Benn Limited, 1956); Richard K. P. Pankhurst, **William Thompson** (London: C. A. Watts & Co. Ltd., 1954); M. Hasbach, **W. Thompson** (Stuttgart: Gustav Fischer Verlag, 1922); Janet Kimball, **The Economic Doctrines of John Gray** (Washington, D.C.: The Catholic University of America Press, 1948), which discloses new biographical material. On the whole group, see also Esther Lowenthal, **The Ricardian Socialists** (New York: Columbia University Press, 1911), and on Hodgskin and Thompson, W. Stark, **The Ideal Foundations of Economic Thought** (London: Routledge & Kegan Paul Ltd., 1943), pp.

51–148. See also, about a possible Gray-Friedman connection, G. S. Tavlas, "Some Initial Formulations of the Monetary Growth-Rate Rule," **History of Political Economy**, Vol. 9, No. 4 (Winter, 1977), 535–47.

• Oncken, Hermann, **Ferdinand Lassalle**, 4th ed. (Stuttgart: Deutsche Verlaganstalt GMBH, 1923), is the standard biography of Lassalle. See also Gustav Mayer, **Lassalle als Nationalökonom** (Berlin: Mayer & Müller, 1894); Shlomo Na'aman, **Lassalle** (Hanover: Verlag für Literatur und Zeitgeschehen, 1970). Works in English about Lassalle include Eduard Bernstein, **Ferdinand Lassalle as a Social Reformer** (New York: Charles Scribner's Sons, 1893); David Footman, **Ferdinand Lassalle: Romantic Revolutionary** (New Haven, Conn.: Yale University Press, 1947).

• Owen, Robert, **A New View of Society and Other Writings**, with an introduction by G. D. H. Cole (New York: E. P. Dutton & Co., Inc., Everyman's Library, 1927). This useful selection contains the most important writings of Owen, as does Owen's **A New View of Society and Report to the County of Lanark**, ed. with an introduction by V. A. C. Gatrell (New York: Penguin Books, 1970). **A Bibliography of Robert Owen, The Socialist**, 2nd edition, has been prepared under the auspices of the National Library of Wales (London: Oxford University Press, 1925). The standard biography is Frank Podmore, **Robert Owen**, 2 vols. (Des Moines, Iowa: Meredith Corporation, Appleton-Century-Crofts, 1907). Appraisals include G. D. H. Cole, **Robert Owen**, 2nd ed. (London: Ernest Benn Ltd., 1930); Margaret Cole, **Robert Owen of New Lanark** (London: Batchworth Press, 1953); and A. L. Morton, **The Life and Ideas of Robert Owen** (London: Lawrence & Wishart Ltd., 1962), the latter with extracts from Owen's works. Bicentenary studies memorializing the 200th return of Owen's birth include John Butt, ed., **Robert Owen: Prince of Cotton Spinners** (Newton Abbot: David and Charles, 1971); Sidney Pollard and John Salt, eds., **Robert Owen** (London: Macmillan and Company, 1971); Donald E. Pitzer, ed.,

Robert Owen's American Legacy (Indianapolis: Indiana Historical Society, 1972). The contributions by Owen and other early socialists to the development of town planning are reviewed by Leonardo Benevolo, **The Origins of Modern Town Planning**, trans. Judith Landry (London: Routledge & Kegan Paul Ltd., 1967). On Owenite settlements see J. F. C. Harrison, **Robert Owen and the Owenites in Britain and America** (London: Routledge & Kegan Paul Ltd., 1969). On Owen's educational theories see **Robert Owen on Education**, edited with an introduction and notes by Harold Silver (London: Cambridge University Press, 1969).

• Proudhon, Pierre-Joseph, **What Is Property?**, trans. Benjamin R. Tucker (Princeton, Mass.: B. R. Tucker, 1876). There is also an English translation of the first part of the other principal contribution of Proudhon's to economic thought, published under the title **System of Economic Contradictions: or the Philosophy of Poverty**, trans. Benjamin R. Tucker (Princeton, Mass.: B. R. Tucker, 1888). Still another work, **General Idea of the Revolution in the Nineteenth Century**, has been translated by John Beverley Robinson (London: Freedom Press, 1923), and there is a selection of articles, mainly on banking, edited with introduction by Henry Cohen and published under the title **Proudhon's Solution of the Social Problem** (New York: Vanguard Press, Inc., 1927). Wider in scope is **Selected Writings of P.-J. Proudhon**, ed. Stewart Edwards, trans. Elizabeth Fraser (Garden City, N.Y.: Doubleday & Company, Inc., Anchor Books, 1969). Books about Proudhon include George Woodcock, **Pierre-Joseph Proudhon** (New York: The Macmillan Company, 1956); Henri de Lubac, **The Un-Marxian Socialist: A Study of Proudhon**, trans. by R. E. Scantlebury (London: Sheed and Ward Ltd., 1948), which discusses Proudhon's attitude to religion; Georges Gurvitch, **Pour le centenaire de la mort de Pierre-Joseph Proudhon** (Cours public 1963–64) (Paris: Centre de documentation universitaire, 1964); **L'actualité de Proudhon**, Colloque de novembre 1965 (Brussels: Centre national d'étude des problèmes de sociologie et d'économie européennes, 1967); Alan Ritter, **The Political Thought of Pierre-Joseph Proudhon** (Princeton, N.J.: Princeton University Press, 1969); Jacques Langlois, **Défense et actualité de Proudhon** (Paris: Payot, 1976); Constance M. Hall, **The Sociology of Pierre-Joseph Proudhon** (New York: Philosophical Library, 1971); Robert L. Hoffman, **Revolutionary Justice: The Social and Political Theory of P.-J. Proudhon** (Urbana: University of Illinois Press, 1972); Edward Hyams, **Pierre-Joseph Proudhon: His Revolutionary Life, Mind and Works** (New York: Taplinger, 1979). Proudhon, who considered himself "a man of paradoxes," has been the subject of varied interpretations indicated by the titles of these articles: J. Selwyn Schapiro, "Pierre Joseph Proudhon, Harbinger of Fascism" **American Historical Review**, Vol. 50, No. 4 (July, 1945), 714–37, reprinted in his **Liberalism and the Challenge of Fascism** (New York: McGraw-Hill Book Company, 1949); Dudley Dillard, "Keynes and Proudhon," **Journal of Economic History**, Vol. 2, No. 1 (May, 1942), 63–76. Dillard considers Proudhon a forerunner of Keynes. Both Proudhon and Keynes attacked financial capital while accepting private industrial enterprise, and in their theoretical argument both integrated monetary theory into the general body of economic principles.

• Rodbertus, Karl, **Overproduction and Crises**, trans. Julia Franklin, with an introduction by John B. Clark (London: Swan Sonnenschein and Company, 1898). This translation of a study originally published in 1850–51 sheds light on Rodbertus's views about depressions, which he ascribes to the diminution of labor's share in an increasing national output and which in part converge with those of Marx. There is a book-length study, **The Social Philosophy of Rodbertus**, by E. C. K. Gonner (New York: The Macmillan Company, 1899).

• Saint-Simon, Henri de, **Social Organization, the Science of Man, and Other Writings**, edited and translated, with a preface and introduction, by Felix Markham (New York: Harper & Row, Publishers, Torchbooks, 1964). This selection from the writings of Saint-Simon may be supplemented by a systematic restatement of his views, published first in 1831 and available in an English translation under the title **The Doctrine of Saint-Simon: An Exposition. First Year, 1828–1829**. Translated with notes and an introduction by George G. Iggers, preface by G. D. H. Cole (Boston: Beacon Press, 1958). A book-length appraisal of Saint-Simon by a distinguished sociologist is Émile Durkheim, **Socialism and Saint-Simon**, edited and with an introduction by Alvin W. Gouldner, translated by Charlotte Sattler from the edition originally edited, with a preface, by Marcel Mauss (Yellow Springs, O.: Antioch Press, 1958). See also Frank E. Manuel, **The New World of Henri Saint-Simon** (Cambridge, Mass.: Harvard University Press, 1956); the same author's **The Prophets of Paris** (Cambridge, Mass.: Harvard University Press, 1962), which treats also of Fourier and other French writers; Mathurin Dondo, **The French Faust** (New York: Philosophical Library, Inc., 1955); F. A. Hayek, **The Counter-Revolution of Science** (New York: Free Press, 1955), Part 2; R. P. Fehlbaum, **Saint-Simon und die Saint-Simonisten** (Tübingen: J. C. B. Mohr, 1970); Keith Taylor, **Henri Saint-Simon** (London: Croom Helm, 1975); Ghita Ionescu, ed., **The Political Thought of Saint-Simon** (New York: Oxford University Press, 1976); Edward S. Mason, "Saint-Simonism and the Rationalisation of Industry," **Quarterly Journal of Economics**, Vol. 45 (1931), 640–83; Georges Gurvitch, **Les Fondateurs français de la sociologie contemporaine, I: Saint-Simon sociologue** (Paris: Centre de documentation universitaire, 1955); P. V. Lyon, "Saint-Simon and the Origins of Scientism and Historicism," **Canadian Journal of Economics and Political Science**, Vol. 27

(February, 1961), 55–63; René König, "Das Amerika-Bild von Claude-Henri de Saint Simon und seine Bedeutung für die Entwicklung der europäischen Soziologie," in **Spirit of a Free Society: Essays in Honor of Senator J. W. Fulbright** (Heidelberg: Quelle & Meyer, 1962), pp. 13–29.

• Seligman, Edwin R. A., **Essays in Economics** (New York: The Macmillan Company, 1925). Chapter 2 contains an essay on "Owen and the Christian Socialists." The standard work about the latter is C. E. Raven, **Christian Socialism, 1848–1854** (London: Macmillan & Co. Ltd., 1920). See also Torben Christensen, **Origin and History of Christian Socialism, 1848–54** (Aarhus: Universitetsforlaget, 1962); N.C. Masterman, **John Malcolm Ludlow** (New York: Cambridge University Press, 1963). Olive T. Brose, **Frederic Denison Maurice** (Athens, Ohio: Ohio University Press, 1972). Maurice's great-granddaughter is Joan Robinson.

• Vidler, A. R., **Prophecy and Papacy: A Study of Lamennais, the Church and the Revolution** (New York: Charles Scribner's Sons, 1954); Peter N. Stearns, **Priest and Revolutionary: Lamennais and the Dilemma of French Catholicism** (New York: Harper & Row, Publishers, 1967). These works about Lamennais may be supplemented by Jean Baptiste Duroselle, **Les Débuts du catholicisme social en France (1822–1870)** (Paris: Presses Universitaires de France, 1951); A. R. Vidler, **A Century of Social Catholicism, 1820–1920** (London: The Society for Promoting Christian Knowledge, 1964); Bernard Reardon, **Liberalism and Tradition: Aspects of Catholic Thought in Nineteenth-Century France** (New York: Cambridge University Press, 1975).

CHAPTER 20

• Berlin, Isaiah, **Karl Marx: His Life and Environment**, 4th ed. (New York: Oxford University Press, 1978). An assessment by an outstanding authority on intellectual history, which traces the sources of Marx's

thought but deliberately abstains from commenting on his economics. The standard biography of Marx, written by a follower, is Franz Mehring, **Karl Marx**, trans. Edward Fitzgerald (London: George

Allen & Unwin Ltd., 1936); that of Engels, Gustav Mayer, **Friedrich Engels**, abr. and trans. G. and H. Highet, ed. R. H. S. Crossman (New York: Alfred A. Knopf, Inc., 1936). Another notable biography is Edward Hallett Carr, **Karl Marx: A Study in Fanaticism** (London: J. M. Dent & Sons Ltd., 1934). Robert Payne, **Marx** (New York: Simon & Schuster, Inc., 1968), introduces some hitherto little known detail. More recent biographies and appraisals include David McLellan, **Karl Marx: His Life and Thought** (New York: Harper & Row, 1973); Saul K. Padover, **Karl Marx: An Intimate Biography** (New York: McGraw-Hill Book Company, 1978); Jerrold Seigel, **Marx's Fate: The Shape of a Life** (Princeton: Princeton University Press, 1978), a psycho-history; Fritz J. Raddatz, **Karl Marx: A Political Biography**, trans. by Richard Barry (Boston: Little, Brown and Company, 1979); McLellan, **Karl Marx** (New York: The Viking Press, 1976, in the Modern Masters series); W. O. Henderson, **The Life of Friedrich Engels**, 2 vols. (London: Frank Cass, 1974); McLellan, **Engels** (New York: The Viking Press, 1978, in the Modern Masters series). There is an abundance of Russian and lately also of French studies devoted to the founders of Marxism. An example of the former is D. B. Ryazanov, **Karl Marx and Friedrich Engels**, trans. J. Kunitz (New York: International Publishers Co., Inc., 1927), the author of which perished during the Soviet purges of the 1930s. For French studies, see Auguste Cornu, **Karl Marx et Friedrich Engels**, 4 vols. (Paris: Presses Universitaires de France, 1955–70), the work of a Marxist; Jean-Yves Calvez, **La Pensée de Karl Marx** (Paris: Editions du Seuil, 1956), written from a Catholic point of view; Maximilien Rubel, **Karl Marx: Essai de biographie intellectuelle** (Paris: Marcel Rivière, 1957). A notable interpretation by an American, considered by some the greatest literary critic of his time, is Edmund Wilson, **To the Finland Station**, with a new introduction (New York: Farrar, Straus & Giroux, 1972), which takes its title from the scene of Lenin's return to Russia in April, 1917 (first published in 1940).

• Bober, M. M., **Karl Marx's Interpretation of History**, 2nd ed., rev. (Cambridge, Mass.: Harvard University Press, 1948; New York: W. W. Norton & Company Inc., 1965). This work by a professional economist ranges widely over Marx's economic thought and is not limited to Marx's interpretation of history. More recent works that take account of the publication of the **Grundrisse** and which vacillate between a strictly deterministic interpretation of Marx's theory of historical development and a more relaxed view reflecting the persistent influence of Hegel on Marx's thought include Melvin Rader, **Marx's Interpretation of History** (New York: Oxford University Press, 1979); William H. Shaw, **Marx's Theory of History** (Stanford, Calif.: Stanford University Press, 1978); G. A. Cohen, **Karl Marx's Theory of History: A Defense** (Princeton: Princeton University Press, 1978). See also Anthony Giddens, **A Contemporary Critique of Historical Materialism**, Vol. 1, **Power, Property and the State** (Berkeley: University of California Press, 1981); Shlomo Avineri, **The Social and Political Thought of Karl Marx** (New York: Cambridge University Press, 1968); Z. A. Jordan, **The Evolution of Dialectical Materialism** (New York: St. Martin's Press, Inc., 1968) Nicholas Lobkowicz, **Theory and Practice: History of a Concept from Aristotle to Marx** (Notre Dame, Ind.: University of Notre Dame Press, 1968). Nathan Rothenstreich, **Theory and Practice** (The Hague: Martinus Nijhoff Publisher, 1977).

• Böhm-Bawerk, Eugen von, **Karl Marx and the Close of His System** and **Böhm-Bawerk's Criticism of Marx** by Rudolf Hilferding, edited together, with an introduction by Paul M. Sweezy, and with an appendix consisting of an article by Ladislaus von Bortkiewicz, "The Transformation of Values into Prices in the Marxian System" (New York: Augustus M. Kelley, Publisher, 1949). This contains Böhm-Bawerk's famous critique of Marx, which was originally published in 1896 and at its time constituted the authoritative reply to Marx by a leading economist, The principal target of Böhm-Bawerk's

774

attack was Marx's labor theory of value and his attempted solution of the transformation problem. The author of the leading Marx critique of the next generation was Böhm-Bawerk's pupil, Ludwig von Mises, with his **Socialism**, originally published in 1922, trans. J. Kahane, 2nd ed. (London: Jonathan Cape Ltd., 1951), who argued that economic calculation, as based on the price system, would be impossible under socialism, a system without a rational device for the allocation of productive resources.

The translations of Hilferding and Bortkiewicz contain further contributions to the debate about the labor theory of value and the transformation problem. Bortkiewicz tackled the latter with the help of a system of equations and thereby gave direction to the further discussion of the matter. The translation of another article by him, "Value and Price in the Marxian System," may be found in **International Economic Papers**, No. 2 (1952). The highlights of the more recent discussion are Paul A. Samuelson, "Understanding the Marxian Notion of Exploitation: A Summary of the So-called Transformation Problem Between Marxian Values and Competitive Prices," **Journal of Economic Literature**, Vol. 9, No. 2 (June, 1971), 399–431, with subsequent comments by A. P. Lerner, M. Bronfenbrenner, and Joan Robinson, same journal, Vol. 10, No. 1 (March, 1972), 50–56; Vol. 11, No. 1 (March, 1973), 56–63; Vol. 11, No. 4 (December, 1973), 1367; Colloquium by William J. Baumol et al., "On Marx, the Transformation Problem, and Opacity," same journal, Vol. 12, No. 1 (March, 1974), 51–77; M. Morishima and G. Catephores, "Is There an Historical Transformation Problem?" **Economic Journal**, Vol. 85, No. 338 (June, 1975), 309–28; T. Sowell, "Marxian Value Reconsidered," **Economica**, new series, Vol. 30 (August, 1963), 297–308; H. Gottlieb, "Marx's *Mehrwert* Concept and the Theory of Pure Capitalism," **Review of Economic Studies**, Vol. 18, No. 3 (1951), 164–78; and, for a defense by a follower of Marx, Ronald L. Meek, **Studies in the Labour Theory of Value** (London: Lawrence & Wishart Ltd., 1956).

• Cole, G. D. H., **The Meaning of Marxism** (London: Victor Gollancy Ltd., 1950). A new edition of a widely used, popular interpretation, formerly entitled "What Marx Really Meant," by an author who was one of Britain's leading socialist academics.

Other recent expositions and interpretations of Marx's economics at different levels of complexity and detachment are Murray Wolfson, **Karl Marx** (New York: Columbia University Press, 1971); Alexander Balinky, **Marx's Economics: Origin and Development** (Lexington, Mass.: D. C. Heath and Company, 1970); James F. Becker, **Marxian Political Economy: An Outline** (New York: Cambridge University Press, 1977); Antony Cutler et al., **Marx's 'Capital' and Capitalism Today**, 2 vols. (London and Boston: Routledge & Kegan Paul, 1977–78); Meghmad Desai, **Marxian Economics** (Totowa, N.J.: Littlefield, Adams & Company, 1979); Karl Kühne, **Economics and Marxism**, trans. by Robert Shaw, 2 vols. (New York: St. Martin's Press, 1980); Michael Howard and John King, **The Political Economy of Marx** (New York: Longman, Inc., 1975); Michio Morishima, **Marx's Economics: A Dual Theory of Value and Growth** (New York: Cambridge University Press, 1973); Roman Rosdolsky, **The Making of Marx's 'Capital'**, trans. by Pete Burgess (Atlantic Highlands, N.J.: Humanities Press, 1977), a convenient guide through Marx's main work.

• Giddens, Anthony, **The Class Structure of the Advanced Societies** (New York: Harper & Row, 1975); Frank Parkin, **Marxism and Class Theory: A Bourgeois Critique** (New York: Columbia University Press, 1979). The preceding works are sociological studies. For a related matter see Martin Seliger, **The Marxist Conception of Ideology** (New York: Cambridge University Press, 1977); Hans Barth, **Truth and Ideology**, trans. F. Lilge (Berkeley: University of California Press, 1977).

• Gottheil, Fred M., **Marx's Economic Predictions** (Evanston, Ill.: Northwestern University Press, 1967). This work examines the extent to which Marx's predictions, which are listed and classified, flow logically from his analysis. Some of the predictions, in particular those relating to increasing circular disorders of the economy are found to be logical conclusions of Marx's theories, but the larger part of them are not. See also William Fellner, "Marxian Hypotheses and Observable Trends under Capitalism," **Economic Journal**, Vol. 67 (March, 1957), 16–25; Gottfried Haberler, "Marxian Economics in Retrospect and Prospect," **Zeitschrift für Nationalökonomie**, Vol. 26, No. 1–3 (1966), 69–82; Paul Craig Roberts and Matthew A. Stephenson, **Marx's Theory of Exchange, Alienation and Crisis** (Stanford, Calif.: Hoover Institution Press, 1973.

• Hook, Sidney, **From Hegel to Marx: Studies in the Intellectual Development of Karl Marx** (New York: Humanities Press, Inc., 1958). An examination of the philosophical foundations of Marx's thought by one of America's leading philosophers. See also, by the same author, **Towards the Understanding of Karl Marx** (Scranton: Pa.: In text, 1933); **Revolution Reform and Social Justice: Studies in the Theory and Practice of Marxism** (New York: New York University Press, 1975). K. R. Popper, **The Open Society and Its Enemies**, Vol. 2: The High Tide of Prophecy; Hegel and Marx, rev. and enl. ed. (London: Routledge & Kegan Paul Ltd., 1957), contains a searching critique of the Hegelian elements in Marx's work. On this, see also Herbert Marcuse, **Reason and Revolution: Hegel and the Rise of Social Theory** (Boston: Beacon Press, 1960). Eugene Kamenka, **The Ethical Foundations of Marxism** (New York: Encyclopaedia Britannica, Inc., Frederick A. Praeger, Inc., 1962), discusses the nature of "alienation" in the thought of Hegel and Marx: the human mind creates configurations that assume an existence independent of their creator and oppress man. This idea, which appears in the early manuscripts of Marx, has served as the foundation of his interpretation as a humanist. There is a reflex of it in **Das Kapital**, Vol. 1, Chap. 1, Sec. 4 on "The Fetishism of Commodities and the Secret Thereof," where Marx writes of the replacement of relations between persons by relations between commodities in the market, which is man's creation but dominates his economic existence. See also Robert Tucker, **Philosophy and Myth in Karl Marx** (New York: Cambridge University Press, 1961); Erich Fromm, **Marx's Concept of Man** (New York: Frederick Ungar Publishing Co., Inc.,1961), which contains the first American publication of Marx's philosophical manuscripts of 1844. The interpretation of Marx as a humanist, which is based on these, is highly controversial. It is designed, on the one hand, to make Marx's thought more attractive to Western minds, and, on the other, to legitimate the libertarian aspirations in the countries of Eastern Europe. For the background of Marx's early writings see David McLellan, **Marx before Marxism** (London: Macmillan & Co., 1970). See also Bertell Ollman, **Alienation** (New York: Cambridge University Press, 1971); John E. Elliott, "Continuity and Change in the Evolution of Marx's Theory of Alienation," **History of Political Economy**, Vol. 11, No. 3 (Fall, 1979), 317–62.

• Lichtheim, George, **Marxism** (London: Routledge & Kegan Paul Ltd., 1961). A historical and critical study of the rise of Marxist thought, its origins and later developments, which has become the standard work on the subject. See also Robert L. Heilbroner, **Marxism: For and Against** (New York: W. W. Norton and Company, 1980); Robert G. Wesson, **Why Marxism? The Continuing Success of a Failed Theory** (New York: Basic Books, 1976); T. W. Hutchison, **The Politics and Philosophy of Economics: Marxians, Keynesians, and Austrians** (New York: New York University Press, 1981). For a critique of Marxism by a philosopher see H. B. Acton, **The Illusions of the Epoch** (London: Cohen & West Ltd., 1955), which contains a cogently argued demolition. More sympathetic and also more pedestrian is Rudolf Schlesinger, **Marx: His Time and Ours** (London: Routledge & Kegan Paul Ltd., 1950). See also Henry B. Mayo, **Introduction to Marxist Theory** (New York: Oxford University Press, Inc.,

1960), a textbook informed by insight and fairness; and the works by a leading American Marxologist, Bertram D. Wolfe, for example, his **Marxism: 100 Years in the Life of a Doctrine** (New York: Dell Publishing Company, Delta Books, 1965), who draws attention to the ambivalent attitude of Marx and his followers to nationalism and war.

• Marx, Karl, **Capital**, ed. Frederick Engels, 3 vols. (New York: International Publishers Co., Inc., 1967). This is a recent edition in English translation of the unabridged work, with vols. 2 and 3 freshly translated. Another recent translation of the same work is published by Vintage Books (New York: Random House, Vol. 1, 1977; Vol. 2, 1981). A useful edition of Vol. 1 is that by Dana Torr (London: George Allen & Unwin Ltd., 1946). Selections from the intended fourth volume have been translated by G. A. Bonner and Emile Burns and published under the title **Theories of Surplus Value** (London: Lawrence & Wishart Ltd., 1951).

A complete edition of Marx's works would go into many volumes. One that is being prepared in English is supposed to reach 51 volumes (London: Lawrence & Wishart Ltd.; New York: International Publishers). Another edition, of 100 volumes, is supposed to reach completion in the year 2000, when it is scheduled for publication in Moscow and East Berlin. Meanwhile there is available an eight volume **Vintage Marx Library** (New York: Random House, 1974 ff.), consisting of Marx's principal works, and a seven volume **Karl Marx Library**, ed. Saul K. Padover (New York: McGraw-Hill Book Company, 1971 ff.), with each volume covering specific subjects such as revolution, religion, America, etc. For editions of the **Grundrisse** in English translations (notes and excerpts that Marx used in other writings but did not publish separately; first published in 1939) see the substantial excerpts translated and ed. by David McLellan (New York: Harper & Row, 1972), and another edition, trans. by M. Nicolaus (New York: Random House, 1974).

See also **Karl Marx-Friedrich**

Engels: Selected Letters, ed. Fritz J. Raddatz, trans. by Ewald Osers (Boston: Little, Brown and Company, 1982); **The Letters of Karl Marx**, ed. and trans. by Saul K. Padover (Englewood Cliffs, N.J.: Prentice-Hall, 1979).

Useful selections include Robert C. Tucker, ed., **The Marx-Engels Reader**, 2nd ed. (New York: W. W. Norton and Company, 1978); David McLellan, ed., **Karl Marx: Selected Writings** (New York: Oxford University Press, 1977); Michael Howard and John King, eds., **The Economics of Marx: Selected Readings of Exposition and Criticism** (New York: Penguin Books, 1976); Z. A. Jordan, ed., **Karl Marx: Economy, Class and Social Revolution** (New York: Charles Scribner's Sons, 1975); W. O. Henderson, ed., **Engels: Selected Writings** (New York: Penguin Books, 1967).

For a bibliography see Maximilien Rubel, **Bibliographie des oeuvres de Karl Marx** (Paris: Marcel Rivière, 1956, Supplement 1960).

• Robinson, Joan, **An Essay on Marxian Economics**, originally published 1942, 2nd ed. with a new preface (New York: St. Martin's Press, Inc., 1967). This is a pioneering attempt by a leading economic theorist to build a bridge between Marxian and orthodox economics. While by no means uncritical of the former, especially of the labor theory of value and of profits, she nevertheless expresses the opinion that the questions asked by Marx were the right ones, and that modern economics, with its sharpened tools of analysis, should attempt to solve the problem that Marx posed, that is, should try to unravel the law of motion of capitalism. As for the discredited labor theory of value, Professor Robinson holds that no point of substance in Marx's argument depends upon it (p. 22).

Mrs. Robinson's pamphlet, **On Rereading Marx** (Cambridge, Eng.: Students' Bookshop, 1953), contains an ingenious attempt to reveal the common analytical structure that is hidden under the different ideologies of Ricardo, Marx, and modern economic theorists. There are further comments on Marxian economics in her **Collected Economic Papers**, 5 vols. (Oxford: Basil Blackwell & Mott Ltd., 1951 ff.).

• Samuelson, Paul A., "Wages and Interest: a Modern Dissection of Marxian Economic Models," **American Economic Review**, Vol. 47, No. 6 (December, 1957), 884–912. In this continuation of the debate initiated by Professor Robinson, an outstanding American economic theorist applies the tools of modern analysis to a searching critique of Marx's principal propositions. The labor theory of value, he holds, has been an unnecessary detour. The surplus-value approach sheds no light on market situations characterized by imperfections of competition. The transformation problem should treat of the transformation of prices into values, not vice versa; values grounded in equal rates of surplus value, which are assumed in Marx's model, have no solid basis. The "deduction" or "withholding" theory of wages employed by interpreters of Marx does not differ essentially from the conventional "discounted" productivity theories. Falling profit is incompatible with falling wages. The strongest competition does not bring real wages down to the level of subsistence in modern Western societies but at worst to the discounted marginal product of labor.

For a transformation of the Marxian system into a general-equilibrium system, see Martin Bronfenbrenner, "*Das Kapital* for the Modern Man," **Science and Society**, Vol. 29, No. 4 (Fall, 1965), 419–38. To Professor Bronfenbrenner, "the besetting weakness of the Marxian system, omissions apart," is its "structuralism, which is to say, its tendency to take important relations as technically determined behind the back of the price system, leaving the latter with few functions beyond equating profit rates in industries with different organic compositions of capital" (p. 436). As for the omissions, the Marxian system has no public expenditure, revenue, and debt policy. It has no monetary policy. Its treatment of innovations is sketchy, particularly with regard to capital-saving innovations, with Marx invariably stressing the labor-saving character of innovations. "Marx cannot be blamed for anticipating only partially monetary and fiscal policy developments which came generations after his manuscripts were written. It is however unfortu-

nate that his followers have been more vituperative than analytical or convincing in filling the gaps he left behind." See also Paul A. Samuelson, "Marx as Mathematical Economist: Steady-State and Exponential Growth Equilibrium," in **Trade, Stability and Macroeconomics**, Essays in Honor of Lloyd A. Metzler, ed. G. Horwich and P. A. Samuelson (New York: Academic Press, 1974); M. Morishima, "Marx in the Light of Modern Economic Theory," **Econometrica**, Vol. 42, No. 4 (July, 1974), 611–32; Gerard Maarek, **Introduction to Karl Marx's 'Das Kapital': A Study in Formalisation**, trans. by M. Evans (New York: Oxford University Press, 1979); Samuel Hollander, "Marxian Economics as 'General Equilibrium' Theory," **History of Political Economy**, Vol. 13, No. 1 (Spring, 1981), 121–55.

• Schumpeter, Joseph A., **Ten Great Economists: From Marx to Keynes** (New York: Oxford University Press, Inc., 1951; also same publisher, Galaxy Books). Chap. 1, pp. 3–73, contains Schumpeter's appraisal of Marx, reprinted from his **Capitalism, Socialism, and Democracy** (New York: Harper & Row, Publishers, 1942; also same publisher, Torchbooks). Schumpeter's interpretation of Marx is ambivalent, combining criticism with admiration. He finds an affinity between Marx's view of the downfall of capitalism and his own, which ascribes it to the success rather than the failure of the capitalist engine of production (p. 70), and he points out that the Marxian theory of revolution, which is to come only in the fullness of time, has "a distinctly conservative implication" and thus "can be taken seriously" (p. 73). See also Schumpeter's article, "The Communist Manifesto in Sociology and Economics," **Journal of Political Economy**, Vol. 57 (June, 1949), 199–212.

• Sowell, T., "Marx's 'Increasing Misery' Doctrine," **American Economic Review**, Vol. 50 (March, 1960), 111–20. See on the same topic also F. M. Gottheil, "Increasing Misery of the Proletariat: An Analysis of Marx's Wage and Employment Theory," **Canadian Journal of Economics and Political Science**, Vol. 28 (February, 1962),

103–13; R. L. Meek, "Marx's Doctrine of Increasing Misery," **Science and Society**, Vol. 26, No. 4 (1962), 422–41.

• Sweezy, Paul M., **The Theory of Capitalist Development: Principles of Marxian Political Economy** (New York: Oxford University Press, Inc., 1942). An exposition of Marx's economics by the leading Marxist economist in the United States. Sweezy's systematic work may be supplemented by various studies by his counterpart in England, Maurice Dobb, to be found in the latter's **Political Economy and Capitalism** (London: Routledge & Kegan Paul Ltd., 1937), and **On Economic Theory and Socialism** (same publisher, 1955). See also Dobb, **Theories of Value and Distribution Since Adam Smith: Ideology and Economic Theory** (New York: Cambridge University Press, 1973), a doctrinal history from a Marxist point of view. There is also a brief pamphlet by Dobb, **Marx as an Economist** (New York: International Publishers Co., Inc., 1945). For an incisive statement by a Marxist economist who was willing to relinquish the labor theory of value see Oscar Lange, "Marxian Economics and Modern Economic Theory," **Review of Economic Studies**, Vol. 2 (June, 1935), 189–201.

In recent years, France has become a center of Marxist studies of Marx's economics. For examples, see Ernest Mandel, **Traité d'Économie marxiste**, 2 vols. (Paris: Éditions René Jullard, 1962); an English translation was published under the title **Marxist Economic Theory**, 2 vols., (London: The Merlin Press Ltd., 1969); Louis Althusser, Jacques Rancière, Pierre Macherey, **Lire le Capital**, 2 vols. (Paris: François Maspéro Éditeur, 1965); Maurice Godelier, **Rationality and Irrationality in Economics**, trans. by Brian Pearce (New York: Monthly Review Press, 1972; originally published in 1966); same author, **Perspectives in Marxist Anthropology** (New York: Cambridge University Press, 1977). Mandel's work takes account of the further development of Marx's economic thought throughout the world. That of Althusser, Rancière, and Macherey is mainly a philosophical analysis of Marx's ideas. Godelier, in the concluding section of his book, attempts to develop an *anthropologie économique* that lays bare the structure of economic systems and their differences. See also Louis Althusser, **For Marx**, trans. by Ben Brewster (Harmondsworth, Middlesex: Allen Lane, The Penguin Press, 1970), a contribution to the debate about the humanism of the young Marx by an "orthodox" communist; S. de Brunhoff, **Marx on Money** (New York: Urizen Books, 1976; originally published in 1967), who relates Marx's theories of money and credit to other nineteenth-century thinkers.

• Tucker, G. S. L., "Ricardo and Marx," **Economica**, new series, Vol. 28 (August, 1961), 252–69. On Marx's indebtedness to Mill see B. A. Balassa, "Karl Marx and John Stuart Mill," **Weltwirtschaftliches Archiv**, Vol. 83, No. 2 (1959), 147–63; Graeme Duncan, **Marx and Mill** (New York: Cambridge University Press, 1973). See also B. Shoul, "Karl Marx and Say's Law," **Quarterly Journal of Economics**, Vol. 71 (November, 1957), 611–29.

• Wolfson, Murray, **A Reappraisal of Marxian Economics** (New York: Columbia University Press, 1966). A fresh interpretation of Marx's thought, containing a revision of the labor theory of value relating it to demand as well as supply. If demand is ignored, so the author argues, supply would have to be infinitely elastic, an assumption impossible to maintain in the labor market. See also, on various related topics, D. J. Harris, "On Marx's Scheme of Reproduction and Accumulation," **Journal of Political Economy**, Vol. 80, No. 3 (May-June, 1972), 505–22; R. Stanfield, **The Economic Surplus and Neo-Marxism** (Lexington, Mass.,: D. C. Heath and Company, 1973), an attempt at measuring economic surplus; L. Cuyvers, "A Mathematical Interpretation of Marxian Unproductive Labor," **Economica**, Vol. 45, No. 177 (February, 1978), 71–81; N. Rosenberg, "Karl Marx on the Economic Role of Science," **Journal of Political Economy**, Vol. 82, No. 4 (July-August, 1974), 713–28; Joan Robinson, "The Organic Composition of Capital," **Kyklos**, Vol. 31, No. 1 (1978), 5–20; Arun Bose, **Marx on Exploitation and Inequality** (New York: Oxford University Press, 1980).

• Baron, Samuel H., **Plekhanov: The Father of Russian Marxism** (Stanford, Calif.: Stanford University Press, 1963). G. V. Plekhanov (1857–1918) was an influential Russian radical, who during the closing decades of the nineteenth century turned the Russian radical movement to Marxism and away from the Populists who deprecated political action and proposed to rely on the grass-roots movement of the peasantry.

• Barone, E., "The Ministry of Production in the Collectivist State," in F. A. Hayek, ed., **Collectivist Economic Planning** (London: Routledge & Kegan Paul Ltd., 1935). This volume contains an English translation of Barone's article of 1908 as well as related studies and a bibliography. Leading contributions to the later discussion include Oskar Lange and Fred M. Taylor, **On the Economic Theory of Socialism,** ed. Benjamin E. Lippincott (Minneapolis: University of Minnesota Press, 1938) and A. P. Lerner, **The Economics of Control** (New York: The Macmillan Company, 1944). The discussion is reviewed by Abram Bergson, "Socialist Economics," in Howard S. Ellis, ed., **A Survey of Contemporary Economics: Published for the American Economic Association** (Homewood, Ill.: Richard D. Irwin, Inc., Blakiston Books, 1948), pp. 412–48, and by Carl Landauer, **European Socialism** (Berkeley and Los Angeles: University of California Press, 1959), Vol. 2, Chap. 46. Bergson's essay has been reprinted, together with a postscript, in his **Essays in Normative Economics** (Cambridge, Mass.: Harvard University Press, 1966), pp. 193–242.

• Bernstein, Eduard, **Evolutionary Socialism,** trans. Edith C. Harvey (New York: Schocken Books, Inc., 1961). A new edition of the English translation, first published in 1909, of the classic statement of German revisionism as it originally appeared in 1899. The standard appraisal of Bernstein is Peter Gay, **The Dilemma of Democratic Socialism: Ed-ward Bernstein's Challenge to Marx** (New York: Columbia University Press, 1952; New York: The Macmillan Company, Collier Books, 1962). See also Erika Rikli, **Der Revisionismus** (Zurich: H. Girsberger, 1936); Carl E. Schorske, **German Social Democracy, 1905–1917: The Development of the Great Schism** (Cambridge, Mass.: Harvard University Press, 1955); Helmut Hirsch, ed., **Ein revisionistisches Sozial-ismusbild** (Hanover: J. H. W. Dietz Nachfolger, 1967). These works contain references also to Karl Kautsky (1854–1938), the leading theorist of German social democracy and a more orthodox follower of Marx than was Bernstein. Kautsky opposed Bernstein's revisionism, but their paths converged twice: first when they denounced Germany's aggressive aims during World War I, and later in their denunciation of the spread of Lenin's totalitarian dictatorship in Russia. About Kautsky's espousal of democratic socialism see William Ebenstein, **Great Political Thinkers,** 3rd ed. (New York: Holt, Rinehart & Winston, Inc., 1960), pp. 748–51, 759–70; Gary P. Steenson, **Karl Kautsky, 1854–1938** (Pittsburgh: University of Pittsburgh Press, 1978). See also Benedict Kautsky et al., **Ein Leben für den Sozialismus: Erinnerungen an Karl Kautsky** (Hannover: J. H. W. Dietz Nachfolger, 1954).

• Bukharin, N. I., **Economics of the Transformation Period** (New York: Bergman Publishers, Lyle Stuart Inc., 1971), an English translation of Bukharin's exposition of liquidationism, originally published in 1920. A number of other works by Bukharin are available in English translations, including his **Economic Theory of the Leisure Class** (New York: International Publishers Co., Inc., 1927), which contains Bukharin's critique of marginal utility economics, according to his interpretation a doctrinal development that reflects the interests of a coupon-cutting *rentier* class. See also N. Bukharin and E. Preobrazhensky, **The ABC of**

780

Communism, originally published during the early 1920s and reprinted with an introduction by E. H. Carr (Baltimore: Penguin Books, Inc., 1969); **Imperialism and World Economy** (London: Merlin Press, 1972), a work originally published in 1915, that is, by more than a year ahead of Lenin's **Imperialism**. For appraisals see Stephen Cohen, **Bukharin and the Bolshevik Revolution** (New York: Alfred A. Knopf, 1973); Peter Knirsch, **Die ökonomischen Anschauungen Nikolaj I. Bucharins** (Berlin-West: Ost-Europa Institut, 1959), Wirtschaftswissenschaftliche Veröffentlichungen, Band 9. See also "A Note on Bukharin's Ideas," by Rudolf Schlesinger, **Soviet Studies,** Vol. 9 (1959–60), 415–20. The eventual fate of Bukharin, which he shared with a generation of Soviet economists, is described in George Katkov, **The Trial of Bukharin** (London: Batsford, 1969).

• Cole, G. D. H., **Self-Government in Industry** (London: G. Bell & Sons, Ltd., 1917); **Guild Socialism Restated** (London: L. Parsons, 1920). These books are samples of Cole's writings on guild socialism. This matter is also discussed in **The Acquisitive Society** by R. H. Tawney (London: G. Bell & Sons, Ltd., 1921). Tawney (1880–1961), another leading socialist academic, was best known for his contributions to economic history. His socialist writings include **Equality,** 4th rev. ed. (London: George Allen & Unwin Ltd., 1952), and **The Radical Tradition** (London: George Allen & Unwin Ltd., 1964).

About Cole see Margaret Cole, **The Life of G. D. H. Cole** (New York: St. Martin's Press, 1971); Luther P. Carpenter, **G. D. H. Cole: An Intellectual Biography** (New York: Cambridge University Press, 1973); A. W. Wright, **G. D. H. Cole and Socialist Democracy** (New York: Oxford University Press, 1979); S. T. Glass, **The Responsible Society: The Ideas of the English Guild Socialists** (London: Longmans, Green and Company, Ltd., 1966). About Tawney see Ross Terrill, **R. H. Tawney and His Times: Socialism as Fellowship** (Cambridge: Harvard University Press, 1973).

The concluding volumes of Cole's monumental **History of Socialist Thought,** 5 vols. in 7 (New York: St. Martin's Press, Inc., 1953–60) cover all phases of socialism after Marx. They are especially valuable for their treatment of developments in England, which Cole knew first hand and in which he played a noteworthy role.

Cole's **Socialist Economics** (London: Victor Gollancz Ltd., 1950), attempts to establish the socialist position and draws a line of demarcation between the pursuit of socialist goals and the new economic policies inspired by Keynes. Further representative contributions to the discussion of socialist goals and policies in the England of the 1950s and 1960s are R. H. S. Crossman, ed., **New Fabian Essays** (London: Turnstile Press, 1952); C. A. R. Crosland, **The Future of Socialism** (London: Jonathan Cape Limited, 1956); same author, **The Conservative Enemy** (New York: Schocken Books, Inc., 1962); R. H. S. Crossman, **The Politics of Socialism** (New York: Atheneum Publishers, 1965); C. A. R. Crosland, **Socialism Now and Other Essays** (London: Jonathan Cape, 1974). Since the mid-sixties the influence of communists and Trotskyites has increased in Britain, especially in the labor movement. See about this Blake Baker, **The Far Left: an Exposé of the Extreme Left in Britain** (London: Weidenfeld & Nicolson, 1982).

• Freemantle, Anne, ed., **The Papal Encyclicals in Their Historical Context** (New York: The New American Library Inc., 1956). The principal documents indicating the Catholic reaction to the rise of socialist thought may be found in this survey of Catholic teaching on social and economic matters, which includes the leading papal pronouncements: the Encyclical Letter **Rerum Novarum** of 1891, which condemned socialism but upheld the right of workers to form labor unions, and the Encyclical **Quadragesimo Anno** of 1931, which reviewed the matter forty years later. For a more recent statement, see the Encyclical Letter **Mater et Magistra** of 1961, Vatican trans. (Boston: Daughters of St. Paul). See also Philip Hughes, **The Popes' New Order: A Systematic Study of the Social Encyclicals and Addresses** from Leo XIII to Pius XII (London: Burns & Oates Limited, 1943); Christopher Hollis, **The Church and Economics** (same publisher, 1961).

• George, Henry, **Progress and Poverty** (San Francisco, 1879). George's principal work as well as his other books, **Protection or Free Trade, Social Problems, The Land Question, The Science of Political Economy**, have been kept in print (New York: Robert Schalkenbach Foundation); this source also has published **Significant Paragraphs from Henry George's Progress and Poverty**, selected and compiled by Harry Gunnison Brown, with an introduction by John Dewey (1935). The standard biography is Charles A. Barker, **Henry George** (New York: Oxford University Press, Inc., 1955). Earlier works include a biography by his son, Henry George, Jr., **The Life of Henry George** (Garden City, N.Y.: Doubleday & Company, Inc., 1900), and one by his daughter, Anna George de Mille, **Henry George** (Chapel Hill, N.C.: University of North Carolina Press, 1950); also Louis F. Post, **The Prophet of San Francisco** (New York: Vanguard Press, Inc., 1930), the personal memories of a friend and disciple. For a general appraisal of his work, by an enthusiastic follower, see George R. Geiger, **The Philosophy of Henry George** (New York: The Macmillan Company, 1933); also Ernest Teilhac, **Pioneers of American Economic Thought in the Nineteenth Century**, trans. E. A. J. Johnson (New York: The Macmillan Company, 1936), Chap. 3; Steven B. Cord, **Henry George: Dreamer or Realist?** (Philadelphia: University of Pennsylvania Press, 1965); Elwood P. Lawrence, **Henry George in the British Isles** (East Lansing, Mich.: Michigan State University Press, 1957); John A. Hobson, "The Influence of Henry George in England," **Fortnightly Review**, Vol. 62 (December 1, 1897); George J. Stigler, "Alfred Marshall's Lectures on Progress and Poverty," **Journal of Law and Economics**, Vol. 12, No. 1 (April, 1969), 181–83; the lectures, on pp. 184–226, originally delivered in 1883 and published in newspapers, express Marshall's critical reaction to Henry George; Jacob Oser, **Henry George** (New York: Twayne Publishers, 1974); in the Great

Thinkers series); Robert V. Andelson, ed., **Critics of Henry George** (Rutherford, N.J.: Fairleigh Dickinson University Press, 1979); Charles Collier, "Henry George's System of Political Economy," **History of Political Economy**, Vol. 11, No. 1 (Spring, 1979), 64–93.

• Grossman, Gregory, ed., **Value and Plan: Economic Calculation and Organization in Eastern Europe** (Berkeley and Los Angeles: University of California Press, 1960); S. Wellisz, **The Economies of the Soviet Bloc** (New York: McGraw-Hill Book Company, 1964); A. Waterston, **Planning in Yugoslavia** (Baltimore: The Johns Hopkins Press, 1962); Branco Horvat, **Towards a Theory of Planned Economy** (Belgrad: Institute of Economic Research, 1964); same author, **The Political Economy of Socialism: A Marxist Social Theory** (Armonk, N. Y.: M. E. Sharpe, Inc., 1982); W. Brus, **The Market in a Socialist Economy** (London and Boston: Routledge and Kegan Paul, 1972). This is but a small sample of the substantial literature devoted to problems of economic organization in Yugoslavia, Poland, and other countries of Eastern Europe, problems that in turn have given rise to new theories of socialist planning and the construction of models of growth.

• Hayek, F. A., "The London School of Economics, 1895–1945," **Economica**, February, 1946, pp. 1–31. A historical sketch by a well-known economist with conservative leanings, for many years associated with The London School of Economics. The personnel of the school was never selected from any narrowly partisan point of view, and while it included a number of famous Socialist professors, there were also Liberals and Conservatives of great distinction. During the 1930s. when the school's influence reached a peak, its director was William Beveridge (1879–1963), then a Liberal in politics, who later authored a famous social-security scheme, **Social Insurance and Allied Services** (New York: The Macmillan Company, 1942). See also, by Beveridge, **The London School of Economics and Its Problems, 1919–1937** (London: George Allen & Unwin Ltd., 1960); Janet Beveridge, **An Epic of Clare Market: The Birth and**

Early Years of The London School of Economics (London: G. Bell and Sons, Ltd., 1960); Sir Sydney Caine, The History of the Foundations of The London School of Economics and Political Science (London: G. Bell and Sons, Ltd., 1963); José Harris, William Beveridge: A Biography (New York: Oxford University Press, 1977).

• Hilferding, Rudolf, Finance Capital: A Study of the Latest Phase of Capitalist Development, ed. with an introduction by Tom Bottomore (London & Boston: Routledge & Kegan Paul, 1981). See also Austro-Marxism, texts trans. and edited by Bottomore and Patrick Goode, with an introduction by Bottomore (New York: Oxford University Press, 1978); E. Kauder, "Austro-Marxism versus Austro-Marginalism," History of Political Economy, Vol. 2, No. 2 (Fall, 1970), 398–418.

• Kantorovich, L. V., The Best Use of Economic Resources, English edition G. Morton, trans. from the Russian by P. F. Knightsfield (Cambridge, Mass.: Harvard University Press, 1965). An expanded version of Kantorovich's ideas about linear programming and their application to the whole economy. An English translation of Kantorovich's original work of 1939, which initiated linear programming, may be found in Management Science, 1961, and in V. S. Nemchinov, ed., The Use of Mathematics in Economics, English edition A. Nove (Edinburgh: Oliver and Boyd Limited, 1964), pp. 225–79. Nemchinov (died 1964) was one of the pioneers of mathematical economics in the Soviet Union, who contributed various articles to this volume, which also includes a detailed study of "Cost–Benefit Comparisons in a Socialist Economy" by V. V. Novozhilov, another leading mathematical economist in the Soviet Union. Earlier articles by Novozhilov may be found in English translation in International Economic Papers, No. 6 (1956); they treat of the inclusion of an interest rate among cost estimates of investment projects.

For Western reactions to the rise of mathematical economics in the Soviet Union see Leif Johansen, "Soviet Mathematical Economics," Economic Journal, Vol. 76 (September, 1966), 593–601;

Robert W. Campbell, "Marx, Kantorovich and Novozhilov: Stoimost' versus Reality," Slavic Review, Vol. 20 (1961), 402–18; Alfred Zauberman, Aspects of Planometrics (New Haven, Conn.: Yale University Press, 1968); same author, The Mathematical Revolution in Soviet Economics (New York: Oxford University Press, 1975); Michael Ellman, Soviet Planning Today (New York: Cambridge University Press, 1971); same author, Planning Problems in the USSR (same publisher, 1973); A. Katsenelinboigen, Soviet Economic Thought and Political Power in the USSR: The Development of Soviet Mathematical Economics (Oxford: Pergamon Press, 1979); Benjamin Ward, "Kantorovich on Economic Calculation," Journal of Political Economy, Vol. 68 (1960), 545–56; Eugène Zaleski. Planning Reforms in the Soviet Union, 1962–1966, trans. Marie-Christine MacAndrew and G. Warren Nutter, (Chapel Hill, N.C.: University of North Carolina Press, 1967); John P. Hardt et al., eds., Mathematics and Computers in Soviet Economic Planning (New Haven, Conn.: Yale University Press, 1967).

• Kondratieff, N. D., "The Long Waves in Economic Life," trans. W. F. Stolper, Review of Economic Statistics, Vol. 17, Part 2 (November, 1935), 105–15, reprinted in Readings in Business Cycle Theory, selected by a committee of the American Economic Association (Homewood, Ill.: Richard D. Irwin, Inc., Blakiston Books, 1944). Besides this exposition of long cycles, Kondratieff also published a number of other articles in German and American periodicals during the 1920s. For an appraisal see George Garvy, "Kondratieff's Theory of Long Cycles," Review of Economic Statistics, Vol. 25, No. 4 (November, 1943), 203–20. See also James Shuman and David Rosenau, The Kondratieff Wave (New York; World Publishing Company, 1972) and a recent reprint of Kondratieff's article on long waves in Lloyds Bank Review, No. 129 (July, 1978), 41–60. About Kondratieff and some lesser known economists of his time see also Naum Jasny, Soviet Economists of the 20's: Names to be Remembered (New York: Cambridge University Press, 1972).

Kondratieff's interest in business cycles continued an earlier tradition of which M. Tugan-Baranovsky (1865–1919) was the best known exponent in the West. There Tugan has been credited with having pioneered with a business-cycle theory stressing fluctuations in investment in the face of a rather stable rate of saving. Among neo-Marxists and in the Soviet Union, Tugan's views were a frequent target of attacks because of his rejection of underconsumption theories and his opinion that there are no limits to capitalist expansion in the form of continued production of capital. See his **Les Crises industrielles en Angleterre**, originally published 1894, French translation by J. Schapiro (Paris: M. Giard et E. Brière, 1913); Alvin H. Hansen, **Business Cycles and National Income** (New York: W. W. Norton & Company, Inc., 1951), pp. 277–91; A Nove, "M. I. Tugan-Baranowsky, 1865–1919," **History of Political Economy**, Vol. 2, No. 2 (Fall, 1970), 246–62.

• Lange, O. and F. M. Taylor, **On the Economic Theory of Socialism**, contains Lange's articles, reprinted with additions and changes from the **Review of Economic Studies**, Vol. 4, Nos. 1 and 2 (October, 1936 and February, 1937), in which the socialist planning authorities are instructed, by means of a trial and error procedure, to establish a system of prices that would emulate the competitive one. Lange taught at American universities during the thirties and early forties and later returned to his native Poland, where he held important teaching and administrative posts. His views on socialist pricing were of considerable influence in Yugoslavia. He did much to introduce Western methods of economics in the Communist countries of Eastern Europe. See his **Introduction to Econometrics**, revised and enlarged from the first Polish edition by the author, trans. Eugene Lepa (Elmsford, N.Y.: Pergamon Press, Inc., 1959), which contains observations about the Western origin of econometrics and the suitability of this approach for Soviet-type economies. Lange's **Political Economy**, Vol. 1: General Problems, translated from Polish by A. H. Walker (Elmsford, N.Y.: Pergamon Press, Inc., 1963), offers a wide-ranging analysis of the nature and scope of economics as seen through the eyes of an economist intimately acquainted both with Eastern and Western thought, but critical only of the latter. His **Wholes and Parts: A General Theory of System Behavior**, translated from Polish by E. Lepa (Elmsford, N.Y.: Pergamon Press, Inc., 1965), attempts to present dialectic materialism in mathematical garb by drawing on cybernetics and systems analysis. See also Lange in collaboration with A. Banasinski, **Theory of Reproduction and Accumulation** (1969); Lange, **Papers in Economics and Sociology 1930–1960** (1970); **Introduction to Economic Cybernetics** (1970), all published Pergamon Press, Inc. Certain aspects of Lange's thought are discussed in A. Novicki, **L'Économie "généralisée" et la pensée actuelle d'Oskar Lange** (Paris: Cahiers de l'Institut de science économique appliquée, No. 114, 1961).

On Political Economy and Econometrics, Essays in Honor of Oskar Lange (Elmsford, N.Y.: Pergamon Press, Inc., 1965), contains more than forty contributions, most of which are illustrative of current work in Soviet-type economies. There are further examples here of the mathematical transformation of Marx's ideas, such as in the article by Michal Kalecki on "Econometric Model and Historical Materialism," pp. 233–44, in which ways are explored to construct economic models that reflect historical materialism with its distinction between superstructure and productive relations.

A collection of articles of similar type is offered under the title **Problems of Economic Dynamics and Planning, Essays in Honor of Michal Kalecki** (Elmsford, N.Y.: Pergamon Press, Inc., 1966).

• Lenin, V. I., **Imperialism, the Highest Stage of Capitalism**, originally published 1917 and reprinted often, for example, in Lenin's **Selected Works**, Vol. 1 (Moscow: Foreign Languages Publishing House, 1946), pp. 643–740. J. A. Hobson's **Imperialism** was the starting point of the series of denunciations culminating in Lenin's book (London: Constable & Co. Ltd., 1902). Hobson's fallacies are examined by Richard Koebner and Helmut

Dan Schmidt, **Imperialism: The Story and Significance of a Political Word, 1840–1960** (London: Cambridge University Press, 1964), who trace the rise of imperialism as a political slogan from Gladstone to Hobson and beyond. After World War I, the imperialist became "the twentieth-century version of the devil," and imperialism "rose to global eminence as the leading slogan of three world struggles, against capitalism, against Anglo-Saxon domination, and against white colonial power." The theories of imperialism by Hilferding, Luxemburg, Fritz Sternberg, and Henryk Grossmann are ably reviewed by Carl Landauer, **European Socialism**, Vol. 2 (Berkeley and Los Angeles: University of California Press, 1959), Chap. 45. See also Charles Gulick, **Austria from Habsburg to Hitler** (Berkeley and Los Angeles: University of California Press, 1948), Chap. 27 on the Austro-Marxists; Paul M. Sweezy, **The Theory of Capitalist Development: Principles of Marxian Political Economy** (New York: Oxford University Press, Inc., 1942), Chap. 11; Lionel Robbins, **The Economic Causes of War** (London: Jonathan Cape Limited, 1939); B. J. Hovde, "Socialistic Theories of Imperialism Prior to the Great War," **Journal of Political Economy**, Vol. 36 (1928), 569–91; E. M. Winslow, **The Pattern of Imperialism** (New York: Columbia University Press, 1948); Adolf Grabowsky, **Der Sozialimperialismus als letzte Etappe des Imperialismus** (Basel: Weltpolitisches Archiv, 1939); J. A. Schumpeter, **Imperialism: Social Classes,** introduction by Bert Hoselitz, trans. Heinz Norden (New York: The World Publishing Company, Meridian Books, 1955); John Strachey, **The End of Empire** (New York: Random House, Inc., 1959); H. W. Kettenbach, **Lenins Theorie des Imperialismus**, Teil 1: Grundlagen und Voraussetzungen (Cologne: Verlag Wissenschaft und Politik Berend von Nottbeck, 1965); Tom Kemp, **Theories of Imperialism**, (London: Dennis Dobson [Dobson Books, Ltd.], 1968); George Lichtheim, **Imperialism** (New York: Frederick A. Praeger Inc., 1971); Kenneth Boulding and Tapan Mukerjee, eds., **Economic Imperialism: A Book of Readings** (Ann Arbor: University of Michigan Press, 1972); D. K. Fieldhouse, **Economics and Empire, 1830–1914** (Ithaca: Cornell University Press, 1973); V. G. Kiernan, **Marxism and Imperialism** (London: Edward Arnold, 1974); Anthony Brewer, **Marxist Theories of Imperialism** (London and Boston: Routledge & Kegan Paul, 1980); Wolfgang J. Mommsen, **Theories of Imperialism**, trans. by P. S. Falla (New York: Random House, 1980).

• Lichtheim, George, **Marxism in Modern France** (New York: Columbia University Press, 1966). This work offers the best account in English of the intricate history of French socialism. In France as well as in Italy there occurred an upsurge of communism after the Second World War, which continued during the postwar decades. See also Annie Kriegel, **The French Communists**, trans. by E. P. Halperin (Chicago: University of Chicago Press, 1972); Donald L. M. Blackmer and Sidney Tarrow, eds., **Communism in Italy and France** (Princeton: Princeton University Press, 1975); Keith Middlemas, **Power and the Party: Changing Faces of Communism in Western Europe** (London: André Deutsch, 1980).

The numerical strength of French communism had its counterpart in the permeation with Marxist thought of a wide sample of leading French intellectuals. Marxism, in the words of a critical observer, became the "the opiate of the intellectuals," who inside and outside of institutions of higher learning and inside and outside of the Communist party carried on Marxist studies, mainly oriented along philosophical and historical lines but not neglecting economics. This trend was reinforced by the belated discovery of Hegel and by the traditional emphasis, in French secondary education, on the study of the philosophy of history. Jean-Paul Sartre (1905–1980), France's leading man of letters during the decades following the Second World War, attempted to fuse with Marxism his existentialist philosophy, which considers man as a lonely but free and responsible being, cast into a universe devoid of meaning. Sartre's **Critique of Dialectical Reasoning** (Atlantic Highlands, N. J.: Humanities Press, 1976; originally published in 1960) was to express this fusion, which, however, is more Sartrean than Marxist and has greater affinity with ideas of Hobbes and Rousseau than of Marx. In this work Sartre made scarcity one of the central concepts of his philosophy. Scarcity, which arises from the tension—"dialectical interaction"—between man and matter, is an invariant feature of the human condition. It has been the driving force in historical development and is the decisive factor in forming the structure of human relations. Scarcity accounts for the dialectical relationship in which man stands to man, one which unites him with others in attempts to cope with scarcity, but which also divides him from others, in whose absence there would be plenty. Conflict is thus given an economic interpretation, and economic life viewed as a zero-sum game in which the gain of one player is the loss of another, but also as a cooperative venture in which the joint effort brings gain to all. It is a thought general enough to include much of the history of economics; but in Sartre's dialectics, which by its nature underlines tension and struggle, economic warfare such as was typical under mercantilism is coordinated with economic cooperation under conditions of rising productivity, which is more characteristic of modern economic life than is economic warfare. By coordinating both in a timeless dimension, Sartre snuffs out the idea of progress, hitherto a beacon in Western thought.

Of Sartre's **Critique**, an abridged English translation has been published under the title **Reason and Violence**, by R. D. Laing and D. G. Cooper (London: Tavistock Publications Ltd., 1964). See also Walter Odajnyk, **Marxism and Existentialism** (Garden City, N.Y.: Doubleday & Company, Inc., Anchor Books, 1965); Wilfrid Desan, **The Marxism of Jean-Paul Sartre** (same publisher, 1965); Raymond Aron, **Marxism and the Existentialists** (New York: Harper & Row, Publishers, 1969); Mark Poster, **Existential Marxism in France** (Princeton: Princeton University Press, 1975).

Examples of French studies of Marx's economics are cited above, p. 778.

An account of the ideas of a leading figure in Italian communism before World War II, whose influence is still noticeable, may be found in John M. Cammett, **Antonio Gramsci and the Origins of Italian Communism** (Stanford, Calif.: Stanford University Press, 1967); James Joll, **Antonio Gramsci** (New York: Penguin Books, 1978).

On the emancipation of the Italian and other communist movements from the Soviet Union see Roy Godson and Stephen Haseler, **Eurocommunism: Implications for East and West** (New York: St. Martin's Press, 1979); G. R. Urban, ed., **Eurocommunism** (New York: Universe Books, 1978).

On the so-called "new philosophers" who in the 1970's opposed Marxism in France, see Thomas Sheehan, "Paris: Moses and Polytheism," **New York Review of Books**, January 24, 1980, pp. 13–17.

• Leontief, Wassily, "The Decline and Rise of Soviet Economic Science," **Foreign Affairs**, January, 1960, pp. 261–72. The discoverer of input–output analysis comments on the development of Soviet economic thought and on the origins of input–output analysis. An English translation of Leontief's paper of 1925 may be found in Nicolai Spulber, ed., **Foundations of Soviet Strategy for Economic Growth: Selected Soviet Essays, 1924–1930** (Bloomington, Ind.: Indiana University Press, 1964). For other comments see H. S. Levine, "Input–Output Analysis and Soviet Planning," **American Economic Review**, Vol. 52, Supplement (1962), 127–37; Naum Jasny, "The Russian Economic 'Balance' and Input-Output Analysis: A Historical Comment," **Soviet Studies**, Vol. 14 (1962–63), 75–80; Rudolf Schlesinger, "A Note on the Context of Early Soviet Planning," **Soviet Studies**, Vol. 16 (1964–65), 22–44, especially 22–24.

• Lowenthal, Richard, **World Communism** (New York: Oxford University Press, Inc., 1964). A collection of essays tracing the replacement of monolithic by pluralistic communism. Recent transformations of the thought and action of those who claim to be the legatees of Marx are the subject of a number of symposia that investigate the matter from various points of view, with occasional references to

786

economics. Thus the replacement of miscellaneous orthodoxies is interpreted as the rise of a new kind of **Revisionism** in a book by this title, ed. Leopold Labedz (New York: Encyclopaedia Britannica, Inc., Frederick A. Praeger, Inc., 1962), which contains a chapter on "Revisionism in Soviet Economics" by Alfred Zauberman. In **Socialist Humanism**, ed. Erich Fromm (Garden City, N.Y.: Doubleday & Company, Inc., 1965) the attempt is made to disassociate from communism a humanist Marxism derived from Marx's early philosophical writings. One of the essays, by Paul Medow, treats of the relationship between humanistic ideals and mathematical economics. **Toward a Marxist Humanism**, by Leszek Kolakowski, translated from the Polish by Jane Zielonko Peel (New York: Grove Press, Inc., 1968), documents the opposition of a Polish philosopher to the renascent Stalinism. Another symposium, **Marxist Ideology in the Contemporary World**, ed. Milorad M. Drachkovitch, The Hoover Institution (New York: Encyclopaedia Britannica, Inc., Frederick A. Praeger, Inc., 1966), includes articles by such noted economists as P. T. Bauer and G. Haberler. **Marxism in the Modern World**, by the same editor (Stanford, Calif.: Stanford University Press, 1965), contains essays on various revolutionary figures—Lenin, Stalin, Tito, Mao Tse-tung, Castro, and so on—who claim the Marxist label. Similar in scope is **Marx and the Western World**, ed. N. Lobkowicz (Notre Dame, Ind.: University of Notre Dame Press, 1967). See also "Marxism Today," an issue of **Survey** (Journal of Soviet and East European Studies), No. 62 (January, 1962); Wolfgang Leonhard, **Three Faces of Marxism**, trans. by E. Oser (New York: Holt, Rinehart and Winston, 1974); Kolakowski and Stuart Hampshire, eds., **The Socialist Idea** (London: Weidenfeld and Nicolson, 1974); Walter Laqueur and George Mosse, eds., **Conflict and Compromise: Socialists and Socialism in the 20th Century**, special issue of **Journal of Contemporary History**, June, 1976; David McLellan, **Marxism After Marx** (New York: Harper & Row, 1980); George Lichtheim, **From Marx to Hegel and Other Essays** (New York: Herder &

Herder/McGraw-Hill Book Company, 1971); Neil McInnes, **The Western Marxists** (Freeport, N. Y.: Library Press, 1972); Shlomo Avineri, ed., **Varieties of Marxism** (The Hague: Martinus Nijhoff Publisher, 1977); Kolakowski, **Main Currents of Marxism**, Vol. 3.

There are a number of readers, some with extended commentaries. See C. Wright Mills, **The Marxists** (New York: Dell Publishing Co., Inc., Laurel Leaf Library, 1962); Massimo Salvadori, ed., **Modern Socialism** (New York: Harper & Row, 1968); Dick Howard and Karl L. Klare, eds., **The Unknown Dimension: European Marxism Since Lenin** (New York: Basic Books, 1972).

• Lukács, Georg (1885–1971) was a major philosophical interpreter of Marx, who strengthened the Hegelian dimension of Marx's philosophy. Lukács's principal works include **History and Class Consciousness**, trans. by Rodney Livingstone (Cambridge: MIT Press, 1971; originally published in 1923); **The Young Hegel: Studies in the Relations between Dialectics and Economics,** trans by Livingstone (same publisher, 1976), which sheds light on Hegel's economic studies and their influence on his philosophy; **Marxism and Human Liberation**, ed. with an introduction by E. San Juan, Jr. (New York: Dell Publishing Company, 1973); **Realism in Our Time: Literature and the Class Struggle**, with a preface by George Steiner (New York: Harper & Row, 1964). This is Lukács's formulation of the quintessence of Marxism, as stated by Steiner (**Times Library Supplement**, January 22, 1982, p. 68): "The humanization of man as the content of the process of history which—very variously—is realized in the course of every human life. Thus, every individual—no matter how consciously—is an active ingredient in this total historical process, of which he is at the same time the product." For interpretations of Lukács see Kolakowski, **Main Currents of Marxism**, Vol. 3, Chap. VII; George Lichtheim. **Georg Lukács** (New York: The Viking Press, 1970, Modern Masters series), George H. Parkinson, **Georg Lukács** (New York: Random House, 1977).

• Luxemburg, Rosa, **The Accumulation

of **Capital**, translated from the German by Agnes Schwarzschild, with an introduction by Joan Robinson (London: Routledge & Kegan Paul Ltd., 1951). Rosa Luxemburg's contribution to economics was a by-product of an active political life, in which she became a leader of the extreme left wing of the German Social Democratic Party and of the European Socialist movement. She was equally opposed to Bernstein's revisionism, to World War I, and to the political tactics of Lenin, whose employment of a tightly controlled and centralized party organization and of the terror she denounced in no uncertain terms. Unlike Lenin, she identified the dictatorship of the proletariat "with the practice of democracy, not with its abolition." Her murder by German right-wing vigilantes in 1919 meant the unchallenged ascendancy of the Soviets in the affairs of the Third International. For an English translation of Luxemburg's reply to criticism of **The Accumulation of Capital** and a rebuttal by N. Bukharin see Luxemburg and Bukharin, **Imperialism and the Accumulation of Capital**, ed. Kenneth J. Tarbuck, trans. by Rudolf Wichman (New York: Monthly Review Press, 1973).

The definitive biography by J. P. Nettl, **Rosa Luxemburg**, 2 vols. (New York: Oxford University Press, Inc., 1966), contains an appendix, pp. 828–41, on "Rosa Luxemburg as an Economist," with further references. Luxemburg's opposition to Lenin's political tactics has for long had adverse effects on the evaluation of her contribution to economics by Communist writers following the Soviet line. See also Norman Geras, **The Legacy of Rosa Luxemburg** (New York: Schocken Books, 1976); S. Rousseas, "Rosa Luxemburg and the Origins of Capitalist Catastrophe Theory," **Journal of Post-Keynesian Economics**, Vol. 1, No. 4 (Summer, 1979), 3–23.

• Lynd, Helen M., **England in the 1880s** (New York: Oxford University Press, Inc., 1945). A historical narrative explaining the background of the revival of British socialism in the 1880s. See also Royden Harrison, **Before the Socialists: Studies in Labour and Politics, 1861–1881** (London:

Routledge & Kegan Paul Ltd., 1965), which draws attention to the role of the English positivists in this revival; Henry Collins and Chimen Abramsky, **Karl Marx and the British Labor Movement: Years of the First International** (New York: St. Martin's Press, Inc., 1965); Henry Pelling, **The Origins of the Labour Party, 1880–1900**, rev. ed. (New York: Oxford University Press, Inc., 1965). James W. Hulse, **Revolutionists in London: A Study of Five Unorthodox Socialists** (London: Oxford University Press, 1970), examines the activities of Shaw, Morris, Bernstein, Kropotkin, et al.; Stanley Pierson, **Marxism and the Origins of British Socialism** (Ithaca: Cornell University Press, 1973).

• Marcuse, Herbert, **One-Dimensional Man** (Boston: Beacon Press, 1964). Marcuse (1898–1979) became a well-known spokesman of the New Left during the 1960's. He depicts industrial man as alienated or one-dimensional, enslaved by an Establishment which so manipulates his thought that he willingly accepts a "life of toil and fear" to satisfy the "false needs" the system imposes upon him. Marcuse makes a plea for greater spontaneity, release from unnecessary repression, and the transformation of work into play. He addresses his message no longer to a proletariat which has all but vanished but instead to "the substratum of the outcasts and outsiders, the exploited and the persecuted of other races and other colors, the unemployed and the unemployable." He has little use for the ordinary political processes, the employment of which, in his opinion, only confirms the rules of the game, and instead envisages the application of violence and the suppression of thought considered repressive by him. At the same time he admits that the affluence of the industrial society has brought "a good way of life—much better than before." For a critical review of Marcuse's thought, with references to his other writings, see Maurice Cranston, "Herbert Marcuse," **Encounter**, Vol. 32, No. 3 (March, 1969), 38–50. See also, about Marcuse and other members of the Frankfurt School, entries by Martin Jay on Marcuse and Max Horkheimer, **Interna-**

tional **Encyclopedia of the Social Sciences**, Vol. 18, Biographical Supplement (New York: The Free Press, 1979), pp. 497–500, 321–25; Morton Schoolman, **The Imaginary Witness: The Critical Theory of Herbert Marcuse** (New York: Free Press, 1980); Raymond Geuss, **The Idea of a Critical Theory: Habermas and the Frankfurt School** (New York: Cambridge University Press, 1982). About Soviet hostility to Marcuse see Klaus Mehnert, **Moscow and the New Left**, trans. by H. Fischer and L. Wilson (Berkeley: University of California Press, 1975).

• Morris, William, **Selected Writings and Designs**, edited with an introduction by Asa Briggs (Baltimore: Penguin Books, Inc., 1962); R. Page Arnot, **William Morris, the Man and the Myth** (New York: Monthly Review Press, 1964); Philip Henderson, **William Morris: His Life, Work, and Friends** (New York: McGraw-Hill Book Company, 1967); Jack Lindsay, **William Morris** (London: Constable, 1975); Paul Meier, **William Morris: The Marxist Dreamer**, 2 vols. (Atlantic Highlands, N. J.: Humanities Press, 1977); Edward P. Thompson,, **William Morris: Romantic Revolutionary**, rev. ed. (New York: Pantheon, 1977); Peter Faulkner, **Against the Age: An Introduction to William Morris** (London: George Allen & Unwin, 1980). The first of these works contains representative selections from Morris's writings about socialism. Some of these may also be found in the centenary edition of a selection of Morris's works (London: Nonesuch Press, 1948), and in the second volume of a supplement—**William Morris: Artist, Writer, Socialist**, 2 vols. (Oxford: Basil Blackwell & Mott Ltd., 1936)—to Morris's **Collected Works**, which carry an introduction by his daughter May Morris, 24 vols. (London: Longmans, Green & Co. Ltd., 1910–15).

• Nove, Alec, **The Soviet Economy**, rev. ed. (New York: Encyclopaedia Britannica, Inc., Frederick A. Praeger, Inc., 1966). Chap. 11 of this book contains a brief doctrinal history of Soviet economics, with references to primary and secondary source material. Much of the latter can be found in **Soviet Studies,** a periodical that contains frequent comments on Soviet economic thought. A book-length treatment is supplied by I. Guelfat, **Economic Thought in The Soviet Union: Concepts and Aspects. A Comparative Outline** (The Hague: Martinus Nijhoff's N. V., 1969). See also Vladimir G. Treml, "Interaction of Economic Thought and Economic Policy in the Soviet Union," **History of Political Economy,** Vol. 1, No. 1 (Spring, 1969), 187–216. Still of value for the earlier period is Adam Kaufman, "The Origin of 'The Political Economy of Socialism,'" **Soviet Studies**, Vol. 4 (1953), 243–72. Material relating to the doctrinal history of Soviet economics can also be gleaned from Nove's article, "Towards a Theory of Planning," in **Soviet Planning: Essays in Honour of Naum Jasny**, ed. Jane Degras (New York: Encyclopaedia Britannica, Inc., Frederick A. Praeger, Inc., 1964), pp. 193–204; from P. J. D. Wiles, **The Political Economy of Communism** (Cambridge, Mass.: Harvard University Press, 1962); and from Abram Bergson, **The Economics of Soviet Planning** (New Haven, Conn.: Yale University Press, 1964), which contains an extended discussion of the treatment of interest in Soviet economics.

On Lenin as an economist see Alec Nove's contribution to **Lenin: the Man, the Theorist, the Leader: A Reappraisal**, ed. Leonard Schapiro and Peter Reddaway, published in association with the Hoover Institution on War, Revolution, and Peace (Stanford, Calif.: Stanford University Press, 1967).

About Trotsky see Robert Wistrich, **Trotsky: Fate of a Revolutionary** (Totowa, N. J.: Rowman & Littlefield, 1980); Baruch Knei-Paz, **The Social and Political Thought of Leon Trotsky** (New York: Oxford University Press, 1978); Irving Howe, **Leon Trotsky** (New York: The Viking Press, 1979, Modern Masters series).

For an impressionistic picture of the nineteenth- and early twentieth-century background of pre-Soviet Russian economics see J. F. Normano, **The Spirit of Russian Economics** (Scranton, Pa.: Intext, 1945). For studies of still earlier periods, see **A History of Russian Economic Thought, Ninth Through Eigh-**

teenth Centuries, ed. and trans. from the Russian by John M. Letiche (Berkeley, and Los Angeles: University of California Press, 1964); Boris Ischboldin, **History of the Russian Non-Marxian Social-Economic Thought** (New Delhi: New Book Society of India, 1971); Franco Venturi, **Roots of Revolution: A History of the Populist and Socialist Movements in 19th Century Russia**, trans. by Francis Haskell, with an introduction by Isaiah Berlin (New York: Alfred A. Knopf, 1966), a major work of scholarship.

• Preobrazhensky, E., **The New Economics**, trans. by Brian Pearce, with an introduction by A. Nove (London: Oxford University Press, Clarendon Press, 1965). An English translation of Preobrazhensky's contribution to the industrialization debate of the 1920s. For translations of other contributions to this debate, and comments, see Spulber, ed., **Foundations of Soviet Strategy for Economic Growth**. For further comments, see Alexander Ehrlich, **The Soviet Industrialization Debate, 1924–1928** (Cambridge, Mass.: Harvard University Press, 1960); Nicolas Spulber, **Soviet Strategy for Economic Growth** (Bloomington, Ind.: Indiana University Press, 1964); S. Swianiewicz, **Forced Labour and Economic Development. An Inquiry into the Experience of Soviet Idustrialization** (London, Oxford University Press, for Chatham House, 1965); Preobrazhensky, **The Crisis of Soviet Industrialization: Selected Essays**, trans. with an introduction by D. A. Filtzer (White Plains, N. Y.: M. E. Sharpe, 1979); Richard B. Day, **Leon Trotsky and the Politics of Economic Isolation** (New York; Cambridge University Press, 1973); Moshe Lewin, **Political Undercurrents in Soviet Economic Debates: From Bukharin to the Modern Reformers** (Princeton: Princeton University Press, 1974).

• Schwartz, Benjamin, **Chinese Communism and the Rise of Mao** (Cambridge, Mass.: Harvard University Press, 1951), traces the adaptation of Marxism to Chinese conditions. Among the influences working on Mao there were the writings of Yen Fu (1853–1921), who acquainted Chinese intellectuals with the writings of Spencer, Huxley, Mill, Montesquieu, and others, as well as the work of Li Ta-chao (1888–1927), who was the first to spread Marx's ideas in China and blended them with militant nationalism. On the former, see Benjamin Schwartz, **In Search of Wealth and Power: Yen Fu and the West** (Cambridge, Mass.: Harvard University Press, 1964); on the latter, Maurice Meisner, **Li Ta-chao and the Origins of Chinese Marxism** (same publisher, 1967). About Mao see Arthur A. Cohen, **The Communism of Mao Tse-tung** (Chicago: The University of Chicago Press, 1964); Stuart Schram, **Mao Tse-tung** (New York: Simon & Schuster, Inc., 1967); Dick Wilson, ed., **Mao Tse-tung in the Scales of History** (New York: Cambridge University Press, 1977) is an assessment of Mao's thought and influence, with essays by Schram on Mao as a Marxist and by Christopher Howe and Kenneth R. Walker on Mao as an economist. Helene Carrere d'Encausse and Stuart R. Schram, **Marxism and Asia** (Harmondsworth, Middlesex: Allen Lane, The Penguin Press, 1970), contains copious extracts from original sources.

See also Donald W. Treadgold, **The West in Russia and China: Religious and Secular Thought in Modern Times**, 2 vols. (New York: Cambridge University Press, 1973), on the responsibility of Western thinkers and missionaries who disparaged capitalism and prepared the ground for the victory of Marxism in the Soviet Union and China.

• Sharpe, Myron E., ed., **Planning, Profit and Incentives in the USSR**, Vol.1: The Liberman Discussion; A New Phase in Soviet Economic Thought (White Plains, N.Y.: International Arts and Sciences Press, 1966). Translations of contributions to the discussion of Professor E. G. Liberman's proposal to lay greater stress on the profits of the state enterprises as success indicators. Profits have for long been part of the receipts of the state enterprises in the Soviet Union, and Professor Liberman's proposal, which was widely commented upon in the West, does in no way constitute a rehabilitation of profits. Its aim is to assign to them a more prominent role among the success indi-

790

cators—indexes of physical output, and so on—which are employed to ascertain managerial efficiency on the enterprise level. See also Liberman's **Economic Methods and the Effectiveness of Production** (Garden City, N. Y.: Doubleday and Company, 1973; Doubleday Anchor Books); Jan A. Dellenbrant, **Reformists and Traditionalists: A Study of Soviet Discussions about Economic Reform, 1960–1965** (Uppsala: Raben & Sjogren, 1972); J. Wilczynski, **Socialist Economic Development and Reforms** (London: Macmillan and Company, 1972).

• Shaw, George Bernard, ed., **Fabian Essays in Socialism**, first published in 1889, 6th ed., with a new introduction by Asa Briggs (London: George Allen & Unwin Ltd., 1962). This contains a reprint of the original edition as well as the prefaces written by Shaw and Webb to subsequent editions, including Shaw's "Sixty Years of Fabianism." See also R. H. S. Crossman, ed., **New Fabian Essays** (London: J. M. Dent and Sons Ltd., 1970). For the **History of the Fabian Society**, see the book by Edward R. Pease, its secretary for many years, with a new introduction by Margaret Cole, 3rd ed. (London: Frank Cass & Co. Ltd., 1963); also G. D. H. Cole, **Fabian Socialism** (London: George Allen & Unwin Ltd., 1943); Margaret Cole, **The Story of Fabian Socialism** (Stanford, Calif.: Stanford University Press, 1961); A. M. McBriar, **Fabian Socialism and English Politics** (London: Cambridge University Press, 1962); Anne Freemantle, **This Little Band of Prophets: The Story of the Gentle Fabians** (New York: The Macmillan Company, 1960); Norman and Jeanne MacKenzie, **The Fabians** (New York: Simon & Schuster, 1977), a major work on the early Fabians; Willard Wolfe, **From Radicalism to Socialism: Men and Ideas in the Formation of Fabian Socialist Doctrine 1881–1889** (New Haven: Yale University Press, 1975).

About Shaw's economics see T. A. Knowlton, **The Economic Theory of George Bernard Shaw** (Orono, Me.: Maine University Press, 1936); William Irvine, "George Bernard Shaw and Karl Marx," **Journal of Economic History**,

Vol. 6, No. 1 (May, 1946), 53–72; George J. Stigler, "Bernard Shaw, Sidney Webb, and the Theory of Fabian Socialism," in his **Essays in the History of Economics** (Chicago: The University of Chicago Press, 1965), Chap. 9. Also relevant is R. F. Harrod's criticism of ideas of Hobson's paralleling those of Shaw, in John A. Hobson, **The Science of Wealth**, rev. by R. F. Harrod, 4th ed. (New York: Oxford University Press, Inc., 1950), pp. 204–9.

See also Shaw, **Practical Politics**, ed. Lloyd J. Hubenka (Lincoln, Nebraska: University of Nebraska Press, 1976); Shaw, **The Road to Equality: Ten Unpublished Lectures and Essays 1884–1918** (Boston: Beacon Press, 1971). Shaw's later socialist writings include **The Intelligent Woman's Guide to Socialism and Capitalism** (New York: Crowell Collier & Macmillan, Inc., Brentano's, Inc., 1928), and **Everybody's Political What's What?** (New York: Dodd, Mead & Co., 1944).

About Graham Wallas, another early Fabian and for long associated with the London School of Economics, see Terence H. Qualter, **Graham Wallas and the Great Society** (New York: St. Martin's Press, 1980).

On the Fabians' attitude to imperial expansion see Bernard Semmel, **Imperialism and Social Reform** (Cambridge, Mass.: Harvard University Press, 1960).

• Sigmund, Paul E., Jr., ed., **The Ideologies of the Developing Nations,** 2nd rev. ed. (New York: Encyclopaedia Britannica, Inc., Frederick A. Praeger, Inc., 1972), contains a wide-ranging selection of statements documenting the ideologies prevailing in the underdeveloped countries. In the introduction there are incisive comments on the "socialism" of the new nations in Africa and elsewhere. See also William H. Friedland and Carl G. Rosberg, Jr., eds., **African Socialism** (Stanford, Calif.: Stanford University Press, 1967); Saul Rose, **Socialism in Southern Asia** (New York: Oxford University Press, Inc., 1960); Umberto Melotti, **Marx and the Third World**, trans. by Pat Ransford (Atlantic Highlands, N. J.: Humanities Press, 1977); Stephen Clarkson, **The Soviet Theory of Development** (Buffalo: University of Toronto Press,

1978); Luis E. Aguilar, ed., **Marxism in Latin America,** rev. ed. (Philadelphia: Temple University Press, 1978); Daniel P. Moynihan, "The United States in Opposition," **Commentary,** Vol. 59, No. 3 (March, 1975), 31–44, on the influence of British socialist thought in underdeveloped countries.

• Slutsky, Eugen E., "On the Theory of the Budget of the Consumer," **Readings in Price Theory,** selected by a committee of the American Economic Association (Homewood, Ill.: Richard D. Irwin, Inc., 1953), pp. 27–56. English translation of Slutsky's article, originally published in the **Giornale degli Economisti** for 1915. Slutsky's paper, written before the advent of the Soviets, is a contribution to pure mathematical economics, which he wanted to develop "completely independent of psychological assumptions and philosophical hypotheses" (p. 27). The questions that it raised relate to the equilibrium of the consumer and to demand theory. They were on the whole beyond the range of interests considered relevant in Soviet economics. Slutsky also published another paper, one which dealt with economic methodology, "Ein Beitrag zur formal-praxeologischen Grundlegung der Oeko-nomie," **Annales de la classe des sciences sociales et économiques** (Kiev: Académie Oukrainienne des Sciences, 1926), Vol. 4, 238–49, in which he interprets pure economics as constituting part of praxeology, that is, of the science of (rational) human action: "Pure economics is no independent science but only a part of a discipline within the framework of formal praxeology" (p. 249). This is a point of view of which the best known exponent in the West in Ludwig von Mises, the famous critic of socialism. See his **Human Action: A Treatise on Economics** (New Haven, Conn.: Yale University Press, 1949). About Mises's praxeology see Murray N. Rothbard, "Lange, Mises and Praxeology: The Retreat from Marxism," in **Toward Liberty: Essays in Honor of Ludwig von Mises on the Occasion of His 90th Birthday,** 2 vols. (Menlo Park, Calif.: Institute for Humane Studies, 1971), Vol. 2, pp. 307–21; R. A. Gonce, "Natural Law and Ludwig von Mises' Praxeology and Eco-

nomic Science," **Southern Economic Journal,** Vol. 39, No. 4 (April, 1973), 490–507. Cognate ideas have been developed by the Polish logician and philosopher of science, T. Kotarbinski; see Lange, **Political Economy** (cited above, p. 783), p. 189, and a contribution of Kotarbinski to the **Essays in Honour of Oskar Lange** (cited above, p. 783), pp. 303–12, where he attempts to demonstrate "the dependence of concepts used in economics on more general concepts, praxiological in nature" (p. 304). See also Kotarbinski's **Praxiology,** trans. by O. Wojtasiewicz (Elmsford, N.Y.: Pergamon Press, Inc., 1967), reviewed by Anthony Quinton in **N.Y. Review of Books,** April 25, 1968, p. 24. Karol Wojtyla (Pope John Paul II), **The Acting Person,** trans. by A. Potocki (Boston: D. Reidel Publishing Company, 1979; original Polish ed., 1969).

Slutsky's were not the only contributions to mathematical economics in the early decades of the twentieth century. Soviet writers refer to V. K. Dmitriev, author of a collection of essays published in 1904, which carried the subtitle, "attempt at a synthesis of the labor theory of value and of the marginal utility theory," Dmitriev's work is available in English translation under the title **Economic Essays on Value, Competition and Utility,** ed. D. M. Nuti (New York: Cambridge University Press, 1974). For comment see R. M. Larsen, "Dmitriev's Smithian Model," **Scottish Journal of Political Economy,** Vol. 24, No. 3 (November, 1977), 227–33. In the late twenties G. A. Feldman constructed a growth model that was based on Marx's reproduction scheme and has been commented upon by Evsey D. Domar, **Essays in the Theory of Economic Growth** (New York: Oxford University Press, Inc., 1957), pp. 223–61. An English translation of Feldman's work may be found in Spulber, ed., **Foundations of Soviet Strategy for Economic Growth.** The last surviving link with the prerevolutionary generation of mathematical economists is A. A. Konüs, one of the editors of the Russian translation of Slutsky's article of 1915, which was published in 1963, and himself the author of contributions to the theory of index numbers that have found attention in the

West; see his article, "The Problem of the True Index of the Cost of Living," **Econometrica**, Vol. 7 (January, 1939), 10–29.

• Sorel, Georges, **Reflections on Violence**, trans. T. E. Hulme and J. Roth, with an introduction by A. Shils (New York: The Macmillan Company, Collier Books, 1961). Sorel's principal work, originally published in 1908 and translated in 1914. See also **From Georges Sorel: Essays in Socialism and Philosophy**, ed. John Stanley (New York: Oxford University Press, 1976). About Sorel see J. L. Talmon, "The Legacy of Georges Sorel: Marxism, Violence, Fascism," **Encounter**, Vol 34, No. 2 (February, 1970), 47–60; Richard D. Humphrey, **Georges Sorel, Prophet Without Honor: a Study in Anti-Intellectualism** (Cambridge, Mass.: Harvard University Press, 1951); J. H. Meisel, **The Genesis of Georges Sorel: An Account of his Formative Period followed by a Study of his Influence** (Ann Arbor, Mich.: The University of Michigan Press, 1951); Isaiah Berlin, "Georges Sorel," in **Against the Current: Essays in the History of Ideas** (New York: The Viking Press, 1980), pp. 296–332; F. F. Ridley, **Revolutionary Syndicalism in France** (New York: Cambridge University Press, 1970); David D. Roberts, **The Syndicalist Tradition and Italian Fascism** (Chapel Hill: University of North Carolina Press, 1979).

• Thomas, Norman, **Socialism Reexamined** (New York: W. W. Norton & Company, Inc., 1963). A statement by a leader of democratic socialism in the United States. See also the biographies by Murray B. Seidler, **Norman Thomas: Respectable Rebel**, 2nd ed. (Syracuse, N.Y.: Syracuse University Press, 1967); W. A. Swanberg, **Norman Thomas: The Last Idealist** (New York: Charles Scribner's Sons, 1976). For recent statements see Michael Harrington, **Socialism** (New York: Saturday Review Press, 1972) and **The Twilight of Capitalism** (New York: Simon & Schuster, 1977). See also George Fischer, ed., **The Revival of American Socialism**. Selected Papers of the Socialist Scholars Conference (New York: Oxford University Press, 1971); John H. M. Laslett and Seymour M. Lipset, eds., **Failure of a Dream? Essays in the History of American Socialism**

(Garden City, N.Y.: Doubleday and Company, 1975).

A survey of the various brands of American socialism may be found in the work edited by Egbert and Persons, cited above, p. 767. See also Philip Taft, **Movements for Economic Reform** (New York: Holt, Rinehart & Winston, Inc., 1950); Thomas H. Greer, **American Social Reform Movements** (Englewood Cliffs, N.J.: Prentice-Hall, Inc., 1949); Sidney Lens, **Radicalism in America** (New York: Thomas Y. Crowell Company, 1966); David Herreshoff, **American Disciples of Marx: From the Age of Jackson to the Progressive Era** (Detroit: Wayne State University Press, 1967), an account of Orestes Brownson, Daniel De Leon, et al. About the latter see L. Glen Seretan, **Daniel DeLeon: The Odyssey of an American Marxist** (Cambridge: Harvard University Press, 1979).

• Webb, Sidney and Beatrice, **The History of Trade Unionism** (1894); **Industrial Democracy** (1897); **Problems of Modern Industry** (1898); **English Local Government**, 6 vols. (1906–22); **English Poor Law Policy** (1910); **The Prevention of Destitution** (1911); **A Constitution for the Socialist Commonwealth of Great Britain** (1920); **The Consumers' Cooperative Movement** (1921); **English Poor Law History**, 3 vols. (1927–30); **Soviet Communism: A New Civilization?**, 2 vols. (1935), (London: Longmans, Green & Co. Ltd.), mostly available in more recent editions. Also **The Decay of Capitalist Civilization** (London: George Allen & Unwin Ltd., 1923).

See also Beatrice Webb's autobiographical works, **My Apprenticeship** (London: Longmans, Green & Co. Ltd., 1926), and **Our Partnership** (same publisher, 1948); and her **Diaries, 1912–1924**, edited by Margaret Cole, with an introduction by Lord Beveridge (London: Longmans, Green & Co. Ltd., 1952); **Diaries, 1924–1932**, edited with an introduction by Margaret Cole (same publisher, 1956); **American Diary 1898**, ed. David A. Shannon (Madison, Wis.: University of Wisconsin Press, 1963), with interesting observations on the powers of an expert bureaucracy and on university life (pp.

Webb (New York: Alfred A. Knopf, Inc., 1968).

Beatrice Webb's fact-finding method owed much to that practiced by Charles Booth, a religiously inspired humanitarian and pioneer of the survey method. See T. S. and M. B. Simey, **Charles Booth: Social Scientist** (New York: Oxford University Press, Inc., 1960).

On the role of the Webbs in the rise of the welfare state see Bentley B. Gilbert, **The Evolution of National Insurance in Great Britain: The Origins of the Welfare State** (London: Michael Joseph Ltd., 1966). Related developments in the United States are traced in Roy Lubove, **The Struggle for Social Security, 1900–1935** (Cambridge, Mass.: Harvard University Press, 1968).

38f.). **The Letters of Sidney and Beatrice Webb**, 3 vols. (New York: Cambridge University Press, 1978) have been edited by Norman MacKenzie, who put them to good use in his work on the Fabians, cited earlier.

For appraisals see Margaret Cole, **Beatrice Webb** (New York: Harcourt, Brace & World, Inc., 1946); Margaret Cole, ed., **The Webbs and Their Work** (London: Frederick Muller, Ltd., 1949); R. H. Tawney, **The Webbs in Perspective** (London: University of London, Athlone Press, 1953); same author, **The Webbs and Their Work** (London: Fabian Society, ca. 1945), reprinted in Henry W. Spiegel, ed., **The Development of Economic Thought**, abr. ed. (New York: John Wiley & Sons, Inc., 1964), pp. 200–218; Kitty Muggeridge and Ruth Adam, **Beatrice**

CHAPTER 22

• Cournot, Augustin, **Researches into the Mathematical Principles of the Theory of Wealth** (1838), trans. Nathaniel T. Bacon, with an essay on Cournot and mathematical economics and a bibliography of mathematical economics by Irving Fisher (New York: The Macmillan Company, 1897). This is Cournot's principal contribution to economics in an English translation, which was reprinted, with additional material, in 1927 and later. About Cournot see Irving Fisher, "Cournot and Mathematical Economics," **Quarterly Journal of Economics**, Vol. 12 (January, 1898), 119-38, 238-44; Henry L. Moore, "The Personality of Antoine Augustin Cournot," **Quarterly Journal of Economics**, Vol. 19 (May, 1905), 370-99; R. Roy, "Cournot et la théorie des richesses," **Revue d'économie politique**, Vol. 52 (1938), pp. 1547–60; L. Amoroso et al., **Cournot nella economia e la filosofia** (Padua: Milani, 1939), which was published under the auspices of the Reale Istituto Superiore di Economia e Commercio di Venezia, and forms part of the Collana ca'Foscari; Henri Guitton, art. "Cournot," **International Encyclopedia of the Social Sciences** (New York: The Macmillan Company and The Free Press, 1968); Claude Ménard, **La Formation d'une rationalité économique: A. A.**

Cournot (Paris: Librairie E. Flammarion & Cie, 1978). There is a substantial literature dealing with Cournot's solution of the duopoly problem. On this see Edward H. Chamberlin, **The Theory of Monopolistic Competition**, 7th ed. (Cambridge, Mass.: Harvard University Press, 1956), Chap. 3; A. J. Nichol, "A Re-Appraisal of Cournot's Theory of Duopoly Price," **Journal of Political Economy**, Vol. 42 (February, 1934), 80–105. Parallels in the works of Cournot and Walras are elucidated by L. Hecht, "A. Cournot und L. Walras, ein formaler und materialer Vergleich wirtschaftstheoretischer Ableitungen," (Dissertation, Heidelberg, 1931).

• Edgeworth, F. Y., **Mathematical Psychics: An Essay on the Application of Mathematics to the Social Sciences** (London: Routledge & Kegan Paul Ltd., 1881). This work, which was reprinted (London: The London School of Economics; New York: Augustus M. Kelley, Publishers), is Edgeworth's only contribution to economics in book form. His periodical articles, book reviews, and so on, were assembled by him and published as **Papers Relating to Political Economy**, 3 vols. (London: Macmillan & Co. Ltd. for the Royal Economic Society, 1925; reprinted New

York: Burt Franklin). About Edgeworth see John M. Keynes, **Essays in Biography** (New York: Horizon Press, 1951), pp. 218–38; Arthur L. Bowley, "Francis Ysidro Edgeworth," **Econometrica**, Vol. 2 (April, 1934), 113–24. About Edgeworth's contributions to statistics, see Bowley's **F. Y. Edgeworth's Contributions to Mathematical Statistics** (London: Royal Statistical Society, 1928).

Edgeworth contributed appraisals of Cournot and Gossen to Palgrave's **Dictionary of Political Economy** (London: Macmillan & Co. Ltd., 1894–99).

See also D. Collard, "Edgeworth's Propositions on Altruism," **Economic Journal**, Vol. 85, No. 338 (June, 1975), 355–60.

• FitzPatrick, Paul J., "Leading British Statisticians of the Nineteenth Century," **Journal of the American Statistical Association**, Vol. 55 (March, 1960), 38–70. This survey includes an account of the statistical work of Jevons and Edgeworth. On the related matter of graphic presentation see H. Gray Funkhouser, "Historical Development of the Graphical Representation of Statistical Data," **Osiris**, Vol. 3 (1937), 280–90. See also Claude Ménard, "Three Forms of Resistance to Statistics: Say, Cournot, Walras," **History of Political Economy**, Vol. 12, No. 4 (Winter, 1980), 524–41.

• Gossen, Hermann Heinrich, **Entwicklung der Gesetze des menschlichen Verkehrs und der daraus fliessenden Regeln für menschliches Handeln** (Braunschweig: Friedr. Vieweg & Sohn GMBH, 1854); new edition with an introduction by F. A. von Hayek (Berlin: Prager, 1927). About Gossen see W. Stanley Jevons, **The Theory of Political Economy**, 2nd ed. (London: Macmillan & Co. Ltd., 1879), preface (reprinted in the later editions); L. Walras, "Un Économiste inconnu: H. H. Gossen," **Journal des économistes**, 1885, reprinted in his **Études d'économie sociale** (Lausanne: F. Rouge, 1896), pp. 351–74, and published in translation in H. W. Spiegel, ed., **The Development of Economic Thought** (New York: John Wiley & Sons, Inc., 1952); M. Pantaleoni, **Pure Economics**, trans. by T. Boston Bruce (London: Macmillan & Co.

Ltd., 1898), pp. 28ff.; Gisbert Beyerhaus, "H. H. Gossen und seine Zeit," **Zeitschrift für Volkswirtschaft und Sozialpolitik**, new series, Vol. 5 (1926), 522–39; F. Behrens, **H. H. Gossen oder die Geburt der "wissenschaftlichen Apologetik" des Kapitalismus** (Leipzig: Bibliographisches Institut, 1949)—Marxist interpretation; H. W. Spiegel, art. "Gossen," **International Encyclopedia of the Social Sciences.**

• Jenkin, Fleeming, **The Graphic Presentation of the Laws of Supply and Demand and other Essays on Political Economy** (London: The London School of Economics, 1931). This is a partial reprint of Vol. 2 of Jenkin's **Papers, Literary, Scientific etc.**, originally published in 1887. About Jenkin see A. D. Brownlie and M. F. Lloyd Prichard, "Professor Fleeming Jenkin, 1833–1885: Pioneer in Engineering and Political Economy," **Oxford Economic Papers,** new series, Vol. 15, No. 3 (November, 1963), 204–16.

• Jevons, W. Stanley, **The Theory of Political Economy**, 1st ed., 1871, 4th ed. H. Stanley Jevons (1911); **Investigations in Currency and Finance** (1884); **The Coal Question**, 1st ed. 1865, 3rd ed. A. W. Flux (1906); **Methods of Social Reform** (1883); **The Principles of Economics** (1905); (all originally published London: Macmillan & Co. Ltd.; reprints New York: Augustus M. Kelley, Publishers). Other economic works by Jevons include **Money and the Mechanism of Exchange** (Des Moines, Iowa: Meredith Corporation, Appleton-Century-Crofts, 1875); **Primer of Political Economy** (same publisher, 1878); and **The State in Relation to Labour** (London: Macmillan & Co. Ltd., 1882). There is a recent reprint of **The Theory of Political Economy,** ed. with an introduction by R. D. Collison Black, the foremost Jevons scholar of our time (New York: Penguin Books, 1970).

Details about Jevons's career and his opinions can be gleaned from his **Papers and Correspondence,** ed. Black, 7 vols. (Clifton, N. J.: Augustus M. Kelley, Publishers, 1972 ff.) as well as from his **Letters and Journals,** edited by his wife (London: Macmillan & Co. Ltd., 1886); Harriet W. Jevons, "William Stanley Jevons: His Life," **Econometrica**, Vol. 2

(July, 1934), 225–31; Rosamond Köne-kamp (his granddaughter), "William Stanley Jevons (1835–1882): Some Biographical Notes," **The Manchester School,** Vol. 30, No. 3 (September, 1962), 251–73; J. A. L. La Nauze, **Political Economy in Australia,** (Victoria: Melbourne University Press, 1949), which contains a chapter on "Jevons in Sydney."

About Jevons see the memorial issue of **The Manchester School,** Vol. 40, No. 1 (March, 1972), celebrating the centenary of the publication of **The Theory of Political Economy;** J. M. Keynes memorial allocution on the occasion of the centenary of Jevons's birth, published in the **Journal of the Royal Statistical Society,** 1936, and reprinted in J. M. Keynes, **Essays in Biography** (New York: Horizon Press, 1951), 255–309, also in Henry W. Spiegel, ed., **The Development of Economic Thought** (New York: John Wiley and Sons, 1952), pp. 489–525; Black, "Jevons, Bentham and De Morgan," **Economica,** Vol. 39, No. 154 (May, 1972), 119–34, on De Morgan's mathematics; Lionel Robbins, "The Place of Jevons in the History of Economic Thought" **Manchester School,** Vol. 7, No. 1 (1936), 1–17; Allyn A. Young, "Jevons's 'Theory of Political Economy,' " **American Economic Review,** Vol. 2, No. 3 (September, 1912), reprinted in his **Economic Problems New and Old** (Boston: Houghton Mifflin Company, 1927), pp. 213–31; Benjamin H. Higgins, "W. S. Jevons: A Centenary Estimate," **Manchester School,** Vol. 6, No. 2 (1935), 103–11; Ross M. Robertson, "Jevons and His Precursors," **Econometrica,** Vol. 19, No. 3 (July, 1951), 229–49; J. A. L. La Nauze, "The Conception of Jevons' Utility Theory," **Economica,** new series, Vol. 20 (November, 1953), 356–58; H. S. Jevons, "William Stanley Jevons: His Scientific Contributions," **Econometrica,** Vol. 2 (July, 1934), 231–37; E. W. Eckard, **Economics of W. S. Jevons** (Washington, D.C.: American Council on Public Affairs, 1940).

About the background of the economics of Jevons's time and reactions to his work see S. G. Checkland, "Economic Opinion in England as Jevons Found It," **Manchester School,** Vol. 19 (May, 1951), 143–69; T. W. Hutchison, "Economists and Economic Policy in Britain after 1870," **History of Political Economy,** Vol. 1, No. 2 (Fall, 1969), 231–55; R. D. Collison Black, "W. S. Jevons and the Economists of His Time," **Manchester School,** Vol. 30, No. 3 (September, 1962), 203–21; same author, "Jevons and Cairnes," **Economica,** new series, Vol. 27 (August, 1960), 214–32. Marshall's unappreciative review of Jevons's **Theory of Political Economy** is reprinted in **Memorials of Alfred Marshall,** ed. A. C. Pigou (London: Macmillan & Co. Ltd., 1925), pp. 93ff.

About Jevons's contributions to logic and scientific method see Ernest Nagel's introduction to the Dover edition of Jevons's **Principles of Science,** originally published 1874; Frédéric Gillot, **Algèbre et logique, d'après des textes originaux de G. Boole et W.-S. Jevons** (Paris: Albert Blanchard, 1962), and the same author's **Eléments de logique appliquée d'après Wronski, Jevons, Solvay** (Paris: Albert Blanchard, 1964); W. Mays, "Jevons' Conception of Scientific Method," **Manchester School,** Vol. 30, No. 3 (September, 1962), 223–49; W. Mays and D. P. Henry, "Jevons and Logic," **Mind,** new series, Vol. 62, No. 248 (October, 1953), 484–505.

• Robertson, Ross M., "Mathematical Economics before Cournot," **Journal of Political Economy,** Vol. 57, No. 6 (December, 1949), 523–36. This account of pioneering work in mathematical economics may be supplemented by Reghinos D. Theocharis, **Early Developments in Mathematical Economics** (New York: St. Martin's Press, Inc., 1961), and O. Weinberger, **Mathematische Volkswirtschaftslehre** (Stuttgart-Vaihingen: B. G. Teubner, 1930), which is broader in scope and covers also later developments. See also **Precursors in Mathematical Economics: An Anthology,** selected and edited by William J. Baumol and Stephen M. Goldfeld (London: The London School of Economics and Political Science, 1968). The history of econometrics is traced in Joseph J. Spengler, "Quantification in Economics: Its History," in Daniel Lerner, ed., **Quantity and Quality** (New York: The Free Press, 1960), pp. 129–211, and in Spengler's essay "On the Progress of

Quantification in Economics," in Harry Woolf, ed., **Quantification** (Indianapolis: The Bobbs-Merrill Co., Inc., 1961), pp. 128–46.

About Charles Ellet, the American pioneer of marginal analysis, see C. D. Calsoyas, "The Mathematical Theory of Monopoly in 1839: Charles Ellet, Jr.," **Journal of Political Economy**, Vol. 58 (April, 1950), 162–70; about William Whewell see J. L. Cochrane, "The First Mathematical Ricardian Model," **History of Political Economy**, Vol. 2, No. 2 (Fall, 1970), 419–31.

• Stigler, George J., "The Development of Utility Theory," **Journal of Political Economy**, Vol. 58 (August–October, 1950), reprinted in **Essays in the History of Economics** (Chicago: The University of Chicago Press, 1965), pp. 66–155. The doctrinal history of utility theory presented here is supplemented by Stigler's **Production and Distribution Theories: The Formative Period** (New York: The Macmillan Company, 1941), where references may be found to Jevons, Edgeworth and Wicksteed. See also Jacob Viner, "The Utility Concept in Value Theory and Its Critics," **Journal of Political Economy**, Vol. 33 (August–September, 1925), 369–87, 638–59, reprinted in **The Long View and the Short** (New York: The Free Press, 1958), pp. 177–212; Paul Rosenstein-Rodan, "Marginal Utility," **International Economic Papers**, No. 10 (New York: The Macmillan Company, 1960), pp. 71–106; R. S. Howey, **The Rise of the Marginal Utility School, 1870–1889** (Lawrence, Kans.: The University Press of Kansas, 1960); Emil Kauder, **A History of Marginal Utility Theory** (Princeton, N.J.: Princeton University Press, 1965); T. W. Hutchison, **A Review of Economic Doctrines, 1870–1929** (New York: Oxford University Press, Inc., 1953), Chaps. 1–2 (Jevons), 5–6 (Wicksteed and Edgeworth); Ben B. Seligman, **Main Currents in Modern Economics** (New York: The Free Press, 1962), pp. 257–70 (Jevons), 442–55 (Wicksteed and Edgeworth); Hutchison, **On Revolutions and Progress in Economic Knowledge** (New York: Cambridge University Press, 1978), on the Jevonian revolution; Dudley Dillard, "Revolutions in Economic

Theory," **Southern Economic Journal**, Vol. 44, No. 4 (April, 1978), 705–24; Black et al., eds., **The Marginal Revolution in Economics** (Durham, N. C.: Duke University Press, 1972; reprinted from **History of Political Economy**, Vol. 4, No. 2 [Fall, 1972]); William Jaffé, "Menger, Jevons and Walras De-Homogenized," **Economic Inquiry**, Vol. 14, No. 4 (December, 1976), 511–24; Robert B. Ekelund, Jr., et al., eds., **The Evolution of Modern Demand Theory** (Lexington, Mass.: D. C. Heath and Company, 1972), on French and other predecessors of Marshall. An English translation of Charles Dupuit's "On Toll and Transport Charges," originally published in 1849, may be found in **International Economic Papers**, No. 11 (New York: The Macmillan Company, 1962), pp. 7–31. W. Stark, **The Ideal Foundations of Economic Thought**, (London: Routledge & Kegan Paul Ltd., 1943), gives attention to Gossen as well as to Richard Jennings, one of the lesser-known precursors of Jevons.

• Thünen, J. H. von, **Von Thünen's Isolated State**, translated from German by C. M. Wartenberg (Elmsford, N.Y.: Pergamon Press, Inc., 1966). A translation of the second part of the **Isolated State** may also be found in Bernard W. Dempsey, **The Frontier Wage** (Chicago: Loyola University Press, 1960), which contains a generous appraisal of von Thünen's wage theory and of its potential usefulness as a guide to profit-sharing plans. On this subject see also Henry L. Moore, "Von Thünen's Theory of Natural Wages," **Quarterly Journal of Economics**, Vol. 9 (April–July, 1895), 291–304, 388–408; Arthur H. Leigh, "Von Thünen's Theory of Distribution and the Advent of Marginal Analysis," **Journal of Political Economy**, Vol. 54 (December, 1946), 481–502; Mark Blaug, "The German Hegemony of Location Theory: A Puzzle in the History of Economic Thought," **History of Political Economy**, Vol. 11, No. 1 (Spring, 1979), 21–29. See also Erich Schneider's essay on von Thünen, **Econometrica**, January, 1934, reprinted in Spiegel, **Development of Economic Thought**, pp. 445–57. There is a large von

Thünen literature in German, by Asmus Petersen and others. Petersen's **Von Thünens isolierter Staat: Die Landwirtschaft als Glied der Volkswirtschaft** (Hamburg: Verlag Paul Parey, 1944), contains a detailed commentary to von Thünen's principal work.

• Wicksteed, Philip H., **The Common Sense of Political Economy and Selected Papers and Reviews on Economic Theory**, edited with an introduction by Lionel Robbins, 2 vols. (London: Routledge & Kegan Paul Ltd., 1933). Wicksteed's **Alphabet of Economic Science**, originally published in 1888, has been reprinted (New York: Augustus M. Kelley, Pub-

lishers, 1955). His **Essay on the Coordination of the Laws of Distribution** of 1894 was also reprinted (London: The London School of Economics, 1932). About Wicksteed see Robbins's introduction to the **Common Sense of Political Economy**. There is a book-length biography by C. H. Herford, **Philip Henry Wicksteed** (London: J. M. Dent and Sons, Ltd., 1931). For continuing contributions to the "adding-up" problem first raised by Wicksteed, see J. R. Hicks, **The Theory of Wages** (London: Macmillan & Co. Ltd., 1932), pp. 233ff.; Joan Robinson, **Collected Economic Papers**, Vol. 1 (Oxford: Basil Blackwell & Mott Ltd., 1951), 1–19.

CHAPTER 23

• Böhm-Bawerk, Eugen von, **Capital and Interest**, trans. George D. Huncke and Hans F. Sennholz, 3 vols. (South Holland, Ill.: Libertarian Press, 1959). This new translation of Böhm's principal works contains, in Vol. 1, his "History and Critique of Interest Theories," in Vol. 2 his "Positive Theory of Capital," and in Vol. 3 "Further Essays on Capital and Interest." Under the same auspices there has also been published Vol. 1 of **Shorter Classics of Eugen von Böhm-Bawerk** (1962), which includes translations of Böhm's article on "Control or Economic Law?" and of his critique of Marx. Another edition of the latter was cited above, p. 773.

The "Further Essays" are made up of replies, hitherto untranslated, by Böhm to his critics. This discussion, which began in the closing decades of the nineteenth century and continued intermittently for many years, was revived by a new generation in the 1930s, with Frank H. Knight regarding capital as maintaining itself permanently and denying the existence of a period of production of determinate length, and F. A. Hayek upholding a modified Austrian doctrine. See, for references, Nicholas Kaldor, "The Controversy on the Theory of Capital," originally published in 1937 and reprinted in **Essays on Value and Distribution** (New York: The Free Press, 1960), pp. 153–205. Later

contributions include Hayek's **The Pure Theory of Capital** (London: Routledge & Kegan Paul Ltd., 1941); L. M. Lachmann, **Capital and Its Structure** (London: G. Bell & Sons, Ltd., 1956); Donald Dewey, **Modern Capital Theory** (New York: Columbia University Press, 1965). For an attempt to relate the period of production to the capital–output ratio of modern growth theory see Robert Dorfman, "A Graphical Exposition of Böhm-Bawerk's Interest Theory," **Review of Economic Studies**, Vol. 26 (February, 1959), 153–58; "Waiting and the Period of Production," **Quarterly Journal of Economics**, Vol. 73 (August, 1959), pp. 351–72.

For modern appraisals of Böhm-Bawerk's interest theory see Friedrich A. Lutz, **The Theory of Interest**, trans. C. Wittich (Dordrecht, Holland: D. Reidel Publishing Company, 1967), Chap. 1; Joseph W. Conard, **Introduction to the Theory of Interest** (Berkeley and Los Angeles: University of California Press, 1959), Chap. 3; J. Hirshleifer, "A Note on the Böhm-Wicksell Theory of Interest," **Review of Economic Studies**, Vol. 34, No. 98 (April, 1967).

For generous accounts of Böhm-Bawerk's work see "Schumpeter on Böhm-Bawerk," in Henry W. Spiegel, ed., **The Development of Economic Thought**, abr. ed. (New York: John Wiley & Sons, Inc., 1964), pp. 369–80; Joseph A. Schumpeter,

Ten Great Economists (New York: Oxford University Press, Inc., 1951), pp. 143–90; Robert E. Kuenne, **Eugen von Böhm-Bawerk** (New York; Columbia University Press, 1971).

• Ellis, Howard S., **German Monetary Theory 1905–1933** (Cambridge, Mass.: Harvard University Press, 1934). Includes in Chapter 5 an account of the marginal-utility theories of money developed by Mises, Wieser et al., and in Chapter 19 one of the Mises-Hayek analyses of business cycles.

• Hayek, Friedrich A. For a listing of works by and about Hayek see the article by Fritz Machlup, **International Encyclopedia of the Social Sciences**, Vol. 18, Biographical Supplement, pp. 274–82; also Norman P. Barry, **Hayek's Social and Economic Philosophy** (Atlantic Highlands, N. J.: Humanities Press, 1979); Samuel Brittan, "Hayek, The New Right, and the Crisis of Social Democracy," **Encounter**, Vol. 54, No. 1 (January, 1980), 31–46. For critiques of **The Road to Serfdom** see Herman Finer, **The Road to Reaction** (Boston: Little, Brown and Company, 1946); Barbara Wootton, **Freedom Under Planning** (Chapel Hill: University of North Carolina Press, 1945).

• Menger, Carl, **Principles of Economics**, trans. James Dingwall and Bert F. Hoselitz, with an introduction by Frank H. Knight (New York: The Free Press, 1950); **Problems of Economics and Sociology**, edited and with an introduction by Louis Schneider, trans. Francis J. Nock (Urbana, Ill.: University of Illinois Press, 1963). These are translations of Menger's **Grundsätze** (1871) and of his methodological work (1883), which were reprinted in the original German as the first two volumes of **The Collected Works of Carl Menger** (London: The London School of Economics and Political Science, 1934–36). The two concluding volumes of the **Collected Works** contain Menger's essays on methodology, doctrinal history, and monetary theory and policy.

About Menger, see "Hayek on Menger," in Spiegel, **Development of Economic Thought**, pp. 341–68; H. S. Bloch, **La Théorie des besoins de Carl Menger**

(Paris: R. Pichon et R. Durand-Auzias, 1937); same author, "Carl Menger: the Founder of the Austrian School," **Journal of Political Economy**, Vol. 48 (June, 1940), 428–33; A. R. Sweezy, "Collected Works of Carl Menger," **Quarterly Journal of Economics**, Vol. 50 (August, 1936), 719–30; Schumpeter, **Ten Great Economists**, pp. 80–90; J. R. Hicks and W. Weber, eds., **Carl Menger and the Austrian School of Economics** (New York: Oxford University Press, 1973); Laurence S. Moss and John M. Virgo, eds., "Carl Menger and Austrian Economics," **Atlantic Economic Journal**, Vol. 6, No. 3 (September, 1978), 1–69.

Like Jevons, Foxwell, and Keynes, Menger was a great book collector. After his death his library went to the Hitotsubashi University in Tokyo, which has published a number of volumes relating to Menger's work, including **Katalog der Carl Menger-Bibliothek**, 2 vols. (1926 and 1955); **Carl Menger's Zusätze zu Grundsätze der Volkswirtschaftslehre** (1961); **Carl Menger's Erster Entwurf zu seinem Hauptwerk "Grundsätze"** (1963). The last two items contain notes appended to and a first draft of his **Grundsätze**.

• Mises, Ludwig von, **The Theory of Money and Credit**, original edition 1912 (1953); **Socialism**, original edition 1922 (1951); **Bureaucracy** (1944); **Omnipotent Government** (1944); **Human Action** (1949); **Theory and History** (1957) (New Haven, Conn.: Yale University Press); **The Anti-Capitalistic Mentality** (1956); **Epistemological Problems of Economics** (1960); **The Free and Prosperous Commonwealth** (1962); **The Ultimate Foundation of Economic Science** (1962) (New York: Litton Educational Publishing, Inc., Van Nostrand Reinhold Company). See also Mary Sennholz, ed., **On Freedom and Free Enterprise: Essays in Honor of Ludwig von Mises** (New York: Litton Educational Publishing, Inc., Van Nostrand Reinhold Company, 1956); **Toward Liberty**. Essays in Honor of Ludwig von Mises on the Occasion of His 90th Birthday, 2 vols. (Menlo Park, Calif.: Institute for Humane Studies, 1971).

Other notable economists who make up the "younger" Austrian School include Gottfried von Haberler, known for his **Theory of International Trade** (Edinburgh: William Hodge and Company Limited, 1936), and **Prosperity and Depression** (Geneva: League of Nations, 1937), and Fritz Machlup. About the latter see the article by John S. Chipman, **International Encyclopedia of the Social Sciences**, Biographical Supplement, Vol. 18, pp. 486–91; Jacob S. Dreyer, ed., **Breadth and Depth in Economics: Fritz Machlup. The Man and His Ideas** (Lexington, Mass: D. C. Heath and Company, 1978). About the former see J. N. Bhagwati and J. Chipman, "Salute to Gottfried Haberler on the Occasion of His 80th Birthday," **Journal of International Economics**, Vol. 10, No. 3 (August, 1980), 313–18. See also K. I. Vaughn, "Economic Caluculation under Socialism: The Austrian Contribution," **Economic Inquiry**, Vol. 18, No. 4 (October, 1980), 535–54.

• Schumpeter, Joseph A., **The Theory of Economic Development**, first published 1912, trans. Redvers Opie (Cambridge, Mass.: Harvard University Press, 1934); **Economic Doctrine and Method**, first published 1914, trans. R. Aris (New York: Oxford University Press, Inc., 1954); **Business Cycles**, 2 vols. (New York: McGraw-Hill Book Company, 1939); **Capitalism, Socialism and Democracy** (New York: Harper & Row, Publishers, 1942); **Rudimentary Mathematics for Economists and Statisticians**, with W. L. Crum (New York: McGraw-Hill Book Company, 1946); **Imperialism and Social Classes** (New York: Augustus M. Kelley, Publishers, 1951); **Essays**, ed. Richard V. Clemence (Reading, Mass.: Addison-Wesley Publishing Co., Inc., 1951); **Ten Great Economists** (New York: Oxford University Press, Inc., 1951); **History of Economic Analysis** (New York: Oxford University Press, Inc., 1954); **Das Wesen des Geldes** (Göttingen: Vandenhoeck & Ruprecht, 1969). The last item, a posthumous publication, has been edited by Fritz Karl Mann.

About Schumpeter see Seymour E. Harris, ed., **Schumpeter: Social Scientists** (Cambridge, Mass.: Harvard University Press, 1951); "Haberler on Schumpeter," in Spiegel, **Development of Economic Thought**, pp. 432–60; Richard V. Clemence and Francis S. Doody, **The Schumpeterian System** (Reading, Mass.: Addison-Wesley Publishing Co., Inc., 1950); Allen M. Sievers, **Revolution, Evolution and the Economic Order** (Englewood Cliffs, N.J.: Prentice-Hall, Inc., 1962), pp. 26–58; François Perroux, **La Pensée économique de Joseph Schumpeter: Les Dynamiques du capitalisme** (Geneva: Librairie Droz S. A., 1965); Erich Schneider, **Joseph A. Schumpeter**, trans. with an introduction by W. E. Kuhn (Lincoln, Nebraska: University of Nebraska, Bureau of Business Research, 1975); Arnold Heertje, ed., **Schumpeter's Vision: Capitalism, Socialism and Democracy After 40 Years** (New York: Frederick A. Praeger, Inc., 1981), with contributions by Samuelson, Haberler, and others; John E. Elliott, "Marx and Schumpeter on Capitalism's Creative Destruction," **Quarterly Journal of Economics**, Vol. 95, No. 1 (August, 1980), 45–68.

• Stigler, George J., **Production and Distribution Theories: The Formative Period** (New York: The Macmillan Company, 1941), Chaps. 6–8, and the works cited on p. 796 by Viner, Howey, Kauder, Hutchinson (Chaps. 9–12, 23) and Seligman (Chaps. 4, 9) contain appraisals of the Austrians. See also Maffeo Pantaleoni, **Pure Economics**, trans. T. Boston Bruce (New York: The Macmillan Company, 1898), which forms a link with the Lausanne School; William Smart, **An Introduction to the Theory of Value, on the Lines of Menger, Wieser and Böhm-Bawerk**, 4th ed. (London: Macmillan & Co. Ltd., 1926); J. Bonar, "The Austrian Economists and Their View of Value," **Quarterly Journal of Economics**, Vol. 3 (October, 1888), 1–31; A. R. Sweezy, "The Interpretation of Subjective Value Theory in the Writings of the Austrian Economists," **Review of Economic Studies**, Vol. 1 (June, 1934), 176–85; H. Brems, "The Austrian Theory of Value and the Classical One," **Zeitschrift für Nationalökonomie**, Vol. 22 (October, 1962), 261–70; J. R. Hicks, **Capital and Time: A Neo-Austrian Theory** (New York: Oxford University Press, 1973). L. M. Lachmann, "Die geistesgeschichtliche Bedeutung der österreichischen Schule in der Volkswirtschaftslehre," **Zeitschrift für Nationalökonomie**, Vol. 26, Nos. 1–3 (1966), 152–67. About Rudolf Auspitz and Richard Lieben, two Austrian financiers who in the 1880s developed a utility theory on a mathematical basis of which both Menger and Walras disapproved, see Hutchison, pp. 188–91; Howey, pp. 168–72.

See also Hutchison, **The Politics and Philosophy of Economics: Marxians, Keynesians and Austrians** (New York: New York University Press, 1981); see also Emil Kauder, "The Retarded Acceptance of the Marginal Utility Theory," **Quarterly Journal of Economics**, Vol. 67 (November, 1953), 564–75; same author, "Intellectual and Political Roots of the Older Austrian School," **Zeitschrift für Nationalokonomie**, Vol. 17 (December, 1957), 411–25. William M. Johnston, **The Austrian Mind: An Intellectual and Social History, 1848–1938** (Berkeley: University of California Press, 1971).

• Wieser, Friedrich von, **Natural Value**, ed. William Smart, trans. Christian A. Malloch (London: Macmillan & Co. Ltd., 1893); **Social Economics**, trans. A. Ford Hinrichs, with a preface by Wesley Clair Mitchell (New York: Adelphi Company, 1927). See "Hayek on Wieser," in Spiegel, **Development of Economic Thought**, 1952 ed., pp. 554–67; R. B. Ekelund, Jr., "Power and Utility: The Normative Economics of Friedrich von Wieser," **Review of Social Economy**, Vol. 28, No. 2 (September, 1970), 179–96.

CHAPTER 24

• Kaldor, Nicholas, "The Determinateness of Static Equilibrium" (1934), **Essays on Value and Distribution** (New York: The Free Press, 1960), pp. 14–33; John R. Hicks, **Value and Capital** (New York: Oxford University Press, Inc., 1939); Paul A. Samuelson, **Foundations of Economic Analysis** (Cambridge, Mass.: Harvard University Press, 1947). All these works contain further contributions to general-equilibrium theory. For a readable introduction see William J. Baumol, **Economic Dynamics** 2nd ed. (New York: The Macmillan Company, 1959). See also Robert E. Kuenne, **The Theory of General Economic Equilibrium** (Princeton, N.J.: Princeton University Press, 1963) and articles by Kuenne cited on pp. 575f. of that work; Vivian Walsh and Harvey Gram, **Classical and Neoclassical Theories of Economic Equilibrium** (New York: Oxford University Press, 1980).

• Leontief, Wassily. See the article by William H. Miernyk about him in **International Encyclopedia of the Social Sciences**, Biographical Supplement, Vol. 18, pp. 435–38. For a readable introduction see Miernyk, **The Elements of Input-Output Analysis** (New York: Random House, Inc., 1965); for an appraisal of this analysis in doctrinal history, see G. L. S. Shackle, **The Years of High Theory** (London: Cambridge University Press, 1967), Chap. 17.

• Pareto, Vilfredo, **Cours d'économie politique**, 2 vols. (Lausanne: F. Rouge, 1896–97); **Manuel d'économie politique** (Paris: V. Giard et E. Brière, 1909); "Mathematical Economics" (1911), **International Economic Papers**, Vol. 5 (1955), 58–102. For a translation of the **Manuel** see **Manual of Political Economy**, trans. by Anne S. Schwier, ed. Anne S. Schwier and Alfred N. Page (Clifton, N.J.: Augustus M. Kelley, 1971); see about this the review article by William Jaffé, **Journal of Economic Literature**, Vol. 10, No. 4 (December, 1972), 1190–1201, with further discussion, same journal, Vol. 12, No. 1 (March, 1974), 78–96. Selections from Pareto's writings have been published under the title **The Other Pareto**, ed. and trans. by Bucolo Placido (New York: St. Martin's Press, 1980).

For general appraisals see Renato Cirillo, **The Economics of Vilfredo Pareto** (Totowa, N.J.: Frank Cass, 1979); Warren J. Samuels, **Pareto on Policy** (New York: Elsevier Scientific Publishing Company, 1974); G. H. Bousquet, **Vilfredo Pareto:**

son vie et son oeuvre (Paris: Éditions Payot, 1928); **Pareto (1848–1923): Le Savant et l'homme** (Lausanne: Librairie Payot S.A., 1960); Schumpeter, **Ten Great Economists** (New York: Oxford University Press, Inc., 1951), pp. 110–42; "Demaria on Pareto," in Henry W. Spiegel, ed., **The Development of Economic Thought** (New York: John Wiley & Sons, Inc., 1952), pp. 628–51; Gottfried Eisermann, **Vilfredo Pareto als National-ökonom und Soziologe** (Tübingen: J. C. B. Mohr [Paul Siebeck], 1961); U. Ricci, "Pareto and Pure Economics," **Review of Economic Studies**, Vol. 1, No. 1 (October, 1933), 3–21; L. Amoroso, "Vilfredo Pareto," **Econometrica**, Vol. 6 (January, 1938), 1–21; Erich Schneider, "Vilfredo Pareto: The Economist in Light of His Letters to Maffeo Pantaleoni," Banca Nazionale del Lavoro, **Review**, Vol. 14 (September, 1961), 247–95. There are further articles about Pareto in **Revue d'économie politique**, Vol. 59, Nos. 5–6, (September–December, 1949), and other relevant material is listed in a new edition of his **Cours**, forming Vol. 1 of Pareto's **Oeuvres complètes** (Geneva: Librairie Droz S.A., 1964), pp. xxvii*–xxx*.

On the indifference curve see G. L. S. Shackle, **The Years of High Theory** (London: Cambridge University Press, 1967), Chap. 7. On the Pareto optimum, Abram Bergson, **Essays in Normative Economics** (Cambridge, Mass.: Harvard University Press, 1966), pp. 203ff.; Oskar Lange, **On the Economic Theory of Socialism** (Minneapolis: University of Minnesota Press, 1938), pp. 65ff.; A. P. Lerner, **The Economics of Control** (New York: The Macmillan Company, 1944), Chaps. 6 and 9; Enrico Barone, "The Ministry of Production in the Collectivist State," in F. A. Hayek, ed., **Collectivist Economic Planning** (London: Routledge & Kegan Paul Ltd., 1935), pp. 245–90. On the compensation principle, Nicholas Kaldor, "Welfare Propositions in Economics" (1939), in **Essays on Value and Distribution** (New York: The Free Press, 1960), pp. 143–46. On Pareto's sociology, Morris Ginsberg, **Reason and Unreason in Society** (London: William Heinemann Ltd., 1947), pp. 84–103; Talcott Parsons, **The Structure of Social Action** (New York:

McGraw-Hill Book Company, 1937), Chaps. 5–7; S. E. Finer, "Pareto and Pluto-Democracy: The Retreat to Galapagos," **American Political Science Review**, Vol. 62, No. 2 (June, 1968), 440–50.

About Pareto's law of income distribution see Frederick R. Macaulay, "The Personal Distribution of Income in the United States," in Wesley C. Mitchell, ed., **Income in the United States: Its Amount and Distribution, 1909–19**, Vol. 2 (New York: National Bureau of Economic Research, 1922), Part 3, Chap. 28; C. Bresciani-Turroni, "On Pareto's Law," **Journal of the Royal Statistical Society**, Vol. 100, No. 3 (1937), 421–32; "Annual Survey of Statistical Data: Pareto's Law and the Index of Inequality of Incomes," **Econometrica**, Vol. 7 (April, 1939), 107–33; N. O. Johnson, "The Pareto Law," **Review of Economic Statistics**, Vol. 19 (February, 1937), 20–26; D. H. Macgregor, "Pareto's Law," **Economic Journal**, Vol. 46 (March, 1936), 80–87; E. C. Rhodes, "The Pareto Distribution of Incomes," **Economica**, new series, Vol. 11 (February, 1944), 1–11. See also Joseph J. Spengler, "Pareto on Population," **Quarterly Journal of Economics**, Vol. 58 (August, 1944), 571–601 and Vol. 59 (November, 1944), 107–33.

About Pareto's attempts to develop an economics ostensibly purged of non-scientific elements see Vincent J. Tarascio, **Pareto's Methodological Approach to Economics** (Chapel Hill, N.C.: University of North Carolina Press, 1967). See also, by the same author, "The Monetary and Employment Theories of Vilfredo Pareto," **History of Political Economy**, Vol. 1, No. 1 (Spring, 1969), 101–22.

• Stigler, George J., **Production and Distribution Theories: The Formative Period** (New York: The Macmillan Company, 1941), Chap. 9, and the works cited on p. 796 above by Hutchison (Chaps. 13–14) and Seligman (Chap. 5) contain appraisals of the Lausanne School. See also Gaëtan Pirou, **Les Théories de l'équilibre économique: Walras et Pareto**, 3rd ed. (Paris: Domat-Montchrestien, 1946); F. Bompaire, **Économie mathématique: Du principe de la liberté économique dans l'ouvrage de Cournot et dans celle de** l'École de Lausanne (Walras, Pareto), (Paris: Éditions Sirey, 1931); F. Oulès, **L'École de Lausanne: Textes choisies de L. Walras et V. Pareto** (Paris: Librairie Dalloz S. A., 1950); Eraldo Fossati, **The Theory of General Static Equilibrium** (Oxford: Basil Blackwell & Mott Ltd., 1957); J. O. Clerk, "Walras and Pareto: Their Approach to Applied Economics and Social Economics," **Canadian Journal of Economics and Political Science**, Vol. 8 (November, 1942), 584–94.

On the controversies relating to the theory of production, see Stigler, above; Henry Schultz, "Marginal Productivity and the Lausanne School," **Economica**, Vol. 12 (August, 1932), 285–300; Cecil G. Phipps, "Pareto and Walras on Production," **Metroeconomica**, Vol. 6 (April, 1954), 31–38; William Jaffé, "New Light on an Old Quarrel," **Cahiers Vilfredo Pareto**, Vol. 3 (Geneva: Librairie Droz S.A., 1964), 61–102.

• Wald, Abraham, "On Some Systems of Equations of Mathematical Economics," **Econometrica,** Vol. 19 (October, 1951), 368–403. A fundamental critique, from the mathematical point of view, of the suitability of the Walrasian equations for an equilibrium system.

• Walras, Auguste, **De la nature de la richesse et de l'origine de la valeur** (Paris: Félix Alcan, 1938). New edition, with an introduction by Gaston Leduc, of the principal contribution of the older Walras to economics, first published in 1831. About Auguste Walras see Louis Modeste Leroy, **Auguste Walras: Sa vie, son oeuvre** (Paris: Librairie générale de droit et de jurisprudence, 1923).

• Walras, Léon, **Elements of Pure Economics**, trans. William Jaffé (Homewood, Ill.: Richard D. Irwin, Inc., 1954). An English translation of the "definitive edition" of 1926 of Walras's principal work, collated with the previous editions and with valuable notes by the translator. Professor Jaffé has also edited **Correspondence of Léon Walras and Related Papers**, 3 vols. (Amsterdam: North-Holland Publishing Company, 1965), which contains a wealth of interesting material shedding light on the genesis of Walras's thought,

on the intellectual influences working on him, and on his attempts to find recognition of his doctrine. The publication of the **Correspondence**, a signal contribution of our time to doctrinal history, makes it possible to trace the evolution of Walras's leading ideas. At age nineteen a then popular textbook on mechanics impressed him with an exposition of an equilibrium system that became the pattern for his own work. Later on, in 1871, a mathematician at Lausanne would guide him in the development of his utility theory. Still later, in 1877, another colleague rendered similar services in connection with the marginal productivity theory. For a summary account of these matters, see William Jaffé, "Biography and Economic Analysis," **Western Economic Journal**, Vol. 3, No. 3 (Summer, 1965), 223–32. See also, by the same author, numerous valuable articles shedding light on various phases of Walrasian economics, listed in the bibliography of Jaffé's writings in **History of Political Economy**, Vol. 13, No. 3 (Summer, 1981), 311–12. Jaffé (1898–1980) was the leading authority on Walras.

Further works about Walras include Michio Morishima, **Walras' Economics: A Pure Theory of Capital and Money** (New York: Cambridge University Press, 1977); D. Collard, "Léon Walras and the Cambridge Caricature," **Economic Journal**, Vol. 83, No. 330 (June, 1973), 465–76; John R. Hicks, "Léon Walras," **Econometrica**, Vol. 2 (October, 1934), 338–48; Milton Friedman, "Léon Walras and His Economic System," **American Economic Review**, Vol. 45 (December, 1955), 900–909; R. F. Harrod, "Walras: A Reappraisal," **Economic Journal**, Vol. 66 (June, 1956), 307–16; Marcel Boson, **Léon Walras: Fondateur de la politique économique scientifique** (Paris: Librairie générale de droit et de jurisprudence, 1951). The last work, as its title indicates, concentrates attention on Walras's economic policy proposals rather than on his pure economics.

There are numerous expositions of varying degrees of difficulty of Walras's system of equations; for examples, see Robert Dorfman, Paul A. Samuelson and Robert M. Solow, **Linear Programming and Economic Analysis** (New York:

McGraw-Hill Book Company, 1958), Chap. 13; F. Zeuthen, **Economic Theory and Method** (Cambridge, Mass.: Harvard University Press, 1955), Chap. 11; George J. Stigler, **The Theory of Price**, rev. ed. (New York: The Macmillan Company, 1952), Chap. 16; John F. Due and Robert W. Clower, **Intermediate Economic Analysis**, 5th ed. (Homewood, Ill.: Richard D. Irwin, Inc., 1966), Chap. 18; E. H. Phelps Brown, **The Framework of the Pricing System** (London: Chapman and Hall Ltd., 1936); Gustav Cassel, **The Theory of Social Economy**, trans. Joseph McCabe (New York: Harcourt, Brace & World, Inc., 1924), Chap. 4; R. A. Murray, **Leçons d'économie politique suivant la doctrine de l'école de Lausanne** (Paris: Éditions Payot, 1920).

On Walras's monetary theories see Arthur W. Marget, "Léon Walras and the 'Cash-Balance Approach' to the Problem of the Value of Money," **Journal of Political Economy**, Vol. 39, No. 5 (October, 1931), 569–600; "The Monetary Aspects of the Walrasian System," same journal, Vol. 43 (April, 1935), 145–86. For a different interpretation see Don Patinkin, "The Indeterminacy of Absolute Prices in Classical Economic Theory," **Econometrica**, Vol. 17 (January, 1949), 1–27 and his **Money, Interest, and Prices**, 2nd ed. (New York: Harper & Row, Publishers, 1965), which contains comments also on many other aspects of Walrasian economics. So does Arthur W. Marget, **The Theory of Prices**, 2 vols. (Englewood Cliffs, N.J.: Prentice-Hall, Inc., 1938–1942), which sheds light on many phases of the doctrinal history of monetary theory. On Walras's contribution to the marginal productivity theory of distribution see Jaffé, "New Light on an Old Quarrel," cited p. 802.

See Jean Piaget, **Structuralism**, trans. and ed. Chaninah Maschler (New York: Basic Books, 1970), p. 77 about a connection between the thought of Ferdinand de Saussure, one of the founders of modern synchronic linguistics, and the ideas of Walras.

CHAPTER 25

• Arrow, Kenneth J., **Social Choice and Individual Values** (New York: John Wiley & Sons, Inc., 1951). This important contribution to welfare economics contains a statement of the "paradox of voting." Other works about the rationality of collective decision making include Anthony Downs, **An Economic Theory of Democracy** (New York: Harper & Row, Publishers, 1957); Duncan Black, **The Theory of Committees and Elections** (London: Cambridge University Press, 1958); Robert A. Dahl and Charles E. Lindblom, **Politics, Economics and Welfare** (New York: Harper & Row, Publishers, 1953); J. M. Buchanan and G. Tullock, **The Calculus of Consent** (Ann Arbor, Mich.: The University of Michigan Press, 1962); G. Tullock, **Toward a Mathematics of Politics** (same publisher, 1967); Mancur Olson, Jr., **The Logic of Collective Action** (Cambridge, Mass.: Harvard University Press, 1965); T. W. Hutchison, **Markets and the Franchise** (London: Institute of Economic Affairs, 1966); Robin Farquharson, **Theory of Voting** (Oxford: Basil Blackwell & Mott Ltd., 1970). For a recent statement of Arrow's views see his contribution, "Public and Private Values," to Sidney Hook, ed., **Human Values and Economic Policy** (New York: New York University Press, 1967), pp. 3–21. For an appraisal of Arrow's work see the article by C. C. von Weizsäcker on Arrow in Henry W. Spiegel and Warren J. Samuels, eds., **Contemporary Economists in Perspective** (Greenwich, Ct.: JAI Press, forthcoming).

• Chamberlin, Edward H. See the article by Jesse W. Markham about Chamberlin, with bibliography of works by and about him, **International Encyclopedia of the Social Sciences**, Biographical supplement, Vol. 18, pp. 117–21.

In addition to Joan Robinson's work, pioneer writings about imperfect competition by other authors include Frederick Zeuthen, **Problems of Monop-**

oly and Economic Warfare, translated from the Danish, with a foreword by J. A. Schumpeter, (London: Routledge & Kegan Paul Ltd., 1930); Erich Schneider, **Reine Theorie monopolistischer Wirtschaftsformen** (Tübingen: J. C. B. Mohr [Paul Siebeck], 1932); Heinrich von Stackelberg, **Marktform und Gleichgewicht** (Vienna: Springer-Verlag KG, 1934); Ragnar Frisch, "Monopoly-Polypoly: The Concept of Force in the Economy," originally published 1933, translated in **International Economic Papers**, No. 1 (1951). About Zeuthen see Hans Brems, "From the Years of High Theory: Frederick Zeuthen (1888–1959)," **History of Political Economy**, Vol. 8, No. 3 (Autumn, 1976), 400–411; about Frisch see the article by Leif Johansen in Spiegel and Samuels, **Contemporary Economists in Perspective.**

• Coats, A. W. "The Origins and Early Development of the Royal Economic Society," **Economic Journal**, Vol. 78 (June, 1968), 349–71.

• Harrod, Roy. About Harrod see the articles by Ivan C. Johnson in **International Encyclopedia of the Social Sciences**, Biographical Supplement, Vol. 18, pp. 271–74; G. L. S. Shackle in Spiegel and Samuels, **Contemporary Economists in Perspective**.

• Hawtrey, Ralph G., **Good and Bad Trade** (London: Constable & Co. Ltd., 1913). **Currency and Credit** (1919, 4th ed. 1950); **Monetary Reconstruction** (1923); **The Economic Problem** (1926); **The Gold Standard in Theory and Practice** (1927, 5th ed. 1947); **Trade and Credit** (1928); **Economic Aspects of Sovereignty** (1930); **Trade Depression and the Way Out** (1931); **The Art of Central Banking** (1932); **Capital and Employment** (1937); **A Century of Bank Rate** (1938); **Economic Destiny** (1944); **Bretton Woods: For Better or Worse** (1946); **Economic Rebirth** (1946); **Towards the Rescue of Sterling** (1954); **Cross Purposes in Wage Policy** (1955); **Incomes and Money** (1967) (London: Longmans, Green & Co. Ltd.). **Western European Union: Implications for the United Kingdom** (1949); **The Balance of Payments and the Standard of Living**

(1950) (London: Royal Institute of International Affairs).

About Hawtrey see references in Arthur W. Marget, **The Theory of Prices**, 2 vols. (Englewood Cliffs, N.J.: Prentice-Hall, Inc., 1938, 1942); Raymond J. Saulnier **Contemporary Monetary Theory** (New York: Columbia University Press, 1938), Part 1. About the income theory see Alvin H. Hansen, **Monetary Theory and Fiscal Policy** (New York: McGraw-Hill Book Company, 1949), Chap. 6.

• Hicks, John R. About Hicks see the articles by G. C. Reid and J. N. Wolfe in **International Encyclopedia of the Social Sciences**, Biographical Supplement, Vol. 18, pp. 300–302; William Baumol in Spiegel and Samuels, **Contemporary Economists in Perspective.**

• Hutchison, T. W., **A Review of Economic Doctrines, 1870–1929** (London: Oxford University Press, 1953), Chaps. 4 (Marshall), 18 (welfare economics), 19 (imperfect competition), 21 (monetary theory), 23 (Hawtrey and Robertson); Ben B. Seligman, **Main Currents in Modern Economics** (New York: The Free Press, 1962), pp. 403–20 (Hicks), 456–525 (Marshall, Pigou, Robertson, Hawtrey, Robbins), 694–729 (imperfect competition); Erich Schneider, **Einführung in die Wirtschaftstheorie**, Part 4, Vol. 1 (Tübingen: J. C. B. Mohr [Paul Siebeck], 1962), Chaps. 7 (Marshall), 8 (imperfect competition); G. L. S. Shackle, **The Years of High Theory** (New York: Cambridge University Press, 1967), Chaps. 3–6 (imperfect competition); George J. Stigler, **Production and Distribution Theories** (New York: The Macmillan Company, 1941), Chap. 4 (Marshall); Paul T. Homan, **Contemporary Economic Thought** (New York: Harper & Row, Publishers, 1928), pp. 193–280 (Marshall).

• Marshall, Alfred, **Principles of Economics**, first published 1890, 8th ed. 1920; a 9th, variorum edition, with annotations by C. W. Guillebaud, 2 vols. (1961). Marshall's earliest work in book form, **The Pure Theory of Foreign Trade: The Pure Theory of Domestic Values**, which introduced his offer curves, was privately printed and circulated in 1879 and reprinted (London: The London School of Economics, 1930). With his wife he published in 1879 **Economics of Industry**, which contained an early treatment of the essentials of labor economics. Other works by Marshall include **Elements of Economics of Industry** (1892, 3rd ed. 1899); **Industry and Trade** (1919), largely devoted to industrial organization; **Money, Credit and Commerce** (1923), with an important Appendix J on international trade theory, where the relation between demand elasticities and currency depreciation, later designated as Marshall-Lerner condition, was explored; **Official Papers** (1926), which contain contributions to monetary theory. **Memorials of Alfred Marshall**, ed. A. C. Pigou (1925) is a volume of memorial articles, selections from Marshall's writings, and letters. There may be found Keynes's famous obituary, reprinted from the **Economic Journal** for 1924, and reprinted again later in Keynes's **Essays in Biography** (first pub. 1933), (London: Macmillan & Co. Ltd.). See also **The Early Economic Writings of Alfred Marshall 1867–1890**, ed. with an introduction by J. K. Whitaker, 2 vols. (New York: The Free Press, 1975).

In addition to Keynes's obituary, other noted appraisals of Marshall's work include Jacob Viner, "Marshall's Economics, in Relation to the Man and to His Times," **American Economic Review**, Vol. 31 (June, 1941), 223–35; Joseph A. Schumpeter, **Ten Great Economists** (New York: Oxford University Press, Inc., 1951), Chap. 4; G. F. Shove, "The Place of Marshall's 'Principles' in the Development of Economic Theory," **Economic Journal**, Vol. 52 (December, 1942), 294–329.

The periodical literature treating of special phases and aspects of Marshall's thought is immense. Only a small selection is given here. The gradual development of his thought is traced in C. W. Guillebaud, "The Evolution of Marshall's Principles of Economics," **Economic Journal**, Vol. 52 (December, 1942), 330–49. See also a number of articles by Whitaker: "Alfred Marshall: The Years 1877 to 1885," **History of Political Economy**, Vol. 4, No. 1 (Spring, 1972), 1–61; "Some Neglected

Aspects of Alfred Marshall's Economic and Social Thought," same journal, Vol. 9, No. 2 (Summer, 1977), 161–97; "The Marshallian System in 1881: Distribution and Growth," **Economic Journal**, Vol. 84, No. 333 (March, 1974), 1–17. On Marshall's treatment of wants and the general scope of his analysis see Talcott Parsons, **The Structure of Social Action** (New York: McGraw-Hill Book Company, 1937), Chap. 4. On the demand curve see Sidney Weintraub, "The Foundations of the Demand Curve," **American Economic Review**, Vol. 32 (September, 1942), 538–52; Frank H. Knight, "Realism and Relevance in the Theory of Demand," **Journal of Political Economy**, Vol. 52, No. 4 (December, 1944), 289–318; Milton Friedman, **Essays in Positive Economics** (Chicago: The University of Chicago Press, 1953), pp. 47–99; Paul A. Samuelson, "Constancy of the Marginal Utility of Income," in **Studies in Mathematical Economics and Econometrics: In Memory of Henry Schultz,** ed. Oskar Lange, Francis McIntyre, and Theodore O. Yntema (Chicago: The University of Chicago Press, 1942), pp. 75–91. On the later discussion of demand theory see John R. Hicks, **Value and Capital**, 2nd ed. (London: Oxford University Press, 1946); René Roy, **De l'utilité** (Paris: Hermann, 1942); D. H. Robertson, **Utility and All That and Other Essays** (London: George Allen & Unwin Ltd., 1952), Chap. 1; J. R. Hicks, **A Revision of Demand Theory** (London: Oxford University Press, 1956); Tapas Majumdar, **The Measurement of Utility** (London: Macmillan & Co. Ltd., 1958); Paul A. Samuelson, **Collected Scientific Papers**, ed. Joseph E. Stiglitz (Cambridge, Mass.: The M. I. T. Press, 1966), Vol. 1, Part 1.

On consumer surplus see the articles by John R. Hicks, "The Rehabilitation of Consumers' Surplus," **Review of Economic Studies**, Vol. 8 (February, 1941), 108–16; "Consumers' Surplus and Index Numbers," same review, Vol. 9, No. 2 (Summer, 1942), 126–37; "The Four Consumer's Surpluses," same review, Vol. 11, No. 1 (Winter, 1943), 31–41; Kenneth E. Boulding, "The Concept of Economic Surplus," **American Economic Review**, Vol.

35 (December, 1945), 851–69, reprinted in American Economic Association, **Readings in the Theory of Income Distribution** (Homewood, Ill.: Richard D. Irwin, Inc., Blakiston Books, 1946), pp. 638–59; R. W. Pfouts, "A Critique of Some Recent Contributions to the Theory of Consumers' Surplus," **Southern Economic Journal**, Vol. 19, No. 3 (January, 1953), 315–33.

On Marshall's theory of the firm see Lionel Robbins, "The Representative Firm," **Economic Journal**, Vol. 38 (1928), 387–404; D. H. Robertson, "Increasing Returns and the Representative Firm," same journal, Vol. 40 (March, 1930), 80–89; Frank H. Knight, **The Ethics of Competition** (New York: Harper & Row, Publishers, 1935), Chaps. 7, 8; Jacob Viner, "Cost Curves and Supply Curves," **Zeitschrift für Nationalökonomie**, 1931, reprinted in American Economic Association, **Readings in Price Theory** (Homewood, Ill.: Richard D. Irwin, Inc., 1953), pp. 198–232; George J. Stigler, "Production and Distribution in the Short Run," **Journal of Political Economy**, Vol. 47 (1939), 305–27; William Fellner and Howard S. Ellis, "External Economies and Diseconomies," **American Economic Review**, Vol. 33 (September, 1943), 493–511; Ragnar Frisch, "Alfred Marshall's Theory of Value," **Quarterly Journal of Economics**, Vol. 64, No. 4 (November, 1950), 495–524; Edith T. Penrose, **The Theory of the Growth of the Firm** (Oxford: Basil Blackwell & Mott Ltd., 1959); B. J. Loasby, "Whatever Happened to Marshall's Theory of Value?" **Scottish Journal of Political Economy**, Vol. 25, No. 1 (February, 1978), 1–12; H. M. Robertson, "Alfred Marshall's Aims and Methods Illustrated From His Treatment of Distribution," **History of Political Economy**, Vol. 2, No. 1 (Spring, 1970), 1–64; articles by Laurence Moss and others, **Eastern Economic Journal**, Vol. 8, No. 1 (January, 1982).

On Marshall's rent theory see F. W. Ogilvie, "Marshall on Rent," with reply by M. Tappan Hollond, **Economic Journal**, Vol. 40 (1930), 1–24, 369–83; R. Opie, "Die Quasirente in Marshalls Lehrgebäude," **Archiv für Sozialwissenschaft und Sozialpolitik**, Vol. 40 (1928), 251–79; same author, "Marshall's Time Analysis," **Economic Journal**, Vol. 41 (1931), 199–215. On miscellaneous topics see Joseph J. Spengler, "Marshall on the Population Question," **Population Studies**, Vol. 8, Part 3, and Vol. 9, Part 1 (March, 1955–July, 1955), 264–87, 56–66; Bruce Glassburner, "Alfred Marshall on Economic History and Historical Development," **Quarterly Journal of Economics**, Vol. 69 (November, 1955), 577–95; A. J. Youngson, "Marshall on Economic Growth," **Scottish Journal of Political Economy**, Vol. 3 (February, 1956), 1–18.

About Marshall's contribution to monetary theory and its later transformation by his followers see Alvin H. Hansen, **Monetary Theory and Fiscal Policy** (New York: McGraw-Hill Book Company, 1949), Chaps. 1 and 3; Eprime Eshag, **From Marshall to Keynes: An Essay on the Monetary Theory of the Cambridge School** (Oxford: Basil Blackwell & Mott Ltd., 1963). The respective roles of Marshall and Marx in the rise of the mixed economy are explored by Clark Kerr, **Marshall, Marx and Modern Times** (London: Cambridge University Press, 1970).

Book-length appraisals of Marshall include Herbert J. Davenport, **The Economics of Alfred Marshall** (Ithaca, N.Y.: Cornell University Press, 1935); H. Hirsch, **Alfred Marshalls Beitrag zur modernen Theorie der Unternehmung** (Berlin: Duncker & Humblot, 1966), Sozialwissenschaftliche Abhandlungen No. 10.

Joan Robinson concludes her **Collected Economic Papers**, Vol. 1 (Oxford: Basil Blackwell & Mott Ltd., 1951), with a delightful parody, telling the story of "The Beauty and the Beast" in the style of Marshall's victorian prose.

• Pigou, Arthur Cecil, **The Economics of Welfare** (first published 1912, 4th ed. 1932). This is Pigou's most important contribution, a revision of his earlier **Wealth and Welfare** (1912). Altogether he wrote nearly thirty books and over a hundred pamphlets and articles. Some of these were about subjects that he had treated in earlier editions of his welfare economics, but that subsequently became themes of separate works. His principal publications about **Unemployment** include a book of this title (1913), as well as **The Theory of Unemployment** (1933) and **Employment and Equilibrium** (2nd ed. 1949). He also wrote full-fledged treatises on **Industrial Fluctuations** (2nd ed. 1929) and **A Study in Public Finance** (3rd ed. 1947). Works smaller in compass were **Principles and Methods of Industrial Peace** (1905); **Protective and Preferential Import Duties** (1906); **Essays in Applied Economics** (1923); **Economic Essays and Addresses** (London: P. S. King and Son, 1931), with Dennis H. Robertson, and containing Pigou's programmatic "The Function of Economic Analysis"; **Economics of Stationary States** (1935); **Economics in Practice** (1935); **Socialism versus Capitalism** (1937); **The Political Economy of War** (rev. ed. 1941); **Lapses from Full Employment** (1945); **Income** (1946); **Aspects of British Economic History, 1918–1925** (1947); **The Veil of Money** (1949); **Essays in Economics** (1952); **Income Revisited** (1955). There are appraisals of Marshall's and Keynes's work in **Alfred Marshall and Current Thought** (1953), and **Keynes's General Theory** (1950). About Pigou's view of the welfare state see "Some Aspects of the Welfare State," **Diogenes**, No. 7 (Summer, 1954), 1–11, reprinted in William Ebenstein, ed., **Great Political Thinkers**, 3rd ed. (New York: Holt, Rinehart & Winston, Inc., 1960), pp. 836–43.

Pigou's early interests are indicated by such publications as **Robert Browning as a Religious Teacher** (1901); **The Problem of Theism and Other Essays** (1908). About Pigou see the obituary notice by Harry G. Johnson, **Canadian Journal of Economics and Political Science**, Vol. 26 (February, 1960), 150–55.

Unless otherwise indicated, Pigou's books were published in London: Macmillan & Co., Ltd.

For later discussions of the Pigou, or real balance, effect, see Don Patinkin, **Money, Interest, and Prices**, 2nd ed. (New York: Harper & Row, Publishers, 1965); Gardner Ackley, **Macroeconomic Theory** (New York: The Macmillan Company, 1961), pp. 269ff.; Edward Shapiro, **Macroeconomic Analysis** (New York: Harcourt, Brace & World, Inc., 1966), pp. 230ff., 482ff., with further references to the periodical literature.

• Robbins, Lionel. See the article about Robbins, with bibliography of works by and about him, by T. W. Hutchison, **International Encyclopedia of the Social Sciences**, Biographical Supplement, Vol. 18, pp. 660–63. See also Robbins's article "Economics and Political Economy," **American Economic Review**, Vol. 71, No. 2 (May, 1981), 1–10, where he traces his definition in economics to Hume and Menger (p. 2). On Robbins's and other definitions of economics see Israel M. Kirzner, **The Economic Point of View**, 2nd ed, (New York: New York University Press, 1976).

• Robertson, Dennis H., **A Study of Industrial Fluctuation** (1915); **Banking Policy and the Price Level** (1926); **Economic Fragments** (1931) (London: P. S. King and Son). **Money** (1922, rev. 1928); **The Control of Industry** (1923) (Welwyn, Hertfordshire: James Nisbet & Co. Ltd.; also London: Cambridge University Press). **Economic Essays and Addresses**, with A. C. Pigou (1931); **Essays in Monetary Theory** (1940) (London: P. S. King and Son). **Utility and All That** (New York: The Macmillan Company, 1952); **Britain in the World Economy** (London: George Allen & Unwin Ltd., 1954); **Economic Commentaries** (London: Staples Press Limited, 1956); **Lectures on Economic Principles**, 3 vols. (London: Staples Press Limited, 1957–59); **Growth, Wages, Money** (London: Cambridge University Press, 1961); **Essays in Money and Interest**, selected with a memoir, by Sir John Hicks (London: William Collins Sons & Co. Ltd., Fontana Library, 1966). About Robertson see, in addition to Hicks's memoir, Paul A. Samuelson, "D. H. Robertson (1890–1963)," **Quarterly Journal of Economics**, Vol. 77, No. 4 (November, 1963), 517–36 and references in Marget, **Theory of Prices**. See also John R. Presley, **Robertsonian Economics** (New York: Holmes & Meier, 1979).

• Robinson, Joan. See the articles, with bibliographies, by Geoffrey C. Harcourt, **International Encyclopedia of the Social Sciences**, Biographical Supplement, Vol. 18, pp. 663–71; Spiegel and Samuels, **Contemporary Economists in Perspective**.

• Sraffa, Piero, "The Laws of Returns

under Competitive Conditions," originally published in **Economic Journal**, 1926, and reprinted in American Economic Association, **Readings in Price Theory** (Homewood, Ill.: Richard D. Irwin, Inc., 1953), Chap. 9. In subsequent years Sraffa published but little, being occupied with the preparation of his magnificent edition of the **Works and Correspondence of Ricardo**, 10 vols. (London: Cambridge University Press, 1951–55). In 1960 he published **Production of Commodities by Means of Commodities** (London: Cambridge University Press), the central ideas of which had taken shape during the late 1920s. This work, which is grounded in the premarginalist approach of the classics and in which the laws of return are suspended, traces the effects on relative prices of changes in the division of the product between profits and wages. Its findings converge in part with those of modern activity analysis. For a comment see the last essay in Maurice Dobb, **Papers on Capitalism, Development and Planning** (London: Routledge & Kegan Paul Ltd., 1967); A. Roncaglia, **Sraffa and the Theory of Prices**, trans. by J. A. Kregel (New York: John Wiley and Sons, 1978); article on Sraffa by Luigi L. Pasinetti, **International Encyclopedia of the Social Sciences**, Biographical Supplement, Vol. 18, pp. 736–39.

CHAPTER 26

• Keynes, John Maynard. The Royal Economic Society has sponsored the publication of **The Collected Writings of John Maynard Keynes**, ed. Austin Robinson and Donald Moggridge, a work that will eventually include thirty volumes and of which the bulk has been published (New York: Cambridge University Press, 1971 ff.). A full-length biography has been written by Roy F. Harrod, **The Life of John Maynard Keynes** (London: Macmillan & Co. Ltd., 1951). A shorter biography, together with an exposition of Keynes's thought, may be found in Seymour E. Harris, **John Maynard Keynes, Economist and Policy Maker** (New York: Charles Scribner's Sons, 1955). For a description of the intellectual circle in which Keynes moved see Quentin Bell, **Bloomsbury** (London: George Weidenfeld & Nicolson Ltd., 1968). Indiscretions about a private phase of his life are revealed in Michael Holroyd, **Lytton Strachey: A Critical Biography**, 2 vols. (New York: Holt, Rinehart & Winston, Inc., 1968).

Among the voluminous literature interpreting and commenting on Keynes's work the following stand out: Dudley Dillard, **The Economics of John Maynard Keynes** (Englewood Cliffs, N.J.: Prentice-Hall, Inc., 1948); Alvin H. Hansen, **A Guide to Keynes** (New York: McGraw-Hill Book Company, 1953); Seymour E. Harris, ed., **The New Economics: Keynes' Influence on Theory and Public Policy** (New York: Alfred A. Knopf, Inc., 1947); Lawrence R. Klein, **The Keynesian Revolution** (New York: The Macmillan Company, 1947); Kenneth K. Kurihara, ed., **Post-Keynesian Economics** (New Brunswick; N.J.: Rutgers University Press, 1954); Robert Lekachman, ed., **Keynes's General Theory: Reports of Three Decades** (New York: St. Martin's Press, Inc., 1964); same author, **The Age of Keynes** (New York, Random House, Inc., 1966); Herbert Stein, **The Fiscal Revolution in America** (Chicago: The University of Chicago Press, 1969); G. Schmölders, R. Schröder, H. St. Seidenfus, **John Maynard Keynes als "Psychologe"** (Berlin: Duncker & Humblot, 1956); Paul Lambert, **L'Oeuvre de John Maynard Keynes**, Vol. 1 (The Hague: Martinus Nijhoff's N.V., 1963); Axel Leijonhufvud, **On Keynesian Economics and the Economics of Keynes** (London: Oxford University Press, 1968); Donald Winch, **Economics and Policy** (New York: Walker and Company, 1970); A. G. Hines, **A Reappraisal of Keynesian Economics** (London: Martin Robertson and Company Ltd., 1971); D. E. Moggridge, ed., **Keynes: Aspects of the Man and His Work** (New York: St. Martin's Press, 1974); James Tobin, **The**

New Economics One Decade Older (Princeton: Princeton University Press, 1974); G. L. S. Shackle, **Keynesian Kaleidics: The Evolution of a General Political Economy** (Chicago: Aldine Publishing Company, 1974); Milo Keynes, ed., **Essays on John Maynard Keynes** (New York: Cambridge University Press, 1975); Hyman P. Minsky, **John Maynard Keynes** (New York: Columbia University Press, 1975); John R. Hicks, **The Crisis in Keynesian Economics** (New York: Basic Books, 1975); Don Patinkin, **Keynes' Monetary Thought: A Study of Its Development** (Durham, N.C.: Duke University Press, 1976); Robert Skidelsky, ed., **The End of the Keynesian Era** (New York: Holmes & Meier, Publishers, 1977); Patinkin and J. Clark Leith, eds., **Keynes, Cambridge and the General Theory** (Buffalo: University of Toronto Press, 1978); Brian Morgan, **Monetarists and Keynesians** (New York: John Wiley and Sons, Halsted Press, 1978); Sidney Weintraub, **Keynes, Keynesians and Monetarists** (Philadelphia: University of Pennsylvania Press, 1978); Elizabeth and Harry Johnson, **The Shade of Keynes** (Chicago: University of Chicago Press, 1979); Paul A. Samuelson, "Lord Keynes and the General Theory," **Econometrica**, Vol. 14 (July, 1946), 187–200; Richard Kahn, "Some Aspects of the Development of Keynes's Thought," **Journal of Economic Literature**, Vol. 16 No. 2 (June, 1978), 545–59; Dudley Dillard, "A Monetary Theory of Production: Keynes and the Institutionalist," **Journal of Economic Issues**, Vol. 14, No. 2 (June, 1980), 255–73.

G. L. S. Shackle's theory of expectations is developed in his **Expectations in Economics** (London: Cambridge University Press, 1949). About Shackle see article by Mark Perlman in Spiegel and Samuels, **Contemporary Economists in Perspective**. Etienne Mantoux's critique of Keynes's views may be found in his **The Carthaginian Peace** (New York: Charles Scribner's Sons, 1952). Richard Kahn's article developing the multiplier concept was published under the title "The Relations of Home Investment to Unemployment." **Economic Journal**, 1931, pp. 173–98, which has been reprinted in Kahn's **Selected Essays on Employment and**

Growth (New York: Cambrige University Press, 1972). On this matter see also Hugo Hegeland, "The Genesis of the Multiplier Theory," in **Money, Growth and Methodology, and Other Essays in Economics: In Honour of Johan Åkerman** (Lund: AB C. W. K. Gleerup Bokfoerlag, 1961), pp. 211–32, who calls attention to the converging views of a number of writers, including Vernon A. Mund, who pioneered in developing the multiplier concept.

References to writers anticipating Keynes's views may also be found in Chapter 23 of his **General Theory** and in Robert T. Nash and William P. Gramm, "A Neglected Early Statement of the Paradox of Thrift," **History of Political Economy**, Vol. 1, No. 2 (Fall, 1969), 395–400. On J. A. Hobson see Michael Freeden. **The New Liberalism: An Ideology of Social Reform** (New York: Oxford University Press, 1978); John A. Garraty, **Unemployment in History: Economic Thought and Public Policy** (New York: Harper & Row, 1978), who refers to Hobson as "the most original of the new students of unemployment" at the close of the nineteenth century (p. 123). For an account of converging contributions to macroeconomics in Germany during the 1930's by Ferdinand Grünig and Carl Föhl see K. W. Rothschild, "The Old and the New—Some Recent Trends in the Literature of German Economics," **American Economic Review**, Vol. 54, No. 2, Part 2, supplement (March, 1964), 8–11.

For a review of the contributions of Duesenberry, Modigliani and Friedman to the further development of the consumption function see Gardner Ackley, **Macroeconomic Theory** (New York: The Macmillan Company, 1961), pp. 242ff. Nicholas Kaldor's "Alternative Theories of Distribution" originally published in the **Review of Economic Studies**, Vol. 23 (1955–56), has been reprinted in his **Essays on Value and Distribution** (New York: The Free Press, 1960), pp. 209–36. About Kaldor see the article by Luigi L. Pasinetti in **International Encyclopedia of the Social Sciences**, Biographical Supplement, Vol. 18, pp. 367–69. The early development of fiscal policy can be traced to William H. Beveridge, **Full Employment in a Free Society** (New York: W. W. Norton &

Company, Inc., 1945), and to T. Balogh et al., **The Economics of Full Employment: Studies prepared at the Oxford University Institute of Statistics** (Oxford: Basil Blackwell & Mott Ltd., 1944), which includes a contribution, entitled "Three Ways to Full Employment," by M. Kalecki, a Polish economist then residing in England. A number of articles by Kalecki, originally written in Polish during the 1930s and anticipating in part Keynes's **General Theory,** have been made available in English translation under the title **Studies in the Theory of Business Cycles, 1933–1939** (Oxford: Basil Blackwell & Mott Ltd., 1966). About Kalecki see George R. Feiwel, **The Intellectual Capital of Michal Kalecki** (Knoxville: University of Tennessee Press, 1975), where references to other writings by Kalecki may be found.

For a conservative critique of Keynes's views see Henry Hazlitt, **The Failure of the "New Economics,"** (New York: Litton Educational Publishing, Inc., Van Nostrand Reinhold Company, 1959); Hazlitt, ed., **The Critics of Keynesian Economics** (same publisher, 1960); W. H. Hutt, **Keynesianism—Retrospect and Prospect** (Chicago: Henry Regnery Co., 1963); David McCord Wright, **The Keynesian System** (Bronx, N.Y.: Fordham University Press, 1961). Lekachman, **Keynes' General Theory,** contains more recent views of some of Keynes's early critics, whose original statements are assembled in Hazlitt, **Keynesian Economics**. See also James M. Buchanan and Richard E. Wagner, **Democracy in Deficit: The Political Legacy of Lord Keynes** (New York: Academic Press, 1977). Marxist criticism of Keynes is reviewed in Carl B. Turner, **An Analysis of Soviet Views on John Maynard Keynes** (Durham, N.C.: Duke University Press, 1970).

• Shackle, G. L. S., **The Years of High Theory: Invention and Tradition in Economic Thought, 1926–1939** (London: Cambridge University Press, 1967). Chaps. 9–18, the larger part of the book, treat of Keynes and his forerunners. See also T. W. Hutchison, **A Review of Economic Doctrines, 1870–1929** (London: Oxford University Press, 1953), Chaps. 15 (Wick-sell and Cassel), 21 and 24 (early contributions of Keynes); same author, **On Revolutions and Progress in Economic Knowledge** (New York: Cambridge University Press, 1978), on the Keynesian revolution; same author, **The Politics and Philosophy of Economics: Marxians, Keynesians and Austrians** (New York: New York University Press, 1981); Ben B. Seligman, **Main Currents in Modern Economics** (New York: The Free Press, 1962), Chaps. 7 (Swedish contributions), 9, sec. 4–5 (Keynes); George J. Stigler, **Production and Distribution Theories** (New York: The Macmillan Company, 1941), Chap. 10 (Wicksell); Joseph A. Schumpeter, **Ten Great Economists** (New York: Oxford University Press, Inc., 1951), Chap. 10 (Keynes); Emile James, **Histoire de la pensée économique au xxᵉ siècle,** 2 vols. (Paris: Presses Universitaires de France, 1955). The first volume of this comprehensive survey, which is organized by topics, treats of the period from 1900 to Keynes's **General Theory;** the second reviews later developments.

• Wicksell, Knut, **Lectures on Political Economy,** translated from Swedish by E. Classen and edited with an introduction by Lionel Robbins, 2 vols. (London: Routledge & Kegan Paul Ltd., 1934–35); **Interest and Prices,** trans. R. F. Kahn, with an introduction by Bertil Ohlin (London: Macmillan & Co. Ltd., 1936); **Value, Capital and Rent,** with a foreword by G. L. S. Shackle, trans. S. H. Frowein (New York: Holt, Rinehart & Winston, Inc., 1954). These are the translations of Wicksell's principal works, originally published in 1901–06, 1898, and 1893 respectively. Except for excerpts, Wicksell's **Finanztheoretische Untersuchungen** (Stuttgart: Gustav Fischer Verlag, 1896), is available only in the original German. Miscellaneous essays have been reprinted under the title **Selected Papers on Economic Theory,** edited with an introduction by Erik Lindahl (Cambridge, Mass.: Harvard University Press, 1958). There is a full-length biography by Torsten Gårdlund, **The Life of Knut Wicksell,** translated from Swedish by Nancy Adler (Stockholm: Almqvist & Wiksell Gebers Foerlag AB, 1958). For appraisals of Wicksell's work see the introductions to the English translations of his writings as well as Don Patinkin, **Studies in Monetary Economics** (New York: Harper & Row, 1972) on Wicksell's cumulative process; Steinar Strom and Björn Thalberg, eds., **The Theoretical Contributions of Knut Wicksell** (London: Macmillan Press, 1979) reprinted from **Scandinavian Journal of Economics**, Vol. 80, No. 2 (1978), a special issue devoted to Wicksell; Carl G. Uhr, **Economic Doctrines of Knut Wicksell** (Berkeley and Los Angeles: University of California Press, 1960); same author, "Knut Wicksell—A Centennial Evaluation," **American Economic Review**, Vol. 41, No. 5 (December, 1951), 829–60; "Frisch on Wicksell," in Henry W. Spiegel, ed., **The Development of Economic Thought** (New York: John Wiley and Sons, Inc., 1952), pp. 652–99. The work of Ragnar Frisch (1895–1973), a distinguished student of econometrics who in fact gave this new approach its name, exemplifies the flourishing of economics also in Norway, as does Frederick Zeuthen, **Problems of Monopoly and Economic Warfare** (London: Routledge & Kegan Paul Ltd., 1930) for Denmark. About Frisch see articles by Leif Johansen in **International Encyclopedia of the Social Sciences**, Biographical Supplement, Vol. 18, pp. 211–15, and in Spiegel and Samuels, **Contemporary Economists in Perspective**.

About David Davidson see Carl G. Uhr, **Economic Doctrines of David Davidson** (Stockholm: Almqvist & Wiksell, 1975).

About Wicksell's views on the theory of public finance see Richard A. Musgrave, **The Theory of Public Finance** (New York: McGraw-Hill Book Company, 1959), index under "Wicksell"; James M. Buchanan, "Wicksell on Fiscal Reform," **American Economic Review**, September, 1952, pp. 599–602; Duncan Black, "Wicksell's Principle in the Distribution of Taxation," in J. K. Eastham, ed., **Dundee Economic Essays**, School of Economics. Dundee, 1955, pp. 7–23. G. J. Gröbner, **Verteilung von Einkommen und Ressourcen: Knut Wicksells finanztheoretische Leistung in neuerer Sicht** (Göttingen: Vandenhoeck & Ruprecht, 1970); P.

Hennipman, "Wicksell and Pareto; Their Relationship in the Theory of Public Finance," **History of Political Economy**, Vol. 14, No. 1 (Spring, 1982), 37–64. Wicksell's work in this field was continued by Erik Lindahl, **Die Gerechtigkeit der Besteuerung** (Lund: AB C. W. K. Gleerup Bokfoerlag, 1919). Excerpts from Wicksell's and Lindahl's writings may be found in English translation in R. A. Musgrave and Alan T. Peacock, eds., **Classics in the Theory of Public Finance** (London: Macmillan & Co. Ltd., 1958).

Gustav Cassel's principal writings include **The Nature and Necessity of Interest** (London: Macmillan & Co. Ltd., 1903); **Money and Foreign Exchange after 1914** (New York: The Macmillan Company, 1922); **The Theory of Social Economy** (New York: Harcourt, Brace & World, Inc., 1924, rev. ed. 1932); **Fundamental Thoughts in Economics** (London: George Allen & Unwin Ltd., 1925); **On Quantitative Thinking in Economics** (London: Oxford University Press, 1935); **The Downfall of the Gold Standard** (London: Oxford University Press, 1936). Cassel was honored with a **Festschrift** that included contributions by the foremost economists of the time; see **Economic Essays in Honour of Gustav Cassel** (London: George Allen & Unwin Ltd., 1933). For a frank appraisal of Cassel's work by his foremost pupil see Gunnar Myrdal, "Gustav Cassel in Memoriam (1866–1945)," Oxford, Institute of Economics and Statistics, **Bulletin**, Vol. 25, No. 1 (February, 1963), 1–10. See also E. Lundberg, "L'influenza di Gustav Cassel sulla teorie economica e sulla politica economica," **Economia Internazionale**, (August, 1967), pp. 478–90; Joseph J. Spengler, "Cassel on Population," **History of Political Economy**, Vol. 1, No. 1 (Spring, 1969), 150–72.

"A Survey of Economic Thought in Sweden, 1875–1950," has been contributed by Eli F. Heckscher, himself an outstanding member of the Swedish group (**The Scandinavian Economic History Review**, Vol. 1, No. 1 (1953), 105–25). See also Karl-Gustav Landgren, **Economics in Modern Sweden**, trans. Paul Gekker (Washington, D.C.: Library of Congress, Reference Department, 1957), and, for the work of the Stockholm School in income and employment analysis, Bertil Ohlin, "Some Notes on the Stockholm Theory of Saving and Investment,"**Economic Journal**, Vol. 47 (March, 1937), reprinted in American Economic Association, **Readings in Business Cycle Theory** (Homewood, Ill.: Richard D. Irwin, Inc., Blakiston Books, 1944); Tord Palander, "On the Concepts and Methods of the Stockholm School," **International Economic Papers**, No. 3 (1953), pp. 5–57; A. P. Lerner, "Some Swedish Stepping Stones in Economic Theory," **Canadian Journal of Economics and Political Science**, Vol. 6, No. 4 (November, 1940), 574–91, a review from the Keynesian point of view of Gunnar Myrdal, **Monetary Equilibrium** (Edinburgh: William Hodge and Company Limited, 1939); and Erik Lindahl, **Studies in the Theory of Money and Capital** (New York: Holt, Rinehart & Winston, Inc., 1939); Brinley Thomas, **Monetary Policy and Crises: A Study of Swedish Experience** (London: Routledge & Kegan Paul Ltd., 1936); articles by Otto Steiger, Bertil Ohlin and Bent Hansen about the Stockholm School in a memorial issue of **History of Political Economy**, Vol 13, No. 2 (Summer, 1981).

Johan Åkerman's works include **Das Problem der sozialökonomischen Synthese** (Lund: AB C. W. K. Gleerup Bokfoerlag, 1938); **Structures et cycles économiques**, 2 vols. in 3 (Paris: Presses Universitaires de France, 1955–57); **Theory of Industrialism** (Lund: AB C. W. K. Gleerup Bokfoerlag, 1960).

Bertil Ohlin, **Interregional and International Trade** (Cambridge, Mass.: Harvard University Press, 1933), is the contribution of the Stockholm School to international-trade theory. For reactions, see Jacob Viner, **Studies in the Theory of International Trade** (New York: Harper & Row, Publishers, 1937), pp. 500ff.; Gottfried Haberler, **A Survey of International Trade Theory** (Princeton, N.J.: Princeton University Press, International

Finance Section, 1955), pp. 17ff.; Richard E. Caves, **Trade and Economic Structure** (Cambridge, Mass.: Harvard University Press, 1963), pp. 23ff. About Ohlin see a symposium issue of **History of Political Economy**, Vol. 10, No. 3 (Fall, 1978) and articles by Harald Dickson, **International Encyclopedia of the Social Sciences**, Biographical Supplement, Vol. 18, pp. 603–607; Richard Caves in Spiegel and Samuels, **Contemporary Economists in Perspective**.

Ohlin's work and Tord Palander, **Beiträge zur Standortstheorie** (Uppsala: Almqvist & Wiksell Gebers Foerlag AB, 1935) have stimulated the growing literature about spatial location and regional economics; see, for example, August Lösch, **The Economics of Location**, translated from the 2nd revised edition by William H. Woglom with the assistance of Wolfgang F. Stolper (New Haven, Conn.: Yale University Press, 1954); Edgar M. Hoover, **The Location of Economic Activity** (New York: McGraw-Hill Book Company, 1948); Walter Isard, **Location and Space Economy** (New York: John Wiley & Sons, Inc., 1956); Walter Isard et al., **Methods of Regional Analysis** (New York: John Wiley & Sons, Inc., 1960).

About Gunnar Myrdal see articles by Paul Streeten, **International Encyclopedia of the Social Sciences**, Biographical Supplement, Vol. 18 pp. 571–78; Erik Lundberg and Lloyd Reynolds in Spiegel and Samuels, **Contemporary Economists in Perspective**.

The **Festschriften** for Åkerman, Lindahl and Zeuthen contain samples of a rich variety of Scandinavian contributions to economics; see **Money, Growth and Methodology**, cited above; **Twenty-Five Economic Essays in Honour of Erik Lindahl** (Stockholm: Ekonomisk Tidskrift, 1956); **Festskrift til Frederik Zeuthen** (Copenhagen: Nationaløkonomisk Forening, 1958).

CHAPTER 27

The bibliographies of the works of writers listed here and in the following chapters are not intended to be complete.

• Ayres, Clarence E. (1891–1972) was an American institutional economist who emphasized institutional obstacles to technological change. For an appraisal see William Breit and William Patton Culbertson, Jr., eds., **Science and Ceremony: The Institutional Economics of C. E. Ayres** (Austin: University of Texas Press, 1976).

• Boulding, Kenneth. For an appraisal see article by Robert A. Solo in Henry W. Spiegel and Warren J. Samuels, eds., **Contemporary Economists in Perspective** (Greenwich, Ct.: JAI Press, forthcoming).

• Clark, John Bates; a list of works by and about Clark is appended to the article about Clark by John Maurice Clark in **International Encyclopedia of the Social Sciences** (New York: The Macmillan Company, The Free Press, 1968), Vol. 2, 504–8.

• Clark, John Maurice; a list of works by and about Clark may be found in the article about Clark by Jesse W. Markham, **International Encyclopedia of the Social Sciences**, Vol. 2, 508–11. See also C. Addison Hickman, **J. M. Clark** (New York: Columbia University Press, 1975).

• Coats, A. W., "The First Two Decades of the American Economic Association," **American Economic Review**, Vol. 50 (1960), 555–74.

• Commons, John R.; for a bibliography, see article by Joseph Dorfman, **International Encyclopedia of the Social Sciences**, Vol. 3, 22–24; also **John R. Commons: Addresses delivered on October 10, 1950,** in commemoration of his achievements as a teacher, economist, and administrator (Madison, Wis.: State Historical Society of Wisconsin, 1952); W. F. Kennedy, "John R. Commons, Conservative Reformer," **Western Economic Journal**, Vol. 1, No. 1 (Fall, 1962), 29–42; Gerald G. Somers, ed., **Labor, Management and Social Policy: Essays in the John R. Commons Tradition** (Madison, Wis.: University of Wisconsin Press, 1963). See also Paul J. McNulty, **The Origin and Development of Labor Economics** (Cambridge: MIT Press, 1980). Commons's influence has been acknowledged not only by labor economists but also by scholars active in a wide variety of fields, for example, Chester I. Barnard, Oliver E. Williamson, and Herbert A. Simon.

• Davenport, Herbert J., see article by Henry W. Spiegel, with bibliography, in **International Encyclopedia of the Social Sciences**, Vol. 4, 16–17.

• Fetter, Frank A., see John A. Coughlan, "The Contributions of Frank Albert Fetter (1863–1949) to the Development of Economic Theory" (Ph.D. dissertation, The Catholic University of America, Washington, D.C., 1965; Ann Arbor, Mich.: University Microfilms).

• Fisher, Irving, see article by Maurice Allais, with bibliography, in **International Encyclopedia of the Social Sciences**, Vol. 5, 475–85; also William Fellner et al., **Ten Economic Studies in the Tradition of Irving Fisher** (New York: John Wiley & Sons, Inc., 1967).

• Friedman, Milton. See article, by Niels Thygesen in Spiegel and Samuels, **Contemporary Economists in Perspective**.

• Galbraith, John K. See articles by M. E. Sharpe, **International Encyclopedia of the Social Sciences**, Biographical Supplement, Vol. 18, pp. 223–26; Daniel R. Fusfeld in Spiegel and Samuels, **Contemporary Economists in Perspective**. About one of Galbraith's forerunners, the American economist Simon N. Patten (1852–1922), who was an early prophet of the economy of abundance, see Daniel M. Fox, **The Discovery of Abundance** (Ithaca, N.Y.: Cornell University Press, 1968). About prophets of the affluent society in France see Alfred Sauvy, "La Pensée économique en France sur l'idée d'abondance et de besoin," **History of Political Economy**, Vol. 1, No. 2 (Fall, 1969), 279–305.

• Hansen, Alvin H., **Business Cycle Theory** (Boston: Ginn and Company, 1927); **Full Recovery or Stagnation?** (New York: W. W. Norton & Company, Inc., 1938); **Fiscal Policy and Business Cycles** (same publisher, 1941); **America's Role in the World Economy** (same publisher, 1945); **Monetary Theory and Fiscal Policy** (New York: McGraw-Hill Book Company, 1949); **Business Cycles and National Income** (New York: W. W. Norton & Company, Inc., 1951); **A Guide to Keynes** (New York: McGraw-Hill Book Company,

1953); **The American Economy** (same publisher, 1957); **Economic Issues of the 1960s** (same publisher, 1960). See also Lloyd A. Metzler et al., **Income, Employment and Public Policy, Essays in Honor of Alvin H. Hansen** (New York: W. W. Norton & Company, Inc., 1948).

• Knight, Frank H.; see article by James M. Buchanan, with bibliography, **International Encyclopedia of the Social Sciences**, Vol. 8, 424–28.

• Kuznets, Simon. See articles, with bibliography, by Richard A. Easterlin in **International Encyclopedia of the Social Sciences**, Biographical Supplement, Vol. 18, pp. 393–97; Erik Lundberg in Spiegel and Samuels, **Contemporary Economists in Perspective**. See also J. W. Kendrick, "The Historical Development of National-Income Accounts," **History of Political Economy**, Vol. 2, No. 2 (Fall, 1970), 284–315.

• Laughlin, J. Laurence; see the book-length appraisal, **J. Laurence Laughlin** by Alfred Bornemann (Washington, D.C.: American Council on Public Affairs, 1940), which contains a bibliography. See also Richard J. Storr, **Harper's University: The Beginnings**, A History of the University of Chicago (Chicago: The University of Chicago Press, 1966).

• Mitchell, Wesley Clair; see article by Victor Zarnowitz, with bibliography, in **International Encyclopedia of the Social Sciences**, Vol. 10, 373–78.

• Newcomb, Simon; see article by A. W. Coats, with bibliography, in **International Encyclopedia of the Social Sciences**, Vol. 11, 172–74; also Loretta M. Dunphy, **Simon Newcomb: His Contribution to Economics** (Washington, D.C.: The Catholic University of America Press, 1956).

• Samuelson, Paul A. See article by Assar Lundbeck in Spiegel and Samuels, **Contemporary Economists in Perspective**.

• Schumpeter, Joseph A., **Ten Great Economists** (New York: Oxford University Press, Inc., 1951), on Taussig, Fisher, and Mitchell; T. W. Hutchinson, **A Review of Economic Doctrines, 1870–1929** (London: Oxford University Press, 1953), on J. B.

Clark, Veblen, Fisher, Newcomb, and so on; Joseph Dorfman, **The Economic Mind in American Civilization**, Vols. 3–5 (New York: The Viking Press, Inc., 1949, 1959); Ben B. Seligman, **Main Currents in Modern Economics** (New York: The Free Press, 1962); Henry W. Spiegel, ed., **The Rise of American Economic Thought** (Philadelphia: Chilton Book Company, 1960); Paul T. Homan, **Contemporary Economic Thought** (New York: Harper & Row, Publishers, 1928), on Clark, Veblen, Mitchell, and Hobson; Rexford G. Tugwell, ed., **The Trend of Economics** (New York: Alfred A. Knopf Inc., 1924); Allan G. Gruchy, **Modern Economic Thought: The American Contribution** (Englewood Cliffs, N.J.: Prentice-Hall, Inc., 1947), on the institutional economists; same author, **Contemporary Economic Thought: The Contribution of Neo-Institutional Economics** (Clifton, N.J.: Augustus M. Kelley, 1972), on Galbraith, Ayres, Myrdal and Gerhard Colm; Abram L. Harris, **Economics and Social Reform** (New York: Harper & Row, Publishers, 1958), on Veblen and Commons. For a view of the advances during the later part of the period, organized by topics rather than by writers, see **A Survey of Contemporary Economics**, Vol. 1, ed. Howard S. Ellis, and Vol. 2, ed. Bernard F. Haley (Homewood, Ill.: Richard D. Irwin, Inc., 1948, 1952).

• Simons, Henry C.; see article by Herbert Stein, with bibliography, in **International Encyclopedia of the Social Sciences**, Vol. 14, 260–62; also J. Ronnie Davis, "Chicago Economists, Deficit Budgets, and the Early 1930s," **American Economic Review**, Vol. 58, No. 3, Part 1 (June, 1968), 476–82, where attention is drawn to certain parallels between Keynes's views and those of the Chicago economists; same author, "Henry Simons, the Radical: Some Documentary Evidence," **History of Political Economy**, Vol. 1, No. 2 (Fall, 1969), 388–94; same author, **The New Economics and the Old Economists** (Ames: Iowa State University Press, 1971).

On the Chicago School in general see Don Patinkin, **Studies in Monetary Economics** (New York: Harper & Row, 1972); same author, **Essays On and In the**

Chicago Tradition (Durham: Duke University Press, 1981); various articles about "The Chicago School of Political Economy," **Journal of Economic Issues**, Vol. 9, No. 4 (December, 1975); Melvin W. Reder, "Chicago Economics: Permanence and Change," **Journal of Economic Literature**, Vol. 20, No. 1 (March, 1982), 1–38.

• Stigler, George J., **Production and Distribution Theories: The Formative Period** (New York, The Macmillan Company, 1941); **The Theory of Price**, originally published 1942 (3rd ed., same publisher, 1966); **The Intellectual and the Market Place, and Other Essays** (New York: The Free Press, 1963); **Essays in the History of Economics** (Chicago: The University of Chicago Press, 1965); **The Organization of Industry** (Homewood, Ill.: Richard D. Irwin Inc., 1968). Stigler also has done empirical studies, for example, **Trends in Employment in the Service Industries** (New York: National Bureau of Economic Research, 1956).

• Taussig, Frank W., see article by Gottfried Haberler, with bibliography, in **International Encyclopedia of the Social Sciences**, Vol. 15, 516–18; also Warren Samuels, "Taussig on the Psychology of Economic Policy," **Indian Economic Journal**, Vol. 15, No. 1 (July–September, 1967), 1–13.

• Veblen, Thorstein, see article, with bibliography of writings by and about Veblen, contributed by Arthur K. Davis to **International Encyclopedia of the Social Sciences**, Vol. 16, 303–8; also Annie Vinokur, **Thorstein Veblen et la tradition dissidente dans la pensée économique américaine** (Paris: Librairie générale de droit et de jurisprudence, 1969); Joseph Dorfman,

ed., **Thorstein Veblen: Essays, Reviews and Reports** (Clifton, N.J.: Augustus M. Kelley, 1973); David Seckler, **Thorstein Veblen and the Institutionalists** (London: Macmillan Press, 1974); Leonard A. Dente, **Veblen's Theory of Social Change** (New York: New York Times, Arno Press, 1977; Dissertations in American Economic History series); John P. Diggins, **The Bard of Savagery: Thorstein Veblen and Modern Social Theory** (New York: Seabury Press, 1978); C. C. Qualey, ed., **Thorstein Veblen** (New York: Columbia University Press, 1968); D. A. Walker, "Thorstein Veblen's Economic System," **Economic Inquiry**, Vol. 15, No. 2 (April, 1977), 213–37.

• Viner, Jacob. See the article, with bibliography, by William Baumol and Ellen Viner Seiler in **International Encyclopedia of the Social Sciences**, Biographical Supplement, Vol. 18, pp. 783–87; also Donald Winch, "Jacob Viner," **American Scholar**, Vol. 50, No. 4 (Autumn, 1981), 519–25.

• Walker, Francis A.; see article, with bibliography, by Spiegel, **International Encyclopedia of the Social Sciences**, Vol. 16, 438–40; Bernard Newton, **F. A. Walker** (New York: Augustus M. Kelley, Publishers, 1968).

• White, Morton, **Social Thought in America: The Revolt against Formalism** (New York: The Viking Press, Inc., 1949); Richard Hofstadter, **Social Darwinism in American Thought** (Philadelphia: University of Pennsylvania Press, 1945); Arthur M. Schlesinger, Jr., and Morton White, eds., **Paths of American Thought** (Boston: Houghton Mifflin Company, 1963). The intellectual background of various strands of thought in American economics.

CHAPTER 28

• Allais, Maurice, **Économie et intérêt**, 2 vols. (Paris: Librairie des publications officielles, 1947); **Traité d'économie pure** (Paris: Imprimerie Nationale, 1952). Further references in Jacques H. Drèze, "Some Postwar Contributions of French Economists to Theory and Public Policy, with Special Emphasis on Resource Allo-

cation," **American Economic Review**, Vol. 54, No. 4, Part 2, Supplement (June, 1964), 1–64; also Allais, "A Restatement of the Quantity Theory of Money," **American Economic Review**, Vol. 56, No. 5 (December, 1966), 1123–57 with additional references; Allais, "Economics as a Science," **Cahiers Vilfredo Pareto et Revue**

816   européenne d'histoire des sciences sociales, Vol. 16 (1968), 5–24.

• Arrow, Kenneth J., "Mathematical Models in the Social Sciences," in Daniel Lerner and Harold D. Lasswell, eds., **The Policy Sciences** (Stanford, Calif.: Stanford University Press, 1951), pp. 129–54. Similarly oriented surveys may be found in James C. Charlesworth, ed., **Mathematics and the Social Sciences** (Philadelphia: American Academy of Political and Social Science, 1963) with contributions by Leonid Hurwicz and Oskar Morgenstern; Daniel Lerner, ed., **Quantity and Quality** (New York: The Free Press, 1960), contributions by W. Leontief and Joseph J. Spengler; Harry Woolf, ed., **Quantification** (Indianapolis: The Bobbs-Merrill Co., Inc., 1961), contribution by Spengler; Richard Stone, **Mathematics in the Social Sciences and Other Essays** (London: Chapman and Hall Ltd., 1966), Chap. 1; Paul F. Lazarsfeld, ed., **Mathematical Thinking in the Social Sciences** (New York: The Free Press, 1954).

• Divisia, François, see article, with bibliography, by René Roy, **International Encyclopedia of the Social Sciences**, Biographical Supplement, Vol. 4 (1968), 241–43.

• Douglas, Paul H. See the article, with bibliography of works by and about Douglas, by Glen G. Cain in **International Encyclopedia of the Social Sciences,** Biographical Supplement, Vol. 18, pp. 153–57. See also Carl-Axel Olsson, "The Cobb-Douglas or the Wicksell Function?" **Economy and History** (University of Lund, Sweden), Vol. 14 (1971), pp. 64–69, which points to another multiple discovery.

• Gibrat, R., **Les Inégalités économiques** (Paris: Éditions Sirey, 1931).

• Haavelmo, Trygve, "The Probability Approach to Econometrics," **Econometrica**, Supplement, 1944; **A Study of the Theory of Investment** (Chicago: The University of Chicago Press, 1960); "Business Cycles: Mathematical Models," **International Encyclopedia of the Social Sciences**, Vol. 2 (1968), 245–49.

• Hotelling, Harold. See article by Ralph W. Pfouts and M. R. Leadbetter in **International Encyclopedia of the Social Sciences**, Biographical Supplement, Vol. 18, pp. 325–28.

• Koopmans, Tjalling C. See articles by Lars Werin and Karl G. Jungenfeld in Spiegel and Samuels, **Contemporary Economists in Perspective**.

• Malinvaud, Edmond, **Statistical Methods of Econometrics**, trans. by Mrs. A. Silvey (Skokie, Ill.: Rand McNally & Co., 1966). See also Drèze, "Theory and Public Policy," p. 61.

• Massé, Pierre, **Optimal Investment Decisions**, trans. from French (Englewood Cliffs, N.J.: Prentice-Hall, Inc., 1962). See Drèze, "Theory and Public Policy," pp. 61f., for further references.

• Moore, Henry L., **Laws of Wages; An Essay in Statistical Economics** (1911); **Economic Cycles: Their Law and Cause** (1914); **Forecasting the Yield and Price of Cotton** (1917); **Generating Economic Cycles** (1923); **Synthetic Economics** (1929) (New York: The Macmillan Company). About Moore, see George J. Stigler, **Essays in the History of Economics** (Chicago: The University of Chicago Press, 1965), Chaps. 7, 13.

• Perroux, François, **L'Économie du xxᵉ siècle**, 3rd ed. (1969); **La Valeur** (1943); **Le Capitalisme** (1948); **Les Comptes de la nation** (1949); **L'Europe sans rivages** (1954); **Théorie générale du progrès économique** (1956–57); **La Coexistence pacifique**, 3 vols. (1958); **L'Economie des jeunes nations** (1962); **Economie et société: contrainte, échange, don**, 2nd ed. (1963); **Industrie et création collective**, Vol. 1 (1964); **Les Techniques quantitatives de la planification** (1966) (Paris: Presses Universitaires de France); **Le Pain et la parole** (Paris: Éditions du Cerf, 1969); "Indépendance" de la nation (Paris: Aubier Montaigne, 1969); **Pouvoir et économie** (Paris: Dunod, 1973); **Unités actives et mathématiques nouvelles** (same publisher, 1975); **Pour une philosophie du nouveau développement** (Paris: Aubier Montaigne, 1981). **Théorie générale** was published as Cahiers de l'Institute de science économique appliquée, of which Perroux is the director. Drèze, "Theory and Public Policy," lists on p. 63 a number of other writings by Perroux, including a few English translations, to which may be added "The Domination Effect and Modern Economic Theory," **Social Research**, Vol. 17 (June, 1950), 188–206, and "Information, a Factor of Economic Progress," **Diogenes**, 1958. See also, **Hommage à François Perroux**, ed. Philippe Hardouin (Grenoble: Presses Universitaires de Grenoble, 1977); article by Pierre Uri about Perroux in Spiegel and Samuels, **Contemporary Economists in Perspective**.

• Schultz, Henry, **Theory and Measurement of Demand** (Chicago: The University of Chicago Press, 1938). See also Oskar Lange, Francis McIntyre, and Theodore O. Yntema, eds., **Studies in Mathematical Economics and Econometrics: In Memory of Henry Schultz** (same publisher, 1942); Herman Wold, **Demand Analysis** (New York: John Wiley & Sons, Inc., 1952).

• Simon, Herbert A. See articles by William Baumol and Albert Ando in Spiegel and Samuels, **Contemporary Economists in Perspective**.

• Tinbergen, Jan. See articles by Henk C. Bos in **International Encyclopedia of the Social Sciences**, Biographical Supplement, Vol. 18, pp. 766–70; Bent Hansen in Spiegel and Samuels, **Contemporary Economists in Perspective**.

• Von Neumann, John, and Oskar Morgenstern, **Theory of Games and Economic Behavior** (Princeton, N.J.: Princeton University Press, 1944), 3rd ed. 1953. The two articles by von Neumann that exerted a profound influence on mathematical economics were "On the Theory of Games of Strategy," first published in German in 1928, translated in A. W. Tucker and R. Duncan, eds., **Contributions to the Theory of Games** (Princeton, N.J.: Princeton University Press, 1959), Vol. 4, 13–42; "A Model of General Economic Equilibrium," first published in German in 1937, translated in **Review of Economic Studies**, Vol. 13, No. 1 (1945), 1–9. See entry on "John von Neumann," by Oskar Morgenstern, in **International Encyclopedia of the Social Sciences**, Vol. 16 (1968), 385–87; also the articles on "Game Theory" by Morgenstern and Martin Shubik, same encyclopedia, Vol. 6, 62–74, and the article on "Statics and Dynamics in Economics," by William J. Baumol, same encyclopedia, Vol. 15, 169–77. On games within a broader perspective see J. Huizinga, **Homo Ludens: A Study of the Play Element in Culture**, trans. R. F. C. Hull (London: Routledge & Kegan Paul Ltd., 1949).

About Morgenstern see article by Martin Shubik in **International Encyclopedia of the Social Sciences**, Biographical Supplement, Vol. 18, pp. 541–44; also by Andrew Schotter in Spiegel and Samuels, **Contemporary Economists in Perspective**.

• Wald, Abraham; see article, with bibliography, by Harold Freeman, in **International Encyclopedia of the Social Sciences**, Vol. 16 (1968), 435–38. On "The Intellectual Migration: Europe and America, 1930–1960," of which both von Neumann and Wald formed part, see **Perspectives in American History**, Vol. 2 (September, 1968), which contains a number of memoirs published by the Charles Warren Center for Studies in American History, Harvard University, dedicated to von Neumann.

CHAPTER 29

• Becker, Gary S., **A Treatise on the Family** (Cambridge: Harvard University Press, 1981) is the most recent account of Becker's approach. It has a lengthy bibliography. See also Yoram Ben-Porath and Michael T. Hannan, "Two Views of Becker's **A Treatise on the Family**," **Journal of Economic Literature**, Vol. 20, No. 1 (March, 1982), 52–72; Theodore W. Schultz, ed., **Economics of the Family** (Chicago: University of Chicago Press for National Bureau of Economic Research, 1974), where the quotation from Becker may be found on p. 299; Harvey Leibenstein, "An Interpretation of The Economic Theory of Fertility: Promising

818

Path or Blind Alley?" **Journal of Economic Literature**, Vol. 12, No. 2 (June, 1974), 457–79; Paul A. Samuelson, "An Economist's Non-Linear Model of Self-Generated Fertility Waves," **Population Studies**, Vol. 30, No. 2 (July, 1976), 243–47 (about Richard A. Easterlin's theory of fertility). On the application of demand analysis to animal behavior see J. H. Kagel et al., "Demand Curves for Animal Consumers," **Quarterly Journal of Economics**, Vol. 96, No. 1 (February, 1981), 1–15.

• Bell, J. F., "Origins of Japanese Academic Economics," **Monumenta Nipponica** (Sophia University, Tokyo), Vol. 16, Nos. 3–4 (1960–61), 43–68.

• Brooks, John, "The Supply Side," **The New Yorker**, April 19, 1982, pp. 96–150. A review of the field by an able financial journalist. See also Jude Wanniski, "The Mundell-Laffer Hypothesis," **The Public Interest**, No. 39 (Spring, 1975); same author, **The Way the World Works** (New York: Basic Books, 1978); George Gilder, **Wealth and Poverty** (New York: Basic Books, 1981); David A. Stockman, "The Social Pork Barrel," **The Public Interest**, No. 39 (Spring, 1975); William Greider, "The Education of David Stockman," **Atlantic Monthly**, December, 1981; David G. Raboy, ed., **Essays in Supply Side Economics** (Washington: Institute for Research on the Economics of Taxation, 1982); Lewis Beman, "Supply-Side Economics," **Encyclopedia of Economics**, ed. Douglas Greenwald (New York: McGraw-Hill Book Company, 1982), pp. 910–12; Robert Lekachman, **Greed Is Not Enough: Reaganomics** (New York: Pantheon, 1982).

• Dillard, Dudley, "Neo-Keynesian Economics," in **Encyclopedia of Economics**, ed. Douglas Greenwald, pp. 703–706, with further references. See also Paul Davidson, "Post-Keynesian Economics," same encyclopedia, pp. 738–44.

• Kaldor, N., "The Irrelevance of Equilibrium Economics," **Economic Journal**, Vol. 82, No. 328 (December, 1972), 1237–55; O. Morgenstern, "Thirteen Critical Points in Contemporary Economic Theory," **Journal of Economic Literature**, Vol. 10, No. 4 (December, 1972), 1163–89; E. H. Phelps Brown, "The Underdevelopment

of Economics," **Economic Journal**, Vol. 82, No. 325 (March, 1972), 1–10; G. D. N. Worswick, "Is Progress in Economic Science Possible?" same journal, same number, 73–86; G. Myrdal, "Response to Introduction," **American Economic Review**, Vol. 62, No. 2 (May, 1972), 456–62; J. Robinson, "The Second Crisis in Economic Theory," same journal, same number, 1–16. See also Benjamin Ward, **What's Wrong With Economics?** (New York: Basic Books, 1972), and the reply by W. W. Heller, "What's Right With Economics?" same journal, Vol. 65, No. 1 (March, 1975), 1–26.

• Kuhn, Thomas, **The Structure of Scientific Revolutions**, second ed. enlarged (Chicago: The University of Chicago Press, 1970; originally published 1962). For comments and the views of Imre Lakatos see Lakatos and Alan Musgrave, eds., **Criticism and the Growth of Knowledge** (New York: Cambridge University Press, 1970). For criticism see Paul Feyerabend, **Against Method** (London: Verso, 1978). See also Gary Gutting, ed., **Paradigms and Revolutions: Applications and Appraisals of Thomas Kuhn's Philosophy of Science** (Notre Dame: University of Notre Dame Press, 1980), which contains reprints of useful articles, including Mark Blaug's "Kuhn versus Lakatos, or Paradigms versus Research Programmes in the History of Economics", pp. 137–159, originally published in **History of Political Economy**, Vol. 7 (1975), 399–433; and a list of sixteen other articles about the application of Kuhn's concept to the history of economics, pp. 336–37. See also S. J. Latsis, ed., **Method and Appraisal in Economics** (New York: Cambridge University Press, 1976). On "Revolutions in Economic Theory" see the article by Dudley Dillard, **Southern Economic Journal**, Vol. 44, No. 4 (April, 1978), 705–24; T. W. Hutchison, **On Revolutions and Progress in Economic Knowledge** (New York: Cambridge University Press, 1978).

• Leibenstein, Harvey, **Beyond Economic Man: A New Foundation for Microeconomics** (Cambridge: Harvard University Press, 1976); Fred Hirsch, **Social Limits to Growth** (same publisher, 1976); Mancur Olson, **The Rise and Decline of**

Nations (New Haven: Yale University Press, 1982).

• Machlup, Fritz, "Austrian Economics," in **Encyclopedia of Economics**, ed. Douglas Greenwald, pp. 38–43, with bibliography. See also Alex H. Shand, **Subjectivist Economics: The New Austrian School** (London: Pica Press, 1981); Louis M. Spadaro, ed., **New Directions in Austrian Economics** (1978); Edwin G. Dolan, ed., **The Foundations of Modern Austrian Economics** (1976); Ludwig M. Lachmann, **Capital, Expectations and the Market Process** (1977); Gerald P. O'Driscoll, Jr., **Economics as a Coordination Problem: The Contributions of Fredrich A. Hayek** (1977); Laurence S. Moss, ed., **The Economics of Ludwig von Mises** (1976); Murray N. Rothbard, ed., **Frank A. Fetter, Capital, Interest and Rent: Essays in the Theory of Distribution** (1977); Israel M. Kirzner, **The Economic Point of View** (1976), all published by Sheed, Andrews and McMeel, Kansas City, Mo.

• Myrdal, Gunnar, "The Nobel Prize in Economic Science," **Challenge**, Vol. 20, No. 1 (March-April, 1977), 50–52.

• Patinkin, Don, "Keynes and Econometrics," **Econometrica**, Vol. 44, No. 6 (November, 1976), 1091–1123; M. G. Phelps, "Laments, Ancient and Modern: Keynes on Mathematical and Econometric Methodology," **Journal of Post Keynesian Economics**, Vol. 2, No. 4 (Summer, 1980), 482–93.

• Selden, Richard T., "Monetarism," in **Modern Economic Thought**, ed. Sidney Weintraub (Philadelphia: University of Pennsylvania Press, 1977), pp. 253–74.

• Sheridan, Alan, **Michel Foucault: The Will to Truth** (New York: Methuen, Inc., 1980). A useful introduction to Foucault's work, with bibliography of publications by and about Foucault.

• Spiegel, Henry W., and Warren J. Samuels, eds., **Contemporary Economists in Perspective** (Greenwich, Ct.: JAI Press, forthcoming). Appraisals of some forty leading economists, including all Nobelists, by their peers. **Modern Economic Thought**, ed. Sidney Weintraub (Philadelphia: University of Pennsylvania Press, 1977), is systematically organized and contains well-informed contributions on twenty-eight topics. See also **The Crisis in Economic Theory**, ed. Irving Kristol and Nathan Glazer (New York: Basic Books, 1981), originally published as a special issue, **The Public Interest**, 1980; with contributions by Kenneth J. Arrow and other authorities; Benjamin Ward, **The Liberal Economic World View, The Radical Economic World View, The Conservative Economic World View** (all published New York; Basic Books, 1979), which contain appraisals of leading exponents of the respective views.

• Walras, Léon. **Correspondence of Léon Walras and Related Papers**, ed. William Jaffé, 3 vols. (Amsterdam: North-Holland Publishing Company, 1965). See the index under Nobel Peace Prize for correspondence relating to Walras's pursuit of this award. Frédéric Passy (1822–1912), a French economist well known at his time, a follower of Bastiat and the founder of the first French peace organization, shared the first Nobel Peace Prize in 1901. A year later Herbert Spencer was a leading candidate for the literature prize. Encouraged by the selection of Passy, Walras actively promoted his own candidacy for the peace prize in 1905 and subsequent years, but his efforts were in vain. In letters to the Nobel Peace Prize Committee he would refer to his pioneering work in mathematical economics that furnished scientific proof supporting free trade and economic justice and thereby served the cause of peace.

Frederick Soddy, a monetary reformer on the side but better known as a chemist, won the chemistry prize in 1921. Occasionally the liberal German economist Lujo Brentano is mistakenly credited with having won the peace prize in 1927.

• Weisskopf, Thomas E., "Radical Economics," **Encyclopedia of Economics**, ed. Douglas Greenwald, pp. 799–801, and the literature there cited; also Howard Sherman, **Radical Political Economy** (New York: Basic Books, 1972); Jesse Schwartz, ed., **The Subtle Anatomy of Capitalism** (Santa Monica, Calif.: Goodyear Publishing Company, 1977); William Ebenstein and Edwin Fogelman, **Today's Isms**, 8th ed. (Englewood Cliffs, N.J.: Prentice-Hall, Inc., 1980).

INDEX

*Italic figures refer to pages
in which the subject is singled out for special attention.*

A

Absentee ownership, 498, 545
Absolute advantage, 255, 329
Absolutism, 199, 417
Abstinence, 353
Academic economics
    Austria, 531
    Britain, 288, 290–91, 639
    France, 275, 655–58
    Germany, 97, 425, 655
    Netherlands, 655
    Scandinavia, 655
United States, 364, 627, 641–42, 665
Academic freedom, 291
Acceleration principle, 610, 635, 640, 643
Accounting, 99, 569, 623
Accumulation of wealth, 164–66
Activity analysis, 653
Acton, Lord, 428
Actuarial science, 135–37
Adding-up problem, 526–27
Advance economics, 619
Advertising, 568, 641
Affluent society, 259, 389, 475–76, 502–503,
    606, 640–41

Aftalion, A., 351, 584, 640
Age of economists, 579
Aggregate demand, adequacy of, 265–66,
    291–306
Aggregate equilibium, 586, 595, 609, 612
Aggregation (*see* Macroeconomics)
Agio theory of interest, 539–42
Agricultural economics, 427
Åkerman, J., 594–95, 812
Albert the Great, 62
Alienation, 240, 416
Allais, M., 656, 815–16
Allen, R. G. D., 493, 557
Allocation of resources, 62–63, 505, 528,
    572, 577, 584, 586–87, 611–12
Alphabet, 8
Ambrose, 44–45, 689
America, 87–92, 102, 112, 114, 147, 150–51,
    258, 272, 301, 709, 722 (*see also* United
    States)
American Economic Association, 426, 432,
    617, 621, 627, 630, 813
American Revolution, 436
American Statistical Association, 617
American system, 362
Analytical geometry, 121, 143, 509, 621

Henry William Spiegel is Professor Emeritus of Economics, The Catholic University of America. His other books include *Land Tenure Policies at Home and Abroad*, *The Economics of Total War*, *The Brazilian Economy*, *Current Economic Problems*, *Introduction to Economics*, *Development of Economic Thought*, *Du Pont on Economic Curves*, and *The Rise of American Economic Thought*.

Books of related interest

Keynes' Monetary Thought
A Study of its Development
Don Patinkin

Essays On and In the Chicago Tradition
Don Patinkin

Economists in Government
An International Comparative Study
Edited by A. W. Coats

The Economist in Parliament, 1780–1868
Frank Whitson Fetter

The Marginal Revolution in Economics
Interpretation and Evaluation
Edited by R. D. Collison Black, A. W. Coats, *and* Craufurd Goodwin

Economists' Papers, 1750–1950
A Guide to Archive and other Manuscript Sources for the History of British and Irish Economic Thought
Compiled by R. P. Sturges